WEBSTER'S
Student Dictionary

WEBSTER'S
Student Dictionary

Edited by P. H. Collin

BARNES
&NOBLE
BOOKS
NEW YORK

American Edition Copyright © 1992, 1999 by Barnes & Noble, Inc.
Appendices Copyright © 1999 by Market House Books Ltd.
Copyright © 1983, 1991, 1992 by the Harrap Publishing Group Ltd.

This edition published by Barnes & Noble, Inc.,
by arrangement with the Harrap Publishing Group Ltd.

1999 Barnes & Noble Books

ISBN 0-7607-1492-4

Printed and bound in the United States of America

02 03 04 05 MP 20 19 18 17 16 15 14 13 12 11 10 9 8 7 6 5 4

OPM

Contents

About This Dictionary

This entirely revised dictionary lists the words most commonly used in English, giving definitions and in many cases examples of use. Grammar notes are given in many entries – irregular plurals for nouns, comparatives and superlatives for adjectives, past forms for verbs. Where a word is commonly used with a preposition, that preposition is given in bold letters.

To make the dictionary as compact as possible, many derived words are listed under the main headwords and do not appear separately: so *package* is to be found under *pack*, *secrecy* under *secret*, etc.

Abbreviations Used in the Dictionary

adj.	adjective	*inter.*	interjection
adv.	adverb	*n.*	noun
approx.	approximately	*pl.*	plural
Brit.	British	*prep.*	preposition
def.	definite	*sl.*	slang
e.g.	for example	*s.o.*	someone
esp.	especially	*sth.*	something
indef.	indefinite	*usu.*	usually
inf.	informal	*v.*	verb

Pronunciation

The following signs are used to show the pronunciation of words in the dictionary.

Where there are several pronunciations that are current only the most common are indicated, -**r** is never pronounced at the end of words, but when a word ending in -**r** is followed by a vowel the -**r** can be pronounced.

Words are also marked with a sign (') to show where the strong beat should be placed, but this is only a guide; the pronunciation of a word can change depending on the position of the word in a sentence.

æ	back	ə	afraid	ð	then	p	penny
ɑː	farm	əu	boat	dʒ	just	r	round
ɒ	top	əuə	lower	f	fog	s	some
aɪ	pipe	ɜː	word	g	go	ʃ	short
au	how	iː	heap	h	hand	t	too
aɪə	fire	ɪ	hit	j	yes	tʃ	chop
auə	flower	ɪə	hear	k	catch	θ	thing
ɔː	bought	uː	school	χ	loch	v	voice
ɔɪ	toy	u	book	l	last	w	was
e	fed	ʌ	but	m	mix	z	zoo
eə	hair	b	back	n	nut	ʒ	treasure
eɪ	take	d	dog	ŋ	sing		

Alphabet

These are the letters of the English alphabet, showing their pronunciation.

Aa	eɪ	**Hh**	eɪtʃ	**Oo**	əʊ	**Vv**	viː
Bb	biː	**Ii**	aɪ	**Pp**	piː	**Ww**	dʌbljuː
Cc	siː	**Jj**	dʒeɪ	**Qq**	kjuː	**Xx**	eks
Dd	diː	**Kk**	keɪ	**Rr**	ɑː	**Yy**	waɪ
Ee	iː	**Ll**	el	**Ss**	es	**Zz**	zee
Ff	ef	**Mm**	em	**Tt**	tiː		
Gg	dʒiː	**Nn**	en	**Uu**	juː		

Aa

a, an [*stressed* eɪ, æn; *unstressed* ə, ən] (**a** *before words beginning with a consonant, and before words beginning with* **u** *pronounced* juː; **an** *before* **a, e, i, o** *or* **u** *and before* **h** *where* **h** *is not pronounced*) indefinite article (a) one; **give me a stamp and an envelope.** (b) not a particular one; **he has a big nose.** (c) for each one/in each one; **thirty miles an hour.** (d) a certain; **I know a Dr. Smith.**

A1 [eɪ'wʌn] in very good condition.

aard•vark ['ɑːdvɑːk] *n.* ant-eating animal of South America.

AB ['eɪ'biː] *n.* able seaman.

a•back [ə'bæk] *adv.* **taken aback** = surprised, usu. unpleasantly.

ab•a•cus ['æbəkəs] *n.* (*pl.* **-ses, -ci**) device for counting, made of small beads which slide along rods in a frame.

a•baft [ə'bɑːft] *adv.* (*of ships*) at/toward the stern; aft.

ab•a•lo•ne [æbə'ləʊnɪ] *n.* type of Pacific shellfish.

a•ban•don [ə'bændən] *v.* (a) to leave. (b) to give up. **a•ban•don•ment,** *n.* giving up.

a•base [ə'beɪs] *v.* (a) (*formal*) to lower the rank, esteem or position of (s.o.); **to a. oneself** = to grovel/to apologize. (b) to humiliate.

a•bashed [ə'bæʃt] *adj.* ashamed.

a•bate [ə'beɪt] *v.* to become less strong. **a•bate•ment,** *n.* reduction (in amount, force, etc.); **a. in taxes** = reduction in taxes.

ab•at•toir ['æbətwɑː] *n.* slaughterhouse/place where animals are killed for meat.

ab•bess ['æbes] *n.* (*pl.* **-es**) woman in charge of nuns in a convent.

ab•bey ['æbɪ] *n.* Christian religious establishment with living quarters, etc., grouped around a church.

ab•bot ['æbət] *n.* man in charge of monks in an abbey.

ab•bre•vi•ate [ə'briːvɪeɪt] *v.* to shorten (words, names, etc.). **ab•bre•vi•a•tion**

[əbriːvɪ'eɪʃn] *n.* group of letters representing a larger word.

ABC [eɪbiː'siː] *n.* the alphabet.

ab•di•cate ['æbdɪkeɪt] *v.* to give up the throne. **ab•di•ca•tion** [æbdɪ'keɪʃn] *n.* giving up (of a throne).

ab•do•men ['æbdəmen] *n.* lower part of the body, containing the stomach, bowels, etc. **ab•dom•i•nal** [æb'dɒmɪnl] *adj.* referring to the abdomen.

ab•duct [æb'dʌkt] *v.* to remove or carry off (s.o.) by force. **ab•duc•tion,** *n.* removal (of s.o.) by force. **ab•duc•tor,** *n.* person who abducts s.o.

a•beam [ə'biːm] *adv.* (*of ships*) side by side.

ab•er•ra•tion [æbə'reɪʃn] *n.* (a) change from what is usual. (b) sudden attack of forgetfulness; **mental a.** = slight confusion. **ab•er•rant** [ə'berənt] *adj.* abnormal/not usual.

a•bet [ə'bet] *v.* (**abetted**) to aid and a. s.o. = to be s.o.'s accomplice in a crime. **a•bet•tor,** *n.* person who abets s.o.

a•bey•ance [ə'beɪəns] *n.* suspension (of a law, etc.); **in a.** = not being applied.

ab•hor [əb'hɔː] *v.* to feel hatred/horror for (sth). **ab•hor•rent** [əb'hɒrənt] *adj.* disgusting/which makes you shudder. **ab•hor•rence,** *n.* horror/great dislike.

a•bide [ə'baɪd] *v.* (a) to stick to/to follow; **to a. by a promise** = to stand by what you have promised. (b) (*only with negative*) to like; **I can't a. the smell of garlic. a•bid•ing,** *adj.* which stays/remains.

a•bil•i•ty [ə'bɪlɪtɪ] *n.* power to do sth; capability; **to the best of my a.** = as best I can.

ab in•i•ti•o [æbɪ'nɪʃɪəʊ] *adj.* (course) which starts from the beginning.

ab•ject ['æbdʒekt] *adj.* (a) very miserable. (b) cowardly/extremely humble. **ab•ject•ly,** *adv.* in a miserable/humble way.

ab•jure [æb'dʒʊə] *v.* to swear not to do sth.

æ back, ɑː farm, ɒ top, aɪ pipe, aʊ how, aɪə fire, aʊə flower, ɔː bought, ɔɪ toy, e fed, eəhair, eɪ take, ə afraid, əʊ boat, əʊə lower, ɜː word, iː heap, ɪ hit, ɪə hear, uː school, ʊ book, ʌ but, b back, d dog, ð then, dʒ just, f fog, g go, h hand, j yes, k catch, l last, m mix, n nut, ŋ sing, p penny, r round, s some, ʃ short, t too, tʃ chop, θ thing, v voice, w was, z zoo, ʒ treasure

ab•la•tion [æ'bleɪʃn] *n.* operation to remove an organ.

a•blaze [ə'bleɪz] *adv.* in flames.

a•ble ['eɪbl] *adj.* having the ability (to do sth). **a. seaman** = experienced seaman. **a•ble•ism**, *n.* bias against disabled people. **a•bly** ['eɪblɪ] *adv.* very efficiently.

ab•lu•tions [ə'bluːʃənz] *n. pl.* (*formal*) washing (face/hands, etc.).

ab•nor•mal [æb'nɔːml] *adj.* not normal. **ab•nor•mal•ly**, *adv.* not normally/unusually. **ab•nor•mal•i•ty** [æbnɔː'mælɪtɪ] *n.* (*pl.* **abnormalities**) being abnormal; unusualness/peculiarity.

a•board [ə'bɔːd] *adv. & prep.* on/in (a ship/aircraft/train/bus).

a•bode [ə'bəʊd] *n.* (*formal*) home; **of no fixed a.** = with no permanent address; **right of a.** = the right to live in a country.

a•bol•ish [ə'bɒlɪʃ] *v.* to cancel/to remove. **ab•o•li•tion** [æbə'lɪʃn] *n.* act of abolishing. **ab•o•li•tion•ist**, *n.* person who is in favor of abolition (esp. of slavery/capital punishment).

a•bom•i•na•ble [ə'bɒmɪnəbl] *adj.* horrible/disgusting; **the a. snowman** = yeti. **a•bom•i•na•bly**, *adv.* in a horrible way. **a•bom•i•nate** [ə'bɒmɪneɪt] *v.* to dislike intensely. **a•bom•i•na•tion** [əbɒmɪ'neɪʃn] *n.* unpleasant/disgusting thing.

ab•o•rig•i•ne [æbə'rɪdʒɪnɪ] *n.* member of a race which was living in a country before the country was settled: original inhabitant. **ab•o•rig•i•nal.** 1. *adj.* referring to aborigines. 2. *n.* aborigine.

a•bor•tion [ə'bɔːʃn] *n.* (deliberate) termination of a pregnancy. **a•bort**, *v.* (a) to cause an abortion to (s.o.). (b) to stop (a project) taking place. **a•bor•tion•ist**, *n.* person who carries out an illegal abortion. **a•bor•tive**, *adj.* (plan) which fails.

ABO sys•tem [eɪbiː'əʊ] *n.* system of classifying blood by the letters A, B and O.

a•bound [ə'baʊnd] *v.* (**in**) to be full of.

a•bout [ə'baʊt] *adv. & prep.* (a) in various places; **clothes lying a. on the floor; there's a lot of flu a.** (b) concerning; **tell me a. your book; what do you want to speak to me a.? how a. a cup of tea?** = would you like a cup of tea? (c) (*in the army*) round; **a. turn** = facing the opposite direction. (d) approximately; **a. three feet deep; at a. four o'clock.** (e) on the point (of doing sth); **just a. to go out.** (f) in the process of doing sth; **while you're a. it, can you mail this letter?**

a•bove [ə'bʌv] *adv. & prep.* (a) higher than; **a. the clouds; the temperature was a. 40°.** (b) louder than; **I can't hear you a. the noise.** (c) **they're living a. their means** = more extravagantly than they can afford. (d) earlier on (in a book); higher up (on a page). **a•bove•board**, *adj.* open/honest; not corrupt.

ab•ra•ca•dab•ra [æbrəkə'dæbrə] *n.* traditional magic spell.

a•brade [æ'breɪd] *v.* to scrape off (a surface).

a•bra•sion [ə'breɪʒn] *n.* scraping off (of the skin). **a•bra•sive** [ə'breɪzɪv] 1. *adj.* (a) grinding (substance). (b) sharp/rude (manner, comment). 2. *n.* rough substance for smoothing a surface.

a•breast [ə'brest] *adv.* in a row; level (with sth); **walking three a.** = three people side by side; **to keep a. of/with sth** = to keep up with the latest developments.

a•bridged [ə'brɪdʒd] *adj.* shortened. **a•bridg•ment**, *n.* shortened version (of a long book).

a•broad [ə'brɔːd] *adv.* in or to another country.

ab•ro•gate ['æbrəgeɪt] *v.* (*formal*) to end (a law, a treaty). **ab•ro•ga•tion** [æbrə'geɪʃn] *n.* ending (of a treaty).

ab•rupt [ə'brʌpt] *adj.* sudden (departure); brusque (way of speaking). **ab•rupt•ly**, *adv.* suddenly; brusquely. **ab•rupt•ness**, *n.* suddenness; brusqueness.

ab•scess ['æbses] *n.* (*pl.* **-es**) collection of pus in the body.

ab•scond [æb'skɒnd] *v.* to run away.

ab•seil ['æbseɪl] *v.* to come down a cliff or wall by means of a fixed rope coiled around one's body.

ab•sence ['æbsəns] *n.* (a) not being there; **she was sentenced in her a.** (b) lack; **in the a. of a map we had to ask our way. ab•sent** 1. *adj.* ['æbsənt] not present. 2. *v.* [æb'sent] **to a. oneself** = to stay away (from class/a meeting) deliberately. **ab•sen•tee** [æbsən'tiː] *n.* person who is absent; **a. landlord** = landlord/owner who does not live near the property owned and takes no interest in it. **ab•sen•tee•ism**, *n.* deliberately staying away from work. **ab•sent-mind•ed**, *adj.* forgetful. **ab•sent-mind•ed•ly**, *adv.* forgetfully. **ab•sent-mind•ed•ness**, *n.* being often forgetful.

ab•so•lute ['æbsəluːt] *adj.* complete; **the president assumed a. power** = became a dictator. **ab•so•lute•ly**, *adv.* totally. **ab•so•lut•ism**, *n.* political theory that governments should have absolute power.

ab•so•lu•tion [æbsə'luːʃn] *n.* blessing by a priest to forgive sin.

ab•solve [əb'zɒlv] *v.* to remove blame for a sin from (s.o.); to release (s.o.) from a promise.

ab•sorb [əb'zɔ:b] v. (a) to soak up (liquid); to deaden (a shock); to accept (a stranger/outside body) into a group. (b) absorbed in = completely busy with; it's an absorbing story = it holds your attention. **ab•sorb•ent**, adj. which absorbs. **ab•sorb•er**, n. shock a. = part of a car which softens the shock of a bump to the passengers. **ab•sorp•tion** [əb'zɔːpʃn] n. act of absorbing.

ab•stain [əb'stein] v. (from) not to do sth deliberately; **Mr. Smith abstained** = refused to vote. **ab•stain•er**, n. person who does not drink alcohol.

ab•ste•mi•ous [əb'sti:miəs] adj. not drinking (or eating) too much. **ab•ste•mi•ous•ness**, n. not drinking (or eating) too much.

ab•sten•tion [əb'stenʃn] n. refusal to do sth; **several abstentions** = several people did not vote.

ab•sti•nence ['æbstinəns] n. not drinking/eating to excess; **total a.** = not drinking any alcohol.

ab•stract 1. adj ['æbstrækt] not concrete; (painting) which does not reproduce sth recognizable. 2. n. ['æbstrækt] (a) quality of not being concrete; **in the a.** = without mentioning specific cases. (b) abstract picture. (c) summary. 3. v. [əb'strækt] (a) to remove; to steal. (b) to summarize. **ab•stract•ed**, adj vague/dreamy; thoughtful. **ab•strac•tion**, n. (a) removing; stealing. (b) vague idea.

ab•struse [əb'stru:s] adj. very difficult to understand.

ab•surd [əb'sɜːd] adj. very odd; ridiculous. **ab•surd•i•ty**, n. fact of being absurd. **ab•surd•ly**, adv. ridiculously.

a•bun•dant [ə'bʌndənt] adj. in large quantities. **a•bun•dance**, n. large quantity. **a•bun•dant•ly**, adv. plentifully; very much.

a•buse 1. n. [ə'bju:s] (a) wrong use/bad use. (b) evil. (c) rude words/insults; **term of a.** = rude/insulting word. (d) very bad treatment (often sexual, of a person, such as a child). 2. v. [ə'bju:z] (a) to put to wrong use; **he abused my confidence** = he took advantage of my confidence. (b) to insult. (c) to mistreat; to make bad use of. **a•bu•sive** [ə'bju:siv] adj. insulting.

a•but [ə'bʌt] v. (abutted) (formal) to a. on a **property** = to be next to a property.

a•bys•mal [ə'bizml] adj. extremely large; **the weather was a.** = very bad. **a•bys•mal•ly**, adv. extremely badly.

a•byss [ə'bis] n. (pl. -es) very deep hole; very deep part of the sea.

Ac symbol for actinium.

AC abbrev. for alternating current.

A/C = account.

a•ca•cia [ə'keiʃə] n. common tropical tree which produces gum.

ac•a•dem•ic [ækə'demik] 1. adj. (a) abstract (idea, question). (b) relating to study at a school, college, or university; **a. staff** = teaching staff at school, college, or university. 2. student/teacher at a college or university. **ac•a•dem•i•cal•ly**, adv. referring to academic matters/to teaching at a school, college, or university. **ac•a•de•mi•cian** [ækædə'miʃn] n. member of an academy. **a•cad•e•my** [ə'kædəmi] n. (a) school giving specialized instruction or training. **military a.** = training school for officers in the armed forces. **a. of music** = school for musicians. (b) society for the promotion of literature/art/science.

ac•cede [ək'si:d] v. (a) **to a. to the throne** = to become king or queen. (b) (formal) to agree (to).

ac•cel•er•ate [æk'seləreit] v. (to cause to) go faster. **ac•cel•er•a•tion** [ækselə'reiʃn] n. going faster. **ac•cel•er•a•tor** [æk'seləreitə] n. pedal (in a car) which allows more fuel into the engine, and increases speed.

ac•cent ['æksənt] n. (a) way of pronouncing; **an Irish a.** (b) small sign over a letter to show that it is pronounced differently. (c) stress. **ac•cen•tor**, n. small brown singing bird. **ac•cen•tu•ate** [ək'sentjueit] v. to stress/to make more obvious. **ac•cen•tu•a•tion** [əksentju'eiʃn] n. stressing.

ac•cept [ək'sept] v. (a) to take (thing which is offered). (b) to agree (to do sth). (c) **accepted custom** = sth which is usually done. **ac•cept•a•bil•i•ty**, n. being acceptable. **ac•cept•a•ble**, adj. which you can easily accept. **ac•cept•ance**, n. (a) receiving (of thing offered). (b) agreement (to do sth).

ac•cess ['ækses] 1. n. way of getting to person/place; **a. road** = road leading off a main road to buildings; **to have easy a. to** = to be able to get sth easily. 2. v. to call up information which is stored in a computer. **ac•ces•si•ble** [ək'sesibl] adj. able to be reached easily. **ac•ces•si•bil•i•ty** [əksesi'biliti] n. being accessible.

ac•ces•sion [ək'seʃn] n. **a. (to the throne)** = becoming king or queen. **ac•ces•sion,** *n.* sth. added; **a. to a library** = new books added to a library.

ac•ces•so•ry [ək'sesərɪ] 1. *n.* (a) piece of minor equipment which is added to main items; **a. bag** = bag for carrying extra items to attach to a camera. (b) nonessential items of clothing (handbag, gloves, hat, etc.). (c) **charged with being an a. to the crime** = with helping to commit the crime. 2. *adj.* nonessential.

ac•ci•dent ['æksɪdənt] *n.* thing which happens by chance, often with unfortunate results; **I discovered the documents by a.; fatal a.** = accident where s.o. is killed. **ac•ci•den•tal** [æksɪ'dentl] 1. *adj.* by accident; not on purpose. 2. *n.* (*in music*) additional sharp, flat or natural. **ac•ci•den•tal•ly,** *adv.* by accident; not on purpose. **ac•ci•dent-prone,** *adj.* (of a person) likely to have a lot of accidents.

ac•claim [ə'kleɪm] 1. *n.* great shout of praise. 2. *v.* to greet with a shout of praise. **ac•cla•ma•tion** [æklə'meɪʃn] *n.* act of acclaiming.

ac•cli•mate [ə'klaɪmət] *v.* to make (sth/s.o.) used to a new climate or a new way of living. **ac•cli•ma•tion** [əklaɪ'meɪʃn] *n.* becoming acclimated.

ac•co•lade ['ækʊleɪd] *n.* sign of praise or approval.

ac•com•mo•date [ə'kɒmədeɪt] *v.* (a) to adapt; to supply (s.o.) with sth. (b) to provide lodging for (s.o.). **ac•com•mo•dat•ing,** *adj.* helpful; giving satisfaction; always ready to help. **ac•com•mo•da•tion** [əkɒmə'deɪʃn] *n.* (a) place to live/to sleep; **all the a. in the town have been booked.** (b) agreement/compromise. (c) adjustment.

ac•com•pa•ny [ə'kʌmpnɪ] *v.* (a) to go with; **sauce to a. the fish** = to be served with the fish. (b) to play (usu. the piano) while s.o. sings or plays another instrument. **ac•com•pa•ni•ment,** *n.* (a) thing which accompanies. (b) music played to accompany a soloist. **ac•com•pa•nist,** *n.* person who accompanies a soloist.

ac•com•plice [ə'kʌmplɪs] *n.* person who helps another person commit a crime.

ac•com•plish [ə'kʌmplɪʃ] *v.* to finish/to carry out (a plan, etc.). **ac•com•plished,** *adj.* gifted/talented; skilled. **ac•com•plish•ment,** *n.* (a) finishing (of a task). (b) **accomplishments** = talents.

ac•cord [ə'kɔːd] *n.* (a) agreement; **with one a.** = all together/in agreement. (b) **of your own a.** = spontaneously/with no prompting. **ac•cord•ance,** *n.* agreement; **in a. with your instructions** = following your instructions. **ac•cord•ing•ly,** *adv.* in accordance; correspondingly. **ac•cord•ing to,** *adv.* (a) as s.o. says or writes; as stated by s.o. (b) by/in relation to; **separate the children into groups a. to their ages.**

ac•cor•di•on [ə'kɔːdɪən] *n.* **(piano) a.** = musical instrument with a bellows and a keyboard. **ac•cor•di•on•ist,** *n.* person who plays an accordion.

ac•cost [ə'kɒst] *v.* to go/to come up to (s.o.) and speak to him/her.

ac•count [ə'kaʊnt] 1. *n.* (a) story/description; **by all accounts** = according to what everyone said. (b) statement of money; **bank a.** = money deposited in a bank; **checking a.** = account from which you can draw money without giving notice; **savings a.** = account where you leave money for some time and on which interest is paid; **to pay money on a.** = to pay part of the total bill in advance; **expense a.** = money which an employee of a business is allowed to spend on entertainment and personal expenses which are paid for by the business. (c) statement or record showing the financial position of a business. (d) **he turned the accident to a.** = he was able to profit from the accident. (e) **he was called to a.** = he was asked to explain; **she gave a good a. of herself** = she came out of the game/examination, etc., very well. (f) **to take sth into a.** = to make allowances for sth. (g) **on a. of** = because of; **I was worried on her a.** = I was afraid sth might happen to her; **on no a.** = not under any circumstances. 2. *v.* **to a. for sth** = to explain. **ac•count•a•bil•i•ty** [əkaʊntə'bɪlɪtɪ] *n.* being accountable **(for** sth). **ac•count•a•ble,** *adj.* responsible. **ac•count•an•cy,** *n.* principles/profession of being an accountant. **ac•count•ant,** *n.* person who deals with the accounts (of a business). **ac•count•ing,** *n.* accountancy.

ac•cou•ter•ments [ə'kuːtrəmənts] *n. pl.* (usu. bulky or complicated) equipment which is carried.

ac•cred•it [ə'kredɪt] *v.* to authorize.

ac•cre•tion [ə'kriːʃn] *n.* increase in size by gradual additions.

ac•crue [ə'kruː] *v.* to increase by addition. **ac•cru•al,** *n.* increase made by addition.

acct. *abbrev. for* account.

ac•cu•mu•late [ə'kjuːmjʊleɪt] *v.* to pile up. **ac•cu•mu•la•tion** [əkjuːmjʊ'leɪʃn] *n.* act of accumulating; pile/heap. **ac•cu•mu•la•tor** [ə'kjuːmjʊleɪtə] *n.* a person or thing which accumulates.

ac•cu•rate ['ækjʊrət] *adj.* completely correct. **ac•cu•ra•cy,** *n.* being accurate; complete correctness. **ac•cu•rate•ly,** *adv.* completely correctly.

ac•cuse [ə'kju:z] v. to say that s.o. has done sth wrong; **the police accused him of stealing the car. ac•cu•sa•tion** [ækju'zeɪʃn] n. saying that s.o. has done sth wrong. **ac•cu•sa•tive** [ə'kju:zətɪv] adj. & n. (in grammar) (case) which shows the object of a verb. **ac•cused,** n. person who has been accused of a crime. **ac•cus•er,** n. person who accuses s.o. **ac•cus•ing,** adj. in an a. tone = as if accusing. **ac•cus•ing•ly,** adv. as if accusing.

ac•cus•tom [ə'kʌstəm] v. to make (s.o.) used (to sth).

ace [eɪs] n. (a) playing card which shows only one spot; **the a. of diamonds.** (b) person who is very brilliant at doing sth; **an a. pilot.** (c) (in tennis) shot which your opponent cannot return.

ac•er•bate ['æsəbeɪt] v. to make worse.

a•cer•bi•ty [ə'sɜ:bɪtɪ] n. (formal) sharpness (of flavor/character).

ac•e•tate ['æsɪteɪt] n. type of synthetic fiber.

a•ce•tic [ə'si:tɪk] adj. referring to vinegar.

ac•e•tone ['æsɪtəʊn] n. colorless liquid, used to dissolve solids.

a•cet•y•lene [ə'setɪli:n] n. gas which burns with a very bright light.

ache [eɪk] 1. n. pain; (see **toothache, headache,** etc.). 2. v. to hurt. **ach•ing,** adj. which hurts.

a•chieve [ə'tʃi:v] v. to succeed in doing (sth); to reach (a goal). **a•chieve•ment,** n. what you achieve; successful undertaking/exploit.

A•chil•les' heel [ə'kɪli:z'hi:l] n. weak spot. **A•chil•les' tendon,** n. tendon at the back of the ankle.

ach•ro•mat•ic [ækrəʊ'mætɪk] adj. without color.

ac•id ['æsɪd] 1. n. usually liquid chemical substance which contains hydrogen, corrodes some metals, and turns litmus paper red; **the a. test** = test which will show the true value of s.o. or sth. 2. adj. bitter/unpleasant. **a•cid•i•fy,** v. to make substances acid. **a•cid•i•ty** [ə'sɪdɪtɪ] n. (a) acid contents. (b) bitterness. **ac•id rain,** n. rain with a high level of acidity, caused by pollution.

ac•knowl•edge [ək'nɒlɪdʒ] v. (a) to admit (that sth is true). (b) to reply to say you have received (a letter). **ac•knowl•edg•ment,** n. admission (that sth is true); reply stating that you have received sth; **my letter has not had any a.** = no one has replied to it; (in a book) **ac-**

knowledgments = the list of people the author wants to thank for help.

ac•me ['ækmɪ] n. highest point.

ac•ne ['æknɪ] n. skin disease, with spots on the face/neck, etc.

ac•o•lyte ['ækəlaɪt] n. person who helps a priest during religious ceremonies.

ac•o•nite ['ækənaɪt] n. small spring flower which is poisonous.

a•corn ['eɪkɔ:n] n. fruit of an oak tree.

a•cous•tic [ə'ku:stɪk] 1. adj. referring to sound; **a. coupler** = device for linking a computer to a telephone handset, allowing data to be transmitted; **a. guitar** = ordinary guitar (as opposed to an electric guitar). 2. n. **acoustics** = (i) study of sound; (ii) ability to carry sound without distortion.

ac•quaint [ə'kweɪnt] v. (a) to inform. (b) **to be acquainted with** = to know. **ac•quaint•ance,** n. (a) knowing; **to make the a. of** = to get to know. (b) person you know (slightly).

ac•qui•esce [ækwɪ'es] v. (formal) to agree. **ac•qui•es•cence,** n. agreement. **ac•qui•es•cent,** adj. in agreement.

ac•quire [ə'kwaɪə] v. to get into your possession; **acquired immune deficiency syndrome (AIDS)** = condition, caused by the human immunodeficiency virus (HIV), in which the body's immune system breaks down, making the patient susceptible to any infection. **ac•qui•si•tion** [ækwɪ'zɪʃn] n. (a) act of acquiring. (b) thing you have acquired. **ac•quis•i•tive** [ə'kwɪzɪtɪv] adj. always ready to acquire things. **ac•quis•i•tive•ness,** n. love of acquiring things.

ac•quit [ə'kwɪt] v. (**acquitted**) (a) to decide that someone is innocent. (b) **he acquitted himself well** = he did well. **ac•quit•tal,** n. decision that a person is innocent.

a•cre ['eɪkə] n. unit for measuring the area of land (43,560 square feet or 4047 square meters). **a•cre•age** ['eɪkrɪdʒ] n. area in acres.

ac•rid ['ækrɪd] adj. bitter/pungent (smell).

ac•ri•mo•ni•ous [ækrɪ'məʊnɪəs] adj. bitter (argument). **ac•ri•mo•ny** ['ækrɪmənɪ] n. bitterness (of argument).

ac•ro•bat ['ækrəbæt] n. person who does spectacular physical exercises. **ac•ro•bat•ic** [ækrə'bætɪk] adj. referring to spectacular exercises. **ac•ro•bat•ics,** n. pl. spectacular physical exercises.

æ back, ɑ: farm, ɒ: top, aɪ pipe, aʊ how, aɪe fire, aʊə flower, ɔ: bought, ɔɪ toy, e fed, eəhair, eɪ take, ə afraid, əʊ boat, əʊə lower, ɜ: word, i: heap, ɪ hit, ɪə hear, u: school, ʊ book, ʌ but, b back, d dog, ð then, dʒ just, f fog, g go, h hand, j yes, k catch, l last, m mix, n nut, ŋ sing, p penny, r round, s some, ʃ short, t too, tʃ chop, θ thing, v voice, w was, z zoo, ʒ treasure

ac•ro•nym ['ækrənɪm] n. word (like NATO) formed from the initials of other words.

a•crop•o•lis [æ'krɒpəlɪs] n. castle protecting a town in ancient Greece.

a•cross [ə'krɒs] adv. & prep. (a) from one side to the other; **it is twelve inches a.** (b) on the other side; **a. the street.** (c) **I came/ran a. this** = I found it. **across-the-board,** adj. which applies to everything or everyone.

a•cros•tic [ə'krɒstɪk] n. poem/puzzle in which the first letters of each line form a word.

a•cryl•ic [ə'krɪlɪk] adj. & n. (material/paint) made from acid.

act [ækt] 1. n. (a) thing which is done; **we caught him in the a.** = as he was doing it; **a. of God** = natural disaster which cannot be prevented. (b) large section of a play. 2. v. (a) to play (a part in a play). (b) to do sth; **to a. on behalf of** = represent; **to a. as** = do the work of. (c) to behave. (d) to take effect/to work. **act•ing.** 1. adj. **a. president** = person who is taking the place of the president. 2. n. profession of an actor. **ac•tion** ['ækʃn] n. (a) doing; **out of a.** = not working. (b) thing done. (c) **the a. of the play** = what happens in it. (d) mechanism (of a gun, watch, etc.). (e) lawsuit; **an a. for libel.** (f) warfare; **killed in a.** = on the battlefield. **ac•tion•a•ble,** adj. (sth) for which s.o. could bring a lawsuit against you. **ac•ti•vate** ['æktɪveɪt] v. to put into action. **ac•tive** ['æktɪv] adj. vigorous/agile; (volcano) which still erupts; **on a. duty** = serving full-time military duty. **ac•tive•ly,** adv. in an active way. **ac•tiv•ist,** n. person who actively supports a political policy. **ac•tiv•i•ty** [æk'tɪvɪtɪ] n. (a) movement/being active. (b) occupation. **ac•tor, actress** ['æktə, 'æktrəs] n. (pl. -es) person who acts in the theater/motion pictures/on television.

ac•tin•i•um [æk'tɪnɪəm] n. (element: Ac) radioactive metal.

ac•tu•al ['æktjuəl] adj. real; **in a. fact** = really. **ac•tu•al•i•ty** [æktju'ælɪtɪ] n. reality. **ac•tu•al•ly,** adv. really.

ac•tu•ary ['æktjuərɪ] n. person who calculates insurance rates. **ac•tu•ar•i•al** [æktju'eərɪəl] adj. referring to insurance rates.

ac•tu•ate ['æktjueɪt] v. to set in motion/to start off.

a•cu•i•ty [ə'kju:ɪtɪ] n. sharpness (of sight).

a•cu•men ['ækju:mən] n. ability to make shrewd decisions.

ac•u•punc•ture ['ækjupʌŋktʃə] n. way of healing and curing by placing the tips of needles in the skin. **ac•u•punc•tur•ist,** n. doctor who practices acupuncture.

a•cute [ə'kju:t] adj. (a) very sharp (angle). (b) sudden serious (illness/pain). (c) perceptive.

a•cute•ly, adv. very sharply (aware). **a•cute•ness,** n. sharpness (of pain); seriousness (of illness); clearness (of hearing).

ad [æd] n. inf. advertisement.

A.D. ['eɪ'di:] abbreviation for Anno Domini (Latin for in the year of our Lord) (used to show dates after the birth of Christ) **A.D. 923.**

ad•age ['ædɪdʒ] n. wise old saying.

a•da•gio [ə'dɑ:dʒɪəu] n. slow piece of music.

Ad•am ['ædəm] n. inf. **I don't know him from A.** = I have no idea who he is; **A.'s apple** = lump in the front of a person's neck.

ad•a•mant ['ædəmənt] adj. fixed in your opinion/intentions.

a•dapt [ə'dæpt] v. to change (sth) so that it fits; to make (sth) more suitable. **a•dapt•a•bil•i•ty** [ədæptə'brlrtɪ] n. ease of adapting yourself to new circumstances. **a•dapt•a•ble,** adj. able to (be) adapt(ed) easily. **ad•ap•ta•tion** [ædæp'teɪʃn] n. written work which is adapted from another. **a•dapt•er, adaptor,** n. electric plug which allows several plugs to be fitted to the same socket; small disk which allows a record with a large central hole to be fitted on a turntable.

add [æd] v. (a) to join (sth to sth else). (b) to say/to write sth more. (c) to make a total. **ad•den•dum** [ə'dendəm] n. (pl. addenda) piece added, as at the end of a book. **add up,** v. to make a total of (figures); **these figures don't add up** = the total given is incorrect.

ADD ['eɪ'di:'di:] abbrev. for attention deficit disorder.

ad•der ['ædə] n. viper.

ad•dict ['ædɪkt] n. person who cannot stop from doing sth (usu. which is harmful); **drug a.** = person who cannot stop taking a drug; **TV a.** = person who is always watching television. **ad•dict•ed** [ə'dɪktɪd] adj. (to) (person) who cannot stop (taking a drug). **ad•dic•tion** [ə'dɪkʃn] n. **drug a.** = inability to stop taking a drug. **ad•dic•tive,** adj. which causes addiction.

ad•di•tion [ə'dɪʃn] n. (a) act of adding; **in a.** = added to this; also. (b) thing added. **ad•di•tion•al,** adj. further. **ad•di•tive** ['ædɪtɪv] n. substance, usu. chemical, which is added.

ad•dled ['ædld] adj. (a) confused. (b) rotten (egg).

ad•dress [ə'dres] 1. n. (pl. -es) (a) number of house, name of street, town, county, etc., where a person lives/where an office is situated; **a. book** = book containing a list of addresses. (b) formal speech. 2. v. (a) to write the name and address of the person/the business to whom sth is being sent. (b) to speak to (s.o.). (c) (in golf) to aim at the ball.

ad•dress•ee [ædre'siː] *n.* person to whom a letter is addressed.

ad•duce [ə'djuːs] *v.* (*formal*) to bring added proof (of sth).

ad•e•noids ['ædənɔɪdz] *n. pl.* small growths in the back of the throat. **ad•e•noi•dal** [ædɪ'nɔɪdl] *adj.* referring to the adenoids.

a•dept ['ædept] *adj. & n.* (person who is) clever (at doing sth).

ad•e•quate ['ædɪkwət] *adj.* (large) enough. **ad•e•quate•ly**, *adv.* enough.

ad•here [əd'hɪə] *v.* to stick (to). **ad•her•ence**, *n.* sticking/attachment. **ad•her•ent**, *n.* person who belongs to (a society, etc.).

ad•he•sion [əd'hiːʒn] *n.* attachment/sticking; ability to stick. **ad•he•sive** [əd'hiːzɪv] 1. *adj.* which sticks; **a. tape** = tape coated on one side with a substance which sticks. 2. *n.* glue.

ad hoc [æd'hɒk] *adj.* which applies to a particular case.

a•dieu [ə'djuː] *n.* (*poetic*) goodbye.

ad in•fi•ni•tum [ædɪnfɪ'naɪtəm] *adv.* for ever.

ad•i•pose ['ædɪpəʊs] *adj.* fatty (tissue).

ad•ja•cent [ə'dʒeɪsənt] *adj.* (to) next to/touching/side by side.

ad•jec•tive ['ædʒəktɪv] *n.* word used to describe a noun. **ad•jec•ti•val** [ædʒek'taɪvl] *adj.* used like an adjective. **ad•jec•ti•val•ly**, *adv.* like an adjective.

ad•join [ə'dʒɔɪn] *v.* to be next to sth/to touch sth.

ad•journ [ə'dʒɜːn] *v.* to put off (a meeting) to a later date; **let's a. to the bar** = let's stop talking here and continue in the bar. **ad•journ•ment**, *n.* putting off (a meeting) to a later date.

ad•ju•di•cate [ə'dʒuːdɪkeɪt] *v.* to give a decision (in a dispute); to be the judge (in a competition). **ad•ju•di•ca•tion** [ədʒuːdɪ'keɪʃn] *n.* decision (in a dispute); judging (of a competition). **ad•ju•di•ca•tor** [ə'dʒuːdɪkeɪtə] *n.* judge.

ad•junct ['ædʒʌŋkt] *n.* thing additional (to sth).

ad•just [ə'dʒʌst] *v.* to put right by making a slight change. **ad•just•a•ble**, *adj.* which can be changed slightly. **ad•just•er, adjustor** *n.* person who calculates the extent of losses in an insurance claim. **ad•just•ment**, *n.* slight change made (to a mechanism).

ad•ju•tant ['ædʒətənt] *n.* military officer who assists in administration.

ad-lib ['æd'lɪb] *v.* (**ad-libbed**) *inf.* to speak without a script.

ad•min•is•ter [əd'mɪnɪstə] *v.* to govern/to rule (a country/an office); to run (a business/an estate); **to a. an oath to s.o.** = to make s.o. swear an oath. **ad•min•is•tra•tion** [ədmɪnɪ'streɪʃn] *n.* ruling (of a country); the government. **ad•min•is•tra•tive**, *adj.* which administers; referring to administration. **ad•min•is•tra•tor**, *n.* person who administers.

ad•mi•ra•ble ['ædmərəbl] *adj. see* **admire**.

ad•mi•ral ['ædmərəl] *n.* highest-ranking officer in the navy; **red a.** = type of red and black butterfly. **ad•mi•ral•ty**, *n.* court or laws that deal with maritime affairs. **the Admiralty**, *n.* British government department dealing with the navy.

ad•mire [əd'maɪə] *v.* to look at (sth) with pleasure. **ad•mi•ra•ble** ['ædmərəbl] *adj.* remarkable; excellent. **ad•mi•ra•bly**, *adv.* remarkably; excellently. **ad•mi•ra•tion** [ædmə'reɪʃn] *n.* feeling of pride/pleasure. **ad•mir•er** [əd'maɪərə] *n.* person who admires. **ad•mir•ing**, *adj.* (look) showing admiration. **ad•mir•ing•ly**, *adv.* in an admiring way.

ad•mis•sion [əd'mɪʃn] *n.* (a) being allowed to enter; **no a.** = no one can enter. (b) saying that sth is true. **ad•mis•si•ble** [əd'mɪsɪbl] *adj.* (evidence) that can be admitted.

ad•mit [əd'mɪt] *v.* (**admitted**) (a) to allow to enter. (b) to say that sth is true. (c) to accept (evidence/idea, etc.). **ad•mit•tance**, *n.* entrance. **ad•mit•ted•ly**, *adv.* according to general opinion.

ad•mix•ture [æd'mɪkstʃə] *n.* thing which is added to make a mixture.

ad•mon•ish [əd'mɒnɪʃ] *v.* to scold s.o./to tell s.o. off. **ad•mo•ni•tion** [ædmə'nɪʃn] *n.* scolding.

ad nau•se•am [æd'nɔːzɪəm] *adv.* until one is sick of it.

a•do [ə'duː] *n.* **without any more a.** = without any more fuss.

a•do•be [ə'dəʊbɪ] *n.* bricks made from clay dried in the sun.

ad•o•les•cence [ædə'lesns] *n.* period between childhood and being an adult. **ad•o•les•cent**, *adj. & n.* (referring to) a young person between child and adult.

æ back, aː farm, ɒ top, aɪ pipe, aʊ how, aɪə fire, aʊə flower, ɔ bought, ɔɪ toy, e fed, eəhair, eɪ take, ə afraid, əʊ boat, əʊə lower, ɜː word, iː heap, ɪ hit, ɪə hear, uː school, ʊ book, ʌ but, b back, d dog, ð then, dʒ just, f fog, g go, h hand, j yes, k catch, l last, m mix, n nut, ŋ sing, p penny, r round, s some, ʃ short, t too, tʃ chop, θ thing, v voice, w was, z zoo, ʒ treasure

a•dopt [ə'dɒpt] v. (a) to take (s.o.) legally as your son or daughter. (b) to follow/to take up (a line of argument); to put on (an air). (c) to prescribe (a book) for use in class. **a•dop•tion** [ə'dɒpʃn] n. (a) legal taking of a child as your own. (b) prescribing (of a book) for use in class. **a•dop•tive**, adj. who has (been) adopted.

a•dore [ə'dɔː] v. to love very strongly. **a•dor•a•ble**, adj. pretty/lovely. **ad•o•ra•tion** [ædə'reɪʃn] n. strong love/worship. **a•dor•er**, n. person who adores.

a•dorn [ə'dɔːn] v. to cover with ornaments/to decorate. **a•dorn•ment**, n. adorning; ornament.

ad•re•nal [ə'driːnəl] adj. referring to the kidneys. **a•dren•a•line** [ə'drenəlɪn] n. secretion which is produced by a gland when s.o. is excited/afraid.

a•drift [ə'drɪft] adv. to cast a boat a. = to let a boat float without control; to cut yourself a. = to separate yourself.

a•droit [ə'drɔɪt] adj. skillful/clever (with your hands). **a•droit•ly**, adv. smartly.

ad•sorb [æd'zɔːb] v. to form a thin film on the surface of sth.

ad•u•la•tion [ædju'leɪʃn] n. wild praise/excessive flattery.

a•dult ['ædʌlt, ə'dʌlt] adj. & n. grown-up (person); fully grown (animal).

a•dul•ter•ate [ə'dʌltəreɪt] v. to water down; to add sth of inferior quality to (a substance).

a•dul•ter•er, a•dul•ter•ess [ə'dʌltərə, ə'dʌltərəs] n. person who commits adultery. **a•dul•ter•ous**, adj. referring to adultery. **a•dul•ter•y**, n. (of married person) having sexual intercourse with s.o. to whom he/she is not married.

ad va•lo•rem [ædvə'lɔːrəm] adj. (tax) calculated on the value of the thing being taxed.

ad•vance [əd'vɑːns] 1. n. (a) forward movement: **a. guard** = troops sent ahead of the main force. (b) **in a.** = early; beforehand. (c) **to make advances to** = to try to attract. (d) payment made early. 2. v. (a) to go forward. (b) to put forward; **he advanced me ten dollars** = he gave me ten dollars as an early payment. **ad•vanced**, adj. (a) (subject) which is studied after several years' initial study; **a. student** = student who has studied for several years. (b) **the season is well a.** = the season is coming to an end; **in an a. state of decay** = very decayed. **ad•vance•ment**, n. progress (of science, etc.).

ad•van•tage [əd'vɑːntɪdʒ] n. useful thing which will help you to be successful; **to take a. of** = to profit from; **to take a. of s.o.** = to use or cheat for your own benefit; **her dress shows off** her figure to a. = makes her figure look perfect. **ad•van•ta•geous** [ædvən'teɪdʒəs] adj. profitable/useful.

ad•vent ['ædvent] n. (a) coming; arrival. (b) **Advent** = church season before Christmas.

ad•ven•ti•tious [ædven'tɪʃəs] adj. (root) which develops from a plant's stem and not from another root.

ad•ven•ture [əd'ventʃə] n. new, exciting and dangerous experience. **ad•ven•tur•er**, n. person who aims to make a fortune by taking risks. **ad•ven•tur•ous**, adj. bold (person); exciting (life). **ad•ven•tur•ous•ly**, adv. boldly. **ad•ven•tur•ous•ness**, n. being adventurous.

ad•verb ['ædvɜːb] n. word used to describe a verb/an adjective/another adverb. **ad•ver•bi•al** [əd'vɜːbɪəl] adj. used as an adverb. **ad•ver•bi•al•ly**, adv. like an adverb.

ad•ver•sar•y ['ædvəsrɪ] n. person you are fighting against.

ad•verse ['ædvɜːs] adj. (a) contrary (winds). (b) bad; unfavorable (conditions). **ad•verse•ly**, adv. badly. **ad•ver•si•ty** [əd'vɜːsɪtɪ] n. difficulty.

ad•vert [æd'vɜːt] v. (formal) to refer to.

ad•ver•tise ['ædvətaɪz] v. to show that sth is for sale/to publicize sth; **she advertised for a new secretary** = put an advertisement in the paper asking people to apply for the job; **there's no need to a. the fact** = there's no need to tell everyone the secret. **ad•ver•tise•ment** [əd'vɜːtɪsmənt] n. announcement that sth is for sale/is wanted. **ad•ver•tis•er**, n. person who advertises. **ad•ver•tis•ing**, n. action of announcing the sale of sth; business of describing goods for sale; **a. agency** = company which designs and places advertisements. **ad•ver•to•ri•al** [ˌædvə'tɔːrɪəl] n. advertisement in the style of an editorial.

ad•vice [əd'vaɪs] n. (a) suggestion as to what should be done; **a piece of a.** (b) official notification.

ad•vise [əd'vaɪz] v. to suggest what should be done. **ad•vis•a•bil•i•ty**, n. being recommended. **ad•vis•a•ble**, adj. which you would recommend. **ad•vis•ed•ly**, adv. after a lot of thought; deliberately. **ad•vis•er, ad•visor**, n. person who gives advice. **ad•vi•so•ry**, adj. in an a. capacity = as an adviser.

ad•vo•ca•cy ['ædvəkəsɪ] n. pleading for; support for.

ad•vo•cate 1. n. ['ædvəkət] (a) person who pleads for a cause. (b) lawyer who pleads in certain courts. 2. ['ædvəkeɪt] v. to recommend/to plead.

adz [ædz] *n.* ax with the blade at right angles to the handle.

ae•gis ['iːdʒɪs] *n. (formal)* **under the a. of** = supported/patronized by.

ae•o•li•an [iːˈəʊlɪən] *adj.* caused by the wind.

ae•on ['iːɒn] *n. see* eon.

aer•ate [eəˈreɪt] *v.* to fill sth with air or gas.

aer•i•al ['eərɪəl] 1. *adj.* referring to the air. 2. *n.* device for sending or receiving radio or TV signals.

aer•ie ['iːrɪ] *n.* nest of an eagle; high and inaccessible house.

aer•o•bat•ics [eərəˈbætɪks] *n. pl.* trick flying (as a display).

aer•o•bic [eəˈrəʊbɪk] *adj.* needing oxygen to take place or to exist. **aer•o•bics,** *n. pl.* exercises to improve the body's use of oxygen.

aer•o•drome ['eərədrəʊm] *n. Brit* small airfield.

aer•o•dy•nam•ics [eərədaɪˈnæmɪks] *n.* science of movement of flying bodies in the air.

aer•o•nau•ti•cal [eərəˈnɔːtɪkl] *adj.* referring to aircraft flying. **aer•o•nau•tics,** *n.* science of flying aircraft.

aer•o•pha•gia [eərəʊˈfeɪdʒɪə] *n.* habit of swallowing air.

aer•o•plane ['eərəpleɪn] *n. Brit.* airplane.

aer•o•sol ['eərəsɒl] *n.* canister filled under pressure, which sends out a spray when the button is pushed.

aer•o•space ['eərəʊspeɪs] *n.* the space around the earth, including the atmosphere.

aes•thete ['iːsθiːt] *n.* person who appreciates beauty in art. **aes•thet•ic** [iːsˈθetɪk] *adj.* pleasing from an artistic point of view. **aes•thet•i•cal•ly,** *adv.* from an artistic point of view.

a•far [əˈfɑː] *adv.* **from a.** = from a long way away.

af•fa•ble ['æfəbl] *adj.* pleasant/courteous. **af•fa•bil•i•ty** [æfəˈbɪlɪtɪ] *n.* pleasantness/courtesy. **af•fa•bly,** *adv.* in a pleasant/friendly way.

af•fair [əˈfeə] *n.* (a) business; **that's my a.** = it's my business and not yours; **his affairs** = his business. (b) **he's having an a. with her** = he's her lover. (c) **the present state of affairs** = how things are at present.

af•fect [əˈfekt] *v.* (a) to pretend/to put on. (b) to touch/to change sth. **af•fec•ta•tion** [æfekˈteɪʃn] *n.* pretense. **af•fect•ed,** *adj.* pretended/put on. **af•fect•ing,** *adj.* touching/which makes you feel emotion.

af•fec•tion [əˈfekʃn] *n.* liking/love.

af•fec•tion•ate, *adj.* showing love or fondness for s.o. **af•fect•ive dis•or•der,** *n.* any mental disorder, e.g. depression, characterized by abnormal moods. **af•fec•tion•ate•ly,** *adv.* in a loving way.

af•fi•da•vit [æfɪˈdeɪvɪt] *n.* written sworn statement.

af•fil•i•ate [əˈfɪlɪeɪt] *v.* to link (a small group to a larger one). **af•fil•i•a•tion** [əfɪlɪˈeɪʃn] *n.* **political a.** = political link.

af•fin•i•ty [əˈfɪnɪtɪ] *n. (pl.* affinities) closeness/similarity of character; strong attraction. **affinity card,** *n.* card that gives a discount to members of a club, college, etc. when used to buy goods.

af•firm [əˈfɜːm] *v.* (a) to state. (b) to make a statement (in court, but not under oath). **af•fir•ma•tion** [æfəˈmeɪʃn] *n.* statement. **af•firm•a•tive** [əˈfɜːmətɪv] 1. *adj.* agreeing. 2. *n.* **the answer is in the a.** = the answer is yes. **af•firm•a•tive•ly,** *adj.* **she answered a.** = she answered yes. **affirmative ac•tion,** *n.* policy to counter discrimination, esp. in employment, by providing special opportunities for women and minorities.

af•fix [əˈfɪks] *v. (formal)* to attach.

af•flict [əˈflɪkt] *v.* to torture/to torment. **af•flic•tion** [əˈflɪkʃn] *n.* torment; cause of distress.

af•flu•ence ['æflʊəns] *n.* wealth. **af•flu•ent,** *adj.* rich; **a. society** = society where most people have enough money.

af•ford [əˈfɔːd] *v.* to have enough money to pay for (sth).

af•for•est•a•tion [æfɒrɪˈsteɪʃn] *n.* planting trees to make a forest.

af•fray [əˈfreɪ] *n. (formal)* fight between several people in public.

af•front [əˈfrʌnt] 1. *n.* offense. 2. *v.* to insult.

a•field [əˈfiːld] *adv.* **to go far a.** = to go a long way.

a•fire [əˈfaɪə] *adj.* on fire.

a•flame [əˈfleɪm] *adj. (formal)* on fire.

af•la•tox•in [æfləˈtɒksɪn] *n.* poison substance which forms on seeds and nuts.

a•float [əˈfləʊt] *adv.* floating.

a•foot [əˈfʊt] *adv.* **there's a plan a.** = a plan is being prepared; **there's sth a.** = sth is being plotted.

a•fore•said [əˈfɔːsed] *adj. (formal)* which has been mentioned before.

a•fore•thought [əˈfɔːθɔːt] *adj. (formal)* **with**

æ back, ɑː farm, ɒ top, aɪ pipe, aʊ how, aɪə fire, aʊə flower, ɔː bought, ɔɪ toy, e fed, eəhair, eɪ take, ə afraid, əʊ boat, əʊə lower, ɜː word, iː heap, ɪ hit, ɪə hear, uː school, ʊ book, ʌ but, b back, d dog, ð then, dʒ just, f fog, g go, h hand, j yes, k catch, l last, m mix, n nut, ŋ sing, p penny, r round, s some, ʃ short, t too, tʃ chop, θ thing, v voice, w was, z zoo, ʒ treasure

malice a. = having planned the crime beforehand.

a•fraid [ə'freɪd] *adj.* (a) frightened (by); **she's a. of the dark.** (b) sorry to have to say; **I'm a. she's ill.**

a•fresh [ə'freʃ] *adv.* (all over) again.

Af•ri•can ['æfrɪkən] *adj. & n.* (person) from Africa; **A. violet** = small houseplant with blue or pink flowers.

Afro- ['æfrəʊ] *prefix meaning* African/between Africa and another country.

Af•ro ['æfrəʊ] *adj. & n.* **A. (hairstyle)** = type of bouffant hairstyle.

aft [ɑːft] *adv.* at/toward the back of a ship.

af•ter ['ɑːftə] 1. *adv.* next/later. 2. *prep.* next to/following; **the police are a. you** = the police are looking for you; **what's he a.?** = what does he want? **a. you** = please go first. 3. *conj.* following the time when. **af•ter•birth**, *n.* placenta which comes out of the womb after the birth of young. **af•ter•care**, *n.* care for people after an operation, etc. **aftereffects**, *n. pl.* effects that follow on sth. **af•ter•glow**, *n.* glow in the sky after the sun has set. **af-ter-hours**, *adj.* open for business after the usual or legal time for closing. **af•ter•math**, *n.* what takes place after a catastrophe. **af•ter•noon**, *n.* part of the day between 12 noon and evening. **af•ter•shave**, *n.* **a. (lotion)** = lotion for soothing the face after shaving. **af•ter•shock**, *n.* lighter earth tremor felt after a major earthquake. **af•ter•thought**, *n.* thing which you think of later. **af•ter•ward, afterwards**, *adv.* after that; next/later.

Ag *symbol for* silver.

a•gain [ə'geɪn, ə'gen] *adv.* once more; **once a.** = another time; **a. and a.** = several times; **now and a.** = sometimes; *inf.* **come a.?** = could you repeat that?

a•gainst [ə'genst] *prep.* (a) touching. (b) contrary to (rules, etc.); **he's a. lending her any more money** = he's opposed to lending her money.

ag•a•ric [ə'gærɪk] *n.* type of fungus.

ag•ate ['ægət] *n.* semi-precious stone, usu. with bands of different colors.

age [eɪdʒ] 1. *n.* (a) number of years you have lived; **under a.** = below the legal age (to do sth). (b) period; **the Stone A.** (c) **for ages** = for a very long time. 2. *v.* to become old. **aged** 1. *adj.* [eɪdʒd] **a. 74** = 74 years old. 2. ['eɪdʒɪd] (a) *adj.* very old. (b) *n.* **the a.** = old people. **age•ism**, *n.* bias against the elderly. **age•less**, *adj.* which does not grow old or look old.

a•gen•cy ['eɪdʒənsɪ] *n.* (a) office which represents a larger company/which works on behalf of another company; **we are the a. for Ford cars** = we are the distributors for Ford cars. (b) means.

a•gen•da [ə'dʒendə] *n.* list of things to be discussed at a meeting.

a•gent ['eɪdʒənt] *n.* (a) person who represents s.o. else; **secret a.** = spy. (b) substance which has an effect on another; **a. provocateur** = person who provokes people to commit crimes, esp. crimes against the state.

ag•glom•er•a•tion [əglɒmə'reɪʃn] *n.* a jumbled mass or collection.

ag•gran•dize•ment [ə'grændɪzmənt] *n.* making larger/more powerful.

ag•gra•vate ['ægrəveɪt] *v.* to make worse. **ag•gra•va•ting**, *adj. inf.* annoying. **ag•gra•va•tion** [ægrə'veɪʃn] *n.* worsening (of a quarrel); *inf.* annoyance.

ag•gre•gate ['ægrɪgət] *n.* (a) total; **in the a.** = as a total. (b) mixture of sand, gravel, etc., with cement.

ag•gres•sion [ə'greʃn] *n.* hostility; attacking; **act of a.** = attack. **ag•gres•sive** [ə'gresɪv] *adj.* hostile; attacking. **ag•gres•sive•ly**, *adv.* violently. **ag•gres•sive•ness**, *n.* being aggressive. **ag•gres•sor**, *n.* attacker.

ag•grieved [ə'griːvd] *adj.* upset; hurt.

a•ghast [ə'gɑːst] *adj.* horrified.

ag•ile ['ædʒaɪl] *adj.* lightfooted; (animal/person) who can climb/swing/run, etc., very easily. **a•gil•i•ty** [ə'dʒɪlɪtɪ] *n.* being agile.

a•gi•o ['ædʒɪəʊ] *n.* charge made for converting money to another currency.

ag•i•tate ['ædʒɪteɪt] *v.* to stir up public opinion **(for/against** sth). **ag•i•ta•tion** [ædʒɪ'teɪʃn] *n.* (a) worry. (b) **political a.** = political unrest. **ag•i•ta•tor** ['ædʒɪteɪtə] *n.* person who stirs up political unrest.

ag•nos•tic [æg'nɒstɪk] *adj. & n.* (person) who believes that nothing can be known about God. **ag•nos•ti•cism**, *n.* belief that nothing can be known about God.

a•go [ə'gəʊ] *adv.* in the past; **three years a.**

a•gog [ə'gɒg] *adj.* **all a.** = very eager.

ag•o•nize ['ægənaɪz] *v.* to worry **(over** a decision). **a•go•nized**, *adj.* as if in pain/in agony. **a•go•niz•ing**, *adj.* (a) very sharp (pain). (b) upsetting, painful (decision).

ag•o•ny ['ægənɪ] *n.* extreme pain/extreme discomfort; **a. column** = letters and advice about personal problems in a newspaper.

ag•o•ra•pho•bi•a [ægərə'fəʊbɪə] *n.* irrational fear of public places or open spaces.

a•grar•i•an [ə'greərɪən] *adj.* dealing with the land.

a•gree [ə'griː] *v.* (a) **(with)** to say that you think the same way as (s.o.). (b) **(to)** to say yes to (a suggestion). (c) **eggs don't a. with me** = make me feel ill. **a•gree•a•ble,** *adj.* (a) pleasant. (b) in agreement; **are you a. to this?** = do you agree? **a•gree•a•bly,** *adv.* pleasantly. **a•gree•ment,** *n.* act of saying yes; **to be in a. with** = to agree with.

ag•ri•cul•ture ['ægrɪkʌltʃə] *n.* use of the land for growing crops/raising animals, etc. **ag•ri•cul•tur•al** [ægrɪ'kʌltʃərəl] *adj.* referring to agriculture. **ag•ri•busi•ness,** *n.* farming and making products for farmers, seen as a business.

a•gron•o•my [ə'grɒnəmɪ] *n.* study of agriculture.

a•ground [ə'graund] *adv.* no longer afloat; **the ship went a.**

a•head [ə'hed] *adv.* in front; in advance (of a time); **full speed a.** = go forward as fast as possible.

a•hoy [ə'hɔɪ] *inter. used by sailors in order to call a ship.*

AI *abbreviation for* (a) artificial insemination. (b) artificial intelligence.

aid [eɪd] 1. *n.* (a) help; **first a.** = help to injured/sick people; **first-a. kit** = box with bandages/medicines, etc.; **in a. of the Red Cross** = to help the Red Cross. (b) instrument to help; **a hearing a.** 2. *v.* to help.

aide [eɪd] *n.* assistant (of a president, etc.).

aide-de-camp [eɪddə'kɒn] *n.* (*pl.* **aides-**) officer who assists a senior officer.

AIDS [eɪdz] = acquired immune deficiency syndrome.

ail [eɪl] *v.* (*old*) to be ill. **ail•ing** ['eɪlɪŋ] *adj.* sick. **ail•ment** ['eɪlmənt] *n.* A minor illness.

ai•ler•on ['eɪlərɒn] *n.* flap on the edge of an aircraft's wing.

aim [eɪm] 1. *n.* target; what you are trying to do; **he took a.** = he pointed his gun at the target. 2. *v.* (a) to plan/to intend to do. (b) to point (**at**). **aim•less,** *adj.*, **aim•less•ly,** *adv.* with no particular plan.

air ['eə] 1. *n.* (a) mixture of gases which we breathe, and which surrounds the earth; **travel by a.** = in an aircraft; **in the a.** = not yet decided; **on the a.** = speaking live on TV/on radio. (b) little tune. (c) appearance/feeling. 2. *v.* to freshen (a room, clothes, etc.) by giving more air. **air base,** *n.* military airfield. **air bed,** *n.* inflatable plastic/rubber mattress. **air•borne,** *adj.* carried in the air. **air brake,** *n.* (a) movable part on an aircraft to slow it down. (b) brake (on trucks) which works by compressed air. **air-con•di•tioned,** *adj.*

cooled by an air conditioner. **air con•di•tion•er,** *n.* machine which keeps a room at the right temperature. **air con•di•tion•ing,** *n.* cooling of the air by an air conditioner. **air-cooled,** *adj.* (engine) cooled by air, not by water. **air•craft,** *n.* (*pl.* aircraft) machine which flies. **air•craft car•ri•er,** *n.* large warship which carries aircraft and has a long deck for landing and taking off. **air•crew,** *n.* the crew of an aircraft. **air•field,** *n.* small landing field for aircraft. **air force,** *n.* military air defense branch of a country's armed forces. **air•freight.** 1. *n.* shipping goods by air. 2. *v.* to ship goods by air. **air•gun,** *n.* gun which shoots pellets using compressed air. **air•i•ly,** *adv.* in an airy way. **air•less,** *adj.* with no air or wind; stuffy. **air let•ter,** *n.* very light piece of writing paper which, when folded and stuck down, becomes its own envelope. **air•lift.** 1. *n.* transport of emergency supplies/people by air. 2. *v.* to transport emergency supplies/people by air. **air•line,** *n.* company which runs passenger or cargo air services. **air lock,** *n.* blockage in the flow of a liquid in a pipe (caused by air). **air•mail,** *n. & adv.* (mail) sent by air. **air•man,** *n.* (*pl.* -men) man serving in an air force. **air mat•tress,** *n.* mattress which can be inflated. **Air Miles,** *n. pl.* points awarded to buyers of certain products that can be used to purchase airline tickets. **air•plane,** *n.* machine that flies. **air pock•et,** *n.* sudden turbulence in air. **air•port,** *n.* commercial installation where passenger and cargo planes land and take off. **air raid,** *n.* attack by military aircraft. **air•ship,** *n.* large inflated balloon driven by an engine. **air•sick,** *adj.* sick because of traveling by air. **air•sick•ness,** *n.* feeling of being airsick. **airspeed,** *n.* speed of an aircraft in the air. **air•strip,** *n.* small runway where planes can land and take off. **air•tight,** *adj.* not letting in any air. **air traf•fic con•trol,** *n.* control of the movement of aircraft by people on the ground. **air•way,** *n.* passage (such as the throat) through which air passes in the body. **air•wor•thi•ness,** *n.* safety of an aircraft for use. **air•y,** *adj.* (-ier, -iest) (a) full of air. (b) vague (promise). **air•y-fair•y,** *adj.* impractical (plan).

aisle [aɪl] *n.* passageway; side part in a church parallel to the nave.

æ back, a: farm, ɒ top, aɪ pipe, aʊ how, aɪə fire, aʊə flower, ɔ: bought, ɔɪ toy, e fed, eəhair, eɪ take, ə afraid, əʊ boat, əʊə lower, v: word, i: heap, ɪ hit, ɪə hear, u: school, ʊ book, ʌ but, b back, d dog, ð then, dʒ just, f fog, g go, h hand, j yes, k catch, l last, m mix, n nut, ŋ sing, p penny, r round, s some, ʃ short, t too, tʃ chop, θ thing, v voice, w was, z zoo, ʒ treasure

a•jar [ə'dʒɑː] *adj.* (of door/window) slightly open.

aka [eɪkeɪ'eɪ] = also known as.

a•kim•bo [ə'kɪmbəʊ] *adv.* **with her arms a.** = with her hands on her hips.

a•kin [ə'kɪn] *adj.* similar (**to**).

Al *symbol for* aluminum.

al•a•bas•ter ['æləbɑːstə] *n.* smooth white stone.

à la carte [ælæ'kɑːt] *adv. & adj.* (meal) made of several dishes ordered separately from a menu.

a•lac•ri•ty [ə'lækrɪtɪ] *n.* speed.

à la mode [ælæ'mɒd] *adv.* served with ice cream.

a•larm [ə'lɑːm] 1. *n.* thing which gives a loud warning; **false a.** = warning signal which is false; **fire a.** = bell which rings when a fire breaks out; **a. (clock)** = clock which rings at a certain time. 2. *v.* to warn (s.o.); to frighten (s.o.). **a•larm•ist,** *adj. & n.* (person) who is unnecessarily worried by sth.

a•las [ə'læs] *inter. showing sadness.*

al•ba•tross ['ælbətrɒs] *n.* (*pl.* **-es**) very large white sea bird.

al•be•do [æl'biːdəʊ] *n.* ability to reflect light.

al•be•it [ɔːl'biːɪt] *conj.* (*formal*) although.

al•bi•no [æl'biːnəʊ] *n.* animal or person born with pale skin, white hair, and pink eyes.

al•bum ['ælbəm] *n.* (a) large book for sticking things in. (b) long-playing record.

al•bu•men ['ælbjumən] *n.* white part of an egg.

al•che•my ['ælkəmɪ] *n.* medieval chemistry, aimed at converting metals to gold. **al•che•mist,** *n.* person who studied alchemy.

al•co•hol ['ælkəhɒl] *n.* intoxicating liquid distilled from a fermented mixture. **al•co•hol•ic** [ælkə'hɒlɪk] 1. *adj.* referring to alcohol. 2. *n.* person who is addicted to drinking alcohol. **al•co•hol•ism,** *n.* addiction to drinking alcohol. **al•co•pop** ['ælkəʊ,pɒp] *n. inf.* alcoholic drink that resembles a soft drink.

al•cove ['ælkəʊv] *n.* small recess in a wall.

al•der ['ɔːldə] *n.* tree which often grows near water.

ale [eɪl] *n.* type of beer.

a•lert [ə'lɜːt] 1. *adj.* watchful; lively. 2. *n.* **to be on the a.** = to be watchful/to watch out for sth; **he gave the a.** = he gave a warning signal. 3. *v.* **to a. s.o. to** = to warn s.o. of. **a•lert•ness,** *n.* watchfulness; promptness (in doing sth).

al•fal•fa [æl'fælfə] *n.* cloverlike plant used as fodder.

al•fres•co [æl'freskəʊ] *adj. & adv.* in the open air; **an a. meal.**

al•gae ['ældʒiː] *n. pl.* tiny water plants with no stems or leaves.

al•ge•bra ['ældʒɪbrə] *n.* branch of mathematics where numbers are replaced by letters. **al•ge•bra•ic** [ældʒɪ'breɪk] *adj.* referring to algebra.

al•go•rithm ['ælgərɪðm] *n.* plan for working out a complicated calculation.

a•li•as ['eɪlɪəs] 1. *adv.* otherwise known as. 2. *n.* (*pl.* **-es**) assumed name.

al•i•bi ['ælɪbaɪ] *n.* proof that you were somewhere else when a crime was committed.

al•ien ['eɪlɪən] 1. *adj.* foreign (**to**). 2. *n.* foreigner.

al•ien•ate ['eɪlɪəneɪt] *v.* to turn away/to repel. **al•ien•a•tion** [eɪlɪə'neɪʃn] *n.* turning away/repelling.

a•light [ə'laɪt] 1. *v.* (*formal*) **to a. from** = to get off (a train/bus, etc.). 2. *adj.* on fire.

a•lign [ə'laɪn] *v.* to put (yourself/sth) in line; to put (yourself) on the same side as. **a•lign•ment,** *n.* row (of objects); putting (countries) on the same side.

a•like [ə'laɪk] *adv.* almost the same.

al•i•men•ta•ry [ælɪ'mentərɪ] *adj.* which feeds; **a. canal** = tube by which food goes into the stomach, and passes through the body.

al•i•mo•ny ['ælɪmənɪ] *n.* money paid regularly by a person to that person's former spouse.

a•live [ə'laɪv] *adj.* (a) living/not dead. (b) **a. to** = aware of. (c) lively.

al•ka•li ['ælkəlaɪ] *n.* substance which will neutralize an acid, and which turns litmus paper blue. **al•ka•line,** *adj.* not acid.

all [ɔːl] 1. *adj. & pron.* (a) everything; everyone; **a. the children; a. of us prefer beer.** (b) (*in tennis*) **fifteen a.** = fifteen points each. (c) **once (and) for a.** = for the last time; **not at a.** = certainly not; **a. but** = nearly. 2. *adv.* completely; **dressed a. in blue; a. at once/a. of a sudden** = suddenly; *inf.* **not a. there** = mad. **all in,** *adj. inf.* worn out. **all-night,** *adj.* which goes on for the whole night. **all-out,** *adj.* complete (strike); **we must make an a.-out effort** = we must do everything. **all right** [ɔːl'raɪt] *adj.* (a) fine; well. (b) yes, I will. **all-a•round, all-round,** *adj.* general; **a.-around athlete** = person who is good at all sorts of sports. **all-star,** *adj.* with many stars appearing. **all-time,** *adj.* (greatest level, etc.) ever.

Al•lah ['ælæ] *n.* Muslim name for God.

al•lay [ə'leɪ] *v.* to calm (fear/anger).

al•le•ga•tion [ælɪ'geɪʃn] *n.* suggestion as if it were fact. **al•lege** [ə'ledʒ] *v.* to suggest (as a fact that). **al•leged,** *adj.* suggested. **al•leg•ed•ly** [ə'ledʒɪdlɪ] *adv.* as is alleged.

al•le•giance [ə'liːdʒəns] *n.* faithfulness; **they**

swore a. to the President = they swore to obey him.

al•le•go•ry ['ælɪgərɪ] *n.* piece of writing where the characters represent abstract qualities or defects. **al•le•gor•i•cal** [ælɪ'gorɪkl] *adj.* referring to allegory.

al•le•gro [ə'legrəʊ] *adv. & adj. (in music)* played quite fast.

al•ler•gy ['ælədʒɪ] *n.* illness caused by a reaction to irritant substances. **al•ler•gen**, *n.* substance (such as pollen) which produces an allergic reaction. **al•ler•gic** [ə'lɜːdʒɪk] *adj.* reacting badly against; **I am a. to grass pollen; she is a. to jazz** = dislikes it intensely.

al•le•vi•ate [ə'liːvɪeɪt] *v.* to lessen/to soften. **al•le•vi•a•tion** [əliːvɪ'eɪʃn] *n.* lessening.

al•ley ['ælɪ] *n.* (a) very narrow street. (b) **bowling a.** = long narrow area for bowling or playing bowls.

al•li•ance [ə'laɪəns] *n.* link between two groups or countries.

al•lied ['ælaɪd] *adj.* (a) linked by an alliance; **the a. powers** = western countries linked against communist states. (b) linked.

al•li•ga•tor ['ælɪgeɪtə] *n.* large flesh-eating reptile living in tropical rivers.

al•lit•er•a•tion [əlɪtə'reɪʃn] *n.* use of repeated consonants at the beginning of words in poetry.

al•lo•cate ['æləkeɪt] *v.* to give (sth) as a share (for a particular purpose). **al•lo•ca•tion** [ælə'keɪʃn] *n.* division/giving as a share; amount allocated.

al•lot [ə'lɒt] *v.* (**allotted**) to share out between several people. **al•lot•ment**, *n.* sharing out.

al•low [ə'laʊ] *v.* (a) **to a. s.o. to do sth** = to let (s.o. do sth). (b) to give; **we will a. you six weeks to pay. al•low•a•ble**, *adj.* which is permitted; **a. expenses** = expenses which are allowed against tax. **al•low•ance**, *n.* (a) money paid regularly. (b) **to make allowances for** = take into account.

al•loy ['ælɔɪ] 1. *n.* mixture of two or more metals. 2. *v.* to mix (metals).

all•spice ['ɔːlspaɪs] *n.* small round tropical seed used as a spice.

al•lude [ə'luːd] *v.* **to a. to sth** = to refer to sth indirectly or briefly.

al•lure [ə'ljʊə] *v.* to attract. **al•lur•ing**, *adj.* attractive.

al•lu•sion [ə'luːʒn] *n.* slight reference. **al•lu•sive**, *adj.* which makes reference to sth.

al•lu•vi•al [ə'luːvɪəl] *adj.* (soil/land) which has been deposited by rivers. **al•lu•vi•um**, *n.* soil which has been deposited by a river.

al•ly 1. *n.* ['ælaɪ] person/country who is on the same side as you in a quarrel or war. 2. *v.* [ə'laɪ] **to a. oneself to** = to join forces with/to support.

al•ma ma•ter [ælmə'meɪtə] *n.* school or college which s.o. has attended.

al•ma•nac ['ɔːlmənæk] *n.* calendar which also contains advice or information.

al•might•y [ɔːl'maɪtɪ] 1. *adj. inf.* very powerful; **an a. row** = a very loud noise. 2. *n.* **the A.** = God.

al•mond ['ɑːmənd] *n.* nut from a tree of the peach family.

al•mon•er ['ɑːmənə] *n.* (*old*) person who distributes alms for a church, royal family, etc.

al•most ['ɔːlməʊst] *adv.* nearly; not quite.

alms [ɑːmz] *n. pl.* (*old*) gift to old/sick/poor people. **alms•hous•es**, *n. pl.* houses formerly built as homes for the poor.

al•oe ['æləʊ] *n.* desert plant with thick leaves and bitter juice.

a•loft [ə'lɒft] *adv.* (*formal*) high up (in the air).

a•lone [ə'ləʊn] *adj. & adv.* with no one else.

a•long [ə'lɒŋ] 1. *prep.* **a. the road** = from one end of the road to the other; for some distance down the road. 2. *adv.* **come a. with me** = come with me; **all a.** = from the beginning; **they don't get a. very well together** = they do not agree. **a•long•side**, *adv. & prep.* beside.

a•loof [ə'luːf] *adj. & adj.* coldly/unfriendly; **they kept a.** = they did not mix with others. **a•loof•ness**, *n.* cold and haughty.

a•o•pe•ci•a [æləʊ'piːsɪə] *n.* baldness.

a•loud [ə'laʊd] *adv.* loud enough to be heard; in a loud voice.

alp [ælp] *n.* mountain or mountain meadow in Switzerland.

al•pac•a [æl'pækə] *n.* wool from a llama.

al•pha ['ælfə] *n.* first letter of the Greek alphabet.

al•pha•bet ['ælfəbet] *n.* letters used to write words, laid out in a set order (A, B, C, etc.). **al•pha•bet•i•cal** [ælfə'betɪkl] *adj.* **in a. order** = in order based on the first letter of each word. **al•pha•bet•i•cal•ly**, *adv.* in alphabetical order.

al•pine ['ælpaɪn] *adj. & n.* referring to high mountains; (plant) which grows on high mountains. **al•pin•ist** *n.* person who climbs mountains.

al•read•y [ɔːl'redɪ] *adv.* by now.

æ back, ɑː farm, ɒ top, aɪ pipe, aʊ how, aɪə fire, aʊə flower, ɔː bought, ɔɪ toy, e fed, eəhair, eɪ take, ə afraid, əʊ boat, əʊə lower, ɜː word, iː heap, ɪ hit, ɪə hear, uː school, ʊ book, ʌ but, b back, d dog, ð then, dʒ just, f fog, g go, h hand, j yes, k catch, l last, m mix, n nut, ŋ sing, p penny, r round, s some, ʃ short, t too, tʃ chop, θ thing, v voice, w was, z zoo, ʒ treasure

al•right [ɔːl'raɪt] *adj. & inter. inf.* = **all right.**

al•sa•tian [æl'seɪʃn] *n.* large dog (of German origin) often used as a guard dog.

al•so ['ɔːlsəʊ] *adv.* as well/at the same time.

al•tar ['ɒltə] *n.* table in church/temple for religious ceremonies.

al•ter ['ɒltə] *v.* to change. **al•ter•a•tion** [ɒltə-'reɪʃn] *n.* change.

al•ter•ca•tion [ɔːltə'keɪʃn] *n. (formal)* argument.

al•ter•nate 1. *adj.* [ɔːl'tɜːnət] every other/missing one each time. 2. *v.* ['ɔːltəneɪt] to put (sth) in place of sth else, and then switch them around. **al•ter•nate•ly** [ɔːl'tɜːnətlɪ] *adv.* in turns; one first and then the other. **al•ter•nat•ing,** *adj.* (electric current) which flows one way and then the other. **al•ter•na•tive** [ɔːl'tɜːnətɪv] *n. & adj.* thing in place of sth else. **al•ter•na•tive•ly,** *adv.* on the other hand. **al•ter•na•tor** ['ɔːltəneɪtə] *n.* device which produces alternating current.

al•though [ɔːl'ðəʊ] *conj.* in spite of the fact that.

al•tim•e•ter ['æltɪmiːtə] *n.* instrument for measuring altitude.

al•ti•tude ['æltɪtjuːd] *n.* height (measured above the level of the sea).

al•to ['æltəʊ] *n. (pl. -os)* (man with a) high-pitched voice; (woman with a) low-pitched voice.

al•to•geth•er [ɔːltə'geðə] *adv.* considering everything together.

al•tru•ism ['æltruːɪzəm] *n.* being unselfish. **al•tru•is•tic,** *adj.* unselfish.

a•lum ['æləm] *n.* natural mineral salt.

a•lu•mi•num [ə'luːmɪnəm], *Brit.* **a•lu•min•i•um** [ælju'mɪnjəm] *n. (element: Al)* light white metal.

a•lum•nus [ə'lʌmnəs] *n. (pl.* **alumni** [ə-'lʌmnaɪ]) graduate (of a college/university).

al•ways ['ɔːlweɪz] *adv.* every time/all the time.

a•lys•sum ['ælɪsəm] *n.* low garden plant with small white flowers.

Alz•heim•er's dis•ease ['æltseɪməz dɪ'ziːz] *n.* condition where a patient becomes prematurely senile.

am [æm] *v. see* **be.**

a.m. ['eɪ'em] *adv.* in the morning.

a•mal•gam [ə'mælgəm] *n. (formal)* mixture of substances. **a•mal•ga•mate** [ə'mælgəmeɪt] *v.* to mix together/to link up. **a•mal•ga•ma•tion** [əmælgə'meɪʃn] *n.* amalgamating; things amalgamated.

a•man•u•en•sis [æmænjuː'ensɪs] *n.* person who writes for s.o. else.

am•a•ryl•lis [æmərɪlɪs] *n.* lily.

a•mass [ə'mæs] *v.* to pile up (a fortune).

am•a•teur ['æmətɜː] *n. & adj.* (person) who is not paid to do sth; (person) who does sth because he likes doing it. **am•a•teur•ish,** *adj.* not very well done.

am•a•to•ry ['æmətərɪ] *adj.* referring to love.

a•maze [ə'meɪz] *v.* to surprise. **a•mazed,** *adj.* surprised. **a•maze•ment,** *n.* surprise. **a•maz•ing,** *adj.* very surprising.

am•bas•sa•dor, am•bas•sa•dress [æm-'bæsədə, -dres] *n.* person who represents a country in another country.

am•ber ['æmbə] *n.* yellow or orange translucent stone made of fossilised resin.

am•ber•gris ['æmbəgrɪ] *n.* substance from sperm whales, used in making perfume.

am•bi•dex•trous [æmbɪ'dekstrəs] *adj.* (person) who can use either right or left hand equally well.

am•bi•ence ['æmbɪəns] *n.* surroundings. **am•bi•ent,** *adj.* which surrounds; **a. temperature** = temperature of the air around sth.

am•big•u•ous [æm'bɪgjʊəs] *adj.* which has two possible meanings. **am•bi•gu•i•ty** [æmbɪ'gjuːɪtɪ] *n.* state of having two possible meanings; vagueness.

am•bit ['æmbɪt] *n.* general area covered by sth.

am•bi•tion [æm'bɪʃn] *n.* desire to improve your status in the world. **am•bi•tious,** *adj.* wanting to be successful; (project) which aims very high.

am•biv•a•lent [æm'bɪvələnt] *adj.* undecided/with two points of view.

am•ble ['æmbl] *v.* **he was ambling along** = walking slowly along.

am•bro•sia [æm'brəʊzɪə] *n.* delectable food.

am•bu•lance ['æmbjʊləns] *n.* vehicle for taking sick people to a hospital.

am•bush ['æmbʊʃ] 1. *n. (pl. -es)* surprise attack. 2. *v.* to attack by surprise.

a•me•ba [ə'miːbə] *n. (pl.* **amebas, amebae** [-biː]) tiny organism consisting of a single cell.

a•mel•io•rate [ə'miːljəreɪt] *v. (formal)* to make better. **a•mel•io•ra•tion** [əmiːljə-'reɪʃn] *n.* becoming better.

a•men [ɑː'men, eɪ'men] *inter.* word (meaning let this be so) which is used at the end of Christian prayers; **I say a. to that** = I agree entirely.

a•me•na•ble [ə'miːnəbl] *adj.* docile/easy-going; **a. to new ideas** = willing to accept new ideas.

a•mend [ə'mend] *v.* to change (for the better). **a•mend•ment,** *n.* change, esp. suggested change to a proposal. **a•mends** *n.* **to make a. for something** = to compensate for an injury, etc.

a•men•i•ty [ə'miːnɪtɪ] *n.* (a) pleasantness (of a place). (b) pleasant or agreeable feature.

A•mer•i•can [ə'merɪkən] 1. *adj.* referring to

America; **A. plan** = full board (in a hotel). 2. *n.* person from the United States.

am•e•thyst ['æməθɪst] *n.* purple precious stone.

a•mi•a•ble ['eɪmɪəbl] *adj.* pleasant. **a•mi•a•bil•i•ty** [eɪmɪə'bɪlɪtɪ] *n.* being amiable. **a•mi•a•bly,** *adv.* pleasantly.

am•i•ca•ble ['æmɪkəbl] *adj.* friendly. **am•i•ca•bly,** *adv.* in a friendly way.

a•mid(st) [ə'mɪd(st)] *prep.* in the middle of. **a•mid•ships,** *adv. & prep.* in the middle of a ship.

a•mi•no ac•id [ə'miːnəu 'æsɪd] *n.* acid found in protein, necessary for growth.

a•miss [ə'mɪs] *adv. & adj.* **don't take it a.** = don't be annoyed; **something is a.** = has gone wrong.

am•i•ty ['æmɪtɪ] *n.* friendship.

am•me•ter ['æmɪtə] *n.* device for measuring electricity in amperes.

am•mo•nia [ə'məunɪə] *n.* gas made of hydrogen and nitrogen, which has a strong smell.

am•mo•nite ['æmənaɪt] *n.* fossil shell like that of a large snail.

am•mu•ni•tion [æmju'nɪʃn] *n.* (*no pl.*) bullets/shells, etc., for using in warfare/hunting, etc.

am•ne•sia [æm'niːzɪə] *n.* medical state when you forget everything.

am•nes•ty ['æmnəstɪ] 1. *n.* pardon (to criminals). 2. *v.* to offer (criminals) a pardon.

am•ni•ot•ic flu•id ['æmnɪɒtɪk 'fluːɪd] *n.* liquid surrounding a baby in the womb.

a•moe•ba [ə'miːbə] *n.* (*pl.* amœbas, amœbae [ə-'miːbiː]) *see* ameba.

a•mok [ə'mɒk] *adv.* **to run a.** = to run wild killing people.

a•mong(st) [ə'mʌŋ(st)] *prep.* (a) in the middle of. (b) out of.

a•mor•al [eɪ'mɒrəl] *adj.* with no sense of values/of morality.

am•o•rous ['æmərəs] *adj.* tending to fall in love; showing (sexual) love.

a•mor•phous [ə'mɔːfəs] *adj.* having no particular shape.

am•or•tize ['æmɔːtaɪz] *v.* to write off (a debt).

a•mount [ə'maunt] 1. *n.* (a) quantity. (b) sum (of money). 2. *v.* to add up (to); **it amounts to the same thing** = it means the same.

a•mour pro•pre [æmuː 'prɒpr] *n.* respect for oneself.

amp, am•pere [æmp, 'æmpeə] *n.* quantity of electricity flowing in a current.

am•per•sand ['æmpəsænd] *n.* printing sign (&) meaning 'and.'

am•phet•a•mine [æm'fetəmiːn] *n.* drug which stimulates.

am•phib•i•an [æm'fɪbɪən] *n.* (a) animal which lives both in water and on land. (b) (military) vehicle that moves in water and on land. **am•phib•i•ous,** *adj.* which lives/travels in water and on land.

am•phi•the•a•ter, am•phi•the•a•tre ['æmfɪθɪətə] *n.* (a) Greek or Roman circular theater. (b) lecture hall with rows of seats rising in tiers.

am•pho•ra ['æmfərə] *n.* Greek or Roman wine jar.

am•ple ['æmpl] *adj.* (a) large. (b) enough/sufficient. **am•ply,** *adv.* in large enough quantity.

am•pli•fy ['æmplɪfaɪ] *v.* (a) to make (a sound, etc.) louder. (b) to develop (sth) in more detail. **am•pli•fi•ca•tion** [æmplɪfɪ'keɪʃn] *n.* development; making louder. **am•pli•fi•er,** *n.* machine which amplifies a sound.

am•pule, am•poule ['æmpuːl] *n.* small container containing liquid for injections.

am•pu•tate ['æmpjutert] *v.* to cut off (a limb). **am•pu•ta•tion** [æmpju'teɪʃn] *n.* cutting off.

a•muck [ə'mʌk] *adv. see* amok

am•u•let ['æmjulet] *n.* lucky charm.

a•muse [ə'mjuːz] *v.* to give (s.o.) pleasure; **to a. yourself** = to spend time happily. **a•muse•ment,** *n.* pleasure; **a•muse•ment park,** outdoor area with games, rides, and entertainment. **a•mus•ing,** *adj.* which makes you laugh.

an [æn, ən] *see* **a.**

an•a•bol•ic ster•oids ['ænə'bɒlɪk 'sterɔɪdz] *n.* chemical substances which make the body create more tissue.

a•nach•ro•nism [ə'nækrənɪzəm] *n.* thing which is out of keeping with the period. **a•nach•ro•nis•tic** [ənækrə'nɪstɪk] *adj.* which is not in keeping with the period.

an•a•con•da [ænə'kɒndə] *n.* very large snake.

a•nae•mi•a [ə'niːmɪə] *n. see* anemia.

an•aer•o•bic [æneə'rəubɪk] *adj.* not needing oxygen to take place.

an•aes•thet•ic [ænəs'θetɪk] *n. see* anesthetic.

an•a•gram ['ænəgræm] *n.* word or phrase containing the letters of another word or phrase jumbled up (e.g. *Cathy* and *yacht*).

a•nal ['eɪnl] *adj.* referring to the anus.

æ back, ɑː farm, ɒ top, aɪ pipe, au how, aɪə fire, auə flower, ɔː bought, ɔɪ toy, e fed, eəhair, eɪ take, ə afraid, əu boat, əuə lower, ɜː word, iː heap, ɪ hit, ɪə hear, uː school, u book, ʌ but, b back, d dog, ð then, dʒ just, f fog, g go, h hand, j yes, k catch, l last, m mix, n nut, ŋ sing, p penny, r round, s some, ʃ short, t too, tʃ chop, θ thing, v voice, w was, z zoo, ʒ treasure

an•al•ge•sic [ænəl'dʒiːzɪk] *adj. & n.* (drug) which relieves pain. **an•al•ge•si•a**, *n.* absence of pain.

a•nal•o•gous [ə'næləgəs] *adj.* similar/parallel. **an•a•log** ['ænəlɒg] *adj.* (computer) working on a more or less continuous signal. **a•nal•o•gy** [ə'nælədʒɪ] *n.* similarity/parallel.

an•a•lyze ['ænəlaɪz] *v.* to examine (sth) closely to see how it is formed. **a•nal•y•sis** [ə'nælɪsɪs] *n.* (*pl.* **analyses** [ə'nælɪsiːz]) close examination. **an•a•lyst** ['ænəlɪst] *n.* (a) person who carries out analyses. (b) psychoanalyst. **an•a•lyt•i•cal** [ænə'lɪtɪkl] *adj.* which examines closely in detail.

an•ar•chy ['ænəkɪ] *n.* total lack of order or government. **an•ar•chic** [ə'nɑːkɪk] *adj.* lacking in order. **an•ar•chist**, *n.* person who believes in anarchy.

a•nath•e•ma [ə'næθəmə] *n.* curse; **it's a. to him** = he dislikes it intensely.

a•nat•o•my [ə'nætəmɪ] *n.* structure (esp. of a body). **an•a•tom•i•cal** [ænə'tɒmɪkl] *adj.* relating to the structure of the body.

an•ces•tor ['ænsestə] *n.* member of your family many generations ago. **an•ces•tral** [æn'sestrəl] *adj.* **a. home** = home of a family for many generations. **an•ces•try** ['ænsestrɪ] *n.* origin (of a family).

an•chor ['æŋkə] 1. *n.* (a) heavy metal hook dropped to the bottom of the sea to hold a ship in one place; **they dropped a. in the bay; the ship was at a.** (b) thing which holds secure/which gives security. 2. *v.* to drop anchor; hold (a ship) with an anchor. **an•chor•age**, *n.* place where ships can anchor safely. **an•chor•man, anchorwoman**, *n.* main presenter on a TV news program.

an•cho•vy ['æntʃəvɪ, æn'tʃəuvɪ] *n.* small fish with a strong taste.

an•cient ['eɪnʃənt] *adj.* very old.

an•cil•lar•y [æn'sɪlərɪ] *adj.* secondary.

and [ænd, ənd] *conj. showing connection between two things;* **try a. sing** = try to sing.

an•dan•te [æn'dæntɪ] *adv. & adj.* (*in music*) played quite slowly.

and•i•ron ['ændaɪən] *n.* metal stand to hold logs in a hearth.

an•droid ['ændrɔɪd] *adj.* shaped like a human being.

an•drol•o•gy [æn'drɒlədʒɪ] *n.* study of diseases of men, esp. of the reproductive system.

an•ec•dote ['ænɪkdəʊt] *n.* short humorous story told by s.o.

a•ne•mi•a [ə'niːmɪə] *n.* illness caused by lack or red cells in the blood. **a•ne•mic** [ə'niːmɪk] *adj.* looking pale; suffering from anemia.

an•e•mom•e•ter [ænɪ'mɒmɪtə] *n.* instrument for measuring wind. **a•nem•o•graph**, *n.* instrument which records wind force on paper.

a•nem•o•ne [ə'nemənɪ] *n.* small flower; **sea a.** = animal which looks like a flower, living in the sea.

an•er•oid ['ænərɔɪd] *adj.* **a. barometer** = barometer which measures atmospheric pressure by the movement of a vacuum box.

an•es•thet•ic [ænɪs'θetɪk] *n.* substance which makes you lose consciousness; **local a.** = substance which numbs part of the body. **an•es•the•sia** [ænɪs'θiːzɪə] *n.* loss of consciousness from being given an anesthetic. **an•es•the•tist** [ə'niːsθətɪst] *n.* doctor who gives anesthetics. **an•es•the•tize** [ə'niːsθətaɪz] *v.* to give (s.o.) an anesthetic.

an•eu•rysm, an•eu•rism ['ænjʊrɪzəm] *n.* swelling of an artery.

a•new [ə'njuː] *adv.* (*formal*) again.

an•gel ['eɪndʒl] *n.* heavenly being with wings; *inf.* kind person. **an•gel•ic** [æn'dʒelɪk] *adj.* looking innocent/like an angel.

an•gel•i•ca [æn'dʒelɪkə] *n.* sweet-smelling plant of which the green stalks are preserved in sugar and used in desserts.

an•ge•lus ['ændʒələs] *n.* service said in Roman Catholic churches, esp. at the sunset.

an•ger ['æŋgə] 1. *n.* great annoyance. 2. *v.* to make (s.o.) annoyed.

an•gi•na [æn'dʒaɪnə] *n.* pains in the chest.

an•gle ['æŋgl] 1. *n.* (a) corner; **right a.** = angle of 90°; **acute a.** = angle of less than 90°; **obtuse a.** = angle of more than 90°. (b) point of view. 2. *v.* (a) to kick a ball/to shoot at an angle and not straight. (b) **to a. for a raise** = to try to get an increase in salary by dropping hints. **an•gler**, *n.* person who fishes with a hook and line. **an•gling**, *n.* fishing with a hook and line.

An•gli•can ['æŋglɪkən] *adj. & n.* (person) belonging to the Church of England or a church affiliated with it.

An•gli•cism ['æŋglɪsɪzəm] *n.* way of saying sth which is English or influenced by English.

Anglo- ['æŋgləʊ] *prefix meaning* English/between England and another country. **an•glo•phile**, *n.* person who likes England. **an•glo•phobe**, *n.* person who hates England.

an•go•ra [æn'gɔːrə] *n. & adj.* (animal) with thick very soft wool; **a. cat; a. rabbit; a. jumper.**

an•gos•tu•ra [æŋgɒ'stuːrə] *n.* bitter substance used to flavor drinks.

an•gry ['æŋgrɪ] *adj.* (**-ier, -iest**) very annoyed. **an•gri•ly**, *adv.* in an angry way.

ang•strom ['æŋstrɒm] *n.* unit of measurement of wavelengths.

an•guish ['æŋgwɪʃ] *n.* great suffering. **an•guished,** *adj.* showing great suffering.

an•gu•lar ['æŋgjulə] *adj.* (*of rock*) sharp/with sharp angles; (*of person*) with prominent bones.

an•i•line ['ænɪliːn] *n.* liquid produced from coal, used to make paint and plastics.

an•i•mal ['ænɪml] *n.* living creature which is not a plant.

an•i•mate ['ænɪmeɪt] *v.* (a) to make lively. (b) to draw on a film a series of cartoon figures, each with slightly different poses, so that when the film is projected the figures appear to move; **animated cartoon. an•i•ma•tion** [ænɪ'meɪʃn] *n.* (a) liveliness/vivacity. (b) act of making an animated cartoon.

an•i•mos•i•ty, an•i•mus [ænɪ'mɒsɪtɪ, 'ænɪməs] *n.* unfriendly attitude/hostility (**to-ward**).

an•i•on [æ'naɪən] *n.* negative ion.

an•i•seed ['ænɪsiːd] *n.* plant whose seeds are used to flavor sweets and drinks.

an•kle ['æŋkl] *n.* part of your body joining the foot to the leg; **a. socks** = short socks which stop just above the ankles; **a.-deep** = up to one's ankles.

an•nals ['ænlz] *n. pl.* written yearly account of events/discoveries, etc., which have taken place.

an•neal [ə'niːl] *v.* to strengthen (sth) by heating and cooling.

an•nex [ə'neks] 1. *v.* to join (one country to another). 2. *n.* (a) building attached to another building. (b) document attached to another document. **an•nex•a•tion** [ænek'seɪʃn] *n.* joining of one country to another.

an•ni•hi•late [ə'naɪəleɪt] *v.* to destroy completely. **an•ni•hi•la•tion** [ənaɪə'leɪʃn] *n.* complete destruction.

an•ni•ver•sa•ry [ænɪ'vɜːsərɪ] *n.* day which falls on the same date as an important event in the past.

an•no•tate ['ænəteɪt] *v.* to make notes on (sth); to add notes to (a book). **an•no•ta•tion,** *n.* adding of notes; note added.

an•nounce [ə'naʊns] *v.* to tell publicly. **an•nounce•ment,** *n.* public statement. **an•nounc•er,** *n.* person on radio or TV who announces programs, reads the news, etc.

an•noy [ə'nɔɪ] *v.* to make (s.o.) angry.

an•noy•ance, *n.* state of being annoyed. **an•noyed,** *adj.* angry; irritated.

an•nu•al ['ænjuəl] 1. *adj.* which happens once a year. 2. *n.* plant that lives for one year only; book which comes out in a new edition each year. **an•nu•al•ized,** *adj.* shown on an annual basis. **an•nu•al•ly,** *adv.* every year.

an•nu•i•ty [ə'njuɪtɪ] *n.* sum of money which is paid annually.

an•nul [ə'nʌl] *v.* (**annulled**) to end/to cancel. **an•nul•ment,** *n.* cancellation.

an•nu•lar ['ænjuːlə] *adj.* shaped like a ring.

an•ode ['ænəud] *n.* positive electric terminal. **an•o•dize,** *v.* to cover (metal) with a film by using it in electrolysis.

an•o•dyne ['ænədaɪn] *adj. & n.* (medicine) which makes pain less strong; (thing) which stops you worrying.

a•noint [ə'nɔɪnt] *v.* to put oil on (a person) as part of a religious ceremony.

a•nom•a•ly [ə'nɒməlɪ] *n.* thing which is unusual/which does not fit into the normal pattern. **a•nom•a•lous,** *adj.* abnormal/strange.

a•non [ə'nɒn] *adv.* soon.

a•non. = anonymous.

a•non•y•mous [ə'nɒnɪməs] *adj.* (person) who does not give his/her name; **a. letter** = a letter with no signature. **an•o•nym•i•ty** [ænə-'nɪmɪtɪ] *n.* hiding of your name. **a•non•y•mous•ly,** *adv.* without giving your name.

a•noph•e•les [æ'ɒfeliːz] *n.* mosquito which transmits malaria.

an•o•rak ['ænəræk] *n.* waterproof jacket with a hood.

an•o•rex•i•a ner•vo•sa [ænə'reksɪə nɜː-'vəusə] *n.* condition where you refuse to eat because of worry that you may become fat.

an•oth•er [ə'nʌðə] *adj. & pron.* (a) (one) more. (b) a different one. (c) **one a.** = each other.

an•swer ['ɑːnsə] 1. *n.* reply. 2. *v.* to reply; **to a. back** = reply rudely. **an•swer•a•ble,** *adj.* responsible (**for** something **to** a person). **an•swer•ing,** *adj.* in answer; **a. machine** = machine having a recorded message on the telephone which answers automatically for s.o. who is out.

ant [ænt] *n.* small insect living in large communities. **ant•eat•er,** *n.* animal which eats ants. **ant•hill,** *n.* mound of earth containing an ants' nest.

an•tag•o•nize [æn'tægənaɪz] *v.* to arouse s.o.'s hostility. **an•tag•o•nism,** *n.* hostil-

---

æ back, ɑː farm, ɒ top, aɪ pipe, aʊ how, aɪə fire, aʊə flower, ɔː bought, ɔɪ toy, e fed, eəhair, eɪ take, ə afraid, əʊ boat, əʊə lower, vː word, iː heap, ɪ hit, ɪə hear, uː school, ʊ book, ʌ but, b back, d dog, ð then, dʒ just, f fog, g go, h hand, j yes, k catch, l last, m mix, n nut, ŋ sing, p penny, r round, s some, ʃ short, t too, tʃ chop, θ thing, v voice, w was, z zoo, ʒ treasure

ity/opposition. **an•tag•o•nist**, *n.* opponent. **an•tag•o•nis•tic** [æntægə'nɪstɪk] *adj.* hostile.

ant•arc•tic [æn'tɑːktɪk] *adj. & n.* (referring to) the area around the South Pole. **Ant•arc•ti•ca**, *n.* region around the South Pole.

an•te ['æntɪ] *n.* money gambled by a player at the beginning of a game of poker.

ante- ['æntɪ] *prefix meaning* before.

an•te•ced•ent [æntɪ'siːdənt] *n.* earlier form of sth; thing which comes before.

an•te•date ['æntɪdeɪt] *v.* to put an earlier date on (a check); to happen earlier.

an•te•di•lu•vi•an [æntɪdɪ'luːvɪən] *adj.* very ancient.

an•te•lope ['æntɪləup] *n.* type of deer found in Africa.

an•te•na•tal [æntɪ'neɪtl] *adj.* before birth; **a. clinic** = clinic for pregnant women.

an•ten•na [æn'tenə] *n.* (a) (*pl.* **-ae** [æn'teniː]) feeler/sensitive apparatus for sensing. (b) (*pl.* **-as**) aerial.

an•te•ri•or [æn'tɪərɪə] *adj.* which comes earlier.

an•te•room ['æntɪruːm] *n.* small room leading to a larger room.

ant•hel•min•tic [ænθel'mɪntɪk] *adj. & n.* (substance) to remove worms.

an•them ['ænθəm] *n.* choral music (for a special occasion); **national a.** = official music of a country, played to honor the state.

an•ther ['ænθə] *n.* tip of a stamen which carries pollen.

an•thol•o•gy [æn'θɒlədʒɪ] *n.* collection of poems/stories, etc., by various people in one book. **an•thol•o•gize**, *v.* to put (a poem) into an anthology.

an•thra•cite ['ænθrəsaɪt] *n.* hard coal which gives off a lot of heat but not much smoke or flame.

an•thrax ['ænθræks] *n.* serious disease of cattle, which can be caught by people.

an•thro•poid ['ænθrəpɔɪd] *adj. & n.* (ape) which is like a human being.

an•thro•pol•o•gy [ænθrə'pɒlədʒɪ] *n.* study of human beings. **an•thro•po•log•i•cal** [ænθrəpə'lɒdʒɪkl] *adj.* referring to the study of human beings. **an•thro•pol•o•gist** [ænθrə'pɒlədʒɪst] *n.* scientist who studies human beings.

an•thro•po•mor•phic [ænθrəpə'mɔːfɪk] *adj.* (religion, etc.) which gives gods, animals, etc., the form of human beings.

anti- ['æntɪ] *prefix meaning* against; **anti-tank gun; anti-malaria tablet; anti-inflationary measures. anti-se•mit•ic**, *adj.* against Jews.

an•ti•bi•ot•ic [æntɪbaɪ'ɒtɪk] *adj. & n.* (drug) which kills bacteria.

an•ti•bod•y ['æntɪbɒdɪ] *n.* chemical substance built up in the body to fight a particular disease.

an•tic•i•pate [æn'tɪsɪpeɪt] *v.* (a) to act because you see sth is about to happen. (b) to expect sth to happen. **an•tic•i•pa•tion** [æntɪsɪ'peɪʃn] *n.* expectation that sth will happen. **an•tic•i•pa•to•ry**, *adj.* which anticipates.

an•ti•cli•max [æntɪ'klaɪmæks] *n.* (*pl.* **-es**) feeling of being let down when sth exciting does not happen.

an•tics ['æntɪks] *n. pl.* playing around; fooling.

an•ti•cy•clone [æntɪ'saɪkləun] *n.* area of high atmospheric pressure.

an•ti•dote ['æntɪdəut] *n.* **(to)** thing which counteracts the effects of a poison.

an•ti•freeze ['æntɪfriːz] *n.* liquid put in the radiator of a car to prevent it freezing in cold weather.

an•ti•gen ['æntɪdʒən] *n.* substance which produces antibodies.

an•ti•his•ta•mine [æntɪ'hɪstəmiːn] *n.* medicine which prevents allergies.

an•ti•mo•ny ['æntɪmənɪ] *n.* (*element*: Sb) white metal used to make alloys.

an•ti•ox•i•dant [æntɪ'ɒksɪdənt] *n.* (a) any substance that slows deterioration by oxidation of a material. (b) any substance, e.g. vitamin E, that inhibits oxidation in the body.

an•ti•pa•thy [æn'tɪpəθɪ] *n.* **(to)** feeling of not liking s.o./sth.

an•ti•per•spi•rant [æntɪ'pɜːspɪrənt] *n.* spray which stops you perspiring.

an•ti•phon ['æntɪfɒn] *n.* (religious) chant for two sets of singers, each singing in turn. **an•tiph•o•nal**, *adj.* (sung) like an antiphon.

an•tip•o•des [æn'tɪpədiːz] *n. pl.* two places which are on opposite sides of the earth from one another **an•tip•o•de•an** [æntɪpə'diːən] *adj.* from the antipodes.

an•ti•py•ret•ic [æntɪpaɪə'retɪk] *adj. & n.* (substance) which reduces fever.

an•ti•quar•y [æn'tɪkwərɪ] *n.* person who collects, studies, or sells antiques. **an•ti•quar•i•an** [æntɪ'kweərɪən] *adj.* **a. bookseller** = bookseller who sells old books.

an•ti•quat•ed ['æntɪkweɪtɪd] *adj.* old (and decrepit).

an•tique [æn'tiːk] 1. *adj.* very old (and valuable). 2. *n.* old and valuable object; **a. shop** = shop which sells old objects.

an•tiq•ui•ty [æn'tɪkwɪtɪ] *n.* ancient times.

an•ti•sep•tic [æntɪ'septɪk] *adj. & n.* (substance) which prevents a wound becoming septic.

an•ti•so•cial [æntɪ'səuʃl] *adj.* disliking society; bad for society.

an•ti•stat•ic [æntɪ'stætɪk] *adj.* which stops the effect of static electricity.

an•tith•e•sis [æn'tɪθəsɪs] *n.* (*pl.* -theses) [-θəsi:z] opposite.

an•ti•tox•in [æntɪ'tɒksɪn] *n.* substance which counteracts the effects of a toxin. **an•ti•tox•ic,** *adj.* which counteracts a toxin.

an•ti•ven•in [æntɪ'veni:n] *n.* substance which counteracts snake bites.

an•ti•vi•ral [æntɪ'vaɪrəl] *adj. & n.* (drug) which inhibits the growth of viruses.

an•ti•viv•i•sec•tion•ist [æntɪvɪvɪ'sekʃənɪst] *n.* person who is opposed to using live animals for experiments.

ant•ler ['æntlə] *n.* horn (on deer).

an•to•nym ['æntənɪm] *n.* word which means the opposite of another word.

a•nus ['eɪnəs] *n.* (*pl.* -es) hole through which animals produce waste matter from the bowels.

an•vil ['ænvɪl] *n.* (a) block on which a blacksmith beats hot metal. (b) one of the ossicles in the ear.

anx•i•e•ty [æŋ'zaɪətɪ] *n.* *(a)* great worry (**about**). (b) eagerness (**to**). **anx•ious** ['æŋkʃəs] *adj.* (a) very worried. (b) eager (**to**). **anx•ious•ly,** *adv.* worriedly.

an•y ['enɪ] 1. *adj. & pron.* (a) it does not matter which. (b) some; **have you a. sugar? I haven't got a.; he hasn't a. money.** 2. *adv.* **I can't go a. further** = I can go no further.

an•y•bod•y ['enɪbɒdɪ] *pron.* (a) it does not matter who. (b) some person; **hardly a.** = very few.

an•y•how ['enɪhaʊ] 1. *adv.* carelessly. 2. *conj.* = **an•y•way.**

an•y•one ['enɪwʌn] *pron.* = **an•y•bod•y.**

an•y•thing ['enɪθɪŋ] *pron.* (a) it does not matter what; **hardly a.** = almost nothing. (c) *inf.* **like a.** = very strongly; **raining like a.** = pouring down.

an•y•way ['enɪweɪ] *adv. & conj.* in any case.

an•y•where ['enɪweə] *prep.* (a) it does not matter where. (b) somewhere; **can you see it a.?**

a•or•ta [eɪ'ɔ:tə] *n.* (*pl.* -as, -ae) main artery taking blood from the heart.

a•pace [ə'peɪs] *adv.* (*formal*) fast.

a•part [ə'pɑ:t] *adv.* (a) separated. (b) separate; **the watch came a.** = fell to pieces; **can you tell them a.?** = can you say which is which? (c) **a. from** = except.

a•part•heid [ə'pɑ:taɪt] *n.* (formerly) policy in South Africa of racial segregation.

a•part•ment [ə'pɑ:tmənt] *n.* set of rooms in a building, usu. on one floor, as a separate living unit.

ap•a•thy ['æpəθɪ] *n.* lack of interest. **ap•a•thet•ic** [æpə'θetɪk] *adj.* uninterested.

ape [eɪp] 1. *n.* large manlike monkey with no tail. 2. *v.* to imitate (s.o.).

a•per•i•ent [ə'pɪərɪənt] *adj. & n.* substance which makes the bowels work.

a•pe•ri•tif [ə'perɪti:f] *n.* drink taken before a meal to give you an appetite.

ap•er•ture ['æpətʃə] *n.* hole; opening.

a•pex ['eɪpeks] *n.* (*pl.* apexes, apices) top (of a triangle).

a•pha•sia [ə'feɪzjə] *n.* being unable to speak, caused by brain damage.

a•phid, a•phis ['eɪfɪd, 'eɪfɪs, 'æfɪs] *n.* (*pl.* aphids, aphides) small insect which sucks the sap from plants.

aph•o•rism ['æfərɪzəm] *n.* short wise saying.

aph•ro•dis•i•ac [æfrə'dɪzɪæk] *n. & adj.* (substance) which increases sexual desire.

a•pi•ar•y ['eɪpɪərɪ] *n.* place where bees are kept. **a•pi•a•rist,** *n.* (*formal*) beekeeper.

a•pi•cul•ture ['æpɪkʌltʃə] *n.* keeping of bees (for honey).

a•piece [ə'pi:s] *adv.* each.

a•plomb [ə'plɒm] *n.* calmness/self-confidence.

a•poc•a•lyp•tic [əpɒkə'lɪptɪk] *adj.* which prophesies doom. **A•poc•a•lypse,** *n.* last book of the New Testament, prophesying doom.

a•poc•ry•phal [ə'pɒkrɪfl] *adj.* probably untrue. **A•poc•ry•pha,** *npl.* collection of texts of the Old Testament which are not accepted as genuine.

ap•o•gee ['æpədʒi:] *n.* highest point (in the orbit of a planet/in the career of a diplomat, politician, etc.).

a•pol•o•get•ic [əpɒlə'dʒetɪk] *adj.* making excuses; saying you are sorry. **a•pol•o•get•i•cal•ly,** *adv.* in an apologetic way. **a•pol•o•gist,** *n.* person who writes or speaks on behalf of a cause. **a•pol•o•gize** [ə'pɒlədʒaɪz] *v.* to say you are sorry. **a•pol•o•gy,** *n.* saying you are sorry; **my apologies for being late** = I'm sorry I'm late.

ap•o•plex•y ['æpəpleksɪ] *n.* sudden inability to move caused by a stroke. **ap•o•plec•tic** [æpə'plektɪk] *adj.* (a) referring to apoplexy. (b) red-faced.

æ back, ɑ: farm, ɒ: top, aɪ pipe, aʊ how, aɪə fire, aʊə flower, ɔ: bought, ɔɪ toy, ə fed, eəhair, eɪ take, ə afraid, əʊ boat, əʊə lower, v: word, i: heap, ɪ hit, ɪə hear, u: school, ʊ book, ʌ but, b back, d dog, ð then, dʒ just, f fog, g go, h hand, j yes, k catch, l last, m mix, n nut, ŋ sing, p penny, r round, s some, ʃ short, t too, tʃ chop, θ thing, v voice, w was, z zoo, ʒ treasure

a•pos•ta•sy [æ'pɒstəsɪ] *n.* abandoning a religious belief.

a•pos•tle [ə'pɒsl] *n.* one of the twelve men who were the original disciples of Jesus; **a. spoon** = small spoon with the figure of an apostle on the end of the handle. **a•pos•tate** [ə'pɒsteɪt] *n.* person who has given up his/her beliefs. **ap•os•tol•ic** [æpəs'tɒlɪk] *adj.* of the apostles.

a pos•te•ri•o•ri [eɪpɒsteri'ɔːrɪ] *adj.* based on observed facts.

a•pos•tro•phe [ə'pɒstrəfɪ] *n.* printing sign (') which shows either that a letter has been left out (**weren't**) or with **s** to show possession (**a boy's coat, the girls' team**).

a•poth•e•o•sis [æpɒθɪ'əʊsɪs] *n.* making s.o. into a god.

ap•pall, ap•pal [ə'pɔːl] *v.* to frighten/to make horrified. **ap•pal•ling,** *adj.* horrible/frightening. **ap•pall•ing•ly,** *adv.* frighteningly.

ap•pa•rat•us [æpə'reɪtəs] *n.* (*no pl.*) equipment (for doing scientific tests, etc.

ap•par•el [ə'pærəl] *n.* (*formal*) clothes.

ap•par•ent [ə'pærənt] *adj.* which seems. **ap•par•ent•ly,** *adv.* as it seems.

ap•pa•ri•tion [æpə'rɪʃn] *n.* ghost; thing which seems strange.

ap•peal [ə'piːl] 1. *n.* (a) asking for (help, etc.). (b) request to the law courts to reconsider a verdict. (c) attraction; **sex a.** = physical attraction. 2. *v.* (a) to ask **for.** (b) **to a. to** = (i) to ask (s.o.) to judge; (ii) to attract. **ap•peal•ing,** *adj.* attractive; as if asking for help. **ap•pel•lant,** *n.* person who appeals.

ap•pear [ə'pɪə] *v.* (a) to come into sight. (b) to be present (**at**). (c) to act (**in** a play). (d) to seem. **ap•pear•ance,** *n.* (a) how a thing or person looks. (b) being present; **to put in an a.** = to be present.

ap•pease [ə'piːz] *v.* to try to avoid/to soothe. **ap•pease•ment,** *n.* policy of avoiding conflict.

ap•pel•la•tion [æpə'leɪʃn] *n.* (*formal*) name.

ap•pend [ə'pend] *v.* to attach/to join. **ap•pend•age,** *n.* thing attached.

ap•pen•dix [ə'pendɪks] *n.* (a) (*pl.* **appendixes, appendices** [ə'pendɪsiːz]) small tube attached to main intestine. (b) section at the back of a book giving information which is additional to the text. **ap•pen•dec•to•my** [æpen-'dektəmɪ] *n.* operation to remove an appendix. **ap•pen•di•ci•tis** [əpendɪ'saɪtɪs] *n.* illness caused by inflammation of the appendix.

ap•per•tain [æpə'teɪn] *v.* (*formal*) to be relevant.

ap•pe•tite ['æpɪtaɪt] *n.* desire to eat, etc. **ap•pe•tiz•er,** *n.* snack taken with drinks before the main meal. **ap•pe•tiz•ing,** *adj.* which makes you want to eat.

ap•plaud [ə'plɔːd] *v.* to clap or cheer to show you appreciate sth. **ap•plause,** *n.* clapping and cheering.

ap•ple ['æpl] *n.* common hard fruit, growing on a tree; tree which bears this fruit.

ap•plet ['æplɪt] *n.* computer program that runs within a page on the Internet.

ap•pli•ance [ə'plaɪəns] *n.* machine/device.

ap•pli•qué [ə'pliːkeɪ] *n.* decoration made by sewing shaped pieces of cloth on to a larger piece.

ap•ply [ə'plaɪ] *v.* (a) to put (sth) on sth. (b) to be relevant. (c) to ask s.o. **for** sth (esp. a job). (d) **to a. yourself** = to work hard. **ap•pli•ca•ble** [ə'plɪkəbl] *adj.* which refers to. **ap•pli•cant** ['æplɪkənt] *n.* person who applies for a job; candidate. **ap•pli•ca•tion** [æplɪ'keɪʃn] *n.* (a) action of putting something on something; **for external a. only** = only to be used on the skin. (b) asking for (a job, etc.); **a. form** = form to be filled in when applying. **ap•plied,** *adj.* (science) which is put to practical use.

ap•point [ə'pɔɪnt] *v.* to give (s.o.) a job (**as**). **ap•point•ed,** *adj.* (a) arranged/stated. (b) equipped/furnished. **ap•point•ment,** *n.* (a) being given a job. (b) meeting time which has been agreed. (c) **appointments** = furniture and equipment.

ap•por•tion [ə'pɔːʃn] *v.* (*formal*) to divide up/to share out.

ap•po•site ['æpəzɪt] *adj.* fitting/appropriate (remark). **ap•po•si•tion,** *n.* putting a word next to another; **noun in a.** = noun used as an adjective to describe another noun.

ap•praise [ə'preɪz] *v.* to judge the value of (sth). **ap•prais•al,** *n.* evaluation.

ap•pre•ci•ate [ə'priːʃɪeɪt] *v.* (a) to feel the value of (sth). (b) to increase in value. **ap•pre•ci•a•ble,** *adj.* which can be felt. **ap•pre•ci•a•bly,** *adv.* in a way which could be felt. **ap•pre•ci•a•tion** [əpriːʃɪ'eɪʃn] *n.* (a) estimation (of the value of sth). (b) increase in value. **ap•pre•cia•tive** [ə'priːʃjətɪv] *adj.* praising.

ap•pre•hend [æprɪ'hend] *v.* to arrest (a criminal). **ap•pre•hen•sion** [æprɪ'henʃn] *n.* fear. **ap•pre•hen•sive,** *adj.* afraid/nervous. **ap•pre•hen•sive•ly,** *adv.* nervously.

ap•pren•tice [ə'prentɪs] *n.* youth who works with a skilled man to learn from him. **ap•pren•tice•ship,** *n.* time you spend as an apprentice.

ap•prise [ə'praɪz] *v.* (*formal*) to inform (s.o. **of** sth).

ap•proach [ə'prəʊtʃ] 1. *n.* (*pl.* -**es**) (a) way of

dealing (with a problem). (b) **he made approaches to her to join his company** = he contacted her to ask her to join his company. (c) way into. 2. *v.* (a) to go near. (b) to deal with (a question). **ap•proach•a•ble**, *adj.* easy to talk to. **ap•proach•ing**, *adj.* which is coming closer.

ap•pro•ba•tion [æprə'beɪʃn] *n.* (*formal*) approval.

ap•pro•pri•ate 1. *adj.* [ə'prəupriət] suitable/which fits. 2. *v.* [ə'prəuprieit] to seize (sth which belongs to s.o. else). **ap•pro•pri•a•tion** [əprəupri'eɪʃn] *n.* (a) seizure. (b) money voted to a budget.

ap•prove [ə'pruːv] *v.* to express agreement with (sth); to allow; **to a. of sth** = to be in agreement with sth. **ap•prov•al**, *n.* allowing (sth); **on a.** = on trial. **ap•prov•ing**, *adj.* which shows agreement. **ap•prov•ing•ly**, *adv.* showing agreement.

ap•prox•i•mate 1. *adj.* [ə'prɒksɪmət] rough (calculation). 2. *v.* [ə'prɒksɪmeɪt] to be nearly correct. **ap•prox•i•mate•ly**, *adv.* roughly. **ap•prox•i•ma•tion** [əprɒksɪ'meɪʃn] *n.* rough estimate.

ap•pur•te•nance [ə'pɜːtənəns] *n.* (*formal*) thing which is connected to or belongs to sth else.

APR = annual percentage rate.

ap•ri•cot ['eɪprɪkɒt] *n.* yellow fruit with large stone, grown in warm countries; tree which bears apricots.

A•pril ['eɪprəl] *n.* 4th month of the year. **April Fool**, *n.* person who is tricked on April 1st. **April Fool's Day**, *n.* April 1st/day when people are tricked.

a pri•o•ri [eɪpraɪ'ɔːri] *adj.* based on theory or assumptions.

a•pron ['eɪprən] *n.* (a) piece of cloth, worn over clothes to protect them when working. (b) area in an airport where aircraft are parked.

ap•ro•pos [æprə'pəu] *adv.* referring to.

apse [æps] *n.* rounded end of a church.

apt [æpt] *adj.* (a) expression which fits well. (b) likely (**to**). **ap•ti•tude**, *n.* ability; **a. test** = test to see if you are fitted for a job. **apt•ly**, *adv.* fittingly. **apt•ness**, *n.* fitness (of an expression).

aq•ua•lung ['ækwəlʌŋ] *n.* skindiver's portable oxygen equipment.

aq•ua•ma•rine [ækwəmə'riːn] 1. *adj.* dark blue-green. 2. *n.* semi-precious blue stone.

aq•ua•plane ['ækwəpleɪn] *v.* (*of car*) to slide along the wet surface of a road.

a•quar•i•um [ə'kweərɪəm] *n.* (a) tank for keeping fish. (b) exhibition where fish are displayed.

A•quar•i•us [ə'kweərɪəs] *n.* one of the signs of the Zodiac, shaped like a man carrying water.

a•quat•ic [ə'kwætɪk] *adj.* which lives in water; **a. plants.**

aq•ua•tint ['ækwətɪnt] *n.* print which has been shaded to look like a drawing.

aq•ue•duct ['ækwɪdʌkt] *n.* channel which takes water over land.

a•que•ous ['ækwɪəs] *adj.* containing water.

aq•ui•fer ['ækwɪfə] *n.* layer of porous rock in which water gathers.

aq•ui•line ['ækwɪlaɪn] *adj.* hooked (nose).

Ar *symbol for* argon.

Ar•ab ['ærəb] 1. *adj.* referring to Arabia. 2. *n.* Muslim person living in Arabia or some other Near Eastern countries. **A•ra•bi•an** [ə'reɪbɪən] *adj.* referring to Arabia. **Ar•a•bic** ['ærəbɪk] 1. *n.* language spoken by Arabs. 2. *adj.* **arabic numerals** = signs for numbers written 1, 2, 3, 4, etc. **a•ra•bis**, *n.* small garden plant, with little white flowers.

ar•a•besque [ærə'besk] *n.* complicated design of leaves/flowers.

ar•a•ble ['ærəbl] *adj. & n.* (land) which is good for growing crops.

a•rach•nid [ə'ræknɪd] *n.* type of animal with eight legs, such as a spider.

ar•bi•trage ['ɑːbɪtrɑːdʒ] *n.* buying shares in a company which is likely to be taken over, so as to sell them later at a profit. **ar•bi•tra•geur**, *n.* person whose business is arbitrage.

ar•bi•trate ['ɑːbɪtreɪt] *v.* to judge between two parties in a quarrel. **ar•bi•ter**, *n.* person who decides (usu. on questions of fashion). **ar•bi•trar•i•ly**, *adv.* at random. **ar•bi•trar•y**, *adj.* (decision) taken at random. **ar•bi•tra•tion** [ɑːbɪ'treɪʃn] *n.* judgement in a dispute. **ar•bi•tra•tor** ['ɑːbɪtreɪtə] *n.* person who judges a dispute.

ar•bo•re•al [ɑː'bɔːrɪəl] *adj.* living in trees.

ar•bo•re•tum [ɑːbə'riːtəm] *n.* collection of trees grown for study.

ar•bor, *Brit.* **ar•bour** ['ɑːbə] *n.* shady place where trees are trained to form a shelter.

arc [ɑːk] *n.* (a) part of a circle. (b) electric spark jumping between two points. **arc lamp, arc light**, *n.* very bright light. **arc weld•ing**, *n.* welding by an electric arc.

æ back, ɑː farm, ɒ top, aɪ pipe, aʊ how, aɪə fire, aʊə flower, ɔː bought, ɔɪ toy, e fed, eə hair, eɪ take, ə afraid, əʊ boat, əʊə lower, ɜː word, iː heap, ɪ hit, ɪə hear, uː school, ʊ book, ʌ but, b back, d dog, ð then, dʒ just, f fog, g go, h hand, j yes, k catch, l last, m mix, n nut, ŋ sing, p penny, r round, s some, ʃ short, t too, tʃ chop, θ thing, v voice, w was, z zoo, ʒ treasure

ar•cade [ɑːˈkeɪd] *n.* covered area with an arched roof; **shopping a.** = row of stores covered by a roof.

ar•cane [ɑːˈkeɪn] *adj.* mysterious/secret.

arch [ɑːtʃ] 1. *n.* (*pl.* -es) (a) vault/rounded structure forming a roof, or top of a door. (b) **triumphal a.** = large construction with a rounded vault over a carriageway, usu. built to celebrate a victory. (c) rounded part under the foot. 2. *v.* to make (sth) round. 3. *adj.* wicked and playful. **arch•ed,** *adj.* made with an arch. **arch•way,** *n.* passage/entrance with an arch.

arch- [ɑːtʃ] *prefix meaning* greatest; **arch-enemy.**

ar•chae•ol•o•gy, ar•che•ol•o•gy [ɑːkɪˈɒlədʒɪ] *n.* study of ancient civilization. **ar•chae•o•log•i•cal** [ɑːkɪəˈlɒdʒɪkl] *adj.* referring to archaeology. **ar•chae•ol•o•gist** [ɑːkɪˈɒlədʒɪst] *n.* person who studies archaeology.

ar•cha•ic [ɑːˈkeɪɪk] *adj.* very ancient.

arch•an•gel [ˈɑːkeɪndʒl] *n.* highest rank of angel.

arch•bish•op [ɑːtʃˈbɪʃəp] *n.* very important bishop/leader of bishops.

arch•er [ˈɑːtʃə] *n.* person who shoots with a bow and arrow. **ar•cher•y,** *n.* sport of shooting arrows at a target.

ar•che•type [ˈɑːkɪtaɪp] *n.* original version from which other versions can be copied. **ar•che•typ•al,** *adj.* original; perfect (example).

ar•chi•pel•a•go [ɑːkɪˈpeləgəʊ] *n.* (*pl.* -os, -oes) group of islands.

ar•chi•tect [ˈɑːkɪtekt] *n.* person who designs buildings. **ar•chi•tec•ture,** *n.* design of buildings. **ar•chi•tec•tur•al,** *adj.* referring to architecture.

ar•chi•trave [ˈɑːtʃɪtreɪv] *n.* molding around a door or window.

ar•chives [ˈɑːkaɪvz] *n. pl.* collection of documents, esp. public or historical records. **ar•chi•vist** [ˈɑːkɪvɪst] *n.* librarian who looks after archives.

arc•tic [ˈɑːktɪk] *adj. & n.* (referring to) the area around the North Pole; extremely cold (weather).

ar•dent [ˈɑːdənt] *adj.* very strenuous; keen. **ar•dent•ly,** *adj.* strenuously/fiercely.

ar•dor, *Brit.* **ar•dour** [ˈɑːdə] *n.* violence (of emotions).

ar•du•ous [ˈɑːdjʊəs] *adj.* very difficult/hard (task). **ar•du•ous•ly,** *adv.* with great difficulty.

are [ɑː] *v. see* **be.**

ar•e•a [ˈeərɪə] *n.* (a) space; measure of the surface of sth. (b) region. (c) **ar•e•a code,** *n.*

number which you dial in addition to the telephone number to call a particular town or country. (d) general subject.

a•re•ca [əˈriːkə] *n.* type of tropical nut.

a•re•na [əˈriːnə] *n.* space where sports and fights take place.

Ar•gen•tine, Ar•gen•tin•i•an [ˈɑːdʒəntaɪn, ɑːdʒənˈtɪnjən] 1. *adj.* referring to Argentina. 2. *n.* person from Argentina.

ar•gon [ˈɑːgɒn] *n.* (element: Ar) inert gas.

ar•gue [ˈɑːgjuː] *v.* to discuss without agreeing; to quarrel. **ar•gu•a•ble,** *adj.* which is open to discussion. **ar•gu•ment,** *n.* (a) quarrel/discussion without agreement. (b) reasoning. **ar•gu•men•ta•tive** [ɑːgjuˈmentətɪv] *adj.* (person) who likes to quarrel.

a•ri•a [ˈɑːrɪə] *n.* long solo song in opera.

ar•id [ˈærɪd] *adj.* very dry. **a•rid•i•ty** [əˈrɪdɪtɪ] *n.* extreme dryness.

Ar•ies [ˈeəriːz] *n.* one of the signs of the Zodiac, shaped like a ram.

a•rise [əˈraɪz] *v.* (**arose; arisen**) (a) to appear; to start. (b) to result **from.**

a•ris•to•crat [ˈærɪstəkræt] *n.* person who is born into the aristocracy. **ar•is•toc•ra•cy** [ærɪˈstɒkrəsɪ] *n.* top rank (by birth) of society. **a•ris•to•crat•ic** [ærɪstəˈkrætɪk] *adj.* referring to the aristocracy; superior (attitude).

a•rith•me•tic [əˈrɪθmetɪk] *n.* calculations with figures. **ar•ith•met•i•cal** [ærɪθˈmetɪkl] *adj.* referring to arithmetic.

arm [ɑːm] 1. *n.* (a) part of the body between the hand and shoulder; **a. in a.** = with their arms linked. (b) thing shaped like an arm; piece at the side of a chair to rest your arms on. (c) narrow stretch of water running inland. (d) **arms** = weapons; **up in arms about** = very angry/furious. 2. *v.* to equip with weapons. **ar•ma•ments,** *n. pl.* heavy weapons/war equipment. **arm•band,** *n.* piece of cloth worn around your arm. **arm•chair,** *n.* chair with arms. **armed,** *adj.* equipped with weapons; **the a. forces** = the army, navy and air force of a country. **arm•ful,** *n.* load carried in your arms. **arm•hole,** *n.* hole in a piece of clothing through which you put your arms. **ar•mor,** *Brit.* **ar•mour** *n.* (a) metal protective clothes for medieval soldiers. (b) thick protecting material covering ships or tanks. **armored,** *adj.* protected by metal; **a. car** = military car made of thick metal which carries a small gun. **armor-plat•ed,** *adj.* protected by thick metal plates. **ar•mor•y,** *n.* place where weapons are kept; arsenal. **arm•pit,** *n.* part of your body under where your arm joins the shoulder. **arm•rest,** *n.* thing which you rest your arm on. **ar•my,** *n.* all the soldiers of a country.

ar•ma•da [ɑːˈmɑːdə] n. fleet of warships.

ar•ma•dil•lo [ɑːməˈdɪləʊ] n. small South American animal covered with a flexible shell.

ar•ma•ged•don [ɑːməˈgedən] n. great final battle.

ar•ma•ture [ˈɑːmətjə] n. moving part of an electric motor; coil in a dynamo.

ar•mi•stice [ˈɑːmɪstɪs] n. decision to stop fighting temporarily.

a•ro•ma [əˈrəʊmə] n. (pleasant) smell (of coffee/wine, etc.). ar•o•mat•ic [ærəˈmætɪk] adj. (herb) with a strong pleasant smell.

a•rose [əˈrəʊz] v. see arise.

a•round [əˈraʊnd] 1. adv. (a) surrounding a place, person, or thing, in a circle. (b) in an indefinite place. (c) on all sides; he looked a. him; she handed around the letters; is there enough cake to go around? 2. prep. (a) surrounding. (b) approximately.

a•rouse [əˈraʊz] v. (a) to wake. (b) to excite (emotion).

ar•peg•gi•o [ɑːˈpedʒɪəʊ] n. (pl. -os) chord with the notes played one after the other and not all together.

ar•range [əˈreɪndʒ] v. (a) to put in order. (b) to adapt (a piece of music). (c) to organize. ar•range•ment, n. (a) way in which something is laid out. (b) organizing. (c) agreement.

ar•rant [ˈærənt] adj. complete, unmitigated.

ar•ray [əˈreɪ] 1. n. display. 2. v. (a) to set out in order. (b) (formal) to dress (in fine costume).

ar•rears [əˈrɪəz] n. to be in a. = to be late (in doing sth).

ar•rest [əˈrest] 1. n. being held (by the police) on a charge; he's under a.; cardiac a. = stoppage of the heart. 2. v. to hold (s.o.) for breaking the law. ar•rest•ing, adj. which attracts the attention.

ar•rive [əˈraɪv] v. to reach a place; (of baby) to be born. ar•ri•val, n. (a) reaching a place. (b) person who has arrived.

ar•ro•gant [ˈærəgənt] adj. very proud. ar•ro•gance, n. being very proud; thinking that you are superior. ar•ro•gant•ly, adv. proudly.

ar•row [ˈærəʊ] n. (a) long stick with a sharp point which is shot by a bow. (b) sign showing the way to a place. ar•row•root, n. flour made from the root of a tropical American plant.

arse [ɑːs] n. (vulgar) buttocks.

ar•se•nal [ˈɑːsənl] n. store of weapons.

ar•se•nic [ˈɑːsnɪk] n. (element: As) powerful poison.

ar•son [ˈɑːsn] n. criminal act of setting fire to a property. ar•son•ist, n. person who sets fire to property.

art [ɑːt] n. painting, drawing, sculpture and music; a. gallery = museum of paintings, sculptures, etc.; arts subjects = subjects (such as languages, history, etc.) which are not sciences. art•ful, adj. clever; up to the latest tricks. art•ful•ly, adv. cleverly. art•less, adj. natural/not forced; naive.

ar•te•fact [ˈɑːtɪfækt] n. see artifact.

ar•te•ri•o•scle•ro•sis [ɑːtərɪəʊsklərəʊsɪs] n. hardening of the arteries (esp. in old age).

ar•ter•y [ˈɑːtərɪ] n. (a) tube that blood flows through from the heart to other parts of the body. (b) important road. ar•te•ri•al [ɑːˈtɪərɪəl] adj. referring to an artery.

ar•te•sian [ɑːˈtiːʒn] adj. a. well = well drilled in the ground which does not require a pump to make the water rise.

ar•thri•tis [ɑːˈθraɪtɪs] n. illness where joints become swollen and stiff. ar•thrit•ic [ɑːˈθrɪtɪk] adj. stiff from arthritis.

ar•thro•de•sis [ɑːθrəʊˈdiːsɪs] n. operation to fix a hip joint so that it does not move. ar•thro•plas•ty [ˈɑːθrəʊplæstɪ] n. operation to replace a hip joint with an artificial one. ar•thro•pod, n. animal with a body formed of joined sections, such as a spider.

ar•ti•choke [ˈɑːtɪtʃəʊk] n. (a) (globe) a. = green vegetable like the flower of a thistle. (b) (Jerusalem) a. = root vegetable.

ar•ti•cle [ˈɑːtɪkl] n. (a) clause (in agreement). (b) piece of writing in a newspaper, etc. (c) thing/object. (d) part of speech; "the" is a definite a.; "a" is an indefinite a.

ar•tic•u•late 1. v. [ɑːˈtɪkjuleɪt] (a) to speak (a word). (b) to join. 2. adj. [ɑːˈtɪkjulət] clear-speaking. ar•tic•u•la•tion [ɑːtɪkjuˈleɪʃn] n. (Med.) joint.

ar•ti•fice, n. trick. ar•tif•i•cer, n. skilled craftsman.

ar•ti•fact [ˈɑːtɪfækt] n. object (usu. a tool) made by a human being.

ar•ti•fi•cial [ɑːtɪˈfɪʃl] adj. which is an imitation/not the real thing; a. respiration = reviving s.o. who is nearly dead. ar•ti•fi•ci•al•i•ty, n. falseness/not being sincere. ar•ti•fi•cial•ly, adv. unnaturally.

ar•til•ler•y [ɑːˈtɪlərɪ] n. section of the army concerned with guns; the a. = the guns.

æ back, aː farm, ɒ top, aɪ pipe, aʊ how, aiə fire, aʊə flower, ɔː bought, ɔɪ toy, e fed, eəhair, eɪ take, ə afraid, əʊ boat, əʊə lower, vː word, iː heap, ɪ hit, ɪə hear, uː school, ʊ book, ʌ but, b back, d dog, ð then, dʒ just, f fog, g go, h hand, j yes, k catch, l last, m mix, n nut, ŋ sing, p penny, r round, s some, ʃ short, t too, tʃ chop, θ thing, v voice, w was, z zoo, ʒ treasure

ar•til•ler•y•man, *n.* (*pl.* -men) soldier working with guns.

ar•ti•san [ɑːtɪˈzæn] *n.* skilled workman/craftsman.

art•ist [ˈɑːtɪst] *n.* person who draws, paints, or plays music. **ar•tis•tic** [ɑːˈtɪstɪk] *adj.* (person) who has a feeling or skill for art; (thing) which looks good because it is made by an artistic person. **ar•tis•ti•cal•ly,** *adv.* with art. **art•ist•ry** [ˈɑːtɪstrɪ] *n.* skill in art.

ar•tiste [ɑːˈtiːst] *n.* performer in a theater (esp. dancer/acrobat).

art•y [ˈɑːtɪ] *adj. inf.* pretending to be artistic.

ar•um [ˈeərəm] *n.* lily with a tall white flower.

as [æz, əz] *conj.* (a) like. (b) because. (c) at the same time that. (d) doing the job of; acting the part of. (e) in a certain way. (f) **as for** = referring to/concerning. (g) **as from** = starting from. (h) **as if/as though** = like/seeming. (i) **as long as** = on condition that. (j) **as soon as** = immediately. (k) **as to** = referring to. (l) **as well as** = in addition to.

As *symbol for* arsenic.

ASAP [eɪeɪseɪˈpiː] = as soon as possible.

as•bes•tos [æsˈbestəs] *n.* mineral substance which is fireproof. **as•bes•to•sis** [æsbes-ˈtəʊsɪs] *n.* lung disease caused by breathing in particles of asbestos.

as•cend [əˈsend] *v.* (*formal*) to go up. **as•cend•an•cy,** *n.* influence. **as•cend•ant,** *n.* rising; **in the a.** = becoming powerful/popular. **as•cen•sion** [əˈsenʃn], **as•cent** [əˈsent] *n.* going up.

as•cer•tain [æsəˈteɪn] *v.* (*formal*) to check/to find out (the facts). **as•cer•tain•a•ble,** *adj.* which can be checked.

as•cet•ic [əˈsetɪk] 1. *adj.* (way of life) where you do not allow yourself any comfort or pleasure. 2. *n.* religious person who does not allow himself any pleasures. **as•cet•i•cism,** *n.* belief in an ascetic way of life.

ASCII [ˈæski] American Standard Code for Information Interchange.

a•scor•bic [æˈskɔːbɪk] *adj.* **a. acid** = vitamin C occurring in oranges, vegetables, etc.

as•cot [ˈæskət] *n.* type of scarf worn around the neck.

as•cribe [əˈskraɪb] *v.* (*formal*) to attribute (sth **to** s.o.). **a•scrib•a•ble,** *adj.* which can be ascribed.

a•sep•tic [əˈseptɪk] *adj.* sterilized/with no infection.

a•sex•u•al [ˈeɪseksjuəl] *adj.* not involving sex.

ash [æʃ] *n.* (*pl.* **ashes**) (a) common tree in northern countries; wood of this tree. (b) dust left after something has burned. (c) **ashes** = remains of a person's body after cremation. **ash•can,** *n.* container for putting ashes or trash in. **ash•en** [ˈæʃən] *adj.* very pale.

ash•tray, *n.* small bowl for putting ash from cigarettes, etc.

a•shamed [əˈʃeɪmd] *adj.* sorry because of sth wrong.

ash•lar [ˈæʃlə] *n.* (*no pl.*) building stones cut square.

a•shore [əˈʃɔː] *adv.* on land.

A•sian [ˈeɪʒn] *adj. & n.* (person) from Asia. **A•si•at•ic** [eɪsɪˈætɪk] *adj.* referring to Asia.

a•side [əˈsaɪd] 1. *adv.* to one side; **a. from** = apart from. 2. *n.* words spoken in a play which the other characters are not supposed to hear.

as•i•nine [ˈæsɪnaɪn] *adj.* stupid.

ask [ɑːsk] *v.* (a) to put a question (**about**); **to a. after** s.o. = to inquire about s.o.'s health. (b) **to a. for** = to request/to want (sth) to be given to you. (c) to invite (s.o. **to** a party, etc.). **ask•ing,** *n.* **it's yours for the a.** = you only have to ask for it and you will get it.

a•skance [əˈskɑːns] *adv.* **to look at sth/s.o. a.** = to be suspicious of.

a•skew [əˈskjuː] *adv.* not straight.

a•slant [əˈslɑːnt] *adv.* sloping.

a•sleep [əˈsliːp] *adj.* sleeping.

asp [æsp] *n.* small poisonous snake.

as•par•a•gus [əˈspærəgəs] *n.* cultivated plant of which you eat the new shoots as a vegetable.

as•pect [ˈæspekt] *n.* (a) direction which a house faces. (b) side; way of looking at sth.

as•pen [ˈæspn] *n.* small tree with leaves which tremble in the wind.

as•per•i•ty [æˈsperɪtɪ] *n.* sharpness.

as•per•sions [əˈspɜːʃnz] *n. pl.* bad comments (**on** s.o.).

as•phalt [ˈæsfælt] 1. *n.* mixture of tar and sand which is used for surfacing roads. 2. *v.* to cover with asphalt.

as•phyx•i•ate [əsˈfɪksɪeɪt] *v.* to stifle/to kill (s.o.) by preventing them from breathing. **as•phyx•i•a, asphyxiation** [əsfɪksɪˈeɪʃn] *n.* being unable to breathe.

as•pic [ˈæspɪk] *n.* jelly made from meat, fish, poultry, or vegetable juices.

as•pi•dis•tra [æspɪˈdɪstrə] *n.* type of indoor plant.

as•pi•rate [ˈæspɪrət] *adj. & n.* (sound) which has to be breathed (as "h" in "horse").

as•pire [əˈspaɪə] *v.* (**to**) to have the ambition to do sth. **as•pir•ant** [ˈæspərənt] *n.* person who aspires to do sth. **as•pi•ra•tion** [æspɪˈreɪʃn] *n.* ambition. **as•pir•ing,** *adj.* ambitious/hopeful.

as•pi•rin [ˈæsprɪn] *n.* (tablet of) common drug taken to stop headaches/colds, etc.

ass [æs] *n.* (*pl.* -es) (a) donkey. (b) stupid person. (c) *Sl.* buttocks.

as•sail•ant [ə'seɪlənt] *n.* person who attacks (s.o.).

as•sas•si•nate [ə'sæsɪneɪt] *v.* to kill (s.o.) for political reasons. as•sas•sin, *n.* person who kills for political reasons. as•sas•si•na•tion [əsæsɪ'neɪʃn] *n.* political murder.

as•sault [ə'sɔ:lt] 1. *n.* attack. 2. *v.* to attack.

as•say [ə'seɪ] 1. *n.* test to see how pure metal is. 2. *v.* to test (metal) to see how pure it is.

as•se•gai ['æsəgaɪ] *n.* native spear from Southern Africa.

as•sem•ble [ə'sembl] *v.* to get together; to put together. as•sem•bly, *n.* (a) meeting. (b) putting together; a. line = continuous moving line in a factory, where machines, etc., are put together.

as•sent [ə'sent] 1. *n.* agreement. 2. *v.* to agree (to).

as•sert [ə'sɜ:t] *v.* to state firmly; to a. yourself = take a firm position. as•ser•tion [ə'sɜ:ʃn] *n.* statement (of rights). as•ser•tive, *adj.* forceful.

as•sess [ə'ses] *v.* (a) to calculate the amount of damages/of tax which should be paid. (b) to value. (c) to estimate. as•sess•ment, *n.* (a) calculation of damages/of tax. (b) calculation of value. (c) estimate. as•ses•sor, *n.* person who assesses.

as•set ['æset] *n.* (a) valuable thing which belongs to you. (b) *pl.* assets = anything owned which can be sold to pay debts.

as•sid•u•ous [ə'sɪdjʊəs] *adj.* regular and very careful. as•si•du•i•ty [æsɪ'djuːɪtɪ] *n.* regularity of work. as•sid•u•ous•ly, *adv.* regularly and very carefully; without fail.

as•sign [ə'saɪn] *v.* (a) to appoint (s.o. to do sth). (b) to transfer sth to s.o. as•sig•na•tion [æsɪg'neɪʃn] *n.* (a) transfer (of property). (b) lovers' meeting. as•sign•ment, *n.* (a) delegation (of a task to s.o.). (b) work which you have been told to do.

as•sim•i•late [ə'sɪmɪleɪt] *v.* to digest (food); to learn and understand (facts). as•sim•i•la•tion [əsɪmɪ'leɪʃn] *n.* act of assimilating food or information.

as•sist [ə'sɪst] *v.* to help (s.o.). as•sis•tance, *n.* help. as•sis•tant. 1. *n.* person who helps. 2. *adj.* deputy.

as•siz•es [ə'saɪzɪz] *n. pl.* (*old*) local courts held in various parts of England and Wales at regular intervals (now the Crown Courts).

as•so•ci•ate 1. *v.* [ə'səʊsɪeɪt] (with) to link

(with s.o.)/to be linked (to s.o./sth). 2. *n.* [ə'səʊsɪət] person who is linked to s.o. as•so•ci•a•tion [əsəʊsɪ'eɪʃn] *n.* group/society.

as•so•nance ['æsənəns] *n.* rhyme using vowels only.

as•sort•ed [ə'sɔ:tɪd] *adj.* (a) matched. (b) mixed. as•sort•ment, *n.* collection/mixture.

as•suage [ə'sweɪdʒ] *v.* (*formal*) to calm/to soothe.

as•sume [ə'sjuːm] *v.* (a) to take (power, responsibility) upon yourself. (b) to suppose. as•sumed, *adj.* false. as•sump•tion [ə'sʌmpʃn] *n.* (a) taking up (of office). (b) belief that sth is true, even if it has not been proved.

as•sure [ə'ʃʊə] *v.* (a) to make safe/certain. (b) to state/to affirm. as•sur•ance, *n.* (a) promise. (b) calm; feeling of certainty. as•sured *adj.* certain. as•sur•ed•ly [ə'ʃʊərədlɪ] *adv.* certainly.

as•ter ['æstə] *n.* garden plant with star-shaped flowers.

as•ter•isk ['æstərɪsk] *n.* sign (*) to indicate some special mention.

a•stern [ə'stɜːn] *adv.* behind a ship; (*of ship*) to go a. = to go backward.

as•ter•oid ['æstərɔɪd] *n.* very small planet.

asth•ma ['æsmə] *n.* wheezing, usu. caused by allergy. asth•mat•ic [æs'mætɪk] *adj. & n.* (person) who suffers from asthma.

a•stig•ma•tism [ə'stɪgmətɪzəm] *n.* condition of the eyes where the image focuses correctly at one angle but not at another. as•tig•mat•ic [æstɪg'mætɪk] *adj.* referring to astigmatism.

as•ton•ish [ə'stɒnɪʃ] *v.* to surprise. as•ton•ish•ing, *adj.* surprising. as•ton•ish•ing•ly, *adv.* surprisingly. as•ton•ish•ment, *n.* surprise.

as•tound [ə'staʊnd] *v.* to surprise completely. as•tound•ing, *adj.* very surprising.

as•tra•khan [æstrə'kæn] *n.* dark fur from the skin of black lambs.

as•tral ['æstrəl] *adj.* referring to stars.

a•stray [ə'streɪ] *adv.* lost; to go a. = get lost; to lead a. = to lead into bad habits.

a•stride [ə'straɪd] *adv. & prep.* with your legs on either side (of).

as•trin•gent [ə'strɪndʒənt] 1. *adj.* harsh/severe (comments, etc.). 2. *n.* medicine/cosmetic for closing pores, etc. as•trin•gen•cy, *n.* being astringent.

as•trol•o•gy [ə'strɒlədʒɪ] *n.* art of foretelling

æ back, ɑ: farm, ɒ: top, aɪ pipe, aʊ how, aɪə fire, aʊə flower, ɔ: bought, ɔɪ toy, ə fed, eəhair, eɪ take, ə afraid, əʊ boat, əʊə lower, v: word, i: heap, ɪ hit, ɪə hear, u: school, ʊ book, ʌ but, b back, d dog, ð then, dʒ just, f fog, g go, h hand, j yes, k catch, l last, m mix, n nut, ŋ sing, p penny, r round, s some, ʃ short, t too, tʃ chop, θ thing, v voice, w was, z zoo, ʒ treasure

events from the stars and planets.
as•trol•o•ger, *n.* person who gives advice based on reading the position of the stars.

as•tro•log•i•cal [æstrə'lɒdʒɪkl] *adj.* referring to astrology.

as•tro•naut ['æstrənɔːt] *n.* person who travels in a spacecraft.

as•tron•o•my [ə'strɒnəmɪ] *n.* science of studying the stars, the sun and the universe. **as•tron•o•mer,** *n.* person who studies astronomy. **as•tro•nom•i•cal** [æstrə'nɒmɪkl] *adj.* (a) referring to astronomy. (b) *inf.* very large. **as•tro•nom•i•cal•ly,** *adv.* (a) using astronomy. (b) *inf.* enormously.

as•tro•phys•ics [æstrəʊ'fɪzɪks] *n.* study of the physics of the universe.

as•tute [ə'stjuːt] *adj.* clever/wise. **as•tute•ly,** *adv.* cleverly. **as•tute•ness,** *n.* being astute.

a•sun•der [ə'sʌndə] *adv.* (*old*) apart.

a•sy•lum [ə'saɪləm] *n.* (a) place of refuge; **political a.** = permission to stay in a country when one is politically undesirable in one's own. (b) (*old*) mental hospital.

a•sym•me•try [ə'sɪmətrɪ] *n.* lack of symmetry. **a•sym•met•ri•cal** [æsɪ'metrɪkl] *adj.* not symmetrical.

at [æt, ət] *prep.* (a) (*showing time or place*) **at the office; at night.** (b) (*showing speed or rate*) **at 100 miles an hour; at fifty cents a pound.** (c) (*showing cause*) **she laughed at my old coat.** (d) busy; **at work.** (e) **at first** = at the beginning; **at once** = immediately.

at•a•rax•i•a [ætə'ræksɪə] *n.* excessive calmness.

at•a•vis•tic [ætə'vɪstɪk] *adj.* reverting to the characteristics of one's ancestors.

a•tax•i•a [æ'tæksɪə] *n.* being unable to coordinate the use of muscles.

ate [et] *v. see* eat.

a•the•ism ['eɪθɪzəm] *n.* believing there is no god. **a•the•ist,** *n.* person who believes there is no god. **a•the•is•tic** [eɪθɪ'ɪstɪk] *adj.* referring to atheism.

ath•lete ['æθliːt] *n.* person who takes part in a sport, in particular, running, jumping, throwing; **athlete's foot** = skin infection on the feet. **ath•let•ic** [æθ'letɪk] *adj.* referring to sport. **ath•let•ics,** *n.* organized sports where you run, jump or throw.

At•lan•tic [ət'læntɪk] *n.* **the A. (Ocean)** = ocean separating Europe and Africa from North and South America.

at•las ['ætləs] *n.* (*pl.* -es) book of maps.

at•mos•phere ['ætməsfɪə] *n.* (a) air which surrounds the earth. (b) general feeling (at a party, etc.). **at•mos•pher•ic** [ætməs'ferɪk] *adj.* referring to the atmosphere. **at•mos•pher•ics,** *n. pl.* electric distur-

bances which interfere with radio or TV signals.

at•oll ['ætɒl] *n.* tropical coral island.

at•om ['ætəm] *n.* (a) basic particle of matter. (b) very small thing. **a•tom•ic** [ə'tɒmɪk] *adj.* referring to physical atoms; **a. bomb** = bomb which uses nuclear energy; **a. number** = number of protons in one atom of a chemical element; **a. weight** = ratio of the mass of an atom of an element to the mass of carbon 12. **at•om•ize** ['ætəmaɪz] *v.* to reduce to very fine particles. **at•om•iz•er,** *n.* device for atomizing, esp. a spray for scent.

a•ton•al [,eɪtəʊnəl] *adj.* without any tones.

a•tone [ə'təʊn] *v.* to make amends (**for**). **a•tone•ment,** *n.* making amends (**for** a sin).

a•tri•um ['ætrɪəm] *n.* (a) central court of a large building, usu. with a glass roof. (b) one of the chambers of the heart.

a•tro•cious [ə'trəʊʃəs] *adj.* (a) very wicked. (b) very bad. **a•tro•cious•ly,** *adv.* very badly. **a•troc•i•ty** [ə'trɒsɪtɪ] *n.* very wicked deed.

at•ro•phy ['ætrəfɪ] 1. *n.* wasting away (of a limb). 2. *v.* to waste away.

at•tach [ə'tætʃ] *v.* to fasten. **at•ta•ché** [ə-'tæʃeɪ] *n.* specialized member of the staff of an embassy. **attaché case,** *n.* small case for carrying papers. **at•tach•ment,** *n.* (a) device which is attached to something else. (b) affection.

at•tack [ə'tæk] 1. *n.* (a) starting to fight. (b) sudden start of a disease. 2. *v.* to start fighting (s.o.). **at•tack•er,** *n.* person who attacks.

at•tain [ə'teɪn] *v.* to reach (an age, an ambition). **at•tain•a•ble,** *adj.* which can be reached. **at•tain•ment,** *n.* (a) reaching. (b) **attainments** = talents/intellectual capacities.

at•tain•der [æ'teɪndə] *n.* loss of a person's civil rights as a result of having been convicted of a felony or treason and sentenced to death.

at•tempt [ə'tempt] 1. *n.* try. 2. *v.* to try.

at•tend [ə'tend] *v.* (a) **to a. to s.o.** = to look after s.o. (b) to be present at. **at•tend•ance,** *n.* being present. **at•tend•ant,** *n.* (a) person who waits on or goes with another person. (b) person who is on duty (in a public restroom, etc.).

at•ten•tion [ə'tenʃn] *n.* (a) careful thought about sth.; **a. deficit disorder** = condition, esp. of children, characterized by a short concentration span and hyperactivity. (b) (*of soldiers*) **to stand at a.** = to stand straight with heels together. **at•ten•tive** [ə'tentɪv] *adj.* (a) paying attention; careful. (b) taking care of (s.o.). **at•ten•tive•ly,** *adv.* with attention.

at•ten•u•ate [ə'tenjueɪt] *v.* (*formal*) to make thinner/weaker; **attenuating circumstances** = circumstances which reduce the blame attached to a crime. **at•ten•u•a•tion,** *n.* becoming weaker.

at•test [ə'test] *v.* (*formal*) (**to**) to say that sth is true.

at•tic ['ætɪk] *n.* room under the roof of a house.

at•tire [ə'taɪə] *n.* (*no pl.*) (*formal*) clothing. **at•tired,** *adj.* (**in**) wearing.

at•ti•tude ['ætɪtjuːd] *n.* (a) way of standing/sitting, etc. (b) way of thinking.

at•tor•ney [ə'tɜːnɪ] *n.* (a) lawyer. (b) **power of a.** = power to act on behalf of s.o. else.

at•tract [ə'trækt] *v.* to make (sth) come towards you. **at•trac•tion** [ə'trækʃn] *n.* (a) pull. (b) ability to attract (s.o.)/to make (s.o.) interested. (c) thing which attracts people. **at•trac•tive,** *adj.* pleasant-looking. **at•trac•tive•ly,** *adv.* in an attractive way.

at•trib•ute 1. *n.* ['ætrɪbjuːt] (a) quality. (b) symbol. 2. *v.* [ə'trɪbjuːt] **to a. sth to s.o.** = to say that sth belongs to s.o. **at•trib•ut•a•ble** [ə-'trɪbjʊtəbl] *adj.* which can be attributed to s.o.

at•tri•tion [ə'trɪʃn] *n.* wearing down; **war of a.** = war to be won by wearing down your enemy's forces.

at•tuned to [ə'tjuːnd tʊ] *adj.* aware of (latest fashions, etc.).

Au *symbol for* gold.

au•ber•gine ['əʊbəʒiːn] *n.* eggplant.

au•brie•tia [ɔː'briːʃə] *n.* low growing plant with bright purple flowers.

au•burn ['ɔːbən] *adj.* reddish chestnut-colored (hair).

auc•tion ['ɔːkʃn] 1. *n.* sale where the item is sold to the highest bidder. 2. *v.* to sell (sth) to the highest bidder. **auc•tion•eer** [ɔːkʃə'nɪə] *n.* person who is in charge of an auction. **auc•tion off,** *v.* to sell (sth) by auction to get rid of it. **auction gal•ler•y,** *n.* place where auctions are carried out.

au•da•cious [ɔː'deɪʃəs] *adj.* very daring. **au•da•cious•ly,** *adv.* daringly. **au•dac•i•ty** [ɔː'dæsɪtɪ] *n.* daring.

au•di•ble ['ɔːdɪbl] *adj.* which can be heard. **au•di•bil•i•ty** [ɔːdɪ'bɪlɪtɪ] *n.* capacity for being heard. **au•di•bly** ['ɔːdɪblɪ] *adv.* in an audible way.

au•di•ence ['ɔːdɪəns] *n.* (a) people listening to a concert/watching a movie or play, etc. (b) (*formal*) hearing.

au•di•o book ['ɔːdɪəʊ bʊk] *n.* tape or compact disk of a recording of the reading aloud of a book.

au•di•o-vis•u•al [ɔːdɪəʊ'vɪzjʊəl] *adj.* referring to a method of teaching using tapes, records, films, etc.

au•dit ['ɔːdɪt] 1. *n.* official checking of accounts. 2. *v.* to check (the accounts of a company). **au•di•tor,** *n.* expert accountant who checks the accounts of a company, etc.

au•di•tion [ɔː'dɪʃn] 1. *n.* testing of the suitability of actors/dancers, etc., for a job. 2. *v.* (a) to test the suitability of (an actor/dancer, etc., for a job). (b) (*of actor*) **to a. for a part** = to go to a test for a part.

au•di•to•ri•um [ɔːdɪ'tɔːrɪəm] *n.* huge hall for meetings/concerts, etc.

au fait [əʊ'feɪ] *adj.* (*French*) familiar (**with**).

auf Wie•der•seh•en [aʊf'viːdəzeɪn] (*German*) goodbye.

au•ger ['ɔːgə] *n.* tool for boring holes.

aug•ment [ɔːg'ment] *v.* to increase. **aug•men•ta•tion** [ɔːgmen'teɪʃn] *n.* increase.

au•gur ['ɔːgə] *v.* to be a sign for the future.

au•gust [ɔː'gʌst] *adj.* solemn and dignified.

Au•gust ['ɔːgəst] *n.* 8th month of the year.

auk [ɔːk] *n.* large black and white sea bird.

aunt [ɑːnt] *n.* sister of your mother or father; wife of an uncle.

au pair [əʊ'peə] *adj. & n.* (*pl.* **au pairs**) **she is going to France as an au pair (girl)** = she is going to live with a French family to do light housework (and learn French).

au•ra ['ɔːrə] *n.* general feeling surrounding a person/a place.

au•ral ['ɔːrəl] *adj.* using the ear. **au•ral•ly,** *adv.* by listening.

au re•voir [əʊrə'vwɑːr] (*French*) goodbye.

au•ri•cle ['ɔːrɪkl] *n.* (a) outside part of the ear. (b) space in the heart which fills with blood and then pumps it into the ventricles.

au•ro•ra [ə'rɔːrə] *n.* **a. borealis** = the Northern lights/bright lights seen in the sky in the far North.

aus•cul•ta•tion [ɔːskəl'teɪʃn] *n.* listening to the chest of a patient, using a stethoscope.

aus•pic•es ['ɔːspɪsɪz] *n. pl.* (a) forecast/signs of the future. (b) patronage; **under the a. of** = subsidized/organized by. **aus•pi•cious** [ɔː-'spɪʃəs] *adj.* favorable/lucky. **aus•pi•cious•ly,** *adv.* favorably.

Aus•sie ['ɒzɪ] *n. & adj. inf.* Australian.

aus•tere [ɔː'stɪə] *adj.* cold/severe; without luxury. **aus•ter•i•ty** [ɔː'sterɪtɪ] *n.* absence of luxury.

Aus•tral•ian [ɒs'treɪlɪən] 1. *adj.* referring to

æ back, aː farm, ɒ top, aɪ pipe, aʊ how, aɪə fire, aʊə flower, ɔː bought, ɔɪ toy, e fed, eəhair, eɪ take, ə afraid, əʊ boat, əʊə lower, ɜː word, iː heap, ɪ hit, ɪə hear, uː school, ʊ book, ʌ but, b back, d dog, ð then, dʒ just, f fog, g go, h hand, j yes, k catch, l last, m mix, n nut, ŋ sing, p penny, r round, s some, ʃ short, t too, tʃ chop, θ thing, v voice, w was, z zoo, ʒ treasure

Australia. 2. *n.* person from Australia.
Aus•tral•a•sian, *adj.* referring to
Australasia (the part of the Southern Hemisphere including Australia, New Zealand, and the Pacific Islands.

Aus•tri•an ['ɒstrɪən] 1. *adj.* referring to Austria. 2. *n.* person from Austria.

au•tar•chy ['ɔːtɑːkɪ] *n.* self rule, situation where a state rules itself.

au•tar•ky ['ɔːtɑːkɪ] *n.* self-sufficiency.

au•then•tic [ɔː'θentɪk] *adj.* real; genuine.
au•then•ti•cate [ɔː'θentɪkeɪt] *v.* to swear that sth is true. **au•then•tic•i•ty** [ɔːθen-'tɪsɪtɪ] *n.* being authentic.

au•thor ['ɔːθə] *n.* person who writes books, etc.
au•thor•ship, *n.* identity of the author.

au•thor•i•ty [ɔː'θɒrɪtɪ] *n.* (a) power. (b) permission. (c) source. (d) ruling committee or group. (e) expert. **au•thor•i•tar•i•an** [ɔːθɒrɪ'teərɪən] *adj.* exercising strict control.
au•thor•i•ta•tive [ɔː'θɒrɪtətɪv] *adj.* (a) commanding. (b) which sounds as if it is correct. **au•thor•i•ta•tive•ly**, *adv.* in an authoritative way.

au•thor•ize ['ɔːθəraɪz] *v.* to give (s.o.) permission. **au•thor•i•za•tion** [ɔːθəraɪ'zeɪʃn] *n.* permission.

au•tis•tic [ɔː'tɪstɪk] *adj.* suffering from autism. **au•tism**, *n.* mental illness which makes you withdrawn and unable to communicate.

auto- ['ɔːtəʊ] *prefix meaning* self; **automatic; automobile.**

au•to•bi•og•ra•phy [ɔːtəbaɪ'ɒgrəfɪ] *n.* life story of a person written by himself/herself.
au•to•bi•o•graph•i•cal [ɔːtəbaɪə'græfɪkl] *adj.* referring to the life of the writer.

au•toc•ra•cy [ɔː'tɒkrəsɪ] *n.* system of government by one person. **au•to•crat** ['ɔːtəkræt] *n.* dictator/person who does not allow anyone else to rule him. **au•to•crat•ic** [ɔːtə'krætɪk] *adj.* ruled by one person.
au•to•crat•i•cal•ly, *adv.* like a dictator.

au•tog•a•my [ɔː'tɒgəmɪ] *n.* self-fertilization.

au•to•graph ['ɔːtəgrɑːf] 1. *n.* signature (of a famous person). 2. *v.* **to a. a book for s.o.** = to write your signature in it.

au•to•mat•ed *adj.* controlled by automation. **a. teller machine** = machine that automatically dispenses cash when a plastic card is inserted and certain buttons are pushed.
au•to•mat•ic [ɔːtə'mætɪk] *adj. & n.* (device) which works by itself. **au•to•mat•i•cal•ly**, *adv.* working by itself. **au•to•ma•tion** [ɔːtə'meɪʃn] *n.* installation of machinery to make a process more automatic. **au•tom•a•ton** [ɔː-'tɒmətən] *n.* (*pl.* **-ta**) doll which moves with a motor inside it; person who acts like a robot.

au•to•mo•bile ['ɔːtəməbiːl] *n.* car.

au•to•mo•tive [ɔːtə'məʊtɪv] *adj.* referring to cars.

au•ton•o•my [ɔː'tɒnəmɪ] *n.* self-government.
au•ton•o•mous, *adj.* (region) which governs itself.

au•top•sy ['ɔːtɒpsɪ] *n.* cutting up of a dead body to discover the cause of death.

au•to•sug•ges•tion [ɔːtəʊsə'dʒeʃtʃən] *n.* state where a person makes himself/herself believe sth. about himself/herself.

au•tumn ['ɔːtəm] *n.* season of the year when the leaves fall off the trees. **au•tum•nal** [ɔː-'tʌmnl] *adj.* referring to autumn.

aux•il•ia•ry [ɔːg'zɪlɪərɪ] 1. *n.* (a) helper. (b) verb which is used to form part of another verb. 2. *adj.* (person/machine) which helps.

a•vail [ə'veɪl] 1. *v.* **to a. oneself of** = to use. 2. *n.* **of no a.** = no use. **a•vail•a•bil•i•ty** [əveɪlə-'bɪlɪtɪ] *n.* being available. **a•vail•a•ble**, *adj.* ready to be used; which can be obtained.

av•a•lanche ['ævəlɑːnʃ] *n.* fall of snow down a mountainside.

a•vant-garde [ævɒŋ'gɑːd] *adj.* experimental (music/drama).

av•a•rice ['ævərɪs] *n.* state of not wanting to spend money. **av•a•ri•cious** [ævə'rɪʃəs] *adj.* wanting to hoard money and not spend it.

a•venge [ə'vendʒ] *v.* to pay s.o. back for (a crime). **a•veng•er**, *n.* person who pays back a crime.

av•e•nue ['ævənjuː] *n.* (a) wide, tree-lined, road in a city. (b) two parallel rows of trees. (c) way of approaching a problem.

a•ver [ə'vɜː] *v.* (*formal*) to state.

av•er•age ['ævərɪdʒ] 1. *n.* (a) figure arrived at when a total is divided by the number of figures added. (b) **on a.** = as a general rule. 2. *adj.* general; ordinary. 3. *v.* to work out as an average.

a•verse [ə'vɜːs] *adj.* **he is a. to hard work** = he dislikes it. **a•ver•sion** [ə'vɜːʃn] *n.* (a) (to) dislike. (b) **my pet a.** = thing I dislike most.

a•vert [ə'vɜːt] *v.* (a) to turn away (one's eyes). (b) to prevent (a disaster).

a•vi•a•ry ['eɪvɪərɪ] *n.* building for keeping birds in.

a•vi•a•tion [eɪvɪ'eɪʃn] *n.* art/technology of flying (aircraft). **a•vi•a•tor** ['eɪvɪeɪtə] *n.* airplane pilot.

av•id ['ævɪd] *adj.* eager/enthusiastic. **av•id•ly**, *adv.* eagerly.

av•o•ca•do (pear) [ævə'kɑːdəʊ ('peə)] *n.* (*pl.* -os) green tropical fruit with a large stone in the middle, eaten as a vegetable.

av•o•cet ['ævəset] *n.* white wader with a long bill which is curved upwards.

a•void [ə'vɔɪd] *v.* (a) to try not to do (sth). (b) to keep away from. **a•void•a•ble**, *adj.*

which you could have avoided. **a•void•ance,** *n.* act of avoiding.

av•oir•du•pois [ævədə'pɔɪz] *n.* system of weights based on ounces, pounds, etc.

a•vow•al [ə'vauəl] *n.* (*formal*) admission. **a•vowed** [ə'vaud] *adj.* stated; admitted.

a•vun•cu•lar [ə'vʌŋkjulə] *adj.* like an uncle.

a•wait [ə'weɪt] *v.* to wait for.

a•wake [ə'weɪk] 1. *v.* (**awoke; awoken**) (a) to wake (s.o.) up. (b) to become aware of. 2. *adj.* not sleeping.

a•wak•en [ə'weɪkn] *v.* to wake/to arouse. **a•wak•en•ing,** *n.* **a rude a.** = a disturbing realization.

a•ward [ə'wɔːd] 1. *n.* (a) prize. (b) decision which settles a dispute. 2. *v.* to give (a prize, etc.).

a•ware [ə'weə] *adj.* knowing. **a•ware•ness,** *n.* state of being aware.

a•wash [ə'wɒʃ] *adj.* covered with a liquid.

a•way [ə'weɪ] *adv.* (a) not here/far; **a. game** = at another team's field. (b) **the birds were singing a.** = they were going on singing; **right a.** = immediately.

awe [ɔː] *n.* fear/terror. **awe-in•spir•ing, awesome,** *adj.* frightening. **awe-struck,** *adj.* frightened/full of terror. **aw•ful** ['ɔːfl] *adj.* (a) (*old*) very frightening. (b) very bad/very strong; unpleasant. **aw•ful•ly,** *adv. inf.* very.

a•while [ə'waɪl] *adv.* for a short time.

awk•ward ['ɔːkwəd] *adj.* (a) difficult. (b) embarrassing. (c) clumsy. **awk•ward•ly,** *adv.* with difficulty; inconveniently. **awk•ward•ness,** *n.* (a) embarrassment. (b) difficulty.

awl [ɔːl] *n.* tool used for making small holes.

awn•ing ['ɔːnɪŋ] *n.* canvas roof stretched out to protect from the sun or rain.

a•woke, a•wok•en [ə'wəuk, ə'wəukn] *v. see* **awake.**

AWOL ['eɪwɒl] = absent without leave.

a•wry [ə'raɪ] *adv.* not straight.

ax, axe [æks] 1. *n.* instrument with a sharp metal head for chopping wood; **to have an a. to grind** = a particular point of view to put across. 2. *v.* to reduce (expenditure); to fire (staff).

ax•il ['æksɪl] *n.* place where a leaf joins a stem.

ax•i•om ['æksɪəm] *n.* well-known saying/obviously true statement. **ax•i•o•mat•ic** [æksɪə-'mætɪk] *adj.* obvious; well-known.

ax•is ['æksɪs] *n.* (*pl.* **axes** ['æksiːz]) imaginary line through center of a sphere.

ax•le ['æksl] *n.* rod going through the middle of a wheel.

a•ya•tol•lah [aɪə'tɒlə] *n.* Muslim leader.

aye [aɪ] *n.* yes; **the ayes have it** = more people have voted yes than no.

a•zal•ea [ə'zeɪlɪə] *n.* small shrub with showy scented flowers.

azo ['eɪzəu] *n.* **a. dyes** = dyes added to food to give it a better color.

az•ure ['eɪʒə] *adj.* blue like the sky.

æ back, ɑː farm, ɒ top, aɪ pipe, au how, aɪe fire, auə flower, ɔː bought, ɔɪ toy, e fed, eəhair, eɪ take, ə afraid, əu boat, əuə lower, vː word, iː heap, ɪ hit, ɪə hear, uː school, u book, ʌ but, b back, d dog, ð then, dʒ just, f fog, g go, h hand, j yes, k catch, l last, m mix, n nut, ŋ sing, p penny, r round, s some, ʃ short, t too, tʃ chop, θ thing, v voice, w was, z zoo, ʒ treasure

Bb

Ba *symbol for* barium.

BA [biːˈeɪ] Bachelor of Arts.

bab•ble [ˈbæbl] 1. *n.* (a) trickling sound (of water). (b) chatter. 2. *v.* (a) to make a trickling sound. (b) to chatter.

babe [beɪb] *n.* (*formal*) baby.

ba•bel [ˈbeɪbl] *n.* loud noise of talking.

ba•boon [bəˈbuːn] *n.* large African monkey.

ba•by [ˈbeɪbɪ] *n.* (a) very young child; **to have a b.** = to give birth to a baby; **the b. of the family** = the youngest of the children. (b) small animal. (c) small object; **b. grand** (piano). **baby carriage,** *n.* small carriage in which you can push a baby. **baby car•ri•er,** *n.* canvas cot with handles for carrying a baby. **ba•by•ish,** *adj.* like a baby. **ba•by-sit,** *v.* (baby-sat) to look after children while their parents are out. **ba•by-sit•ter,** *n.* person who baby-sits.

bach•e•lor [ˈbætʃələ] *n.* (a) unmarried man; **b. pad** = small apartment for a single person; **b. girl** = unmarried woman. (b) holder of a bachelor's degree from a university, having completed a four-year course of study.

ba•cil•lus [bəˈsɪləs] *n.* (*pl.* bacilli [bæˈsɪlaɪ]) type of bacterium.

back [bæk] 1. (a) part of the body down the spine between the neck and buttocks; **he did it behind my b.** = without my knowing; **I was glad to see the b. of him** = I was glad to see him go; **to put s.o.'s b. up** = to annoy s.o.; **we've broken the b. of the work** = we have done most of the work. (b) opposite part/side to the front; **he knows Chicago like the b. of his hand** = very well; **I have an idea at the b. of my mind** = I have the beginnings of an idea; **b. to front** = the wrong way round. (c) sportsman who plays in a defensive position in football/hockey, etc. 2. *adj.* (a) referring to the rear; **he's had to take a b. seat** = he's had to take a less prominent position; **b. seat driver** = passenger in a car who offers the driver unwanted advice. (b) in arrears; **b. pay** = pay which is owed to s.o. 3. *adv.* (a) to the rear; **stand b.** = move backward; **please sit b., I can't see** = please lean backward in your chair. (b) in return; **I'll call you b.** = I'll phone you again; **as soon as I get b. to the office** = as soon as I return to the office. (c) ago; **a few years b.** 4. *v.* (a) to (make sth) go backward; **can you b. the** car into the garage? he backed away from the fire. (b) to support (with money). (c) to gamble on (a horse). (d) (*of wind*) to blow in another direction. **back•ache,** *n.* pain in the back. **back bench•er,** *n.* any member of a legislature. **back•bit•ing,** *n.* sharp criticism. **back•bone,** *n.* spine/column of bones forming the main support of the back. **back•break•ing,** *adj.* very hard (work). **back•date,** *v.* to put an earlier date than true on (a check). **back down,** *v.* to retreat from your former position. **back•drop,** *n.* (*in theater*) painted sheet at the back of the stage. **back•er,** *n.* person who supports sth with money; person who gambles money on horse racing. **back•fire,** *v.* (*of a car*) to make a small bang, due to misfiring of the ignition; (*of a plan*) to go wrong with unfortunate consequences for the planner. **back•gam•mon,** *n.* game like checkers played on a special board. **back•ground,** *n.* the back part of a painting against which the foreground stands out; **he comes from a working class b.** = his family is working class; **b. music** = music played quietly in a movie or in a restaurant. **back•hand,** *adj. & n.* (tennis/table tennis shot) played with the back of the racket/paddle. **back•hand•ed,** *adj.* (compliment) that could be taken also as an insult. **back•hand•er,** *n.* blow/shot with the back of the hand. **back•ing,** *n.* (a) material used on the back of sth to strengthen it. (b) musical accompaniment to a singer or instrument. (c) (financial) support. (d) reversing (of a car). **back•lash,** *n.* reverse effect (of a political or social move); **white b.** = reaction among white people against measures taken to protect black people. **back•less,** *adj.* (dress, etc.) with no back. **back•log,** *n.* work not done/bills not paid. **back num•ber,** *n.* old copy of a magazine or newspaper. **back out,** *v.* to decide not to continue (with a project). **back•pack,** *n.* bag carried on a walker's back. **back•pack•er,** *n.* person who goes backpacking. **back•pack•ing,** *n.* going for a long walk, carrying your clothes, food, tent, etc., in a backpack. **back•ped•al,** *v.* (-pedaled) (a) to pedal backwards. (b) to reverse your opinions. **back•side,** *n. inf.* buttocks.

back•slid•ing, *n.* going back to a bad habit after having reformed. **back•space,** *n.* moving a cursor back one space on a computer monitor. **back•stage,** *adv. & adj.* in the parts of a theater where the audience can't go; behind the scenes/hidden from view. **back•stairs,** *n.* stairs (for servants) in the back part of a large house. **back•stroke,** *n.* style of swimming on your back. **back talk,** *n.* replying rudely. **back•track,** *v.* to change your opinion. **back up,** *v.* (a) to support (s.o.). (b) to make a copy of a computer file, for security reasons. (c) to reverse a car. **back•up (copy)** *n.* copy of a computer file or disk. **back•ward,** *adj.* (a) slow/retarded (child); (country) which is not industrially advanced. (b) **b. in paying bills** = slow in paying. **back•ward•ness,** *n.* being backward. **back•ward, backwards,** *adv.* in reverse/toward the rear; **he knows the song b.** = extremely well. **back•wa•ter,** *n.* (a) small slow-moving branch of a river. (b) quiet/old-fashioned place. **back•woods,** *n. pl.* forest; **they live in the b.** = they live far from other houses. **back•woods•man,** *n.* (*pl.* -men) person who lives in the forest. **back•yard,** *n.* small, usu. grassy area behind a house.

ba•con ['beɪkn] *n.* pork which has been salted or smoked; *inf.* **it saved his b.** = it got him out of the difficult situation.

bac•te•ri•um [bæk'tɪərɪəm] *n.* (*pl.* **bacteria**) microscopic organism which produces germs or decay. **bac•te•ri•al, bacteriological** [bæktɪərɪə'lɒdʒɪkl] *adj.* referring to bacteria; **b. warfare** = method of conducting war by using bacteria to kill the enemy. **bac•ter•i•ol•o•gist** [bæktɪərɪ'ɒlədʒɪst] *n.* scientist who specializes in bacteriology. **bac•te•ri•ol•o•gy,** *n.* study of bacteria.

bad [bæd] 1. *adj.* (**worse, worst**) (a) not good; **b. meat; b. driver.** (b) wicked. (c) unpleasant; **b. news; she's in a b. temper.** (d) serious; **b. accident.** (e) diseased; injured; **b. leg.** 2. *n.* (a) s.o. which is bad. (b) **I'm $50 to the b.** = I have lost/wasted $50. **bad•die, baddy,** *n. inf.* villain. **bad•lands,** *n.* land which cannot be cultivated. **bad•ly,** *adv.* (**worse, worst**) (a) not well (done). (b) seriously (wounded). (c) very much; **he b. needs a shave.**

bade [bæd] *v. see* **bid.**

badge [bædʒ] *n.* small sign worn to show that you belong to a group, or simply as a decoration.

badg•er ['bædʒə] 1. *n.* wild animal with striped black and white head which lives underground and comes out at night. 2. *v.* to bother (s.o.); **he badgered me into helping him.**

bad•i•nage [bædɪ'nɑːʒ] *n.* light teasing talk.

bad•min•ton ['bædmɪntən] *n.* game for two or four people, played with rackets and a shuttlecock.

baf•fle ['bæfl] 1. *n.* shield (to cut out noise). 2. *v.* (a) to puzzle. (b) to frustrate. **baf•fle•ment,** *n.* being baffled.

bag [bæg] 1. *n.* (a) thing made of paper/cloth/plastic which you can carry things in; **shopping b.** = large bag for carrying shopping; *inf.* **bags of money** = lots of money. (b) **bags under the eyes** = puffy layer of skin beneath the eyes showing that you are ill or tired. (c) *inf.* **it's in the b.** = the deal is agreed. (d) animals killed while hunting. (e) *inf.* **old b.** = dirty old woman. 2. *v.* (**bagged**) to catch (an animal when hunting). **bag•gy,** *adj.* (**-ier, -iest**) (*of clothes*) too big/hanging in folds.

bag•asse [bæ'gæs] *n.* residue left after crushing sugar cane.

bag•a•telle [bægə'tel] *n.* (a) game where small metal balls are sent round a board. (b) unimportant thing.

bag•gage ['bægɪdʒ] *n.* (*no pl.*) luggage.

bag•pipes ['bægpaɪps] *n. pl.* musical instrument made of an air sack attached to pipes.

bail [beɪl] *n.* (a) money paid to a court as security for a prisoner's temporary release; **he was released on b. of $5000.** (b) small piece of wood resting on the top of stumps in cricket. **bail•er,** *n.* scoop for removing water from a boat. **bail out,** *v.* (a) to scoop water out of (a boat); to help (s.o.) who is in financial difficulties. (b) to jump out of a crashing aircraft with the help of a parachute. (c) to pay money to let a prisoner out temporarily between hearings.

Bai•ley bridge ['beɪlɪ'brɪdʒ] *n.* prefabricated bridge which is supported by boats.

bail•iff ['beɪlɪf] *n.* court official who can seize property in payment of debts. (b) landowner's agent on an estate.

bairn ['beən] *n.* (*in Scotland*) child.

bait [beɪt] 1. *n.* fly, worm, etc., used to at-

æ back, ɑː farm, ɒ top, aɪ pipe, aʊ how, aɪə fire, aʊə flower, ɔː bought, ɔɪ toy, e fed, eəhair, eɪ take, ə afraid, əʊ boat, əʊə lower, vː word, iː heap, ɪ hit, ɪə hear, uː school, ʊ book, ʌ but, b back, d dog, ð then, dʒ just, f fog, g go, h hand, j yes, k catch, l last, m mix, n nut, ŋ sing, p penny, r round, s some, ʃ short, t too, tʃ chop, θ thing, v voice, w was, z zoo, ʒ treasure

tract fish or animals. 2. *v.* to attach bait to (a hook or trap).

baize [beɪz] *n.* green cloth made of wool.

bake [beɪk] *v.* to cook (in an oven). **bake•house,** *n.* building with ovens for baking. **bak•er,** *n.* person who makes bread and cakes; **baker's dozen** = thirteen. **bak•er•y,** *n.* place where baked goods are sold. **bak•ing.** *n.* cooking (in an oven); **b. dish** = fireproof dish which can be put in the oven; **b. sheet** = flat sheet of metal for baking cookies, biscuits, etc. on. **bak•ing pow•der,** *n.* powder which when added to a cake mix helps it to rise.

bal•a•cla•va [bælə'klɑːvə] *n.* **b. (helmet)** = knitted woolen helmet covering the whole head and neck, with a round opening for the face.

bal•a•lai•ka [bælə'laɪkə] *n.* Russian stringed instrument like a small guitar.

bal•ance ['bæləns] 1. *n.* (a) machine which weighs; **the result hangs in the b.** = you cannot tell which way the result will turn out. (b) staying steady; **to keep/to lose one's b.; the b. of power** = the division of power between countries. (c) what remains after all payments have been made; **we have a b. of $25 in the bank; b. of payments** = difference between money obtained from exports and money paid for imports by a country; **b. sheet** = statement drawn up at the end of a year showing the financial situation of a company. 2. *v.* (a) to remain in one position without falling. (b) to make (sth) stand without falling. (c) to counteract the effect of (sth). (d) **to make the accounts b.** = to make the total of income and expenditure cancel each other out. **bal•anced,** *adj.* level; sensible.

bal•co•ny ['bælkənɪ] *n.* (a) small terrace jutting out from an upper floor. (b) upper terrace of seats in a theater/auditorium, etc.

bald [bɔːld] *adj.* (a) with no hair. (b) not elaborate; **a b. statement of fact. bald•ing,** *adj.* becoming bald. **bald•ly,** *adv.* plainly; drily. **bald•ness,** *n.* lack of hair.

bal•der•dash ['bɔːldədæʃ] *n.* nonsense.

bale [beɪl] 1. *n.* large bundle. 2. *v.* **to b. hay** = to make hay into large bundles.

bale•ful ['beɪlful] *adj.* threatening/unpleasant; **a b. look. bale•ful•ly,** *adv.* in a baleful way.

balk [bɔːlk] *v.* (a) to prevent s.o. from doing sth. (b) **to b. at sth** = to refuse to do sth.

ball [bɔːl] *n.* (a) round object for playing games; **keep the b. rolling** = keep everything moving; **I'll start the b. rolling** = I'll start things off; **he's on the b.** = he knows his job very well/he is up to date; **they won't play b.** = they won't cooperate with us. (b) thing with a round shape; **b. of wool.** (c) formal dance. (d) game like (baseball) played with a ball. **b. park** = area set aside for playing baseball. **ball-and-**

sock•et, *adj.* (joint) where a ball at the end of one rod/bone fits a socket at the end of another. **ball bear•ing,** *n.* bearing using a ring of little steel balls; one of these steel balls. **ball boy, ball girl,** *n.* boy or girl who picks up the balls during a tennis match. **ball cock,** *n.* mechanism with a valve operated by a floating ball (for filling tanks/cisterns). **ball•point,** *adj.* **b. pen** = pen with a tiny ball which is automatically coated with ink from a tube. **ball•room,** *n.* large room for formal dances; **b. dancing** = formal dancing.

bal•lad ['bæləd] *n.* romantic popular song or poem telling a story. **bal•lade,** *n.* form of poetry, with a repeated refrain.

bal•last ['bæləst] *n.* (a) material carried in ship/balloon to give extra weight. (b) stones used to bed down railroad ties.

bal•let ['bæleɪ] *n.* (a) dancing as a spectacle for public performance; **b. dancer.** (b) piece danced for performance; **the ballet "Swan Lake."** (c) company which performs ballets. **bal•le•ri•na** [bælə'riːnə] *n.* woman ballet dancer.

bal•lis•tics [bə'lɪstɪks] *n.* science of shooting bullets or shells.

bal•loon [bə'luːn] *n.* large round object which is inflated; **hot-air b.** = large passenger-carrying balloon inflated with hot air. **bal•loon•ing,** *n.* sport of racing large passenger-carrying balloons.

bal•lot ['bælət] 1. *n.* voting by pieces of paper; **a secret b.** = election where the votes of individual voters are not disclosed; **absentee b.** = election where voters can mail in their votes; **b. box** = sealed box for putting ballot papers in. 2. *v.* to vote by pieces of paper. **bal•lot•rig•ging,** *n.* illegal arrangement of votes in a ballot, so that one side wins.

bal•ly•hoo [bælɪ'huː] *n.* energetic publicity/advertising (during an election campaign, etc.).

balm•y ['bɑːmɪ] *adj.* fragrant/soft (air/breeze).

bal•sa ['bɔːlsə] *n.* very light wood (used for making models).

bal•sam ['bɔːlsəm] *n.* fragrant flowering plant.

bal•us•trade [bælə'streɪd] *n.* stone fence made of small carved pillars along the edge of a terrace/balcony, etc. **bal•us•ter** ['bæləstə] *n.* small pillar.

bam•boo [bæm'buː] *n.* tropical plant which provides tall, strong, jointed canes; **b. shoots** = young shoots of bamboo which can be eaten.

bam•boo•zle [bæm'buːzl] *v.* to trick/to puzzle (s.o.).

ban [bæn] 1. *n.* law/instruction which forbids sth; **a b. on smoking in public places.** 2. *v.* **(banned)** to forbid (sth).

ba•nal [bə'nɑːl] *adj.* ordinary/trivial. **ban•al•i•ty** [bə'nælɪtɪ] *n.* ordinariness.

ba•nan•a [bə'nɑːnə] *n.* long yellow tropical fruit; **b. republic** = corrupt central American state.

band [bænd] 1. *n.* (a) thin loop of material for tying things together. (b) group of frequencies in radio transmission. (c) group of people. (d) group of musicians, esp. playing brass and percussion instruments. 2. *v.* to form a group. **band•mas•ter,** *n.* leader of a brass band. **bands•man,** *n.* (*pl.* **bandsmen**) musician playing in a band. **band•stand,** *n.* small stage (in public gardens) for outdoor concerts. **band•wag•on,** *n.* **to jump on the b.** = to join a popular movement/to start to do sth which is already proving popular.

band•age ['bændɪdʒ] 1. *n.* piece of cloth to tie around a wound/around a twisted ankle, etc. 2. *v.* to tie a cloth around a wound.

ban•dan•na [bæn'dænə] *n.* large silk handkerchief.

ban•deau ['bændəʊ] *n.* ribbon to tie back the hair.

ban•dit ['bændɪt] *n.* robber/brigand.

ban•dy ['bændɪ] 1. *adj.* **he has b. legs** = when he stands with feet together, his knees do not touch. 2. *v.* (**bandied**) **to b. about** = to shout/write (words to several people).

bane [beɪn] *n.* **it's the b. of my life** = it's what annoys me most.

bang [bæŋ] 1. *n.* (a) loud noise; **supersonic b.** = loud noise made when an aircraft goes faster than the speed of sound. (b) sharp blow. (c) hair cut straight across the forehead. 2. *v.* to make a bang (by hitting sth). 3. *inter. showing noise of an explosion;* **the gun suddenly went b.; b. in the middle** = right in the middle. **bang•er,** *n. Brit. inf.* sausage. **bang•ing,** *n.* noise of repeated bangs.

ban•gle ['bæŋgl] *n.* bracelet made of metal or rigid material.

ban•ish ['bænɪʃ] *v.* to send (s.o.) away/to exile (s.o.); to get rid of (sth).

ban•is•ters ['bænɪstəz] *n. pl.* set of vertical rods with a handrail along the side of stairs.

ban•jo ['bændʒəʊ] *n.* stringed instrument with a round body.

bank [bæŋk] 1. *n.* (a) long pile or mound of earth/sand/snow, etc. (b) edge of a river or canal. (c) row (of lights). (d) institution for keeping or lending money; **b. charges** = charges made by a bank for its services; **b. holiday** = public holiday when the banks are closed. 2. *v.* (a) to pile up in a long mound; **the snow banked up along the road** = the wind blew

the snow into banks. (b) (*of plane*) to roll to one side. (c) to put money into a bank; to use a bank; **where do you b.?** = which bank do you use? (d) **I'm banking on taking two weeks off next month** = I'm counting on/relying on taking two weeks off. **bank•er,** *n.* person who directs a bank. **bank•ing,** *n.* the profession of being a banker. **bank note,** *n.* paper money issued by a bank. **bank•roll,** *v. inf.* to pay for (a project). **bank•rupt,** *adj. & n.* (person) whose debts exceed his assets and who has been declared incapable of meeting his debts; **he has been declared b. bank•rupt•cy,** *n.* state of being bankrupt.

bank•sia ['bæŋksɪə] *n.* Australian shrub with yellow flowers.

ban•ner ['bænə] *n.* (a) long flag; **b. headlines** = very large headlines in a newspaper. (b) large piece of material with a slogan written on it, carried in a procession or protest march.

banns [bænz] *n. pl.* official statement in church of intention to marry.

ban•quet ['bæŋkwɪt] *n.* large formal dinner. **ban•quet•ing hall,** *n.* large room where banquets are held.

ban•tam ['bæntəm] *n.* breed of very small chickens.

ban•tam•weight, *n.* light weight in boxing between flyweight and featherweight.

ban•ter ['bæntə] *n.* sarcastic teasing comments. **ban•ter•ing,** *adj.* (tone of voice) used when making light sarcastic comments.

ban•yan ['bænjæn] *n.* tropical tree with roots which come down from the branches.

ba•o•bab ['bæʊbæb] *n.* very large tropical tree, found in Africa.

bap•tize [bæp'taɪz] *v.* to admit s.o. to the church and give them a Christian name. **bap•tism** ['bæptɪzəm] *n.* church ceremony where s.o. is given a Christian name. **bap•tis•mal** [bæp'tɪzml] *adj.* referring to baptism.

bar [bɑː] 1. *n.* (a) long piece (of metal/chocolate, etc.). (b) obstacle; **harbor b.** = ridge of sand at the entrance to a harbor; **color b.** = objection to persons because of the color of their skin. (c) place where drinks are served; **snack b./sandwich b.** = counter/shop where food/drinks are served. (e) officially recognized lawyers; legal profession. (f) division (in music). (g) unit of atmospheric pressure. 2. *v.* (**barred**) to block (a road); to stop (s.o. **from** doing sth). 3. *prep.* **b. none** = with no exceptions. **bar code,** *n.* system of lines printed on a product which can be read by a computer. **bar•ring,** *prep.* excepting.

barb [bɑ:b] *n.* small tooth (on a fish-hook or arrow). **barbed,** *adj.* with sharp points; **b. comment** = sharp critical comment; **b. wire** = wire (for fences) with sharp spikes.

bar•bar•i•an [bɑ:'beərɪən] *n.* wild/uncivilized person. **bar•bar•ic** [bɑ:'bærɪk] *adj.* cruel/uncivilized. **bar•bar•i•ty** [bɑ:'bærɪtɪ] *n.* cruelty. **bar•ba•rous** ['bɑ:bərəs] *adj.* cruel/uncivilized.

bar•be•cue ['bɑ:bɪkju:] 1. *n.* (a) charcoal fire/grill for cooking food outdoors. (b) meal cooked on a barbecue. 2. *v.* to cook on a barbecue.

bar•ber ['bɑ:bə] *n.* man who cuts men's hair.

bar•bi•tu•rate [bɑ:'bɪtjʊrət] *n.* drug which makes you sleep.

bard [bɑ:d] *n.* (*formal*) poet.

bare ['beə] 1. *adj.* (a) naked/not covered with clothes or leaves. (b) just enough; **a b. living** = just enough to live on; **b. necessities** = absolutely essential items for existence; **elected with a b. majority** = with a very small majority. 2. *v.* to strip naked; **he bared his soul** = he told all his innermost thoughts. **bare•back,** *adj. & adv.* riding a horse with no saddle. **bare•faced,** *adj.* crude/cynical (lie). **bare•foot,** *adv.* with no shoes on. **bare•foot•ed,** *adj.* with no shoes on. **bare•head•ed,** *adv. & adj.* with no hat on. **bare•ly,** *adv.* hardly/scarcely; **I b. had enough money to pay the bill. bare•ness,** *n.* nakedness.

bar•gain ['bɑ:gɪn] 1. *n.* (a) thing bought; sale agreed; **to strike a b.** = to agree on a sale; **he drives a hard b.** = he is a tough negotiator. (b) thing bought more cheaply than it usually is; **into the b.** = as well as everything else; **b. basement** = part of a store where cheap items are sold; 2. *v.* (a) to negotiate a sale; **I got more than I bargained for** = more than I expected. (b) to haggle. **bar•gain•ing,** *n.* discussion about prices/wages, etc.: **collective b.** = discussion between management and unions to fix new salaries for union members.

barge [bɑ:dʒ] 1. *n.* large flat-bottomed cargo boat on inland waters. 2. *v.* to bump heavily (into). **barge•man** (*pl* **-men**) *n.* man in charge of a barge. **barge pole,** *n.* long pole for moving a barge along.

bar•i•tone ['bærɪtəʊn] *adj. & n.* (singer with a) voice between tenor and bass.

bar•i•um ['beərɪəm] *n.* (*element:* Ba) white soft metal; **b. cocktail** = liquid which you drink before having your stomach X-rayed, which will show up clearly on the X-ray.

bark [bɑ:k] 1. *n.* (a) outer part of a tree. (b) loud noise made by dog; **his b. is worse than his bite** = he is not as terrifying as he sounds. 2. *v.* (a) **he barked his shin on the rock** = he scraped the skin off his shin. (b) to make a loud call like a dog; **to b. up the wrong tree** = to get the wrong idea. **bark•er,** *n.* person who calls out to advertise sth in the street. **bark•ing,** *n.* continuous calls of dogs.

bar•ley ['bɑ:lɪ] *n.* cereal crop; **pearl b.** = grains of barley used in cooking; **b. sugar** = candy made of boiled sugar.

bar•maid ['bɑ:meɪd] *n.* woman who serves drinks in a bar. **bar•man** ['bɑ:mən] *n.* (*pl.* -men) bartender.

barm•y ['bɑ:mɪ] *adj.* (-ier, -iest) *inf.* mad.

barn [bɑ:n] *n.* large farm building for storing grain or hay. **barn•yard,** *n.* yard in a farm.

bar•na•cle ['bɑ:nəkl] *n.* (a) small shellfish which clings to the bottoms of ships/to submerged wooden posts, etc. (b) **b. goose** = common northern goose.

bar•ney ['bɑ:nɪ] *n. sl.* argument.

ba•rom•e•ter [bə'rɒmɪtə] *n.* instrument for measuring atmospheric pressure, and therefore for forecasting the weather. **bar•o•met•ric** [bærə'metrɪk] *adj.* referring to a barometer; **b. pressure.**

bar•on ['bærən] *n.* lowest rank of hereditary peers, now also title of life peers. **bar•on•ess,** *n.* wife of a baron; title of a life peeress. **bar•on•et,** *n.* hereditary knight. **ba•ro•ni•al** [bə'rəʊnɪəl] *adj.* large/sumptuous (castle).

ba•roque [bə'rɒk] *adj.* in the ornate style of architecture of the late 17th and 18th centuries.

bar•racks [] *n.* buildings where military personnel are housed.

bar•ra•cu•da [bærə'kju:də] *n.* large tropical fish.

bar•rage ['bærɑ:ʒ] *n.* (a) dam across a river, etc. (b) rapid fire (of guns/questions).

bar•rel ['bærəl] *n.* (a) large wooden container (for wine/oil/fish/oysters, etc.); **he's got me over a b.** = in a very awkward situation. (b) firing tube (on a gun). (c) **b. organ** = machine for making music when a handle is turned.

bar•ren ['bærən] *adj.* unproductive (land); (woman/animal) who cannot have young; (tree) which does not produce fruit. **bar•ren•ness,** *n.* being barren.

bar•ri•cade [bærɪ'keɪd] 1. *n.* makeshift heap of cars/rubbish, etc., made to block a street. 2. *v.* to block (a street/a door).

bar•ri•er ['bærɪə] *n.* thing which stops you moving forward.

bar•ris•ter ['bærɪstə] *n. Brit.* lawyer who is allowed to speak in court.

bar•row ['bærəu] *n.* (a) small wheeled truck which is pushed by hand. (b) mound of earth piled over a prehistoric tomb.

bar•tend•er ['bɑːtendə] *n.* man who serves drinks in a bar.

bar•ter ['bɑːtə] 1. *n.* exchange (of one product for another). 2. *v.* to exchange (one product for another).

ba•salt ['bæsɔːlt] *n.* black volcanic rock.

base [beɪs] 1. *n.* (a) bottom part. (b) military camp; **air force b.** (c) substance which is the main part of a mixture. (d) chemical compound which reacts with an acid to form a salt. 2. *v.* **to b. sth on** = to use sth as a base. 3. *adj.* low/cheap; **b. metal** = not a precious metal.

base•ball ['beɪsbɔːl] *n.* team game played with a bat and ball. **base•board,** *n.* decorative board running along the bottom edge of a wall in a room. **base•less,** *adj.* (accusation) without any basis in fact. **base•ment,** *n.* floor beneath the ground floor.

bash [bæʃ] 1. *n.* (*pl.* -es) **a b. on the head** = you bumped your head. 2. *v.* to hit (sth) hard.

bash•ful ['bæʃful] *adj.* shy/modest. **bash•ful•ly,** *adv.* shyly. **bash•ful•ness,** *n.* being bashful.

ba•sic ['beɪsɪk] *adj.* elementary; **b. vocabulary** = most commonly used words. **ba•si•cal•ly,** *adv.* at bottom. **ba•sics** *pl. n.* simple and important facts; **to get back to b.** = to consider the basic points again.

BASIC ['beɪsɪk] Beginners All-purpose Symbolic Instruction Code.

bas•il ['bæzl] *n.* type of scented herb.

ba•sil•i•ca [bə'zɪlɪkə] *n.* (a) large rectangular church. (b) large catholic church.

ba•sin ['beɪsn] *n.* large bowl; **wash b.** = bowl in a bathroom with faucets giving running water for washing the hands.

ba•sis ['beɪsɪs] *n.* (*pl.* bases) (scientific) reason.

bask [bɑːsk] *v.* to lie (in the sun/in glory).

bas•ket ['bɑːskɪt] *n.* container made of woven straw/cane, etc.; **b. chair** = chair made of woven cane. **bas•ket•ball** ['bɑːskɪtbɔːl] *n.* team game where you try to throw a ball into a small net high up. **bas•ket•work,** *n.* making of baskets; objects made of woven straw/cane, etc.

bas-re•lief ['bæsrɪliːf] *n.* type of carving in stone where the figures stand out against (but are joined to) the background.

bass 1. [bæs] *n.* type of edible freshwater fish. 2.

[beɪs] *adj. & n.* (*pl.* -es) low/deep voice or music; **double b.** = instrument like a very large cello; **b. guitar/trombone** = large guitar/trombone tuned to play low notes; **b. clef** = sign in music showing that the notes are lower.

bas•set ['bæsɪt] *n.* **b. (hound)** = breed of dog with short legs and long ears.

bas•soon [bə'suːn] *n.* low-pitched wind instrument. **bas•soon•ist,** *n.* person who plays a bassoon.

bas•tard ['bɑːstəd] *adj. & n.* (person) not born of married parents; (thing) which is not pure; *inf.* hateful person/thing.

baste [beɪst] *v.* (a) to sew (material) loosely. (b) to spread juices over (meat which is cooking).

bas•tion ['bæstɪən] *n.* fortified part/stronghold.

bat [bæt] 1. *n.* (a) small mammal which flies by night and hangs upside down to rest. (b) instrument for hitting a ball (in some games). 2. *v.* (**batted**) (a) to be one of the two batsmen (in baseball, cricket, etc.); (*of a baseball/cricket team, etc.*) to have the turn to bat. (b) **she never batted an eyelid** = she did not show any surprise. **bats•man,** *n.* (*pl.* -men) person (esp. in cricket) who is batting.

batch [bætʃ] *n.* (*pl.* -es) quantity of bread/cakes baked at one time; group of letters/goods taken together.

bat•ed ['beɪtɪd] *adj.* **with b. breath** = holding your breath.

bath [bɑːθ] 1. *n.* (a) water used for washing all the body. (b) container for such water; container full of a liquid; **will you run my b. for me?** = will you fill the bath tub with water for me? (c) act of washing all the body; **to take a b.** (d) **public baths** = large (public) building with a swimming pool. 2. *v.* to wash (s.o./yourself) all over; **he is bathing the baby. bath mat,** *n.* small mat to step on as you get out of the bath. **bath oil,** *n.* scented oil to put in a bath. **bath•robe,** *n.* loose coatlike garment worn before or after a bath or for relaxing in. **bath•room,** *n.* room with a toilet, wash basin and usu. a bathtub or shower. **bath salts,** *n. pl.* scented crystals to put in a bath. **bath towel,** *n.* very large towel for drying yourself after a bath. **bath•tub,** *n.* tub/container for washing all the body.

bathe [beɪð] 1. *n.* swim. 2. *v.* (a) to swim. (b) to wash (a wound) carefully. (c) to take a bath. **bath•er,** *n.* person who is swimming. **bath•ing,** *n.* swimming (in the sea, river or a

æ back, aː farm, ɒ top, aɪ pipe, aʊ how, aɪe fire, aʊə flower, ɔː bought, ɔɪ toy, e fed, eəhair, eɪ take, ə afraid, əʊ boat, əʊə lower, vː word, iː heap, ɪ hit, ɪə hear, uː school, ʊ book, ʌ but, b back, d dog, ð then, dʒ just, f fog, g go, h hand, j yes, k catch, l last, m mix, n nut, ŋ sing, p penny, r round, s some, ʃ short, t too, tʃ chop, θ thing, v voice, w was, z zoo, ʒ treasure

pool); **b. suit** = piece of clothing worn when swimming.

ba•thos ['beɪθɒs] *n.* sudden drop from a serious subject to a trivial one.

bath•y•sphere ['bæθɪsfɪə] *n.* round pressurized cabin for exploring deep parts of the sea. **bath•y•scaph,** *n.* type of small submarine, used for underwater research.

ba•tik [bæ'tiːk] *n.* type of cloth, colored in patterns by dyeing it with wax designs on it.

ba•ton ['bætn] *n.* stick (of orchestra conductor or police officer).

ba•tra•chi•an [bə'treɪkɪən] *n.* amphibian, such as a toad.

bat•tal•ion [bə'tælɪən] *n.* part of the army often commanded by a lieutenant-colonel.

bat•ten ['bætn] 1. *n.* thin strip of wood. 2. *v.* (*on ship*) **to b. down the hatches** = to close down the hatch covers before a storm.

bat•ter ['bætə] 1. *n.* thin liquid mixture of flour/eggs/milk, for making pancakes, etc. 2. *v.* to hit hard and continuously. **bat•tered,** *adj.* which has been hit hard; **b. babies/wives** = babies/wives who have been constantly ill-treated. **bat•ter•ing ram,** *n.* long beam used to break down castle gates.

bat•ter•y ['bætərɪ] *n.* (a) group of artillery guns. (b) container with a cell or several cells charged with electricity. (c) **assault and b.** = criminal charge of attacking s.o. with violence. **bat•ter•y-pow•ered** *adj.* worked by an electric battery.

bat•tle ['bætl] 1. *n.* important fight between large enemy forces; **a b. royal** = a great struggle. 2. *v.* to fight (**against**). **bat•tle•ax, battleaxe,** *n. inf.* large fierce woman. **bat•tle•field,** *n.* site of a battle. **bat•tle•front,** *n.* line along which fighting is taking place. **bat•tle•ments,** *n. pl.* top part of a castle wall, with a walk for soldiers. **bat•tle•ship,** *n.* very large warship.

bat•ty ['bætɪ] *adj. inf.* mad.

bau•ble ['bɔːbl] *n.* (*formal*) cheap piece of jewelery.

baud rate ['bɔːdreɪt] *n.* number of signal changes transmitted per second.

baulk [bɔːlk] *v. see* **balk.**

baux•ite ['bɔːksaɪt] *n.* mineral from which aluminum is produced.

bawd•y ['bɔːdɪ] *adj.* rude/coarse.

bawl [bɔːl] *v.* to shout loudly. **bawl out,** *v.* to criticize (s.o.).

bay [beɪ] 1. *n.* (a) fragrant shrub whose leaves are used in cooking. (b) large rounded inlet in a coast; **the B. of Biscay.** (c) arch of a bridge; section of a church between pillars; **b. window** = window which projects from an outside wall. (d) **parking b.** = place marked for park-

ing; **loading b.** = place where trucks can be parked with a high platform for loading. (e) light brown horse. (f) **to keep attackers at b.** = to keep them away. 2. *v.* (*of hunting dog*) to bark.

bay•o•net ['beɪənət] *n.* sharp blade attached to the end of a rifle.

ba•zaar [bə'zɑː] *n.* (a) oriental market. (b) market selling goods for charity.

ba•zoo•ka [bə'zuːkə] *n.* small anti-tank gun.

b. & b. = bed and breakfast.

BBC [biːbiː'siː] British Broadcasting Corporation.

B.C. ['biː'siː] *abbrev. for* before Christ; **Julius Caesar died in 44 B.C.**

be [biː] *v.* (**I am, you are, he is, we/they are; I/he was, we/you/they were; he has been**) 1. (a) (*describing a person or thing*) **the house is big.** (b) to add up to; **two and three are five.** (c) to exist/to live; **where are we? there he is; how are you today? tomorrow is Friday.** (d) to feel; **I am cold; they are hungry.** (e) to go; **have you ever been to New York? the police had been into every room.** (f) (*showing time*) **it is four o'clock.** (g) (*showing future*) **he is to see the doctor tomorrow.** 2. (*used to make part of verbs*) **I am coming; he has been waiting for hours;** (*passive use*) **he was killed by a train. be•ing.** 1. *adj.* **for the time b.** = temporarily/for now. 2. *n.* (a) existence; **the association came into b. in 1946.** (b) **human b.** = person.

beach [biːtʃ] 1. *n.* (*pl.* **-es**) stretch of sand/pebbles by the side of the sea. 2. *v.* to bring (a boat) on to the beach. **beach•comb•er,** *n.* person who collects things thrown up on the beach by the sea. **beach•head,** *n.* small area occupied by troops at the beginning of an invasion from the sea. **beach•wear,** *n.* (*no pl.*) clothes to wear on the beach.

bea•con ['biːkən] *n.* light (used as a signal); **radio b.** = radio transmitter which guides aircraft into an airport.

bead [biːd] *n.* (a) small ornament with a hole so that it can be threaded. (b) small drop of liquid. **bead•ing,** *n.* thin strip of wood (usu. carved in a pattern) used to decorate. **bead•y,** *adj.* **b. eyed** = with eyes small and bright like beads.

bea•gle ['biːgl] *n.* breed of dog used for hunting.

beak [biːk] *n.* hard covering of a bird's mouth.

beak•er ['biːkə] *n.* metal/plastic cup, usu. with no handle; glass container used in scientific experiments.

beam [biːm] 1. (a) large block of wood used in building. (b) ray (of light/sound); **radio b.** = wavelength for radio transmission. (c) width of a ship; *inf.* **he's broad in the b.** = rather fat. 2. *v.* (a) to send out rays. (b) to smile.

beam•ing, *adj.* radiant (sunshine/smile/face).

bean [bi:n] *n.* (a) vegetable with edible seeds (and pods); *inf.* full of beans = full of vigor. (b) coffee beans = fruit of the coffee plant which, when roasted and ground, are used to make coffee.

bear ['beə] 1. *n.* (a) large furry wild animal; polar b. = large white bear living in Arctic regions; teddy b. = toy bear. (b) person who believes the stock market prices will fall. 2. *v.* (bore; has borne) (a) to carry; this tree has borne fruit every year; the deposit bears interest at 5%. (b) to stand/to put up with; I can't b. noise. (c) to support; will this branch b. my weight? (d) to turn; b. right at the crossroads. (e) to aim; the enemy brought their guns to b. on our ship. **bear•a•ble,** *adj.* which you can put up with. **bear down on,** *v.* to advance heavily toward (s.o.). **bear•er,** *n.* person who carries sth. **bear•ing,** *n.* (a) ball bearings = set of small balls around an axle to spread the weight evenly and make the wheel turn smoothly. (b) to get your bearings = to find out where you are; to lose your bearings = to lose all idea of where you are. (c) stately b. = stately way of standing/walking. **bear out,** *v.* to confirm. **bear•skin,** *n.* tall fur hat worn by a soldier in some armies. **bear up,** *v.* to survive cheerfully. **bear with,** *v.* to endure patiently.

beard ['biəd] *n.* hair on the lower part of a man's face; whiskers on a mussel/oyster, etc. **beard•ed,** *adj.* with a beard. **beard•less,** *adj.* with no beard.

beast [bi:st] *n.* (a) wild animal; b. of burden = donkey/horse, etc., trained to carry loads. (b) nasty, difficult, or unpleasant person. **beast•li•ness,** *n.* nastiness/unpleasantness (of person). **beast•ly,** *adj.* nasty; unpleasant.

beat [bi:t] 1. *n.* (a) regular sound; heart b. (b) regular measure in music. (c) area regularly patrolled by a policeman. 2. *v.* (beat; has beaten) (a) to hit hard several times. (b) to chase (birds); we b. a hasty retreat = we went away very quickly; don't b. about the bush = get to the point quickly; *Sl.* b. it! = go away! (c) to defeat. (d) to do better than (a record). (e) to stir (eggs, etc.) vigorously. **beat back,** *v.* to push back. **beat down,** *v.* (a) to flatten. (b) I beat down his price = I reduced the price he was asking by haggling; he beat me down = he made me reduce my price. (c) (*of the sun*) to strike hard on. **beat•en,** *adj.* off the b. track

= away from other houses. **beat•er,** *n.* (a) person who drives birds towards the people who will shoot them. (b) machine for beating eggs. **beat•ing,** *n.* act of hitting. **beat up,** *v.* (a) to whip (cream). (b) to attack (s.o.).

be•at•i•fy [bi:'ætɪfaɪ] *v.* to declare (s.o.) blessed (as the first step to declaring s.o. a saint). **be•at•i•fi•ca•tion** [bi:ætɪfɪ'keɪʃn] *n.* declaring s.o. blessed.

Beau•fort scale ['bəufət'skeɪl] *n.* scale for measuring wind strengths.

beau•ti•ful ['bju:tɪful] *adj.* very pleasing to look at. **beau•ti•cian,** *n.* person who makes people beautiful (by applying makeup, etc.). **beau•ti•ful•ly,** *adv.* in a very pleasing way. **beau•ti•fy,** *v.* to make sth beautiful. **beau•ty,** *n.* state of being beautiful; b. salon = establishment specializing in women's appearance; b. spot = dark spot, usu. on the face.

bea•ver ['bi:və] *n.* small American mammal which lives in water and makes dams with trees which it gnaws down.

be•calmed [bi:'ka:md] *adj.* (*of a sailing ship*) not able to move because there is no wind.

be•came [bɪ'keɪm] *v. see* **be•come.**

be•cause [bɪ'kɒz] *conj.* for the reason that; owing to the fact that. **because of,** *prep.* on account of.

beck [bek] *n.* (a) (*in northern England*) mountain stream. (b) he is always at her b. and call = he always does exactly what she wants him to do.

beck•on ['bekən] *v.* to make a sign (to s.o.) to come.

be•come [bɪ'kʌm] *v.* (became; has become) to change into sth different; what became of him? = what happened to him? **be•com•ing,** *adj.* her dress is very b. = her dress suits her very well.

bec•que•rel ['bekərel] *n.* SI unit of radiation.

bed [bed] *n.* (a) piece of furniture for sleeping on; double b. = bed for two people; single b. = bed for one person; to go to b. = to lie down in bed to sleep for the night; he took to his b. = he was ill and had to stay in bed; to make the b. = to straighten the bedclothes after getting out of bed. (b) bottom (of a river/lake); oyster b. = collection of oysters at the bottom of the sea; watercress b. = mass of watercress growing in a river. (c) area of garden kept for plants. 2. *v.* (bedded) to b. down = to give (horses) fresh straw. **bed•clothes,** *n. pl.* sheets/blankets, etc., on a bed. **bed•cov•er,** *n.* cloth which

---

æ back, ɑ: farm, ɒ top, aɪ pipe, aʊ how, aiə fire, aʊə flower, ɔ: bought, ɔɪ toy, e fed, eəhair, eɪ take, ə afraid, əʊ boat, əʊə lower, ɜ: word, i: heap, ɪ hit, ɪə hear, u: school, ʊ book, ʌ but, b back, d dog, ð then, dʒ just, f fog, g go, h hand, j yes, k catch, l last, m mix, n nut, ŋ sing, p penny, r round, s some, ʃ short, t too, tʃ chop, θ thing, v voice, w was, z zoo, ʒ treasure

covers a bed during the daytime. **bed•ding**, n. (a) bedclothes (mattress/pillows, etc.); straw (for horses). (b) **bedding plants** = plants suitable for putting into flower beds. **bed•fel•low**, n. person who sleeps in the same bed; person who is associated with s.o. **bed jack•et**, n. warm jacket worn in bed. **bed•pan**, n. bowl for passing waste water into when lying in bed. **bed•rid•den**, adj. forced to stay in bed because of illness. **bed•rock**, n. bottom rock beneath various mineral seams. **bed•room**, n. room for sleeping in. **bed•side**, n. side of a bed; **b. manner** = attitude of a doctor to his sick patient. **bed•sore**, n. sore which is caused by lying in bed for long periods. **bed•spread**, n. decorative cloth to put over a bed. **bed•stead**, n. solid frame of a bed. **bed•time**, n. time to go to bed; **it's past your b.** = it's later than the time you usually go to bed.

be•dev•iled [bɪ'devld] adj. surrounded (with difficulties).

bed•lam ['bedləm] n. loud noise; chaos.

be•drag•gled [bɪ'drægld] adj. wet and dirty.

bee [biː] n. small insect which makes honey. **bee•eat•er**, n. small tropical bird, which eats insects such as bees. **beehive**, n. box in which a colony of bees lives. **bee•keep•er**, n. person who keeps bees. **bee•keep•ing**, n. keeping of bees (for honey). **bee•line**, n. straight line; **he made a b. for the drinks** = he went straight to the drinks. **bees•wax**, n. wax produced by bees, used as a polish.

beech [biːtʃ] n. (pl. -es) large northern tree; wood of this tree.

beef [biːf] 1. n. (a) meat from a bull or cow; **corned b.** = beef which has been salted. (b) inf. grumble. 2. v. inf. to grumble (**about**). **beef•burg•er** ['biːfbɜːgə] n. hamburger. **beef•y**, adj. (-ier, -iest) muscular.

beep [biːp] 1. n. short high sound made by an electronic device, such as a computer. 2. v. to make a short high-pitched sound. **beep•er**, n. small radio receiver that emits a beep (or vibrates) when signaled in order to call the person carrying it.

beer ['bɪə] n. alcoholic drink made from malt, flavored with hops; a glass of this drink. **beer•y**, adj. referring to beer.

beet [biːt] n. (a) sugar b. root vegetable grown for processing into sugar. (b) beetroot. **beet•root**, n. dark red root vegetable.

bee•tle ['biːtl] n. small winged insect with a hard cover over its wings.

beet•ling ['biːtlɪŋ] adj. (cliff) which is high and looks threatening.

be•fall [bɪ'fɔːl] v. (befell; has befallen) (formal) to happen (to).

be•fit [bɪ'fɪt] v. (formal) (befitted) to suit.

be•fore [bɪ'fɔː] adv., prep. & conj. (a) in front (of). (b) earlier (than). **be•fore•hand**, adv. in advance.

be•friend [bɪ'frend] v. to be friendly to and help (s.o.).

beg [beg] v. (begged) (a) to ask for money. (b) to ask; **to b. a favor of s.o.** = to ask s.o. a favor; **I b. your pardon** = excuse me. **beg•gar**, n. person who asks for money; inf. **lucky beggar!** = what a lucky person! **beg•gar•ly**, adj. small/poor (wage). **beg•ging**, n. asking for money; **it's going b.** = no one wants it.

be•get [bɪ'get] v. (beget; begot; has begotten) (old) to give birth to; to produce.

be•gin [bɪ'gɪn] v. (began; has begun) to start; **b. again** = start from the beginning. **be•gin•ner**, n. person who is starting to do sth. **be•gin•ning**, n. first part/start; **at the b.** = to start with.

be•go•nia [bɪ'gəʊnɪə] n. pot plant with large bright flowers.

be•grudge [bɪ'grʌdʒ] v. to feel resentment because of sth s.o. has or does; **I don't b. him his money.**

be•guile [bɪ'gaɪl] v. to make (time) pass quickly and pleasantly.

be•half [bɪ'hɑːf] n. (a) **I am speaking on b. of the association** = I am speaking to get support for the association. (b) **acting on my b.** = acting for me. (c) **don't worry on my b.** = do not worry about me.

be•have [bɪ'heɪv] v. to act; **b. yourself** = be good. **be•haved**, adj. **well-behaved child** = polite/quiet child; **badly-behaved child** = child who is rude/dirty/noisy. **be•hav•ior**, Brit. **be•hav•iour**, n. conduct/way of acting. **be•hav•ior•al**, adj. concerning the behavior of human beings.

be•head [bɪ'hed] v. to cut off a head.

be•hind [bɪ'haɪnd] 1. adv. (a) after; **he stayed b.** = he stayed at the place everyone started from. (b) late; **I am b. with my work.** 2. prep. (a) at the back of; **what is really b. it all?** = what is the real cause of it all? **I'm b. you completely** = I'm in full support. (b) late/retarded (by comparison with s.o. else); less advanced than (s.o.). 3. n. inf. buttocks. **be•hind•hand**, adv. late.

be•hold [bɪ'həʊld] v. (beheld) (formal) to see. **be•hold•er**, n. person who sees.

be•hold•en [bɪ'həʊldən] adj. (formal) grateful (**to** s.o. **for** sth).

be•hoove [bɪ'həʊv] v. to be fitting.

beige [beɪʒ] adj. pale fawn color.

be•lat•ed [bɪ'leɪtɪd] adj. late. **be•lat•ed•ly**, adv. late.

be•lay [bɪ'leɪ] v. to attach a rope.

belch [beltʃ] 1. n. (pl. -es) noise made when

bringing up gas from the stomach. 2. *v.* (a) to make a noise by bringing up gas from the stomach through the mouth. (b) to pour **out** (smoke, flames).

be•lea•guered [bɪ'liːgəd] *adj.* in a difficult position; surrounded by enemies.

bel•fry ['belfrɪ] *n.* tower for bells.

Bel•gian ['beldʒən] 1. *adj.* referring to Belgium. 2. *n.* person from Belgium.

be•lie [bɪ'laɪ] *v.* (*formal*) to hide/to show (sth) wrongly.

be•lieve [bɪ'liːv] *v.* to feel sure of (sth), without any proof; **I b. so** = I think that is correct; **to b. in sth** = to believe that sth exists. **be•lief**, *n.* feeling sure of sth. **be•liev•a•ble**, *adj.* which one can believe. **be•liev•er**, *n.* person who believes in sth, esp. God.

be•lit•tle [bɪ'lɪtl] *v.* to make (sth) seem small or unimportant.

bell [bel] *n.* metal cup-shaped object which makes a ringing sound when hit; mechanism to make a ringing sound; **that rings a b.** = that reminds me of something. **bell•boy, bell-hop**, *n.* messenger boy employed in a hotel. **bell push**, *n.* button which rings a bell when pushed. **bell tow•er**, *n.* tower for bells.

bel•la•don•na ['belə'dɒnə] *n.* deadly nightshade, a poisonous plant.

belle [bel] *n.* beautiful woman.

bel•li•cose ['belɪkəʊs] *adj.* (*formal*) warlike.

bel•lig•er•ent [bə'lɪdʒərənt] 1. *adj.* warlike. 2. *n.* country fighting a war. **bel•lig•er•en•cy**, *n.* being belligerent.

bel•low ['beləʊ] 1. *n.* loud cry (of bull/angry person). 2. *v.* to make a loud cry.

bel•lows ['beləʊz] *n. pl.* apparatus for blowing air into a fire to make it burn brightly.

bel•ly ['belɪ] *n.* (*pl.* **-ies**) *inf.* abdomen. **bel•ly•ache**. 1. *n.* pain in the stomach. 2. *v. inf.* to complain bitterly (**about** sth). **bel•ly flop**, *n. inf.* **to do a b.** = to fall flat on to the water instead of diving into it. **bel•ly•ful**, *n. inf.* **I've had a b. of his complaints** = I've had as many of his complaints as I can stand.

be•long [bɪ'lɒŋ] *v.* (a) **to b. to s.o.** = to be s.o.'s property. (b) **to be to a club** = to be a member (of a club). **be•long•ings**, *n. pl.* personal property.

be•lov•ed [bɪ'lʌvɪd] 1. *adj.* whom s.o. loves. 2. *n.* person who is loved by s.o.

be•low [bɪ'ləʊ] 1. *adv.* lower down. 2. *prep.* lower than; **the temperature never goes b. 25°.**

belt [belt] 1. *n.* (a) strap which goes around your waist; **seat b.** = belt in a car or aircraft which holds you safely in place. (b) zone; **green b.** = area around a town having woods/parks where building is not permitted. 2. *v. inf.* **they were belting out a song** = singing a song very loudly.

be•moan [bɪ'məʊn] *v.* (*formal*) to complain about (sth).

be•mused [bɪ'mjuːzd] *adj.* bewildered/puzzled.

bench [bentʃ] *n.* (*pl.* **-es**) (a) long hard seat (for several people). (b) **the b.** = judge or judges who try cases in court. (c) table (for working). **bench mark**, *n.* standard against which something can be tested.

bend [bend] 1. *n.* (a) curve; **S-bend** = double curve in a pipe; *inf.* **around the b.** = quite mad. (b) **the bends** = illness in divers caused by coming up from a deep dive too quickly. 2. *v.* (**bent**) to make (a straight object) curved; to curve. **bend down**, *v.* to stoop.

be•neath [bɪ'niːθ] 1. *adv.* underneath/below. 2. *prep.* under; **he thinks it is b. him** = he thinks it is too unimportant for him to deal with.

ben•e•dic•tion [benɪ'dɪkʃn] *n.* blessing (in church).

ben•e•fac•tor, benefactress ['benɪfæktə, 'benɪfæktrəs] *n.* person who gives s.o./a society money.

ben•ef•i•cent [bɪ'nefɪsənt] *adj.* (*formal*) (person) who does good.

ben•e•fi•cial [benɪ'fɪʃl] *adj.* which does good; useful.

ben•e•fi•ci•ar•y [benɪ'fɪʃərɪ] *n.* (*pl.* **-ies**) person who inherits sth from a person who has died.

ben•e•fit ['benɪfɪt] 1. *n.* (a) profit/advantage. (b) payment; **unemployment b.** = payment (by the state) to unemployed people; **maternity b.** = payment to a woman who has had a baby. 2. *v.* to be of profit.

be•nev•o•lence [bə'nevələns] *n.* goodness/charity. **be•nev•o•lent**, *adj.* good/charitable. **be•nev•o•lent•ly**, *adv.* in a benevolent way.

be•night•ed [bɪ'naɪtəd] *adj.* uneducated.

be•nign [bɪ'naɪn] *adj.* (a) pleasant (person). (b) non-malignant (growth).

bent [bent] 1. *adj.* (a) curved. (b) **he is b. on becoming a sailor** = he is very eager to become a sailor. (c) *Sl.* dishonest. 2. *n.* **she has a natural b. to be a doctor** = she has an instinct to become a doctor. 3. *v. see also* **bend**.

æ back, aː farm, ɒː top, aɪ pipe, aʊ how, aiə fire, aʊə flower, ɔː bought, ɔɪ toy, e fed, eəhair, eɪ take, ə afraid, əʊ boat, əʊə lower, vː word, iː heap, ɪ hit, ɪə hear, uː school, ʊ book, ʌ but, b back, d dog, ð then, dʒ just, f fog, g go, h hand, j yes, k catch, l last, m mix, n nut, ŋ sing, p penny, r round, s some, ʃ short, t too, tʃ chop, θ thing, v voice, w was, z zoo, ʒ treasure

ben•zene ['benziːn] *n.* liquid obtained from coal, which is used as a fuel and causes cancer. **ben•zine** ['benziːn] *n.* liquid mixture obtained from petroleum, and used for cleaning.

be•queath [bɪ'kwiːð] *v.* to leave (property/money) to s.o. when you die. **be•quest** [bɪ'kwest] *n.* property left to s.o.

ber•ber•is ['bɜːbərɪs] *n.* plant with small red berries, grown for decoration.

be•reaved [bɪ'riːvd] *n.* **the b.** = (i) widow/widower; (ii) family of a person who has died. **be•reave•ment,** *n.* loss of member of the family through death.

be•ret ['bereɪ] *n.* round cloth or felt cap with no peak.

ber•i•ber•i [berɪ'berɪ] *n.* tropical disease of the nervous system.

ber•ry ['berɪ] *n.* (*pl.* **-ies**) fruit of a shrub.

ber•serk [bə'zɜːk] *adj.* **to go b.** = to go wild/mad.

berth [bɜːθ] 1. *n.* (a) place where a ship ties up to a quay or dock; **to give sth a wide b.** = to avoid sth at all costs. (b) bed (in a ship/train). 2. *v.* to tie up (a ship).

ber•yl ['berɪl] *n.* type of precious stone.

be•seech [bɪ'siːtʃ] *v.* (**beseeched/besought** [bɪ'sɔːt]) (*formal*) to ask (s.o. **to do** sth).

be•set [bɪ'set] *v.* (**beset**) to surround, causing problems. **be•set•ting sin,** *n.* defect which is always present.

be•side [bɪ'saɪd] *prep.* at the side of; **b. the point** = nothing to do with the subject.

be•sides [bɪ'saɪdz] 1. *prep.* other than. 2. *adv.* also/in any case.

be•siege [bɪ'siːdʒ] *v.* (*of troops/newspaper reporters*) to surround.

be•sought [bɪ'sɔːt] *v. see* **be•seech.**

best [best] (*superlative of* **good** *and* **well**) 1. *adj. & n.* very good; better than anyone/anything else; **b. man** = friend of the bridegroom who helps him at a wedding; **the b. of it is that** = the most interesting/funniest part of the story is that; **do your b.** = do as well as you can; **for the b. part of an hour** = for almost a whole hour; **to the b. of my knowledge** = as far as I know. 2. *adv.* in a way which is better than anyone else; **best-dressed** = wearing the most fashionable clothes. **best•sel•ler,** *n.* book/article that sells in very large numbers.

bes•tial ['bestjəl] *adj.* like a beast. **bes•ti•al•i•ty** [bestɪ'ælɪtɪ] *n.* being bestial.

be•stir [bɪ'stɜː] *v.* (*formal*) **to b. yourself** = to get the energy to do sth.

be•stow [bɪ'stəʊ] *v.* (*formal*) to give.

bet [bet] 1. *n.* money put down as a pledge when you try to forecast the result of a race, etc., and which you lose if you guess wrongly. 2. *v.* (**bet**) to offer to pay money if what you think

will happen does not happen; **I b. you he's going to be late** = I am quite sure. **bet•tor, better,** *n.* person who bets. **bet•ting,** *n.* placing of bets; **b. parlor** = place where you can bet money on horse races.

be•ta ['biːtə] *n.* second letter of the Greek alphabet. **be•ta block•er** *n.* drug which reduces the heart's activity.

be•take [bɪ'teɪk] *v.* (**betook**) (*formal*) to take.

be•tel ['biːtl] *n.* type of tropical nut.

bête noire [bet'nwɑː] *n.* thing which you dislike particularly.

be•tide [bɪ'taɪd] *v.* (*formal*) to happen to (s.o.).

be•tray [bɪ'treɪ] *v.* to reveal a secret about s.o. to his enemies. **be•tray•al,** *n.* giving s.o. up to his enemies.

be•troth [bɪ'trəʊð] *v.* (*formal*) to engage s.o. to marry. **be•troth•al,** *n.* act of betrothing s.o.

bet•ter ['betə] (*comp. of* **good** *and* **well**) 1. *adj.* superior; of higher quality; less ill; finer (weather). 2. *adv.* **I'm feeling b.** = I'm feeling less ill; **he thought b. of it** = he decided not to do what he had planned; **you'd b. be going** = it's time you went; **he's b. off where he is** = he's in a better position where he is. 3. *v.* **to b. oneself/one's position** = to improve one's position.

be•tween [bɪ'twiːn] *prep.* with things on both sides; **b. you and me** = privately; **in b.** = in the middle of.

be•twixt [bɪ'twɪkst] *prep* (*old*) between.

bev•el ['bevl] 1. *n.* angled edge of a flat surface. 2. *v.* (**beveled, bevelled**) to give a flat surface an angled edge.

bev•er•age ['bevərɪdʒ] *n.* drink.

bev•y ['bevɪ] *n.* (*pl.* **-ies**) group (esp. of girls).

be•wail [bɪ'weɪl] *v.* (*formal*) to complain about (sth).

be•ware [bɪ'weə] *v.* **to b. of** = to watch out for.

be•wil•der [bɪ'wɪldə] *v.* to puzzle. **be•wil•der•ment,** *n.* puzzle/surprise.

be•witch [bɪ'wɪtʃ] *v.* to charm/to cast a spell on. **be•witch•ing,** *adj.* charming (girl).

be•yond [bɪ'jɒnd] 1. *adv.* further than; on the other side of; **it's b. a joke** = it's no longer funny.

bi•an•nu•al [baɪ'ænjʊəl] *adj.* which happens twice a year. **bi•an•nu•al•ly,** *adv.* twice a year.

bi•as ['baɪəs] *n.* (a) **to cut material on the b.** = slantwise/diagonally. (b) slant/strong opinion in one direction. **bi•ased,** *adj.* showing strong opinion in one direction/prejudiced.

bib [bɪb] *n.* small cloth tied under a baby's chin.

bi•ble ['baɪbl] *n.* (a) book of Christian or Jewish scriptures. (b) important book of reference. **bib•li•cal** ['bɪblɪkl] *adj.* referring to the bible.

bib•li•og•ra•phy [bɪblɪ'ɒgrəfɪ] *n.* list of

books/articles referring to a special subject.
bib•li•og•ra•pher, *n.* person who writes a
bibliography. **bib•li•o•graph•i•cal**
[bɪblɪəˈgræfɪkl] *adj.* (details) referring to a particular subject. **bib•li•o•phile** [ˈbɪblɪəʊfaɪl]
n. person who loves books.

bib•u•lous [ˈbɪbjuːləs] *adj.* fond of drinking.

bi•cam•er•al•ism [baɪˈkæmərəlɪzm] *n.* system of government where there are two legislative parts or branches.

bi•car•bo•nate [baɪˈkɑːbənət] *n.* **b. of soda** =
chemical used as a medicine for stomach pains
or as an ingredient in cooking.

bi•cen•ten•ar•y [baɪsenˈtiːnərɪ] *n.* anniversary of 200 years. **bi•cen•ten•ni•al** [baɪsen-
ˈtenɪəl] *adj.* referring to a bicentenary.

bi•ceps [ˈbaɪseps] *n.* large muscle in the top
part of the arm.

bick•er [ˈbɪkə] *v.* to quarrel.

bi•coast•al [baɪˈkəʊstl] *adj.* referring to both
the east and west coasts of the U.S.

bi•cy•cle [ˈbaɪsɪkl] 1. *n.* two-wheeled vehicle
driven by pedals. 2. *v.* to ride on a bicycle.

bid [bɪd] 1. *n.* offer/attempt; **he made a b. for
power** = he tried to seize power; **takeover b.** =
attempt to take over a company. 2. *v.* (a)
(**bid/bade** [bæd]; **has bidden**) to wish; **he bade
me farewell.** (b) (**bid; has bid**) to make an offer
at an auction. **bidder,** *n.* person who makes an
offer at an auction. **bid•ding,** *n.* (a) command; **I did it at his b.** = I did it because he told
me to do it. (b) offers made at an auction.

bide [baɪd] *v.* **to b. your time** = to wait for the
right moment.

bi•det [ˈbiːdeɪ] *n.* low washbasin for washing
the genitals.

bi•en•ni•al [baɪˈenjəl] *adj. & n.* (plant) which
flowers in its second year; (event) which occurs every two years. **bi•en•ni•al•ly,** *adv.*
every two years.

bier [ˈbɪə] *n.* table/hearse for carrying a coffin.

biff [bɪf] 1. *n. inf.* hit. 2. *v. inf.* to hit.

bi•fo•cal [baɪˈfəʊkl] *adj. & n.* **b. glasses/bifocals**
= glasses with two types of lens in each frame,
one for reading and one for long distance.

bi•fur•cate [ˈbaɪfəkeɪt] *v.* to split.
bi•fur•ca•tion [baɪfəˈkeɪʃn] *n.* splitting (of a
road).

big [bɪg] 1. *adj.* (**bigger, biggest**) large; **b. game** =
large animals (lions, etc.) which are hunted for
sport. 2. *adv.* **to talk b.** = to pretend to be important. **big•head,** *n. inf.* person who is

proud of himself and shows off. **big•wig,** *n.*
important person in an official position.

big•a•my [ˈbɪgəmɪ] *n.* action of illegally mar-
rying a second wife/husband, when the first is
still alive and has not been divorced.
big•a•mist, *n.* person who is illegally married
to two people at the same time. **big•a•mous,**
adj. **b. marriage** = illegal marriage when you
are already married to s.o. else.

bight [baɪt] *n.* (a) loop of a rope. (b) wide
curved bay.

big•ot [ˈbɪgət] *n.* person with a narrow-minded
attitude to religion/politics; fanatic.
big•ot•ed, *adj.* with very unbending ideas
about religion/politics, etc. **big•ot•ry,** *n.* narrow-minded attitude to religion/politics, etc.

bike [baɪk] *n. inf.* bicycle.

bi•ki•ni [bɪˈkiːnɪ] *n.* brief two-piece bathing
suit for women.

bi•lat•er•al [baɪˈlætərəl] *adj.* on two sides; **b.
agreement** = agreement between two sides.

bil•ber•ry [ˈbɪlbərɪ] *n.* small edible blue berry
growing in northern mountains; plant which
bears these berries.

bile [baɪl] *n.* bitter fluid produced by the liver to
digest fat.

bilge [bɪldʒ] *n.* dirty water (in a ship's hull); *inf.*
nonsense.

bi•lin•gual [baɪˈlɪŋgwəl] *adj.* using two languages; (person) who can speak two languages equally fluently.

bil•ious [ˈbɪlɪəs] *adj.* sick. **bil•ious•ness,** *n.*
feeling sick.

bilk [bɪlk] *v.* to cheat (s.o.) **of** sth.

bill [bɪl] *n.* (a) hard covering of a bird's mouth.
(b) note showing the amount of money you
have to pay. (c) draft of a proposed law or act.
(d) bank note. (e) poster (showing what is on
at a theater); **that will fill the b.** = will be very
suitable. (f) **b. of fare** = menu. **bill•board,** *n.*
large wooden panel for posters. **bill•fold,** *n.*
wallet for paper money, etc. **bill•hook,** *n.*
large hooked knife, used for cutting small
branches.

bil•la•bong [ˈbɪləbɒŋ] *n.* (*in Australia*) loop in
a river where there is no current.

bil•let [ˈbɪlɪt] 1. *n.* lodgings (for soldiers). 2. *v.*
to lodge (soldiers).

bil•liards [ˈbɪljədz] *n.* game involving hitting
balls with a long rod on a smooth
green-covered table. **bil•liard ball, billiard
table,** *n.* ball/table used in the game of billiards.

æ back, ɑː farm, ɒ top, aɪ pipe, aʊ how, aɪə fire, aʊə flower, ɔː bought, ɔɪ toy, e fed, eə hair, eɪ take, ə
afraid, əʊ boat, əʊə lower, ɜː word, iː heap, ɪ hit, ɪə hear, uː school, ʊ book, ʌ but, b back, d dog, ð then,
dʒ just, f fog, g go, h hand, j yes, k catch, l last, m mix, n nut, ŋ sing, p penny, r round, s some, ʃ short, t
too, tʃ chop, θ thing, v voice, w was, z zoo, ʒ treasure

bil•lion ['bɪljən] *n.* *U.S.* one thousand millions; *Brit.* (formerly) one million millions; **billions of letters** = a great many letters.

bil•low ['bɪləu] 1. *n.* large wave. 2. *v.* to move in large waves.

bil•ly goat ['bɪlɪgəut] *n.* male goat.

bim•bo ['bɪmbəu] *n.* *Sl.* attractive young girl.

bi•month•ly [baɪ'mʌnθlɪ] 1. *adj.* every two months; twice a month. 2. *n.* bimonthly magazine.

bin [bɪn] *n.* storage box.

bi•na•ry ['baɪnərɪ] *adj.* in twos; **b. system** = where numbers are shown by the figures 1 and 0 only.

bind [baɪnd] *v.* (**bound** [baund]) (a) to tie. (b) to cover (a book). (c) to oblige (s.o.) to do sth.; **to b. (s.o.) over** = to make s.o. legally obligated to do sth. **bind•er,** *n.* (a) bookbinder. (b) stiff cover for holding and protecting loose sheets of paper/magazines. **bind•er•y,** *n.* factory which binds books. **bind•ing,** 1. *adj.* **this contract is b. on both parties** = both parties have to do what it says. 2. *n.* outside cover of a book. **bind•weed,** *n.* type of climbing weed.

binge [bɪndʒ] *n.* *inf.* wild drunken party.

bin•go ['bɪŋgəu] *n.* game (played in public) where the aim is to cover up all the numbers on a card as they are called out.

bin•na•cle ['bɪnəkl] *n.* box containing the compass on a ship.

bin•oc•u•lar [bɪ'nɒkjulə] 1. *adj.* **b. vision** = ability to see the same object with two eyes, and therefore to judge distance. 2. *n. pl.* **binoculars** = double glasses for seeing long distances.

bi•no•mi•al [baɪ'nəumɪəl] *adj.* (theory) based on two figures; **b. classification** = way of classifying plants and animals, using two Latin names.

bi•o•chem•is•try [baɪəu'kemɪstrɪ] *n.* science of the chemical constituents of animals or plants. **bi•o•chem•i•cal,** *adj.* referring to biochemistry. **bi•o•chem•ist,** *n.* person who studies the chemical composition of animals or plants.

bi•o•de•grad•a•ble [baɪəudɪ'greɪdəbl] *adj.* which decomposes naturally to form harmless material.

bi•o•eth•ics [baɪəu'eθɪks] *n.* the study of the moral issues arising from biological and medical research.

bi•og•ra•phy [baɪ'ɒgrəfɪ] *n.* story of the life of s.o. **bi•og•ra•pher,** *n.* person who writes a biography. **bi•o•graph•i•cal** [baɪə'græfɪkl] *adj.* referring to a biography.

bi•ol•o•gy [baɪ'ɒlədʒɪ] *n.* study of living things. **bi•o•log•i•cal** [baɪə'lɒdʒɪkl] *adj.* referring to living things; **b. warfare** = war in which germs are used. **bi•ol•o•gist,** *n.* person who studies biology.

bi•o•mass ['baɪəumæs] *n.* all living organisms in a certain place.

bi•o•me•chan•ics [baɪəumɪ'kænɪks] *n.* the study of the mechanics of the movement/structure of living organisms.

bi•on•ic [baɪ'ɒnɪk] *adj.* with powers reinforced by electronic devices.

bi•o•phys•ics [baɪəu'fɪzɪks] *n.* science of the physics of living things.

bi•op•sy ['baɪɒpsɪ] *n.* operation to remove a growth/a piece of tissue.

bi•o•rhythms ['baɪəurɪðmz] *n. pl.* cycles of activity which are said to recur regularly in each person's life.

bi•par•tite [baɪ'pɑːtaɪt] *adj.* with two sides taking part.

bi•ped ['baɪped] *n.* animal with two legs.

bi•plane ['baɪpleɪn] *n.* aircraft with two sets of wings, one above the other.

birch [bɜːtʃ] 1. *n.* (*pl.* **-es**) **silver b.** = common northern tree with white bark. 2. *v.* to beat with a bundle of twigs.

bird [bɜːd] *n.* (a) animal with wings and feathers. (b) *inf.* person. **bird's-eye view,** *n.* view from high up looking down. **bird watch•er,** *n.* person who studies birds. **bird watch•ing,** *n.* study of birds.

bi•ret•ta [bɪ'retə] *n.* small cap worn by a Catholic priest.

birth [bɜːθ] *n.* being born; **he is French by b.** = he has French nationality because his parents are French; **b. certificate** = official document showing date and place of s.o.'s birth; **b. control** = method of preventing pregnancy; **b. rate** = average number of children born per thousand population; **to give b. to** = to have (a child)/to produce (young). **birth•day,** *n.* date on which you were born; **in his b. suit** = naked/with no clothes on. **birth•mark,** *n.* mark on the skin which is there from birth. **birth•place,** *n.* place where s.o. was born/sth was invented. **birth•right,** *n.* right which you inherit at birth.

bis•cuit ['bɪskɪt] *n.* small soft cake or bread. **water biscuits** = biscuits made of flour and water.

bi•sect [baɪ'sekt] *v.* to cut into two equal parts.

bi•sex•u•al [baɪ'seksjuəl] *adj.* who is attracted to both sexes.

bish•op ['bɪʃəp] *n.* (a) church leader in charge of a diocese. (b) piece in chess shaped like a bishop's hat. **bish•op•ric,** *n.* post of bishop.

bis•muth ['bɪzməθ] *n.* (*element:* Bi) white metal used in medicine.

bi•son ['baɪsn] *n.* (*pl.* **bison**) large wild ox or cow.

bis•tro ['biːstrəu] *n.* (*pl.* -os) small restaurant/café.

bit [bɪt] *n.* (a) small piece; **a b. longer** = a little while longer; **the chair has fallen to bits** = has come apart; **she's thrilled to bits** = very pleased; **he is a b. of a nuisance** = he is rather a nuisance; **b. by b.** = in stages; **not a b. of use** = of no use at all; **he's every b. as ugly as you said** = just as ugly; **b. part** = small part (in a play). (b) piece of metal for making holes which is placed in a drill. (c) piece of metal going through a horse's mouth to which the reins are attached. (d) small piece of information (in a computer) represented by 0 or 1. **bit•map** ['bɪt mæp] *n.* image created on a visual display unit where the number of bits per pixel determines the number of possible colors. (e) *v. see also* **bite.**

bitch [bɪtʃ] 1. *n.* (*pl.* -es) (a) female dog. (b) *inf.* unpleasant woman. 2. *v. inf.* to complain.

bite [baɪt] 1. *v.* (**bit; has bitten**) to cut with teeth; **he bit my head off** = he spoke angrily to me. 2. *n.* (a) mouthful. (b) place where you have been bitten. **bit•ing,** *adj.* sharp (wind); piercing (cold); sharp (remark).

bit•ten ['bɪtn] *v. see* **bite.**

bit•ter ['bɪtə] *adj.* (a) not sweet; sour. (b) resentful/cruel; **to the b. end** = right to the very end. (c) very cold. **bit•ter•ly,** *adv.* sharply/resentfully. **bit•ter•ness,** *n.* resentment.

bit•tern ['bɪtən] *n.* marsh bird which makes a booming call.

bi•tu•men ['bɪtjumən] *n.* black substance, like tar. **bi•tu•mi•nous** [bɪ'tjuːmɪnəs] *adj.* referring to bitumen.

bi•valve ['baɪvælv] *n.* shellfish with two shells hinged together.

biv•ou•ac ['bɪvuæk] *v.* (**bivouacked**) to camp out in the open without a tent.

bi•zarre [bɪ'zɑː] *adj.* very strange.

blab [blæb] *v.* (**blabbed**) *inf.* to talk too much/to gossip.

black [blæk] 1. *adj.* (-er, -est) (a) of a very dark color, the opposite of white; **b. coffee** = coffee without milk or cream; **b. ice** = dangerous layer of thin ice on a road; **b. box** = device which stores information about an aircraft's flight; **b. market** = selling illegally, at high prices, products which are not normally available. (b) bad; **b. deeds** = evil deeds. 2. *n.* (a) very dark color, opposite to white; **to be in the b.** = to have money in a bank account. (b) member of a dark-skinned race of people orig-inating in Africa. **black•ball,** *v.* to vote against (s.o.) joining a club. **black•ber•ry,** *n.* common wild fruit, growing on long prickly stems. **black•bird,** *n.* common northern bird, the male of which has black feathers and yellow beak. **black•board,** *n.* board on the wall which can be written on. **black cur•rant,** *n.* common black soft fruit grown in the garden. **black•en,** *v.* to make black. **black fly,** *n.* small black aphis. **black•guard** ['blægɑːd] *n.* scoundrel/wicked person. **black•head,** *n.* blocked pore which shows up as a black dot on the skin. **black•ish,** *adj.* rather black. **black•list.** 1. *n.* list of undesirable things or people. 2. *v.* to put (s.o.'s name) on a list of undesirable people. **black•mail.** 1. *v.* to make s.o. pay money by threatening to reveal some unpleasant or shameful detail about them. 2. *n.* act of blackmailing. **black•mail•er,** *n.* person who blackmails. **Black Ma•ri•a,** *n. Sl.* patrol wagon. **black•ness,** *n.* total darkness. **black out,** *v.* (a) to wipe off/to suppress. (b) to faint/to lose consciousness. (c) to cut off the electricity. **black•out,** *n.* (a) loss of consciousness. (b) sudden stoppage of electricity supply. **black•smith,** *n.* man who makes horseshoes, gates, etc., out of metal. **black•thorn,** *n.* wild prickly bush, with white flowers.

blad•der ['blædə] *n.* (a) bag in the body where urine is stored. (b) bag inside a ball which is inflated.

blade [bleɪd] *n.* (a) cutting part of knife, etc. (b) thin leaf of grass. (c) one arm of a propeller. (d) flat part at the end of an oar.

blame [bleɪm] 1. *n.* criticism of s.o. for having done sth; **to get the b. for** = to be said to be responsible for. 2. *v.* **to b. s.o. for sth** = to say that sth was caused by s.o.; **he is to b. for the accident** = he is responsible for the accident; **I don't b. you** = I think you were quite right. **blame•less,** *adj.* Pure or innocent. **blame•wor•thy,** *adj.* (person) who can rightly be blamed.

blanch [blɑːntʃ] *v.* (a) to put quickly into boiling water. (b) to turn white.

blanc•mange [blə'mɒnʒ] *n.* dessert like a cream jelly flavored with chocolate/strawberry, etc.

bland [blænd] *adj.* smooth/not striking; (food) without much flavor. **bland•ly,** *adv.* in a smooth casual way. **bland•ness,** *n.* smoothness; lack of any striking features.

æ back, ɑː farm, ɒ top, aɪ pipe, aʊ how, aɪə fire, aʊə flower, ɔː bought, ɔɪ toy, e fed, eə hair, eɪ take, ə afraid, əʊ boat, əʊə lower, ɜː word, iː heap, ɪ hit, ɪə hear, uː school, ʊ book, ʌ but, b back, d dog, ð then, dʒ just, f fog, g go, h hand, j yes, k catch, l last, m mix, n nut, ŋ sing, p penny, r round, s some, ʃ short, t too, tʃ chop, θ thing, v voice, w was, z zoo, ʒ treasure

blan•dish•ments ['blændɪʃmənts] *n. pl.* attractive flattery.

blank [blæŋk] 1. *adj.* (**-er, -est**) (a) (paper, etc.) with nothing on it; **b. check** = check where the figures are not written in; **b. verse** = poetry which does not rhyme; **he looked b.** = he looked lost/surprised. (b) **b. cartridge** = with no bullet in it. 2. *n.* (a) white space (with nothing printed on it); **my mind is a b.** = I cannot remember anything; **he drew a b.** = he failed to make any progress. (b) cartridge with no bullet in it. **blank•ly,** *adv.* with vacant expression.

blan•ket ['blæŋkɪt] 1. *n.* woolen bed covering; **electric b.** = electrically heated pad to warm a bed; **b. order** = order which covers many items. 2. *v.* to cover (with fog, etc.).

blare ['bleə] 1. *n.* loud noise. 2. *v.* to make a loud noise.

blar•ney ['blɑːnɪ] *n.* talk which is intended to trick.

bla•sé ['blɑːzeɪ] *adj.* with a couldn't-care-less attitude.

blas•pheme [blæs'fiːm] *v.* to swear; to talk without respect for God. **blas•phem•er,** *n.* person who swears. **blas•phe•mous** ['blæsfəməs] *adj.* showing no respect for religion; antireligious (talk). **blas•phe•my,** *n.* disrespect for religion; swearing.

blast [blɑːst] 1. *n.* (a) sharp blowing of wind. (b) short whistle. (c) **going full b.** = working at full power. (d) explosion; shock wave from an explosion. 2. *v.* (a) to blow up. (b) to ruin. **blast fur•nace,** *n.* furnace used to make steel. **blast off,** *v.* (*of rocket*) to take off. **blast-off,** *n.* departure of a rocket.

bla•tant ['bleɪtənt] *adj.* obvious/unmistakable. **bla•tant•ly,** *adv.* obviously/unmistakably.

blath•er [missing] *n.* silly talk.

blaze [bleɪz] 1. *n.* (a) fierce fire; **she worked like blazes** = she worked extremely hard. (b) white mark made by cutting away the bark of a tree; white mark on the forehead of an animal. 2. *v.* (a) to burn fiercely. (b) **to b. a trail** = to mark a path by cutting the bark on trees/to be the first to do something. **blaz•ing,** *adj.* fiery.

blaz•er ['bleɪzə] *n.* jacket with metal buttons, originally worn with a badge to show membership of a club/school.

bla•zon ['bleɪzn] 1. *n.* coat of arms. 2. *v.* to proclaim (sth).

bleach [bliːtʃ] 1. *n.* substance which takes the color out of something. 2. *v.* to take the color out of sth. **bleach•ers,** *n. pl.* raised tiers of seats at a sports stadium.

bleak [bliːk] *adj.* (**-er, -est**) cold/inhospitable. **bleak•ly,** *adv.* in a cold/inhospitable way.

blear•y ['blɪərɪ] *adj.* watery/dim (eyes). **blear•y-eyed,** *adj.* with watery eyes.

bleat [bliːt] 1. *n.* noise made by a sheep or goat. 2. *v.* (a) to make a noise like a goat/sheep. (b) to complain; **what is he bleating about?** = what does he keep complaining about?

bleed [bliːd] 1. *n.* a nose b. = loss of blood from the nose. 2. *v.* (**bled**) to lose blood; **my heart bleeds for you** = I am very sorry for you.

bleep [bliːp] 1. *n.* small noise made by a radio/a radar screen. 2. *v.* (*of a radio*) to make a small noise. **bleep•er,** *n.* machine which makes a bleep.

blem•ish ['blemɪʃ] 1. *n.* (*pl.* **-es**) imperfection/mark. 2. *v.* to spoil.

blench [blenʃ] *v.* to tremble with fear.

blend [blend] 1. *n.* mixture (of coffee/tea/tobacco). 2. *v.* to mix. **blend•er,** *n.* machine for mixing food.

bless [bles] *v.* to make sacred; to bring happiness/wealth to (s.o.); *inf.* **b. you!** = *phrase said when someone sneezes.* **bless•ed** ['blesɪd] *adj.* (a) protected by God. (b) *inf.* cursed/annoying. **bless•ing,** *n.* (a) thing which is useful/which brings happiness; **it's a b. in disguise** = it doesn't look like it, but it is very useful. (b) short prayer, esp. before or after a meal.

bleth•er ['bleðə] *n. see* **blath•er.**

blew [bluː] *v. see* **blow.**

blight [blaɪt] 1. *n.* fungoid disease (attacking vegetables/leaves, etc.). 2. *v.* to spoil/to ruin.

blimp [blɪmp] *n.* small airship.

blind [blaɪnd] 1. *n.* (a) covering (over a window); **Venetian b.** = blind made of many horizontal flat strips of wood or plastic. (b) **the b.** = people who cannot see. 2. *adj.* not able to see; **to turn a b. eye to sth** = pretend not to notice; **b. alley** = (i) alley with no way out; (ii) position with no prospect of progress; **b. spot** = (i) part of the road which a motorist cannot see; (ii) thing which s.o. is incapable of understanding. 3. *v.* to prevent s.o. from seeing; to make s.o. blind. 4. *adv.* **flying b.** = flying an aircraft, using the instruments only. **blind•fold.** 1. *n.* bandage put over s.o.'s eyes to prevent him from seeing. 2. *v.* to put a bandage over s.o.'s eyes. **blind•ly,** *adv.* without being able to see. **blind•ness,** *n.* not being able to see.

blink [blɪŋk] 1. *n. inf.* **on the b.** = not working properly. 2. *v.* to close your eyelids very quickly. **blink•ers,** *n.* shades put on a horse's eyes to prevent it from looking sideways.

blip [blɪp] *n.* small dot of light on a radar screen.

bliss [blɪs] *n.* great happiness. **bliss•ful,** *adj.* extremely happy. **bliss•ful•ly,** *adv.* happily.

blis•ter ['blɪstə] 1. *n.* bump on the skin (with

water underneath) made by rubbing; **b. pack** = type of container, where the product is covered by a stiff plastic bubble. 2. *v.* to make bumps on the surface (of sth).

blithe•ly ['blaɪðlɪ] *adv.* in a happy carefree way.

blith•er•ing ['blɪðərɪŋ] *adj. inf.* carrying on or talking foolishly.

blitz [blɪts] 1. *n.* (*pl.* **-es**) (a) bombing (of a town). (b) *inf.* **b. on sth** = sudden campaign to clear sth up. 2. *v.* to bomb.

bliz•zard ['blɪzəd] *n.* heavy snowstorm with strong winds.

bloat•ed ['bləʊtɪd] *adj.* full; too fat.

bloat•er ['bləʊtə] *n.* dried salt herring.

blob [blɒb] *n.* large spot.

bloc [blɒk] *n.* (*political*) group; **b. vote** = vote by a group voting together.

block [blɒk] 1. *n.* (a) piece/lump (of stone or wood). (b) large building; **he lives two blocks away** = there are two crossroads between here and his house. (c) **b. capitals/letters** = capital letters. (d) **b. and tackle** = arrangement of pulleys and ropes for lifting heavy objects. 2. *v.* to prevent sth going past; **the truck blocked the road for hours. block•ade** [blɒ'keɪd] 1. *n.* preventing supplies being brought into a place. 2. *v.* to prevent supplies being brought into a place. **block•age,** *n.* blocking. **block up,** *v.* to stop (a hole), to fill (a pipe).

bloke [bləʊk] *n. Brit. inf.* man.

blond, blonde [blɒnd] *adj. & n.* (man/woman) with fair hair.

blood [blʌd] *n.* red liquid in the body; **b. group** = type of blood a person has; **b. donor** = person who gives blood to be used in operations; **b. pressure** = pressure at which the heart pumps blood; **b. transfusion** = giving blood to a sick person. **it makes my b. boil** = it makes me very angry; **his b. ran cold** = he was scared. **blood bank,** *n.* place where blood is stored until it is needed for transfusions. **blood•bath,** *n.* massacre. **blood•cur•dling,** *adj.* very frightening. **blood•hound,** *n.* dog trained to follow tracks. **blood•less,** *adj.* with no blood; **b. revolution** = revolution where no one was killed. **blood•shed,** *n.* killing. **blood•shot,** *adj.* red (eyes). **blood•sports,** *n. pl.* sports which involve killing animals. **blood•stain,** *n.* stain caused by blood. **blood•stained,** *adj.* stained with blood. **blood•stock,** *n.* race horses. **blood•stream,** *n.* flow of blood through the body. **blood•suck•er,** *n.* animal

which sucks your blood. **blood test,** *n.* test to show the condition of the blood. **blood•thirst•y,** *adj.* cruel/liking gory details. **blood ves•sel,** *n.* vein/artery which carries blood. **blood•y,** *adj.* (**-ier, -iest**) (a) covered with blood; where much blood has been shed; (b) *Brit. Sl.* awful. **blood•y-mind•ed,** *adj. inf.* awkward/uncooperative.

bloom [bluːm] 1. *n.* (a) flower; **the apple trees are in full b.** = all the apple flowers are out. (b) velvety skin (of a peach); dust (on skin of a grape). (c) **b. of youth** = healthy glow of a young person. (d) layer of algae on the surface of the water. 2. *v.* to flower/to flourish. **bloo•mers** *inf.* wide knickers.

blos•som ['blɒsəm] 1. *n.* flower (on trees). 2. *v.* to flower.

blot [blɒt] 1. *n.* dirty spot; drop (of ink on paper). 2. *v.* (**blotted**) to drop a spot (of ink) on sth; to dry the ink on a letter. **blot•ter,** *n.* pad of blotting paper. **blot•ting pa•per,** *n.* thick absorbent paper for drying ink. **blot•to** ['blɒtəʊ] *adj. inf.* drunk.

blotch [blɒtʃ] *n.* large patch of color. **blotch•y,** *adj.* (face) with patches of red.

blouse [blaʊz] *n.* (woman's) shirt.

blow [bləʊ] 1. *n.* knock/punch. 2. *v.* (**blew** [bluː]; **has blown**) to make air move; (*of air*) to move; **it's blowing hard** = there is a strong wind; **he blew his nose** = he cleared his nose by blowing down it into a handkerchief; **to b. a fuse** = to burn out a fuse by overloading it. **blow away,** *v.* to move (sth) away by blowing. **blow down,** *v.* to fall down/to make (sth) fall down by blowing. **blow dry,** *v.* (**blow drying**) to dry (s.o.'s hair) with a blower. **blow-dry,** *n.* act of drying hair with a blower. **blow•er,** *n.* device which blows. **blow•fly,** *n.* large blue-green fly that is attracted by meat. **blow•gun,** *n.* pipe through which poison arrows can be blown. **blow off,** *v.* to go off/to make (sth) go off by blowing. **blow out,** *v.* to go out/to make (sth) go out by blowing. **blow•out,** *n.* (a) *inf.* huge meal. (b) bursting (of a tire). **blow over,** *v.* (*of storm*) to end; to knock (sth) down by blowing. **blow•torch,** *n.* device with a strong gas flame used in metalworking. **blow up,** *v.* (a) to explode. (b) to destroy by explosives. (c) to fill (sth) with air. (d) to enlarge (a photograph). **blow•y,** *adj.* windy.

blowz•y ['blaʊzɪ] *adj.* common, redfaced (woman).

æ back, ɑː farm, ɒ top, aɪ pipe, aʊ how, aɪə fire, aʊə flower, ɔː bought, ɔɪ toy, e fed, eəhair, eɪ take, ə afraid, əʊ boat, əʊə lower, vː word, iː heap, ɪ hit, ɪə hear, uː school, ʊ book, ʌ but, b back, d dog, ð then, dʒ just, f fog, g go, h hand, j yes, k catch, l last, m mix, n nut, ŋ sing, p penny, r round, s some, ʃ short, t too, tʃ chop, θ thing, v voice, w was, z zoo, ʒ treasure

blub•ber ['blʌbə] 1. *n.* fat (of a whale/seal). 2. *v.* to cry noisily.

bludg•eon ['blʌdʒən] 1. *n.* large stick for hitting people. 2. *v.* to beat (s.o.) with a stick.

blue [bluː] 1. *adj.* (-er, -est) (a) colored like the sky; **b. baby** = baby with blue skin caused by heart disease; **once in a b. moon** = very seldom. (b) pornographic; **b. movies.** (c) sad. 2. *n.* (a) color like that of the sky; **out of the b.** = as a complete surprise. (b) **blues** = Afro-American folk music, the basis of jazz. **blue•bell,** *n.* common blue wild flower/wild hyacinth. **blue be•ret** *n. inf.* soldier of a United Nations peacekeeping force. **blue•ber•ry,** *n.* small blue berry; plant which bears this berry. **blue•bot•tle,** *n.* large blue-green fly that is attracted to meat. **blue chip (share),** *n.* share in a safe company. **blue col•lar work•er,** *n.* manual laborer. **blue-eyed,** *adj.* with blue eyes; **blue-eyed boy** = favorite. **Blue laws,** *n.* laws which regulate what can be done on a Sunday. **blue jeans,** *n.* pants or trousers, usu. made of blue denim, worn for work or casual wear. **blue-pen•cil,** *v.* (-penciled, -pencilled) to change or correct. **blue•print,** *n.* detailed plan. **blu•ish,** *adj.* rather blue.

bluff [blʌf] 1. *n.* (a) steep rocky hill. (b) trick; **to call s.o.'s b.** = to claim (successfully) that s.o. is tricking/is lying. 2. *adj.* down-to-earth/straightforward (person). 3. *v.* to trick/to pretend. **bluff•ly,** *adv.* in a straightforward way. **bluff•ness,** *n.* being blunt/straightforward.

blun•der ['blʌndə] 1. *n.* mistake. 2. *v.* (a) to make a mistake. (b) **to b. into** = to bump into. **blun•der•ing,** *adj.* clumsy.

blunt [blʌnt] 1. *adj.* (a) not sharp. (b) straightforward/frank/almost rude. 2. *v.* to make blunt. **blunt•ly,** *adv.* frankly/almost rudely. **blunt•ness,** *n.* being blunt.

blur [blɜː] 1. *n.* indistinct picture. 2. *v.* (**blurred**) to make indistinct.

blurb [blɜːb] *n.* piece of publicity describing sth. as a book.

blurt [blɜːt] *v.* to let out (a secret).

blush [blʌʃ] 1. *n.* (*pl.* -es) red shade (on skin). 2. *v.* to go red (with embarrassment).

blus•ter ['blʌstə] 1. *n.* swaggering talk; attitude of defiance. 2. *v.* to swagger/to show off. **blus•ter•y,** *adj.* strong (wind/gale).

bo•a ['bəʊə] *n.* **b. constrictor** = large tropical snake which kills animals by wrapping itself round them and squeezing them; **feather b.** = type of scarf made of feathery material.

boar [bɔː] *n.* male pig, usu. wild.

board [bɔːd] 1. *n.* (a) large flat piece of wood, etc.; **ironing b.** = narrow table for ironing. (b) food; **full b.** = room and all meals (in a hotel). (c) group of people in charge of a business. (d) **to go on b.** = to go on to a ship/into an aircraft. 2. *v.* (a) to go on to a (ship/bus), into (an aircraft). **board•er,** *n.* person who receives regular meals and usu. lodging for a fixed rate. **board•ing,** *adj.* (a) **b. card** = card which allows you to go into an aircraft. (b) **b. house** = house where you pay a fixed rate for regular meals and lodging. **b. school** = school where the children receive food and lodging during the term. **board•room,** *n.* room where a board of directors meets. **board up,** *v.* to cover (windows/doors) with boards for protection.

boast [bəʊst] 1. *n.* act of boasting. 2. *v.* (a) (**of/about**) to talk about how clever/strong/handsome, etc., you are. (b) to possess (sth), and be proud. **boast•er,** *n.* person who is always boasting. **boast•ful,** *adj.* very proud; always boasting.

boat [bəʊt] *n.* (small) ship; **b. train** = train which connects with a boat; **we're all in the same b.** = we're all in equal circumstances. **boat•er,** *n.* flat straw hat. **boat•house,** *n.* shed for storing boats. **boat•ing,** *n.* rowing (for pleasure). **boat•man,** *n.* (*pl.* -men) man in charge of boats. **boat•swain** ['bəʊsn] *n.* (*at sea*) man in charge of the boats and sails.

bob [bɒb] 1. *n.* (a) little curtsy. (b) hair tied in a knot. 2. *v.* (**bobbed**) to move quickly up and down.

bob•bin ['bɒbɪn] *n.* small reel for holding thread (for a sewing machine/a spinning wheel).

bob•ble [bɒbl] *n.* little fluffy ball used for decoration.

bob•by ['bɒbɪ] *n. Brit.* policeman. **bob•by-pin,** *n.* flat type of hairpin. **bob•by-socks,** *n. pl.* girls' ankle socks.

bob•sled, bobsleigh ['bɒbsleɪ] *n.* sled with two runners, used for racing.

bode [bəʊd] *v.* **it bodes ill** = it promises to bring ruin.

bod•ice ['bɒdɪs] *n.* top part (of a dress).

bod•kin ['bɒdkɪn] *n.* large thick needle used for threading tape or elastic.

bod•y ['bɒdɪ] *n.* (*pl.* -ies) (a) main structure of an animal or person; main part of an animal or person not including the head and limbs; **dead b.** = corpse. (b) group of people. (c) main part (of a building/a car, etc.). (d) strength (of wine). **bod•i•ly.** 1. *adj.* of the body; **to cause s.o. grievous b. harm** = to attack s.o. and beat him up. 2. *adv.* **they carried him out b.** = they lifted him up and carried him. **bod•y•guard,** *n.* person or group of people who guards s.o. **bod•y•work,** *n.* outer covering of a car.

bog [bɒg] 1. *n.* area of marshland. 2. *v.* (**bogged**) **to get bogged down** = to get stuck (in mud); **the discussion got bogged down in details** = they got stuck in details. **bog•gy**, *adj.* marshy.

bo•gey ['bəʊgɪ] *n.* (a) (*also* **bogeyman**) thing which frightens children. (b) (*in golf*) normal number of strokes which a player should take to play a hole.

bog•gle ['bɒgl] *v.* to be reluctant (**at** = to do sth); **the mind boggles** = it is impossible to imagine.

bo•gus ['bəʊgəs] *adj.* false.

bo•he•mi•an [bəʊ'hiːmɪən] *adj. & n.* (person) living a wild/unconventional life.

boil [bɔɪl] 1. *n.* (a) swelling in the body full of pus. (b) **bring the water to a b.** = make the water boil. 2. *v.* (a) to heat (a liquid) until it bubbles. (b) to cook in boiling water; **hard-boiled egg** = egg which has been cooked until it is solid (usu. eaten cold). **boil away**, *v.* to evaporate (through boiling). **boil down**, *v.* (a) to evaporate (through boiling); to reduce (a piece of writing). (b) to be reduced to; **it all boils down to whether he will resign willingly or not** = the main question is, will he resign willingly or not. **boil•er**, *n.* large metal container for boiling water; large metal container and arrangement of tubes for supplying heat or power. **boil•ing.** 1. *n.* action of heating a liquid until it bubbles; **212°F (100°C) is the b. point of water.** 2. *adj.* (liquid) which is boiling or very hot; **it is b. in this room** = it is very hot. 3. *adv.* **b. hot** = very hot. **boil over**, *v.* to rise in a pan when boiling, and run over the sides.

bois•ter•ous ['bɔɪstrəs] *adj.* noisy/violent (crowd/wind/sea, etc.). **bois•ter•ous•ly,** *adv.* in a boisterous way. **bois•ter•ous•ness,** *n.* noise/violence.

bold [bəʊld] *adj.* (-**er**, -**est**) (a) strongly marked (color/outline). (b) daring/brave. **bold•ly,** *adv.* bravely/defiantly. **bold•ness,** *n.* daring/bravery.

bole [bəʊl] *n.* tree trunk.

bo•le•ro *n.* (a) [bə'leərəʊ] type of Spanish dance. (b) ['bɒlərəʊ] short sleeveless jacket worn by women.

boll [bɒl] *n.* seed head of the cotton plant.

bol•lard ['bɒlɑːd] *n.* low post on a wharf quay for attaching a ship's rope.

bol•ster ['bəʊlstə] 1. *n.* long pillow going right across a bed. 2. *v.* (*also* **to bolster up**) to support or uphold; **to b. s.o. spirits** = to make s.o. feel better.

bolt [bəʊlt] 1. *n.* (a) flash of lightning with thunder; **it came as a b. from the blue** = it came as a complete surprise. (b) metal rod which slides into a hole to secure a door. (c) metal rod with a screw which fastens with a nut. (d) **to make a b. for** = to rush toward. 2. *v.* (a) to run fast/to escape; **the horse bolted** = the horse got out of control. (b) to eat quickly and with big mouthfuls. (c) to fasten (a door) with a bolt. (d) to fasten with a bolt and nut. 3. *adv.* **sitting b. upright** = sitting straight upright.

bomb [bɒm] 1. *n.* (a) large explosive weapon, often dropped from an aircraft; **b. disposal** = removing the fuse from an unexploded bomb. (b) *inf.* complete failure. 2. *v.* (a) to drop bombs on. (b) to fail completely. **bom•bard** [bɒm'bɑːd] *v.* to attack (repeatedly). **bom•bard•ment,** *n.* attack (with bombs/shells/questions). **bomb•er,** *n.* special aircraft for dropping bombs. **bomb•shell,** *n.* great (usu. unpleasant) surprise.

bom•bast•ic [bɒm'bæstɪk] *adj.* flowery/boasting (way of speaking).

bo•na fide ['bəʊnə'faɪdɪ] 1. *adj.* made in good faith; **a bona fide offer.** 2. *n.* **the police are checking on his bona fides** = they are checking that he is speaking the truth.

bo•nan•za [bə'nænzə] *n.* great wealth (discovered suddenly).

bond [bɒnd] 1. *n.* (a) link; joining together. (b) paper showing that money has been lent to the government; (c) in **b.** (goods held) in a customs warehouse until taxes or duties are paid. 2. *v.* to link/to join (with glue). **bond•age,** *n.* slavery. **bond•ed ware•house,** *n.* warehouse containing goods in bond.

bone [bəʊn] 1. *n.* one of the solid white pieces which make up the framework of the body; **b. dry** = completely dry; **I've got a b. to pick with you** = I want to complain about sth which you've done. 2. *v.* to take the bones out of (meat, fish). **bone•less,** *adj.* with no bones. **bon•y,** *adj.* with big bones; with many bones.

bon•fire ['bɒnfaɪə] *n.* outdoor fire for burning leaves, etc. or as a celebration.

bon•go ['bɒngəʊ] *n.* small drum, tapped with the hand.

bon•kers ['bɒŋkəz] *adj. Sl.* mad.

bon•net ['bɒnɪt] *n.* (a) child's/woman's hat, with a brim framing the face. (b) *Brit.* hinged cover for the front part of a car.

bon•ny ['bɒnɪ] *adj.* (-**ier**, -**iest**) good-looking and healthy.

æ **back**, ɑː **farm**, ɒ **top**, aɪ **pipe**, aʊ **how**, aɪə **fire**, aʊə **flower**, ɔː **bought**, ɔɪ **toy**, e **fed**, eə **hair**, eɪ **take**, ə **afraid**, əʊ **boat**, əʊə **lower**, ɜː **word**, iː **heap**, ɪ **hit**, ɪə **hear**, uː **school**, ʊ **book**, ʌ **but**, b **back**, d **dog**, ð **then**, dʒ **just**, f **fog**, g **go**, h **hand**, j **yes**, k **catch**, l **last**, m **mix**, n **nut**, ŋ **sing**, p **penny**, r **round**, s **some**, ʃ **short**, t **too**, tʃ **chop**, θ **thing**, v **voice**, w **was**, z **zoo**, ʒ **treasure**

bon•sai ['bɒnsaɪ] n. (art of growing) trees in small pots, pruned so that they remain small.

bo•nus ['bəʊnəs] n. (pl. -es) extra money.

boo [buː] 1. inter. call to show disapproval or to surprise. 2. v. to show disapproval by saying "boo."

boob [buːb] n. Sl. (a) stupid, silly person. (b) breast.

boo•by ['buːbɪ] n. silly person. **boo•by prize**, n. (silly) prize given to the last person in a competition. **boo•by trap**. n. trap to catch s.o. unawares. **boob•y-trap**, v. (**boobytrapped**) to set a trap (in a place).

book [bʊk] 1. n. (a) printed pages attached together with a cover. (b) **exercise b.** = book of blank pages with lines for writing on; **check b.** = book of blank checks; (c) script (of musical). (d) **b. of tickets** = several tickets fastened together and sold as a unit; **b. of matches** = matches fastened together in a cardboard holder. 2. v. (a) to reserve (a place/seat/table) on plane/in theater/in restaurant. (b) **he was booked for speeding** = the police have made a charge against him for speeding. **book•a•ble**, adj. which can be reserved in advance. **book•bind•er**, n. person who puts covers on printed sheets to make a book. **book•bind•ing**, n. art of binding books. **book•case**, n. cabinet/set of shelves for keeping books. **book•ie**, n. inf. person who collects bets before a race. **book in**, v. to register (at a hotel). **book•ing**, n. (a) reservation (of seats/places); **b. office** = office (at railway station, theater, etc.) where you can book seats in advance. (b) arrangement (for actor, etc.) to appear at a theater. **book•ish**, adj. learned/studious. **book•keep•er**, n. person who keeps systematic records of money transactions. **book•keep•ing**, n. skill or work of being a bookkeeper. **book•let**, n. small book with only a few pages. **book•lov•er**, n. person who loves (and collects) books. **book•mak•er**, n. person who collects bets before a race. **book•mark•(er)**, n. (a) long, narrow, piece of card/cloth/leather used to keep your place in a book. (b) a marker put on a site on the Internet so that the computer user can find the site again easily and quickly. **book•mo•bile** ['bʊkməbiːl] n. traveling library. **book•sell•er**, n. person who sells books. **book•shelf**, n. shelf for keeping books. **book•shop**, n. bookstore. **book•stall, bookstand**, n. stand or stall selling books, usu. outdoors. **book•store**, n. store selling books. **book up**, v. to reserve. **book•worm**, n. person who reads many books.

bool•e•an adj. referring to a system of symbolic logic that is used in computer programming.

boom [buːm] 1. n. (a) floating barrier across a harbor. (b) long rod attached to the lower edge of a sail; long rod (for holding a microphone over speakers' heads). (c) low muffled sound. (d) sudden increase (in value/sales/general prosperity). 2. v. (a) to make a low muffled sound. (b) to increase suddenly/to become more prosperous.

boo•mer•ang ['buːməræŋ] 1. n. curved piece of wood which, when thrown, comes back to the thrower. 2. v. to backfire/to rebound.

boon [buːn] 1. n. advantage/blessing. 2. adj. **b. companion** = great friend.

boor [bɔː, 'bʊə] n. rough/uncouth man. **boor•ish**, adj. rude/uncouth.

boost [buːst] 1. n. help/publicity. 2. v. (a) to help/to promote. (b) to increase (voltage in electricity cable). **boost•er**, n. (a) apparatus for increasing voltage. (b) **b. rocket** = rocket which helps keep up the speed of the main rocket; **b. shot** = injection which keeps up the protection given by a former injection.

boot [buːt] 1. n. (a) footwear which goes above the ankle. (b) Brit. back part of a car (where the luggage can be put). 2. v. (a) to kick. (b) (computers) to carry out a set of instructions automatically. **boot camp**, n. Sl. (a) basic training camp in the U.S. Marine Corps/Navy. (b) prison for juvenile offenders with a military-style regime. **boot•ee**, n. small knitted boot for babies. **boot•la•ces**, n. pl. very long laces for boots. **boot•leg**, adj. illegal (whisky, etc.). **boot•leg•ger**, n. person who makes/transports illegal spirits.

booth [buːð] n. (a) stall for display of goods at a market/fair/exhibition. (b) small enclosed space for a specific use by one person.

boo•ty ['buːtɪ] n. treasure captured in a war.

booze [buːz] 1. n. inf. alcoholic drink. 2. inf. to drink (alcohol). **booz•er**, n. inf. person who drinks a lot.

bo•rac•ic [bə'ræsɪk] adj. chemical substance used in ointments.

bo•rax ['bɔːræks] n. white powder used in making glass and as an antiseptic.

Bor•deaux mix•ture ['bɔːdəʊ'mɪkstʃə] n. sulfur spray, used on plants.

bor•der ['bɔːdə] 1. n. frontier/edge; **flower b.** = edging of flowers along a flower bed. 2. v. **France borders on Germany** = France touches Germany; **it is a movie which borders on the indecent** = which is almost indecent. **bor•der•ing**, adj. close to. **bord•er•line**, n. line between two surfaces; **b. case** = case which is on the dividing line (between two types).

bore [bɔː] 1. n. (a) width of a tube. (b) person/thing which is dull and tiresome. **what a b.** = what a nuisance. (c) wave in a river caused by the tide. 2. *v.* (a) to make (a hole). (b) to tire (s.o.) by being dull. **I'm bored stiff** = very bored. (c) *see also* **bear. bore•dom,** *n.* being bored. **bor•ing,** *adj.* which makes you lose interest completely.

born [bɔːn] *adj.* **he was b. in 1962** = his birth took place in 1962; **she's a b. actress** = she has always had a gift for acting; **I wasn't b. yesterday** = I'm not as stupid as you think.

borne [bɔːn] *v. see* **bear.**

bo•ron ['bɔːrɒn] *n.* (*element:* B) brown powder which resists high temperatures and is used to make borax.

bor•ough ['bʌrə] *n.* incorporated municipality which is smaller than a city, in some U.S. states.

bor•row ['bɒrəʊ] *v.* to take (sth) for a short time with the owner's permission; to take (money) from a bank, etc., for a time, usu. paying interest on it. **bor•row•er,** *n.* person who borrows (money, etc.). **bor•row•ing,** *n.* (a) act of borrowing money. (b) money borrowed.

bor•zoi [bɔː'zɔɪ] *n.* breed of long-haired hound.

bos•om ['bʊzəm] *n.* breast; **b. friend** = close friend.

boss [bɒs] 1. *n.* (*pl.* -es) *inf.* (a) person who is in charge. (b) round knob. 2. *v. inf.* to command/to give orders; **she bosses him around** = she is always telling him what to do. **boss•i•ness,** *n.* being bossy. **boss•y,** *adj.* (-ier, -iest) (person) always giving orders.

bo•sun ['bəʊsn] *n.* (*at sea*) man in charge of the boats and sails.

bot•a•ny ['bɒtənɪ] *n.* study of plants. **bo•tan•i•cal** [bə'tænɪkl] *adj.* relating to plants; **b. gardens** = gardens scientifically arranged to show different species of plants. **bot•a•nist** ['bɒtənɪst] *n.* person who studies plants.

botch [bɒtʃ] *v.* to ruin/to make a mess of (a job).

both [bəʊθ] 1. *adj. & pron.* two persons/objects together. 2. *adv.* at the same time.

both•er ['bɒðə] 1. *n.* worry/annoyance. 2. *v.* (a) to annoy (s.o.). (b) to take trouble (**to do sth**). **both•ered,** *adj.* worried/embarrassed.

bot•tle ['bɒtl] 1. *n.* tall glass/plastic container for liquids; **hot water b.** = container for hot water which is used for warming a part of the body. 2. *v.* to put/pour (sth) into a bottle.

bot•tle-feed•ing, *n.* feeding of babies by a bottle, not at the breast. **bot•tle•neck,** *n.* (a) narrow part of a bottle. (b) place where traffic or progress is hindered. **bot•tle up,** *v.* (a) to hold back (one's feelings). (b) to hinder, as traffic. **bot•tling,** *n.* putting into bottles.

bot•tom ['bɒtəm] 1. *n.* (a) lowest part; base; **prices have touched rock b.** = they are at their lowest; **he finished at the b. of the class** = he had the worst marks. (b) buttocks. 2. *adj.* lowest. **bot•tom•less,** *adj.* with no bottom. **bot•tom•ry,** *n.* mortgage on a ship.

bot•u•lism ['bɒtjʊlɪzəm] *n.* illness caused by bacteria in food.

bou•clé ['buːkleɪ] *n.* wool with many loops in it.

bou•doir ['buːdwɑː] *n.* small private room for a woman.

bouf•fant ['buːfɒn] *adj.* fluffy (hairstyle).

bou•gain•vil•le•a [buːgən'vɪlɪə] *n.* tropical climbing plant with purple or pink flowers.

bough [baʊ] *n.* large branch.

bought [bɔːt] *v. see* **buy.**

boul•der ['bəʊldə] *n.* large rock.

boul•e•vard ['buːləvɑːd] *n.* wide road.

bounce [baʊns] 1. *n.* (a) springiness; **the bed has a lot of b. in it.** (b) **he's got a lot of b.** = he is full of energy. 2. *v.* (a) to spring up and down; to make (sth) spring up and down; **the ball bounced down the stairs.** (b) *inf.* **his check bounced** = there was not enough money in the account to pay the sum on the check. **bounc•er,** *n.* person who throws undesirable customers out of a restaurant/club, etc. **bounc•ing,** *adj.* (ball) which bounces; **b. baby** = healthy-looking baby. **bounc•y,** *adj.* (a) which bounces well. (b) (person) who is full of energy.

bound [baʊnd] 1. *n.* leap. 2. *adj.* (a) **b. for South America** = leaving for/on the way to South America; **homeward b.** = on the way home. (b) tied up. (c) obliged. (d) very likely; **they are b. to be late.** (e) *see also* **bind.** 3. *v.* to leap. **bound•en,** *adj.* **b. duty** = obligation. **bound•less,** *adj.* without any limits. **bounds,** *n.* limits/edges; **out of b.** = (place) where people are not allowed to go.

bound•a•ry ['baʊndrɪ] *n.* frontier/outer limit of sth.

boun•ty ['baʊntɪ] *n.* (a) giving (as of money); generosity. (b) money given as a reward or in excess of usual wages. **boun•ti•ful,** *adj.* generous.

æ **back,** ɑː **farm,** ɒ **top,** aɪ **pipe,** aʊ **how,** aɪə **fire,** aʊə **flower,** ɔː **bought,** ɔɪ **toy,** e **fed,** eə **hair,** eɪ **take,** ə **afraid,** əʊ **boat,** əʊə **lower,** ɜː **word,** iː **heap,** ɪ **hit,** ɪə **hear,** uː **school,** ʊ **book,** ʌ **but,** b **back,** d **dog,** ð **then,** dʒ **just,** f **fog,** g **go,** h **hand,** j **yes,** k **catch,** l **last,** m **mix,** n **nut,** ŋ **sing,** p **penny,** r **round,** s **some,** ʃ **short,** t **too,** tʃ **chop,** θ **thing,** v **voice,** w **was,** z **zoo,** ʒ **treasure**

bou•quet [bu'keɪ] *n.* artistically arranged bunch of flowers.

bour•bon ['bɜːbən] *n.* corn whisky.

bour•geois ['buəʒwɑː] *adj. & n.* middle-class (person). **bour•geoi•sie** [buəʒwɑ'zi:] *n.* the middle class.

bout [baʊt] *n.* (a) sports contest. (b) attack (of illness).

bou•tique [bu:'ti:k] *n.* small store selling fashionable clothes/perfume, etc.; small clothing department in a large store.

bo•vine ['bəʊvaɪn] *adj.* referring to cows and bulls; **b. spongiform encephalopathy** = fatal disease of the nervous system in cattle, caused by an abnormal prion protein in the brain.

bow¹ ['bəʊ] *n.* (a) long piece of wood with taut string joining both ends, used for shooting arrows. (b) wooden rod with hair stretched taut between its ends, used for playing a violin or other stringed instrument. (c) ribbon/tie knotted to look like a butterfly. **bow•leg•ged**, *adj.* with legs which curve apart at the knee. **bow tie**, *n.* short necktie tied in a bow. **bow win•dow**, *n.* window projecting out from the wall in a curve.

bow² [baʊ] 1. *n.* (a) salute made by bending the body forward. (b) (*usu.* **bows**) front part of a ship. (c) rower who sits nearest the bow of a rowing boat. 2. *v.* to bend forward. **bow•sprit**, *n.* horizontal mast going forward from the bows of a ship.

bowd•ler•ize ['baʊdləraɪz] *v.* to cut indecent parts from (a book).

bow•els (*sometimes* **bowel**) ['baʊəlz] *n.* intestines; **in the b. of the earth** = deep underground.

bow•er ['baʊə] *n.* shelter covered by trees or plants.

bowl [bəʊl] 1. *n.* (a) wide container (of china/plastic, etc.). (b) wooden ball for playing game of bowls. (c) **bowls** = game where wooden balls are rolled to try to get nearest to small target ball. 2. *v.* (a) to throw a ball, esp. in cricket. (b) to roll a bowl (in a game of bowls). **bowl•er**, *n.* (a) person who plays bowls. (b) (*in cricket*) person who throws the ball to the opposing batsman. (c) **b.** (**hat**) = black round-topped man's hat. **bowl•ing**, *n.* (a) game of bowls; **b. green** = level grassy area for playing bowls. (b) game of knocking down wooden pins with a large ball; **b. alley** = establishment for bowling. **bowl over**, *v.* to knock down/to surprise.

box [bɒks] 1. *n.* (*pl.* **-es**) (a) container with a lid; **mailbox** = box in the street for mailing letters. (b) evergreen tree, with very small leaves; hard wood from this tree. (c) small balcony room in a theater; cubicle for a horse; place where a witness gives evidence in court. (d) smack (on the ear). 2. *v.* (a) **to b. s.o.'s ears** = to smack s.o. on the ears. (b) to fight an opponent in the boxing ring. **box•er**, *n.* (a) man who practices the sport of boxing. (b) breed of large dog with short hair. **box•ing**, *n.* sport of fighting with gloves in a ring; *Brit.* **B. Day** = day after Christmas Day, December 26. **box of•fice**, *n.* office in a theater where you buy tickets.

boy [bɔɪ] *n.* male child; **old b.** = old friend/old man/former pupil of a school. **boy•friend**, *n.* young male friend. **boy•hood**, *n.* youth/time of life when you are a boy. **boy•ish**, *adj.* like a boy. **Boy Scouts**, *n.* social/educational organization for boys.

boy•cott ['bɔɪkɒt] 1. *n.* act of boycotting. 2. *v.* to refuse to have anything to do with s.o./sth.

bra [brɑː] *n. inf.* brassiere/woman's undergarment for supporting the breasts.

brace [breɪs] 1. *n.* (a) support; (*on teeth*) metal clamp to make teeth grow straight. (b) *Brit.* **braces** = elastic straps over the shoulders to hold up trousers. (c) pair; **a b. of grouse** = two grouse. (d) tool for holding a bit to drill holes. 2. *v.* to support/to strengthen; **he braced himself for the ordeal** = he stiffened his muscles to prepare himself for the ordeal. **brac•ing**, *adj.* invigorating/healthy (climate).

brace•let ['breɪslət] *n.* ornamental chain/band worn round the wrist.

brack•en ['brækən] *n.* wild fern growing often in open country.

brack•et ['brækɪt] 1. *n.* (a) support (for shelf, etc., against a wall). (b) printing symbol showing that sth is separated from the rest of the text. (c) (administrative) group; **the middle-income b.** 2. *v.* (a) to put (words) into brackets. (b) to link; **his name was bracketed with that of the mayor.**

brack•ish ['brækɪʃ] *adj.* salty/undrinkable water.

bract [brækt] *n.* part of a plant which is shaped like a leaf but can be colored like a flower.

brad [bræd] *n.* small nail with a flat head.

brad•awl ['brædɔːl] *n.* boring tool for making holes (esp. in leather).

brag [bræg] *v.* (**bragged**) to boast.

Brah•min ['brɑːmɪn] *n.* (a) highest-ranking Hindu; (b) very important person.

braid [breɪd] 1. *n.* plaited decoration. 2. *v.* to plait (hair) with ribbon.

braille [breɪl] *n.* system of raised dots on paper for the blind to read by touch.

brain [breɪn] 1. *n.* nervous center of the head which thinks and directs the body; **use your b.** = think hard; **she's got brains** = she's intelligent; *inf.* **b. drain** = departure of highly intelligent people to other countries in order to work for higher salaries. 2. *v.* to knock s.o. out by hitting him on the head. **brain•child,** *n.* original idea/plan thought up by s.o. **brain•i•ness,** *n.* intelligence. **brain•less,** *adj.* idiotic/stupid. **brain•pow•er,** *n.* intelligence/ability to think or reason. **brain•storm,** *n.* sudden mad idea. **brain•wash,** *v.* to indoctrinate (s.o.)/to make s.o. think in a totally different manner from before. **brain wave,** *n.* brilliant idea. **brain•y,** *adj.* (-ier, -iest) *inf.* intelligent.

braise [breɪz] *v.* to cook (meat/vegetables) in a covered pot with very little liquid.

brake [breɪk] 1. *n.* mechanism for stopping a car/bicycle, etc.; **hand b.** = brake operated by a hand lever. 2. *v.* to stop/to slow down by applying the brakes. **brak•ing,** *n.* putting on the brakes; **b. distance** = distance a car travels after the brakes are applied before it comes to a halt.

bram•ble ['bræmbl] *n.* wild blackberry.

bran [bræn] *n.* skins of wheat seeds which are separated from the flour.

branch [brɑːntʃ] 1. *n.* (*pl.* **-es**) (a) limb of a tree. (b) offshoot; **b. of a river; b. line** = minor railroad line. (c) office (of a bank, etc.); store (of a chain of stores). 2. *v.* **to b. out** = to spread out/to diversify.

brand [brænd] 1. *n.* (a) identification mark made (on cattle) by a hot iron. (b) named product made by one manufacturer. 2. *v.* (a) to mark (cattle) with a hot iron. (b) **he was branded as a thief** = he was called a thief. **brand•ed,** *adj.* (a) marked (cattle, etc.). (b) (goods) with a brand name. **brand name,** *n.* name applied to one product. **brand-new,** *adj.* completely new.

brand•ish ['brændɪʃ] *v.* to wave (sth) about.

bran•dy ['brændɪ] *n.* strong alcohol distilled from wine; glass of this alcohol.

brash [bræʃ] *adj.* vulgar, pushy.

brass [brɑːs] *n.* yellow metal made from copper and zinc; **top b.** = directors/high-ranking officers; **to get down to b. tacks** = to discuss the basic problem. (b) musical instruments made of brass; **a b. band.** (c) *inf.* money. (d) something, as ornamental hardware, made of brass. **brass-rub•bing,** *n.* reproduction of a brass plate by covering it with paper and rubbing with wax. **brass•y,** *adj.* (a) (noise) like that of brass instruments. (b) rude, loud-mouthed (person).

bras•si•cas ['bræsɪkəz] *n. pl.* plants of the cabbage family.

bras•siere ['bræzɪə] *n.* woman's undergarment for supporting the breasts.

brat [bræt] *n.* rude child.

bra•va•do [brə'vɑːdəʊ] *n.* reckless bravery.

brave [breɪv] 1. *adj.* (-er, -est) not afraid; courageous. 2. *v.* to defy. 3. *n.* male American Indian warrior. **brave•ly,** *adv.* with courage. **brav•er•y,** *n.* courage.

bra•vo [brɑː'vəʊ] *inter. showing approval.*

brawl [brɔːl] 1. *n.* wild fight. 2. *v.* to fight wildly. **brawl•er,** *n.* person who is fighting wildly.

brawn [brɔːn] *n.* (a) muscle power. (b) flesh of a boar, esp. boiled and pickled. **brawn•y,** *adj.* muscular/strong.

bray [breɪ] *v.* to make a loud call like a donkey.

bra•zen ['breɪzn] 1. *adj.* (a) like brass/made of brass. (b) shameless. 2. *v.* **he brazened it out** = he impudently got through the awkward situation.

bra•zier ['breɪzɪə] *n.* metal basket for burning coal.

Bra•zil•i•an [brə'zɪlɪən] 1. *adj.* referring to Brazil. 2. *n.* person from Brazil.

breach [briːtʃ] 1. *n.* (*pl.* **-es**) (a) crack (in a defense/dam). (b) breaking (of a law/promise); **b. of the peace** = disorderly behavior; **b. of faith** = going back on what has been promised; **b. of promise** = refusing to marry s.o. after having promised to do so. 2. *v.* to split; to make a crack in (a wall).

bread [bred] *n.* (*no pl.*) food made from flour, water and yeast baked in an oven; **wholemeal b.** = bread made from flour which contains the whole grain; **bread-and-butter letter** = letter written to say thank you for hospitality; **b. box** = metal/plastic container for keeping bread fresh. **bread•crumbs,** *n. pl.* bread broken up into very small pieces. **bread•win•ner,** *n.* person who earns money to feed the family.

breadth [bredθ] *n.* (a) measurement of how broad or wide sth is. (b) wideness (of views).

break [breɪk] 1. *n.* (a) split/crack (where two parts have broken). (b) quarrel. (c) **b. in the weather** = change in the weather. (d) rest period; **coffee b.** = period where you stop work for a cup of coffee; **morning b.** = short period of play during the morning at school. (e) **he had a lucky b.** = his bad luck changed. (f) **at b. of day** = at dawn. (g) series of shots in billiards or pool. 2. *v.* (**broke; has broken**) (a) to fall to pieces/to smash (sth) into pieces; **my watch is broken** = my watch has stopped working; **it**

æ back, ɑː farm, ɒ top, aɪ pipe, aʊ how, aɪə fire, aʊə flower, ɔː bought, ɔɪ toy, e fed, eəhair, eɪ take, ə afraid, əʊ boat, əʊə lower, ɜː word, iː heap, ɪ hit, ɪə hear, uː school, ʊ book, ʌ but, b back, d dog, ð then, dʒ just, f fog, g go, h hand, j yes, k catch, l last, m mix, n nut, ŋ sing, p penny, r round, s some, ʃ short, t too, tʃ chop, θ thing, v voice, w was, z zoo, ʒ treasure

broke her heart = she was extremely upset; **he broke the record for the high jump** = did better than anyone had ever done before. (b) **we are breaking even** = we are not making a loss or a profit. (c) not to keep (a promise/a rule). (d) **the storm broke** = storm suddenly started; **the day was breaking** = daylight was coming. (e) (*of boy's voice*) to become deeper as the boy grows older. (f) to cushion (a fall). (g) (*of wave*) to grow tall and crash down. **break•a•ble**, *adj.* which can easily be broken. **break•a•bles**, *n. pl.* fragile objects (glasses/cups, etc.). **break•a•ges**, *n. pl.* breaking (of glass, etc.); things which have been broken. **break away**, *v.* to escape/to be detached (**from**). **break•a•way**, *adj.* which has become detached; **the b. nationalist party** = the nationalist party which has split off from a larger party. **break down**, *v.* (a) to smash (sth). (b) to collapse; to go wrong. (c) to list (items). **break•down**, *n.* (a) collapse; **nervous b.** = state where you become severely depressed. (b) list under various headings. (c) **we had a b. on the highway** = our car stopped working; **b. lane** = lane for cars which do not work. **break•er**, *n.* big wave which is breaking. **break•fast** ['brekfəst] 1. *n.* first meal of the day; food eaten at this meal; **continental b.** = breakfast of bread and coffee; 2. *v.* to eat the first meal of the day; **break in**, *v.* (a) to enter forcibly. (b) to interrupt. (c) to train (a horse). **break-in**, *n.* burglary. **break•ing**, *n.* (a) action of smashing/falling to pieces. (b) **b. and entering** = crime of breaking into s.o.'s property. **break in•to**, *v.* to enter forcibly. **break loose**, *v.* to escape. **break•neck**, *adj.* at **b. speed** = extremely fast. **break off**, *v.* (a) to split away/to crack; to remove (sth) by breaking. (b) to stop; **they have broken off negotiations. break o•pen**, *v.* to smash (in order to open). **break out**, *v.* (a) to start; **war has broken out**. (b) to escape; **three prisoners broke out from prison. break•out**, *n.* escape. **break through**, *v.* to smash in order to go through. **break•through**, *n.* sudden success or new development. **break up**, *v.* (a) to smash to pieces. **break it up!** = stop fighting; **they had a quarrel and broke up** = did not work/live together any more. (b) to come to an end; **the meeting broke up at noon. break•up**, *n.* coming to pieces/an end. **break•wa•ter**, *n.* wall/fence going into the sea to prevent waves from battering the coast.

bream [briːm] *n.* (*pl.* **bream**) type of fat edible fish.

breast [brest] *n.* (a) one of two milk-giving organs in a woman's body; **b. feeding** = feeding a child with milk from the breast. (b) chest/front part of the top of the body; **b. pocket** = pocket

on the front of a jacket; **b. stroke** = swimming stroke where both arms stretch out together and are brought back to the chest.

breath [breθ] *n.* air which goes into and out of the body; **out of b./gasping for b.** = having difficulty in breathing; **don't waste your b. on them** = don't waste time talking to them; **it took my b. away** = I was completely astonished; **he muttered under his b.** = quietly; **a b. of wind** = a slight breeze. **breath•a•lyz•er**, *n.* instrument for testing if a driver has drunk too much alcohol. **breath•less**, *adj.* out of breath/panting. **breath•less•ly**, *adv.* in a rush/without taking time to breathe. **breath•tak•ing**, *adj.* so exciting/beautiful that it takes your breath away.

breathe [briːð] *v.* to suck air in or out through the nose or mouth; **b. deeply** = take in lots of air; **don't b. a word about it!** = don't say anything about it. **breath•er**, *n.* rest period; **I'm going out for a b.** = I'm going out to get some fresh air. **breath•ing**, *n.* act of taking air in and out of the body; **b. apparatus** = mask, etc., which allows you to breathe when in gas/smoke, etc.; **b. space** = rest period.

bred [bred] *v. see* **breed.**

breech [briːtʃ] *n.* (*pl.* **-es**) (a) back part of a gun where the ammunition is loaded. (b) **b. birth, breech delivery** = birth in which the baby's feet or buttocks appear first. (c) **breeches** = trousers which come down to below the knees; **breeches buoy** = device, like a canvas seat, used to rescue people at sea.

breed [briːd] 1. *n.* particular race of animal. 2. *v.* (**bred**) to produce young animals/plants; **I was born and bred in the country** = I was born and grew up in the country; **well-bred person** = s.o. who is polite/who has been well educated. **breed•er**, *n.* (a) person who breeds (animals). (b) (**fast**) **b. reactor** = nuclear machine which makes a surplus of nuclear material. **breed•ing**, *n.* (a) production of animals. (b) training in good manners.

breeze [briːz] 1. *n.* slight wind; **a stiff breeze** = quite a strong wind. 2. *v.* **he breezed into the restaurant** = he rushed in looking very pleased with himself. **breez•i•ly**, *adv.* in a happy-go-lucky way. **breez•y**, *adj.* (a) windy. (b) happy-go-lucky.

breth•ren ['breðrən] *n. pl.* (*religious*) brothers.

breve [briːv] *n.* long note in music.

bre•vi•ar•y ['briːvjərɪ] *n.* book of Roman Catholic prayers.

brev•i•ty ['brevɪtɪ] *n.* conciseness/shortness.

brew [bruː] 1. *n.* liquid which has been brewed. 2. *v.* (a) to make (beer/coffee/tea). (b) **there's trouble brewing** = there is trouble coming. **brew•er**, *n.* person who makes beer; **brewer's yeast** = yeast used in brewing beer, and taken

in tablet form as a source of vitamin B.
brew•er•y, *n*. place where beer is made.

bri•ar ['braɪə] *n. see* **bri•er.**

bribe [braɪb] 1. *n*. money given illegally to s.o.
to get sth done. 2. *v*. to give (s.o.) money illegally to get sth done. **brib•er•y**, *n*. act of
bribing.

bric-à-brac ['brɪkəbræk] *n*. (*no pl.*) ornaments
or furniture of little value.

brick [brɪk] *n*. block of baked clay, used for
building; **he dropped a b.** = he made an unfortunate remark by mistake. **brick•lay•er**, *n*.
person who builds with bricks. **brick up**, *v*. to
fill in (window/doorway) with bricks.
brick•work, *n*. bricks built up into a wall.
brick•yard, *n*. place where bricks are made,
sold, or kept.

bride [braɪd] *n*. woman who is about to get
married or who has just got married. **brid•al**,
adj. referring to a wedding. **bride•groom**, *n*.
man who is about to get married or who has
just got married. **brides•maid**, *n*. woman
who is the bride's attendant at a wedding.

bridge [brɪdʒ] 1. *n*. (a) construction to take a
road/railroad across a river/road/railroad
line. (b) top part of a ship where a captain
stands. (c) top of the nose. (d) (*in a violin*) support for the strings. (e) type of card game for
four people. 2. *v*. to put a bridge across (a
river, etc.). **bridge•head**, *n*. preliminary position held by attackers who have attacked
across water. **bridge loan**, *n*. short-term
loan, esp. one to help s.o. buy a house before
he has sold his old one.

bri•dle ['braɪdl] 1. *n*. headstraps (for a horse).
2. *v*. (a) to hold back (a horse). (b) to take
offense. **bri•dle path**, *n*. path for
horseriders.

brief [bri:f] 1. *adj*. short. 2. *n*. (a) papers concerning a legal case. (b) instructions. (c) **briefs**
= underpants. 3. *v*. to give a case to (a lawyer);
to give (s.o.) information/instructions.
brief•case, *n*. small case for carrying papers.
brief•ing, *n*. conference where information
is given. **brief•ly**, *adv*. shortly/speaking for a
short time.

bri•er [braɪə] *n*. prickly wild bush, esp. a rose.

bri•gade [brɪ'geɪd] *n*. (a) army group, smaller
than a division. (b) **fire b.** = group of people
whose job is to fight fires. **brig•a•dier**
[brɪgə'dɪə] *n*. army officer in charge of a brigade; rank in the army above colonel.

brig•and ['brɪgənd] *n*. robber.

bright [braɪt] *adj*. (**-er, -est**) (a) shining very
strongly/having a very vivid color; **to look on
the b. side of things** = to be optimistic. (b) intelligent. **bright•en**, *v*. (a) to make bright. (b)
she brightened up when she saw him = she became more cheerful; **the weather is brightening
up** = it is getting nicer. **bright•ly**, *adv*. (a)
with a strong light. (b) in an intelligent/cheerful tone of voice. **bright•ness**, *n*. strength (of
light); intelligence (of person).

brill [brɪl] *n*. (*pl.* **brill**) type of flat white edible
sea fish.

bril•liant ['brɪljənt] 1. *adj*. (a) very shiny. (b)
very clever. 2. *n*. gem, esp. a diamond.
bril•liance, *n*. brightness; intelligence.

brim [brɪm] 1. *n*. edge. 2. *v*. (**brimmed**) **the glass
was brimming over with wine** = the glass was
overflowing. **brim•ful**, *adj*. very full/full to
overflowing.

brin•dled ['brɪndld] *adj*. (*of animals*) brown
with streaks of another color.

brine [braɪn] *n*. salt water.

bring [brɪŋ] *v*. (**brought** [brɔ:t]; **has brought**) to
take (sth/s.o.) to this place. **bring about**, *v*.
to cause/to make (sth) happen. **bring along**,
v. to bring with you. **bring back**, *v*. to return
(here); **that picture brings it all back to me** =
makes me remember it all. **bring down**, *v*. to
make (sth/s.o.) fall down; to lower (sth).
bring forward, *v*. **to bring forward the date
of the meeting** = to arrange an earlier date for
it. **bring in**, *v*. to make (sth/s.o.) come in.
bring off, *v*. to succeed in; **he brought it off** =
he did it successfully. **bring on**, *v*. to produce/to make grow; **you've brought it on yourself** = it's your own fault. **bring out**, *v*. to
make (sth/s.o.) come out; **to b. out a new book**
= to publish a new book; **to b. out the color** =
to make the color more noticeable/more effective. **bring a•round** or **round**, *v*. (a) to take
(sth) to s.o.'s house. (b) to revive (s.o.) who is
unconscious. **bring up**, *v*. (a) to raise (a subject). (b) to vomit. (c) to educate in manners.

brink [brɪŋk] *n*. edge (of cliff); **on the b. of a nervous breakdown** = very close to having a nervous breakdown.

brin•y ['braɪnɪ] *adj*. salty; *inf*. **the b.** = the sea.

brisk [brɪsk] *adj*. (**-er, -est**) rapid. **brisk•ly**, *adv*.
rapidly.

bris•ket ['brɪskɪt] *n*. beef from the breast of an
animal.

bris•ling ['brɪzlɪŋ] *n*. small sea fish, like a sardine.

æ back, a: farm, ɒ: top, aɪ pipe, aʊ how, aɪə fire, aʊə flower, ɔ: bought, ɔɪ toy, e fed, eəhair, eɪ take, ə
afraid, əʊ boat, əʊə lower, v: word, i: heap, ɪ hit, ɪə hear, u: school, ʊ book, ʌ but, b back, d dog, ð then,
dʒ just, f fog, g go, h hand, j yes, k catch, l last, m mix, n nut, ŋ sing, p penny, r round, s some, ʃ short, t
too, tʃ chop, θ thing, v voice, w was, z zoo, ʒ treasure

bris•tle ['brɪsl] 1. *n.* short stiff hair (on animal/brush). 2. *v.* (a) to take offense. (b) **to b. with** = to be full of/covered with; **to bristle with excitement. brist•ly,** *adj.* covered with short stiff hair.

Brit•ish ['brɪtɪʃ] *adj. & n.* referring to Great Britain; **the B.** = the people of Great Britain. **the B. Isles** = group of islands off the north coast of Europe, including England, Wales, Scotland, Ireland, and many smaller islands. **Brit,** *n. Sl.* a Briton, **Brit•on** ['brɪtn] *n.* person from Great Britain.

brit•tle ['brɪtl] *adj.* which breaks easily. **brit•tle•ness,** *n.* fragility.

broach [brəʊtʃ] *v.* (a) to open (a cask of wine, etc.). (b) to start talking about (a problem).

broad [brɔːd] *adj.* (**-er, -est**) very wide; **in b. daylight** = in full daylight; **a b. Scottish accent** = a strong accent; **b. beans** = type of beans with large flat seeds. **broad•cast.** 1. *n.* radio/television program; 2. *v.* (**broadcast**) (a) to sow (by throwing seed by hand). (b) to send out by radio/television; **they b. an appeal to the people.** (c) to tell everyone (the news); **don't b. the fact** = keep it a secret. 3. *adv.* (sowing) by throwing the seed by hand. 4. *adj.* sent by radio/television. **broad•cast•er,** *n.* person who speaks on the radio/television. **broad•en,** *v.* to make wider; **travel broadens the mind** = travel makes your knowledge/interest more extensive. **broad•loom,** *adj.* (carpet) woven in a very wide strip. **broad•ly,** *adv.* **b. speaking** = in a general way. **broad•mind•ed,** *adj.* tolerant; not easily taking offense. **broad-shoul•der•ed,** *adj.* with wide shoulders. **broad•side,** *n.* (a) firing of all the guns on one side of a ship. (b) sharp written or spoken criticism.

bro•cade [brə'keɪd] *n.* thick cloth with a raised pattern.

broc•co•li ['brɒkəlɪ] *n.* (*pl.* **broccoli**) cabbagelike vegetable of which the flowerheads are eaten.

bro•chure ['brəʊʃə] *n.* small book; small publicity pamphlet.

brogue [brəʊg] *n.* (a) heavy shoe with patterned leather top. (b) accent (usu. Irish).

broil [brɔɪl] *v.* to grill. **broil•er,** *n.* chicken specially bred for roasting.

broke [brəʊk] *adj. inf.* **to be flat b.** = to have no money; *see also* **break.**

bro•ken ['brəʊkən] *adj.* (a) in pieces; **a b. home** = home where the parents have separated. (b) spoken with a foreign accent and with many mistakes. (c) *see also* **break. bro•ken-down,** *adj.* not working. **bro•ken-heart•ed,** *adj.* very upset/sad.

bro•ker ['brəʊkə] *n.* person who deals in stocks/insurance. **bro•ker•age,** *n.* fee charged by a broker for his work.

bro•mide ['brəʊmaɪd] *n.* (a) chemical used to make a calming medicine. (b) photographic paper.

bron•chi•al ['brɒŋkɪəl] *adj.* referring to the respiratory tubes; **b. asthma** = asthma in the lungs. **bron•chi,** *n. pl.* air passages leading into the lungs. **bron•chi•tis** [brɒŋ'kaɪtɪs] *n.* disease of the respiratory tubes.

bronze [brɒnz] *n.* metal made from copper and tin; **B. Age** = prehistoric period when weapons of bronze were used. **bronzed,** *adj.* tanned/sunburned.

brooch [brəʊtʃ] *n.* ornament to pin on to clothing.

brood [bruːd] 1. *n.* group of chicks/small children. 2. *v.* to have gloomy thoughts; **she's brooding sth.** = she is thinking about something. **brood•y,** *adj.* (a) (hen) preparing to sit on a clutch of eggs. (b) (person) who has gloomy thoughts.

brook [brʊk] 1. *n.* small stream. 2. *v.* to allow/to accept.

broom [bruːm] *n.* (a) shrub with yellow flowers. (b) brush with long handle for sweeping the floor. **broom•stick,** *n.* long handle of a broom.

bros. [brɒs] *abbreviation for* brothers.

broth [brɒθ] *n.* light soup; **Scotch b.** = thick soup with barley, vegetables and lamb.

broth•el ['brɒθl] *n.* house of prostitutes.

broth•er ['brʌðə] *n.* (a) male child of the same parents as another child. (b) man belonging to a monastic order. **broth•er•hood,** *n.* fraternity; companionship (between men). **broth•er-in-law,** *n.* (*pl.* **brothers-in-law**) brother of your husband or wife; husband of your sister; husband of the sister of your husband or wife. **broth•er•ly,** *adj.* as of brothers.

brought [brɔːt] *v. see* **bring.**

brow [braʊ] *n.* (a) forehead/top part of the face above the eyes. (b) line of hair above each eye. (c) rounded top of a hill. **brow•beat,** *v.* (**browbeat; has browbeaten**) to intimidate (s.o.).

brown [braʊn] 1. *adj.* (**-er, -est**) colored like the color of wood or soil. 2. *n.* color of wood or soil. 3. *v.* to become brown; to make brown. **brown•field** *adj. & n.* (urban site) that has previously been built on. **Brown•ie,** *n.* (a) girl in the junior section of the Girl Scouts. (b) chocolate cookie. **brown•ish,** *adj.* rather brown.

browse [braʊz] *v.* (a) (*of animal*) to wander about eating grass. (b) (*of person*) to wander round a store. looking at goods for sale.

brows•er, *n.* person who is browsing in a store.

bru•cel•lo•sis [brəsel'əʊsɪs] *n.* disease caught from drinking infected milk.

bruise [bruːz] 1. *n.* mark made on the skin by a blow. 2. *v.* to get/to make marks on the skin from a blow. **bruis•er,** *n.* bully; fighter.

brunch [brʌntʃ] *n.* large meal (as a combination of breakfast and lunch) taken in the middle of the morning.

bru•nette [bruː'net] *adj. & n.* (woman) with brown hair.

brunt [brʌnt] *n.* **to bear the b. of** = to suffer most from.

brush [brʌʃ] 1. *n.* (*pl.* -es) (a) instrument with a handle and hair/wire/nylon bristles for painting or cleaning. (b) scrub land. (c) cleaning with a brush. (d) short argument/fight with an opponent. (e) piece of carbon which makes an electric contact. (f) tail (of a fox). 2. *v.* (a) to clean with a brush. (b) to go past sth touching it gently. **brush aside,** *v.* to reject. **brush away,** *v.* to clear away with a brush. **brush down,** *v.* to brush (sth) vigorously. **brush off,** *v.* to clean (sth) off with a brush. **brush-off,** *n. inf.* **to give s.o. the b.-off** = to send s.o. away without listening or agreeing to what they want. **brush up,** *v.* (a) to make (yourself) smart. (b) to improve (your knowledge of). **brush•wood,** *n.* low undergrowth.

brusque [bruːsk] *adj.* abrupt/impolite. **brusque•ly,** *adv.* rudely.

Brus•sels sprouts ['brʌslz'sprauts] *n. pl.* vegetable like tiny cabbages.

brute [bruːt] *n.* (a) animal. (b) rude/violent person; **to use b. force** = to use rough methods. **bru•tal,** *adj.* violent. **brut•al•i•ty** [bruː'tælɪtɪ] *n.* violent action. **bru•tal•ize,** *v.* to beat (s.o.). **bru•tal•ly,** *adv.* in a brutal way. **brut•ish,** *adj.* rude/violent.

bry•o•ny ['braɪənɪ] *n.* type of climbing plant with poisonous berries.

BS [biːs'siː] Bachelor of Science.

BSE [biːs'iː] *abbrev. for* bovine spongiform encephalopathy.

bub•ble ['bʌbl] 1. *n.* small amount of air trapped in liquid. 2. *v.* to make bubbles. **bub•bly.** 1. *adj.* with bubbles. 2. *n. inf.* champagne.

bu•bon•ic plague [bjuː'bɒnɪk 'pleɪg] *n.* fatal disease, transmitted by rats.

buck [bʌk] 1. *n.* (a) male deer/rabbit. (b) *inf.* dollar. (c) *inf.* **to pass the b.** = to hand responsibility on to s.o. else. 2. *v.* (*of horse*) to jump in

the air (with rounded back). **buck•teeth,** *n. pl.* teeth which stick out in front. **buck up,** *v. inf.* to make (s.o.) feel more lively.

buck•et ['bʌkɪt] *n.* round container with an open top and a handle. **buck•et•ful,** *n.* quantity contained in a bucket. **buck•et seat,** *n.* rounded seat (in a car).

buck•le ['bʌkl] 1. *n.* metal fastener for attaching a belt/strap/shoe. 2. *v.* (a) to attach (sth) with a metal clasp. (b) to bend/to collapse.

buck•ram ['bʌkrəm] *n.* thick cloth for covering books.

buck•wheat ['bʌkwiːt] *n.* dark grain, giving a brown flour.

bu•col•ic [bjuː'kɒlɪk] *adj.* referring to the countryside.

bud [bʌd] 1. *n.* (a) point on a plant where a new shoot is appearing; flower not yet opened; **the roses are in b.** = the flowers are ready to open. (b) buddy. 2. *v.* (**budded**) (a) to make buds. (b) to graft a bud. **bud•ding,** *adj.* (flower) not yet open; **b. concert pianist** = person who hopes to be a concert pianist.

Bud•dhism ['budɪzəm] *n.* religion following the teaching of Buddha. **Bud•dhist,** *adj. & n.* (person) who follows the teaching of Buddha.

bud•dle•ia ['bʌdlɪə] *n.* garden shrub with long purple flowers.

bud•dy ['bʌdɪ] *n. inf.* friend.

budge [bʌdʒ] *v.* to move.

budg•er•i•gar ['bʌdʒərɪgɑː] *n.* blue or green tropical bird like a small parrot.

budg•et ['bʌdʒɪt] 1. *n.* list of proposed expenditure. 2. *v.* **to b. for** = to plan how to spend money on sth.

budg•ie ['bʌdʒɪ] *n. inf.* budgerigar.

buff [bʌf] 1. (a) *adj. & n.* (of a) pale yellowy-brown color. (b) *n. inf.* enthusiast. 2. *v.* to polish/to shine.

buf•fa•lo ['bʌfələʊ] *n.* (*pl.* -oes/-o) large wild ox or cow (in America and parts of Africa and Asia).

buff•er ['bʌfə] *n.* shock-absorbing pad; **b. state** = small country between two larger states, which may be antagonistic to each other; **b. zone** = area between two areas of fighting.

buf•fet¹ ['bufeɪ] *n.* (a) counter or snack bar (in railroad station, etc.) where light meals or refreshments are sold; **b. car** = railroad car containing a buffet. (b) self-service meal. (c) sideboard.

buf•fet² ['bʌfɪt] *v.* to bang/to jolt.

æ back, ɑ: farm, ɒ: top, aɪ pipe, aʊ how, aɪə fire, aʊə flower, ɔ: bought, ɔɪ toy, e fed, eəhair, eɪ take, ə afraid, əʊ boat, əʊə lower, v: word, i: heap, ɪ hit, ɪə hear, u: school, ʊ book, ʌ but, b back, d dog, ð then, dʒ just, f fog, g go, h hand, j yes, k catch, l last, m mix, n nut, ŋ sing, p penny, r round, s some, ʃ short, t too, tʃ chop, θ thing, v voice, w was, z zoo, ʒ treasure

buf•foon [bə'fuːn] *n.* fool/clown. **buf•foon•er•y,** *n.* foolish action.

bug [bʌg] 1. *n.* (a) small insect which sucks. (b) any small insect. (c) *inf.* germ. (d) hidden microphone. (e) defect in a computer program. 2. *v.* (**bugged**) (a) to install a hidden microphone in (a room). (b) *inf.* **what's bugging you?** = what's bothering you? **bug•bear,** *n.* thing which you hate.

bu•gle ['bjuːgl] *n.* military trumpet. **bu•gler,** *n.* person who blows a bugle.

build [bɪld] 1. *n.* size/shape (of person). 2. *v.* (**built** [bɪlt]; **has built**) to construct; to make by putting pieces together. **build•er,** *n.* person who constructs houses, etc. **build•ing,** *n.* (a) constructing; **b. land** = land for construction of houses. (b) construction; house/office block. **build up,** *v.* to construct/to create/to increase. **built-in,** *adj.* (cupboards, etc.) which are constructed as part of a building. **built-up,** *adj.* **built-up area** = area of a town where there are many buildings.

bulb [bʌlb] *n.* (a) fleshy underground stem of a plant, which produces leaves and flowers in spring. (b) glass globe full of gas which produces light when an electric current passes through it. **bul•bous,** *adj.* fat and rounded.

bulge [bʌldʒ] 1. *n.* swelling. 2. *v.* to swell out (with).

bu•lim•i•a [buˈlimiə] *n.* disease where you have a craving to eat and force yourself to vomit.

bulk [bʌlk] 1. *n.* large quantity; size; **in b.** = in large quantities; **b. purchase** = purchase in large quantities; **the b. of our sales** = most of our sales. 2. *v.* **to b. large** = to be important; to take up a lot of room. **bulk•head,** *n.* dividing wall in a ship or aircraft. **bulk•i•ness,** *n.* being bulky. **bulk•y,** *adj.* (**-ier, -iest**) very large/taking up an inconvenient amount of room.

bull [bʊl] *n.* (a) male ox. (b) male of certain species. (c) person who believes the stock market prices will rise. (d) official pronouncement by the pope. (e) *Sl.* foolish or exaggerated talk; nonsense. **bull•dog,** *n.* breed of squat, flatfaced dogs. **bull•doze,** *v.* (a) to knock down/to clear using a bulldozer. (b) to force; **he bulldozed his proposal through the committee** = forced them to agree to it. **bull•doz•er,** *n.* large tractor with a shovel in front for moving earth. **bull•fight,** *n.* entertainment in Spain, where a man fights a bull. **bull•fight•er,** *n.* man who fights bulls. **bull•finch,** *n.* small finch with red breast. **bull•frog,** *n.* large frog. **bul•lock,** *n.* castrated bull. **bull•ring,** *n.* arena where bullfights take place. **bull's-eye,** *n.* center point of a target.

bul•let ['bʊlɪt] *n.* piece of metal fired from a revolver or small gun. **bul•let•proof,** *adj.* (jacket/window) specially made so that bullets cannot pierce it.

bul•le•tin ['bʊlɪtɪn] *n.* piece of information; report on a situation.

bul•lion ['bʊljən] *n.* gold or silver bars.

bul•ly ['bʊlɪ] 1. *n.* person who frightens people who are weaker than he is; = thugs. 2. *v.* to intimidate (s.o.). **bul•ly beef,** *n. inf.* corned beef.

bul•rush ['bʊlrʌʃ] *n.* (*pl.* **-es**) tall reed with a brown furry head.

bul•wark ['bʊlwək] *n.* side of a ship which rises higher than the deck.

bum [bʌm] 1. *n.* tramp; person who loafs about doing nothing. 2. *v.* (**bummed**) *inf.* **to b. off s.o.** = to live at s.o.'s expense.

bum•ble ['bʌmbl] *v.* to move/do things in a clumsy way. **bum•ble•bee,** *n.* large furry bee.

bump [bʌmp] 1. *n.* (a) slight shock from hitting sth lightly. (b) small bulge on the body (from being hit). 2. *v.* to hit sth (lightly); **I bumped into him at the station** = I met him by chance. **bump off,** *v. inf.* to murder. **bump•y,** *adj.* (**-ier, -iest**) uneven (path/flight).

bump•er ['bʌmpə] *n.* (a) something very large; **a b. crop.** (b) metal or rubber strip at front and rear of a car to protect it when it is hit.

bump•tious ['bʌmpʃəs] *adj.* (person) full of his own importance.

bun [bʌn] *n.* (a) small cake; (b) hair wound round in a knot at the back of the head.

bunch [bʌntʃ] 1. *n.* (*pl.* **-es**) (a) cluster (of things) tied together; (b) group of people. 2. *v.* to gather together in a group.

bun•dle ['bʌndl] 1. *n.* parcel (of papers, etc.); group of nerves. 2. *v.* to tie (several things) together.

bung [bʌŋ] 1. *n.* stopper; thing which stops up a hole (in a cask). 2. *v.* to block/to stop up a hole.

bun•ga•low ['bʌŋɡələʊ] *n.* house with only a ground floor.

bun•gle ['bʌŋɡl] *v.* to do (sth) badly. **bun•gler,** *n.* person who has done a job badly.

bun•ion ['bʌnjən] *n.* painful swelling at the base of the big toe.

bunk [bʌŋk] *n.* (a) bed attached to a wall; **b. beds** = two beds, one on top of the other. (b) *inf.* nonsense.

bun•ker ['bʌŋkə] *n.* (a) storage area or bin for coal, as on a ship. (b) sandy pit on a golf course. (c) fortified gun emplacement.

bun•ny ['bʌnɪ] *n.* pet name for a rabbit.

bunt•ing ['bʌntɪŋ] *n.* (a) type of small singing bird. (b) (*no pl.*) strings of small flags.

bu•oy [bɔɪ] 1. *n.* floating marker showing a channel (in a river/at the entrance to a harbor). 2. *v.* **to b. s.o. up** = to cheer s.o. up. **buoy•an•cy**, *n.* ability to float; **buoy•ant**, *adj.* (a) which can float easily. (b) full of vigor.

bur•ble ['bɜːbl] 1. *n.* low murmur. 2. *v.* to murmur softly.

bur•den ['bɜːdn] 1. *n.* (a) heavy load; sth which is hard to do/to bear; **beast of b.** = animal (like a donkey) used to carry loads; **to make s.o.'s life a b.** = to make things difficult for s.o. (b) theme music of a song. 2. *v.* to load.

bu•reau [bjuərəu] *n.* (*pl.* **bureaus, bureaux** ['bjuərəuz]) (a) office; **information b.** = office which collects and hands out information. (b) (*old*) desk; (c) chest of drawers.

bu•reauc•ra•cy [bjuə'rɒkrəsɪ] *n.* rule by civil servants. **bu•reau•crat** ['bjuərəkræt] *n.* civil servant. **bu•reau•crat•ic** [bjuərə'krætɪk] *adj.* referring to the civil service.

bur•geon ['bɜːdʒn] *v.* to begin to grow.

burgh ['bʌrə] *n.* (*Scotland*) chartered town.

bur•glar ['bɜːglə] *n.* person who enters a house to steal; **b. alarm** = electric alarm which rings if a burglar attempts to enter the house. **bur•gla•ry**, *n.* robbery committed by a burglar. **bur•gle**, *v.* to steal from (a house).

bur•gun•dy ['bɜːgəndɪ] *n.* type of French red wine.

bur•i•al ['berɪəl] *n.* act of burying (a dead body); **b. ground** = cemetery.

bur•lap ['bɜːlæp] *n.* thick canvas.

bur•lesque [bɜː'lesk] 1. *adj. & n.* light satirical (play). 2. *v.* to satirize.

bur•ly ['bɜːlɪ] *adj.* (**-ier, -iest**) strong/solid (man).

Bur•mese [bɜː'miːz] 1. *adj.* coming from Burma. 2. *n.* (a) person from Burma. (b) language spoken in Burma.

burn [bɜːn] 1. *n.* (a) place (on the body) which has been burned. (b) (*in Scotland*) stream. 2. *v.* (**burned/burnt; has burned/burnt**) (a) to destroy by fire; **he got his fingers burned** = he suffered a loss/he did not do at all as well as he expected; **he's burned his bridges** = he can't go back now. (b) to use as a fuel. **burn down**, *v.* to destroy by fire. **burn•er**, *n.* apparatus for burning. **burn out**, *v.* **the fire has burned itself out** = the fire has gone out because there was nothing left to burn. **burned**, *adj.* which has gone black with fire.

bur•nish ['bɜːnɪʃ] *v.* to make (sth) shine by rubbing.

burp [bɜːp] 1. *n.* noise made when bringing up gas from the stomach through the mouth. 2. *v.* to make a burp.

burr [bɜː] *n.* (a) prickly part of a plant, containing seeds, which clings to clothes, etc. (b) country accent with a strongly pronounced "r." (c) rough edge to a piece of cut metal.

bur•row ['bʌrəu] 1. *n.* hole in the ground where rabbits live. 2. *v.* to make a long hole underground.

bur•sar ['bɜːsə] *n.* person in charge of the finances of a school/college/university. **bur•sa•ry**, *n.* scholarship/money given to a student to help him pay for his studies.

burst [bɜːst] 1. *n.* (a) sudden explosion; **b. of gunfire; b. of laughter.** (b) sudden attack; **b. of speed.** 2. *v.* (**burst; has burst**) to explode/to break open; **she b. into the room** = she rushed into the room; **the boy b. into tears** = he started to cry; **he was bursting to tell everyone the secret** = he was eagerly waiting to tell the secret. **burst o•pen**, *v.* to (make sth) come open with a bang. **burst out**, *v.* to shout out; **he burst out laughing.**

bur•y ['berɪ] *v.* to put (sth) into a hole in the ground.

bus [bʌs] 1. *n.* (*pl.* **-es**) motor vehicle for carrying passengers; **school b.** = bus which takes children to school. 2. *v.* (**bussed**) to take (children) to school in a different part of the town in order to mix racial groups. **bus driv•er**, *n.* person who drives a bus; **a busman's holiday** = spending your spare time doing sth similar to your normal job. **bus•sing**, *n.* action of sending children to school in a different part of the town in order to mix racial groups. **bus stop**, *n.* place where a bus stops regularly to let people on or off.

bus•by ['bʌzbɪ] *n.* tall fur hat worn by some soldiers.

bush [buʃ] *n.* (*pl.* **-es**) (a) plant which is smaller than a tree. (b) **the b.** = wild uncultivated land (in Africa/Australia); **b. fire** = fire in wild uncultivated land; **b. pilot** = pilot of a plane flying in the bush. **bushed**, *adj. inf.* tired out. **bush•man**, *n.* (*pl.* **-men**) native of the African bush. **bush•y**, *adj.* growing thickly.

bush•el ['buʃl] *n.* measure for grain (= 8 gallons).

busi•ness ['bɪznəs] *n.* (*pl.* **-es**) (a) affair; **it's none of your b.** = it has nothing to do with you. (b) commercial work; **to do b. with s.o.** = trade with s.o.; **do you think he means b.?** = do you think he is serious? (c) commercial or in-

---

æ back, aː farm, ɒ top, aɪ pipe, au how, aiə fire, auə flower, ɔː bought, ɔɪ toy, e fed, eəhair, eɪ take, ə afraid, əu boat, əuə lower, vː word, iː heap, ɪ hit, ɪə hear, uː school, u book, ʌ but, b back, d dog, ð then, dʒ just, f fog, g go, h hand, j yes, k catch, l last, m mix, n nut, ŋ sing, p penny, r round, s some, ʃ short, t too, tʃ chop, θ thing, v voice, w was, z zoo, ʒ treasure

dustrial organization. **busi•ness•like,** *adj.* practical/serious. **busi•ness•man, busi- nesswoman,** *n.* (*pl.* **-men/-women**) person who works in a business.

bust [bʌst] 1. *n.* (a) sculpture of head and shoul- ders. (b) measurement round a woman's breasts. 2. *adj. inf.* broken. 3. *v.* (**busted/bust**) *inf.* to break.

bus•tard ['bʌstəd] *n.* large brown bird, which runs fast.

bus•tle ['bʌsl] 1. *n.* (a) pad at the back of a dress (in Victorian times). (b) rushing around. 2. *v.* to rush around.

bus•y ['bɪzɪ] *adj.* (**-ier, -iest**) occupied with doing sth; **he is b. fixing the lawnmower; b. street** = street with lots of pedestrians and traffic. **bus•i•ly,** *adv.* in a busy way. **bus•y•bod•y,** *n.* person who interferes in other people's affairs.

but [bʌt] *conj., adv. & prep.* (suggesting the op- posite/a reservation) **he is tall b. his sister is short; nothing b.** = only; **b. for his letter, we would not have known he was here** = if it had not been for his letter.

bu•tane ['bjuːteɪn] *n.* gas (often used for cook- ing or heating).

butch [bʊtʃ] *adj. Sl.* (of woman) very mascu- line.

butch•er ['bʊtʃə] 1. *n.* person who prepares and sells meat. 2. *v.* (a) to kill in cold blood. (b) to ruin by doing badly; **they butchered the play. shop, butcher's shop,** *n.* store which sells meat and poultry. **butch•er•y,** *n.* mas- sacre/brutal killing.

but•ler ['bʌtlə] *n.* main male servant in a large house.

butt [bʌt] 1. *n.* (a) large barrel for keeping a liq- uid. (b) end of a cigarette. (c) shoulder end of a rifle. (d) place where you practice shooting. (e) person who is often teased. (f) push (with the head). (g) *inf.* buttocks. 2. *v.* (a) to push (s.o.) with your head. (b) **to b. in** = to interrupt a conversation.

but•ter ['bʌtə] 1. *n.* solid yellow fat made from cream. 2. *v.* to spread butter on (sth); **to b. s.o. up** = to flatter s.o. **but•ter•cup,** *n.* common bright yellow wild flower. **but•ter•fin•gers,** *n.* person who can't catch/who drops things. **but•ter•fly,** *n.* in- sect with brightly colored wings. **but•ter•milk,** *n.* thin milk left after butter has been churned. **but•ter•scotch,** *n.* sweet made from butter and sugar.

but•tock(s) ['bʌtək(s)] *n.* fleshy part of the body which you sit on.

but•ton ['bʌtn] 1. *n.* small object stitched to clothes for attaching one part of clothing to another; small round object which you press to make a machine work; **b. mushroom** = small round mushroom which is not fully grown. 2. *v.* to close or attach with buttons. **but•ton•hole.** 1. *n.* hole for putting a but- ton through. 2. *v.* **to b. s.o.** = to trap s.o. and talk to him at length.

but•tress ['bʌtrəs] 1. *n.* (*pl.* **-es**) supporting pil- lar (reinforcing a wall). 2. *v.* to support.

bux•om ['bʌksəm] *adj.* plump and attractive (woman).

buy [baɪ] 1. *v.* (**bought** [bɔːt] **has bought**) to get by paying money. 2. *n.* thing which you have bought/which you might buy; **a good b.** = a bargain. **buy•er,** *n.* person who buys, esp. person who buys stock for a large store. **buy out,** *v.* to buy a partner's share in a business.

buzz [bʌz] 1. *n.* (a) (*pl.* **-es**) noise like a bee. (b) *inf.* telephone call; **give me a b. tomorrow.** 2. *v.* (a) to make a noise like a bee. (b) (*of aircraft*) to fly low and close to (sth, as a house or an- other aircraft). **buzz•er,** *n.* device which makes a buzzing noise. **buzz off,** *v. inf.* to go away. **buzz word,** *n.* word which is fre- quently used.

buz•zard ['bʌzəd] *n.* kind of bird of prey.

by [baɪ] 1. *prep.* (a) near. (b) before; **by ten o'clock.** (c) using; **by airmail; by car.** (d) **paint- ing by Rembrandt** = which Rembrandt painted; **play by Shakespeare** = which Shake- speare wrote. (e) **by yourself** = alone. (f) **by the dozen** = a dozen at a time. 2. *adv.* (a) near; **put some money by for a rainy day** = put money to one side/save money. (b) past; **he drove by without stopping. by•gone.** 1. *adj.* past/for- mer. 2. *n.* thing which comes from the past; **let bygones be bygones** = forget past insults. **by•law,** *n.* law which is passed by a munici- pal council. **by•pass.** 1. *n.* (a) road which goes around a town. (b) **heart b.** = operation to insert a tube to go around a diseased part of an artery. 2. *v.* to go around (a town), avoid- ing the center; to avoid (sth) by going around it. **by-prod•uct,** *n.* secondary product made as a result of manufacturing something else. **by-road,** *n.* small local road. **by•stand•er,** *n.* person standing near the scene of action. **by•way,** *n.* small path/road. **by•word,** *n.* (**for**) famous or common saying or phrase.

bye [baɪ] *n.* (a) right to pass to the next round of a sporting tournament without having to play. (b) (*in cricket*) run scored without the batsman having hit the ball.

bye(-bye) [baɪ(baɪ)] *inter. used when leaving someone.*

byte [baɪt] *n.* series of bits processed by a com- puter as one piece.

Cc

C *symbol for* carbon.

Ca *symbol for* calcium.

cab [kæb] *n.* taxi. **cab•driv•er,** *n.* person who drives a taxi.

ca•bal [kæ'bɑːl] *n.* small group of politicians who plot in secret.

cab•a•ret ['kæbəreɪ] *n.* entertainment given in a restaurant or club.

cab•bage ['kæbɪdʒ] *n.* green leafy vegetable; **c. white** = common type of white butterfly.

cab•in ['kæbɪn] *n.* (a) small room on a ship. (b) small hut. (c) interior of an aircraft; **c. crew** = air hostesses and stewards.

cab•i•net ['kæbɪnət] *n.* (a) piece of furniture with shelves. (b) central committee of advisers or ministers in a government; **cab•i•net•mak•er,** *n.* woodworker who makes furniture.

ca•ble ['keɪbl] 1. *n.* (a) thick rope/wire; **c. railway** = railway where railroad cars are pulled up a steep hill by a cable. (b) telegraph wire for sending messages underwater. (c) message sent by underwater cable. (d) **c. TV** = television sent by cable. 2. *v.* to send a message to (s.o.) by cable. **ca•ble•car,** *n.* cabin on a cable railway. **ca•ble•gram,** *n.* telegram sent by cable.

ca•boo•dle [kə'buːdl] *n. inf.* **the whole c.** = everything.

ca•ca•o [kə'kɑːəʊ] *n.* tropical tree, of which the seeds provide cocoa and chocolate.

cache [kæʃ] *n.* hidden store.

ca•chet ['kæʃeɪ] *n.* special mark.

cack•le ['kækl] 1. *n.* noise made by hens; *Sl.* **cut the c.** = stop chattering. 2. *v.* to chatter.

ca•coph•o•ny [kə'kɒfənɪ] *n.* loud unpleasant mixture of sounds. **ca•coph•o•nous,** *adj.* unpleasantly noisy.

cac•tus ['kæktəs] *n.* (*pl.* **cacti** ['kæktaɪ], **cactuses, cactus**) prickly plant which grows in the desert.

cad [kæd] *n.* (*old*) unpleasant/dishonest person. **cad•dish,** *adj.* like a cad.

ca•dav•er [kə'dɑːvə] *n.* corpse. **ca•dav•er•ous,** *adj.* looking like a corpse.

CAD/CAM = computer-assisted design/computer-assisted manufacture.

cad•die ['kædɪ] 1. *n.* person who carries the clubs for a golfer. 2. *v.* to act as a caddie (**for** s.o.).

cad•dis fly ['kædɪsflaɪ] *n.* insect living near water.

cad•dy ['kædɪ] *n.* (*pl.* **caddies**) box for keeping tea in.

ca•dence ['keɪdəns] *n.* rhythm (of music/poetry).

ca•den•za [kə'denzə] *n.* flowery piece for a solo instrument in the middle of concerto/symphony, etc.

ca•det [kə'det] *n.* young person training for the armed forces.

cadge [kædʒ] *v.* to scrounge/to try to get (sth) without having to pay for it. **cadg•er,** *n.* person who cadges.

cad•mi•um ['kædmɪəm] *n.* (*element:* Cd) gray metal which can be poisonous to human beings.

ca•dre ['kɑːdə] *n.* (a) small group of expert people in a political party or the military. (b) active specialist working in a cadre.

cae•cum ['siːkəm] *see* **ce•cum.**

cae•sar•e•an [sɪ'zeərɪən] *n.* **c. (section)** = operation on a pregnant woman to deliver her baby through the wall of the womb.

ca•fé ['kæfeɪ] *n.* (a) small restaurant. (b) bar or nightclub.

caf•e•te•ri•a [kæfɪ'tɪərɪə] *n.* self-service restaurant.

caf•feine ['kæfiːn] *n.* stimulating substance in coffee, tea, and cola drinks

caf•tan ['kæftæn] *n.* long Arab-style gown.

cage [keɪdʒ] 1. *n.* enclosure of wire or with metal bars for keeping birds or animals. 2. *v.* to put in a cage.

cag•ey ['keɪdʒɪ] *adj.* (**cagier, cagiest**) secretive/unwilling to reveal sth. **cag•i•ly,** *adv.* in a cagey way. **cag•i•ness,** *n.* being cagey.

æ **back,** ɑː **farm,** ɒ **top,** aɪ **pipe,** aʊ **how,** aɪə **fire,** aʊə **flower,** ɔː **bought,** ɔɪ **toy,** e **fed,** eə **hair,** eɪ **take,** ə **afraid,** əʊ **boat,** əʊə **lower,** ɜː **word,** iː **heap,** ɪ **hit,** ɪə **hear,** uː **school,** ʊ **book,** ʌ **but,** b **back,** d **dog,** ð **then,** dʒ **just,** f **fog,** g **go,** h **hand,** j **yes,** k **catch,** l **last,** m **mix,** n **nut,** ŋ **sing,** p **penny,** r **round,** s **some,** ʃ **short,** t **too,** tʃ **chop,** θ **thing,** v **voice,** w **was,** z **zoo,** ʒ **treasure**

ca•hoots [kə'huːts] *n. inf.* **to be in c. with s.o.** = to work with s.o., against another person.

cairn [keən] *n.* heap of stones to mark an important spot.

cais•son [kə'suːn] *n.* watertight enclosure, as in a dry dock.

ca•jole [kə'dʒəul] *v.* to persuade by flattering. **ca•jol•er•y**, *n.* act of flattering.

cake [keɪk] 1. *n.* (a) cooked food made of eggs, flour and sugar, usu. eaten cold; *Sl.* **it's a piece of c.** = it is very easy; **you can't have your c. and eat it** = you can't benefit from two quite opposite things. (b) block of soap. 2. *v.* to form a dry crust.

cal•a•mine ['kæləmaɪn] *n.* **c. lotion** = pink liquid put on skin to soothe and stop itching.

ca•lam•i•ty [kə'læmɪtɪ] *n.* disaster. **ca•lam•i•tous**, *adj.* very unfortunate/disastrous.

cal•car•e•ous [kæl'keərɪəs] *adj.* (soil) containing chalk.

cal•ce•o•lar•i•a [kælsɪəu'leərɪə] *n.* house plant, with colored boat-shaped flowers.

cal•cin•ate ['kælsɪneɪt] *v.* to burn to ashes.

cal•ci•um ['kælsɪəm] *n.* (a) (*element:* Ca) gray metal which forms bones. (b) white substance found in water, lime, etc. **cal•ci•fy**, *v.* to turn (sth) into calcium.

cal•cu•late ['kælkjuleɪt] *v.* to work out (a sum); to estimate (quite accurately); **calculated insult** = deliberate insult. **cal•cu•la•ble**, *adj.* which can be calculated. **cal•cu•lat•ing**, *adj.* (person) who plans clever schemes. **cal•cu•la•tion** [kælkju'leɪʃn] *n.* act of calculating; sum which has been calculated. **cal•cu•la•tor**, *n.* electronic machine for doing sums. **cal•cu•lus**, *n.* (a) mathematical way of calculating. (b) stone formed inside the body.

cal•dron ['kɔːldrən] *n. see* **caul•dron.**

cal•en•dar ['kælendə] *n.* sheet showing the days and months of a year; **c. month, c. year** = month/year as shown on a calendar.

ca•len•du•la [kə'lendjuːlə] *n.* yellow flower, the marigold.

calf [kɑːf] *n.* (*pl.* **calves** [kɑːvz]) (a) young cow/bull; young (of elephant, etc.). (b) leather (from cow's skin). (c) fleshy back part of the leg between the ankle and the knee.

cal•i•ber, *Brit.* **cal•i•bre** ['kælɪbə] *n.* (a) interior diameter of a gun. (b) standing/intellectual ability. **cal•i•brate,** *v.* to mark/to correct degrees on (a thermometer)/to mark units on (a scale). **cal•i•bra•tion,** *n.* marking of degrees; degree marked.

cal•i•co ['kælɪkəu] *n.* thick cotton cloth.

cal•i•pers, callipers ['kælɪpəz] *n. pl.* instrument for measuring the diameter of sth. round (like a pipe).

call [kɔːl] *n.* (a) shout/cry; song of a bird; **I want a c. at 7 o'clock** = I want to be waked at 7 o'clock; **on c.** = available for duty. (b) conversation on the telephone. (c) visit. (d) need; **there's no c. for alarm.** 2. *v.* (a) to shout; **c. me at 7 o'clock** = wake me at 7 o'clock. (b) to telephone. (c) to give (s.o.) a name. (d) to visit. **call back,** *v.* (a) to telephone in reply; to telephone again. (b) to come back to visit again. **call•box,** *n.* street telephone or signal box for calling the police or fire department. **call•boy,** *n.* (a) young man in a theater who tells performers when it is time for them to go on stage. (b) young man in a hotel who runs messages; bellhop. **call•er,** *n.* (a) person who comes to visit. (b) person who telephones. **call for,** *v.* (a) **he called for help** = he shouted to ask for help. (b) **to c. for s.o.** = to go to s.o.'s house to pick them up. (c) to need/to require. **call girl,** *n.* prostitute who can be called by telephone. **call in,** *v.* to call (s.o.) to make them come in; **they called in the police. call•ing,** *n.* vocation; job. **call off,** *v.* to cancel. **call on,** *v.* (a) to visit. (b) to appeal to (s.o.). **call out,** *v.* (a) to shout. (b) to ask (police/military) to come to help. **call sign,** *n.* letters/words which identify a radio station. **call up,** *v.* (a) to telephone. (b) to order (s.o.) to join the military. **call-up,** *n.* order to join the military.

cal•lig•ra•phy [kə'lɪɡrəfɪ] *n.* art of fine handwriting. **cal•li•graph•ic** [kælɪ'ɡræfɪk] *adj.* referring to calligraphy.

cal•li•pers ['kælɪpəz] *see* **cal•i•pers.**

cal•lis•then•ics [kælɪs'θenɪks] *n.* exercises which are supposed to make the body strong and beautiful.

cal•lous ['kæləs] *adj.* hard/unfeeling. **cal•lous•ly,** *adv.* cruelly. **cal•lous•ness,** *n.* cruelty.

cal•low ['kæləu] *adj.* young and inexperienced.

cal•lus ['kæləs] *n.* (*pl.* **-es**) hard patch on the skin.

calm [kɑːm] 1. *adj.* (**-er, -est**) quiet/not rough. 2. *n.* period of quiet. 3. *v.* to become/to make quiet. **calm•ly,** *adv.* quietly. **calm•ness,** *n.* period of quiet.

cal•o•rie ['kælərɪ] *n.* measure of heat/of energy-giving value of food. **cal•o•rif•ic** [kælə'rɪfɪk] *adj.* referring to heat.

cal•um•ny ['kæləmnɪ] *n.* lie/false statement. **ca•lum•ni•ate** [kə'lʌmnɪeɪt] *v.* to tell lies about (s.o.).

calve [kɑːv] 1. *v.* to give birth to a calf. 2. *n. pl. see* **calf.**

ca•lyp•so [kə'lɪpsəu] *n.* type of topical song sung in the West Indies.

ca•lyx ['kælɪks] *n.* (*pl.* -es) outer covering of a flower bud.

cam [kæm] *n.* ring on a camshaft, which makes pistons move up and down.

ca•ma•ra•de•rie [kæmə'rædərɪ] *n.* friendship among comrades, esp. in the armed forces.

cam•ber ['kæmbə] *n.* bend/curve (in a surface); way in which the road slopes. **cam•bered,** *adj.* sloping/rounded (surface).

cam•bric ['kæmbrɪk] *n.* thin cotton cloth.

cam•cord•er ['kæmkɔːdə] *n.* portable cine-camera which records pictures for video.

came [keɪm] *v. see* **come.**

cam•el ['kæml] *n.* desert animal with one or two humps, used for riding. **cam•el's hair** (*also* **cam•el•hair,** *n.* thick pale brown wool, used for making coats, etc.

ca•mel•lia [kə'miːlɪə] *n.* evergreen bush with pink or white flowers.

cam•e•o ['kæmɪəu] *n.* (a) small stone with a design of a head which stands out against a darker background. (b) small but sharply defined part in a play/film.

cam•er•a ['kæmərə] *n.* (a) machine for taking photographs or pictures to be shown on a screen. (b) **in c.** = in closed session/in secret. **cam•er•a•man,** *n.* (*pl.* -men) man who operates a movie or television-camera.

cam•o•mile ['kæməmaɪl] *n.* fragrant plant, of which the dried leaves are used for making hot drinks.

cam•ou•flage ['kæməflɑːʒ] 1. *n.* hiding (sth) by means of coloring, so that it is difficult to see it against the background. 2. *v.* to hide (sth) so that it is difficult to see it against the background.

camp [kæmp] 1. *n.* place where people live in tents or cabins in the open temporarily; **c. bed** = folding bed; **c. fire** = fire round which campers sit at night. 2. *v.* (a) to live or sleep in a tent temporarily. (b) **to c. it up** = to put on an affected style. 3. *adj.* in an affected (often playful) style. **camp•er,** *n.* (a) small van equipped with beds, tables, cooking facilities, etc. (b) person who lives in a tent or camper. **camp•ing,** *n.* going on vacation with a tent or camper. **camp•site,** *n.* area specially laid out for tents and campers.

cam•paign [kæm'peɪn] 1. *n.* (a) organized military movement. (b) organized method of working; **a sales c.** 2. *v.* (a) to take part in a war. (b) (**for**) to work in an organized fashion to achieve an end. **cam•paign•er,** *n.* person who campaigns.

cam•pa•nol•o•gy [kæmpə'nɒlədʒɪ] *n.* study of ringing church bells.

cam•pan•u•la [kæm'pænjuːlə] *n.* the bell flower, with blue bell-shaped flowers.

cam•phor ['kæmfə] *n.* strong-smelling substance which comes from certain trees; **c. balls** = small white balls impregnated with camphor which prevent moths from attacking clothes. **cam•pho•rat•ed,** *adj.* impregnated with camphor.

cam•pi•on ['kæmpjən] *n.* wild plant with small pink flowers.

cam•pus ['kæmpəs] *n.* (*pl.* -es) land on which a school/college/university is built.

cam•shaft ['kæmʃɑːft] *n.* shaft with projecting rings which open and close pistons in turn.

can [kæn] 1. *n.* (a) metal box for liquids, esp. for preserving food or drink. (b) **watering c.** = bucket with a long spout for watering plants. 2. *v.* (a) (**I/he can;** *neg.* **cannot;** *short form* **can't;** *past* **I/he could;** *neg.* **could not;** *short form* **couldn't**) able to do sth/knowing how to do sth. (b) (**canned**) to put (fruit/vegetables, etc.) into cans to preserve them. **canned,** *adj.* in a metal box; **c. music** = recorded music. **can•ner•y,** *n.* canning factory.

Can•a•da goose [kænədə'guːs] *n.* large wild goose, with black neck and white chin, originally native of N. America.

Ca•na•di•an [kə'neɪdjən] 1. *adj.* referring to Canada. 2. *n.* person from Canada.

ca•nal [kə'næl] *n.* (a) artificial waterway. (b) passage in the body.

can•a•pé ['kænəpeɪ] *n.* small cocktail snack.

ca•nar•y [kə'neərɪ] *n.* small yellow singing bird.

can•can ['kænkæn] *n.* French cabaret dance, where the dancers kick their legs in the air.

can•cel ['kænsl] *v.* (**canceled, cancelled**) (a) to stop (sth which had been planned). (b) to mark a postage stamp with a rubber stamp. **can•cel•la•tion** [kænsə'leɪʃn] *n.* act of canceling; seat/ticket which is on sale because a purchaser cannot use it. **can•cel out,** *v.* to balance (sth) and so remove its force.

can•cer ['kænsə] *n.* (a) disease of the blood or tissue. (b) **Cancer** = one of the signs of the Zodiac, shaped like a crab; **Tropic of C.** = imaginary line 23° 28 north of the equator. **can•cer•ous,** *adj.* referring to cancer.

æ back, ɑː farm, ɒ top, aɪ pipe, aʊ how, aɪə fire, aʊə flower, ɔː bought, ɔɪ toy, e fed, eəhair, eɪ take, ə afraid, əʊ boat, əʊə lower, vː word, iː heap, ɪ hit, ɪə hear, uː school, ʊ book, ʌ but, b back, d dog, ð then, dʒ just, f fog, g go, h hand, j yes, k catch, l last, m mix, n nut, ŋ sing, p penny, r round, s some, ʃ short, t too, tʃ chop, θ thing, v voice, w was, z zoo, ʒ treasure

can•de•la•bra [kændi'lɑːbrə] *n. pl.* branched candlesticks; chandeliers.

can•did ['kændɪd] *adj.* frank/open. **can•did•ly**, *adv.* in a candid way.

can•di•date ['kændɪdət] *n.* person seeking election; person who has entered a competition/an examination. **can•di•da•cy**, *n.* act of standing as a candidate.

can•died ['kændɪd] *adj.* dried and sugared; c. **peel** = dried orange/lemon peel.

can•dle ['kændl] *n.* stick of wax with a wick in the center; **to burn the c. at both ends** = to work hard during the day and enjoy yourself late into the night. **can•dle•light**, *n.* light from a candle. **can•dle•lit**, *adj.* lit by candles. **can•dle•stick**, *n.* holder for a candle. **can•dle•wick**, *n.* cotton material for bedcovers, with patterns of tufts.

can•dor, *Brit.* **can•dour** ['kændə] *n.* frankness/openness.

can•dy ['kændɪ] *n.* something sweet to eat. **can•dy-striped**, *adj.* with stripes of color on a white background like certain fabrics. **can•dy•tuft**, *n.* plant with pink or blue flowers.

cane [keɪn] 1. *n.* (a) stem (esp. of jointed plants like bamboo). (b) walking stick (cut from such plants). 2. *v.* to hit with a cane. **can•ing**, *n.* beating with a cane.

ca•nine ['keɪnaɪn] 1. *adj.* referring to dogs. 2. *n.* **c. (tooth)** = round pointed tooth.

can•is•ter ['kænɪstə] *n.* round metal box.

can•ker ['kæŋkə] *n.* disease/sore which eats into flesh/into wood of trees.

can•na ['kænæ] *n.* tropical plant, with large leaves and red or orange flowers.

can•na•bis ['kænəbɪs] *n.* plant, parts of which can be smoked to give a pleasant feeling of relaxation.

can•nel•o•ni [kæne'ləʊnɪ] *n.* type of pasta, like small pancakes with a meat or spinach filling.

can•ni•bal ['kænɪbl] *n.* person who eats people. **can•ni•bal•ism**, *n.* custom of eating people. **can•ni•bal•ize**, *v.* to take pieces of old machinery to repair another machine.

can•non ['kænən] 1. *n.* (a) large gun; gun in an aircraft. (b) (*in billiards*) hitting of one ball off the other two. 2. *v.* to bounce off (another ball/the cushion); to bump (**into** sth). **can•non•ball**, *n.* large metal ball fired by a cannon.

can•not ['kænət] *v. see* **can.**

can•ny ['kænɪ] *adj.* (-ier, -iest) wise/clever. **can•ni•ly**, *adv.* cleverly.

ca•noe [kə'nuː] 1. *n.* boat propelled by one or more people with paddles. 2. *v.* (**canoed**) to travel in a canoe. **ca•noe•ing**, *n.* sport of going in a canoe. **ca•noe•ist**, *n.* person who paddles a canoe.

can•on ['kænən] *n.* (a) religious rule or instructions; c. **law** = the church's laws. (b) clergyman attached to a cathedral. **ca•non•i•cal**, *adj.* referring to a canon. **can•on•i•za•tion**, *n.* declaring s.o. a saint. **can•on•ize**, *v.* to declare (s.o.) a saint.

can•o•py ['kænəpɪ] *n.* small roof over a platform/balcony, etc.

cant [kænt] *n.* (a) hypocrisy/insincere language. (b) jargon/language of a certain group of people.

can't [kɑːnt] *v. see* **can.**

can•ta•loupe ['kæntəluːp] *n.* type of melon with pink flesh.

can•tan•ker•ous [kæn'tæŋkrəs] *adj.* bad-tempered. **can•tan•ker•ous•ness**, *n.* continual bad temper.

can•ta•ta [kæn'tɑːtə] *n.* musical piece for several voices and orchestra (usu. on a religious theme).

can•teen [kæn'tiːn] *n.* (a) self-service restaurant, as on a military base. (b) portable container for water.

can•ter ['kæntə] 1. *n.* gentle gallop. 2. *v.* to go at a canter.

can•ti•cle ['kæntɪkl] *n.* religious song.

can•ti•le•ver ['kæntɪliːvə] *n.* projecting support which holds up a balcony/a bridge. **can•ti•le•vered**, *adj.* held up by a cantilever.

can•to ['kæntəu] *n.* (*pl.* -os) long section of an epic poem.

can•ton ['kænton] *n.* administrative division of Switzerland.

can•vas ['kænvəs] *n.* (*pl.* -es) thick cloth (for making tents/sails, or for painting on); a painting on canvas.

can•vass ['kænvəs] *v.* to try to persuade people to vote for s.o./to buy sth. **can•vass•er**, *n.* person who canvasses. **can•vas•sing**, *n.* going from door to door to persuade people to vote.

can•yon ['kænjən] *n.* large valley with perpendicular sides.

cap [kæp] 1. *n.* (a) hat with a peak; **c. and gown** = hat and robes worn by graduates of a school/college/university. (b) top/cover (of a bottle, pen, etc.). (c) small piece of paper with gunpowder. 2. *v.* (**capped**) (a) to top with a cap; to fix a cover on (a pipe) to stop it leaking. (b) to surpass/to do better than.

ca•pa•ble ['keɪpəbl] *adj.* competent/able. **ca•pa•bil•i•ty** [keɪpə'bɪlɪtɪ] *n.* ability. **ca•pa•bly** ['keɪpəblɪ] *adv.* competently/efficiently.

ca•pac•i•ty [kə'pæsɪtɪ] *n.* (a) amount which a

container can hold; **seating c.** = number of seats (in a bus/theater, etc.). (b) **engine c.** = power of an engine. (c) ability to do something. (d) position; **in his c. as manager.** **ca•pac•i•tor,** *n.* device for storing an electric charge. **ca•pa•cious** [kə'peɪʃəs] *n.* very large/which contains a lot.

cape [keɪp] *n.* (a) long cloak. (b) headland jutting into the sea.

ca•per ['keɪpə] 1. *n.* (a) jumping/leaping. (b) small bitter seed used in cooking. (c) *inf.* trick. 2. *v.* **to c. about** = to jump/to leap.

cap•il•lar•y [kə'pɪlərɪ] *adj. & n.* very thin (tube); very thin blood vessel; **c. attraction** = physical phenomenon where water is drawn up in a thin tube.

cap•i•tal ['kæpɪtl] 1. *n.* (a) decorated stone on the top of a column. (b) large letter. (c) main city of a country/a state, etc. (d) money which is invested. (e) **c. punishment** = execution/legal killing of a criminal. 2. *adj.* (a) very important. (b) *inf.* very good. **cap•i•tal•ism,** *n.* economic system based on ownership of resources by individuals or companies and not by the state. **cap•i•tal•ist,** *adj. & n.* (person) who supports the theory of capitalism; businessman. **cap•i•tal•i•za•tion** [kæpɪtəlaɪ'zeɪʃn] *n.* amount of capital invested in a company. **cap•i•tal•ize** ['kæpɪtəlaɪz] *v.* (a) to invest capital in a company. (b) **to c. on** = to take advantage of (sth).

cap•i•ta•tion [kæpɪ'teɪʃn] *n.* tax or payment accrued uniformly on each individual.

Cap•i•tol ['kæpɪtəl] *n.* building where the U.S. Congress meets; **on C. Hill** = in the U.S. Congress.

ca•pit•u•late [kə'pɪtjuleɪt] *v.* to give in/to surrender. **ca•pit•u•la•tion** [kəpɪtju'leɪʃn] *n.* surrendering.

ca•pon ['keɪpɒn] *n.* fat castrated chicken.

cap•pu•ci•no [kæpu:'tʃi:nəu] *n.* frothy Italian coffee, with milk and sometimes chocolate.

ca•price [kə'pri:s] *n.* whim/sudden fancy. **ca•pri•cious** [kə'prɪʃəs] *adj.* whimsical/prone to change your mind. **ca•pri•cious•ness,** *n.* tendency to change your mind suddenly.

Cap•ri•corn ['kæprɪkɔ:n] *n.* one of the signs of the Zodiac, shaped like a goat; **Tropic of C.** = imaginary line 23° 28 south of the equator.

cap•si•cum ['kæpsɪkəm] *n.* green pepper (plant).

cap•size [kæp'saɪz] *v.* (*of boats*) to turn over.

cap•stan ['kæpstən] *n.* machine which turns to haul in a rope or anchor.

cap•sule ['kæpsju:l] *n.* enclosed case; small case for a dose of medicine which melts when swallowed; **space c.** = living compartment in a spacecraft.

cap•tain ['kæptɪn] 1. *n.* (a) officer in charge of a ship or aircraft. (b) rank in the army, airforce, etc. above lieutenant; rank in the navy above commander. (c) leader of sports team. 2. *v.* to lead (an expedition/a team). **cap•tain•cy,** *n.* (a) rank of captain (in the military). (b) post of leader of a sports team.

cap•tion ['kæpʃn] *n.* phrase printed beneath a picture.

cap•tious ['kæpʃəs] *adj.* continually finding fault.

cap•ti•vate ['kæptɪveɪt] *v.* to charm/to seduce.

cap•tive ['kæptɪv] 1. *n.* prisoner. 2. *adj.* **held c.** = held as a prisoner. **cap•tiv•i•ty** [kæp'tɪvɪtɪ] *n.* imprisonment. **cap•tor,** *n.* person who captures s.o. **cap•ture** ['kæptʃə] 1. *n.* taking of s.o./sth captive. 2. *v.* (a) to take (s.o./sth) captive. (b) **they have captured 10% of the market** = they have taken 10% of the possible sales.

cap•y•ba•ra [kæp'bɑ:rə] *n.* very large rodent, native of S. America.

car [kɑ:] *n.* (a) private motor vehicle; *Brit.* **c. park** = parking lot. (b) railroad car. **car pool,** *n.* group of people who each take turns in driving all their children to school, etc. **car•port,** *n.* shelter for a car. **car•sick,** *adj.* feeling ill when traveling by motor vehicle. **car wash,** *n.* place where cars are washed automatically.

ca•rafe [kə'ræf] *n.* glass jug for serving wine.

car•a•mel ['kærəmel] *n.* (a) sweet made with sugar and butter. (b) burned sugar; **c. custard** = pudding of egg custard topped with browned sugar. **car•a•mel•ize,** *v.* to heat sugar until it becomes brown.

car•a•pace ['kærəpeɪs] *n.* outside shell (of an animal).

car•at ['kærət] *n.* (a) *see* **karat.** (b) weight of a diamond.

car•a•van ['kærəvæn] *n.* (*a*) group of vehicles/animals traveling together (esp. across a desert). (b) *Brit.* van with beds, table, washing facilities, etc., which can be towed by a car.

car•a•way ['kærəweɪ] *n.* spicy seed used to flavor cakes and biscuits.

car•ba•mate ['kɑ:bəmeɪt] *n.* type of pesticide.

car•bine ['kɑ:baɪn] *n.* type of light rifle.

æ back, a: farm, ɒ: top, aɪ pipe, aʊ how, aɪe fire, aʊə flower, ɔ: bought, ɔɪ toy, e fed, eəhair, eɪ take, ə afraid, əʊ boat, əʊə lower, v: word, i: heap, ɪ hit, ɪə hear, u: school, ʊ book, ʌ but, b back, d dog, ð then, dʒ just, f fog, g go, h hand, j yes, k catch, l last, m mix, n nut, ŋ sing, p penny, r round, s some, ʃ short, t too, tʃ chop, θ thing, v voice, w was, z zoo, ʒ treasure

car•bo•hy•drate [kɑːbəʊ'haɪdreɪt] *n.* chemical substance containing carbon, hydrogen and oxygen, and derived from sugar; **she eats too many carbohydrates** = too much fattening food.

car•bol•ic [kɑː'bɒlɪk] *adj.* referring to an acid used to disinfect; **c. soap.**

car•bon ['kɑːbən] *n.* (*element:* C) substance found in charcoal, soot, diamonds; **c. dioxide** = colorless gas (CO_2) forming a small part of the atmosphere; **c. monoxide** = colorless poisonous gas (CO) present in car exhaust fumes; **c. paper** = paper with black substance on one side, used to make copies, as in typing; **c. copy** = identical copy. **car•bo•nate,** *n.* salt of carbonic acid. **car•bon•ic** [kɑː'bɒnɪk] *adj.* referring to carbon; **c. acid** = acid formed when carbon dioxide is dissolved in water. **car•bon•if•er•ous** [kɑːbə'nɪfərəs] *adj.* coal-bearing. **car•bon•ize** ['kɑːbənaɪz] *v.* to make into carbon by burning.

car•bo•run•dum [kɑːbə'rʌndəm] *n.* hard substance used for polishing or sharpening.

car•boy ['kɑːbɔɪ] *n.* very large glass bottle for containing corrosive liquids.

car•bun•cle ['kɑːbʌŋkl] *n.* (a) red precious stone. (b) large inflamed spot on the skin.

car•bu•re•tor [kɑːbə'retə] *n.* device in a car for changing liquid fuel into vapor.

car•case/car•cass ['kɑːkəs] *n.* (a) body of a dead animal ready for the butcher; bones left after you have eaten a cooked bird. (b) body (of a person).

car•cin•o•gen [kɑː'sɪnədʒən] *n.* substance which causes cancer.

car•ci•no•ma [kɑːsɪ'nəʊmə] *n.* cancer.

card [kɑːd] 1. *n.* (a) small rectangle of stiff paper for writing on. (b) rectangle of stiff paper with a design on it, used for playing games; **playing cards** = ordinary cards, marked in four designs (diamonds, hearts, clubs, spades); **c. games** = games using packs of special cards; **they were playing cards** = they were playing games of cards. (c) (**calling/business/business**) **c.** = small piece of stiff paper with your name and address printed on it; **credit c.** = plastic card which allows you to buy goods without paying for them immediately; 2. *v.* to comb (raw wool). **card•board,** *n.* thick card, used for packing. **card in•dex.** 1. *n.* series of small cards classified into alphabetical or numerical order. 2. *v.* to classify (sth) on to small filing cards. **card•sharpe,** *n.* person who cheats at cards to win money.

car•di•ac ['kɑːdɪæk] *adj.* referring to the heart; **c. arrest** = heart attack.

car•di•gan ['kɑːdɪgən] *n.* woolen jacket which buttons at the front.

car•di•nal ['kɑːdɪnl] 1. *adj.* (a) very important

(rule, etc.). (b) **c. numbers** = numbers which show quantity (1, 2, 3, etc.). 2. *n.* (a) high dignitary of the Catholic church. (b) bright red North American bird.

car•di•o•gram ['kɑːdɪəgræm] *n.* chart showing heart beats. **car•di•o•graph,** *n.* machine for recording heart beats in the form of cardiograms. **car•di•ol•o•gy** [kɑːdɪ'ɒlədʒɪ] *n.* study of the heart and its diseases. **car•di•ol•o•gist,** *n.* doctor specializing in cardiology. **car•di•o•vas•cu•lar,** *adj.* referring to the heart and the blood circulation system.

care ['keə] 1. *n.* (a) worry. (b) looking after s.o./sth; **to take c.** = to watch out/to be careful; **in the c. of** = being looked after by; 2. *v.* (a) to worry; **I don't c. if I never see you again.** (b) to like; **would you c. for a cake?** (c) **to c. for** = to look after. **care•free,** *adj.* without any worries. **care•ful,** *adj.* cautious/taking care. **care•ful•ly,** *adv.* with care. **care•less,** *adj.* not paying attention/not taking care. **care•less•ly,** *adv.* in a careless way. **care•less•ness,** *n.* being careless. **care•tak•er,** *n.* (a) person who looks after a building; (government) which runs a country temporarily (until a permanent one is elected). (b) person who looks after another person. **care•worn,** *adj* tired because of worries.

ca•reen [kə'riːn] *v.* (a) to tilt (a boat) over, so as to clean the bottom. (b) *inf.* to go along very fast.

ca•reer [kə'rɪə] 1. *n.* (a) life of professional work. (b) forward rush. 2. *v.* to rush forward out of control. **ca•reer•ist,** *adj. & n.* (person) only aiming at advancing his career.

ca•ress [kə'res] 1. *n.* (*pl.* -es) gentle touch. 2. *v.* to stroke gently.

car•et ['kærɪt] *n.* mark (∧) used to show that sth is missing.

car•go ['kɑːgəʊ] *n.* (*pl.* -oes, gos) goods carried (esp. on a ship).

car•i•bou ['kærɪbuː] *n.* (*pl.* **caribou**) reindeer of North America.

car•i•ca•ture ['kærɪkətjʊə] 1. *n.* amusing drawing which satirizes by emphasizing s.o.'s particular features. 2. *v.* to satirize by emphasizing s.o.'s bad features.

car•ies ['keəriːz] *n.* (*pl.* **caries**) decayed place in a tooth.

car•il•lon ['kærɪlɒn] *n.* set of bells, usu. in a tower, on which tunes can be played.

car•min•a•tive ['kɑːmɪnətɪv] *n.* medicine which relieves indigestion.

car•mine ['kɑːmɪn] *adj. & n.* bright red (color).

car•nage ['kɑːnɪdʒ] *n.* bloodshed/massacre/killing.

car•nal ['kɑːnl] *adj.* referring to the body; sensual.

car•na•tion [kɑː'neɪʃn] *n.* strongly scented flower often worn in a buttonhole.

car•net ['kɑːneɪ] *n.* customs permit to take a car from one country to another at no charge.

car•ni•val ['kɑːnɪvl] *n.* festival often with dancing and eating in the open air.

car•ni•vore ['kɑːnɪvɔː] *n.* animal which eats flesh. **car•niv•o•rous** [kɑː'nɪvərəs] *adj.* flesh-eating.

car•ol ['kærəl] 1. *n.* special song sung at a particular time of the year; **Christmas c.** 2. *v.* (**caroled**) to sing Christmas carols. **car•ol•er,** *n.* person singing Christmas carols.

ca•rot•id [kæ'rɒtɪd] *n.* artery in the neck.

ca•rouse [kə'raʊz] *v.* to drink alcohol and enjoy yourself. **ca•rous•al,** *n.* (*formal*) drunken party.

car•ou•sel [kæru:'sel] *n.* (a) circular conveyor belt which distributes luggage. (b) merry-go-round.

carp [kɑːp] 1. *n.* (*pl.* **carp**) fat edible fish often bred in captivity for eating. 2. *v.* to keep on finding fault with things.

car•pel ['kɑːpəl] *n.* female part of a flower.

car•pen•ter ['kɑːpəntə] *n.* person who works with wood, esp. in building. **car•pen•try,** *n.* art of working with wood.

car•pet ['kɑːpɪt] 1. *n.* woven or knotted covering for the floor; *inf.* **to call on the c.** = to criticize s.o. 2. *v.* to cover (as) with a carpet. **car•pet•bag•ger,** *n.* politician who tries to make his fortune in a part of the country which is not his home. **car•pet•ing,** *n.* covering with a carpet; wide piece of carpet. **car•pet sweep•er,** *n.* device which cleans carpets by means of rotating brushes.

car•riage ['kærɪdʒ] *n.* (a) action of carrying goods. (b) open vehicle pulled by a horse. (c) way of walking. (d) movable part on a typewriter which goes from side to side. (e) small, light vehicle in which you can push a baby.

car•ri•er ['kærɪə] *n.* (a) thing/person who carries; **c. pigeon** = pigeon specially trained for carrying messages; (b) person who carries the germ of a disease without suffering and can infect others with it. (c) **aircraft c.** = ship which carries aircraft.

car•ri•on ['kærɪən] *n.* (*no pl.*) rotting meat. **car•ri•on crow,** *n.* type of large black crow.

car•rot ['kærət] *n.* bright orange root vegetable.

car•ry ['kærɪ] *v.* (a) to lift (sth) up and move it from one place to another. (b) to win (a vote).

(c) (*of sound*) to be heard at a distance. (d) to keep (in a store). **car•ry a•long,** *v.* to carry (sth) which cannot prevent it. **car•ry a•way,** *v.* (a) to take away/to demolish. (b) **to get carried away** = to get overcome with emotion/excitement. **car•ry for•ward,** *v.* (*in bookkeeping*) to take (a sum) on to the next page or column. **carry off,** *v.* (a) to win/to take away; **to carry off first prize. (b) he carried it off very well** = he got through a potentially embarrassing situation very well. **carry on,** *v.* (a) to continue/to go on. (b) *inf.* to be very angry; make a fuss. **carry out,** *v.* to do (sth) successfully. **carry through,** *v.* to bring (sth) to a finish.

cart [kɑːt] 1. *n.* vehicle pulled by a horse; **to put the c. before the horse** = not to put first things first. 2. *v.* to carry (sth heavy). **car•ter,** *n.* person or company which transports goods. **cart horse,** *n.* large strong horse. **cart•load,** *n.* quantity carried in a cart. **cart•wheel,** *n.* (a) wheel of a cart. (b) **to turn cartwheels** = to turn over and over sideways on your outstretched hands and feet.

carte blanche [kɑːt'blɒnʃ] *n.* **to have c. b. to do sth** = to be able to do whatever you want.

car•tel [kɑː'tel] *n.* group of companies which try to fix the price of sth.

car•ti•lage ['kɑːtɪlɪdʒ] *n.* strong flexible material which acts as a cushion in joints in the body. **car•ti•lag•i•nous** [kɑːtɪ'lædʒɪnəs] *adj.* made of cartilage.

car•tog•ra•pher [kɑː'tɒgrəfə] *n.* person who draws maps. **car•to•graph•ic,** *adj.* referring to maps. **car•tog•ra•phy,** *n.* science of drawing maps.

car•ton ['kɑːtən] *n.* cardboard box.

car•toon [kɑː'tuːn] *n.* (a) funny drawing in a newspaper, magazine, etc. (b) movie made of moving drawings. (c) sketch for a painting. **car•toon•ist,** *n.* person who draws cartoons.

car•tridge ['kɑːtrɪdʒ] *n.* (a) tube packed with gunpowder and a bullet for firing from a gun. (b) film/recording tape enclosed in a plastic case which fits directly into the camera/tape recorder; tube of ink which fits into a pen. (c) part of a record player which holds the stylus.

carve [kɑːv] *v.* (a) to cut (meat) up. (b) to cut (stone/wood) to make a shape. **car•ver,** *n.* (a) person who carves. (b) carving knife. **carv•ing,** *n.* (a) cutting up cooked meat; **c. knife** = large sharp knife for cutting meat. (b)

æ back, ɑː farm, ɒ top, aɪ pipe, aʊ how, aɪə fire, aʊə flower, ɔː bought, ɔɪ toy, e fed, eəhair, eɪ take, ə afraid, əʊ boat, əʊə lower, vː word, iː heap, ɪ hit, ɪə hear, uː school, ʊ book, ʌ but, b back, d dog, ð then, dʒ just, f fog, g go, h hand, j yes, k catch, l last, m mix, n nut, ŋ sing, p penny, r round, s some, ʃ short, t too, tʃ chop, θ thing, v voice, w was, z zoo, ʒ treasure

art of cutting stone/wood into shapes. (c) an object which has been made by carving.

car•y•at•id [kær'jætɪd] *n.* statue of a female figure, which acts as a column holding up a roof.

cas•cade [kæs'keɪd] 1. *n.* (artificial) waterfall. 2. *v.* to fall in large quantities.

case [keɪs] 1. *n.* (a) box (of goods). (b) protective box or covering. (c) suitcase. (d) way in which sth happens; example; **in any c.** = anyway; **in c. of fire** = if fire breaks out; **just in c.** = to guard against a possible emergency. (e) sick person; **c. history** = details of a patient's past history, progress, etc. (f) legal affair. 2. *v.* to put (sth) in a case.

ca•sein [keɪ'siːɪn] *n.* protein found in milk.

case•ment ['keɪsmənt] *n.* window that opens on hinges; frame around such a window.

cash [kæʃ] 1. *n.* money (in coins and notes); **c. crop** = crop grown for sale; **c. register** = machine which shows the amount to be paid and has a drawer for keeping money. 2. *v.* to change (a check) into cash; **to c. in on** = to make a lot of money by profiting from sth. **cash and car•ry**, *adj* selling items for cash only and no delivery. **cash•back**, *n.* service in which customers paying for goods by debit card can draw cash. **cash flow**, *n.* rate at which money comes into and is paid out of a business.

cash•ew [kə'ʃuː] *n.* small sweetish nut, often eaten salted.

cash•ier [kə'ʃiːə] 1. *n.* person who deals with money. 2. *v.* to expel (an officer) from the armed forces.

cash•mere ['kæʃmɪə] *adj. & n.* (made of) fine soft goat's wool.

cas•ing ['keɪsɪŋ] *n.* hard covering which protects something.

ca•si•no [kə'siːnəʊ] *n.* (*pl.* **-os**) building where you can gamble.

cask [kɑːsk] *n.* large barrel.

cas•ket ['kɑːskɪt] *n.* (a) ornamental box (for jewels). (b) coffin.

cas•sa•ta [kə'sɑːtə] *n.* Italian ice cream with dried fruit in it.

cas•se•role ['kæsərəʊl] *n.* (a) oven-proof covered dish. (b) food cooked in a covered dish in the oven.

cas•sette [kə'set] *n.* (a) magnetic tape in a plastic case which can fit directly into a playing or recording machine; **c. player** = machine for playing cassettes; **c. recorder** = machine for recording and playing back cassettes. (b) film in a plastic case which fits directly into a camera.

cas•sock ['kæsək] *n.* long, usu. black, gown worn by priests, choirboys, etc.

cast [kɑːst] 1. *n.* (a) throwing (of a fishing line). (b) plaster shape made from a mold. (c) list of actors in a play/movie; all the actors in a play/movie. (d) **c. of mind** = way of thinking. (e) squint (in an eye). 2. *v.* (**cast**) (a) to throw. (b) to mold metal/plaster. (c) to choose actors for a play/movie. 3. *adj.* which has been cast in a mold; **a cast-iron alibi** = a perfect alibi. **cast a•bout for**, *v.* to look for. **cast a•drift**, *v.* to abandon (a boat/a family). **cast a•side**, *v.* to throw away. **cast a•way**, *v.* to throw away; **cast away on a desert island** = shipwrecked on a desert island. **cast•a•way**, *n.* person who has been shipwrecked. **cast down**, *v.* to throw down; **they were cast down** = they were miserable. **cast•ing**. 1. *n.* (a) molding of a shape/thing which has been molded. (b) choosing of actors. 2. *adj.* **c. vote** = vote which decides when the other votes are equal. **cast off**, *v.* (a) to calculate roughly the number of pages in (a book), before it is printed. (b) to untie the ropes holding a boat. (c) (*in knitting*) to finish stitches. **cast•off cloth•ing**, *n.*, **cast•offs**, *n. pl.* clothes which have been thrown away. **cast on**, *v.* to put (stitches) on to the needles when knitting.

cas•ta•nets [kæstə'nets] *n. pl.* hollow clappers made of wood which are held in the hand and clicked in time to music by Spanish dancers.

caste [kɑːst] *n.* hereditary class (in Indian society).

cas•ti•gate ['kæstɪgeɪt] *v.* (*formal*) to punish/to beat s.o. as a punishment; to criticize s.o. sharply.

cas•tle ['kɑːsl] *n.* (a) large fortified building. (b) piece in chess which looks like a castle.

cast•or/cast•er ['kɑːstə] *n.* (a) container with holes in the lid for sprinkling sugar, pepper, etc. (b) wheel screwed on to the leg of a chair. **cas•tor oil**, *n.* oil from a palm which is used as a laxative.

cas•trate [kæ'streɪt] *v.* to remove the testicles from (a male animal). **cas•tra•tion** [kæ'streɪʃn] *n.* act of castrating.

cas•u•al ['kæʒjʊəl] *adj.* (a) not formal. (b) not serious. **cas•u•al•ly**, *adv.* by chance; in an informal way. **cas•u•al•ness**, *n.* being casual.

cas•u•al•ty ['kæʒjʊəltɪ] *n.* person injured or killed in a battle/an accident; person or thing destroyed or damaged.

cas•u•ist•ry ['kæzjuːɪstrɪ] *n.* debating problems in very fine detail.

cat [kæt] *n.* (a) furry domestic pet, which purrs and has a long tail; wild animal of the same family as the domestic cat; *inf.* **he let the c. out of the bag** = he revealed the secret; **c. burglar** = burglar who climbs walls or drainpipes to enter a house. (b) *inf.* woman who makes spiteful remarks. **cat•call**, *n.* whistle/hoot (to show displeasure). **cat•fish**, *n.* (*pl.* **catfish**) large ugly freshwater fish with whiskers. **cat•gut**, *n.* gut used as thread. **cat•nap**, *n.* short nap. **cat•nip**, *n.* plant much liked by cats. **cat•walk**, *n.* open metal gangway running along the outside of a ship/building.

ca•tab•o•lism [kæ'tæbɒlɪzm] *n.* breaking down of complex substances into simple chemicals.

cat•a•clysm ['kætəklɪzəm] *n.* disaster. **cat•a•clys•mic** [kætə'klɪzmɪk] *adj.* disastrous.

cat•a•combs ['kætəku:mz] *n. pl.* underground rooms (used in ancient times for burying the dead).

cat•a•lep•sy ['kætəlepsɪ] *n.* state where s.o. becomes unconscious and stiff. **cat•a•lep•tic**, *adj.* referring to catalepsy.

cat•a•log, catalogue ['kætəlɒg] 1. *n.* list of things for sale/in a library/in a museum. 2. *v.* to make a list of books in a library/of treasures in a museum/of things for sale. **cat•a•log•er**, *n.* person who specializes in the making of catalogs.

ca•tal•y•sis [kə'tælɪsɪs] *n.* chemical reaction which is helped by a substance which does not itself change. **cat•a•lyst** ['kætəlɪst] *n.* chemical substance which helps to produce a chemical reaction; anything which helps sth to take place. **cat•a•lyt•ic**, *adj.* referring to catalysis; **c. converter** = device attached to the exhaust pipe of a car to reduce carbon monoxide.

cat•a•ma•ran [kætəmə'ræn] *n.* boat with two parallel hulls.

cat•a•pult ['kætəpʌlt] 1. *n. Brit.* slingshot. **c. launching gear** = mechanism on an aircraft carrier for sending an aircraft into the air. 2. *v.* to send (an aircraft, etc.) into the air; to put (s.o.) into a new job quickly.

cat•a•ract ['kætərækt] *n.* (a) waterfall on a river. (b) film which grows over the eye and eventually prevents you from seeing.

ca•tarrh [kə'tɑ:] *n.* type of cold caused by inflammation of the nose and bronchial tubes. **ca•tarrh•al** [kə'tɑ:rəl] *adj.* referring to catarrh.

ca•tas•tro•phe [kə'tæstrəfɪ] *n.* disaster. **cat•a•stroph•ic** [kætə'strɒfɪk] *adj.* disastrous.

cat•a•ton•ic [kætə'tɒnɪk] *adj.* (condition) where a patient is either violent or stays without moving at all.

catch [kætʃ] 1. *n.* (*pl.* -es) (a) things which have been caught; **we had a good c.** = we caught a lot

of fish; **he's/she's a good c.** = he/she is a good prospective husband/worker. (b) action of catching (a ball, etc.). (c) awkwardness/hitch; **there must be a c. to it** = there must be something wrong with it/there must be a trap; **c. 22** = vicious circle which cannot be escaped from. 2. *v.* (**caught**) (a) to grab hold of (sth) which is moving; **I didn't c. what you said** = I was not able to hear. (b) to get (a disease). (c) to find (s.o.) by surprise. **catch•ing**, *adj.* (disease) which can be caught/which is infectious. **catch•ment area**, *n.* (a) land from which a river gets its water. (b) area served by a government agency, hospital, etc. **catch on**, *v.* (a) to understand. (b) to become fashionable. **catch phrase**, *n.* popular phrase, usu. associated with an entertainer or advertisement. **catch up**, *v.* to move faster than s.o. so as to draw level with. **catch•word**, *n.* popular phrase. **catch•y**, *adj.* (tune) which is easy to remember.

cat•e•chize ['kætɪkaɪz] *v.* to ask questions. **cat•e•chism** ['kætɪkɪzəm] *n.* book of religious instruction; religious classes.

cat•e•go•ry ['kætɪgərɪ] *n.* classification of things/people. **cat•e•gor•ic(al)** [kætɪ'gɒrɪk(l)] *adj.* straightforward/definite. **cat•e•gor•i•cal•ly**, *adv.* definitely.

ca•ter ['keɪtə] *v.* to supply food and drink (at a party, etc.). **ca•ter•er**, *n.* person who supplies food. **cater for**, *v.* to provide for. **ca•ter•ing**, *n.* supplying of food.

cat•er•pil•lar ['kætəpɪlə] *n.* insect larva which turns into a moth or butterfly; **c. track** = endless metal belt running round a pair of wheels (on a tank, etc.); **c. tractor** = tractor which runs on caterpillar tracks.

cat•er•waul ['kætəwɔːl] *v.* to howl (like cats at night).

ca•the•dral [kə'θi:drəl] *n.* large church which is the seat of a bishop.

cath•er•ine wheel ['kæθrɪnwi:l] *n.* firework which spins around and around.

cath•e•ter ['kæθɪtə] *n.* very thin tube which can be inserted into the body to remove fluid.

cath•ode ['kæθəʊd] *n.* negative electric pole; **c. ray tube** = tube (as in a television set) where a stream of electrons hits a screen.

cath•o•lic ['kæθlɪk] 1. *adj.* (a) wide/general (taste). (b) **Catholic** referring to the Roman Catholic Church. 2. *n.* **Catholic** = s.o. who is a member of the Roman Catholic Church.

æ back, ɑ: farm, ɒ top, aɪ pipe, aʊ how, aɪə fire, aʊə flower, ɔ: bought, ɔɪ toy, ə fed, eəhair, eɪ take, ə afraid, əʊ boat, əʊə lower, v: word, i: heap, ɪ hit, ɪə hear, u: school, ʊ book, ʌ but, b back, d dog, ð then, dʒ just, f fog, g go, h hand, j yes, k catch, l last, m mix, n nut, ŋ sing, p penny, r round, s some, ʃ short, t too, tʃ chop, θ thing, v voice, w was, z zoo, ʒ treasure

ca•thol•i•cism [kə'θɒlɪsɪzəm] *n.* beliefs of the Roman Catholic church.

cat•kin ['kætkɪn] *n.* flower of a willow or hazel tree.

cat•sup ['kætsəp] *n. see* **ketchup.**

cat•tle ['kætl] *n. pl.* animals of the cow family (such as bulls, calves, oxen, etc.).

cat•ty ['kætɪ] *adj.* (**-ier, -iest**) nasty/sharp-tongued (woman).

cau•cus ['kɔːkəs] *n.* (*pl.* **-es**) group of party leaders who plan electoral strategy and choose candidates.

caught [kɔːt] *v. see* **catch.**

caul•dron, caldron ['kɔːldrən] *n.* large deep pan for cooking.

cau•li•flow•er ['kɒlɪflaʊə] *n.* cabbagelike vegetable with a large white flower head which is eaten; **c. ear** = permanently swollen ear, found in boxers.

caulk ['kɔːk] *v.* to fill the cracks in a boat's hull to make it watertight.

cause [kɔːz] 1. *n.* (a) thing which makes sth happen; **he died from natural causes** = he died naturally, and was not killed in an accident or murdered. (b) reason for doing sth. (c) area of interest/principle/charity to which s.o. gives support. 2. *v.* to make (sth) happen. **cause cé•lèbre,** *n.* famous court case. **caus•al,** *adj.* referring to a cause.

cause•way ['kɔːzweɪ] *n.* road/path built up on a bank above marshy ground or water.

caus•tic ['kɔːstɪk] *adj.* (a) burning; **c. soda** = chemical used for cleaning. (b) sharp (wit). **caus•ti•cal•ly,** *adv.* in a sharp/witty way.

cau•ter•ize ['kɔːtəraɪz] *v.* to burn (a wound) to stop infection. **cau•ter•i•za•tion** [kɔːtərəɪ'zeɪʃn] *n.* cauterizing.

cau•tion ['kɔːʃn] 1. *n.* care/precaution. 2. *v.* to warn. **cau•tion•ar•y,** *adj.* which warns. **cau•tious,** *adj.* careful/prudent. **cau•tious•ly,** *adv.* in a cautious way. **cau•tious•ness,** *n.* being cautious.

cav•al•cade ['kævəlkeɪd] *n.* procession (usu. of horseriders/cars).

cav•a•lier [kævə'lɪə] *adj.* high-handed/with no respect for other people or customs.

cav•al•ry ['kævəlrɪ] *n.* soldiers on horseback.

cave [keɪv] 1. *n.* large underground hole in rock or earth; **c. bears** = prehistoric bears which lived in caves; **c. paintings** = paintings on walls of caves done by cavemen. 2. *v.* **to c. in** = to collapse. **cave•man,** *n.* (*pl.* **-men**) primitive person who lived in caves.

ca•ve•at ['kævɪæt] *n.* warning (esp. against doing sth); **c. emptor** = let the buyer beware.

cav•ern ['kævən] *n.* very large cave. **cav•ern•ous,** *adj.* like a cavern.

cav•i•ar(e) ['kævɪɑː] *n.* very expensive delicacy consisting of the eggs of a sturgeon.

cav•il ['kævɪl] *v.* (**cavilled**) **to c. at sth** = to object to sth.

cav•i•ty ['kævɪtɪ] *n.* hole; **c. wall** = wall made of two rows of bricks with a gap in between.

ca•vort [kə'vɔːt] *v.* to behave in an excited, merry way.

caw [kɔː] *v.* to make a croaking sound like a crow.

cay•enne ['keɪen] *n.* type of hot red pepper.

cay•man ['keɪmən] *n.* alligator.

CB ['siː'biː] *abbrev. for* citizens' band.

cc ['siːsiː] *abbrev. for* cubic centimeter.

Cd *symbol for* cadmium.

CD ['siː'diː] *abbrev. for* compact disk.

CD-ROM ['siːdiː'rɒm] *abbrev. for* compact disk read-only memory; compact disk that can be read by a computer.

cease [siːs] *v.* to stop. **cease•fire,** *n.* agreement to stop shooting (in a war). **cease•less,** *adj.* without stopping. **cease•less•ly,** *adv.* without stopping.

ce•cum ['siːkəm] *n.* wide part of the large intestine.

ce•dar ['siːdə] *n.* large evergreen tree, with sweet-smelling wood; wood from this tree. **ce•dar•wood,** *n.* wood from a cedar.

cede [siːd] *v.* to pass (property/land) **to** s.o. else.

ce•dil•la [sɪ'dɪlə] *n.* accent placed under the letter "c," showing that it is pronounced "s."

cei•lidh ['keɪlɪ] *n.* (*in Scotland, Ireland*) party with performances of songs and dances.

ceil•ing ['siːlɪŋ] *n.* (a) inside roof over a room. (b) upper limit.

cel•an•dine ['seləndaɪn] *n.* small wild plant with yellow flowers.

cel•e•brate ['selɪbreɪt] *v.* (a) to remember a special day with parties and feasts. (b) to perform (a mass). **cel•e•brant,** *n.* priest who celebrates mass. **cel•e•brat•ed,** *adj.* very famous. **cel•e•bra•tion** [selɪ'breɪʃn] *n.* festivity. **ce•leb•ri•ty** [sə'lebrɪtɪ] *n.* (a) famous person. (b) being famous.

ce•ler•i•ac [sɪ'lerɪæk] *n.* vegetable with a thick root tasting like celery.

ce•ler•i•ty [sə'lerɪtɪ] *n.* speed.

cel•er•y ['selərɪ] *n.* white- or green-stemmed plant, eaten as a vegetable, esp. raw.

ce•les•tial [sə'lestjəl] *adj.* (*formal*) heavenly/referring to the sky.

cel•i•bate ['selɪbət] *adj.* not married, esp. because of religious vows. **cel•i•ba•cy,** *n.* state of being celibate.

cell [sel] *n.* (a) room in a prison/in a monastery; (b) basic unit of an organism. (c) basic political group. (d) part of an electric battery. **cel•lu•lar,** *adj.* made up of many small cells.

cel•lu•li•tis, *n.* inflammation of tissue under the skin.

cel•lar ['selə] *n.* underground room or rooms beneath a house.

cel•lo ['tʃeləu] *n.* large stringed instrument, smaller than a double bass. **cel•list**, *n.* person who plays the cello.

cel•lo•phane ['seləfeɪn] *n.* trademark for transparent flexible sheet for wrapping or covering.

cel•lu•lose ['seljuləus] *n.* chemical substance found in plants, used for making paper and paint.

Cel•si•us ['selsɪəs] *adj. & n.* (scale for) measuring temperature, where the boiling point of water is 100°, and the freezing point 0°.

Celt [kelt] *n.* descendant of a European people now found in Scotland, Ireland, Wales, Brittany, etc. **Celt•ic**, *adj.* referring to ancient or modern Celts.

ce•ment [sɪ'ment] 1. *n.* (a) powder made from limestone heated with clay, which when mixed with water dries hard. (b) mortar. (c) strong glue. 2. *v.* (a) to stick together with cement. (b) to strengthen/to make close. **ce•ment mix•er**, *n.* machine for mixing cement.

cem•e•ter•y ['semətrɪ] *n.* burial ground.

ce•no•taph ['senətɑːf] *n.* war memorial; empty tomb.

cen•ser ['sensə] *n.* (*in church*) metal receptacle on a chain for burning incense.

cen•sor ['sensə] 1. *n.* official who inspects letters/newspaper articles/plays/books, etc., to see if they can be sent or published. 2. *v.* to forbid the publication of (sth) because it may be obscene or may reveal secrets. **cen•so•ri•ous** [sen'sɔːrɪəs] *adj.* critical/which criticizes. **cen•sor•ship**, *n.* office of censor; act of censoring.

cen•sure ['senʃə] 1. *n.* condemnation/criticism. 2. *v.* to condemn/to criticize (s.o.)

cen•sus ['sensəs] *n.* (*pl.* -es) official counting of the population of a country.

cent [sent] *n.* small coin/one-hundredth part of a dollar.

cen•taur ['sentɔː] *n.* mythical animal, half man, half horse.

cen•ten•ar•y [sen'tiːnərɪ] *n.* hundredth anniversary. **cen•te•nar•i•an** [sentɪ'neərɪən] *n.* person who is 100 years old or more. **cen•ten•ni•al** [sen'tenjəl] *adj.* referring to a centenary.

cen•ti•grade ['sentɪgreɪd] *adj. & n.* Celsius.

cen•ti•li•ter, *Brit.* **cen•ti•li•tre** ['sentɪliːtə] *n.* liquid measure, one hundredth part of a liter.

cen•ti•me•ter, *Brit.* **cen•ti•me•tre** ['sentɪmiːtə] *n.* measure of length, one hundredth part of a meter.

cen•ti•pede ['sentɪpiːd] *n.* creeping animal with a large number of legs.

cen•ter, *Brit.* **cen•tre** ['sentə] 1. *n.* (a) middle; **c. party** = political party in the center, neither right nor left. (b) large building containing several different units. (c) player who plays in the middle of the field. 2. *v.* (a) to place in the center. (b) to put the main emphasis (**on**). **cen•tral**, *adj.* in the middle; **c. heating** = heating for a whole building which comes from one heating apparatus. **cen•tral•i•za•tion** [sentrəlaɪ'zeɪʃn] *n.* act of centralizing. **cen•tral•ize**, *v.* to put under the control of a central system. **cen•tral•ly**, *adv.* in the middle.

cen•trif•u•gal [sentrɪ'fjuːgl] *adj.* which tends to go away from the center.

cen•trip•e•tal [sentrɪ'piːtl] *adj.* which tends to go toward the center.

cen•tu•ry ['sentʃərɪ] *n.* hundred years.

ce•ram•ic [sə'ræmɪk] *adj.* made of pottery. **ce•ram•ics**, *n.* art of working in pottery.

ce•re•al ['sɪərɪəl] *n.* (a) grain crop such as wheat, barley, corn, etc. (b) (**breakfast**) **c.** = grain foods eaten with sugar and milk for breakfast.

ce•re•bel•lum [serɪ'beləm] *n.* back part of the brain, which governs balance.

ce•re•bral ['serɪbrəl] *adj.* (a) referring to the brain. (b) intellectual (rather than emotional). **c. palsy** = disorder of the brain which affects control of the voluntary muscles. **ce•re•brum**, *n.* main part of the brain.

cer•e•mo•ny ['serɪmənɪ] *n.* official occasion; solemn behavior on an official occasion; **don't stand on c.** = be informal. **cer•e•mo•ni•al** [serɪ'məunɪəl] 1. *n.* way of conducting a ceremony. 2. *adj.* referring to a ceremony. **cer•e•mo•ni•al•ly**, *adv.* with ceremony. **cer•e•mo•ni•ous**, *adj.* with a lot of ceremony. **cer•e•mo•ni•ous•ly**, *adv.* with a lot of ceremony.

ce•rise [sə'riːz] *n.* bright cherry pink color.

cer•tain ['sɜːtn] *adj.* (a) sure. (b) particular. **cer•tain•ly**, *adv.* of course. **cer•tain•ty**, *n.* (a) being certain. (b) sure/certain thing.

cer•tif•i•cate [sə'tɪfɪkət] *n.* official document

æ back, ɑː farm, ɒ top, aɪ pipe, aʊ how, aɪə fire, aʊə flower, ɔː bought, ɔɪ toy, ə fed, eəhair, eɪ take, ə afraid, əʊ boat, əʊə lower, vː word, iː heap, ɪ hit, ɪə hear, uː school, ʊ book, ʌ but, b back, d dog, ð then, dʒ just, f fog, g go, h hand, j yes, k catch, l last, m mix, n nut, ŋ sing, p penny, r round, s some, ʃ short, t too, tʃ chop, θ thing, v voice, w was, z zoo, ʒ treasure

which proves/shows sth. **cer•ti•fi•a•ble** [sɜː'tɪ'faɪəbl] *adj.* (person) who should be declared insane; (thing) which should be certified. **cer•ti•fi•ca•tion** [sɜːtɪfɪ'keɪʃn] *n.* act of certifying. **cer•ti•fy** ['sɜːtɪfaɪ] *v.* to write a certificate; to put in writing an official declaration; to declare (s.o.) insane.

cer•ti•tude ['sɜːtɪtjuːd] *n.* certainty.

cer•vix ['sɜːvɪks] *n.* (*pl.* -es) neck, esp. the neck of the womb. **cer•vi•cal**, *adj.* referring to the cervix.

ces•sa•tion [se'seɪʃn] *n.* stopping.

ces•sion ['seʃn] *n.* ceding.

cess•pool, cesspit ['sespɪt, 'sespuːl] *n.* underground tank for collecting sewage.

cf. *abbrev for* confer, meaning to compare.

CFS [siːef'es] *abbrev. for* chronic fatigue syndrome.

cg *abbrev for* centigram.

chafe [tʃeɪf] *v.* (a) to rub/to wear out by rubbing. (b) to become irritated/annoyed. **chaf•ing dish,** *n.* dish which keeps food hot.

chaff [tʃɑːf] *n.* (a) dried corn stalks left after the grain is extracted. (b) good-humored teasing.

chaf•finch ['tʃæfɪntʃ] *n.* common pink-breasted finch.

cha•grin ['ʃægrɪn] *n.* annoyance/sadness.

chain [tʃeɪn] 1. *n.* (a) series of rings joined together; **c. reaction** = events/chemical reactions which build up rapidly. (b) row (of mountains). (c) **c. store** = group of stores belonging to the same company. 2. *v.* to attach with a chain. **chain•saw,** *n.* saw where the teeth are set in a continuous chain driven by a motor. **chain-smoke,** *v.* to smoke (cigarettes) one after the other. **chain-smok•er,** *n.* person who chain-smokes.

chair ['tʃeə] 1. *n.* (a) piece of furniture for one person to sit on. (b) position of chairman at a meeting; position of professor at a university; **in the c.** = in position of authority. 2. *v.* to be in charge of (a meeting). **chair•lift,** *n.* chairs on a cable which take skiers up a mountain. **chair•man,** *n.* (*pl.* -men) person who is in charge of a meeting; head of a company. **chair•man•ship,** *n.* position of chairman; art of being a chairman. **chair•per•son,** *n.* person who is in charge of a meeting. **chair•wom•an,** *n.* (*pl.* -women) woman who is in charge of a meeting.

chaise longue [ʃeɪz'lɒŋg] *n.* chair with a long seat.

chal•ced•o•ny [kæl'sedənɪ] *n.* whitish stone, a variety of quartz.

cha•let ['ʃæleɪ] *n.* small (vacation) house, usu. made of wood.

chal•ice ['tʃælɪs] *n.* metal cup in which wine is offered at a communion service.

chalk [tʃɔːk] 1. *n.* (a) soft white rock. (b) stick of white or colored material for writing on a blackboard. 2. *v.* to mark or write with chalk. **chalk up,** *v.* to mark (a score/a victory). **chalk•y,** *adj.* white like chalk; gritty like chalk.

chal•lenge ['tʃæləndʒ] 1. *n.* invitation to fight/struggle; **to take up the c.** = accept the invitation to fight. 2. *v.* to ask (s.o.) to fight; to ask (s.o.) to prove that they are right. **chal•leng•er,** *n.* person who challenges. **chal•leng•ing,** *adj.* provocative.

cham•ber ['tʃeɪmbə] *n.* (a) room/hall. **c. of commerce** = official group of businessmen in a town; **judge's chambers** = office of a judge. (b) space in a piece of machinery, esp. one of the spaces for cartridges in a revolver. (c) space in an organ, such as the heart. (d) **c. music** = music for a few instruments, originally played in a small room. **cham•ber•maid,** *n.* woman who cleans rooms in a hotel. **cham•ber pot,** *n.* pot in which you can urinate, and which is usu. kept in the bedroom.

cha•me•le•on [kə'miːlɪən] *n.* lizard which changes its color according to its natural surroundings.

cham•fer ['ʃæmfə] *v.* to bevel the edge of (sth).

cham•my cloth ['ʃæmɪleðə] *n.* very soft leather used for washing windows, etc.

cham•ois, *n.* (a) ['ʃæmwɑː] mountain goat. (b) ['ʃæmɪ] very soft leather.

champ [tʃæmp] 1. *n. inf.* champion. 2. *v.* to chew hard and noisily; **c. at the bit** = to be impatient to go.

cham•pagne [ʃæm'peɪn] *n.* sparkling French white wine.

cham•pi•on ['tʃæmpɪən] 1. *n.* best person/animal in a particular competition. 2. *v.* to support (a cause) strenuously. **cham•pi•on•ship,** *n.* (a) support of a cause. (b) contest to determine who is the champion.

chance [tʃɑːns] 1. *n.* (a) luck; **games of c.** = games where you gamble on the possibility of winning; **to take chances** = to take risks. (b) possibility/opportunity. 2. *v.* (a) to happen unexpectedly. (b) to risk. **chanc•y,** *adj. inf.* risky.

chan•cel ['tʃɑːnsl] *n.* part of a church near the altar where a choir sits.

chan•cel•ler•y ['tʃɑːnsəlrɪ] *n.* office of a chancellor; office attached to an embassy.

chan•cel•lor ['tʃɑːnsələ] *n.* (a) government minister; (*in Germany/Austria*) = Prime Minister; **C. of the Exchequer** = British finance minister. (b) chief administrative head of a university.

Chan•ce•ry ['tʃɑːnsərɪ] *n.* one of the divisions of the British High Court.

chan•de•lier [ˌʃændə'lɪə] *n.* lighting device hanging from the ceiling with several branches for holding lights.

chan•dler ['tʃɑːndlə] *n.* person who deals in food and other supplies for ships.

change [tʃeɪndʒ] 1. *n.* (a) difference from what was before; **c. of clothes** = new set of clothes to wear; **to ring the changes** = (i) to ring peals of bells; (ii) to try several alternatives to see which works best. (b) money given back when you pay a larger amount than the price asked; **(small) c.** = money in coins. 2. *v.* (a) to make (sth) different; to become different. (b) to put on different clothes; **changing room** = room where you can change clothes. (c) **(for)** to give sth in place of sth else; **to c. (trains)** = get off one train to catch another. **change•a•bil•i•ty** [tʃeɪndʒə'bɪlɪtɪ] *n.* being changeable. **change•a•ble,** *adj.* which changes often/is likely to change. **change•less,** *adj.* which never changes. **change•ling,** *n.* baby supposed to have been substituted for another by fairies.

chan•nel ['tʃænl] 1. *n.* (a) piece of water connecting two seas. (b) bed (of a stream); ditch/gutter along which liquid can flow. (c) means/ways; **channels of communication** = ways of communicating. (d) frequency band for radio or TV. 2. *v.* **(channeled, channelled)** to direct/to persuade to take a certain direction.

chant [tʃɑːnt] 1. *n.* regular singing of a repeated phrase; monotonous song. 2. *v.* to sing to a regular beat.

chant•ey ['ʃæntɪ] *n* song sung by sailors; **sea c.**

cha•os ['keɪɒs] *n.* confusion. **cha•ot•ic** [keɪ'ɒtɪk] *adj.* confused/disorderly.

chap [tʃæp] 1. *n. inf.* man. 2. *v.* to crack (skin). **chaps,** *n. pl.* wide leggings worn by cowboys.

chap•el ['tʃæpl] *n.* (a) small church; part of a large church with a separate altar. (b) local branch of a union (in the printing and publishing industry).

chap•er•on(e) ['ʃæpərəʊn] 1. *n.* (a) older woman who goes around with a young girl on social visits. (b) older person who is with or supervises young people at social gatherings. 2. *v.* to act as a chaperon.

chap•lain ['tʃæplɪn] *n.* priest (attached to a private individual or in the armed forces). **chap•lain•cy,** *n.* position of chaplain.

chapped [tʃæpt] *adj.* (of skin) cracked (with cold).

chap•ter ['tʃæptə] *n.* (a) division of a book. (b) group of priests who administer a cathedral.

char [tʃɑː] 1. *n.* (a) small freshwater fish. (b) *Brit. inf.* charwoman. 2. *v.* **(charred)** (a) *Brit. inf.* to do housework for s.o.. (b) to burn black.

char•ac•ter ['kærəktə] *n.* (a) central being of a person which makes him/her an individual who is different from all others. (b) person in a play/novel. (c) odd person. (d) letter/symbol used in writing or printing. **char•ac•ter•is•tic** [kærəktə'rɪstɪk] 1. *adj.* special/typical. 2. *n.* special/typical feature. **char•ac•ter•is•ti•cal•ly,** *adv.* typically. **char•ac•ter•i•za•tion** [kærəktəraɪ'zeɪʃn] *n.* indication of character. **char•ac•ter•ize** ['kærəktəraɪz] *v.* to be a typical feature of (sth). **char•ac•ter•less,** *adj.* ordinary/with no special features.

cha•rade [ʃə'rɑːd] *n.* (a) game where spectators have to guess a word from a scene acted by others. (b) action which has no meaning/which is simply a pretense.

char•coal ['tʃɑːkəʊl] *n.* black material formed by partly burned wood; **c. gray** = dark, dull gray color.

chard [tʃɑːd] *n.* (*pl.* **chard**) green vegetable like spinach.

charge [tʃɑːdʒ] 1. *n.* (a) money to be paid; **free of c.** (b) care (of s.o./sth). (c) accusation (of an offense). (d) attack (by soldiers running forward). (e) amount of gunpowder in a cartridge/bomb. (f) amount of electric current. 2. *v.* (a) to make (s.o.) pay **for** sth. (b) **(with)** to accuse (of an offense). (c) to put a cartridge in (a gun); to put electricity into (a battery). (d) to attack (by running forward). **charge•a•ble,** *adj.* which can be charged. **charg•er,** *n.* (a) battle horse. (b) device for putting electricity into a car battery.

char•gé d'af•faires [ʃɑːʒeɪdæ'feə] *n.* deputy of an ambassador; an official who takes the place of an ambassador.

char•i•ot ['tʃærɪət] *n.* two-wheeled vehicle pulled by horses. **char•i•ot•eer** [tʃærɪə'tɪə] *n.* person who drives a chariot.

cha•ris•ma [kə'rɪzmə] *n.* personal appeal. **char•is•mat•ic** [kærɪz'mætɪk] *adj.* which appeals to the people.

char•i•ty ['tʃærɪtɪ] *n.* (a) organization which collects money to help the poor or support some cause; giving of money to the poor. (b)

æ back, ɑː farm, ɒ top, aɪ pipe, aʊ how, aɪə fire, aʊə flower, ɔː bought, ɔɪ toy, e fed, eəhair, eɪ take, ə afraid, əʊ boat, əʊə lower, vː word, iː heap, ɪ hit, ɪə hear, uː school, ʊ book, ʌ but, b back, d dog, ð then, dʒ just, f fog, g go, h hand, j yes, k catch, l last, m mix, n nut, ŋ sing, p penny, r round, s some, ʃ short, t too, tʃ chop, θ thing, v voice, w was, z zoo, ʒ treasure

kindness (to the poor/the oppressed). **char•i•ta•ble,** *adj.* (a) which refers to a charity. (b) kind/not critical. **char•i•ta•bly,** *adv.* in a charitable way.

char•la•dy ['tʃɑːleɪdɪ] *n. Brit.* charwoman.

char•la•tan ['ʃɑːlətən] *n.* person who pretends to be an expert, but really is not.

char•lotte ['ʃɑːlɒt] *n.* pudding with fruit and wafers on the outside.

charm [tʃɑːm] 1. *n.* (a) supposedly magic object; **c. bracelet** = bracelet hung with little ornaments. (b) attractiveness. 2. *v.* (a) to bewitch/to put under a spell; **he has a charmed life** = he is very lucky. (b) to attract (s.o.)/to make (s.o.) pleased. **charm•er,** *n.* person who charms. **charm•ing,** *adj.* attractive.

chart [tʃɑːt] 1. *n.* (a) map of the sea, a river or lake. (b) diagram showing statistics; **the charts** = the list of most popular records. 2. *v.* (a) to make a map of (the sea, a river or lake). (b) to make a diagram of; to show (information) in a diagram.

char•ter ['tʃɑːtə] 1. *n.* (a) aircraft hired for a particular flight. (b) legal document giving rights or privileges to (a town/a university). 2. *v.* to hire (an aircraft or boat).

char•wom•an ['tʃɑːwʊmən] *n. Brit.* (*pl.* -women) woman who does housework for s.o.

char•y ['tʃeərɪ] *adj.* reluctant to do sth; cautious.

chase [tʃeɪs] 1. *n.* hunt; **wild goose c.** = useless search. 2. *v.* to run after (s.o.) to try to catch them. **chas•er,** *n.* alcoholic drink such as beer, drunk after another, stronger, alcoholic drink.

chasm ['kæzəm] *n.* huge crack in the ground.

chas•sis ['ʃæsɪ] *n.* (*pl.* chassis ['ʃæsɪz]) metal framework of a car; undercarriage of an aircraft.

chaste [tʃeɪst] *adj.* (sexually) pure. **chas•ti•ty** ['tʃæstɪtɪ] *n.* being chaste.

chas•ten ['tʃeɪsn] *v.* to reprimand; to make (s.o.) less proud. **chas•tened,** *adj.* meek/less proud.

chas•tise [tʃæ'staɪz] *v.* (*formal*) to punish. **chas•tise•ment,** *n.* punishing.

chas•u•ble ['tʃæzjʊbl] *n.* long sleeveless coat worn by priests at ceremonies.

chat [tʃæt] 1. *n.* casual friendly talk. 2. *v.* (**chatted**) to talk in a casual and friendly way; *inf.* **to c. s.o. up** = to get into conversation/to flirt with. **chat•ty,** *adj.* (person) who likes to chat; (letter) full of unimportant news.

chat•tel ['tʃætl] *n.* object which you possess.

chat•ter ['tʃætə] 1. *n.* quick talking. 2. *v.* to talk quickly and not seriously; **his teeth were chattering** = were rattling because of cold.

chat•ter•box, *n.* person who cannot stop talking.

chauf•feur ['ʃəʊfə] *n.* person who is paid to drive a car for s.o. else.

chau•vin•ism ['ʃəʊvɪnɪzəm] *n.* excessive pride in your native country. **chau•vin•ist,** *n.* person who is excessively proud of his/her native country; **male c.** = man who feels that men are superior to women. **chau•vin•is•tic** [ʃəʊvɪ-'nɪstɪk] *adj.* nationalistic.

cheap [tʃiːp] *adj.* (**-er, -est**) (a) not costing a lot of money; **on the c.** = in the cheapest possible way. (b) low/sly (joke, etc.). **cheap•en,** *v.* to reduce the value of (sth). **cheap•ly,** *adv.* not expensively/for a low price. **cheap•ness,** *n.* low cost.

cheat [tʃiːt] 1. *n.* person who tricks s.o. so that he loses. 2. *v.* (a) to trick (s.o.) so that he loses. (b) to try to win by trickery.

check [tʃek] 1. *n.* (a) making sure; examination/test. (b) sudden halt. (c) (*in chess*) state where your opponent has to move to protect his king. (d) pattern of squares in different colors. (e) ticket. (f) bill (in a restaurant). (g) note to a bank asking them to pay money from one account to another; **c. book** = book of blank checks; **blank c.** = check which has no details filled. 2. *v.* (*a*) to make sure; to examine. (b) to bring (s.o.) to a halt. (c) (*in chess*) to put the opponent's king in danger. (d) to hold back. (e) to mark with a sign to show that sth is correct. **checked,** *adj.* with a squared pattern. **check•ers,** *n.* game for two people played with counters on a board marked with sixty-four alternately colored squares. **check in,** *v.* (a) to register when you arrive at a hotel/at an airport/at work. (b) to hand in (luggage) for safe keeping. **check•list,** *n.* list which is used for checking. **check•mate,** (*in chess*) 1. *n.* position where the king cannot move. 2. *v.* to put your opponent's king in a position from which he cannot escape. **check out,** *v.* (a) to leave a hotel; to take (luggage) out of safe keeping. (b) to verify/to see if sth is correct. **check•out,** *n.* cash register in a supermarket. **check o•ver,** *v.* to look over sth to make sure it is all there/all in working order. **check•room,** *n.* place where you leave your coat in a restaurant, theater, etc. **check up on,** *v.* to verify/to see if sth is correct. **check•up,** *n.* complete medical examination; general examination (of a car).

check•ers ['tʃekəz] *n. pl.* squares in a pattern. **check•ered,** *adj.* (a) laid out in a pattern of squares; **c. flag** = flag used to show the end of a motor race. (b) varied/with good and bad parts.

cheek [tʃiːk] 1. *n.* (a) fat side of the face on either side of the nose and below the eye. (b) *inf.*

rudeness. (c) *Sl.* buttock. 2. *v. inf.* to be rude to (s.o.). **cheek•i•ly,** *adv.* in a cheeky way. **cheek•i•ness,** *n.* being cheeky. **cheek•y,** *adj.* **(-ier, -iest)** rude.

cheep [tʃiːp] 1. *n.* little cry, like that made by a baby bird. 2. *v.* to make a little cry.

cheer ['tʃɪə] 1. *n.* (a) shout of praise or encouragement. **cheers!** = (*when drinking*) here's to you; 2. *v.* (a) to shout encouragement. (b) to comfort; to make happier. (c) **to c. up** = to make or become happier; **c. up!** = don't be miserable. **cheer•ful,** *adj.* happy. **cheer•ful•ly,** *adv.* in a cheerful way. **cheer•ful•ness,** *n.* being cheerful. **cheer•i•ly,** *adv.* in a cheery way. **cheer•ing,** *n.* cheers of encouragement. **cheer•i•o,** *inter. Brit. inf.* goodbye. **cheer•lead•er,** *n.* person who directs the cheering of a crowd. **cheer•less,** *adj.* gloomy/sad. **cheer•y,** *adj.* happy.

cheese [tʃiːz] *n.* solid food made from milk. **cheese•burg•er,** *n.* hamburger with melted cheese on top. **cheese•cake,** *n.* cake of sweet pastry and cream cheese, sometimes with fruit. **cheese•cloth,** *n.* thin cotton cloth such as cheeses are wrapped in. **chees•y,** *adj. inf.* smelling of cheese.

chee•tah ['tʃiːtə] *n.* large animal like a leopard, which can run very fast.

chef [ʃef] *n.* (chief) cook (in a restaurant). **chef d'œu•vre,** *n.* masterpiece.

chem•i•cal ['kemɪkl] 1. *adj.* referring to chemistry. 2. *n.* substance (either natural or man-made) which is formed by reactions between elements. **chem•i•cal•ly,** *adj.* by a chemical process. **chem•ist,** *n.* person who specializes in chemistry. **chem•is•try,** *n.* science of chemical substances, elements, compounds, and their reactions.

che•mo•ther•a•py ['kiːməʊ'θerəpɪ] *n.* using chemical drugs to fight disease.

che•nille [ʃə'niːl] *n.* soft cotton cloth, with a tufted surface.

cheque [tʃek] *n. see* **check.**

cher•ish ['tʃerɪʃ] *v.* to love/to treat kindly; to nourish (a hope).

che•root [ʃə'ruːt] *n.* long thin cigar with both ends open.

cher•ry ['tʃerɪ] *n.* small summer fruit, growing on a long stalk; **c. (tree)** = tree which bears cherries.

cher•ub ['tʃərəb] *n.* small fat childlike angel; child who looks like an angel. **che•ru•bic** [tʃə'ruːbɪk] *adj.* round and innocent (face).

cher•vil ['tʃɜːvɪl] *n.* herb used to flavor soups.

chess [tʃes] *n.* (*no pl.*) game for two people played on a board with sixteen pieces on each side. **chess•board,** *n.* black and white squared board you play chess on. **chess•men,** *n. pl.* pieces used in chess.

chest [tʃest] *n.* (a) piece of furniture, like a large box; **c. of drawers** = piece of furniture with several drawers for keeping clothes in. (b) top front part of the body, where the heart and lungs are; **to get sth off your c.** = to speak frankly about sth which is worrying you.

ches•ter•field ['tʃestəfiːld] *n.* sofa with soft back and arms.

chest•nut ['tʃesnʌt] *n.* (a) bright red-brown nut; large tree which grows these nuts; wood of this tree. (b) red-brown color. (c) red-brown horse. (d) *inf.* old joke; cliché.

chev•ron ['ʃevrən] *n.* sign shaped like a V.

chew [tʃuː] *v.* to make (sth) soft with your teeth. **chew•ing gum,** *n.* sweet gum which you chew but do not swallow. **chew•y,** *adj.* which can be chewed for a long time.

chi•an•ti [ki'æntɪ] *n.* Italian red wine.

chic [ʃiːk] *adj.* elegant; **radical c.** = fashionable left-wing opinions or people who hold them.

chi•cane [ʃɪ'keɪn] 1. *n.* trickery. 2. *v* to deceive by trickery. **chi•can•er•y,** *n.* trickery.

chick [tʃɪk] *n.* baby bird, esp. hen. **chick•pea,** *n.* type of yellow pea. **chick•weed,** *n.* common weed with small yellow flowers.

chick•en ['tʃɪkɪn] 1. *n.* young farmyard bird, esp. young hen; meat from a (young) hen. 2. *v. inf.* **to c. out** = to back out of a fight/argument because you are afraid. **chick•en•feed,** *n.* not much money/profit. **chick•en-liv•ered,** *adj.* scared/frightened. **chick•en•pox,** *n.* disease (usu. of children) which gives red itchy spots.

chic•o•ry ['tʃɪkərɪ] *n.* vegetable of which the leaves are used for salads, and the roots are dried and ground to mix with coffee to make it bitter.

chide [tʃaɪd] *v.* (**chided/chid; was chided**) (*formal*) to criticize.

chief [tʃiːf] 1. *adj.* most important; **commander-in-chief** = commander above all other officers. 2. *n.* leader. **chief•ly,** *adv.* mainly. **chief•tain** ['tʃiːftən] *n.* leader of a tribe.

chiff•chaff ['tʃɪftʃæf] *n.* European warbler.

chif•fon ['ʃɪfɒn] *n.* type of very thin material.

æ back, ɑː farm, ɒ top, aɪ pipe, aʊ how, aɪə fire, aʊə flower, ɔː bought, ɔɪ toy, e fed, eəhair, eɪ take, ə afraid, əʊ boat, əʊə lower, ɜː word, iː heap, ɪ hit, ɪə hear, uː school, ʊ book, ʌ but, b back, d dog, ð then, dʒ just, f fog, g go, h hand, j yes, k catch, l last, m mix, n nut, ŋ sing, p penny, r round, s some, ʃ short, t too, tʃ chop, θ thing, v voice, w was, z zoo, ʒ treasure

chi•gnon ['ʃiːnjɒn] *n.* hair tied together in a knot at the back of the head.

chi•hua•hua [tʃɪ'wɑːwɑː] *n.* breed of very small dog.

chil•blain ['tʃɪlbleɪn] *n.* painful swelling on hands, feet, etc., caused by the cold.

child [tʃaɪld] *n.* (*pl.* **children** ['tʃɪldrən]) young boy or girl; **it's child's play** = it's very easy. **child•birth,** *n.* act of giving birth to a child. **child•hood,** *n.* state of being a child; time when you are a child. **child•ish,** *adj.* like a child; silly/foolish. **child•ish•ly,** *adv.* in a childish way. **child•ish•ness,** *n.* being childish. **child•less,** *adj.* with no children. **child•like,** *adj.* innocent like a child.

Chil•e•an ['tʃɪlɪən] 1. *adj.* referring to Chile. 2. *n.* person from Chile.

chil•i, chilli ['tʃɪlɪ] *n.* dried seed pod of the pepper plant, used to make very hot sauces.

chill [tʃɪl] 1. *n.* (a) coldness in the air. (b) illness caused by cold. 2. *v.* to cool. **chill•i•ness,** *n.* coldness. **chill•y,** *adj.* cold; not very welcoming.

chime [tʃaɪm] 1. *n.* ringing of bells. 2. *v.* (*of bells*) to ring. **chime in,** *v. inf.* to enter a conversation.

chim•ney ['tʃɪmnɪ] *n.* tall tube or brick column for taking smoke away from a fire. **chim•ney pot,** *n. Brit.* round top to a chimney on a house. **chim•ney stack,** *n.* tall chimney rising above the roof of a factory; group of chimneys on the roof of a house. **chim•ney sweep,** *n.* person who cleans chimneys.

chim•pan•zee, *inf.* **chimp** [tʃɪmpæn'ziː, tʃɪmp] *n.* type of intelligent ape from Africa.

chin [tʃɪn] *n.* front part of the bottom jaw.

chi•na ['tʃaɪnə] *n.* (*no pl.*) porcelain; cups, plates, etc. made of fine white clay. **c. clay** = fine white clay, used for making china.

chin•chil•la [tʃɪn'tʃɪlə] *n.* gray fur from a small American animal.

chine [tʃaɪn] *v.* to cut the rib bones from the backbone of (a joint of meat).

Chi•nese [tʃaɪ'niːz] 1. *adj.* referring to China. **C. lantern** = garden plant, whose seed pods form bright red balls. 2. *n.* (a) (*pl.* **Chinese**) person from China. (b) language spoken in China.

chink [tʃɪŋk] 1. *n.* (a) little crack. (b) noise of chinking. 2. *v.* to make a noise by knocking glasses/metal objects together.

chintz [tʃɪnts] *n.* thick cotton cloth with bright flower patterns, used for upholstery.

chip [tʃɪp] 1. *n.* (a) little piece of wood/stone, etc.; **to have a c. on your shoulder** = to be permanently indignant about sth where you feel you have been treated unfairly. (b) long piece

of potato fried in oil. (c) small, usu. thin, piece of food; **chocolate chips** = small pieces of chocolate. (d) **silicon c.** = small piece of silicon, able to store data, used in computers. 2. *v.* (**chipped**) to break off a small piece of.

chip•board, *n.* thick board made of small chips of wood glued together, and used in building. **chip in,** *v.* (a) to contribute. (b) to interrupt. **chip off,** *v.* to break off.

chip•munk ['tʃɪpmʌŋk] *n.* small North American animal, like a striped squirrel.

chi•po•la•ta [tʃɪpə'lɑːtə] *n.* long thin sausage.

chi•rop•o•dist [kɪ'rɒpədɪst] *n.* person who specializes in chiropody. **chi•rop•o•dy,** *n.* treatment of feet.

chi•ro•prac•tor ['kaɪrəpræktə] *n.* person who heals by massage and manipulation of joints.

chirp [tʃɜːp] 1. *n.* sharp short call of birds/grasshoppers. 2. *v.* (*of birds/grasshoppers*) to call. **chirp•y,** *adj. inf.* bright and cheerful.

chis•el ['tʃɪzl] 1. *n.* metal tool for cutting small pieces of wood/stone, when hit with a hammer. 2. *v.* (**chiseled, chiselled**) (a) to cut wood/stone with a chisel. (b) *Sl.* to swindle.

chit [tʃɪt] *n.* (a) note/small invoice. (b) young girl.

chit•chat ['tʃɪttʃæt] *n.* gossip/talk.

chit•ter•lings ['tʃɪtəlɪŋz] *n. pl.* pig's intestines prepared as food.

chiv•al•rous ['ʃɪvəlrəs] *adj.* courteous/very polite. **chiv•al•ry,** *n.* politeness/courtesy.

chives [tʃaɪvz] *n. pl.* onionlike plant with small green leaves.

chlo•rine ['klɔːriːn] *n.* (*element:* Cl) greenish gas used to disinfect swimming pools, etc. **chlo•ride** ['klɔːraɪd] *n.* compound of chlorine with another substance. **chlo•ri•nate** ['klɔːrɪneɪt] *v.* to disinfect with chlorine. **chlo•ri•na•tion** [klɔrɪ'neɪʃn] *n.* disinfecting with chlorine.

chlo•ro•fluor•o•car•bon [klɔrəʊflu'ɔːrəʊ-'kɑːbən] *n.* compound of chlorine fluorine, used in aerosols, which remains in the upper atmosphere and contributes to the greenhouse effect.

chlo•ro•form ['klɒrəfɔːm] 1. *n.* chemical, whose vapor when breathed makes you unconscious. 2. *v.* to make unconscious with chloroform.

chlo•ro•phyll ['klɒrəfɪl] *n.* substance which makes plants green.

chock [tʃɒk] *n.* small block of wood which prevents wheels turning. **chock-a-block, chock-full,** *adj.* completely full.

choc•o•late ['tʃɒklət] *n.* (a) food made from cacao tree seeds; **plain c.** = bitter chocolate; **milk c.** = sweet chocolate made with milk; **hot c.** = hot drink made of powdered chocolate.

(b) small sweet made from chocolate. (c) dark brown color.

choice [tʃɔɪs] *n.* thing which you choose; **I haven't any c.** = I have to do it; **c. peaches** = peaches which have been specially selected.

choir ['kwaɪə] *n.* (a) group of people singing together. (b) part of the church where the choir sits. **choir•boy**, *n.* boy who sings in a church choir. **choir•mast•er**, *n.* person who conducts and rehearses a choir.

choke [tʃəuk] 1. *n.* (a) blockage in the throat. (b) (*in a car engine*) valve which increases the flow of air to the engine; knob on the dashboard which activates this valve. (c) central inedible part of a globe artichoke. 2. *v.* (a) to block (a pipe, etc.). (b) to stop breathing because you have swallowed sth. **choke back,** *v.* to hold back (tears). **chok•er**, *n.* piece of ribbon, etc., worn tightly round the neck. **chok•ing**, *adj.* stifling.

chol•er•a ['kɒlərə] *n.* serious infectious disease causing severe diarrhea.

cho•les•ter•ol [kɒ'lestərɒl] *n.* substance in fats and eggs, also produced by the liver, which deposits fat in the arteries.

chomp [tʃɒmp] *v.* to chew noisily.

choose [tʃuːz] *v.* (**chose; chosen**) to decide to take (sth)/to do one particular thing. **choos•ing**, *n.* act of making a choice. **choos•y**, *adj.* difficult to please.

chop [tʃɒp] 1. *n.* (a) piece of meat with a rib bone. (b) jaw, esp. in animals. 2. *v.* (**chopped**) to cut into small pieces with an ax/a knife. **chop down,** *v.* to cut down (a tree) with an ax. **chop off,** *v.* to cut off. **chop•per**, *n.* (a) ax for cutting meat. (b) *inf.* helicopter. **chop•py**, *adj.* quite rough (sea). **chop su•ey**, *n.* Chinese dish of fried meat and bean sprouts. **chop up,** *v.* to cut up into little bits. **chop•sticks** ['tʃɒpstɪks] *n. pl.* long sticks used by oriental people for eating food.

cho•ral ['kɔːrəl] *adj.* referring to a choir.

cho•rale [kɒ'rɑːl] *n.* piece of music for a choir, based on a hymn.

chord [kɔːd] *n.* (a) several notes played together in harmony. (b) line which joins two points on the circumference of a circle.

chore [tʃɔː] *n.* piece of routine work, esp. housework.

cho•re•og•ra•phy [kɒrɪ'ɒgrəfɪ] *n.* art of working out the steps for a ballet. **cho•re•og•ra•pher**, *n.* person who works out the steps for a ballet.

chor•is•ter ['kɒrɪstə] *n.* person who sings in a choir.

chor•tle ['tʃɔːtl] *v.* to chuckle loudly.

cho•rus ['kɔːrəs] 1. *n.* (a) group of people who sing or dance together. (b) part of a song which is repeated by everyone together. 2. *v.* to say sth all together. **chor•us-girl**, *n.* girl who appears as a member of a chorus in a variety show.

chose [tʃəuz], **cho•sen** ['tʃəuzən] *v. see* **choose.**

chough [tʃʌf] *n.* large black bird with a red bill.

chow [tʃau] *n.* (a) type of Chinese dog with thick fur. (b) *inf.* food.

chow•der ['tʃaudə] *n.* fish soup.

chris•ten ['krɪsn] *v.* (a) to give a name to (a baby) in church; to give a name to (a ship/a bell, etc.) at a ceremony. (b) to use (sth) for the first time. **chris•ten•ing**, *n.* ceremony in church where a baby is given a name.

Chris•tian ['krɪstʃən] 1. *n.* person who believes in Christianity. 2. *adj.* referring to Christianity; **C. name** = first name given at a ceremony in church. **Chris•ti•an•i•ty** [krɪstɪ'ænɪtɪ] *n.* religion based on the doctrine preached by Jesus Christ and followed by Christians ever since.

Christ•mas ['krɪsməs] *n.* Christian holiday on December 25th; **C. Day** = December 25th; **Father C.** = **Santa Claus. Christ•mas•sy**, *adj.* like Christmas.

chro•mat•ic [krə'mætɪk] *adj.* referring to colors or to a musical scale.

chrome [krəum] *n.* chromium; **c. yellow** = bright yellow. **chro•mi•um** ['krəumɪəm] *n.* (*element:* Cr) hard shiny metal which does not rust.

chro•mo•some ['krəuməsəum] *n.* one of several elements which form a biological cell, and which carries the genes.

chron•ic ['krɒnɪk] *adj.* continual/repeating (illness, etc.); *inf.* very bad. **chron•i•cal•ly**, *adv.* very badly.

chron•ic fa•tigue syn•drome *n.* (= myalgic encephalomyelitis/postviral syndrome) longlasting condition, sometimes occurring after a viral infection, characterized by muscular pain, weakness, and exhaustion.

chron•i•cle ['krɒnɪkl] 1. *n.* record of things which take place; news story. 2. *v.* to write the history of (events) in the order in which they took place. **chron•i•cler**, *n.* person who writes a chronicle.

æ back, ɑː farm, ɒ top, aɪ pipe, au how, aɪə fire, auə flower, ɔː bought, ɔɪ toy, e fed, eə hair, eɪ take, ə afraid, əu boat, əuə lower, ɜː word, iː heap, ɪ hit, ɪə hear, uː school, u book, ʌ but, b back, d dog, ð then, dʒ just, f fog, g go, h hand, j yes, k catch, l last, m mix, n nut, ŋ sing, p penny, r round, s some, ʃ short, t too, tʃ chop, θ thing, v voice, w was, z zoo, ʒ treasure

chro•nol•o•gy [krɒ'nɒlədʒɪ] *n.* statement of the order in which things happened. **chron•o•log•i•cal** [krɒnə'lɒdʒɪkl] *adj.* in order of when the events happened. **chron•o•log•i•cal•ly,** *adv.* in chronological order.

chro•nom•e•ter [krə'nɒmɪtə] *n.* very accurate watch (as used for timing races).

chrys•a•lis ['krɪsəlɪs] *n. (pl.* **-es**) hard-cased stage through which a caterpillar passes before turning into a butterfly or moth.

chry•san•the•mum [krɪ'sænθəməm] *n.* bright-colored autumn flower.

chub [tʃʌb] *n. (pl.* **chub**) fat river fish.

chub•by ['tʃʌbɪ] *adj.* (**-ier, -est**) quite plump.

chuck [tʃʌk] 1. *n.* (a) part of a drill which holds the bit. (b) type of beef steak. 2. *v. inf.* to throw.

chuck•le ['tʃʌkl] 1. *n.* quiet laugh. 2. *v.* to give a quiet laugh.

chug [tʃʌg] *v.* (**chugged**) to make a regular puffing noise like a steam engine.

chuk•ka ['tʃʌkə] *n.* period of play in a polo match.

chum [tʃʌm] *n. inf.* friend. **chum•my,** *adj.* friendly.

chump [tʃʌmp] *n.* silly fool.

chunk [tʃʌŋk] *n.* large thick piece. **chunk•y,** *adj.* made of large pieces.

church [tʃɜːtʃ] *n. (pl.* **-es**) (a) large building for Christian religious ceremonies. (b) group of Christians together. **church•go•er,** *n.* person who goes to church (regularly). **church•ward•en,** *n.* senior member of a parish. **church•yard,** *n.* cemetery round a church.

churl•ish ['tʃɜːlɪʃ] *adj.* rude. **churl•ish•ly,** *adv.* rudely. **churl•ish•ness,** *n.* rudeness.

churn [tʃɜːn] 1. *n.* large metal container for milk; container in which cream is churned. 2. *v.* to turn cream to make butter. **churn out,** *v. inf.* to produce in a series. **churn up,** *v.* to mix/stir up.

chute [ʃuːt] *n.* (a) slide into water (in a swimming pool). (b) slide for sending things to a lower level.

chut•ney ['tʃʌtnɪ] *n.* highly-flavored sauce usu. made with tomatoes, onions, vinegar and spices.

CIA [siːaɪ'eɪ] *abbreviation for* Central Intelligence Agency.

CID [siːaɪ'diː] *abbreviation for* Criminal Investigation Department of Scotland Yard.

ci•der ['saɪdə] *n.* alcoholic drink made from fermented apple juice.

c.i.f. [siːaɪ'ef] *abbrev for* cost, insurance, freight.

ci•gar [sɪ'gɑː] *n.* tight roll of tobacco leaves which you can light and smoke.

cig•a•rette [sɪgə'ret] *n.* chopped tobacco rolled in very thin paper which you can light and smoke. **cigarette case,** *n.* special case for holding cigarettes. **cigarette end,** *n.* end of a cigarette which has been smoked. **cig•ar•ette hold•er,** *n.* holder for putting cigarettes in to smoke.

cinch [sɪntʃ] *n. inf.* (a) thing which is very easy to do. (b) sth. which is certain to work.

cin•ders ['sɪndəz] *n. pl.* lumps of coarse ash left after coal has been burned.

cine- [sɪnɪ] *prefix* referring to motion pictures. **cin•e•ma** ['sɪnəmə] *n.* (a) theater for showing motion pictures. (b) art of making motion pictures.

cin•e•ra•ri•a [sɪnə'reərɪə] *n.* houseplant with blue, pink, or purple flowers.

cin•na•mon ['sɪnəmən] *n.* spice made from the bark of a tropical tree.

ci•pher ['saɪfə] *n.* (a) code/secret message. (b) monogram/initials of a name linked together artistically. (c) zero; person of no importance.

cir•ca ['sɜːkə] *prep.* (used of dates) about.

cir•cle ['sɜːkl] 1. *n.* (a) line forming a round shape. (b) row of seats in a theater. (c) group of people/society. 2. *v.* (a) to go around in a ring. (b) to draw a circle around (sth).

cir•cuit ['sɜːkɪt] *n.* (a) trip around sth. (b) area visited by a judge who travels from court to court. (c) path of electricity; **printed c. board =** flat card with metal tracks printed on it to form an electric circuit; **short c. =** fault (caused by crossed wires, etc.) when electricity follows a shorter path than usual; **closed c. television =** private television operating over a short area by cable. **cir•cu•i•tous** [sə'kjuːɪtəs] *adj.* roundabout (way).

cir•cu•lar ['sɜːkjulə] *adj. & n.* (sth) round in shape; publicity leaflet given out to many people. **cir•cu•lar•ize,** *v.* to send circulars to (people).

cir•cu•late ['sɜːkjuleɪt] *v.* (a) to distribute/to pass around. (b) to move around. **cir•cu•la•tion** [sɜːkju'leɪʃn] *n.* (a) act of circulating; **bank notes in c. =** notes which are in use. (b) movement of blood around the body. (c) number of copies of a newspaper, etc., which are sold. **cir•cu•la•to•ry,** *adj.* referring to circulation of the blood.

cir•cum•cise ['sɜːkəmsaɪz] *v.* to remove the foreskin of (a male person). **cir•cum•ci•sion** [sɜːkəm'sɪʒn] *n.* act of removing the foreskin.

cir•cum•fer•ence [sə'kʌmfərəns] *n.* (distance around) the edge of a circle.

cir•cum•lo•cu•tion [sɜːkəmlə'kjuʃn] *n.* roundabout way of saying sth.

cir•cum•nav•i•gate [sɜːkəm'nævɪgeɪt] *v.* (*formal*) to sail around (the world).

cir•cum•nav•i•ga•tion [sɜːkəmnævɪ- 'geɪʃn] *n.* sailing around the world.

cir•cum•scribe [sɜːkəm'skraɪb] *v.* (*formal*) to draw a line around sth; to set limits to sth. **cir•cum•scrip•tion** [sɜːkəm'skrɪpʃən] *n.* limiting; a limited area.

cir•cum•spect ['sɜːkəmspekt] *adj.* very careful.

cir•cum•stan•ces ['sɜːkəmstənsɪz] *n. pl.* (a) way in which something took place; **under the c.** = as things have turned out like this/as it happens. (b) state of one's finances. **cir•cum•stan•tial** [sɜːkəm'stænʃl] *adj.* giving details; **c. evidence** = evidence which suggests sth but does not offer firm proof. **cir•cum•stan•ti•ate**, *v.* to give details to prove (sth).

cir•cum•vent [sɜːkəm'vent] *v.* to avoid. **cir•cum•ven•tion**, *n.* avoidance.

cir•cus ['sɜːkəs] *n.* (*pl.* -es) traveling show, often given under a large tent, with animals, clowns, etc.

cir•rho•sis [sɪ'rəʊsɪs] *n.* disease of the liver caused esp. by alcohol.

cir•rus ['sɪrəs] *n.* small very high fleecy cloud.

CIS [siːaɪ'es] *abbrev. for* Commonwealth of Independent States.

cis•tern ['sɪstən] *n.* water tank.

cit•a•del ['sɪtədəl] *n.* fort guarding a town.

cite [saɪt] *v.* (a) to quote (a reference, a person) as proof. (b) to call (s.o.) to appear in court. **ci•ta•tion** [saɪ'teɪʃn] *n.* (a) official document recognizing an act of bravery. (b) quotation of sth as a reference or proof. (c) summons to appear in court.

cit•i•zen ['sɪtɪzn] *n.* (a) inhabitant of a town. (b) person with full rights as an inhabitant of a country; **citizen's arrest** = arrest of a suspected criminal by an ordinary citizen; **citizens' band** = private radio, mainly used by drivers of road vehicles. **cit•i•zen•ship**, *n.* state of being a citizen.

cit•ric ['sɪtrɪk] *adj.* **c. acid** = acid found in citrus fruit. **cit•rus** ['sɪtrəs] *n.* **c. fruit** = fruit such as oranges, lemons or grapefruit.

cit•y ['sɪtɪ] *n.* (a) very large town. (b) (*U.S.*) incorporated municipality with a charter from the state.

civ•et ['sɪvɪt] *n.* wild cat, which provides a substance used in making perfume.

civ•ic ['sɪvɪk] *adj.* referring to a city; **c. center** = social/sports center run by a city; **c. authorities** = leaders of a city. **civ•ics**, *n.* study of municipal affairs.

civ•il ['sɪvl] *adj.* (a) belonging to the general public, not to the military; **c. service** = the government bureaucracy; **c. servant** = person who works in a government department. (b) referring to the ordinary citizen; **c. rights** = the rights of a citizen; **c. rights movement** = campaign to ensure that all citizens have equal rights; **c. war** = war between groups in the same country; **c. defense** = defense by ordinary citizens, not the military; **c. law** = law referring to the private matters, rather than criminal or military matters. **c. action** = court action brought by one citizen against another; **c. engineer** = person who designs roads, bridges, etc. (c) polite. **ci•vil•ian** [sɪ'vɪljən] *adj. & n.* (person) not belonging to the armed forces; private citizen. **ci•vil•i•ty**, *n.* politeness. **civ•il•ly**, *adv.* politely.

civ•i•lize ['sɪvɪlaɪz] *v.* (a) to educate (primitive people) to a higher level of society. (b) to make (s.o.) less rude/uncouth. **civ•i•li•za•tion** [sɪvɪlaɪ'zeɪʃn] *n.* regular civilized way of conducting society; making s.o. civilized.

civ•vy (*usu.* ['sɪvɪ] **civ•vies**), *n. pl. inf.* civilian clothes.

CJD ['siːdʒeɪ'diː] *abbrev. for* Creutzfeldt-Jakob Disease.

Cl *symbol for* chlorine.

clad [klæd] *adj.* covered. **clad•ding**, *n.* material used for the outside covering of walls.

claim [kleɪm] **1.** *n.* (*a*) demand. (b) statement/assertion. **2.** *v.* (a) to demand as one's right. (b) to state/to assert (without any proof). (c) to say you own (sth) which has been left/lost. **claim•ant**, *n.* person who claims a right.

clair•voy•ant [kleə'vɔɪənt] *n.* person who can see in his mind things which are happening elsewhere/who can foretell the future. **clair•voy•ance**, *n.* act of communicating with spirits/of foretelling the future.

clam [klæm] *n.* large shellfish with a hinged shell.

clam•ber ['klæmbə] *v.* to climb with difficulty.

clam•my ['klæmɪ] *adj.* (-ier, -iest) damp and cold; humid (weather). **clam•mi•ness**, *n.* being clammy.

clam•or, *Brit.* **cla•mour** ['klæmə] **1.** *n.* shouting. **2.** *v.* to shout/to demand loudly. **clam•or•ous**, *adj.* noisy/shouting.

clamp [klæmp] **1.** *n.* metal pieces which are

æ back, ɑː farm, ɒ top, aɪ pipe, aʊ how, aɪə fire, aʊə flower, ɔː bought, ɔɪ toy, e fed, eəhair, eɪ take, ə afraid, əʊ boat, əʊə lower, vː word, iː heap, ɪ hit, ɪə hear, uː school, ʊ book, ʌ but, b back, d dog, ð then, dʒ just, f fog, g go, h hand, j yes, k catch, l last, m mix, n nut, ŋ sing, p penny, r round, s some, ʃ short, t too, tʃ chop, θ thing, v voice, w was, z zoo, ʒ treasure

screwed tightly to hold sth together. 2. *v.* (a) to hold tight with a clamp. (b) **to c. down on** = to stop (petty crime, etc.). **clamp▪down**, *n.* **(on)** severe action to stop sth.

clan [klæn] *n.* Scottish family tribe. **clan▪nish,** *adj.* loyal to the clan; supporting your own group. **clan▪nish▪ness,** *n.* being clannish. **clans▪man,** *n.* (*pl.* **-smen**) member of a clan.

clan▪des▪tine [klæn'destɪn] *adj.* secret/undercover.

clang [klæŋ] 1. *n.* loud noise of metal ringing. 2. *v.* to make a loud ringing noise.

clank [klæŋk] 1. *n.* noise of metal hitting metal. 2. *v.* to make a noise of metal hitting other metal.

clap [klæp] 1. *n.* (a) beating of hands against each other to show pleasure. (b) friendly tap (with the hand). (c) loud noise (of thunder). (d) *Sl.* gonorrhea. 2. *v.* **(clapped)** (a) to beat your hands together to show you are pleased. (b) to give (s.o.) a friendly tap with the hand. (c) to put (s.o. in jail) suddenly. **clap▪per,** *n.* swinging metal piece inside a bell which strikes the bell. **clap▪board,** *n.* black board with a striped hinged section at the top, used in film-making to indicate the start of a scene. **clap▪ping,** *n.* applause.

clap▪trap ['klæptræp] *n. inf.* nonsense.

clar▪et ['klærət] *n.* red Bordeaux wine.

clar▪i▪fy ['klærɪfaɪ] *v.* (a) to make clear. (b) to heat (butter, etc.) until it becomes transparent. **clar▪i▪fi▪ca▪tion** [klærɪfɪ'keɪʃn] *n.* making clear/explanation.

clar▪i▪net [klærɪ'net] *n.* wind instrument in the woodwind group. **clar▪i▪net▪ist,** *n.* person who plays a clarinet.

clar▪i▪on ['klærɪən] *n.* trumpet; **c. call** = loud clear call.

clar▪i▪ty ['klærɪtɪ] *n.* clearness.

clash [klæʃ] 1. *n.* (*pl.* **-es**) (a) loud noise of things hitting each other. (b) battle/conflict; shock of two colors placed side by side. 2. *v.* (a) to bang together making a loud noise. (b) not to agree/to be in conflict. (c) to fight.

clasp [klɑːsp] 1. *n.* (a) device for holding sth shut. (b) brooch. (c) act of holding in your hand. 2. *v.* to hold (sth) tight. **clasp▪knife,** *n.* (*pl.* **-knives**) pocket knife which folds.

class [klɑːs] 1. *n.* (*pl.* **-es**) (a) group of people with the same position in society; **middle c.** = class of professional people/bourgeoisie; **working c.** = class of people who do mainly manual labor; **upper c.** = the rich/the aristocracy. (b) group of people (usu. children) who study together. (c) category/group into which things are classified; **first c.** = very good; **to travel first c.** = in the most expensive seats; **tourist c./economy c.** = less expensive seats on aircraft and ships. 2. *v.* to put (sth) in a cate-

gory. **class ac▪tion,** *n.* legal action taken by one or more individuals representing the interests of a large group, e.g. smokers. **clas▪si▪fi▪a▪ble,** *adj.* which can be classified. **clas▪si▪fi▪ca▪tion** [klæsɪfɪ'keɪʃn] *n.* way of ordering things into categories. **clas▪si▪fy** ['klæsɪfaɪ] *v.* to arrange things into groups; **classified information** = information which is officially secret. **class▪less,** *adj.* with no division into social classes. **class▪room,** *n.* room in which a class is taught. **class▪y,** *adj.* **(-ier, -iest)** *inf.* chic/expensive-looking.

clas▪sic ['klæsɪk] 1. *n.* (a) great book/play/piece of music/writer/composer, etc. (b) **the classics** = Ancient Greek and Roman literature, culture, etc. 2. *adj.* (a) (style) which is elegant and based on that of Greek or Roman architecture/literature, etc. (b) typical. **clas▪si▪cal,** *adj.* (a) referring to the classics. (b) serious (music). **clas▪si▪cist,** *n.* person who studies the classics.

clat▪ter ['klætə] 1. *n.* noise of things hitting together. 2. *v.* to make a noise.

clause [klɔːz] *n.* (a) paragraph in a treaty or legal document. (b) part of a sentence; **main c.** = the central part of a sentence; **subordinate clauses** = clauses which depend on the main clause.

claus▪tro▪pho▪bi▪a [klɒstrə'fəubɪə] *n.* terror of being shut inside a closed place. **claus▪tro▪pho▪bic,** *adj.* referring to claustrophobia.

clav▪i▪chord ['klævɪkɔːd] *n.* old musical instrument like a small piano, with a very quiet sound.

clav▪i▪cle ['klævɪkl] *n.* collarbone.

claw [klɔː] 1. *n.* (a) nail (of animal/bird). (b) pincer/part of a crab or lobster which pinches. 2. *v.* to scratch with a claw. **claw ham▪mer,** *n.* hammer with the back of the head curved and split for removing nails.

clay [kleɪ] *n.* stiff soil found in river valleys; stiff earth used for making bricks or china. **clay▪ey,** *adj.* containing clay. **clay▪more,** *n.* sword used in Scotland.

clean [kliːn] 1. *adj.* **(-er, -est)** not dirty; **c. break** = complete break; **to come c.** = to confess (to a crime, etc.). 2. *adv.* completely. 3. *v.* to remove dirt. **clean▪er,** *n.* person/thing which removes dirt; **vacuum c.** = machine for sucking up dirt; **(dry) cleaner's** = store where clothes can be taken to be cleaned; **oven c.** = strong substance for cleaning dirty ovens. **clean▪ing,** *n.* removing dirt. **clean▪li▪ness, cleanness** ['klenlɪnəs, 'kliːnnəs] *n.* state of being clean. **clean▪ly,** *adv.* in a clean way. **clean▪shav▪en,** *adj.* with no beard or mustache.

cleanse [klenz] *v.* to make very clean; **cleansing cream** = cream for cleansing the skin. **cleans•er**, *n.* material which removes dirt.

clear ['klɪə] 1. *adj.* (**-er, -est**) (a) pure; transparent. (b) with nothing in the way. (c) easily understood. (d) complete. (e) free (**of**). 2. *adv.* in a clear way. 3. *v.* (a) to remove (obstacles); **to c. the table** = to remove dirty dishes and cutlery; **to c. one's throat** = to cough slightly to get ready for speaking. (b) to make clear/pure; to become clear/pure. (c) to show that s.o. is innocent. (d) not to hit. **clear•ance**, *n.* (a) act of removing obstacles; act of removing plants from land; **c. sale** = sale where all the goods are reduced in price to clear them from the shelves. (b) space for sth to pass through. **clear a•way**, *v.* to remove (sth) which is in the way; to remove (dirty dishes) from a table. **clear-cut,** *adj.* definite/distinct. **clear-head•ed,** *adj.* clever/with a sharp understanding. **clear•ing,** *n.* (a) act of removing obstacles. (b) area in a wood where the trees have been cut down. **clear•ly,** *adv.* (a) in a way which is easily understood or heard. (b) obviously. **clear•ness,** *n.* being clear. **clear off,** *v.* (a) to pay off (one's debts). (b) to run away. **clear out,** *v.* (a) to empty by throwing out. (b) to go away. **clear up,** *v.* (a) to make clear/pure. (b) to become brighter.

cleat [kli:t] *n.* wooden/metal device for attaching ropes on ships.

cleave [kli:v] *v.* (**clove/cleft; has cloven/cleft**) (*old*) (a) to split. (b) to cling (to). **cleav•age** ['kli:vɪdʒ] *n.* space between the breasts. **cleav•er** ['kli:və] *n.* large ax used by butchers.

clef [klef] *n.* sign at the beginning of a piece of music which shows whether it is bass or treble.

cleft [kleft] *adj. & n.* split; **c. palate** = split roof of the mouth.

clem•a•tis [klə'meɪtɪs] *n.* climbing garden plant with large purple or pink flowers.

clem•ent ['klemənt] *adj.* (*formal*) kind/soft (weather). **clem•en•cy,** *n.* mercy (to a criminal).

clem•en•tine ['klemənti:n] *n.* small sweet orange with a skin which is easily removed.

clench [klentʃ] *v.* to close tightly.

clere•sto•ry ['klɪəstɔːrɪ] *n.* high row of windows in a medieval church.

cler•gy ['klɜːdʒɪ] *n.* persons ordained to perform religious services. **cler•gy•man,** *n.* (*pl.* **-men**) member of the clergy, as a priest or minister.

cler•ic ['klerɪk] *n.* (*formal*) clergyman. **cler•i•cal** ['klerɪkl] *adj.* (a) referring to a clerk. (b) referring to clergy; **c. collar** = stiff white collar fastening at the back, worn by some members of the clergy.

cler•i•hew ['klerɪ'hjuː] *n.* short four-lined humorous poem.

clerk [klɜːk] *n.* (a) person who works in an office; (b) official in charge of records, as for a town, court, etc. (c) salesperson in a store.

clev•er ['klevə] *adj.* intelligent/able to learn quickly; **c. with one's hands** = good at making things. **clev•er•ly,** *adv.* in a clever way. **clev•er•ness,** *n.* being clever.

cli•ché ['kli:ʃeɪ] *n.* saying/phrase which is frequently used.

click [klɪk] 1. *n.* short sharp sound. 2. *v.* (a) to make a short sharp sound; **to c. one's heels** = to bring the heels of one's boots together to make a noise. (b) to be surprisingly successful; **it suddenly clicked** = it was suddenly understood. (c) to press and release a button on a mouse linked to a computer in order to select a function.

cli•ent ['klaɪənt] *n.* person with whom you do business/to whom you give a service. **cli•en•tele** [kli:ɒn'tel] *n.* all the customers (of a business).

cliff [klɪf] *n.* high rock face, usu. by the sea. **cliff•hang•er,** *n.* suspense story; situation where one does not know what will happen.

cli•mac•ter•ic [klaɪ'mæktərɪk] *n.* critical point in life, when changes take place in your body.

cli•mate ['klaɪmət] *n.* general weather conditions. **cli•mat•ic** [klaɪ'mætɪk] *adj.* referring to climate. **cli•ma•tol•o•gy** [klaɪmə'tɒlədʒɪ] *n.* study of climate.

cli•max ['klaɪmæks] *n.* (*pl.* **-es**) peak/greatest amount/highest point. **cli•mac•tic** [klaɪ'mæktɪk] *adj.* referring to a climax.

climb [klaɪm] 1. *n.* act of going up; place where you go up. 2. *v.* to go up. **climb down,** *v.* to come down a mountain/a ladder. **climb•er,** *n.* person who climbs; plant which climbs. **climb•ing,** *n.* sport of climbing mountains.

clime [klaɪm] *n.* (*formal*) country.

clinch [klɪntʃ] 1. *n.* (*pl.* **-es**) (a) (*in boxing*) a position where both boxers hold on to each other. (b) *inf.* close embrace. 2. *v.* (a) (*in boxing*) to hold tight to the other boxer. (b) to settle (a deal).

cling [klɪŋ] *v.* (**clung**) to hold tight **to** (sth).

æ back, aː farm, ɒ top, aɪ pipe, aʊ how, aɪə fire, aʊə flower, ɔː bought, ɔɪ toy, e fed, eəhair, eɪ take, ə afraid, əʊ boat, əʊə lower, ɜː word, iː heap, ɪ hit, ɪə hear, uː school, ʊ book, ʌ but, b back, d dog, ð then, dʒ just, f fog, g go, h hand, j yes, k catch, l last, m mix, n nut, ŋ sing, p penny, r round, s some, ʃ short, t too, tʃ chop, θ thing, v voice, w was, z zoo, ʒ treasure

clin•ic ['klɪnɪk] *n.* specialized medical office or hospital. **clin•i•cal**, *adj.* involving direct observation and treatment of patients as opposed to experimentation and research. **c. thermometer** = thermometer for taking a person's temperature; **to take a c. view of something** = to look at it coolly. **clin•i•cal•ly**, *adv.* in a clinical way. **cli•ni•cian**, *n.* doctor who treats patients directly, as in a hospital.

clink [klɪŋk] 1. *n.* (a) noise of glasses/metal objects hitting each other. (b) *Sl.* prison. 2. *v.* (*of glasses/metal objects*) to make a noise (when hitting together).

clink•er ['klɪŋkə] *n.* hard waste material after coal has been burned.

clip [klɪp] 1. *n.* (a) piece of bent wire for attaching papers, etc., together. (b) *inf.* sharp blow; smack. (c) *inf.* **at a good c.** = quite fast. 2. *v.* (**clipped**) (a) to attach (papers) together. (b) to cut with scissors or shears. **clip•per**, *n.* (*old*) fast sailing vessel, used mainly for carrying tea. **clip•pers**, *n. pl.* small scissors; instrument with a movable blade for cutting hair. **clip•ping**, *n.* small piece cut out of a newspaper, cut off a hedge, etc.

clique [kli:k] *n.* small select group of people. **cli•quey, cliquish**, *adj.* like a clique.

clit•o•ris ['klɪtərɪs] *n.* small erectile part (in female genitals).

cloak [kləuk] 1. *n.* long outer coat with no sleeves. 2. *v.* to cover/to hide as if with a cloak. **cloak•room**, *n.* place where you leave your coat in a restaurant/theater, etc.

clob•ber ['klɒbə] *v. sl.* to hit hard, esp. many times.

cloche [klɒʃ] *n.* (a) a type of close-fitting women's hat. (b) small glass or polythene tent used in gardening for covering young plants.

clock [klɒk] 1. *n.* machine for telling the time; **alarm c.** = clock which rings a bell to wake you up; **to work right around the c.** = to work all day long. 2. *v.* **to c. in/out,** = to record your time of arrival or departure at work. **clock•wise**, *adv.* in the same direction as the hands of a clock. **clock•work**, *n.* (*no pl.*) machine which works on a spring which is wound up with a key; **like c.** = smoothly.

clod [klɒd] *n.* large lump of earth.

clog [klɒg] 1. *n.* wooden shoe. 2. *v.* (**clogged**) to block.

cloi•son•né ['klwæzɒneɪ] *n.* type of enamel decoration, where the sections of enamel are separated by little ridges of metal.

clois•ter ['klɔɪstə] *n.* (*in a monastery*) covered walk round a courtyard. **clois•tered**, *adj.* shut up (as in a monastery).

clone [kləun] *n.* plant/animal which is grown from a piece of another plant/animal, and not from a seed.

close¹ [kləus] 1. *adj.* (**-er, -est**) (a) very near (**to**); **to keep a c. watch on someone** = to watch someone attentively; **c. election** = election where the winner is separated from the loser by only a small number of votes. (b) shut. (c) stuffy. (d) very friendly. 2. *adv.* near; **she is c. to** forty. **close-fist•ed,** *adj.* miserly. **close-fit•ting,** *adj.* tight (dress). **close•ly,** *adv.* (a) attentively. (b) tightly. **close•ness,** *n.* (a) nearness. (b) stuffiness. **close-up,** *n.* photograph taken at very close range.

close² [kləuz] 1. *n.* end. 2. *v.* (a) to shut. (b) to end (an argument/a debate). **closed,** *adj.* shut; **c. shop** = system whereby a factory or business can only employ members of a certain labor union. **close down,** *v.* to shut a factory or business, etc., (permanently); to stop transmitting radio/TV programs. **close in,** *v.* (a) **the days are closing in** = the period of daylight is becoming shorter. (b) **to close in on s.o.** = to run s.o. to earth/to come close to s.o. one is chasing. **clos•ing,** 1. *adj.* final; **c. bid** = last bid at an auction. 2. *n.* shutting (of a store, etc.); **c. time** = time when a store, etc., closes. **clo•sure** ['kləuʒə] *n.* shutting.

clos•et ['klɒzɪt] 1. *n.* (a) small, private room. (b) small room or cupboard, as for clothes, linens, etc. 2. *v.* to shut oneself up **with** s.o.

clot [klɒt] 1. *n.* lump of solidified blood, etc. 2. *v.* (**clotted**) to form lumps; **clotted cream** = cream which has been heated until it solidifies.

cloth [klɒθ] *n.* (a) piece of woven material. (b) woven material.

clothe [kləuð] *v.* to dress. **clothes** [kləuðz] *n. pl.* things you wear; **c. brush** = brush for cleaning clothes; **c. line** = long rope for hanging wet clothes to dry; **c. horse** = wooden or metal frame for hanging clothes to air or dry; **c. pin** = small plastic or wooden clip for attaching wet clothes to a clothes line. **cloth•ing** ['kləuðɪŋ] *n.* (*no pl.*) clothes.

cloud [klaud] 1. *n.* mass of vapor/smoke (in the air); **under a c.** = (a) gloomy; (b) unpopular with the authorities. 2. *v.* to hide with a cloud. **cloud•burst,** *n.* sudden downpour of rain. **cloud-capped,** *adj.* (mountain) topped with clouds. **cloud•i•ness,** *n.* being cloudy. **cloud•less,** *adj.* (sky) with no clouds. **cloud•y,** *adj.* (**-ier, -iest**) covered with clouds; not clear/not transparent.

clout [klaut] 1. *n.* (a) blow (with the fist). (b) *inf.* power/influence. 2. *v.* to give (s.o.) a blow with the fist.

clove [kləuv] *n.* (a) spice formed by small dried flower buds of a tropical tree. (b) piece of garlic. **clove hitch,** *n.* type of knot.

clo•ven ['kləuvn] *adj.* split.

clo•ver ['kləuvə] *n.* common weed, used as fodder for cattle; **to be in c.** = to live very comfortably; **c. leaf intersection** = crossroads formed by two highways and their linking roads, which when seen from above looks like the leaf of clover.

clown [klaʊn] 1. *n.* (a) man who makes people laugh in a circus. (b) stupid fool. 2. *v.* (**about, around**) to play the fool.

cloy [klɔɪ] *v.* to be sickly sweet.

club [klʌb] 1. *n.* (a) large stick; **golf c.** = long stick with which you hit the ball when playing golf. (b) one of the four suits in a pack of cards. (c) group of people who allow others to join them (usu. on payment of a fee); **golf c.; drama c.** 2. *v.* (**clubbed**) (a) to hit with a club. (b) to unite; join **together. club•foot,** *n.* deformed foot. **club•house,** *n.* house where members of a club meet.

cluck [klʌk] *v.* (*of hen*) to make a low noise in the throat.

clue [kluː] *n.* information which helps you solve a mystery/puzzle; **I haven't a c.** = I do not know at all. **clue•less,** *adj. inf.* stupid.

clump [klʌmp] 1. *n.* group of shrubs, trees, etc. 2. *v.* to move making a dull noise.

clum•sy ['klʌmzɪ] *adj.* (**-ier, -iest**) not graceful; frequently breaking things. **clum•si•ly,** *adv.* in a clumsy way. **clum•si•ness,** *n.* being clumsy.

clung [klʌŋ] *v. see* **cling.**

clunk [klʌŋk] *n.* noise of heavy metal objects hitting each other.

clus•ter ['klʌstə] 1. *n.* group of small objects together. 2. *v.* to group (**together**).

clutch [klʌtʃ] 1. *n.* (*pl.* **-es**) (a) several eggs laid together in a nest. (b) clasp; **into his clutches** = into his hands. (c) mechanism for changing the gears in a car; pedal which works the clutch; **to let in the c.** = to make the gears connect; **to let out the c.** = to disengage the engine from the gears. 2. *v.* to grab.

clut•ter ['klʌtə] 1. *n.* mass of things left lying about. 2. *v.* to fill (a room) with a mass of things.

cm *abbrev. for* centimeter.

co- [kəʊ] *prefix meaning* together.

co. [kəʊ, 'kʌmpənɪ] *abbrev. for* company.

Co *symbol for* cobalt.

CO ['siː'əʊ] commanding officer.

c/o *abbrev. for* care of.

coach [kəʊtʃ] 1. *n.* (*pl.* **-es**) (a) large bus for long distance traveling. (b) passenger car (on a train). (c) person who trains sportsmen, etc. 2.

v. (a) to train (sportsmen). (b) to give private lessons to.

co•ag•u•late [kəʊ'ægjʊleɪt] *v.* to form into lumps/to cake. **co•ag•u•la•tion** [kəʊægjʊ'leɪʃn] *n.* forming into lumps/caking.

coal [kəʊl] *n.* black mineral used as fuel; **coal-fired boiler** = boiler which is heated by coal. **coal•field,** *n.* area of coal underground. **coal•mine,** *n.* mine where coal is dug. **coal•min•er,** *n.* person who mines coal. **coal scut•tle,** *n.* metal receptacle for keeping and carrying coal.

co•a•lesce [kəʊə'les] *v.* to join together. **co•a•les•cence,** *n.* joining together.

co•a•li•tion [kəʊə'lɪʃn] *n.* joining together; combination of political parties forming a government.

coarse [kɔːs] *adj.* (**-er, -est**) (a) not fine/rough (laugh, etc.). (b) rude. **coarse•ly,** *adv.* in a coarse way. **coars•en,** *v.* to make coarse. **coarse•ness,** *n.* being coarse.

coast [kəʊst] 1. *n.* land by the sea; **from c. to c.** = across an area of land from one sea to another. 2. *v.* (a) to ride a vehicle without using the engine or the pedals. (b) to sail along the coast. **coast•al,** *adj.* referring to the coast. **coast•er,** *n.* (a) ship which sails from port to port along the coast. (b) flat dish or small mat for standing a bottle/glass on. **coast guard,** *n.* member of a government organization which patrols a country's coast (watching out for wrecks/smugglers, etc.). **coast•line,** *n.* line of the coast.

coat [kəʊt] 1. *n.* (a) long piece of outdoor clothing which covers the top part of the body. (b) fur of an animal. (c) layer (of paint, etc.). (d) **c. of arms** = symbolic design on the shield of a family/town, etc. 2. *v.* to cover (sth) with a layer. **coat hang•er,** *n.* piece of wood/wire/plastic on which you hang clothes. **coat hook,** *n.* hook (on a wall/door) for hanging a coat. **coat•ing,** *n.* covering (of paint, etc.). **coat•rack,** *n.* pole where several coats can be hung.

coax [kəʊks] *v.* to persuade (s.o.) to do sth.

co•ax•i•al [kəʊ'æksɪəl] *adj.* **c. cable** = electric cable where several wires are laid parallel to each other.

cob [kɒb] *n.* (a) seed head (of corn); (b) male swan. (c) short horse.

co•balt ['kəʊbɔːlt] *n.* (*element:* Co) white metal; blue color obtained from the metal.

cob•ble ['kɒbl] *v.* to put things **together**

roughly. **cobbled,** *adj.* covered with cobble-stones. **cob•ble•(stone),** *n.* rounded stone formerly used for paving streets.

cob•bler ['kɒblə] *n.* person who mends shoes.

co•bra ['kəubrə] *n.* large poisonous tropical snake.

cob•web ['kɒbweb] *n.* net of fine thread made by a spider.

co•caine [kə'keɪn] *n.* painkilling drug, also used as a stimulant.

coc•cus ['kɒkəs] *n.* (*pl.* **cocci**) ball-shaped bacterium.

coc•cyx ['kɒksɪks] *n.* (*pl.* **-es**) small bone at the end of the spine.

coch•i•neal [kɒtʃɪ'ni:l] *n.* red coloring used in cooking.

coch•le•a ['kɒtʃlɪə] *n.* spiral tube in the inner ear.

cock [kɒk] **1.** *n.* (a) male bird (esp. a domestic chicken); rooster. (b) tap. (c) hammer on a gun which fires the cartridge. **2.** *v.* (a) to prick up (your ears). (b) to put (your head) to one side. (c) to set (a gun) ready for firing. **cock-a-doo•dle doo!** *inter. showing* the noise made by a cock. **cock•crow,** *n.* early morning.

cock•ade [kɒ'keɪd] *n.* rosette of ribbons worn on a hat.

cock•a•too [kɒkə'tu:] *n.* type of large parrot.

cock•chaf•er ['kɒktʃeɪfə] *n.* large beetle.

cock•er ['kɒkə] *n.* type of spaniel.

cock•er•el ['kɒkrəl] *n.* young cock.

cock-eyed ['kɒkaɪd] *adj. inf.* stupid/odd (idea).

cock•le ['kɒkl] **1.** *n.* small edible shellfish with a double shell. **2.** *v.* (*of paper*) to curl up/wrinkle.

cock•ney ['kɒknɪ] *adj. & n.* (person) who comes from the east part of London; way of speaking of a person from the east part of London.

cock•pit ['kɒkpɪt] *n.* place where the pilot sits in an aircraft or boat.

cock•roach ['kɒkrəutʃ] *n.* (*pl.* **-es**) large brown or black beetle.

cock•sure [kɒk'ʃuə] *adj.* very sure/self-confident.

cock•tail ['kɒkteɪl] *n.* mixed alcoholic drink; **c. lounge** = lounge or room where drinks are served in a hotel, restaurant, etc. **fruit c./shrimp c.** = mixture of fruit/shrimp in salad; **Molotov c.** = grenade made of a bottle of fuel and a fuse which you light before throwing.

cock•y ['kɒkɪ] *adj.* unpleasantly proud and conceited.

co•coa ['kəukəu] *n.* (*no pl.*) brown powder ground from the seeds of the cacao tree, used for making a drink; drink made from this.

co•co•nut ['kəukənʌt] *n.* large nut from a palm tree; **c. matting** = rough matting made from the outer fibers of a coconut.

co•coon [kə'ku:n] **1.** *n.* protective case of thread made by a larva before it turns into a moth or butterfly. **2.** *v.* to wrap (sth) up for protection (**in**).

cod [kɒd] *n.* (*pl.* **cod**) large sea fish; **c. liver oil** = oil from the livers of cod.

c.o.d. [si:əu'di:] *abbreviation for* cash on delivery.

co•da ['kəudə] *n.* last part of a piece of music.

cod•dle ['kɒdl] *v.* (a) to spoil/to pamper (s.o.). (b) to cook (eggs) in warm, but not boiling, water.

code [kəud] **1.** *n.* (a) set of laws/of rules of behavior; (b) secret signs agreed in advance for sending messages; **the Morse c.** = series of dots and dashes used for sending telegraphic messages; **c. word** = secret agreed word. **2.** *v.* to write (a message) in code.

co•deine ['kəudi:n] *n.* drug used to relieve pain and produce sleep.

co•dex ['kəudeks] *n.* very ancient manuscript of the Bible.

codg•er ['kɒdʒə] *n. inf.* man.

cod•i•cil ['kəudɪsɪl] *n.* additional clause to a will.

cod•i•fy ['kəudɪfaɪ] *v.* to write (rules of conduct/laws) as a code. **cod•i•fi•ca•tion** [kəudɪfɪ'keɪʃn] *n.* act of codifying.

co-di•rect•or [kəudaɪ'rektə] *n.* one of two or more directors.

cod•ling ['kɒdlɪŋ] *n.* small apple used for cooking; **c. moth,** moth whose larvae feed on apples.

co-ed•u•ca•tion•al [kəuedju'keɪʃənl] *adj.* (school) where boys and girls are taught together. **co-ed.** **1.** *adj.* co-educational. **2.** *n.* girl who goes to a co-educational school.

co•ef•fi•cient [kəuɪ'fɪʃənt] *n.* factor in mathematics.

coe•la•canth ['si:ləkænθ] *n.* prehistoric type of fish which is not extinct.

coel•i•ac ['si:lɪæk] *adj.* referring to the abdomen.

co•erce [kəu'ɜ:s] *v.* to force. **co•er•cion** [kəu'ɜ:ʃn] *n.* force. **co•er•cive,** *adj.* using force.

co•e•val [kəu'i:vəl] *adj.* belonging to the same generation.

co•ex•ist [kəuɪg'zɪst] *v.* to exist/to live together. **co•ex•ist•ence,** *n.* living together; **peaceful c.** = where countries with different types of government exist side by side in peace. **co•ex•ist•ent,** *adj.* living at the same time (as sth else).

cof•fee ['kɒfɪ] *n.* (a) seeds of a tropical plant, roasted and ground to make a drink. (b) drink made from these beans; **instant c.** = powdered extract of coffee which makes a drink when hot water is poured on it; **c. table** = low table for putting cups/glasses, etc., on; **c. table book** = large colorful art book. **cof•fee shop**, *n.* small restaurant (often in a hotel) serving light meals and snacks.

cof•fers ['kɒfəz] *n. pl.* money chests. **cof•fer dam**, *n.* watertight wall which allows work to be done on the bed of a river or the sea.

cof•fin ['kɒfɪn] *n.* long wooden box in which a dead person is buried or cremated.

cog [kɒg] *n.* tooth (on a toothed wheel). **cog rail•way**, *n.* railway with engines driven by a toothed wheel connecting with a central toothed rail. **cog•wheel**, *n.* wheel with teeth round the edge which fit into the teeth on another wheel and make it turn.

co•gent ['kəʊdʒənt] *adj.* valid (argument); powerful (reason). **co•gen•cy**, *n.* being cogent.

cog•i•tate ['kɒdʒɪteɪt] *v.* to ponder/to think deeply. **cog•i•ta•tion** [kɒdʒɪ'teɪʃn] *n.* deep thought.

co•gnac ['kɒnjæk] *n.* French brandy.

cog•nate ['kɒgneɪt] *adj.* (*formal*) with the same origin.

cog•ni•zance ['kɒgnɪzəns] *n.* knowledge (of a fact). **cog•ni•zant**, *adj.* (of) knowing/being aware.

co•gno•scen•ti [kɒnjə'ʃentɪ] *n. pl.* specialists in the arts.

co•hab•it [kəʊ'hæbɪt] *v.* to live together as man and wife, esp. when not married.

co•here [kəʊ'hɪə] *v.* to hold together; to form a whole. **co•her•ence**, *n.* being coherent. **co•her•ent**, *adj.* clear/logical (ideas). **co•her•ent•ly**, *adv.* clearly/logically. **co•he•sion** [kəʊ'hiːʒn] *n.* sticking together. **co•he•sive** [kəʊ'hiːsɪv] *adj.* which stick together.

co•hort ['kəʊhɔːt] *n.* division of a Roman army; large group of people.

coif•fure [kwɑː'fjʊə] *n.* hairstyle. **coif•feur** [kwɑ'fɜː] *n.* hairdresser.

coil [kɔɪl] 1. *n.* (a) roll (of rope); one loop (in sth coiled). (b) **electric c.** = wire wrapped round a shaft which conducts electricity. (c) contraceptive device. 2. *v.* to roll up; to make loops.

coin [kɔɪn] 1. *n.* piece of metal money. 2. *v.* (a) to strike/to produce (metal money). (b) to invent (a new word). **coin•age**, *n.* (a) system of money (of a country). (b) new word.

co•in•cide [kəʊɪn'saɪd] *v.* to happen (by chance) at the same time as sth else. **co•in•ci•dence** [kəʊ'ɪnsɪdəns] *n.* two things

which happen at the same time by chance. **co•in•ci•den•tal** [kəʊɪnsɪ'dentl] *adj.* happening by coincidence.

coir ['kɔɪə] *n.* coconut fiber.

co•i•tion, coitus [kəʊ'ɪʃn, 'kəʊɪtəs] *n.* (*formal*) act of sexual intercourse.

coke [kəʊk] *n.* (a) (*no pl.*) fuel processed from coal, which gives a very fierce heat. (b) *inf.* Coca-Cola/trademark for a type of soft drink. (c) *inf.* cocaine.

col [kɒl] *n.* high pass between mountains.

col•an•der ['kɒləndə] *n.* bowl with holes in it for draining water from pasta, fruit, or vegetables.

cold [kəʊld] 1. *adj.* (-er, -est) (a) not hot; **he got c. feet** = he was not brave enough to continue; **c. chisel** = hard steel chisel; **c. war** = fight for power between countries without actually using weapons. (b) unfriendly (reception, manner). 2. *n.* (a) state of being cold; **left out in the c.** = left on one side. (b) infectious illness when you sneeze and cough; **to catch a c.** **cold-blood•ed**, *adj.* (a) (animal such as fish) with blood whose temperature varies with its surroundings. (b) with no feelings. **cold•ly**, *adv.* in an unfriendly way. **cold•ness**, *n.* state of being cold. **cold-shoul•der**, *v.* to be deliberately unfriendly to (s.o.).

cole•slaw ['kəʊlslɔː] *n.* cabbage salad.

col•ic ['kɒlɪk] *n.* severe pain in the abdomen. **co•li•tis** [kə'laɪtɪs] *n.* inflammation of the colon.

col•lab•o•rate [kə'læbəreɪt] *v.* to work together. **col•lab•o•ra•tion** [kəlæbə'reɪʃn] *n.* collaborating. **col•lab•o•ra•tor**, *n.* person who collaborates.

col•lage [kɒ'lɑːʒ] *n.* picture made from pieces of paper, etc., which are stuck on to a backing.

col•la•gen ['kɒlədʒən] *n.* fibers which form tissue.

col•lapse [kə'læps] 1. *n.* falling down/ruin. 2. *v.* to fall down suddenly. **col•laps•i•ble**, *adj.* which can be folded up.

col•lar ['kɒlə] 1. *n.* part of clothing which goes around the neck. 2. *v. inf.* to grab/to catch (s.o.). **col•lar•bone**, *n.* bone from the top of the ribs to the shoulder blade.

col•late [kə'leɪt] *v.* to compare texts, etc. **col•la•tion** [kə'leɪʃn] *n.* (a) (*formal*) light cold lunch. (b) comparison of texts. **col•la•tor**, *n.* someone who compares texts.

col•lat•er•al [kə'lætərəl] *adj. & n.* parallel; (security) which is used as an additional guarantee.

col•league ['kɒliːg] *n.* person who works with you.

col•lect 1. ['kɒlɪkt] *n.* short prayer used on a particular day. 2. [kə'lekt] *v.* (a) to fetch and bring together. (b) to gather money for charity. (c) **to call c.** = to ask the person you are phoning to pay for the call. **col•lect•ed,** *adj.* calm/not flustered. **col•lec•tion,** *n.* (a) group of objects brought together. (b) gathering of money; money which has been gathered; **to take a c. for sth. col•lec•tive,** *adj.* brought together; **c. farm** = farm where everything belongs to and is run by the workers on behalf of the state; **c. bargaining** = negotiations for new salaries carried out between union and management. **col•lec•tive•ly,** *adv.* all together. **col•lec•tor,** *n.* person who collects; **ticket c.** = person who takes tickets from railroad passengers, etc.

col•leen [kɒ'liːn] *n.* (in Ireland) girl.

col•lege ['kɒlɪdʒ] *n.* institution of higher education which gives degrees for specialized study. **col•le•giate** [kə'liːdʒɪət] *adj.* belonging to/referring to a college.

col•lide [kə'laɪd] *v.* **to c. with** = to bump into.

col•lie ['kɒlɪ] *n.* type of sheepdog.

col•li•sion [kə'lɪʒən] *n.* bumping into sth.

col•lo•ca•tion [kɒlə'keɪʃn] *n.* (formal) group.

col•loid ['kɒlɔɪd] *n.* viscuous liquid.

col•lo•qui•al [kə'ləʊkwɪəl] *adj.* as is commonly spoken; conversational. **col•lo•qui•al•ism,** *n.* colloquial expression. **col•lo•qui•al•ly,** *adv.* as in conversational speech.

col•lu•sion [kə'luːʒn] *n.* secret illegal agreement.

co•lon ['kəʊlən] *n.* (a) large part of the intestines. (b) punctuation sign (:) to show a break in a sentence.

colo•nel ['kɜːnl] *n.* military officer above lieutenant-colonel.

col•on•nade [kɒlə'neɪd] *n.* row of columns.

col•o•ny ['kɒlənɪ] *n.* (a) territory ruled by another country. (b) group of animals/humans living together. **co•lo•ni•al** [kə'ləʊnɪəl] *adj.* referring to a colony. **co•lo•ni•al•ism,** *n.* exploitation of colonies. **co•lo•ni•al•ist,** *n.* person who advocates colonialism. **col•o•nist** ['kɒlənɪst] *n.* person sent from the home country to settle in a colony. **col•o•ni•za•tion** [kɒlənar'zeɪʒn] *n.* act of making a colony out of a territory. **col•o•nize,** *v.* to occupy (land) and make it a colony.

col•o•phon ['kɒləfən] *n.* printed device which identifies a publisher or printer.

col•or *Brit.* **col•our** ['kʌlə] 1. *n.* (a) shade/tint which an object has in light; **c. TV** = not black and white; **c. scheme** = arrangement of colors (as in the furnishing of a room); (b) shade (of a person's skin); **c. bar** = bar to s.o. because of the color of his/her skin. (c) paint; **water colors** = paints which have to be mixed with water. (d) **color(s)** = flag; **with flying colors** = with great success; **in his true colors** = as he really is. 2. *v.* to paint with color; to make (sth) colored. **col•or•ant,** *n.* coloring material. **col•or•a•tion;** *n.* coloring. **col•or-blind,** *adj.* unable to distinguish same colors (usu. red and green). **col•or-blind•ness,** *n.* being color-blind. **col•ored,** (a) *adj.* (illustration) in color. (b) *adj. & n.* (person) whose skin is not white. **col•or•ful,** *adj.* brightly colored; picturesque/full of local color. **col•or•ing,** *n.* way in which sth is colored; substance which gives color to sth (such as food). **color•less,** *adj.* pale/uninteresting.

Col•o•ra•do bee•tle [kɒlərɑː'dəʊ'biːtl] *n.* striped beetle which attacks potato plants.

co•los•sal [kə'lɒsl] *adj.* (a) very large/huge. (b) splendid. **co•los•sal•ly,** *adv.* greatly/enormously. **co•los•sus,** *n.* (pl. -es) huge statue; huge man.

co•los•to•my [kɒ'lɒstəmɪ] *n.* operation to attach a colon to an artificial hole in the belly.

col•our ['kʌlə] *n. & v. Brit. see* **col•or.**

colt [kəʊlt] *n.* young male horse. **colts•foot,** *n.* wild plant with small yellow flowers.

col•ter ['kəʊltə] *n.* blade of a plow.

co•lum•bine ['kɒləmbaɪn] *n.* garden plant with delicate pink or blue flowers.

col•umn ['kɒləm] *n.* (a) tall pillar. (b) thing which is round and long; **spinal c.** = backbone; **steering c.** = shaft with a wheel on top for steering an aircraft/a car. (c) line of soldiers; **fifth c.** = subversive elements working behind the enemy lines to weaken the morale of the population. (d) long thin block of printing on a page; regular article in a newspaper. **col•um•nist** ['kɒləmɪst] *n.* journalist who writes regularly for a paper.

co•ma ['kəʊmə] *n.* state of unconsciousness. **com•a•tose** ['kəʊmətəʊs] *adj.* (a) in a coma. (b) sleepy/half awake.

comb [kəʊm] 1. *n.* (a) long-toothed instrument for disentangling hair. (b) red crest on the head of a bird (such as a cock). (c) honeycomb. 2. *v.* (a) to disentangle (hair). (b) to search (an area).

com•bat ['kɒmbæt] 1. *n.* fighting. 2. *v.* to fight. **com•bat•ant** ['kɒmbətənt] *adj. & n.* (person) who takes part in a fight. **com•bat•ive,** *adj.* quarrelsome/argumentative.

com•bine 1. *n.* ['kɒmbaɪn] (a) financial/commercial group. (b) **c. (harvester)** = large machine for cutting and threshing grain. 2. *v.* [kəm'baɪn] to join together.

com•bi•na•tion [kɒmbɪ'neɪʃn] *n.* (a) several things joined together. (b) series of numbers which open a lock; **a c. lock.** (c) long one-piece winter underwear.

com•bus•tion [kəm'bʌstʃən] *n.* burning.

com•bus•ti•ble [kəm'bʌstɪbl] *adj. & n.* (substance) which can easily catch fire and burn.

come [kʌm] *v.* **(came; has come)** (a) to arrive here; **c. and see us; c. up to my room.** (b) to happen; **how does the door c. to be open?** *inf.* **how c.?** = why/how did it happen? (c) to add up to; **it comes to $5; c. to that** = by the way/while we are talking of that. (d) **to c.** = in the future. **come a•cross,** *v.* to find. **come af•ter,** *v.* to follow. **come a•long,** *v.* to arrive. **come back,** *v.* to return. **come•back,** *n.* (a) retort. (b) return (of a singer/sportsman) after retirement. **come by,** *v.* to obtain. **come down,** *v.* to descend. **come•down,** *n.* humiliation. **come into,** *v.* (a) to enter. (b) to inherit (money). **come off,** *v.* (a) to fall off. (b) to result; **he came off badly** = the result was bad for him. **come on,** *v.* (a) to hurry. (b) to arrive. **come out,** *v.* (a) to move outside. (b) (*of photograph, etc.*) to result/to show. (c) **to c. out (on strike)** = to strike. **come o•ver,** *v.* (a) to cross. (b) to start to feel; **what has c. over him?** = what is the matter with him? **com•er,** *n.* person who comes; **late comers; all comers. come a•round,** *v.* (a) to visit. (b) to recover from unconsciousness. (c) to change one's way of thinking; to agree with s.o. else. **come to,** *v.* to recover (from unconsciousness). **come•up•pance,** *n. inf.* **he got his c.** = he was punished. **com•ing,** 1. *adj.* approaching. 2. *n.* arrival; **comings and goings.**

com•e•dy ['kɒmədɪ] *n.* play or movie which makes you laugh; funny aspect (of an event). **co•me•di•an** [kə'miːdɪən] *n.* man who tells jokes to make people laugh. **co•me•di•enne** [kəmiːdɪ'en] *n.* woman who tells jokes to make people laugh.

come•ly ['kʌmlɪ] *adj.* attractive (woman).

co•mes•ti•bles [kʌ'mestɪbəlz] *n. pl.* (*formal*) food.

com•et ['kɒmɪt] *n.* body which moves visibly through space with a bright tail.

com•fort ['kʌmfət] 1. *n.* (a) thing which helps to relive suffering. (b) ease of living; **c. station**

= public toilet. 2. *v.* to relieve the suffering of (s.o. who is miserable, etc.). **com•fort•a•ble,** *adj.* soft/relaxing, giving ease. **com•fort•a•bly,** *adv.* in a soft/relaxing way; **c. off** = having plenty of money. **com•fort•er,** *n.* (a) person who comforts. (b) long woolen scarf. (c) bed covering made of a large bag full of feathers. **com•fort•ing,** *adj.* consoling. **com•fort•less,** *adj.* harsh/hard. **com•fy,** *adj.* (-ier, -iest) *inf.* comfortable.

com•frey ['kʌmfrɪ] *n.* herb, used both medicinally and also to make compost.

com•ic ['kɒmɪk] 1. *adj.* funny, amusing. 2. *n.* (a) person who tells jokes to make people laugh. (b) (*usu.* **comics**) children's paper with cartoon stories. **com•i•cal,** *adj.* funny. **com•i•cal•ly,** *adv.* in a funny way.

com•ma ['kɒmə] *n.* punctuation mark (,) showing a break in a sentence around a clause; **inverted commas (" ")** = quotation marks

com•mand [kə'mɑːnd] 1. *n.* (a) order; **c. performance** = play, motion picture, etc. put on at the command of a monarch. **second-in-c.** = officer/person directly under the main commander/director; **in c. of** = in charge of. (b) knowledge (of a language). 2. *v.* (a) to order. (b) to be in charge of. (c) to demand (a price). **com•man•dant** [kɒmən'dænt] *n.* officer in charge of a military base, etc. **com•man•deer** [kɒmən'dɪə] *v.* to order that (sth) should be given over to the armed forces. **com•mand•er** [kə'mɑːndə] *n.* officer in charge (of a military unit/ship); rank in the navy below captain. **com•mand•ing,** *adj.* in command. **com•mand•ment,** *n.* rule; **the Ten Commandments** = rules given by God to Moses. **com•man•do,** *n.* (*pl.* **-os**) group troops specially trained to raid inside enemy territory; member of such a group.

com•mem•o•rate [kə'meməreɪt] *v.* to celebrate (the memory of something/a special occasion, etc.). **com•mem•o•ra•tion** [kəmemə'reɪʃn] *n.* commemorating. **com•mem•o•ra•tive** [kə'memərətɪv] *adj.* which commemorates.

com•mence [kə'mens] *v.* (*formal*) to begin. **com•mence•ment,** *n.* (a) beginning. (b) day when degrees are awarded at a school, college, or university.

com•mend [kə'mend] *v.* (*formal*) to praise. **com•mend•a•ble,** *adj.* praiseworthy. **com•mend•a•bly,** *adv.* in a praiseworthy

---

æ **back,** ɑ: **farm,** ɒ: **top,** aɪ **pipe,** aʊ **how,** aɪə **fire,** aʊə **flower,** ɔ: **bought,** ɔɪ **toy,** e **fed,** eəhair, eɪ **take,** ə **afraid,** əʊ **boat,** əʊə **lower,** vː **word,** iː **heap,** ɪ **hit,** ɪə **hear,** u: **school,** ʊ **book,** ʌ **but,** b **back,** d **dog,** ð **then,** dʒ **just,** f **fog,** g **go,** h **hand,** j **yes,** k **catch,** l **last,** m **mix,** n **nut,** ŋ **sing,** p **penny,** r **round,** s **some,** ʃ **short,** t **too,** tʃ **chop,** θ **thing,** v **voice,** w **was,** z **zoo,** ʒ **treasure**

way. **com•men•da•tion** [kɒmen'deɪʃn] *n.* official praise. **com•mend•a•to•ry** [kə-'mendətri] *adj.* which praises.

com•men•su•rate [kə'mensjurət] *adj.* **c. with** = in proportion to.

com•ment ['kɒment] 1. *n.* remark/what you feel about something; **no c.** = I refuse to discuss the matter. 2. *v.* to make remarks (**on**). **com•men•tar•y**, *n.* (a) remarks about a book, etc. (b) spoken report on a sports event. **com•men•ta•tor**, *n.* person who reports on events on the radio or television.

com•merce ['kɒmɜːs] *n.* business transactions; **chamber of c.** = association of businessmen. **com•mer•cial** [kə'mɜːʃl] 1. *adj.* dealing with business; **c. vehicle** = vehicle used for business purposes. 2. *n.* piece of publicity of television. **com•mer•cial•i•za•tion** [kəmɜːʃəlaɪ'zeɪʃn] *n.* making sth into a business proposition. **com•mer•cial•ize**, *v.* to make into a business proposition. **com•mer•cial•ly**, *adv.* in a commercial way.

com•mis•er•ate [kə'mɪzəreɪt] *v.* to sympathize (**with** s.o.). **com•mis•er•a•tion** [kəmɪzə'reɪʃn] *n.* sympathizing.

com•mis•sar [kɒmɪ'sɑː] *n.* political leader (in a communist state).

com•mis•sar•i•at [kɒmɪ'seərɪət] *n.* department (esp. in the army) dealing with the supply of food.

com•mis•sion [kə'mɪʃn] 1. *n.* (a) group of people which investigates problems of national importance. (b) document naming someone an officer. (c) order for sth to be made/to be used; **out of c.** = not in working order. (d) percentage of sales value given to a salesperson. 2. *v.* (a) to authorize (s.o.) to be an officer/to authorize (an artist/architect, etc.) to do a piece of work; to put (a ship) into commission. (b) to authorize (a piece of work) to be done. **com•mis•sion•aire** [kəmɪʃə-'neə] *n. Brit.* doorkeeper (in a hotel/office building). **com•mis•sion•er** [kə'mɪʃnə] *n.* (a) representative of authority; **c. of police** = highest-ranking police officer; (b) member of a commission.

com•mit [kə'mɪt] *v.* (**committed**) (a) to carry out (a crime). (b) to put in official custody; **to c. to prison** = to send to prison. (c) **to c. oneself** = to promise to do sth. **com•mit•ted**, *adj.* firmly believing in (sth). **com•mit•ment**, *n.* (a) promise. (b) agreement to do sth. (c) promise to pay money. **com•mit•tal**, *n.* act of committing.

com•mit•tee [kə'mɪtɪ] *n.* official group of people who organize or discuss on behalf of a larger body; **to be on a c.** = to be a member of it.

com•mode [kə'məʊd] *n.* (a) chest of drawers. (b) chair with a chamberpot in the seat.

com•mo•di•ous [kə'məʊdɪəs] *adj.* spacious/large (room/house, etc.).

com•mod•i•ty [kə'mɒdɪtɪ] *n.* merchandise; thing sold; **basic commodities** = basic foodstuffs and raw materials.

com•mo•dore ['kɒmədɔː] *n.* (a) rank in the navy above captain. (b) person who directs a yacht club.

com•mon ['kɒmən] 1. *adj.* (**-er, -est**) (a) belonging to everyone/to the public in general; **it is c. knowledge** = everyone knows it. (b) belonging to two or more people; **we have two things in c.**; **C. Market** (formerly) = European Union. (c) ordinary/which happens frequently. (d) vulgar/of the lower class. 2. *n.* land which belongs to a community. **com•mon•er**, *n.* ordinary citizen/not a noble. **com•mon law**, *n.* law which is derived from decisions of courts, rather than from statutes; **c.-l. wife** = woman who lives with a man as his wife, without being married to him. **com•mon•ly**, *adv.* frequently. **com•mon•place**, *adj. & n.* (thing) which happens frequently. **com•mons**, *n.* **the (House of) C.** = the lower (elected) house of the British parliament. **com•mon•sense**, *n.* ordinary good sense. **com•mon•wealth**, *n.* republic; group of states; **the (British) C.** = association of countries, most of which were formerly colonies of Britain but are now independent; **C. of Independent States** = association of countries that were formerly part of the Soviet Union.

com•mo•tion [kə'məʊʃən] *n.* confusion/trouble.

com•mune 1. *n.* ['kɒmjuːn] group of people who work together sharing everything. 2. *v.* [kə'mjuːn] to be in touch (**with** s.o./sth) in spirit. **com•mu•nal** [kə'mjuːnəl] *adj.* (property) held in common/belonging to several people. **com•mu•nal•ly**, *adv.* done by several people together.

com•mu•ni•cate [kə'mjuːnɪkeɪt] *v.* (**with**) to pass information to s.o./to be in touch with s.o. **com•mu•ni•ca•ble**, *adj.* which can be passed on to s.o. **com•mu•ni•cant**, *n.* person who takes Holy Communion. **com•mu•ni•ca•tion** [kəmjuːnɪ'keɪʃn] *n.* act of communicating/passing of information. **com•mu•ni•ca•tive** [kə'mjuːnɪkətɪv] *adj.* talkative; (person) who is willing to give information. **com•mun•ion**, *n.* (a) fellowship with s.o.; (b) **Holy C.** = central Christian religious ceremony, celebrating the Last Supper. **com•mu•ni•qué** [kə'mjuːnɪkeɪ] *n.* official news item given to the press.

com•mu•nism ['kɒmjunɪzəm] *n.* political

doctrine whereby the state owns all industry and land. **com•mu•nist.** 1. *adj.* referring to communism. 2. *n.* (a) person who believes in communism. (b) member of the Communist Party.

com•mu•ni•ty [kə'mju:nɪtɪ] *n.* (a) group of people living in one place; **an urban c.** = a town and its inhabitants; **c. center** = sports/arts center belonging to a town; **the European Economic C.,** *n.* organization linking several European countries for purposes of trade. **religious c.** = group of monks or nuns. (b) the population as a whole. (c) group of organisms living in an area.

com•mute [kə'mju:t] *v.* (a) to reduce (a legal penalty). (b) to travel to work every day for some distance. **com•mut•a•ble,** *adj.* which can be commuted. **com•mu•ta•tion** [kɒmju'teɪʃn] *n.* act of commuting a sentence. **com•mut•er,** *n.* person who travels to work every day for some distance; **c. train** = train for commuters.

com•pact 1. *n.* ['kɒmpækt] (a) agreement. (b) small box for carrying face powder. (c) small car. 2. *adj* [kəm'pækt] small; tight/close together. 3. *v.* to make (sth) compact. **com•pact disk,** *n.* metal recording disk, which can hold a larger amount of music than a plastic record, and which is read by a laser in a special player. **com•pact•ly,** *adv.* tightly/close together.

com•pan•ion [kəm'pænjən] *n.* (a) person who travels or lives with s.o. (b) handbook; **travel companion** = travel handbook. **com•pan•ion•a•ble,** *adj.* friendly. **com•pan•ion•ship,** *n.* friendship. **com•pan•ion•way,** *n.* stairway on a ship.

com•pa•ny ['kʌmpənɪ] *n.* (a) being together with other people; **he is good c.** = he is an entertaining companion; **to part c.** = to split up; **to get into bad c.** = to get in with bad companions. (b) group of soldiers within a battalion; crew of a ship. (c) **theatrical c.** = group of actors who play together. (d) (*usu. written* **Co.** *in names*) commercial or industrial company.

com•pare [kəm'peə] *v.* to put two things side by side to see how they differ; **he compared our bread to a lump of concrete** = he said it was like a lump of concrete; **his work doesn't c. very well with his brother's** = is not as good as his brother's. **com•pa•ra•bil•i•ty** [kɒmpərə-'bɪlɪtɪ] *n.* being comparable. **com•pa•ra•ble** ['kɒmprəbl] *adj.* which can

be compared. **com•par•a•tive** [kəm-'pærətɪv] 1. *adj.* relative. 2. *n.* form of an adjective/adverb showing an increase in level; "better" and "more stupidly" are the comparatives of "good" and "stupidly." **com•par•a•tive•ly,** *adv.* more or less; relatively. **com•par•i•son,** *n.* act of comparing; **there is no c.** = you cannot compare them, one is so much better than the other.

com•part•ment [kəm'pɑ:tmənt] *n.* division inside a box; separate section in a railroad car/in a ship.

com•pass ['kʌmpəs] *n.* (*pl.* **-es**) (a) device which indicates the north by means of a needle. (b) **a pair of compasses** = instrument for drawing a circle. (c) scope/range.

com•pas•sion [kəm'pæʃn] *n.* pity; **to have c. on s.o.** = to take pity on s.o. **com•pas•sion•ate,** *adj.* merciful/pitying. **com•pas•sion fa•tigue,** *n.* indifference towards a humanitarian crisis/disaster due to previous overexposure to such situations.

com•pat•i•ble [kəm'pætəbl] *adj.* able to fit with sth. **com•pat•i•bil•i•ty** [kəmpætə-'bɪlɪtɪ] *n.* ability to fit together.

com•pa•tri•ot [kəm'pætrɪət] *n.* person who comes from the same country.

com•pel [kəm'pel] *v.* (**compelled**) to force. **com•pel•ling,** *adj.* which forces; very exciting (story/film).

com•pen•di•um [kəm'pendɪəm] *n.* collection (of paper/notes/games).

com•pen•sate ['kɒmpensert] *v.* to pay (s.o.) for damage done; to pay **for** a loss. **com•pen•sa•tion** [kɒmpen'seɪʃn] *n.* payment for damage. **com•pen•sa•to•ry,** *adj.* which compensates.

com•pete [kəm'pi:t] *v.* to try to beat others in a race/a game/a business.

com•pe•tent ['kɒmpɪtənt] *adj.* able (to do sth)/capable (of doing sth); efficient. **com•pe•tence,** *n.* (a) capability/efficiency. (b) professional responsibilities; **the case is outside the c. of this court. com•pe•tent•ly,** *adv.* in a capable/efficient way.

com•pe•ti•tion [kɒmpə'tɪʃn] *n.* (a) game where several teams or people try to win. (b) commercial rivalry/trying to sell more than another company. **com•pet•i•tive** [kəm-'petɪtɪv] *adj.* (person) who likes entering competitions; (sport) which is based on competitions; (prices) which aim to compete with those of rival companies. **com•pet•i•tor,** *n.*

æ back, ɑ: farm, ɒ: top, aɪ pipe, aʊ how, aɪə fire, aʊə flower, ɔ: bought, ɔɪ toy, e fed, eəhair, eɪ take, ə afraid, əʊ boat, əʊə lower, ʌ: word, i: heap, ɪ hit, ɪə hear, u: school, ʊ book, ʌ but, b back, d dog, ð then, dʒ just, f fog, g go, h hand, j yes, k catch, l last, m mix, n nut, ŋ sing, p penny, r round, s some, ʃ short, t too, tʃ chop, θ thing, v voice, w was, z zoo, ʒ treasure

person who goes in for a competition; rival company.

com•pile [kəm'paɪl] v. to draw up (a list); to make a collection (of poetry); to write (a dictionary). **com•pi•la•tion** [kɒmpɪ'leɪʃn] n. act of compiling; work which has been compiled. **com•pil•er** [kəm'paɪlə] n. (a) person who compiles. (b) computer program which converts coded data to a machine-readable program.

com•pla•cent [kəm'pleɪsnt] adj. self-satisfied. **com•pla•cen•cy**, n. being complacent. **com•pla•cent•ly**, adv. in a complacent way.

com•plain [kəm'pleɪn] v. to grumble because sth is wrong. **com•plaint**, n. (a) grumble/statement that sth is wrong. (b) illness.

com•plai•sant [kəm'pleɪznt] adj. eager to please.

com•ple•ment 1. n. ['kɒmplɪmənt] (a) number of people needed to fill sth. (b) thing which adds to or fits in with sth else. 2. v. [kɒmplɪ'ment] to complete/to fit in (with sth). **com•ple•men•ta•ry** [kɒmplɪ'mentəri] adj. which fills/completes sth.

com•plete [kəm'pli:t] 1. adj. (a) full/whole. (b) finished. 2. v. (a) to finish. (b) to fill in (a form). **com•plete•ly**, adv. wholly. **com•plete•ness**, n. fullness (of success). **com•ple•tion** [kəm'pli:ʃn] n. finishing; finish; **c. of a contract** = signing of a contract.

com•plex ['kɒmpleks] 1. adj. complicated. 2. n. (pl. -es) series of buildings. (b) repressed emotions/obsessions; **inferiority c.** = feeling that you are inferior; **Œdipus c.** = feeling of hatred for one's father and love for one's mother. **com•plex•i•ty** [kəm'pleksɪti] n. complicated nature.

com•plex•ion [kəm'plekʃn] n. color of the skin on your face; general way things are.

com•pli•cate ['kɒmplɪkeɪt] v. to make things complicated. **com•pli•cat•ed**, adj. with many small details/difficult to understand. **com•pli•ca•tion** [kɒmplɪ'keɪʃn] n. being complicated; second illness which makes the first illness worse.

com•plic•i•ty [kəm'plɪsɪti] n. being an accomplice to a crime.

com•pli•ment 1. n. ['kɒmplɪmənt] praise; **send him my compliments** = send him my good wishes. 2. v. ['kɒmplɪment] to praise. **com•pli•men•ta•ry** [kɒmplɪ'mentəri] adj. which praises; **c. ticket** = free ticket.

com•pline ['kɒmplɪn] n. last service of the day.

com•ply [kəm'plaɪ] v. (**with**) to observe (a rule); to obey (an order). **com•pli•ance**, n. agreement to do sth. **com•pli•ant**, adj. (person) who agrees to do sth/who obeys the rules.

com•po•nent [kəm'pəʊnənt] adj. & n. (piece) which forms part of sth.

com•pose [kəm'pəʊz] v. (a) to make up (music); to write (a letter/a poem). (b) **c. yourself** = be calm. **com•posed**, adj. calm/unflustered. **com•pos•er**, n. person who writes music. **com•pos•ite** ['kɒmpəzɪt] adj. made of several different parts. **com•po•si•tion** [kɒmpə'zɪʃn] n. (a) way in which sth is formed. (b) piece of music/poem/long essay. (c) mixture of several things. **com•pos•i•tor** [kəm'pɒzɪtə] n. person who sets type for printing. **com•po•sure** [kəm'pəʊʒə] n. calmness. **com•pos men•tis** ['kɒmpɒs'mentɪs] adj. sane.

com•post ['kɒmpɒst] n. rotted vegetable matter used as a fertilizer.

com•pound 1. adj. ['kɒmpaʊnd] made up of several parts; **c. fracture** = fracture where the broken bone pierces the skin; **c. interest** = interest calculated on the total sum including the previous year's interest. 2. n. ['kɒmpaʊnd] (a) chemical made up of two or more elements. (b) yard enclosed by a fence. 3. v. [kəm'paʊnd] (a) to come to an agreement with people to whom you owe money. (b) to increase/to aggravate (a crime/a feeling).

com•pre•hend [kɒmprɪ'hend] v. (a) to understand. (b) to include. **com•pre•hen•si•ble**, adj. which can be understood/understandable. **com•pre•hen•sion**, n. understanding. **com•pre•hen•sive**, adj. which includes everything; **com•pre•hen•sive•ness**, n. wide range (of knowledge, etc.).

com•press 1. n. ['kɒmpres] pad of material put on a bruise/sore. 2. v. [kəm'pres] to squeeze into a small space; **compressed air** = air under pressure. **com•pres•sor**, n. machine which compresses air/gas, etc.

com•prise [kəm'praɪz] v. to be formed of.

com•pro•mise ['kɒmprəmaɪz] 1. n. agreement of two opposing points of view, where each side gives way to some extent. 2. v. (a) to come to an agreement by giving way. (b) to embarrass/to put in a difficult position. **com•pro•mis•ing**, adj. embarrassing.

comp•trol•ler [kən'trəʊlə] n. (old) person who controls the finances in an establishment.

com•pul•sion [kəm'pʌlʃn] n. force/urge. **com•pul•sive**, adj. (person) who cannot stop himself doing sth; **a c. smoker**. **com•pul•so•ry**, adj. which you are forced to do.

com•punc•tion [kəm'pʌŋkʃn] n. remorse/regret.

com•pute [kəm'pju:t] v. to calculate. **com•pu•ta•tion** [kɒmpju'teɪʃn] n. calculation. **com•put•er,** *n.* electronic machine which calculates and keeps information automatically; **c. fraud** = fraud committed by using a computer. **com•pu•ter-as•sist•ed,** *adj.* helped by using a computer; **c.-a. design. com•put•er•i•za•tion,** *n.* act of computerizing. **com•put•er•ize,** *v.* (a) to process by computer. (b) to equip (a business, etc.) with a computer.

com•rade ['kɒmreɪd] *n.* friend/companion; fellow member of a socialist or communist party. **com•rade•ship,** *n.* fellowship/friendliness.

con [kɒn] 1. *n.* (a) *inf.* deception; **c. man** = trickster. (b) argument against. 2. *v.* (**conned**) *inf.* to deceive/to trick (s.o.).

con•cat•e•na•tion [kɒnkætɪ'neɪʃən] *n.* chain of events.

con•cave [kɒn'keɪv] *adj.* (surface) which is hollowed in the middle like a spoon.

con•ceal [kən'siːl] *v.* to hide. **con•cealed,** *adj.* hidden; **c. entrance** = entrance which is difficult to see. **con•ceal•ment,** *n.* hiding.

con•cede [kən'siːd] *v.* (a) to admit (that you are wrong). (b) to admit that you have lost.

con•ceit [kən'siːt] *n.* high opinion of oneself. **con•ceit•ed,** *adj.* (person) who thinks too much of himself.

con•ceive [kən'siːv] *v.* (a) to become pregnant. (b) to think up (an idea). **con•ceiv•a•ble,** *adj.* which can be imagined. **con•ceiv•a•bly,** *adv.* in a conceivable way.

con•cen•trate ['kɒnsəntreɪt] 1. *n.* concentrated substance. 2. *v.* (a) (**on**) to pay great attention to (sth). (b) to put (all one's resources) together in one place. **con•cen•trat•ed,** *adj.* very strong (juice after water has been extracted). **con•cen•tra•tion** [kɒnsən'treɪʃn] *n.* (a) attentiveness. (b) putting all your resources into one area. (c) **c. camp** = camp where many political prisoners are held in captivity.

con•cen•tric [kən'sentrɪk] *adj.* (circles) inside each other, each with the same central point.

con•cept ['kɒnsept] *n.* idea/philosophical notion. **con•cep•tion** [kən'sepʃn] *n.* (a) becoming pregnant. (b) idea. **con•cep•tu•al,** *adj.* referring to concepts. **con•cep•tu•al•ize,** *v.* to form a concept of (sth).

con•cern [kən'sɜːn] 1. *n.* (a) worry. (b) interest; **it is no c. of yours** = it is none of your business. (c) company/business; **a big industrial c.** 2. *v.* (a) to deal with; **this concerns you** = is about

you; **that does not c. him** = it has nothing to do with him; **as far as money is concerned** = with reference to money. (b) **to be concerned (about)** = to worry (about). **con•cern•ing,** *prep.* about/referring to.

con•cert ['kɒnsət] *n.* program of music played in public. **con•cert•ed** [kən'sɜːtɪd] *adj.* (effort/attack) done or planned jointly. **concert hall,** *n.* large hall for giving concerts.

con•cer•ti•na [kɒnsə'tiːnə] 1. *n.* portable musical instrument with bellows and a set of keys at either end. 2. *v.* to become crushed/crumpled.

con•cer•to [kən'tʃeətəʊ] *n.* (*pl.* **-os**) piece of music for a solo instrument and orchestra, or for a small group of instruments.

con•ces•sion [kən'seʃn] *n.* act of conceding/of admitting sth; **to make a c.** = to change what you planned to fit in with s.o. else's wishes.

conch [kɒntʃ] *n.* (*pl.* **-es**) type of sea shell, like a a large snail shell. **con•chol•o•gy** [kɒŋ'kɒlədʒɪ] *n.* study of shells.

con•cil•i•ate [kən'sɪlɪeɪt] *v.* to win over (s.o.) who was previously unfriendly; to reconcile. **con•cil•i•a•tion** [kənsɪlɪ'eɪʃn] *n.* act of conciliating. **con•cil•i•a•tor** [kən'sɪlɪeɪtə] *n.* person who tries to reconcile people of opposing views. **con•cil•i•a•to•ry** [kən'sɪlɪətrɪ] *adj.* which is aimed at conciliating.

con•cise [kən'saɪs] *adj.* short; meaning a lot, but using few words. **con•cise•ly,** *adv.* in a concise way. **con•cise•ness, concision** [kən'sɪʒn] *n.* briefness.

con•clave ['kɒŋkleɪv] *n.* religious assembly, esp. meeting of cardinals to elect a pope.

con•clude [kən'kluːd] *v.* (a) to come to an end. (b) to deduce/to come to an opinion. (c) to arrange (a treaty). **con•clud•ing,** *adj.* final. **con•clu•sion** [kən'kluːʒn] *n.* (a) end. (b) opinion reached by reasoning. **con•clu•sive,** *adj.* decisive/which offers firm proof. **con•clu•sive•ly,** *adv.* in a decisive way.

con•coct [kən'kɒkt] *v.* (a) to make (a dish of food). (b) to make up/to invent (a story). **con•coc•tion,** *n.* curious mixture of food or drink.

con•com•i•tant [kən'kɒmɪtənt] *adj.* (*formal*) which accompanies/goes with.

con•cord ['kɒŋkɔːd] *n.* harmony/peace.

con•cord•ance [kən'kɔːdəns] *n.* alphabetical list of words used in a book.

æ back, ɑː farm, ɒ top, aɪ pipe, aʊ how, aɪə fire, aʊə flower, ɔː bought, ɔɪ toy, e fed, eəhair, eɪ take, ə afraid, əʊ boat, əʊə lower, ɜː word, iː heap, ɪ hit, ɪə hear, uː school, ʊ book, ʌ but, b back, d dog, ð then, dʒ just, f fog, g go, h hand, j yes, k catch, l last, m mix, n nut, ŋ sing, p penny, r round, s some, ʃ short, t too, tʃ chop, θ thing, v voice, w was, z zoo, ʒ treasure

con•cor•dat [kɒn'kɔːdæt] *n.* agreement (between church and state).

con•course ['kɒŋkɔːs] *n.* (a) crowd/mass of people. (b) large open space inside a railroad station/concert hall, etc.

con•crete ['kɒnkriːt] 1. *adj.* real/firm. 2. *adj. & n.* (made of) hard stonelike substance made by mixing sand, gravel, cement and water. **con•crete mix•er,** *n.* machine for mixing concrete. **con•cre•tion** [kən'kriːʃn] *n.* mass of things which have solidified together.

con•cu•bine ['kɒŋkjubaɪn] *n.* woman who lives with a man as his second wife, but who is not married to him.

con•cur [kən'kɜː] *v.* (**concurred**) to agree. **con•cur•rence** [kən'kʌrəns] *n.* agreement. **con•cur•rent** [kən'kʌrənt] *adj.* which happen at the same time. **con•cur•rent•ly,** *adv.* happening at the same time.

con•cus•sion [kən'kʌʃn] *n.* shock to the brain caused by being hit on the head. **con•cussed,** *adj.* in a state of concussion.

con•demn [kən'dem] *v.* to blame; to sentence (a criminal); to declare (buildings) to be unfit to use or live in. **con•dem•na•tion** [kɒndem'neɪʃn] *n.* blame.

con•dense [kən'dens] *v.* (a) to reduce the size of (sth); **condensed milk** = milk which has been concentrated and sweetened. (b) (*of steam*) to form drops of water. **con•den•sa•tion** [kɒnden'seɪʃn] *n.* act of condensing; steam which has formed into a film on a cold surface. **con•dens•er,** *n.* part of a machine which turns gas into liquid.

con•de•scend [kɒndɪ'send] *v.* to speak/to act as if you are superior to s.o. else. **con•de•scend•ing,** *adj.* unpleasantly superior (voice/smile, etc.). **con•de•scen•sion,** *n.* acting with a feeling of superiority.

con•di•ment ['kɒndɪmənt] *n.* seasoning for food, such as salt, pepper, mustard.

con•di•tion [kən'dɪʃn] 1. *n.* (a) state. (b) term (of a bargain); **on c. that** = provided that. (c) bad state; **a heart c.** = a weak heart. 2. *v.* (a) to put into good condition. (b) to make (s.o.) used to sth.; **conditioned reflex** = reaction to a stimulus which has been repeated many times. **con•di•tion•al,** *adj. & n.* provided that certain things happen; part of a verb which shows this; "**I would come**" is a conditional form of "**to come.**" **con•di•tion•al•ly,** *adv.* under certain conditions. **con•di•tion•er,** *n.* lotion which puts sth (esp. hair) into good condition.

con•dole [kən'dəʊl] *v.* **to c. with s.o.** = to express your regrets for some tragedy which has happened. **con•do•lences,** *n. pl.* expressions of regret (at the death of s.o.).

con•dom ['kɒndəm] *n.* rubber contraceptive sheath.

con•do•min•i•um [kɒndə'mɪnɪəm] *n.* (a) joint ownership or rule. (b) building held in joint ownership.

con•done [kən'dəʊn] *v.* to excuse/forgive (a crime, etc.).

con•dor ['kɒndɔː] *n.* large South American vulture.

con•du•cive [kən'djuːsɪv] *adj.* favorable (**to**).

con•duct 1. *n.* ['kɒndʌkt] way of behaving. 2. *v.* [kən'dʌkt] (a) to lead/to guide/to control (a business, an orchestra); **conducted tour** = tour led by a guide. (b) to allow (electricity/heat) to pass through. (c) **to c. yourself** = to behave. **con•duc•tion** [kən'dʌkʃn] *n.* passing of heat/electricity. **con•duc•tiv•i•ty** [kɒndʌk-'tɪvɪtɪ] *n.* ability to conduct electricity or heat. **con•duc•tor,** *n.* (a) substance (such as metal) which conducts heat/electricity. (b) person who directs an orchestra. (c) **bus c.** = person who collects money from the passengers on a bus, train, etc. **con•duc•tress,** *n.* (*pl.* **-es**) woman who is a conductor.

con•duit ['kɒndɪt] *n.* tube along which liquids can be passed.

cone [kəʊn] *n.* geometrical figure, round at the base, rising to a point; **ice cream c.** = cone-shaped biscuit for holding ice cream; **pine c.** = fruit of a pine tree; **nose c.** = pointed end of a rocket. **cone-shaped,** *adj.* shaped like a cone.

con•fab ['kɒnfæb] *n. inf.* chat/discussion.

con•fec•tion [kən'fekʃən] *n.* food made of a mixture of sweet things. **con•fec•tion•er•y** [kən'fekʃənrɪ] *n.* sweets and cakes. **con•fec•tion•er's,** *n.* shop selling candy and cakes.

con•fed•er•ate [kən'fedərət] *n.* person who has joined with others (usu. to do a crime). **con•fed•er•a•cy,** *n.* joining together. **con•fed•er•a•tion** [kənfedə'reɪʃn] *n.* group (of states/labor unions, etc.).

con•fer [kən'fɜː] *v.* (**conferred**) (a) to discuss. (b) **to c. an honor on s.o.** = to award s.o. an honor. **con•fer•ence** ['kɒnfərəns] *n.* discussion; meeting of a group/society.

con•fess [kən'fes] *v.* to admit that you have done sth wrong. **con•fes•sion** [kən'feʃn] *n.* admission of fault; **to make your c.** = to admit your sins to a priest. **con•fes•sion•al,** *n.* small private box in a church where a priest hears confessions. **con•fes•sor,** *n.* priest who hears confessions.

con•fet•ti [kən'fetɪ] *n.* small pieces of colored paper thrown over the bride and bridegroom after a wedding.

con•fi•dant, confidante [kɒnfɪ'dænt] *n.* man/woman you tell secrets to.

con•fide [kən'faɪd] *v.* **to c. in s.o.** = to tell s.o. a secret. **con•fi•dence** ['kɒnfɪdəns] *n.* (a) feeling sure. (b) secrecy; **in c.** = as a secret. (c) **c. trick** = trick whereby a trickster gains s.o.'s confidence to steal money from him. **con•fi•dent**, *adj.* sure (of yourself). **con•fi•dent•ly**, *adv.* in a sure way. **con•fi•den•tial** [kɒnfɪ'denʃl] *adj.* secret/private; (secretary) entrusted with confidential matters. **con•fi•den•ti•al•i•ty**, *n.* being secret/private. **con•fi•den•tial•ly**, *adv.* in a confidential way.

con•fig•u•ra•tion [kənfɪgə'reɪʃn] *n.* (a) (*formal*) shape. (b) way in which computer hardware or software are planned.

con•fine [kən'faɪn] *v.* to restrict/to shut up; **confined to bed** = forced to stay in bed. **con•fine•ment**, *n.* (a) imprisonment. (b) period when a woman gives birth to a baby.

con•firm [kən'fɜːm] *v.* (a) to make definite/to make sure. (b) **to be confirmed** = to be made a full member of a church. **con•fir•ma•tion** [kɒnfə'meɪʃn] *n.* (a) making sure. (b) ceremony in which s.o. is made a full member of the church. **con•firm•a•to•ry**, *adj.* which confirms. **con•firmed**, *adj.* permanent; **he is a c. bachelor** = he will never get married.

con•fis•cate ['kɒnfɪskeɪt] *v.* to take away s.o.'s possessions as a punishment. **con•fis•ca•tion** [kɒnfɪs'keɪʃn] *n.* act of confiscating.

con•fla•gra•tion [kɒnflə'greɪʃn] *n.* (*formal*) big fire.

con•flate [kən'fleɪt] *v.* to put together.

con•flict 1. *n.* ['kɒnflɪkt] battle/fight. 2. *v.* [kən'flɪkt] to clash/to contradict.

con•flu•ence ['kɒnfluəns] *n.* (*formal*) place where two rivers join together.

con•form [kən'fɔːm] *v.* to fit in (**to** a pattern); to act in the same way as other people. **con•form•ist**, *n.* person who conforms. **con•form•i•ty**, *n.* conforming.

con•found [kən'faʊnd] *v.* to confuse/to bother.

con•front [kən'frʌnt] *v.* to face up to (a danger); **to c. s.o. with** = to bring s.o. face to face with. **con•fron•ta•tion** [kɒnfrʌn'teɪʃn] *n.* bringing face to face; meeting between opposing sides.

con•fuse [kən'fjuːz] *v.* to mix/to muddle. **con•fused**, *adj.* mixed-up/muddled.

con•fus•ed•ly [kən'fjuːzɪdlɪ] *adv.* in a muddled way. **con•fus•ing**, *adj.* muddling. **con•fu•sion** [kən'fjuːʒn] *n.* muddle/disorder.

con•fute [kən'fjuːt] *v.* (*formal*) to prove (sth) wrong. **con•fu•ta•tion** [kɒnfjuː'teɪʃn] *n.* proving wrong.

con•geal [kən'dʒiːl] *v.* to set solid; to become solid (as of dried blood).

con•gen•ial [kən'dʒiːnɪəl] *adj.* sympathetic/friendly.

con•gen•i•tal [kən'dʒenɪtl] *adj.* (illness/defect) present in a person since birth. **con•gen•i•tal•ly**, *adv.* from birth.

con•ger eel ['kɒŋgə iːl] *n.* very large type of eel.

con•gest•ed [kən'dʒestɪd] *adj.* blocked/crowded. **con•ges•tion** [kən'dʒestʃn] *n.* blocking (of streets); filling (of the lungs) with liquid.

con•glom•er•a•tion [kənglɒmə'reɪʃn] *n.* mass of things heaped together. **con•glom•er•ate** [kən'glɒmərət] *n.* (a) rock made of small pieces fused together. (b) many subsidiary companies linked together.

Con•go•lese [kɒŋgə'liːz] *adj. & n.* (person) from the Congo.

con•grat•u•late [kən'grætjuleɪt] *v.* to give (s.o.) good wishes on a special occasion; to praise (s.o.) for some achievement. **con•grat•u•la•tions** [kəngrætju'leɪnz] *n.* good wishes. **con•grat•u•la•to•ry** [kən'grætjulətrɪ] *adj.* which gives good wishes.

con•gre•gate ['kɒŋgrɪgeɪt] *v.* to gather together. **con•gre•ga•tion** [kɒŋgrɪ'geɪʃn] *n.* people gathered together; people meeting together in a church.

con•gress ['kɒŋgres] *n.* meeting of a group of people; **Congress** = the elected legislative body of the United States. **con•gres•sion•al**, *adj.* referring to the U.S. Congress. **con•gress•man, congresswoman**, *n.* (*pl.* -men -women) member of the Congress of the United States.

con•gru•ent ['kɒŋgruənt] *adj.* which fit together.

con•i•cal ['kɒnɪkl] *adj.* shaped like a cone.

co•ni•fer ['kɒnɪfə] *n.* tree which bears cones. **con•if•er•ous** [kə'nɪfərəs] *adj.* referring to conifers.

con•jec•ture [kən'dʒektʃə] 1. *n.* guess. 2. *v.* to guess. **con•jec•tur•al**, *adj.* possible/which has been guessed at.

con•ju•gal ['kɒndʒʊgl] *adj.* referring to marriage.

con•ju•gate ['kɒndʒʊgeɪt] *v.* to show the different parts of (a verb). **con•ju•ga•tion** [kɒndʒʊ'geɪʃn] *n.* way in which a verb changes according to tense and person.

con•junc•tion [kən'dʒʌŋkʃn] *n.* word which links different parts of a sentence; **in c. with** = together with.

con•junc•ti•vi•tis [kəndʒʌŋktɪ'vaɪtɪs] *n.* inflammation of the eyes.

con•junc•ture [kən'dʒʌŋktʃə] *n.* circumstances.

con•jure ['kʌnʒə] *v.* (a) to do tricks with cards/rabbits, etc. (b) to call **up** (a spirit/a picture). **con•jur•er, conjuror,** *n.* person who does tricks. **con•jur•ing,** *n.* magic tricks.

conk [kɒŋk] *n. Sl.* head. **conk out,** *v. inf.* to stop working.

con•nect [kə'nekt] *v.* to join/to link; **this train connects with the 3:06** = this train arrives in time for you to get off it and catch the 3:06; **they are connected to the Williams family** = they are related to them. **con•nect•ed,** *adj.* joined/linked; **well c.** = with influential friends and relations. **con•nec•tion,** *Brit.* **connexion,** *n.* join/link; **in c. with your visit** = with reference to/concerning your visit; **there is a connection to Chicago** = there is a train which connects with this one for Chicago; **he has connections in the theater** = he has friends/relations in the theater.

conn•ing tow•er ['kɒnɪ̩taʊə] *n.* highest part of a submarine.

con•nive [kə'naɪv] *v.* **to c. at sth** = to allow it to take place. **con•niv•ance,** *n.* conniving (**at sth**).

con•nois•seur [kɒnə'sɜː] *n.* expert/person who knows a lot (about sth).

con•note [kə'nəʊt] *v.* to imply sth in addition. **con•no•ta•tion,** *n.* additional meaning.

con•nu•bi•al [kə'njuːbɪəl] *adj.* (*formal*) referring to marriage.

con•quer ['kɒŋkə] *v.* to defeat by force. **con•quer•ing,** *adj.* triumphant/victorious. **con•quer•or,** *n.* person who leads the invasion of a country; state which captures another country. **con•quest** ['kɒŋkwest] *n.* (a) capturing. (b) thing/country which has been captured.

con•san•guin•i•ty [kɒnsæŋ'gwɪnɪtɪ] *n.* (*formal*) connection by blood.

con•science ['kɒnʃəns] *n.* feeling which tells you if you have done right or wrong. **con•sci-ence-strick•en,** *adj.* ashamed. **con•sci•en•tious** [kɒnʃɪ'enʃəs] *adj.* who works carefully and well; **c. objector** = person who refuses to join the armed forces because

he feels war is wrong. **con•sci•en•tious•ly,** *adv.* in a conscientious way.

con•scious ['kɒnʃəs] *adj.* aware of things around you; **a c. decision** = a deliberate decision. **con•scious•ly,** *adv.* in a conscious way. **con•scious•ness,** *n.* being conscious; **to lose c.** = to become unconscious.

con•script 1. *n.* ['kɒnskrɪpt] person who has been ordered to join the armed forces. 2. *v.* [kən'skrɪpt] to order (people) to join the armed forces. **con•scrip•tion** [kən'skrɪpʃn] *n.* legal obligation to join the armed forces.

con•se•crate ['kɒnsɪkreɪt] *v.* to bless (a new church/a ruler); to devote (one's life to sth). **con•se•cra•tion** [kɒnsɪ'kreɪʃn] *n.* blessing; devoting (of your life).

con•sec•u•tive [kən'sekjʊtɪv] *adj.* following one after the other. **con•sec•u•tive•ly,** *adv.* in order.

con•sen•sus [kən'sensəs] *n.* generally agreed opinion.

con•sent [kən'sent] 1. *n.* agreement. 2. *v.* to agree (**to sth**).

con•se•quence ['kɒnsɪkwəns] *n.* (a) result. (b) importance; **it is of no c.** = it does not matter: **con•se•quent,** *adj.* **c. on** = resulting from. **con•se•quen•tial** [kɒnsɪ'kwenʃl] *adj.* resulting. **con•se•quent•ly,** *adv.* because of this/for this reason.

con•serve [kən'sɜːv] *v.* to save. **con•serv•an•cy,** *n.* body which controls a river, etc. **con•ser•va•tion** [kɒnsə'veɪʃn] *n.* preservation/saving (of energy, natural resources, old buildings, etc.). **con•ser•va•tion•ist,** *n.* person who is interested in conservation. **con•serv•a•tism,** *n.* (a) being conservative. (b) (*in politics*) policies of the Conservative party. **con•serv•a•tive** [kən'sɜːvətɪv] *adj.* (a) not wanting to change; **C. party** = political party in Great Britain which does not want to change the existing system of government, and which does not favor state control of industry; **a C.** = member of the Conservative Party. (b) **at a c. estimate** = at the lowest/most moderate estimate. **con•serv•a•tive•ly,** *adv.* moderately. **con•serv•a•to•ry,** *n.* (a) room with large windows, where you keep tropical flowers and plants. (b) *also* **con•ser•va•toire** [kən'sɜːvətwɑːr] academy of music, art, etc.

con•sid•er [kən'sɪdə] *v.* to think deeply about (sth). **con•sid•er•a•ble,** *adj.* quite large. **con•sid•er•a•bly,** *adv.* to a great extent. **con•sid•er•ate,** *adj.* full of feeling/understanding toward s.o. **con•sid•er•ate•ly,** *adv.* thoughtfully. **con•sid•er•a•tion** [kənsɪdə'reɪʃn] *n.* (a) being thought about. (b) small sum of money. **con•sid•er•ing,** *prep.* when you think of/taking into account.

con•sign [kən'saɪn] *v.* to give (goods) into s.o.'s care. **con•sign•ee,** *n.* (*formal*) person who receives goods from s.o. **con•sign•ment,** *n.* (a) sending of goods. (b) goods which have been sent. **con•sign•or,** *n.* person who consigns goods to s.o.

con•sist [kən'sɪst] *v.* (a) (**in**) to have as a basis. (b) (**of**) to be made up of. **con•sist•en•cy,** *n.* (a) being the same throughout. (b) thickness (of a paste, etc.). **con•sist•ent,** *adj.* which does not contradict; always the same/unchanging. **con•sist•ent•ly,** *adv.* always/permanently.

con•sis•to•ry [kən'sɪstəri:] *n.* meeting of the Pope and cardinals at which a decision is taken.

con•sole 1. *n.* ['kɒnsəʊl] (a) flat table with the keyboard (of an organ/telex machine, etc.). (b) cabinet for a TV set. 2. *v.* [kən'səʊl] to comfort (s.o.) after a loss. **con•so•la•tion** [kɒnsə'leɪʃn] *n.* comfort; **c. prize** = prize given to s.o. who did not win, but who tried hard.

con•sol•i•date [kən'sɒlɪdeɪt] *v.* to make firm/solid. **con•sol•i•da•tion** [kənsɒlɪ'deɪʃn] *n.* making firm.

con•som•mé [kən'sɒmeɪ] *n.* thin clear soup.

con•so•nant ['kɒnsənənt] 1. *n.* (letter representing) a sound which is not a vowel. 2. *adj.* which agrees with.

con•sort 1. *n.* ['kɒnsɔːt] husband or wife (of a queen or king). 2. *v.* [kən'sɔːt] to go around with s.o.

con•sor•ti•um [kən'sɔːtɪəm] *n.* (*pl.* **-tia**) group of companies who work together.

con•spic•u•ous [kən'spɪkjʊəs] *adj.* very obvious; **he was c. by his absence** = everyone noticed that he was not there. **con•spic•u•ous•ly,** *adv.* very obviously.

con•spire [kən'spaɪə] *v.* to plot (**to do** sth). **con•spir•a•cy** [kən'spɪrəsɪ] *n.* plot. **con•spir•a•tor,** *n.* plotter. **con•spir•a•to•ri•al** [kənspɪrə'tɔːrɪəl] *adj.* like s.o. who is plotting.

con•sta•ble ['kʌnstəbl] *n.* (a) a peace officer in a town, rural area, etc. (b) *Brit.* police officer. **con•stab•u•lar•y** [kən'stæbjʊlərɪ] *n.* constables of a district.

con•stant ['kɒnstənt] *adj.* (a) not changing or stopping. (b) faithful. **con•stan•cy,** *n.* faithfulness. **con•stant•ly,** *adv.* all the time.

con•stel•la•tion [kɒnstə'leɪʃn] *n.* group of stars forming a pattern in the sky.

con•ster•na•tion [kɒnstə'neɪʃn] *n.* shock/surprise.

con•sti•pat•ed ['kɒnstɪpeɪtɪd] *adj.* unable to empty the bowels regularly. **con•sti•pa•tion** [kɒnstɪ'peɪʃn] *n.* slow working of the bowels.

con•stit•u•ent [kən'stɪtjʊənt] 1. *adj.* (part) which makes up a whole. 2. *n.* (a) part which goes to make up a whole. (b) voter who lives in a district served by a particular elected official. **con•stit•u•en•cy,** *n.* district of voters served by a particular elected official.

con•sti•tute ['kɒnstɪtjuːt] *v.* to make up; to establish. **con•sti•tu•tion** [kɒnstɪ'tjuːʃn] *n.* (a) bodily health. (b) laws and principles which form the basis of a country's organization. **con•sti•tu•tion•al.** 1. *adj.* referring to the legal basis of a state; (monarchy) where the power is held by an elected government. 2. *n.* short walk which is supposed to be good for the health. **con•sti•tu•tion•al•ly,** *adv.* according to the constitution.

con•strain [kən'streɪn] *v.* to force. **con•straint,** *n.* force.

con•strict [kən'strɪkt] *v.* to squeeze/to strangle. **con•stric•tion** [kən'strɪkʃn] *n.* constricting.

con•struct [kən'strʌkt] *v.* to build. **con•struc•tion** [kən'strʌkʃn] *n.* (a) act of building; way in which sth is made up. (b) thing which has been built. **con•struc•tive,** *adj.* which aims at improving. **con•struc•tive•ly,** *adv.* in a constructive way. **con•struct•or,** *n.* person who constructs.

con•strue [kən'struː] *v.* to take to mean.

con•sul ['kɒnsəl] *n.* country's representative abroad, particularly looking after the business interests and personal affairs of its citizens. **con•su•lar** ['kɒnsjʊlə] *adj.* referring to a consul. **con•su•late,** *n.* house/offices of a consul.

con•sult [kən'sʌlt] *v.* to ask for advice. **con•sult•ant,** *n.* specialist who gives advice, esp. medical specialist attached to a hospital. **con•sul•ta•tion** [kɒnsʌl'teɪʃn] *n.* act of consulting. **con•sul•ta•tive** [kən'sʌltətɪv] *adj.* which gives advice. **con•sult•ing,** *n.* asking for advice.

con•sume [kən'sjuːm] *v.* (a) to eat or drink. (b) to use up. **con•sum•a•bles,** *n.* (a) consumer

æ back, ɑː farm, ɒ top, aɪ pipe, aʊ how, aɪə fire, aʊə flower, ɔː bought, ɔɪ toy, e fed, eə hair, eɪ take, ə afraid, əʊ boat, əʊə lower, vː word, iː heap, ɪ hit, ɪə hear, uː school, ʊ book, ʌ but, b back, d dog, ð then, dʒ just, f fog, g go, h hand, j yes, k catch, l last, m mix, n nut, ŋ sing, p penny, r round, s some, ʃ short, t too, tʃ chop, θ thing, v voice, w was, z zoo, ʒ treasure

goods. (b) (*computers*) paper, ribbons, etc., which are used in peripherals. **con•sum•er,** *n.* person who uses goods or eats food; **c. goods** = goods which are bought by ordinary members of the public (and not by industry). **con•sum•er•ism,** *n.* fighting for the rights of the consumer.

con•sum•mate 1. *adj.* [kən'sʌmɪt] perfect (artist, etc.). 2. *v.* ['kɒnsəmeɪt] to complete; to **c. a marriage** = to have sexual intercourse for the first time after marriage. **con•sum•ma•tion** [kɒnsə'meɪʃn] *n.* completion; end.

con•sump•tion [kən'sʌmpʃn] *n.* (a) act of consuming; quantity consumed. (b) (*old*) tuberculosis. **con•sump•tive,** *adj.* looking as though one is suffering from tuberculosis.

cont. *abbrev for* continued.

con•tact ['kɒntækt] 1. *n.* (a) touch; **c. lenses** = tiny lenses worn on the eyeballs, replacing glasses. (b) person whom you know/whom you have contacted. 2. *v.* to get into communication with (s.o.).

con•ta•gion [kən'teɪdʒn] *n.* passing on of a disease by touching. **con•ta•gious** [kən'teɪdʒəs] *adj.* (disease) which is transmitted by touching.

con•tain [kən'teɪn] *v.* (a) to hold/to have inside. (b) to hold back/to restrain (an attack, anger). **con•tain•er,** *n.* (a) box/bottle, etc., which holds sth else. (b) large case for easy loading on a ship, truck, etc. **con•tain•er•i•za•tion,** *n.* using containers for shipping goods. **con•tain•ment,** *n.* holding back (an enemy).

con•tam•i•nate [kən'tæmɪneɪt] *v.* to make bad/dirty. **con•tam•i•nant,** *n.* substance which contaminates. **con•tam•i•na•tion** [kəntæmɪ'neɪʃn] *n.* act of contaminating.

con•tem•plate ['kɒntempleɪt] *v.* (a) to look at (sth) intently. (b) to plan to do sth. **con•tem•pla•tion** [kɒntem'pleɪʃn] *n.* meditation/deep thought. **con•tem•pla•tive** [kən'templətɪv] *adj.* which meditates.

con•tem•po•rar•y [kən'tempɹəɹɪ] *adj. & n.* (a) (**with**) (person) who lives at the same time or is (about) the same age as another; (thing) which dates back to the same period as another thing. (b) modern/up-to-date. **con•tem•po•ra•ne•ous** [kəntempə'reɪnɪəs] *adj.* of the same date/period.

con•tempt [kən'tempt] *n.* feeling of hatred/disrespect for s.o.; **c. of court** = conduct which a judge rules is offensive to a court. **con•tempt•i•ble,** *adj.* which deserves contempt. **con•temp•tu•ous,** *adj.* scornful (**of**).

con•tend [kən'tend] *v.* (a) (**with**) to fight. (b) to state/to believe. **con•tend•er,** *n.* person who challenges s.o. to a fight; person who fights.

con•tent 1. *adj.* [kən'tent] (**with**) satisfied/happy. 2. *n.* (a) [kən'tent] satisfaction; **to your heart's c.** = as much as you like. (b) ['kɒntent] thing which is contained/which is in a container; **table of contents** = list of chapters/sections in a book; **the contents of the letter** = what was written in it; **mineral c. of water** = percentage of minerals in water. 3. *v.* [kən'tent] to satisfy. **con•tent•ed,** *adj.* satisfied/happy. **con•tent•ed•ly,** *adv.* in a contented way. **con•tent•ed•ness, con•tent•ment,** *n.* being contented.

con•ten•tion [kən'tenʃn] *n.* (a) dispute; **bone of c.** = source of argument. (b) statement/belief. **con•ten•tious** [kən'tenʃəs] *adj.* (person) who likes arguments; (problem) which is a frequent source of dispute.

con•ter•mi•nous [kəʊ'tɜːmɪnəs] *adj.* which has the same boundaries as sth. else.

con•test 1. *n.* ['kɒntest] fight; competition. 2. *v.* [kən'test] (a) to fight (an election). (b) to query; argue that (a will) is invalid. **con•test•ant,** *n.* competitor/person who enters a contest.

con•text ['kɒntekst] *n.* phrase in which a word occurs, which helps show its meaning; **out of c.** = without the surrounding text. **con•tex•tu•al** [kən'tekstjʊəl] *adj.* referring to a context.

con•tig•u•ous [kən'tɪgjʊəs] *adj.* (*formal*) next to/touching. **con•ti•gu•i•ty** [kɒntɪ'gjuːɪtɪ] *n.* being contiguous.

con•ti•nent ['kɒntɪnənt] 1. *n.* large mass of land; **on the C.** = in Europe. 2. *adj.* able to control the passing of urine or excreta. **con•ti•nen•tal** [kɒntɪ'nentl] *adj.* (a) referring to a continent. (b) referring to Europe (excluding the British Isles); **a Continental** = a European (but not an inhabitant of the British Isles); **c. breakfast** = coffee and rolls or bread; **c. climate** = climate with hot dry summers and very cold winters, found in the central parts of continents; **c. quilt** = a duvet, a bag stuffed with feathers, used as the only covering for a bed.

con•tin•gent [kən'tɪndʒənt] 1. *adj.* which depends on sth. 2. *n.* group of soldiers, etc. **con•tin•gen•cy,** *n.* emergency.

con•tin•ue [kən'tɪnjuː] *v.* to go on doing sth. **con•tin•u•al,** *adj.* which goes on all the time without stopping. **con•tin•u•al•ly,** *adv.* very frequently; all the time. **con•tin•u•a•tion** [kəntɪnju'eɪʃn] *n.* (a) (*also* **con•tin•u•ance**) going on without stopping. (b) extension/thing which has been continued. **con•ti•nu•i•ty** [kɒntɪ'njuːɪtɪ] *n.* state of continuing without a break; **c. girl** = girl who ensures that each scene in a motion picture follows on smoothly. **con•tin•u•ous** [kən'tɪnjuəs] *adj.* with no break. **con•tin•u•ous•ly,** *adv.* one after the other with no break in between. **con•tin•u•um,** *n.* thing which continues.

con•tort [kən'tɔːt] *v.* to twist unnaturally. **con•tor•tion** [kən'tɔːʃn] *n.* twisting unnaturally. **con•tor•tion•ist,** *n.* person in a show who twists his body into odd shapes.

con•tour ['kʊntuə] *n.* shape of the outline of sth; **c. (line)** = line on a map drawn through points at the same height above sea level.

con•tra ['kɒntræ] *prep.* against.

con•tra•band ['kɒntrəbænd] *n.* (*no pl.*) goods on which customs duty has not been paid.

con•tra•cep•tion [kɒntrə'sepʃn] *n.* prevention of pregnancy. **con•tra•cep•tive,** *adj. & n.* (thing) which prevents pregnancy.

con•tract 1. *n.* ['kɒntrækt] legal agreement. 2. *v.* [kən'trækt] (a) to get smaller; to make smaller; to tighten. (b) to sign an agreement to do some work. (c) to catch (a disease). **con•trac•tion** [kən'trækʃn] *n.* shortening; shrinking. **con•trac•tor,** *n.* person who does work according to a signed agreement. **con•trac•tu•al,** *adj.* according to a contract.

con•tra•dict [kɒntrə'dɪkt] *v.* to deny what s.o. else says. **con•tra•dic•tion** [kɒntrə'dɪkʃn] *n.* saying the opposite. **con•tra•dic•to•ry,** *adj.* which says the opposite.

con•tral•to [kən'træltəʊ] *n.* (*pl.* -os) (woman with a) low-pitched singing voice.

con•trap•tion [kən'træpʃn] *n.* machine/device.

con•tra•pun•tal [kɒntrə'pʌntl] *adj.* using counterpoint.

con•trar•y ['kɒntrərɪ] 1. *adj.* (a) opposite; **c. winds** = winds blowing in the opposite direction to the one you want. (b) [kən'treərɪ] rude; always doing the opposite of what you want. 2. *n.* **the c.** = the opposite; **on the c.** = quite the opposite; **to the c.** = stating sth different/opposite. 3. *adv.* in an opposite way (**to**). **con•trar•i•ly,** *adv.* in a contrary way. **con•trar•i•ness** [kən'treərɪnəs] *n.* always doing the opposite of what people want/awkwardness (of a child).

con•trast 1. *n.* ['kɒntrɑːst] sharp difference. 2. *v.* [kən'trɑːst] to show up the difference between.

con•tra•vene [kɒntrə'viːn] *v.* to break the

law/the regulations. **con•tra•ven•tion** [kɒntrə'venʃn] *n.* breaking of a law.

con•trib•ute [kən'trɪbjuːt] *v.* (a) to help with; **to c. to** = write articles for (a newspaper, etc.). (b) to give money (**to** a charity). **con•tri•bu•tion** [kɒntrɪ'bjuːʃn] *n.* (a) article submitted to a newspaper. (b) money, etc., given to help sth. **con•trib•u•tor** [kən'trɪbjutə] *n.* a person who contributes. **con•trib•u•to•ry,** *adj.* which helps; **c. factors** = factors which have helped produce the situation.

con•trite ['kɒntraɪt] *adj.* (person) who is sorry. **con•tri•tion** [kən'trɪʃn] *n.* regret.

con•trive [kən'traɪv] *v.* to manage; to plan. **con•triv•ance,** *n.* machine/device. **con•trived,** *adj.* artificial/not natural.

con•trol [kən'trəʊl] 1. *n.* (a) authority/power; keeping in order; **under c.** = in order; **birth c.** = limiting of the number of babies born. (b) **the controls** = the gears/levers, etc., for directing a machine. (c) standard with which the results of an experiment can be compared. 2. *v.* (**controlled**) (a) to direct. (b) to limit/to regulate. **con•trol•la•ble,** *adj.* which can be controlled. **con•trol•ler,** *n.* person who controls. **con•trol tow•er,** *n.* high building at an airport, which houses the radio operators who direct planes on landing or takeoff.

con•tro•ver•sy [kən'trɒvəsɪ] *n.* violent discussion. **con•tro•ver•sial** [kɒntrə'vɜːʃl] *adj.* (subject) which provokes violent discussions. **con•tro•vert,** *v.* (*formal*) to deny. **con•tro•vert•i•ble,** *adj.* which can be denied.

con•tu•ma•cious [kɒntju'meɪʃəs] *adj.* (*formal*) persistently disobedient. **con•tu•me•ly** ['kɒntjumlɪ] *n.* (*formal*) rudeness/insults.

con•tu•sion [kən'tjuːʒn] *n.* (*formal*) bruise.

co•nun•drum [kə'nʌndrəm] *n.* riddle.

con•ur•ba•tion [kɒnə'beɪʃn] *n.* very large spread of a built-up area.

con•va•lesce [kɒnvə'les] *v.* to recover after an illness/an operation. **con•va•les•cence,** *n.* period when you are convalescing. **con•va•les•cent,** *adj. & n.* (person) who is convalescing; **c. home** = rest home for people who are convalescing.

con•vec•tion [kən'vekʃn] *n.* upward movement of heat in air/liquid. **con•vec•tor,** *n.* heater which warms the air moving through it.

æ back, a: farm, ɒ: top, aɪ pipe, aʊ how, aɪe fire, aʊə flower, ɔ: bought, ɔɪ toy, e fed, eəhair, eɪ take, ə afraid, əʊ boat, əʊə lower, v: word, i: heap, ɪ hit, ɪə hear, u: school, ʊ book, ʌ but, b back, d dog, ð then, dʒ just, f fog, g go, h hand, j yes, k catch, l last, m mix, n nut, ŋ sing, p penny, r round, s some, ʃ short, t too, tʃ chop, θ thing, v voice, w was, z zoo, ʒ treasure

con•vene [kən'viːn] v. to call together (a meeting). con•ve•nor, n. person who convenes.

con•ven•ience [kən'viːnɪəns] n. (a) suitableness; at your earliest c. = as soon as it suits you. (b) public toilet. (c) all modern conveniences = all modern comforts (in a house). (d) c. foods = dishes which are easy/quick to prepare. con•ven•ient, adj. suitable; practical. con•ven•ient•ly, adv. handily.

con•vent ['kɒnvənt] n. religious house for women.

con•ven•tion [kən'venʃn] n. (a) custom/usual way of doing things. (b) contract. (c) congress/general meeting of an association/political party. con•ven•tion•al, adj. ordinary/usual; c. weapons = ordinary (not nuclear) weapons. con•ven•tion•al•ly, adv. in a conventional/ordinary/usual way.

con•verge [kən'vɜːdʒ] v. to come together at a certain place. con•ver•gence, n. meeting. con•ver•gent, adj. meeting at a certain point.

con•ver•sant [kən'vɜːsənt] adj. familiar (with a subject).

con•verse 1. n. ['kɒnvɜːs] the opposite. 2. v. [kən'vɜːs] to talk. con•ver•sa•tion [kɒnvə-'seɪʃn] n. talk. con•ver•sa•tion•al, adj. in conversation. con•ver•sa•tion•al•ist, n. person who converses well. con•verse•ly, adv. in the opposite way.

con•ver•sion [kən'vɜːʃn] n. (a) changing (of one thing into another). (b) turning of a person to another religion.

con•vert 1. n. ['kɒnvɜːt] person who has changed religion. 2. v. [kən'vɜːt] (a) to turn (s.o.) from one religion to another. (b) to change. con•vert•er, n. machine which converts. con•vert•i•bil•i•ty [kənvɜːtɪ'bɪlɪtɪ] n. easiness of change of one currency to another. con•vert•i•ble [kən'vɜːtəbl] 1. adj. which can easily be changed (esp. of a currency). 2. n. car with a roof which folds back.

con•vex ['kɒnveks] adj. (surface) which is rounded outward like the back of a spoon.

con•vey [kən'veɪ] v. to transport/to carry; to give (greetings, etc.). con•vey•ance, n. (a) transporting. (b) means of transport. (c) transfer of property from one owner to another. con•vey•anc•ing, n. transferring of property. con•vey•or, n. person who transports/thing which transports; c. belt = long moving surface used in a factory to move products through the production processes.

con•vict 1. n. ['kɒnvɪkt] criminal who has been sentenced to prison. 2. v. [kən'vɪkt] to find (s.o.) guilty; to sentence (a criminal) to prison. con•vic•tion [kən'vɪkʃn] n. (a) being found guilty. (b) firm belief.

con•vince [kən'vɪns] v. to c. s.o. of sth = to persuade/to make (s.o.) believe sth. con•vinc•ing, adj. (argument) which convinces. con•vinc•ing•ly, adv. in a convincing way.

con•viv•i•al [kən'vɪvɪəl] adj. lively/jolly. con•viv•i•al•i•ty [kənvɪvɪ'ælɪtɪ] n. liveliness.

con•voke [kən'vəʊk] v. to call (a meeting). con•vo•ca•tion [kɒnvə'keɪʃn] n. (a) calling of a meeting. (b) meeting of a church assembly/university.

con•vo•lut•ed ['kɒnvəluːtɪd] adj. (a) twisted. (b) very complicated (story, etc.). con•vo•lu•tion [kɒnvə'luːʃn] n. twisting; complication.

con•vol•vu•lus [kən'vɒlvjuləs] n. common climbing weed.

con•voy ['kɒnvɔɪ] 1. n. group of ships/trucks traveling together in line under protection. 2. v. to escort/to protect (esp. a line of merchant ships).

con•vulse [kən'vʌls] v. to make (sth/s.o.) shake. con•vul•sions, n. pl. violent shaking of the body; violent spasms which make the body twitch. con•vul•sive, adj. which causes violent shaking.

coo [kuː] v. to make soft noises (like a pigeon). coo•ing, n. noise made by a pigeon.

cook [kʊk] 1. n. person who prepares food by heating it. 2. v. (a) to prepare (food) by heating. (b) (of food) to be prepared; dinner is cooking. (c) sl. to c. the books = to falsify the entries in account books. cook•book, n. book of recipes. cook•er, n. stove or receptacle for cooking. cook•er•y, n. (no pl.) art of cooking; c. book = cookbook. cook•ie, n. small, sweet cake which is baked. cook•ing, n. action of preparing food, usu. by heating; c. apple = apple for cooking.

cool [kuːl] 1. adj. (-er, -est) (a) quite cold. (b) calm. (c) unfriendly (reception). 2. n. (a) state of being cool; place where it is cool; in the c. of the evening. (b) Sl. calmness; she lost her c. = she lost her temper. 3. v. to make cool; to become cool. cool•ant, n. substance (usu. water) used to keep engines cool. cool down, v. (a) to become cool. (b) to become calm. cool•er, n. (a) thing/machine which cools. (b) Sl. prison. cool•ing. 1. adj. refreshing (drink, etc.). 2. n. action of becoming cool. cool•ly, adv. in a cool/calm way. cool•ness, n. (a) being cool. (b) calmness. (c) unfriendliness (of a reception, etc.). cool off, v. to become cooler.

coo•lie ['kuːlɪ] n. workman/porter (in the Far East).

coop [kuːp] 1. *n.* cage for chickens. 2. *v.* **to be cooped up** = to be shut up inside.

co-op ['kəʊɒp] *n. inf.* cooperative store, apartment building, etc.

coop•er ['kuːpə] *n.* person who makes barrels.

co•op•er•ate [kəʊ'ɒpəreɪt] *v.* to work with s.o. **co•op•er•a•tion** [kəʊɒpə'reɪʃn] *n.* working together. **co•op•er•a•tive** [kəʊ'ɒprətɪv] 1. *adj. & n.* (store, etc.) which works on a profit-sharing basis. 2. *adj.* willing to work with s.o.

co-opt [kəʊ'ɒpt] *v.* to elect (s.o.) to join a committee by votes from those who are already members. **co-op•tion**, *n.* act of co-opting.

co-or•di•nate 1. *n.* [kəʊ'ɔːdɪnət] (a) set of figures which fix a point on a map/graph. (b) **co-ordinates** = matching outer clothes for women. 2. *v.* [kəʊ'ɔːdɪneɪt] to make things work together/fit in with each other. **co-or•di•na•tion** [kəʊɔːdɪ'neɪʃn] *n.* co-ordinating. **co-or•di•nat•or**, *n.* person who co-ordinates.

coot [kuːt] *n.* black water bird with a white forehead.

co-own•er•ship [kəʊ'əʊnəʃɪp] *n.* ownership by several people or groups.

cop [kɒp] *n. inf.* police officer.

cope [kəʊp] 1. *n.* long colored cloak worn by a priest. 2. *v.* to deal **with**.

co•pi•lot ['kəʊpaɪlət] *n.* pilot who is second in command to the captain of an aircraft.

cop•ing ['kəʊpɪŋ] *n.* **c. stone** = top stone on a wall, which protects the wall from the weather.

co•pi•ous ['kəʊpɪəs] *adj.* plentiful/in good supply. **co•pi•ous•ly**, *adv.* in large quantities.

cop•per ['kɒpə] *n.* (a) (*element:* Cu) reddish metal which turns green when exposed to air. (b) large container or pan made of copper. (c) *inf.* policeman. (d) small coin made of copper or other brown metal. **cop•per•plate**, *n.* old-fashioned neat round handwriting.

cop•pice, copse ['kɒpɪs, kɒps] *n.* wood of young trees.

cop•ra ['kɒprə] *n.* dried coconut kernel used to make oil.

cop•u•late ['kɒpjuleɪt] *v.* to have sexual intercourse. **cop•u•la•tion** [kɒpju'leɪʃn] *n.* sexual intercourse.

cop•y ['kɒpɪ] 1. *n.* (a) an imitation/reproduction. (b) book; newspaper. (c) material to be used in a newspaper article/in an advertise-

ment, etc. 2. *v.* to imitate/to make a reproduction of (sth). **cop•y•ed•it**, *v.* to correct (what s.o. has written before it is printed). **cop•y•ed•i•tor**, *n.* person who copyedits. **cop•i•er**, *n.* machine which makes copies. **cop•y•ing**, *n.* imitation. **cop•y•right**, *n.* right to publish a book/put on a play, etc., and not to have it copied without permission; **under c.** = protected by the laws of copyright. **cop•y•writ•er**, *n.* person who writes copy for advertisements.

co•quette [kɒ'ket] *n.* woman who flirts. **co•quet•tish**, *adj.* flirtatious. **co•quet•ry** ['kɒketrɪ] *n.* being coquettish.

cor•a•cle ['kɒrəkl] *n.* light round boat, covered with animal skin.

cor•al ['kɒrəl] *n.* (a) rocklike substance formed of the skeletons of tiny animals in the sea.

cor an•glais [kɔːr'ɒŋgleɪ] *n.* bass oboe.

cor•bel ['kɔːbl] *n.* piece of stone or wood which juts out from a wall and supports sth (usu. a roof beam).

cord [kɔːd] *n.* (a) string/thin rope. (b) stringlike part of the body; **spinal c.** (c) *inf.* **cords** = corduroy trousers.

cor•dial ['kɔːdɪəl] 1. *adj.* friendly. 2. *n.* sweet, aromatic alcoholic drink; liquer. **cor•dial•i•ty** [kɔːdɪ'ælɪtɪ] *n.* friendliness. **cor•dial•ly**, *adv.* in a cordial way.

cord•ite ['kɔːdaɪt] *n.* type of explosive.

cor•don ['kɔːdən] 1. *n.* (a) barrier to prevent s.o. escaping; line of police/soldiers surrounding a point. (b) fruit tree grown as a single stem, with side shoots cut back. 2. *v.* **to c. off a street** = to put up a cordon across a street. **cor•don bleu** [kɔːdɒn'blɜː] *adj.* top quality (cooking).

cor•du•roy ['kɔːdjʊrɔɪ] *n.* velvetlike cloth with ribs.

core [kɔː] 1. *n.* central part; **rotten to the c.** = rotten right through; **to take a c. sample** = to cut a long round sample of rock with a drill. 2. *v.* to scoop out the core of (an apple, etc.).

co-re•spond•ent [kəʊrɪ'spɒndənt] *n.* person cited in a divorce case.

cor•gi ['kɔːgɪ] *n.* breed of small dogs, with short hair and pointed faces.

co•ri•an•der [kɒrɪ'ændə] *n.* small plant, whose seeds and leaves are used for flavoring.

cork [kɔːk] 1. *n.* (a) (material made from) very light bark of a type of oak tree; **c. oak** = oak tree with very light bark. (b) stopper which closes wine bottles. 2. *v.* to put a cork into (a

---

æ back, aː farm, ɒ top, aɪ pipe, aʊ how, aɪə fire, aʊə flower, ɔː bought, ɔɪ toy, e fed, eə hair, eɪ take, ə afraid, əʊ boat, əʊə lower, ɜː word, iː heap, ɪ hit, ɪə hear, uː school, ʊ book, ʌ but, b back, d dog, ð then, dʒ just, f fog, g go, h hand, j yes, k catch, l last, m mix, n nut, ŋ sing, p penny, r round, s some, ʃ short, t too, tʃ chop, θ thing, v voice, w was, z zoo, ʒ treasure

bottle). **cork•age**, *n.* charge made by a restaurant for uncorking a customer's own wine bottle. **corked**, *adj.* (wine) which has an unpleasant taste because of a rotting cork. **cork•screw**, *n.* special screwing device for taking corks out of bottles.

corm [kɔːm] *n.* fat root which can be planted like a bulb.

cor•mo•rant ['kɔːmərənt] *n.* large dark seabird which eats fish.

corn [kɔːn] *n.* (a) cereal crops. (b) tall plant having spiky ears which contain rows of kernels; **sweet c.** = corn grown for human consumption; **c. cob** = core of corn with many rows of kernels. (c) painful hard growth (on a foot). **corn•crake**, *n.* small bird which lives in cornfields. **corn•field**, *n.* field in which corn is grown. **corn•flakes**, *n. pl.* breakfast cereal of crisp pieces of toasted corn. **corn•flow•er**, *n.* blue flower growing in corn fields. **corn•starch**, *n.* powdery starch made from corn, used in cooking. **corn•y**, *adj.* (-ier, -iest) *inf.* old/out-of-date (joke).

cor•ne•a ['kɔːnɪə] *n.* transparent covering of the eyeball. **cor•ne•al**, *adj.* referring to the cornea.

corned [kɔːnd] *adj.* salted/preserved (beef).

cor•ner ['kɔːnə] 1. *n.* angle made by two flat surfaces joining; **she has turned the c.** = she is beginning to recover from an illness. 2. *v.* (a) to turn a corner. (b) to monopolize (a market). (c) to drive (s.o.) into a corner. **cor•ner•stone**, *n.* (a) stone at the bottom of a corner of a building which records the start of building. (b) strong foundation/basis.

cor•net ['kɔːnɪt] *n.* (a) cone-shaped piece of paper for holding candy, nuts, etc. (b) trumpetlike brass musical instrument.

cor•nice ['kɔːnɪs] *n.* decorated molding around a ceiling/around the eaves (of a building).

cor•nu•co•pi•a [kɔːnjuˈkəupɪə] *n.* (*formal*) horn overflowing with fruit and flowers, the symbol of rich harvest.

co•rol•la [kəˈrɒlə] *n.* petals near the center of a flower.

cor•ol•lar•y [kəˈrɒlərɪ] *n.* natural result/thing which follows naturally.

co•ro•na [kəˈrəunə] *n.* ring of light; ring of light visible when the sun is totally eclipsed.

cor•o•nar•y ['kɒrənrɪ] *adj.* referring to the arteries to the heart; **c. thrombosis,** *inf.* **a c.** = heart attack caused by blocking of an artery.

cor•o•na•tion [kɒrəˈneɪʃn] *n.* crowning (of a king/queen/emperor).

cor•o•ner ['kɒrənə] *n.* public official who investigates sudden or accidental deaths.

cor•o•net ['kɒrənət] *n.* small crown.

cor•po•ral ['kɔːprəl] 1. *adj.* referring to the body; **c. punishment** = beating/whipping/caning. 2. *n.* non-commissioned rank in the army below sergeant.

cor•po•rate ['kɔːpərət] *adj.* forming a body; **c. culture** = ethos of a company that is reflected in the behavior of its employees; **c. plan** = overall plan for a whole company. **cor•po•ra•tion** [kɔːpəˈreɪʃn] *n.* (a) town council. (b) large company. (c) *inf.* large stomach.

corps [kɔː] *n.* (*pl.* **corps** [kɔːz]) military or organized group.

corpse [kɔːps] *n.* dead body.

cor•pu•lent ['kɔːpjulənt] *adj.* fat. **cor•pu•lence,** *n.* fatness.

cor•pus ['kɔːpəs] *n.* all the works (of an author).

cor•pus•cle ['kɔːpʌsl] *n.* red or white cell in blood.

cor•ral [kɒˈrɑːl] 1. *n.* fence to enclose cattle. 2. *v.* to enclose (cattle).

cor•rect [kəˈrekt] 1. *adj.* accurate/right/true. 2. *v.* to show the mistakes in (sth); to remove the mistakes from (sth). **cor•rec•tion** [kəˈrekʃn] *n.* making correct. **cor•rec•tive,** *adj. & n.* (thing) which corrects. **cor•rect•ly,** *adv.* accurately. **cor•rect•ness,** *n.* accuracy (of answer, etc.); rightness (of clothes).

cor•re•late ['kɒrəleɪt] *v.* to correspond to/to be linked to. **cor•re•la•tion** [kɒrəˈleɪʃn] *n.* correspondence/link.

cor•re•spond [kɒrɪˈspɒnd] *v.* (a) (to) to fit in with; to match. (b) to write letters; to exchange letters (with s.o.). **cor•re•spond•ence,** *n.* (a) matching. (b) exchange of letters; letters which have come; **c. course** = course of study taken at home with lessons sent by mail. **cor•re•spond•ent,** *n.* person who writes letters; journalist who writes articles for newspapers on particular subjects. **cor•res•pond•ing,** *adj.* which fits/matches. **cor•re•spond•ing•ly,** *adv.* in a similar way.

cor•ri•dor ['kɒrɪdɔː] *n.* long, narrow passage.

cor•ri•gen•da [kɒrɪˈdʒendə] *pl. n.* corrections (in a text).

cor•rob•o•rate [kəˈrɒbəreɪt] *v.* to confirm (a statement). **cor•rob•o•ra•tion** [kərɒbəˈreɪʃn] *n.* confirmation of a statement. **cor•rob•o•ra•to•ry,** *adj.* which corroborates.

cor•rode [kəˈrəud] *v.* to rot (metal); to rust. **cor•ro•sion** [kəˈrəuʒn] *n.* rusting/eating away (of metal). **cor•ro•sive** [kəˈrəusɪv] *adj. & n.* (substance) which eats away metal.

cor•ru•gat•ed ['kɒrəgeɪtɪd] *adj.* bent into waves; **c. paper.**

cor•rupt [kəˈrʌpt] 1. *adj.* not honest; (judge,

etc.) who takes bribes. 2. *v.* to make dishonest/to bribe. **cor•rupt•i•bil•i•ty** [kərʌptə-'bɪlɪtɪ] *n.* being corruptible. **cor•rupt•i•ble**, *adj.* (person) who can be bribed. **cor•rup•tion** [kə'rʌpʃn] *n.* dishonesty/bribery.

cor•sage [kɔː'saːʒ] *n.* flowers worn on the front of a dress.

cor•set ['kɔːsɪt] *n.* tight underwear worn by women to support their bodies.

cor•tege [kɔː'teɪʒ] *n.* (*formal*) procession at a funeral.

cor•tex ['kɔːteks] *n.* outer covering of part of the body, esp. the brain.

cor•ti•sone ['kɔːtɪzəʊn] *n.* hormone medicine used against skin allergies/arthritis, etc.

cor•vette [kɔː'vet] *n.* small naval gunboat.

co•sine ['kəʊsaɪn] *n.* (*in mathematics*) ratio between the length of a side forming an acute angle to that of the hypotenuse in a right-angled triangle.

cos•met•ic [kɒz'metɪk] *adj. & n.* (substance) used in beautifying the face/in improving the look of sth.; **c. surgery** = surgery to improve someone's appearance.

cos•mic ['kɒzmɪk] *adj.* referring to the universe. **cos•mo•naut**, *n.* Soviet astronaut. **cos•mos**, *n.* (*formal*) the universe.

cos•mo•pol•i•tan [kɒzmə'pɒlɪtən] *adj.* (a) made up of people from different parts of the world. (b) at ease in different cities/with people of different nationalities.

cos•set ['kɒsɪt] *v.* to spoil (s.o.) with comfort.

cost [kɒst] 1. *n.* amount which you have to pay for sth; **at all costs** = at no matter what price; **c. of living** = money paid for food, clothing, housing, etc., shown as a monthly index figure. 2. *v.* (a) (**cost**) to have a price of. (b) (**costed**) to calculate the price for (sth). **cost•ing**, *n.* calculation of a selling price. **cost•li•ness**, *n.* expensiveness. **cost•ly**, *adj.* (**-ier, -iest**) expensive.

co-star ['kəʊstɑː] 1. *n.* famous actor/actress starring in a motion picture, play, etc. with other famous actors/actresses. 2. *v.* (**co-starred**) to act in a motion picture, play, etc. as a co-star.

cos•tume ['kɒstjuːm] *n.* (a) set of clothes; **c. jewelery** = cheap imitation jewelery. (b) set of clothes worn in a motion picture, play, etc.

co•sy ['kəʊzɪ] 1. *adj.* (**-ier, -iest**) warm and comfortable. 2. *n.* cover (for a teapot, etc.).

co•si•ly, *adv.* comfortably/warmly. **co•si•ness**, *n.* being cosy.

cot [kɒt] *n.* child's bed with sides.

cot•tage ['kɒtɪdʒ] *n.* little house in the country; **c. cheese** = soft white cheese made from curds; **c. industry** = handicrafts made in people's houses. **cot•tag•er**, *n.* person who lives or vacations in a cottage.

cot•ter pin ['kɒtəpɪn] *n.* pin with a split end, used to hold parts of a machine together.

cot•ton ['kɒtn] 1. *n.* (a) fiber from the downy seed heads of a tropical plant. (b) cloth made of this fiber. (c) thread (for sewing). 2. *v. inf.* **to c. to** = to take a liking to. **cot•ton can•dy**, *n.* molten sugar spun to make a fluffy mass, eaten as a sweet. **cot•ton bat•ting**, *n.* fluffy thin layers or pads of cotton, used for wiping wounds, applying ointment, filling quilts, etc.

cot•y•le•don [kɒtɪ'liːdən] *n.* first leaf on a seedling.

couch [kaʊtʃ] *n.* (*pl.* **-es**) sofa/low bed. **couch grass** [kuːtʃ] *n.* weedlike grass which spreads from underground roots.

cou•chette [kuː'ʃet] *n.* folding bed in a train.

cou•gar ['kuːgə] *n.* large brown American wild cat.

cough [kɒf] 1. *n.* sending air out of the lungs suddenly because of an irritation in the throat; **c. drop** = medicated sweet sucked to relieve irritation in the throat. 2. *v.* to send air out of the lungs suddenly because of irritation; *Sl.* **to c. up** = to pay. **cough•ing**, *n.* series of coughs.

could, couldn't [kʊd, 'kʊdnt] *v. see* **can.**

cou•lomb ['kuːlɒm] *n.* unit of the quantity of electricity passed in one second over a given point by a current of one ampere.

coul•ter ['kuːltə] *n. see* **colter**

coun•cil ['kaʊnsl] *n.* elected or appointed committee, esp. one which acts as an administrative, legislative, or advisory group in a town, city, etc. **coun•cil•lor**, *n.* elected member of a council.

coun•sel ['kaʊnsl] 1. *n.* (a) advice. (b) lawyer. **to lose c.** = to have no longer any idea of what the total is. **coun•sel•ing**, *n.* giving advice. **coun•se•lor, counsellor**, *n.* adviser.

count [kaʊnt] 1. *n.* (a) action of counting/adding figures; **to lose c.** = to have no longer any idea of what the total is. (b) accusation. (c) lower rank of noble. 2. *v.* (a) to add up a total. (b) to say numbers in order. (c) to rely (**on**). (d) to be important. **count down**, *v.* to count backwards (9, 8, 7, 6, etc.). **count•down**, *n.*

æ back, aː farm, ɒ top, aɪ pipe, aʊ how, aɪe fire, aʊə flower, ɔː bought, ɔɪ toy, e fed, eəhair, eɪ take, ə afraid, əʊ boat, əʊə lower, vː word, iː heap, ɪ hit, ɪə hear, uː school, ʊ book, ʌ but, b back, d dog, ð then, dʒ just, f fog, g go, h hand, j yes, k catch, l last, m mix, n nut, ŋ sing, p penny, r round, s some, ʃ short, t too, tʃ chop, θ thing, v voice, w was, z zoo, ʒ treasure

counting backwards. **count•ing**, n. action of adding up a total. **count•less**, adj. which cannot be counted/numerous.

coun•te•nance ['kaʊntnəns] 1. n. (formal) face. 2. v. (formal) to approve of (s.o.'s action).

coun•ter ['kaʊntə] 1. n. (a) machine which counts. (b) small round disk used in games. (c) long flat surface in a store for displaying goods, or in a bank for placing money. 2. adj., adv. & prefix. opposite (**to**). 3. v. (a) to stop/to block. (b) to reply with an opposing response. **coun•ter•act**, v. to neutralize/to stop the effects of (sth). **coun•ter•at•tack**. 1. n. attack in return/attack against s.o. who has just attacked you. 2. v. to attack in return. **coun•ter•bal•ance**, v. to compensate for a force in one direction by going in the opposite direction. **coun•ter•blast**, n. strong written or spoken reply to an attack. **coun•ter•charge**, n. accusation against s.o. who has just accused you. **coun•ter•claim**, n. claim made in response to another claim. **coun•ter•clock•wise**, adj. & adv. in the opposite direction to the hands of a clock. **coun•ter-dem•on•stra•tion**, n. rival/opposed demonstration in reply to a demonstration. **coun•ter•es•pi•o•nage**, n. secret service working against spies. **coun•ter•feit** ['kaʊntəfɪt] 1. adj. false/forged (money). 2. v. to forge/to make false money. **coun•ter•foil**, n. slip of paper which you retain after giving s.o. a check/an invoice, etc. **coun•ter•mand**, v. to say that (an order) should not be carried out. **coun•ter•meas•ure**, n. way of stopping the effects of sth. **coun•ter•pane**, n. bedcover. **coun•ter•part**, n. person who has a similar job/is in a similar situation; parallel thing. **coun•ter•point**, n. combination of melodies in a piece of music. **coun•ter•poise**, n. heavy weight which counterbalances. **coun•ter-pro•duc•tive**, adj. which produces a contrary effect to the one intended. **Coun•ter Ref•or•ma•tion**, n. movement in the Catholic church in the 16th century, a response to the Protestant Reformation. **coun•ter-rev•o•lu•tion**, n. revolt against a revolution. **coun•ter-rev•o•lu•tion•ar•y**, adj. & n. (person who is) in revolt against a revolution. **coun•ter•sign**, v. to sign (a document) which s.o. else has signed, in order to authorize it. **coun•ter•sink**, v. (**countersank; countersunk**) to make a hole for the head of (a nail or screw) to fit into so that it is level with the surface.

coun•try ['kʌntrɪ] n. (a) political or geographical unit of land. (b) region. (c) not town; **to** live in the c. **coun•tri•fied**, adj. like the country. **coun•try•man**, n. (pl. **-men**) person who comes from the same country as you. **coun•try•side**, n. the country/the land (excluding towns and cities).

coun•ty ['kaʊntɪ] n. (a) largest local administrative district of a U.S. state. (b) the people who live in a county.

coup [kuː] n. (pl. **coups** [kuːz]) (a) coup d'état. (b) successful move. **coup d'état** [kuːdeɪ'tɑː] n. armed overthrow of a government.

coupe ['kuːpeɪ] n. car with two doors and a fixed roof.

cou•ple ['kʌpl] 1. n. pair/two things/two people together; two people together, esp. a man and woman; a husband and wife; **a c. of** = (i) two; (ii) a few. 2. v. to link together. **cou•plet**, n. two lines of poetry which rhyme. **cou•pling**, n. metal links for joining two pieces of machinery/two wagons together.

cou•pon ['kuːpɒn] n. piece of paper which acts in place of money/in place of a ticket.

cour•age ['kʌrɪdʒ] n. (no pl.) bravery. **cou•ra•geous** [kə'reɪdʒəs] adj. brave. **cou•ra•geous•ly**, adv. bravely.

cour•i•er ['kʊrɪə] n. (a) person who carries messages; (b) guide for a person/persons traveling, who takes care of hotel reservations, luggage, etc.

course [kɔːs] 1. n. (a) passing of time; **in the c. of** =during; **in due c.** = eventually. (b) road; direction. (c) **of c.** = naturally; **as a matter of c.** = in the usual way. (d) series of lessons; book/series of books for studying. (e) series of treatments for an illness. (f) dish of food for a meal. (g) track (for racing). (h) **golf c.** = area of land specially designed for playing golf. (i) line of bricks (in a wall). 2. v. to flow fast.

court [kɔːt] 1. n. (a) legal proceeding where a judge (and jury) try criminals. (b) group of people living around a king or queen. (c) area where a game of tennis/squash, etc., is played. 2. v. (a) to try to persuade (a woman) to marry you. (b) to look for; to try to win (praise, etc.); to risk (disaster). **cour•te•ous** ['kɜːtjəs] adj. very polite. **cour•te•ous•ly**, adv. politely. **cour•te•sy** ['kɜːtəsɪ] n. politeness; **by c. of** = with the kind permission of; **c. car** = free car waiting for hotel guests at an airport. **cour•ti•er** ['kɔːtjə] n. member of a royal court. **court-mar•tial** [kɔːt'mɑːʃl] 1. n. trial of a soldier by other soldiers. 2. v. (**court-martialed, court-martialled**) to try (a soldier). **court•room**, n. room where a trial is held. **court•ship**, n. courting a woman. **court•yard**, n. square yard surrounded by buildings.

cous•in ['kʌzn] n. son or daughter of an uncle or aunt.

cou•tu•ri•er [ku:'tjʊrɪeɪ] n. dress-designer.

cove [kəʊv] n. small bay.

cov•en ['kʌvn] n. group of witches.

cov•e•nant ['kʌvənənt] 1. n. contract/agreement. 2. v. to agree by contract.

Cov•en•try ['kɒvəntrɪ] n. **to send s.o. to C.** = to refuse to speak to s.o.

cov•er ['kʌvə] 1. n. (a) thing which is put over sth to protect it; **under c. of night** = under the protection of the dark. (b) lid. (c) (cardboard) binding of a book; outer pages of a magazine. (d) shelter; **to take c.** 2. v. (a) to put sth over (sth) to protect it. (b) to travel (a certain distance). (c) to point a gun at. (d) to be enough to pay for. (e) to deal with. (f) to protect with insurance. (g) to be a reporter at (an event). **cov•er•age**, n. amount of space/time devoted to an event in a newspaper/on TV. **cov•er•ing.** 1. n. thing which covers. 2. adj. **c. letter** = explanatory letter sent with a form/with another letter, etc. **cov•er•mount**, n. gift attached to the cover of a magazine. **cov•er up**, v. to hide completely. **cov•er-up**, n. hiding (of a scandal).

cov•er•let ['kʌvələt] n. cover for a bed.

co•vert ['kʌvət] adj. (formal) hidden/secret.

cov•et ['kʌvɪt] v. to want (sth which belongs to s.o. else). **cov•et•ous**, adj. wanting sth which belongs to s.o. else.

cov•ey ['kʌvɪ] n. group (of partridges).

cow [kaʊ] 1. n. (a) female animal of the bull family kept to give milk. (b) female of certain animals, e.g. the elephant. 2. v. to frighten. **cow•boy**, n. man who drives herds of cattle. **cow•hand, cowherd, cowman**, n. man who looks after cattle. **cow flop**, n. round flat cake of cow dung. **cow•shed**, n. shed for cows. **cow•slip**, n. common yellow wild flower.

cow•ard ['kaʊəd] n. person who is not brave. **cow•ard•ice**, n. lack of bravery. **cow•ard•ly**, adj. not brave.

cow•er ['kaʊə] v. to crouch down because of fear.

cowl [kaʊl] n. hood (for a monk's habit); cover for a chimney. **cowl•ing**, n. cover for an airplane engine, airplane part, etc.

cow•rie ['kaʊrɪ] n. colorful seashell.

cox [kɒks] 1. n. (pl. **-es**) person who steers a rowing boat. 2. v. to steer a rowing boat.

cox•swain ['kɒksn] n. (a) sailor in charge of a ship's boat. (b) person who steers a rowing boat. **cox•wain•less**, adj. coxless.

coy [kɔɪ] adj. timid; shy. **coy•ly**, adv. in a coy way. **coy•ness**, n. being coy.

coy•o•te [kɔɪ'əʊtɪ] n. small American wolf.

coy•pu ['kɔɪpu:] n. small animal like a beaver.

CPU [si:pi:'ju:] central processing unit.

crab [kræb] n. edible ten-footed crustacean with large pincers, which walks sideways; **c. apple** = bitter wild or cultivated apple. **crabbed**, adj. (a) bad-tempered. (b) (handwriting) which is difficult to read. **crab•by**, adj. inf. bad-tempered.

crack [kræk] 1. n. (a) sharp dry sound. (b) sharp blow. (c) thin break; split; **at c. of dawn** = at daybreak. (d) inf. **to have a c. at sth** = to try to do sth. (e) Sl. strong form of cocaine. 2. adj. inf. first-class. 3. v. (a) to make a sharp sound. (b) to make a thin split in (sth). (c) **to c. jokes** = to tell jokes. (d) inf. **get cracking!** = start (working, etc.). (e) to decipher (a code). **crack down on**, v. inf. to campaign against. **crack•er**, n. (a) small firework which makes a bang. (b) paper tube which makes a little explosion when it is pulled. (c) dry unsweetened biscuit. **crack•ers**, adj. inf. mad. **crack•pot**, adj. & n. inf. mad (person). **crack up**, v. inf. (a) to praise (sth) extravagantly. (b) to collapse.

crack•le ['krækl] 1. n. small explosive sounds. 2. v. to make little explosive sounds. **crack•ling**, n. hard cooked pork skin.

cra•dle ['kreɪdl] 1. n. (a) baby's bed which can be rocked. (b) support (for a piece of machinery). (c) starting point (for civilization, etc.). 2. v. to rock (in your arms).

craft [krɑ:ft] n. (a) artistry; skill; **crafts** = types of work done by hand. (b) ship. (c) cunning; slyness. **craft•i•ly**, adv. cunningly. **craft•i•ness**, n. cunning; slyness. **crafts•man**, n. (pl. **-men**) artist; person who is expert in using his hands. **crafts•man•ship**, n. skill of a craftsman. **craft•y**, adj. (-ier, -iest) sly.

crag [kræg] n. steep rock cliff. **crag•gy**, adj. rough (rock or person's face).

cram [kræm] v. (**crammed**) (a) to squeeze (**into**). (b) to learn facts hurriedly before an examination.

cramp [kræmp] 1. n. sudden pain where the muscles tighten up and cannot be relaxed. 2. v. to hinder; to squeeze tight. **cram•pon**, n.

æ back, ɑ: farm, ɒ: top, aɪ pipe, aʊ how, aɪə fire, aʊə flower, ɔ: bought, ɔɪ toy, ə fed, eəhair, eɪ take, ə afraid, əʊ boat, əʊə lower, ɜ: word, i: heap, ɪ hit, ɪə hear, u: school, ʊ book, ʌ but, b back, d dog, ð then, dʒ just, f fog, g go, h hand, j yes, k catch, l last, m mix, n nut, ŋ sing, p penny, r round, s some, ʃ short, t too, tʃ chop, θ thing, v voice, w was, z zoo, ʒ treasure

metal hook/spike attached to boots for climbing in ice and snow.

cran•ber•ry ['krænbərɪ] *n.* wild red edible berry.

crane [kreɪn] 1. *n.* (a) tall metal construction for lifting heavy weights. (b) long-legged tropical bird. 2. *v.* to stretch (one's neck). **crane•fly**, *n.* common insect with long legs.

cra•ni•um ['kreɪnɪəm] *n.* bones covering the top part of the skull. **cra•ni•al**, *adj.* referring to the cranium; **c. nerves** = the nerves which link the brain with the head and neck.

crank [kræŋk] 1. *n.* (a) shaft with a right-angled bend, used for transmitting motion. (b) very odd person; irritable person. 2. *v.* to turn or lift with a crank. **crank•shaft**, *n.* rod which is turned by a crank. **crank•y**, *adj.* odd/bizarre/irritable (person).

cran•ny ['krænɪ] *n.* small crack/small gap.

crap [kræp] *n. sl.* shit/trash. **craps** [kræps] *n.* game played with two dice.

crash [kræʃ] 1. *n.* (*pl.* -es) (a) loud noise. (b) accident; **c. helmet** = helmet worn by motorcyclists to protect them in case of a crash. (c) financial collapse. (d) complete breakdown of a computer. 2. *v.* (a) to explode; to make a great noise. (b) to be damaged/destroyed in an accident; **to c. into** = to hit in an accident. (c) to collapse financially. (d) (*of a computer*) to break down completely. 3. *adj.* urgent; **a c. course** = very rapid course. **crash-land**, *v.* to land heavily, without using the undercarriage, so that the aircraft is damaged. **crash-land•ing**, *n.* act of landing heavily.

crass [kræs] *adj.* (a) rude/coarse. (b) obviously materialistic.

crate [kreɪt] 1. *n.* large rough wooden box. 2. *v.* to put into a crate.

cra•ter ['kreɪtə] *n.* hole at the top of a volcano; hole made by a bomb.

cra•vat [krə'væt] *n.* type of scarf worn by men knotted round the neck in place of a tie.

crave [kreɪv] *v.* to want (sth) very much. **crav•ing**, *n.* strong desire (**for**).

cra•ven ['kreɪvn] *adj.* cowardly.

crawl [krɔːl] 1. *n.* (a) creeping on hands and knees. (b) fast swimming stroke with arms going overarm. (c) very slow progress. 2. *v.* (a) to move around on hands and knees. (b) to creep along slowly. (c) to be covered (**with** creeping things).

cray•fish ['kreɪfɪʃ] *n.* (*pl.* crayfish) kind of fresh-water crustacean like a small lobster.

cray•on ['kreɪɒn] *n.* stick of colored material for drawing.

craze [kreɪz] *n.* mania (**for** sth). **cra•zi•ly**, *adv.* madly. **cra•zi•ness**, *n.* madness. **cra•zy**, *adj.* (-ier, -iest) mad.

creak [kriːk] 1. *n.* squeaky cracking noise. 2. *v.* to make a squeaky cracking noise. **creak•y**, *adj.* which makes a creaking noise.

cream [kriːm] 1. *n.* (a) rich fatty part of milk; **c. cheese** = rich soft cheese; **the c. of the undergraduates** = the top few. (b) smooth paste; **face c.** 2. *adj.* colored like cream; very pale fawn. 3. *v.* to whip into a smooth paste. **cream•er•y**, *n.* dairy. **cream•y**, *adj.* (-ier, -iest) smooth; full of cream.

crease [kriːs] 1. *n.* fold made by ironing; fold made accidentally. 2. *v.* (a) to iron a fold into (sth). (b) to make folds accidentally in (sth).

cre•ate [krɪ'eɪt] *v.* (a) to make; to invent. (b) *inf.* to make a disturbance/a fuss. **cre•a•tion** [krɪ'eɪʃn] *n.* thing which has been made. **cre•a•tive**, *adj.* full of ideas; always making sth. **cre•a•tiv•i•ty** [krɪeɪ'tɪvɪtɪ] *n.* aptitude for creating. **cre•a•tor**, *n.* person who makes/invents sth.

crea•ture ['kriːtʃə] *n.* animal; person.

crèche [kreʃ] *n.* model scene representing the birth of Jesus Christ, including a stable with figures, usu. displayed at Christmas.

cre•dence ['kriːdəns] *n.* belief (that sth is correct/true).

cre•den•tials [krɪ'denʃəlz] *n. pl.* papers which prove your identity or rank so that people can trust you.

cred•i•ble ['kredɪbl] *adj.* which can be believed. **cred•i•bil•i•ty** [kredɪ'bɪlɪtɪ] *n.* ability to be believed; **he suffers from a c. gap** = people do not believe him. **cred•i•bly**, *adv.* reliably.

cred•it ['kredɪt] 1. *n.* (a) merit; recognition of quality; **it does you c.** = you are to be praised for it; **he's a c. to the school** = he has made the school proud of him. (b) belief; faith. (c) time given to pay; **c. card** = card which allows you to buy goods without having to pay immediately; **on c.** = without paying immediately. (d) side of an account showing money in hand or which is owed to you; (e) **credits** = list of actors'/directors' names which appear at the beginning or end of a motion picture/TV program. 2. *v.* (**credited**) (a) **to c. s.o. with** = to attribute a quality, etc., to s.o.; to believe. (c) to promise to pay (s.o.); to pay money into (an account). **cred•it•a•ble**, *adj.* honorable (deed). **cred•it•a•bly**, *adv.* honorably. **cred•i•tor**, *n.* person who is owed money.

cred•u•lous ['kredjuləs] *adj.* (person) who believes anything easily. **cre•du•li•ty** [krɪ'djuːlɪtɪ], **cred•u•lous•ness**, *n.* belief/trust. **cred•u•lous•ly**, *adv.* in a credulous way.

creed [kriːd] *n.* statement of what you believe; **the Apostles' C.** = the statement of Christian faith.

creek [kriːk] *n.* small stream.

creel [kri:l] *n.* basket to put fish in.

creep [kri:p] 1. *n.* (a) *inf.* sly, unpleasant person. (b) **he gives me the creeps** = he makes me shudder. 2. *v.* (**crept** [krept]) (a) to move around stealthily. (b) **creeping plant** = plant which spreads close to the ground/which climbs up a wall. **creep•er**, *n.* plant which climbs over walls. **creep•y**, *adj.* (**-ier, -iest**) *inf.* which makes you shudder. **creep•y-crawl•y** *n. inf.* insect.

cre•mate [krɪ'meɪt] *v.* to burn (a dead body). **cre•ma•tion**, *n.* burning of a dead body. **cre•ma•to•ri•um** [kremə'tɔːrɪəm] *n.* (*pl.* -ia) place where bodies are burned.

cren•el•at•ed, crenellated ['krənəleɪtɪd] *adj.* (castle wall) with openings to shoot through.

cre•ole ['kri:əʊl] *adj. & n.* (person) of mixed West Indian and European descent.

cre•o•sote ['krɪəsəʊt] 1. *n.* dark brown liquid, used for protecting wood from rotting. 2. *v.* to paint with creosote.

crepe [kreɪp] *n.* (a) **c. paper** = slightly crinkly colored paper; (b) **c. soles** = thick wrinkled rubber soles for shoes.

crept [krept] *v. see* **creep.**

cre•scen•do [krɪ'ʃendəʊ] *n.* (*pl.* -os) increasing noise (esp. in music).

cres•cent ['kresnt] *n.* (a) curved shape, like a new moon. (b) street which forms a semicircle.

cress [kres] *n.* (*no pl.*) small green salad plant, usu. eaten with seedlings of mustard.

crest [krest] *n.* (a) top (of hills/waves). (b) plumes/fleshy growth on the head of a bird. (c) coat of arms. **crest•fal•len**, *adj.* discouraged/depressed.

cre•tin ['kretɪn] *n.* person who is mentally weak; *inf.* very stupid person. **cre•tin•ous**, *adj.* very stupid.

Creutz•feldt-Ja•kob Dis•ease ['krɔɪtsfəlt 'jɑːkɒp] *n.* fatal disease of the nervous system, caused by an abnormal prion protein in the brain, characterized by progressive dementia and loss of physical co-ordination.

cre•vasse [krɪ'væs] *n.* deep crack in a glacier.

crev•ice ['krevɪs] *n.* small crack in a rock/wall.

crew [kru:] *n.* (a) people who work a boat/aircraft/bus, etc. (b) gang. **crew•cut**, *n.* very short haircut.

crib [krɪb] 1. *n.* (a) manger/box for food for horses or cows. (b) baby's bed. (c) word-for-word translation/list of answers to help a bad student with homework. (d) **c.**

death = sudden unexplained death of a sleeping baby, possibly caused by overheating. 2. *v.* (**cribbed**) to copy.

crib•bage ['krɪbɪdʒ] *n.* card game where the points are marked by pegs on a special board.

crick [krɪk] 1. *n.* **c. in the neck** = sprain/pulled muscle in the neck. 2. *v.* to pull a muscle in (one's neck).

crick•et ['krɪkɪt] *n.* (a) small jumping insect, like a grasshopper. (b) game played between two teams of eleven players using bats, hard balls and wickets as targets, played esp. in Great Britain and Commonwealth countries. *inf.* **it isn't c.** = it is not fair. **crick•et•er**, *n.* person who plays cricket.

crime [kraɪm] *n.* illegal act. **crim•i•nal** ['krɪmɪnl] 1. *adj.* referring to an illegal act. 2. *n.* person who commits a crime. **crim•i•nal•ly**, *adv.* so bad as to be against the law. **crim•i•nol•o•gy** [krɪmɪ'nɒlədʒɪ] *n.* study of crime.

crimp [krɪmp] *v.* to press into waves or folds.

crim•son ['krɪmzn] *adj. & n.* deep red color.

cringe [krɪndʒ] *v.* (a) to bend to avoid a blow. (b) to be excessively humble.

crin•kle ['krɪŋkl] *v.* to fold making many small creases. **crin•kly**, *adj.* (**-ier, -iest**) with many creases/curls.

crin•o•line ['krɪnəli:n] *n.* (*old*) very wide skirt.

crip•ple ['krɪpl] 1. *n.* person who is disabled or lame. 2. *v.* (a) to make (s.o.) disabled. (b) to prevent (a machine/a factory) from working.

cri•sis ['kraɪsɪs] *n.* (*pl.* **crises** ['kraɪsi:z]) critical moment; turning point.

crisp [krɪsp] 1. *adj.* (**-er, -est**) dry and brittle; sharp/cold (air); crunchy (lettuce). 2. *n.* piece of food that is thin and crisp. **crisp•ness**, *n.* being crisp. **crisp•y**, *adj.* very crisp.

criss-cross ['krɪskrɒs] 1. *adj.* with lines crossing in two directions. 2. *v.* to go backward and forward in different directions.

cri•te•ri•on [kraɪ'tɪərɪən] *n.* (*pl.* **criteria**) standard by which things are judged.

crit•ic ['krɪtɪk] *n.* (a) person who examines sth and comments on it, esp. person who writes comments on new plays and motion pictures for a newspaper. (b) person who comments unfavorably on sth/who finds fault with sth. **crit•i•cal**, *adj.* dangerous (situation); extremely urgent/important (decision); very serious (medical condition). (b) unfavorable (comment). **crit•i•cal•ly**, *adv.* in a critical way. **crit•i•cism** ['krɪtɪsɪzəm] *n.* (a) com-

---

æ **back**, ɑː **farm**, ɒ **top**, aɪ **pipe**, aʊ **how**, aɪə **fire**, aʊə **flower**, ɔː **bought**, ɔɪ **toy**, e **fed**, eə **hair**, eɪ **take**, ə **afraid**, əʊ **boat**, əʊə **lower**, ɜː **word**, iː **heap**, ɪ **hit**, ɪə **hear**, uː **school**, ʊ **book**, ʌ **but**, b **back**, d **dog**, ð **then**, dʒ **just**, f **fog**, g **go**, h **hand**, j **yes**, k **catch**, l **last**, m **mix**, n **nut**, ŋ **sing**, p **penny**, r **round**, s **some**, ʃ **short**, t **too**, tʃ **chop**, θ **thing**, v **voice**, w **was**, z **zoo**, ʒ **treasure**

ment; **literary c.** = comment on a work of literature. (b) unfavorable comment. **crit•i•cize**, *v.* to comment unfavorably on (sth). **cri•tique** [krɪ'tiːk] *n.* piece of careful literary criticism.

croak [krəʊk] 1. *n.* hoarse noise (like that made by frogs). 2. *v.* to make a hoarse sound. **croak•y**, *adj.* (**-ier, -iest**) hoarse (voice).

cro•chet ['krəʊʃeɪ] 1. *n.* type of knitting using one needle with a hook at the end. 2. *v.* (**crocheted** ['krəʊʃeɪd]; **crocheting** ['krəʊʃeɪɪŋ]) to make (sth) using a hooked needle. **cro•chet-hook**, *n.* hooked needle for crocheting.

crock [krɒk] *n.* rough earthenware pot. **crock•er•y**, *n.* (*no pl.*) rough pottery tableware.

croc•o•dile ['krɒkədaɪl] *n.* large meat-eating reptile living in rivers in Africa; **she wept c. tears** = she pretended to cry when she was not in any way sad.

cro•cus ['krəʊkəs] *n.* (*pl.* **-es**) purple, yellow or white spring flower.

croft [krɒft] *n.* (*in Scotland*) small farm held by a tenant. **croft•er**, *n.* farmer who holds a croft.

crois•sant ['krwæsɒŋ] *n.* rolled pastry, made in the shape of a crescent.

crone [krəʊn] *n.* ugly old witch.

cro•ny ['krəʊnɪ] *n.* old friend.

crook [krʊk] *n.* (a) bend. (b) long stick with a bent top; (c) *inf.* criminal. **crook•ed** ['krʊkɪd] *adj.* (a) bent. (b) dishonest. **crook•ed•ly**, *adv.* in a bent way; not straight.

croon [kruːn] *v.* to sing in a low voice. **croon•er**, *n.* person who croons.

crop [krɒp] 1. *n.* (a) vegetables/grain, etc., grown for food. (b) part of a bird's throat shaped like a bag. (c) small whip used by a rider. (d) short haircut. 2. *v.* (**cropped**) (a) to cut (a hedge/s.o.'s hair) short. (b) (*of sheep*) to eat (grass) so that it is very short. **crop•per**, *n. inf.* **he came a c.** = (i) he fell badly; (ii) his plans did not succeed. **crop up**, *v.* to occur.

cro•quet ['krəʊkeɪ] *n.* lawn game played with hoops, balls and mallets.

cro•quette [krə'ket] *n.* small ball of mashed potato, covered with breadcrumbs and fried.

cro•sier ['krəʊzɪə] *n.* staff (like a crook) carried by a bishop.

cross [krɒs] 1. *n.* (a) shape with two lines cutting across each other at right angles. (b) shape of a vertical line, with another cutting across it at right angles, forming the symbol of the Christian church; wooden construction of this shape; **the Red C.** = international rescue and medical organization. (c) thing which is hard to bear. (d) mixture of two breeds; mixture of two different things. 2. *v.* (a) **to c. oneself** = to make a sign of the cross on oneself. (b) to go across; to place across; **crossed line** = telephone connection where you can hear other people talking. (d) to breed (two animals/plants) together. 3. *adj.* (a) opposed/contrary; **they are at c. purposes** = they are in disagreement; **to talk at c. purposes** = to misunderstand what each other is saying. (b) bad-tempered/angry. **cross•bar**, *n.* beam which goes across a space. **cross•bill**, *n.* type of bird, with a bill of which the top part crosses over the bottom. **cross•breed**, *n.* animal produced by crossing two animals of different breeds. **cross•check**, *v.* to check again to make sure. **cross-coun•try**, *adj.* & *n.* (race) across fields and along roads, not on a track. **cross-ex•am•i•na•tion**, *n.* searching questioning by an opposing lawyer. **cross-ex•am•ine**, *v.* to ask (s.o.) searching questions. **cross•eyed**, *adj.* (person) whose eyes do not face forward; (person) with a squint. **cross-fer•ti•lize**, *v.* to fertilize (one plant) with another variety. **cross•fire**, *n.* gunfire from two directions, so that the fire crosses. **cross-grained**, *adj.* bad-tempered. **cross•ing**, *n.* (a) act of going across. (b) place where you cross; **pedestrian c.** = crosswalk. **cross•legged**, *adj.* & *adv.* with one ankle over the other. **cross•ly**, *adv.* in an angry way. **cross off, cross out**, *v.* to draw a line through (sth written). **cross•o•ver**, 1. *n.* book/play/recording, etc. that is transposed into a different genre. 2. *adj.* (a) (book/play/recording, etc.) existing in more than one genre. (b) (author/performer, etc.) working in more than one genre. (c) (writing/art/music, etc.) combining two or more styles. **cross-ques•tion**, *v.* to cross-examine. **cross-ques•tion•ing**, *n.* cross-examining. **cross-ref•er•ence**, *n.* line in a reference book telling you to look in another section for further information. **cross•roads**, *n. pl.* place where two roads cross. **cross-sec•tion**, *n.* (a) diagram as if a cut had been made across sth. (b) sample. **cross•walk**, *n.* pedestrian crossing. **cross•wind**, *n.* wind blowing across a road, etc. **cross•wise**, *adv.* in the shape of a cross. **cross•word**, *n.* puzzle where small squares have to be filled with letters forming words to which clues are given.

crosse [krɒs] *n.* stick with a net, used in playing lacrosse.

crotch [krɒtʃ] *n.* (*pl.* **-es**) place where the two legs fork.

crotch•et ['krɒtʃɪt] *n.* note in music lasting two quavers or half as long as a minim.

crotch•et•y, *adj.* (a) bad-tempered. (b) odd/slightly mad; capricious.

crouch [kraʊtʃ] *v.* to bend down low.

croup [kruːp] *n.* (a) infection in the throat, which makes children cough noisily. (b) rear part of a horse.

croup•i•er ['kruːpɪə] *n.* person who is in charge of a gaming table.

crow [krəʊ] 1. *n.* large common black bird; **as the c. flies** = in a straight line. 2. *v.* (a) (*of a cockerel*) to call. (b) **to c. over s.o.** = to exclaim happily because you have beaten s.o. **crow•bar**, *n.* large metal lever for opening boxes. **crow's-feet**, *n.* little wrinkles at the outer corners of the eyes. **crow's nest**, *n.* platform on top of a mast for a lookout.

crowd [kraʊd] 1. *n.* mass of people. 2. *v.* to group together.

crown [kraʊn] 1. *n.* (a) gold and jeweled headdress for a king/queen, etc. (b) symbol of monarchy; (c) top (of the head, a tooth, etc.). (d) type of coin. 2. *v.* (a) to make (s.o.) king/queen/emperor, etc. by placing a crown on his head. (b) to be a splendid end to (sth). (c) *inf.* to hit (s.o.) on the head. (d) to reward. (e) to put a false top on (a tooth). **Crown Prince**, *n.* eldest son of a monarch, who will inherit the throne.

cru•cial ['kruːʃl] *adj.* extremely important/critical. **cru•cial•ly**, *adv.* vitally/critically.

cru•ci•ble ['kruːsɪbl] *n.* small pot used for heating substances in chemical experiments.

cru•ci•fix ['kruːsɪfɪks] *n.* (*pl.* -es) statue representing Jesus Christ on the cross. **cru•ci•fix•ion** [kruːsɪ'fɪkʃn] *n.* killing by nailing to a cross. **cru•ci•fy**, *v.* to kill (s.o.) by nailing to a cross.

crude [kruːd] 1. *adj.* (-er, -est) (a) unpurified; unrefined (oil). (b) rude/ill-mannered. 2. *n.* unrefined oil. **crude•ly**, *adv.* in a crude way. **crude•ness, crudity**, *n.* being crude.

cru•el ['kruːəl] *adj.* (crueler, cruelest) which causes pain/suffering. **cru•el•ly**, *adv.* savagely/unkindly. **cru•el•ty**, *n.* being cruel.

cru•et ['kruːɪt] *n.* set of containers for salt, pepper, mustard, etc.

cruise [kruːz] 1. *n.* long pleasure voyage in a ship calling at different ports. 2. *v.* (a) to go about steadily (in a boat) visiting places. (b) to travel at an even speed. **cruis•er**, *n.* large warship, smaller than a battleship; **cabin c.** = motor boat with a cabin for living in.

crumb [krʌm] *n.* small piece (of bread, etc.).

crum•ble ['krʌmbl] 1. *n.* dessert made of fruit covered with a mixture of flour, shortening and sugar. 2. *v.* to break into small pieces. **crum•bly**, *adj.* which easily falls to pieces.

crum•my ['krʌmɪ] *adj.* (-ier, -iest) *inf.* rotten/no good.

crum•pet ['krʌmpɪt] *n.* thick round batter cake, served toasted with butter.

crum•ple ['krʌmpl] *v.* to crush/to screw up into a ball. **crum•ple zones**, *pl. n.* areas at the front and rear of a vehicle that absorb some of the impact of a crash by crumpling.

crunch [krʌntʃ] 1. *n.* (*pl.* -es) (a) sound of sth crisp being crushed. (b) *inf.* crisis point; **when it comes to the c.** 2. *v.* to crush (sth crisp); to chew (sth hard). **crunch•y**, *adj.* hard and crisp.

crup•per ['krʌpə] *n.* piece of leather which fastens around a horse's tail to keep the saddle in place.

cru•sade [kruː'seɪd] 1. *n.* (a) medieval campaign by Christians against Muslims who occupied the Holy Land. (b) campaign. 2. *v.* to campaign/to fight (**against** or **for**). **cru•sad•er**, *n.* person who goes on a crusade.

crush [krʌʃ] 1. *n.* (a) drink made of fruit juice. (b) mass of people squeezed together. (c) infatuation. 2. *v.* to squash.

crust [krʌst] *n.* hard exterior (of bread/cake/the earth, etc.). **crust•y**, *adj.* (-ier, -iest) (bread) with a hard crust.

crus•ta•cean [krʌ'steɪʃn] *n.* one of many types of animals with hard shells, mainly living in the sea, such as lobsters, crabs, etc.

crutch [krʌtʃ] *n.* (*pl.* -es) (a) lame person's long stick which goes under the armpit. (b) (*old*) crotch.

crux [krʌks] *n.* central point of a problem; **the c. of the matter.**

cry [kraɪ] 1. (a) act of making tears. (b) shout; exclamation (esp. of pain). (c) call (of a bird/animal). 2. *v.* (a) to make tears. (b) (*also* **cry out**) to shout; to exclaim (in pain). **cry•ing**, *adj.* scandalous/which needs putting right.

cry•o•gen•ics [kraɪəʊ'dʒenɪks] *n.* study of very low temperatures.

crypt [krɪpt] *n.* cellar under a church.

cryp•tic ['krɪptɪk] *adj.* secret; mysterious.

crypto- ['krɪptəʊ] *prefix* hidden.

æ back, aː farm, ɒ top, aɪ pipe, aʊ how, aɪə fire, aʊə flower, ɔː bought, ɔɪ toy, e fed, eəhair, eɪ take, ə afraid, əʊ boat, əʊə lower, vː word, iː heap, ɪ hit, ɪə hear, uː school, ʊ book, ʌ but, b back, d dog, ð then, dʒ just, f fog, g go, h hand, j yes, k catch, l last, m mix, n nut, ŋ sing, p penny, r round, s some, ʃ short, t too, tʃ chop, θ thing, v voice, w was, z zoo, ʒ treasure

cryp•to•gam ['krɪptəgæm] *n.* plant (like moss) which has no flowers.

cryp•to•gram ['krɪptəgræm] *n.* message written in a secret language; coded message. **cryp•tog•ra•phy,** *n.* study of codes.

crys•tal ['krɪstl] *n.* (a) chemical formation of regular-shaped solids. (b) very clear bright glass. **crys•tal•line,** *adj.* shaped like a crystal; clear as a crystal. **crys•tal•li•za•tion** [krɪstəlaɪ'zeɪʃn] *n.* formation of crystals. **crys•tal•lize** ['krɪstəlaɪz] *v.* (a) to form crystals. (b) to preserve fruit in sugar. (c) to take shape. **crys•tal•log•ra•phy** [krɪstə'lɒgrəfɪ] *n.* study of crystals.

Cu *symbol for* copper.

cub [kʌb] *n.* (a) young animal (esp. bear/fox). (b) **C. Scout** = boy in the younger section of the Boy Scouts.

Cu•ban ['kjuːbn] 1. *adj.* referring to Cuba. 2. *n.* person from Cuba.

cub•by-hole ['kʌbɪhəʊl] *n.* small dark cupboard/hiding place.

cube [kjuːb] 1. *n.* (a) geometric solid shape where all six sides are square and join each other at right angles. (b) the result where a number is multiplied by itself twice; **c. root** = number which when multiplied by itself twice produces a given number. 2. *v.* (a) to multiply (a number) by itself twice. (b) **cubed sugar** = sugar in square lumps. **cu•bic,** *adj.* solid; **c. capacity** = capacity to hold something; **c. centimeter** = (i) cube where each side measures one centimeter; (ii) the volume of this size.

cu•bi•cle ['kjuːbɪkl] *n.* small room (in a dormitory); small space (in an office); changing room (in a store, etc.).

cub•ism ['kjuːbɪzəm] *n.* art movement where geometric shapes predominate. **cub•ist,** *adj. & n.* (painter) using geometric shapes.

cuck•oo ['kʊkuː] 1. *n.* common summer bird, which lays its eggs in other birds' nests. 2. *adj. inf.* stupid. **cuck•oo clock,** *n.* clock where a small bird makes a noise like a cuckoo to call the time.

cu•cum•ber ['kjuːkʌmbə] *n.* long vegetable used in salads or for pickling.

cud [kʌd] *n.* food chewed a second time.

cud•dle ['kʌdl] 1. *n.* a hug. 2. *v.* to hug and kiss (s.o.). **cud•dle•some, cuddly,** *adj.* warm and soft.

cudg•el ['kʌdʒl] 1. *n.* large stick for hitting people with; **to take up the cudgels for** = to go to defend s.o. 2. *v.* (**cudgelled**) **to c. one's brains** = to think hard.

cue [kjuː] *n.* (a) (*in a play*) the line which indicates that you speak or act next; **to take your c. from s.o.** = to follow s.o. closely/to do as s.o. does. (b) long stick for playing billiards/pool.

cuff [kʌf] 1. *n.* (a) end of the sleeve round the wrist; **speaking off the c./an off the c. speech** = speech made without any notes; impromptu speech. (b) folded part at the bottom of each leg of a pair of trousers. (c) smack (with an open hand). 2. *v.* to give (s.o.) a smack. **cuff-links,** *n. pl.* fasteners for attaching shirt cuffs.

cui•rass [kwiː'ræs] *n.* armor for the top part of the body.

cui•sine [kwɪ'ziːn] *n.* style of cooking.

cul-de-sac ['kʌldəsæk] *n.* small street open at only one end.

cu•li•nar•y ['kʌlɪnərɪ] *adj.* referring to cooking.

cull [kʌl] *v.* to kill (some animals in a herd) when there are too many of them.

cul•let ['kʌlɪt] *n.* broken glass for recycling.

cul•mi•nate ['kʌlmɪneɪt] *v.* to reach a climax/to end (**in**). **cul•mi•na•tion** [kʌlmɪ'neɪʃn] *n.* final point/grand ending.

cu•lottes [kjuː'lɒts] *n. pl.* woman's wide shorts, like a split skirt.

cul•pa•ble ['kʌlpəbl] *adj.* guilty. **cul•pa•bil•i•ty** [kʌlpə'bɪlɪtɪ] *n.* guilt.

cul•prit ['kʌlprɪt] *n.* person who has done something wrong.

cult [kʌlt] *n.* religious or semi-religious worship; **c. hero** = person worshipped by a group of admirers.

cul•ti•vate ['kʌltɪveɪt] *v.* (a) to dig and water (the land) to grow plants; to grow (plants). (b) to do everything to win (s.o.'s friendship). **cul•ti•vat•ed,** *adj.* (person) who has been educated/who is civilized. **cul•ti•va•tion** [kʌltɪ'veɪʃn] *n.* (a) act of cultivating. (b) education. **cul•ti•va•tor,** *n.* (a) farmer/person who cultivates. (b) small motor-powered plow.

cul•ture ['kʌltʃə] *n.* (a) cultivation of plants/pearls. (b) growing (of germs in a laboratory). (c) civilization. **cul•tur•al,** *adj.* referring to culture. **cul•tured,** *adj.* (a) civilized; well educated (person). (b) (pearl) which has been artificially grown.

cul•vert ['kʌlvət] *n.* drain which goes under a road in a pipe.

cum•ber•some ['kʌmbəsəm] *adj.* large and heavy.

cum•in ['kʌmɪn] *n.* herb whose seeds are used for flavoring.

cum•mer•bund ['kʌməbʌnd] *n.* type of decorative belt, usu. worn by men with formal clothes.

cu•mu•la•tive ['kjuːmjʊlətɪv] *adj.* which accumulates; which grows by adding new parts.

cu•mu•lus ['kjuːmjʊləs] *n.* type of large white cloud; rounded masses of clouds.

cu•ne•i•form ['kjuːnɪfɔːm] *adj. & n.* type of ancient writing done on wet clay with a stick.

cun•ning ['kʌnɪŋ] 1. *n.* (a) cleverness. (b) trickery. 2. *adj.* (a) clever. (b) tricky/sly.

cup [kʌp] 1. *n.* (a) bowl with a handle for drinking coffee or tea, etc. (b) silver goblet or vase given as a prize in sporting events/competitions, etc.; **c. final** = final match for a championship. 2. *v.* (**cupped**) to put (hands) in the shape of a cup. **cup•ful,** *n.* quantity held by a cup.

cup•board ['kʌbəd] *n.* large piece of furniture with shelves and doors; alcove in a wall with shelves and doors.

cu•pid•i•ty [kjuː'pɪdɪtɪ] *n.* greed; desire for sth.

cu•po•la ['kjuːpələ] *n.* small dome.

cur [kɜː] *n.* dirty dog.

cu•ra•re [kjʊə'rɑːrɪ] *n.* S. American poison, now used to relax the muscles.

cu•rate ['kjʊərət] *n.* minor priest who helps the parish priest. **cu•ra•cy,** *n.* post of curate.

cu•ra•tor [kjʊ'reɪtə] *n.* person in charge of a museum.

curb [kɜːb] 1. *n.* (a) stone edging to a pavement/path. (b) thing which holds you back. 2. *v.* to control; to hold back.

curd [kɜːd] *n.* solid food made from sour milk. **cur•dle** ['kɜːdl] *v.* to (cause to) go sour.

cure ['kjʊə] 1. *n.* (a) making better. (b) remedy. 2. *v.* (a) to make better. (b) to preserve (fish/pork, etc.) by salting/smoking, etc.; to preserve (skins) to make leather. **cur•a•ble,** *adj.* (disease) which can be cured. **cur•a•tive,** *adj.* which can cure.

cu•ret•tage [kjure'tɑːʒ] *n.* scraping of the inside of part of the body. **cu•rette,** *n.* surgical instrument for scraping.

cur•few ['kɜːfjuː] *n.* period when no one is allowed on the streets.

cu•rie ['kjuərɪ] *n.* unit of measurement of radioactivity.

cu•ri•o ['kjuərɪəʊ] *n.* (*pl.* -os) old/rare object.

cu•ri•os•i•ty [kjuərɪ'ɒsɪtɪ] *n.* (a) desire for knowledge. (b) odd/rare object. **cu•ri•ous** ['kjuərɪəs] *adj.* (a) wanting to know. (b) odd/peculiar. **cu•ri•ous•ly,** *adv.* oddly.

curl [kɜːl] 1. *n.* lock of wavy twisted hair. 2. *v.* (a) to make (hair) wave/twist. (b) to grow in waves/twists naturally. **curl•er,** *n.* small tube for wrapping hair round to make it curl. **curl•ing,** *n.* team game where heavy weights are slid across ice towards a target. **curl up,** *v.*

to roll up into a ball. **curl•y,** *adj.* (-ier, -iest) with natural waves, twists.

cur•lew ['kɜːljuː] *n.* brown wading bird with a long curved beak.

cur•rant ['kʌrənt] *n.* (a) small black or red soft fruit; bush of this fruit. (b) small dried grape.

cur•ren•cy ['kʌrənsɪ] *n.* (a) (system of) money; **hard c.** = money which can be easily exchanged internationally. (b) being well known; **to gain c.** = to become more frequently heard.

cur•rent ['kʌrənt] 1. *n.* flow of water/air/electricity. 2. *adj.* of the present time; frequent; **c. affairs** = things which are happening at the present moment. **cur•rent•ly,** *adv.* at the present time.

cur•ric•u•lum [kə'rɪkjʊləm] *n.* list of subjects studied in a school, etc. **c. vitae** ['viːtɪ] = summary of biographical details, esp. details of education and work experience.

cur•ry ['kʌrɪ] 1. *n.* hot spice; dish made with hot spice; **c. powder. 2.** *v.* (a) to cook with hot spices. (b) to brush down (a horse). (c) **to c. favor with s.o.** = to try to make s.o. favor you. **cur•ry•comb,** *n.* stiff brush for brushing a horse.

curse [kɜːs] 1. *n.* (a) evil magic spell. (b) swear word. (c) calamity/evil. (d) *inf.* **the c.** = woman's menstrual periods. 2. *v.* (a) to cast an evil spell on (s.o.). (b) to swear.

cur•sive ['kɜːsɪv] *adj.* (writing) with the letters joined together.

cur•sor ['kɜːsə] *n.* spot of light which moves round a computer screen, showing where work is being done.

cur•so•ry ['kɜːsərɪ] *adj.* rapid/superficial (inspection/glance). **cur•so•ri•ly,** *adv.* rapidly.

curt [kɜːt] *adj.* (-er, -est) abrupt. **curt•ly,** *adv.* abruptly. **curt•ness,** *n.* being curt.

cur•tail [kɜː'teɪl] *v.* to shorten; to reduce. **cur•tail•ment,** *n.* act of curtailing.

cur•tain ['kɜːtn] *n.* long piece of material hanging by hooks from a pole, covering a window or cutting off the stage in a theater. 2. *v.* (*also* **c. off**) to hide/to cover with a curtain. **cur•tain-call,** *n.* calling of an actor to take a bow after the end of a performance. **cur•tain-rod,** *n.* rod on which a curtain is hung.

curt•sy ['kɜːtsɪ] 1. *n.* respectful movement made by women/girls, by bending the knees

---

æ back, ɑː farm, ɒ top, aɪ pipe, aʊ how, aɪə fire, aʊə flower, ɔː bought, ɔɪ toy, e fed, eəhair, eɪ take, ə afraid, əʊ boat, əʊə lower, ɜː word, iː heap, ɪ hit, ɪə hear, uː school, ʊ book, ʌ but, b back, d dog, ð then, dʒ just, f fog, g go, h hand, j yes, k catch, l last, m mix, n nut, ŋ sing, p penny, r round, s some, ʃ short, t too, tʃ chop, θ thing, v voice, w was, z zoo, ʒ treasure

and putting one foot forward. 2. *v*. **to c. to s.o.** = to make a curtsy to s.o.

curve [kɜːv] 1. *n*. rounded shape like a semi-circle. 2. *v*. to make a rounded shape. **cur•va•ceous** [kɜːˈveɪʃəs] *adj*. (girl) with a rounded figure. **cur•va•ture** [ˈkɜːvətʃə] *n*. bending of something into a curve; **c. of the spine** = abnormal bending of the spine. **curved,** *adj*. rounded.

cush•ion [ˈkuʃn] 1. *n*. bag filled with feathers, etc., for sitting/leaning on. 2. *v*. to soften (a blow).

cush•y [ˈkuʃɪ] *adj*. (**-ier, -iest**) *inf*. easy (job).

cusp [kʌsp] *n*. point where two curves meet.

cus•pi•dor [ˈkʌspɪˈdɔː] *n*. bowl into which one can spit.

cuss•ed [ˈkʌsɪd] *adj. inf*. awkward and contrary. **cuss•ed•ness** [ˈkʌsɪdnəs] *n. inf*. being cussed.

cus•tard [ˈkʌstəd] *n*. sweet dessert made with eggs, milk and flavoring, baked or boiled.

cus•to•dy [ˈkʌstədɪ] *n*. keeping. **cus•to•di•an** [kʌˈstəʊdɪən] *n*. person who keeps sth safe; guardian of an ancient monument, etc.

cus•tom [ˈkʌstəm] *n*. (a) habit. (b) patronizing a business establishment. **custom-built/custom-made** = made to special order. **cus•tom•ar•i•ly,** *adv*. usually. **cus•tom•ar•y,** *adj*. habitual. **cus•tom•er,** *n*. client/person who patronizes a business establishment. **cus•tom•ize,** *v*. to convert (car) to a customer's special and peculiar requirements. **cus•toms,** *n*. tax on goods imported into a country.

cut [kʌt] 1. *n*. (a) reduction (in salary); breaking off (electricity supply). (b) opening made with a sharp blade; small wound. (c) **short c.** = way which is shorter than usual. (d) way in which a suit/jacket, etc., is made. (e) piece/slice of meat. (f) share (of profits, etc.). 2. (**cut**) (a) to make an opening (using a sharp blade); to wound (with a knife); to shorten; to reduce. (b) to divide (a pack of playing cards) in half. (c) not to look at (s.o.) whom you know. (d) to miss (a lecture). 3. *adj*. which has been cut. **cut down,** *v*. to chop down (a tree); to reduce (an amount). **cut in,** *v*. to interrupt a conversation; to move in quickly in front of another car in traffic. **cut off,** *v*. to disconnect (electricity supply); to remove; to stop (s.o.) reaching a place. **cut out,** *v*. (a) to stop (eating sth, etc.). (b) to remove a small piece by cutting it from a large piece (of paper, etc.); **he is not cut out for the army** = he does not fit in with/is not suitable for the army. **cut-rate,** *adj*. cheap. **cut•ter,** *n*. (a) person who cuts. (b) machine which cuts. (c) small, fast boat. **cut•throat,**

adj. vicious/intense. **cut•ting,** 1. *adj*. which cuts; sharply critical (remark). 2. *n*. (a) small piece of paper cut out of a newspaper. (b) little piece of a plant which will take root if stuck in dirt or the ground. **cut up,** *v*. to make into small pieces by cutting; *inf*. **cut up** = very upset.

cu•ta•ne•ous [kjuːˈteɪnɪəs] *adj*. referring to the skin.

cute [kjuːt] *adj. inf*. nice. **cute•ness,** *n*. niceness.

cu•ti•cle [ˈkjuːtɪkl] *n*. skin round a fingernail or toenail.

cut•lass [ˈkʌtləs] *n*. short sword, used in the navy and in cavalry.

cut•ler•y [ˈkʌtlərɪ] *n*. (*no pl*.) knives, forks and spoons.

cut•let [ˈkʌtlət] *n*. (a) thin slice of meat (usu. with the rib bone attached). (b) fried patty made with meat, etc.

cut•tle•fish [ˈkʌtlfɪʃ] *n*. animal (like a squid) which lives in the sea and squirts ink when attacked.

CV [siːˈviː] *n*. curriculum vitae.

cwt *abbrev for* hundredweight.

cy•a•nide [ˈsaɪənaɪd] *n*. strong poison.

cyber- [ˈsaɪbə] *prefix meaning* computer; **cybercafé; cyberspace.**

cy•ber•ca•fé [ˈsaɪbəkæfeɪ] *n*. café with computers offering customers access to the Internet.

cy•ber•net•ics [saɪbəˈnetɪks] *n*. science of the communication of information.

cy•ber•space [ˈsaɪbəspeɪs] *n*. a three-dimensional representation of information stored in a computer/computer network.

cy•cla•men [ˈsɪkləmən] *n*. common indoor plant with pink flowers which grow from a corm.

cy•cle [ˈsaɪkl] 1. *n*. (a) period during which sth returns. (b) series of songs or poems. (c) bicycle. 2. *v*. to go on a bicycle. **cy•clic, cyclical** [ˈsɪklɪk(l)] *adj*. occuring in cycles. **cy•cling,** *n*. riding a bicycle as a sport. **cy•clist,** *n*. person who rides a bicycle.

cy•clone [ˈsaɪkləʊn] *n*. tropical storm.

cy•clo•styled [ˈsaɪkləʊstaɪld] *adj*. (copy) produced from a stencil.

cy•clo•tron [ˈsaɪkləʊtron] *n*. machine which accelerates the spiral movement of particles, used in nuclear processes.

cyg•net [ˈsɪgnət] *n*. baby swan.

cyl•in•der [ˈsɪlɪndə] *n*. shape like a tube; part of an engine, of this shape, in which a piston moves. **cy•lin•dri•cal** [sɪˈlɪndrɪkl] *adj*. tube-shaped.

cym•bals [ˈsɪmbəlz] *n. pl*. pair of round metal plates which are banged together to make a loud noise in music.

cyn•ic ['sɪnɪk] *n.* person who mocks/who doubts that anything is good. **cyn•i•cal**, *adj.* referring to a cynic. **cyn•i•cal•ly**, *adv.* in a cynical, mocking way. **cyn•i•cism** ['sɪnɪsɪzəm] *n.* being cynical.

cy•no•sure ['saɪnəsjuə] *n.* center of attraction.

cy•press ['saɪprəs] *n.* (*pl.* **-es**) tall slim evergreen tree.

Cyp•ri•ot ['sɪprɪət] 1. *adj.* referring to Cyprus. 2. *n.* person from Cyprus.

cyst [sɪst] *n.* small growth on or inside the body. **cys•ti•tis** [sɪs'taɪtɪs] *n.* inflammation of the bladder. **cys•tos•co•py**, *n.* operation to examine the bladder by means of a very small telescope on the end of a tube.

cy•tol•o•gy [saɪ'tɒlədʒɪ] *n.* study of cells.

Czech [tʃek] 1. *adj.* referring to the Czech Republic. 2. *n.* (a) person from the Czech Republic. (b) language spoken in the Czech Republic.

æ back, aː farm, ɒ top, aɪ pipe, aʊ how, aiə fire, aʊə flower, ɔː bought, ɔɪ toy, e fed, eəhair, eɪ take, ə afraid, əʊ boat, əʊə lower, vː word, iː heap, ɪ hit, ɪə hear, uː school, ʊ book, ʌ but, b back, d dog, ð then, dʒ just, f fog, g go, h hand, j yes, k catch, l last, m mix, n nut, ŋ sing, p penny, r round, s some, ʃ short, t too, tʃ chop, θ thing, v voice, w was, z zoo, ʒ treasure

Dd

dab [dæb] 1. *n.* (a) light tap. (b) small flat fish. (c) small quantity. 2. *v.* (**dabbed**) to give (sth) a light tap; **to d. (sth) on** = to apply (paint, etc.) by pressing lightly.

dab•ble ['dæbl] *v.* to paddle (in water); **he dabbles in politics** = he does a little political work.

dab•chick ['dæbtʃɪk] *n.* common small dark waterbird with a red forehead.

dace [deɪs] *n.* (*pl.* **dace**) small edible freshwater fish.

dachs•hund ['dækshʊnd] *n.* breed of long low dog (originally from Germany).

dac•tyl ['dæktɪl] *n.* measure (one long and two short syllables) used in poetry.

dad [dæd], **dad•dy** ['dædɪ] *n. inf.* father. **dad•dy-long-legs,** *n.* insect with very long legs.

da•do ['deɪdəʊ] *n.* (*pl.* **-os**) lower part of a wall, which is paneled or painted differently from the upper part.

daf•fo•dil ['dæfədɪl] *n.* spring flower in shades of yellow, with a trumpet-shaped center.

daft [dɑːft] *adj. inf.* silly.

dag•ger ['dægə] *n.* short knife; **to look daggers at** = to look at angrily.

da•guerre•o•type [də'gerɪəʊtaɪp] *n.* photographic process, where the image is captured on silver-coated plate.

dahl•ia ['deɪlɪə] *n.* autumn garden flower (produced from a bulbous root).

Dail [dɔɪl] *n.* lower house of the Irish Parliament.

dai•ly ['deɪlɪ] 1. *adj.* every day. 2. *adv.* **twice d.** = two times a day. 3. *n.* newspaper published every weekday.

dain•ty ['deɪntɪ] *adj.* (**-ier, -iest**) delicate; small. **dain•ti•ly,** *adv.* delicately.

dair•y ['deərɪ] *n.* place where milk, cream and butter are processed or sold; **d. produce** = milk, butter, cream and cheese. **d. farm** = farm which produces milk. **dair•y•man,** *n* (*pl.* **-men**) man who looks after dairy cows.

da•is ['deɪɪs] *n.* low platform (in large hall).

dai•sy ['deɪzɪ] *n.* small pink and white summer flower; **d. wheel printer** = typewriter/computer printer, where the characters are on the ends of spokes of a wheel.

dale [deɪl] *n.* (*in north of England*) valley.

dal•ly ['dælɪ] *v.* to idle; to spend time doing nothing. **dal•li•ance,** *n.* (*old*) idling.

dal•ma•tian [dæl'meɪʃn] *n.* large white dog with black spots.

dam [dæm] 1. *n.* (a) wall (of earth or concrete) blocking a river, etc. (b) female mammal which is a mother. 2. *v.* (**dammed**) to block (a river) by building a wall across it.

dam•age ['dæmɪdʒ] 1. *n.* (a) harm (done to things, not to people). (b) **damages** = payment ordered by a court to a victim. (c) *inf.* total of a bill. 2. *v.* to spoil or harm (sth).

dam•ask ['dæməsk] *n.* kind of patterned material, used esp. for tableclothes, etc. **dam•a•scene,** *adj.* (steel) decorated with patterns of silver or gold.

dame [deɪm] *n.* (a) *inf.* woman. (b) *Brit.* title given to women (*equivalent to* Sir *for men*).

damn [dæm] 1. *n.* curse. 2. *v.* to condemn; to curse; to criticize. 3. *inter. inf. expressing annoyance.* **dam•na•ble,** *adj.* cursed. **dam•na•tion** [dæm'neɪʃn] *n.* state of being eternally condemned. **damned,** *adj. inf.* very annoying. **damn•ing,** *adj.* which shows that sth is wrong.

damp [dæmp] 1. *n.* wetness. 2. *adj.* (**-er, -est**) rather wet. 3. *v.* to wet; to reduce (enthusiasm). **damp•en,** *v.* to damp. **damp•er,** *n.* (a) plate at the back of a fireplace which regulates the draft. (b) soft pad which touches a piano string to soften the tone. **damp•ness,** *n.* state of being wet. **damp-proof,** *adj.* resistant to wet.

dam•sel ['dæmzl] *n.* (*old*) girl.

dam•son ['dæmzən] *n.* small purple plum; tree which bears this fruit.

dance [dɑːns] 1. *n* (a) way of moving to music. (b) evening entertainment where people dance. 2. *v.* (a) to move (in time to music). (b) to jump up and down (with excitement). **danc•er,** *n.* person who dances; **ballet d.** = person who dances in ballet.

dan•de•li•on ['dændɪlaɪən] *n.* wild plant with yellow flowers and bitter sap.

dan•druff ['dændrʌf] *n.* small pieces of dry skin (in the hair).

dan•dy ['dændɪ] *n.* man who is too interested in clothes. **dan•di•fied,** *adj.* like a dandy.

Dane [deɪn] *n.* person from Denmark; **Great D.** = breed of very large short-haired dog.

dan•ger ['deɪndʒə] *n.* risk; possibility of harm or death; **in d.** = at risk; **out of d./off the d. list** = no longer likely to die. **dan•ger•ous,** *adj.* which can cause injury or death. **dan•ger•ous•ly,** *adv.* in a dangerous way.

dan•gle ['dæŋgl] *v.* to (cause to) hang limply.

Dan•ish ['deɪnɪʃ] 1. *adj.* referring to Denmark; **D. pastry** = sweet pastry cake with jam or fruit folded in it. 2. *n.* language spoken in Denmark.

dank [dæŋk] *adj.* cold and damp.

daph•ne ['dæfnɪ] *n.* small shrub with pink flowers which appear very early in the spring.

dap•per ['dæpə] *adj.* smart/elegant.

dap•pled ['dæpld] *adj.* covered with patches of light and dark color.

dare ['deə] 1. *n.* act of daring s.o. to do sth. 2. *v.* (a) to be brave enough (to do sth); **I d. say** = perhaps/probably. (b) to challenge (s.o.) to do sth by suggesting it is cowardly not to do it. **dare•dev•il,** *adj. & n.* (person) full of reckless bravery. **dar•ing.** 1. *adj.* brave but foolish. 2. *n.* foolish bravery.

dark [dɑːk] 1. *adj.* (**-er, -est**) (a) with little or no light. (b) not a light color; **d. horse** = person/thing which succeeds though not expected to do so; **D. Ages** = period between the end of the Roman civilization in Northern Europe and the Middle Ages. (c) gloomy. 2. *n.* (a) absence of light. (b) **to keep s.o. in the d.** = to keep sth a secret from s.o. **dark•en,** *v.* to become dark. **dark•ly,** *adv.* in a gloomy way. **dark•ness,** *n.* absence of light. **dark•room,** *n.* room with a special light, in which you can develop and print films.

dar•ling ['dɑːlɪŋ] *n. & adj.* (person) loved; lovable.

darn [dɑːn] 1. *v.* to mend (holes in clothes). 2. *n.* place where clothes have been mended. **darn•ing,** *n.* action of mending; clothes which are waiting to be mended.

dart [dɑːt] 1. *n.* (a) light arrow with a sharp point. (b) small heavy arrow with feathers (for playing a game with); **darts** = games where two teams throw small heavy arrows at a round target. (c) small tuck sewn into a garment to make it fit. (d) quick rush. 2. *v.* to run fast. **dart•board,** *n.* round target at which darts are thrown.

dash [dæʃ] 1. *n.* (*pl.* **-es**) (a) small amount. (b) little line. (c) sudden rush. 2. *v.* (a) to rush. (b) to smash (sth). **dash•board,** *n.* instrument panel in a car. **dash•ing,** *adj.* very smart and energetic (person).

das•tard•ly ['dɑːstədlɪ] *adj.* cowardly and unpleasant.

da•ta ['deɪtə] *n.* statistical information; **d. bank** = store of information in a computer; **d. protection** = keeping information or computer records safely, so that they cannot be copied. *see also* **da•tum. da•ta•base,** *n.* data stored in a computer, which can be used to provide information of various kinds. **da•ta pro•cess•ing,** *n.* analysis of statistical information using a computer.

date [deɪt] 1. *n.* (a) number of a day, month or year; **up to d.** = recent; **he is bringing the book up to d.** = he is revising the book to put in the most recent information; **out of d.** = not modern; **the book is three years out of d.** (b) agreed meeting time. (c) fruit of a date palm. 2. *v.* (a) to write the number of the day on (sth). (b) to give the date of (an antique, etc.). (c) to agree to meet (s.o. of the opposite sex) at a particular time. (c) **this house dates from 1600** = this house has existed since 1600. (d) to seem old-fashioned. **dat•a•ble,** *adj.* which can be dated. **dat•ed,** *adj.* old-fashioned. **date•less,** *adj.* with no date. **date•line,** *n.* heading (with date and place) of a report from a foreign correspondent. **date line,** *n.* line of longitude (in the Pacific Ocean) which indicates the change in date from east to west. **date palm,** *n.* palm tree which provides small, very sweet brown fruit.

da•tive ['deɪtɪv] *adj. & n.* (*in grammar*) (case) showing giving.

da•tum ['deɪtəm] *n.* (*pl.* **data**) piece of information.

daub [dɔːb] 1. *n.* (a) smear. (b) *inf.* bad painting. 2. *v.* to smear with paint/with mud, etc.

daugh•ter ['dɔːtə] *n.* female child (of a parent). **daugh•ter-in-law,** *n.* (*pl.* **daughters-in-law**) son's wife.

daunt [dɔːnt] *v.* to discourage. **not daunted** = not frightened. **daunt•less,** *adj.* fearless.

dav•en•port ['dævənpɔːt] *n.* (a) sofa. (b) small writing desk.

da•vit ['dævɪt] *n.* (*on a ship*) small crane for lowering the lifeboats into the sea.

daw•dle ['dɔːdl] *v.* to walk slowly and aimlessly.

æ back, ɑː farm, ɒ top, aɪ pipe, aʊ how, aɪə fire, aʊə flower, ɔː bought, ɔɪ toy, e fed, eəhair, eɪ take, ə afraid, əʊ boat, əʊə lower, vː word, iː heap, ɪ hit, ɪə hear, uː school, ʊ book, ʌ but, b back, d dog, ð then, dʒ just, f fog, g go, h hand, j yes, k catch, l last, m mix, n nut, ŋ sing, p penny, r round, s some, ʃ short, t too, tʃ chop, θ thing, v voice, w was, z zoo, ʒ treasure

dawn [dɔ:n] 1. *n.* (a) beginning of day, when the sun rises. (b) beginning (of civilization). 2. *v.* (a) (*of day*) to begin. (b) **it dawned on him that** = he began to realize that.

day [deɪ] *n.* (a) period of time lasting 24 hours. (b) period of time from morning to night. (c) light. (d) **two apples a d.** = every day. (e) **one d./some d.** = sometime in the future. (f) period (in the past). **day•break,** *n.* early morning when the sun is about to rise. **day care cen•ter,** *n.* place where elderly or disabled people can meet and be looked after or where young children can be cared for during the day. **day•dream.** 1. *n.* dream which you have during the day when you are not asleep. 2. *v.* to think about other things; not to concentrate. **day•light,** *n.* light of day; **d. saving time** = system of advancing the clocks in summer to take advantage of the longer daylight period. **day•time,** *n.* **in the d.** = during the day.

daze [deɪz] 1. *n.* state of not being mentally alert. 2. *v.* to stun (s.o.).

daz•zle ['dæzl] *v.* to blind (temporarily). **daz•zling,** *adj.* very bright (light).

db, dB *abbrev. for* decibel.

D & C *abbrev. for* dilation and curettage.

DC *abbrev. for* direct current.

DDT [di:di:'ti:] *n.* insecticide, highly damaging to the environment.

dea•con ['di:kən] *n.* minor priest. **dea•con•ess,** *n.* woman who can direct services (in some Protestant churches).

dead [ded] 1. *adj.* (a) not alive; (telephone line, etc.) not working. (b) complete (silence, etc.). (c) no longer used. 2. *n.* (a) **the d.** =dead people. (b) **in the d. of night** = in the middle of the night. 3. *adv.* (a) completely. (b) exactly. **dead•beat,** *n. sl.* person who does not pay his debts. **dead•en,** *v.* to make (a sound) quieter; to make (a blow) soft. **dead end,** *n.* (street/way) leading nowhere. **dead heat,** *n.* race where two contestants come in equal first. **dead let•ter,** (a) letter which cannot be delivered. (b) law which is no longer obeyed. **dead•line,** *n.* date by which sth has to be done. **dead•li•ness,** *n.* being deadly. **dead•lock.** 1. *n.* state where two sides cannot agree. 2. *v.* to (cause to) be unable to agree. **dead•ly,** *adj.* (-ier, -iest) so strong as to kill; **d. nightshade** = very poisonous plant. **dead•pan,** *adj.* not showing any emotion.

deaf [def] 1. *adj.* (-er, -est) unable to hear; having difficulty in hearing. 2. *n.* **the d.** = people who cannot hear. **deaf•en,** *v.* to make deaf (by a loud noise). **deaf•en•ing,** *adj.* so loud as to make you deaf. **deaf•ness,** *n.* state of being deaf.

deal [di:l] 1. *n.* (a) large quantity; **a good d. better** = much better. (b) handing out (playing cards). (c) (business) affair. (d) wood from a pine tree. 2. *v.* (**dealt** [delt]) (a) to hand out. (b) **to d. with** = to organize to solve a problem. (c) **to d. in** = to buy and sell. **deal•er,** *n.* person who buys and sells. **deal•er•ship,** *n.* business of a dealer. **deal•ings,** *n. pl.* business/affairs.

dean [di:n] *n.* person in charge of lecturers or priests. **dean•er•y,** *n.* position or house of a dean (in a cathedral).

dear ['dɪə] *adj.* (-er, -est) (a) well liked; loved. (b) (*addressing someone at the beginning of a letter*) **D. Mr. Smith; D. Sir.** (c) expensive. 2. *inter.* **oh d.!** = how annoying! **dear•ly,** *adv.* tenderly; very much.

dearth [dɜ:θ] *n.* scarcity.

death [deθ] *n.* act of dying. **d. duty** = tax paid on money left by dead person; **d. mask** = plaster mask made of s.o.'s face, after death; **d. rate** = number of people who die (as a percentage of the population). **death•bed,** *n.* bed on which s.o. is dying. **death•less,** *adj.* which will live for ever. **death•ly,** *adv.* as if dead. **death•trap,** *n.* dangerous place. **death watch bee•tle,** *n.* beetle which bores holes in wood and makes a clicking sound.

deb [deb] *n. inf.* debutante.

de•ba•cle [deɪ'bɑ:kl] *n.* (a) sudden defeat/collapse. (b) breakup of ice on a river in spring.

de•bar [dɪ'bɑ:] *v.* (**debarred**) **to d. s.o. from sth** = to forbid s.o. to do sth.

de•base [dɪ'beɪs] *v.* to degrade; to reduce the value of (sth, esp. the value of the metal in coinage). **de•base•ment,** *n.* act of debasing.

de•bate [dɪ'beɪt] 1. *n.* formal discussion. 2. *v.* to discuss. **de•bat•a•ble,** *adj.* not absolutely certain.

de•bauched [dɪ'bɔ:tʃt] *adj.* (person) who spends his time in wild living and enjoys immoral pleasures. **de•bauch•er•y,** *n.* wild living.

de•ben•ture [dɪ'bentʃə] *n.* document showing that a company agrees to repay a debt, and to pay a fixed interest on it, the money being secured on the company's assets.

de•bil•i•tate [dɪ'bɪlɪteɪt] *v.* to make weak. **de•bil•i•ty,** *n.* Weakness.

deb•it ['debɪt] 1. *n.* (money) which is owed; **on the d. side** = against (a proposal). 2. *v.* to deduct money from (an account). **deb•it card,** *n.* card that allows customers to pay for goods by deducting money from their bank accounts via an electronic link through telephone networks.

deb•o•nair [debə'neə] *adj.* carefree/relaxed (air).

de•brief ['di:'bri:f] *v.* to ask (s.o.) questions to obtain information about a mission which he has just completed. **de•brief•ing,** *n.* obtaining information about a mission by questioning the person who carried it out.

de•bris ['debri:] *n.* pieces (of a demolished building/crashed aircraft, etc.).

debt [det] *n.* money owed to s.o.; **he is in d.** = he owes money. **debt•or,** *n.* person who owes money.

de•bug [di:'bʌg] *v.* (**debugged**) to remove bugs from (sth); to correct errors in a computer program.

de•bunk [di'bʌŋk] *v. inf.* to disprove.

de•but ['deibju:] *n.* first appearance (of an artist/actor, etc.). **deb•u•tante,** *n.* girl who goes into adult society for the first time.

deca- ['dekə] *prefix meaning* ten.

dec•ade ['dekeid] *n.* period of ten years.

dec•a•dence ['dekədəns] *n.* decline in moral values. **dec•a•dent,** *adj.* declining in moral values.

de•caf•fein•at•ed [di:'kæfineitid] *adj.* (coffee) which has had the caffeine removed.

de•cal ['di:kæl] *n.* sticker/piece of plastic or paper with a pattern or slogan which you can stick to a surface as a decoration.

de•camp [di:'kæmp] *v. inf.* to go away.

de•cant [di'kænt] *v.* to pour (liquid, esp. wine) from a bottle into another container. **de•cant•er,** *n.* glass bottle which wine is poured into before serving.

de•cap•i•tate [di'kæpiteit] *v.* to cut off the head of (s.o.). **de•cap•i•ta•tion** [dikæpi-'teiʃn] *n.* act of cutting off a head.

de•car•bon•ize [de'kɑ:bənaiz] *v.* to remove carbon deposits from (a gas engine).

de•cath•lon [di'kæθlən] *n.* sporting competition where each athlete competes in ten different types of sport.

de•cay [di'kei] 1. *n.* falling into ruin; rotting. 2. *v.* to fall into ruin; to rot.

de•cease [di'si:s] *n.* (*formal*) death. **de•ceased,** *n.* dead person.

de•ceit [di'si:t] *n.* trickery. **de•ceit•ful,** *adj.* tricking. **de•ceit•ful•ly,** *adv.* in a deceitful way. **de•ceive** [di'si:v] *v.* to trick; to make (s.o.) believe sth which is not true.

de•cel•er•ate [di:'seləreit] *v.* to (make sth) go slower. **de•cel•er•a•tion** [di:selə'reiʃn] *n.* going slower.

De•cem•ber [di'sembə] *n.* 12th month of the year.

de•cent ['di:sənt] *adj.* (a) honest. (b) quite good. **de•cen•cy,** *n.* honor; good morals. **de•cent•ly,** *adv.* in a decent way.

de•cen•tral•ize [di:'sentrəlaiz] *v.* to move (authority/offices) from the center. **de•cen•tral•i•za•tion** [di:sentrəlai'zeiʃn] *n.* act of decentralizing.

de•cep•tion [di'sepʃn] *n.* fraud; making s.o. believe sth which is not true. **de•cep•tive,** *adj.* not as it looks. **de•cep•tive•ly,** *adv.* in a way which deceives.

dec•i•bel ['desibel] *n.* unit of measurement of noise.

de•cide [di'said] *v.* to make up your mind (to do sth). **de•cid•ed,** *adj.* (a) firm (tone, manner). (b) certain/obvious (difference, etc.). **de•cid•ed•ly,** *adv.* (a) in a firm manner. (b) certainly.

de•cid•u•ous [di'sidjuəs] *adj.* (tree) which loses its leaves in winter.

dec•i•mal ['desiml] 1. *adj.* (system of mathematics) based on the number 10; **d. point** = dot indicating the division between units and parts which are less than one unit (such as 2.05). 2. *n.* figure expressed on the base of 10. **dec•i•mal•ize,** *v.* to change to decimals. **dec•i•mate,** *v.* to remove one out of ten of; to cut down/to remove/to kill in large numbers.

de•ci•pher [di'saifə] *v.* to make out (sth badly written, or written in code). **de•ci•pher•ment,** *n.* act of deciphering.

de•ci•sion [di'siʒn] *n.* making up your mind; ability to make up your mind. **de•ci•sive** [di-'saisiv] *adj.* firm (voice); (contest, etc.) which brings about a result. **de•ci•sive•ly,** *adv.* in a decisive way; firmly.

deck [dek] *n.* (a) floor (of ship/bus). **flight deck** = (i) control cabin (of plane); (ii) flat surface on an aircraft carrier where aircraft land and take off. (b) pack (of playing cards). (c) apparatus for playing records, tapes, cassettes. **deck•chair,** *n.* collapsible canvas chair (for sitting in the sun). **decked,** *adj.* decorated/covered with.

deck•le-edged [dekl'edʒd] *adj.* (paper) with a ragged edge.

de•claim [di'kleim] *v.* to recite in a loud voice. **de•clam•a•to•ry** [di'klæmətəri] *adj.* as if in a loud voice.

de•clare [di'kleə] *v.* (a) to state (officially). (b)

æ back, ɑ: farm, ɒ: top, ai pipe, aʊ how, aiə fire, aʊə flower, ɔ: bought, ɔi toy, e fed, eəhair, ei take, ə afraid, əʊ boat, əʊə lower, v: word, i: heap, i hit, iə hear, u: school, ʊ book, ʌ but, b back, d dog, ð then, dʒ just, f fog, g go, h hand, j yes, k catch, l last, m mix, n nut, ŋ sing, p penny, r round, s some, ʃ short, t too, tʃ chop, θ thing, v voice, w was, z zoo, ʒ treasure

(*at customs*) to say what (dutiable goods) one has. (c) (*at cards*) to say which suit is trumps.

dec•la•ra•tion [deklə'reɪʃn] *n.* (official) statement.

de•cline [dɪ'klaɪn] 1. *n.* downward trend. 2. *v.* (a) to refuse (an invitation). (b) to become weaker. (c) (*in grammar*) to show the different cases of (a word). **de•clen•sion**, *n.* form of the different cases of a word.

de•cliv•i•ty [dɪ'klɪvɪtɪ] *n.* slope downwards.

de•code [di:'kəud] *v.* to translate (a message) out of code. **de•cod•er**, *n.* person who decodes.

de•col•late ['dekəleɪt] *v.* to separate copies. **de•col•la•tor**, *n.* machine which separates copies (of computer printouts).

de•com•pose [di:kəm'pəuz] *v.* to rot. **de•com•po•si•tion** [di:kɒmpə'zɪʃn] *n.* act of rotting.

de•com•pres•sion [di:kəm'preʃn] *n.* reducing the pressure in sth; **d. chamber** = room where divers stay to get used gradually to normal pressures after working in very deep water.

de•con•ges•tant [di:kən'dʒestənt] *n.* medicine which unblocks, esp. a blocked nose.

de•con•tam•i•nate [di:kən'tæmɪneɪt] *v.* to remove infection/radioactivity from (sth). **de•con•tam•i•na•tion** [di:kəntæmɪ'neɪʃn] *n.* act of decontaminating.

de•con•trol [di:kən'trəul] *v.* to remove controls from sth.

de•cor ['deɪkɔ:] *n.* (a) scenery (for a play). (b) interior decoration (of a room).

dec•o•rate ['dekəreɪt] *v.* (a) to paint (a building); to put new wallpaper in (a room); to put up flags/lights (to celebrate an occasion). (b) to award (s.o.) a medal. **dec•o•ra•tions** [dekə'reɪʃnz] *n.pl.* (a) flags/lights, etc., used to celebrate an occasion. (b) medals. **dec•o•ra•tive** ['dekərətɪv] *adj.* pleasant to look at; serving as a decoration. **dec•o•ra•tive•ly**, *adv.* in a decorative way. **dec•o•ra•tor**, *n.* person who paints houses; **interior d.** = person who designs ways of decorating the inside of buildings.

de•co•rum [dɪ'kɔ:rʌm] *n.* being decorous. **dec•o•rous** ['dekərəs] *adj.* very well-behaved.

de•coy 1. *n.* ['di:kɔɪ] object to attract and trap sth. 2. *v.* [dɪ'kɔɪ] to attract and trap (sth/s.o.).

de•crease 1. *n.* ['di:kri:s] fall; lessening. 2. *v.* [di:'kri:s] to fall; to become less.

de•cree [dɪ'kri:] 1. *n.* official legal order, as of a government, church, etc. 2. *v.* to state as a legal order.

de•crep•it [dɪ'krepɪt] *adj.* falling to pieces; old and feeble (person). **de•crep•i•tude**, *n.* being decrepit.

de•cry [dɪ'kraɪ] *v.* to say that (sth) is bad.

ded•i•cate ['dedɪkeɪt] *v.* to place (a church) under the patronage of a saint; to write a book for/to offer a book to (s.o.); to spend (all your life) on sth. **ded•i•cat•ed**, *adj.* (computer/program) reserved for a particular task. **ded•i•ca•tion** [dedɪ'keɪʃn] *n.* (a) devotion. (b) inscription at the beginning of a book showing to whom it is dedicated.

de•duce [dɪ'dju:s] *v.* to conclude (from examining evidence).

de•duct [dɪ'dʌkt] *v.* to remove (from a sum of money). **de•duct•i•ble**, *adj.* which can be deducted. **de•duc•tion** [dɪ'dʌkʃn] *n.* (a) thing which is deduced; conclusion. (b) thing which is deducted; sum of money which is taken away.

deed [di:d] *n.* (a) (noble) act. (b) legal document; **the deeds of a house** = papers showing who owns the house.

deem [di:m] *v.* (*formal*) to consider.

deep [di:p] 1. *adj.* (**-er, -est**) (a) which goes down a long way. (b) rich/dark (color). (c) low-pitched/bass (voice). 2. *adv.* a long way down. 3. *n.* **the d.** = the sea. **deep•en**, *v.* to go further down; to become deeper; to make (sth) deeper. **deep-freeze**, *n.* refrigerator for freezing food and keeping it frozen. **deep-fried**, *adj.* cooked in deep oil. **deep•ly**, *adv.* profoundly; very much. **deep-root•ed**, *adj.* which goes down a long way. **deep-seat•ed**, *adj.* solid/firm.

deer [dɪə] *n.* (*pl.* deer) wild animal which runs fast, and of which the male usually has horns. **deer•hound**, *n.* large fast-running dog, bred for chasing deer. **deer•stalk•er**, *n.* round tweed hat, with small peaks at the front and back.

de•face [dɪ'feɪs] *v.* to spoil the surface of (sth); to write on (a wall); to mutilate (a statue). **de•face•ment**, *n.* act of defacing.

de fac•to [di:'fæktəu] *adj.* existing in fact/real.

def•a•ma•tion [defə'meɪʃn] *n.* **d. of character** = saying bad things about s.o. **de•fam•a•to•ry** [dɪ'fæmətrɪ] *adj.* which says bad things about s.o. **de•fame**, [dɪ'feɪm] *v.* to say bad things about s.o.

de•fault [dɪ'fɔ:lt] 1. *n.* (a) failing to carry out the terms of a contract. (b) (*computers*) set way of working; **d. drive** = the drive which is set to be accessed first. 2. *v.* to fail to carry out the terms of a contract. **de•fault•er**, *n.* person who defaults.

de•feat [dɪ'fi:t] 1. *n.* loss (of fight/vote). 2. *v.* to beat (s.o. in a fight/vote). **de•feat•ism**, *n.* feeling sure that you will lose. **de•feat•ist**, *adj.* sure that you will lose.

def•e•cate ['defəkeɪt] *v.* to pass waste matter from the bowels.

de•fect 1. *n.* ['diːfekt] fault. 2. *v.* [dɪ'fekt] to leave the armed forces/your country, to go over to the enemy side. **de•fec•tion,** *n.* going over to the side of the enemy. **de•fec•tive,** *adj.* faulty. **de•fec•tor,** *n.* person who defects.

de•fend [dɪ'fend] *v.* (a) to protect (from attack). (b) to speak on behalf of (an accused person). **de•fend•ant,** *n.* person who is accused of doing sth illegal/person who is sued in a civil law suit. **de•fend•er,** *n.* person who defends.

de•fense, *Brit.* **de•fence** [dɪ'fens] *n.* (a) protection. (b) **the d.** = lawyers who speak on behalf of an accused person. **de•fense•less,** *adj.* unprotected. **de•fen•si•bil•i•ty,** *n.* being defensible. **de•fen•si•ble,** *adj.* which can be defended. **de•fen•sive.** 1. *adj.* which protects. 2. *n.* **on the d.** = feeling one has to justify oneself. **de•fen•sive•ly,** *adv.* in a defensive way.

de•fer [dɪ'fɜː] *v.* (**deferred**) (a) to put off/to put back. (b) **to d. to s.o./to s.o.'s opinion** = to accept the advice of s.o. who knows better. **def•er•ence** ['defərəns] *n.* respect. **def•er•en•tial,** *adj.* respectful. **de•fer•ment,** *n.* postponement.

de•fi•ance [dɪ'faɪəns] *n.* acting against (law/authority). **de•fi•ant,** *adj.* very proud and antagonistic.

de•fib•ril•la•tor [diː'fɪbrɪleɪtə] *n.* machine which stimulates a weak heart by giving it electric shocks.

de•fi•cien•cy [dɪ'fɪʃənsɪ] *n.* lack. **de•fi•cient,** *adj.* (**in**) lacking (sth). **mentally deficient** = below normal intelligence.

def•i•cit ['defɪsɪt] *n.* amount by which expenditure is larger than receipts (in a company's/a country's accounts).

de•file 1. *n.* ['diːfaɪl] narrow pass between mountains. 2. *v.* [dɪ'faɪl] to dirty/to pollute. **de•file•ment,** *n.* act of polluting.

de•fine [dɪ'faɪn] *v.* (a) to explain clearly/to give the meaning of. (b) to state the boundary of. **de•fin•a•ble,** *adj.* which can be defined. **def•i•nite** ['defɪnət] *adj.* very clear; **d. article** = "the" (*as opposed to the indefinite article,* "a" *or* "an"). **def•i•nite•ly,** *adv.* certainly. **def•i•ni•tion** [defɪ'nɪʃn] *n.* (a) clear explanation (of a word). (b) clearness (of a picture).

de•fin•i•tive [dɪ'fɪnɪtɪv] *adj.* final/which cannot be improved.

de•flate [dɪ'fleɪt] *v.* (a) to let the air out of (a tire). (b) to reduce inflation in (the economy). **de•fla•tion** [dɪ'fleɪʃn] *n.* reducing inflation. **de•fla•tion•ar•y,** *adj.* which leads to deflation.

de•flect [dɪ'flekt] *v.* to turn aside (an arrow/a bullet, etc.). **de•flec•tion,** *n.* act of deflecting.

de•fo•li•ate [diː'fəʊlɪeɪt] *v.* to remove the leaves of (a tree, etc.). **de•fo•li•a•tion,** *n.* act of defoliating. **de•fo•li•ant,** *n.* chemical used to defoliate.

de•for•est•a•tion [diːfores'teɪʃn] *n.* removal of trees from an area of land.

de•formed [dɪ'fɔːmd] *adj.* badly shaped. **de•for•ma•tion** [defɔː'meɪʃn] *n.* spoiling the shape of sth. **de•form•i•ty,** *n.* badly shaped part of the body.

de•fraud [dɪ'frɔːd] *v.* to cheat.

de•fray [dɪ'freɪ] *v.* to pay (costs).

de•freeze [diː'friːz] *v.* to thaw (frozen food).

de•frock [diː'frɒk] *v.* to remove (a priest) from holy orders.

de•frost [diː'frɒst] *v.* to melt the ice or frost from (as the inside of a refrigerator). **de•frost•er,** *n.* blower in a car or truck which prevents the windows fogging up.

deft [deft] *adj.* (**-er, -est**) very agile/clever (with your hands). **deft•ly,** *adv.* in a deft way. **deft•ness,** *n.* being deft.

de•funct [dɪ'fʌŋkt] *adj.* dead (person); (law) which is no longer applied.

de•fuse [dɪ'fjuːz] *v.* to take the fuse out of (a bomb) so that it cannot explode; to make (a situation) less tense.

de•fy [dɪ'faɪ] *v.* (a) to refuse to obey (law). (b) to challenge (s.o. **to** sth).

de•gen•er•ate 1. *adj.* [dɪ'dʒenerət] which has degenerated/become depraved. 2. *v.* [dɪ'dʒenereɪt] (a) to become depraved. (b) to get worse. **de•gen•er•a•cy,** *n.* being degenerate. **de•gen•er•a•tion** [dɪdʒenə'reɪʃn] *n.* becoming degenerate; becoming worse.

de•grade [dɪ'greɪd] *v.* (a) to humiliate (s.o.); to make (s.o.) like an animal. (b) to make (a chemical compound) simpler. **de•grad•a•ble,** *adj.* which can be degraded. **deg•ra•da•tion** [degre'deɪʃn] *n.* becoming like an animal. **de•grad•ing,** *adj.* lowering; which humiliates/which makes a person like an animal.

æ back, ɑː farm, ɒ top, aɪ pipe, aʊ how, aɪə fire, aʊə flower, ɔː bought, ɔɪ toy, e fed, eəhair, eɪ take, ə afraid, əʊ boat, əʊə lower, vː word, iː heap, ɪ hit, ɪə hear, uː school, ʊ book, ʌ but, b back, d dog, ð then, dʒ just, f fog, g go, h hand, j yes, k catch, l last, m mix, n nut, ŋ sing, p penny, r round, s some, ʃ short, t too, tʃ chop, θ thing, v voice, w was, z zoo, ʒ treasure

de•gree [dɪ'griː] n. (a) division of an angle or scale. (b) level; amount; **to a certain d.** = to some extent. (c) diploma (of a university).

de•his•cence [diː'hɪsəns] n. bursting of a seed pod.

de•hu•mid•i•fi•er [diːhjuː'mɪdɪfaɪə] n. device which removes humidity from the air.

de•hy•drate [diː'haɪ'dreɪt] v. to remove water from (sth). **de•hy•dra•tion,** n. becoming dehydrated.

de-ice [diː'aɪs] v. to remove the ice from (sth). **de-ic•er,** n. thing which de-ices.

de•i•fy ['deɪɪfaɪ] v. to make (sth/s.o.) into a god. **de•i•fi•ca•tion** [deɪɪfɪ'keɪʃn] n. making into a god.

deign [deɪn] v. to condescend (**to** to sth).

de•i•ty ['deɪɪtɪ] n. god.

dé•jà vu [dɪːʒæ'vuː] adv. feeling that you have already seen sth before.

de•ject•ed [dɪ'dʒektɪd] adj. depressed/unhappy. **de•ject•ed•ly,** adv. in a gloomy way. **de•jec•tion** [dɪ'dʒekʃn] n. gloom/depression.

de ju•re [diː'jʊərɪ] adv. correct according to the law.

de•lay [dɪ'leɪ] 1. n. time during which one is late. 2. v. (a) to make late. (b) to wait; to put (sth) off until later.

de•lec•ta•ble [dɪ'lektəbl] adj. very pleasant; very attractive. **de•lec•ta•tion** [dɪlek'teɪʃn] n. pleasure/enjoyment.

del•e•gate 1. n. ['delɪgət] person who represents others at a meeting. 2. v. ['delɪgeɪt] to pass (authority/responsibility) on to a subordinate. **del•e•ga•tion** [delɪ'geɪʃn] n. (a) group of representatives. (b) passing of authority to a subordinate.

de•lete [dɪ'liːt] v. to cross out (a word/text). **de•le•tion** [dɪ'liːʃn] n. word/phrase which has been crossed out.

del•e•te•ri•ous [delɪ'tɪərɪəs] adj. (formal) harmful.

de•lib•er•ate 1. adj. [dɪ'lɪbərət] (a) done on purpose. (b) slow and thoughtful (speech/manner). 2. v. [dɪ'lɪbəreɪt] to debate/to discuss. **de•lib•er•ate•ly,** adv. (a) on purpose. (b) slowly and thoughtfully. **de•lib•er•a•tion** [dɪlɪbə'reɪʃn] n. (a) thought; consideration. (b) **the deliberations of a meeting** = the debate/discussion.

del•i•ca•cy ['delɪkəsɪ] n. (a) sensitivity. (b) state of being delicate. (c) rare thing to eat. **del•i•cate,** adj. (a) easily damaged; very thin. (b) liable to get illnesses. (c) very fine. **del•i•cate•ly,** adv. with care.

del•i•ca•tes•sen [delɪkə'tesn] n. store selling cold meat, salads, cheeses, etc.

de•li•cious [dɪ'lɪʃəs] adj. which tastes very good. **de•li•cious•ly,** adv. in a delicious way.

de•light [dɪ'laɪt] 1. n. pleasure. 2. v. to take pleasure (**in**). **de•light•ed,** adj. very pleased. **de•light•ful,** adj. very pleasant.

de•lin•e•ate [dɪ'lɪnɪeɪt] v. (formal) to draw. **de•lin•e•a•tion** [dɪlɪnɪ'eɪʃn] n. (formal) drawing.

de•lin•quen•cy [dɪ'lɪŋkwənsɪ] n. minor crime; **juvenile d.** = crimes committed by young people. **de•lin•quent,** adj. & n. criminal, esp. one who is young.

de•lir•i•ous [dɪ'lɪrɪəs] adj. mad with fever/with happiness. **de•lir•i•um,** n. madness caused by fever; great excitement.

de•liv•er [dɪ'lɪvə] v. (a) to bring (sth) to s.o. (b) to make (a speech). (c) to help the mother give birth to (a baby). **de•liv•er•ance,** n. (formal) rescue. **de•liv•er•y,** n. (a) bringing sth to s.o. (b) birth (of a child).

dell [del] n. small hollow filled with trees.

del•phin•i•um [del'fɪnɪəm] n. garden plant with tall blue flowers.

del•ta ['deltə] n. (a) land around the mouth of a river made of mud brought by the river. (b) fourth letter of the Greek alphabet. **d. wing aircraft** = with wings forming a triangle.

de•lude [dɪ'luːd] v. to make (s.o.) believe sth which is wrong. **de•lu•sion** [dɪ'luːʒn] n. wrong belief.

del•uge ['deljuːdʒ] 1. n. flood. 2. v. to flood (**with**).

de luxe [dɪ'lʌks] adj. very expensive; of very high quality.

delve [delv] v. to dig (**into** the past/archives, etc.).

dem•a•gogue ['deməgɒg] n. politician who appeals to the crowd for support. **dem•a•gogu•er•y,** n. appealing for support from the crowd as a means of obtaining political power.

de•mand [dɪ'mɑːnd] 1. n. asking for sth; **it is in d.** = many people want it. 2. v. to ask insistently for sth. **de•mand•ing,** adj. (job) which takes up much time and energy.

de•mar•ca•tion [diːmɑː'keɪʃn] n. showing of boundaries.

dé•marche ['deɪmɑː] n. official, often diplomatic, approach to another party.

de•mean [dɪ'miːn] v **to d. yourself** = to make yourself appear undignified or contemptible.

de•mean•or [dɪ'miːnə] n. behavior/manner.

de•ment•ed [dɪ'mentɪd] adj. mad. **de•men•tia** [dɪ'menʃə] n. (formal) madness.

de•mer•it [diː'merɪt] n. fault; unattractive point.

demi- ['demɪ] prefix meaning half.

dem•i•john ['demɪdʒɒn] *n.* large bottle for al-coholic drink.

de•mil•i•ta•rized [diːˈmɪlɪtəraɪzd] *adj.* (zone) which no longer has armed forces in it.

de•mise [dɪˈmaɪz] *n.* (*formal*) death.

dem•o ['deməʊ] *n. inf.* demonstration.

de•mo•bi•lize [diːˈməʊbɪlaɪz] *v.* to release (s.o.) from the armed forces. **de•mo•bi•li•za•tion** [diːməʊbɪlaɪˈzeɪʃn] *n.* being demobilized.

de•moc•ra•cy [dɪˈmɒkrəsɪ] *n.* system of government by freely elected representatives of the people. **dem•o•crat** ['deməkræt] *n.* (a) person who believes in democracy. (b) **Demo-crat** = member of one of the two main political parties in the U.S. **dem•o•crat•ic** [deməˈkrætɪk] *adj.* referring to democracy. **dem•o•crat•i•cal•ly**, *adv.* in a democratic way.

dem•o•graph•ic [deməˈgræfɪk] *adj.* referring to demography. **de•mog•ra•phy** [dɪˈmɒgrəfɪ] *n.* study of population figures.

de•mol•ish [dɪˈmɒlɪʃ] *v.* to knock down. **dem•o•li•tion** [deməˈlɪʃn] *n.* knocking down.

de•mon ['diːmən] *n.* devil. **de•mo•ni•a•cal** [diːməˈnaɪəkl], **de•mon•ic** [diːˈmɒnɪk] *adj.* like a devil.

dem•on•strate ['demənstreɪt] *v.* (a) to show. (b) to form a crowd to protest (**against** sth). **de•mon•stra•ble**, *adj.* which can be demonstrated. **dem•on•stra•tion** [demənˈstreɪʃn] *n.* (a) showing. (b) march to protest against sth; crowd which is protesting against sth. **dem•on•stra•tor**, *n.* person who marches/who forms part of a crowd to protest against sth; person who shows how to do sth. **de•mon•stra•tive** [dɪˈmɒnstrətɪv] *adj* (person) who shows his feelings openly.

de•mor•al•ize [dɪˈmɒrəlaɪz] *v.* to lower the morale/confidence of (s.o.). **de•mor•al•i•za•tion** [dɪmɒrəlaɪˈzeɪʃn] *n.* lowering of morale. **de•mor•al•ized**, *adj.* doubtful that you can win.

de•mote [diːˈməʊt] *v.* to give (s.o.) a less important job. **de•mo•tion**, *n.* act of demoting.

de•mur [dɪˈmɜː] *v.* (**demurred**) **to d. at** = to object to sth.

de•mure [dɪˈmjʊə] *adj.* quiet and serious (girl). **de•mure•ly**, *adv.* in a demure way.

de•mur•rage [diːˈmʌrɪdʒ] *n.* payment for keeping a ship in dock when unloading.

den [den] *n.* (a) place to hide away in. (b) *inf.* small room where you can hide away to work.

de•na•tion•al•ize [diːˈnæʃnəlaɪz] *v.* to put (a nationalized industry) into private ownership. **de•na•tion•al•i•za•tion** [dɪnæʃnlaɪˈzeɪʃn] *n.* act of denationalizing.

den•dro•chro•nol•o•gy [dendrəʊkrɒˈnɒlədʒɪ] *n.* finding the age of wood by the study of the tree rings.

den•gue ['deng] *n.* tropical fever.

de•ni•al [dɪˈnaɪəl] *n.* statement that sth is not true.

den•i•grate ['denɪgreɪt] *v.* to say that (an action) is worse than it is.

den•im ['denɪm] *n.* thick cotton cloth; **denims** = clothes made of this cloth.

den•i•zen ['denɪzən] *n.* (*formal*) inhabitant of a particular place.

de•nom•i•na•tion [dɪnɒmɪˈneɪʃn] *n.* (a) unit of money (on a bank note/coin). (b) religious sect; church. **de•nom•i•na•tion•al**, *adj.* belonging to a particular sect. **de•nom•i•na•tor** [dɪˈnɒmɪneɪtə] *n.* figure beneath the line in a fraction.

de•note [dɪˈnəʊt] *v.* to mean.

de•noue•ment, dénouement [deɪˈnuːmɒn] *n.* ending (of a plot).

de•nounce [dɪˈnaʊns] *v.* to blame/to accuse (s.o./sth) openly.

dense [dens] *adj.* (**-er, -est**) (a) very thick; crowded together. (b) stupid. **dense•ly**, *adv.* thickly. **dense•ness**, *n.* being dense. **den•si•ty**, *n.* (a) physical degree of mass per unit of volume. (b) **high d. of population** = many people per unit of area.

dent [dent] 1. *n.* slight hollow (as made by a blow). 2. *v.* to make a slight hollow in (sth).

den•tist ['dentɪst] *n.* person who looks after teeth. **den•tal**, *adj.* referring to teeth; **d. floss** = thin thread for cleaning between teeth. **den•ti•frice**, *n.* toothpaste. **den•tis•try**, *n.* work of a dentist. **den•ti•tion**, *n.* arrangement of a person's teeth. **den•tures** ['dentʃəz] *n.pl.* false teeth.

de•nude [dɪˈnjuːd] *v.* to make (sth) bare; to remove all the covering from (sth).

de•nun•ci•a•tion [dɪnʌnsɪˈeɪʃn] *n.* public accusation/blame.

de•ny [dɪˈnaɪ] *v.* to state that (sth) is not correct; to prevent (s.o.) having sth; **to d. oneself** = not to eat/drink, etc., very much.

de•o•dor•ant [dɪˈəʊdərənt] *n.* preparation which removes unpleasant smells.

æ back, ɑː farm, ɒ top, aɪ pipe, aʊ how, aɪe fire, aʊə flower, ɔː bought, ɔɪ toy, e fed, eəhair, eɪ take, ə afraid, əʊ boat, əʊə lower, vː word, iː heap, ɪ hit, ɪə hear, uː school, ʊ book, ʌ but, b back, d dog, ð then, dʒ just, f fog, g go, h hand, j yes, k catch, l last, m mix, n nut, ŋ sing, p penny, r round, s some, ʃ short, t too, tʃ chop, θ thing, v voice, w was, z zoo, ʒ treasure

de•o•dor•ize, v. to remove unpleasant smells from (sth).

de•ox•y•ri•bo•nu•cle•ic ac•id [diːɒksɪraɪbəunjuːˈklɛɪkˈæsɪd] n. DNA, the basic genetic material in a cell.

de•part [dɪˈpɑːt] v. to go away. **de•part•ed.** n. **the d.** = the dead. **de•par•ture** [dɪˈpɑːtʃə] n. leaving. **d. lounge** = large waiting room at an airport for passengers about to leave.

de•part•ment [dɪˈpɑːtmənt] n. section of a large organization; **d. store** = large store with many different sections. **dé•parte•ment**, n. administrative division of France. **de•part•men•tal** [dɪpɑːtˈmentl] adj. referring to a department.

de•pend [dɪˈpend] v. (a) (**on**) to be decided according to sth. (b) to rely (**on** sth). **de•pend•a•ble**, adj. that can be relied on. **de•pend•ant**, n. member of family supported by another. **de•pend•ence**, n. being dependent. **de•pend•en•cy**, n. country which is ruled by another. **de•pend•ent**, adj. (a) supported by s.o. else; relying on s.o. else. (a) addicted to (a drug).

de•pict [dɪˈpɪkt] v. (formal) to show. **de•pic•tion**, n. showing.

de•pil•a•to•ry [dɪˈpɪlətrɪ] adj. & n. (substance) which removes hair from the body.

de•plete [dɪˈpliːt] v. to run down/to use up (stores).

de•plore [dɪˈplɔː] v. to be extremely sorry that sth has happened; to dislike (an action/an attitude). **de•plor•a•ble**, adj. very bad (behavior).

de•ploy [dɪˈplɔɪ] v. to spread out (soldiers, etc.) for action. **de•ploy•ment**, n. act of deploying.

de•pop•u•late [diːˈpɒpjuleɪt] v. to reduce the number of people living in an area. **de•pop•u•la•tion** [diːpɒpjuˈleɪʃn] n. act of being depopulated.

de•port [dɪˈpɔːt] v. to expel (s.o.) from a country. **de•por•ta•tion** [diːpɔːˈteɪʃn] n. expulsion (of a foreigner). **de•port•ment**, n. way of walking/sitting.

de•pose [dɪˈpəʊz] v. (a) to force (s.o.) to leave his position; to force (a king, etc.) to give up his throne. (b) to state (in court). **dep•o•si•tion** [depəˈzɪʃn] n. (a) forcing s.o. to leave his position. (b) statement (by a witness).

de•pos•it [dɪˈpɒzɪt] 1. n. (a) money placed in a bank; money given to secure sth you want to buy. (b) mineral layer (in the ground); sediment/chemical left at the bottom of a container. 2. v. to put (money) in a bank. **de•pos•i•tar•y**, n. person who receives something which is deposited for safe keeping.

de•pos•i•tor, n. person with money in a bank. **de•pos•i•to•ry**, n. place for storing furniture, etc.

de•pot [ˈdepəʊ] n. central warehouse; central garage; central place for assembling military personnel.

de•praved [dɪˈpreɪvd] adj. corrupted/wicked. **de•prav•i•ty** [dɪˈprævɪtɪ] n. state of living a wicked life.

dep•re•cate [ˈdeprəkeɪt] v. to disapprove of (sth).

de•pre•ci•ate [dɪˈpriːʃɪeɪt] v. to lose value. **de•pre•ci•a•tion** [dɪprɪʃɪˈeɪʃn] n. regular loss in value. **de•pre•ci•a•to•ry**, adj. which depreciates.

dep•re•da•tion [deprəˈdeɪʃn] n. attack/ruining.

de•press [dɪˈpres] v. (a) to make miserable. (b) to push down (a button). **de•pressed**, adj. miserable. **de•press•ing**, adj. gloomy. **de•pres•sion** [dɪˈpreʃn] n. (a) miserable feeling. (b) low pressure area bringing bad weather. (c) economic crisis. (d) hollow (in the ground). **de•pres•sive**, adj. which makes s.o. depressed.

de•prive [dɪˈpraɪv] v. **to d. s.o. of sth** = to take sth away from s.o. **dep•ri•va•tion** [deprɪˈveɪʃn] n. being deprived of sth. **de•prived**, adj. (person) who has not enjoyed any of society's benefits.

dept. = department.

depth [depθ] n. (a) how deep sth is; distance downwards; **he's out of his d.** = (i) the water is too deep for him; (ii) it is too difficult for him to understand. (b) very deep point. **depth charge**, n. type of bomb dropped into the sea which explodes deep beneath the surface.

dep•u•ta•tion [depjuˈteɪʃn] n. group of people who speak on behalf of others. **de•pute** v. [dɪˈpjuːt] to give responsibility (**to** s.o.). **dep•u•tize** [ˈdepjutaɪz] v. to stand in (**for** s.o.). **dep•u•ty** [ˈdepjutɪ] n. person who can take the place of another person.

de•rail [dɪˈreɪl] v. to make (a train) leave the rails. **de•rail•ment**, n. leaving the rails. **de•rail•leur** [dɪˈreɪljə] n. bicycle gear system, where the chain goes round a movable sprocket.

de•ranged [dɪˈreɪndʒd] adj. mad.

der•by [ˈdɜːrbɪ] n. (a) sporting contest. (b) bowler hat.

de•reg•u•late [dɪˈregjuleɪt] v. to remove government restrictions from an industry. **de•reg•u•la•tion**, n. removal of official restrictions.

der•e•lict [ˈderəlɪkt] 1. n. tramp. 2. adj. ruined and abandoned. **der•e•lic•tion** [derəˈlɪkʃən] n. neglecting (to do your duty).

de•ride [dɪˈraɪd] *v.* to laugh at (s.o.). **de•ri•sion** [dɪˈrɪʒn] *n.* mockery. **de•ri•sive** [dɪˈraɪsɪv] *adj.* mocking (laughter). **de•ri•so•ry** [dɪˈraɪzərɪ] *adj.* laughably small (amount).

de ri•gueur [dərɪˈgɛːə] *adv.* obligatory.

de•rive [dɪˈraɪv] *v.* to come originally (from sth). **der•i•va•tion** [derɪˈveɪʃn] *n.* origin (of a word). **de•riv•a•tive** [dɪˈrɪvətɪv] *n.* thing which is derived.

der•ma•ti•tis [dɜːməˈtaɪtɪs] *n.* disease of the skin. **der•ma•tol•o•gist** [dɜːməˈtɒlədʒɪst] *n.* person who studies dermatology. **der•ma•tol•o•gy,** *n.* study of skin diseases.

de•rog•a•to•ry [dɪˈrɒgətrɪ] *adj.* showing contempt.

der•rick [ˈderɪk] *n.* large metal construction (like a crane); **oil d.** = metal frame which holds the drilling equipment for an oil well.

de•sal•i•nate [diːˈsælɪneɪt] *v.* to remove salt (from sea water).

des•cant [ˈdeskænt] *n.* musical part which is played/sung much higher than the rest.

de•scend [dɪˈsend] *v.* (a) to go down (a staircase, etc.). (b) **to d. from s.o.** = to have s.o. as an ancestor. (c) **to d. upon** = to attack; *inf.* to visit unexpectedly. **de•scend•ant,** *n.* person whose family goes back to a certain ancestor. **de•scent,** *n.* (a) going down. (b) **he is of Irish descent** = his family was Irish.

de•scribe [dɪˈskraɪb] *v.* to say what (sth/s.o.) is like. **de•scrip•tion** [dɪˈskrɪpʃn] *n.* picture in words of what sth is like. **de•scrip•tive,** *adj.* which says what sth is like.

des•e•crate [ˈdesɪkreɪt] *v.* to use (a church/a grave) in a disrespectful way. **des•e•cra•tion,** *n.* act of desecrating.

de•seg•re•gate [dɪˈsegrəgeɪt] *v.* to end the segregation of (a group of people, or institution). **de•seg•re•ga•tion,** *n.* action of desegregating.

des•ert 1. *adj. & n.* [ˈdezət] very dry, usu. sandy (place). 2. *v.* [dɪˈzɜːt] to leave the armed forces without permission; to leave (s.o.) all by himself. **de•sert•ed,** *adj.* abandoned; with no inhabitants. **de•sert•er,** *n.* person who leaves the armed forces without permission. **de•ser•tion,** *n.* act of deserting. **de•serts** [dɪˈzɜːts] *n. pl. (formal)* **just d.** = rightful reward.

de•serve [dɪˈzɜːv] *v.* to merit (sth). **de•serv•ed•ly** [dɪˈzɜːvɪdlɪ] *adv.* in a way

which is right. **de•serv•ing,** *adj.* which ought to be supported/helped.

des•ic•cate [ˈdesɪkeɪt] *v.* to dry.

de•sign [dɪˈzaɪn] 1. *n.* plan; drawing of sth, before it is constructed; **to have designs on** = to plan to attack/take (sth). 2. *v.* to plan (sth). **de•sign•er,** *n.* artist who plans sth. **de•sign•ing,** *adj.* crafty (person).

des•ig•nate [ˈdezɪgneɪt] 1. *v.* to appoint (s.o.) to a post. 2. *suffix showing* person who has been appointed but has not started work; **the ambassador-designate. des•ig•na•tion,** *n.* act of designating.

de•sire [dɪˈzaɪə] 1. *n.* want. 2. *v.* to want. **de•sir•a•bil•i•ty,** *n.* being desirable. **de•sir•a•ble,** *adj.* which a lot of people want. **de•sir•ous,** *adj.* (of) wanting.

de•sist [dɪˈzɪst] *v. (formal)* **(from)** to stop doing (sth).

desk [desk] *n.* table for writing. **desk•top pub•lish•ing,** *n.* creating finished printed documents using a computer and a special program.

des•o•late [ˈdesələt] *adj.* bleak inhospitable (place). **des•o•la•tion** [desəˈleɪʃn] *n.* bleakness; ruin (of a place).

de•spair [dɪˈspeə] 1. *n.* hopelessness. 2. *v.* **he despaired of being rescued** = he had given up all hope of being rescued.

des•per•ate [ˈdesprət] *adj.* (a) hopeless. (b) wild (through being in despair). **des•per•ate•ly,** *adv.* urgently; wildly. **des•per•a•tion** [despəˈreɪʃn] *n.* hopelessness.

des•pi•ca•ble [dɪˈspɪkəbl] *adj.* worthless/which you can look down on.

de•spise [dɪˈspaɪz] *v.* to look down on (s.o.)/to think (s.o.) is not worth much.

de•spite [dɪˈspaɪt] *prep.* in spite of.

de•spoil [dɪˈspɔɪl] *v.* to ruin, to plunder.

de•spond•en•cy [dɪˈspɒndənsɪ] *n.* discouragement. **de•spond•ent,** *adj.* discouraged.

des•pot [ˈdespɒt] *n.* tyrant/dictator. **des•pot•ic** [dɪˈspɒtɪk] *adj.* like a dictator. **des•pot•ism** *n.* tyranny/dictatorship.

des•sert [dɪˈzɜːt] *n.* sweet course (in a meal). **dessert spoon,** *n.* spoon for eating dessert.

des•ti•na•tion [destɪˈneɪʃn] *n.* place a person/vehicle is going to. **des•tine** [ˈdestɪn] *v.* to aim (s.o.) for a certain position. **des•ti•ny,** *n.* what may happen in the future.

des•ti•tute [ˈdestɪtjuːt] *adj.* with no money or

æ back, aː farm, ɒ top, aɪ pipe, aʊ how, aɪə fire, aʊə flower, ɔː bought, ɔɪ toy, e fed, eəhair, eɪ take, ə afraid, əʊ boat, əʊə lower, vː word, iː heap, ɪ hit, ɪə hear, uː school, ʊ book, ʌ but, b back, d dog, ð then, dʒ just, f fog, g go, h hand, j yes, k catch, l last, m mix, n nut, ŋ sing, p penny, r round, s some, ʃ short, t too, tʃ chop, θ thing, v voice, w was, z zoo, ʒ treasure

belongings. **des•ti•tu•tion** [destɪ'tjuːʃn] *n.* being destitute.

de•stroy [dɪ'strɔɪ] *v.* to remove/to kill/to ruin completely. **de•stroy•er,** *n.* medium-sized naval ship.

de•struc•tion [dɪ'strʌkʃn] *n.* complete ruining. **de•struc•tive** [dɪ'strʌktɪv] *adj.* which destroys. **de•struc•tive•ness,** *n.* tendency to destroy things.

des•ul•to•ry ['dezəltrɪ] *adj.* haphazard/with no connecting links.

de•tach [dɪ'tætʃ] *v.* to separate; **detached house** = house which is not attached to another. **de•tach•a•ble,** *adj.* which you can separate. **de•tach•ment,** *n.* (a) indifference; lack of immediate interest. (b) small group of military personnel, etc.

de•tail ['diːteɪl] 1. *n.* small item. 2. *v.* (a) to list all the small items. (b) **to d. s.o. to do sth** = to give a task or duty to s.o.

de•tain [dɪ'teɪn] *v.* (a) to keep (s.o. in prison). (b) to hold (s.o.) back; to stop (s.o.) from leaving. **de•tain•ee** [diːteɪ'niː] *n.* person held in prison.

de•tect [dɪ'tekt] *v.* to discover; to notice. **de•tec•tion** [dɪ'tekʃn] *n.* discovery. **de•tec•tive,** *n.* police officer who investigates crimes. **de•tec•tor,** *n.* instrument which discovers sth.

dé•tente, detente [deɪ'tɑːnt] *n.* friendly atmosphere between two formerly hostile countries.

de•ten•tion [dɪ'tenʃn] *n.* imprisonment; keeping s.o. from leaving; **d. home** = place where young criminals are imprisoned for a short time.

de•ter [dɪ'tɜː] *v.* (**deterred**) to discourage (s.o. **from** doing sth).

de•ter•gent [dɪ'tɜːdʒənt] *n.* chemical used instead of soap for washing clothes or dishes.

de•te•ri•o•rate [dɪ'tɪərɪəreɪt] *v.* to go bad; to get worse. **de•te•ri•o•ra•tion** [dɪtɪərɪə'reɪʃn] *n.* worsening.

de•ter•mine [dɪ'tɜːmɪn] *v.* (a) to fix (a date, etc.). (b) to decide finally (**to**). **de•ter•mi•nant,** *n.* thing which determines. **de•ter•mi•na•tion** [dɪtɜːmɪ'neɪʃn] *n.* firm intention. **de•ter•mined,** *adj.* resolved (**to**).

de•ter•rent [dɪ'terənt] *n.* thing which discourages; **nuclear d.** = nuclear weapon which it is hoped will discourage the enemy from attacking.

de•test [dɪ'test] *v.* to dislike intensely. **de•test•a•ble,** *adj.* very unpleasant. **de•tes•ta•tion** [dɪtes'teɪʃn] *n.* strong dislike.

det•o•nate ['detəneɪt] *v.* to set off (an explo-

sive). **det•o•na•tion** [detə'neɪʃn] *n.* explosion. **det•o•na•tor,** *n.* small explosive charge which will set off a large explosion.

de•tour ['diːtʊə] *n.* roundabout road taken to avoid an obstacle/to see sth not on the direct route.

de•tract [dɪ'trækt] *v.* (**from**) to remove part of sth/to make sth less important. **de•trac•tor,** *n.* person who criticizes sth.

det•ri•ment ['detrɪmənt] *n.* hurt; damage; **to the d. of** = damaging to. **det•ri•men•tal** [detrɪ'mentl] *adj.* which damages.

de•tri•tus [diː'trɪtəs] *n.* debris which is formed by the weathering of rock; any waste matter.

deuce [djuːs] *n.* (a) score in tennis when both players are at 40 points. (b) score of two (in cards).

deu•te•ri•um [djuː'tɪərɪəm] *n.* heavy form of hydrogen.

Deutsch•mark ['dɔɪtʃmɑːk] *n.* currency used in Germany.

de•val•ue [diː'væljuː] *v.* to reduce value of (a currency) in relationship to that of other countries. **de•val•u•a•tion** [diːvæljuː'eɪʃn] *n.* reducing the international value of currency.

dev•as•tate ['devəsteɪt] *v.* to wreck/to lay waste (countryside). **dev•as•tat•ing,** *adj* overwhelming. **dev•as•ta•tion** [devə'steɪʃn] *n.* widespread damage.

de•vel•op [dɪ'veləp] *v.* (a) to use to good purpose. (b) to expand. (c) to start (a disease, etc.). (d) to produce and fix (a photograph) from film. (e) to grow. **de•vel•op•er,** *n.* (a) liquid for developing photographs. (b) person who builds property. **de•vel•op•ing,** *adj.* growing; **d. countries** = countries which are becoming industrialized. **de•vel•op•ment,** *n.* (a) growth. (b) **developments** = what will happen.

de•vi•ate ['diːvɪeɪt] *v.* to swerve/to turn away (from a direct line). **de•vi•a•tion** [diːvɪ'eɪʃn] *n.* moving away from a direct or normal line. **de•vi•ance,** *n.* deviation from normal human behavior. **de•vi•ant,** *adj. & n.* (person) who deviates from normal human behavior.

de•vice [dɪ'vaɪs] *n.* (a) small (useful) machine. (b) **left to his own devices** = left to do whatever he wanted. (c) emblem (on a coat of arms).

dev•il ['devl] *n.* (a) evil spirit; *inf.* **what the devil?** = what on earth? **d.'s advocate** = person who argues the opposite point of view, in order to oppose a widely held opinion. (b) *inf.* person; **lucky d.! dev•il•ish,** *adj.* referring to the devil. **dev•iled,** *adj.* cooked in a spicy sauce. **dev•il•ment, devilry,** *n.* wicked behavior.

de•vi•ous ['diːvɪəs] *adj.* not straightforward; roundabout. **de•vi•ous•ly,** *adv.* in a devious way. **de•vi•ous•ness**, *n.* not being straight-forward.

de•vise [dɪˈvaɪz] *v.* to think up; to invent.

de•void [dɪˈvɔɪd] *adj.* empty (**of**).

dev•o•lu•tion [diːvəˈljuːʃn] *n.* removing of power from the center. **de•volve** [dɪˈvɒlv] *v.* to pass on (responsibility, duty, etc.).

de•vote [dɪˈvəʊt] *v.* **to d. time to sth** = to spend time on sth. **de•vot•ed**, *adj.* (person) who spends all his time on sth. **de•vo•tee** [devəˈtiː] *n.* (**of**) person who is very enthusiastic about sth. **de•vo•tion** [dɪˈvəʊʃn] *n.* (religious) attachment; **devotions** = prayers. **de•vo•tion•al**, *adj.* religious.

de•vour [dɪˈvaʊə] *v.* (*formal*) to eat (greedily).

de•vout [dɪˈvaʊt] *adj.* pious; deeply concerned with religion.

dew [djuː] *n.* water which forms at night on objects in the open air. **dew•drop**, *n.* drop of dew. **dew claw**, *n.* small claw on the side of a dog's foot. **dew•lap**, *n.* skin which hangs in folds on the throat. **dew•y**, *adj.* covered in dew. **dew•y-eyed**, *adj.* innocent and sentimental.

dex•ter•i•ty [dekˈsterətɪ] *n.* skill (with hands). **dex•trous** [ˈdekstrəs] *adj.* clever (with one's hands).

dex•trose [ˈdekstrəʊz] *n.* sweet substance found naturally.

dhow [daʊ] *n.* Arab sailing boat.

di•a•be•tes [daɪəˈbiːtiːz] *n.* (*no pl.*) illness where the sugar content of the blood rises because of lack of insulin. **di•a•be•tic** [daɪəˈbetɪk] 1. *adj.* referring to diabetes; **d. food** = food with a low sugar content which can be eaten by people suffering from diabetes. 2. *n.* person suffering from diabetes.

di•a•bol•ic(al) [daɪəˈbɒlɪk(l)] *adj.* referring to the devil; evil.

di•a•crit•ic [daɪəˈkrɪtɪk] *n.* sign written above a character to show pronunciation.

di•a•dem [ˈdaɪədem] *n.* crown.

di•ag•nose [daɪəgˈnəʊz] *v.* to identify (an illness). **di•ag•no•sis**, *n.* (*pl.* **-ses**) identification (of an illness). **di•ag•nos•tic** [daɪəgˈnɒstɪk] *adj.* referring to diagnosis. **di•ag•nos•tics**, *pl. n.* test to find faults in computer hardware/software.

di•ag•o•nal [daɪˈægənl] *adj. & n.* (line) going from one corner to another slantwise. **di•ag•o•nal•ly**, *adv.* slantwise.

di•a•gram [ˈdaɪəgræm] *n.* sketch/plan.

di•a•gram•mat•ic [daɪəgrəˈmætɪk] *adj.* in the form of a diagram.

di•al [ˈdaɪəl] 1. *n.* round face (of a clock/meter/telephone). 2. *v.* (**dialed**) to make a telephone call; **to call the police you must dial 911. di•a•ling**, *n.* making a call on the telephone; **d. tone** = sound on the telephone which shows that you can dial.

di•a•lect [ˈdaɪəlekt] *n.* variety of a language spoken in a particular area. **di•a•lec•tal**, *adj.* referring to a dialect.

di•a•lec•tic [daɪəˈlektɪk] *n.* reasoned investigation of philosophical truth.

di•a•logue [ˈdaɪəlɒg] *n.* conversation between two people/two groups.

di•al•y•sis [daɪˈælɪsɪs] *n.* cleaning of the blood by passing it through a filter.

di•am•e•ter [daɪˈæmɪtə] *n.* distance across the center of a circle. **di•a•met•ri•cal•ly** [daɪəˈmetrɪklɪ] *adv.* **d. opposed to** = completely against/opposite.

dia•mond [ˈdaɪəmənd] *n.* (a) very hard transparent precious stone; **d. wedding** = 60th wedding anniversary. (b) one of the four suits in a pack of cards.

di•an•thus [daɪˈænθəs] *n.* Latin name for carnations or pinks.

dia•per [ˈdaɪəpə] *n.* cloth or absorbent fabric used to cover a baby's bottom.

di•aph•a•nous [daɪˈæfənəs] *adj.* (cloth) which is so thin that you can see through it.

di•a•phragm [ˈdaɪəfræm] *n.* (a) thin sheet which vibrates with noise. (b) thin wall of muscle separating the chest and the abdomen.

di•ar•rhe•a, di•ar•rhoe•a [daɪəˈrɪə] *n.* illness of the intestines where your bowel movements are very fluid.

di•a•ry [ˈdaɪərɪ] *n.* (a) description of what has happened in your life day by day; **he has kept a d. for years.** (b) small book in which you write notes/appointments for each day of the week. **di•a•rist**, *n.* person who writes a diary.

di•a•stase [daɪəˈsteɪz] *n.* enzyme which breaks down starch and converts it to sugar.

di•as•to•le [daɪəˈstəʊl] *n.* phase in the beating of the heart when the heart swells and fills with blood.

di•a•tom [daɪˈætəm] *n.* type of microscopic sea creature.

di•a•tribe [ˈdaɪətraɪb] *n.* violent spoken or written criticism.

dib•ble [ˈdɪbl] *n.* tool used to make holes in the ground for planting.

æ back, ɑː farm, ɒ top, aɪ pipe, aʊ how, aɪe fire, aʊə flower, ɔː bought, ɔɪ toy, e fed, eəhair, eɪ take, ə afraid, əʊ boat, əʊə lower, ɜː word, iː heap, ɪ hit, ɪə hear, uː school, ʊ book, ʌ but, b back, d dog, ð then, dʒ just, f fog, g go, h hand, j yes, k catch, l last, m mix, n nut, ŋ sing, p penny, r round, s some, ʃ short, t too, tʃ chop, θ thing, v voice, w was, z zoo, ʒ treasure

dice [daɪs] 1. n. (pl. **dice**) small cube with one to six dots on each face (for games). 2. v. (a) to cut up (vegetables, etc.) into very small cubes. (b) to gamble. **dic•ey**, adj. inf. dangerous/difficult.

di•chot•o•my [daɪ'kɒtəmɪ] n. splitting into two (usu. contradictory) parts.

dick•ens ['dɪkɪnz] n. inf. **what the d.?** = what on earth?

dick•er ['dɪkə] v. inf. **to d. about** = to barter or bargain.

dick•y ['dɪkɪ] n. inf. false shirt front.

di•cot•y•le•don [daɪkɒtɪ'liːdən] n. plant whose seedlings have two fleshy leaves.

dic•tate [dɪk'teɪt] v. (a) to say (sth) to s.o. who writes down your words. (b) to tell s.o. what to do. **dic•ta•tion** [dɪk'teɪʃn] n. act of dictating (sth to be written down). **dic•ta•tor**, n. person who rules a country alone. **dic•ta•to•ri•al** [dɪktə'tɔːrɪəl] adj. like a dictator. **dic•ta•tor•ship**, n. rule of a country by one person.

dic•tion ['dɪkʃn] n. way of speaking.

dic•tion•ar•y ['dɪkʃənrɪ] n. (a) book which lists words in alphabetical order, giving their meanings or translations. (b) list of correctly spelled words in a spelling check program.

dic•tum ['dɪktəm] n. (pl. -ta) saying (made by a notable person).

did [dɪd] v. see **do**.

di•dac•tic [daɪ'dæktɪk] adj. which teaches.

did•dle ['dɪdl] v. inf. to trick/to cheat.

die [daɪ] 1. n. metal stamp for making coins. 2. v. to stop living; inf. **I'm dying to read his book** = I am very eager to read his book; **I'm dying for a cup of coffee** = I'd love a cup of coffee; **the sound died away** = became fainter; **the wind died down** = became less strong; **the old customs are dying out** = not being continued. **die•cast**, adj. cast from metal in a mold. **die•hard**, adj. & n. inf. very reactionary (person).

diel•drin [daɪ'eldrɪn] n. powerful insecticide.

di•er•e•sis [daɪ'ɪərɪsɪs] n. (pl. -ses) two dots (¨) put over a vowel to show that it is pronounced separately from another.

die•sel ['diːzl] n. **d. engine** = engine which runs on thicker fuel than gas; **d. oil** = oil used in diesel engines.

di•et ['daɪət] 1. n. (a) kind of food you eat; **to be on a d.** = to eat only one sort of food/to eat less. (b) (in some countries) parliament. 2. v. to eat less food/only one sort of food. **di•e•tar•y**, adj. referring to a diet. **di•et•er**, n. person who is on a diet. **di•e•tet•ics**, n. study of food and its nutritional value. **di•e•ti•cian** [daɪə'tɪʃn] n. person who specializes in the study of diets.

dif•fer ['dɪfə] v. **to d. from** = not to be the same as; **I beg to d.** = I must disagree.

dif•fer•ence ['dɪfrəns] n. way in which two things are not the same; **it doesn't make any d.** = it does not change the situation. **dif•fer•ent**, adj. not the same; **that is quite a d. thing** = it is not at all the same. **dif•fer•en•tial** [dɪfə'renʃl] 1. adj. showing up the difference; **d. equation.** 2. n. (a) part of the axle of a car which allows wheels to turn at different speeds at corners. (b) difference in rate, amount, etc. **dif•fer•en•ti•ate**, v. to make/to tell the difference (between). **dif•fer•en•ti•a•tion**, n. act of differentiating. **dif•fer•ent•ly**, adv. not in the same way.

dif•fi•cult ['dɪfɪkʌlt] adj. not easy. **dif•fi•cul•ty**, n. thing which is not easy; **she got into difficulties when swimming** = she was in danger of drowning; **he is in financial difficulties** = he has problems to do with money.

dif•fi•dence ['dɪfɪdəns] n. being diffident. **dif•fi•dent**, adj. shy; lacking confidence. **dif•fi•dent•ly**, adv. shyly.

dif•fract [dɪ'frækt] v. to split light into its different colors. **dif•frac•tion** [dɪ'frækʃn] n. splitting up of light into its different colors.

dif•fuse 1. adj. [dɪ'fjuːs] vague/unclear; **d. lighting** = soft lighting, not giving any sharp shadows. 2. v. [dɪ'fjuːz] to spread out; to send out; **diffused lighting** = soft lighting, not giving any sharp shadows. **dif•fu•sion**, n. act of diffusing.

dig [dɪg] 1. n. (a) poke; **he gave me a d. in the ribs** = he nudged me with his elbow. (b) satirical attack. (c) archaeological excavation. 2. v. (dug; has dug) to make a hole in the ground; **we dug up an old bottle in the garden** = we found the bottle when digging. **dig•ger**, n. person/machine that digs. **dig•ging**, n. action of making a hole in the ground. **dig in**, v. inf. to start eating. **digs**, n. pl. inf. living quarters.

di•gest 1. n. ['daɪdʒest] summary. 2. v. [daɪ'dʒest] (a) to turn (food) into energy in the stomach and intestine; **I cannot d. my dinner** = I am feeling unwell after my dinner. (b) to ponder over (a piece of information). **di•gest•i•ble**, adj. which can be digested. **di•ges•tion**, n. action of turning food into energy. **di•ges•tive**, adj. which helps you to digest.

dig•it ['dɪdʒɪt] n. (a) single figure (from 0 to 9). (b) finger or toe. **dig•it•al**, adj. which involves figures; **d. watch** = watch where the time is shown by figures (such as 11:52); **d. camera** = camera that produces pictures that can be saved, viewed, and printed on a computer; **d. computer** = computer which works on a varied signal; **d. television** = television transmitted as digital rather than analog signals; **d. video** = video in digital rather than analog form; **d. video disk** = computer disk that contains large amounts of digitized audio and video information. **dig•i•tize,** *v.* to convert information to digital form.

dig•i•tal•in, digitalis [dɪdʒɪ'teɪlɪn, -ɪs] *n.* drugs made from foxgloves.

dig•ni•fied ['dɪgnɪfaɪd] *adj.* solemn/important-looking. **dig•ni•fy,** *v.* to honor (s.o.) with a title; to give dignity to (s.o.). **dig•ni•tar•y,** *n.* important person. **dig•ni•ty,** *n.* solemn/serious way of behaving; **it is beneath his d. to clean his own shoes** = he is too proud to clean them.

di•gress [daɪ'gres] *v.* to wander away from the subject when speaking. **di•gres•sion,** *n.* speech/writing which does not deal with the subject.

di•hed•ral [daɪ'hi:drəl] *n.* angle at which an aircraft's wing varies from the horizontal.

dike, dyke [daɪk] *n.* (a) long wall of earth to keep out water. (b) long ditch.

dik•tat ['dɪktæt] *n.* official command.

di•lap•i•dat•ed [dɪ'læpɪdeɪtɪd] *adj.* falling into ruin. **di•lap•i•da•tion,** *n.* being in ruins.

di•late [daɪ'leɪt] *v.* to make (eyes) grow larger; (*of the eyes*) to grow larger. **di•late up•on,** *v.* to talk at length about. **di•la•ta•tion** [dɪlə'teɪʃn], **di•la•tion** [daɪ'leɪʃn] *n.* act of dilating. **di•la•tor,** *n.* drug used to make a part of the body (such as the eyes) grow larger.

dil•a•to•ry ['dɪlətərɪ] *adj.* slow (to act). **dil•a•to•ri•ness,** *n.* slowness.

di•lem•ma [dɪ'lemə] *n.* serious problem, where a choice has to be made between several bad alternatives; **in a d.** = not knowing which course of action to follow.

dil•et•tante [dɪlɪ'tæntɪ] *n.* person who is interested in a subject, but not very seriously.

dil•i•gence ['dɪlɪdʒəns] *n.* hard work/taking care. **dil•i•gent,** *adj.* hard-working.

dill [dɪl] *n.* herb used for flavoring fish and pickles.

dil•ly-dal•ly ['dɪlɪ'dælɪ] *v.* to hang back; to loiter.

di•lute [daɪ'lju:t] 1. *v.* to add water to (another liquid) to make it weaker. 2. *adj.* with water added. **di•lu•tion,** *n.* act of diluting.

dim [dɪm] 1. *adj.* **(dimmer, dimmest)** (a) weak

(light); **I have a d. recollection of it** = I can remember it vaguely. (b) rather stupid. 2. *v.* **(dimmed)** to turn down (a light); **the house lights dimmed** = the lights in the theater were turned down (as the play started). **dim•ly,** *adv.* vaguely; unclearly. **dim•mer,** *n.* light switch which dims a light. **dim•ness,** *n.* weakness (of light); vagueness (of memory).

dime [daɪm] *n. U.S.* ten cent coin.

di•men•sion [dɪ'menʃn] *n.* measurement (in figures). **di•men•sion•al,** *adj.* **two-dimensional** = having two dimensions, flat; **three-dimensional** = having three dimensions/in the round.

di•min•ish [dɪ'mɪnɪʃ] *v.* to make (sth) smaller; to become smaller. **dim•i•nu•tion** [dɪmɪ'nju:ʃn] *n.* becoming smaller. **di•min•u•tive** [dɪ'mɪnjutɪv] 1. *adj.* very small. 2. *n.* word used to show that sth is small; **"Kate" is a d. of "Catherine".**

di•min•u•en•do [dɪmɪnju'endəu] *n.* (*in music*) decreasing noise.

dim•ple ['dɪmpl] *n.* small hollow (in cheeks/in babies' fat elbows). **dim•pled,** *adj.* with dimples.

din [dɪn] 1. *n.* loud noise. 2. *v.* **(dinned)** to force (a piece of information **into** s.o.'s head) by frequently repeating it.

dine [daɪn] *v.* to have dinner; **to d. out** = to have dinner away from home. **din•er,** *n.* (a) person eating dinner. (b) dining car. (c) small restaurant selling hot food. **din•ing car,** *n.* restaurant car (on a train). **din•ing room,** *n.* room where people usually eat.

ding-dong ['dɪŋdɒŋ] *n.* sound made by a bell.

din•ghy ['dɪŋgɪ] *n.* small boat.

din•go ['dɪŋgəu] *n.* Australian wild dog.

din•gy ['dɪndʒɪ] *adj.* **(-ier, -iest)** dirty. **din•gi•ness,** *n.* dirt.

din•ner ['dɪnə] *n.* main meal (usu. the evening meal); **d. table** = table (where people eat); **d. party** = dinner to which guests are invited; **d. jacket** = formal (usu. black) jacket worn for dinner with a black bow tie.

di•no•saur ['daɪnəsɔ:] *n.* large prehistoric reptile.

dint [dɪnt] *n.* **by d. of** = through; by means of.

di•o•cese ['daɪəsɪs] *n.* area under the charge of a bishop. **di•oc•e•san** [daɪ'ɒsɪzn] *adj.* referring to a diocese.

di•ox•ide [daɪ'ɒksaɪd] *n.* oxide with two parts of oxygen to one part of another substance.

dip [dɪp] 1. *n.* (a) quick covering with liquid. (b)

æ back, ɑ: farm, ɒ top, aɪ pipe, aʊ how, aɪə fire, aʊə flower, ɔ: bought, ɔɪ toy, ə fed, eəhair, eɪ take, ə afraid, əʊ boat, əʊə lower, v: word, i: heap, ɪ hit, ɪə hear, u: school, ʊ book, ʌ but, b back, d dog, ð then, dʒ just, f fog, g go, h hand, j yes, k catch, l last, m mix, n nut, ŋ sing, p penny, r round, s some, ʃ short, t too, tʃ chop, θ thing, v voice, w was, z zoo, ʒ treasure

sudden drop (of a road/of land). (c) soft mixture into which crackers, raw vegetables, etc. can be dipped as cocktail snacks. (d) short bathe/swim. (e) **sheep d.** = place where sheep are dipped in pesticide to kill ticks. 2. *v.* (**dipped**) (a) to put (sth) quickly **into** a liquid. (b) to dive. (c) **to d. a flag** = to lower a flag. (d) **to d. into a book** = to read a few lines here and there. **dip•per,** *n.* small brown bird which dives into water. **dip•stick,** *n.* rod (in the engine of a car) which shows the level of oil in the engine.

diph•the•ri•a [dɪf'θɪərɪə] *n.* (*no pl.*) serious infectious disease of babies.

diph•thong ['dɪfθɒŋ] *n.* two vowel sounds which are pronounced together.

di•plo•ma [dɪ'pləʊmə] *n.* certificate showing that you have passed an examination.

di•plo•ma•cy [dɪ'pləʊməsɪ] *n.* art of negotiating between different parties, esp. between different countries. **dip•lo•mat** #ɪpləmæt] *n.* person (such as an ambassador) who represents his country abroad. **dip•lo•mat•ic** [dɪplə'mætɪk] *adj.* (a) representing one's country. (b) careful not to give offense. **dip•lo•mat•i•cal•ly,** *adv.* in a diplomatic way. **dip•lo•ma•tist** [dɪ'pləʊmətɪst] *n.* diplomat.

dip•so•ma•ni•a [dɪpsə'meɪnɪə] *n.* habitual drinking of alcohol. **dip•so•ma•ni•ac,** *n.* person who wants to drink alcohol all the time.

dire ['daɪə] *adj.* very serious; **d. necessity** = urgent necessity.

di•rect [daɪ'rekt/dɪ'rekt] 1. *v.* (a) to aim toward a point. (b) to tell (s.o.) to do sth; to manage/organize (a motion picture, play, etc.). 2. *adj.* straight; **d. hit** = hit on the target; **there is a d. flight to Paris** = the plane does not stop between here and Paris. 3. *adv.* straight; without stopping. **d. debit,** *n.* arrangement made by a bank account holder for the regular (usu. monthly) payment of any amount demanded by a specified party. **di•rec•tion** [daɪ'rekʃn] *n.* (a) point to which you are going/at which you are aiming. (b) instruction. (c) guiding (of the making of a motion picture). **di•rec•tion•al,** *adj.* going in one direction. **di•rec•tive,** *n.* official instruction. **di•rect•ly.** 1. *adv.* immediately; straight. 2. *conj.* **I will write the letter d. I get home** = as soon as I get home. **di•rect•ness,** *n.* frankness (of a reply). **di•rec•tor** [daɪ'rektə] *n.* (a) person who is appointed by the shareholders to help run a company; **managing d.** = person who is in charge of a company. (b) person in charge of making a motion picture/a play. **di•rec•to•rate,** *n.* group of directors. **di•rec•tor•ship,** *n.* position of director.

di•rec•to•ry, *n.* list of people/businesses showing their telephone numbers and addresses; book giving lists of people/businesses with their addresses and telephone numbers; **classified d.** = telephone directory where companies are classified into various groups.

dirge [dɜːdʒ] *n.* funeral song.

dir•i•gi•ble [dɪ'rɪdʒɪbl] *n.* large airship which can be steered.

dirk [dɜːk] *n.* short dagger.

dirn•dl ['dɜːndl] *n.* wide skirt gathered tight at the waist.

dirt [dɜːt] *n.* mud; earth; filth; **d. cheap** = extremely cheap. **dirt•i•ness,** *n.* being dirty/not being clean. **dirt•y.** 1. *adj.* (**-ier, -iest**) (a) not clean; covered with dirt. (b) **d. trick** = low/unpleasant trick. 2. *v.* to cover with dirt.

dis, diss [dɪs] *v. Sl.* to treat with contempt/disrespect.

dis•a•bil•i•ty [dɪsə'bɪlɪtɪ] *n.* physical handicap. **dis•a•bled** [dɪs'eɪbld] 1. *adj.* physically handicapped. 2. *n.* **the d.** = physically handicapped people.

dis•a•buse [dɪsə'bjuːz] *v.* to make (s.o.) see that he was wrong.

dis•ad•van•tage [dɪsəd'vɑːntɪdʒ] *n.* handicap; drawback; lack of advantage. **dis•ad•van•taged,** *adj.* handicapped. **dis•ad•van•ta•geous** [dɪsædvɑːn'teɪdʒəs] *adj.* which does not give an advantage; unfavorable.

dis•af•fect•ed [dɪsə'fektɪd] *adj.* discontented/rebellious.

dis•a•gree [dɪsə'griː] *v.* not to agree; **cabbage disagrees with me** = makes me feel ill. **dis•a•gree•a•ble,** *adj.* unpleasant. **dis•a•gree•ment,** *n.* lack of agreement.

dis•al•low [dɪsə'laʊ] *v.* to refuse to accept; **the team's second goal was disallowed** = was not counted.

dis•ap•pear [dɪsə'pɪə] *v.* to vanish. **dis•ap•pear•ance,** *n.* vanishing.

dis•ap•point [dɪsə'pɔɪnt] *v.* to let (s.o.) down; not to turn out as expected. **dis•ap•point•ing,** *adj.* unsatisfactory; not coming up to expectations. **dis•ap•point•ment,** *n.* sadness because what was expected did not take place.

dis•ap•prove [dɪsə'pruːv] *v.* not to approve (of sth). **dis•ap•prov•al, disapprobation** [dɪsæprəʊ'beɪʃn] *n.* lack of approval. **dis•ap•prov•ing•ly,** *adv.* in a way which shows you do not approve.

dis•arm [dɪs'ɑːm] *v.* to remove weapons from (s.o.). **dis•ar•ma•ment,** *n.* abolition of weapons by a country. **dis•arm•ing,** *adj.*

charming (manner) which prevents people from criticizing.

dis•ar•range [dɪsə'reɪndʒ] v. to put (sth) into disorder.

dis•ar•ray [dɪsə'reɪ] n. lack of order.

dis•as•ter [dɪ'zɑːstə] n. catastrophe; very bad accident; **air d.** = crash of an aircraft killing many people. **dis•as•trous,** adj. very bad/catastrophic. **dis•as•trous•ly,** adv. very badly.

dis•band [dɪs'bænd] v. to send (soldiers) back home; to split up (a group of soldiers/musicians, etc.).

dis•bar [dɪs'bɑː] v. **(disbarred)** (formal) to remove (a lawyer) from the legal profession.

dis•be•lief [dɪsbɪ'liːf] n. lack of belief. **dis•be•liev•er,** n. person who does not believe.

dis•bud [dɪs'bʌd] v. **(disbudded)** to remove some of the buds from (a plant).

dis•burse [dɪs'bɜːs] v. to pay out (money).

disc [dɪsk] n. round flat object, esp. a record for playing on a record-player; **slipped d.** = painful condition where one of the cushioning discs in the spine has become displaced; **d. brakes** = round, flat brakes in a car. **d. harrow** = type of harrow, formed of a series of circular metal blades; **d. jockey** = person who plays records on the radio/in a club, etc.

dis•card 1. n. ['dɪskɑːd] thing which has been discarded. 2. v. [dɪs'kɑːd] to put (sth) aside; to reject.

dis•cern [dɪ'sɜːn] v. to see/to make out. **dis•cern•i•ble,** adj. which can be seen. **dis•cern•ing,** adj. (person) who has good judgement. **dis•cern•ment,** n. ability to judge correctly.

dis•charge 1. n. ['dɪstʃɑːdʒ] (a) liquid (coming out of a pipe, etc.); pus (coming out of a wound). (b) payment (of a debt). (c) release (of a prisoner). 2. v. [dɪs'tʃɑːdʒ] (a) to unload (a cargo); to let off (a gun). (b) to send (s.o.) away; **he was discharged from the hospital** = he was allowed to go home because he was better. (c) to release (a prisoner). (d) to pay (a debt).

dis•ci•ple [dɪ'saɪpl] n. follower (of a religious leader).

dis•ci•pline ['dɪsɪplɪn] 1. n. keeping people under control. 2. v. to control/to punish (s.o.). **dis•ci•pli•nar•i•an** [dɪsɪplɪ'neərɪən] n. person who believes in strict discipline. **dis•ci•pli•nar•y** [dɪsɪ'plɪnərɪ] adj. (action) which keeps s.o. under control.

dis•claim [dɪs'kleɪm] v. not to admit/to deny; **he disclaims all knowledge of the payment** = he says he knows nothing about the payment. **dis•claim•er,** n. statement in which you disclaim all knowledge of sth.

dis•close [dɪs'kləuz] v. to reveal (a secret). **dis•clo•sure** [dɪs'kləuʒə] n. revealing (of a secret).

dis•co ['dɪskəu] n. (pl. -os) inf. discotheque; place where people dance to recorded music; dancing to pop/rock music.

dis•col•or, Brit. **dis•col•our** [dɪs'kʌlə] v. to change the color of (sth). **dis•col•or•a•tion** [dɪskʌlə'reɪʃn] n. change of color.

dis•com•fort [dɪs'kʌmfət] n. lack of comfort.

dis•con•cert [dɪskən'sɜːt] v. to surprise/to embarrass. **dis•con•cert•ing,** adj. worrying/surprising.

dis•con•nect [dɪskə'nekt] v. to undo (two things which are connected); **they disconnected the refrigerator** = they unplugged the refrigerator. **dis•con•nect•ed,** adj. disjointed; with no links.

dis•con•so•late [dɪs'kɒnsələt] adj. very sad. **dis•con•so•late•ly,** adv. very sadly.

dis•con•tent [dɪskən'tent] n. state of not being satisfied. **dis•con•tent•ed,** adj. not satisfied.

dis•con•tin•ue [dɪskən'tɪnjuː] v. not to continue to do/produce (sth). **dis•con•ti•nu•i•ty** [dɪskɒntɪ'njuɪtɪ] n. being discontinuous. **dis•con•tin•u•ous,** adj. which stops and starts; intermittent.

dis•cord ['dɪskɔːd] n. lack of agreement. **dis•cord•ant** [dɪs'kɔːdənt] adj. (a) not in agreement. (b) out of harmony.

dis•co•theque ['dɪskətek] n. place where people dance to recorded music.

dis•count 1. n. ['dɪskaunt] percentage less than the normal price; **d. store** = shop where goods are cheaper than elsewhere. 2. v. [dɪs'kaunt] (a) not to pay any attention to (sth). (b) to put a discount on (a price).

dis•cour•age [dɪs'kʌrɪdʒ] v. not to encourage; **to d. s.o. from doing sth** = to stop s.o. doing sth. **dis•cour•age•ment,** n. being discouraged; thing which stops you doing sth. **dis•cour•ag•ing,** adj. not encouraging.

dis•course 1. n. ['dɪskɔːs] (formal) talk/speech. 2. v. [dɪs'kɔːs] (formal) to speak.

dis•cour•te•ous [dɪs'kɜːtɪəs] adj. rude. **dis•cour•te•ous•ly,** adv. rudely. **dis•cour•te•sy,** n. rudeness.

---

dis•cov•er [dɪs'kʌvə] v. to find (sth new).
dis•cov•er•er, n. person who finds sth.
dis•cov•er•y, n. act of finding sth new.

dis•cred•it [dɪs'kredɪt] 1. n. doubt/lack of belief (in s.o.). 2. v. to make people doubt (s.o./sth); **he has been discredited** = no one believes him any more. **dis•cred•it•a•ble,** adj. not honorable (conduct). **dis•cred•it•a•bly,** adv. dishonorably.

dis•creet [dɪs'kri:t] adj. quiet; not allowing anyone to notice. **dis•creet•ly,** adv. quietly; without anyone noticing.

dis•crep•an•cy [dɪs'krepənsɪ] n. lack of agreement (between figures/accounts).

dis•crete [dɪs'kri:t] adj. separate/not connected.

dis•cre•tion [dɪs'kreʃn] n. wisdom/good sense; **I leave it to your d.** = I leave it for you to decide. **dis•cre•tion•ar•y,** adj. (powers) used at s.o.'s discretion.

dis•crim•i•nate [dɪs'krɪmɪneɪt] v. to distinguish; **to d. between** = to treat (two things) differently; **to d. against** = to prefer (one thing to another). **dis•crim•i•nat•ing,** adj. able to distinguish/judge. **dis•crim•i•na•tion** [dɪskrɪmɪ'neɪʃn] n. (a) judgment; **a person of d.** = of good taste. (b) preference (for or against sth); **racial d.** = preference for or against a race.

dis•cur•sive [dɪs'kɜ:sɪv] adj. not succinct/not to the point.

dis•cus ['dɪskəs] n. (pl. -es) flat round disk which is thrown as a sport.

dis•cuss [dɪs'kʌs] v. to talk about (a problem). **dis•cus•sion** [dɪs'kʌʃn] n. talking about (a problem); **the question under d.** = the problem we are talking about.

dis•dain [dɪs'deɪn] 1. n. looking down; feeling that s.o./sth is inferior. 2. v. to look down on (sth); to refuse to do (sth) because it is beneath you. **dis•dain•ful,** adj. superior (air). **dis•dain•ful•ly,** adv. with a superior air.

dis•ease [dɪ'zi:z] n. serious illness (of animals, plants, etc.). **dis•eased,** adj. sick.

dis•em•bark [dɪsɪm'bɑ:k] v. to get off a ship. **dis•em•bar•ka•tion** [dɪsembɑ:'keɪʃn] n. getting off a ship.

dis•em•bod•ied [dɪsɪm'bɒdɪd] adj. not connected to a body.

dis•em•bow•el [dɪsɪm'baʊəl] v. to remove the intestines from (s.o.).

dis•en•chant•ed [dɪsɪn'tʃɑ:ntɪd] adj. (with) feeling that sth has not turned out as well as expected. **dis•en•chant•ment,** n. feeling that sth has not turned out as well as expected.

dis•en•fran•chise [dɪsɪn'fræntʃaɪz] v. see **dis•fran•chise.**

dis•en•gage [dɪsɪn'geɪdʒ] v. (a) to break off; **the troops disengaged** = the troops broke off the fighting. (b) to separate (the gears of a car).

dis•en•tan•gle [dɪsɪn'tæŋgl] v. to untie (knotted string, etc.).

dis•fa•vor, Brit. **dis•fa•vour** [dɪs'feɪvə] n. shame; lack of favor; **the senator fell into d.** = he was disgraced; **the minister incurred the king's d.** = he fell into disgrace with the king.

dis•fig•ure [dɪs'fɪgə] v. to make ugly. **dis•fig•ure•ment,** n. act of disfiguring.

dis•fran•chise [dɪs'fræntʃaɪz] v. to remove the right to vote from (s.o.). **dis•fran•chise•ment,** n. removal of the right to vote.

dis•gorge [dɪs'gɔ:dʒ] v. (a) to pour out. (b) to give up (things which have been stolen).

dis•grace [dɪs'greɪs] 1. n. shame; being out of favor with s.o.; **the mayor fell into d.** = he was out of favor. 2. v. to bring shame on. **dis•grace•ful,** adj. which you should be ashamed of. **dis•grace•ful•ly,** adv. in a disgraceful way.

dis•grun•tled [dɪs'grʌntld] adj. annoyed/discontented.

dis•guise [dɪs'gaɪz] 1. n. costume, wig, etc., to make a person look like s.o. else; **in d.** = dressed to look like s.o. else. 2. v. to dress so as to look like s.o. else; to make (sth) look/sound different; **there is no disguising the fact** = you cannot hide the fact.

dis•gust [dɪs'gʌst] 1. n. (at) strong dislike; feeling sick/very discontented. 2. v. to make (s.o.) feel sick. **dis•gust•ing,** adj. which makes you feel sick.

dish [dɪʃ] 1. n. (pl. -es) (a) large plate (for serving food); (b) part of a meal; (plate of) prepared food. 2. v. inf. **he is dishing out the food** = he is serving the meal; **they are dishing out tickets** = they are handing out tickets. **dish•cloth,** n. cloth for washing dishes. **dish•wash•er,** n. machine for washing dishes. **dish•wa•ter,** n. water which has been used for washing dishes.

dis•har•mo•ny [dɪs'hɑ:mənɪ] n. not being in agreement/in harmony.

dis•heart•en [dɪs'hɑ:tn] v. to discourage. **dis•heart•en•ing,** adj. discouraging.

di•shev•elled [dɪ'ʃevəld] adj. untidy (appearance)/uncombed (hair).

dis•hon•est [dɪs'ɒnɪst] adj. not honest. **dis•hon•est•ly,** adv. not honestly; illegally. **dis•hon•es•ty,** n. lack of honesty.

dis•hon•or, Brit. **dis•hon•our** [dɪs'ɒnə] 1. n. lack of honor. 2. v. (a) to treat rudely. (b) not to honor; **dishonored check** = check which the bank will not pay. **dis•hon•or•a•ble,** adj. not honorable; shameful.

dis•hon•or•a•bly, *adv.* in a dishonorable way.

dis•il•lu•sion [dɪsɪˈluːʒn] *n.* feeling of being let down/that sth has not turned out as you expected. **dis•il•lu•sion•ed**, *adj.* feeling that sth has not turned out as expected. **dis•il•lu•sion•ment**, *n.* feeling of being let down/that sth has not turned out as expected.

dis•in•cen•tive [dɪsɪnˈsentɪv] *n.* thing which discourages; **the low salary is a d. to work** = the salary does not encourage people to work.

dis•in•clin•ed [dɪsɪnˈklaɪnd] *adj.* not inclined; **she is feeling d. to go to work today** = she does not want to go to work today. **dis•in•cli•na•tion** [dɪsɪnklɪˈneɪʃn] *n.* not wanting to do sth.

dis•in•fect [dɪsɪnˈfekt] *v.* to remove/to prevent infection. **dis•in•fect•ant**, *n.* chemical liquid for fighting infection.

dis•in•for•ma•tion [dɪsɪnfəˈmeɪʃən] *n.* false information to confuse an enemy.

dis•in•gen•u•ous [dɪsɪnˈdʒenjʊəs] *adj.* false; lacking frankness; pretending to be naive.

dis•in•her•it [dɪsɪnˈherɪt] *v.* to change your will so that s.o. will no longer inherit your money when you die.

dis•in•te•grate [dɪsˈɪntɪɡreɪt] *v.* to fall to pieces. **dis•in•te•gra•tion** [dɪsɪntɪˈɡreɪʃn] *n.* falling to pieces.

dis•in•ter [dɪsɪnˈtɜː] *v.* (**disinterred**) to dig up (sth) which has been buried.

dis•in•ter•est•ed [dɪsˈɪntrəstɪd] *adj.* not in favor of one side or the other; **he is a totally d. observer** = he is an impartial observer. **dis•in•ter•est•ed•ness**, *n.* being disinterested.

dis•joint•ed [dɪsˈdʒɔɪntɪd] *adj.* without any links; unconnected.

disk [dɪsk] *n.* any round flat object, especially a piece of magnetized plastic used in computers to record information; **floppy d.** = small disk which can be inserted and removed from a computer; **hard d.** = disk with a large capacity, which is permanently fixed in a computer. **disk•ette**, *n.* small floppy disk. **disk drive**, *n.* device which spins a disk in a computer and controls the access of information.

dis•like [dɪsˈlaɪk] 1. *n.* lack of liking; **to take a d. to** = to start to hate. 2. *v.* not to like; **I don't d. honey** = I like honey.

dis•lo•cate [ˈdɪsləkeɪt] *v.* (a) to put (an arm/leg, etc.) out of joint. (b) to disorganize. **dis•lo•ca•tion** [dɪsləˈkeɪʃn] *n.* (a) disorganization. (b) putting an arm/leg, etc., out of joint.

dis•lodge [dɪsˈlɒdʒ] *v.* to detach/to remove.

dis•loy•al [dɪsˈlɔɪəl] *adj.* not loyal. **dis•loy•al•ty**, *n.* being disloyal.

dis•mal [ˈdɪzməl] *adj.* miserable. **dis•mal•ly**, *adv.* miserably; (to fail a test) very badly.

dis•man•tle [dɪsˈmæntl] *v.* to take to pieces.

dis•may [dɪsˈmeɪ] 1. *n.* horror/consternation. 2. *v.* to strike (s.o.) with horror.

dis•mem•ber [dɪsˈmembə] *v.* to cut up (a body) into parts; to take apart.

dis•miss [dɪsˈmɪs] *v.* (a) to send (s.o.) away. (b) to remove (s.o.) from a job. (c) to refuse or disregard. **dis•miss•al**, *n.* removal from a job.

dis•mount [dɪsˈmaʊnt] *v.* to get off a horse/bicycle, etc.

dis•o•bey [dɪsəˈbeɪ] *v.* to refuse to obey. **dis•o•be•di•ence** [dɪsəˈbiːdɪəns] *n.* lack of obedience. **dis•o•be•di•ent**, *adj.* not obedient.

dis•or•der [dɪsˈɔːdə] *n.* (a) lack of order; untidiness. (b) riot; disturbance. (c) illness. **dis•or•der•ly**, *adj.* wild (crowd).

dis•or•gan•ize [dɪsˈɔːɡənaɪz] *v.* to put (sth) out of its usual order.

dis•o•ri•en•tate [dɪsˈɔːrɪənteɪt] *v.* to make (s.o.) lose their sense of direction; to confuse (s.o.). **dis•o•ri•en•ta•tion**, *n.* feeling lost.

dis•own [dɪsˈəʊn] *v.* to refuse to acknowledge (sth) is yours.

dis•par•age [dɪsˈpærɪdʒ] *v.* to say that sth is bad. **dis•par•age•ment**, *n.* act of disparaging. **dis•par•ag•ing**, *adj.* critical; saying that sth is bad.

dis•pa•rate [ˈdɪspərət] *adj.* varied/different. **dis•par•i•ty** [dɪsˈpærɪtɪ] *n.* difference.

dis•pas•sion•ate [dɪsˈpæʃnət] *adj.* calm and without emotion. **dis•pas•sion•ate•ly**, *adv.* calmly.

dis•patch [dɪsˈpætʃ] 1. *n.* (*pl.* **-es**) (a) sending. (b) speed (of doing sth). (c) message. 2. *v.* (a) to send. (b) to finish quickly. (c) to kill off.

dis•pel [dɪsˈpel] *v.* (**dispelled**) to clear away.

dis•pense [dɪsˈpens] *v.* (a) to distribute. (b) to prepare and sell (medicine). (c) **to d. with** = to do without. **dis•pen•sa•ble**, *adj.* which can be dispensed with. **dis•pen•sa•ry**, *n.* place where medicines, etc. are dispensed. **dis•pen•sa•tion** [dɪspənˈseɪʃn] *n.* permission not to follow a rule, etc. **dis•pens•er**, *n.* automatic machine/box with a hole to allow one object to come out at a time.

dis•perse [dɪs'pɜːs] *v.* to clear away; to scatter in different directions. **dis•per•sal, disper•sion,** *n.* act of dispersing.

dis•pir•it•ed [dɪ'spɪrɪtɪd] *adj.* sad/discouraged; feeling disappointed.

dis•place [dɪs'pleɪs] *v.* to move (sth) from its usual place; **displaced persons** = refugees who have fled from their home lands. **dis•place•ment,** *n.* moving (of sth); amount of water removed by a ship, (hence) the volume of the ship.

dis•play [dɪs'pleɪ] 1. *n.* show/exhibition; **d. screen** = screen on which data is displayed. **d. unit** = special stand for showing goods for sale. 2. *v.* to put (sth) on show.

dis•please [dɪs'pliːz] *v.* not to please. **dis•pleas•ure** [dɪs'pleʒə] *n.* annoyance.

dis•port [dɪs'pɔːt] *v.* (*formal*) **to d. oneself** = to amuse oneself.

dis•pose [dɪs'pəuz] *v.* **to d. of sth** = to get rid of sth. **dis•pos•a•ble,** *adj.* which can be thrown away after use; **d. income** = amount of income left over after personal taxes have been deducted. **dis•pos•al,** *n.* (a) machine attached to a sink which grinds up waste. (b) **I am at your d.** = you can ask me to do anything you wish. **dis•posed,** *adj.* **he is well d. towards us** = he favors us. **dis•po•si•tion** [dɪspə'zɪʃn] *n.* (a) character. (b) act of passing property to another person.

dis•pos•sess [dɪspə'zes] *v.* **to d. s.o. of** = to remove possessions from s.o.

dis•pro•por•tion [dɪsprə'pɔːʃn] *n.* being out of proportion. **dis•pro•por•tion•ate,** *adj.* unusual; out of proportion. **dis•pro•por•tion•ate•ly,** *adv.* in a disproportionate way.

dis•prove [dɪs'pruːv] *v.* to prove (sth) is wrong.

dis•pute [dɪs'pjuːt] 1. *n.* argument. 2. *v.* to argue that (sth) is incorrect. **dis•put•a•ble,** *adj.* which can be disputed. **dis•pu•tant,** *n.* person who disputes. **dis•pu•ta•tion,** *n.* (*formal*) argument.

dis•qual•i•fy [dɪs'kwɒlɪfaɪ] *v.* to rule that (s.o.) is incapable of doing sth/not qualified to do sth. **dis•qual•i•fi•ca•tion** [dɪskwɒlɪfɪ'keɪʃn] *n.* rule that s.o. is disqualified.

dis•qui•et [dɪs'kwaɪət] *n.* worry. **dis•qui•et•ing,** *adj.* which makes you worried.

dis•qui•si•tion [dɪskwɪ'zɪʃn] *n.* (*formal*) long, formal speech.

dis•re•gard [dɪsrɪ'gɑːd] 1. *n.* (**for**) indifference (to sth); lack of worry (about sth). 2. *v.* to take no notice of.

dis•re•pair [dɪsrɪ'peə] *n.* **in d.** = needing to be repaired.

dis•re•pute [dɪsrɪ'pjuːt] *n.* bad reputation.

dis•rep•u•ta•ble [dɪs'repjutəbl] *adj.* with a bad reputation; **he is a d. character** = a wicked person.

dis•re•spect [dɪsrɪ'spekt] *n.* lack of respect. **dis•re•spect•ful,** *adj.* lacking respect; rude.

dis•robe [dɪs'rəub] *v.* (*formal*) to undress.

dis•rupt [dɪs'rʌpt] *v.* to break up/to interrupt (a meeting). **dis•rup•tion** [dɪs'rʌpʃn] *n.* breaking up; interruption (of a meeting). **dis•rup•tive,** *adj.* which disrupts.

dis•sat•is•fac•tion [dɪssætɪs'fækʃn] *n.* lack of satisfaction. **dis•sat•is•fied** [dɪs'sætɪsfaɪd] *adj.* not satisfied.

dis•sect [dɪ'sekt] *v.* to cut up (a dead body/plant) in order to examine the inside. **dis•sec•tion,** *n.* cutting up (a body or plant).

dis•sem•ble [dɪ'sembl] *v.* (*formal*) to hide one's feelings.

dis•sem•i•nate [dɪs'semɪneɪt] *v.* to spread (news) around. **dis•sem•i•na•tion,** *n.* act of spreading news around.

dis•sen•sion [dɪ'senʃn] *n.* lack of agreement. **dis•sent** [dɪ'sent] 1. *n.* lack of agreement. 2. *v.* **to d. from** = not to agree with. **dis•sent•er,** *n.* person who does not agree (esp. with the established church).

dis•ser•ta•tion [dɪsə'teɪʃn] *n.* short (university) thesis.

dis•serv•ice [dɪs'sɜːvɪs] *n.* unintentional harm; **you do yourself a d.** = you are harming your reputation.

dis•si•dent ['dɪsɪdənt] *adj. & n.* (person) who does not agree with the opinion of his political party/with the state, etc. **dis•si•dence,** *n.* disagreement (with the state).

dis•sim•i•lar [dɪ'sɪmɪlə] *adj.* not the same; **they are not d.** = they are quite alike.

dis•sim•u•late [dɪ'sɪmjuleɪt] *v.* (*formal*) to hide one's feelings. **dis•sim•u•la•tion,** *n.* (*formal*) hiding one's feelings.

dis•si•pate ['dɪsɪpeɪt] *v.* to clear away; to get rid of. **dis•si•pa•tion** [dɪsɪ'peɪʃn] *n.* throwing away (a fortune); wild living.

dis•so•ci•ate [dɪ'səusɪeɪt] *v.* **to d. yourself from** = to say that you have nothing to do with. **dis•so•ci•a•tion,** *n.* act of dissociating oneself.

dis•so•lute ['dɪsəljuːt] *adj.* depraved; undisciplined.

dis•solve [dɪ'zɒlv] *v.* (a) to make (a solid substance) become part of a liquid; to become part of a liquid. (b) to bring to an end. **dis•so•lu•tion,** *n.* act of dissolving a government organization, partnership, etc. **dis•sol•vent,** *n.* substance which can dissolve other substances.

dis•so•nant ['dɪsənənt] *adj.* out of harmony.

dis•suade [dɪ'sweɪd] *v.* **to d. s.o. from sth** = to

persuade s.o. not to do sth. **dis•sua•sion**, *n.* persuading s.o. not to do sth.

dis•tal ['dɪstəl] *adj.* away from the center of the body.

dis•tance ['dɪstəns] 1. *n.* space from one point to another; **in the d.** = quite a long way away. 2. *v.* **to d. yourself from** = to put yourself at a distance from. **dis•tant**, *adj.* far away; **he is a d. relative** = he is related to me, but not of my close family. **dis•tant•ly**, *adv.* in a distant way.

dis•taste [dɪs'teɪst] *n.* dislike. **dis•taste•ful**, *adj.* unpleasant.

dis•tem•per [dɪs'tempə] 1. *n.* (a) water color paint for walls. (b) sickness of dogs, cats, and horses. 2. *v.* to put distemper on (a wall).

dis•tend [dɪs'tend] *v.* to swell. **dis•ten•sion**, *n.* swelling.

dis•til [dɪ'stɪl] *v.* (**distilled**) to make pure water/alcohol by heating and collecting the vapor; **distilled water** = pure water. **dis•til•la•tion**, *n.* act of distilling (water/alcohol). **dis•till•er**, *n.* person who distils alcohol. **dis•till•er•y**, *n.* factory for distilling alcohol.

dis•tinct [dɪ'stɪŋkt] *adj.* (a) separate. (b) clear. **dis•tinc•tion** [dɪ'stɪŋkʃn] *n.* (a) difference. (b) special excellence. **dis•tinc•tive**, *adj.* very noticeable; particular to one thing; which makes one thing different from others. **dis•tinct•ly**, *adv.* clearly. **dis•tinct•ness**, *n.* being distinct.

dis•tin•guish [dɪ'stɪŋgwɪʃ] *v.* (a) to see clearly; to make out (detail). (b) to see a difference (**between** two things). (c) **he distinguished himself** = he made himself noticed. **dis•tin•guish•a•ble**, *adj.* which can be distinguished. **dis•tin•guished**, *adj.* important/well-known (writer/painter, etc.).

dis•tort [dɪ'stɔːt] *v.* to twist; to give a false impression of. **dis•tor•tion** [dɪ'stɔːʃn] *n.* twisting; giving a false impression.

dis•tract [dɪ'strækt] *v.* to attract attention from. **dis•tract•ed**, *adj.* wild (with worry/grief). **dis•trac•tion** [dɪ'strækʃn] *n.* (a) amusement. (b) worry; **he loved her to d.** = he was wild about her.

dis•train [dɪs'treɪn] *v.* to seize goods to pay for debts.

dis•traught [dɪs'trɔːt] *adj.* wild (with worry/grief, etc.).

dis•tress [dɪ'stres] 1. *n.* (a) great sorrow/pain. (b) difficulty; trouble; **d. signal** = signal sent out by ship/aircraft in trouble. 2. *v.* to make (s.o.) very sad. **dis•tress•ing**, *adj.* very sad; worrying.

dis•trib•ute [dɪ'strɪbjuːt] *v.* to give to several people; **we d. Japanese cars** = we are the agents for Japanese cars. **dis•tri•bu•tion** [dɪstrɪ'bjuːʃn] *n.* giving to several people. **dis•trib•u•tive** [dɪ'strɪbjutɪv] *adj.* which distributes. **dis•trib•u•tor**, *n.* (a) company which sells goods for another (usu. overseas) company. (b) (*in a car engine*) mechanism which passes the electric spark to each sparking plug in turn.

dis•trict ['dɪstrɪkt] *n.* area/region; **d. attorney** = government official who acts as a lawyer in prosecuting cases for the government or the people in a certain region.

dis•trust [dɪs'trʌst] 1. *n.* lack of trust. 2. *v.* to have no trust in.

dis•turb [dɪ'stɜːb] *v.* to bother/to worry (s.o.); to interrupt (s.o.). **dis•tur•bance**, *n.* (a) noise. (b) public disorder. **dis•turb•ing**, *adj.* worrying.

dis•u•nit•ed [dɪsjuː'naɪtəd] *adj.* no longer united.

dis•use [dɪs'juːs] *n.* **to fall into d.** = not to be used any more. **dis•used** ['dɪsjuːzd] *adj.* not used.

ditch [dɪtʃ] 1. *n.* long trench for taking away water. 2. *v.* (a) to make a ditch. (b) (*of aircraft*) to come down in the sea. (c) *inf.* to abandon; **he ditched his car and walked** = he left his car by the side of the road.

dith•er ['dɪðə] 1. *n.* **all of a d.** = very agitated. 2. *v.* not to be able to make up one's mind.

dit•to ['dɪtəu] *n.* the same thing; printer's sign (.) meaning that the same thing is to be repeated.

dit•ty ['dɪtɪ] *n.* little song.

di•u•ret•ic [daɪju'retɪk] *adj. & n.* (substance) which makes you produce more urine.

di•ur•nal [daɪ'ɜːnəl] *adj.* (*poetic*) daily.

di•van [dɪ'væn] *n.* low couch; bed with a solid base and no back or ends.

dive [daɪv] 1. *n.* (a) plunge downward head first. (b) *inf.* disreputable bar/club. 2. *v.* (**dived, dove** [dəuv]) to plunge head first. **div•er**, *n.* person who works underwater. **div•ing board**, *n.* plank at swimming pool from which people dive. **div•ing suit**, *n.* heavy suit for divers working at great depths.

di•verge [daɪ'vɜːdʒ] *v.* to split; to go in different ways. **di•ver•gence**, *n.*

æ back, ɑː farm, ɒ top, aɪ pipe, aʊ how, aɪə fire, aʊə flower, ɔː bought, ɔɪ toy, e fed, eəhair, eɪ take, ə afraid, əʊ boat, əʊə lower, ɜː word, iː heap, ɪ hit, ɪə hear, uː school, ʊ book, ʌ but, b back, d dog, ð then, dʒ just, f fog, g go, h hand, j yes, k catch, l last, m mix, n nut, ŋ sing, p penny, r round, s some, ʃ short, t too, tʃ chop, θ thing, v voice, w was, z zoo, ʒ treasure

split/difference. **di•ver•gent**, *adj.* which split/which are different. **di•verg•ing**, *adj.* splitting; **d. opinions** = opinions which are quite different.

di•verse [daɪ'vɜːs] *adj.* varied. **di•ver•si•fi•ca•tion** [daɪvɜːsɪfɪˈkeɪʃn] *n.* act of diversifying. **di•ver•si•fy**, *v.* to vary; to do other sorts of work. **di•ver•si•ty**, *n.* great variety.

di•ver•sion [daɪ'vɜːʃn] *n.* (a) sending traffic another way. (b) amusement. (c) **to create a d.** = to do sth to distract s.o.'s attention from another thing which you do not want him to see. **di•vert**, *v.* (a) to send traffic another way. (b) to amuse. (c) **I am trying to d. his attention** = to distract his attention.

di•vest [daɪ'vest] *v.* (*formal*) **to d. s.o. of sth** = to take sth away from s.o.

di•vide [dɪ'vaɪd] *v.* (a) to cut into parts. (b) to calculate how many of one number there are in another. **di•vid•ers**, *n. pl.* pair of compasses for measuring.

div•i•dend ['dɪvɪdend] *n.* part of profits shared out among shareholders.

di•vine [dɪ'vaɪn] 1. *adj.* referring to God. 2. *v.* to predict the future; to search for hidden sources of water. 3. *n.* (*formal*) learned priest. **div•i•na•tion** [dɪvɪˈneɪʃn] *n.* predicting what will happen in the future. **di•vin•er**, *n.* person who finds hidden sources of water. **di•vin•i•ty** [dɪ'vɪnɪtɪ] *n.* god; state of being a god.

di•vi•sion [dɪ'vɪʒn] *n.* (a) splitting up into parts; calculation of how many of one number there are in another; **long d.** = working out of a complicated division (such as 2,894 divided by 19) on paper. (b) important part (of army/company). **di•vi•sion•al**, *adj.* referring to a division. **di•vis•i•ble** [dɪ'vɪzəbl] *adj.* which can be divided. **di•vi•sive**, *adj.* which produces quarrels. **di•vi•sor** [dɪ'vaɪzə] *n.* number which divides another.

di•vorce [dɪ'vɔːs] 1. *n.* legal separation of husband and wife leaving each free to remarry. 2. *v.* (a) to separate (two ideas, etc.). (b) to break off a marriage legally. **di•vor•cee** [dɪvɔːˈsiː] *n.* person who is divorced.

div•ot ['dɪvət] *n.* small piece of turf.

di•vulge [daɪ'vʌldʒ] *v.* to reveal (a secret).

diz•zy ['dɪzɪ] *adj.* (**-ier, -iest**) feeling that everything is spinning around; **I feel d.** = my head is turning; **d. heights** = such great heights that they make your head turn. **diz•zi•ly**, *adv.* in a dizzy way. **diz•zi•ness**, *n.* feeling that everything is turning around you.

DJ ['diːdʒeɪ] *abbrev. for* disc jockey.

DNA [diːenˈeɪ] *abbrev. for* deoxyribonucleic acid; **DNA fin•ger•print•ing, DNA pro•fi•ling** *see* **genetic fingerprinting.**

do [duː] 1. *n.* (*pl.* **dos**) party; social gathering. 2. *v.* (**did; done**) (a) to work at (sth); to make/to complete (sth); **I'm doing my hair** = I am combing my hair; **she was doing the laundry; he hasn't done the dishes; can you do today's crossword? well done!** = congratulations, you have worked/run, etc., well! (b) **the potatoes aren't done yet** = aren't cooked yet; **the meat is done to a turn** = the meat is well cooked; *inf.* **I feel done in** = I am tired out. (c) to be satisfactory; **will this color do? we will have to make do with paper plates** = we will have to accept paper plates because there is no alternative. (d) to go (at a certain speed). (e) (*used in negatives, questions and answers*) **it doesn't matter; we didn't laugh; do you live in town?**—yes, **I do; but your parents don't live there, do they?**—no, **they do not.** (f) (*takes the place of another verb*) **can you swim as fast as he does? he speaks French better than I do; she arrived before we did.** (g) (*telling someone not to do something*) **don't throw that paper away!** (h) **how do you do?** = hello! (i) (*to emphasize*) **why don't you work?**—**I do work! why didn't she tell you?**—**she did tell me! do a•way**, *v.* **to do away with sth** = to abolish sth; **to do away with s.o.** = to murder s.o. **do for**, *v. inf.* to kill/to destroy. **do-good•er**, *n.* (*pl.* **do-gooders**) *inf.* person who tries to help others, but in an ineffectual or officious way. **do in**, *v. inf.* to kill. **do•ing**, *n.* (a) **it takes some d.** = it is quite difficult to do. (b) *inf.* **doings** = things. **do-it-your•self**, *n.* repairing/building/painting by yourself, without employing a professional. **do up**, *v.* (a) to fasten. (b) to renovate; **they bought an old cottage and did it up. do with**, *v.* (a) *inf.* to need; **I could do with a drink.** (b) to concern; **it is nothing to do with me** = it is not my business; **it is to do with the new book** = it concerns/it is about the new book; **what have you done with my hat?** = where have you put my hat? **do with•out**, *v.* to manage without.

doc•ile ['dəʊsaɪl] *adj.* quiet/not aggressive. **do•cil•i•ty** [dəʊ'sɪlɪtɪ] *n.* being docile.

dock [dɒk] 1. *n.* (a) artificial harbor; **the docks** = the whole harbor; **dry d.** = dock where the water is pumped out to allow repairs to be done to a ship. (b) box in a court of law, where the prisoner sits. (c) wild plant with very large leaves. 2. *v.* (a) to put a ship into harbor; (*of ship*) to arrive in harbor. (b) to link two spacecraft together in space. (c) to cut off/to remove. **dock•er**, *n.* man who works in the docks. **dock•yard**, *n.* place where ships are built.

dock•et ['dɒkɪt] 1. *n.* list of cases to be tried in a court of law. 2. *v.* to enter in a docket.

doc•tor ['dɒktə] 1. *n.* (*shortened in names to* **Dr.**) person who looks after people's health; learned person with the highest degree from a university. 2. *v.* (a) to look after (a patient/a sick animal). (b) to change figures in (accounts). **doc•tor•al**, *adj.* referring to a doctorate. **doc•tor•ate** ['dɒktərət] *n.* highest degree from a university.

doc•trine ['dɒktrɪn] *n.* statement of what a group of people believe. **doc•tri•naire** [dɒktrɪ'neə] *adj.* very dogmatic. **doc•tri•nal** [dɒk'traɪnl] *adj.* referring to a doctrine.

doc•u•ment ['dɒkjumənt] *n.* paper with writing on it. **doc•u•men•ta•ry** [dɒkju-'mentərɪ] 1. *n.* factual film about a real subject. 2. *adj.* referring to documents. **doc•u•men•ta•tion**, *n.* all the documents which refer to sth.

dod•der ['dɒdə] *v.* to walk uncertainly/to totter. **dod•der•y**, *adj.* old and trembly.

dodge [dɒdʒ] 1. *n.* trick. 2. *v.* to avoid/to get out of the way. **dodg•ems**, *n. pl.* ride at an amusement park where small electric cars are driven around and bump into each other.

do•do ['dəudəu] *n.* large extinct bird.

doe [dəu] *n.* female (deer/rabbit).

doff [dɒf] *v.* to take off (one's hat/clothes).

dog [dɒg] 1. *n.* (a) carnivorous animal which barks, often kept as a pet; **let sleeping dogs lie** = not to disturb the existing state of affairs. (b) male fox. (c) **the dogs** = dog races; **to go to the dogs** = to go to ruin. (d) **d. days** = very hot period in late summer. 2. *v.* (**dogged**) **to d. s.o.'s footsteps** = to follow s.o. **dog-col•lar**, *n.* (a) leather band to go around a dog's neck. (b) *sl.* white collar worn by members of the clergy. **dog-eared**, *adj.* (book) with its pages bent or torn. **dog-fish**, *n.* huss/small white sea fish. **dog•ged** ['dɒgɪd] *adj.* not giving in easily. **dog•ged•ly**, *adv.* in a dogged way. **dog•house**, *n.* kennel; *inf.* **in the d.** = in disgrace. **dog rose**, *n.* wild pink rose. **dog-tired**, *adj.* worn out. **dog•watch**, *n.* (*in the navy*) one of two watches in the evening. **dog•wood**, *n.* shrub with bright red stems.

dog•ger•el ['dɒgərəl] *n.* bad poetry.

dog•ma ['dɒgmə] *n.* official belief. **dog•mat•ic** [dɒg'mætɪk] *adj.* insistent that what you say is right. **dog•mat•i•cal•ly**, *adv.* in a dogmatic way. **dog•ma•tism**, *n.* insistence that you are right. **dog•ma•tize**, *v.* to insist that you are right.

doi•ly ['dɔɪlɪ] *n.* decorated paper/lace mat to put under a cake on a plate.

dol•drums ['dɒldrəmz] *n. pl.* **in the d.** = in a gloomy, depressed mood.

dole [dəul] 1. *n.* money given by the government to people without work; **on the d.** = unemployed and receiving government payments. 2. *v.* **to d. out** = to hand out.

dole•ful ['dəulful] *adj.* gloomy. **dole•ful•ly**, *adv.* gloomily.

doll [dɒl] *n.* toy which looks like a baby. **dolled up**, *adj. inf.* very smartly dressed. **dol•ly**, *n.* (a) *inf.* doll. (b) wheeled platform for a TV camera/for moving heavy loads.

dol•lar ['dɒlə] *n.* unit of money used in the United States and certain other countries.

dol•lop ['dɒləp] *n. inf.* large lump (of sth soft).

dol•men ['dɒlmən] *n.* prehistoric tomb with a flat stone supported by uprights.

dol•phin ['dɒlfɪn] *n.* mammal like a small whale living in the sea.

do•main [də'meɪn] *n.* (a) area controlled by s.o. (b) area of knowledge.

dome [dəum] *n.* semi-spherical roof. **domed**, *adj.* with a dome.

Domes•day Book ['du:mzdeɪ buk] *n.* record of land and population in England, made for William I in 1086.

do•mes•tic [də'mestɪk] *adj.* (a) referring to the home; **d. animals** = animals kept by humans for wool/milk/meat, etc. (b) **d. flights** = flights inside a country. **do•mes•ti•cat•ed** [də-'mestɪkeɪtɪd] *adj.* (animal) trained to live in the house. **do•mes•tic•i•ty** [dɒme'stɪsɪtɪ] *n.* life at home.

dom•i•cile ['dɒmɪsaɪl] *n.* (*formal*) place where s.o. lives. **dom•i•cil•i•ary**, *adj.* which takes place in the home. **dom•i•ciled**, *adj.* (*formal*) living; resident.

dom•i•nant ['dɒmɪnənt] *adj.* most important; supreme; commanding. **dom•i•nance**, *n.* being dominant. **dom•i•nate** ['dɒmɪneɪt] *v.* (a) to rule. (b) to be very obvious. **dom•i•nat•ing**, *adj.* ruling; over-shadowing. **dom•i•na•tion** [dɒmɪ-'neɪʃn] *n.* act of dominating. **dom•i•neer** [dɒmɪ'nɪə] *v.* to rule (s.o.); **a domineering wife** = a wife who rules her husband.

do•min•ion [də'mɪnjən] *n.* (a) self-governing state in the British Commonwealth. (b) rule (over a territory).

dom•i•no ['dɒmɪnəu] *n.* (*pl.* **-oes**) one of a set of small flat blocks, each divided into two sec-

æ back, ɑː farm, ɒ top, aɪ pipe, au how, aiə fire, auə flower, ɔ: bought, ɔɪ toy, e fed, eəhair, eɪ take, ə afraid, əu boat, əuə lower, vː word, iː heap, ɪ hit, ɪə hear, uː school, u book, ʌ but, b back, d dog, ð then, dʒ just, f fog, g go, h hand, j yes, k catch, l last, m mix, n nut, ŋ sing, p penny, r round, s some, ʃ short, t too, tʃ chop, θ thing, v voice, w was, z zoo, ʒ treasure

tions, with up to six dots in each section; **d. theory** = theory that if one event occurs, others will inevitably follow.

don [dɒn] 1. *n.* head, tutor, or fellow of a college at Oxford or Cambridge University. 2. *v.* (**donned**) to put on (a piece of clothing). **don•nish**, *adj.* like a don.

do•nate [dəu'neɪt] *v.* to give. **do•na•tion** [dəu'neɪʃn] *n.* gift.

done [dʌn] *v. see* **do**.

don•key ['dɒŋkɪ] *n.* farm animal like a small horse but with long ears; *inf.* **I haven't seen him for donkey's years** = I have not seen him for a long time; **d. work** = hard dull work.

do•nor ['dəunə] *n.* person who gives; **blood d.** = person who gives blood for blood transfusions.

doo•dle ['du:dl] *v.* to make meaningless drawings/patterns on paper.

doom [du:m] 1. *n.* (a) fate. (b) unhappy ending/ruin. 2. *v.* to condemn (s.o./sth). **Dooms•day**, *n.* end of the world.

door [dɔ:] *n.* barrier of wood/metal, etc., which closes an entrance; **front d.** = main door of a house; **back d.** = door at the back of a house; **he lives two doors down the street** = he lives two houses away. **door•keep•er**, *n.* person who is on guard at a main door. **door•knob**, *n.* handle or knob for opening/shutting a door. **door•man**, *n.* (*pl.* **-men**) person who is in attendance at a door (of a restaurant/hotel, etc.). **door•mat**, *n.* mat or carpet in front of a door. **door•step**, *n.* block of stone/wood, etc., forming the base of a doorway. **door•way**, *n.* space filled by a door.

dope [dəup] *n.* (a) *inf.* drug. (b) strong glue/varnish for making models. (c) *inf.* information. (d) *inf.* stupid fool. **dop•ey**, *adj. inf.* stupid/silly.

dor•mant ['dɔ:mənt] *adj.* sleeping; **d. account** = bank account which is not used; **d. plant** = plant which is not growing because it is winter; **d. volcano** = volcano which is not erupting, but which is not extinct.

dor•mer ['dɔ:mə] *n.* **d.** (**window**) = window with a small gable roof jutting out from a sloping roof.

dor•mi•to•ry ['dɔ:mɪtrɪ] *n.* (a) long room full of beds. (b) building which has many bedrooms and provides living quarters for students, etc.

dor•mouse ['dɔ:maus] *n.* (*pl.* **dormice**) small mouselike animal.

dor•sal ['dɔ:sl] *adj.* (muscle/fin) on the back of an animal.

DOS [dɒs] disk operating system.

dose [dəus] 1. *n.* (a) quantity of medicine. (b) *inf.* attack of a disease. (c) *Sl.* attack of venereal disease. 2. *v.* to give (s.o.) medicine. **dos•age**, *n.* amount of medicine to be given.

dos•si•er ['dɒsɪə] *n.* collection of relevant papers.

dot [dɒt] 1. *n.* small round spot; **he arrived at three o'clock on the d.** = exactly at three o'clock. 2. *v.* (**dotted**) to mark with small spots; **dotted line** = line made up of small spots; **the hillside is dotted with houses** = there are houses here and there on the hillside. **dot-ma•trix print•er**, *n.* computer printer which forms letters from many small dots. **dot•ty**, *adj.* (**-ier, -iest**) *inf.* slightly mad.

dote [dəut] *v.* **to d. on s.o.** = to be very fond of s.o. **dot•age**, *n.* feebleness of mind from old age.

dot•ter•el ['dɒtərəl] *n.* type of field bird.

dot•tle ['dɒtl] *n.* mass of unburned tobacco at the bottom of a pipe.

dou•ble ['dʌbl] 1. *adj.* (a) with two parts; **d. bed** = bed for two people; **d. chin** = chin with a second fold of flesh beneath. (b) twice as big; **a d. whisky** = two measures of whisky; **it takes d. the time** = twice as long; **it is d. the distance** = twice as far. 2. *adv.* **I am seeing d.** = I can see two things when there is only one there. 3. *n.* (a) **on the d.** = at a run. (b) **he is my d.** = he and I look exactly alike. (c) **men's/women's/mixed doubles** = tennis matches for two men or two women or one man and one woman on each side. 4. *v.* (a) to multiply by two. (b) **he doubled back** = he turned around and came back along the same way. (c) **she was doubled up in pain** = was bent forward. **dou•ble-bar•rel•led**, *adj.* (a) (gun) with two barrels. (b) having two purposes. **dou•ble bass**, *n.* very large stringed musical instrument. **dou•ble-breast•ed**, *adj.* (jacket) which overlaps in front. **dou•ble-cross**, *v.* to trick (s.o.) when he thinks that you are working on his side. **dou•ble-cross•er**, *n.* trickster/cheat. **dou•ble deal•ing**, *n.* trickery. **dou•ble-deck•er**, *n.* (a) bus with an upper as well as a lower deck. (b) *inf.* sandwich made with three slices of bread. **dou•ble den•si•ty**, *adj. & n.* (computer disk) having twice the standard storage capacity. **dou•ble Dutch**, *n. inf.* nonsense. **dou•ble-edged**, *adj.* (a) with two sharp edges. (b) which has two quite different meanings. **dou•ble glaz•ing**, *n.* two panes of glass in windows, which insulate. **dou•ble he•lix**, *n.* structure of DNA molecules, comprising two parallel helical chains with a common axis. **dou•ble-joint•ed**, *adj.* with very flexible joints. very flexibly. **dou•ble-park**, *v.* to park alongside a car which is already parked at the side of the street. **dou•ble-park•ing,**

n. parking alongside a car which is already parked at the side of the street. **dou•ble-quick,** *adj. & adv.* extremely fast. **dou•ble take,** *n.* second reaction which comes after a first. **dou•ble-talk,** *n.* words which mean sth quite different from what they seem. **dou•bly,** *adv.* twice.

dou•blet ['dʌblət] *n.* (a) tight-fitting jacket. (b) word of the same origin as another word.

doubt [daut] 1. *n.* not being sure; **to have doubts about** = not to be sure; **no d.** = of course/certainly; **in d.** = uncertain. 2. *v.* not to be sure of. **doubt•ful,** *adj.* uncertain. **doubt•ful•ly,** *adv.* hestitatingly. **doubt•less,** *adv.* certainly.

douche [duːʃ] *n.* spray of water to clean part of the body.

dough [dəu] *n.* (a) uncooked mixture of water and flour for making bread, etc. (b) *Sl.* money. **dough•nut,** *n.* small round or ring-shaped cake cooked by frying in oil. **dough•y,** *adj.* soft and wet (like uncooked dough).

dough•ty ['dauti] *adj.* (*poetic*) brave.

dour ['duə] *adj.* gloomy/silent. **dour•ly,** *adv.* gloomily.

douse [daus] *v.* to throw water on (sth).

dove [dʌv] *n.* (a) white domesticated pigeon. (b) politician who is in favor of negotiating for peace. (c) [dəuv] *v. see* **dive. dove•tail,** *v.* (a) to join (wood) together with a V-shaped joint. (b) to fit in neatly. **dove•cote,** *n.* house for doves.

dow•a•ger ['dauədʒə] *n.* widow of a nobleman who has kept her title and property.

dow•dy ['daudi] *adj.* (**-ier, -iest**) badly-dressed (person); dull/unfashionable (clothes). **dow•di•ly,** *adv.* in a dowdy way.

dow•el ['dauəl] *n.* round wooden peg like a nail for attaching pieces of wood together. **dow•el•ling,** *n.* **a piece of d.** = a long round stick of wood from which dowels can be cut.

dow•er ['dauə] *n.* share of property which belongs to a widow.

down [daun] 1. *adv., adj. & prep.* (a) toward the bottom; **he fell d.** = fell to the ground; **d. with examinations!** = let's do away with examinations; **he tried to go up the d. escalator** = the one which was going downward. (b) at the bottom; **she is d. with influenza** = she has gone to bed with influenza; *inf.* **d. under** = in Australia and New Zealand; **inflation is d. again** = inflation is lower again. 2. *n.* (a) soft feathers

(of a duck). (b) **the downs** = rounded chalk hills in the south of England. 3. *v.* to swallow quickly. **down-and-out,** *n.* tramp/person with no money who lives in the street. **down-at-heel,** *adj.* looking worn/shabby (clothes). **down•cast,** *adj.* gloomy/depressed. **down•fall,** *n.* collapse/ruin. **down•grade,** *v.* to reduce the status of (s.o.). **down•heart•ed,** *adj.* depressed/gloomy. **down•hill,** *adv.* toward the bottom (of a hill). **down•load,** *v.* to load data/program into a computer. **down pay•ment,** *n.* part of a total cost paid in advance. **down•pour,** *n.* heavy fall of rain. **down•right.** 1. *adj.* complete/distinct. 2. *adv.* completely/distinctly. **down•shift•ing,** *n.* changing to a less busy/materialistic lifestyle, usu. by moving house and job. **down•side,** *n.* negative/pessimistic view. **down•size,** *v.* (a) to make smaller. (b) to reduce a company's costs by reducing the size of its workforce. **down•stage,** *adv.* toward the front of a stage. **down•stairs,** *adv. & n.* on/to a lower, esp. the ground, floor. **down•stream,** *adj. & adv.* toward the mouth of a river. **down-to-earth,** *adj.* straightforward/matter-of-fact (way of speaking, etc.). **down•town,** *adv. & n.* (in/to the) central business district of a town. **down•trod•den,** *adj.* oppressed/badly treated. **down•ward,** *adj.* (movement) toward the bottom. **down•ward, downwards,** *adv.* toward the bottom. **down•y,** *adj.* covered with down/with soft feathers.

Down•ing Street ['dauniŋstriːt] *n.* residence of the British Prime Minister; *inf.* the British government.

Down's syn•drome ['daunz'sindrəum] *n.* congenital defect, where the patient has slanting eyes, a wide flat face, and has difficulty in speaking.

dow•ry ['dauri] *n.* money or goods which a bride brings to her husband.

dowse [dauz] *v.* to look for water using a forked twig which moves above water. **dows•er,** *n.* person who dowses.

doy•en ['dɔiən] *n.* senior member of a group.

doze [dəuz] 1. *n.* short sleep. 2. *v.* to be half asleep; **he dozed off** = he went into a light sleep. **doz•y,** *adj.* sleepy.

doz•en ['dʌzn] *n.* twelve; **half a d. apples** = six apples; **dozens of people/times** = many people/times.

æ back, aː farm, ɒ top, aɪ pipe, au how, aiə fire, auə flower, ɔː bought, ɔɪ toy, e fed, eəhair, eɪ take, ə afraid, əu boat, əuə lower, vː word, iː heap, ɪ hit, ɪə hear, uː school, u book, ʌ but, b back, d dog, ð then, dʒ just, f fog, g go, h hand, j yes, k catch, l last, m mix, n nut, ŋ sing, p penny, r round, s some, ʃ short, t too, tʃ chop, θ thing, v voice, w was, z zoo, ʒ treasure

Dr. ['dɒktə] *abbreviation for* Doctor.

drab [dræb] *adj.* lacking bright colors; brown, gray.

drach•ma ['drækmə] *n.* unit of money used in Greece.

dra•co•ni•an [drə'kəʊnɪən] *adj.* very severe/harsh (law, etc.).

draft [drɑːft] 1. *n.* (a) rough plan (of a document). (b) obligatory military service. (c) order for money to be paid by a bank. (*also Brit.* **draught**) (d) pulling; **d. horse** = horse trained to pull heavy loads; **beer on d./d. beer** = beer which is pumped out of a barrel, by hand. (e) mouthful/swallow. (f) amount of a ship's bottom which is under water; **boat with a shallow draft** = boat which does not go very deep into the water. (g) breeze (in a room). 2. *v.* (a) to draw up a rough plan of. (b) to call (s.o.) for service; **drafts•man**, *Brit.* **draughtsman** ['drɑːftsmən] *n.* (*pl.* **-men**) person who draws plans. **drafts•man•ship**, *Brit.* **draughtsmanship** *n.* skill at drawing. **draft•y**, *Brit.* **draughty** *adj.* (**-ier, -iest**) full of breezes.

drag [dræg] 1. *n.* (a) long uphill climb; *Sl.* **what a d.!** = how boring! (b) *Sl.* wearing of women's clothes by a man; **he was in d.** (c) *inf.* one puff on a cigarette. 2. *v.* (**dragged**) (a) to pull sth heavy along. (b) to hang back/to stay behind; to go slowly. (c) to pull a net along the bottom of (a lake) to try to find sth. **drag•net**, *n.* net used to drag a lake; full search for criminals. **drag on**, *v.* to continue slowly. **drag out**, *v.* to pull out; to make (a story) last a long time.

drag•on ['drægən] *n.* mythological animal which breathes fire. **drag•on•fly**, *n.* common insect with brilliant transparent wings. **dragon mar•ket**, *n. inf.* an emerging market on the Pacific rim, e.g. Malaysia.

dra•goon [drə'guːn] 1. *n.* (*old*) soldier on horseback. 2. *v.* to force.

drain [dreɪn] 1. *n.* (a) pipe for carrying waste water; *inf.* **it's like pouring money down the d.** = it is a waste of money. (b) **d. on resources** = gradual loss of money; **brain d.** = movement of professional people to work for other companies or overseas for better pay. 2. *v.* (a) to remove (a liquid). (b) to drink the contents of (a glass). **drain•age**, *n.* system of pipes for taking away waste water. **drain•ing**, *n.* removal of excess liquid; **d. board** = sloping surface next to a sink for draining water off dishes. **drain•pipe**, *n.* pipe which takes away waste water.

drake [dreɪk] *n.* male duck.

dram [dræm] *n.* small drink (of spirits).

dra•ma ['drɑːmə] *n.* (a) serious theatrical performance; **d. department** = department which deals with plays. (b) series of serious events. **dra•mat•ic** [drə'mætɪk] *adj.* (a) referring to

drama. (b) surprising; giving a shock. **dra•mat•i•cal•ly**, *adv.* very surprisingly. **dra•mat•ics**, *n. pl.* putting on plays. **dram•a•tist** ['dræmətɪst] *n.* person who writes plays. **dram•a•ti•za•tion**, [dræmətaɪ'zeɪʃn] *n.* adaptation (of a novel) for the stage/for TV. **dram•a•tize** ['dræmətaɪz] *v.* (a) to adapt (a novel) for the stage/for TV. (b) to make (sth) seem much more dramatic than it really is.

drank [dræŋk] *v. see* **drink.**

drape [dreɪp] 1. *n.* **drapes** = long curtains. 2. *v.* to hang (clothes) around sth.

dra•per•y ['dreɪpərɪ] *n.* (a) (*usu.* **draperies**) long curtains. (b) cloth which is hung or falls in long, loose folds.

dras•tic ['dræstɪk] *adj.* severe/sudden. **dras•ti•cal•ly**, *adv.* suddenly.

draught [drɑːft] *n. Brit. see also* **draft.** **draughts** = game played with black and white counters on a board with black and white squares.

draw [drɔː] 1. *n.* (a) lottery. (b) attraction. (c) **he is quick on the d.** = he pulls out his gun and shoots quickly. (d) game where neither side wins. 2. *v.* (**drew, drawn**) (a) to make a picture with a pen or pencil. (b) to pull; **he drew the curtains** = he opened/closed the curtains; **to d. lots** = take a piece of paper/stick, etc., from a bundle, the person taking the marked paper/stick being the one selected; **he drew a blank** = he was unsuccessful in his search. (c) to move (sth) closer, etc. (d) not to have a winner in a game; **the match was drawn** = neither side won. (e) to collect liquid; **to d. blood** = to cut s.o. so that they bleed. (f) to take (money) from an account. **draw a•side**, *v.* to take (s.o.)/to move to one side. **draw back**, *v.* **he drew back the curtains** = he opened the curtains; **she drew back** = she moved backward. **draw•back**, *n.* inconvenient thing; obstacle. **draw•bridge**, *n.* bridge which can be raised or lowered to give access across water. **draw•er**, *n.* sliding compartment in a desk or cupboard which you open by pulling on a handle; **chest of drawers** = piece of bedroom furniture made of several sliding compartments. **draw•ing**, *n.* picture done with pen or pencil; **d. board** = large board used by designers, on which paper is laid for drawing on; **it was back to the d. board** = he had to start the project all over again. **draw•ing room**, *n.* sitting room; room for sitting and talking in, but not eating. **drawn**, *adj.* looking tired. **draw out**, *v.* to pull (sth) out; to make (sth) last a long time. **draw•string**, *n.* string which, when pulled, closes a bag. **draw up**, *v.* to make (a plan, etc.).

drawl [drɔ:l] 1. *n.* slow way of speaking. 2. *v.* to speak slowly, dragging the words.

drawn [drɔ:n] *v. see* **draw.**

dray [dreɪ] *n.* low flat truck or cart for carrying barrels.

dread [dred] 1. *n.* great fear. 2. *v.* to fear greatly. **dread•ful,** *adj.* awful. **dread•ful•ly,** *adv.* awfully/extremely.

dream [dri:m] 1. *n.* (a) things which you think you see happening when you are asleep. (b) lovely thing. 2. *v.* (**he dreamed/he dreamt** [dremt]) to think you see things happening while you are asleep; **I wouldn't d. of wearing pink socks** = I wouldn't ever think of wearing pink socks. **dream•er,** *n.* person who thinks a lot/who is out of touch with practical things. **dream•i•ly,** *adv.* as in a dream. **dream•less,** *adj.* without dreams. **dream tick•et,** *n.* partnership, usu. of two election candidates, thought to be perfect. **dream up,** *v.* to invent. **dream•y,** *adj.* like a dream.

drear•y ['drɪərɪ] *adj.* (-ier, -iest) sad/gloomy; not interesting. **drear•i•ly,** *adv.* sadly/gloomily. **drear•i•ness,** *n.* being dreary; dreary appearance.

dredge [dredʒ] *v.* (a) to scrape the bottom of (a river or lake) to remove sand or mud. (b) to sprinkle (a cake) with sugar, etc. **dredg•er,** *n.* (a) machine for removing sand or mud from the bottom of a river or lake; boat with such a machine in it. (b) container with holes in the top for sprinkling (sugar, etc.).

dregs [dregz] *n. pl.* sediment at the bottom of a bottle; rubbish.

drench [drentʃ] *v.* to soak; **drenched** = wet through.

dress [dres] 1. *n.* (*pl.* -es) (a) piece of woman's/girl's clothing, covering more or less all the body. (b) special clothes; **d. rehearsal** = rehearsal where the actors wear their costumes; **d. circle** = first balcony of seats above the orchestra in a theater; **d. coat** = man's formal black coat. 2. *v.* (a) to put on clothes. (b) to clean (a wound)/to put a bandage on (a wound). (c) to arrange a display in (a store window). (d) to prepare (meat or fowl) for cooking. **dress down,** *v.* to criticize. **dress•er,** *n.* (a) person in a theater who helps the actors with their costumes; **window d.** = person who arranges displays in store windows. (b) piece of kitchen furniture with open shelves above and cupboards below. **dress•ing,** *n.* (a) putting on clothes; **d. room** = room for getting dressed, esp. room where an actor puts on his costume; **d. gown** = long robe worn over pyjamas or nightdress; **d. table** = bedroom table with mirrors. (b) sauce (for salad); **French d.** = sauce made of oil and vinegar. (c) bandage (for a wound). **dress•mak•er,** *n.* person who makes women's clothes. **dress•mak•ing,** *n.* making of women's clothes by hand. **dress up,** *v.* to put on a costume. **dress•y,** *adj.* very showily dressed; showy (clothes).

dres•sage ['dresɑ:ʒ] *n.* training of a horse which shows how obedient it is.

drew [dru:] *v. see* **draw.**

drib•ble ['drɪbl] *v.* (a) to let drops of liquid run out of your mouth. (b) to move a ball by little amounts along as you are walking or running.

drib•lets, dribs and drabs ['drɪbləts, 'drɪbzən'dræbz] *n. pl.* little bits; **in dribs and drabs** = a little at a time.

dri•er ['draɪə] *n.* = **dry•er.**

drift [drɪft] 1. *n.* (a) general direction; **I got the general d. of his argument** = I understood the general sense of his argument. (b) pile of snow blown by the wind. (c) **North Atlantic D.** = current which crosses the North Atlantic. 2. *v.* (a) to let yourself move. (b) (*of snow*) to pile up. **drift•er,** *n.* person with no set plan in life/person who moves aimlessly from job to job. **drift•wood,** *n.* (*no pl.*) wood which floats and blows on to the shore.

drill [drɪl] 1. *n.* (a) machine for making holes (in wood/metal, etc.); **pneumatic d.** = machine driven by compressed air for making holes in roads. (b) military practice in marching, etc.; *inf.* **fire d.** = practice in reaching the life boats on a ship/practice in evacuating a building in case of fire. (c) small furrow in the ground in which you sow seeds. (d) thick cotton cloth. 2. *v.* (a) to make holes; **he is drilling for oil** = he is making holes in the ground in the hope of finding oil. (b) to do military practice.

dri•ly ['draɪlɪ] *adv.* = **dry•ly.**

drink [drɪŋk] 1. *n.* liquid which you swallow; alcohol; **soft drinks** = non-alcoholic drinks; **he has a d. problem** = he suffers from alcoholism; **he was much the worse for d.** = he was drunk. 2. *v.* (**drank; has drunk**) to swallow (liquid); **he was drinking at the bar** = he was drinking alcohol at the bar; **she doesn't d.** = she never drinks alcohol; **let's d. to the success of the expedition** = let us raise our glasses and wish it success. **drink•a•ble,** *adj.* nice to drink. **drink•er,** *n.* person who drinks (too much alcohol).

æ back, ɑ: farm, ɒ: top, aɪ pipe, aʊ how, aɪə fire, aʊə flower, ɔ: bought, ɔɪ toy, e fed, eəhair, eɪ take, ə afraid, əʊ boat, əʊə lower, ɜ: word, i: heap, ɪ hit, ɪə hear, u: school, ʊ book, ʌ but, b back, d dog, ð then, dʒ just, f fog, g go, h hand, j yes, k catch, l last, m mix, n nut, ŋ sing, p penny, r round, s some, ʃ short, t too, tʃ chop, θ thing, v voice, w was, z zoo, ʒ treasure

drink•ing, *n.* action of swallowing liquid; consumption of alcohol; alcoholism; **d. water** = water which is safe to drink.

drip [drɪp] 1. *n.* (a) small drop of water. (b) (*in a hospital*) **intravenous d.** = device which allows liquid to drip regularly into the bloodstream of a patient. 2. *v.* (**dripped**) to fall in drops; **the faucet is dripping** = drops of water are coming out of the faucet which has not been turned off tightly enough; **drip-dry shirt** = shirt which does not crease if hung to dry while wet.

drip•pings, *n.* fat left in a pan after roasting meat.

drive [draɪv] 1. *n.* (a) ride in a motor vehicle. (b) way in which a car is propelled or guided; **car with front-wheel d.** = car where the engine is connected directly to the front wheels; **car with right-hand d.** = car where the driver sits on the right-hand side. (c) device in a computer which spins a disk. (d) short private road leading to a house. (e) stroke (in golf or cricket) where the ball is hit hard and far. (f) energy. (g) campaign (to collect money for charity). 2. *v.* (**drove; has driven**) (a) to make a motor vehicle travel in a certain direction; **I will d. you to the airport** = I will take you to the airport in my car. (b) to force/to push; **he was driven to it** = he was forced to do it; **she drives a hard bargain** = she is a very tough businesswoman; **the pressure of work was driving her frantic** = making her become frantic. (c) (*in golf, etc.*) to hit the ball hard and far. **drive a•long,** *v.* to ride along a road in a motor vehicle. **drive at,** *v.* **what is he driving at?** = what is he trying to say? **drive a•way,** *v.* (a) to force (sth/s.o.) to go away. (b) to ride away in a motor vehicle. **drive back,** *v.* (a) to force back. (b) to go/to come back in a motor vehicle. **drive in,** *v.* to go in by car; **drive-in movie theater/restaurant** = movie theater/restaurant where you can drive in in a car and watch a motion picture or eat while still sitting in the car. **drive on,** *v.* to continue one's journey. **driv•er,** *n.* person who drives (a motor vehicle); **driver's license** = permit which allows you to drive. **drive•way,** *n.* short private road leading to a house. **driv•ing.** 1. *adj.* (rain/snow) blown by the wind. 2. *n.* action of driving a motor vehicle; **d. test** = test taken before you can have a driving license; **d. school** = school where you learn to drive; **d. wheel** = wheel which moves a part of the machinery (in a machine)/steering wheel (in a car/truck, etc.).

driv•el [ˈdrɪvl] *n.* nonsense.

driv•en [ˈdrɪvn] *v. see* **drive**.

driz•zle [ˈdrɪzl] 1. *n.* thin continuous rain. 2. *v.* to rain in a thin mist. **driz•zly,** *adj.* (weather) where it is raining in thin mist.

drogue [drəʊg] *n.* (*a*) funnel-shaped object, made of cloth, used to pull behind an aircraft for target practice. (b) parachute used as a brake.

droll [drəʊl] *adj.* funny in an odd way.

drom•e•dar•y [ˈdrɒmədərɪ] *n.* camel with only one hump.

drone [drəʊn] 1. *n.* (a) male bee. (b) lazy person. (c) buzz (of an insect/an engine); monotonous noise. 2. *v.* to buzz; to talk slowly and in a monotonous voice.

drool [druːl] *v.* (a) to slobber. (b) *inf.* to show excessive pleasure about something.

droop [druːp] *v.* to hang down; **his spirits drooped** = he was feeling miserable.

drop [drɒp] 1. *n.* (a) tiny quantity of liquid which falls; **the doctor has given me some drops for my eyes** = liquid to be put in the eyes in small quantities. (b) small round jewel; small round candy. (c) fall. (d) jumping by a group of people with parachutes. 2. *v.* (**dropped**) to fall; to let (sth) fall; **she dropped a stitch** = she let a stitch slip in her knitting; *inf.* **d. me a line when you are in Paris** = send me a short letter when you are in Paris; **shall I d. you at your door?** = shall I drive you back and leave you at your door? **he has dropped the idea of going to live in Greece** = he has given up the idea; **the whole project has been dropped** = has been stopped; **d. it** = stop talking about it. **drop in,** *v.* to call on s.o. **drop-kick,** *n.* kick in football where you drop the ball to the ground and kick it as it is falling. **drop•let,** *n.* little drop. **drop off,** *v.* to fall off; **he dropped off** = he fell asleep. **drop out,** *v.* to stop competing; **he has dropped out** = he has given up his studies/has stopped living conventionally. **drop-out,** *n.* person who has stopped studying/stopped living conventionally. **drop•per,** *n.* glass tube for putting drops in eyes, etc. **drop•pings,** *n. pl.* solid waste matter from birds/animals.

drop•sy [ˈdrɒpsɪ] *n.* disease where liquid forms in parts of the body. **drop•si•cal,** *adj.* suffering from dropsy.

dross [drɒs] *n.* worthless matter; refuse.

drought [draʊt] *n.* long period when there is no rain/when the land is dry.

drove [drəʊv] 1. *n.* large number (of people/animals). 2. *v. see* **drive**.

drown [draʊn] *v.* (a) to die by being unable to breathe in water. (b) to flood (a field). (c) to cover up (a noise).

drowse [draʊz] *v.* to be half asleep. **drow•si•ly,** *adv.* sleepily. **drow•si•ness,** *n.* feeling of wanting to go to sleep. **drow•sy,** *adj.* sleepy.

drub•bing [ˈdrʌbɪŋ] *n.* beating.

drudge [drʌdʒ] *n.* person who does hard/boring work. **drudg•er•y,** *n.* hard/boring work.

drug [drʌg] 1. *n.* (a) medicine. (b) substance which affects the nerves, and which can be habit forming. 2. *v.* (**drugged**) to give a drug to (s.o.); **his coffee had been drugged** = s.o. had put a drug in his coffee. **drug•gist,** *n.* person who makes or sells medicines. **drug•store,** *n.* store having a druggist and usu. selling cosmetics, medical supplies, and a variety of other items.

dru•id ['druːɪd] *n.* priest of the old Celtic religion.

drum [drʌm] 1. *n.* (a) large round percussion instrument, covered with tightly stretched material and played with a stick; **d. major** = head of a military band. (b) large barrel; cylindrical container. 2. *v.* (**drummed**) (a) to bang on a drum; to tap your fingers quickly on a surface. (b) **to d. up support** = to encourage people vigorously to give their support. (c) **to d. sth into s.o.** = to make s.o. learn sth by constantly repeating it. **drum•mer,** *n.* person who plays the drums. **drum•stick,** *n.* (a) wooden stick for playing a drum. (b) lower part of a leg (of a cooked chicken/turkey, etc.).

drunk [drʌŋk] 1. *adj.* excited/incapable because of drinking alcohol. 2. *n.* person who is drunk. **drunk•ard,** *n.* person who is often drunk. **drunk•en,** *adj.* referring to an excess of alcohol. **drunk•en•ly,** *adv.* in a drunken way. **drunk•en•ness,** *n.* (habit of) being drunk.

drupe [druːp] *n.* fruit with a large stone (like a peach).

dry [draɪ] 1. *adj.* (**drier, driest**) (a) not wet; **he only had d. bread to eat** = bread with no butter or jam; **d. land** = solid land; **at the end of the play there wasn't a d. eye in the house** = the play made all the audience cry. (b) (*of wine*) not sweet. (c) (area) where alcohol is forbidden. (d) uninteresting/boring (book). (e) **d. sense of humor** = where you make jokes without seeming to know they are funny. 2. *v.* to stop being wet; to wipe (sth) until it is dry. **dry-clean,** *v.* to clean (clothes) with chemicals. **dry-clean•er's,** *n.* business establishment where clothes are dry-cleaned. **dry•er,** *n.* machine for drying; **spin d.** = machine which dries wet clothes by spinning them around very fast. **dry-goods store,** *n.* store which sells fabric and related merchandise, as opposed to groceries or hardware. **dry ice,** *n.*

solid carbon dioxide, used to produce very cold temperatures. **dry•ing,** *n.* action of making something dry; **I'll do the d.** = I'll dry the dishes. **dry•ly,** *adv.* in a sharp, sarcastic way. **dry•ness,** *n.* state of being dry. **dry out,** *v.* to make (sth) dry. **dry rot,** *n.* disease in wood which makes the wood powdery. **dry run,** *n.* practice. **dry up,** *v.* to stop flowing; **he dried up in the middle of his speech** = he stopped talking and could not continue.

dry•ad ['draɪæd] *n.* mythological wood goddess.

du•al ['djuəl] *adj.* double; in a pair; **he has d. nationality** = he is a citizen of two countries; **du•al•i•ty** [djuˈælɪtɪ] *n.* being dual.

dub [dʌb] *v.* (**dubbed**) (a) to make (s.o.) a knight. (b) to add a dialogue to (a motion picture) in another language from the original.

dub•bin ['dʌbɪn] *n.* type of thick oil for making leather soft and waterproof.

du•bi•ous ['djuːbɪəs] *adj.* (a) doubtful/vague; suspicious. (b) hesitant. **du•bi•ous•ly,** *adv.* doubtfully. **du•bi•e•ty** [djuːˈbaɪətɪ], **du•bi•ous•ness,** *n.* doubt.

duch•ess ['dʌtʃes] *n.* wife/widow of a duke. **duch•y,** *n.* land ruled by a duke.

duck [dʌk] 1. *n.* (a) common water bird; female of this bird; meat of this bird used a food; **lame d.** = elected official who has lost an election but continues in office until his/her successor takes over. (b) strong cotton cloth. 2. *v.* (a) to lower your head quickly (to avoid hitting sth). (b) to push (s.o.) under water. (c) to avoid (an unpleasant job). **duck•boards,** *n. pl.* boards placed as a path across wet ground. **duck•ling,** *n.* baby duck. **duck•weed,** *n.* green weed which floats on the surface of ponds.

duct [dʌkt] *n.* tube for carrying air/liquid, etc.

duc•tile ['dʌktaɪl] *adj.* (metal) which can be pulled to form thin wires.

dud [dʌd] *n. inf.* failure; (shell) which will not explode.

dude [djuːd] *n.* dandy; visitor to a ranch.

dudg•eon ['dʌdʒən] *n.* **to leave in high d.** = to leave feeling very indignant.

due [djuː] 1. *adj.* (a) expected; **when is the baby d.?** = when is the baby expected to be born? (b) (money which is) owed. (c) just/deserved. (d) **d. to** = caused by. (e) **in d. course** = subsequently. 2. *adv.* **the plane flew d. west** = straight in a westerly direction. 3. *n.* what is

æ back, ɑː farm, ɒ top, aɪ pipe, aʊ how, aɪə fire, aʊə flower, ɔː bought, ɔɪ toy, e fed, eəhair, eɪ take, ə afraid, əʊ boat, əʊə lower, ɜː word, iː heap, ɪ hit, ɪə hear, uː school, ʊ book, ʌ but, b back, d dog, ð then, dʒ just, f fog, g go, h hand, j yes, k catch, l last, m mix, n nut, ŋ sing, p penny, r round, s some, ʃ short, t too, tʃ chop, θ thing, v voice, w was, z zoo, ʒ treasure

owed/deserved; **to give s.o. his d.** = to be fair to s.o.

du•el ['djuəl] *n.* fight between two people (with swords/guns). **du•el•ist,** *n.* person who fights a duel.

du•en•na [dju:'enə] *n.* elderly Spanish lady, who acts as chaperone.

du•et [dju'et] *n.* piece of music played/sung by two people.

duf•fel, duffle ['dʌfl] *n.* **d. coat** = thick coat (often with a hood) fastened with toggles; **d. bag** = large bag, usu. canvas, which is closed by a string.

dug [dʌg] *v. see* **dig. dug•out,** *n.* hole in the ground, made as a shelter for soldiers; **d. canoe** = boat made from a tree trunk which has been hollowed out.

duke [dju:k] *n.* highest rank of nobleman.

dul•cet ['dʌlsɪt] *adj.* (voice, etc.) which sounds pleasant.

dul•ci•mer ['dʌlsɪmə] *n.* musical instrument with strings hit with little hammers.

dull [dʌl] *adj.* (**duller, dullest**) (a) not exciting/not interesting. (b) gloomy (weather). (c) not sharp (sound). (d) not bright; gloomy (color). (e) rather stupid. **dull•ard,** *n.* stupid person. **dull•ness,** *n.* (a) lack of excitement. (b) gloominess (of color/weather). (c) boredom. (d) slowness; stupidity. **dul•ly,** *adv.* in a dull way.

du•ly ['dju:lɪ] *adv.* properly; as you should.

dumb [dʌm] *adj.* (a) unable to speak. (b) stupid. **dumb•bell** ['dʌmbel] *n.* bar with weights on each end used by weightlifters. **dumb down,** *v.* to make sth, such as a TV program, less mentally challenging. **dumb•found** [dʌm'faund] *v.* to surprise/to flabbergast; **I am dumbfounded at the news** = I am astonished by the news. **dumb•ly,** *adv.* silently/without saying anything.

dum•dum ['dʌmdʌm] *n.* soft-nosed bullet which flattens out when it hits its target.

dum•my ['dʌmɪ] *n.* (a) false thing; (b) stupid person; (c) model of a human figure used to show clothes (in a store or store window).

dump [dʌmp] 1. *n.* place to put garbage and other refuse; **what a d.!** = what an awful place. 2. *v.* (a) to put (sth) heavily on the ground. (b) to throw away; to get rid of. (c) to sell (surplus goods) at a very cheap price (usu. overseas).

dump•ling ['dʌmplɪŋ] *n.* small ball of dough served in stew; **apple dumplings** = apples baked in dough.

dumps [dʌmps] *n. pl. inf.* **down in the d.** = miserable.

dump•y ['dʌmpɪ] *adj.* short and squat.

dun [dʌn] 1. *n.* (a) debt collector. (b) demand to

be paid. 2. *adj.* dull brown color. 3. *v.* (**dunned**) to demand that (a debtor) pay you.

dunce [dʌns] *n.* stupid person.

dune [dju:n] *n.* **sand dunes** = grass-covered sandy ridges by the seashore.

dung [dʌŋ] *n.* solid waste matter (of animals).

dun•ga•rees [dʌngə'ri:z] *n. pl.* overalls/working clothes, usu. of thick blue cloth.

dun•geon ['dʌndʒən] *n.* dark and unpleasant underground prison.

dunk [dʌŋk] *v.* to dip (bread, etc.) into a liquid.

dun•lin ['dʌnlɪn] *n.* small shore bird.

dun•no [də'nəu] *v. inf.* = (**I) don't know.**

du•o ['dju:əu] *n.* two people (usu. two performers).

du•o•dec•i•mal [dju:əu'desɪml] *adj.* (system of calculating) based on the number 12.

du•o•de•num [dju:əu'di:nəm] *n.* part of the intestine immediately below the stomach. **du•o•de•nal,** *adj.* referring to the duodenum.

dupe [dju:p] 1. *n.* person who has been tricked. 2. *v.* to trick (s.o.).

du•plex ['dju:pleks] *n.* (*pl.* **-es**) two-family house; **d. apartment** = apartment with rooms on two floors.

du•pli•cate 1. *n. & adj.* ['dju:plɪkət] copy/double. 2. *v.* ['dju:plɪkeɪt] to make a copy (of a letter, etc.); **you are just duplicating his work** = you are simply doing his work all over again. **du•pli•cat•ing,** *n.* action of making a copy. **du•pli•ca•tion** [dju:plɪ'keɪʃn] *n.* copying; repetition. **du•pli•ca•tor,** *n.* machine which makes copies of documents.

du•plic•i•ty [dju:'plɪsɪtɪ] *n.* dishonesty; tricking s.o.

du•ra•ble ['djuərəbl] *adj.* which lasts/which does not wear away. **du•ra•bil•i•ty** [djuərə'bɪlɪtɪ] *n.* ability to last/not wear out. **du•ra•bly,** *adv.* in a durable way.

du•ra•tion [dju'reɪʃn] *n.* period of time for which sth lasts.

du•ress [dju'res] *n.* force/illegal threats used to make s.o. do sth.

dur•ing ['djuərɪŋ] *prep.* for the time sth lasts.

du•rum ['djuərəm] *n.* hard wheat, used for making pasta.

dusk [dʌsk] *n.* twilight/period in the evening just before it gets dark. **dusk•y,** *adj.* dark-skinned.

dust [dʌst] 1. *n.* thin layer of dry dirt. 2. *v.* (a) to remove dust from (sth). (b) to sprinkle (sugar) on a cake. **dust bowl,** *n.* area where the dry surface soil has been blown away. **dust cov•er,** *n.* dust jacket. **dust•er,** *n.* cloth for removing dust; **feather d.** = brush made of feathers for removing dust. **dust•ing,** *n.* (a) removing of dust. (b) sprinkling (of snow, sugar, etc.). **dust jack•et**, *n.* paper cover around a book. **dust•pan**, *n.* small wide shovel with a handle, for sweeping dirt into. **dust•y**, *adj.* (**-ier, -iest**) covered with dust.

Dutch [dʌtʃ] 1. *adj.* referring to the Netherlands; **D. courage** = courage which comes from being drunk; **D. treat** = party where each person pays his share. 2. *n.* (a) language spoken in the Netherlands. (b) **the Dutch** = the people of the Netherlands. (c) **to go d.** = to split the expenses. **Dutch•man, Dutchwoman,** (*pl.* **-men, -women**) man/woman from the Netherlands.

du•ty ['djuːtɪ] *n.* (a) what one has to do; service; **to be on d. all day; d. officer** = officer who is in charge at a particular time. (b) money which has to be paid; **d. free shop** = shop at an airport/on a boat where goods can be bought free of local tax. **du•ti•a•ble**, *adj.* (goods) on which a customs duty must be paid. **dut•i•ful**, *adj.* (person) who does what they should do. **dut•i•ful•ly**, *adv.* as one should.

du•vet ['duːveɪ] *n.* bag stuffed with feathers, used as the only covering for a bed.

DVD ['diːviːdiː] *abbrev. for* digital video disk.

dwarf [dwɔːf] 1. *n.* person who is much smaller than normal; variety of plant or animal which is smaller than usual; 2. *v.* to make (sth) appear small.

dwell [dwel] *v.* (**dwelt/dwelled**) to live. **dwell•er**, *n. & suffix* person who lives (in a place). **dwell•ing**, *n.* house. **dwell on**, *v.* to refer at length to (a subject).

dwin•dle ['dwɪndl] *v.* to get less. **dwin•dling**, *adj.* which is getting less.

dye [daɪ] 1. *n.* color used to stain cloth; 2. *v.* to stain with a color. **dye•ing**, *n.* staining (of cloth).

dy•ing ['daɪɪŋ] *adj.* about to die.

dyke [daɪk] *n. see* **dike**.

dy•na•mic [daɪ'næmɪk] *adj.* energetic/forceful (person). **dy•nam•ics**, *n. pl.* study of objects in movement.

dy•na•mite ['daɪnəmaɪt] 1. *n.* high explosive. 2. *v.* to blow up with dynamite.

dy•na•mo ['daɪnəməu] *n.* (*pl.* **-os**) small electricity generator.

dy•nas•ty ['dɪnəstɪ] *n.* several generations of one family, esp. a family of rulers.

dys•en•ter•y ['dɪsəntrɪ] *n.* disease of the intestines.

dys•func•tion [dɪs'fʌŋkʃən] *n.* (a) abnormal functioning of an organ. (b) abnormal functioning/breakdown of a family/relationship/groups, etc. **dys•func•tion•al**, *adj.* functioning abnormally.

dys•lex•i•a [dɪs'leksɪə] *n.* being dyslexic. **dys•lex•ic**, *adj.* (person) who has great difficulty in reading and writing.

dys•pep•sia [dɪs'pepsɪə] *n.* inability to digest food properly. **dys•pep•tic**, *adj.* unable to digest food properly.

dys•tro•phy ['dɪstrəfɪ] *n.* **muscular d.** = disease causing gradual weakening of the muscles. **dys•troph•ic** [dɪs'trofɪk] *adj.* (lake) with acid peaty water.

æ back, aː farm, ɒ top, aɪ pipe, aʊ how, aɪə fire, aʊə flower, ɔː bought, ɔɪ toy, e fed, eəhair, eɪ take, ə afraid, əʊ boat, əʊə lower, vː word, iː heap, ɪ hit, ɪə hear, uː school, ʊ book, ʌ but, b back, d dog, ð then, dʒ just, f fog, g go, h hand, j yes, k catch, l last, m mix, n nut, ŋ sing, p penny, r round, s some, ʃ short, t too, tʃ chop, θ thing, v voice, w was, z zoo, ʒ treasure

Ee

each [iːtʃ] 1. *adj.* every. 2. *pron.* every person; everything. 3. **e. other** = both of two people or things; **we write to e. other.**

ea•ger ['iːgə] *adj.* very willing to do sth. **ea•ger•ly**, *adv.* in an eager way. **ea•ger•ness**, *n.* being eager.

ea•gle ['iːgl] *n.* large bird of prey. **ea•gle-eyed**, *adj.* (person) who can see very clearly/who notices small details.

ear ['ɪə] *n.* (a) part of the head, used for hearing; **middle e.** = space inside the head beyond the eardrum; **inner e.** = space inside the head, beyond the middle ear, which controls balance and hearing. (b) sense of hearing; sense of correct tone. (c) **e. of corn** = head of the corn plant, with rows of kernels. **ear•ache** ['ɪəreɪk] *n.* pain in an ear. **ear•drum**, *n.* tight skin inside the ear which resonates to sound waves and so allows you to hear. **ear•lobe**, *n.* lobe on an ear. **ear•mark**, *v.* to reserve (sth such as money) for a special purpose. **ear•phone**, *n.* part of a pair of headphones which fits over one ear. **ear•ring**, *n.* ring attached to the earlobe as an ornament. **ear•shot**, *n.* **within e./out of e.** = near enough to be heard/too far away to be heard.

earl [ɜːl] *n.* high-ranking nobleman.

ear•ly ['ɜːlɪ] (-ier, -iest) 1. *adv.* before the proper time; at the beginning of a period of time; **the train left five minutes e.; e. in the afternoon.** 2. *adj.* which happens at the beginning of a period of time; which happens before the usual time; **at an e. date** = soon.

earn [ɜːn] *v.* to be paid money for working. **earn•ings** ['ɜːnɪŋz] *n. pl.* amount of money earned; salary/wages.

ear•nest ['ɜːnɪst] 1. *adj.* serious. 2. *n.* (a) money paid as a guarantee. (b) **in e.** = seriously/really. **ear•nest•ly**, *adv.* seriously. **ear•nest•ness**, *n.* being earnest.

earth [ɜːθ] *n.* (a) planet on which we live; *inf.* **why on e. did you say that?** = whatever made you say that? (b) soil. **to run s.o. to e.** = to find s.o. after a difficult search. **earth•en** ['ɜːθən] *adj.* made of clay. **earth•en•ware**, *n. & adj.* (pottery) made of clay. **earth•ly**, *adj. inf.* **of no e. use** = of no possible use. **earth•quake**, *n.* shaking of the earth caused by a fault or un-derground volcanic activity. **earth-shat•ter•ing**, *adj. inf.* momentous or upsetting (news). **earth•works**, *n. pl.* walls of earth built as defenses. **earth•worm**, *n.* worm/small animal which looks like a very small snake and lives in earth. **earth•y**, *adj.* (-ier, -iest) coarse/rude (humor).

ear•wig ['ɪəwɪg] *n.* small insect with curved pincers on its tail.

ease [iːz] 1. *n.* absence of difficulty; **ill at e.** = nervous/uncomfortable. 2. *v.* (a) to make less painful. (b) to make easy. (c) to make less tight. **ease off**, *v.* to become less. **ease up**, *v.* to slow down.

ea•sel ['iːzl] *n.* vertical frame on legs (to support a blackboard/painting, etc.).

ease•ment ['iːzmənt] *n.* right to use a path across someone else's property.

e•ast [iːst] 1. *n.* one of the points of the compass, the direction of the rising sun; the eastern part of a country; **the Far E.** = countries to the east of India; **the Middle E.** = countries to the east of Egypt and west of Pakistan; **the Near E.** = countries at the eastern end of the Mediterranean. 2. *adj.* of the east; **E. coast** = eastern part of the United States, on the Atlantic Ocean. 3. *adv.* toward the east. **east•bound**, *adj.* going toward the east. **east•er•ly**, *adj.* (a) **e. wind** = wind from the east. (b) toward the east. **east•ern**, *adj.* of the east. **east•ern•most**, *adj.* furthest east. **east•ward**. 1. *adj.* toward the east. 2. *adv.* (*also* **eastwards**) toward the east.

Eas•ter ['iːstə] *n.* Christian festival (in March or April); **E. Sunday** = Sunday celebrating Christ's rising from the dead; **E. egg** = chocolate or sugar egg eaten at Easter.

eas•y ['iːzɪ] (-ier, -iest) 1. *adj.* not difficult; **the house is an e. walk from the station** = is conveniently close to the station; **my boss is very e. to get along with** = not difficult to work for. 2. *adv.* **to take things e.** = to rest/to do only light work; **e. now!** = be careful/don't get excited! **go e. on/with the jam!** = don't take too much of it. **eas•i•ly**, *adv.* without difficulty. **eas•i•ness**, *n.* state of being easy/of not being difficult. **eas•y chair**, *n.* large comfortable armchair. **eas•y-go•ing**, *adj.* (person who is) easy to get on with/not very critical.

eat [i:t] v. (**ate** [et]; **has eaten**) to chew and swallow (food); **eating apple** = apple to be eaten raw, rather than cooked; **I had him eating out of my hand** = he did everything I told him to do; **he had to e. his words** = to take back what he had said. **eat•a•ble**, adj. edible. **eat•a•bles**, n. pl. things to eat. **eat away**, v. (of acid) to corrode. **eat•er**, n. person who eats. **eat in•to**, v. to reduce gradually. **eat up**, v. to finish eating all of sth; inf. **car that eats up gas** = car that uses a lot of gas.

eau de Co•logne [əʊdəkə'ləʊn] n. liquid with a light scent.

eaves [i:vz] n. pl. edge of a roof overhanging the wall. **eaves•drop**, v. (**eavesdropped**) to listen to a conversation which you are not supposed to hear. **eaves•drop•per**, n. person who eavesdrops.

ebb [eb] 1. n. (of tide) going down. 2. v. (of tide) to go down.

Eb•o•la vi•rus [i:'bəʊlə] n. virus causing a serious contagious disease characterized by internal bleeding and fever.

eb•on•y ['ebənɪ] n. black tropical wood.

e•bul•lient [ɪ'bʌljənt] adj. very excited/full of life. **e•bul•lience**, n. high spirits.

EC ['i:si:] n. European Community.

ec•cen•tric [ɪk'sentrɪk] adj. odd (person). **ec•cen•tri•cal•ly**, adv. in an eccentric way. **ec•cen•tric•i•ty** [eksen'trɪsɪtɪ] n. being eccentric.

ec•cle•si•as•ti•cal [ɪkli:zɪ'æstɪkl] adj. belonging to the church.

ECG ['i:si:'dʒi:] n. electrocardiogram.

ech•e•lon ['eʃəlɒn] n. (a) arrangement of separate things in steps, and not in a straight line. (b) group of people at a certain level in an organization.

ech•o ['ekəʊ] 1. n. (pl. **echoes**) repeated sound reverberating in a cave, etc. 2. v. (of sound) to repeat.

éclair [eɪ'kleə] n. long cake made of pastry, filled with cream and covered with chocolate.

ec•lec•tic [ɪ'klektɪk] adj. taking ideas, etc., from several different sources.

e•clipse [ɪ'klɪps] 1. n. temporary disappearance of (part of) the sun or moon, because another body passes across them. 2. v. (a) to hide (another planet) by passing in front of it. (b) to be more brilliant/successful than s.o.

eco- ['i:kəʊ] prefix meaning ecology/ecological; **ecocentric; ecotourism.**

e•co•cen•tric [i:kəʊ'sentrɪk] adj. concerned for the environment; e.g. ecocentric planning.

e•co•friend•ly ['i:kəʊfrendlɪ] adj. having a positive (or negligible negative) impact on the environment.

E. coli [i:'kəʊlaɪ] n. abbrev. for Escherichia coli.

e•col•o•gy [ɪ'kɒlədʒɪ] n. study of the relationship between plants and animals and their environment. **ec•o•log•i•cal** [i:kə'lɒdʒɪkl] adj. referring to ecology. **e•col•o•gist**, n. person who studies ecology.

e•con•o•my [ɪ'kɒnəmɪ] n. (a) saving (of money or resources); **e. pack** = cheaper packet of goods. (b) way in which a country makes money; financial state of a country. **ec•o•nom•ic** [i:kə'nɒmɪk] adj. referring to economy. **ec•o•nom•i•cal**, adj. which saves money or resources. **ec•o•nom•i•cal•ly**, adv. without waste. **ec•o•nom•ics**, n. (a) study of the finance of industry/of a country. (b) financial structure. **e•con•o•mist** [ɪ'kɒnəmɪst] n. person who specializes in the study of finance. **e•con•o•mize**, v. to e. (on) = to save/avoid waste.

e•co•ter•ror•ist ['i:kəʊterərɪst] n. person who uses violence in an attempt to further environmentalist goals.

e•co•tour•ism ['i:kəʊtʊərɪzəm] n. tourism that has a positive (or negligible negative) impact on the environment.

ec•ru [eɪ'kru:] n. pale fawn color.

ec•sta•sy ['ekstəsɪ] n. great happiness. **ec•sta•tic** [ɪk'stætɪk] adj. very happy. **ec•stat•i•cal•ly**, adv. extremely happy.

ECT [i:si:'ti:] n. electroconvulsive therapy.

ec•to•plasm ['ektəʊplæzəm] n. substance said to come from the body of a person in a trance.

ECU ['ekju] n. European Currency Unit.

ec•u•men•i•cal [i:kju:'menɪkl] adj. referring to Christian unity/concerned with joining together all Christian groups.

ec•ze•ma ['eksɪmə] n. skin disease which causes itchy red spots.

ed•dy ['edɪ] 1. n. small swirl of water (in a stream). 2. v. to swirl around.

e•del•weiss ['eɪdəlveɪs] n. alpine plant with white flowers.

e•de•ma [ɪ'di:mə] n. excess liquid gathering in tissues, causing a swelling.

edge [edʒ] 1. n. (a) (sharp) side of flat object;

the scraping noise set my teeth on e. = made me shudder; **on e.** = nervous/jumpy. (b) sharpened side of a knife/ax, etc. (c) point at the outside of sth; **a house at the e. of the forest. 2.** *v.* (a) to creep sideways. (b) to put along the edge; **a dress edged with silk. edge•wise, edgeways,** *adv.* sideways. **edg•ing,** *n.* material used to edge with. **edg•y,** *adj.* nervous/jumpy.

ed•i•ble ['edɪbl] *adj.* which can be safely eaten.

e•dict ['iːdɪkt] *n.* official order.

ed•i•fice ['edɪfɪs] *n.* large building.

ed•i•fy ['edɪfaɪ] *v.* (*formal*) to instruct and improve (s.o.). **ed•i•fi•ca•tion** [edɪfɪ'keɪʃn] *n.* instruction and improvement.

ed•it ['edɪt] *v.* to make notes on (a text); to change (a text) to make it more acceptable; to prepare (a text) for publication; to cut up (motion-picture film/tape) and stick it together in correct order to make it ready to be shown/played. **e•di•tion** [ɪ'dɪʃn] *n.* (a) number of books/papers printed at the same time; **first e.** = copy of the first printing of a book. (b) form in which a book is published. **ed•i•tor,** *n.* (a) person who makes notes on a text/who prepares a text for publication. (b) director or head of a newspaper or a department of a newspaper; **the sports e.** (c) device for editing. **ed•i•to•ri•al** [edɪ'tɔːrɪəl] **1.** *adj.* referring to editors/to editing. **2.** *n.* leading article written by the editor of a newspaper.

ed•u•cate ['edjukeɪt] *v.* to teach/to instruct (s.o.); **an educated person** = person who is cultivated. **ed•u•ca•tion** [edju'keɪʃn] *n.* (system of) teaching/being taught; **adult e.** = teaching of adults. **ed•u•ca•tion•al,** *adj.* referring to education/teaching/schools; **e. publisher** = publisher who produces school books. **ed•u•ca•tion•ist,** *n.* person who specializes in the study of teaching methods.

ed•u•tain•ment [edju'teɪnmənt] *n.* communication of educational material in an entertaining manner.

Ed•ward•i•an [ed'wɔːdjən] *adj.* referring to the time of Edward VII of England (1901–1910).

eel [iːl] *n.* long thin fish like a snake.

ee•rie ['ɪərɪ] *adj.* (**eerier, eeriest**) frightening/weird. **ee•ri•ly,** *adv.* in an eerie way. **ee•ri•ness,** *n.* being eerie.

ef•face [ɪ'feɪs] *v.* to rub out. **ef•face•ment,** *n.* rubbing out.

ef•fect [ɪ'fekt] **1.** *n.* (a) result/influence; **this rule takes e./comes into e. on November 1st** = starts to be applied. (b) meaning; **words to that e.** = words with that meaning. (c) (*in theater/motion pictures/on radio*) **sound effects** = artificial or reproduced sounds (such as thunder, horses, creaking doors). **2.** *v.* to pro-

duce/to carry out. **ef•fec•tive,** *adj.* (a) which produces a (good) result. (b) which takes effect; **a rule e. on November 1st.** **ef•fec•tive•ly,** *adv.* in a way which produces a good result. **ef•fec•tu•al,** *adj.* (*formal*) which produces the intended effect. **ef•fec•tu•al•ly,** *adv.* in an effectual way. **ef•fec•tu•ate,** *v.* to carry out (sth) effectively.

ef•fem•i•nate [ɪ'femɪnət] *adj.* (*of man*) behaving in a feminine way. **ef•fem•i•na•cy,** *n.* being effeminate.

ef•fer•vesce [efə'ves] *v.* (*of liquid*) to make bubbles giving off gas. **ef•fer•ves•cence,** *n.* bubbles in liquid; act of making bubbles. **ef•fer•ves•cent,** *adj.* which bubbles.

ef•fete [e'fiːt] *adj.* weak/with no strength left.

ef•fi•ca•cious [efɪ'keɪʃəs] *adj.* (medicine, etc.) which produces the correct result. **ef•fi•ca•cy** ['efɪkəsɪ] *n.* being effective; power to produce the correct result.

ef•fi•cien•cy [ɪ'fɪʃənsɪ] *n.* ability to produce the required result. **ef•fi•cient,** *adj.* able to work well/to produce the required result. **ef•fi•cient•ly,** *adv.* in an efficient way.

ef•fi•gy ['efɪdʒɪ] *n.* statue/model of s.o.

ef•flu•ent ['efluənt] *n.* sewage; liquid waste (from a factory). **ef•flu•vi•um,** *n.* hidden liquid which has a strong unpleasant smell.

ef•fort ['efət] *n.* use of physical energy. **ef•fort•less,** *adj.* without apparently using any energy.

ef•fron•ter•y [ɪ'frʌntərɪ] *n.* rudeness.

ef•fu•sive [ɪ'fjuːsɪv] *adj.* too enthusiastic (in thanks). **ef•fu•sive•ly,** *adv.* very enthusiastically.

e.g. [iː'dʒiː] *abbreviation for* exempli gratia, *meaning* for example.

e•gal•i•tar•i•an [ɪgælɪ'teərɪən] *adj. & n.* (person) who believes in equality for everyone.

egg [eg] **1.** *n.* (a) ovum produced by a female animal. (b) hard-shelled cell, produced by a bird, esp. that of a hen. **2.** *v.* **to e. s.o. on** = to encourage s.o. to do sth. **egg•cup,** *n.* holder for a boiled egg. **egg•head,** *n. inf.* intellectual. **egg•plant,** *n.* aubergine/purple fruit eaten as vegetable. **egg•shell,** *n.* shell around an egg; **e. paint** = paint with a slightly shiny matt finish. **egg•tim•er,** *n.* device for timing how long an egg is boiled.

e•go ['iːgəu] *n.* yourself; high opinion of yourself; **e. trip** = action which boosts your opinion of yourself. **e•go•cen•tric** [egəu'sentrɪk] *adj.* thinking only about yourself. **e•go•ism** ['egəuɪzəm] *n.* thinking about oneself. **e•go•ist,** *n.* person who only thinks of himself/herself. **e•go•tism** ['egəutɪzəm] *n.* talking only about oneself. **e•go•tist,** *n.* person who only talks about himself/herself. **e•go•tis•tic(al)** [egəu'tɪstɪk(l)] *adj.* conceited.

e•gre•gious [ɪ'griːdʒəs] *adv.* very bad; shocking.

e•gret ['iːgrət] *n.* type of heron with beautiful white tail feathers.

E•gyp•tian [ɪ'dʒɪpʃn] 1. *adj.* referring to Egypt. 2. *n.* person from Egypt.

eh [eɪ] *inter.* showing surprise/inquiry.

ei•der ['aɪdə] *n.* type of duck. **ei•der•down** ['aɪdədaun] *n.* bed covering made of a large bag full of feathers.

eight [eɪt] (a) number 8. **he is e. (years old); come to see us at e. (o'clock).** (b) eight people (the crew of a rowing boat). **eight•een,** number 18; **the e. hundreds** = the years between 1800 and 1899. **eight•eenth, 18th,** *adj. & n.* referring to eighteen; **the e. century** = period from 1700 to 1799. **eighth, 8th,** *adj. & n.* referring to eight. **eight•i•eth, 80th,** *adj. & n.* referring to eighty. **eight•y,** number 80.

Eire ['ʒərə] *n.* Irish Republic.

ei•ther ['aɪðə, 'iːðə] 1. *adj. & pron.* (a) one or the other; **I don't believe e. of you.** (b) both; **there are trees on e. side of our house. 2.** *conj. & adv.* (*showing choice*) **e. you come here or I will come to you;** (*emphatic*) **he isn't French and he isn't American e.**

e•jac•u•late [ɪ'dʒækjuleɪt] *v.* (a) (*formal*) to exclaim/to say (sth) suddenly. (b) (*of male*) to produce sperm. **e•jac•u•la•tion** [ɪdʒækju-'leɪʃn] *n.* act of ejaculating; sperm which has been ejaculated.

e•ject [ɪ'dʒekt] *v.* to throw out. **ejection/ejector seat,** *n.* seat in an aircraft which throws the pilot out in an emergency.

eke [iːk] *v.* to **e. out** = to economize (savings)/to try not to use up (resources).

e•lab•o•rate 1. *adj.* [ɪ'læbərət] very detailed, very complicated. 2. *v.* [ɪ'læbəreɪt] to go into details. **e•lab•o•ra•tion** [ɪlæbʊ'reɪʃn] *n.* being elaborate; detailed explanation. **e•lab•o•rate•ly,** *adv.* in a complicated/detailed way.

e•land ['iːlənd] *n.* large S. African antelope.

e•lapse [ɪ'læps] *v.* (*of time*) to pass.

e•las•tic [ɪ'læstɪk] 1. *adj.* which stretches and contracts; not rigid. 2. *n.* rubber band. **e•las•tic•i•ty** [ɪlæ'stɪsɪtɪ] *n.* ability to stretch.

e•lat•ed [ɪ'leɪtɪd] *adj.* very excited and pleased.

e•la•tion [ɪ'leɪʃn] *n.* feeling of excitement and pleasure.

el•bow ['elbəu] *n.* joint in the arm. **el•bow•room,** *n.* space to move about.

eld•er ['eldə] 1. *adj.* older (person); **e. statesman** = statesman who is older (and wiser) than others. 2. *n.* (a) older person. (b) common tree with white flowers and bunches of small purple berries. **eld•er•ber•ry,** *n.* (a) elder tree. (b) fruit of an elder. **eld•er•ly,** *adj.* quite old. **eld•est,** *adj.* oldest (of a group).

El Do•ra•do [eldʊ'rɑːdəu] *n.* legendary country of gold.

e•lect [ɪ'lekt] 1. *v.* (a) to choose by voting. (b) to **e. to do sth** = to choose to do sth. 2. *suffix showing* person who has been elected to a post, but who has not taken it up officially; **the mayor-elect. e•lec•tion** [ɪ'lekʃn] *n.* process of choosing by voting; **general e.** = regularly scheduled election for local, state, or national office. **e•lec•tion•eer•ing,** *n.* working for an election campaign. **e•lec•tive,** *adj.* which can be chosen. **e•lec•tor,** *n.* person who is qualified to vote in an election. **e•lec•tor•al,** *adj.* referring to an election; **e. college** = group of people elected to elect s.o. (such as a president). **e•lec•tor•ate,** *n.* all the people in a country who are qualified to vote.

e•lec•tric [ɪ'lektrɪk] *adj.* (a) generating/worked by electricity. (b) **the atmosphere was e.** = full of excitement. **e•lec•tri•cal,** *adj.* referring to electricity. **e•lec•tri•cal•ly,** *adj.* by electricity. **e•lec•tric chair,** *n.* chair used to execute criminals by passing a strong electric current through their bodies. **e•lec•tri•cian** [elek'trɪʃn] *n.* person who installs or works on electrical wiring or equipment. **e•lec•tric•i•ty** [elek'trɪsɪtɪ] *n.* form of energy used for power. **e•lec•tri•fi•ca•tion** [ɪlektrɪfɪ'keɪʃn] *n.* changing to an electric source of power. **e•lec•tri•fy** [ɪ'lektrɪfaɪ] *v.* (a) to convert to an electric source of power. (b) to startle and excite. **e•lec•tro•car•di•o•gram,** *n.* chart made by an electrocardiograph. **e•lec•tro•car•di•o•graph,** *n.* device for recording the electric impulses made by a beating heart. **e•lec•tro•con•vul•sive ther•a•py,** *n.* treatment of mental disorders by giving the patient small electric shocks. **e•lec•tro•cute,** *v.* to kill by electricity. **e•lec•tro•cu•tion** [ɪlektrə'kjuːʃn] *n.* killing by electricity. **e•lec•trode,** *n.* rod which

---

æ back, ɑː farm, ɒ top, aɪ pipe, aʊ how, aɪə fire, aʊə flower, ɔː bought, ɔɪ toy, e fed, eəhair, eɪ take, ə afraid, əʊ boat, əʊə lower, vː word, iː heap, ɪ hit, ɪə hear, uː school, ʊ book, ʌ but, b back, d dog, ð then, dʒ just, f fog, g go, h hand, j yes, k catch, l last, m mix, n nut, ŋ sing, p penny, r round, s some, ʃ short, t too, tʃ chop, θ thing, v voice, w was, z zoo, ʒ treasure

leads the electric current into or out of a cell. **e•lec•tro•en•ceph•a•lo•gram,** *n.* chart made by an electroencephalograph. **e•lec•tro•en•ceph•a•lo•graph,** *n.* device for recording the electric impulses made by the brain. **e•lec•trol•y•sis** [ɪlek'trɒlɪsɪs] *n.* (a) separation of the parts of a compound liquid by passing an electric current through it. (b) removal of unwanted hair by electric current. **e•lec•tro•lyte** [ɪ'lektrəlaɪt] *n.* chemical solution which can be broken into its parts by electrolysis. **e•lec•tro•mag•net,** *n.* magnet made of material wound with a coil of wire with an electric current passing through it. **e•lec•tro•mag•net•ic,** *adj.* made by an electromagnet. **e•lec•tro•mo•tive,** *adj.* (force) which produces an electric current. **e•lec•tron,** *n.* basic particle in an atom. **e•lec•tron•ic** [ɪlek'trɒnɪk] *adj.* referring to electrons or electronics. **e•lec•tron•ic mail,** *n.* system of sending messages from one computer to another, using telephone lines. **e•lec•tron•i•cal•ly,** *adv.* in an electronic way. **e•lec•tron•ic or•gan•iz•er,** *n. see* **personal organizer. e•lec•tron•ics,** *n.* science of conduction of electrons; industry which makes TV sets/radios/calculators, etc. **e•lec•tro•plate,** *v.* to coat (a metal, usu. copper), with a thin layer of silver by means of electrolysis.

el•ee•mos•y•nar•y [eli:məʊ'saɪnəri] *adj.* referring to charity.

el•e•gant ['elɪgənt] *adj.* well dressed; very fashionable. **el•e•gance,** *n.* being elegant. **el•e•gant•ly,** *adv.* fashionably.

el•e•gy ['elədʒɪ] *n.* sad poem about s.o. who is dead. **el•e•gi•ac** [elɪ'dʒaɪək] *adj.* sad and regretful.

el•e•ment ['elɪmənt] *n.* (a) basic chemical substance. (b) basic part (of sth). (c) natural environment; **he's in his e. when he's talking about gardening.** (d) **the elements** = bad weather (wind/rain, etc.). (e) wire which heats in an electric heater/stove, etc. **el•e•men•ta•ry** [elɪ'mentrɪ] *adj.* basic/simple; **e. mathematics. el•e•men•ta•ry school,** *n.* school which includes the first through the sixth or eighth grades.

el•e•phant ['elɪfənt] *n.* very large African or Indian animal, with a trunk and tusks; **white e.** = expensive but useless thing. **el•e•phan•ti•a•sis** [elɪfən'taɪəsɪs] *n.* tropical disease where parts of the body become huge. **el•e•phan•tine** [elɪ'fæntaɪn] *adj.* very large, heavy and difficult to move.

el•e•vate ['elɪveɪt] *v.* to raise up. **el•e•va•tion** [elɪ'veɪʃn] *n.* (a) raising. (b)

(drawing of) one side of a building. (c) height (above sea-level). **el•e•va•tor,** *n.* (a) device for lifting people or goods from one floor of a building to another; **grain e.** = large building for hoisting and storing grain. (b) part of the tail of an aircraft.

e•lev•en [ɪ'levn] *adj. & n.* (a) number 11; **he arrived at e. (o'clock); he is e. (years old).** (b) eleven people (as in a sports team). **e•lev•enth, 11th,** *adj. & n.* referring to eleven; **at the e. hour** = at the last minute; **the e. century** = period from 1000 to 1099.

elf [elf] *n.* (*pl.* **elves** [elvz]) small, usu. male, supernatural being. **elf•in,** *adj.* referring to elves.

e•lic•it [ɪ'lɪsɪt] *v.* to obtain (information) (**from** s.o.).

e•lide [ɪ'laɪd] *v.* to omit a sound when speaking. **e•li•sion** [ɪ'lɪʒn] *n.* omitting of a sound.

el•i•gi•ble ['elɪdʒɪbl] *adj.* able to be chosen (**for** sth); **e. bachelor** = man who has all the qualifications (esp. money) to be married. **el•i•gi•bil•i•ty** [elɪdʒə'bɪlɪtɪ] *n.* being eligible.

e•lim•i•nate [ɪ'lɪmɪneɪt] *v.* (a) to remove (waste, etc.). (b) to exclude (s.o.) after a test. **e•lim•i•na•tion** [ɪlɪmɪ'neɪʃn] *n.* act of eliminating. **e•lim•i•na•tor,** *n.* game, etc., which decides who is eliminated.

e•lite [eɪ'liːt] *n.* group of privileged people/the best people. **e•lit•ism,** *n.* rule by an elite.

e•lix•ir [ɪ'lɪksə] *n.* medicine which people imagine will cure everything.

E•liz•a•be•than [elɪzə'biːbən] *adj.* referring to the time of Elizabeth I of England (1558–1603).

elk [elk] *n.* (*pl.* **elk**) large European deer with flat antlers.

el•lipse [ɪ'lɪps] *n.* oval shape. **el•lip•sis,** *n.* absence of a word which is needed to complete the meaning of a phrase. **el•lip•tic(al),** *adj.* (a) oval. (b) difficult to understand because of a missing word or phrase.

elm [elm] *n.* large deciduous tree; **Dutch e. disease** = disease which kills elms.

el•o•cu•tion [elə'kjuːʃn] *n.* clear and elegant way of speaking.

e•lon•gate ['iːlɒŋgeɪt] *v.* to stretch out to make longer. **e•long•a•tion** [iːlɒŋ'geɪʃn] *n.* act of elongating.

e•lope [ɪ'ləʊp] *v.* to run away from home to get married (**with** s.o.). **e•lope•ment,** *n.* act of eloping.

el•o•quence ['eləkwəns] *n.* art of speaking well. **el•o•quent,** *adj.* good and persuasive (speech). **el•o•quent•ly,** *adv.* in an eloquent way.

else [els] *adv.* (a) otherwise; **you had better pay,**

or e. = or I will force you to pay. (b) other; **anyone e.** = any other person; **nobody e.** = no other person; **anything e.** = any other thing; **nowhere e.** = no other place; **somewhere e./someplace e.** = in some other place. **else•where**, adv. somewhere else; in other places.

e•lu•ci•date [ɪˈluːsɪdeɪt] v. to make clear/to make easy to understand. **e•lu•ci•da•tion** [ɪluːsɪˈdeɪʃn] n. making clear.

e•lude [ɪˈluːd] v. to escape/to avoid (capture). **e•lu•sion**, n. act of eluding. **e•lu•sive** [ɪˈluːsɪv] adj. difficult to find.

el•ver [ˈelvə] n. baby eel.

em [em] n. space in printing equal to the width of the letter "m".

e•ma•ci•at•ed [ɪˈmeɪsɪeɪtɪd] adj. extremely thin. **e•ma•ci•a•tion**, n. being emaciated.

e•mail [ˈiːmeɪl] n. see **e•lec•tron•ic mail**.

em•a•nate [ˈeməneɪt] v. to come **from**. **em•a•na•tion**, n. thing which comes.

e•man•ci•pate [ɪˈmænsɪpeɪt] v. to make (s.o.) free. **e•man•ci•pa•tion** [ɪmænsɪˈpeɪʃn] n. setting free.

e•mas•cu•late [ɪˈmæskjuleɪt] v. to make feeble. **e•mas•cu•la•tion** [ɪmæskjuˈleɪʃn] n. making feeble.

em•balm [ɪmˈbɑːm] v. to treat (a dead body) with chemicals to prevent it from decaying.

em•bank•ment [ɪmˈbæŋkmənt] n. artificial bank (along a river); road along such a bank.

em•bar•go [ɪmˈbɑːgəʊ] 1. n. (pl. **-oes**) official prohibition (**on** goods/traffic/information). 2. v. to prohibit (sth) officially.

em•bark [ɪmˈbɑːk] v. 1. to go on board a ship; **the passengers embarked at New York. 2. to e. on sth** = to start doing sth. **em•bar•ka•tion** [embɑːˈkeɪʃn] n. act of going on board a ship or aircraft.

em•bar•rass [ɪmˈbærəs] v. to make (s.o.) feel uncomfortable (by rudeness/indecency, etc.). **em•bar•rass•ment**, n. act of making s.o. feel uncomfortable.

em•bas•sy [ˈembəsɪ] n. home or offices of an ambassador.

em•bat•tled [ɪmˈbætld] adj. under attack; constantly criticized.

em•bed [ɪmˈbed] v. (**embedded**) to fix (sth) into a mass of concrete/flesh, etc.

em•bel•lish [ɪmˈbelɪʃ] v. to decorate/to make beautiful. **em•bel•lish•ments**, n. pl. decorations/beautiful improvements.

em•bers [ˈembəz] n. pl. pieces of wood/coal which are red hot.

em•bez•zle [ɪmˈbezl] v. to steal (money which you are looking after for s.o.). **em•bez•zle•ment**, n. act of embezzling. **em•bez•zler**, n. person who embezzles.

em•bit•tered [ɪmˈbɪtəd] adj. (of person) made angry and sad (by disappointment/envy).

em•blem [ˈembləm] n. design which is adopted as the characteristic of a country/team/town, etc. **em•blem•at•ic** [emblə-ˈmætɪk] adj. which acts as an emblem.

em•bod•y [ɪmˈbɒdɪ] v. to show (an idea) in a physical form. **em•bod•i•ment**, n. physical expression of an idea.

em•bo•lism [ˈembəlɪzəm] n. blocking of a blood vessel by a blood clot or a bubble of air.

em•boss [ɪmˈbɒs] v. to raise (a design) above a flat surface; **embossed letterhead** = address pressed on writing paper so that it stands above the surface.

em•brace [ɪmˈbreɪs] v. (a) to hold and kiss (s.o.) as a gesture of affection. (b) to become a convert to (a belief).

em•bro•ca•tion [embrəˈkeɪʃn] n. liquid which you rub into parts of the body which are stiff.

em•broi•der [ɪmˈbrɔɪdə] v. to make artistic patterns by sewing with colored threads. **em•broi•der•y**, n. art of sewing flower designs/patterns.

em•broil [emˈbrɔɪl] v. to involve (s.o.) in a quarrel.

em•bry•o [ˈembrɪəʊ] n. (pl. **-os**) earliest state of a living organism; rudimentary idea. **em•bry•ol•o•gy**, n. study of embryos. **em•bry•on•ic** [embrɪˈɒnɪk] adj. original/in a very early state.

e•mend [iːˈmend] v. to change/to make correct. **e•men•da•tion** [iːmenˈdeɪʃn] n. change/correction.

em•er•ald [ˈemrəld] adj. & n. green precious stone; color of this stone.

e•merge [ɪˈmɜːdʒ] v. to come out (**from** inside sth); to become apparent/known. **e•mer•gence**, n. act of emerging. **e•mer•gent**, adj. **e. nations** = countries which are slowly becoming economically independent.

e•mer•gen•cy [ɪˈmɜːdʒənsɪ] n. dangerous state where decisions have to be made quickly (such as fire/accident/breakdown of law and order); **state of e.** = when normal administra-

---

æ back, ɑ: farm, ɒ: top, aɪ pipe, aʊ how, aɪə fire, aʊə flower, ɔ: bought, ɔɪ toy, e fed, eəhair, eɪ take, ə afraid, əʊ boat, əʊə lower, vː word, iː heap, ɪ hit, ɪə hear, uː school, ʊ book, ʌ but, b back, d dog, ð then, dʒ just, f fog, g go, h hand, j yes, k catch, l last, m mix, n nut, ŋ sing, p penny, r round, s some, ʃ short, t too, tʃ chop, θ thing, v voice, w was, z zoo, ʒ treasure

tive processes are taken over by the police or armed forces; **e. exit** = door used when a fire breaks out; **e. operation** = operation carried out at short notice because the patient is seriously ill; **e. services** = the police, fire and ambulance services.

e•mer•i•tus [ɪ'merɪtəs] *adj.* (professor) who has retired but keeps his title.

em•er•y ['eməri] *n.* fine crystals used for polishing. **em•er•y board,** *n.* thin stick of cardboard covered with fine crystals, used for filing fingernails. **em•er•y pa•per,** *n.* fine sandpaper.

e•met•ic [ɪ'metɪk] *n.* substance which makes you vomit.

em•i•grate ['emɪgreɪt] *v.* to leave a country to live in another. **em•i•grant,** *n.* person who emigrates. **em•i•gra•tion** [emɪ'greɪʃn] *n.* act of leaving a country to live in another. **em•i•gré** ['emɪgreɪ] *n.* person who has emigrated for political reasons.

em•i•nence ['emɪnəns] *n.* high place; high rank. **em•i•nent** ['emɪnənt] *adj.* very highly respected because of position or work. **em•i•nent•ly,** *adv.* remarkably; particularly.

e•mir ['emɪə] *n.* Muslim ruler. **e•mir•ate,** *n.* country ruled by an emir.

em•is•sar•y ['emɪsəri] *n.* person sent to negotiate on s.o.'s behalf.

e•mit [ɪ'mɪt] *v.* (**emitted**) to send out (a sound/smoke, etc.). **e•mis•sion,** *n.* act of emitting; thing emitted.

e•mol•lient [ɪ'mɒlɪənt] *adj. & n.* (substance) which softens.

e•mol•u•ment [ɪ'mɒljumənt] *n.* (*formal*) payment/salary.

e•mo•tion [ɪ'məʊʃn] *n.* (strong) feeling. **e•mo•tion•al,** *adj.* showing emotion. **e•mo•tion•al•ly,** *adv.* in an emotional way. **e•mo•tive,** *adj.* which is likely to cause strong feeling.

em•pan•el [ɪm'pænəl] *v. see* **impanel.**

em•pa•thy ['empəθi] *n.* being able to share the feelings of another person, by imagining yourself as that person.

em•per•or ['emprə] *n.* ruler of an empire.

em•pha•size ['emfəsaɪz] *v.* to stress the importance of (sth). **em•pha•sis** ['emfəsɪs] *n.* stress (usu. in speech). **em•phat•ic** [ɪm-'fætɪk] *adj.* using emphasis. **em•phat•i•cal•ly,** *adv.* in a forceful way.

em•pire ['empaɪə] *n.* large number of territories ruled by a central government.

em•pir•i•cal [em'pɪrɪkl] *adj.* based on practical experiment and not on theory.

em•place•ment [ɪm'pleɪsmənt] *n.* place where guns are set.

em•ploy [ɪm'plɔɪ] *v.* (a) to give (s.o.) regular work. (b) to use. **em•ploy•ee** [emplɔɪ'iː] *n.* person who is employed. **em•ploy•er,** *n.* person who gives work to people and pays them. **em•ploy•ment,** *n.* regular paid work.

em•po•ri•um [ɪm'pɔːrɪəm] *n.* large store, usu. selling a large variety of merchandise.

em•pow•er [ɪm'paʊə] *v.* to give (s.o.) the authority to do sth.

em•press ['emprəs] *n.* woman ruler of an empire; wife/widow of an emperor.

emp•ty ['emti] 1. *adj.* with nothing inside. 2. *n.* thing, usu. bottle, which has nothing in it. 3. *v.* to make (sth) empty; to remove (the contents) from sth. **emp•ti•ness,** *n.* being empty. **emp•ty-hand•ed,** *adj.* with no results; having received nothing.

EMS [iːem'es] *n.* European Monetary System.

e•mu ['iːmjuː] *n.* large Australian bird which cannot fly.

em•u•late ['emjʊleɪt] *v.* to try to do as well as or better than (s.o.). **em•u•la•tion** [emjʊ-'leɪʃn] *n.* act of emulating.

e•mul•sion [ɪ'mʌlʃn] *n.* mixture of two liquids which do not unite completely, such as oil and water. **e•mul•si•fi•er,** *n.* thing which emulsifies. **e•mul•si•fy,** *v.* to make into an emulsion.

en [en] *n.* space in printing equal to the width of the letter "n".

en•a•ble [ɪ'neɪbl] *v.* to make it possible for s.o. to do sth.

en•act [ɪ'nækt] *v.* to make (a law). **en•act•ment,** *n.* making (of a law).

e•nam•el [ɪ'næml] 1. *n.* (a) very hard covering of color. (b) hard colored coating fixed to metal by heating. (c) hard coating on the teeth. 2. *v.* (**enameled**) to cover with very hard color.

en•am•oured [ɪ'næməd] *adj.* **I'm not e. of her hair style** = I don't like it very much.

en bloc [ɒn'blɒk] *adv. French.* all together as a group.

en•camped [ɪn'kæmpd] *adj.* in a camp. **en•camp•ment,** *n.* large camp.

en•cap•su•late [ɪn'kæpsjʊleɪt] *v.* to put in a capsule; to put in a shortened form.

en•case [ɪn'keɪs] *v.* to surround as if in a case.

en•chant [ɪn'tʃɑːnt] *v.* to charm. **en•chant•ing,** *adj.* very beautiful/magical. **en•chant•ment,** *n.* magic spell.

en•cir•cle [ɪn'sɜːkl] *v.* to surround completely.

en•clave ['enkleɪv] *n.* small group/small area completely surrounded by another quite different and larger group/mass.

en•close [ɪn'kləʊz] *v.* to put (an object) inside sth; **I am enclosing a bill with my letter. en•clo•sure** [ɪn'kləʊʒə] *n.* (a) fenced area for keeping animals. (b) paper enclosed with a letter in an envelope.

en•code [en'kəud] *v.* to put data/a message into code.

en•co•mi•um [ɪn'kəumɪəm] *n.* (*formal*) praise.

en•com•pass [ɪn'kʌmpəs] *v.* to surround.

en•core ['ɒŋkɔː] 1. *n.* (a) calling (by the audience) for a performer to repeat a song, a piece of music. (b) song/piece of music repeated at the request of the audience. 2. *v.* to call for a song, etc., to be repeated.

en•coun•ter [ɪn'kauntə] 1. *n.* (a) meeting. (b) short conflict. 2. *v.* to meet.

en•cour•age [ɪn'kʌrɪdʒ] *v.* to give (s.o.) the confidence to do sth. **en•cour•age•ment,** *n.* giving s.o. the confidence to do sth. **en•cour•ag•ing,** *adj.* which encourages.

en•croach [ɪn'krəutʃ] *v.* **to e. on** = to occupy space belonging to s.o. else. **en•croach•ment,** *n.* act of encroaching.

en•crust [ɪn'krʌst] *v. see* **incrust**.

en•cum•ber [ɪn'kʌmbə] *v.* (*formal*) to weigh down (s.o.) **with** sth. **en•cum•brance,** *n.* thing which encumbers.

en•cyc•li•cal [ɪn'sɪklɪkl] *n.* solemn letter from the Pope.

en•cy•clo•pe•di•a, encyclopaedia [ɪnsaɪklə'piːdɪə] *n.* reference book which gives facts about things/people/events, etc. **en•cy•clo•pe•dic,** encyclopaedic, *adj.* like an encyclopedia.

end [end] 1. *n.* (a) final part; *inf.* **no e. of** = very many; **to go off the deep e.** = to act in an irrational way; **to be at a loose e.** = to have nothing to do; **to make ends meet** = to have enough money to live on. (b) final part of a period of time. (c) aim; **to this e.** = in order to do this. 2. *v.* to finish. **end•game,** *n.* way of playing the last moves in chess game. **end•ing,** *n.* way a story, etc., finishes. **end•less,** *adj.* with no apparent end. **end•less•ly,** *adv.* with no apparent end. **end•pa•pers,** *n.* pages (usually left blank) at the beginning and end of a book. **end•ways, endwise,** *adv.* with the end first.

en•dan•ger [ɪn'deɪndʒə] *v.* to put in danger.

en•dear [ɪn'dɪə] *v.* **to e. s.o. to s.o.** = to make s.o. loved by s.o. **en•dear•ment,** *n.* term of e. = word showing that you love.

en•deav•or, *Brit.* **en•deav•our** [ɪn'devə] 1. *n.* (*formal*) attempt. 2. *v.* (*formal*) to try hard.

en•dem•ic [en'demɪk] *adj.* (disease) which is often found in a particular place.

en•dive ['endɪv] *n.* salad vegetable with curly leaves.

en•do•car•di•um [endəu'kɑːdɪəm] *n.* membrane lining the heart.

en•do•crine ['endəkraɪn] *adj.* **e. gland** = gland which makes hormones and passes them directly into the bloodstream without using ducts.

en•dorse [ɪn'dɔːs] *v.* to show approval; **to e. a check** = to sign it on the back to show it is yours. **en•dorse•ment,** *n.* approval.

en•dow [ɪn'dau] *v.* (a) to give a regular income to (a school/hospital, etc.). (b) **endowed with** = having (naturally) certain qualities. **en•dow•ment,** *n.* (a) giving of money (to a school, etc.) to provide a regular income. (b) **e. insurance** = type of insurance policy where a sum of money is paid to the insured person on a certain date, or to his heirs if he dies.

en•dure [ɪn'djuə] *v.* (a) to suffer. (b) to stay/to last. **en•dur•a•ble,** *adj.* which can be endured. **en•dur•ance,** *n.* ability to suffer hardship; **e. test** = test of a machine/person to see if it/he works well under bad conditions.

en•e•ma ['enɪmə] *n.* liquid medicine put into the rectum with a syringe.

en•e•my ['enəmɪ] *n.* opponent (in war).

en•er•gy ['enədʒɪ] *n.* force/strength; **atomic e.** = power from atomic reactions. **en•er•get•ic** [enə'dʒetɪk] *adj.* having or using energy; lively. **en•er•get•i•cal•ly,** *adv.* having or using much force. **en•er•gize,** *v.* to make (sth) vigorous.

en•er•vate ['enəveɪt] *v.* to make (s.o.) lazy/sluggish.

en•fee•ble [ɪn'fiːbl] *v.* to make (s.o.) feeble.

en•fold [ɪn'fəuld] *v.* to wrap (sth) **up in** sth.

en•force [ɪn'fɔːs] *v.* to make sure (a law) is obeyed. **en•force•a•ble,** *adj.* which can be enforced. **en•force•ment,** *n.* act of enforcing.

en•fran•chise [ɪn'fræntʃaɪz] *v.* to give (s.o.) the right to vote in elections.

en•gage [ɪn'geɪdʒ] *v.* (a) to attach together (legally); to employ (new staff). (b) to make parts of a machine fit into each other; **e. first gear** = put your car into first gear. (c) to be occupied (in doing sth). (d) to attack (the enemy). **en•gaged,** *adj.* (a) having officially stated one's intention to marry. (b) busy; occupied. **en•gage•ment,** *n.* (a) appointment. (b) statement of intention to marry; **e. ring** = ring given by man to woman when they agree to

æ back, ɑː farm, ɒ top, aɪ pipe, au how, aiə fire, auə flower, ɔː bought, ɔɪ toy, e fed, eəhair, eɪ take, ə afraid, əu boat, əuə lower, vː word, iː heap, ɪ hit, ɪə hear, uː school, u book, ʌ but, b back, d dog, ð then, dʒ just, f fog, g go, h hand, j yes, k catch, l last, m mix, n nut, ŋ sing, p penny, r round, s some, ʃ short, t too, tʃ chop, θ thing, v voice, w was, z zoo, ʒ treasure

marry. (c) battle. **en•gag•ing**, *adj*. charming.

en•gen•der [ɪn'dʒendə] *v*. (*formal*) to produce.

en•gine ['endʒɪn] *n*. (a) machine/large motor which produces power. (b) locomotive/vehicle for pulling trains. **en•gined**, *adj*. with an engine; **single-e. aircraft. en•gi•neer** [endʒɪ'nɪə] 1. *n*. (a) person who looks after technical equipment, esp. engines. (b) (*in the armed forces*) person who specializes in construction of bridges/defenses, etc.; **civil e.** = person who specializes in construction of roads/bridges, etc. (c) person who drives a locomotive. 2. *v*. to arrange (sth) by plotting. **en•gi•neer•ing**, *n*. science/study of technical equipment; **civil e.** = science of construction (esp. of roads/bridges, etc.).

Eng•lish ['ɪŋglɪʃ] 1. *adj*. referring to England; **I think he is E. although he speaks with an American accent. 2.** *n*. (a) **the E.** = the people of England. (b) language spoken in the United States, England, Australia, and many other countries; **can you speak E.? what is that in E.? Eng•lish•man, Englishwoman**, *n*. (*pl*. -men, -women) person from England.

en•grave [ɪn'greɪv] *v*. to cut (a pattern/a letter) on to a hard surface. **en•grav•er**, *n*. artist who engraves. **en•grav•ing**, *n*. picture printed from an engraved plate.

en•gross [ɪn'grəʊs] *v*. to take up all the attention of.

en•grossed [ɪn'grəʊst] *adj*. **e. in** = very interested/busy in.

en•gulf [ɪn'gʌlf] *v*. to swallow up.

en•hance [ɪn'hɑːns] *v*. to increase (beauty/value). **en•hance•ment**, *n*. increase (in value, etc.).

e•nig•ma [ɪ'nɪgmə] *n*. mystery/puzzle. **en•ig•mat•ic** [enɪg'mætɪk] *adj*. difficult to explain/difficult to understand.

en•join [ɪn'dʒɔɪn] *v*. (*formal*) to command.

en•joy [ɪn'dʒɔɪ] *v*. to take pleasure in (sth); **to e. yourself** = to have a good time. **en•joy•a•ble**, *adj*. pleasing. **en•joy•ment**, *n*. pleasure.

en•large [ɪn'lɑːdʒ] *v*. (a) to make bigger. (b) **to e. upon** = to give more details about. **en•large•ment**, *n*. bigger photograph (than the original negative). **en•larg•er**, *n*. device for enlarging photographs.

en•light•en [ɪn'laɪtn] *v*. **to e. s.o. on/about sth** = to give s.o. a clear picture of sth. **en•light•ened**, *adj*. free of prejudice; holding approved ideas. **en•light•en•ment**, *n*. knowledge/absence of ignorance; **the Enlightenment** = period in the 18th century when many scientific discoveries were made.

en•list [ɪn'lɪst] *v*. (a) to join the armed forces. (b) **to e. s.o.'s help** = to get help from s.o. **en•list•ment**, *n*. joining the armed forces.

en•liv•en [ɪn'laɪvn] *v*. to make more lively.

en masse [ɒn'mæs] *adv*. all together in a crowd.

en•mi•ty ['enmɪtɪ] *n*. hatred **toward** s.o.

en•no•ble [ɪ'nəʊbl] *v*. (a) to make more excellent, dignified, or respected. (b) to make (s.o.) a peer.

e•nor•mous [ɪ'nɔːməs] *adj*. very large. **e•nor•mi•ty**, *n*. seriousness (of a crime). **e•nor•mous•ly**, *adv*. very much.

e•nough [ɪ'nʌf] 1. *adj*. sufficient; as much as is needed; **have you got e. money? 2.** *n*. sufficient quantity; **have you had e. to eat? 3.** *adv*. sufficiently; **it is not light e. to take pictures.**

en•quire [ɪŋ'kwaɪə] *v*. *see* **inquire**. **en•quir•y**, *n*. *see* **inquiry**.

en•rage [ɪn'reɪdʒ] *v*. to make (s.o.) very annoyed.

en•rap•ture [ɪn'ræptʃə] *v*. to charm (s.o.).

en•rich [ɪn'rɪtʃ] *v*. to make richer. **en•rich•ment**, *n*. making richer.

en•roll, enrol [ɪn'rəʊl] *v*. (**enrolled**) to admit (new members/new students); **he enrolled in a cooking class. en•roll•ment, enrolment**, *n*. action of admitting new members/students; list of all new students.

en route [ɒn'ruːt] *adv*. on the way.

en•sconced [ɪn'skɒnst] *adj*. firmly settled.

en•sem•ble [ɒn'sɒmbl] *n*. (a) group (of musicians/singers). (b) set of women's clothes which match. (c) group of things which fit together.

en•shrine [ɪn'ʃraɪn] *v*. to enclose as if in a shrine.

en•sign ['ensaɪn] *n*. (a) national flag used by a ship. (b) junior naval officer.

en•slave [ɪn'sleɪv] *v*. to make a slave of (s.o.).

en•snare [ɪn'snɛə] *v*. to catch in a trap.

en•sue [ɪn'sjuː] *v*. to follow. **en•su•ing**, *adj*. which follows.

en suite [ɒn'swiːt] *adv*. joined in a series.

en•sure [ɪn'ʃʊə] *v*. to make sure of.

en•tail [ɪn'teɪl] *v*. to involve/to include.

en•tan•gle [ɪn'tæŋgl] *v*. to be caught up in (in string/bushes/problems). **en•tan•gle•ment**, *n*. state of being entangled.

en•tente [ɒn'tɒnt] *n*. peaceful agreement (between countries).

en•ter ['entə] *v*. (a) to go in/to come in. (b) to write down (a name, etc.). (c) to type information on a keyboard, and put it into a computer system. (d) to put your name on a list as a competitor. **en•ter into**, *v*. to take part in (an agreement).

en•ter•i•tis [entə'raɪtɪs] *n.* infection of the intestines. **en•ter•ic** [en'terɪk] *adj.* referring to the intestines.

en•ter•prise ['entəpraɪz] *n.* (a) new plan/adventure. (b) ability to plan. (c) method of working in business; **private e.** = business companies which are not state-owned. **en•ter•pris•ing,** *adj.* with initiative.

en•ter•tain [entə'teɪn] *v.* (a) to amuse. (b) to offer (s.o.) a meal. (c) to consider (a suggestion/an idea). **en•ter•tain•er,** *n.* person/performer who entertains. **en•ter•tain•ing,** *adj.* amusing. **en•ter•tain•ment,** *n.* (a) amusement. (b) hospitality.

en•thral•ling [ɪn'θrɔːlɪŋ] *adj.* extremely interesting.

en•throne [ɪn'θrəʊn] *v.* to put (s.o.) on a throne.

en•thu•si•asm [ɪn'θjuːzɪæzəm] *n.* great interest. **en•thuse** [ɪn'θjuːz] *v. inf.* to show great interest (over sth). **en•thu•si•ast,** *n.* person who shows great interest in sth. **en•thu•si•as•tic** [ɪnθjuːzɪ'æstɪk] *adj.* showing great interest; **he was very e. about my book. en•thu•si•as•ti•cal•ly,** *adv.* with enthusiasm.

en•tice [ɪn'taɪs] *v.* to attract/to tempt. **en•tice•ment,** *n.* act of enticing; thing which entices.

en•tire [ɪn'taɪə] *adj.* whole. **en•tire•ly,** *adv.* wholly; **I e. agree with you. en•tire•ty** [ɪn-'taɪərətɪ] *n.* being whole; **he translated the book in its e.** = completely.

en•ti•tle [ɪn'taɪtl] *v.* (a) to give the right to; **he is entitled to two weeks' vacation a year.** (b) to give a title to; **a book entitled** *War and Peace.* **en•ti•tle•ment,** *n.* right to have.

en•ti•ty ['entɪtɪ] *n.* thing which exists as a separate unit.

en•tomb [ɪn'tuːm] *v.* to bury.

en•to•mol•o•gy [entə'mɒlədʒɪ] *n.* study of insects. **en•to•mo•log•i•cal** [entəmə-'lɒdʒɪkl] *adj.* referring to entomology. **en•to•mol•o•gist** [entə'mɒlədʒɪst] *n.* person who studies insects.

en•tou•rage [ɒntu:'rɑːʒ] *n.* group of people (secretaries/assistants/advisers, etc.) surrounding an important person.

en•trails ['entreɪlz] *n. pl.* intestines of an animal.

en•trance¹ ['entrəns] *n.* (act of) going in; (door for) going in; **main e.** = main doorway.

en•trance² [ɪn'trɑːns] *v.* to bewitch. **en•tranc•ing,** *adj.* very attractive/beautiful.

en•trant ['entrənt] *n.* person who enters a race/a competition.

en•treat [ɪn'triːt] *v.* to plead. **en•treat•ing,** *adj.* pleading. **en•treat•ing•ly,** *adv.* pleadingly. **en•treat•y,** *n.* plea.

en•trée ['ɒntreɪ] *n.* (a) freedom to go in. (b) small dish served before the main dish (in a formal meal).

en•trench [ɪn'trenʃ] *v.* to dig trenches/to dig in. **en•trenched,** *adj.* **firmly e.** = firmly established.

en•tre•pre•neur [ɒntrəprə'nɜː] *n.* (a) person who directs a company and speculates commercially. (b) contractor who acts as a middleman. **en•tre•pre•neur•i•al** [ɒntrəprə'nɜːrɪəl] *adj.* speculative.

en•trust [ɪn'trʌst] *v.* **to e. sth to s.o./to e. s.o. with sth** = to give s.o. the responsibility for sth.

en•try ['entrɪ] *n.* (a) going in. (b) written information in a reference book/accounts ledger/computer system.

en•twine [ɪn'twaɪn] *v.* to twist around.

e•nu•mer•ate [ɪ'njuːməreɪt] *v.* to mention one by one/to make a list of. **e•nu•mer•a•tion,** *n.* list; act of enumerating.

e•nun•ci•ate [ɪ'nʌnsɪeɪt] *v.* to speak (words) clearly. **e•nun•ci•a•tion** [ɪnʌnsɪ'eɪʃn] *n.* clear pronunciation.

en•vel•op [ɪn'veləp] *v.* to cover/to surround with a covering. **en•vel•ope** ['envələʊp] *n.* paper covering for sending letters.

en•vi•ron•ment [ɪn'vaɪərənmənt] *n.* surroundings (in which you live). **en•vi•ron•men•tal** [ɪnvaɪərən'mentl] *adj.* which refers to the surroundings of sth; **e. audit** = assessment of a company's impact on the environment, esp. in relation to pollution reduction targets; **E. Protection Agency** = official U.S. government agency which oversees protection of the environment and pollution control. **en•vi•ron•men•tal•ist,** *n.* person concerned with conservation of the environment. **en•vi•rons** [ɪn'vaɪərənz] *n. pl.* area surrounding a place.

en•vis•age [ɪn'vɪzɪdʒ] *v.* to foresee; to plan (sth) which may take place.

en•voy ['envɔɪ] *n.* person sent officially (by a country)/high-ranking diplomat.

en•vy ['envɪ] **1.** *n.* feeling of wishing to have sth which s.o. else has/of wanting to be or do sth

---

æ back, ɑː farm, ɒ top, aɪ pipe, aʊ how, aɪə fire, aʊə flower, ɔː bought, ɔɪ toy, e fed, eəhair, eɪ take, ə afraid, əʊ boat, əʊə lower, vː word, iː heap, ɪ hit, ɪə hear, uː school, ʊ book, ʌ but, b back, d dog, ð then, dʒ just, f fog, g go, h hand, j yes, k catch, l last, m mix, n nut, ŋ sing, p penny, r round, s some, ʃ short, t too, tʃ chop, θ thing, v voice, w was, z zoo, ʒ treasure

else. 2. *v.* **to e. s.o. sth** = to wish to have sth belonging to s.o.; to be unhappy because you want to be like s.o. else. **en•vi•a•ble,** *adj.* which one can envy. **en•vi•ous,** *adj.* feeling envy.

en•zyme ['enzaɪm] *n.* substance which can make other substances change (as in digestion).

e•on ['iːən] *n.* very long time.

ep•au•let, epaulette ['epəlet] *n.* decorative strip on the shoulder of a uniform.

e•phem•er•al [ɪ'fiːmərəl] *adj.* which disappears quickly/does not last long. **e•phem•er•a,** *n. pl.* printed papers (like tickets) which are thrown away after use.

ep•ic ['epɪk] 1. *n.* long story/poem/motion picture. 2. *adj.* long and difficult.

ep•i•cen•ter ['epɪsentə] *n.* point on the surface of the earth which an earthquake reaches first.

ep•i•cure ['epɪkjuə] *n.* person who is fond of, and knows a lot about, food. **e•pi•cu•re•an** [epɪkju'riːən] *adj. & n.* (referring to) an epicure.

ep•i•dem•ic [epɪ'demɪk] *n.* wave of disease which affects a lot of people.

ep•i•der•mis [epɪ'dɜːmɪs] *n.* outer layer of skin.

ep•i•du•ral [epɪ'djuərəl] *adj.* (anaesthetic) given in the spine.

ep•i•glot•tis [epɪ'glɒtɪs] *n.* cartilage at the back of the throat which prevents food from being taken into the windpipe.

ep•i•gram ['epɪgræm] *n.* short, witty saying. **ep•i•gram•mat•ic** [epɪgrə'mætɪk] *adj.* witty, like an epigram. **ep•i•graph,** *n.* text used to illustrate sth. (as at the end of a book).

ep•i•lep•sy ['epɪlepsɪ] *n.* disease usu. characterized by convulsive fits. **ep•i•lep•tic** [epɪ'leptɪk] 1. *adj.* referring to epilepsy. 2. *n.* person who suffers from epilepsy.

ep•i•logue, epilog ['epɪlɒg] *n.* short text at the end of a longer work.

E•piph•a•ny [ɪ'pɪfənɪ] *n.* Christian festival on January 6th, celebrating the visit of the Kings to the Christ child.

e•pis•co•pal [ɪ'pɪskəpl] *adj.* referring to bishops; (church) which has bishops. **e•pis•co•pa•lian** [ɪpɪskə'peɪlɪən] *adj. & n.* (member) of an episcopal church.

ep•i•sode ['epɪsəud] *n.* (a) short piece of action in longer story. (b) short period (in your life).

e•pis•te•mol•o•gy [epɪstə'mɒlədʒɪ] *n.* study of knowledge.

e•pis•tle [ɪ'pɪsl] *n.* (*formal*) long letter.

ep•i•taph ['epɪtɑːf] *n.* writing on a gravestone.

ep•i•thet ['epɪθet] *n.* special name describing s.o.; **William I has the e. of "the Conqueror."**

e•pit•o•me [ɪ'pɪtəmɪ] *n.* person who shows a particular quality very strongly. **e•pit•o•mize,** *v.* to show (a quality) very strongly.

ep•och ['iːpɒk] *n.* major period of time. **ep•och-mak•ing,** *adj.* very important historically.

eq•ua•ble ['ekwəbl] *adj.* calm/not easily upset.

e•qual ['iːkwəl] 1. *v.* (**equaled, equalled**) to be exactly the same as/to add up to; **two plus two equals four.** 2. *adj.* (a) exactly the same as/level with something; **all things being e.** = having considered everything carefully. (b) **he wasn't e. to the task** = he wasn't strong enough/brave enough to do it. 3. *n.* person who is on the same level as s.o. else. **e•qual•i•ty** [ɪ'kwɒlɪtɪ] *n.* state of being equal. **e•qual•ize** ['iːkwəlaɪz] *v.* to make equal; to score and make the points of both teams the same. **e•qual•iz•er,** *n.* goal, etc., which makes the score equal. **e•qual•ly,** *adv.* in exactly the same way.

e•qua•nim•i•ty [ekwə'nɪmɪtɪ] *n.* not getting flustered/calmness.

e•quate [ɪ'kweɪt] *v.* to see (two things) as equal. **e•qua•tion** [ɪ'kweɪʒn] *n.* mathematical or chemical formula showing two parts are equal.

e•qua•tor [ɪ'kweɪtə] *n.* imaginary line around the circumference of the earth which is the same distance from the North and South Poles. **e•qua•tor•i•al** [ekwə'tɔːrɪəl] *adj.* referring to the equator.

eq•uer•ry ['ekwərɪ] *n.* man who is in attendance on a king/queen.

e•ques•tri•an [ɪ'kwestrɪən] *adj. & n.* (person) riding on a horse.

e•qui•dis•tant [iːkwɪ'dɪstənt] *adj.* at an equal distance from sth.

e•qui•lat•er•al [iːkwɪ'lætərəl] *adj.* (triangle) with all sides of the same length.

e•qui•lib•ri•um [iːkwɪ'lɪbrɪəm] *n.* state of being perfectly balanced.

e•quine ['ekwaɪn] *adj.* referring to horses.

e•qui•nox ['iːkwɪnɒks] *n.* time of the year when the day and night are of equal length. **e•qui•noc•tial** [iːkwɪ'nɒkʃl] *adj.* referring to an equinox.

e•quip [ɪ'kwɪp] *v.* (**equipped**) to provide (sth/s.o.) **with** arms/machinery/furniture; **well equipped** = with all the arms/machinery, etc., which are thought necessary. **e•quip•ment,** *n.* things which are provided to equip sth.

eq•ui•ty ['ekwɪtɪ] *n.* (a) quality of being fair, just. (b) value of a property in addition to what is owed on it as a mortgage, etc. **eq•ui•ta•ble,** *adj.* fair/just. **eq•ui•ta•bly,** *adv.* in an equitable way.

e•quiv•a•lent [ɪ'kwɪvələnt] *adj. & n.* (thing) of the same value/same strength (as sth). e•quiv•a•lence, *n.* being equivalent.

e•quiv•o•cate [ɪ'kwɪvəkeɪt] *v.* to mislead/to give an ambiguous answer. e•quiv•o•cal, *adj.* uncertain/ambiguous. e•quiv•o•cal•ly, *adv.* in an equivocal way. e•quiv•o•ca•tion, *n.* ambiguous reply.

e•ra ['ɪərə] *n.* long period of history; **the Victorian e.**

e•rad•i•cate [ɪ'rædɪkeɪt] *v.* to wipe out/to destroy completely. e•rad•i•ca•tion [ɪrædɪ-'keɪʃn] *n.* wiping out.

e•rase [ɪ'reɪz] *v.* to rub out (writing)/to remove (recorded material) from a tape; to remove data on a disk. e•ras•er, *n.* piece of rubber for removing pencil/pen/chalk marks. e•ra•sure [ɪ'reɪʒə] *n.* place where a piece of writing has been erased.

ere [ɛːə] *prep.* (*poetic*) before.

e•rect [ɪ'rekt] 1. *adj.* straight upright. 2. *v.* to put up a building, tent, etc. e•rec•tile, *adj.* (tissue) which can become erect. e•rec•tion, *n.* (a) action of putting up; thing which has been erected. (b) state where the penis becomes erect.

erg [ɜːg] *n.* unit of measurement of work.

er•go•nom•ics [ɜːgə'nɒmɪks] *n.* study of people at work and their working environment.

er•got ['ɜːgɒt] *n.* poisonous disease of rye.

er•i•ca ['erɪkə] *n.* heather.

er•mine ['ɜːmɪn] *n.* white fur (from the winter coat of a stoat).

e•rode [ɪ'rəʊd] *v.* to wear away. e•ro•sion [ɪ-'rəʊʒn] *n.* act of wearing away.

e•rog•e•nous [ɪ'rɒdʒənəs] *adj.* very sensitive sexually.

e•rot•ic [ɪ'rɒtɪk] *adj.* strongly sexual. e•rot•i•cism, *n.* erotic quality.

err [ɜː] *v.* to make a mistake/to be at fault.

er•rand ['erənd] *n.* being sent out (esp. to buy sth); **to run errands for s.o.**

er•rant ['erənt] *adj.* (knight) wandering in search of adventure.

er•rat•ic [ɪ'rætɪk] *adj.* irregular/wild. er•rat•i•cal•ly, *adv.* in a wild manner.

er•ra•tum [ɪ'rɑːtəm] *n.* (*pl.* **errata**) mistake in a printed book.

er•ror ['erə] *n.* mistake; **in e.** = by mistake. er•ro•ne•ous [ɪ'rəʊnɪəs] *adj.* wrong. er•ro•ne•ous•ly, *adv.* by mistake.

er•satz ['eəzæts] *adj.* artificial; imitated.

erst•while [ɜːstwaɪl] *adj.* former.

e•ruc•ta•tion [erʌk'teɪʃn] *n.* (*formal*) belching.

er•u•dite ['erjuːdaɪt] *adj.* learned. er•u•di•tion [erjuː'dɪʃn] *n.* learning/knowledge.

e•rupt [ɪ'rʌpt] *v.* (*of volcano*) to throw out lava, ash, etc.; (*of person*) to become angry suddenly. e•rup•tion, *n.* (a) (*of volcano*) throwing out of lava/ash. (b) appearance of a rash on the skin.

er•y•sip•e•las [erɪ'sɪpələs] *n.* red rash on the skin.

es•ca•late ['eskəleɪt] *v.* to get worse/more violent; to increase steadily. es•ca•la•tion [eskə'leɪʃn] *n.* getting worse/bigger. es•ca•la•tor, *n.* moving stairs.

es•ca•lope [eskæ'lɒp] *n.* thin slice of meat, esp. veal.

es•ca•pade ['eskəpeɪd] *n.* wild act.

es•cape [ɪ'skeɪp] 1. *n.* (a) action of getting away from prison/from an awkward situation; **we had a narrow e.** = we were almost killed; **e. clause** = part of a contract which allows one party to avoid the obligations of the contract. (b) key/program which controls the actions of a computer. 2. *v.* (a) to get away (**from** prison/**from** an awkward situation); **he escaped through the window.** (b) to avoid/to miss; **his name escapes me** = I cannot remember his name. es•cap•ee [eskeɪ'piː] *n.* person who has escaped from prison. es•cape•ment, *n.* device in a watch or clock which regulates the movement. es•cap•ism, *n.* retreat from reality. es•cap•ist *adj. & n.* (person) who retreats from reality.

es•carp•ment [ɪ'skɑːpmənt] *n.* steep slope.

es•chew [es'tʃuː] *v.* (*formal*) to avoid.

es•cort 1. *n.* ['eskɔːt] person or group of people accompanying s.o. 2. *v.* [es'kɔːt] to accompany (s.o.).

Es•ki•mo ['eskɪməʊ] *n. & adj.* (*pl.* **-o** *or* **-os**) one of a people living in the north of Canada and Greenland.

e•soph•a•gus [ə'sɒfəgəs] *n.* part of the throat down which food passes from the mouth to the stomach.

es•o•ter•ic [ɪsəʊ'terɪk] *adj.* understood by very few people; difficult to understand.

es•pa•drille [espə'driːj, -drɪl] *n.* canvas rope-soled shoe.

es•pal•ier [ɪ'spælɪə] *n.* artificial shape of a

æ back, ɑː farm, ɒ top, aɪ pipe, aʊ how, aɪə fire, aʊə flower, ɔː bought, ɔɪ toy, e fed, eəhair, eɪ take, ə afraid, əʊ boat, əʊə lower, ɜː word, iː heap, ɪ hit, ɪə hear, uː school, ʊ book, ʌ but, b back, d dog, ð then, dʒ just, f fog, g go, h hand, j yes, k catch, l last, m mix, n nut, ŋ sing, p penny, r round, s some, ʃ short, t too, tʃ chop, θ thing, v voice, w was, z zoo, ʒ treasure

fruit tree, with a central stem and branches which form the shape of a ladder.

es•par•to [ɪ'spɑːtəʊ] n. type of grass.

es•pe•cial [e'speʃl] adj. particular. **es•pe•cial•ly,** adv. particularly/very.

es•pi•o•nage ['esprɪənɑːʒ] n. spying; **industrial e.** = spying on a rival company to try to find out trade secrets.

es•pla•nade ['espləneɪd] n. level place (along a seashore) where people can walk.

es•pouse [es'pauz] v. (formal) to support (a cause).

es•pres•so [ɪ'spresəʊ] n. coffee made by forcing boiling water through ground coffee.

es•prit de corps [esprɪːdə'kɔː] n. feeling of loyalty to a group (usually a military unit).

es•py [ɪ'spaɪ] v. (old) to see.

Esq. [es'kwaɪə] abbreviation for esquire (very polite form of address written after man's name on envelope) **George Martin, Esq.**

es•say. 1. n. ['eseɪ] piece of prose writing on a particular subject. 2. v. [e'seɪ] (formal) to attempt. **es•say•ist,** n. person who writes essays.

es•sence ['esəns] n. pure extract taken from sth; central part (of an argument). **es•sen•tial** [ɪ'senʃl] adj. & n. (thing) which is very important/indispensable; **the bare essentials** = the things which are absolutely necessary. **es•sen•tial•ly,** adv. basically/for the most important part.

es•tab•lish [ɪ'stæblɪʃ] v. (a) to set up/to create. (b) to show sth to be true. **es•tab•lish•ment,** n. (a) creation/setting up. (b) sth established, as a business, household, organization, etc. (c) **the E.** = (small) group of people in positions of authority or influence.

es•tate [ɪ'steɪt] n. (a) large area of land belonging to one person. (b) property owned by a person at the time of death.

es•teem [ɪ'stiːm] 1. n. respect; **to hold s.o. in (high) e.** = to respect s.o. (very much). 2. v. (formal) to consider; **I esteem it an honor. es•teemed,** adj. highly respected. **es•ti•ma•ble,** adj. which can be respected.

es•ter ['estə] n. compound of an acid and an alcohol.

es•ti•mate 1. n. ['estɪmət] calculation which shows the worth/cost/number of sth; price quoted by a supplier; **rough e.** = an approximate calculation. 2. v. ['estɪmeɪt] to calculate (approximately) the cost/the number, etc., of sth; to calculate a price (before supplying the item). **es•ti•ma•tion** [estɪ'meɪʃn] n. calculation of how much sth is worth; judgment of how valuable a person is.

es•ter ['estə] n. compound of an acid and an alcohol.

es•trange [ɪ'streɪndʒ] v. to make unfriendly. **es•trange•ment,** n. becoming estranged.

es•tro•gen [estrədʒen] n. female hormone, controlling bodily changes in the reproductive cycle.

es•tu•ar•y ['estjuərɪ] n. wide part of a river where the sea comes in at high tide.

etc. [et'setərə] abbreviation for et cetera meaning and so on/and the others. **et•cet•er•as** [et'setərəz] n. pl. other things.

etch [etʃ] v. to engrave on metal with acid. **etch•ing,** n. picture reproduced from a metal plate which has been engraved with acid.

e•ter•ni•ty [ɪ'tɜːnɪtɪ] n. never-ending period of time; inf. **it will take an e.** = it will take a very long time. **e•ter•nal,** adj. everlasting. **e•ter•nal•ly,** adv. for ever; inf. all the time.

e•ther ['iːθə] n. very volatile liquid which burns easily and is used as an anesthetic.

e•the•re•al [ɪ'θiːərɪəl] adj. very light like a fairy.

eth•ics ['eθɪks] n. moral principles. **eth•i•cal,** adj. morally right; **e. investment** = investment in companies considered ethical by the investor.

eth•nic ['eθnɪk] adj. relating to a particular race; **e. minority** = minority of a different racial origin than that of the majority. **eth•nog•ra•phy,** n. writing about different races. **eth•no•log•i•cal** [eθnə'lɒdʒɪkl] adj. referring to ethnology. **eth•nol•o•gist** [eθ'nɒlədʒɪst] n. person who studies ethnology. **eth•nol•o•gy** [eθ'nɒlədʒɪ] n. study of the customs of different races.

e•thos ['iːθɒs] n. beliefs or characteristics (esp. of a group of people).

eth•yl ['eθɪl] n. liquid formed from ether and alcohol, used to boost gasoline.

et•i•quette ['etɪket] n. correct way of behaving in society; **professional e.** = the rules of behavior of a particular group of professional people.

et•y•mol•o•gy [etɪ'mɒlədʒɪ] n. way in which a word and its meaning have developed historically. **et•y•mo•log•i•cal** [etɪmə'lɒdʒɪkl] adj. referring to etymology.

EU [iː'juː] abbrev. for European Union.

eu•ca•lyp•tus [juːkə'lɪptəs] n. evergreen tree which gives a strong-smelling oil used to treat colds.

eu•char•ist ['juːkərɪst] n. Christian ceremony of taking consecrated bread and wine. **eu•char•is•tic** [juːkə'rɪstɪk] adj. referring to the eucharist.

eu•gen•ics [juː'dʒenɪks] n. science of breeding strong human beings.

eu•lo•gy ['juːlədʒɪ] n. (formal) speech or writing praising s.o. **eu•lo•gize,** *v.* to praise (s.o.) strongly. **eu•lo•gis•tic** [ju:lə'dʒɪstɪk] *adj.* which eulogizes.

eu•nuch ['ju:nək] *n.* castrated man, usu. a servant.

eu•phe•mism ['ju:fəmɪzəm] *n.* word or phrase used in place of a more offensive or unpleasant word. **eu•phe•mis•tic** [ju:fə-'mɪstɪk] *adj.* referring to euphemism. **eu•phe•mis•ti•cal•ly,** *adv.* as a euphemism.

eu•pho•ni•um [ju:'fəunɪəm] *n.* large brass wind instrument.

eu•pho•ny ['ju:fəni] *n.* pleasant sound.

eu•pho•ri•a [ju:'fɔːrɪə] *n.* extreme happiness. **eu•phor•ic** [ju:'fɒrɪk] *adj.* very happy.

eu•re•ka [ju:'ri:kə] *interj.* meaning a discovery has been made.

eu•ro ['juərəu] *n.* unit of money used in those EU countries who are participating in European Monetary Union.

Euro- ['juərəu] *prefix referring to* Europe; **Eurocurrency, Eurodollar.**

Eu•ro•pe•an [juərə'pi:ən] *adj. & n.* (person) from Europe; **the E. Union** = group of European countries forming a single market and having some common social, monetary, foreign, and security policies; **the E. Parliament** = the parliament to which members (MEPs) are elected from each country of the EU; **the E. monetary system** = system of controlled exchange rates between some member states of the EU; **E. Currency Unit** = accounting unit of E. Monetary System; **E. Monetary Union** = currency union of those EU countries who choose to participate.

Eu•sta•chian [ju:'steɪʃn] *adj.* **E. tube** = tube which connects the middle ear to the throat.

eu•tha•na•sia [ju:θə'neɪzɪə] *n.* painless killing of s.o./sth (as a sick animal) to put them out of their misery.

eu•troph•ic [ju:'trɒfɪk] *adj.* (lake) which is rich in nutrients.

e•vac•u•ate [ɪ'vækjueɪt] *v.* (a) to make (people) leave a dangerous place; to remove (troops) from a place; to remove people from (a place). (b) to empty (the bowels). **e•vac•u•a•tion** [ɪvækju'eɪʃn] *n.* (a) leaving a dangerous place. (b) emptying of the bowels. **e•vac•u•ee** [ɪvækju'i:] *n.* person who has been evacuated.

e•vade [ɪ'veɪd] *v.* to avoid.

e•val•u•ate [ɪ'væljueɪt] *v.* to calculate value.

e•val•u•a•tion [ɪvælju'eɪʃn] *n.* act of calculating.

ev•a•nes•cent [ɪvə'nesənt] *adj.* (*formal*) which fades quickly.

e•van•gel•i•cal [i:væn'dʒelɪkl] *adj.* referring to certain Protestant churches and their teaching of the Bible. **e•van•ge•list** [ɪ-'vændʒəlɪst] *n.* (a) one of the four men who wrote the Gospels. (b) preacher.

e•vap•o•rate [ɪ'væpəreɪt] *v.* (a) to turn liquid into vapor. (b) to disappear. **e•vap•o•ra•tion** [ɪvæpə'reɪʃn] *n.* process of turning liquid into vapor. **e•vap•o•rat•ed,** *adj.* **e. milk** = milk which has been reduced in volume by evaporation.

e•va•sion [ɪ'veɪʒn] *n.* avoiding (a direct answer). **e•va•sive** [ɪ'veɪsɪv] *adj.* which tries to avoid. **e•va•sive•ly,** *adj.* trying to avoid a direct answer. **e•va•sive•ness,** *n.* trying to avoid a direct answer.

eve [i:v] *n.* night before; short time before; **on the e. of our departure** = just before we were due to leave; **Christmas E.** = December 24th/day before Christmas; **New Year's E.** = December 31st.

e•ven ['i:vn] **1.** *adj.* (a) flat/level. (b) regular; **a man of very e. temper** = who never gets very excited. (c) equal (in a competition); **to get e. with s.o.** = try to have revenge on s.o.; **the company is just breaking e.** = it is making no profit, but no loss either. (d) **e. number** = number which can be divided by 2. **2.** *v.* (a) to flatten/to smooth (sth). (b) to make equal; **to e. things up** = to make things equal. **3.** *adv.* not only; **he doesn't e. like strawberries** = most people like strawberries, but he doesn't; **e. worse** = worse than before; **e. so** = however/if you consider everything; **e. now** = right at this minute. **e•ven•ly,** *adv.* (a) in a level way. (b) equally; **they are e. matched** = they are equals (in competition). **e•ven•ness,** *n.* being even.

eve•ning ['i:vnɪŋ] *n.* late part of the day, as night falls; **this e.** = today in the evening. **eve•ning-dress,** *n.* clothes worn to special occasions in the evening (long dress for women, black clothes and black or white bow tie for men).

e•ven•song ['i:vənsɒŋ] *n.* Anglican church service held in the evening.

e•vent [ɪ'vent] *n.* (a) happening; **happy e.** = birth of a child; **in the course of events** = as things turned out; **in the e. of his refusing** = if he should refuse. (b) result; **in any e.** = what-

---

æ back, a: farm, ɒ: top, aɪ pipe, aʊ how, aɪə fire, aʊə flower, ɔ: bought, ɔɪ toy, e fed, eəhair, eɪ take, ə afraid, əʊ boat, əʊə lower, v: word, i: heap, ɪ hit, ɪə hear, u: school, ʊ book, ʌ but, b back, d dog, ð then, dʒ just, f fog, g go, h hand, j yes, k catch, l last, m mix, n nut, ŋ sing, p penny, r round, s some, ʃ short, t too, tʃ chop, θ thing, v voice, w was, z zoo, ʒ treasure

ever happens; **at all events** = in any case. (c) sporting competition; **field events** = jumping and throwing competitions; **track events** = running and hurdling. **e•vent•ful,** *adj.* exciting/full of unexpected happenings.

e•ven•tide [iːvnˈtaɪd] *n.* (*old*) evening.

e•ven•tu•al [ɪˈventjʊəl] *adj.* final. **e•ven•tu•al•i•ty** [ɪventjuˈælɪtɪ] *n.* thing which might happen; **in that e.** = if that should happen. **e•ven•tu•al•ly,** *adv.* in the end.

ev•er [ˈevə] *adv.* (a) at any time; **I hardly e. see her** = almost never see her; **louder than e.** = louder than before. (b) always; **e. since then** = from that time onward; **they lived happily e. after** = always, from then on; **I will love you for e. and e.** = always. (c) *inf.* **e. so** = extremely. (d) (*emphatic*) **what e. is the matter?** = what on earth is the matter? **what e. is it for?** = what can it be used for? **ev•er•more,** *adv.* always. **ev•er•green** [ˈevəgriːn] 1. *adj.* (plant) which keeps its leaves all winter. 2. *n.* tree which keeps its leaves all winter. **ev•er•last•ing** [evəˈlɑːstɪŋ] *adj.* going on for ever.

eve•ry [ˈevrɪ] *adj.* each; all (taken separately); **e. other day** = each alternate day. **eve•ry•bod•y,** *pron.* all people. **eve•ry•day,** *adj.* ordinary/very common. **eve•ry•one,** *pron.* everybody. **eve•ry•thing,** *pron.* all things. **eve•ry•where,** *adv.* in all places.

e•vict [ɪˈvɪkt] *v.* to put (s.o.) out of his/her home. **e•vic•tion** [ɪˈvɪkʃn] *n.* act of putting s.o. out of his/her home.

ev•i•dence [ˈevɪdəns] *n.* (a) traces (of crime). (b) written or spoken report (at a trial); **the criminal turned State's e.** = gave information to the court which proved that his accomplices were guilty. (c) **in e.** = visible. **ev•i•dent,** *adj.* obvious. **ev•i•dent•ly,** *adv.* obviously; presumably.

e•vil [ˈiːvl] 1. *adj.* very wicked. 2. *n.* wickedness; injustice.

e•vince [ɪˈvɪns] *v.* (*formal*) to show (a certain quality/feeling).

e•voke [ɪˈvəʊk] *v.* to call up (an image). **ev•o•ca•tion** [ɪvəʊˈkeɪʃn] *n.* act of evoking. **e•voc•a•tive** [ɪˈvɒkətɪv] *adj.* which calls up a sensation in the mind of the onlooker or reader.

e•volve [ɪˈvɒlv] *v.* (a) to work out gradually (a scientific theory/a way of working). (b) to develop (gradually). **ev•o•lu•tion** [iːvəˈluːʃn] *n.* gradual development; **the theory of e.** = theory that human beings and other living organisms developed gradually from primitive forms of life. **ev•o•lu•tion•ar•y,** *adj.* referring to evolution.

ewe [juː] *n.* female sheep.

ew•er [ˈjuːə] *n.* large jug.

ex- [eks] *prefix meaning* (a) former; who used to be; **my ex-girlfriend.** (b) out of; **export.**

ex•ac•er•bate [ɪɡˈzæsəbeɪt] *v.* (*formal*) to make worse/more painful. **ex•ac•er•ba•tion** [ɪɡzæsəˈbeɪʃn] *n.* making worse.

ex•act [ɪɡˈzækt] 1. *adj.* precise. 2. *v.* to force (sth) **from** s.o. **ex•act•ing,** *adj.* (person) who demands a lot (of effort). **ex•ac•tion,** *n.* (*formal*) demand (for money). **ex•ac•ti•tude,** *n.* precision. **ex•act•ly,** *adv.* precisely; **e.!** = that's right.

ex•ag•ger•ate [ɪɡˈzædʒəreɪt] *v.* to make things seem larger/worse/better than they really are. **ex•ag•ger•a•tion** [ɪɡzædʒəˈreɪʃn] *n.* (statement, etc.) making things seem larger/worse/better; **without e.** = quite truthfully.

ex•al•ted [ɪɡˈzɔːltɪd] *adj.* in a high position in authority; very happy. **ex•al•ta•tion** [egzəlˈteɪʃn] *n.* exalted feeling.

ex•am•ine [ɪɡˈzæmɪn] *v.* to inspect (sth) to see if it is correct; to test (a student); to ask (a witness) questions. **ex•am** [ɪɡˈzæm] *n. inf.* written or spoken test. **ex•am•i•na•tion** [ɪɡzæmɪˈneɪʃn] *n.* inspection; written or spoken test. **ex•am•in•ee** [ɪɡzæmɪˈniː] *n.* person being tested. **ex•am•in•er** [ɪɡˈzæmɪnə] *n.* person who inspects or tests.

ex•am•ple [ɪɡˈzɑːmpl] *n.* case selected to show sth; **to set an e.** = to act well, so that others may copy you; **to make an e. of s.o.** = to punish s.o. so that others will learn not to do what he did; **for e.** = to name one thing out of many.

ex•as•per•ate [ɪɡˈzɑːspəreɪt] *v.* to make (s.o.) furious. **ex•as•per•a•tion** [ɪɡzɑːspəˈreɪʃn] *n.* fury.

ex•ca•vate [ˈekskəveɪt] *v.* to dig (a hole in the ground); to carry out an archaeological investigation of (a place). **ex•ca•va•tion** [ekskəˈveɪʃn] *n.* large hole; archaeological investigation. **ex•ca•va•tor,** *n.* machine for making holes in the ground.

ex•ceed [ɪkˈsiːd] *v.* to go beyond (a limit). **ex•ceed•ing•ly,** *adv.* very.

ex•cel [ɪkˈsel] *v.* (excelled) to be very good (at sth). **ex•cel•lence** [ˈeksələns] *n.* very good quality. **Ex•cel•len•cy,** *n.* title given to high officials, as ambassadors and Roman Catholic bishops. **ex•cel•lent,** *adj.* very good.

ex•cept [ɪkˈsept] 1. *prep. & conj.* not including; other than; **all went well e. that James was sick** = apart from the fact that. 2. *v.* not to include (sth). **ex•cep•tion** [ɪkˈsepʃn] *n.* thing not included; **he took e. to what she said** = he was annoyed at what she said. **ex•cep•tion•a•ble,** *adj.* not to be approved of. **ex•cep•tion•al,**

adj. outstanding. **ex•cep•tion•al•ly,** *adv.* particularly.

ex•cerpt ['eksɜːpt] 1. *n.* small part (of a larger piece of music/writing). 2. *v.* to make an excerpt.

ex•cess [ɪk'ses] *n.* (a) too much (of sth); **in e. of** = more than; **to e.** = too much; **e. baggage** = more baggage than one is allowed to carry. (b) action or behavior which is worse than is normally acceptable. **ex•ces•sive,** *adj.* more than is normal. **ex•ces•sive•ly,** *adv.* too much.

ex•change [ɪks'tʃeɪndʒ] 1. *n.* giving of one thing for another; **foreign e.** = exchange of the money of one country for that of another; **e. rate** = rate at which one money is given for another; **telephone e.** = central place or station where telephone calls are linked; **stock e.** = place where stocks and shares are bought and sold. 2. *v.* to swap/to give (sth) **for** sth else; **they exchanged addresses** = each of them gave the other his address. **ex•change•a•ble,** *adj.* which can be exchanged.

ex•cheq•uer [eks'tʃekə] *n.* British government department dealing with public money.

ex•cise 1. *n.* ['eksaɪz] tax on certain goods (as alcohol or tobacco). 2. *v.* [ɪk'saɪz] to cut out. **ex•ci•sion** [ɪk'sɪʒn] *n.* cutting out.

ex•cite [ɪk'saɪt] *v.* to arouse (s.o./sth); to make (s.o.) very emotional; **he was excited at/by the thought of going on vacation.** **ex•cit•a•bil•i•ty** [ɪksaɪtə'bɪlɪti] *n.* ease with which you are made very excited. **ex•cit•a•ble** [ɪk'saɪtəbl] *adj.* easily excited. **ex•cite•ment,** *n.* state of being excited. **ex•cit•ing,** *adj.* which makes s.o. excited.

ex•claim [ɪk'skleɪm] *v.* to say (sth) loudly and suddenly. **ex•cla•ma•tion** [eksklə'meɪʃn] *n.* shouting out; **exclamation mark** = written sign (!) to show exclamation.

ex•clude [ɪk'skluːd] *v.* to shut out (s.o./sth from somewhere). **ex•clud•ing,** *prep.* without; other than; not including. **ex•clu•sion** [ɪk'skluːʒn] *n.* act of shutting out. **ex•clu•sive.** 1. *adj.* (a) very select; not open to everyone. (b) **e. right** = right to do sth which no one else is allowed to do. 2. *adv.* not including. **ex•clu•sive•ly,** *adv.* solely/only.

ex•com•mu•ni•cate [ekskə'mjuːnɪkeɪt] *v.* to expel from membership in a church; refuse communion to (a member of a church). **ex•com•mu•ni•ca•tion** [ekskəmjuːnɪ-'keɪʃn] *n.* being excommunicated.

ex•cre•ment ['ekskrəmənt] *n.* solid waste matter produced by the body.

ex•cres•cence [ɪk'skresns] *n.* ugly growth/lump.

ex•crete [ɪk'skriːt] *v.* to produce (waste matter). **ex•cre•ta,** *n. pl.* (*formal*) waste matter produced by the body.

ex•cru•ci•at•ing [ɪk'skruːʃieɪtɪŋ] *adj.* very painful.

ex•cul•pate ['ekskʌlpeɪt] *v.* (*formal*) to remove blame from (s.o.).

ex•cur•sion [ɪk'skɜːʃn] *n.* short pleasure trip; **e. ticket** = special round-trip ticket at a reduced rate.

ex•cuse 1. *n.* [ɪk'skjuːs] reason; apology. 2. *v.* [ɪk'skjuːz] to pardon (s.o.); to allow (s.o.) not to do sth; **e. me** = I am sorry. **ex•cus•a•ble,** *adj.* which can be pardoned. **ex•cus•a•bly,** *adv.* in an excusable way.

ex•e•crate ['eksɪkreɪt] *v.* (*formal*) to curse/to hate (s.o.). **ex•e•cra•ble,** *adj.* extremely bad. **ex•e•cra•bly,** *adv.* extremely badly.

ex•e•cute ['eksɪkjuːt] *v.* to carry out (an official order), esp. to kill s.o. who has been condemned to death. **ex•ec•u•tant** [eg-'zekjutənt] *n.* performer (of a piece of music). **ex•e•cu•tion** [eksɪ'kjuːʃn] *n.* carrying out (of plan); legal killing of person sentenced to death. **ex•e•cu•tion•er** [eksɪ'kjuːʃənə] *n.* official who executes people. **ex•ec•u•tive** [ɪg'zekjutɪv] 1. *adj.* responsible for carrying out plans, laws, official policies, etc.; which puts things into practice; **e. committee** = committee which runs the business, etc. 2. *n.* (a) person in business who makes decisions/plans, etc. (b) **Chief E.** = person having executive power in a government; **the Chief E. in the United States is the president.** **ex•ec•u•tor** [ɪg'zekjutə] *n.* person who sees that a dead person's will is carried out. **ex•ec•u•trix** [ɪg'zekjutrɪks] *n.* woman who sees that a dead person's will is carried out.

ex•e•ge•sis [eksɪ'dʒiːsɪs] *n.* commentary (on the Bible).

ex•em•pla•ry [ɪg'zemplərɪ] *adj.* which serves as an example. **ex•em•plar,** *n.* perfect example. **ex•em•pli•fy,** *v.* to show as an example.

ex•empt [ɪg'zempt] 1. *adj.* not forced to obey (law, etc.). 2. *v.* to free (s.o.) **from** having to obey a rule or law/**from** doing sth. **ex•emp•tion** [ɪg'zempʃn] *n.* (**from**) ruling that s.o. does not have to do sth.

ex•er•cise ['eksəsaɪz] 1. *n.* use of physical or

æ back, ɑː farm, ɒ top, aɪ pipe, aʊ how, aɪə fire, aʊə flower, ɔː bought, ɔɪ toy, e fed, eəhair, eɪ take, ə afraid, əʊ boat, əʊə lower, vː word, iː heap, ɪ hit, ɪə hear, uː school, ʊ book, ʌ but, b back, d dog, ð then, dʒ just, f fog, g go, h hand, j yes, k catch, l last, m mix, n nut, ŋ sing, p penny, r round, s some, ʃ short, t too, tʃ chop, θ thing, v voice, w was, z zoo, ʒ treasure

mental powers; **e. book** = book for writing out work at school. 2. *v.* (a) to make (an animal) take exercise. (b) to use (power); **he exercised his right of veto.**

ex•ert [ɪg'zɜːt] *v.* to use (force/pressure, etc.). **ex•er•tion** [ɪg'zɜːʃn] *n.* effort.

ex gra•ti•a [eks'greɪʃə] *adj.* (payment) made as a present, with no obligation implied.

ex•hale [eks'heɪl] *v.* (*formal*) to breathe out.

ex•haust [ɪg'zɔːst] 1. *n.* escape (of steam/gas); **e. (pipe)** = pipe in a car which carries away fumes from the engine. 2. *v.* to wear out; to finish. **ex•haust•ed,** *adj.* (a) tired out. (b) completely used up. **ex•haus•tion** [ɪg-'zɔːstʃn] *n.* state of being very tired. **ex•haus•tive,** *adj.* very thorough. **ex•haus•tive•ly,** *adv.* thoroughly.

ex•hib•it [ɪg'zɪbɪt] 1. *n.* object displayed (in court/at an exhibition). 2. *v.* to display. **ex•hi•bi•tion** [eksɪ'bɪʃn] *n.* display (of works of art, flowers, etc.). **ex•hi•bi•tion•ist,** *n.* person who acts in a strange way so that people will look at him. **ex•hib•i•tor,** *n.* person who displays sth at an exhibition.

ex•hil•a•rate [ɪg'zɪləreɪt] *v.* to make extremely happy. **ex•hil•ar•at•ing,** *adj.* which makes you full of energy. **ex•hil•a•ra•tion** [ɪgzɪlə'reɪʃn] *n.* extreme happiness.

ex•hort [ɪg'zɔːt] *v.* (*formal*) to urge/to encourage (s.o. to do sth). **ex•hor•ta•tion** [ɪgzɔː-'teɪʃn] *n.* encouragement.

ex•hume [ɪg'zjuːm] *v.* to dig up (a dead person who has been buried). **ex•hu•ma•tion** [eksju'meɪʃn] *n.* act of digging up a dead body which has been buried.

ex•i•gent ['egzɪdʒənt] *adj.* (*formal*) very urgent. **ex•i•gen•cy** [eg'zɪdʒənsɪ] *n.* (*formal*) urgent need.

ex•ig•u•ous [eg'zɪgjʊəs] *adj.* very small.

ex•ile ['egzaɪl] 1. *n.* (a) banishment (from one's native country); **he went into e.** (b) person who is banished. 2. *v.* to send (s.o.) away from his native country as a punishment.

ex•ist [ɪg'zɪst] *v.* to live/to be. **ex•ist•ence,** *n.* life/being. **ex•ist•ent, existing,** *adj.* actual/which is present at this moment.

ex•it ['egzɪt, 'eksɪt] 1. *n.* way out; going out; **he made his e. by the window** = he went out by the window; **emergency e.** = door used in emergency; **fire e.** = door used in case of fire. 2. *v.* (*in a play*) goes out; **e. Mr. Smith.**

ex lib•ris [eks'liːbrɪs] *n.* printed label stuck in a book to show who it belongs to.

ex•o•crine ['eksəʊkriːn] *adj.* (gland) with ducts.

ex•o•dus ['eksədəs] *n.* departure/leaving (usu. of a crowd).

ex of•fi•ci•o [eksɒ'fɪʃɪəʊ] *adv. & adj.* because of your position.

ex•on•er•ate [ɪg'zɒnəreɪt] *v.* to state that no blame should be attached to (s.o.). **ex•on•er•a•tion** [ɪgzɒnə'reɪʃn] *n.* statement that no blame is attached to s.o.

ex•or•bi•tant [ɪg'zɔːbɪtənt] *adj.* very high (price).

ex•or•cise, exorcize ['egzɔːsaɪz] *v.* to drive (a devil/a ghost) from a place. **ex•or•cism** ['egzɔːsɪzəm] *n.* driving away a devil/a ghost. **ex•or•cist,** *n.* person who exorcises.

ex•ot•ic [ɪg'zɒtɪk] *adj.* unusual; referring to a tropical place; from a foreign place. **ex•ot•i•cal•ly,** *adv.* in an exotic way.

ex•pand [ɪk'spænd] *v.* to increase in size/to become larger.

ex•panse [ɪk'spæns] *n.* wide extent. **ex•pan•sion** [ɪk'spænʃn] *n.* increase in size. **ex•pan•sive,** *adj.* (person) who talks freely. **ex•pan•sive•ness,** *n.* being expansive.

ex•pa•ti•ate [ɪk'speɪʃɪeɪt] *v.* (*formal*) to talk at great length **on** sth.

ex•pa•tri•ate 1. *n.* [ɪk'spætrɪət] person who is not living in his native country. 2. *v.* [ɪk-'spætrɪeɪt] to send (s.o.) away from his native country.

ex•pect [ɪk'spekt] *v.* to think/to hope/to assume sth is going to happen; **I e. she is tired; he expects me to do all the housework; is it going to rain?—I e. so; we're expecting visitors =** we are waiting for visitors to arrive; **she's expecting =** she is pregnant. **ex•pect•an•cy,** *n.* hope; **life e. =** number of years a person will probably live. **ex•pect•ant,** *adj.* expecting; **e. mother =** pregnant woman. **ex•pect•ant•ly,** *adv.* hopefully. **ex•pec•ta•tion** [ekspek'teɪʃn] *n.* hope.

ex•pec•to•rant [ɪk'spektərənt] *n.* cough medicine which makes you cough up phlegm. **ex•pec•to•rate,** *v.* (*formal*) to cough up phlegm.

ex•pe•di•en•cy [ɪk'spiːdɪənsɪ] *n.* most simple/straightforward way of doing sth. **ex•pe•di•ent.** 1. *n.* simple way of doing sth. 2. *adj.* simple/straightforward.

ex•pe•dite ['ekspɪdaɪt] *v.* to make sth happen faster. **ex•pe•di•tion** [ekspɪ'dɪʃn] *n.* (a) rapidity. (b) journey of exploration; **to go on an e. to the North Pole. ex•pe•di•tion•ar•y,** *adj.* (army) which is on a journey. **ex•pe•di•tious,** *adj.* prompt/rapid. **ex•pe•di•tious•ly,** *adv.* rapidly.

ex•pel [ɪk'spel] *v.* (**expelled**) to throw (s.o.) out; to send (s.o.) away.

ex•pend•a•ble [ɪk'spendəbl] *adj.* which is not

worth keeping after it has been used; **he is e.** = he can be fired/left behind/killed.

ex•pend•i•ture [ɪk'spendɪtʃə] *n.* amount spent.

ex•pense [ɪk'spens] *n.* amount of money spent; **e. account** = money which a businessman is allowed to spend on entertainment and personal expenses which are paid for by his firm; **they had a good laugh at his e.** = they laughed at him. **ex•pen•sive**, *adj.* which costs a lot of money.

ex•pe•ri•ence [ɪk'spɪərɪəns] 1. *n.* thing lived through; wisdom gained by living through various situations; **I have no e. of traveling in the desert.** 2. *v.* to live through (sth). **ex•pe•ri•enced**, *adj.* wise from plenty of practice.

ex•per•i•ment [ɪk'sperɪmənt] 1. *n.* scientific test. 2. *v.* to carry out a scientific test. **ex•per•i•men•tal** [ɪksperɪ'mentl] *adj.* used as part of a test. **ex•per•i•men•tal•ly**, *adv.* as an experiment. **ex•per•i•men•ta•tion**, *n.* carrying out of experiments.

ex•pert ['ekspɜːt] 1. *adj.* referring to s.o. who knows a great deal about a subject; **e. system** = computer program which has been devised for a particular purpose. 2. *n.* person who knows a great deal about a subject. **ex•per•tise** [ekspə'tiːz] *n.* specialist knowledge.

ex•pi•ate ['ekspɪeɪt] *v.* (*formal*) to make amends for (a crime). **ex•pi•a•tion** [ekspɪ-'eɪʃn] *n.* making amends.

ex•pire [ɪk'spaɪə] *v.* (a) to come to an end. (b) (*formal*) to die. **ex•pi•ra•tion, expiry,** *n.* coming to an end; **the e. date of a ticket.**

ex•plain [ɪk'spleɪn] *v.* to give reasons for (sth); to make (sth) clear. **ex•pla•na•tion** [eksplə-'neɪʃn] *n.* reason for sth. **ex•plan•a•to•ry** [ɪk'splænətərɪ] *adj.* which gives reasons; which makes clear.

ex•ple•tive [ɪk'spliːtɪv] *n.* swear word.

ex•pli•ca•ble [ɪk'splɪkəbl] *adj.* which can be explained.

ex•plic•it [ek'splɪsɪt] *adj.* straightforward/clear. **ex•plic•it•ly,** *adv.* clearly.

ex•plode [ɪk'spləʊd] *v.* (a) (*of bombs, etc.*) to go off/to blow up. (b) to make (bombs) go off; to discredit (a theory).

ex•ploit 1. *n.* ['eksplɔɪt] great/daring achievement. 2. *v.* [ɪk'splɔɪt] to take commercial advantage of (sth); **to e. mineral resources.** **ex•ploi•ta•tion** [eksplɔɪ'teɪʃn] *n.* taking advantage.

ex•plore [ɪk'splɔː] *v.* to investigate/to travel and discover (esp. unknown lands). **ex•plo•ra•tion** [eksplə'reɪʃn] *n.* investigation (of unknown lands). **ex•plor•a•to•ry** [ɪk'splɒrətərɪ] *adj.* tentative/preliminary. **ex•plor•er,** *n.* person who explores unknown lands.

ex•plo•sion [ɪk'spləʊʒn] *n.* blowing up (of bombs/oil tanks, etc.); **population e.** = rapid increase in population. **ex•plo•sive** [ɪk-'spləʊsɪv] 1. *adj.* liable to blow up. 2. *n.* material (like gunpowder) which can blow up.

ex•po•nent [ɪk'spəʊnənt] *n.* person who practices a certain belief/a certain art. **ex•po•nen•tial** [ekspə'nenʃəl] *adj.* growing in proportion to the original number (i.e. growing faster as numbers increase).

ex•port 1. *n.* ['ekspɔːt] goods sent to a foreign country for sale. 2. *v.* [ɪk'spɔːt] to send (goods) to a foreign country for sale. **ex•port•er,** *n.* person or company which sells goods to foreign countries.

ex•pose [ɪk'spəʊz] *v.* (a) to show. (b) to let light go onto photographic film or plate. (c) to reveal (a scandal). **exposed,** *adj.* (a) open; **in a very e. position** = not sheltered from the wind. (b) **e. film** = where the pictures have been taken but not developed. **ex•po•si•tion** [ekspə'zɪʃn] *n.* detailed explanation. **ex•po•sure** [ɪk'spəʊʒə] *n.* (a) state of not being sheltered from cold/danger, etc. (b) time and amount of light needed for a picture to be taken on film; **e. meter** = device for calculating the exposure for a photograph. (c) revealing (of corruption, etc.). (d) direction in which (a house) faces.

ex•pos•é [ɪk'spəʊzeɪ] *n.* newspaper/magazine report revealing corruption/wrongdoing, etc.

ex•pos•tu•late [ɪk'spɒstjuleɪt] *v.* (*formal*) to protest/to reason (**with** s.o.). **ex•pos•tu•la•tion** ['ɪkspɒstjuˈleɪʃn] *n.* protest.

ex•pound [ɪk'spaʊnd] *v.* to explain in detail.

ex•press [ɪk'spres] 1. *adj.* done on purpose; **I did it with the e. intention of embarrassing him.** 2. *adj. & n.* rapid (train/postal service). 3. *v.* (a) to put into words; **I expressed myself badly** = I did not make clear what I wanted to say. (b) to put into symbols; **to e. a fraction in decimals.** **ex•pres•sion** [ɪk'spreʃn] *n.* (a) way of showing feeling on the face. (b) phrase. **ex•pres•sive,** *adj.* showing feeling. **ex•press•ly,** *adv.* on purpose.

æ **back,** ɑː **farm,** ɒ **top,** aɪ **pipe,** aʊ **how,** aɪə **fire,** aʊə **flower,** ɔː **bought,** ɔɪ **toy,** e **fed,** eə **hair,** eɪ **take,** ə **afraid,** əʊ **boat,** əʊə **lower,** ɜː **word,** iː **heap,** ɪ **hit,** ɪə **hear,** uː **school,** ʊ **book,** ʌ **but,** b **back,** d **dog,** ð **then,** dʒ **just,** f **fog,** g **go,** h **hand,** j **yes,** k **catch,** l **last,** m **mix,** n **nut,** ŋ **sing,** p **penny,** r **round,** s **some,** ʃ **short,** t **too,** tʃ **chop,** θ **thing,** v **voice,** w **was,** z **zoo,** ʒ **treasure**

ex•press•way, *n.* fast road with few points of access or exit.

ex•pro•pri•ate [ɪk'sprəuprɪeɪt] *v.* (*of the state/a local authority*) to take away (property) from a private owner. **ex•pro•pri•a•tion** [ɪksprəuprɪ'eɪʃn] *n.* taking of property away from a private owner.

ex•pul•sion [ɪk'spʌlʃn] *n.* act of being thrown out/sent away.

ex•punge [ek'spʌndʒ] *v.* (*formal*) to wipe out/to cross out.

ex•pur•gate ['ekspəgeɪt] *v.* to remove rude/offensive expressions from (a book). **ex•pur•ga•tion** [ekspə'geɪʃn] *n.* act of expurgating.

ex•quis•ite [ɪk'skwɪzɪt] *adj.* very finely made/very refined. **ex•quis•ite•ly,** *adv.* finely.

ex•ser•vice•man [eks'sɜːvɪsmən] *n.* (*pl.* -men) man who used to be a member of the armed forces.

ex•tant [ɪk'stænt] *adj.* still in existence.

ex•tem•po•re [ɪk'stempəri] *adv. & adj.* without notes; **he spoke for ten minutes e.; an e. speech. ex•tem•po•rize,** *v.* to speak without preparation/without notes.

ex•tend [ɪk'stend] *v.* (a) to stretch out; **extended family** = family group which includes various relatives. (b) to make longer. **ex•tend•a•ble, extensible,** *adj.* which can be extended. **ex•ten•sion,** *n.* (a) act of extending; thing added on. (b) subsidiary telephone in a home/office. **ex•ten•sive,** *adj.* very widespread; very vast. **ex•ten•sive•ly,** *adv.* very greatly/widely. **ex•ten•sor,** *n.* muscle which makes a joint become straight.

ex•tent [ɪk'stent] *n.* degree; size; range; area.

ex•ten•u•at•ing [ɪk'stenjueɪtɪŋ] *adj.* which lessens or explains a crime; **e. circumstances. ex•ten•u•a•tion** [ɪkstenju'eɪʃn] *n.* lessening (of the seriousness of a crime).

ex•te•ri•or [ɪk'stɪərɪə] 1. *adj.* outside. 2. *n.* outside; **the e. of a house.**

ex•ter•mi•nate [ɪk'stɜːmɪneɪt] *v.* to kill (large number of living things). **ex•ter•mi•na•tion** [ɪkstɜːmɪ'neɪʃn] *n.* act of killing (large numbers).

ex•ter•nal [ɪk'stɜːnl] *adj.* outside; **medicine for e. use only** = which must not be drunk or eaten. **ex•ter•nal•ly,** *adv.* outside.

ex•tinct [ɪk'stɪŋkt] *adj.* (volcano) which no longer erupts; (species) which has died out. **ex•tinc•tion** [ɪk'stɪŋkʃn] *n.* putting out (of a fire); dying out (of a species).

ex•tin•guish [ɪk'stɪŋgwɪʃ] *v.* to put out (a fire). **ex•tin•guish•er,** *n.* **fire e.** = apparatus for putting out fires.

ex•tir•pate ['ekstɜːpeɪt] *v.* (*formal*) to destroy completely.

ex•tol [ɪk'stəul] *v.* (**extolled**) (*formal*) to praise very highly.

ex•tort [ɪk'stɔːt] *v.* to get (money) **from** s.o. by threats. **ex•tor•tion** [ɪk'stɔːʃn] *n.* getting money from s.o. by threats. **ex•tor•tion•ate,** *adj.* excessive (demands); very high (price).

ex•tra ['ekstrə] 1. *adj.* more than normal; additional. 2. *adv.* (a) more than usual; **e. strong string.** (b) in addition; **the service charge is e.** 3. *n.* (a) person (not a star) appearing in crowd scenes in a motion picture. (b) sth more than usual. 4. *extra- prefix meaning* outside; **extracurricular** = outside the curriculum; **extramarital** = outside marriage; **extrasensory** = (perception) by other means than the five senses; **extraterritorial** = outside the territory.

ex•tract 1. *n.* ['ekstrækt] thing reduced from sth larger; **meat e.** = substance concentrated from meat. 2. *v.* [ɪk'strækt] to pull (sth) out; to produce (sth). **ex•trac•tion** [ɪk'strækʃn] *n.* (a) pulling out (of a tooth); production (of coal, etc.). (b) origin; **he is of French e.** = his family originally was French.

ex•tra•dite ['ekstrədaɪt] *v.* to bring back (a criminal) to his own state or country for trial (by agreement with the state or country where he was arrested). **ex•tra•dit•a•ble,** *adj.* (crime) for which you can be extradited. **ex•tra•di•tion** [ekstrə'dɪʃn] *n.* return of a criminal to his own state or country.

ex•tra•ne•ous [ɪk'streɪnɪəs] *adj.* not directly connected with sth.

ex•traor•di•nar•y [ɪk'strɔːdnrɪ] *adj.* marvelous; quite different from everything else; strange/unusual. **ex•traor•di•nar•i•ly,** *adv.* in an extraordinary way.

ex•trap•o•late [ɪk'stræpəleɪt] *v.* to calculate (sth unknown) on the basis of available information. **ex•trap•o•la•tion** [ɪkstræpə'leɪʃn] *n.* calculating sth unknown on the basis of available information.

ex•trav•a•gance [ɪk'strævəgəns] *n.* excessive expense and luxury. **ex•trav•a•gant,** *adj.* (a) (person) who spends a lot of money. (b) expensive and luxurious. **ex•trav•a•gant•ly,** *adv.* in an extravagant way. **ex•trav•a•gan•za** [ɪkstrævə'gænzə] *n.* expensive and luxurious party/show/motion picture.

ex•treme [ɪk'striːm] 1. *adj.* very great; excessive; **at the e. end** = at the outermost end. 2. *n.* **to go to extremes** = to do everything in an excessive way. **ex•treme•ly,** *adv.* very; excessively. **ex•trem•ist,** *n.* person who has extreme views (usu. about politics).

ex•trem•i•ty [ɪkˈstremɪtɪ] *n.* end point; **the extremities** = the hands and feet.

ex•tri•cate [ˈekstrɪkeɪt] *v.* to get (s.o.) out of a difficult situation.

ex•tro•vert [ˈekstrəvɜːt] *n.* person who is very outgoing and active. **ex•tro•vert•ed** *adj.* referring to an extrovert.

ex•trude [ɪkˈstruːd] *v.* to squeeze out under pressure. **ex•tru•sion** [ɪkˈstruːʒn] *n.* squeezing (of metal) under pressure.

ex•u•ber•ance [ɪgˈzjuːbərəns] *n.* wild enthusiasm. **ex•u•ber•ant,** *adj.* wildly enthusiastic.

ex•ude [ɪgˈzjuːd] *v.* to send out/to give off (a smell/a feeling) in all directions; **he exudes self-confidence.**

ex•ult [ɪgˈzʌlt] *v.* to rejoice/to be glad; **he exulted over his victory** = he showed great pleasure at winning. **ex•ult•ant,** *adj.* full of triumph. **ex•ul•ta•tion,** *n.* great rejoicing.

eye [aɪ] 1. *n.* (a) part of the head, used for seeing; **keep your eyes open!** = watch out! **to set/clap eyes on sth** = to see sth (suddenly); **it catches the e.** = it is very noticeable; **to keep an e. on** = to guard; **they don't see e. to e.** = they do not agree. (b) *inf.* **private e.** = private detective. (c) small hole in a needle for passing the thread through; small loop for attaching a hook; bud on a potato through which sprouts grow. 2. *v.* to look at (s.o./sth) carefully. **eye•ball,** *n.* ball of the eye; *inf.* **I'm up to my eyeballs in work** = I have masses of work to do. **eye•bath,** *n.* small cup for bathing the eye. **eye•brow,** *n.* small arch of hair above the eye. **eye•ful,** *n. inf.* good look at sth. **eye•glass•es,** *n. pl.* pair of glass lenses in a frame, for correcting poor vision. **eye•lash,** *n.* one of the hairs growing round the rim of the eye. **eye•let,** *n.* small hole (as in a shoe, for passing the lace through). **eye•lid,** *n.* skin that covers and uncovers the eye. **eye•lin•er,** *n.* cosmetic substance for drawing a line around the eye. **eye-o•pen•er,** *n.* thing which surprises you. **eye•piece,** *n.* lens at the end of a telescope through which you look. **eye•shade,** *n.* shade worn on the forehead for keeping bright light out of the eyes. **eye•shad•ow,** *n.* cosmetic substance for coloring the eyelids. **eye•sight,** *n.* (*no pl.*) ability to see; **his e. is failing** = he can see less well. **eye•sore,** *n.* thing which is hideous/unpleasant to look at. **eye•strain,** *n.* (*no pl.*) tiredness of the eyes. **eye•tooth,** *n.* (*pl.* **-teeth**) canine. **eye•wash,** *n.* (*no pl.*) liquid for bathing the eyes; *inf.* **it's all e.** = it is nonsense. **eye•wit•ness,** *n.* person who has seen sth happen.

ey•rie [ˈɪərɪ] *n. see* **aerie.**

æ back, ɑː farm, ɒ top, aɪ pipe, aʊ how, aɪə fire, aʊə flower, ɔː bought, ɔɪ toy, e fed, eəhair, eɪ take, ə afraid, əʊ boat, əʊə lower, ɜː word, iː heap, ɪ hit, ɪə hear, uː school, ʊ book, ʌ but, b back, d dog, ð then, dʒ just, f fog, g go, h hand, j yes, k catch, l last, m mix, n nut, ŋ sing, p penny, r round, s some, ʃ short, t too, tʃ chop, θ thing, v voice, w was, z zoo, ʒ treasure

Ff

F *symbol for* fluorine.

fa•ble ['feɪbl] *n.* moral story usu. about animals, making them seem like human beings.

fab•ric ['fæbrɪk] *n.* (a) material. (b) basic structure (of society). **fab•ri•cate** ['fæbrɪkeɪt] *v.* to invent (an untrue story); to forge (a paper). **fab•ri•ca•tion** [fæbrɪ'keɪʃn] *n.* invention.

fab•u•lous ['fæbjʊləs] *adj.* (a) imaginary, as in a fable. (b) *inf.* marvelous/wonderful. **fab•u•lous•ly**, *adv. inf.* wonderfully.

fa•cade [fə'sɑːd] *n.* front of a large building; outward appearance which is intended to give a false impression.

face [feɪs] 1. *n.* (a) front part of the head; **f. to f.** = talking and looking at each other; **to make a f.** = to make a rude expression; **to lose f.** = to feel humiliated. (b) front of an object. 2. *v.* (a) to put a facing/an outward covering on (sth). (b) to turn your head toward; **the house faces east** = the house looks toward the east; **to f. up to** = to accept bravely. **face•cloth,** *n.* washcloth. **face•less,** *adj.* threateningly anonymous. **face•lift,** *n.* operation to remove wrinkles from your face. **face pack,** *n.* cream which is left on the face to improve the skin. **face val•ue,** *n.* value written on a banknote/stock/bond; **to take sth at f. v.** = to assume that the first/obvious meaning is the correct one. **fac•ing,** *n.* material covering the surface of a building/the edges of a garment.

fac•et ['fæsɪt] *n.* (a) one of the flat sides on a cut gem. (b) aspect (of a problem, etc.).

fa•ce•tious [fə'siːʃəs] *adj.* funny/joking (in an offensive way). **fa•ce•tious•ly,** *adv.* not seriously/in a joking way. **fa•ce•tious•ness,** *n.* being facetious.

fa•cial ['feɪʃl] 1. *adj.* referring to a face. 2. *n.* beauty treatment to make your face more beautiful.

fac•ile ['fæsaɪl] *adj.* done too easily. **fa•cil•i•ty** [fə'sɪlɪtɪ] *n.* (a) ease/absence of difficulty. (b) sth, as a building or equipment, which can be used for a specific purpose; **hospital facilities, sports facilities. fa•cil•i•tate,** *v.* to make (sth) easy.

fac•sim•i•le [fæk'sɪmɪlɪ] *n.* (a) perfect reproduction; perfect copy. (b) fax.

fact ['fækt] *n.* thing that is true; **in f./as a matter of f.** = really/actually.

fac•tion ['fækʃn] *n.* group of people linked together in opposition to a leader/a government. **fac•tion•al,** *adj.* referring to factions.

fac•tor ['fæktə] *n.* (a) one of the numbers which produce a given number when multiplied. (b) thing which is influential/important. (c) person who buys the debts of a company at a discount and then tries to reclaim the full amount from the debtor.

fac•to•ry ['fæktrɪ] *n.* building where things are made; **f. ship** = ship which freezes or cans fish which are caught by smaller fishing boats.

fac•to•tum [fæk'təʊtəm] *n.* person who does all types of work.

fac•tu•al ['fæktjʊəl] *adj.* containing facts. **fac•tu•al•ly,** *adv.* in a factual way.

fac•ul•ty ['fækəltɪ] *n.* (a) special ability. (b) teaching staff (of a school/university/college, etc.).

fad [fæd] *n.* strange temporary mania. **fad•dist,** *n.* person who follows a fad. **fad••dy,** *adj. inf.* (person) who has odd likes and dislikes about food.

fade [feɪd] *v.* to lose color, brightness or strength; to make (sth) lose color.

fag [fæg] 1. *n.* (a) *Sl.* cigarette. (b) *Sl.* male homosexual. 2. *v.* to tire by working hard; exhaust; *Sl.* **fagged out** = tired out.

fag•ot ['fægət] *n.* bundle of sticks for lighting a fire.

Fahr•en•heit ['færənheɪt] *adj.* (scale for) measuring heat where the boiling point of water is 212° and the freezing point 32°.

fa•ience [faɪ'ɑːns] *n.* thick glazed earthenware.

fail [feɪl] 1. *v.* (a) to be unsuccessful in doing sth. (b) to grow weaker. (c) not to pass (a candidate) in an examination. 2. *n.* **without f.** = certainly. **fail•ing.** 1. *n.* weakness/bad point. 2. *prep.* **f. that** = if that does not work. **fail-safe,** *adj.* (machine) made so that if anything goes wrong it will stop working and therefore not be dangerous. **fail•ure** ['feɪljə] *n.* (a) breakdown/stoppage; **heart f.** = dangerous condition when the heart has stopped beating; **power f.** = breakdown in the supply of electricity. (b) thing which did not work out satisfactorily.

faint [feɪnt] 1. *adj.* (a) not clear; difficult to see or hear; weak. 2. *v.* to lose consciousness for a short time. **faint•heart•ed,** *adj.* timid. **faint•ly,** *adv.* weakly. **faint•ness,** *n.* being faint.

fair ['feə] 1. *n.* (a) group of sideshows/amusements/food booths, etc., set up in one place for a short time. (b) market for selling and advertising goods. 2. *adj.* (-er, -est) (a) light-colored (skin, hair). (b) honest/correct. (c) not bad. (d) (*of weather*) dry and warm. **fair•ground,** *n.* place in the open air where a fair is held. **fair•ly,** *adv.* (a) quite/not completely. (b) justly/correctly. **fair•ness,** *n.* (a) light coloring. (b) honesty/correctness. **fair•way,** *n.* (a) part of a golf course where the grass is kept cut. (b) navigable channel.

fair•y ['feərɪ] *n.* (a) small supernatural creature who is able to work magic; **f. story** = fairytale. (b) *Sl.* male homosexual. **fair•y•land,** *n.* land where fairies are supposed to live. **fair•y•tale,** *n.* story about fairies/princesses/giants, etc.

faith [feɪθ] *n.* belief/trust; **f. healer** = person who heals by prayer; **in good f.** = honorably, even though wrongly. **faith•ful,** *adj.* (a) trusting/loyal. (b) completely correct. **faith•ful•ness,** *n.* being faithful. **faith•ful•ly,** *adv.* loyally. **faith•less,** *adj.* disloyal.

fake [feɪk] 1. *n.* imitation/forgery; not the real thing. 2. *v.* to make an imitation of (sth).

fa•kir ['feɪkɪə] *n.* Indian holy man.

fal•con ['fɔːlkən] *n.* small bird of prey, sometimes trained to catch other birds in sport. **fal•con•ry,** *n.* sport of hunting with falcons.

fall [fɔːl] 1. *n.* (a) drop/collapse. (b) the autumn. (c) **falls** = waterfall. (d) **f. from power** = loss of a powerful position. 2. *v.* (**fell; has fallen**) to drop down. **fall back,** *v.* to retreat/to go back. **fall back on,** *v.* to use (sth) which was kept as a reserve. **fall down,** *v.* to drop to the ground. **fall•en,** *adj.* dropped. **fall for,** *v.* (a) to fall in love with (s.o.). (b) to be tricked by (sth). **fall in,** *v.* (*in the military*) to stand in line. **fall in with,** *v.* to join with (s.o.); to agree with (an idea). **fall off,** *v.* to become less. **fall out,** *v.* (a) to drop. (b) to have an argument. **fall•out,** *n.* radioactive dust from a nuclear explosion. **fall through,** *v.* to fail. **fall to,** *v.* to start to do sth (esp. eat or work).

fal•la•cy ['fæləsɪ] *n.* false argument; error. **fal•la•cious** [fə'leɪʃəs] *adj.* wrong.

fal•li•bil•i•ty [fælɪ'bɪlɪtɪ] *n.* being fallible. **fal•li•ble** ['fælɪbl] *adj.* (person) who can make a mistake.

Fal•lo•pi•an [fə'ləupɪən] *adj.* **F. tube** = tube in a woman from an ovary to the womb.

fal•low ['fæləu] *adj.* (land) which is purposely not used for crops for a time so that it can regain its goodness. **fallow deer,** *n.* small deer with white spots.

false [fɔːls] *adj.* (-er, -est) (a) not true. (b) not real; **f. teeth** = artificial teeth; **f. alarm** = signal for an emergency when there isn't one. **false•hood,** *n.* lie. **false•ly,** *adv.* in a false way. **false mem•o•ry syn•drome,** *n.* supposed syndrome in which a person in psychotherapy is mistakenly convinced that he/she has recovered a repressed memory of childhood trauma. **false•ness,** *n.* being false. **fal•si•fi•ca•tion,** *n.* act of falsifying. **fal•si•fy,** *v.* to change (sth) thus making it invalid.

fal•set•to [fɒl'setəu] *n.* unnaturally high voice (used by a man singing).

fal•ter ['fɔːltə] *v.* to move or speak hesitantly.

fame [feɪm] *n.* being well known. **famed,** *adj.* well known.

fa•mil•iar [fə'mɪljə] *adj.* (a) heard or seen before; well known; **I am f. with that type of machine** = I know that type of machine. (b) very informal/(too) friendly. **fa•mil•iar•i•ty** [fəmɪlɪ'ærɪtɪ] *n.* (a) (with) good knowledge of s.o./sth. (b) excessively informal way of speaking to s.o. **fa•mil•iar•i•za•tion** [fəmɪljərar-'zeɪʃn] *n.* act of familiarizing. **fa•mil•iar•ize** [fə'mɪljəraɪz] *v.* **to f. yourself with sth** = to become informed about sth. **fa•mil•iar•ly,** *adv.* in a familiar way.

fam•i•ly ['fæmɪlɪ] *n.* (a) group of people who are closely related, esp. mother, father and their children; **f. planning** = birth control; **f. tree** = table of the family going back over many generations. (b) group of animals/plants, etc., which are closely related.

fam•ine ['fæmɪn] *n.* very serious lack/shortage of food. **fam•ished,** *adj. inf.* very hungry.

fa•mous ['feɪməs] *adj.* well known.

fan [fæn] 1. *n.* (a) object/machine for moving air, to make things cooler or warmer; **f. belt** = loop of rubber which turns a fan to cool the engine of a car. (b) passionate admirer. 2. *v.* (**fanned**) to make the air move. **fan club,** *n.* organized group of admirers (of an actor, singer, athlete, etc.). **fan mail,** *n.* admiring

æ back, ɑ: farm, ɒ: top, aɪ pipe, aʊ how, aɪə fire, aʊə flower, ɔ: bought, ɔɪ toy, e fed, eəhair, eɪ take, ə afraid, əʊ boat, əʊə lower, v: word, i: heap, ɪ hit, ɪə hear, u: school, ʊ book, ʌ but, b back, d dog, ð then, dʒ just, f fog, g go, h hand, j yes, k catch, l last, m mix, n nut, ŋ sing, p penny, r round, s some, ʃ short, t too, tʃ chop, θ thing, v voice, w was, z zoo, ʒ treasure

letters received by an actor, etc. **fan out,** *v.* to spread out (like a fan).

fa•nat•ic [fə'nætɪk] *adj. & n.* (person) who is madly enthusiastic about sth, esp. religion. **fa•nat•i•cal,** *adj.* too enthusiastic. **fa•nat•i•cal•ly,** *adv.* in a fanatical way. **fa•nat•i•cism,** *n.* being fanatical.

fan•ci•er ['fænsɪə] *n.* person who has an interest (in a certain type of plant or animal); **pigeon f.** = person who breeds and races pigeons.

fan•cy ['fænsɪ] 1. *n.* (a) imagination. (b) desire; **it took his f.** = made him want it. 2. *adj.* pretty/decorated. 3. *v.* (a) to imagine/to believe. (b) to like/to want to have; *inf.* **I think she fancies you** = she is attracted to you. **fancy dress,** *n.* unusual costume (worn to a party). **fan•ci•ful,** *adj.* imaginative.

fan•fare ['fænfeə] *n.* piece of music played on trumpets to signal the entrance of an important person/the start of a show.

fang [fæŋ] *n.* animal's long tooth.

fan•light ['fænlaɪt] *n.* small window over a door or a large window.

fan•ta•sy ['fæntəsɪ] *n.* invented story/not a true story. **fan•ta•size,** *v.* to imagine/to dream. **fan•tas•tic** [fæn'tæstɪk] *adj.* (a) strange/like a dream. (b) *inf.* wonderful/amazing. **fan•tas•ti•cal•ly,** *adv.* in a fantastic way.

far [fɑː] **(farther/further; farthest/furthest)** 1. *adv.* (a) a long way away/not near; **so f.** = up to now. (b) much; **by f. the best.** 2. *adj.* distant/not near. **far•a•way,** *adj.* distant/remote. **far-fetched,** *adj.* difficult to believe. **far-reach•ing,** *adj.* which has important results. **far-sight•ed,** *adj.* looking to the future.

far•ad ['færæd] *n.* unit of electrical capacity.

farce [fɑːs] *n.* comedy based on slapstick and ridiculous situations; absurd situation. **far•ci•cal,** *adj.* absurd.

fare [feə] 1. *n.* (a) price to be paid for a journey; **roundtrip f.** = fare from one place to another and back again. (b) passenger in a bus/taxi. (c) food. 2. *v.* to get on; to do (well/badly).

fare•well [feə'wel] *inter. & n.* (*formal*) goodbye.

far•i•na•ceous [færɪ'neɪʃəs] *adj.* made of flour.

farm [fɑːm] 1. *n.* land used for growing crops and keeping animals. 2. *v.* to look after a farm; to grow crops/to keep animals for sale. **farm•er,** *n.* person who looks after a farm. **farm•house,** *n.* house where the farmer and his family live. **farm•ing,** *n.* job of looking after a farm/growing crops/keeping animals for sale. **farm out,** *v.* to hand over

(work/child, etc.) to another person. **farm•stead,** *n.* farm and all its buildings. **farm•yard,** *n.* space outside a farmhouse, usu. surrounded by farm buildings or a wall.

far•ra•go [fə'rɑːgəʊ] *n.* tangled, confused mass.

far•ri•er ['fɑrɪə] *n.* blacksmith who shoes horses.

far•row ['færəʊ] *v.* to have a litter of piglets.

fart [fɑːt] 1. *n.* (*vulgar*) noise made when passing gas from the intestines through the anus. 2. *v.* (*vulgar*) to make a fart.

far•ther ['fɑːðə] *adj. & adv.* to a greater distance; more distant. **far•thest** ['fɑːðəst] *adj. & adv.* to the greatest distance; most distant.

fas•ci•cle ['fæsɪkl] *n.* section of a large book, which is published in sections.

fas•ci•nate ['fæsɪneɪt] *v.* to attract/to charm. **fas•ci•nat•ing,** *adj.* attractive/very interesting. **fas•ci•na•tion** [fæsɪ'neɪʃn] *n.* attraction/charm. **fas•ci•na•tor,** *n.* person who fascinates.

fas•cism ['fæʃɪzəm] *n.* extreme right-wing political movement. **fas•cist,** *adj. & n.* (person) supporting fascism.

fash•ion ['fæʃn] 1. *n.* (a) manner/way; **after/in a f.** = not very well. (b) most admired style at a particular moment. 2. *v.* to make. **fash•ion•a•ble,** *adj.* in fashion. **fash•ion•a•bly,** *adv.* (dressed) in a fashionable way.

fast [fɑːst] 1. *adj. & adv.* (-er, -est) (a) quick; **my watch is five minutes f.** = my watch shows a time five minutes later than it really is; **f. film** = film which requires very short exposure times; **f. food** = food which is prepared and served quickly. (b) tightly fixed; **f. colors** = colors in fabric which do not run when washed; **to make sth f.** = to attach sth tightly. (c) **f. asleep** = soundly sleeping. 2. *n.* period when you stop eating. 3. *v.* to stop eating (for a time).

fast•en ['fɑːsn] *v.* to fix tightly. **fast•en•er,** *n.* device which fastens/attaches. **fast•en•ing,** *n.* thing which fastens.

fas•tid•i•ous [fæ'stɪdrəs] *adj.* hard to please; easily shocked. **fas•tid•i•ous•ly,** *adv.* in a fastidious way. **fas•tid•i•ous•ness,** *n.* being fastidious.

fast•ness ['fɑːsnəs] *n.* (*pl.* -es) secure place; stronghold (as in the mountains).

fat [fæt] 1. *adj.* (**fatter, fattest**) (a) big and round; overweight; *inf.* **a f. lot of good** = very little good. (b) thick. (c) full of grease. 2. *n.* (a) grease/white layer on an animal's body under the skin. (b) **cooking f.** = refined oil (either vegetable or animal) used in frying, etc. **fat•ness,** *n.* being fat.

fate [feɪt] n. destiny; thing that is certain to happen as we think it has been decided by a power beyond human control. **fa•tal**, adj. deadly/causing death. **fa•tal•ism**, n. accepting fate. **fa•tal•ist**, n. person who accepts what happens, knowing that it is usually bad and cannot be avoided. **fa•tal•is•tic** [feɪtə-'lɪstɪk] adj. like a fatalist. **fa•tal•i•ties** [fə-'tælɪtɪz] n. pl. deaths. **fa•tal•ly**, adv. causing death. **fat•ed**, adj. destined/condemned by fate. **fate•ful**, adj. (decision, etc.) important for its serious consequences in the future.

fa•ther ['fɑːðə] 1. n. (a) male parent; **f. figure** = older man who is consulted for advice. (b) originator. (c) title given to a priest. 2. v. to be the father of. **fa•ther-in-law**, n. (pl. fathers-in-law) father of your wife or husband. **fa•ther•land**, native country. **fa•ther•less**, adj. with no father. **fa•ther•ly**, adj. like a father.

fath•om ['fæðəm] 1. n. measure of depth of water (6 feet or 1.8 meters). 2. v. to find the meaning or truth of.

fa•tigue [fə'tiːg] 1. n. (a) tiredness; **metal f.** = wearing out of metal used in a construction, causing weak points. (b) (also **fatigue duty**) cleaning duty in the military; **fatigues** = uniform worn when doing this. 2. v. to tire (s.o.) out.

fat•ten ['fætn] v. to make fat. **fat•ten•ing**, adj. (foods) which make you fat. **fat•ty**, adj. (food/tissue) which has a lot of fat in it.

fat•u•ous ['fætjuəs] adj. stupid/silly. **fat•u•ous•ly**, adv. in a fatuous way. **fat•u•ous•ness, fatuity** [fə'tjuɪtɪ] n. being fatuous.

fau•cet ['fɔːsɪt] n. apparatus with a twisting knob and a valve which, when you turn it, allows liquid to come out of a pipe/container; tap.

fault [fɔːlt] 1. n. (a) mistake; **she's at f.** = has made a mistake. (b) imperfection/thing which is not as it should be. (c) (in geology) break in a rock layer where a section of rock slips down and another section rises. (d) (in tennis) error in serving. 2. v. to criticize/to find (sth) wrong. **fault•i•ness**, n. being faulty. **fault•less**, adj. perfect. **fault•less•ly**, adv. perfectly. **fault•y**, adj. (-ier, -iest) with mistakes or imperfections.

faun [fɔːn] n. mythical creature, like a man with goat's legs and horns.

fau•na ['fɔːnə] n. wild animals (of an area).

faux pas [fəu'pɑː] n. piece of embarrassing behavior.

fa•vor, Brit. **fa•vour** ['feɪvə] 1. n. (a) friendly act/kindness. (b) support for one group/one person at the expense of others; **out of f.** = disliked; **the score is 3-2 in his f.** = he is leading 3-2. (c) preference/liking; **to be in f. of** = to prefer. (d) ribbon/badge (worn by a supporter). 2. v. (a) to like/to prefer. (b) to make things easy for (s.o.). **fa•vor•a•ble** ['feɪvrəbl] adj. helpful/kind; good (impression). **fa•vor•a•bly**, adv. in a favorable way. **fa•vored**, adj. preferred/liked. **fa•vor•ite**. 1. adj. preferred/most liked. 2. n. (a) most liked thing/person. (b) horse, team, etc., which most people think will win. **fa•vor•it•ism**, n. prejudice/preference for one thing/person.

fawn [fɔːn] 1. n. young deer. 2. adj. brownish cream color. 3. v. **to f. on s.o.** = to try to get s.o.'s favor by doing everything they ask.

fax [fæks]. 1. n. (pl. **faxes**) copy of a text or image sent by telephone. 2. v. to send an image by telephone.

FBI [efbiː'aɪ] n. Federal Bureau of Investigation.

Fe symbol for iron.

fear ['fɪə] 1. n. terror/worry/feeling of being afraid. 2. v. to be afraid of (sth). **fear•ful**, adj. terrible. **fear•ful•ly**, adv. terribly/very. **fear•less**, adj. with no feeling of terror. **fear•less•ly**, adv. not feeling afraid. **fear•some**, adj. frightening.

fea•si•ble ['fiːzəbl] adj. (a) which can be done. (b) likely/probable. **fea•si•bil•i•ty** [fiːzə-'bɪlɪtɪ] n. ability to be done; **f. study** = study to see if sth can be done. **fea•si•bly**, adv. possibly.

feast [fiːst] 1. n. (a) special religious day when we remember a saint or special event. (b) very large meal. 2. v. (a) to eat expensive food. (b) to eat a very large meal.

feat [fiːt] n. unusually difficult act.

feath•er ['feðə] 1. n. one of many growths which form the covering of a bird's body; **light as a f.** = very light. 2. v. (a) **to f. one's nest** = to make a lot of money (usu. fraudulently). (b) to make the blade of an oar skim fast across the surface of the water. **feather-brained**, adj. silly and forgetful. **feath•ered**, adj. with feathers. **feath•er•weight**, n. weight in boxing between bantamweight and lightweight. **feath•er•y**, adj. light/delicate (like a feather).

fea•ture ['fiːtʃə] 1. n. (a) special part of the face

æ back, ɑː farm, ɒ top, aɪ pipe, aʊ how, aɪə fire, aʊə flower, ɔː bought, ɔɪ toy, e fed, eəhair, eɪ take, ə afraid, əʊ boat, əʊə lower, ɜː word, iː heap, ɪ hit, ɪə hear, uː school, ʊ book, ʌ but, b back, d dog, ð then, dʒ just, f fog, g go, h hand, j yes, k catch, l last, m mix, n nut, ŋ sing, p penny, r round, s some, ʃ short, t too, tʃ chop, θ thing, v voice, w was, z zoo, ʒ treasure

(such as nose/mouth, etc.); important aspect of sth. (b) important item in a news program or article; important article on a special subject. (c) **f. film** = main motion picture in a program. 2. *v.* (a) to have as the main actor/as the main subject, esp. on TV, or in a motion picture or newspaper. (b) to play an important part. **fea•ture•less,** *adj.* with no striking features.

Feb•ru•ar•y ['februərɪ] *n.* 2nd month of the year.

fe•ces ['fiːsiːz] *n. pl.* (*formal*) solid waste matter from the body. **fe•cal,** *adj.* referring to feces.

feck•less ['fekləs] *adj.* (person) who has no sense of responsibility/who is incompetent.

fe•cund ['fekənd] *adj.* fertile/fruitful. **fe•cun•di•ty** [fɪ'kʌndɪtɪ] *n.* being fecund.

fed [fed] *v. see* **feed. fed up,** *adj. inf.* bored/tired (**with**).

fed•er•a•tion [fedə'reɪʃn] *n.* group of states or societies which have joined together. **fed•er•al** ['fedərəl] *adj.* referring to a system where a group of semi-independent states exist under a central government. **fed•er•ate** ['fedəreɪt] *v.* to join (states) together in a federation.

fee [fiː] *n.* money paid for professional services, to schools, etc.

fee•ble ['fiːbl] *adj.* (**-er, -est**) weak. **fee•ble-mind•ed,** *adj.* of low intelligence. **fee•ble•ness,** *n.* weakness. **fee•bly,** *adv.* weakly.

feed [fiːd] 1. *n.* (a) food given to animals. (b) *inf.* meal; **morning f.** = morning meal given to babies. (c) means of putting material into a machine; device for feeding material into a machine. 2. *v.* (**fed**) (a) to give food to (s.o./sth). (b) (*esp. of animals*) to eat. (c) to put (**in**). **feed•back,** *n.* (a) return of a signal in an electronic circuit causing a high-pitched noise. (b) information/details about sth which has been done. **feed•er,** *n.* s.o./sth that gives food; **sheet f.** = device on a printer for inserting single sheets of paper. **feed•ing,** *adj.* giving food; **f. bottle** = bottle used for giving milk, etc., to a baby. **feed•lot,** *n.* fenced area of land where livestock are fattened.

feel [fiːl] 1. *n.* touch, esp. with the fingers. 2. *v.* (**felt**) (a) to touch, esp. with your fingers; **the knife felt cold; to f. one's way** = act cautiously until one has more experience. (b) to have a feeling/sensation; **he feels it would be unwise** = he thinks it would be unwise; **do you f. like a cup of coffee?** = would you like a cup of coffee? **to f. up to doing sth** = to feel strong enough to do it. **feel•er,** *n.* antenna/long part on an insect's head with which it touches; **to put out a f.** = to explore sth/to see if sth is ac-

ceptable. **feel•ing,** *n.* (a) sense of touch. (b) thing felt inside/emotion.

feet [fiːt] *n. pl. see* **foot.**

feign [feɪn] *v.* (*formal*) to pretend.

feint [feɪnt] 1. *n.* false attack; move to confuse your opponent. 2. *v.* to make a move to confuse your opponent.

feist•y ['feɪstɪ] *adj.* aggressive.

fe•lic•i•ty [fə'lɪsɪtɪ] *n.* (*formal*) happiness. **fe•lic•i•tous,** *adj.* well chosen (words).

fe•line ['fiːlaɪn] 1. *adj.* referring to a cat; like a cat. 2. *n.* member of the cat family.

fell [fel] 1. *n.* (*England*) high moorland. 2. *adj.* (*old*) cruel; **at one f. swoop** = swiftly. 3. *v.* to cut down (a tree); to knock (s.o.) down; *see also* **fall.**

fel•low ['feləʊ] *n.* (a) man. (b) person who is in the same group; **f. workers.** (c) member of a learned society. **fel•low•ship,** *n.* (a) friendly feeling. (b) group of people with similar interests.

fel•on ['felən] *n.* criminal. **fel•o•ny,** *n.* serious crime.

felt [felt] 1. *n.* thick, matted material made of wool; **f. tipped pen** = pen of which the writing end is made of hard felt. 2. *v.* to cover (sth) with felt; *see also* **feel. felt-tip,** *n.* felt tipped pen.

fe•male ['fiːmeɪl] 1. *adj.* (a) referring to women/girls. (b) referring to the sex which has young. 2. *n.* (a) *inf.* woman/girl. (b) animal/insect/bird which gives birth to young or lays eggs; flower which produces seeds.

fem•i•nine ['femənɪn] *adj.* (a) belonging to a woman, like a woman. (b) (*in grammar*) referring to words which have a particular form to indicate the female gender. **fem•i•nin•i•ty** [femɪ'nɪnətɪ] *n.* womanliness; female qualities. **fem•i•nism** ['femɪnɪzəm] *n.* being a feminist. **fem•i•nist,** *n.* person who (usu. woman) who actively supports the right of women to equal status with men.

fem•o•ral ['fiːmərəl] *adj.* referring to the femur.

fe•mur ['fiːmə] *n.* thigh bone.

fen [fen] *n.* large area of marsh.

fence [fens] 1. *n.* (a) barrier, usu. of wood or wire, used to keep people or animals in or out of a place; **to sit on the f.** = to avoid giving a definite answer to a question. (b) *Sl.* person who takes stolen goods to resell them. 2. *v.* (a) **to f. in/off** = to surround with a fence. (b) to fight with swords as a sport. **fenc•er,** *n.* person who fences. **fenc•ing,** *n.* (a) material making up a fence. (b) sport of fighting with swords.

fend [fend] *v.* (a) **to f. off** = to push away. (b) **to f. for yourself** = to look after yourself.

fend•er ['fendə] *n.* (a) low guard around a fireplace to stop coal or wood falling out into the room. (b) rope mat/rubber tire, etc., hung against the side of a boat to protect it from bumps. (c) strip of metal over the wheels of a car, bicycle, or other vehicle to protect against mud or water; mudguard.

feng shui ['fʌŋ 'ʃweɪ] *n.* Chinese art of deciding the optimum location and design of a building/room, etc. so that it is in harmony with energies believed to flow around the earth.

fen•nel ['fenl] *n.* herb with a smell like aniseed.

fe•ral ['fɪərəl] *adj.* (animal) which is wild (having once been domesticated).

fer•ment 1. *n.* ['fɜːmənt] upset/agitation. **2.** *v.* [fə'ment] to change by fermentation. **fer•men•ta•tion** [fɜːmen'teɪʃn] *n.* chemical change brought about in liquids, usu. leading to the production of alcohol.

fern [fɜːn] *n.* green plant often with feathery leaves which does not have flowers or seeds.

fe•ro•cious [fə'rəʊʃəs] *adj.* fierce/angry. **fe•ro•cious•ly,** *adv.* in a ferocious way. **fe•roc•i•ty** [fə'rɒsɪtɪ] *n.* fierceness.

fer•ret ['ferɪt] **1.** *n.* small weasellike animal half-tamed and used to drive rabbits or rats from holes. **2.** *v.* **to f. out** = to find out by endless searching.

Fer•ris wheel ['ferɪswiːl] *n.* large vertical wheel with seats, at an amusement park or fair.

fer•ro•con•crete [ferəʊ'kɒŋkriːt] *n.* concrete reinforced with steel bars.

fer•rous ['ferəs] *adj.* containing iron.

fer•rule ['feruːl] *n.* metal cap on the end of an umbrella or stick.

fer•ry ['ferɪ] **1.** *n.* (a) (*also* **ferryboat**) boat which carries goods or people back and forth across a stretch of water. (b) place where a boat crosses a stretch of water. **2.** *v.* to take (s.o.) across in a boat; **the bus ferried people to and from the station** = took them back and forth. **fer•ry•man,** *n.* (*pl.* **-men**) man in charge of a ferry.

fer•tile ['fɜːtl, *Brit.* 'fɜːtaɪl] *adj.* rich enough to produce crops; (*of female*) able to produce young; **she has a f. imagination** = she is very imaginative/she can imagine things very easily. **fer•til•i•ty** [fə'tɪlɪtɪ] *n.* ability to produce crops or young. **fer•ti•li•za•tion** [fɜːtɪlaɪ'zeɪʃn] *n.* the act of fertilizing. **fer•ti•lize** ['fɜːtɪlaɪz] *v.* (a) to join male and female cells together, so that a new animal/plant will be made. (b) to spread fertilizer on. **fer•ti•liz•er,** *n.* chemical or manure spread over the ground to make it richer and more able to produce crops.

fer•vor, *Brit.* **fer•vour** ['fɜːvə] *n.* passion. **fer•vent, fervid,** *adj.* passionate. **fer•vent•ly,** *adv.* in a fervent way.

fes•cue ['feskjuː] *n.* grass grown in meadows.

fes•ter ['festə] *v.* (*of wound*) to become bad and produce pus.

fes•ti•val ['festɪvl] *n.* (a) religious celebration which comes at the same time each year. (b) artistic celebration/entertainment which is put on at regular intervals; **arts f., music f. fes•tive,** *adj.* happy; fit for a celebration. **fes•tiv•i•ty** [fe'stɪvɪtɪ] *n.* celebration.

fes•toon [fe'stuːn] **1.** *n.* long chain of hanging decorations. **2.** *v.* to hang with decorations.

fetch [fetʃ] *v.* (a) to go and bring (s.o./sth) back. (b) to be sold at (a certain price). **fetch•ing,** *adj.* attractive/pretty. **fetch up,** *v. inf.* to arrive/to end up (in a certain place).

fete, fête [feɪt] **1.** *n.* public celebration/entertainment, often held outdoors. **2.** *v.* to celebrate or honor with a fete.

fet•id ['fiːtɪd] *adj.* bad-smelling (water/breath).

fet•ish ['fetɪʃ] *n.* (a) object worshipped by s.o. (b) obsession.

fet•lock ['fetlɒk] *n.* back part of a horse's leg just above the hoof.

fet•ter ['fetə] *v.* to chain (a prisoner). **fet•ters,** *n. pl.* chains.

fet•tle ['fetl] *n.* **in fine f.** = in very good condition.

fe•tus, *Brit.* **foe•tus** ['fiːtəs] *n.* unborn child/reptile/bird, etc., which is developing from an embryo. **fe•tal,** *adj.* referring to a fetus.

feud [fjuːd] **1.** *n.* bitter quarrel. **2.** *v.* to quarrel bitterly all the time.

feu•dal ['fjuːdl] *adj.* **f. system** = medieval system of holding land in return for services to an overlord or king. **feu•dal•ism,** *n.* feudal system.

fe•ver ['fiːvə] *n.* (a) state when the body's temperature is higher than normal. (b) **f. (pitch)** = great excitement. **fe•ver•ish,** *adj.* suffering from a fever. **fe•ver•ish•ly,** *adv.* excitedly; impatiently.

few [fjuː] *adj. & n.* (a) (**-er, -est**) not many. (b) **a f.** = some/several.

fey [feɪ] *adj.* otherworldly, supernatural.

fez [fez] *n.* round hat worn in some Muslim countries.

æ back, ɑː farm, ɒ top, aɪ pipe, aʊ how, aɪə fire, aʊə flower, ɔː bought, ɔɪ toy, e fed, eəhair, eɪ take, ə afraid, əʊ boat, əʊə lower, ɜː word, iː heap, ɪ hit, ɪə hear, uː school, ʊ book, ʌ but, b back, d dog, ð then, dʒ just, f fog, g go, h hand, j yes, k catch, l last, m mix, n nut, ŋ sing, p penny, r round, s some, ʃ short, t too, tʃ chop, θ thing, v voice, w was, z zoo, ʒ treasure

fi•an•cé, fi•an•cée [fɪˈɒnseɪ] *n.* man/woman who is engaged to be married.

fi•as•co [fɪˈæskəu] *n.* (*pl.* **-os**) total failure.

fib [fɪb] 1. *n.* lie. 2. *v.* (**fibbed**) to tell lies. **fib•ber**, *n.* person who tells lies.

fi•ber, *Brit.* **fi•bre** [ˈfaɪbə] *n.* small thread of material. (b) **moral f.** = strength of moral feelings. **fi•ber•glass**, *n.* (a) glass fiber wool used as insulation. (b) strong material made of woven threads of glass; plastic containing threads of glass. **fi•ber op•tics**, *n.* use of thin strands of material through which light can be passed, in order to convey messages or images over long distances. **fi•broid**, *adj.* (growth, etc.) made of fibers. **fi•bro•my•al•gi•a**, *n.* any of several rheumatoid disorders characterized by pain, tenderness and stiffness of the muscles, fatigue, and headaches. **fi•bro•my•o•si•tis**, *n.* fibromyalgia. **fi•brous**, *adj.* made of fibers.

fib•u•la [ˈfɪbjulə] *n.* thin bone between the knee and the ankle behind the tibia.

fick•le [ˈfɪkl] *adj.* changeable/not steady. **fick•le•ness**, *n.* being fickle.

fic•tion [ˈfɪkʃn] *n.* (a) story that is not true. (b) novels. **fic•tion•al** *adj.* (character) who exists in fiction. **fic•ti•tious** [fɪkˈtɪʃəs] *adj.* untrue/not real.

fid•dle [ˈfɪdl] 1. *n. inf.* (a) violin. (b) dishonest/illegal dealings. 2. *v. inf.* (a) to play the fiddle. (b) to play idly with sth. **fid•dler**, *n. inf.* violin player. **fid•dle•sticks**, *n. inf.* nonsense.

fi•del•i•ty [fɪˈdelɪtɪ] *n.* faithfulness/accuracy (of a reproduction).

fidg•et [ˈfɪdʒɪt] 1. *n.* person who cannot stay still. 2. *v.* to move restlessly. **fidg•et•y**, *adj.* restless.

field [fiːld] 1. *n.* (a) piece of cultivated land surrounded by fences or hedges. (b) large surface/area; **f. day** = busy and exciting time. (c) piece of ground for playing games; **f. events** = jumping and throwing competitions. (d) special area of study. (e) area of influence (of a magnet/of gravity/of a charged particle). 2. *v.* (*in baseball, cricket*) (a) to stop (a ball hit by s.o. at bat). (b) to be part of the side which is not batting. **field•er**, *n.* (*in baseball, cricket*) member of the side which is not batting. **field glas•ses**, *n. pl.* binoculars. **field hock•ey**, *n.* team game played on grass with long curved sticks and a hard ball. **field mar•shal**, *n.* highest rank in the British and certain other armies. **field•mouse**, *n.* (*pl.* **-mice**) small mouse living in fields and meadows. **field•work**, *n.* scientific research done outside, and not in a laboratory.

field•work•er, *n.* person engaged in fieldwork.

fiend [fiːnd] *n.* devil; monster; *inf.* addict; **dope f.** = dope addict. **fiend•ish**, *adj.* devilish; very cruel.

fierce [ˈfɪəs] *adj.* ferocious/angry; which will attack anything; very violent or strong; **f. winds.** **fierce•ly**, *adv.* strongly and angrily. **fierce•ness**, *n.* violence; intensity.

fier•y [ˈfaɪərɪ] *adj.* burning/full of fire; angry.

fi•es•ta [fɪˈestə] *n.* Spanish festival.

fife [faɪf] *n.* small metal flute played in military bands.

fif•teen [fɪfˈtiːn] *n.* (a) number 15. (b) group of fifteen people (as in a sports team). **fif•teenth, 15th**, *adj. & n.* referring to fifteen.

fifth, 5th [fɪfθ] *adj. & n.* referring to five. **Fifth A•mend•ment**, *n.* the Amendment to the Constitution of the United States which allows citizens not to give evidence in court which might incriminate themselves. **fifth col•umn**, *n.* enemy sympathizers inside a country under attack.

fif•ty [ˈfɪftɪ] number 50; **f.-f.** = each paying half of the cost. **fif•ti•eth, 50th**, *adj.* referring to fifty.

fig [fɪg] *n.* juicy sweet fruit of the fig tree.

fight [faɪt] 1. *n.* struggle/battle; boxing match. 2. *v.* (**fought**) to struggle with (s.o./sth). **fight•er**, *n.* (a) person who fights. (b) fast attacking aircraft. **fight•ing**, *n.* action of struggling with s.o.

fig•ment [ˈfɪgmənt] *n.* **f. of the imagination** = thing which has been imagined.

fig•ure [ˈfɪgə, *Am.* ˈfɪgjə] 1. *n.* (a) written number (such as 28). (b) geometric shape such as a triangle or circle; drawing/diagram in a book. (c) shape of a person. (d) **f. of speech** = colorful expression used to illustrate a meaning. (e) pattern of movement (in skating/dancing). 2. *v.* (a) **to f. out** = to try to understand; *inf.* **that figures** = that makes sense. (b) to appear (in a novel, etc.). **fig•ur•a•tive** [ˈfɪgjurətɪv] *adj.* (usage of a word) which is not the literal meaning. **fig•ur•a•tive•ly**, *adv.* in a figurative way. **fig•ure•head**, *n.* (a) wooden figure carved on the front of a ship. (b) person who seems important but who has no real power. **fig•ur•ine** [ˈfɪgjuriːn] *n.* small figure (in china/wood, etc.).

fil•a•ment [ˈfɪləmənt] *n.* thin wire (in an electric bulb).

fil•bert [ˈfɪlbət] *n.* type of hazel nut.

filch [fɪltʃ] *v.* to steal.

file [faɪl] 1. *n.* (a) metal tool used for smoothing rough surfaces. (b) holder for papers and documents. (c) section of data on a computer; **f.**

server = central unit of a computer network that allows other computers access to files. (d) line of people; **in single f.** = one behind the other. 2. *v.* (a) to smooth (a surface) with a file. (b) to put (papers) away in a folder or case. (c) to walk in a line. **fil•ing cab•i•net,** *n.* box with drawers for putting files in. **fil•ings,** *n. pl.* small pieces of metal which come away when metal is filed smooth.

fil•i•al ['fɪlɪəl] *adj.* (*formal*) referring to a son or daughter.

fil•i•bus•ter ['fɪlɪbʌstə] 1. *n.* attempt to prevent a law being passed by speaking for a very long time in the debate. 2. *v.* to delay the passing of a law by speaking for a very long time in the debate.

fil•i•gree ['fɪlɪgriː] *n.* very decorative ornamental work done in precious metals.

Fil•i•pi•no [fɪlɪ'piːnəu] *adj. & n.* (*pl.* -os) (person) from the Philippines.

fill [fɪl] *v.* to put as much as possible into (sth)/to make (sth) full; to become full; to drill a hole in (a bad tooth) and fill it up with metal, etc.; to find s.o. to do (a job). **fill•er,** *n.* material used to fill holes and cracks in walls/woodwork, etc. **fill in,** *v.* (a) to fill a hole. (b) to complete the blank spaces in (a form/document). (c) *inf.* **to f. s.o. in on** = to tell/to inform (s.o.). **fill•ing,** *n.* thing that fills up sth else. **fill•ing sta•tion,** *n.* place where you can buy fuel and oil. **fill out,** *v.* (a) to write everything that is asked for on (a form). (b) to get fatter. **fill up,** *v.* to fill (sth) until it is completely full; to become completely full.

fil•let ['fɪlɪt] 1. *n.* good cut of meat or fish from which all the bones have been removed. 2. *v.* to remove the bones from (a fish).

fil•lip ['fɪlɪp] *n.* sharp stroke.

fil•ly ['fɪlɪ] *n.* young female horse.

film [fɪlm] 1. *n.* (a) motion picture. (b) roll of coated plastic put in a camera and used for taking photographs or pictures to be shown on a screen. (c) thin covering (of dust, etc.). 2. *v.* to take pictures of (sth) with a motion-picture camera. **film star,** *n.* well-known motion-picture actor or actress. **film•strip,** *n.* strip of film with several still pictures which are projected one after the other. **film•y,** *adj.* very thin/almost transparent.

fil•ter ['fɪltə] 1. *n.* (a) device/material for straining liquids or air, stopping any solids from passing through. (b) glass on a camera which allows only certain colors or intensities of light to pass through. 2. *v.* (a) to pass through a filter. (b) to move gradually and quietly. (c) **to f. through/down** = to go/come slowly through or down. **fil•ter pa•per,** *n.* paper used for filtering liquids. **fil•ter-tip cig•a•rettes,** *n. pl.* cigarettes with a filter at the mouth end.

filth [fɪlθ] *n.* dirt; obscene words/books, etc. **filth•y,** *adj.* (-ier, -iest) (a) very dirty. (b) obscene. **filth•i•ly,** *adv.* in a filthy way. **filth•i•ness,** *n.* being filthy; filthy things.

fil•trate ['fɪltreɪt] *n.* liquid which has been filtered. **fil•tra•tion,** *n.* action of filtering.

fin [fɪn] *n.* (a) thin limb on the body of a fish which it moves to swim. (b) piece shaped in a similar way on a bomb, rocket or aircraft.

fi•na•gle [fɪ'neɪgl] *v. inf.* to work dishonestly; to get (sth) dishonestly.

fi•nal ['faɪnl] 1. *adj.* coming at the end; last; **the decision is f.** = cannot be changed. 2. *n.* (a) last competition in a contest between several teams or competitors. (b) **finals** = last examinations at the end of a school/college/university course. **fi•nal•ist,** *n.* person taking part in the final competition. **fi•nal•i•ty** [faɪ'nælɪtɪ] *n.* state of being at the end. **fi•nal•i•za•tion** [faɪnəlaɪ'zeɪʃn] *n.* act of finalizing. **fi•nal•ize** ['faɪnəlaɪz] *v.* to finish making plans for sth. **fi•nal•ly,** *adv.* at last; in the last place.

fi•na•le [fɪ'nɑːlɪ] *n.* last part of a piece of music/of a show.

fi•nance ['faɪnæns] 1. *n.* money, esp. belonging to the public or to a company. 2. *v.* to provide money for. **fi•nan•cial** [fɪ'nænʃl] *adj.* concerning money. **fi•nan•cial•ly,** *adv.* regarding finance. **fin•an•cier** [fɪ'nænsɪə] *n.* person who deals with money on a large scale.

finch [fɪntʃ] *n.* (*pl.* -es) small seed-eating bird.

find [faɪnd] 1 *n.* good thing which you have discovered. 2. *v.* (**found**) to discover (sth hidden or lost); **to be found** = to exist; **to f. out** = to discover; to learn; **to f. s.o. out** = to discover the true nature, character, or identity of s.o.; **it has been found that** = it is a known fact that. **find•er,** *n.* person who finds. **find•ings,** *n. pl.* facts discovered/recommendations.

fine [faɪn] 1. *n.* money to be paid as a punishment for doing wrong. 2. *adj.* (-er, -est) (a) pure. (b) lovely/good. (c) (*of weather*) good; with no precipitation. (d) very thin; very small. 3. *inter.* **f.!** = all right/agreed. 4. *v.* (a) to make (sth) fine. (b) to punish by making s.o. pay a fine. **fine art,** *n.* painting/sculpture, etc.

fine•ly, *adv.* delicately/thinly/beautifully.
fin•er•y, *n.* fine clothes.

fi•nesse [fɪ'nes] *n.* skill (in dealing with awkward situations).

fin•ger ['fɪŋɡə] 1. *n.* (a) one of the five parts at the end of a hand, usu. other than the thumb; **to keep your fingers crossed** = to hope that sth will happen as you want it; **to put your f. on sth** = to identify it. (b) part of a glove into which a finger goes. (c) thing shaped like a finger. 2. *v.* to touch with the fingers. **fin•ger•ing,** *n.* use of the fingers when playing a musical instrument. **fin•ger•nail,** *n.* thin horny substance which grows at the end of the fingers. **fin•ger•print,** *n.* mark left by the end of the fingers. **fin•ger•stall,** *n.* cover put over a finger which has been hurt. **fin•ger•tip,** *n.* end of the finger; **she has the information at her fingertips** = she has the information close at hand or at her disposal.

fin•i•al ['fɪnɪəl] *n.* decoration on a gable.

fin•ick•y ['fɪnɪkɪ] *adj.* (*also* finical) *inf.* (a) awkward and detailed (work). (b) fussy (person) who dislikes things, esp. certain types of food; **f. eater.**

fin•ish ['fɪnɪʃ] 1. *n.* (a) end. (b) way in which sth is completed; appearance of sth when it is finished. 2. *v.* to end. **finish off,** *v.* (a) to complete or use all of sth. (b) to kill. **finish up,** *v.* (a) to end up. (b) to finish completely. **finish with,** *v.* **to f. with s.o.** = to stop being friendly with s.o.; **to f. with sth** = to need sth no longer.

fi•nite ['faɪnaɪt] *adj.* with an end/with a limit; **f. verb** = verb which indicates a tense.

Finn [fɪn] *n.* person from Finland. **Finn•ish** ['fɪnɪʃ] 1. *adj.* referring to Finland. 2. *n.* language spoken in Finland.

fiord ['fjɔːd] *n.* fjord.

fir [fɜː] *n.* **f. (tree)** = evergreen tree with needle-shaped leaves.

fire ['faɪə] 1. *n.* (a) thing that is burning; **to catch f.** = to start burning because of sth else which is in flames; **to set f. to sth** = to make sth start burning. (b) great enthusiasm or excitement. (c) shooting of guns. 2. *v.* (a) to make (sth) burn. (b) to make (s.o.) excited. (c) to bake/to heat. (d) to shoot (a gun); **f. away** = ask your question. (e) to dismiss (s.o.) from a job. **fire a•larm,** *n.* bell/siren which gives warning that a fire has started. **fire•arm,** *n.* any gun held in the hand. **fire•brand,** *n.* agitator. **fire•break,** *n.* strip of land which has been cleared of trees, to prevent forest fires from spreading. **fire bri•gade,** *n.* people whose job is to put out fires. **fire•damp,** *n.* explosive gas in a mine. **fire en•gine,** *n.* vehicle used by the fire brigade to carry pumps/hoses/ladders, etc., to put out fires.

fire es•cape, *n.* stairs/ladder which can be used by people to get out of buildings on fire. **fire ex•tin•guish•er,** *n.* portable cylinder filled with chemicals or foam to put out a small fire. **fire•fight,** *n.* military skirmish involving light weapons. **fire•fly,** *n.* type of insect which glows at night. **fire•guard,** *n.* metal screen put in front of a fireplace. **fire•light,** *n.* light from a fire. **fire•man,** *n.* (*pl.* -men) (a) man whose job it is to put out fires. (b) man who keeps the fire burning in a furnace/a steam train. **fire•place,** *n.* place where a fire is lit indoors. **fire•proof,** *adj.* which will not burn. **fire•side,** *n.* area around a fireplace in a room. **fire sta•tion,** *n.* center where fire engines are based. **fire•ward•en,** *n.* person in charge of putting out fires, as in a forest. **fire•wood,** *n.* (*no pl.*) wood for making fires. **fire•work** (*usu.* fireworks) *n.* small container holding chemicals which will sparkle or explode when lit.

firm [fɜːm] 1. *n.* business/company. 2. *adj.* solid/fixed/strong. 3. *adv.* **to stand f.** = to refuse to change your mind. **firm•ly,** *adv.* in a strong way.

fir•ma•ment ['fɜːməmənt] *n.* (*formal*) sky.

first [fɜːst] 1. *adj. & adv.* (*as a number can be written* 1st) (a) at the beginning/coming before everything else; **at f.** = at the beginning. (b) for the first time. (c) in a first class seat. 2. *n.* thing/person coming before everything else; **in f.** = in first gear. **first aid,** *n.* help given to a person who is hurt before a doctor or ambulance arrives. **First A•mend•ment,** *n.* the Amendment to the Constitution of the United States which grants citizens freedom of speech. **first class.** 1. *adj.* excellent; highest; most expensive. 2. *adv.* (travel) with the most expensive seats. **first day cov•er,** *n.* special stamped envelope canceled on the first day of issue of the stamp on it. **first floor,** *n.* (a) story above the ground floor in a building. (b) ground floor. **first•hand,** *adj. & adv.* direct from the original source. **First La•dy,** *n.* wife of the President of the United States. **first•ly,** *adv.* to start with. **first mate,** *n.* second-in-command of a merchant ship. **first night,** *n.* evening when a play is performed for the first time. **first-rate,** *adj.* excellent.

firth [fɜːθ] *n.* (*in Scotland*) long arm of the sea.

fis•cal ['fɪskl] *adj.* referring to tax/government revenue.

fish [fɪʃ] 1. *n.* (*pl.* **fish,** *occasionally* **fishes**) cold-blooded animal with fins and scales, that lives in water; **he's like a f. out of water** = awkward, because he feels he is not in his usual surroundings. 2. *v.* (a) to try to catch fish; *inf.* **to f. out** = to take out. (b) to try to get (infor-

mation). **fish•bone,** *n.* bone in a fish.
fish•cake, *n.* round cake of fish and potato
mixed together. **fish•er•man,** *n.* (*pl.* **-men**)
man who catches fish, either as his job or for
sport. **fish•er•y,** *n.* business of catching fish.
fish stick, *n.* frozen finger-shaped piece of
fish covered in breadcrumbs. **fish-hook,** *n.*
metal hook at the end of a line which catches
in the mouth of the fish. **fish•ing,** *n.* catching
fish. **fish•ing boat,** *n.* boat used for fishing.
fish•ing rod, *n.* long piece of wood to which
is attached the line and hook. **fish•ing
tack•le,** *n.* all the equipment used by a
fisherman. **fish•y,** *adj.* (a) like a fish. (b) *inf.*
suspicious/odd (story, etc.).

fis•sion ['fɪʃn] *n.* breaking up of sth into parts;
nuclear f. = breaking up of an atom in an explosion.

fis•sure ['fɪʃə] *n.* crack/split, esp. in a rock or in
the ground.

fist [fɪst] *n.* tightly closed hand. **fist•ful,** *n.*
amount you can hold in your fist.
fist•i•cuffs, *n. pl.* (*old*) fighting.

fit [fɪt] 1. *n.* sudden sharp attack of illness, etc.;
by fits and starts = at odd moments/with continual stoppages. 2. *adj.* (**fitter, fittest**) (a)
right/suitable. (b) capable. (c) healthy. 3. *v.*
(**fitted**) (a) to be the right size for. (b) to put in
the right place. (c) to make suitable for.
fit•ful, *adj.* irregular. **fit•ful•ly,** *adv.* irregularly. **fit in,** *v.* (a) to be suitable/to match
(with). (b) to find room/time for (s.o./sth).
fit•ment, *n.* furniture/equipment which is
fixed in a room. **fit•ness,** *n.* being fit. **fit
out, fit up,** *v.* to provide all the equip-
ment/clothing necessary for. **fit•ted,** *adj.*
suitable/right; which has been made to fit.
fit•ter, *n.* (a) skilled mechanic who adjusts
machines and their parts. (b) person who
makes sure clothes fit. **fit•ting,** 1. *adj.* suit-
able/right. 2. *n.* (a) action of making sth fit/of
trying on a new piece of clothing; **f. room** =
small room in a store where you can try on
clothes before you buy them. (b) thing which
is fixed in a building but which could be removed.

five [faɪv] *n.* number 5. **fiv•er,** *n. inf.* five dollar
bill.

fix [fɪks] 1. *n.* (*pl.* **-es**) (a) difficult position. (b)
Sl. injection of a drug such as heroin. 2. *v.* (a)
to fasten/to attach. (b) to arrange. (c) to
make/to prepare (a drink/meal, etc.). (d) to
pass (a photographic plate) through a liquid

to stop the image changing. (e) to mend.
fix•at•ed, *adj.* obsessed. **fix•a•tion** [fɪk-
'seɪʃn] *n.* obsession. **fix•a•tive** ['fɪksətɪv] *n.*
substance which fixes the colors on a painting.
fixed, *adj.* (a) attached firmly. (b) (price, etc.)
arranged or agreed upon. **fix•ed•ly**
['fɪksɪdlɪ] *adv.* with eyes fixed on s.o. **fix•er,**
n. person who can arrange sth. **fix•i•ty,** *n.*
state of being fixed. **fix•ture** ['fɪkstʃə] *n.* object permanently fixed in a house (like a sink,
toilet, radiator). **fix up,** *v.* to arrange.

fizz [fɪz] 1. *n.* sound like a lot of bubbles. 2. *v.* to
bubble up. **fizz•y,** *adj.* bubbly.

fiz•zle out ['fɪzl'aut] *v. inf.* to come to noth-
ing/not to work.

fjord ['fjɔːd] *n.* long arm of the sea among
mountains in Norway.

flab•ber•gast ['flæbəgɑːst] *v.* to amaze.

flab•by ['flæbɪ] *adj.* (**-ier, -iest**) (person) who is
soft and fat. **flab,** *n. inf.* soft excess flesh.
flab•bi•ness, *n.* being flabby.

flac•cid ['flæksɪd] *adj.* hanging loosely.

flag [flæg] 1. *n.* (a) piece of material with the
emblem of a country/club, etc., on it. (b) large
paving stone. (c) iris/marsh plant with long fat
leaves and purple flowers. (d) mark inserted in
a computer text. 2. *v.* (**flagged**) (a) to grow
tired. (b) **to f. down** = to wave to make (a cab)
stop. (c) to insert a mark in a computer file.
flag•pole, flagstaff, *n.* tall pole on which
large flags are flown. **flag•ship,** *n.* ship on
which a high-ranking naval officer (as an ad-
miral) sails, and which therefore flies his special flag. **flag•stone,** *n.* large flat stone used
for making pavements/floors.

flag•el•late ['flædʒəleɪt] *v.* (*formal*) to whip.
flag•el•la•tion [flædʒə'leɪʃn] *n.* (*formal*)
whipping.

flag•on ['flægən] *n.* large round container for
liquids.

fla•grant ['fleɪgrənt] *adj.* (crime) which is obvious. **fla•grance,** *n.* being flagrant.
fla•grant•ly, *adv.* in a flagrant way.

flail [fleɪl] 1. *n.* implement for threshing grain.
2. *v.* to wave (your arms) about.

flair ['fleə] *n.* natural ability (**for** sth).

flak [flæk] *n.* (*no pl.*) gun fire against aircraft;
sharp criticism.

flake [fleɪk] 1. *n.* tiny, thin piece. 2. *v.* **to f.
off/away** = to fall off in little pieces; *Sl.* **to f.
out** = to collapse with tiredness. **flak•y,** *adj.* in
thin pieces.

flam•boy•ant [flæm'bɔɪənt] *adj.* brightly col-

æ back, ɑː farm, ɒ top, aɪ pipe, au how, aiə fire, auə flower, ɔː bought, ɔɪ toy, e fed, eəhair, eɪ take, ə
afraid, əu boat, əuə lower, vː word, iː heap, ɪ hit, ɪə hear, uː school, u book, ʌ but, b back, d dog, ð then,
dʒ just, f fog, g go, h hand, j yes, k catch, l last, m mix, n nut, ŋ sing, p penny, r round, s some, ʃ short, t
too, tʃ chop, θ thing, v voice, w was, z zoo, ʒ treasure

ored; too bright. **flam•boy•ance,** *n.* being flamboyant. **flam•boy•ant•ly,** *adv.* in a flamboyant way.

flame [fleɪm] 1. *n.* (a) bright tongue of fire. (b) *inf.* abusive electronic mail. 2. *v. inf.* to send abusive electronic mail. **flame•proof, flame-resistant,** *adj.* specially treated so that it will not catch fire or melt. **flam•ing,** *adj.* in flames.

fla•min•go [flə'mɪŋgəu] *n.* (*pl.* -os) water bird with long legs and neck, often with pink feathers.

flam•ma•ble ['flæməbl] *adj.* easily set on fire/inflammable.

flan [flæn] *n.* open tart; sweet baked custard.

flange [flændʒ] *n.* rim/edge which sticks out on a pipe or wheel.

flank [flæŋk] 1. *n.* side (esp. of an animal, an army). 2. *v.* to be at the side of (sth).

flan•nel ['flænl] *n.* warm woolen material; **flannels** = flannel trousers. **flan•nel•et, flannelette,** *n.* warm cotton material, which feels like flannel.

flap [flæp] 1. *n.* (a) hinged part (which hangs down). (b) *inf.* excitement and worry. (c) movement like that of a bird's wing. 2. *v.* (**flapped**) to move up and down like a bird's wing. **flap•jack,** *n.* pancake.

flare ['fleə] 1. *n.* (a) device which gives a sudden blaze of light (esp. as a signal). (b) widening bottom part (of a skirt/of trousers) 2. *v.* (a) to burn brightly. (b) (*of a skirt/trousers*) to widen gradually. **flare up,** *v.* (a) to blaze suddenly. (b) to get angry.

flash [flæʃ] 1. *n.* (*pl.* -es) (a) short sudden burst of light or emotion; **in a f.** = very quickly. (b) apparatus for taking photographs in the dark. (c) short item of news. 2. *v.* (a) to light up quickly and suddenly. (b) to show (sth) quickly. (c) **to f. by/past** = to move/to pass by quickly. **flash•back,** *n.* scene in a motion picture, novel, etc., showing what happened at an earlier date. **flash•bulb,** *n.* photographic light bulb which makes a short burst of light when you take a photograph. **flash•cube,** *n.* square block of four flash bulbs. **flash•er,** *n. inf.* man who exposes his private parts. **flash•gun,** *n.* photographic device for holding a flashbulb. **flash•i•ly,** *adv.* in a flashy way. **flash•i•ness,** *n.* being flashy. **flash•ing,** *n.* metal strip which covers a joint in a roof. **flash•light,** *n.* portable electric light which you can hold in your hand. **flash•point,** *n.* temperature at which gas or gasoline vapor will ignite/moment at which a revolution will break out. **flash•y,** *adj.* showy and bright but of poor quality.

flask [flɑːsk] *n.* (small) bottle or other container for liquids.

flat [flæt] 1. *adj. & adv.* (**flatter, flattest**) (a) level/smooth; punctured (tire); **f. rate** = fixed charge which never changes. (b) (*of drink*) no longer sparkling. (c) (*of battery*) no longer producing electricity. (d) (*of music*) below the correct pitch. (e) definite (refusal). (f) **to go f. out** = as fast as you can go; **f. broke** = with no money at all. 2. *n.* (a) place which is level; **f. racing** = horse racing on a level course, not over jumps. (b) flat tire. (c) (*esp. Brit.*) accommodation made up of a set of rooms, usu. on one floor, in a building containing several such groups of rooms. (d) note in music which is a semitone lower. **flat•fish,** *n.* type of fish with a flattened body. **flat•ly,** *adv.* definitely. **flat•ten,** *v.* to make flat. **flat•worm,** *n.* worm with a flat body.

flat•ter ['flætə] *v.* (a) to praise (s.o.) insincerely. (b) to make (s.o.) feel honored. (c) **to f. yourself** = to deceive yourself/to persuade yourself that sth is true, when it is not. **flat•ter•er,** *n.* person who flatters. **flat•ter•y,** *n.* insincere praise.

flat•u•lence ['flætjuləns] *n.* gas in the intestine. **flat•u•lent,** *adj.* suffering from flatulence.

flaunt [flɔːnt] *v.* to display (sth) in a vulgar way to attract attention.

flau•tist ['flɔːtɪst] *n.* flutist.

fla•vor, *Brit.* **fla•vour** ['fleɪvə] 1. *n.* taste. 2. *v.* to add spices and seasoning in cooking; to add a flavor to (sth). **fla•vor•ing,** *n.* substance added to food to give a particular taste.

flaw [flɔː] 1. *n.* fault/mistake; defect. 2. *v.* to spoil. **flaw•less,** *adj.* perfect.

flax [flæks] *n.* (*no pl.*) plant used for making linen cloth. **flax•en-haired,** *adj.* fair-haired.

flay [fleɪ] *v.* (a) to strip the skin off (an animal). (b) to criticize (s.o.) harshly.

flea [fliː] *n.* tiny blood-sucking insect that jumps. **flea bite,** *n.* place where a flea has bitten. **flea mar•ket,** *n.* market for secondhand goods.

fleck [flek] 1. *n.* small spot. 2. *v.* to mark (sth) with spots.

fled [fled] *v. see* **flee.**

fledg•ling ['fledʒlɪŋ] *n.* small bird ready to fly from the nest.

flee [fliː] *v.* (**fled**) to run away (**from**).

fleece [fliːs] 1. *n.* wool of a sheep. 2. *v. Sl.* to cheat (s.o.) and take their money. **fleec•y,** *adj.* made of fleece; covered with fleece; looking like fleece.

fleet [fliːt] 1. *n.* (a) group of ships belonging together. (b) collection of vehicles. 2. *adj.* rapid (footsteps). **fleet•ing** ['fli:tɪŋ] *adj.* short and quick. **fleet•ing•ly**, *adv.* rapidly.

flesh [fleʃ] *n.* (a) soft part of the body covering the bones; **in the f.** = in reality (not on TV or in photographs); **a f. wound** = one which is not too deep; **his own f. and blood** = his relations/his family. (b) soft part of a fruit. **flesh•y**, *adj.* fat/plump.

fleur-de-lys [flɜ:də'li:s] *n.* lily design, formerly the emblem of France.

flew [flu:] *v. see* **fly**.

flex [fleks] 1. *n.* flexible insulated cable for carrying electricity. 2. *v.* to bend. **flex•i•bil•i•ty** [fleksɪ'bɪlɪtɪ] *n.* ability to bend easily/to adapt to new circumstances. **flex•i•ble**, *adj.* (a) easy to bend. (b) adaptable. **flex•i•bly**, *adv.* in a flexible way. **flex•time, flexitime,** *n.* system where workers can start and stop their day's work at various times.

flib•ber•ti•gib•bet ['flɪbətɪdʒɪbrɪt] *n.* silly, empty-headed person.

flick [flɪk] 1. *n.* little sharp blow/tap. 2. *v.* (a) to hit lightly. (b) to move sth with a light, quick movement.

flick•er ['flɪkə] 1. *n.* trembling/quivering. 2. *v.* to tremble/to quiver; to burn unsteadily.

fli•er ['flaɪə] *n. see* **fly**.

flight [flaɪt] *n.* (a) journey through the air; flying. (b) group of birds/aircraft flying together. (c) **f. of stairs** = group of stairs in one direction. (d) running away; **to put to f.** = to chase away; **to take f.** = to run away. **flight deck,** *n.* (a) flat surface on an aircraft carrier on which aircraft land and take off. (b) section at the front of a large aircraft where the pilots sit. **flight•less**, *adj.* (bird) which cannot fly. **flight re•cord•er,** *n.* box carried on a plane where details of the flight are recorded automatically. **flight•y** ['flaɪtɪ] *adj.* silly and empty-headed.

flim•sy ['flɪmzɪ] *adj.* (*of material*) light and thin; poorly made; poor (excuse). **flim•si•ly**, *adv.* in a flimsy way. **flim•si•ness**, *n.* being flimsy.

flinch [flɪntʃ] *v.* to move back in pain/fear.

fling [flɪŋ] 1. *n.* (a) lively dance (esp. as done in Scotland). (b) period of letting off one's high spirits. 2. *v.* (**flung**) to throw wildly.

flint [flɪnt] *n.* (a) very hard type of rock which makes sparks when struck. (b) small piece of metal which makes a spark to light a cigarette lighter. **flint•y**, *adj.* hard/severe (look).

flip [flɪp] *v.* (**flipped**) to hit lightly; **to f. over** = to

turn over quickly. **flip flops,** *n. pl.* rubber sandals held on by a strap between the toes. **flip side,** *n.* second side of a record.

flip•pant ['flɪpənt] *adj.* joking about things which should be taken seriously. **flip•pant•ly**, *adv.* in a flippant way.

flip•per ['flɪpə] *n.* (a) limb of a sea animal used for swimming. (b) long flat piece of rubber which you can attach to your foot to help you swim faster.

flirt [flɜ:t] 1. *n.* person, esp. woman, who flirts. 2. *v.* to play at attracting people of the opposite sex for amusement. **flir•ta•tion** [flɜ:'teɪʃn] *n.* brief love affair. **flir•ta•tious**, *adj.* (person) who flirts a lot.

flit [flɪt] 1. *n.* light, quick movement. 2. *v.* (**flitted**) to move lightly and quickly.

flitch [flɪtʃ] *n.* (*pl.* **-es**) side of bacon.

float [fləʊt] 1. *n.* (a) piece of cork, etc., attached to a fishing line which will float on the surface of the water. (b) decorated vehicle in a parade. 2. *v.* to (make sth) lie on the top of a liquid; to start up (a company) by selling shares in it; to let (a currency) find its own exchange rate internationally and not fix it at a certain amount. **float•ing**, *adj.* resting on the surface of a liquid.

flock [flɒk] 1. *n.* (a) group of similar animals together, esp. sheep/goats/birds. (b) waste cotton. 2. *v.* to move in a group; **to f. together** = to come together in a group.

floe [fləʊ] *n.* large sheet of ice floating on the sea.

flog [flɒg] *v.* (**flogged**) (a) to beat hard, usu. with a whip. (b) *Sl.* to sell.

flood [flʌd] 1. *n.* (a) large amount of water over land which is usu. dry. (b) large amount of (tears/letters, etc.). 2. *v.* to cover with water; **they flooded in** = came in large numbers. **flood•gate,** *n.* part of a lock/sluice/dam in a river, which can be opened or shut and which helps control the flow of the water. **flood•light.** 1. *n.* powerful light often used for lighting the outside of a building or a sports playing field at night. 2. *v.* (**floodlit**) to light with floodlights.

floor [flɔ:] 1. *n.* (a) part of a room on which you walk. (b) story/one level of rooms in a building. (c) part of an assembly room where people discuss; **to take the f.** = to start speaking in a discussion. 2. *v.* (a) to knock to the ground. (b) to amaze and puzzle (s.o.). **floor•board,** *n.* long flat piece of wood used for making wooden floors. **floor•cloth,** *n.* cloth for

---

æ **back**, ɑ: **farm**, ɒ: **top**, aɪ **pipe**, aʊ **how**, aɪə **fire**, aʊə **flower**, ɔ: **bought**, ɔɪ **toy**, e **fed**, eə **hair**, eɪ **take**, ə **afraid**, əʊ **boat**, əʊə **lower**, ɜ: **word**, i: **heap**, ɪ **hit**, ɪə **hear**, u: **school**, ʊ **book**, ʌ **but**, b **back**, d **dog**, ð **then**, dʒ **just**, f **fog**, g **go**, h **hand**, j **yes**, k **catch**, l **last**, m **mix**, n **nut**, ŋ **sing**, p **penny**, r **round**, s **some**, ʃ **short**, t **too**, tʃ **chop**, θ **thing**, v **voice**, w **was**, z **zoo**, ʒ **treasure**

washing floors. **floor•show**, *n.* nightclub entertainment.

flop [flɒp] 1. *n.* (a) *inf.* failure. (b) movement of sth falling limply. 2. *v.* (**flopped**) (a) to fall/to sit/to lie limply or heavily. (b) *inf.* to fail. **flop•py**, *adj.* which hangs limply; **f. disk** = disk used in a computer.

flo•ra ['flɔːrə] *n.* wild plants (of an area). **flo•ral**, *adj.* referring to flowers.

flo•ret ['flɒrɪt] *n.* little flower which is part of a flowerhead.

flo•ri•bun•da [flɒrɪ'bʌndə] *n.* type of rose with many small flowers.

flor•id ['flɒrɪd] *adj.* red (face).

flor•in ['flɒrɪn] *n.* (*old*) British coin worth two shillings.

flo•rist ['flɒrɪst] *n.* person who sells flowers.

floss [flɒs] *n.* waste silk threads; **dental f.** = thin thread for pulling between the teeth to remove pieces of food.

flo•ta•tion [fləu'teɪʃn] *n.* starting of a new company by selling shares in it.

flo•til•la [flə'tɪlə] *n.* small group of boats.

flot•sam ['flɒtsəm] *n.* (*no pl.*) trash or refuse floating in the water.

flounce [flauns] 1. *n.* border of ruffled cloth (attached to a skirt, etc.). 2. *v.* **to f. out** = to go out of a room showing your impatience and annoyance. **flounced**, *adj.* with flounces.

floun•der ['flaundə] 1. *n.* common edible flat fish. 2. *v.* (*also* **flounder about**) to move (in water) with difficulty; to be uncertain of an answer to a question.

flour ['flauə] *n.* grain crushed to powder, used for making bread/cakes, etc. **flour•mill**, *n.* place where grain is ground into flour. **flour•y**, *adj.* like flour.

flour•ish ['flʌrɪʃ] 1. *n.* (*pl.* -es) (a) a wide movement of the arm in the air. (b) large curve in handwriting. (c) fanfare (of trumpets). 2. *v.* (a) to grow well. (b) to wave (sth) in the air.

flout [flaut] *v.* to scorn/to disregard (sth).

flow [fləu] 1. *n.* movement of liquid/air, etc. 2. *v.* to move along smoothly. **flow•chart**, *n.* diagram showing the stages in a process.

flow•er ['flauə] 1. *n.* colorful part of a plant which produces the seed. 2. *v.* to make flowers. **flow•er•bed**, *n.* part of a garden where flowers are grown. **flow•er•pot**, *n.* container to grow plants in. **flow•er•y**, *adj.* (a) (*also* **flowered**) decorated with a pattern of flowers. (b) ornate (style).

flown [fləun] *v. see* **fly.**

flu [fluː] *n.* influenza/common illness like a bad cold, often with a high temperature.

fluc•tu•ate ['flʌktjueɪt] *v.* to move backward and forward/up and down. **fluc•tu•a•tion**

[flʌktju'eɪʃn] *n.* movement backward and forward/up and down.

flue [fluː] *n.* pipe leading to a chimney.

flu•en•cy ['fluənsɪ] *n.* ease of speaking. **flu•ent**, *adj.* able to speak easily. **flu•ent•ly**, *adv.* easily.

fluff [flʌf] 1. *n.* soft pieces of wool or hair. 2. *v. inf.* to do (sth) badly. **fluff•i•ness**, *n.* being fluffy. **fluff•y**, *adj.* like fluff; covered with fluff.

flu•id ['fluːɪd] 1. *n.* liquid. 2. *adj.* (situation/movement) which is not settled; changing. **flu•id•i•ty** [fluː'ɪdɪtɪ] *n.* being fluid.

fluke [fluːk] *n.* (a) *inf.* chance/lucky event. (b) one of the two flat parts of a whale's tail/of an anchor. (c) type of flatworm.

flum•mox ['flʌməks] *v. inf.* to confuse (s.o.).

flung [flʌŋ] *v. see* **fling.**

flunk [flʌŋk] *v. inf.* to fail (an examination/a candidate).

flun•ky, flunkey ['flʌŋkɪ] *n.* (a) person who fawns on s.o. and tries to please. (b) servant.

fluo•res•cence [fluə'resns] *n.* ability to send out a glow of light when an electric current is applied. **fluo•res•cent**, *adj.* giving off light when electric current is applied.

fluor•ine ['fluəriːn] *n.* (*element:* F) pale yellow-green gas. **fluor•i•da•tion** [fluərai-'deɪʃn] *n.* adding fluoride to water (to prevent tooth decay). **fluor•ide** ['fluəraɪd] *n.* compound of fluorine; **f. toothpaste** = toothpaste with small amount of fluoride added in order to prevent tooth decay.

flur•ry ['flʌrɪ] *n.* (a) hurried excitement. (b) sudden small amount of snow, rain or wind.

flush [flʌʃ] 1. *n.* (*pl.* -es) (a) redness of the face. (b) rush of water. (c) (*at cards*) hand with all the cards of the same suit. 2. *v.* (a) to go red in the face. (b) **to f. out** = to drive out of hiding. (c) **to f. a toilet** = to wash it out by moving a handle which makes water rush through. 3. *adj.* (a) **f. with** = level with. (b) *inf.* having plenty of money to spend.

flust•er ['flʌstə] 1. *n.* nervous worry. 2. *v.* to worry/to confuse (s.o.).

flute [fluːt] *n.* (a) wind instrument played by blowing across a small hole at the end of a pipe. (b) long rounded groove. **flut•ed**, *adj.* decorated with grooves or scallops. **flut•ist**, *n.* person who plays the flute.

flut•ter ['flʌtə] 1. *n.* light movement, esp. of wings. 2. *v.* (a) to move (wings, etc.) quickly and lightly. (b) to move softly and quickly.

flu•vi•al ['fluːvɪəl] *adj.* referring to rivers.

flux [flʌks] *n.* (a) constant change. (b) substance used in soldering.

fly [flaɪ] 1. *n.* (*pl.* **flies**) (a) small insect with two wings; **f. fishing** = sport of fishing with an imitation fly as bait. (b) strip of material sewn along one edge, which covers a zipper, buttons, or other fastening on the front of trousers. 2. *v.* (**flew; has flown**) (a) to move through the air. (b) to move fast. (c) to put up (a flag). **fly•blown**, *adj.* rotten (meat). **fly•by**, *n.* flight of aircraft over a certain spot to celebrate sth. **fly-by-night**, *n. inf.* unreliable company. **fly•catch•er**, *n.* bird which catches flies. **fli•er, flyer**, *n.* (a) person who pilots an aircraft. (b) paper advertising sth. **fly•ing club**, *n.* club for people interested in flying aircraft. **fly•ing fish**, *n.* fish which jumps out of the water as it moves. **fly•ing sau•cer**, *n.* unidentified flying object which people claim to see and which they think comes from another planet. **fly•ing squad**, *n.* group of policemen who arrive quickly at the scene of a crime. **fly•ing start**, *n.* good beginning to a race/a new job, etc. **fly•leaf**, *n.* blank leaf of paper at the beginning and end of a book. **fly•past**, *n.* flyby. **fly•weight**, *n.* lightest category of boxer. **fly•wheel**, *n.* large heavy wheel which turns, keeping an engine working at a steady pace.

foal [fəʊl] *n.* young horse.

foam [fəʊm] 1. *n.* mass of small bubbles; **f. rubber** = rubber in blocks with many little holes in it, used for chair cushions, etc. 2. *v.* to make froth. **foam•y**, *adj.* covered with foam.

fob [fɒb] 1. *n.* little ornament attached to a watch-chain. 2. *v.* (**fobbed**) **to f. s.o. off with sth** = to deceive s.o. into accepting sth which they don't really want.

fo'c'sle [ˈfəʊksl] *n.* front part of a ship where the crew lives.

fo•cus [ˈfəʊkəs] 1. *n.* (a) (*pl.* **foci** [ˈfəʊsaɪ]) point where rays of light from an object meet; **in f.** = clearly visible; **out of f.** = blurred/not clear. (b) center of attention. 2. *v.* to adjust so as to be able to see clearly. **fo•cal**, *adj.* referring to a focus.

fod•der [ˈfɒdə] *n.* food for cows/sheep, etc.

foe [fəʊ] *n.* (*formal*) enemy/opponent.

foe•tus [ˈfiːtəs] *n. see* **fe•tus.**

fog [fɒg] *n.* thick mist through which it is difficult to see. **fog•gi•ness**, *n.* being foggy. **fog•gy**, *adj.* misty. **fog•horn**, *n.* horn which makes a deep, loud sound, used in fog as a warning to ships. **fog light**, *n.* headlight on a car, used in fog.

fo•gy, fogey [ˈfəʊgɪ] *n.* **old f.** = reactionary old man.

foi•ble [ˈfɔɪbl] *n.* slight flaw in character; weakness.

foil [fɔɪl] 1. *n.* (a) thin metal sheet; **tin f./aluminum f.** = foil used for wrapping food before cooking or for storage. (b) long thin sword with a button on the end used in the sport of fencing. (c) person who contrasts sharply with another and so makes the other's qualities stand out. 2. *v.* to defeat; to prevent (a plot) being put into effect.

foist [fɔɪst] *v.* **to f. sth on s.o.** = to force s.o. to accept sth which they don't want.

fold [fəʊld] 1. *n.* (a) small enclosure for sheep. (b) crease (in paper/cloth, etc.) 2. *v.* (a) to bend (sth) so that one part is on top of another. (b) **to f. your arms** = to bend your arms together in front of your chest. **fold•er**, *n.* cardboard envelope for holding papers. **fold•ing**, *adj.* able to be folded. **fold up**, *v.* (a) to bend (sth) over to make smaller than before. (b) *inf.* to finish/to end.

fo•li•age [ˈfəʊlɪdʒ] *n.* leaves on a tree or plant. **fo•li•ar**, *adj.* referring to leaves.

fo•li•o [ˈfəʊlɪəʊ] *n.* (a) very large size of book. (b) page number.

folk [fəʊk] *n. pl.* people; **my f.** = my family. **folk dance**, *n.* traditional dance. **folk•lore**, *n.* traditional stories and beliefs. **folk•song**, *n.* traditional song.

fol•li•cle [ˈfɒlɪkl] *n.* small hole (in the skin) out of which a hair grows.

fol•low [ˈfɒləʊ] *v.* (a) to go after/to come after; to continue along (a road). (b) to act in accordance with (a rule). (c) to understand. **fol•low•er**, *n.* supporter. **fol•low•ing**, *adj.* which follows; next. **follow up**, *v.* to investigate/to research (sth) further.

fol•ly [ˈfɒlɪ] *n.* silly behavior.

fo•ment [fəˈment] *v.* (*formal*) to stir up (trouble). **fo•men•ta•tion** [fəʊmenˈteɪʃn] *n.* act of stirring up trouble.

fond [fɒnd] *adj.* loving; **I am f. of music** = I like music. **fond•ly**, *adv.* in a fond way. **fond•ness**, *n.* liking/love.

fon•dle [ˈfɒndl] *v.* to stroke lovingly.

fon•due [ˈfɒndjuː] *n.* dish of melted cheese into which pieces of bread are dipped, or of hot oil into which pieces of meat are dipped, or of chocolate into which pieces of fruit are dipped.

font [fɒnt] *n.* (a) basin holding holy water for baptism in a church. (b) set of type of one particular size and design.

æ back, ɑː farm, ɒ top, aɪ pipe, aʊ how, aɪə fire, aʊə flower, ɔː bought, ɔɪ toy, e fed, eəhair, eɪ take, ə afraid, əʊ boat, əʊə lower, ɜː word, iː heap, ɪ hit, ɪə hear, uː school, ʊ book, ʌ but, b back, d dog, ð then, dʒ just, f fog, g go, h hand, j yes, k catch, l last, m mix, n nut, ŋ sing, p penny, r round, s some, ʃ short, t too, tʃ chop, θ thing, v voice, w was, z zoo, ʒ treasure

fon•ta•nel, fon•ta•nelle [fɒntə'nel] *n.* soft membrane between the pieces of the skull of a baby.

food [fu:d] *n.* substances eaten by people and animals or taken in by plants; **f. poisoning** = illness caused by sth eaten. **food•stuff,** *n.* thing that can be eaten.

fool [fu:l] 1. *n.* idiot/stupid person. 2. *v.* (a) **to f. around** = to play around in a silly way. (b) to trick (s.o.). **fool•har•dy,** *adj.* brave, but taking unnecessary risks. **fool•ish,** *adj.* silly/stupid. **fool•ish•ly,** *adv.* stupidly. **fool•ish•ness,** *n.* silliness/stupidity. **fool•proof,** *adj.* so simple that even an idiot could use it safely; which cannot fail. **fools•cap** ['fu:lskæp] *n.* large size of writing paper.

foot [fut] 1. *n.* (*pl.* **feet**) (a) end part of the leg on which you stand; **on f.** = walking; **under f.** = on the ground; *inf.* **to put your f. in it** = to say sth embarrassing; **to put your f. down** = to be firm/not to give in. (b) base/end of sth. (c) measure of length (= 12 inches or 30.5 cm); **three feet wide.** 2. *v.* (a) **to f. it** = to walk. (b) **to f. the bill** = to pay the bill. **foot-and-mouth dis•ease,** *n.* disease of cows. **foot•age,** *n.* (*no pl.*) length or amount of motion picture which has been exposed. **foot•ball** *n.* (a) game played between two teams with a ball which is kicked; (b) ball used in the game of football. **foot•brake,** *n.* brake (on a machine or car) operated by the foot. **foot•bridge,** *n.* small bridge for people to walk across. **foot•fall,** *n.* footstep. **foot•hills,** *n. pl.* lower slopes. **foot•hold,** *n.* (a) place where you can put your foot when climbing. (b) small position on which you can build. **foot•ing,** *n.* (a) safe place for your feet. (b) **to put things on a firm f.** = to base things firmly. **foot•lights,** *n. pl.* row of lights along the front of the stage in a theater. **foot•loose,** *adj.* free to go anywhere; with no ties. **foot•man,** *n.* (*pl.* **-men**) male servant. **foot•note,** *n.* explanation at the bottom of a page, referring to sth on the page. **foot•path,** *n.* path for walkers. **foot•print,** *n.* mark left by the foot on the ground. **foot sol•dier,** *n.* soldier who travels on foot. **foot•sore,** *adj.* (person) with feet which hurt. **foot•step,** *n.* sound of a foot touching the ground. **foot•stool,** *n.* small stool which supports the feet. **foot•wear,** *n.* (*no pl.*) boots and shoes. **foot•work,** *n.* (*no pl.*) way of using your feet (esp. in sports).

foot•ling ['fu:tlɪŋ] *adj.* silly/insignificant.

for [fɔ:] 1. *prep.* (a) in exchange. (b) in support of. (c) used as. (d) because of. (e) in the direction of; **the train f. Chicago.** (f) toward; **my love f. you.** (g) over a distance of/over a length of time; **f. miles; f. a month.** (h) as a present to; belonging to; **a letter f. you.** (i) in the place of; **can you write this letter f. me?** (j) with the purpose of; **to go f. a walk; run f. the bus** = to catch the bus. (k) **f. all that** = in spite of everything; **as f.** = regarding; **f. sale** = able to be bought; **f. example** = to name one thing out of many; **f. ever/f. good** = always; **f. the most part** = usually. 2. *conj.* because.

for•age ['fɒrɪdʒ] 1. *n.* food for horses and cattle. 2. *v.* (a) to search for food/supplies. (b) to rummage/to look for sth.

for•ay ['fɒreɪ] *n.* sudden attack.

for•bade [fə'bæd] *v. see* **for•bid.**

for•bear•ance [fɔ:'beərəns] *n.* patience. **for•bear•ing,** *adj.* patient/long-suffering.

for•bid [fə'bɪd] *v.* (forbade [fə'bæd]; forbidden) to tell (s.o.) not to do sth. **for•bid•ding,** *adj.* sinister/looking dangerous.

force [fɔ:s] 1. *n.* (a) strength/power; **in f.** = (i) in large numbers; (ii) (law which is) operating/working. (b) organized group of people; **police f; the armed forces** = navy, army and air force. 2. *v.* (a) to move by using strength. (b) to compel/to make (s.o.) do sth. (c) to make (plants) grow faster/earlier than normal. **force back,** *v.* to push sth back very hard. **forced,** *adj.* (a) compelled; **f. landing** = quick landing of an aircraft because sth is wrong. (b) artificial/not real. **force-feed,** *v.* (force-fed) to feed (s.o. on hunger strike) by force. **force•ful,** *adj.* strong/powerful. **force•ful•ly,** *adv.* in a forceful way. **force•ful•ness,** *n.* being forceful. **force ma•jeure,** *n.* thing which happens (such as a war) which cannot be controlled by parties to a contract. **force•meat,** *n.* minced meat used as stuffing (for turkeys, etc.).

for•ceps ['fɔ:seps] *n.* (*no pl.*) pincers used by doctors in surgery.

for•ci•ble ['fɔ:sɪbl] *adj.* done by/with force. **for•ci•bly,** *adv.* using force.

ford [fɔ:d] 1. *n.* shallow part of a river where you can cross by going through the water. 2. *v.* to cross a river by going through a shallow part. **ford•a•ble,** *adj.* (river) which can be forded.

fore [fɔ:] 1. *n.* front part of a ship; **f. and aft** = front and back of a ship. **to come to the f.** = to become prominent. 2. *adj.* front/before (*used as a prefix in words such as* **forearm, foresee**). **fore•arm.** 1. *n.* ['fɔ:rɑ:m] part of the arm between the hand and the elbow. 2. *v.* [fɔ:'ɑ:m] to get ready (as for a fight) beforehand. **fore•bears,** *n. pl.* (*old*) ancestors. **fore•bod•ing** [fɔ:'bəʊdɪŋ] *n.* feeling that sth evil will take place. **fore•cast.** 1. *n.* description of what will happen in the future. 2. *v.*

(forecast) to say what will happen in the future. **fore•cast•er**, *n.* person who says what will happen in the future, esp. concerning the weather. **fore•cas•tle** ['fəuksl] *n.* front part of a ship where the crew live. **fore•close** [fɔː'kləuz] *v.* to take away property because the owner cannot pay back money which he has borrowed on its security. **fore•clo•sure**, *n.* act of foreclosing. **fore•court**, *n.* courtyard in front of a building. **fore•fa•ther**, *n.* ancestor. **fore•fin•ger**, *n.* index finger/first finger next to the thumb. **fore•foot**, *n.* front foot (of an animal). **fore•front**, *n.* **to be in the f. of a campaign** = to be one of the leaders. **fore•go** [fɔː'gəu] *v.* (**forewent, has foregone**) to do without. **fore•go•ing**, *adj.* which has gone before. **fore•gone**, *adj.* decided in advance; **it was a f. conclusion** = everyone knew. **fore•ground**, *n.* part of a picture/scene nearest the viewer. **fore•hand**, *adj.* (*in tennis*) (stroke) played with the palm of the hand facing forward. **fore•head** ['fɒrɪd, 'fɔː'hed] *n.* part of the head between the eyes and the hair. **fore•knowl•edge**, *n.* knowledge in advance. **fore•land**, *n.* headland. **fore•leg**, *n.* front leg of an animal. **fore•man**, *n.* (*pl.* -men) (a) (*in a factory*) workman in charge of several others. (b) **f. of a jury** = spokesperson for the jury. **fore•most**, *adj. & adv.* first/chief; **first and f.** = first of all. **fore•noon**, *n.* morning. **fore•paw**, *n.* front paw. **fore•run•ner**, *n.* person/thing coming before another more important one. **fore•see** [fɔː'siː] *v.* (**foresaw; has foreseen**) to feel in advance that sth will happen. **fore•see•a•ble**, *adj.* which can be foreseen. **fore•shad•ow** [fɔː'ʃædəu] *v.* to be a sign of (sth to come). **fore•shore**, *n.* part of a beach which is covered by the sea at each high tide. **fore•sight**, *n.* ability to see what will probably happen in the future; ability to plan for emergencies. **fore•skin**, *n.* loose skin covering the end of the penis. **fore•stall** [fɔː'stɔːl] *v.* to anticipate/to stop (s.o. doing sth). **fore•taste**, *n.* small bit of sth that will be had later on. **fore•tell** [fɔː'tel] *v.* (**foretold**) to predict/to say what will happen in the future. **fore•thought**, *n.* thinking ahead. **fore•warned**, *adj.* warned in advance. **fore•word**, *n.* short section at the beginning of a book introducing it to the reader.

for•eign ['fɒrən] *adj.* (a) not belonging to your own country. (b) strange; **f. exchange** = ex-

changing the money of one country for money of another; **f. to s.o.'s nature** = very strange for s.o. to do it. (c) **f. body** = thing from outside which lodges in your body. **for•eign•er**, *n.* person who does not belong to your country.

fo•ren•sic [fə'rensɪk] *adj.* referring to or used in courts of law or public discussion and debate; **f. medicine** = use of medicine for purposes of the law, as in solving crimes involving death.

for•est ['fɒrɪst] *n.* large area covered with trees. **for•est•er**, **forest ranger**, *n.* person whose job it is to look after a forest. **for•est•ry**, *n.* job of looking after a forest and its trees; science of growing and maintaining forests.

for•ev•er [fə'revə] *adv.* always.

for•ex ['fɒreks] *n. abbrev. for* foreign exchange.

for•feit ['fɔːfɪt] 1. *n.* thing taken/lost as a punishment. 2. *v.* to lose (sth), esp. as a punishment. **for•fei•ture** ['fɔːfɪtʃə] *n.* act of forfeiting.

for•gath•er [fɔː'gæðə] *v.* (*formal*) to gather together.

for•gave [fə'geɪv] *v. see* **for•give.**

forge [fɔːdʒ] 1. *n.* blacksmith's workshop where he makes horseshoes and other iron objects. 2. *v.* (a) to work (metal) in a forge. (b) to copy (sth) illegally. (c) **to f. ahead** = to go forward quickly. **forged**, *adj.* copied illegally. **forg•er**, *n.* person who copies sth illegally. **forg•er•y**, *n.* (a) making an illegal copy. (b) illegal copy.

for•get [fə'get] *v.* (**forgot; has forgotten**) not (to be able) to remember; to leave (sth) behind. **for•get•ful**, *adj.* often unable to remember. **for•get•ful•ness**, *n.* being forgetful. **for•get-me-not**, *n.* small blue-flowered plant.

for•give [fə'gɪv] *v.* (**forgave** [fə'geɪv]; **has forgiven**) to pardon/to stop being angry with (s.o.). **for•giv•a•ble**, *adj.* able to be pardoned/understandable. **for•give•ness**, *n.* pardon(ing).

for•go [fɔː'gəu] *v.* (**forwent, has forgone**) to do without.

for•got [fə'gɒt] *v. see* **for•get.**

fork [fɔːk] 1. *n.* (a) object with a handle at one end and sharp points at the other, used for picking things up. (b) place where a branch leaves a tree trunk. (c) place where two roads split. 2. *v.* (a) (*of a road*) to split into two parts. (b) *inf.* **to f. out** = to pay for sth, usu. unwillingly. **forked**, *adj.* divided into two. **fork•lift**

æ back, ɑː farm, ɒ top, aɪ pipe, aʊ how, aɪə fire, aʊə flower, ɔː bought, ɔɪ toy, e fed, eəhair, eɪ take, ə afraid, əʊ boat, əʊə lower, vː word, iː heap, ɪ hit, ɪə hear, uː school, ʊ book, ʌ but, b back, d dog, ð then, dʒ just, f fog, g go, h hand, j yes, k catch, l last, m mix, n nut, ŋ sing, p penny, r round, s some, ʃ short, t too, tʃ chop, θ thing, v voice, w was, z zoo, ʒ treasure

truck, *n.* motor vehicle which can lift heavy loads on metal arms.

for•lorn [fə'lɔːn] *adj.* left alone and feeling sad; **f. hope** = very slight hope. **for•lorn•ly,** *adv.* sadly.

form [fɔːm] 1. *n.* (a) shape. (b) paper with blank spaces for you to fill in. (c) condition of an athlete/racing animal; **he's in good f.** = he's in a good mood/he's very amusing. (d) structure/style of a piece of writing/a piece of music. (e) school class, esp. in a private school. (f) custom/behavior. (g) frame in which type is placed for printing. 2. *v.* (a) to shape; to take shape. (b) to be produced. (c) to organize; **they formed a club. for•ma•tion** [fɔː'meɪʃn] *n.* shaping/forming of sth. **for•ma•tive** ['fɔːmətɪv] *adj.* referring to the early years of life when a person's character is being formed.

for•mal ['fɔːml] *adj.* (a) ceremonial/done according to certain rules. (b) regular; clearly written (agreement). **for•mal•i•ty** [fɔː'mælɪtɪ] *n.* thing which has to be done to conform with the rules but which does not mean much. **for•mal•i•za•tion,** *n.* making formal. **for•mal•ize,** *v.* to make (an agreement) formal/regular. **for•mal•ly,** *adv.* according to rules/ceremonially.

form•al•de•hyde [fɔː'mældɪhaɪd] *n.* gas used in solution to make formalin. **for•ma•lin,** *n.* solution used as a disinfectant and preservative.

for•mat ['fɔːmæt] 1. *n.* (a) shape/size (in which sth is made). (b) dimensions of a page/book. 2. *v.* (**formatted**) to arrange text on a computer, so that it is ready for final printing; to prepare a computer disk so that it is ready to receive data.

form•er ['fɔːmə] *adj.* (a) earlier. (b) first thing mentioned (of two). **for•mer•ly,** *adv.* at an earlier time.

for•mic ['fɔːmɪk] *adj.* **f. acid** = acid found in the sting of ants.

For•mi•ca [fɔː'maɪkə] *n.* trademark for a hard plastic.

for•mi•da•ble ['fɔːmɪdəbl] *adj.* frighteningly difficult; very impressive (person).

for•mu•la ['fɔːmjulə] *n.* (*pl.* **-ae** [-iː]) (a) statement, usu. of a scientific fact and often by means of symbols. (b) milky food for babies. **for•mu•late,** *v.* (a) to express (sth) as a formula. (b) to express (an idea) clearly. **for•mu•la•tion,** *n.* expressing clearly.

for•ni•cate ['fɔːnɪkeɪt] *v.* to have sexual intercourse (when not married). **for•ni•ca•tion,** *n.* act of fornicating.

for•sake [fɔː'seɪk] *v.* (**forsook; has forsaken**) to leave behind. **for•sak•en,** *adj.* abandoned/deserted.

for•swear [fɔː'sweə] *v.* (*formal*) to swear not to do (sth).

for•syth•i•a [fɔː'saɪθɪə] *n.* common garden shrub with yellow flowers.

fort [fɔːt] *n.* strong building which can be defended against enemy attacks; **to hold the f.** = to be in charge while s.o. is away.

for•te ['fɔːtɪ] 1. *n.* (a) loud piece of music. (b) particular ability. 2. *adv.* played loudly.

forth [fɔːθ] *adv.* (*formal*) forward; **back and f.** = backward and forward; **and so f.** = and so on. **forth•com•ing,** *adj.* (a) soon to appear. (b) *inf.* friendly/full of information. **forth•right,** *adj.* direct/blunt (way of speaking). **forth•with,** *adv.* immediately.

for•ti•fy ['fɔːtɪfaɪ] *v.* to make strong; **fortified wine** = wine (like sherry/port) with extra alcohol added. **for•ti•fi•ca•tion** [fɔːtɪfɪ'keɪʃn] *n.* (a) making strong. (b) **fortifications** = walls/towers built to defend a city.

for•tis•si•mo [fɔː'tɪsɪməu] *adv.* very loudly (in music).

for•ti•tude ['fɔːtɪtjuːd] *n.* strength of mind/bravery, esp. when in pain.

fort•night ['fɔːtnaɪt] *n.* two weeks. **fort•night•ly,** *adj. & adv.* once every two weeks.

for•tress ['fɔːtrəs] *n.* (*pl.* **-es**) strong building/castle.

for•tu•i•tous [fɔː'tjuɪtəs] *adj.* accidental/happening by chance. **for•tu•i•tous•ly,** *adv.* by chance/accidentally.

for•tune ['fɔːtjuːn] *n.* (a) luck/chance. (b) what will happen in the future. (c) large amount of money. **for•tu•nate** ['fɔːtʃənət] *adj.* lucky. **for•tu•nate•ly,** *adv.* by good luck. **for•tune-tel•ler,** *n.* person who says what will happen in the future by looking at cards or lines on your hand.

for•ty ['fɔːtɪ] *n.* number 40; *inf.* **f. winks** = short sleep in the daytime. **for•ti•eth, 40th,** *adj. & n.* referring to 40.

fo•rum ['fɔːrəm] *n.* (a) place where matters of general interest can be discussed. (b) public discussion.

for•ward ['fɔːwəd] 1. *adj.* (a) toward the front. (b) advanced/well ahead. (c) too confident. 2. *adv.* (a) **from that day f.** = from then on. (b) to the front; **to look f. to sth** = to wait for sth with pleasure. 3. *n.* (*in sports*) player in an attacking/front position. 4. *v.* (a) to send on (a letter) to another address. (b) to help (sth) progress. **for•ward-look•ing,** *adj.* thinking ahead/dealing with the future optimistically. **for•ward, forwards,** *adv.* to the front.

fos•sil ['fɒsl] *n.* remains of an animal/plant left in a rock; *inf.* elderly old-fashioned person. **fos•sil•i•za•tion,** *n.* becoming fossilized.

fos•sil•iz•ed ['fɒsɪlaɪzd] adj. turned into a rock.

fos•ter ['fɒstə] v. (a) to bring up (a child who is not your own). (b) to encourage (an idea, etc.). fos•ter-child, n. (pl. -children) child brought up by parents who are not his own. fos•ter home, n. family/home where a foster-child is brought up. fos•ter-moth•er, n. mother who fosters a child. fos•ter-par•ents, n. pl. parents who foster a child.

fought [fɔːt] v. see fight.

foul [faʊl] 1. adj. (-er, -est) (a) bad/dirty/unpleasant (taste, language, air, etc.). (b) against the rules of a game. (c) f. play = murder. (d) to fall/run f. of = to get into trouble with. 2. n. action against the rules of the game. 3. v. (a) to make dirty. (b) to do sth against the rules of the game. (c) the boat fouled its anchor = its anchor got stuck in weeds, etc.; inf. to f. sth up = to make a mess of sth/to create a problem. foul•ly, adv. in a foul way. foul•mouthed, adj. with foul language. foul•ness, n. being foul.

found [faʊnd] v. (a) to establish/to begin (sth). (b) to base (a story, etc.). (c) to melt (metal); to make (sth) out of molten metal; see also find. foun•da•tion [faʊn'deɪʃn] n. (a) establishing/beginning. (b) base below ground on which a building is laid; f. stone = cornerstone. (c) organization which provides money for certain projects. (d) colored cream put on the face under powder. found•er. 1. n. person who establishes/begins sth. 2. v. (of a boat, scheme) to collapse/to sink. found•ling, n. baby abandoned by its parents and found by s.o. else. found•ry, n. works where things are made from molten metal, etc.

fount [faʊnt] n. (old) fountain.

foun•tain ['faʊntɪn] n. jet of water in a street or garden; f. pen = pen which you can fill up with ink.

four [fɔː] n. (a) number 4; on all fours = on hands and knees. (b) four people (in a rowing boat). four-by-four, n. motor vehicle with four-wheel drive. four•fold, adv. & adj. four times as much. four•post•er (bed), n. bed with a tall post at each corner and curtains. four•some, n. (a) activity/game played by four people. (b) group of four people. four•teen, n. number 14. four•teenth, 14th, adj. referring to fourteen. fourth, 4th. 1. adj. referring to four. 2. n. quarter.

four-wheel drive, n. system powering all four wheels of a motor vehicle.

fowl [faʊl] n. (pl. fowl) domestic birds kept for food or eggs (chickens, ducks, turkeys and geese); wild f. = game birds which are shot for sport. fowl•ing piece, n. gun for shooting wild fowl.

fox [fɒks] 1. n. wild animal with reddish fur and a bushy tail. 2. v. to puzzle/to trick. fox cub, n. young fox. fox•glove, n. tall purple and white flower found in woods. fox•hound, n. dog used for hunting foxes. fox•hunt•ing, n. chasing foxes to catch and kill them, usu. with dogs. fox ter•ri•er, n. type of small dog. fox•trot, n. type of ballroom dance. fox•y, adj. crafty/cunning.

foy•er ['fɔɪeɪ] n. large entrance hall at the front of a hotel/theater/apartment house or in a house or apartment.

fra•cas ['frækɑː] n. noisy disturbance.

frac•tion ['frækʃn] n. (a) very small piece/amount. (b) (in mathematics) less than a whole number. frac•tion•al, adj. very small. frac•tion•al•ly, adv. by a very small amount.

frac•tious ['frækʃəs] adj. bad-tempered/crying (child). frac•tious•ness, n. being fractious.

frac•ture ['fræktʃə] 1. n. break (esp. in bones); simple f. = clean break of a bone; compound f. = one where the broken bone has pierced the skin. 2. v. to break (a bone).

frag•ile ['frædʒaɪl] adj. easily broken/delicate. fra•gil•i•ty [frə'dʒɪlɪti] n. being easily broken.

frag•ment 1. n. ['frægmənt] small piece. 2. v. [fræg'ment] to break into small pieces. frag•men•tar•y, adj. in pieces/not complete. frag•men•ta•tion, n. breaking into small pieces.

fra•grance ['freɪgrəns] n. pleasant smell. fra•grant, adj. sweet-smelling.

frail [freɪl] adj. weak. frail•ty, n. weakness.

frame [freɪm] 1. n. (a) supporting structure of a building/ship/aircraft/bicycle/glasses, etc.; f. house = wooden house. (b) bone structure of a person/animal; f. of mind = temper/mood. (c) border of wood/metal/plastic around a picture/mirror/window. (d) one picture in a length of motion-picture film. (e) glass box for protecting young plants in a garden. 2. v. (a) to put into words. (b) to put a border around (sth). (c) inf. to make (an innocent person) appear guilty. frame-up, n. inf. arrangement

æ back, ɑː farm, ɒ top, aɪ pipe, aʊ how, aɪe fire, aʊə flower, ɔː bought, ɔɪ toy, e fed, eəhair, eɪ take, ə afraid, əʊ boat, əʊə lower, ʌ: word, iː heap, ɪ hit, ɪə hear, uː school, ʊ book, ʌ but, b back, d dog, ð then, dʒ just, f fog, g go, h hand, j yes, k catch, l last, m mix, n nut, ŋ sing, p penny, r round, s some, ʃ short, t too, tʃ chop, θ thing, v voice, w was, z zoo, ʒ treasure

whereby an innocent person is framed.
frame•work, *n.* (a) structure supporting a
building, etc. (b) basis of a plan.

franc [fræŋk] *n.* unit of money in France, Belgium and Switzerland.

fran•chise ['fræntʃaɪz] 1. *n.* (a) right to vote.
(b) permit to sell a company's products in a
certain region/to trade using a well-known
brand name. 2. *v.* to license a product to others who will sell it and pay a fee for its use.
fran•chi•see, *n.* person who runs a business
under franchise. **fran•chis•or,** *n.* person
who licenses s.o. to operate a franchise.

Franco- ['fræŋkəʊ] *prefix meaning* between
France and another country.

frank [fræŋk] 1. *adj.* plain-speaking; (person)
who says what he thinks. 2. *v.* to stamp (a letter) on a special machine. **frank•ly,** *adv.*
speaking truthfully. **frank•ness,** *n.* saying
what you think.

frank•furt•er ['fræŋkfɜːtə] *n.* long spiced sausage, which is boiled and sometimes eaten
with a roll.

frank•in•cense ['fræŋkɪnsens] *n.* gum from a
tree, burned as incense.

fran•tic ['fræntɪk] *adj.* worried and wildly excited. **fran•ti•cal•ly,** *adv.* in an excited and
worried way.

fra•ter•nal [frə'tɜːnl] *adj.* brotherly.
fra•ter•nal•ly, *adv.* in a fraternal way.
fra•ter•ni•ty, *n.* (a) society of men with similar interests. (b) student association for men
at a college or university. (c) brotherly feeling.
frat•er•ni•za•tion [frætənaɪ'zeɪʃn] *n.* act of
fraternizing. **frat•er•nize** ['frætənaɪz] *v.* to
become friendly (with s.o.).

frat•ri•cide ['frætrɪsaɪd] *n.* murder of your
brother.

fraud [frɔːd] *n.* (a) (piece of) dishonesty. (b) person pretending to be sth he is not; thing that is
not what you expect. **fraud•u•lence,** *n.* dishonesty. **fraud•u•lent,** *adj.* dishonest.

fraught [frɔːt] *adj.* (a) (with) full of (problems,
danger). (b) *inf.* full of anxiety; worrying (situation).

fray [freɪ] 1. *n.* fight; **ready for the f.** = ready to
fight/ready to take part in the action. 2. *v.* (of
material) to become worn/to unravel so that
threads are loose.

fraz•zle ['fræzl] *n.* state of exhaustion.

freak [friːk] *n.* (a) unusual type of person/ani-
mal/plant. (b) extraordinary change in the
weather. (c) person who is fanatic about sth.
freak•ish, *adj.* unusual/extraordinary. **freak
out,** *v. inf.* to become very excited (as because
of the effect of drugs).

freck•le ['frekl] *n.* small brown mark on the
skin, often caused by the sun. **freck•led,** *adj.*
covered in freckles.

free [friː] 1. *adj.* (**freer, freest**) (a) not impris-
oned/not tied down. (b) not occupied. (c) not
costing any money. (d) able to do what you
want; **to be f. with sth** = to give sth away generously. (e) **to be f. from/of sth** = to be without
sth (usu. unpleasant). 2. *v.* (a) to get (a person)
out of prison. (b) to release from a difficult situation. **free•dom,** *n.* state of being free; **f. of
speech** = ability to say what you like.
free-for-all, *n.* general fight/general argument among several people. **free•hand,** *adj.
& adv.* (drawing) drawn without the help of
rulers/compasses, etc. **free•hold,** *n. & adj.*
right to own a property for ever.
free•hold•er, *n.* person who owns a free-
hold property. **free•lance.** 1. *adj. & n.* independent (worker), not employed by one
particular company. 2. *adv.* (to work) independently. 3. *v.* to work independently.
free•load•er, *n. inf.* person who lives on
money/gifts, etc. which he gets from other
people. **free•ly,** *adv.* in a frank manner/with-
out being tied. **Free•ma•son,** *n.* member of
a secret society. **free•ma•son•ry,** *n.* broth-
erhood/fraternity. **free-range,** *adj.* (hens)
kept in the open, not in boxes. **free style,** *n.*
(*in sport*) any style; (*in swimming*) any stroke,
usu. crawl. **free trade,** *n.* system of trade
agreements between countries where goods
are imported and exported free of tax.
free•ware, *n.* computer software that is distributed to users without charge. **free•way,**
n. fast highway with few points of access or
exit. **free•wheel** [friː'wiːl] *v.* to go along on a
bicycle without pedaling. **free will,** *n.* ability
to decide for yourself.

free•si•a ['friːʒə] *n.* scented flower grown from
a bulb.

freeze [friːz] 1. *n.* (a) period of frost. (b) **wage
f./price f.** = period of standstill in wages or
prices. 2. *v.* (**froze; has frozen**) (a) to change
from liquid to solid because of the cold. (b) to
become very cold. (c) to stay very still. (d) to
store (food) at below freezing point. (e) to
keep prices or wages at the present level. (f) to
prevent the owner from collecting, using or
selling (assets). **freez•er,** *n.* deep-freeze/re-
frigerator for freezing food and keeping it
frozen. **freez•ing point,** *n.* temperature at
which a liquid becomes solid.

freight [freɪt] 1. *n.* (a) transport of goods by air,
sea or land. (b) goods transported; **f. train** =
train used for transporting goods; **f. car** = car
which carries goods not passengers. 2. *v.* to
transport (goods). **freight•er,** *n.* air-
craft/ship which carries goods.
freight•train, *n.* train of freight cars.

French [frentʃ] 1. *adj.* referring to France; **F.
window** = door made of glass usu. opening on

to a garden; **F. dressing** = salad dressing made of oil and vinegar; **F. fries/F. fried potatoes** = long pieces of potato fried in oil; **to take F. leave** = to go away without permission; **F. horn** = brass instrument with a coiled tube. 2. *n.* (a) language spoken in France and some other countries. (b) **the F.** = the people of France. **French•man, Frenchwoman,** *n.* (*pl.* -**men, -women**) person from France. **French pol•ish,** *v.* to polish (wood) with a resin polish.

fre•net•ic [frəˈnetɪk] *adj.* wildly excited.

fren•zy [ˈfrenzɪ] *n.* wild excitement. **fren•zied,** *adj.* wildly excited. **fren•zied•ly,** *adv.* in a frenzied way.

fre•quent 1. *adj.* [ˈfriːkwənt] happening often/often seen. 2. *v.* [frɪˈkwent] go go (somewhere) very often. **fre•quen•cy,** *n.* (a) rate at which sth happens. (b) number of vibrations per second made by a radio wave. **fre•quent•ly,** *adv.* often.

fres•co [ˈfreskəʊ] *n.* (*pl.* -**oes**) painting done on wet plaster on a wall.

fresh [freʃ] *adj.* (**-er, -est**) (a) new/not used; **f. air** = open air. (b) recent (news); newly-made (cakes). (c) not canned or frozen. (d) quite strong (wind). (e) healthy-looking. (f) rude; impudent. **fresh•en,** *v.* to become/to make fresh. **fresh•man,** *n.* (*pl.* -**men**) new student in his/her first year at a school, college or university. **fresh•ly,** *adv.* newly/recently. **fresh•ness,** *n.* being fresh. **fresh wa•ter,** *n.* water in rivers or lakes. **fresh•wa•ter,** *adj.* referring to river or lake water, not salt water.

fret [fret] 1. *n.* raised metal strip crossing the neck of a guitar against which you press the strings. 2. *v.* (**fretted**) to worry/be unhappy. **fret•ful,** *adj.* crying and unhappy (child). **fret•ful•ly,** *adv.* in a fretful way.

fret•work [ˈfretwɜːk] *n.* patterns in wood cut with a very fine saw. **fret•saw,** *n.* fine saw used for cutting patterns in wood.

Freud•i•an [ˈfrɔɪdɪən] *adj.* referring to Freud and his theories of psychoanalysis; **a F. slip** = a mistake in speaking which seems to show your real feelings, when you are trying to hide them.

fri•a•ble [ˈfraɪəbl] *adj.* (earth) which can be crumbled easily.

fri•ar [ˈfraɪə] *n.* member of a Christian religious order.

fric•as•see [ˈfrɪkæseɪ] *n.* dish of pieces of meat cooked in a rich sauce.

fric•tion [ˈfrɪkʃn] *n.* (a) rubbing one thing against another. (b) disagreement between two or more people.

Fri•day [ˈfraɪdeɪ] *n.* fifth day of the week/day between Thursday and Saturday; **Good F.** = the Friday before Easter Day.

fridge [frɪdʒ] *n. inf.* refrigerator.

fried [fraɪd] *v. see* **fry.**

friend [frend] *n.* person whom you know well and like; supporter (of a cause); **the Society of Friends** = religious society, also called the Quakers. **friend•less,** *adj.* having no friends. **friend•li•ness,** *n.* friendly feeling. **friend•ly,** *adj.* like a friend/kind/helpful. **friend•ship,** *n.* state of being friends.

frieze [friːz] *n.* decorative border around the top of walls, pillars, etc.

frig•ate [ˈfrɪgət] *n.* small fast-moving naval ship.

fright [fraɪt] *n.* (a) fear. (b) *inf.* awful-looking person. **fright•ful,** *adj. inf.* terrible/awful. **fright•ful•ly,** *adv. inf.* extremely/terribly/very. **fright•ful•ness,** *n.* unpleasantness.

fright•en [ˈfraɪtn] *v.* to make (s.o.) afraid. **fright•en•ed,** *adj.* afraid/scared (**of**). **fright•en•ing,** *adj.* causing fear.

frig•id [ˈfrɪdʒɪd] *adj.* (a) very cold/icy. (b) unfriendly/not showing any warm feelings; (woman) not interested in sex. **fri•gid•i•ty** [frɪˈdʒɪdɪtɪ] *n.* (a) great cold. (b) coldness of feelings, esp. lack of interest in sex. **fri•gid•ly,** *adv.* in a cold way.

frill [frɪl] *n.* (a) piece of material gathered together and sewn onto a dress, etc. (b) **frills** = unnecessary ornaments. **frilled,** *adj.* with frills. **frill•y,** *adj.* with many frills.

fringe [frɪndʒ] *n.* (a) hair lying over the forehead. (b) edging of material consisting of loose threads hanging down (on a shawl/dress/carpet, etc.). (c) outer edge of an area; **f. benefits** = extra benefits on top of a salary (such as a free car, etc.).

frip•per•y [ˈfrɪpərɪ] *n.* useless ornament.

frisk [frɪsk] *v.* (a) to jump (**about**). (b) to search (s.o.) by running your hands over him to see if he is carrying a weapon. **frisk•i•ly,** *adv.* in a frisky way. **frisk•i•ness,** *n.* feeling full of life. **frisk•y,** *adj.* lively.

frit•il•lar•y [frɪˈtɪlərɪ] *n.* type of small butterfly.

frit•ter [ˈfrɪtə] 1. *n.* piece of meat/fruit/vegetable dipped in a mixture of flour, egg and milk

---

æ back, ɑː farm, ɒ top, aɪ pipe, aʊ how, aɪə fire, aʊə flower, ɔː bought, ɔɪ toy, e fed, eəhair, eɪ take, ə afraid, əʊ boat, əʊə lower, vː word, iː heap, ɪ hit, ɪə hear, uː school, ʊ book, ʌ but, b back, d dog, ð then, dʒ just, f fog, g go, h hand, j yes, k catch, l last, m mix, n nut, ŋ sing, p penny, r round, s some, ʃ short, t too, tʃ chop, θ thing, v voice, w was, z zoo, ʒ treasure

and fried. 2. *v.* **f. away** = to waste (time, money).

friv•o•lous ['frɪvələs] *adj.* silly/not serious. **friv•o•lous•ly**, *adv.* in a frivolous way. **friv•o•lous•ness, fri•vol•i•ty** [frɪ'vɒlɪtɪ] *n.* silliness/lack of seriousness.

friz•zle ['frɪzl] *v. inf.* (a) (*of hair*) to be very tightly curled. (b) to fry in hot fat.

friz•zy ['frɪzɪ] *adj. inf.* tightly curled (hair). **frizz,** *v. inf.* to put (hair) into tight curls.

fro [frəʊ] *adv.* **to and f.** = backward and forward.

frock [frɒk] *n.* (a) dress/piece of female clothing covering more or less all the body. (b) long robe worn by monks or priests.

frog [frɒg] *n.* (a) small tailless reptile which lives on both land and water; **to have a f. in your throat** = to feel you have sth in your throat which stops you speaking clearly. (b) decorated fastening on a uniform. **frog•man,** *n.* (*pl.* **-men**) underwater diver.

frol•ic ['frɒlɪk] 1. *n.* happy game/party. 2. *v.* (**frolicked**) to play happily.

from [frɒm] *prep.* (a) (*showing movement away*) **the plane f. Paris.** (b) (*showing where something started*) **f. beginning to end; f. now on; f. time to time** = sometimes. (c) (*showing difference*) **I can't tell butter f. margarine.** (d) sent by; **a letter f. Peter.** (e) because of; **he died f. pneumonia.** (f) according to; **f. what I heard.**

frond [frɒnd] *n.* large leaf of a fern or palm tree.

front [frʌnt] 1. *n.* (a) part which faces forward; most prominent part; **in f. of** = before. (b) land which runs along a road, street, shoreline, etc. (c) line of an army nearest the enemy in battle. (d) (*of weather*) line separating cold and warm masses of air. (e) business used to hide an illegal activity. 2. *adj.* foremost/first (seat, door, etc.). 3. *v.* to face (**on to**). **front•age** ['frʌntɪdʒ] *n.* (a) length of a property along a road, street, etc. (b) land between a building and a road, street, body of water, etc. **fron•tal,** *adj.* of/in the front; belonging to the front.

fron•tier ['frʌntɪə] *n.* (a) boundary line between two countries or states. (b) **frontiers** = the outermost limit of human knowledge.

fron•tis•piece ['frʌntɪspiːs] *n.* picture opposite the title page of a book.

frost [frɒst] *n.* (a) weather when the temperature is below the freezing point of water. (b) white covering on the ground/trees, etc., when the temperature is below freezing. **frost•bite,** *n.* damage to a part of the body due to cold. **frost•bit•ten,** *adj.* attacked by frostbite. **frost•ed,** *adj.* (a) covered in frost; damaged by frost. (b) (glass) which has a rough surface through which it is difficult to see. (c) (cake) covered with frosting.

frost•i•ly, *adv.* coldly/in an unfriendly way. **frost•ing,** *n.* icing on a cake. **frost•y,** *adj.* (a) very cold; covered with frost. (b) cold/unfriendly (manner).

froth [frɒθ] 1. *n.* mass of bubbles on top of a liquid. 2. *v.* to have masses of bubbles. **froth•y,** *adj.* having bubbles on top.

frown [fraʊn] 1. *n.* pulling down the eyebrows as a sign of anger/puzzlement, etc. 2. *v.* to pull down the eyebrows; **to f. on (sth)** = to disapprove of sth.

frowz•y ['fraʊzɪ] *adj.* untidy and dirty.

froze [frəʊz] *v. see* **freeze.**

fro•zen ['frəʊzn] *adj.* (a) very cold. (b) at a temperature below freezing point; **f. food** = food stored at a temperature below freezing point; *see also* **freeze.**

fru•gal ['fruːgl] *adj.* spending/costing very little money. **fru•gal•i•ty** [fruː'gælɪtɪ] *n.* being frugal. **fru•gal•ly,** *adv.* in a frugal way.

fruit [fruːt] 1. *n.* (a) (*pl. usu.* **fruit**) part of a plant which contains the seeds and which is often eaten; **f. salad** = pieces of fresh fruit mixed and served cold. (b) product (of hard work). 2. *v.* to carry/to produce edible parts. **fruit•cake,** *n.* cake with a lot of dried fruit in it. **fruit•ful,** *adj.* (work) which produces good results. **fruit•ful•ly,** *adv.* in a fruitful way. **fru•i•tion** [fruː'ɪʃn] *n.* **to come to f.** = to be accomplished with good results. **fruit•less,** *adj.* producing no results. **fruit•less•ly,** *adv.* in a fruitless way. **fruit•y,** *adj.* (a) tasting of fruit. (b) *inf.* deep and tuneful (voice).

frump [frʌmp] *n.* person, usu. a woman, who wears old-fashioned clothes. **frump•ish,** *adj.* (wearing) out-of-date clothes.

frus•trate [frʌ'streɪt] *v.* to prevent (s.o.) doing what he/she wants to do. **frus•tra•tion** [frʌ'streɪʃn] *n.* feeling of anger and impatience when stopped from doing what you want.

fry [fraɪ] 1. *n.* (*pl.* **fry**) baby fish; **small f.** = unimportant people. 2. *v.* to cook in oil/fat. **fry•ing pan,** *n.* shallow, open pan used for frying; **to jump out of the f. p. into the fire** = to go from one difficult situation to sth worse.

ft *abbreviation for* **foot.**

fuch•sia ['fjuːʃə] *n.* garden plant with colorful hanging flowers.

fud•dle ['fʌdl] *v.* to make (s.o.) feel hazy and confused.

fud•dy-dud•dy ['fʌdɪdʌdɪ] *n. inf.* old-fashioned person.

fudge [fʌdʒ] 1. *n.* soft candy made from butter, sugar and milk. 2. *v.* to avoid dealing with sth; **to f. the issue** = to avoid making a decision on an issue.

fuel ['fjuəl] 1. *n.* substance (coal/gas/oil/wood, etc.) which can be burned to give heat/power;

to add f. to the fire = to make matters worse. 2. *v.* (fueled, fuelled) to provide fuel for.

fug [fʌg] *n. inf.* stuffy/hot atmosphere. fug•gi•ness, *n.* being fuggy. fug•gy, *adj.* stuffy/hot.

fu•gi•tive ['fjuːdʒətɪv] *n. & adj.* (person) who is running away.

fugue [fjuːg] *n.* piece of music where a tune is repeated in several patterns.

ful•crum ['fulkrəm] *n.* point on which a lever rests/on which a seesaw balances.

ful•fill, fulfil [ful'fɪl] *v.* (fulfilled) to complete (sth) satisfactorily. ful•fill•ment, *n.* satisfactory ending.

full [ful] 1. *adj.* (-er, -est) (a) containing as much as possible; f. up = with no more room; I'm f. (up) = I have eaten as much as I can; f. skirt = wide skirt made from lots of material. (b) all; as many (as possible). (c) complete; f. year = one complete year. (d) round and plump (face); f. moon = moon when completely round. 2. *n.* in f. = completely/entirely. full back, *n.* (in games) defensive player near the goal. full•blood•ed, *adj.* (a) vigorous (argument). (b) (of horses) strongly typical. full-blown, *adj.* (a) (of a flower) wide open. (b) he is a f.-b. doctor = he has passed all his examinations and is qualified. full-fledged, *adj.* experienced/qualified. full-grown, *adj.* adult. full-length, *adj.* (a) from head to toe. (b) long (story/motion picture). full•ness, *n.* (a) state of containing as much as possible. (b) state when all is completed. full-scale, *adj.* complete/total. full-time, *adj. & adv.* all the time. ful•ly, *adv.* completely/entirely.

ful•mar ['fulmɑː] *n.* gray and white northern seabird.

ful•mi•nate ['fʌlmɪneɪt] *v.* (formal) to protest angrily. ful•min•a•tions [fʌlmɪ'neɪʃnz] *n. pl.* angry protests.

ful•some ['fulsəm] *adj.* excessive/too much.

fu•ma•role ['fjuːmərəul] *n.* hole in the side of a volcano through which smoke escapes.

fum•ble ['fʌmbl] *v.* (with) to touch/to feel clumsily. fum•bling, *adj.* clumsy.

fume [fjuːm] 1. *n. pl.* fumes = smoke/gas. 2. *v.* to be angry.

fu•mi•gate ['fjuːmɪgeɪt] *v.* to clean (a room) by smoking out germs and insects. fu•mi•ga•tion [fjuːmɪ'geɪʃn] *n.* smoking out germs/insects.

fun [fʌn] *n.* amusement/pleasure; to make f. of/to poke f. at = to laugh at/to mock; for f./in

f. = not seriously/as a joke. fun fair, *n.* amusement park.

func•tion ['fʌŋkʃn] 1. *n.* (a) job/duty. (b) gathering of people; party. 2. *v.* (a) to work. (b) to serve (as). func•tion•al, *adj.* useful but not decorative. func•tion•al•ly, *adv.* in a functional way. func•tion•ar•y, *n.* official. function key, *n.* key on a computer keyboard which activates a set of instructions.

fund [fʌnd] 1. *n.* (a) sum of money set aside for a special purpose. (b) collection. 2. *v.* to provide money for (a special purpose).

fun•da•men•tal [fʌndə'mentl] *adj.* basic/essential. fun•da•men•tal•ly, *adv.* basically.

fu•ner•al ['fjuːnərəl] *n.* ceremony where a dead person is buried/cremated. fu•ner•ar•y, *adj.* used in a funeral. fu•ne•re•al [fjuː'nɪərɪəl] *adj.* sad and gloomy.

fun•gus ['fʌŋgəs] *n.* (pl. fungi ['fʌŋgaɪ]) plant which has no green leaves or flowers and which frequently lives on other plants. fun•gi•cide ['fʌndʒɪsaɪd] *n.* chemical which kills fungus. fun•gi•cid•al, *adj.* which kills fungus. fun•goid, *adj.* like a fungus.

fu•nic•u•lar [fə'nɪkjulə] *n.* f. (railway) = railway where cars held by cables travel up a slope.

funk [fʌŋk] 1. *n. inf.* (a) fear. (b) to be in a f. = to be depressed/in low spirits. 2. *v. inf.* to be afraid to do sth.

fun•nel ['fʌnl] 1. *n.* (a) tube with a wide mouth and narrow bottom used when pouring liquids from one container into another. (b) chimney on a ship from which the smoke comes. 2. (funneled, funnelled) *v.* to pass through a funnel/through a narrow space.

fun•ny ['fʌnɪ] *adj.* (a) which makes people laugh. (b) odd/unusual; I feel f. = I feel ill. fun•ni•ly, *adv.* oddly. fun•ny bone, *n. inf.* part of the elbow which hurts sharply if it is hit.

fur [fɜː] 1. *n.* (a) soft coat of an animal. (b) coating like fur, as a deposit in kettles/water pipes, etc., or on the tongue when sick. 2. *v.* (furred) to become covered with a coating like fur. fur•ry, *adj.* covered with fur.

fur•bish ['fɜːbɪʃ] *v.* to polish/to clean.

fu•ri•ous ['fjuərɪəs] *adj.* very angry. fu•ri•ous•ly, *adv.* in a furious way.

furl [fɜːl] *v.* to roll up and tie securely.

fur•long ['fɜːlɒŋ] *n.* measure of length (= 220 yards).

æ back, ɑː farm, ɒ top, aɪ pipe, au how, aiə fire, auə flower, ɔː bought, ɔɪ toy, e fed, eəhair, eɪ take, ə afraid, əu boat, əuə lower, vː word, iː heap, ɪ hit, ɪə hear, uː school, u book, ʌ but, b back, d dog, ð then, dʒ just, f fog, g go, h hand, j yes, k catch, l last, m mix, n nut, ŋ sing, p penny, r round, s some, ʃ short, t too, tʃ chop, θ thing, v voice, w was, z zoo, ʒ treasure

fur•lough ['fɜːləʊ] *n.* leave of absence (esp. from the armed forces).

fur•nace ['fɜːnəs] *n.* large structure with a chamber which can be heated to a very high temperature for heating a building, producing steam, etc.

fur•nish ['fɜːnɪʃ] *v.* (a) to provide with chairs/tables, etc.; **furnished apartment** = rented apartment where the furniture is provided by the owner. (b) to supply (**with**). **fur•nish•ings**, *n. pl.* fittings in a house.

fur•ni•ture ['fɜːnɪtʃə] *n.* (*no pl.*) tables/chairs/cupboards/beds, etc.; **a piece of f.** = one article of furniture.

fu•ror [fju:'rɔː], *Brit.* **fu•ro•re** [fju:'rɔːrɪ] *n.* outburst of anger/excitement.

fur•ri•er ['fʌrɪə] *n.* person who sells fur coats, etc.

fur•row ['fʌrəʊ] 1. *n.* long groove cut in the earth by a plow. 2. *v.* to make furrows in (the land, etc.).

fur•ther ['fɜːðə] 1. *adv. & adj.* (a) farther/to a greater distance/more distant. (b) additional; **f. delays.** 2. *v.* to advance (a plan). **fur•ther•ance**, *n.* advancing (of a plan). **fur•ther•more** [fɜːðə'mɔː] *adv.* also/in addition. **fur•ther•most** ['fɜːðəməʊst] *adj.* most distant. **fur•thest**, *adj. & adv.* to the greatest distance/most distant.

fur•tive ['fɜːtɪv] *adj.* secret; as if hiding something. **fur•tive•ly**, *adv.* in a furtive way. **fur•tive•ness**, *n.* being furtive.

fu•ry ['fjʊərɪ] *n.* fierce anger.

furze [fɜːz] *n.* gorse.

fuse [fjuːz] 1. *n.* (a) length of string attached to a bomb which burns slowly when lit. (b) small piece of wire in an electrical circuit which melts and breaks if the circuit is overloaded, and so prevents further damage; **to blow a f.** = to overload the electric circuit and make the fuse break. 2. *v.* **to f. together** = to join together (wires/companies, etc.). **fuse•box,** *n.* box where the fuses are kept.

fu•se•lage ['fjuːzəlɑːʒ] *n.* body of an aircraft.

fu•sil•lade [fjuːzɪ'leɪd] *n.* rapid gunfire.

fu•sion ['fjuːʒn] *n.* (a) melting together of two pieces of metal. (b) joining together of two different things.

fuss [fʌs] 1. *n.* agitated complaints about little things that do not matter; **to make a f. about sth** = to complain at length about sth unimportant; **to make a f. of s.o.** = to pay great attention to s.o. 2. *v.* to be agitated; to show unnecessary care and attention (over little things). **fuss•i•ly**, *adv.* in a fussy way. **fuss•i•ness**, *n.* being fussy. **fuss•y**, *adj.* (a) unnecessarily careful and demanding about little things. (b) disliking lots of things.

fus•ty ['fʌstɪ] *adj.* smelling of dampness. **fus•ti•ness**, *n.* being fusty.

fu•tile ['fjuːtaɪl, *Am.* 'fjuːtl] *adj.* useless. **fu•til•i•ty** [fjuː'tɪlɪtɪ] *n.* uselessness.

fu•ture ['fjuːtʃə] 1. *n.* time which has not yet happened; **in the f.** = from now on. 2. *adj.* coming/not yet happened. **fu•tures,** *n.* trade in something, such as foreign currency or commodities, for delivery at a later date. **fu•tur•is•tic** [fjuːtʃə'rɪstɪk] *adj.* oddly modern (art).

fuzz [fʌz] *n.* (a) fluffy hair or other matter. (b) *Sl.* **the f.** = the police. **fuzz•i•ness**, *n.* being fuzzy. **fuzz•y**, *adj.* (a) fluffy and curly. (b) not clear/blurred. **fuz•zy log•ic** 1. *n.* logic that accommodates and describes imprecise reasoning and uncertainty in a way that can be processed by a computer. 2. *adj.* (computer program/system) able to process data formulated by fuzzy logic.

Gg

g *abbrev. for* gram.

gab [gæb] *n. inf.* talk/chat; **the gift of g.** = talent for speaking.

gab•ar•dine ['gæbədi:n] *n.* closely woven cotton, wool, or other material, used for making clothes.

gab•ble ['gæbl] 1. *n.* loud, unintelligible talk. 2. *v.* to speak very quickly.

ga•ble ['geɪbl] *n.* triangular upper part of a wall at the end of a roof. **ga•bled**, *adj.* with gables.

gad [gæd] *v.* **(gadded) to g. about** = to be constantly out and about. **gad•a•bout**, *n.* person who is always out and about. **gad•fly**, *n.* fly which attacks cows; irritating person.

gadg•et ['gædʒɪt] *n.* useful machine/tool. **gadg•et•ry**, *n.* lots of gadgets.

Gael•ic ['geɪlɪk, *in Scotland* 'gælɪk] *n.* language of Scots, Manx and Irish Celts.

gaff [gæf] 1. *n.* stick with iron hook for catching large fish. 2. *v.* to catch with a gaff.

gaffe [gæf] *n.* blunder; indiscreet act or remark.

gaf•fer ['gæfə] *n. inf.* old man.

gag [gæg] 1. *n.* (a) soft object put into or tied round the mouth to stop s.o. speaking. (b) joke. 2. *v.* **(gagged)** (a) to bind (s.o.) round the mouth; **to g. the press** = to impose censorship. (b) to retch/to choke.

ga•ga ['gɑ:gɑ:] *adj. inf.* senile/stupid.

gag•gle ['gægl] *n.* flock (of geese).

gai•e•ty ['geɪətɪ] *n.* happiness/cheerfulness. **gai•ly** ['geɪlɪ] *adv.* happily.

gain [geɪn] 1. *n.* increase of possessions; profit. 2. *v.* (a) to obtain/to get; **to g. the upper hand** = to get control. (b) **the clock gains five minutes a day** = it moves five minutes ahead of the correct time in every twenty-four hours. (c) **to g. on s.o./sth** = to get closer to a person or thing you are chasing. **gain•ful**, *adj.* which earns money; **g. employment. gain•ful•ly**, *adv.* **g. employed** = doing work which earns money.

gain•say [geɪn'seɪ] *v.* **(gainsaid)** *(formal)* to deny (sth).

gait [geɪt] *n.* manner of walking.

gait•er ['geɪtə] *n.* covering of cloth or leather worn over the leg below the knee.

gal. *abbrev. for* gallon.

ga•la ['gɑ:lə] *n.* festive occasion.

gal•ax•y ['gæləksɪ] *n.* collection of stars, found singly and in groups and clusters. **ga•lac•tic** [gə'læktɪk] *adj.* belonging to a galaxy.

gale [geɪl] *n.* very strong wind.

ga•le•na [gə'li:nə] *n.* natural form of lead sulfide.

gall [gɔ:l] 1. *n.* (a) bile/bitter liquid produced by the liver to digest fat. (b) growth produced by insects on trees, esp. the oak. (c) painful swelling/blister (esp. on horses). (d) *inf.* rudeness/impudence. 2. *v.* to annoy/to humiliate. **gall•ing**, *adj.* humiliating; annoying. **gall-blad•der**, *n.* bag in the body where bile is stored. **gall•stone**, *n.* small stonelike substance which sometimes forms in the gall-bladder.

gal•lant ['gælənt] *adj.* (a) brave/chivalrous. (b) very polite towards women. **gal•lant•ly**, *adv.* in a gallant way. **gal•lant•ry** ['gæləntrɪ] *n.* bravery.

gal•le•on ['gælɪən] *n.* large Spanish warship in the 16th century.

gal•ler•y ['gælərɪ] *n.* (a) room in which pictures are hung, often for sale. (b) store selling pictures/antiques, etc. (c) *(in a church/hall, etc.)* balcony which runs around part of the main hall; *(in a theater)* highest rows of usu. cheapest seats; **to play to the g.** = to appeal to the public; **minstrels' g.** = balcony above the end of a castle dining hall from where musicians entertained the diners. (d) **shooting g.** = long, narrow room at one end of which is a target for shooting.

gal•ley ['gælɪ] *n.* (a) low, flat, single-decked ship, rowed by slaves. (b) ship's kitchen. (c) *(in printing)* rectangular tray which holds type. **galley proof**, *n.* proof printed on long sheets of paper.

Gal•lic ['gælɪk] *adj.* French. **gall•i•cism**

æ back, a: farm, ɒ: top, aɪ pipe, aʊ how, aiə fire, aʊə flower, ɔ: bought, ɔɪ toy, ɛ fed, eəhair, eɪ take, ə afraid, əʊ boat, əʊə lower, v: word, i: heap, ɪ hit, ɪə hear, u: school, ʊ book, ʌ but, b back, d dog, ð then, dʒ just, f fog, g go, h hand, j yes, k catch, l last, m mix, n nut, ŋ sing, p penny, r round, s some, ʃ short, t too, tʃ chop, θ thing, v voice, w was, z zoo, ʒ treasure

['gælɪsɪzəm] *n.* French word or phrase adopted into another language.

gal•li•vant ['gælɪvænt] *v. inf.* to be always out and about looking for amusement.

gal•lon ['gælən] *n.* liquid measure equal to 4 quarts or 4.5 liters.

gal•lop ['gæləp] 1. *n.* (a) fastest pace of a horse running with all feet off the ground in each stride. (b) fast ride on a horse. 2. *v.* to run/to go fast; **galloping inflation** = rapidly rising inflation.

gal•lows ['gæləʊz] *n.* structure on which criminals are hanged.

Gal•lup poll ['gæləp'pəʊl] *n.* test of public opinion on an important topic, esp. of how a representative sample of the public will vote, in order to forecast an election result.

ga•lore [gə'lɔː] *adv.* (*always after the noun*) plenty; **apples g.**

ga•losh•es [gə'lɒʃɪz] *n. pl.* plastic/rubber shoes worn over other shoes to protect them.

ga•lumph [gə'lʌmf] *v. inf.* to walk about heavily.

gal•va•nize ['gælvənaɪz] *v.* (a) **galvanized iron** = iron coated with zinc to protect it from rust. (b) to rouse by shock into action. gal•va•ni•za•tion [gælvənaɪ'zeɪʃn] *n.* process of galvanizing. gal•va•nom•e•ter [gælvə'nɒmɪtə] *n.* instrument for measuring small electric currents.

gam•bit ['gæmbɪt] *n.* (a) (*in chess*) opening move whereby a player sacrifices a minor piece in order to take a major one later. (b) opening move in some action.

gam•ble ['gæmbl] 1. *n.* risk taken in the hope of getting good results. **it's a bit of a g.** = you can't be sure it will succeed. 2. *v.* to risk (money) on cards or sporting results; **to g. on sth happening** = to act in the hope that it will happen. gam•bler, *n.* person who gambles. gam•bling, *n.* risking money; betting **on** sth.

gam•bol ['gæmbl] *v.* (**gamboled, gambolled**) to run, leap, or jump in play.

game [geɪm] 1. *n.* (a) contest played according to rules and decided by skill, strength or luck; **a g. of tennis/chess; to play the g.** = to act honorably; **so that's his little g.** = now we know what his plans are. (b) (*in tennis/bridge, etc.*) single round. (c) wild animals and birds (deer, rabbits, pheasants, etc.) hunted for sport or food; **g. soup** = soup made from game; **big g.** = large wild animals (lions/elephants, etc.) shot for sport. 2. *adj.* (a) willing/courageous. (b) lame (leg). game•keep•er, *n.* person employed to breed and look after game. game•ly, *adv.* bravely. game•ness, *n.* being game. games•man•ship, *n.* (*no pl.*) the art of winning by devious means, such as

distracting your opponent. gam•ing, *n.* gambling.

gam•ete ['gæmiːt] *n.* plant or animal cell which can link with another to reproduce.

gam•ma ['gæmə] *n.* third letter of the Greek alphabet. gam•ma glob•u•lin, *n.* protein found in blood plasma. **gamma rays** *n. pl.* rays of short wavelength sent out by radioactive substances.

gam•mon ['gæmən] *n.* smoked or cured ham.

gam•ut ['gæmət] *n.* (a) whole range of musical notes. (b) whole range or scope.

gan•der ['gændə] *n.* male goose.

gang [gæŋ] 1. *n.* band of people acting or going about together. 2. *v.* **to g. together** = to join together; **to g. up on (s.o.)** = to take sides with one or more people against s.o. gang•plank, *n.* long piece of wood giving access to a boat from the shore. gang•ster, *n.* member of a gang of violent criminals. gang•way, *n.* (a) passageway. (b) bridge from the shore to a ship.

gan•gling ['gæŋglɪŋ] *adj.* tall (person) with long arms and legs.

gan•gli•on ['gæŋglɪən] *n.* (a) nucleus of nerves in the central nervous system. (b) small lump on a tendon.

gan•grene ['gæŋgriːn] *n.* rotting of body tissue, caused by a blockage of the blood supply. gan•gre•nous ['gæŋgrɪnəs] *adj.* affected by gangrene.

gan•net ['gænɪt] *n.* large white sea bird.

gan•try ['gæntrɪ] *n.* metal bridge for carrying lights/a crane, etc.

gap [gæp] *n.* (a) space/hole in a hedge/wall, etc. (b) gorge or pass (between mountains). (c) space/difference; **age g.** = difference in age; **generation g.** = difference in years between one generation and another, often resulting in intolerance between them.

gape [geɪp] *v.* to open your mouth wide. gap•ing, *adj.* wide open.

ga•rage ['gærɪdʒ, 'gærɑːʒ] 1. *n.* (a) building for storing motor vehicles; **g. sale** = private sale of unwanted household goods (held in the garage or yard of a house). (b) station/place where motor vehicles are repaired and serviced. 2. *v.* to put (a vehicle) into a garage.

garb [gɑːb] *n.* (*no pl.*) (*formal*) clothing. garbed, *adj.* dressed (**in**).

gar•bage ['gɑːbɪdʒ] *n.* refuse/trash; **g. can** = container for refuse/trash.

gar•ble ['gɑːbl] *v.* to select certain items from speeches in order to give an unfair or malicious representation; to distort/confuse.

gar•den ['gɑːdn] 1. *n.* piece of ground used for growing flowers, fruit, or vegetables; **g. center** = place where plants, seeds and garden tools are sold. 2. *v.* to look after a garden.

gar•den•er, *n.* person who looks after a garden. **gar•den•ing**, *n.* looking after a garden.

gar•de•nia [gɑːˈdiːnɪə] *n.* shrub with fragrant white or yellow flowers.

gar•gan•tu•an [gɑːˈgæntjʊən] *adj.* huge/enormous.

gar•gle [ˈgɑːgl] 1. *n.* antiseptic liquid used for washing the throat. 2. *v.* to wash the throat by holding antiseptic liquid in it and breathing out at the same time.

gar•goyle [ˈgɑːgɔɪl] *n.* water spout on a medieval building, carved like a grotesque head.

gar•ish [ˈgeərɪʃ] *adj.* bright/showy/over-decorated. **gar•ish•ly**, *adv.* very brightly.

gar•land [ˈgɑːlənd] 1. *n.* (a) circle of flowers or leaves worn as a decoration. (b) decoration made of linked paper/ribbon, etc. 2. *v.* to hang with garlands.

gar•lic [ˈgɑːlɪk] *n.* plant whose bulb has a strong smell and taste, used as a flavoring. **gar•lick•y**, *adj.* tasting/smelling of garlic.

gar•ment [ˈgɑːmənt] *n.* article of clothing.

gar•ner [ˈgɑːnə] *v.* (*formal*) to collect and store.

gar•net [ˈgɑːnɪt] *n.* semi-precious dark red stone.

gar•nish [ˈgɑːnɪʃ] 1. *n.* thing used to decorate food. 2. *v.* to decorate (esp. food).

gar•ret [ˈgærət] *n.* attic room immediately under the roof of a house.

gar•ri•son [ˈgærɪsn] 1. *n.* (a) troops stationed in a fortress/town, etc., in order to defend it. (b) fortress. 2. *v.* to place troops on garrison duty in (a town).

gar•rotte [gəˈrɒt] *v.* to strangle (s.o.) with a cord.

gar•ru•lous [ˈgærjʊləs] *adj.* talkative. **gar•ru•lous•ly**, *adv.* in a garrulous way. **gar•ru•lous•ness, garrulity** [gæˈruːlɪtɪ] *n.* being garrulous.

gar•ter [ˈgɑːtə] *n.* band worn above or below the knee to keep a stocking or sock up; **Order of the Garter** = highest order of English knighthood.

gas [gæs] 1. *n.* (a) chemical substance like air, which is completely fluid and has no definite shape or volume. (b) substance, produced from coal or extracted naturally from the ground, which is used for cooking or heating; **to cook by g.; g. stove** = stove which uses gas; **natural g.** = gas which is extracted from the earth. (c) substance used as an anesthetic while having a tooth removed, etc. (d) gasoline, *inf.* **to step on the g.** = to accelerate. (e) *inf.*

unimportant talk. 2. *v.* (**gassed**) (a) to poison (s.o.) by making them breathe gas. (b) *inf.* to talk about nothing in particular. **gas•e•ous** [ˈgæsjəs] *adj.* referring to gas. **gas•mask**, *n.* mask used as protection against poison gases. **gas•o•line**, *n.* inflammable liquid produced from petroleum and used as a fuel to drive motor vehicles. **gas•om•e•ter** [gæˈsɒmɪtə] *n.* large container in which gas is stored in a laboratory. **gas sta•tion**, *n.* place where you can buy gasoline. **gas•sy**, *adj.* full of gas/full of bubbles. **gas•works**, *n.* place where gas is manufactured.

gash [gæʃ] 1. *n.* long deep cut/wound. 2. *v.* to make a gash.

gas•ket [ˈgæskɪt] *n.* piece of thin material used to seal two parts of an engine to prevent air/gas, etc., from escaping.

gasp [gɑːsp] 1. *n.* sharp intake of breath. 2. *v.* to struggle to breathe/to catch your breath in surprise.

gas•tric [ˈgæstrɪk] *adj.* referring to the stomach. **gas•trec•to•my**, *n.* operation to remove the stomach. **gas•tro•en•ter•i•tis** [gæstrəʊentəˈraɪtɪs] *n.* illness of the stomach and intestines. **gas•tro•nome** [ˈgæstrənəʊm] *n.* expert on food and drink. **gas•tro•nom•ic** [gæstrəˈnɒmɪk] *adj.* referring to food and drink. **gas•tron•o•my** [gæsˈtrɒnəmɪ] *n.* art of cooking.

gate [geɪt] *n.* (a) barrier, usu. made of wood or iron, closing an opening in a wall/fence, etc. (b) number of people who watch a match/sports competition; money paid by spectators at a match, etc. **gate•crash**, *v.* to go uninvited to (a party). **gate•crash•er**, *n.* uninvited guest. **gate-legged ta•ble**, *n.* table with hinged legs which fold like a gate. **gate•post**, *n.* post to which a gate is attached by hinges. **gate•way**, *n.* (a) gap in a wall/fence, etc., where a gate can be fitted. (b) hardware/software connecting different computer networks.

ga•teau [ˈgætəʊ] *n.* (*pl.* **gateaux** [ˈgætəʊz]) large decorated cake.

gath•er [ˈgæðə] *v.* (a) to bring together/to collect. (b) to gain (speed). (c) to understand; **I g. that you are coming.** (d) to pull (material) into folds by means of tiny stitches. **gath•er•ing**. 1. *n.* (a) group of people who have come together. (b) swelling with pus. 2. *adj.* imminent; **a g. storm. gather up**, *v.* to bring (things) together and pick them up.

æ back, ɑː farm, ɒ top, aɪ pipe, aʊ how, aɪə fire, aʊə flower, ɔː bought, ɔɪ toy, e fed, eəhair, eɪ take, ə afraid, əʊ boat, əʊə lower, vː word, iː heap, ɪ hit, ɪə hear, uː school, ʊ book, ʌ but, b back, d dog, ð then, dʒ just, f fog, g go, h hand, j yes, k catch, l last, m mix, n nut, ŋ sing, p penny, r round, s some, ʃ short, t too, tʃ chop, θ thing, v voice, w was, z zoo, ʒ treasure

gauche [gəʊʃ] *adj.* clumsy/tactless.

gau•cho ['gaʊtʃəʊ] *n.* South American herdsman.

gaud•y ['gɔːdɪ] *adj.* (-ier, -iest) too brightly colored; showy; lacking in taste. **gaud•i•ly**, *adv.* showily. **gaud•i•ness**, *n.* being gaudy.

gauge [geɪdʒ] 1. *n.* (a) standard measure of width/thickness, etc. (b) distance between rails on a railroad track. (c) instrument measuring depth/pressure, etc. 2. *v.* (a) to measure exactly. (b) to estimate/to guess.

gaunt [gɔːnt] *adj.* lean/haggard. **gaunt•ness**, *n.* being gaunt.

gaunt•let ['gɔːntlət] *n.* strong glove with long wrist cover, for driving, fencing, etc.; **to throw down/take up the g.** = to issue/accept a challenge; **to run the g.** = to go through a difficult time.

gauss [gaʊs] *n.* unit for measuring the strength of a magnetic field.

gauze [gɔːz] *n.* thin/transparent material. **gauz•y**, *adj.* thin (material).

gave [geɪv] *v. see* **give.**

gav•el ['gævl] *n.* auctioneer's or chairman's hammer.

gawk•y ['gɔːkɪ] *adj.* (-ier, -iest) awkward/ungainly. **gawk•i•ness**, *n.* being gawky.

gawp [gɔːp] *v. inf.* to stare rudely (**at**).

gay [geɪ] 1. *adj.* (-er, -est) happy; full of fun. 2. *adj. & n. inf.* homosexual. **gay•ness**, *n.* being gay.

gaze [geɪz] 1. *n.* intent look. 2. *v.* to look steadily for a long time.

ga•ze•bo [gə'ziːbəʊ] *n.* small summerhouse.

ga•zelle [gə'zel] *n.* kind of antelope.

ga•zette [gə'zet] *n.* official newspaper, giving details of public appointments, etc. **gaz•et•teer** [gæzə'tɪə] *n.* geographical dictionary.

GDP [dʒiːdiː'piː] *n.* gross domestic product.

gear ['gɪə] 1. *n.* (a) equipment; **landing g.** = undercarriage of an aircraft. (b) *inf.* clothing. (c) **gears** = arrangement of toothed wheels, levers, etc., connecting an engine/pedals, etc., with wheels; **in g.** = with the gears connected. 2. *v.* **to g. sth to** = to fit/to match. **gear•box**, *n.* casing for gears in cars. **gear•shift**, *n.* handle by which the gears are changed in a car. **gear•wheel**, *n.* toothed wheel connecting with another wheel of different diameter to change the power ratio of the engine.

geck•o ['gekəʊ] *n.* (*pl.* -os) small tropical lizard.

gee [dʒiː] *inter. showing surprise.*

geese [giːs] *n. pl. see* **goose.**

gee•zer ['giːzə] *n. Sl.* (old) man.

Gei•ger count•er ['gaɪgəkaʊntə] *n.* device for detecting and recording radioactivity.

gei•sha ['geɪʃə] *n.* Japanese hostess and dancing girl.

gel [dʒel] *n.* substance like a jelly.

gel•a•tin(e) ['dʒelətiːn] *n.* substance obtained after stewing skin, bones, etc., and used to make jellies. **ge•lat•i•nous** [dʒə'lætɪnəs] *adj.* like jelly.

geld [geld] *v.* to castrate.

geld•ing ['geldɪŋ] *n.* castrated animal, esp. horse.

gel•ig•nite ['dʒelɪgnaɪt] *n.* nitroglycerine explosive.

gem [dʒem] *n.* precious stone. **gem•ol•o•gy** [dʒe'mɒlədʒɪ] *n.* the science of gems.

Gem•i•ni ['dʒemɪnaɪ] *n.* one of the signs of the zodiac, shaped like twins.

gen•der ['dʒendə] *n.* grammatical classification of objects roughly corresponding to the two sexes and absence of sex, masculine, feminine, and neuter.

gene [dʒiːn] *n.* part of a chromosome which carries characteristics transmitted by the parent; **g. bank** = gene library; **g. library** = collection of cloned genes representing the entire genetic material of an organism; **g. pool** = all the genes present in a population; **g. therapy** = modification/replacement of defective genes in order to prevent hereditary diseases.

ge•ne•a•log•i•cal [dʒiːnɪə'lɒdʒɪkl] *adj.* referring to genealogy. **ge•ne•al•o•gist** [dʒiːnɪ'ælədʒɪst] *n.* person who studies genealogy. **ge•ne•al•o•gy**, *n.* study of family descent through the generations.

gen•er•a ['dʒenərə] *n. see* **ge•nus.**

gen•er•al ['dʒenrəl] 1. *adj.* completely or approximately universal; including or affecting all or nearly all parts; **g. anesthetic** = anesthetic which makes the patient lose consciousness; **g. election** = local, state, or national election in which the whole country is involved; **in g.** = as a rule. 2. *n.* superior military officer. **gen•er•al•is•si•mo** [dʒenrə'lɪsɪməʊ] *n.* commander-in-chief of the armed forces in some countries. **gen•er•al•i•ty** [dʒenə'rælɪtɪ] *n.* being general; **generalities** = general subjects (for a conversation). **gen•er•al•i•za•tion** [dʒenrəlaɪ'zeɪʃn] *n.* general statement. **gen•er•al•ize** ['dʒenrəlaɪz] *v.* to try to express sth as a general notion. **gen•er•al•ly** ['dʒenrəlɪ] *adv.* as a rule. **gen•er•al prac•ti•tion•er**, *n.* doctor who treats all illnesses/family doctor. **gen•er•al-pur•pose**, *adj.* serving many purposes.

gen•er•ate ['dʒenəreɪt] *v.* to bring into existence; to produce. **gen•er•a•tion** [dʒenə'reɪʃn] *n.* (a) bringing into existence. (b) all people born about the same time; **g. gap** = age difference between one generation and another, often resulting in intolerance between them. (c) period of years separating parents and children. (d) members of a family born about the same time. **gen•er•a•tor** ['dʒenəreɪtə] *n.* apparatus for producing electricity by gas, etc.

ge•ner•ic [dʒə'nerɪk] *adj.* referring to a genus/group/type. **ge•ner•i•cal•ly,** *adv.* in a generic way.

gen•er•ous ['dʒenərəs] *adj.* (a) **g. with sth** = willing to give sth. (b) large; **a g. helping.** **gen•er•os•i•ty** [dʒenə'rɒsɪtɪ] *n.* willingness to give (money, etc.). **gen•er•ous•ly,** *adv.* in a generous way.

gen•e•sis ['dʒenəsɪs] *n.* origin/beginning.

ge•net•ics [dʒə'netɪks] *n.* study of heredity. **ge•net•ic,** *adj.* referring to genes/to genetics. **ge•net•i•cal•ly,** *adv.* in a genetic way. **ge•net•ic en•gi•neer•ing,** *n.* modification/replacement of genes in order to produce an organism with desired characteristics, e.g. pest-resistant plants. **ge•net•ic fin•ger•print•ing, genetic profiling,** *n.* analysis of DNA in a sample of body tissue in order to identify an individual, e.g. in forensic medicine.

ge•ni•al ['dʒiːnɪəl] *adj.* cheerful/kindly. **gen•ial•ly,** *adv.* cheerfully.

ge•nie ['dʒiːniː] *n.* in the Arabian Nights, a magic slave who appears from a bottle or lamp.

gen•i•tal ['dʒenɪtl] 1. *adj.* referring to the sex organs. 2. *n.pl.* **genitals** = external sex organs.

gen•i•tive ['dʒenɪtɪv] *adj. & n.* (*in grammar*) **g.** (**case**) = form of a word showing possession.

gen•ius ['dʒiːnɪəs] *n.* (*pl.* **-es**) (a) a person with very great intelligence. (b) very great intelligence. (c) **g. for** = ability to do sth easily.

gen•o•cide ['dʒenəsaɪd] *n.* mass killing of a race.

gen•re ['ʒɑːnrə] *n.* particular type (of art, etc.).

gent [dʒent] *n. inf.* gentleman.

gen•teel [dʒen'tiːl] *adj.* refined, often excessively so. **gen•teel•ly,** *adv.* in a genteel way. **gen•til•i•ty** [dʒen'tɪlɪtɪ] *n.* refinement (of manners).

gen•tian ['dʒenʃn] *n.* small blue alpine flower.

gen•tile ['dʒentaɪl] *n.* person not of Jewish race.

gen•tle ['dʒentl] *adj.* (**-er, -est**) mild/tender/soft. **gent•le•folk,** *n. pl.* (*old*) people of good breeding. **gent•le•man** ['dʒentlmən]

n. (*pl.* **-men**) (a) man of good breeding and manners; **g.'s agreement** = agreement which is not written down. (b) (*polite way of referring to men*) **Well, gentlemen, shall we begin?** **gen•tle•man•ly,** *adj.* like a gentleman. **gen•tle•ness,** *n.* softness/carefulness. **gent•ly** ['dʒentlɪ] *adv.* softly/carefully.

gen•try ['dʒentrɪ] *n.* people of high class and breeding.

gen•u•flect ['dʒenjʊflekt] *v.* to bend the knee, esp. in worship. **gen•u•flec•tion,** *n.* bending the knee.

gen•u•ine ['dʒenjʊɪn] *adj.* authentic/true. **gen•u•ine•ly,** *adv.* truly. **gen•u•ine•ness,** *n.* being genuine.

ge•nus ['dʒiːnəs] *n.* (*pl.* **genera** ['dʒenərə]) group of animals/plants which have common characteristics, and are distinct from all other groups.

ge•o•cen•tric [dʒiːəʊ'sentrɪk] *adj.* (astronomy, etc.) using the earth as the starting point when measuring distances.

ge•od•e•sy [dʒɪ'ɒdɪsɪ] *n.* science of measurement of the earth. **ge•o•des•ic** [dʒiːəʊ'diːsɪk] *adj.* referring to geodesy; **g. dome** = dome made of set of polygons.

ge•og•ra•phy [dʒɪ'ɒgrəfɪ] *n.* science of the earth's surface/form/physical features/climate, etc. **ge•og•ra•pher** [dʒɪ'ɒgrəfə] *n.* person who studies geography. **ge•o•graph•ic(al)** [dʒɪə'græfɪk(l)] *adj.* referring to geography. **ge•o•graph•i•cal•ly,** *adv.* in a geographical way.

ge•ol•o•gy [dʒɪ'ɒlədʒɪ] *n.* science of the earth's crust, esp. rock formations. **ge•o•log•i•cal** [dʒɪə'lɒdʒɪkl] *adj.* referring to geology. **ge•o•log•i•cal•ly.** *adv.* in a geological way. **ge•ol•o•gist** [dʒɪ'ɒlədʒɪst] *n.* person who studies geology.

ge•om•e•try [dʒɪ'ɒmɪtrɪ] *n.* mathematical science of properties and relations of lines/surfaces/solids, etc., in space. **ge•o•met•ric(al)** [dʒɪə'metrɪk(l)] *adj.* referring to geometry; **a g. design** = design of lines/curves, etc. **ge•o•met•ri•cal•ly,** *adv.* in a geometrical way.

ge•o•phys•ics [dʒiːəʊ'fɪzɪks] *n.* study of the physical properties of the earth. **ge•o•phys•i•cist,** *n.* person who studies geophysics.

geor•gette [dʒɔː'dʒet] *n.* thin silk cloth.

Geor•gian ['dʒɔːdʒɪən] *adj.* referring to the

æ back, ɑ: farm, ɒ: top, aɪ pipe, aʊ how, aiə fire, aʊə flower, ɔ: bought, ɔɪ toy, e fed, eəhair, eɪ take, ə afraid, əʊ boat, əʊə lower, v: word, i: heap, ɪ hit, ɪə hear, u: school, ʊ book, ʌ but, b back, d dog, ð then, dʒ just, f fog, g go, h hand, j yes, k catch, l last, m mix, n nut, ŋ sing, p penny, r round, s some, ʃ short, t too, tʃ chop, θ thing, v voice, w was, z zoo, ʒ treasure

reigns of George I to IV of England (1714–1830).

ge•o•sta•tion•ar•y or•bit [dʒiːʹsteɪʃənrɪʹɔːbɪt] *n.* orbit of a satellite that remains over the same point on the earth's surface.

ge•o•ther•mal [dʒiːəuʹθɜːməl] *adj.* (energy) derived from the earth's heat.

ge•ra•ni•um [dʒəʹreɪnɪəm] *n.* perennial plant with white, pink or red flowers.

ger•bil [ʹdʒɜːbl] *n.* small desert rat which jumps, kept as a pet.

ger•i•at•rics [dʒerɪʹætrɪks] *n.* branch of medical science dealing with old age and its diseases. **ger•i•at•ric**, *adj.* for old people. **ger•i•a•tri•cian** [dʒerɪəʹtrɪʃn] *n.* doctor specializing in geriatrics.

germ [dʒɜːm] *n.* (a) portion of organism capable of developing into a new one; **wheat g.** (b) micro-organism, often causing disease. **ger•mi•cid•al**, *adj.* which kills germs. **ger•mi•cide**, *n.* substance which kills germs. **germ war•fare**, *n.* war fought using germs as a weapon.

Ger•man [ʹdʒɜːmən] *adj.* referring to Germany; **G. measles** = mild disease which gives a red rash and which can affect the development of an unborn child if caught by a pregnant woman; **G. shepherd** = large dog often used as a guard dog. 2. *n.* (a) person from Germany. (b) language spoken in Germany, Austria and parts of Switzerland. **Ger•man•ic** [dʒɜːʹmænɪk] *adj.* referring to the Germans. **Ger•man•o**, *prefix meaning* between Germany and another country.

ger•mane [dʒɜːʹmeɪn] *adj.* relevant.

ger•mi•nate [ʹdʒɜːmɪneɪt] *v.* (*of seeds*) to begin to grow/to sprout. **ger•mi•na•tion** [dʒɜːmɪʹneɪʃn] *n.* beginning of plant growth from a seed.

ger•on•tol•o•gy [dʒerɒnʹtɒlədʒɪ] *n.* scientific study of old age and its problems, illnesses, etc.

ger•ry•man•der [ʹdʒerɪmændə] *v.* to alter the boundaries of voting districts in order to improve the chances of a political party in an election.

ger•und [ʹdʒerʌnd] *n.* noun formed from the *-ing* form of a verb.

ges•ta•tion [dʒeʹsteɪʃn] *n.* period between conception and birth.

ges•tic•u•late [dʒeʹstɪkjʊleɪt] *v.* to make expressive signs with the hands and arms. **ges•tic•u•la•tion** [dʒestɪkjuʹleɪʃn] *n.* sign with arms or hands.

ges•ture [ʹdʒestʃə] 1. *n.* (a) movement of limb or body, esp. hands, to give an expression of feeling. (b) action which expresses some positive feeling; **token g.** = small action which

symbolizes feelings. 2. *v.* to make a movement to express a feeling.

get [get] *v.* (**got; has got** or **has gotten**) (a) to obtain. (b) to receive. (c) **to have/have got** = to possess. (d) go for and bring back. (e) *inf.* to understand; **you've got it!** = you've found the right answer/you understand correctly. (f) to cause to happen; to make (s.o.) do sth; **he got his shoes mended; she got the policeman to show her the way.** (g) to have got to = to be obliged to. (h) to arrive at; **to g. home early.** (i) *inf.* to start; **let's get going** = let's start now. (j) to catch (a disease). (k) to become; **he's getting too old for the job.** (l) to be doing sth; **she's getting dressed. get a•bout,** *v.* (a) to go from place to place. (b) to be rumored. **get a•cross,** *v.* (a) to cross (a road). (b) to make (sth) understood. **get a•long,** *v.* (a) to manage. (b) to be on friendly terms (**with s.o.**). **get at,** *v.* (a) to reach. (b) to suggest; **what are you getting at? get a•way,** *v.* to manage to go away; to escape; **he got away with it** = he wasn't found out. **get•a•way,** *n.* escape; **g. car** = car used to escape in. **get back,** *v.* (a) to return. (b) to recover (sth). **get by,** *v.* (a) to pass. (b) *inf.* to manage. **get down,** *v.* (a) to descend. (b) to bring down. (c) to depress; to make (s.o.) gloomy. (d) to make (sth) be written. (e) **to get down to some hard work** = to start to work hard. **get in,** *v.* (a) to go inside (a car, etc.). (b) to be elected. **get in•to,** *v.* (a) to go inside (a car, etc.). (b) **to g. i. trouble** = to be in a difficult situation. **get off,** *v.* (a) to come down from. (b) **he got off lightly** = he received a light punishment. **get on,** *v.* (a) to mount (a bicycle, etc.). (b) to age; **he is getting on** = he is past middle age. (c) **to g. o. with s.o.** = to be friendly with s.o.; **get out,** *v.* (a) to bring out/to go out; **get out!** = leave the room. (b) **I've gotten out of the habit of eating chocolates** = I don't eat chocolates any more. (c) **to get out of (doing) sth** = to avoid doing sth. **get o•ver,** *v.* (a) to overcome (a difficulty). (b) to recover from (an illness). (c) to climb over. **get a•round/round,** *v.* (a) to go around (a corner). (b) to flatter (s.o.). (c) **to g. a. to (doing) sth** = to find time to do (sth). **get through,** *v.* (a) to pass (a test). (b) **to g. t. to s.o.** = to manage to get in contact with s.o. (by telephone). **get-to•geth•er,** *n. inf.* meeting. **get up,** *v.* to rise (from sitting or lying position); to get out of bed. **get-up,** *n.* odd clothes.

gey•ser [ʹgiːzə] *n.* hot spring of water.

ghast•ly [ʹgɑːstlɪ] *adj.* (**-ier, -iest**) horrible/frightful. **ghast•li•ness,** *n.* being ghastly.

gher•kin [ʹgɜːkɪn] *n.* small vegetable of the cucumber family, used for pickling.

ghet•to ['getəu] *n.* (*pl.* -os) area in a city where deprived people live.

ghost [gəust] 1. *n.* (a) spirit of a dead person; **g. story** = story about ghosts which aims at frightening the reader. (b) **the Holy G.** = third person of the Christian Trinity. (c) ghost writer. (d) **a g. of a smile** = very slight smile. 2. *v.* to write (book/article/speech, etc.) for s.o. else who then takes the credit. **ghost•ly,** *adj.* like a ghost. **ghost writ•er,** *n.* person who writes a book for s.o. else who then takes the credit.

ghoul [gu:l] *n.* evil ghost which haunts graves. **ghoul•ish** ['gu:lɪʃ] *adj.* weird/bloodthirsty.

gi•ant ['dʒaɪənt] 1. *n.* (a) (*in fairy tales and myths*) huge human being. (b) abnormally tall person, animal or plant. (c) very powerful industrial organization. (d) extremely able or important person. 2. *adj.* very large. **gi•ant•ess** [dʒaɪən'tes] *n.* (*pl.* -es) female giant.

gib•ber ['dʒɪbə] *v.* to speak very fast, without any meaning. **gib•ber•ish** ['dʒɪbrɪʃ] *n.* (*no pl.*) fast unintelligible speech.

gib•bet ['dʒɪbɪt] *n.* gallows/structure on which criminals were hanged.

gib•bon ['gɪbən] *n.* long-armed ape.

gibe [dʒaɪb] 1. *n.* sarcastic remark. 2. *v.* to jeer/to mock.

gib•lets ['dʒɪbləts] *n. pl.* liver/heart, etc., of poultry, removed before the bird is cooked.

gid•dy ['gɪdɪ] *adj.* (-ier, -iest) dizzy; feeling as if everything is spinning round. **gid•di•ly,** *adv.* in a giddy way. **gid•di•ness,** *n.* dizzy feeling.

gift [gɪft] *n.* (a) present/thing given; **g. certificate** = certificate given as a present, which allows the person who receives it to buy sth at a store. (b) talent; **she has a g. for music. gift•ed,** *adj.* talented. **gift-wrap,** *v.* (**gift-wrapped**) to wrap (sth) in colored paper to give as a present.

gig [gɪg] *n.* (a) light carriage on two wheels. (b) *inf.* performance by popular musicians.

giga- ['gɪgə] *prefix* one thousand million.

gi•gan•tic [dʒaɪ'gæntɪk] *adj.* huge/colossal.

gig•gle ['gɪgl] 1. *n.* little nervous laugh; **to have a fit of the giggles** = to be unable to stop giggling. 2. *v.* to laugh little nervous laughs.

gig•o•lo ['dʒɪgɒləu] *n.* (*pl.* -os) man who is paid by a woman to be her lover.

gild [gɪld] *v.* to cover with a thin layer of gold.

gill [dʒɪl] *n.* liquid measure equal to a quarter of a pint (140 ml).

gills [gɪlz] *n. pl.* (a) breathing organs in fish and other aquatic creatures. (b) thin vertical folds on the underside of mushrooms.

gilt [gɪlt] 1. *adj.* covered with a thin layer of gold. 2. *n.* (a) young female pig. (b) gilt-edged security. **gilt-edged,** *adj.* (investment) which will not lose its value.

gim•bals ['gɪmbəlz] *n. pl.* device (of several rings balanced inside each other) to keep a compass level at sea.

gim•crack ['dʒɪmkræk] *adj.* cheap and badly made.

gim•let ['gɪmlət] *n.* small tool used for boring holes.

gim•mick ['gɪmɪk] *n.* device adopted for the purpose of attracting attention or publicity.

gin [dʒɪn] *n.* (a) colorless alcoholic drink flavored with juniper; glass of this drink. (b) trap for catching wild animals and game. (c) machine for cleaning raw cotton.

gin•ger ['dʒɪndʒə] 1. *n.* plant with a hot-tasting root used in cooking and medicine. 2. *adj.* (hair) of reddish color. **gin•ger•bread,** *n.* cake made with molasses and flavored with ginger. **gin•ger ale, ginger beer,** *n.* fizzy ginger-flavored drink. **gin•ger•ly,** 1. *adj.* cautious. 2. *adv.* delicately/with caution. **ginger up,** *v.* to stimulate/to enliven.

ging•ham ['gɪŋəm] *n.* checked cotton cloth.

gin•gi•vi•tis [dʒɪndʒɪ'vaɪtɪs] *n.* swelling and bleeding of the gums.

gink•go ['gɪŋgəu] *n.* Chinese tree, which is similar to trees which flourished millions of years ago.

gip•sy ['dʒɪpsɪ] *n. see* **gyp•sy.**

gi•raffe [dʒɪ'rɑ:f] *n.* African animal with a very long neck and spotted skin.

gird [gɜ:d] *v.* (*formal*) (**girded/girt**) to tie a belt round (sth).

gird•er ['gɜ:də] *n.* iron/steel beam used as a support.

gir•dle ['gɜ:dl] *n.* (a) belt/sash. (b) corset. (c) **pelvic g.** = bones around the hips supporting the lower limbs.

girl [gɜ:l] *n.* female child; young woman. **girl•friend,** *n.* female companion (esp. of a man). **girl•hood,** *n.* period when you are a girl (before becoming a woman). **girl•ie,** *adj. inf.* **g. magazine** = one with photographs of naked young women. **girl•ish,** *adj.* like a young girl.

girt [gɜ:t] *v. see* **gird.**

æ back, ɑ: farm, ɒ: top, aɪ pipe, aʊ how, aɪə fire, aʊə flower, ɔ: bought, ɔɪ toy, e fed, eəhair, eɪ take, ə afraid, əʊ boat, əʊə lower, v: word, i: heap, ɪ hit, ɪə hear, u: school, ʊ book, ʌ but, b back, d dog, ð then, dʒ just, f fog, g go, h hand, j yes, k catch, l last, m mix, n nut, ŋ sing, p penny, r round, s some, ʃ short, t too, tʃ chop, θ thing, v voice, w was, z zoo, ʒ treasure

girth [gɜ:θ] n. (a) circumference/distance round sth. (b) band of leather or cloth tied round the body of a horse to secure the saddle.

gist [dʒɪst] n. real point of a matter; basic essentials.

give [gɪv] 1. v. (gave; has given) (a) to hand (sth) to s.o.; to transfer (sth) to s.o. (b) to utter (a cry). (c) to collapse; to bend. 2. n. (a) suppleness; **the plank hasn't enough g.** (b) **g. and take** = agreement between two people/parties to make concessions. **give away**, v. (a) to hand over (sth) without asking for anything in return. (b) to betray/to tell (a secret). (c) to give (a bride) to the bridegroom. **give back**, v. to return. **give in**, v. to surrender/to yield. **giv•en**, adj. (a) **she is g. to crying** = she cries frequently. (b) particular/which has been identified. (c) **g. name** = first name/Christian name. **give off**, v. to let out. **give out**, v. (a) to distribute. (b) inf. to fail. (c) to make known. **give o•ver**, v. inf. to stop. **giv•er**, n. person who gives. **give up**, v. to stop (doing sth); **I give up!** = I cannot think of the answer; **the murderer gave himself up** = surrendered to the police. **give way**, v. (a) to allow s.o. to go first. (b) to yield; to bend; to collapse.

giz•zard ['gɪzəd] n. second stomach of a bird, where its food is ground up into tiny pieces.

gla•brous ['glæbrəs] adj. smooth, with no hair.

gla•cé ['glæseɪ] adj. (cherries) preserved in sugar.

gla•cier ['glæsɪə] n. mass of ice which moves slowly down from a mountain. **gla•cial** ['gleɪʃl] adj. (a) referring to ice. (b) very cold; without emotion. **gla•ci•a•tion** [gleɪsɪ'eɪʃn] n. effect of ice on rocks.

glad [glæd] adj. pleased/happy. **glad•den**, v. to make glad. **glad•ly**, adv. happily. **glad•ness**, n. happiness.

glade [gleɪd] n. (formal) clear open space in the midst of trees.

glad•i•a•tor ['glædɪeɪtə] n. man who fought in an arena (in ancient Rome). **glad•i•a•to•ri•al** [glædɪə'tɔːrɪəl] adj. referring to gladiators.

glad•i•o•lus [glædɪ'əʊləs] n. (pl. **gladioli** [glædɪ'əʊlaɪ]) tall garden plant with sword-shaped leaves and bright flower spikes.

glair [gleːə] n. white of egg, used as a glaze.

glam•or, Brit. **glam•our** ['glæmə] n. (a) magic/enchantment. (b) outward charm/attractiveness (of a woman). **glam•or•ize**, v. to make (sth) appear more appealing than it really is. **glam•or•ous**, adj. attractive/enchanting.

glance [glɑːns] 1. n. quick look. 2. v. (a) to look briefly. (b) to slide off an object instead of striking it fully. **glan•cing**, adj. sliding off to the side; not straight.

gland [glænd] n. organ of the body which produces a liquid which controls bodily changes, such as growth. **glan•du•lar** ['glændjʊlə] adj. referring to glands; **g. fever** = severe illness which affects the glands.

glare ['gleə] 1. n. (a) strong/fierce light. (b) fierce/fixed look. 2. v. (a) to shine too brightly. (b) to look angrily at s.o. **glar•ing**, adj. **g. mistake** = very obvious mistake.

glas•nost ['glæznɒst] n. openness, freedom of information.

glass [glɑːs] n. (a) substance made from sand and soda or potash, usu. transparent, used for making windows, etc. (b) open container made of glass used esp. for drinking; contents of such a glass. (c) mirror; **looking g.; stained g.** = colored glass used frequently in the windows of a church. **glass blow•er**, n. person who blows and shapes molten glass into bottles, etc. **glas•ses**, n. pl. eyeglasses. **glass•ware**, n. (no pl.) articles made of glass. **glass wool**, n. soft substance, made from glass fiber, used as an insulating material in buildings. **glass•y**, adj. (a) resembling glass. (b) dull/unseeing; **a g. stare.**

glau•co•ma [glɔː'kəʊmə] n. disease of the eyes which can cause blindness.

glaze [gleɪz] 1. n. shiny surface (on pottery). 2. v. (a) to fit with glass; to put glass in (a window). (b) to cover with a shiny coating. **gla•zier** ['gleɪzɪə] n. person whose trade is to fit glass in windows. **glaz•ing**, n. fitting with windows; **double g.** = windows with two sheets of glass a small distance apart, which help insulation.

gleam [gliːm] 1. n. (a) short-lived weak light. (b) faint/temporary show of some quality. 2. v. to shine.

glean [gliːn] v. to collect (grain) left after the harvest; to gather or discover (news/information, etc.). **glean•er**, n. person who gleans. **glean•ings**, n. pl. things obtained by gleaning.

glee [gliː] n. (a) short song sung by several singers. (b) joy/gaiety. **glee•ful**, adj. joyful. **glee•ful•ly**, adv. happily.

glen [glen] n. narrow valley.

glib [glɪb] adj. fluent but insincere way of speaking. **glib•ly**, adv. smoothly and insincerely.

glide [glaɪd] 1. n. smooth movement. 2. v. to move smoothly. **glid•er**, n. small aircraft without an engine that relies on wind currents for propulsion. **glid•ing**, n. sport of flying gliders.

glim•mer ['glɪmə] 1. n. (a) feeble light. (b) tiny

quantity; faint/temporary show of (interest, etc.). 2. *v.* to shine feebly/intermittently.

glimpse [glɪmps] 1. *n.* quick/passing sight. 2. *v.* to catch sight of (sth).

glint [glɪnt] 1. *n.* flash/glitter/sparkle. 2. *v.* to flash/to glitter (like metal).

glis•ten ['glɪsn] *v.* (*of something wet*) to shine/to sparkle.

glit•ter ['glɪtə] 1. *n.* bright light/sparkle. 2. *v.* to shine brightly/to sparkle.

gloam•ing ['gləʊmɪŋ] *n.* twilight.

gloat [gləʊt] *v.* **to g. over** = to take pleasure in (s.o.'s misfortune); to look at (sth) greedily.

globe [gləʊb] *n.* (a) **the g.** = the earth. (b) ball with a map of the world on it. (c) round object; glass shade which covers an electric light bulb; **g. artichoke** = tall green thistlelike plant of which you eat parts of the flower head. **glob•al**, *adj.* world-wide. **glob•al•ly**, *adv.* all over the world. **glob•al po•si•tion•ing sys•tem**, *n.* navigation system that can give the location on the earth of a device when it transmits and receives signals from satellites. **glob•al warm•ing**, *n.* increase in the temperature of the earth's atmosphere, thought to be caused by the greenhouse effect. **globe•trot•ter**, *n.* tourist who travels all over the world.

glob•ule ['glɒbjuːl] *n.* small round object (such as a drop of water). **glob•u•lar**, *adj.* shaped like a globe. **glob•u•lin**, *n.* protein found in blood, which contains antibodies.

glock•en•spiel ['glɒknspiːl] *n.* musical instrument like a xylophone with metal bars.

gloom [gluːm] *n.* (a) darkness. (b) despair/melancholy. **gloom•i•ly**, *adv.* in a gloomy way. **gloom•y**, *adj.* (-ier, -iest) melancholy; pessimistic.

glo•ry ['glɔːrɪ] 1. *n.* (a) fame/renown. (b) magnificent sight. 2. *v.* **to g. in** = to get great pleasure from/to pride oneself on. **glo•ri•fi•ca•tion** [glɔːrɪfɪ'keɪʃn] *n.* transforming into sth more splendid. **glo•ri•fy**, *v.* to make glorious/to transform into sth more splendid. **glo•ri•ous** ['glɔːrɪəs] *adj.* splendid. **glo•ri•ous•ly**, *adv.* in a glorious way. **glo•ry•hole**, *n.* cupboard/room where you can keep junk.

gloss [glɒs] 1. *n.* (a) shine on a surface; showy appearance; **g. paint** = paint which is shiny when dry. (b) comment about a text. 2. *v.* **to g. over** = to try to hide (a mistake, etc.). **gloss•i•ness**, *n.* being glossy. **gloss•y**, *adj.*

& *n.* (-ier, -iest) g. magazines/glossies = colorful, expensive magazines printed on shiny paper.

glos•sa•ry ['glɒsərɪ] *n.* short explanation of meanings of words, usu. found at the end of a book.

glot•tis ['glɒtɪs] *n.* space in the vocal cords, which makes sound when opened or closed. **glot•tal**, *adj.* referring to the glottis; **g. stop** = type of clicking sound made by closing the glottis.

glove [glʌv] *n.* article of clothing worn on the hand; **to handle s.o. with kid gloves** = to deal gently with s.o.; **hand in g. with s.o.** = closely associated with s.o.; **g. compartment** = small cupboard on the dashboard of a car, in which you can put small items. **gloved**, *adj.* wearing gloves.

glow [gləʊ] 1. *n.* (a) brightness/warmth. (b) blush/bloom. 2. *v.* to shine; to show warm color. **glow•ing**, *adj.* shining/warm. **glow-worm**, *n.* female beetle which gives off a green light in the dark.

glow•er ['glaʊə] *v.* to frown.

glox•in•i•a [glɒk'sɪnɪə] *n.* type of pot plant with large trumpet-shaped flowers.

glu•cose ['gluːkəʊz] *n.* natural sugar found in fruit.

glue [gluː] 1. *n.* substance which will stick things together. 2. *v.* to stick together. **glue•y**, *adj.* sticky.

glum [glʌm] *adj.* (**glummer, glummest**) sullen; looking dejected/miserable.

glut [glʌt] 1. *n.* too much of (sth); supply exceeding demand. 2. *v.* **to be glutted (with)** = to have too much.

glu•ten ['gluːtən] *n.* protein left when starch is removed from flour. **glu•ti•nous** ['gluːtɪnəs] *adj.* sticky.

glut•ton ['glʌtn] *n.* (a) person who eats too much. (b) person with great enthusiasm **for** sth. **glut•ton•ous**, *adj.* referring to overeating. **glut•ton•y**, *n.* eating too much.

glyc•er•in, glycerine ['glɪsərɪn] *n.* colorless, sweet liquid (used in medicines/in explosives, etc.).

gm *abbrev. for* gram.

GMT [dʒiːem'tiː] *abbreviation for* Greenwich Mean Time.

gnarled [nɑːld] *adj.* twisted/rugged; covered with hard lumps.

gnash [næʃ] *v.* to grind (the teeth).

æ back, ɑː farm, ɒ top, aɪ pipe, aʊ how, aɪə fire, aʊə flower, ɔː bought, ɔɪ toy, e fed, eə hair, eɪ take, ə afraid, əʊ boat, əʊə lower, vː word, iː heap, ɪ hit, ɪə hear, uː school, ʊ book, ʌ but, b back, d dog, ð then, dʒ just, f fog, g go, h hand, j yes, k catch, l last, m mix, n nut, ŋ sing, p penny, r round, s some, ʃ short, t too, tʃ chop, θ thing, v voice, w was, z zoo, ʒ treasure

gnat [næt] *n.* small, two-winged fly which stings.

gnaw [nɔ:] *v.* to chew.

gneiss [naɪs] *n.* type of hard rock.

gnome [nəum] *n.* dwarf/mischievous ugly little man (in fairy stories). **gno•mic**, *adj.* concise and clever (saying).

GNP [dʒi:en'pi:] *n.* gross national product.

gnu [nu:] *n.* large South African antelope.

go [gəu] 1. *n.* (a) act of moving; *inf.* **he's always on the g.** = always moving about. (b) *inf.* energy; **she's full of g.** (c) attempt/try. (d) **to try and make a g. of it** = to try to make the business successful. 2. *v.* **(went; has gone)** (a) to move from one place to another; to travel. (b) to work; **my car won't g.** (c) to leave; **from the word g.** = from the start. (d) **to be going to do sth** = to intend to do sth; to be about to do sth. (e) to fit; **it's too big to g. into the box.** (f) to become; **she went pale.** (g) to make a noise; **the guns went bang.** (h) to have a certain tune/certain words; **how does the song g.?** (i) to fail; **the brakes went. go a•bout,** *v.* (a) to try to do sth/to plan how to do sth. (b) (*of sailing boat*) to turn to sail in another direction. (c) to move around. **go a•head,** *v.* to start to do sth. **go-a•head.** 1. *n.* permission to start. 2. *adj.* enterprising; active. **go a•long with,** *v.* to agree with (s.o./sth). **go back,** *v.* to return. **go back on,** *v.* not to keep (a promise). **go-be•tween,** *n.* person who carries messages from one person to another. **go-cart,** *n.* flat wooden frame with four wheels for children to play with. **go down,** *v.* (a) to descend. (b) **to go down well** = to be accepted. **go for,** *v.* (a) to apply for. (b) to like. (c) to be sold. (d) to attack. **go-get•ter,** *n. inf.* energetic, ambitious person. **go-go danc•er,** *n. inf.* person who performs an energetic (and usu. erotic) dance in a nightclub. **go in,** *v.* to enter; **the sun's gone in** = is hidden by clouds. **go in for,** *v.* (a) to approve of. (b) to do or like to do (sth); **to g. i. f. fishing. go•ing.** 1. *adj.* (a) working. (b) **g. rate** = usual rate/current rate. 2. *n.* **do it while the g. is good** = while you have the chance. (b) **goings-on** = unusual things which are happening. **go in•to,** *v.* (a) to enter. (b) (*in math*) to divide. (c) to examine. **go-kart,** *n.* flat frame with four wheels and an engine, used as a small racing car. **go-kart•ing,** *n.* racing in go-karts. **go off,** *v.* (a) to explode. (b) to turn out; happen. **go on,** *v.* (a) to continue. (b) (*showing disbelief*) *inf.* **go on!** = I don't believe you! (c) to happen; **what's going on here?** (d) **to go on about sth** = to talk all the time; to nag. **go out,** *v.* (a) to leave. (b) to stop operating; **the electricity went off. go out with,** *v.* to go to parties/the theater, etc. with (s.o. of the opposite sex). **go a•round,** *v.* (a) to be enough for all. (b) to visit. **go un•der,** *v.* (a) to drown. (b) to be ruined. **go up,** *v.* to rise; **to g. u. in flames** = to burn. **go with,** *v.* to match/to fit with. **go with•out,** *v.* not to have.

goad [gəud] 1. *n.* long stick for driving cattle. 2. *v.* **to g. s.o. into doing sth** = to urge/to drive s.o. on by annoying him/her.

goal [gəul] *n.* (a) object of effort/ambition; aim. (b) two posts between which a ball has to be driven to score a point in a game. (c) points won (in football/hockey, etc.). **goal•keep•er,** *inf.* **goal•ie,** *n.* player who defends the goal. **goal•mouth,** *n.* area just in front of the goal. **goal•post,** *n.* one of the two posts between which a ball is driven to score a goal.

goat [gəut] *n.* domestic animal with horns and a beard; **to separate the sheep from the goats** = to divide the good from the bad; *inf.* **to get s.o.'s g.** = to annoy s.o. **goat•ee** [gəu'ti:] *n.* small beard, like that of a goat.

gob [gɒb] *n. Sl.* 1. mouth; **shut your g.!** = stop talking! 2. *v. Sl.* to spit.

gob•bet ['gɒbɪt] *n.* large lump (of fat).

gob•ble ['gɒbl] *v.* (a) to eat quickly and greedily. (b) to make a noise like a turkey. **gob•ble•de•gook** ['gɒbldɪgu:k] *n. inf.* meaningless official/technical language.

gob•let ['gɒblət] *n.* metal or glass drinking cup without handles.

gob•lin ['gɒblɪn] *n.* (*in fairy stories*) mischievous ugly little man.

god [gɒd] *n.* (a) deity; superhuman power. (b) **God** = creator and ruler of the Universe, according to Christian/Jewish/Muslim, etc., belief. (c) thing which is worshipped. **god•child,** *n.* (*pl.* -children) child who was sponsored at baptism. **god-daugh•ter,** *n.* girl who was sponsored at baptism. **god•dess,** *n.* female god. **god•fa•ther,** *n.* man who sponsors a child at baptism; *inf.* head of a mafia group. **god-fear•ing,** *adj.* sincerely religious. **god•for•sak•en,** *adj.* bad/awful. **god•like,** *adj.* like a god. **god•li•ness,** *n.* being godly. **god•ly,** *adj.* holy. **god•moth•er,** *n.* woman who sponsors a child at baptism. **god•par•ents,** *n. pl.* people who sponsor a child at baptism. **god•send,** *n.* blessing. **god•son,** *n.* boy who was sponsored at baptism.

go•down ['gəudaun] *n.* warehouse (in the Far East).

gog•gle ['gɒgl] *v.* to stare (at). **gog•gles,** *n. pl.* protective glasses against dust and glare.

goi•ter, *Brit.* **goi•tre** ['gɔɪtə] *n.* disease in which the thyroid gland in the neck swells up.

gold [gəʊld] 1. *n.* (a) (*element:* Au) precious yellow metal. (b) medal made of gold (won in a sports competition). 2. *adj.* made of gold; **g. leaf** = thin covering of gold; **g. plate** = dishes made of gold. **gold•crest**, *n.* very small bird, with an orange crest on its head. **gold-dig•ger**, *n.* (a) person who digs for gold. (b) *inf.* woman who marries a man for his money. **gold•en**, *adj.* made of gold; gold-colored; **g. opportunity** = wonderful chance; **g. rule** = very important rule; **g. wedding** = fiftieth anniversary of marriage; **g. handshake** = sum of money or other benefit given to an employee, usu. older, as an incentive to retire earlier than planned. **gold•field**, *n.* land where gold is mined. **gold•finch**, *n.* brightly colored song bird. **gold•fish**, *n.* (*pl.* **goldfish**) small orange fish kept in ponds/bowls. **gold•mine**, *n.* mine which produces gold; very profitable business. **gold rec•ord**, *n.* award given to a singer whose record has sold one million copies. **gold•smith**, *n.* person who works in gold.

golf [gɒlf] *n.* game for two people, or two couples, where a small hard ball is struck with long-handled clubs into a series of holes, the object being to use as few strokes as possible. **golf club**, *n.* (a) wooden- or metal-headed stick for striking the golf ball. (b) group of people who play golf, and allow others to join them on payment of a fee; clubhouse where golfers meet. **golf course**, *n.* ground on which golf is played. **golf•er**, *n.* person who plays golf.

go•nad ['gəʊnæd] *n.* gland which produces gametes.

gon•do•la ['gɒndələ] *n.* (a) boat used on the canals in Venice. (b) basket/passenger compartment hanging underneath a balloon. **gon•do•lier** [gɒndə'lɪə] *n.* man who pushes a gondola, using a pole.

gone [gɒn] *v. see* **go**. **gon•er** ['gɒnə] *n. inf.* dying person; dead person.

gong [gɒŋ] *n.* metal disk with a turned rim which gives a resonant sound when struck, used esp. to call people to meals.

gon•na ['gɒnə] *v. Sl.* = going to.

gon•or•rhe•a, *Brit.* **gon•or•rhoe•a** [gɒnə-'rɪə] *n.* type of venereal disease.

goo [guː] *n. inf.* (*no pl.*) sticky stuff. **goo•ey**, *adj. inf.* sticky.

good [gʊd] 1. *adj.* (**better, best**) (a) having the right qualities/satisfactory; **did you have a g.**

time? = did you enjoy yourself? (b) able; **he is g. at French.** (c) right/proper; **it is a g. idea.** (d) morally excellent/virtuous; **he is a g. man.** (e) well behaved/not troublesome. (f) efficient/suitable/competent; **he was as g. as his word** = he did what he said he would do. (g) **g. morning! g. afternoon! g. evening!** *interjections used when meeting or leaving someone in the morning, afternoon or evening.* (h) valid/sound/thorough. (i) not less than; **she waited a g. half-hour.** (j) a lot of; **a g. many people; a g. deal of money.** (k) **as g. as** = practically/almost. 2. *n.* (a) **the g.** = virtuous people. (b) profit/advantage; **what g. will it do him? to do g.** = to act kindly; **for g.** = permanently/forever; **he is up to no g.** = he is acting in a suspicious manner. (c) **goods** = movable property. **good•bye** [gʊd'baɪ] *n. & inter. used when leaving someone.* **good-for-noth•ing**, *n.* useless, lazy person. **Good Fri•day**, *n.* Friday before Easter Day. **good-hu•mored**, *adj.* pleasant; in a happy mood. **good•ies**, *n. pl.* good things/money/treasure. **good•ish**, *adj.* quite good. **good-look•ing**, *adj.* handsome/pretty. **good-na•tured**, *adj.* kindly/pleasant. **good•ness**, *n.* virtue/kindness/generosity. **good•night**, *n. & inter. used when leaving someone late at night.* **good•will**, *n.* (a) kindly feeling toward a person. (b) good reputation of a business. **good•y-good•y**, *adj. inf.* (person) who is too good.

goof [guːf] 1. *n. Sl.* stupid person. 2. *v.* to make a stupid mistake. **goof•y**, *adj. inf.* stupid.

goon [guːn] *n.* silly fool.

goos•an•der [guː'sændə] *n.* type of wild duck.

goose [guːs] *n.* (*pl.* **geese**) (a) web-footed water bird, larger than a duck. (b) *inf.* silly person. **goose•ber•ry** ['guːzbrɪ] *n.* small edible green fruit; bush which bears this fruit. **goose•flesh**, *n.* **goose-pim•ples**, *n.pl.* mass of small bumps on the skin caused by fear/by cold, etc. **goose-step.** 1. *n.* way of marching without bending the knees. 2. *v.* (**goosestepped**) to march without bending the knees.

go•pher ['gəʊfə] *n.* North American rodent which lives in burrows.

gore [gɔː] 1. *n.* (a) (*formal*) blood which has thickened after coming from a wound. (b) section of a skirt, shaped like a triangle. 2. *v.* to pierce with a horn. **gored**, *adj.* (skirt) with a gore.

æ **back**, ɑː **farm**, ɒ **top**, aɪ **pipe**, aʊ **how**, aɪə **fire**, aʊə **flower**, ɔː **bought**, ɔɪ **toy**, e **fed**, eə **hair**, eɪ **take**, ə **afraid**, əʊ **boat**, əʊə **lower**, ɜː **word**, iː **heap**, ɪ **hit**, ɪə **hear**, uː **school**, ʊ **book**, ʌ **but**, b **back**, d **dog**, ð **then**, dʒ **just**, f **fog**, g **go**, h **hand**, j **yes**, k **catch**, l **last**, m **mix**, n **nut**, ŋ **sing**, p **penny**, r **round**, s **some**, ʃ **short**, t **too**, tʃ **chop**, θ **thing**, v **voice**, w **was**, z **zoo**, ʒ **treasure**

gorge [gɔːdʒ] 1. *n.* narrow opening between hills. 2. *v.* to eat greedily; **he gorged himself on chocolates.**

gor•geous ['gɔːdʒəs] *adj.* magnificent/splendid; richly colored. **gor•geous•ly**, *adv.* splendidly.

gor•gon ['gɔːgən] *n.* mean, ugly woman.

go•ril•la [gə'rɪlə] *n.* large, powerful African ape.

gor•mand•ize ['gɔːməndaɪz] *v.* to eat far too much.

gorse [gɔːs] *n.* prickly yellow-flowered shrub.

gor•y ['gɔːrɪ] *adj.* (**-ier, -iest**) covered in blood.

gosh [gɒʃ] *inter. showing* surprise.

gos•hawk ['gɒshɔːk] *n.* type of trained hawk.

gos•ling ['gɒzlɪŋ] *n.* baby goose.

gos•pel ['gɒspl] *n.* record of Christ's life in the books of the four evangelists; **it's the g. truth** = it's absolutely true.

gos•sa•mer ['gɒsəmə] *n.* (a) very fine cobweb. (b) very fine material.

gos•sip ['gɒsɪp] 1. *n.* (a) idle talk, esp. about other people; **g. column** = section in a paper which gives news about the private lives of famous people. (b) person who spreads rumors. 2. *v.* to talk idly; to spread rumors. **gos•sip•y**, *adj.* full of gossip.

got [gɒt] *v.* (a) *see* **get.** (b) **to have g. to do sth** = to be obliged/to have to do sth.

goth•ic ['gɒθɪk] *adj.* style of architecture with pointed arches used in Western Europe in 12th–16th centuries.

got•ta ['gɒtə] *v. Sl.* = (have) got to.

got•ten ['gɒtn] *v. see* **get.**

gouache [gʊ'ɑːʃ] *n.* kind of thick watercolor paint.

gouge [gaʊdʒ] 1. *n.* kind of chisel used in carpentry. 2. *v.* to scoop out.

gou•lash ['guːlæʃ] *n.* Hungarian stew flavored with paprika.

gourd [gʊəd] *n.* dried fruit of a climbing plant, used as a bowl.

gour•mand ['gʊəmənd] *n.* person who eats too much.

gour•met ['gʊəmeɪ] *n.* connoisseur of food and wine.

gout [gaʊt] *n.* painful inflammation of the joints, esp. the big toe. **gout•y**, *adj.* afflicted with gout.

gov•ern ['gʌvən] 1. *v.* (a) to rule with authority. (b) to influence/to determine. **gov•ern•ance**, *n.* (*formal*) way of governing. **gov•ern•ess**, *n.* female teacher, usu. in a private household. **gov•ern•ment** ['gʌvənmənt] *n.* group of people ruling a country. **gov•ern•men•tal** [gʌvən'mentl] *adj.* referring to a government. **gov•er•nor**,

n. head of a state government in the United States.

gown [gaʊn] *n.* (a) (*formal*) dress. (b) long official robe (worn by a judge/person with a degree, etc.). (c) **dressing-g.** = long coat worn over night clothes.

G.P. ['dʒiː'piː] *abbreviation for* general practitioner; family doctor.

G.P.O. [dʒiːpiː'əʊ] *abbreviation for* General Post Office.

GPS [dʒiːpiː'es] *abbrev. for* global positioning system.

grab [græb] 1. *n.* sudden seizing with the hands; **to make a g. for** = to try to seize. 2. *v.* (**grabbed**) to seize.

grace [greɪs] 1. *n.* (a) pleasing quality/attractiveness; **with good g.** = with a show of willingness. (b) short prayer of thanksgiving before or after a meal. (c) act of mercy; pardon from all sin. (d) favor shown by granting a delay; **ten days' g.** 2. *v.* to honor. **grace•ful**, *adj.* moving with ease. **grace•ful•ly**, *adv.* moving easily. **grace•ful•ness**, *n.* ease of movement. **grace•less**, *adj.* with no grace. **grace note**, *n.* note in music which need not be played, but which adds to the attraction of the piece. **gra•cious** ['greɪʃəs] *adj.* kind/agreeable; elegant (way of living); **good g.!** = how surprising! **gra•cious•ly**, *adv.* kindly. **gra•cious•ness**, *n.* being gracious.

grade [greɪd] 1. *n.* (a) degree/level/rank; **to make the g.** = to succeed. (b) mark in an exam. (c) class (in school). 2. *v.* to arrange in grades/to sort out. **gra•da•tion** [grə'deɪʃn] *n.* series of steps, passing from one level to another. **grade cross•ing**, *n.* place where a railroad track crosses a road, etc. at the same level.

gra•di•ent ['greɪdɪənt] *n.* amount of slope in a road, railroad, etc.

grad•u•al ['grædjʊəl] *adj.* slow/progressive. **grad•u•al•ly**, *adv.* little by little.

grad•u•ate 1. *n.* ['grædjʊət] person who has obtained a degree; **g. of Yale University.** 2. *v.* ['grædjʊeɪt] (a) to obtain a degree (**from** a university). (b) to arrange in gradations. (c) to mark in a scale; **graduated measuring glass** = one with quantities marked on it. **grad•u•a•tion** [grædjʊ'eɪʃn] *n.* (a) obtaining a degree. (b) act of marking a scale.

graf•fi•ti [grə'fiːtɪ] *n. pl.* unofficial drawings or writing on walls.

graft [grɑːft] 1. *n.* (a) shoot of a plant inserted into another plant from which it receives sap and of which it becomes part. (b) (*in surgery*) piece of transplanted living tissue. (c) *Sl.* bribery; bribe. 2. *v.* to insert (part of a plant) into another plant so that it can grow; to attach (skin, etc.) to other parts of the body.

Grail [greɪl] *n.* **the Holy G.** = precious object (the cup used at the Last Supper) which was sought by medieval knights.

grain [greɪn] *n.* (a) seed of cereal. (b) small particle of sand/gold, etc. (c) texture of particles (in stone); lines of fibers in wood/material; **it goes against the g.** = it goes against natural instincts. (d) measurement of weight. **grain•y,** *adj.* (wood) with a strongly marked grain.

gram [græm] *n.* measurement of weight, one thousandth part of a kilogram.

gram•mar ['græmə] *n.* (a) art and science of a language; rules of the forms of words and their relationship in a language. (b) book which explains/teaches the rules of a language. **gram•mar•i•an** [grə'meərɪən] *n.* specialist in the study of grammar. **gram•mar school,** *n.* elementary school. **gram•mat•i•cal** [grə'mætɪkl] *adj.* conforming to the rules of grammar. **gram•mat•i•cal•ly,** *adv.* according to the rules of grammar.

gram•pus ['græmpəs] *n.* sea animal similar to a dolphin.

gra•na•ry ['grænərɪ] *n.* storehouse for grain.

grand [grænd] 1. *adj.* (-er, -est) (a) important/imposing. (b) final. (c) conducted with solemnity. (d) very good. 2. *n.* (a) *inf.* grand piano. (b) *Sl.* thousand dollars. **gran•dad,** *n. inf.* grandfather. **grand•child,** *n.* (*pl.* -children) child of a son or daughter. **grand•daugh•ter,** *n.* daughter of a son or daughter. **gran•dee** [græn'diː] *n.* proud aristocrat (usu. Spanish). **gran•deur** ['grændʒə] *n.* splendor/majesty. **grand•fa•ther,** *n.* father of a mother or father; **g. clock** = tall clock standing on the floor. **gran•dil•o•quence** [græn'dɪləkwəns] *n.* pompous/wordy speech. **gran•dil•o•quent,** *adj.* speaking in a pompous way. **gran•di•ose** ['grændɪəus] *adj.* very splendid. **grand•ly,** *adv.* in a grand way. **grand•ma** ['grænmɑː] *n. inf.* grandmother. **grand•mas•ter,** *n.* chessplayer of international quality. **grand•moth•er,** *n.* mother of a mother or father. **grand•ness,** *n.* being grand. **grand•pa** ['grænpɑː] *n. inf.* grandfather. **grand•par•ents,** *n. pl.* parents of a mother or father. **grand pi•a•no,** *n.* large horizontal piano. **Grand Prix** [grɒŋ'priː] *n.* motor/motorcycle race. **grand•son,** *n.* son of a son or daughter. **grand•stand,** *n.* building with a sloping bank of seats for spectators at a racetrack or sports stadium.

grange [greɪndʒ] *n.* farm with its buildings.

gran•ite ['grænɪt] *n.* hard light-gray stone used for building.

gran•ny ['grænɪ] *n. inf.* grandmother; **g. knot** = insecure type of reef knot.

grant [grɑːnt] 1. *n.* financial aid. 2. *v.* (a) to agree/to give consent; **to take sth for granted** = not to appreciate it any more. (b) to agree; **I g. you it is a difficult job** = I admit that it is difficult. **grant•ed,** *adj.* admitted/understood.

gran•u•late ['grænjuleɪt] *v.* to form into grains. **gran•u•lar,** *adj.* containing grains; like grains. **gran•ule,** *n.* very small particle.

grape [greɪp] *n.* small green or purple fruit growing in clusters on a vine, eaten as fruit or made into wine. **grape•fruit,** *n.* (*pl.* grapefruit) large round yellow citrus fruit. **grape•vine,** *n.* climbing plant on which grapes grow. **I heard it on the g.** = I learned the news by gossip/unofficially.

graph [grɑːf] *n.* mathematical diagram/curve. **graph•ic** ['græfɪk] *adj.* (a) referring to graphs/diagrams/signs, etc. (c) vivid (description). **graph•i•cal,** *adj.* referring to graphs/diagrams/signs, etc. **graph•i•cal•ly,** *adv.* (a) using graphs/diagrams/signs, etc. (b) in a graphic way. **graph•i•cal us•er in•ter•face (GUI),** *n.* means by which a user interacts with a computer that involves graphics, e.g. by using a mouse to select options on screen. **graph•ics,** *n.* pictures/charts on a printed document or on a computer screen. **graph pa•per,** *n.* paper with small squares for drawing graphs on.

graph•ite ['græfaɪt] *n.* naturally occurring form of carbon; lead (as used in a pencil).

graph•ol•o•gy [græ'folədʒɪ] *n.* science of discovering s.o.'s character from handwriting. **graph•ol•o•gist,** *n.* person who practices graphology.

grap•nel ['græpnl] *n.* small anchor with several hooks.

grap•ple ['græpl] *v.* to wrestle/to fight (**with**). **grap•pling i•ron,** *n.* grapnel.

grasp [grɑːsp] 1. *n.* (a) tight hold/grip. (b) understanding. 2. *v.* (a) to seize; to grab tightly. (b) to understand. **grasp at,** *v.* to try to grab. **grasp•ing,** *adj.* (person) who is eager to get more things.

grass [grɑːs] 1. *n.* (a) low green plant of which the thin leaves and stalks are eaten by cattle, etc.; **don't let the g. grow under your feet** =

æ back, ɑː farm, ɒ top, aɪ pipe, aʊ how, aiə fire, aʊə flower, ɔː bought, ɔɪ toy, e fed, eəhair, eɪ take, ə afraid, əʊ boat, əʊə lower, vː word, iː heap, ɪ hit, ɪə hear, uː school, ʊ book, ʌ but, b back, d dog, ð then, dʒ just, f fog, g go, h hand, j yes, k catch, l last, m mix, n nut, ŋ sing, p penny, r round, s some, ʃ short, t too, tʃ chop, θ thing, v voice, w was, z zoo, ʒ treasure

waste no time in doing sth. (b) plant of a species related to grass (including bamboo, etc.). (c) lawn/piece of ground covered with grass. (d) *Sl.* marijuana. 2. *v.* **to g. over** = to cover with grass. **grass•hop•per,** *n.* green jumping insect with long back legs. **grass•land,** *n.* prairie or pasture. **grass•roots,** *n. pl.* ordinary members of a political party/a labor union; common people; **g. reaction** = reaction by the ordinary members (of a party, etc.). **grass-snake,** *n.* common snake. **grass•wid•ow,** *n.* wife whose husband has temporarily gone away. **grass•wid•ow•er,** *n.* husband whose wife has temporarily gone away. **grass•y,** *adj.* covered with growing grass.

grate [greɪt] 1. *n.* metal frame for holding wood, coal, etc. when burning in a fireplace, etc. 2. *v.* (a) to reduce to small bits by rubbing on a rough surface. (b) to make a noise like two rough surfaces rubbing together. (c) to have an irritating effect upon. **grat•er,** *n.* instrument for grating cheese, etc. **grat•ing.** 1. *n.* grille; framework of wooden or metal bars. 2. *adj.* **a g. sound** = an irritating sound as of the rubbing together of rough surfaces.

grate•ful ['greɪtfʊl] *adj.* thankful. **grate•ful•ly,** *adv.* thankfully.

grat•i•fy ['grætɪfaɪ] *v.* (a) to satisfy/to delight. (b) to please. **grat•i•fi•ca•tion** [grætɪfɪ'keɪʃn] *n.* satisfaction. **gra•ti•fy•ing,** *adj.* pleasing/satisfying.

grat•in ['grætæn] *n.* dish cooked with a crust, often of cheese, on top.

grat•is ['grɑːtɪs] *adv.* free/without charge.

grat•i•tude ['grætɪtjuːd] *n.* appreciation.

gra•tu•i•ty [grə'tjuːɪtɪ] *n.* present of money given in return for services in excess of the cost of the services. **gra•tu•i•tous,** *adj.* unasked for; undeserved.

grave [greɪv] 1. *n.* tomb/hole in the ground to put a dead body in; burial place; **to have one foot in the g.** = to be very near to death. 2. *adj.* (-er, -est) serious/solemn. **grave•dig•ger,** *n.* man who digs graves. **grave•stone,** *n.* memorial stone placed on a grave. **grave•yard,** *n.* cemetery/place where people are buried.

grav•el ['grævl] *n.* mixture of sand and small stones.

grav•en ['greɪvn] *adj.* (*old*) carved.

grav•i•tate ['grævɪteɪt] *v.* to move (**towards** sth). **grav•i•ta•tion** [grævɪ'teɪʃn] *n.* force of the earth's center which attracts and causes objects to fall to the ground if dropped. **grav•i•ty** ['grævɪtɪ] *n.* (a) seriousness. (b) weight; **specific g.** = density of a substance divided by the density of water. (c) force attract-

ing all objects to the earth's center, causing objects to fall to the ground if dropped.

gra•vy ['greɪvɪ] *n.* (*no pl.*) (a) juices that drip from meat during cooking. (b) brown sauce served with meat. **gravy boat,** *n.* small dish for serving gravy.

gray [greɪ] (*also* grey) 1. *adj.* (-er, -est) of a color between black and white; **g. matter** = active part of the brain; *inf.* intelligence. 2. *n.* color between black and white. **gray-haired,** *adj.* with gray hair. **gray•ish,** *adj.* rather gray. **gray•lag,** *n.* common European wild goose. **gray•ling** ['greɪlɪŋ] *n.* (a) type of brown butterfly. (b) gray fish.

graze [greɪz] 1. *n.* slight surface wound/scratch. 2. *v.* (a) to feed on growing grass. (b) to wound slightly in passing. **graz•ing,** *n.* pasture.

grease [griːs] 1. *n.* (a) melted animal fat. (b) oily/fatty substance. 2. *v.* (a) to cover/to coat with oil/fat, etc. (b) *inf.* **to g. s.o.'s palm** = to bribe s.o. **grease•gun,** *n.* device for putting grease into machines. **grease•paint,** *n.* make-up used by actors. **greas•y,** *adj.* smeared with grease; oily.

great [greɪt] 1. *adj.* (-er, -est) (a) large/big. (b) extreme. (c) distinguished/grand. (d) remarkable. (e) *inf.* wonderful. **great-aunt,** *n.* aunt of a father or mother. **Great Dane,** *n.* breed of very large dog. **great-grand•chil•dren,** *n. pl.* grandchildren of a son or daughter. **great-grand•daugh•ter,** *n.* granddaughter of a son or daughter. **great-grand•fa•ther,** *n.* grandfather of a father or mother. **great-grand•moth•er,** *n.* grandmother of a father or mother. **great-grand•par•ents,** *n. pl.* grandparents of a father or mother. **great-grand•son,** *n.* grandson of a son or daughter. **great•ly,** *adv.* very much. **great•ness,** *n.* remarkable ability. **great-un•cle,** *n.* uncle of a father or mother.

grebe [griːb] *n.* type of diving bird with a long neck.

Gre•cian ['griːʃn] *adj.* referring to ancient Greece.

greed [griːd] *n.* too great appetite; desire for more than is necessary. **greed•i•ly,** *adv.* with great appetite. **greed•i•ness,** *n.* being greedy. **greed•y,** *adj.* (-ier, -iest) wanting too much food, etc.; **g. for** = always wanting (power, etc.).

Greek [griːk] 1. *adj.* referring to Greece. 2. *n.* (a) person from Greece. (b) language spoken in Greece.

green [griːn] 1. *adj.* (-er, -est) (a) of a color like grass; **g. light** = light which shows you can go ahead; **g. with envy** = very envious. (b) immature/gullible. (c) referring to a concern about the environment; **g. party** = political party concerned with environmental issues. 2. *n.* (a) color like that of grass. (b) piece of public land covered with grass. (c) piece of land covered with smooth grass on which you can play certain games. **green•back**, *n. inf.* dollar bill. **green belt**, *n.* area of countryside around a town where building is prohibited. **green card**, *n.* work permit given by the U.S. government to s.o. who is going to live in the United States. **green•er•y**, *n.* vegetation. **green•finch**, *n.* bird with yellow and green plumage. **green•fly**, *n.* (*pl.* greenfly) small green aphid. **green•gage**, *n.* kind of green plum. **green•gro•cer**, *n.* person who sells fruit and vegetables. **green•horn**, *n.* inexperienced person. **green•house**, *n.* shelter made of glass and wood or metal for cultivation of delicate plants; **g. effect** = warming effect on the atmosphere, caused by carbon dioxide in the upper atmosphere. **green•ish**, *adj.* rather green. **green mail**, *n.* buying shares in a company, threatening to take the company over, then selling the shares at a profit. **green•room**, *n.* room where actors can rest when they are off-stage. **greens**, *n. pl. inf.* cooked green vegetables. **green•stick frac•ture**, *n.* fracture of a long bone in a child, where the bone bends, but does not break. **green thumb**, *n.* skill in gardening.

greet [gri:t] *v.* to salute/to welcome. **greet•ing**, *n.* reception/way of welcoming s.o. **greet•ings**, *n. pl.* good wishes.

gre•gar•i•ous [grɪ'geərɪəs] *adj.* fond of company/sociable.

grem•lin ['gremlɪn] *n.* imaginary imp, supposed to be responsible for faults in machinery.

gre•nade [grɪ'neɪd] *n.* small bomb thrown by hand.

gren•a•dine [grenə'di:n] *n.* red drink, made from pomegranate juice.

grew [gru:] *v. see* **grow**.

grey [greɪ] *adj. & n. see* **gray**. **greyhound**, *n.* slender, long-legged, swift dog, often used for racing.

grid [grɪd] *n.* (a) grating/frame of spaced parallel bars. (b) system of numbered squares on a map. (c) electricity supply system over a large area. **grid•dle**, *n.* flat frying pan or other surface for cooking pancakes, bacon, etc. **grid•dle•cake**, *n.* pancake. **grid•i•ron**, *n.*

(a) metal frame for cooking food over an open fire. (b) football field.

grief [gri:f] *n.* deep sorrow; **to come to g.** = to meet with disaster. **grief-strick•en**, *adj.* very sad.

griev•ance ['gri:vəns] *n.* real or imagined grounds for complaint; **to air one's grievances** = to tell about one's complaints.

grieve [gri:v] *v.* to feel sad (**for**); **it grieves me** = it makes me sad. **grieve o•ver**, *v.* to mourn; to feel sad because of (sth). **griev•ous**, *adj.* severe; **g. bodily harm** = severe injury to s.o.

grif•fin ['grɪfɪn] *n.* imaginary animal with a lion's head and eagle's wings.

grif•fon ['grɪfən] *n.* (a) type of small terrier. (b) type of vulture.

grill [grɪl] 1. *n.* (a) metal frame for cooking food over a direct source of heat. (b) (*also* **grillroom**) restaurant where most food is cooked on a grill. (c) **mixed g.** = collection of grilled food. (d) framework of metal/wooden bars. 2. *v.* (a) to cook over a grill. (b) *inf.* to interrogate (s.o.)/to ask (s.o.) searching questions.

grille [grɪl] *n.* grating; frame of spaced parallel bars; **radiator g.** = parallel bars in front of a radiator on a car.

grilse [grɪls] *n.* young salmon, returning to the river from the sea for the first time.

grim [grɪm] *adj.* (**grimmer, grimmest**) (a) sinister/severe. (b) bad/gloomy. **grim•ly**, *adv.* tenaciously; with determination. **grim•ness**, *n.* being grim.

grim•ace [grɪ'meɪs] 1. *n.* twisted expression on the face. 2. *v.* to make a grimace.

grime [graɪm] *n.* ingrained dirt. **grim•i•ness**, *n.* being grimy. **grim•y**, *adj.* dirty.

grin [grɪn] 1. *n.* wide smile. 2. *v.* (**grinned**) to smile broadly; **to g. and bear it** = to accept things bravely.

grind [graɪnd] 1. *n.* boring/monotonous work; **the daily g.** = repetitive work to be done every day. 2. *v.* (**ground**) (a) to reduce to small pieces by crushing; **to g. corn/coffee.** (b) to mince; **ground beef** = minced beef. (c) to rub surfaces together; **to g. your teeth** = to rub together the upper and lower teeth, usu. in anger; **to g. to a halt** = to stop. (d) to sharpen (a tool)/to smooth (sth rough); **to have an ax to g.** = to have a particular interest or point of view which makes your judgment biased. **grind•er**, *n.* machine or device for grinding; **coffee g. grind•stone**, *n.* stone which turns to sharpen knives; **to keep one's nose to the g.** = to keep working very hard.

grin•go ['grɪŋgəʊ] *n. inf.* (*esp. in Mexico*) foreigner, usu. American.

grip [grɪp] 1. *n.* (a) firm hold; **to come to grips with** = to deal with; handle; **to keep a g. on** = to remain in control of. (b) (*old*) small bag for carrying clothes, etc. when traveling. 2. *v.* (**gripped**) (a) to seize. (b) to hold (attention). **grip•ping**, *adj.* holding the attention.

gripe [graɪp] *v.* to moan/to complain **about** sth.

gris•ly ['grɪzlɪ] *adj.* (**ier, -iest**) causing horror/dread.

grist [grɪst] *n. inf.* **g. for/to the mill** = it's all useful/it all helps.

gris•tle ['grɪsl] *n.* tough, whitish, flexible tissue in meat. **gris•tly**, *adj.* full of pieces of gristle.

grit [grɪt] 1. *n.* (a) small particles of stone/sand, as in water, food, etc. (b) *inf.* courage. (c) **grits** = type of porridge made of corn or wheat. 2. *v.* (**gritted**) (a) to make a scratchy sound. (b) **to g. your teeth** = to clench your teeth together, usu. in fear/determination. **grit•ti•ness**, *n.* being gritty. **grit•ty**, *adj.* full of grit.

griz•zled ['grɪzld] *adj.* with gray or partly gray hair. **griz•zly** ['grɪzlɪ] 1. *adj.* gray or grayish. 2. *n.* **g.** (**bear**) = large, fierce North American bear.

groan [grəʊn] 1. *n.* deep sound expressing pain/grief/disapproval. 2. *v.* (a) to moan deeply. (b) **to g. under a weight** = to be heavily laden.

groats [grəʊts] *n. pl.* crushed oats.

gro•cer ['grəʊsə] *n.* person who sells canned foods, butter, sugar, eggs, etc., and miscellaneous household supplies. **gro•cer•ies**, *n. pl.* items on sale in a grocery. **gro•cer•y, grocery store**, *n.* grocer's store.

grog [grɒg] *n.* drink of spirits and water. **grog•gi•ly**, *adv.* unsteadily. **grog•gy**, *adj.* unsteady.

groin [grɔɪn] *n.* (a) hollow where the thigh joins the belly. (b) place where two vaults join. **groined**, *adj.* (roof) with joined vaults.

groom [gru:m] 1. *n.* (a) person who looks after horses. (b) bridegroom/new husband. 2. *v.* to look after/to make smart; **well-groomed** = smart and well-dressed.

groove [gru:v] *n.* (a) channel/hollow. (b) routine; **to get into a g.** = to be stuck in a routine. **groov•y**, *adj. Sl.* fine/fashionable.

grope [grəʊp] *v.* to feel with your hands as if you were blind.

gros•beak ['grəʊsbi:k] *n.* small bird with a large beak.

gross [grəʊs] 1. *n.* (*pl.* **gross**) twelve dozen, 144. 2. *adj.* (**-er, -est**) (a) bloated; horribly fat. (b) great/excessive; **g. injustice.** (c) total; **g. weight** = combined weight of container and contents; **g. income** = total income before deductions and allowances are made. **gross•ly**, *adv.* greatly.

gro•tesque [grə'tesk] *adj.* outrageous/fantastic; strange and ugly.

grot•to ['grɒtəʊ] *n.* (*pl.* **-oes**) picturesque cave; room decorated to resemble a cave.

grot•ty ['grɒtɪ] *adj. inf.* dirty.

grouch [graʊtʃ] 1. *n. inf.* grumble. 2. *v. inf.* to grumble. **grouch•y**, *adj. inf.* grumpy.

ground [graʊnd] 1. *n.* (a) soil/earth. (b) surface of the earth; **to go to g.** = to hide away. (c) area of land; **to stand one's g.** = to maintain one's position/authority; **to lose g.** = to become less successful; **to break new g.** = to be the first to start a project; **to get (sth) off the g.** = to start (sth) successfully/to get (a project) going. (d) large area of land set aside for a particular purpose; **picnic g.** (e) **grounds** = land surrounding a large house. (f) reason; **grounds for complaint.** (g) **coffee grounds** = small pieces of ground coffee beans left after the coffee has been made. 2. *v.* (a) to base. (b) to run (a boat) on to the land. (c) to keep (aircraft/pilot) on the ground. (d) *see also* **grind. ground•less**, *adj.* without reason. **ground•nut**, *n.* peanut. **ground rule**, *n.* basic rule of procedure. **grounds•keep•er**, *n.* person who looks after an area of land, as a park, gardens, golfcourse, etc. **ground•speed**, *n.* the speed of an aircraft over the ground. **ground•swell**, *n.* (*no pl.*) large slow-moving waves. **ground•work**, *n.* basic work/preliminary work.

group [gru:p] 1. *n.* (a) number of people or animals gathered close together. (b) classification; **blood g.; age g.** (c) small number of people playing music together. 2. *v.* **to g.** (**together**) = to form into groups. **group•er**, *n.* large tropical sea fish, used as food. **group•ie**, *n. Sl.* girl follower of a rock group, celebrity, etc. **group prac•tice**, *n.* several doctors who share patients between them and usu. work from the same offices. **group•ware**, *n.* computer software that allows many users to share files, etc. and to exchange electronic mail.

grouse [graʊs] 1. *n.* (a) (*pl.* **grouse**) reddish/black bird shot for sport and food. (b) *inf.* grumble. 2. *v. inf.* to grumble (**about** sth).

grout [graʊt] *v.* to fill the spaces between tiles on a floor or wall with cement. **grout•ing**, *n.* cement used to fill spaces between tiles.

grove [grəʊv] *n.* small group of trees.

grov•el ['grɒvl] *v.* (**groveled, grovelled**) to humble yourself; to lie with your face on the ground.

grow [grəʊ] 1. v. (**grew** [gruː], **has grown**) (a) to develop/to exist as a living plant. (b) to increase in size/height. (c) to become/to evolve gradually. (d) to cultivate; **she grows roses.** **grow•er,** n. (a) person who cultivates. (b) plant that grows in a specified way; **a slow g.** **grow•ing,** adj. getting bigger. **grown,** adj. developed to full size. **grown-up,** adj. & n. adult. **grow on,** v. inf. to become accepted; **this picture grows on you** = you gradually come to like it. **grow out of,** v. to become bigger/older (so that clothes no longer fit, etc.). **growth,** n. (a) development; increase in height/size. (b) lump of tissue in the body. **growth rate,** n. speed with which sth grows. **grow up,** v. to become adult.

growl [graʊl] 1. n. sound made in the throat expressing anger, like that made by dogs. 2. v. to murmur angrily.

grown [grəʊn] v. see **grow.**

grub [grʌb] 1. n. (a) larva of an insect; short worm which grows into an insect. (b) Sl. food. 2. v. (**grubbed**) to dig. **grub•bi•ness,** n. dirty appearance. **grub•by,** adj. (**-ier, -iest**) dirty.

grudge [grʌdʒ] 1. n. feeling of resentment/ill will (**against** s.o.). 2. v. to be unwilling to give (s.o. sth). **grudg•ing,** adj. reluctant.

gruel ['grʊəl] n. thin porridge.

gruel•ing ['grʊəlɪŋ] adj. exhausting/tiring; very difficult.

grue•some ['gruːsəm] adj. causing horror/dread.

gruff [grʌf] adj. (**-er, -est**) (a) deep/rough (voice). (b) stern (manner). **gruff•ly,** adv. in a gruff way. **gruff•ness,** n. being gruff.

grum•ble ['grʌmbl] 1. n. moan/complaint. 2. v. to complain (**about** sth). **grum•bler,** n. person who complains.

grump•y ['grʌmpɪ] adj. (**-ier, -iest**) bad-tempered. **grump•i•ly,** adv. in a bad-tempered manner. **grump•i•ness,** n. being grumpy.

grunt [grʌnt] 1. n. low sound, like that made by pigs. 2. v. to make a low snorting sound.

gua•no ['gwɑːnəʊ] n. (no pl.) droppings of sea-birds.

guar•an•tee [gærən'tiː] 1. n. (a) legal document promising that a machine will work for a certain time; **the car is still under g.** (b) person who receives a guarantee. (c) thing that assures a certain result. 2. v. to give assurance (**that** sth will happen). **guar•an•teed,** adj.

assured. **guar•an•tor** [gærən'tɔː] n. person who makes or gives a guarantee.

guard [gɑːd] 1. n. (a) watch/looking out; **to be on g.** = to be watchful; **to be on your g.** = to be prepared against attack/surprise, etc.; **to be caught off g.** = to be taken unawares. (b) soldier/police officer who protects s.o./a building; **g. of honor** (also **honor guard**) = group of soldiers acting as a ceremonial escort to an important person. (c) device to prevent injury or accident. 2. v. (a) to defend/to protect; to watch (prisoners) carefully so that they cannot escape; **closely guarded secret** = secret which is carefully kept secret. (b) to be careful. **guard•ed,** adj. careful/noncommital (reply). **guard•i•an,** n. keeper/protector responsible for the upbringing of a child. **guard•i•an•ship,** n. protection. **guard•room,** n. room used as a prison. **guards•man,** n. (pl. **-men**) members of the National Guard.

gua•va ['gwɑːvə] n. orange-colored tropical fruit.

guel•der rose ['geldə'rəʊz] n. garden shrub with white pompom flowers.

gue•ril•la, guerrilla [gə'rɪlə] n. person (not a regular soldier) engaged in unofficial fighting; group of these soldiers.

guern•sey ['gɜːnzɪ] n. (a) breed of cow, which gives rich milk. (b) heavy knitted shirt.

guess [ges] 1. n. rough estimate; **it is anybody's g.** = no one really knows. 2. v. (a) to estimate. (b) to think. **guess•ti•mate,** n. inf. rough calculation. **guess•work,** n. process of guessing.

guest [gest] n. (a) person entertained at another's house; **paying g.** = lodger/boarder; **g. artist/g. conductor** = person who is invited to play with/to conduct an orchestra. (b) person staying in a hotel. **guest•house,** n. house where guests are lodged.

guff [gʌf] n. inf. words which mean nothing.

guf•faw [gə'fɔː] 1. n. loud/coarse laugh. 2. v. to laugh loudly.

GUI [dʒiːjuː'aɪ] abbrev. for graphical user interface.

guide [gaɪd] 1. n. (a) person who shows the way/who describes buildings/works of art, etc., as you see them. (b) indication. (c) book of helpful advice. 2. v. to conduct/to lead; **guided tour** = tour where the tourists are led by a guide; **guided missile** = missile which is led to the target by a controlling device. **guid•ance,** n. advice. **guide•book,** n.

æ back, ɑː farm, ɒ top, aɪ pipe, aʊ how, aɪə fire, aʊə flower, ɔː bought, ɔɪ toy, e fed, eəhair, eɪ take, ə afraid, əʊ boat, əʊə lower, vː word, iː heap, ɪ hit, ɪə hear, uː school, ʊ book, ʌ but, b back, d dog, ð then, dʒ just, f fog, g go, h hand, j yes, k catch, l last, m mix, n nut, ŋ sing, p penny, r round, s some, ʃ short, t too, tʃ chop, θ thing, v voice, w was, z zoo, ʒ treasure

book of helpful advice/information. **guide dog,** *n.* dog which is specially trained to lead a blind person. **guide•lines,** *n. pl.* advice how to proceed. **guid•ing,** *adj.* directing.

guild [gɪld] *n.* association of people with similar interests or goals.

guile [gaɪl] *n.* treachery/cunning/trickery. **guile•less,** *adj.* honest/straightforward.

guil•le•mot ['gɪlɪmɒt] *n.* black and white sea bird.

guil•lo•tine ['gɪlətiːn] 1. *n.* (a) machine with a sharp blade for beheading criminals. (b) machine with a sharp blade for cutting paper. 2. *v.* (a) to cut the head off (s.o.) with a guillotine. (b) to cut (paper) with a guillotine.

guilt [gɪlt] *n.* having committed a crime; being aware that you have committed a crime. **guilt•i•ly,** *adv.* showing that you know you have done wrong. **guilt•less,** *adj.* innocent. **guilt•y,** *adj.* (**-ier, -iest**) blameworthy/criminal; having done wrong.

guin•ea fowl ['gɪnɪfaʊl] *n.* small black bird with white spots, used for food.

guin•ea pig ['gɪnɪpɪg] *n.* (a) small furry animal with no tail, often kept as a pet. (b) person/animal used in a scientific experiment.

guise [gaɪz] *n.* (*formal*) appearance; **in the g. of** = pretending to be.

gui•tar [gɪ'tɑː] *n.* stringed musical instrument played with the fingers; **electric g.** = guitar which is connected to an amplifier. **gui•tar•ist,** *n.* person who plays a guitar.

gulch [gʌltʃ] *n.* gully.

gulf [gʌlf] *n.* (a) area of ocean or sea partly surrounded by land. (b) wide difference (**between** points of view). **Gulf Stream,** *n.* warm current which crosses the Atlantic from West to East.

Gulf War syn•drome, *n.* supposed condition characterized by debilitating symptoms, experienced by soldiers following the Persian Gulf War (1991).

gull [gʌl] *n.* long-winged, web-footed sea bird.

gul•let ['gʌlɪt] *n.* food tube from the mouth to the stomach; esophagus.

gul•li•ble ['gʌlɪbl] *adj.* easily taken in/ready to believe anything. **gul•li•bil•i•ty** [gʌlɪ'bɪlɪtɪ] *n.* being gullible.

gul•ly ['gʌlɪ] *n.* small ravine/channel, usu. cut by a stream.

gulp [gʌlp] 1. *n.* quick swallow. 2. *v.* (*also* **to gulp down**) to swallow hastily.

gum [gʌm] 1. *n.* (a) sticky substance produced by some trees. (b) thin glue. (c) flesh in which the teeth are set. (d) (**chewing**) **g.** = sweet sticky substance you chew but do not swallow. 2. *v.* (**gummed**) to stick together; **gummed label** = label with dry glue, which sticks if moistened.

gum•boil, *n.* small abcess on a gum. **gum•boot,** *n.* rubber boot. **gum•drop,** *n.* type of candy. **gum•shoe,** *n. Sl.* private detective. **gum tree,** *n.* eucalyptus tree.

gump•tion ['gʌmpʃn] *n.* enterprising spirit/resourcefulness.

gun [gʌn] 1. *n.* weapon which uses an explosive force to send out a bullet; **starting g.** = weapon used to make a bang to start a race; **grease g.** = instrument for injecting a small amount of grease into a part of an engine; **to stick to one's guns** = to maintain one's position; **to jump the g.** = to start doing sth before you should. 2. *v.* (**gunned**) (a) to shoot at. (b) **to be gunning for s.o.** = to be trying to attack s.o. **gun•boat,** *n.* small ship carrying heavy guns. **gun car•riage,** *n.* vehicle which carries a heavy gun. **gun•dog,** *n.* dog trained to accompany hunters shooting birds. **gun•fire,** *n.* firing of a gun. **gun•man,** *n.* (*pl.* **-men**) armed robber. **gun•ner,** *n.* soldier in the artillery; person who fires a gun. **gun•ner•y,** *n.* management of large guns. **gun met•al,** *n.* dark gray metal, made of copper, tin, lead and zinc. **gun•pow•der,** *n.* explosive substance. **gun•room,** *n.* room where you keep sporting guns. **gun run•ner,** *n.* person who brings guns into a country illegally. **gun run•ning,** *n.* illegal importing of guns. **gun•shot,** *n.* bullet from a gun; sound made by a gun being fired. **gun•smith,** *n.* manufacturer of guns. **gun•wale** ['gʌnl] *n.* upper edge of ship's side.

gung-ho [gʌŋ'həʊ] *adj. inf.* wildly enthusiastic.

gun•ny ['gʌnɪ] *n.* thick material for making sacks.

gup•py ['gʌpɪ] *n.* small tropical fish often kept as a pet.

gur•gle ['gɜːgl] 1. *n.* bubbling sound. 2. *v.* to make a bubbling sound.

gu•ru ['guːruː] *n.* notable thinker who has many disciples.

gush [gʌʃ] 1. *n.* sudden stream/sudden rush of liquid. 2. *v.* (a) to flow heavily. (b) to speak effusively; to praise too much. **gush•er,** *n.* oil well where the oil comes out so strongly that it does not need to be pumped. **gush•ing,** *adj.* praising/talking extravagantly.

gus•set ['gʌsɪt] *n.* triangle of cloth inserted in an article of clothing to make it larger. **gus•set•ed,** *adj.* with gussets.

gust [gʌst] 1. *n.* sudden violent rush of wind or rain. 2. *v.* to blow in gusts. **gust•i•ly,** *adv.* in gusts. **gust•y,** *adj.* windy.

gus•to ['gʌstəʊ] *n.* (*no pl.*) zest/enthusiasm.

gut [gʌt] 1. *n.* (a) lower part of the intestine; *inf.* **g. reaction** = natural/instinctive reaction; *inf.* **I hate his guts** = I dislike him a lot. (b) *inf.* **guts** = courage. (c) material made from the intestines of animals and used for violin and tennis racket strings. 2. *v.* (**gutted**) (a) to take out the internal organs of (animal/fish). (b) to remove/to destroy (the contents of sth); **the house was gutted by fire. guts•y,** *adj. inf.* brave.

gut•ta-per•cha [gʌtə'pɜːʃə] *n.* soft rubbery substance from Malaya.

gut•ter ['gʌtə] 1. *n.* shallow trough below the eaves of a house or at the side of a street to carry away rainwater. 2. *v.* (*of a candle*) to flicker so that the molten wax runs down the side. **gut•ter•ing,** *n.* (*no pl.*) curved metal or plastic used to make gutters. **gut•ter•snipe,** *n.* dirty child, living in the poor part of a town.

gut•tur•al ['gʌtərəl] *adj.* produced in the throat. **gut•tur•al•ly,** *adv.* spoken in the throat.

guy [gaɪ] *n.* (a) man/fellow. (b) rope.

guz•zle ['gʌzl] *v.* to eat or drink greedily. **guz•zler,** *n.* person who eats greedily.

gym [dʒɪm], **gym•na•si•um** [dʒɪm'neɪzɪəm] *n.* room or building for indoor athletic events and exercise. **gym•nast** ['dʒɪmnæst] *n.* expert in gymnastics. **gym•nas•tic** [dʒɪm-'næstɪk] *adj.* referring to gymnastics. **gym•nas•tics,** *n.* exercises on wall

bars/wooden horse, etc., to help develop muscles and physical coordination.

gym•kha•na [dʒɪm'kɑːnə] *n.* competition for horse riding and racing; display of driving sports cars on a special course.

gyn•e•col•o•gy [gaɪnə'kɒlədʒɪ] *n.* study of the diseases of women's reproductive system. **gy•ne•col•o•gist,** *n.* doctor specializing in diseases of women's reproductive system. **gyn•e•co•log•i•cal** [gaɪnəkə'lɒdʒɪkl] *adj.* referring to women's diseases.

gyp•soph•i•la [dʒɪp'sɒfɪlə] *n.* garden plant with masses of small white flowers.

gyp•sum ['dʒɪpsəm] *n.* sulfate of lime.

gyp•sy ['dʒɪpsɪ] *n.* member of a wandering race.

gy•rate [dʒaɪ'reɪt] *v.* to turn round; to move rhythmically. **gy•ra•tion** [dʒaɪ'reɪʃn] *n.* circular movement. **gy•ra•to•ry** [dʒaɪ'reɪtərɪ] *adj.* turning round in a circle.

gyro- ['dʒaɪrəʊ] *prefix meaning* revolving; **gyro-compass** = compass which uses a gyroscope to avoid the shock of movement. **gy•ro•scope** ['dʒaɪrəskəʊp] *n.* spinning wheel mounted so that it can rotate on any axis. **gy•ro•scop•ic** [dʒaɪrə'skɒpɪk] *adj.* rapidly spinning.

æ back, ɑː farm, ɒ top, aɪ pipe, aʊ how, aɪə fire, aʊə flower, ɔː bought, ɔɪ toy, e fed, eəhair, eɪ take, ə afraid, əʊ boat, əʊə lower, vː word, iː heap, ɪ hit, ɪə hear, uː school, ʊ book, ʌ but, b back, d dog, ð then, dʒ just, f fog, g go, h hand, j yes, k catch, l last, m mix, n nut, ŋ sing, p penny, r round, s some, ʃ short, t too, tʃ chop, θ thing, v voice, w was, z zoo, ʒ treasure

Hh

H *symbol for* hydrogen.

ha [hɑː] (a) *inter. showing surprise. (b) abbrev. for* hectare.

ha•be•as cor•pus ['heɪbɪəs 'kɔːpəs] *n.* order to bring a prisoner to answer a charge in court.

hab•er•dash•er•y ['hæbədæʃrɪ] *n.* store/department selling men's shirts, ties, etc.

hab•it ['hæbɪt] *n.* (a) custom; regular way of doing sth; **from force of h.** = because it is sth you ordinarily do. (b) dress; **riding h.** = special dress for horse riding. **hab•it-form•ing,** *adj.* (drug) which you can become addicted to. **ha•bit•u•al** [hə'bɪtjʊəl] *adj.* regular/normal. **ha•bit•u•al•ly,** *adv.* ordinarily/in the usual way. **ha•bit•u•ate,** *v.* to accustom (s.o.) to doing sth. **ha•bit•u•é** [hæ'bɪtjʊeɪ] *n.* regular client/visitor.

hab•i•tat ['hæbɪtæt] *n.* place where a certain animal or plant is usually found.

hab•i•ta•tion [hæbɪ'teɪʃn] *n.* place/building where s.o. lives; **not fit for h.** = not fit to live in. **hab•it•a•ble** ['hæbɪtəbl] *adj.* fit to live in.

hack [hæk] 1. *n.* (a) horse which is hired. (b) writer, artist, etc. who sacrifices his/her talent, training, integrity to work solely for money doing dull, unimaginative work. (c) *Sl.* second-rate writer. 2. (a) *v.* to chop roughly. (b) to enter a computer system illegally, using a modem. **hack•er,** *n.* person who hacks into a computer system. **hack•ing,** *adj.* dry and unpleasant (cough).

hack•les ['hæklz] *n. pl.* neck feathers (on a cock); hairs on the neck (of a dog); **to raise s.o.'s h.** = to make s.o. annoyed.

hack•ney ['hæknɪ] *n.* **h. coach** = taxi. **hack•neyed** ['hæknɪd] *adj.* (phrase) which is often used.

hack•saw ['hæksɔː] *n.* saw for cutting metal, which has a narrow blade attached to a frame.

had [hæd] *v. see* **ha•ve.**

had•dock ['hædək] *n.* (*pl.* **haddock**) common white sea fish.

Ha•des ['heɪdiːz] *n.* hell.

haft [hɑːft] *n.* handle (of a knife, etc.).

hag [hæg] *n.* witch; ugly old woman.

hag•gard ['hægəd] *adj.* thin/tired (face).

hag•gis ['hægɪs] *n.* Scottish food, made of sheep's heart, liver, etc., cooked with oatmeal in a bag.

hag•gle ['hægl] *v.* (**over**) to discuss a price to try to reduce it.

hag•i•og•ra•phy ['hægɪɒgrəfɪ] *n.* writing about saints.

ha-ha ['hɑːhɑː] 1. *inter.* to show that you are amused. 2. *n.* fence put at the bottom of a ditch.

hai•ku ['haɪkuː] *n.* very short Japanese poem.

hail [heɪl] 1. *n.* (a) small pieces of ice which fall like frozen rain. (b) small missiles which fall; **a h. of bullets.** (c) call. 2. *v.* (a) to fall as small pieces of ice; to fall in small pieces. (b) to call out to (s.o.); to wave to (a taxi) to stop. (c) to come **from. hail•stone,** *n.* small piece of ice falling from the sky. **hail•storm,** *n.* storm when hailstones fall from the sky.

hair [heə] *n.* (a) single long thread growing on the body of a human or animal. (b) mass of hairs growing on the head; *inf.* **to let your h. down** = to relax/become less formal. **hair•brush,** *n.* special brush for keeping your hair neat. **hair•cut,** *n.* making your hair shorter by cutting. **hair•do,** *n. inf.* style of a woman's hair. **hair•dress•er,** *n.* person who cuts/dyes/styles hair. **hair•dres•ser's,** *n.* business where people can have their hair cut and styled. **hair•dress•ing,** *n.* cutting/dyeing/styling hair. **hair•less,** *adj.* with no hair. **hair•line,** *n.* (a) line where the hair meets the forehead. (b) very thin line/crack. **hair•net,** *n.* light net worn over the hair to keep it in place. **hair•piece,** *n.* small wig; piece of false hair. **hair•pin,** *n.* bent piece of wire used to keep hair in place; **h. turn** = very sharp turn, as on a mountain road. **hair-rais•ing,** *adj.* frightening. **hair•spring,** *n.* spiral spring in a watch. **hair•style,** *n.* way of dressing/cutting, etc., the hair. **hair•y,** *adj.* (-ier, -iest) (a) covered with hairs. (b) *Sl.* frighteningly dangerous.

hake [heɪk] *n.* (*pl.* **hake**) common small white sea fish.

hal•cy•on ['hælsɪən] *adj.* calm/beautiful (weather); carefree (days).

hale [heɪl] *adj.* **h. and hearty** = very healthy.

half [hɑːf] 1. *n.* (*pl.* **halves** [hɑːvz]) one of two equal parts; **first h.** = first part of a sports match; **to go halves** = each pays half. 2. *adj.* being divided into two equal parts; **h. an hour** = 30 minutes. 3. *adv.* partly/not fully; **h. as tall** = smaller by half, 50 per cent of the size. **half-and-half**, *adv.* in two equal quantities. **half-back**, *n.* defense player in football/rugby, etc. **half-baked**, *adj. inf.* (plan) which has not been well thought out. **half-breed**, *n.* person/animal with parents of different races. **half-broth•er**, *n.* brother who has one parent the same as you. **half-caste**, *n.* person with parents of two different races. **half-cocked**, *adj.* **to go off h.-c.** (or **at half cock**) = to behave or have happen hastily or without enough planning. **half-doz•en**, *n.* six. **half-emp•ty**, *adj.* partly empty/not completely empty. **half-fare**, *n.* fare reduced by half. **half-full**, *adj.* partly full/not completely full. **half-heart•ed**, *adj.* lacking conviction/enthusiasm. **half-hour•ly**, *adj. & adv.* every thirty minutes. **half-life**, *n.* time taken for a substance to lose half its radioactivity. **half-mast**, *n.* **the flags are at h.-m.** = the flags are flying halfway up the flagpole as a sign of mourning. **half-nel•son**, *n.* hold in wrestling, where one wrestler twists the arm of his opponent below his back. **half-o•pen**, *adj.* partly open/not completely open. **half•pen•ny** ['heɪpnɪ] *n.* (*pl.* **-pennies** = *coins*, **-pence** = *price*) (*old*) British coin worth half a penny. **half-sis•ter**, *n.* sister who has one parent the same as you. **half-tim•bered**, *adj.* (house) whose walls are made of wooden beams with brick or plaster walls between. **half-time**, *n.* short rest in the middle of a game. **half-tone**, *n.* photograph reproduced by means of dots of varying sizes. **half-track**, *n.* vehicle driven by caterpillar tracks behind and by ordinary wheels in front. **half-vol•ley**, *n.* (*in tennis*) hitting the ball just after it has bounced. **half•way**, *adv.* in the middle of a distance or length; **to meet s.o. h.** = to compromise with s.o. **half•wit**, *n.* idiot. **half-wit•ted**, *adj.* stupid. **half-year**, *n.* six months. **half-year•ly**, *adj. & adv.* (taking place) every six months.

hal•i•but ['hælɪbʌt] *n.* (*pl.* **halibut**) large white flatfish living in the sea.

hal•i•to•sis [hælɪ'təʊsɪs] *n.* bad-smelling breath.

hall [hɔːl] *n.* (a) large room or building for pub-

lic meetings; large building where students live in a college or university. (b) (**entrance**) **h.** = room or passage through which you enter a house or building.

hal•le•lu•jah [hælɪ'luːjə] *inter.* meaning praise to God.

hall•mark ['hɔːlmɑːk] *n.* mark put on gold and silver to show that it has the correct purity. **hall•marked**, *adj.* (silver spoon, etc.) with a hallmark stamped on it.

hal•lo [hə'ləʊ] *inter. showing a greeting.*

hal•loo [hə'luː] 1. *n.* call to dogs when hunting. 2. *v.* to shout halloo.

hal•low ['hæləʊ] *v.* to bless (sth)/to declare (sth) holy; **hallowed ground** = ground (near a church) which has been blessed. **Hal•low•een, Hallowe'en** [hæləʊ'iːn] *n.* the evening of October 31st, the eve of All Saints' Day, when witches and ghosts are said to roam about.

hal•lu•ci•na•tion [həluːsɪ'neɪʃn] *n.* seeing things which are not there; thing seen when you hallucinate. **hal•lu•ci•nate** [hə'luːsɪneɪt] *v.* to see things which are not there. **hal•lu•ci•na•to•ry** [hə'luːsɪnətrɪ] *adj.* (drug) which causes hallucinations. **hal•lu•ci•no•gen** [hə'luːsɪnədʒən] *n.* substance which gives you hallucinations. **hal•lu•ci•no•gen•ic**, *adj.* which causes hallucinations.

ha•lo ['heɪləʊ] *n.* (*pl.* **-oes**) glow of light (around the moon/around the head of a saint).

hal•o•gen ['hælədʒən] *n.* one of a group of chemical elements (including chlorine/fluorine/iodine).

halt [hɔːlt] 1. *n.* complete stop; **to come to a h.** = to stop; **to call a h. to** = to bring to a stop. 2. *v.* to stop. **halt•ing**, *adj.* hesitant.

halt•er ['hɔːltə] *n.* rope put around animal's neck to lead it; **h. top** = woman's top with a piece of material going around the back of the neck, leaving the arms and back bare.

halve [hɑːv] *v.* (a) to divide into two equal parts. (b) to reduce by half. **halves**, *n. pl. see* **half.**

hal•yard ['hæljəd] *n.* rope used to pull up a flag/sail.

ham [hæm] 1. *n.* (a) salted or smoked meat from a pig's leg. (b) *inf.* bad actor. (c) *inf.* amateur radio operator working from home. 2. *v.* (**hammed**) to act badly. **ham-hand•ed**, *adj.* clumsy.

ham•burg•er ['hæmbɜːgə] *n.* flat cake of

æ back, ɑː farm, ɒ top, aɪ pipe, aʊ how, aɪə fire, aʊə flower, ɔː bought, ɔɪ toy, e fed, eəhair, eɪ take, ə afraid, əʊ boat, əʊə lower, ɜː word, iː heap, ɪ hit, ɪə hear, uː school, ʊ book, ʌ but, b back, d dog, ð then, dʒ just, f fog, g go, h hand, j yes, k catch, l last, m mix, n nut, ŋ sing, p penny, r round, s some, ʃ short, t too, tʃ chop, θ thing, v voice, w was, z zoo, ʒ treasure

ground beef, cooked and eaten as a sandwich in a roll.

ham•let ['hæmlət] *n.* small village.

ham•mer ['hæmə] 1. *n.* (a) heavy metal tool for knocking nails into wood/posts into the ground, etc. (b) object which hits sth as part of a machine. (c) metal ball which is thrown in sporting contests. 2. *v.* to hit hard, as with a hammer. **hammer out**, *v.* (a) to make (sth) flat with a hammer. (b) **to h. out an agreement** = to come to an agreement after long difficult discussions. **hammer toe**, *n.* deformed toe which bends downwards.

ham•mock ['hæmək] *n.* hanging bed made of a strong cloth or net.

ham•per ['hæmpə] 1. *n.* large basket. 2. *v.* to stop/to hinder/to get in the way.

ham•ster ['hæmstə] *n.* small rodent, often kept as a pet.

ham•string ['hæmstrɪŋ] *n.* tendon behind the knee. **ham•strung**, *adj.* powerless; unable to do anything.

hand [hænd] 1. *n.* (a) part of the body at the end of each arm; **to have a h. in sth** = to help to make sth happen; **to give a h./lend a h. with** = to help with; **at h.** = near; **in h.** = in reserve; **on h.** = readily available; **out of h.** = uncontrollable. (b) workman; sailor; **an old h.** = very experienced person. (c) cards which have been dealt to you in a game. (d) one of the pointers on a clock or dial. (e) round of applause. (f) unit of measurement of the height of a horse. 2. *v.* to pass (sth) **to** s.o. by hand. **hand•bag**, *n.* woman's bag for carrying money, cosmetics, and other belongings. **hand•bill**, *n.* small announcement or advertisement given out by hand. **hand•book**, *n.* book which gives instructions or information. **hand•brake**, *n.* lever in a vehicle which works the brakes. **hand•clap**, *n.* clapping of the hands. **hand•cuff**, *v.* to attach (s.o.'s hands) with handcuffs. **handc•uffs**, *n. pl.* metal rings linked by a chain for attaching a prisoner's hands together. **hand•ful**, *n.* as much as you can hold in your hand; small number; person who is difficult to control. **hand•gun**, *n.* small gun which is carried in the hand. **hand•i•cap.** 1. *n.* (a) physical/mental disability; thing which puts you at a disadvantage. (b) penalty imposed in a race or competition on opponents who have exceptional ability to make it harder for them to win. 2. *v.* (**handicapped**) to put at a disadvantage; **the mentally handicapped** = people with a disability of the mind. **hand•i•cap•per**, *n.* person who calculates the handicaps in a race or competition. **hand•i•craft**, *n.* work done by hand; **handicrafts** = artistic work done by hand (such as knitting/pottery, etc.).

hand•i•ly, *adv.* in a handy way. **hand in**, *v.* to give in by hand. **hand•i•work**, *n.* work done by a particular person. **hand•ker•chief** ['hæŋkətʃiːf] *n.* square piece of cloth or paper for wiping your nose. **hand•made**, *adj.* made by hand, not by machine. **hand on**, *v.* to pass on. **hand out**, *v.* to distribute. **hand•out**, *n.* (a) money which is given out. (b) printed information sheet given out to people. **hand o•ver**, *v.* to give (sth) to s.o. **hand•picked**, *adj.* carefully selected. **hand•rail**, *n.* bar which you hold on to (next to a staircase, escalator, etc.). **hand a•round**, *v.* to pass around by hand. **hand•shake**, *n.* greeting when you grasp hands. **hand•spring**, *n.* gymnastic exercise where you turn a somersault on your hands and land on your feet. **hand•stand**, *n.* **to do a h.** = to balance on the palms of your hands with your feet in the air. **hand•writ•ing**, *n.* writing done by hand. **hand•writ•ten**, *adj.* written by hand, not typed or printed. **hand•y**, *adj.* (**-ier, -iest**) useful; in a convenient place. **hand•y•man**, *n.* (*pl.* **-men**) person who can do any sort of work, esp. repairs in the house.

han•dle ['hændl] 1. *n.* part of an object which you hold in the hand; *inf.* **to fly off the h.** = to lose your temper. 2. *v.* (a) to move, touch, feel, etc. with the hand or hands. (b) to deal with (sth); **handling charge** = charge which has to be paid to s.o. who has delivered or dealt with sth. **han•dle•bar(s)**, *n.* (*pl.*) bar on the front of a bicycle or motorcycle which steers the front wheel.

hand•some ['hænsəm] *adj.* (a) good-looking. (b) fine/large (profit). **hand•some•ly**, *adv.* elegantly; generously.

hang [hæŋ] 1. *n.* (a) way in which sth hangs/drops/falls; *inf.* **to get the h. of sth** = to understand how sth works. (b) *inf.* **he doesn't give a h.** = he doesn't worry about it at all. 2. *v.* (**hung**) (a) to attach/to be attached above the ground to a nail or by a string/chain, etc. (b) to stick (wallpaper) on a wall. (c) (**hanged**) to kill (s.o.) by tying a rope round his neck and suspending him off the ground. **hang a•bout**, **hang around**, *v. inf.* to wait/to wander aimlessly in a certain place. **hang back**, *v.* to stay behind the others. **hang•dog**, *adj. inf.* sheepish (expression). **hang down**, *v.* to hang in a long piece. **hang•er**, *n.* object for hanging sth; **coat h.** = piece of wood/plastic/metal which is placed inside a coat to hang it up. **hang•er-on**, *n.* (*pl.* **hangers-on**) person who stays near s.o. in the hope of getting money or food. **hang glid•er**, *n.* huge kite used in hang gliding. **hang glid•ing**, *n.* sport of floating through the air by hanging on to a huge kite made of a metal frame covered with plastic. **hang•ing,** *n.* carpet/tapestry which is hung on a wall as decoration. **hang•man,** *n.* (*pl.* **-men**) executioner who kills people by hanging them. **hang•nail,** *n.* torn skin at the root of a fingernail. **hang on,** *v.* (a) **to h. on to sth** = to clutch (sth)/to keep (sth). (b) *inf.* to wait. **hang out,** *v. inf.* to live (in a place). **hang•o•ver,** *n.* (a) unpleasant effects of having drunk too much alcohol. **hang up,** *v.* to hang (sth) on a hook; to replace (a telephone receiver). **hang-up,** *n.* (*pl.* **hang-ups**) *Sl.* thing which worries you and prevents you from acting normally.

hang•ar ['hæŋə] *n.* large shed for keeping aircraft in.

hank [hæŋk] *n.* wool coiled into a loose loop.

hank•er ['hæŋkə] *v.* **to h. after/for** = to want (very much). **hank•er•ing,** *n.* desire.

han•ky ['hæŋkɪ] *n. inf.* handkerchief.

han•ky•pan•ky [hæŋkɪ'pæŋkɪ] *n. inf.* trouble/bad behavior; trickery.

hap•haz•ard [hæp'hæzəd] *adj.* done at random/unplanned. **hap•haz•ard•ly,** *adv.* at random; without any plan.

hap•less ['hæpləs] *adj.* (*formal*) unfortunate/unlucky.

hap•pen ['hæpn] *v.* (a) to take place; **what has happened to him?** = (i) what is he doing now? (ii) what harm has come to him? (b) to take place by chance. **hap•pen•ing,** *n.* event/thing which takes place. **hap•pen•stance,** *n.* **by h.** = by a coincidence.

hap•py ['hæpɪ] *adj.* (**-ier, -iest**) glad/full of joy. **hap•pi•ly,** *adv.* joyfully/gladly. **hap•pi•ness,** *n.* joy/gladness. **hap•py-go-luck•y,** *adj.* easy-going/carefree.

ha•ra-ki•ri [hærə'kɪrɪ] *n.* Japanese form of suicide.

ha•rangue [hə'ræŋ] 1. *n.* long loud, often scolding, speech. 2. *v.* to deliver a harangue to (s.o.).

ha•rass [hə'ræs] *v.* to bother/to worry (s.o.). **ha•rass•ment,** *n.* bothering/worrying; many small attacks on an enemy.

har•bin•ger ['hɑːbɪndʒə] *n.* (*formal*) thing which shows that sth else is approaching.

har•bor, *Brit.* **har•bour** ['hɑːbə] 1. *n.* port/safe place where ships can tie up to load

or unload. 2. *v.* (a) to continue to have (a grudge) against s.o. (b) to protect (a criminal).

hard [hɑːd] 1. *adj.* (**-er, -est**) (a) firm/not soft: (b) **h. currency** = one which does not lose its value compared to other currencies. (c) difficult; **h. times/h. luck** = bad luck; **h. labor** = punishment involving difficult manual work. (d) strict/severe. (e) (*of water*) containing calcium, which makes it difficult to form a lather. (f) strong (drink); (drug) which makes you become addicted; **h. drinker** = person who drinks a lot of alcohol. 2. *adv.* (a) strongly. (b) with difficulty. **hard-and-fast,** *adj.* strict/absolute (rule). **hard•back,** *n.* hardcover. **hard•board,** *n.* artificial board made of small shreds of wood stuck together. **hard-boiled,** *adj.* (a) (egg) which has been boiled until the white and yolk are set solid. (b) (person) without much feeling/who is not easily shocked. **hard by,** *adv.* close. **hard-core.** 1. *n.* central part (of a group) which is totally loyal and dedicated. 2. *adj.* totally loyal and dedicated. **hard•cov•er,** *n.* book with a stiff cover. **hard disk,** *n.* solid disk, fixed in a computer. **hard•en,** *v.* to make hard; **hardened criminal** = regular/permanent criminal. **hard•en off,** *v.* to bring (tender plants) into the open air. **hard hat,** *n.* protective helmet worn by construction workers, etc. **hard-head•ed,** *adj.* practical/sensible. **hard-heart•ed,** *adj.* cruel. **hard•lin•er,** *n.* person who is very antagonistic/stern towards s.o./an enemy, etc. **hard•ly,** *adv.* almost not. **hard•ness,** *n.* being solid/hard/not soft; difficulty; strictness. **hard of hear•ing,** *adj.* (person) who is quite deaf. **hard sell,** *n.* strenuous efforts to sell sth. **hard•ship,** *n.* suffering caused by lack of sth. **hard up,** *adj. inf.* with no money. **hard•ware,** *n.* (*no pl.*) (a) tools, nails, cutlery, and other metal articles; **h. store** = store selling pans/hammers/nails/paint, etc.; **military h.** = guns, tanks, and other military equipment. (b) physical parts/machinery of a computer. **hard-wear•ing,** *adj.* which does not wear out easily. **hard•wood,** *n.* wood which comes from deciduous trees. **hard•work•ing,** *adj.* (person) who works hard. **har•dy,** *adj.* (**-ier, -iest**) which can survive in difficult conditions; (plant) which can stay out of doors all the year round.

hare ['heə] *n.* common field mammal, like a large rabbit. **hare-brained,** *adj.* mad/sense-

æ back, ɑː farm, ɒ top, aɪ pipe, aʊ how, aiə fire, aʊə flower, ɔː bought, ɔɪ toy, e fed, eəhair, eɪ take, ə afraid, əʊ boat, əʊə lower, vː word, iː heap, ɪ hit, ɪə hear, uː school, ʊ book, ʌ but, b back, d dog, ð then, dʒ just, f fog, g go, h hand, j yes, k catch, l last, m mix, n nut, ŋ sing, p penny, r round, s some, ʃ short, t too, tʃ chop, θ thing, v voice, w was, z zoo, ʒ treasure

less (plan). **hare•bell**, *n.* wild flower shaped like a little blue bell. **hare•lip**, *n.* split in the upper lip from birth.

har•em [ha:'ri:m] *n.* women in a Muslim household; women's quarters in a Muslim house.

har•i•cot ['hærɪkəʊ] *n.* **h. (bean)** = dry white bean eaten cooked.

hark [ha:k] 1. *old inter. meaning* listen. 2. *v.* **to h. back to** = to go back to (a subject talked about earlier).

har•le•quin ['ha:lɪkwɪn] *n.* character in old pantomime, wearing a mask and a suit of diamond-patterned cloth.

har•lot ['ha:lət] *n.* (*formal*) prostitute.

harm [ha:m] 1. *n.* damage. 2. *v.* to damage/to hurt. **harm•ful**, *adj.* which hurts/which causes damage. **harm•less**, *adj.* which causes no damage/which does not hurt.

har•mo•ny ['ha:mənɪ] *n.* (a) musical sounds which do not clash. agreeable effect (of music/color, etc.). (b) general agreement. **har•mon•ic** [ha:'mɒnɪk]. 1. *adj.* referring to harmony. 2. *n.* higher note which is heard when a note is played. **har•mon•i•ca** [ha:-'mɒnɪkə] *n.* mouth organ. **har•mo•ni•ous** [ha:'məʊnɪəs] *adj.* (sounds) which are in agreement/which sound well together. **har•mo•ni•ous•ly**, *adv.* in a harmonious way. **har•mo•ni•um** [ha:'məʊnɪəm] *n.* musical instrument like an organ where the sound comes from air pumped through reeds. **har•mo•ni•za•tion**, [ha:mənaɪ'zeɪʃn] *n.* act of harmonizing. **har•mo•nize**, *v.* (a) to be in or bring to agreement. (b) to form chords out of the main tune of a piece of music.

har•ness ['ha:nəs] 1. *n.* (a) leather straps which attach a horse to a cart; **he is still in h.** = he is still working. (b) straps for attaching a parachute to s.o.; straps which have a leash attached to control a small child. 2. *v.* (a) to attach (a horse) to a cart. (b) to use (natural resources/atomic power, etc.) for making energy.

harp [ha:p] 1. *n.* large upright musical instrument, with many strings which are plucked with the fingers. 2. *v.* **to h. on** = keep talking about. **harp•ist**, *n.* person who plays a harp.

har•poon [ha:'pu:n] 1. *n.* long barbed spear used to kill whales. 2. *v.* to kill (a whale) with a harpoon.

harp•si•chord ['ha:psɪkɔ:d] *n.* old musical instrument, like a piano, but with strings which are plucked.

har•py ['ha:pɪ] *n.* (a) cruel mythical monster, with a woman's body and an eagle's claws. (b) cruel person (esp. woman).

har•ri•er ['hærɪə] *n.* (a) dog who hunts hares. (b) long-distance runner. (c) type of falcon.

har•row ['hærəʊ] 1. *n.* large rake pulled by a tractor for breaking up heavy soil. 2. *v.* to break up soil with a harrow. **har•row•ing**, *adj.* very disturbing, causing mental pain.

har•ry ['hærɪ] *v.* to bother/to worry (s.o.) by continual attacks.

harsh [ha:ʃ] *adj.* (**-er, -est**) (a) cruel/sharp (punishment, etc.). (b) rough/unpleasant (voice, etc.). **harsh•ly**, *adv.* in a harsh way. **harsh•ness**, *n.* cruelty/roughness.

hart [ha:t] *n.* male deer.

har•um-scar•um [heərəm'skeərəm] *adj. & n.* wild (young person).

har•vest ['ha:vɪst] 1. *n.* (a) cutting/picking of ripe crops. (b) period of the year when crops are picked. 2. *v.* to cut/to pick ripe crops. **har•vest•er**, *n.* person/machine which cuts crops.

has [hæz] *v. see* **have. has-been** ['hæzbi:n] *n.* (*pl.* **has-beens**) *inf.* person/thing no longer as well known/important as before.

hash [hæʃ] 1. *n.* (a) minced or chopped meat; *inf.* **he made a h. of it** = he did it badly. (b) *inf.* hashish. (c) **h. (mark)** = printed sign (#) used in computers as an indicator. 2. *v.* to mince or chop (meat, etc.); **h. brown potatoes** = fried grated or chopped potatoes.

hash•ish ['hæʃɪʃ] *n.* hemp used as a drug.

hasp [ha:sp] *n.* metal bar, which closes a door or lid by fitting over a loop which is locked with a padlock.

has•sle ['hæsl] 1. *n. inf.* bother/struggle to do sth. 2. *v. inf.* to struggle/to argue.

has•sock ['hæsək] *n.* cushion for the feet or for kneeling on in a church.

haste [heɪst] *n.* speed; **to make h.** = to hurry up. **has•ten** ['heɪsn] *v.* to make (sth) go faster/come faster; to hurry up. **hast•i•ly**, *adv.* rapidly. **hast•i•ness**, *n.* being hasty. **hast•y**, *adj.* (**-ier, -iest**) rapid and with not enough preparation.

hat [hæt] *n.* piece of clothing worn on the head; **keep it under your h.** = keep it secret; **h. trick** = three goals, etc., scored by the same person in the same game. **hat•band**, *n.* piece of ribbon which goes round a hat. **hat•less**, *adj.* not wearing a hat.

hatch [hætʃ] 1. *n.* opening in a ship's deck; opening in the floor or wall of an aircraft. 2. *v.* (a) to warm (eggs) until baby birds appear; (*of a baby bird*) to break out of the egg; to plan a plot). (b) to indicate shade in a sketch by drawing parallel lines close together. **hatch•back**, *n.* type of car with a sloping back and a large rear door which opens upwards. **hatch•er•y**, *n.* place where eggs are kept until they develop into young. **hatch•way**, *n.* opening in a ship's deck.

hatch•et ['hætʃɪt] *n.* small ax; *inf.* **to bury the h.** = to make peace; *Sl.* **h. man** = person brought into a company to fire some of the staff. **hatchet-faced**, *adj.* (person) with a grim pointed face.

hate [heɪt] 1. *n.* great dislike. 2. *v.* to dislike intensely. **hate•ful**, *adj.* horrible/unpleasant. **ha•tred**, *n.* great dislike.

hat•ter ['hætə] *n.* person who makes hats.

haugh•ty ['hɔːtɪ] *adj.* (**-ier, -iest**) very proud. **haugh•ti•ly**, *adv.* in a very proud manner. **haugh•ti•ness**, *n.* being haughty.

haul [hɔːl] 1. *n.* (a) catch (of fish); **the burglars made a good h.** = they stole a lot of valuable property. (b) distance traveled. 2. *v.* to pull with difficulty. **haul•age**, *n.* moving of things. **haul•er**, *n.* person or company who moves goods or things; **trash h.**

haulm [hɔːm] *n.* stems of peas/beans/potatoes.

haunch [hɔːnʃ] *n.* thigh and loin (of an animal); **the dog was sitting on its haunches** = sitting in a squatting position.

haunt [hɔːnt] 1. *n.* place where s.o. goes frequently. 2. *v.* to go to (a place) frequently; (*of ghosts*) to appear in (a place). **haunt•ed**, *adj.* (house) where a ghost appears.

have [hæv] *v.* (**I have, he has; I had, he had**) (a) (*also* **have got**) to possess. **the house has (got) no telephone.** (b) to take (a meal/a bath). (c) to play; **will you h. a game of tennis?** (d) to get (sth) done. (f) (*making the past tense of verbs*) **h. you finished your work?** (g) (*showing compulsion to do something*) **you will h. to sing that song again; you had better say nothing. have got,** *v.* to have got to do sth = to be obliged/to have to do sth. **have had,** *v. inf.* **he's had it** = he is finished/he has missed an opportunity. **have on,** *v.* (a) to be wearing. (b) to have arranged or be occupied with; **have you anything on for tonight?** (c) *inf.* to trick (s.o.); **they're having you on. have it out,** *v.* to settle a quarrel with s.o.

ha•ven ['heɪvn] *n.* safe port; safe place; **tax h.** = country where taxes are low.

hav•er•sack ['hævəsæk] *n.* bag carried on the back.

hav•oc ['hævək] *n.* damage; **to play h. with** = do a lot of damage to.

haw [hɔː] *n.* small red berry on the hawthorn. **haw•finch,** *n.* largest European finch.

hawk [hɔːk] 1. *n.* (a) bird of prey; **she has eyes like a h.** = she has very good eyesight/notices every detail. (b) person who is in favor of military attacks on an enemy/who is prepared to take a hard line in international relations. 2. *v.* (a) to sell goods from door to door. (b) to clear your throat. **hawk•er,** *n.* person who sells things from place to place.

hawse [ɔːz] *n.* bow of a ship, with holes for the anchor cable. **haw•ser** ['hɔːzə] *n.* thick rope for attaching a boat to a mooring.

haw•thorn ['hɔːθɔːn] *n.* common hedge shrub with white flowers and red berries.

hay [heɪ] *n.* long dried grass used as forage; **to make h. while the sun shines** = to enjoy yourself/to make money while you can. **hay•fe•ver,** *n.* running nose/eyes, etc., caused by an allergy to pollen or dust. **hay•field,** *n.* field of grass which will be cut to make hay. **hay•seed,** *n. inf.* unsophisticated country person. **hay•stack,** *n.* pile of hay, usu. cone shaped, stored outdoors. **hay•wire,** *adj. inf.* **he's gone h.** = he's gone mad.

haz•ard ['hæzəd] 1. *n.* (a) risk. (b) rough ground (on a golf course). 2. *v.* to risk; **he hazarded a guess** = he made a rough guess. **haz•ard•ous,** *adj.* dangerous/risky.

haze [heɪz] *n.* light mist. **ha•zi•ly,** *adv.* vaguely. **ha•zi•ness,** *n.* being hazy. **ha•zy,** *adj.* (**-ier, -iest**) (a) misty. (b) vague.

ha•zel ['heɪzl] 1. *n.* tree which bears small nuts. 2. *adj. & n.* light brown (color). **hazel nut,** *n.* nut from a hazel tree.

he [hiː] (a) *pronoun referring to a male person or animal;* **he is my father.** (b) *prefix meaning* male; **he-goat. he-man,** *n.* (*pl.* **he-men**) strong/virile man.

He *symbol for* helium.

head [hed] 1. *n.* (a) part of the body with brain, eyes, ears, mouth, etc., attached to the rest of the body by the neck; **the horse won by a h.** = by the length of a head; **h. over heels** = with the head first; **to fall h. over heels down the stairs.** (b) brain; **a good h. for figures.** (c) top; leafy part (of a cabbage); foam (on the top of a glass of beer). (d) first one (of a group/a procession). (e) most important person; **h. waiter.** (f) **heads** *n. pl.* = top side of a coin; **to play heads or tails** = to spin a coin and try to guess which side will be on top. (g) part of a machine which records/picks up data (as on a tape recorder/computer). (h) (*no pl.*) number of animals; **fifty h. of sheep.** 2. *v.* (a) to be first/to lead. (b) to go toward. (c) (*soccer*) to hit (a ball) with your head. **head•ache,** *n.* (a) pain

æ **back,** ɑː **farm,** ɒ **top,** aɪ **pipe,** aʊ **how,** aɪə **fire,** aʊə **flower,** ɔː **bought,** ɔɪ **toy,** e **fed,** eə **hair,** eɪ **take,** ə **afraid,** əʊ **boat,** əʊə **lower,** ɜː **word,** iː **heap,** ɪ **hit,** ɪə **hear,** uː **school,** ʊ **book,** ʌ **but,** b **back,** d **dog,** ð **then,** dʒ **just,** f **fog,** g **go,** h **hand,** j **yes,** k **catch,** l **last,** m **mix,** n **nut,** ŋ **sing,** p **penny,** r **round,** s **some,** ʃ **short,** t **too,** tʃ **chop,** θ **thing,** v **voice,** w **was,** z **zoo,** ʒ **treasure**

in the head. (b) complicated problem.
head•board, *n.* board/panel at the top of a
bed. **head•dress,** *n.* ornamental covering for
the head. **head•er,** *n.* (a) dive. (b) (*soccer*)
hitting a ball with the head. **head first,** *adv.*
with one's head first. **head•gear,** *n.* hat or
cap. **head•hunt,** *v.* to look for candidates
for important jobs. **head•hunt•er,** *n.* (a)
member of a tribe which cuts off the heads of
enemies and collects them. (b) *inf.* person who
tries to find suitably qualified candidates for
important jobs. **head•ing,** *n.* words at the
top of a text. **head•lamp,** *n.* headlight.
head•land, *n.* (a) promontory. (b) land at
the edge of a field, where the tractor turns.
head•less, *adj.* with no head. **head•light,**
n. main light on the front of a car/bicycle, etc.
head•line, *n.* words in large capitals in a
newspaper; **news headlines** = short summary
of the main items of news on TV/radio.
head•line rate, *n.* rate of inflation/inter-
est/taxation, etc. before adjustment to allow
for distorting factors. **head•long,** *adj. & adv.*
rushing/non-stop; with your head first.
head•mas•ter, *n.* man in charge of a private
school. **head•mis•tress,** *n.* woman in
charge of a private school. **head off,** *v.* to
prevent (sth) from taking place. **head-on,**
adj. & adv. with the front; head first.
head•phones, *n. pl.* apparatus for listening
to radio/records, etc., which fits over your
ears. **head•quar•ters,** *n. pl.* main offices (of
a military force/company). **head•rest,** *n.*
cushion/part of a seat for leaning your head
on. **head•room,** *n.* space to pass upright.
head•scarf, *n.* (*pl.* -scarves) square piece of
cloth worn by women to cover their hair.
head•set, *n.* apparatus for listening to
radio/records, etc., which fits over your ears
with a band across the top of your head.
head•ship, *n.* position of headmaster/head-
mistress. **head•stone,** *n.* gravestone.
head•strong, *adj.* obstinate/self-willed.
head•way, *n.* progress/movement forward.
head•wind, *n.* wind blowing in your face.
head•word, *n.* main word in a dictionary.
head•y, *adj.* (-ier, -iest) (drink) which is
likely to make you drunk; (news) which is
likely to make you excited.
heal [hi:l] *v.* to make (a person/a wound) become healthy; to become healthy. **heal•ing,**
n. making healthy.
health [helθ] *n.* (a) state of the body where
there is no sickness; **h. foods** = natural foods
(such as yogurt/nuts, etc.) which are good for
your health. (b) general state of the body.
health•i•ly, *adv.* in a healthy way.
health•i•ness, *n.* being healthy. **health•y,**

adj. (a) full of good health/not ill. (b) which
gives good health. (c) strong (dislike, etc.).
heap [hi:p] 1. *n.* large pile; *inf.* **heaps** = lots. 2. *v.*
to put in a pile.
hear ['hɪə] *v.* (**heard** [hɜ:'d]) to sense sounds by
the ear; to listen to (sth); **he's never heard of it**
= does not know about it; **he won't h. of it** = he
will not allow it. **hear•er,** *n.* person who
hears. **hear hear!** *inter. used to show agreement.* **hear•ing,** *n.* (a) ability to hear; **h. aid** =
small device for improving the hearing of s.o.
who is nearly deaf; **h. dog** = dog that is specially trained to alert deaf people to sounds,
e.g. alarms. (b) listening to s.o. (c) court case.
hear•say, *n.* what people say, rather than
what is true.
heard [hɜ:d] *v. see* **hear.**
hearse [hɜ:s] *n.* vehicle for carrying a coffin.
heart [hɑ:t] *n.* (a) organ in an animal which
pumps blood round the body; **h. attack** = severe illness when the heart stops temporarily;
h. failure = dangerous condition when the
heart has stopped beating; **to learn by h.** =
learn by memory so that you can repeat it. (b)
center of the emotions; **with all my h.** = with
great emotion. (c) center (of a town/forest).
(d) courage; **to lose h.** = to become discouraged; **to take h.** = to be encouraged. (e) **hearts**
= one of the four suits of playing cards.
heart•beat, *n.* sound of the heart pumping
blood. **heart-break•ing** *adj.* which makes
you very sad/upset. **heart-bro•ken,** *adj.* extremely sad/disappointed. **heart•burn,** *n.*
burning feeling in the chest and stomach after
eating indigestible food. **heart•en,** *v.* to encourage. **heart•felt,** *adj.* sincere.
heart•i•ly, *adv.* vigorously; warmly.
heart•i•ness, *n.* being hearty. **heart•land,**
n. central part of a country. **heart•less,** *adj.*
cruel. **heart•less•ly,** *adv.* in a heartless way.
heart-rend•ing, *adj.* pitiful.
heart•strings, *n. pl.* deepest feelings (of
pity/love, etc.). **heart-throb,** *n.* popular
film-star, etc. **heart-to-heart,** *adj.* earnest
private (conversation). **heart•warm•ing,**
adj. which encourages/pleases. **heart•y,** *adj.*
(-ier, -iest) vigorous/strong; large (meal/appe-
tite).
hearth [hɑ:θ] *n.* floor of a fireplace; fireplace.
hearth•rug, *n.* small rug placed in front of a
fireplace.
heat [hi:t] 1. *n.* (a) great warmth. (b) qualifying
round in a competition; **dead h.** = race where
two competitors reach the finish line at the
same time. (c) (*of female animal*) **in h.** = sexually excited. 2. *v.* to warm to a higher temperature; **heated discussion** = discussion where
people become quite angry. **heat•ed•ly,** *adv.*

angrily. **heat•er**, *n.* apparatus for warming. **heat•ing**, *n.* making sth warm; means of heating; **central h.** = heating system for a whole building from one source. **heat•wave**, *n.* period of very hot weather.

heath [hi:θ] *n.* (a) area of wild country covered with low shrubs. (b) heather.

heath•en ['hi:ðn] *adj. & n.* (person) who is not a Christian; (person) who is not a member of any important religious group.

heath•er ['heðə] *n.* wild plant with small purple or white bell-shaped flowers, which grows on moors and mountains in England and Scotland.

heave [hi:v] 1. *n.* hard pull. 2. *v.* **(heaved)** (a) to pull hard. (b) **(hove)** **to h. to** = to stop a ship; **to h. in sight** = to appear. (c) *inf.* to throw. (d) to breathe noisily.

heav•en ['hevn] *n.* paradise/place where God and the angels live; **the heavens** = the sky; **good heavens!** = how surprising! **heav•en•ly**, *adj.* (a) belonging to heaven. (b) *inf.* beautiful; very fine. **heav•en-sent**, *adj.* coming at an opportune time; lucky.

heav•y ['hevɪ] *adj.* **(-ier, -iest)** (a) weighing a lot; (meal) which is very filling and indigestible. (b) strong/great. (c) rough (sea). (d) full (schedule, etc.). (e) **h. drinker** = person who drinks a lot of alcohol. **heav•i•ly**, *adv.* (a) as if weighing a lot. (b) greatly; **h. underlined** = with thick lines put underneath. (c) (to sleep) soundly. **heav•i•ness**, *n.* being heavy. **heav•y-du•ty**, *adj.* (machine, etc.) specially made for rough work. **heav•y in•dus•try**, *n.* industry which makes large products (like steel/ships/cars, etc.). **heav•y wa•ter**, *n.* water containing deuterium in place of hydrogen. **heav•y•weight**, *n.* heaviest category of boxer.

He•brew ['hi:bru:] *n.* (a) member of Jewish people living in ancient Palestine. (b) language of the Jews.

heck•le ['hekl] *v.* to call out; to interrupt a public speaker. **heck•ler**, *n.* person who interrupts a speaker at a meeting. **heck•ling**, *n.* interrupting a speaker.

hect-, hecto- ['hekt(əu)] *prefix meaning* one hundred. **hec•to•li•ter**, *n.* one hundred liters.

hec•tare ['hektɑ:] *n.* (measure of) area of 10,000 square meters (approx. 2.4 acres).

hec•tic ['hektɪk] *adj.* very busy/active. **hec•ti•cal•ly**, *adv.* in a hectic way.

hec•tor ['hektə] *v.* to bully/to intimidate. **hec•tor•ing**, *adj.* bullying (tone of voice).

hedge [hedʒ] 1. *n.* (a) screen/fence made of growing shrubs. (b) protection (**against**). 2. *v.* (a) to surround with a hedge. (b) to avoid answering a question. (c) **to h. your bets** = to arrange things so that you will be protected against losing. **hedge•hog**, *n.* small mammal covered with prickles. **hedge•row**, *n.* row of shrubs forming a hedge. **hedge spar•row**, *n.* common sparrow found in the country.

he•don•ist ['hi:dənɪst] *n.* person who lives for pleasure. **he•don•is•tic**, *adj.* like a hedonist.

heed [hi:d] 1. *n.* **to take h. of/to pay h. to** = to pay attention to. 2. *v.* to pay attention to. **heed•less**, *adj.* careless/imprudent; without paying attention. **heed•less•ly**, *adv.* in a heedless way.

heel [hi:l] 1. *n.* (a) back part of the foot; back part of a sock/stocking into which the heel of the foot goes; **to take to one's heels** = to run away. (b) raised block under the back of a shoe. (c) *Sl.* unpleasant person. 2. *v.* to put a new heel on (a shoe). (b) (*of a ship*) **to h. over** = to lean to one side.

heft•y ['heftɪ] *adj.* **(-ier, -iest)** large/strong.

he•gem•o•ny [hɪ'gemənɪ] *n.* leadership by one country.

heif•er ['hefə] *n.* young cow.

height [haɪt] *n.* (a) measurement of how tall or high sth is. (b) highest point. **height•en**, *v.* to increase/to make more noticeable.

hei•nous ['heɪnəs] *adj.* wicked (crime).

heir, heiress ['eə, eə'res] *n.* person who is going to inherit money, etc., from s.o. **heir•loom**, *n.* valuable object which has belonged to a family for years.

held [held] *v. see* **hold.**

hel•i•cal ['helɪkl] *adj. see* **he•lix.**

hel•i•cop•ter ['helɪkɒptə] *n.* type of aircraft with revolving blades on top, enabling it to take off vertically. **hel•i•pad**, *n.* small marked area where a helicopter may land. **hel•i•port**, *n.* place where helicopters land and take off.

he•li•o•graph ['hi:lɪəgrɑ:f] *n.* apparatus for signaling, using mirrors which flash in the sun.

he•li•o•trope ['hi:lɪətrəup] *n. & adj.* plant with purple flowers; purple (color).

æ **back**, ɑ: **farm**, ɒ: **top**, aɪ **pipe**, aʊ **how**, aɪe **fire**, aʊə **flower**, ɔ: **bought**, ɔɪ **toy**, e **fed**, eə **hair**, eɪ **take**, ə **afraid**, əʊ **boat**, əʊə **lower**, ɜ: **word**, i: **heap**, ɪ **hit**, ɪə **hear**, u: **school**, ʊ **book**, ʌ **but**, b **back**, d **dog**, ð **then**, dʒ **just**, f **fog**, g **go**, h **hand**, j **yes**, k **catch**, l **last**, m **mix**, n **nut**, ŋ **sing**, p **penny**, r **round**, s **some**, ʃ **short**, t **too**, tʃ **chop**, θ **thing**, v **voice**, w **was**, z **zoo**, ʒ **treasure**

he•li•um ['hi:lɪəm] *n.* (*element:* He) light gas which does not burn.

he•lix ['hi:lɪks] *n.* spiral shape. **hel•i•cal** ['helɪkl] *adj.* spiral.

hell [hel] *n.* (a) place where devils live and wicked people are punished after death. (b) *inf.* **a h. of a noise** = a very loud noise; **one h. of a party** = a very good party; **to give s.o. h.** = to make life difficult for s.o.; *Sl.* **what the h.?** = what on earth? **hell-bent on,** *adj. inf.* very determined to do sth. **hell•ish,** *adj.* like hell; *inf.* unbearable.

hel•le•bore ['helɪbɔ:] *n.* winter plant with greenish white flowers.

Hel•len•ic [he'lenɪk] *adj.* referring to Greece.

hel•lo [hə'ləʊ] *inter. showing a greeting.*

helm [helm] *n.* wheel or handle connecting to the rudder of a ship; **at the h.** = in charge. **helms•man,** *n.* (*pl.* -men) person who is steering a ship.

hel•met ['helmət] *n.* metal or plastic hat used as a protection; **crash h.** = helmet worn by motorcyclists.

help [help] 1. *n.* (a) aid/assistance. (b) person who helps. 2. *v.* (a) to aid (s.o.)/to come to s.o.'s assistance. (b) **to h. yourself** = to serve yourself; *inf.* **to h. yourself to** = to take without asking; steal. (c) **can't h. doing sth** = can't stop (doing sth)/can't avoid (sth). **help•er,** *n.* person who helps. **help•ful,** *adj.* (person) who helps; (thing) which is useful. **help•ful•ly,** *adv.* in a helpful way. **help•ful•ness,** *n.* being helpful. **help•ing.** 1. *adj.* which helps. 2. *n.* serving/portion (of food). **help•less,** *adj.* weak/unable to help yourself. **help•less•ly,** *adv.* unable to help. **help•less•ness,** *n.* being helpless. **help•mate,** *n.* helper. **help out,** *v.* to come to (s.o.'s) assistance in an emergency.

hel•ter-skel•ter ['heltə'skeltə] *adv.* in a confused rush.

hem [hem] 1. *n.* sewn edge on a piece of cloth/a skirt/tablecloth/handkerchief, etc. 2. *v.* (**hemmed**) (a) to sew a hem. (b) **to h. in** = to enclose. (c) **to h. and haw** = to have difficulty in making up your mind. **hem•line,** *n.* bottom edge of a dress/skirt, etc. **hem•stitch.** 1. *n.* stitch used in a hem. 2. *v.* to sew a hem using a hemstitch.

he•ma•tite ['hi:mətaɪt] *n.* iron ore.

hemi- ['hemɪ] *prefix* half. **hem•i•ple•gi•a,** *n.* paralysis affecting one side of the body.

hem•i•sphere ['hemɪsfɪə] *n.* half a sphere, esp. half of the earth's globe; **northern h./southern h.** = parts of the earth north and south of the equator. **hem•i•spher•i•cal** [hemɪ'sferɪkl] *adj.* shaped like half a sphere.

hem•lock ['hemlɒk] *n.* (a) common poisonous plant. (b) type of American evergreen tree.

he•mo•glo•bin [hi:mə'gləʊbɪn] *n.* substance in red blood cells which contains iron and carries oxygen.

he•mo•phil•i•a [hi:mə'fɪlɪə] *n.* hereditary disease, esp. in males, which prevents blood from clotting. **he•mo•phil•i•ac,** *n.* person suffering from hemophilia.

hem•or•rhage ['hemərɪdʒ] 1. *n.* loss of much blood, usu. internally. 2. *v.* to suffer a hemorrhage.

hem•or•rhoids ['hemərɔɪdz] *n. pl.* small swollen veins at the anus.

hemp [hemp] *n.* tropical plant, which gives rough fibers for making sacks/ropes, etc., and which also provides a drug. **hemp•en,** *adj.* (*formal*) made of hemp.

hen [hen] *n.* (a) female chicken. (b) female bird; *inf.* **h. party** = party for women only. **hen•house,** *n.* place for keeping chickens in. **hen•pecked,** *adj.* (husband) whose wife nags him continuously and tells him what to do.

hence [hens] *adv.* (a) from this time; **five years h.** (b) for this reason. **hence•forth, henceforward,** *adv.* from now on.

hench•man ['hentʃmən] *n.* (*pl.* -men) helper/accomplice (of a criminal).

hen•na ['henə] *n.* red dye used to color hair. **hen•naed** ['henəd] *adj.* (hair) colored with henna.

hep•a•ti•tis [hepə'taɪtɪs] *n.* disease of the liver.

hep•ta•gon ['heptəgən] *n.* geometrical figure with seven sides. **hep•tag•o•nal** [hep'tægənl] *adj.* seven-sided.

her [hɜ:] 1. *pronoun referring to a female; object form of* she; **have you seen her? 2.** *adj.* belonging to a female; **have you seen her brother?**

her•ald ['herəld] 1. *n.* messenger sent to announce sth. 2. *v.* to be a sign that sth is approaching; to announce. **he•ral•dic** [he'rældɪk] *adj.* referring to heraldry. **her•ald•ry** ['herəldrɪ] *n.* study of coats of arms.

herb [hɜ:b] *n.* tasty or pungent plant used in cooking or as a medicine. **her•ba•ceous border** [hɜ:'beɪʃəs 'bɔ:də] *n.* flowerbed planted with flowers which sprout up again every year. **herb•age,** *n.* grass or other green plants. **herb•al,** *adj.* containing/using herbs. **herb•al•ist,** *n.* person who sells herbs as medicines. **her•bar•i•um,** *n.* collection of dried plants arranged systematically. **herb•i•cide,** *n.* substance which kills weeds. **her•biv•ore** ['hɜ:bɪvɔ:] *n.* animal which eats plants. **her•biv•o•rous** [hɜː'bɪvərəs] *adj.* (animal) which eats plants.

her•cu•le•an [hɜːkjuː'liːən] *adj.* showing great strength; (task) which needs great effort.

herd [hɜːd] 1. *n.* group of animals; **h. instinct** = tendency of people to do what others do. 2. *v.* to form/to make into a group. **herds•man**, *n.* (*pl.* **-men**) man who looks after a herd of cows, etc.

here ['hɪə] *adv.* to/in this place. **here•a•bouts**, *adv.* around about here/in this area. **here•af•ter**, *adv.* from this time on. **here•by**, *adv.* (*formal*) in this way. **here•to**, *adv.* to this. **here•with** [hɪə'wɪθ] *adv.* with this.

he•red•i•ty [hɪ'redɪtɪ] *n.* passing on of characteristics from parent to child. **her•e•dit•a•ment**, *n.* property which can be inherited. **he•red•i•tar•y**, *adj.* which is passed on from parent to child.

her•e•sy ['herəsɪ] *n.* heretical belief. **her•e•tic**, *n.* person who does not hold generally accepted religious beliefs. **he•ret•i•cal** [hə'retɪkl] *adj.* (belief) which is not generally accepted/which is condemned by the church.

her•it•age ['herɪtɪdʒ] *n.* thing which is passed on from one generation to the next.

her•maph•ro•dite [hɜː'mæfrədaɪt] *n.* animal/plant which is both male and female.

her•met•ic [hɜː'metɪk] *adj.* sealed; airtight. **her•met•i•cal•ly**, *adv.* (sealed) tightly so that no air can get in.

her•mit ['hɜːmɪt] *n.* person who lives alone and refuses to see other people; **h. crab** = small crab which lives in empty sea shells. **her•mit•age**, *n.* place where a hermit lives; secluded place.

her•ni•a ['hɜːnɪə] *n.* condition where part of the bowel has pushed through a weak place in the wall of the abdomen.

he•ro, heroine ['hɪərəu, 'herəuɪn] *n.* (*pl.* **-oes**) person who does brave deeds; main character in a book/motion picture, etc. **he•ro•ic** [hɪ'rəuɪk] *adj.* brave/like a hero. **he•ro•i•cal•ly**, *adv.* like a hero. **her•o•ism** ['herəuɪzəm] *n.* bravery.

her•o•in ['herəuɪn] *n.* drug made from poppies.

her•on ['herən] *n.* common water bird with long legs and neck.

her•pes ['hɜːpiːz] *n.* disease which gives blisters on the skin.

her•ring ['herɪŋ] *n.* common sea fish; **red h.** = distraction/false lead. **herring-bone**, *adj.* (pattern) in a zigzag. **herring gull**, *n.* common large gray and white gull.

hers [hɜːz] *adj.* belonging to her. **her•self** [hɜː'self] *pronoun referring to a female subject;* **she was washing h.; all by h.; she wrote to me h.**

hertz [hɜːts] *n.* (*no pl.*) standard unit of frequency of radio waves.

hes•i•tate ['hezɪteɪt] *v.* to stop for a moment; to be unable to decide. **hes•i•tance, hesitancy**, *n.* being hesitant. **hes•i•tant**, *adj.* doubtful/undecided. **hes•i•tant•ly**, *adv.* in a hesitant way. **hes•i•ta•tion** [hezɪ'teɪʃn] *n.* indecision/doubt.

hes•sian ['hesɪən] *n.* rough cloth like burlap.

het•er•o•ge•ne•ous [hetərəu'dʒiːnjəs] *adj.* of varied sorts.

het•er•o•sex•u•al [hetərəu'seksjuəl] *adj. & n.* (person) who is attracted to people of the opposite sex.

het up ['het 'ʌp] *adj. inf.* excited; anxious.

heu•ris•tic [hjuː'rɪstɪk] *adj.* which stimulates interest or investigation.

hew [hjuː] *v.* (**hewn**) to carve/to cut.

hex•a•gon ['heksəgən] *n.* geometrical figure with six sides. **hex•a•gon•al** [hek'sægənl] *adj.* six-sided.

hex•am•e•ter [hek'sæmɪtə] *n.* line of poetry with six beats.

hey [heɪ] *inter. showing a greeting/surprise.*

hey•day ['heɪdeɪ] *n.* period of greatest glory/success/power.

Hg *symbol for* mercury.

hi [haɪ] *inter. showing a greeting.*

hi•a•tus [haɪ'eɪtəs] *n.* (*pl.* **-uses**) gap/interruption.

hi•ber•nate ['haɪbəneɪt] *v.* (*of animals*) to sleep during the winter. **hi•ber•na•tion** [haɪbə'neɪʃn] *n.* spending the winter asleep.

hi•bis•cus [hɪ'bɪskəs] *n.* tropical shrub with large trumpet-shaped flowers.

hic•cup, hiccough ['hɪkʌp] 1. *n.* repeated spasm in the throat like a small cough. 2. *v.* (**hiccuped, hiccupped**) to make a loud noise because of a hiccup.

hick [hɪk] *n. inf.* stupid person from the country.

hick•o•ry ['hɪkərɪ] *n.* North American tree like a walnut.

hid, hidden [hɪd, 'hɪdn] *v. see* **hide.**

hide [haɪd] 1. *n.* leather; whole skin of an animal. 2. *v.* (**hid, has hidden**) to be out of sight; to

---

æ back, aː farm, ɒ top, aɪ pipe, au how, aiə fire, auə flower, ɔː bought, ɔɪ toy, e fed, eəhair, eɪ take, ə afraid, əu boat, əuə lower, vː word, iː heap, ɪ hit, ɪə hear, uː school, u book, ʌ but, b back, d dog, ð then, dʒ just, f fog, g go, h hand, j yes, k catch, l last, m mix, n nut, ŋ sing, p penny, r round, s some, ʃ short, t too, tʃ chop, θ thing, v voice, w was, z zoo, ʒ treasure

put (a thing) somewhere so that no one can see it. **hide-and-seek,** *n.* children's game, where some hide and the others try to find them. **hide•bound,** *adj.* unwilling to change ideas/narrow-minded. **hide-out,** *n.* secret place where you cannot be found. **hid•ing,** *n.* (a) putting yourself/sth out of sight. (b) *inf.* beating/whipping.

hid•e•ous ['hɪdɪəs] *adj.* horribly ugly. **hid•e•ous•ly,** *adv.* in a hideous way. **hid•e•ous•ness,** *n.* being hideous.

hi•er•ar•chy ['haɪərɑːkɪ] *n.* arrangement in a system of ranks/grades. **hi•er•ar•chi•cal** [haɪə'rɑːkɪkl] *adj.* arranged in a set system of ranks.

hi•er•o•glyph•ics [haɪərəʊ'glɪfɪks] *n. pl.* system of picture writing used by the ancient Egyptians. **hi•er•o•glyph,** *n.* symbol used in hieroglyphics.

hi-fi ['haɪ'faɪ] *adj. & n. inf.* high fidelity radio/stereo (equipment).

hig•gle•dy-pig•gle•dy [hɪgldɪ'pɪgldɪ] *adv.* in disorder/all over the place.

high [haɪ] 1. *adj.* (-er, -est) (a) going far above; tall. (b) great (rank, price, etc.); **h. fidelity =** (radio equipment) which gives excellent reproduction of sound. (c) shrill (note). (d) (*of meat*) going rotten. (e) main; most important. (f) powerful (explosive). (g) *inf.* influenced by drugs. 2. *adv.* (-er, -est) (a) far above. (b) to a great degree. 3. *n.* (a) high-pressure zone in the atmosphere. (b) **an all-time h. =** the highest point ever reached. (c) *inf.* state of intoxication produced by a drug, etc. **high•ball,** *n.* whiskey and soda. **high•brow,** *adj. & n.* intellectual (person). **high chair,** *n.* small chair with very long legs for a baby to sit in to eat. **High Church,** *adj. & n.* (part of the Anglican Church) which regards ritual as very important. **high-fa•lu•tin,** *adj. inf.* which sounds/looks imposing. **high-fi•del•i•ty,** *adj.* which produces sound of a very high quality. **high fli•er, high flyer,** *n.* extravagant, as in goals, ideas, or tastes. **high-hand•ed,** *adj.* (action) done without considering other people. **high•land,** *adj.* coming from the highlands/from a mountain region. **High•land•er,** *n.* person who lives in the Highlands of Scotland. **High•lands,** *n. pl.* mountain region, esp. in northern Scotland. **high•light.** 1. *n.* most interesting event. 2. *v.* to accentuate/to draw attention to. **high•ly,** *adv.* very/greatly. **high-mind•ed,** *adj.* noble/very serious. **high•ness,** *n.* (a) being high/being above other things. (b) title given to princes, etc. **high-pitched,** *adj.* sharp/shrill (sound); steep (roof). **high-pow•ered,** *adj.* very powerful (en-

gine). **high priest,** *n.* most important priest. **high-rise,** *adj.* (building) with many floors. **high school,** *n.* school attended after elementary school or junior high school which includes the ninth or tenth grade through twelfth grade. **high seas,** *n. pl.* the oceans. **high sea•son,** *n.* most popular season for vacation travel. **high-speed,** *adj.* which goes/works very fast. **high-spirit•ed,** *adj.* lively. **high spot,** *n.* most enjoyable part of an entertainment. **high-strung,** *adj.* very emotional/excitable. **high tea,** *n.* (*in North of England and Scotland*) large meal of tea, cold meat, cakes, etc., eaten in the early evening. **high•wa•ter mark,** *n.* highest point (reached by the tide/by sth advancing. **high•way,** *n.* main road. **high•way•man,** *n.* (*pl.* -men) person who attacked travelers and robbed them.

hi•jack ['haɪdʒæk] *v.* to take control of (an aircraft/a train, etc.) with passengers on board, by threatening the pilot/driver. **hi•jack•er,** *n.* person who hijacks.

hike [haɪk] 1. *n.* (a) strenuous walk. (b) increase (in price, etc.). 2. *v.* (a) to go for a strenuous walk. (b) to increase (prices, etc.). **hik•er,** *n.* person who goes for long walks. **hik•ing,** *n.* walking as a relaxation.

hi•lar•i•ous [hɪ'leərɪəs] *adj.* very funny/very happy. **hi•lar•i•ous•ly,** *adv.* in a very funny way. **hi•lar•i•ty** [hɪ'lærɪtɪ] *n.* great laughter.

hill [hɪl] *n.* rise in the land, lower than a mountain. **hill•bil•ly,** *n.* person who lives in a remote area. **h. music =** country style music. **hill•ock,** *n.* little hill. **hill•side,** *n.* side of a hill. **hill•y,** *adj.* (-ier, -iest) (region) with many hills.

hilt [hɪlt] *n.* protective shield on the handle of a sword; **to the h. =** totally.

him [hɪm] *pronoun referring to a male; object form of* he; **have you seen h.? him•self** [hɪm'self] *pronoun referring to a male subject;* **he was washing h.; he is all by h.; he wrote to me h.**

hind [haɪnd] 1. *n.* female deer. 2. *adj.* **h. legs =** back legs (of an animal).

hind•er ['hɪndə] *v.* to prevent (s.o.) from doing sth. **hin•drance,** *n.* obstacle.

hind•most ['haɪndməʊst] *adj.* furthest back.

hind•sight ['haɪndsaɪt] *n.* knowing facts about an event in the past which could have been useful if they had been known at the time.

Hin•du ['hɪnduː] *adj. & n.* (person) following the main religion of India. **Hin•di,** *n.* language spoken in the central part of India.

hinge [hɪndʒ] 1. *n.* (a) metal bracket on which a door/a window hangs and opens. (b) small piece of gummed paper for sticking stamps into a stamp album. 2. *v.* to center/to depend (**on**). **hinged**, *adj.* with hinges.

hint [hɪnt] 1. *n.* (a) hidden suggestion/clue. (b) sign. (c) **hints** = helpful advice. 2. *v.* to suggest/to insinuate.

hin•ter•land ['hɪntəlænd] *n.* area inland from a sea port/around a large town.

hip [hɪp] *n.* (a) projecting bone where the legs join the body; wide part of the body where the legs join it. (b) fruit of a wild rose. (c) **h. h. hooray!** = *words used to give a cheer.* **hipped**, *adj.* (roof) which breaks at an angle.

hip•pie ['hɪpɪ] *n. inf.* person who lives/dresses in a different way from the majority of people in society.

hip•po•pot•a•mus, *inf.* **hip•po** [hɪpə- 'pɒtəməs, 'hɪpəʊ] *n.* (*pl.* **-muses, -mi** [-maɪ]; **-os**) very large African animal living in water and mud.

hire ['haɪə] 1. *n.* renting (of a car, etc.) usu. for a short time. 2. *v.* to rent (a car, etc.); to engage the services of (s.o.); **to h. out** = to offer one's services for a fee. **hire•ling**, *n.* person who is hired to do a job. **hir•er**, *n.* person who hires.

hir•sute ['hɜːsjuːt] *adj.* covered with hair.

his [hɪz] *adj.* (a) belonging to a male. (b) belonging to him; **a friend of h.**

His•pa•no [hɪs'pɑːnəʊ] *prefix meaning* between Spain and another country. **His•pan•ic**, *n.* person living in the United States who is of Spanish or Latin American descent.

hiss [hɪs] 1. *n.* whistling sound like an "s," made by snakes/by gas escaping, etc.; similar sound made to show you do not like sth. 2. *v.* to make a hissing sound.

his•ta•mine ['hɪstəmiːn] *n.* substance which causes an allergy.

his•tol•o•gy [hɪ'stɒlədʒɪ] *n.* science of body cells. **his•tol•o•gist**, *n.* person who specializes in histology.

his•to•ry ['hɪstərɪ] *n.* (a) study of the past; story of what happened in the past. (b) **natural h.** = study of animals and plants. **his•to•ri•an** [hɪ'stɔːrɪən] *n.* person who studies or writes about the past. **his•tor•ic** [hɪ'stɒrɪk] *adj.* (event) which is so important that it will be remembered. **his•tor•i•cal**, *adj.* referring to history; **h. novel** = novel set in the past. **his•tor•i•cal•ly**, *adv.* as in the past. **his•tri•on•ic** [hɪstrɪ'ɒnɪk] *adj.* referring to acting. **his•tri•on•ics**, *n. pl.* dramatic behavior.

hit [hɪt] 1. *n.* (a) blow; **he scored three hits** = he

hit the target three times. (b) song/play, etc. which is very popular. 2. *v.* (**hit; has hit**) (a) to knock against; to touch (sth) hard. (b) to affect (badly). **hit back**, *v.* to defend yourself against attack. **hit-man**, *n.* (*pl.* **-men**) person employed to kill/to hurt s.o. **hit off**, *v. inf.* **to hit it off with s.o.** = to get on well with s.o. **hit-or-miss**, *adj.* erratic/careless. **hit out**, *v.* (**at**) to try to attack (s.o.). **hit on**, *v.* to discover; **to h. o. a new restaurant.**

hitch [hɪtʃ] 1. *n.* awkward delay/unexpected stoppage. 2. *v.* (a) to pull **up**. (b) to hitch-hike. (c) to attach with a rope; *inf.* **to get hitched** = to get married. **hitch-hike**, *v.* to get a free ride in s.o.'s car, stopping the car by pointing your thumb. **hitch-hik•er**, *n.* person who hitch-hikes.

hith•er ['hɪðə] *adv.* (*formal*) to this place; **h. and thither** = all over the place; **h. and yon** = from here to another, farther, place. **hith•er•to**, *adv.* up till now.

HIV ['eɪtʃaɪ'viː] *n.* human immunodeficiency virus.

hive [haɪv] *n.* (a) box in which bees make their nest. (b) **hives** = sore red patches on the skin, usu. on the face.

hoard [hɔːd] 1. *n.* mass/store (of money/food, etc.) which has been collected. 2. *v.* to collect and store (money/food, etc.). **hoard•er**, *n.* person who buys food when supplies are low. **hoard•ing**, *n.* (a) buying food, etc., when supplies are low. (b) temporary fence made of rough planks.

hoar•frost ['hɔːfrɒst] *n.* white frost which covers trees/plants, etc.

hoarse [hɔːs] *adj.* rough (voice). **hoarse•ly**, *adv.* in a hoarse voice. **hoarse•ness**, *n.* roughness/harshness (of voice).

hoar•y ['hɔːrɪ] *adj.* (**-ier, -iest**) (a) (*formal*) white-haired. (b) *inf.* very old (joke).

hoax [həʊks] 1. *n.* trick. 2. *v.* to trick/to deceive. **hoax•er**, *n.* person who hoaxes.

hob [hɒb] *n.* shelf or ledge where a kettle or food can be put by the side of a fire for warmth.

hob•ble ['hɒbl] *v.* (a) to attach the legs of (a horse) so that it cannot move easily. (b) to walk with difficulty.

hob•by ['hɒbɪ] *n.* pastime; thing done as a relaxation. **hob•by•horse**, *n.* subject which s.o. always talks about.

hob•gob•lin [hɒb'gɒblɪn] *n.* goblin.

hob•nail ['hɒbneɪl] *n.* large nail used to protect

æ **back**, ɑː **farm**, ɒ **top**, aɪ **pipe**, aʊ **how**, aɪə **fire**, aʊə **flower**, ɔː **bought**, ɔɪ **toy**, e **fed**, eə **hair**, eɪ **take**, ə **afraid**, əʊ **boat**, əʊə **lower**, ɜː **word**, iː **heap**, ɪ **hit**, ɪə **hear**, uː **school**, ʊ **book**, ʌ **but**, b **back**, d **dog**, ð **then**, dʒ **just**, f **fog**, g **go**, h **hand**, j **yes**, k **catch**, l **last**, m **mix**, n **nut**, ŋ **sing**, p **penny**, r **round**, s **some**, ʃ **short**, t **too**, tʃ **chop**, θ **thing**, v **voice**, w **was**, z **zoo**, ʒ **treasure**

the soles of boots. **hob•nailed,** *adj.* (boots) with large metal nails.

hob•nob ['hɒbnɒb] *v.* (**hobnobbed**) *inf.* to be on friendly terms (**with** s.o. important).

ho•bo ['həʊbəʊ] *n.* person with no home or money.

hock [hɒk] *n.* (a) middle joint of an animal's leg; lower part of a leg of an animal used for food. (b) German white wine. (c) *Sl.* **in h.** = pawned.

hock•ey ['hɒkɪ] *n.* (a) team game played on grass with long curved sticks and a hard ball. (b) ice hockey.

ho•cus-po•cus ['həʊkəs'pəʊkəs] *n.* (a) meaningless words (used by magicians). (b) trickery.

hod [hɒd] *n.* (a) wooden container on the end of a pole, used by builders for carrying bricks. (b) metal container for coal.

hoe [həʊ] 1. *n.* garden tool with a blade on the end of a long handle. 2. *v.* to take out weeds/to loosen the soil with a hoe.

hog [hɒg] 1. *n.* domestic pig, raised for market; *inf.* **to go (the) whole h.** = to do sth completely. 2. *v.* (**hogged**) to monopolize.

hogs•head ['hɒgzhed] *n.* (a) large barrel. (b) liquid measure of about 63 gallons.

hoi pol•loi [hɔɪpə'lɔɪ] *n.* the ordinary people.

hoist [hɔɪst] 1. *n.* apparatus for lifting; goods lift. 2. *v.* to lift up.

hoi•ty-toi•ty ['hɔɪtɪ'tɔɪtɪ] *adj. inf.* snobbish; superior (air).

hold [həʊld] 1. *n.* (a) grip. (b) influence/power. (c) part of a ship/aircraft where cargo is carried. 2. *v.* (**held**) (a) to have in your hand, etc. (b) to contain. (c) to make (sth) take place. (d) to keep in (one's breath, a liquid). (e) to stay. (f) **to h. office** = to have a post (in a government). **hold back,** *v.* to keep back; not to go forward. **hold down,** *v.* to keep (sth) down; to work hard to keep (a job). **hold•er,** *n.* person or thing which holds. **hold forth,** *v.* to talk at great length. **hold•ing,** *n.* number of shares which you own; **h. company** = company formed to control shares in other companies. **hold off,** *v.* not to act. **hold on,** *v.* (a) to cling on to/to take a grip on (sth). (b) to wait. **hold out,** *v.* (a) to offer. (b) to last. **hold o•ver,** *v.* to postpone (sth). **hold up,** *v.* (a) to raise. (b) to support. (c) to hinder/to delay. (d) to attack and rob. **hold-up,** *n.* (a) delay; breakdown. (b) armed attack. **hold with,** *v. inf.* to accept/to agree with/approve of.

hole [həʊl] 1. *n.* opening/space. 2. *v.* (a) to make a hole in. (b) (*in golf*) to send (the ball) into the hole. **hole up,** *v. inf.* to hide away.

hol•i•day ['hɒlɪdeɪ] 1. *n.* period when you do not work, esp. a day when business is legally suspended to celebrate sth or to honor s.o. 2. *v.* (*esp. Brit.*) to go on vacation.

ho•li•ness ['həʊlɪnəs] *n. see* **ho•ly.**

ho•lis•tic [hɒ'lɪstɪk] *adj.* (attitude) which considers many sides to a problem; (medical treatment) which deals with the environment of the patient as well as the illness itself.

hol•ler ['hɒlə] *v. inf.* to shout.

hol•low ['hɒləʊ] 1. *n.* low-lying land; small depression in a flat surface. 2. *adj.* empty/with nothing inside; meaningless (success). 3. *v.* to **h. out** = to make (sth) hollow.

hol•ly ['hɒlɪ] *n.* very prickly evergreen bush with red berries.

hol•ly•hock ['hɒlɪhɒk] *n.* common garden flower which produces very tall spikes of blossom.

holm oak ['hɒlməʊk] *n.* evergreen oak found in temperate climates.

hol•o•caust ['hɒləkɔːst] *n.* destruction by fire.

hol•o•graph ['hɒləgrɑːf] *n.* letter, etc., written by hand by the person whose signature it bears. **hol•o•gram,** *n.* three-dimensional picture produced by lasers. **hol•og•ra•phy,** *n.* science of making holograms.

hol•ster ['həʊlstə] *n.* leather pouch for carrying a revolver.

ho•ly ['həʊlɪ] *adj.* (**-ier, -iest**) sacred (place); very pious (person); **h. orders** = being a priest. **ho•li•ness,** *n.* being holy; **his H.** = title given to the Pope. **Ho•ly Week,** *n.* the week which ends with Easter Sunday.

hom•age ['hɒmɪdʒ] *n.* (a) respect; **to pay h. to s.o.** = to show s.o. signs of respect. (b) (*formal*) duty/service (to a feudal lord).

home [həʊm] 1. *n.* (a) place where you live/place where you come from originally. (b) (*in sports*) **at h.** = playing on one's own sports field, etc. (c) house where people are looked after. 2. *adv.* to/at the place where you live; **to strike h.** = to hit the target. 3. *adj.* (a) referring to the place where you live. (b) not foreign; domestic. (c) (*in sports*) referring to the local team/the local sports field, etc.; (match) played by the local team on their own field, etc. 4. *v.* **to h. in on** = to go to a target. **home-grown,** *adj.* (vegetables) grown in the garden, not bought; (industry) which is developed in a country, and not imported. **home•land,** *n.* land which is the home of a people/one's native country. **home•less,** *adj.* with nowhere to live. **home•li•ness,** *n.* being homely. **home•ly,** *adj.* (a) simple; not ostentatious. (b) plain/ugly (person). **home-made,** *adj.* made at home/not bought. **home page,** *n.* page on the Internet that introduces a website and details its contents. **home run,** *n.* (*in baseball*) run made by a batter who touches all the bases. **home•sick,** *adj.* unhappy because of wanting to go home. **home•sick•ness**, *n*. feeling of being homesick. **home•stead**, *n*. house and its land and buildings. **home•ward**, *adj. & adv*. going toward home. **home•ward**, **homewards**, *adv*. toward home. **home•work**, *n*. work which children take from school to be done at home in the evening. **hom•ing**, *adj*. **h. pigeon** = pigeon trained to return to the place where it usually lives; **h. device** = device (on a missile) which guides it to the target.

hom•i•cide ['hɒmɪsaɪd] *n*. murder. **hom•i•cid•al** [hɒmɪ'saɪdl] *adj*. likely to murder.

hom•i•ly ['hɒmɪlɪ] *n*. sermon/talk, esp. one dealing with morality.

ho•me•op•a•thy [həumɪ'ɒpəθɪ] *n*. method of curing sick people by accustoming them to very small quantities of drugs which would normally make them ill. **ho•me•o•path** ['həumjəpæθ] *n*. doctor who practices homeopathy. **hom•e•o•path•ic**, *adj*. referring to homeopathy.

ho•mo•ge•ne•ous [hɒməu'dʒiːnɪəs] *adj*. of the same sort/quality (as other things). **ho•mo•ge•ne•i•ty** [hɒməudʒə'niːətɪ] *n*. being homogeneous.

ho•mog•e•nize [hə'mɒdʒənaɪz] *v*. to mix various parts until they become a single whole, to the cream mix to the cream into milk. **ho•mog•e•ni•za•tion** [həmɒdʒənaɪ'zeɪʃn] *n*. treatment of milk so that the cream does not separate.

hom•o•nym ['hɒmənɪm] *n*. word which is spelled and pronounced the same as another word but has a different meaning.

ho•mo•phone ['hɒməfəun] *n*. word which is pronounced the same as another, but has a different meaning and usu. spelling.

ho•mo•sex•u•al [həuməu'seksjuəl] *adj. & adj*. (person) who is attracted to persons of the same sex as himself/herself. **ho•mo•sex•u•al•i•ty** [həuməuseksju'ælɪtɪ] *n*. being homosexual.

hone [həun] *v*. to smooth/to sharpen (a blade).

hon•est ['ɒnɪst] *adj*. truthful; not cheating or stealing. **hon•est•ly**, *adv*. truthfully. **hon•es•ty**, *n*. (a) truthfulness. (b) garden flower with silvery seed cases, used as a winter decoration.

hon•ey ['hʌnɪ] *n*. sweet substance produced by bees. **honey-bee**, *n*. type of bee which makes honey. **hon•ey•comb**, *n*. construction of wax cells in which bees store honey; pattern of six-sided shapes like bees' cells. **hon•ey•combed**, *adj*. full of little holes. **hon•ey•dew**, *n*. type of melon which has green flesh. **hon•eyed**, *adj*. sweet/flattering (words). **hon•ey•moon**. 1. *n*. trip or vacation taken by a husband and wife immediately after their wedding. 2. *v*. to go on a honeymoon. **hon•ey•suck•le**, *n*. common climbing plant with scented yellow and pink flowers.

honk ['hɒŋk] 1. *n*. noise made by a goose/by a car horn. 2. *v*. to make a noise like a goose/a car horn.

hon•o•rar•i•um [ɒnə'reərɪəm] *n*. money paid to s.o. for work which is usually done free.

hon•or•ar•y ['ɒnərərɪ] *adj*. given as a mark of respect or honor.

hon•or, *Brit*. **hon•our** ['ɒnə] 1. *n*. (a) self-respect. (b) mark of respect; title given as a mark of respect. (c) **honors course** = university course which involves independent research. (d) title given to a judge. 2. *v*. (a) to respect; to give a title/medal to (s.o.) as a mark of respect. (b) to pay (a bill); (*of a bank*) to pay (a check). **hon•or•a•ble**, *adj*. that can be respected. **hon•or•a•bly**, *adv*. in a way which you can respect.

hooch [huːtʃ] *n*. *Sl*. alcoholic drink.

hood [hud] *n*. (a) loose covering for the head, attached to a coat. (b) folding roof on a car or baby carriage. (c) lid covering the engine of a car. (d) *Sl*. gangster. **hood•ed**, *adj*. wearing a hood.

hood•lum ['huːdləm] *n*. thug/gangster.

hood•wink ['hudwɪŋk] *v*. to trick.

hoof [huːf] *n*. (*pl*. **hooves**) hard part of the foot of a horse, etc. **hoofed**, *adj*. (animal) which has hooves.

hoo-ha ['huːhɑː] *n*. *inf*. fuss/bother.

hook [huk] 1. *n*. (a) bent piece of metal used for holding or pulling, etc.; **to get s.o. off the h.** = to release s.o. from a difficult situation; **by h. or by crook** = by any means available; **h. and eye** = small hook and loop for fastening clothing. (b) very small, bent piece of metal used for catching fish. (c) (*in boxing*) blow/stroke made with the arm bent. 2. *v*. (a) to hang on a hook; to attach with a hook. (b) to catch (a fish) with a hook. **hooked**, *adj*. (a) shaped like a hook. (b) caught with/on a hook. (c) *inf*. **h. on** = very interested in (a book, etc.); addicted to (drugs). **hook•er**, *n*. *inf*. prostitute.

æ **back**, ɑ: **farm**, ɒ: **top**, aɪ **pipe**, au **how**, aiə **fire**, auə **flower**, ɔ: **bought**, ɔɪ **toy**, e **fed**, eə **hair**, eɪ **take**, ə **afraid**, əu **boat**, əuə **lower**, ɜ: **word**, i: **heap**, ɪ **hit**, ɪə **hear**, u: **school**, u **book**, ʌ **but**, b **back**, d **dog**, ð **then**, dʒ **just**, f **fog**, g **go**, h **hand**, j **yes**, k **catch**, l **last**, m **mix**, n **nut**, ŋ **sing**, p **penny**, r **round**, s **some**, ʃ **short**, t **too**, tʃ **chop**, θ **thing**, v **voice**, w **was**, z **zoo**, ʒ **treasure**

hook-up, *n.* radio or TV link. **hook•worm,** *n.* type of parasitic worm.

hook•ah ['hʊkə] *n.* tobacco pipe where the smoke is cooled by being passed through water.

hook•y, hookey ['hʊkɪ] *n.* **to play h.** = to avoid going to school.

hoo•li•gan ['huːlɪgən] *n.* rowdy wild person. **hoo•li•gan•ism,** *n.* wild behavior.

hoop [huːp] *n.* large ring of wood or metal. **hoop-la,** *n.* excitement; bustle.

hoo•poe ['huːpuː] *n.* large cream-colored bird with a crest.

hoo•ray [hʊ'reɪ] *inter. showing great pleasure/excitement.*

hoot [huːt] 1. *n.* call of an owl; **hoots of laughter** = sound like an owl call, made when you are laughing. 2. *v. (of an owl)* to call; **to h. with laughter** = laugh hilariously.

Hoo•ver ['huːvə] *n.* trademark for a type of vacuum cleaner.

hop [hɒp] 1. *n.* (a) little jump. (b) short flight (in a plane). (c) bitter fruit used in making beer; climbing plant which bears this fruit. 2. *v.* **(hopped)** to jump on one leg; *(of birds)* to jump with both feet together.

hope [həʊp] 1. *n.* expectation/wanting sth to happen. 2. *v.* to expect that sth will happen; to want sth to happen. **hope•ful,** *adj.* full of hope/confident; giving hope; **h. signs. hope•ful•ly,** *adv.* (a) confidently. (b) **h. the rain will stop** = let's hope/I hope it will stop. **hope•less,** *adj.* with no hope; **he's h. at chess** = he plays very badly. **hope•less•ly,** *adv.* with no hope. **hope•less•ness,** *n.* being hopeless.

hop•per ['hɒpə] *n.* very large funnel for channeling loose material (like sand/corn, etc.).

hop•sack•ing ['hɒpsækɪŋ] *(also* **hopsack)** *n.* thick rough material.

hop•scotch ['hɒpskɒtʃ] *n.* children's game in which you hop over marked squares on the ground.

horde [hɔːd] *n.* crowd/mass.

ho•ri•zon [hə'raɪzn] *n.* (a) line where the earth seems to meet the sky. (b) layer of soil.

hor•i•zon•tal [hɒrɪ'zɒntl] *adj.* lying flat/not upright. **hor•i•zon•tal•ly,** *adv.* lying flat.

hor•mone ['hɔːməʊn] *n.* substance produced by glands in the body, which causes various physical reactions. **hor•mo•nal,** *adj.* referring to hormones.

horn [hɔːn] *n.* (a) hard bony growth on the head of some animals. (b) feeler on a snail's head. (c) brass musical instrument shaped like an animal's horn. (d) instrument on a car, etc., which makes a loud warning noise. **horned,** *adj.* with horns. **horn in (on),** *v. inf.* to join

(a meeting) uninvited. **horn•pipe,** *n.* vigorous dance danced by sailors. **horn•rimmed,** *adj.* (glasses) with tortoiseshell or tortoiseshell-like frames. **horn•y,** *adj.* hard/rough (hands).

horn•beam ['hɔːnbiːm] *n.* common hedgerow tree.

hor•net ['hɔːnɪt] *n.* large red wasp.

ho•rol•o•gy [hɒ'rɒlədʒɪ] *n.* study of time and clocks.

hor•o•scope ['hɒrəskəʊp] *n.* description of a person's character/forecasting of what will happen to a person in the future, based on the position of the stars when he or she was born.

hor•ren•dous [hɒ'rendəs] *adj.* horrible; dreadful.

hor•ri•ble ['hɒrəbl] *adj.* terrible/frightening. **hor•ri•bly,** *adv.* frighteningly/badly. **hor•rid** ['hɒrɪd] *adj.* offensive/unpleasant. **hor•ri•fic** [hə'rɪfɪk] *adj.* frightening/shocking. **hor•ri•fi•cal•ly,** *adv.* in a horrific way. **hor•ri•fy** ['hɒrɪfaɪ] *v.* to make (s.o.) very frightened/to shock (s.o.).

hor•ror ['hɒrə] *n.* terror/feeling of being very frightened; **h. film** = film which aims to frighten the audience. **horror-struck, horror-stricken,** *adj.* very frightened.

hors-d'œu•vre [ɔː'dɜːv] *n. pl.* cold food served at the beginning of a meal.

horse [hɔːs] 1. *n.* (a) large animal with hooves, which is used for riding or pulling vehicles; **h. racing** = racing of horses; **dark h.** = person you know nothing about and who may win; *inf.* **straight from the horse's mouth** = from a very reliable source. (b) apparatus made of wood over which you jump in gymnastics. (c) **clothes h.** = wooden frame used for drying clothes. 2. *v.* **to h. around** = to play roughly. **horse•back, on h.** = riding on a horse. **horse-chest•nut,** *n.* type of large tree; shiny inedible nut of this tree. **horse•fly,** *n.* large fly which bites animals. **horse•hair,** *n.* hair from the mane or tail of a horse, used for padding furniture. **horse laugh,** *n.* loud unpleasant laugh. **horse•man,** *n. (pl.* **-men)** person riding a horse; person skilled at riding horses. **horse•play,** *n.* rough play. **horse•pow•er,** *n.* unit formerly used when calculating the power of a car engine. **horse•rad•ish,** *n.* plant with a large root used to make a sharp sauce. **horse sense,** *n. inf.* commonsense. **horse•shoe,** *n.* curved metal strip nailed to the hooves of horses. **horse•tail,** *n.* common leafless weed. **horse trad•ing,** *n.* bargaining between parties before coming to an agreement. **horse•wom•an,** *n. (pl.* **-women)** woman riding a horse; woman skilled at riding horses.

hors•y, *adj.* (a) looking like a horse. (b) interested in horses.

hor•ti•cul•ture ['hɔːtɪkʌltʃə] *n.* science of gardening. **hor•ti•cul•tur•al** [hɔːtɪ'kʌltʃərəl] *adj.* referring to horticulture. **hor•ti•cul•tur•ist**, *n.* person who specializes in gardening.

hose [həʊz] 1. *n.* (a) long, flexible tube for carrying liquid, esp. water. (b) stockings/socks; **panty h.** = tights/stockings and briefs in one piece. 2. *v.* (*also* **hose down**) to spray with water, etc., from a hose. **ho•sier•y** ['həʊzjərɪ] *n.* knitted pieces of clothing (esp. stockings/socks).

hos•pice ['hɒspɪs] *n.* place where poor or terminally ill people can live.

hos•pi•ta•ble [hʊ'spɪtəbl] *adj.* welcoming. **hos•pi•ta•bly**, *adv.* in a welcoming way. **hos•pi•tal•i•ty** [hɒspɪ'tælɪtɪ] *n.* welcome to visitors; giving visitors food, drink, etc.

hos•pi•tal ['hɒspɪtl] *n.* place where sick people are treated. **hos•pi•tal•ize**, *v.* to put (s.o.) in a hospital.

host [həʊst] 1. *n.* (a) man who invites guests. (b) hotel keeper. (c) animal/plant on which other animals/plants live. (d) large number. (e) (*in church*) consecrated bread. 2. *v.* to be the host at (a dinner reception/a conference/TV show). **host•ess**, *n.* woman who invites guests.

hos•ta ['hɒstæ] *n.* common garden plant which grows in shade.

hos•tage ['hɒstɪdʒ] *n.* person kept prisoner until the demands of the captor are met.

hos•tel ['hɒstl] *n.* (a) building providing rooms for homeless families/students, etc. (b) **youth h.** = building where young hikers, etc. may stay the night cheaply.

hos•tile ['hɒstl] *adj.* referring to an enemy; unfriendly. **hos•til•i•ty** [hɒ'stɪlɪtɪ] *n.* (a) dislike (of a plan)/opposition (to a plan). (b) **hostilities** = warfare.

hot [hɒt] *adj.* (**hotter, hottest**) (a) very warm; *inf.* **to get into h. water** = to get into trouble; **to make things h. for s.o.** = make life unbearable. (b) highly spiced. (c) very strong; **h. line** = direct telephone link between heads of state; **he's in the h. seat** = his job involves him in awkward decisions. (d) *inf.* very recent (news); (goods) which have just been stolen. **hot air**, *n. inf.* useless excited talk. **hot•bed**, *n.* place where sth unpleasant breeds rapidly. **hot-blood•ed**, *adj.* (person) with a violent temper. **hot-desk•ing**, *n.* office system in which employees do not have their own desks but may work at any unoccupied desk. **hot dog**, *n.* hot frankfurter eaten in a long roll with mustard, pickles, etc. **hot•foot**, *adv.* running fast. **hot•head**, *n.* impetuous person. **hot•house**, *n.* heated greenhouse. **hot link**, *n.* word/phrase in a computer hypertext document that provides an active link to relevant information, which can be displayed by selecting the word/phrase. **hotplate**, *n.* piece of metal heated usu. by electricity, used to heat food. **hot-tem•pered**, *adj.* (person) with a violent temper. **hot-wa•ter bot•tle**, *n.* container filled with hot water which is used to warm a part of the body.

ho•tel [həʊ'tel] *n.* building where you can buy food and drink, and rent a room for the night. **ho•te•lier** [həʊ'telɪə] *n.* person who runs a hotel.

hound [haʊnd] 1. *n.* large hunting dog. 2. *v.* to chase (s.o.)/to victimize (s.o.).

hour ['aʊə] *n.* (a) period of time lasting sixty minutes; *inf.* **they took hours to do it** = a very long time. (b) particular point in time; **on the h.** = at nine o'clock, ten o'clock, etc. exactly. **hour•glass**, *n.* timing device made of two glass containers joined by a narrow tube, through which sand falls. **hour•ly**, *adj. & adv.* every hour.

house 1. *n.* [haʊs, *pl.* 'haʊzɪz] (a) building in which people live; *inf.* **like a h. on fire** = very fast; quickly. (b) dynasty/royal family. (c) commercial establishment; business. (d) audience (at a play); members (of a legislative or other deliberative body). (e) **drinks are on the h.** = drinks offered free by the owner of a restaurant, bar, etc. 2. *v.* [haʊz] to provide accommodation for (s.o./sth). **house ar•rest**, *n.* **under h. arrest** = not allowed to leave one's house which is being guarded by the police. **house•boat**, *n.* large boat which is used for living in. **house•bound**, *adj.* not able to leave the house. **house•break•er**, *n.* burglar/person who breaks into a house to steal. **house•break•ing**, *n.* breaking into a house to steal. **house•coat**, *n.* light coat/dressing gown worn by women in the house. **house•hold**, *n.* family/people who live together in the same house; **h. word** = saying which everybody uses. **house•hold•er**, *n.* head of a family/person who owns/who is in charge of a house. **house•keep•er**, *n.* woman employed to look after and direct the

---

æ back, ɑː farm, ɒ top, aɪ pipe, aʊ how, aɪə fire, aʊə flower, ɔː bought, ɔɪ toy, e fed, eəhair, eɪ take, ə afraid, əʊ boat, əʊə lower, ɜː word, iː heap, ɪ hit, ɪə hear, uː school, ʊ book, ʌ but, b back, d dog, ð then, dʒ just, f fog, g go, h hand, j yes, k catch, l last, m mix, n nut, ŋ sing, p penny, r round, s some, ʃ short, t too, tʃ chop, θ thing, v voice, w was, z zoo, ʒ treasure

management of a house. **house•keep•ing**, *n.* looking after a house; **h. money** = money set aside for paying food/heating, etc., in a house. **house•maid**, *n.* girl employed to do housework. **house•mas•ter, housemistress**, *n.* person in charge of a dormitory in a private school. **House of Com•mons**, *n.* lower house of the British Parliament. **House of Lords**, *n.* upper house of the British Parliament. **House of Rep•re•sen•ta•tives**, *n.* lower house of the U.S. Congress. **house phy•si•cian**, *n.* doctor working and usu. living in a hospital, hotel, or other public institution. **house plant**, *n.* plant which is kept in the house. **house sur•geon**, *n.* doctor working and usu. living in a hospital. **house-trained**, *adj.* (animal) trained not to pass excreta in the house. **house•warm•ing**, *n.* party to celebrate moving into a new house. **house•wife**, *n.* (*pl.* -wives) woman who spends her time looking after a house and usu. has no outside work. **house•work**, *n.* general cleaning work in a house. **hous•ing** [ˈhaʊzɪŋ] *n.* (a) providing accommodation for people; **h. development** = area of houses or apartments built at one time. (b) covering for part of a machine.

hove [həʊv] *v. see* **heave**.

hov•el [ˈhɒvl] *n.* small dirty house.

hov•er [ˈhɒvə] *v.* (a) to fly/to hang in the air without moving forward. (b) to hang (**around** s.o.). **hov•er•craft**, *n.* vehicle which moves over water or land on a cushion of air. **hov•er•fly**, *n.* small insect which hovers.

how [haʊ] *adv.* (a) in what way/to what extent; **h. are you?** (b) the means of; **tell me h. to do it.** (c) (*showing surprise*) **h. green the trees are! how do you do?** *inter. showing a greeting.* **how•ev•er** [haʊˈevə] *adv.* (a) to whatever extent. (b) in spite of this.

how•dah [ˈhaʊdɑː] *n.* seat on an elephant's back.

how•itz•er [ˈhaʊɪtsə] *n.* short gun which fires shells high into the air.

howl [haʊl] 1. *n.* loud wail. 2. *v.* to make a loud wailing noise. **howl down**, *v.* to stop (s.o.) making a speech by shouting at him. **howl•er**, *n. inf.* bad mistake. **howl•ing**, *n.* loud wailing.

hoy•den [ˈhɔɪdn] *n.* boisterous girl. **hoy•den•ish**, *adj.* like a hoyden.

HQ [ˈeɪtʃˈkjuː] *n.* headquarters.

HTML [ˈeɪtʃtiːemˈel] *abbrev. for* hypertext markup language.

hub [hʌb] *n.* (a) center of a wheel where it is connected to the axle. (b) center of activity/business. **hub cap**, *n.* metal plate covering the center of a car wheel.

hub•ble-bub•ble [ˈhʌblbʌbl] *n. inf.* hookah.

hub•bub [ˈhʌbʌb] *n.* confused sound of voices.

hud•dle [ˈhʌdl] 1. *n.* **to go into a h.** = to meet together to discuss sth in secret. 2. *v.* to crowd together.

hue [hjuː] *n.* (a) color. (b) **h. and cry** = public protest of anger/alarm.

huff [hʌf] *n.* **in a h.** = in a bad temper. **huff•y**, *adj. inf.* bad-tempered.

hug [hʌg] 1. *n.* throwing your arms round s.o. 2. *v.* (**hugged**) (a) to throw your arms around (s.o.). (b) to keep close to (sth).

huge [hjuːdʒ] *adj.* very large/enormous. **huge•ly**, *adv. inf.* enormously.

hug•ger-mug•ger [ˈhʌgəmʌgə] *adj. inf.* (a) secret. (b) confused; messy.

hulk [hʌlk] *n.* (a) rotten old ship which is no longer used for sailing. (b) large and clumsy thing/person. **hulk•ing**, *adj.* big and awkward.

hull [hʌl] 1. *n.* (a) main body of a ship. (b) pea or bean pod. 2. *v.* to take (peas) out of their pods.

hul•la•ba•loo [hʌləbəˈluː] *n.* loud disorderly noise or excitement.

hul•lo [həˈləʊ] *inter. showing a greeting.*

hum [hʌm] 1. *n.* low buzzing noise. 2. *v.* (**hummed**) (a) to make a continual low buzzing noise. (b) to sing the tune of a song without using the words. **hum•ming•bird**, *n.* very small brightly colored tropical bird which hovers.

hu•man [ˈhjuːmən] 1. *adj.* referring to people; **a h. being** = a person; **h. immunodeficiency virus (HIV)** = virus which causes AIDS, transmitted through sexual intercourse/blood; **h. nature** = general characteristics of people. 2. *n.* person. **hu•mane** [hjuːˈmeɪn] *adj.* kind/gentle. **hu•mane•ly**, *adv.* kindly/gently. **hu•man•ism** [ˈhjuːmənɪzəm] *n.* concern with human beings rather than with religions. **hu•man•ist**, *n.* person who believes in humanism. **hu•man•is•tic**, *adj.* referring to humanism. **hu•man•i•tar•i•an** [hjuːmænɪˈteərɪən] *adj.* kind toward other humans. **hu•man•i•ty** [hjuːˈmænɪtɪ] *n.* (a) all people. (b) great kindness. (c) **the humanities** = arts subjects (not sciences). **hu•man•i•za•tion**, *n.* act of humanizing. **hu•man•ize**, *v.* to make (more) human. **hu•man•kind**, *n.* people, seen as a biological group. **hu•man•ly**, *adv.* **we will do everything h. possible** = all we can.

hum•ble [ˈhʌmbl] 1. *adj.* (-er, -est) modest/not proud; **to eat h. pie** = to admit you were wrong. 2. *v.* to make (s.o.) less proud/less important. **hum•ble•ness**, *n.* being humble.

hum•bug ['hʌmbʌg] *n.* (a) confidence trick. (b) person who tricks s.o./who pretends to be sth which he is not.

hum•ding•er [hʌm'dɪŋə] *n. inf.* wonderful/remarkable person/thing.

hum•drum ['hʌmdrʌm] *adj.* dull/ordinary.

hu•mer•us ['hjuːmərəs] *n.* bone in the top part of the arm.

hu•mid ['hjuːmɪd] *adj.* damp. **hu•mid•i•fi•er** [hjuː'mɪdɪfaɪə] *n.* machine which dampens the air (in a house). **hu•mid•i•ty** [hjuː'mɪdɪtɪ] *n.* dampness.

hu•mil•i•ate [hjuː'mɪlɪeɪt] *v.* to make (s.o.) feel unimportant/humble/ashamed. **hu•mil•i•a•tion** [hjuːmɪlɪ'eɪʃn] *n.* making s.o. feel unimportant/humble/ashamed. **hu•mil•i•ty** [hjuː'mɪlɪtɪ] *n.* humbleness/being humble.

hum•mock ['hʌmək] *n.* low rise in the ground.

hu•mor, *Brit.* **hu•mour** ['hjuːmə] 1. *n.* (a) seeing the funny aspects of sth. (b) general feeling/mood. 2. *v.* to do what s.o. wants in order to keep him happy. **hu•mor•ist,** *n.* person who makes jokes; writer of funny stories or articles. **hu•mor•ous,** *adj.* funny/amusing. **hu•mor•ous•ly,** *adv.* in a humorous way.

hump [hʌmp] 1. *n.* lump on the back; small rounded bump in the ground. 2. *v. inf.* to carry (on your shoulder). **hump•backed,** *adj.* (person) with a hump.

hu•mus ['hjuːməs] *n.* good soil made rich with decayed animal or vegetable matter.

hunch [hʌntʃ] 1. *n. inf.* feeling that sth is going to happen. 2. *v.* to bend low. **hunch•back,** *n.* person with a hunched back.

hun•dred ['hʌndrəd] *n.* number 100; **hundreds of** = very many. **hun•dred•fold,** *adv.* a hundred times. **hun•dredth, 100th,** *adj.* referring to a hundred. **hun•dred•weight,** *n.* weight of 100 pounds (approx. 45.359 kilos).

hung [hʌŋ] *v. see* **hang; h. jury** = jury which cannot reach a majority decision. **hung o•ver,** *adj. inf.* feeling ill after drinking too much alcohol. **hung up,** *adj. inf.* suffering from an emotional disturbance.

Hun•gar•i•an [hʌŋ'geərɪən] 1. *adj.* referring to Hungary. 2. *n.* (a) person from Hungary. (b) language spoken in Hungary.

hun•ger ['hʌŋgə] *n.* wanting/needing to eat. **hun•ger strike,** *n.* refusing to eat to force s.o. to do sth. **hun•gri•ly,** *adv.* in a hungry way. **hun•gry,** *adj.* feeling hunger.

hunk [hʌŋk] *n.* large rough piece (of bread/cheese).

hunt [hʌnt] 1. *n.* (a) chasing of wild animals for sport; group of people who meet regularly to chase wild animals, esp. foxes. (b) search (**for** s.o.). 2. *v.* (a) to look **for** (s.o./sth). **hunt down,** *v.* to track (a person/an animal) and catch them. **hunt•er,** *n.* person who chases wild animals; horse used in hunting; **bargain h.** = person who is looking for bargains in stores, etc. **hunt•ing,** *n.* (a) chasing wild animals. (b) looking for sth. **hunt•ing ground,** *n.* place where wild animals are often found. **hunts•man,** *n.* (*pl.* **-men**) man who hunts wild animals; man who looks after a pack of hunting hounds.

hur•dle ['hɜːdl] *n.* (a) small fence which has to be jumped over in a race. (b) difficulty; obstacle. **hurd•ler,** *n.* person who takes part in races with hurdles.

hur•dy-gur•dy ['hɜːdɪ'gɜːdɪ] *n.* machine which produces music if a handle is turned.

hurl [hɜːl] *v.* to throw hard. **hurl•ing,** *n.* game similar to hockey, traditionally played in Ireland.

hurl•y-burl•y ['hɜːlɪ'bɜːlɪ] *n.* rough activity.

hur•rah, hurray [hu'rɑː, hu'reɪ] *inter. showing great pleasure/excitement.*

hur•ri•cane ['hʌrɪkən] *n.* violent tropical storm, esp. in the West Indies; **h. lamp** = lamp with a glass shield around the flame.

hur•ry ['hʌrɪ] 1. *n.* rush. 2. *v.* (*also* **hurry up**) (a) to go fast. (b) to make (s.o.) go faster. **hur•ried,** *adj.* quick/rushed. **hur•ried•ly,** *adv.* quickly.

hurt [hɜːt] 1. *n.* pain. 2. *v.* (**hurt**) to give (s.o.) pain/to make (s.o.) sad. **hurt•ful,** *adj.* which is painful to the feelings/which makes s.o. sad.

hur•tle ['hɜːtl] *v.* to move quickly/to rush dangerously.

hus•band ['hʌzbənd] 1. *n.* man who is married to a certain woman. 2. *v.* (*formal*) to look after carefully/not waste (your resources). **hus•band•ry,** *n.* farming; **animal h.** = rearing of animals on a farm.

hush [hʌʃ] 1. *n.* quiet. 2. *v.* to make quiet. **hush-hush,** *adj. inf.* secret. **hush mon•ey,** *n.* money paid to s.o. to stop them from revealing a secret. **hush up,** *v.* to suppress (a scandal).

husk [hʌsk] 1. *n.* hard outside covering of a seed. 2. *v.* to take the husk off (a seed).

husk•y ['hʌskɪ] 1. *adj.* (**-ier, -iest**) rough/hoarse (voice). 2. *n.* dog which pulls sleds in the Arctic. **husk•i•ly,** *adv.* in a husky voice. **husk•i•ness,** *n.* hoarseness of the voice.

hus•sar ['hʌzɑː] *n.* soldier on horseback.

hus•sy ['hʌsɪ] *n.* **brazen h.** = wicked girl/woman.

hust•ings ['hʌstɪŋz] *n.* **on the h.** = on an election campaign trail.

hus•tle ['hʌsl] 1. *n.* rush/violent activity. 2. *v.* to push/to hurry (roughly). **hus•tler,** *n.* person who gets things going/who hurries business along.

hut [hʌt] *n.* small rough house, usu. made of wood.

hutch [hʌtʃ] *n.* enclosure for rabbits.

hy•a•cinth ['haɪəsɪnθ] *n.* strongly-scented spring flower grown from a bulb.

hy•brid ['haɪbrɪd] *adj. & n.* (plant/animal, etc.) produced from two different species.

hy•da•tid ['haɪdætid] *adj.* (cyst) caused by a tapeworm.

hy•dran•gea [haɪ'dreɪndʒə] *n.* garden shrub with large blue, white, or pink flowers.

hy•drant ['haɪdrənt] *n.* water pipe in a street to which a hose can be attached; **fire h.** = one to which firemen can attach fire hoses.

hy•drate ['haɪdreɪt] *n.* chemical compound with water.

hy•drau•lic [haɪ'drɔːlɪk] *adj.* worked by fluid. **hy•drau•li•cal•ly,** *adv.* using hydraulic force. **hy•drau•lics,** *n.* study of fluids used mechanically.

hy•dro ['haɪdrəʊ] *n.* (*pl.* **-os**) *inf.* hydroelectric power.

hydro- ['haɪdrəʊ] *prefix meaning* water.

hy•dro•car•bon [haɪdrəʊ'kɑːbn] *n.* organic compound of hydrogen and carbon.

hy•dro•chlo•ric [haɪdrəʊ'klɒrɪk] *adj.* (acid) made of hydrogen and chlorine.

hy•dro•e•lec•tric [haɪdrəʊɪ'lektrɪk] *adj.* referring to hydroelectricity. **hy•dro•e•lec•tric•i•ty** [haɪdrəʊelek-'trɪsɪtɪ] *n.* electricity produced by water power.

hy•dro•foil ['haɪdrəfɔɪl] *n.* boat which skims over the water on thin legs.

hy•dro•gen ['haɪdrədʒən] *n.* (*element:* H) common gas which combines with oxygen to form water; **h. bomb** = extremely powerful nuclear bomb.

hy•drog•ra•pher [haɪ'drɒgrəfə] *n.* person who makes maps of the ocean/sea or ocean/sea bed.

hy•drol•y•sis [haɪ'drɒlɪsɪs] *n.* decomposition of a chemical substance by water.

hy•drom•e•ter [haɪ'drɒmɪtə] *n.* device for measuring the relative density of water.

hy•dro•pho•bi•a ['haɪdrəfəʊbɪə] *n.* (a) rabies. (b) fear of water (usu. a symptom of rabies).

hy•dro•plane ['haɪdrəpleɪn] *n.* powerful flat-bottomed motorboat which skims over the surface of the water.

hy•dro•pon•ics [haɪdrə'pɒnɪks] *n.* science of growing plants in water, without using soil.

hy•dro•stat•ic [haɪdrəʊ'stætɪk] *adj.* referring to fluids at rest.

hy•dro•ther•a•py [haɪdrə'θerəpɪ] *n.* treatment of sick people with water.

hy•e•na [haɪ'iːnə] *n.* fierce doglike African animal.

hy•giene ['haɪdʒiːn] *n.* keeping clean and free of germs. **hy•gi•en•ic** [haɪ'dʒiːnɪk] *adj.* (which keeps) clean and free of germs. **hy•gi•en•i•cal•ly,** *adv.* in a hygienic way. **hy•gien•ist,** person who specializes in (esp. dental) hygiene.

hy•grom•e•ter [haɪ'grɒmɪtə] *n.* instrument for measuring humidity.

hy•men ['haɪmen] *n.* thin tissue which covers the entrance to the vagina of a girl who has never had sexual intercourse.

hymn [hɪm] *n.* religious song. **hym•nal** ['hɪmnl], **hymn-book,** *n.* book of hymns.

hype [haɪp] 1. *n. inf.* excessive publicity. 2. *v.* to publicize (a product) excessively.

hyper- ['haɪpə] *prefix meaning* to a great degree; **hyperactive** = very active.

hy•per•bo•la [haɪ'pɜːbələ] *n.* type of curve. **hy•per•bol•ic** [haɪpə'bɒlɪk] *adj.* referring to a hyperbola.

hy•per•bo•le [haɪ'pɜːbəlɪ] *n.* exaggerated comparison. **hy•per•bol•i•cal** [haɪpə-'bɒlɪkl] *adj.* referring to hyperbole.

hy•per•crit•i•cal [haɪpə'krɪtɪkl] *adj.* extremely critical.

hy•per•me•di•a ['haɪpəmiːdɪə] *n. pl.* computer software/hardware that provides active links to relevant items of text, graphics, video, and sound, which can be accessed by selecting a particular word/phrase/image, etc.

hy•per•sen•si•tive [haɪpə'sensɪtɪv] *adj.* very easily offended.

hy•per•ten•sion [haɪpə'tenʃn] *n.* very high blood pressure.

hy•per•text ['haɪpətekst] *n.* computer software/hardware that allows the creation and use of active links to relevant information, which can be displayed by selecting a particular image/word/phrase; **h. markup language** = text description language, consisting of markers embedded in the text to control document structure and active links, used in electronic publishing, esp. on the Internet.

hy•phen ['haɪfn] *n.* short line (-) which joins two words or separates one word into parts. **hy•phen•ate,** *v.* to join (words) with a hyphen or separate (one word) into parts with a hyphen. **hy•phen•a•tion** [haɪfə'neɪʃn] *n.* act of hyphenating.

hyp•no•sis [hɪp'nəʊsɪs] *n.* putting s.o. into a trance, so that they obey your orders; **under h.** = while in a trance. **hyp•not•ic** [hɪp'nɒtɪk] *adj.* referring to hypnosis. **hyp•not•i•cal•ly**, *adv.* in a hypnotic way. **hyp•no•tism** ['hɪpnətɪzəm] *n.* use of hypnosis as a medical process or for amusement. **hyp•no•tist**, *n.* person who practices hypnosis. **hyp•no•tize**, *v.* to put (s.o.) into a trance.

hy•po ['haɪpəʊ] *n.* substance used for fixing the picture when developing a photograph.

hypo- ['haɪpəʊ] *prefix meaning* under/below.

hy•po•caust ['haɪpəʊkɔːst] *n.* ancient Roman heating system, where hot air flowed under a raised floor.

hy•po•chon•dri•a [haɪpə'kɒndrɪə] *n.* being permanently worried about your health. **hy•po•chon•dri•ac**, *n.* person who is always worried about his/her health.

hy•poc•ri•sy [hɪ'pɒkrəsɪ] *n.* pretending to be the opposite of what you really are/to feel the opposite of what you really feel. **hyp•o•crite**

['hɪpəkrɪt] *n.* hypocritical person. **hyp•o•crit•i•cal** [hɪpə'krɪtɪkl] *adj.* referring to hypocrisy.

hy•po•der•mic [haɪpə'dɜːmɪk] *adj.* **h. syringe/needle** = medical instrument used for injections just below the surface of the skin.

hy•po•ten•sion [haɪpəʊ'tenʃn] *n.* very low blood pressure.

hy•pot•e•nuse [haɪ'pɒtənjuːz] *n.* longest side of a right-angled triangle.

hy•po•ther•mi•a [haɪpə'θɜːmɪə] *n.* state where the temperature of the body is abnormally low.

hy•poth•e•sis [haɪ'pɒθəsɪs] *n.* (*pl.* **-theses** [-θəsiːz]) suggestion that sth is true, though without proof. **hy•po•thet•i•cal** [haɪpə'θetɪkl] *adj.* suggested as true, but not necessarily so. **hy•po•thet•i•cal•ly**, *adv.* in a hypothetical way.

hys•ter•ec•to•my [hɪstə'rektəmɪ] *n.* surgical operation to remove a woman's womb.

hys•te•ri•a [hɪ'stɪərɪə] *n.* nervous excitement leading to wild fits of laughing or crying. **hys•ter•i•cal** [hɪ'sterɪkl] *adj.* suffering from hysteria; laughing/crying in a wild manner. **hys•ter•i•cal•ly**, *adv.* in an uncontrollable way. **hys•ter•ics**, *n. pl.* attack of hysteria.

æ back, ɑː farm, ɒ top, aɪ pipe, aʊ how, aiə fire, aʊə flower, ɔː bought, ɔɪ toy, e fed, eəhair, eɪ take, ə afraid, əʊ boat, əʊə lower, vː word, iː heap, ɪ hit, ɪə hear, uː school, ʊ book, ʌ but, b back, d dog, ð then, dʒ just, f fog, g go, h hand, j yes, k catch, l last, m mix, n nut, ŋ sing, p penny, r round, s some, ʃ short, t too, tʃ chop, θ thing, v voice, w was, z zoo, ʒ treasure

Ii

I, i [aɪ] **to dot one's i's and cross one's t's** = to be very careful to settle the final details.

I [aɪ] *pronoun referring to the speaker.*

I *symbol for* iodine

i•amb ['aɪæmb] *n.* Greek poetic measure, formed of a short and a long syllable. **i•am•bic,** *adj.* referring to iambs.

I•be•ri•an [aɪ'biːərɪən] *adj.* referring to Spain and Portugal.

i•bex ['aɪbeks] *n. (pl.* ibex(es)) mountain goat with large curved horns.

i•bid, ibidem ['ɪbɪd(em)] *adv.* in the same book/chapter/page.

i•bis ['aɪbɪs] *n.* tropical water bird with long legs and a curved bill.

ice [aɪs] 1. *n.* (a) frozen water; **to break the i.** = to bring an embarrassing silence to an end; **to keep sth on i.** = not do anything about it for the moment. (b) **dry i.** = frozen carbon dioxide. 2. *v.* (a) to cool with ice. (b) to freeze. (c) to cover with sugar icing. **Ice age,** *n.* geological period when parts of the world were covered with ice. **ice ax,** *n.* ax used by mountaineers to cut footholds in ice. **ice•berg,** *n.* large floating mass of ice at sea; **tip of the i.** = small part of sth (usu. unpleasant) which makes you eventually discover the rest. **ice•box,** *n.* (a) box containing ice to keep food or drink cool. (b) *(old)* refrigerator. **ice-break•er,** *n.* boat specially strengthened to break up ice in shipping lanes. **ice cream,** *n.* frozen dessert made of cream and flavoring. **ice•field,** *n.* large area of ice floating on the sea. **ice•floe,** *n.* sheet of ice floating in the sea. **ice hock•ey,** *n.* form of hockey played on ice. **ice•house,** *n.* house for storing ice during the summer. **Ice•land•er,** *n.* person from Iceland. **Ice•lan•dic.** 1. *adj.* referring to Iceland. 2. *n.* language spoken in Iceland. **ice skate,** *n.* shoe with a sharp blade for skating on ice. **ice-skate,** *v.* to move on ice skates. **i•ci•cle,** *n.* long hanging piece of ice formed by dripping water in cold weather. **i•ci•ly,** *adv.* in a cold/unfriendly way. **i•ci•ness,** *n.* bitter coldness (of weather/of greeting). **ic•ing,** *n.* sugar topping for a cake or cookie, etc. **i•cy,** *adj.* (-ier, -iest) (a) covered with ice. (b) very cold/unwelcoming.

ich•neu•mon fly [ɪk'njuːmən 'flaɪ] *n.* insect, whose larvae live on other insects.

i•con ['aɪkən] *n.* (a) picture of Christ or a saint in the Eastern Christian church. (b) little pictorial symbol on a computer screen. **i•con•o•clast** [aɪ'kɒnəklæst] *n.* person who attacks beliefs which are held by many people. **i•con•o•clas•tic** [aɪkɒnə'klæstɪk] *adj.* which attacks beliefs which are held by many people. **i•co•nog•ra•phy,** *n.* the study of icons; the study of pictures of a particular subject.

id [ɪd] *n.* the basic unconscious drives in a person.

I'd [aɪd] *short for* **I would/I had/I should.**

i•de•a [aɪ'dɪə] *n.* thought/plan in the mind; **I had no i.** = I did not know.

i•de•al [aɪ'dɪəl] 1. *n.* summit of perfection; **person of high ideals** = person who has high standards of perfection. 2. *adj.* perfect; very suitable. **i•de•al•ism,** *n.* aiming at achieving an ideal. **i•de•al•ist,** *n.* person who aims at achieving an ideal; impractical person. **i•de•al•is•tic** [aɪdɪə'lɪstɪk] *adj.* aiming at an ideal; too perfect. **i•de•al•ize,** *v.* to make (s.o./sth) seem perfect. **i•de•al•ly,** *adv.* if everything were perfect.

i•den•ti•fy [aɪ'dentɪfaɪ] *v.* (a) to say who s.o. is/what sth is. (b) to state that sth belongs to you. (c) **to i. with** = to feel you have the same characteristics as (s.o.); to have a feeling of sympathy for (s.o./sth). **i•den•ti•cal,** *adj.* **(with/to)** exactly the same as. **i•den•ti•cal•ly,** *adv.* in exactly the same way. **i•den•ti•fi•a•ble,** *adj.* which can be identified. **i•den•ti•fi•ca•tion** [aɪdentɪfɪ'keɪʃn] *n.* saying who so. is/who sth belongs to. **i•den•ti•kit,** *n.* trademark for a method of making a portrait of a criminal using pieces of photographs or drawings of different faces to form a composite picture. **i•den•ti•ty,** *n.* (a) who s.o. is; **i. card** = card which identifies the holder, usu. showing a photograph of the holder, with the name, date of birth and other details. (b) being the same/being identical.

id•e•o•gram ['ɪdɪəʊgræm] *n.* picture/character which represents a word.

i•de•ol•o•gy [aɪdɪ'ɒlədʒɪ] *n.* theory of life based on political or economic philosophy rather than religious belief. **i•de•o•log•i•cal** [aɪdɪə'lɒdʒɪkl] *adj.* referring to ideology.

ides [aɪdz] *npl.* in the Latin calendar, the 15th of some months and the 13th of others.

id•i•o•cy ['ɪdɪəsɪ] *n. see* **id•i•ot.**

id•i•om ['ɪdɪəm] *n.* (a) characteristic way of speaking/of writing. (b) particular expression where the words do not have their literal meaning. **id•i•o•mat•ic** [ɪdɪə'mætɪk] *adj.* referring to a particular way of speaking.

id•i•o•syn•cra•sy [ɪdɪəu'sɪŋkrəsɪ] *n.* particular way of behaving. **id•i•o•syn•crat•ic** [ɪdɪəusɪŋ'krætɪk] *adj.* odd/peculiar; particular to one person.

id•i•ot ['ɪdɪət] *n.* (a) mentally deficient person. (b) person who is stupid. **id•i•o•cy,** *n.* stupidity. **id•i•ot•ic** [ɪdɪ'ɒtɪk] *adj.* stupid. **id•i•ot•i•cal•ly,** *adv.* in a stupid way.

i•dle ['aɪdl] 1. *adj.* (**idler, idlest**) (a) lazy. (b) not working. (c) aimless/not worthwhile. 2. *v.* (a) to spend time doing nothing. (b) (*of an engine*) to run gently. **i•dle•ness,** *n.* laziness. **i•dler,** *n.* person who idles. **i•dly,** *adv.* (a) lazily. (b) without being involved.

i•dol ['aɪdl] *n.* (a) statue of a god. (b) favorite person. (c) star performer (who is worshipped by fans). **i•dol•a•ter,** *n.* person who worships idols. **i•dol•a•try** [aɪ'dɒlətrɪ] *n.* worship of idols. **i•dol•ize,** *v.* to worship.

i•dyll ['ɪdɪl] *n.* pleasant/happy scene. **i•dyl•lic** [ɪ'dɪlɪk] *adj.* pleasant/happy (in a romantic way). **i•dyl•li•cal•ly,** *adv.* in an idyllic way.

i.e. ['aɪ'iː] *abbrev. for* id est, *meaning* that is.

if [ɪf] 1. *conj.* (a) (*showing what might happen*) **if it rains the ground gets wet.** (b) (*showing supposition*) **if only to please her.** (c) (*exclamation*) **if only I had known!** (d) whether; **do you know if the plane is late?** (e) although; **he is nice, if rather lazy.** (f) at any time when. 2. *n. inf.* undecided question.

ig•loo ['ɪgluː] *n.* dome-shaped shelter built by Eskimos out of blocks of snow.

ig•ne•ous ['ɪgnɪəs] *adj.* (rock) which was originally formed from solidified lava.

ig•nite [ɪg'naɪt] *v.* to set fire to; to catch fire. **ig•ni•tion** [ɪg'nɪʃn] *n.* (*in a car*) electrical device which makes the spark which fires the fuel; **i. key** = key used to switch on the ignition.

ig•no•ble [ɪg'nəubl] *adj.* (*formal*) unworthy.

ig•no•min•y ['ɪgnəmɪnɪ] *n.* shame/disgrace.

ig•no•min•i•ous [ɪgnə'mɪnɪəs] *adj.* shame-ful. **ig•no•min•i•ous•ly,** *adv.* in an ignominious way.

ig•nore [ɪg'nɔː] *v.* not notice (on purpose).

ig•no•ra•mus [ɪgnə'reɪməs] *n.* (*pl.* **-es**) person who is stupid/who knows nothing.

ig•no•rance ['ɪgnərəns] *n.* not knowing.

ig•no•rant ['ɪgnərənt] *adj.* not knowing/stupid. **ig•no•rant•ly,** *adv.* stupidly.

i•gua•na [ɪgju'ɑːnə] kind of large tropical lizard.

il•e•um ['ɪlɪəm] *n.* long part of the small intestine.

il•i•um ['ɪlɪəm] *n.* top part of the hip bone.

ilk [ɪlk] *n. inf.* sort/type.

ill [ɪl] 1. *adj.* (**worse, worst**) (a) sick; not well. (b) bad. 2. *n.* bad thing. 3. *adv.* badly. **ill-ad•vised,** *adj.* not recommended. **ill-bred,** *adj.* badly brought up; with bad manners. **ill-fat•ed,** *adj.* fated to fail. **ill-feel•ing,** *n.* resentment; dislike. **ill-got•ten,** *adj.* illegally acquired. **ill-man•nered,** *adj.* badly behaved/with bad manners/rude. **ill•ness,** *n.* sickness. **ill-starred,** *adj.* fated to fail. **ill-treat,** *v.* to treat (animals/children) badly. **ill will,** *n.* to bear s.o. ill will = to want sth bad to happen to s.o.

I'll [aɪl] *short for* **I will/I shall.**

il•le•gal [ɪ'liːgl] *adj.* against the law. **il•le•gal•i•ty,** *n.* being illegal. **il•le•gal•ly,** *adv.* against the law.

il•leg•i•ble [ɪ'ledʒɪbl] *adj.* (writing) which cannot be read. **il•leg•i•bil•i•ty,** *n.* being illegible. **il•leg•i•bly,** *adv.* in an illegible way.

il•le•git•i•mate [ɪlɪ'dʒɪtəmət] *adj.* (a) (person) born of unmarried parents. (b) against the law. **il•le•git•i•mate•ly,** *adv.* in an illegitimate way. **il•le•git•i•ma•cy,** *n.* being illegitimate.

il•lic•it [ɪ'lɪsɪt] *adj.* against the law/illegal. **il•lic•it•ly,** *adv.* in an illicit way.

il•lit•er•a•cy [ɪ'lɪtərəsɪ] *n.* inability to read and write. **il•lit•er•ate,** *adj. & n.* (person) who cannot read or write.

il•log•i•cal [ɪ'lɒdʒɪkl] *adj.* not sensible/not reasonable. **il•log•i•cal•ly,** *adv.* in an illogical way. **il•log•i•cal•i•ty** [ɪlɒdʒɪ'kælɪtɪ] *n.* being illogical.

il•lu•mi•nate [ɪ'luːmɪneɪt] *v.* (a) to light up. (b) to draw colored initials/pictures in a manuscript. **il•lu•mi•nat•ing,** *adj.* which throws light on (a subject).

æ back, ɑː farm, ɒ top, aɪ pipe, aʊ how, aɪə fire, aʊə flower, ɔː bought, ɔɪ toy, e fed, eəhair, eɪ take, ə afraid, əʊ boat, əʊə lower, ɜː word, iː heap, ɪ hit, ɪə hear, uː school, ʊ book, ʌ but, b back, d dog, ð then, dʒ just, f fog, g go, h hand, j yes, k catch, l last, m mix, n nut, ŋ sing, p penny, r round, s some, ʃ short, t too, tʃ chop, θ thing, v voice, w was, z zoo, ʒ treasure

il•lu•mi•na•tion [ɪluːmɪˈneɪʃn] n. (a) decoration using usu. colored lights. (b) colored initial illustration in a manuscript.

il•lu•sion [ɪˈluːʒn] n. impression which is not true; **optical i.** = thing which appears different from what it really is because the eye is being deceived. il•lu•sion•ist, n. person who entertains with optical illusions. il•lu•sive, adj. false. il•lu•so•ry, adj. which is an illusion.

il•lus•trate [ˈɪləstreɪt] v. (a) to add pictures to. (b) to give/to be an example of. il•lus•tra•tion [ɪləˈstreɪʃn] n. (a) picture (in a book). (b) example. il•lus•tra•tive [ˈɪləstrətɪv] adj. which illustrates/which is an example. il•lus•tra•tor [ˈɪləstreɪtə] n. person who draws the pictures for a book.

il•lus•tri•ous [ɪˈlʌstrɪəs] adj. very famous.

I'm [aɪm] short for **I am.**

im•age [ˈɪmɪdʒ] n. (a) portrait/statue; inf. **he's the spitting i. of his father** = he looks exactly like his father. (b) idea which other people have of a person/a company. (c) picture produced by a lens/seen in a mirror. (d) comparison/symbol used esp. in poetry. im•age•ry, n. using comparison/symbols (in writing) as a way of making people imagine things.

im•ag•ine [ɪˈmædʒɪn] v. to picture (sth) in your mind. im•ag•i•na•ble, adj. which you can imagine. im•ag•i•nar•y, adj. false/not real. im•ag•i•na•tion [ɪmædʒɪˈneɪʃn] n. ability to picture things in your mind. im•ag•i•na•tive [ɪˈmædʒɪnətɪv] adj. (artist) with a strong imagination; (drawing/poem) which shows a lot of imagination. im•ag•i•na•tive•ly, adv. in an imaginative way.

i•ma•go [ɪˈmɑːgəʊ] n. final form of an insect (such as a butterfly) after the larval and pupal stages.

i•mam [ˈɪmæm] n. Muslim priest.

im•bal•ance [ɪmˈbæləns] n. lack of balance.

im•be•cile [ˈɪmbəsiːl] n. (a) mentally deficient person. (b) stupid person. im•be•cil•i•ty [ɪmbəˈsɪlɪtɪ] n. being mentally deficient.

im•bibe [ɪmˈbaɪb] v. (formal) to drink.

im•bri•cat•ed [ˈɪmbrɪkeɪtɪd] adj. overlapping.

im•bro•glio [ɪmˈbrəʊljəʊ] n. (pl. -os) complicated dispute/situation.

im•bue [ɪmˈbjuː] v. (formal) to fill with a feeling.

IMF [aɪemˈef] abbrev. for International Monetary Fund.

im•i•tate [ˈɪmɪteɪt] v. to copy/to do like (s.o.). im•i•ta•tion [ɪmɪˈteɪʃn] n. copy; act of imitating. im•i•ta•tive [ˈɪmɪtətɪv] adj. which copies. im•i•ta•tor [ˈɪmɪteɪtə] n. person who copies.

im•mac•u•late [ɪˈmækjʊlət] adj. extremely clean/tidy. im•mac•u•la•cy, n. being immaculate. im•mac•u•late•ly, adv. extremely tidily.

im•ma•nent [ˈɪmənənt] adj. existing as an inherent part.

im•ma•te•ri•al [ɪməˈtɪərɪəl] adj. not important.

im•ma•ture [ɪməˈtʃʊə] adj. not mature/not fully grown/not fully developed. im•ma•tur•i•ty, n. not being mature.

im•meas•ur•a•ble [ɪˈmeʒrəbl] adj. which cannot be measured/very large. im•meas•ur•a•bly, adv. enormously.

im•me•di•ate [ɪˈmiːdjət] adj. (a) close/nearest. (b) very soon. im•me•di•a•cy, n. being immediate. im•me•di•ate•ly, adv. & conj. without delay; at once.

im•me•mo•ri•al [ɪməˈmɔːrɪəl] adj. **from time i.** = from very ancient times.

im•mense [ɪˈmens] adj. huge/very wide/enormous. im•mense•ly, adv. very much. im•men•si•ty, n. vastness/huge size.

im•merse [ɪˈmɜːs] v. to plunge (sth) in a liquid. im•mer•sion [ɪˈmɜːʃn] n. plunging (into a liquid); **i. heater** (also **immersion coil**) = small electrical device immersed in liquid, as water, to heat it.

im•mi•grate [ˈɪmɪgreɪt] v. to come to settle in a country. im•mi•grant, n. person who comes to a country to settle. im•mi•gra•tion [ɪmɪˈgreɪʃn] n. settling in a new country; **i. office** = office dealing with immigrants; **i. controls** = restrictions placed by a country on the numbers of immigrants.

im•mi•nent [ˈɪmɪnənt] adj. which is about to happen. im•mi•nence, n. being about to happen.

im•mo•bile [ɪˈməʊbaɪl] adj. without moving; unable to move. im•mo•bil•i•ty [ɪməˈbɪlɪtɪ] n. state of not moving. im•mo•bi•li•za•tion [ɪməʊbɪlaɪˈzeɪʃn] n. stopping sth moving. im•mo•bi•lize [ɪˈməʊbɪlaɪz] v. to stop (sth) moving.

im•mod•er•ate [ɪˈmɒdərət] adj. extravagant/not moderate. im•mod•er•ate•ly, adv. in an immoderate way.

im•mod•est [ɪˈmɒdɪst] adj. not modest.

im•mo•late [ˈɪməʊleɪt] v. (poetic) to sacrifice.

im•mor•al [ɪˈmɒrəl] adj. not concerned with the principles of good behavior. im•mo•ral•i•ty [ɪməˈrælɪtɪ] n. lack of morality. im•mor•al•ly, adv. in an immoral way.

im•mor•tal [ɪˈmɔːtl] 1. adj. like a god; who never dies. 2. n. god. im•mor•tal•i•ty [ɪmɔːˈtælɪtɪ] n. being immortal/never dying.

im•mor•tal•ize [ɪˈmɔːtəlaɪz] v. to make (s.o.) be remembered forever.

im•mov•a•ble [ɪˈmuːvəbl] adj. which cannot be moved. **im•mov•a•bly**, adv. in an immovable way.

im•mune [ɪˈmjuːn] adj. (to) (person) who cannot catch a disease. **im•mu•ni•ty**, n. (a) protection (**against** a disease). (b) protection against arrest; **diplomatic i.** = protection of diplomats against being arrested. **im•mu•ni•za•tion** [ɪmjunaɪˈzeɪʃn] n. giving protection against a disease. **im•mu•nize** [ˈɪmjunaɪz] v. to give protection **against** a disease. **im•mu•nol•o•gy**, n. study of immunity.

im•mure [ɪˈmjuə] v. to shut (s.o.) in prison.

im•mu•ta•ble [ɪˈmjuːtəbl] adj. (formal) which cannot be changed/which does not change. **im•mu•ta•bil•i•ty**, n. being immutable. **im•mu•ta•bly**, adv. in an immutable way.

imp [ɪmp] n. little devil; mischievous child.

im•pact [ˈɪmpækt] n. forceful shock/effect. **im•pact•ed** [ɪmˈpæktɪd] adj. (tooth) which is stuck in the jawbone and cannot grow.

im•pair [ɪmˈpeə] v. to harm. **im•pair•ment**, n. harm.

im•pal•a [ɪmˈpɑːlə] n. large African antelope.

im•pale [ɪmˈpeɪl] v. to jab a sharp object through (s.o.'s body).

im•pal•pa•ble [ɪmˈpælpəbl] adj. (formal) which cannot be touched.

im•pan•el [ɪmˈpænəl] v. to choose (a jury).

im•part [ɪmˈpɑːt] v. (formal) to pass on/to communicate (sth **to** s.o.).

im•par•tial [ɪmˈpɑːʃl] adj. not biased. **im•par•ti•al•i•ty**, n. being impartial. **im•par•tial•ly**, adv. in an impartial way.

im•pas•sa•ble [ɪmˈpɑːsəbl] adj. which you cannot go through or across.

im•passe [ˈæmpæs] n. deadlock/state where two sides cannot agree.

im•pas•sioned [ɪmˈpæʃnd] adj. very deeply felt/excited (speech).

im•pas•sive [ɪmˈpæsɪv] adj. expressionless. **im•pas•sive•ly**, adv. in an impassive way.

im•pa•tient [ɪmˈpeɪʃnt] adj. (a) (**with**) not patient; unable to wait for sth. (b) in a hurry (to do sth). **im•pa•tience**, n. lack of patience. **im•pa•tient•ly**, adv. in a hurried way/not patiently.

im•peach [ɪmˈpiːtʃ] v. to charge (a public official) with improper conduct or a crime while in office. **im•peach•ment**, n. act of impeaching.

im•pec•ca•ble [ɪmˈpekəbl] adj. perfect/perfectly correct. **im•pec•ca•bly**, adv. perfectly.

im•pe•cu•ni•ous [ɪmpɪˈkjuːnɪəs] adj. (formal) with no money.

im•pede [ɪmˈpiːd] v. to get in the way of (sth); to prevent (sth) happening. **im•ped•ance** [ɪmˈpiːdəns] n. resistance to an electric current. **im•ped•i•ment** [ɪmˈpedɪmənt] n. obstacle; **speech i.** = stammer, etc., which prevents you speaking clearly. **im•ped•i•men•ta**, n. pl. heavy/awkward baggage or equipment.

im•pel [ɪmˈpel] v. (**impelled**) to push/to force.

im•pend•ing [ɪmˈpendɪŋ] adj. imminent/about to happen.

im•pen•e•tra•ble [ɪmˈpenɪtrəbl] adj. which you cannot go through or into. **im•pen•e•tra•bil•i•ty**, n. being impenetrable.

im•pen•i•tent [ɪmˈpenɪtənt] adj. not penitent/not sorry for having done sth wrong.

im•per•a•tive [ɪmˈperətɪv] adj. (a) urgent/obligatory. (b) (in grammar) **i. verb** = verb used as a command.

im•per•cep•ti•ble [ɪmpəˈseptɪbl] adj. which you can hardly notice. **im•per•cep•ti•bly**, adv. scarcely noticeably.

im•per•fect [ɪmˈpɜːfɪkt] adj. not perfect/not complete. **im•per•fec•tion** [ɪmpəˈfekʃn] n. flaw.

im•pe•ri•al [ɪmˈpɪərɪəl] adj. (a) referring to an empire. (b) (weights/measures) conforming to standards used in the United Kingdom and the British Commonwealth. **im•pe•ri•al•ism**, n. belief in the good of building an empire. **im•pe•ri•al•ist**. 1. n. person who builds an empire. 2. adj. (also **imperialistic**) referring to imperialism.

im•per•il [ɪmˈperɪl] v. (**imperiled**) (formal) to put in danger.

im•pe•ri•ous [ɪmˈpɪərɪəs] adj. arrogant (way of behaving/giving orders). **im•pe•ri•ous•ly**, adv. in an imperious way.

im•per•ma•nent [ɪmˈpɜːmənənt] adj. not permanent/not lasting.

im•per•me•a•ble [ɪmˈpɜːmɪəbl] adj. which liquids cannot go through.

im•per•son•al [ɪmˈpɜːsnl] adj. (a) without a personal touch. (b) (verb) used without a person or thing as the subject.

æ back, ɑː farm, ɒ top, aɪ pipe, aʊ how, aiə fire, aʊə flower, ɔː bought, ɔɪ toy, e fed, eəhair, eɪ take, ə afraid, əʊ boat, əʊə lower, vː word, iː heap, ɪ hit, ɪə hear, uː school, ʊ book, ʌ but, b back, d dog, ð then, dʒ just, f fog, g go, h hand, j yes, k catch, l last, m mix, n nut, ŋ sing, p penny, r round, s some, ʃ short, t too, tʃ chop, θ thing, v voice, w was, z zoo, ʒ treasure

im•per•son•al•ly, *adv.* in an impersonal way.

im•per•son•ate [ɪmˈpɜːsəneɪt] *v.* to imitate (s.o.)/to disguise yourself as (s.o.). im•per•son•a•tion, *n.* act of impersonating. im•per•son•a•tor, *n.* person who impersonates.

im•per•ti•nence [ɪmˈpɜːtɪnəns] *n.* rudeness/insolence. im•per•ti•nent, *adj.* rude/insolent. im•per•ti•nent•ly, *adv.* in an impertinent way.

im•per•turb•a•ble [ɪmpəˈtɜːbəbl] *adj.* calm. im•per•turb•a•bil•i•ty, *n.* being imperturbable. im•per•turb•a•bly, *adv.* calmly.

im•per•vi•ous [ɪmˈpɜːvɪəs] *adj.* (to) which liquids cannot go through.

im•pe•ti•go [ɪmpɪˈtaɪɡəʊ] *n.* contagious disease of the skin (esp. in children).

im•pet•u•ous [ɪmˈpetjuəs] *adj.* thoughtless/hasty (act); (person) who rushes to do sth without thinking. im•pet•u•os•i•ty [ɪmpetjuˈɒsɪti] *n.* rushing to do sth without thinking. im•pet•u•ous•ly [ɪmˈpetjuəsli] *adv.* without thinking.

im•pe•tus [ˈɪmpətəs] *n.* (*pl.* -es) movement forward; stimulus.

im•pinge [ɪmˈpɪndʒ] *v.* (on) to affect.

im•pi•ous [ˈɪmpɪəs] *adj.* not pious/not religious. im•pi•e•ty [ɪmˈpaɪəti] *n.* being impious.

imp•ish [ˈɪmpɪʃ] *adj.* like an imp.

im•plac•a•ble [ɪmˈplækəbl] *adj.* who/which cannot be satisfied. im•plac•a•bly, *adv.* in an implacable way.

im•plant [ɪmˈplɑːnt] 1. *n.* tissue which has been implanted. 2. *v.* to fix (sth) in deeply.

im•plau•si•ble [ɪmˈplɔːzəbl] *adj.* not likely to be true.

im•ple•ment 1. *n.* [ˈɪmplɪmənt] tool/instrument. 2. *v.* [ˈɪmplɪment] to put into effect. im•ple•men•ta•tion [ɪmplɪmənˈteɪʃn] *n.* putting into effect.

im•pli•cate [ˈɪmplɪkeɪt] *v.* to i. s.o. in sth = to suggest that s.o. was connected with sth. im•pli•ca•tion [ɪmplɪˈkeɪʃn] *n.* (a) suggestion (that s.o. is connected with a crime). (b) thing which is implied.

im•plic•it [ɪmˈplɪsɪt] *adj.* which is not definitely said, but is suggested. im•plic•it•ly, *adv.* without questioning.

im•plore [ɪmˈplɔː] *v.* to beg (s.o. to do sth).

im•ply [ɪmˈplaɪ] *v.* to suggest.

im•po•lite [ɪmpəˈlaɪt] *adj.* rude/not polite. im•po•lite•ly, *adv.* rudely, im•po•lite•ness, *n.* lack of politeness.

im•pol•i•tic [ɪmˈpɒlɪtɪk] *adj.* (*formal*) not wise.

im•pon•der•a•bles [ɪmˈpɒndrəblz] *n. pl.* things whose importance you cannot easily calculate.

im•port. 1. *n.* [ˈɪmpɔːt] (a) imports = goods which are brought into a country; i. duty = tax paid on goods brought into a country. (b) (*formal*) meaning (of words). 2. *v.* [ɪmˈpɔːt] to bring goods into a country. im•por•ta•tion [ɪmpɔːˈteɪʃn] *n.* act of importing; goods imported. im•port•er [ɪmˈpɔːtə] *n.* person or country which imports.

im•por•tance [ɪmˈpɔːtns] *n.* seriousness/serious effect/influence. im•por•tant, *adj.* (a) serious/with a serious effect/which matters a great deal. (b) with great influence/holding an influential position. im•por•tant•ly, *adv.* seriously/with a serious effect.

im•por•tune [ɪmˈpɔːtjuːn] *v.* (*formal*) to pester/to bother (s.o.). im•por•tu•nate [ɪmˈpɔːtjunət] *adj.* pestering/bothering.

im•pose [ɪmˈpəʊz] *v.* (a) to inflict. (b) to i. on = cause trouble/inconvenience. im•pos•ing, *adj.* grand/solemn. im•po•si•tion [ɪmpəˈzɪʃn] *n.* (a) laying down (of duties/conditions/obligations). (b) taking advantage (of s.o.).

im•pos•si•ble [ɪmˈpɒsɪbl] *adj.* (a) which cannot be done. (b) awkward/difficult (person/situation). im•pos•si•bil•i•ty, *n.* being impossible. im•pos•si•bly, *adv.* in an impossible way; *inf.* greatly.

im•pos•tor [ɪmˈpɒstə] *n.* person who pretends to be s.o. else. im•pos•ture [ɪmˈpɒstʃə] *n.* pretending to be s.o. else.

im•po•tence [ˈɪmpətəns] *n.* (a) lack of strength. (b) (*of man*) inability to have sexual intercourse. im•po•tent, *adj.* (*a*) weak. (b) (*of man*) unable to have sexual intercourse. im•po•tent•ly, *adv.* without being able to act.

im•pound [ɪmˈpaʊnd] *v.* to take (sth) away and put it in a safe place.

im•pov•er•ish [ɪmˈpɒvərɪʃ] *v.* to make poor. im•pov•er•ish•ment, *n.* making poor.

im•prac•ti•ca•ble [ɪmˈpræktɪkəbl] *adj.* (plan) which cannot work; (road) which cannot be used.

im•prac•ti•cal [ɪmˈpræktɪkl] *adj.* (plan) which is not easy to put into practice; (person) who is not good at doing things with his/her hands.

im•pre•ca•tion [ɪmprɪˈkeɪʃn] *n.* (*formal*) oath/curse.

im•pre•cise [ɪmprɪˈsaɪs] *adj.* not precise/not accurate. im•pre•ci•sion, *n.* lack of precision.

im•preg•na•ble [ɪmˈpregnəbl] *adj.* (fortress) which cannot be captured. im•preg•na•bil•i•ty, *n.* being impregnable.

im•preg•nate ['ɪmpregneɪt] v. (a) to soak (with sth). (b) to make pregnant. im•preg•na•tion, n. act of impregnating.

im•pre•sa•ri•o [ɪmprɪ'sɑːrɪəu] n. (pl. -os) person who organizes concerts and operas.

im•press [ɪm'pres] v. (a) to make (s.o.) admire/respect s.o./sth. (b) to i. sth on s.o. = to make s.o. understand. (c) to stamp (a pattern on sth). im•pres•sion [ɪm'preʃn] n. (a) effect on s.o.'s mind. (b) imitation of how s.o. talks/behaves. (c) mark (of a pattern). (d) printing (of a book). im•pres•sion•a•ble, adj. (person) who is easily influenced (by others). im•pres•sion•ism, n. art movement where painters tried to convey an impression of reality, in particular of light. im•pres•sion•ist. 1. adj. referring to impressionism. 2. n. painter in the impressionist movement. im•pres•sion•is•tic [ɪmpreʃə'nɪstɪk] adj. vague/sketchy. im•pres•sive [ɪm'presɪv] adj. which commands respect. im•pres•sive•ly, adv. in an impressive way.

im•pri•ma•tur [ɪmprɪ'mɑːtə] n. official permission to print a book.

im•print. 1. n. ['ɪmprɪnt] (a) mark made by sth pressed down. (b) name of publishing company printed in its books. 2. v. [ɪm'prɪnt] to stamp/to mark.

im•pris•on [ɪm'prɪzn] v. to put/to keep in prison. im•pris•on•ment, n. putting/keeping in prison.

im•prob•a•ble [ɪm'prɒbəbl] adj. not probable; unlikely. im•prob•a•bil•i•ty, n. lack of probability. im•prob•a•bly, adv. not likely.

im•promp•tu [ɪm'prɒmptjuː] adj. & adv. without any rehearsal or practice.

im•prop•er [ɪm'prɒpə] adj. (a) rude. (b) (word) used in a wrong way. im•prop•er•ly, adv. (a) not correctly. (b) (word which is used) wrongly. im•pro•pri•e•ty [ɪmprə'praɪətɪ] n. being improper; improper action.

im•prove [ɪm'pruːv] v. to make/to get better. im•prove•ment, n. thing which makes better/is better.

im•prov•i•dent [ɪm'prɒvɪdənt] adj. (person) who spends too much money or who does not plan for the future. im•prov•i•dence, n. being improvident. im•prov•i•dent•ly, adv. not thinking about saving for the future.

im•pro•vise ['ɪmprəvaɪz] v. to do/to make (sth) without preparation.

im•prov•i•sa•tion [ɪmprəvaɪ'zeɪʃn] n. making sth without any preparation.

im•pru•dent [ɪm'pruːdənt] adj. careless/not prudent. im•pru•dent•ly, adv. in an imprudent way.

im•pu•dent ['ɪmpjudənt] adj. rude/insolent. im•pu•dence, n. rudeness/insolence. im•pu•dent•ly, adv. rudely/insolently.

im•pugn [ɪm'pjuːn] v. (formal) to attack (s.o.'s character/the truth of a statement).

im•pulse ['ɪmpʌls] n. (a) shock (which makes sth move/work). (b) sudden feeling/decision; i. buying = buying goods on the basis of a sudden decision. im•pul•sive [ɪm'pʌlsɪv] adj. acting on a sudden decision/without thinking. im•pul•sive•ly, adv. in an impulsive way. im•pul•sive•ness, n. being impulsive.

im•pu•ni•ty [ɪm'pjuːnɪtɪ] n. with i. = without risk of punishment.

im•pure [ɪm'pjuə] adj. not pure. im•pu•ri•ties [ɪm'pjuərɪtɪz] n. pl. substances which make sth impure.

im•pute [ɪm'pjuːt] v. to attribute (sth to s.o.); to say that (sth) is caused by (s.o./sth). im•pu•ta•tion, n. saying that s.o. is at fault.

in [ɪn] 1. prep. & adv. (a) (showing place) in Russia; in bed. (b) (showing time) in autumn; in January; long skirts are in = fashionable. (c) one in ten = one out of ten. (d) (showing state) dressed in pink; in public; inf. all in = tired out. 2. n. the ins and outs = the intricate details. 3. adj. inf. fashionable. in-box, n. file/basket for incoming letters, messages, etc. in for, adv. to be in for sth = to be about to get sth. in on, adv. to be in on (a secret) = to know a secret.

in. abbreviation for inch.

in•a•bil•i•ty [ɪnə'bɪlɪtɪ] n. being unable (to).

in•ac•ces•si•ble [ɪnək'sesɪbl] adj. impossible to reach.

in•ac•cu•rate [ɪn'ækjurət] adj. not exact/not accurate. in•ac•cu•rate•ly, adv. not accurately. in•ac•cu•ra•cy, n. not being exact; lack of accuracy.

in•ac•tive [ɪn'æktɪv] adj. not active/not doing anything. in•ac•tion, inactivity [ɪnæk'tɪvɪtɪ] n. lack of action/doing nothing.

in•ad•e•quate [ɪn'ædɪkwət] adj. (a) not enough/insufficient. (b) not competent enough. in•ad•e•qua•cy, n. being inadequate. in•ad•e•quate•ly, adv. not enough; insufficiently.

in•ad•mis•si•ble [ɪnəd'mɪsəbl] adj. (evidence) not allowed to be presented in a court.

æ back, ɑː farm, ɒ top, aɪ pipe, aʊ how, aɪə fire, aʊə flower, ɔː bought, ɔɪ toy, e fed, eəhair, eɪ take, ə afraid, əʊ boat, əʊə lower, ɜː word, iː heap, ɪ hit, ɪə hear, uː school, ʊ book, ʌ but, b back, d dog, ð then, dʒ just, f fog, g go, h hand, j yes, k catch, l last, m mix, n nut, ŋ sing, p penny, r round, s some, ʃ short, t too, tʃ chop, θ thing, v voice, w was, z zoo, ʒ treasure

in•ad•vert•ent [ɪnəd'vɜːtənt] adj. said/done by mistake, not on purpose. **in•ad•vert•ence**, n. being inadvertent; thing done inadvertently. **in•ad•vert•ent•ly**, adv. by mistake.

in•ad•vis•a•ble [ɪnəd'vaɪzəbl] adj. unwise/not recommended.

in•al•ien•a•ble [ɪn'eɪljənəbl] adj. (formal) which cannot be taken away or refused.

in•ane [ɪ'neɪn] adj. stupid. **in•an•i•ty** [ɪn'ænɪtɪ] n. being stupid.

in•an•i•mate [ɪn'ænɪmət] adj. not alive.

in•ap•pli•ca•ble [ɪnə'plɪkəbl] adj. unsuitable/which does not apply (to).

in•ap•pro•pri•ate [ɪnə'prəʊprɪət] adj. (to) not appropriate/not suitable/not fitting the circumstances.

in•ap•ti•tude [ɪn'æptɪtjuːd] n. (for) unsuitableness; lack of ability.

in•ar•tic•u•late [ɪnɑː'tɪkjulət] adj. (a) not speaking clearly. (b) unable to speak.

in•ar•tis•tic [ɪnɑː'tɪstɪk] adj. not artistic; not concerned with the arts.

in•as•much as [ɪnəz'mʌtʃæz] conj. (formal) seeing that/owing to the fact that.

in•at•ten•tive [ɪnə'tentɪv] adj. not paying attention/not attentive. **in•at•ten•tion**, n. not paying attention.

in•au•di•ble [ɪn'ɔːdɪbl] adj. which cannot be heard. **in•au•di•bly**, adv. so quietly that it cannot be heard.

in•au•gu•rate [ɪn'ɔːgjureɪt] v. to swear in (a new president); to open officially (a new building/a festival, etc. **in•au•gu•ral**, adj. (speech) given at an opening ceremony; first (use); opening (ceremony). **in•au•gu•ra•tion** [ɪnɔːgju'reɪʃn] n. swearing in (of a new president); official opening.

in•aus•pi•cious [ɪnɔː'spɪʃəs] adj. unlucky/not giving hope for the future.

in•board ['ɪbɔːd] adj. inside a boat.

in•born ['ɪnbɔːn] adj. (feelings/ideas) which a person has had since birth.

in•bred ['ɪnbred] adj. (feelings/ideas) which a person has had since a very young age. **in•breed•ing**, n. breeding between closely related persons/animals, etc.

Inc. [ɪn'kɔːpəreɪtɪd] short for incorporated.

in•cal•cu•la•ble [ɪn'kælkjuləbl] adj. which cannot be calculated/so large that it cannot be measured.

in cam•er•a [ɪn'kæmərə] adv. in secret; not in public.

in•can•des•cent [ɪnkæn'desnt] adj. which burns with a very bright light. **in•can•des•cence**, n. very bright light.

in•can•ta•tion [ɪnkæn'teɪʃn] n. magic words.

in•ca•pa•ble [ɪn'keɪpəbl] adj. (a) (of) not able. (b) not capable; not competent. **in•ca•pa•bil•i•ty** [ɪnkeɪpə'bɪlɪtɪ] n. incompetence/not being capable.

in•ca•pac•i•ty [ɪnkə'pæsɪtɪ] n. lack of strength/ability to do sth. **in•ca•pac•i•tate**, v. to make (s.o.) unable to do sth.

in•car•cer•ate [ɪn'kɑːsəreɪt] v. (formal) to put/to keep in prison. **in•car•cer•a•tion** [ɪnkɑːsə'reɪʃn] n. putting/keeping in prison.

in•car•nate [ɪn'kɑːnət] adj. in human form. **in•car•na•tion** [ɪnkɑː'neɪʃn] n. appearance in human form.

in•cau•tious [ɪn'kɔːʃəs] adj. not prudent. **in•cau•tious•ly**, adv. rashly.

in•cen•di•ar•y [ɪn'sendjərɪ] 1. adj. which causes fire. 2. n. (a) bomb which causes fire. (b) person who sets fire to buildings.

in•cense. 1. n. ['ɪnsens] spice powder which when burned gives a strong smell. 2. v. [ɪn'sens] to make (s.o.) angry.

in•cen•tive [ɪn'sentɪv] n. thing which encourages, as extra money paid when production is increased.

in•cep•tion [ɪn'sepʃn] n. beginning.

in•ces•sant [ɪn'sesnt] adj. unceasing/continuous.

in•cest ['ɪnsest] n. sexual intercourse with a close member of the family. **in•ces•tu•ous** [ɪn'sestjʊəs] adj. referring to incest.

inch [ɪnʃ] 1. n. (pl. -es) measure of length (= 1/12 of a foot or 2.54 cm). 2. v. to go (slowly).

in•cho•ate [ɪn'kəʊeɪt] adj. (formal) not fully developed.

in•ci•dent ['ɪnsɪdənt] n. (a) minor happening. (b) (usu. violent) action/disturbance. **in•ci•dence**, n. rate. **in•ci•den•tal** [ɪnsɪ'dentl] adj. & n. (thing) which happens in connection with sth else, but forming an unimportant part; subsidiary; **i. music** = background music which accompanies a motion picture. **in•ci•den•tal•ly**, adv. by the way. **in•ci•den•tals**, n. pl. minor expenses.

in•cin•er•ate [ɪn'sɪnəreɪt] v. to destroy by burning. **in•cin•er•a•tion** [ɪnsɪnə'reɪʃn] n. destruction by burning. **in•cin•er•a•tor**, n. furnace for burning trash.

in•cip•i•ent [ɪn'sɪpɪənt] adj. which is beginning/coming.

in•cise [ɪn'saɪz] v. to make a cut in (esp. a stone). **in•ci•sion** [ɪn'sɪʒn] n. cut. **in•ci•sive** [ɪn'saɪsɪv] adj. sharp/cutting. **in•ci•sive•ly**, adv. sharply. **in•ci•sor** [ɪn'saɪzə] n. sharp front tooth for cutting.

in•cite [ɪn'saɪt] v. to encourage (s.o. **to** do sth). **in•cite•ment**, n. encouragement (**to**).

in•ci•vil•i•ty [ɪnsɪ'vɪlɪtɪ] n. (formal) rudeness.

in•clem•ent [ɪn'klemənt] adj. (formal) (of weather) bad.

in•cline 1. *n.* ['ɪnklaɪn] slope. 2. *v.* [ɪn'klaɪn] (a) to slope. (b) to encourage or dispose (s.o.) to do sth. (c) to tend. (d) to bend/to bow. **in•cli•na•tion** [ɪnklɪ'neɪʃn] *n.* (a) (angle of) slope. (b) slight bow (of the head). (c) tendency. **in•clined** *adj.* (a) sloping. (b) likely (**to** do sth).

in•clude [ɪn'kluːd] *v.* to count (s.o./sth) along with others. **in•clu•sion** [ɪn'kluːʒn] *n.* counting s.o./sth in among others. **in•clu•sive**, *adj.* which includes everything; **from Monday to Friday i.** = including both Monday and Friday; **i. language** = language that does not use words/phrases that might be seen as excluding certain groups of people, esp. non-sexist language.

in•cog•ni•to [ɪnkɒg'niːtəʊ] *adv. & n.* **to travel i.** = under a false name or identity.

in•co•her•ent [ɪnkəʊ'hɪərənt] *adj.* not coherent; not linked; which does not make sense. **in•co•her•ence**, *n.* being incoherent. **in•co•her•ent•ly**, *adv.* not in a coherent way; in a way which does not make sense.

in•come ['ɪŋkʌm] *n.* money which you receive; **i. tax** = tax on income; **unearned i.** = income from investments/rents.

in•com•ing ['ɪnkʌmɪŋ] 1. *adj.* which is arriving/coming in; **i. calls** = telephone calls received. 2. *n. pl.* **incomings** = revenue.

in•com•mode [ɪnkɒ'məʊd] *v.* (*formal*) to inconvenience (s.o.).

in•com•mu•ni•ca•do [ɪnkəmjuːnɪ'kɑːdəʊ] *adv.* not allowed to see or write to any person.

in•com•pa•ra•ble [ɪn'kɒmprəbl] *adj.* which cannot be compared to anything else. **in•com•pa•ra•bly**, *adv.* vastly; so much that it cannot be compared.

in•com•pat•i•ble [ɪnkəm'pætɪbl] *adj.* (**with**) which cannot live/work/fit together. **in•com•pat•i•bil•i•ty** [ɪnkəmpætə'bɪlɪti] *n.* being incompatible (**with**).

in•com•pe•tent [ɪn'kɒmpɪtənt] *adj.* not good at doing sth/not competent. **in•com•pe•tence**, *n.* lack of competence. **in•com•pe•tent•ly**, *adv.* in an incompetent way.

in•com•plete [ɪnkəm'pliːt] *adj.* not complete/not finished. **in•com•plete•ly**, *adv.* not completely.

in•com•pre•hen•si•ble [ɪnkɒmprɪ'hensɪbl] *adj.* which cannot be understood. **in•com•pre•hen•sion**, *n.* lack of understanding.

in•con•ceiv•a•ble [ɪnkən'siːvəbl] *adj.* which cannot be imagined.

in•con•clu•sive [ɪnkən'kluːsɪv] *adj.* not final; without a definite result. **in•con•clu•sive•ly**, *adv.* in an inconclusive way.

in•con•gru•ous [ɪn'kɒŋgrʊəs] *adj.* which does not fit with the rest; which seems out of place. **in•con•gru•i•ty**, *n.* being out of place.

in•con•se•quen•tial [ɪnkɒnsɪ'kwenʃl] *adj.* not of any importance.

in•con•sid•er•a•ble [ɪnkən'sɪdərəbl] *adj.* small.

in•con•sid•er•ate [ɪnkən'sɪdərət] *adj.* not thinking of other people. **in•con•sid•er•ate•ly**, *adv.* not thinking about other people.

in•con•sist•ent [ɪnkən'sɪstənt] *adj.* (a) which does not follow/which contradicts. (b) (person) who changes his/her mind frequently. **in•con•sist•en•cy**, *n.* lack of consistency.

in•con•sol•a•ble [ɪnkən'səʊləbl] *adj.* (person) who cannot be comforted.

in•con•spic•u•ous [ɪnkən'spɪkjʊəs] *adj.* not very noticeable. **in•con•spic•u•ous•ly**, *adv.* without being noticed.

in•con•stant [ɪn'kɒnstənt] *adj.* (*formal*) not constant; unfaithful. **in•con•stan•cy**, *n.* lack of constancy.

in•con•test•a•ble [ɪnkən'testəbl] *adj.* which cannot be argued with.

in•con•ti•nent [ɪn'kɒntɪnənt] *adj.* unable to control your bladder or bowels. **in•con•ti•nence**, *n.* being incontinent.

in•con•tro•vert•i•ble [ɪnkɒntrə'vɜːtəbl] *adj.* (fact) with which you must agree; which cannot be disputed.

in•con•ven•ience [ɪnkən'viːnɪəns] 1. *n.* which causes difficulty, awkwardness or bother. 2. *v.* to bother (s.o.). **in•con•ven•ient**, *adj.* awkward; not handy. **in•con•ven•ient•ly**, *adv.* awkwardly.

in•cor•po•rate [ɪn'kɔːpəreɪt] *v.* (a) to bring into one main part. (b) to form an official body. (c) to form a corporation. **in•cor•po•ra•tion** [ɪnkɔːpə'reɪʃn] *n.* act of incorporating.

in•cor•rect [ɪnkə'rekt] *adj.* not correct/false. **in•cor•rect•ly**, *adv.* wrongly/falsely.

in•cor•ri•gi•ble [ɪn'kɒrɪdʒəbl] *adj.* (person) who cannot be corrected/improved.

in•cor•ri•gi•bly, *adv.* in an incorrigible way.

in•cor•rupt•i•ble [ɪnkə'rʌptəbl] *adj.* (person) who cannot be corrupted/be persuaded to behave dishonestly. **in•cor•rupt•i•bil•i•ty** [ɪnkərʌptɪ'bɪlɪtɪ] *n.* being incorruptible.

in•crease 1. *n.* ['ɪnkriːs] growth/expansion; rise (in salary). 2. *v.* [ɪn'kriːs] to rise/to grow/to expand. **in•creas•ing**, *adj.* growing. **in•creas•ing•ly**, *adv.* more and more.

in•cred•i•ble [ɪn'kredɪbl] *adj.* which it is difficult to believe. **in•cred•i•bly**, *adv.* unbelievably.

in•cred•u•lous [ɪn'kredjʊləs] *adj.* (person) who does not believe. **in•cre•du•li•ty** [ɪnkrə'djuːlɪtɪ] *n.* lack of belief. **in•cred•u•lous•ly**, *adv.* as if you do not believe.

in•cre•ment ['ɪnkrəmənt] *n.* regular automatic addition (to salary). **in•cre•men•tal** [ɪnkrɪ'mentl] *adj.* referring to increments.

in•crim•i•nate [ɪn'krɪmɪneɪt] *v.* to show that (s.o.) took part in a crime, etc. **in•crim•i•nat•ing**, *adj.* which shows that s.o. took part in a crime. **in•crim•i•na•to•ry** [ɪn'krɪmɪnətərɪ] *adj.* which incriminates.

in•crust [ɪn'krʌst] *v.* to cover with a hard covering. **in•crus•ta•tion**, *n.* layer (of dirt, etc.) incrusted on a surface.

in•cu•bate ['ɪnkjubeɪt] *v.* to keep (eggs) warm until they hatch; to have (the germs of a disease) in your body. **in•cu•ba•tion** [ɪnkju-'beɪʃn] *n.* keeping eggs warm until they hatch; **i. period** = period during which a disease develops in your body. **in•cu•ba•tor**, *n.* warm box in which eggs are kept until they hatch; sterilized receptacle for keeping very small babies in until they are strong.

in•cu•bus ['ɪnkjubəs] *n.* nightmare; problem which causes great worry.

in•cul•cate ['ɪnkʌlkeɪt] *v.* (*formal*) to fix (ideas, etc.) in the mind of a person.

in•cum•bent [ɪn'kʌmbənt] 1. *n.* person who holds an office, position, etc. at the present time. 2. *adj.* (*formal*) **it is i. on you** = it is your responsibility. **in•cum•ben•cy**, *n.* period when s.o. holds an office, position, etc.

in•cur [ɪn'kɜː] *v.* (**incurred**) to run (a risk); to be liable to; to bring (sth) on yourself.

in•cur•a•ble [ɪn'kjʊərəbl] *adj.* which cannot be made better. **in•cur•a•bly**, *adv.* in a way which cannot be made better.

in•cu•ri•ous [ɪn'kjʊərɪəs] *adj.* not curious/not showing any curiosity.

in•cur•sion [ɪn'kɜːʃn] *n.* movement into sth; attack on sth.

in•debt•ed [ɪn'detɪd] *adj.* owing sth **to** s.o. **in•debt•ed•ness**, *n.* being indebted.

in•de•cent [ɪn'diːsnt] *adj.* not decent/rude/offensive. **in•de•cen•cy**, *n.* being indecent. **in•de•cent•ly**, *adv.* not decently; in a way which shocks.

in•de•ci•pher•a•ble [ɪndɪ'saɪfrəbl] *adj.* (writing/message) that cannot be read/understood.

in•de•ci•sion [ɪndɪ'sɪʒn] *n.* (state of) not being able to decide; hesitating. **in•de•ci•sive** [ɪndɪ'saɪsɪv] *adj.* without a positive result; which/who cannot decide anything.

in•dec•o•rous [ɪn'dekərəs] *adj.* (*formal*) slightly improper.

in•deed [ɪn'diːd] *adv.* (a) really/truly. (b) in fact. (c) *inter. meaning* really! **i. not!** = of course not!

in•de•fat•i•ga•ble [ɪndɪ'fætɪgəbl] *adj.* tireless/who cannot be tired out. **in•de•fat•i•ga•bly**, *adv.* tirelessly.

in•de•fen•si•ble [ɪndɪ'fensɪbl] *adj.* which cannot be defended/excused.

in•de•fin•a•ble [ɪndɪ'faɪnəbl] *adj.* which cannot be defined/explained.

in•def•i•nite [ɪn'defɪnɪt] *adj.* vague; not definite; **i. article** = "a"/"an" (*as opposed to the definite article* "the"). **in•def•i•nite•ly**, *adv.* for an indefinite period.

in•del•i•ble [ɪn'delɪbl] *adj.* which cannot be rubbed out. **in•del•i•bly**, *adv.* permanently (marked).

in•del•i•cate [ɪn'delɪkət] *adj.* rude/not polite. **in•del•i•ca•cy**, *n.* being indelicate.

in•dem•ni•fy [ɪn'demnɪfaɪ] *v.* to pay (s.o.) for damage. **in•dem•ni•ty**, *n.* (a) payment (for loss/damage). (b) guarantee (of payment) against loss/damage.

in•dent [ɪn'dent] *v.* to start a line several spaces in from the left-hand margin. **in•den•ta•tion** [ɪnden'teɪʃn] *n.* inward cut along an edge. **in•dent•ed**, *adj.* with a jagged edge.

in•den•ture [ɪn'dentʃə] *n.* contract by which a person is apprenticed to a master craftsman.

in•de•pend•ent [ɪndɪ'pendənt] *adj.* free/not ruled by anyone else; not needing/not relying on anyone else; (candidate) not belonging to a political party. **in•de•pend•ence**, *n.* freedom; not needing/not relying on anyone else. **in•de•pend•ent•ly**, *adv.* freely; separately.

in•de•scrib•a•ble [ɪndɪ'skraɪbəbl] *adj.* which cannot be described. **in•de•scrib•a•bly**, *adv.* in a way which cannot be described.

in•de•struct•i•ble [ɪndɪ'strʌktəbl] *adj.* which cannot be destroyed.

in•de•ter•mi•na•ble [ɪndɪ'tɜːmɪnəbl] *adj.* which cannot be decided/solved.

in•de•ter•mi•nate [ɪndɪ'tɜːmɪnət] *adj.* vague/not precise.

in•dex ['ɪndeks] 1. *n.* (*pl.* **-dexes, -dices** [-dɪsiːz]) (a) **i. (finger)** = first finger (next to the thumb). (b) classified list (showing the contents/references in a book). (c) **cost of living i.** = regular government statistics which show the rises and falls in the cost of living. 2. *v.* (a) to write an index for (a book). (b) to relate (wages, taxes, pensions, etc.) to the cost of living index. **in•dex•er,** *n.* person who compiles indexes. **in•dex•ing,** *n.* (a) (*also* **indexation**) relating sth to the cost of living index. (b) compiling of an index.

In•di•an ['ɪndjən] 1. *adj.* referring to India; referring to the indigenous people of North and South America; **in I. file** = in line/one behind the other; **I. summer** = period of hot weather in autumn. 2. *n.* (a) person from India. (b) member of one of the indigenous tribes of North and South America.

in•di•a rub•ber [ɪndjə'rʌbə] *n.* rubber eraser for rubbing out pencil marks.

in•di•cate ['ɪndɪkeɪt] *v.* to show/to point out. **in•di•ca•tion** [ɪndɪ'keɪʃn] *n.* sign/pointer. **in•dic•a•tive** [ɪn'dɪkətɪv] *adj.* (a) typical/which indicates. (b) (tense of a verb) which shows that the action actually took place/is taking place. **in•di•ca•tor,** *n.* (a) thing which indicates.

in•dict [ɪn'daɪt] *v.* to accuse (s.o.) of a crime. **in•dict•a•ble,** *adj.* (offense) which you can be charged with. **in•dict•ment** [ɪn'daɪtmənt] *n.* detailed accusation.

in•dif•fer•ent [ɪn'dɪfrənt] *adj.* (a) not caring; not interested. (b) ordinary/mediocre; not special. **in•dif•fer•ence,** *n.* lack of interest. **in•dif•fer•ent•ly,** *adv.* (a) not bothering. (b) in a mediocre way.

in•dig•e•nous [ɪn'dɪdʒənəs] *adj.* (to) which is born in/belongs to (a place).

in•di•gent ['ɪndɪdʒənt] *adj.* (*formal*) very poor. **in•di•gence,** *n.* great poverty.

in•di•ges•tion [ɪndɪ'dʒestʃn] *n.* not being able to digest food; pain caused when the body is unable to digest food. **in•di•gest•i•ble,** *adj.* which cannot be digested; which causes pain because the body cannot digest it.

in•dig•nant [ɪn'dɪgnənt] *adj.* feeling offended/angry. **in•dig•nant•ly,** *adv.* in an indignant way. **in•dig•na•tion** [ɪndɪg-'neɪʃn] *n.* being indignant.

in•dig•ni•ty [ɪn'dɪgnɪti] *n.* injury to s.o.'s dignity.

in•di•go ['ɪndɪgəʊ] *n.* blue dye; deep blue color.

in•di•rect [ɪndɪ'rekt, ɪndaɪ'rekt] *adj.* (a) not direct/oblique; (tax) added to the price of goods before they are sold and not paid directly to the government. (b) (discourse) reporting what s.o. has said but not in his exact words. **in•di•rect•ly,** *adv.* not directly.

in•dis•creet [ɪndɪ'skriːt] *adj.* revealing/not discreet. **in•dis•cre•tion** [ɪndɪ'skreʃn] *n.* (a) lack of discretion/being careless about what you do or say. (b) doing sth careless.

in•dis•crim•i•nate [ɪndɪ'skrɪmənət] *adj.* widespread/not selective. **in•dis•crim•i•nate•ly,** *adv.* (a) in every direction. (b) without selecting/without choosing.

in•dis•pen•sa•ble [ɪndɪ'spensəbl] *adj.* which you cannot do without.

in•dis•posed [ɪndɪ'spəʊzd] *adj.* (a) slightly ill. (b) unwilling. **in•dis•po•si•tion** [ɪndɪspə-'zɪʃn] *n.* (a) slight illness. (b) unwillingness.

in•dis•put•a•ble [ɪndɪ'spjuːtəbl] *adj.* which cannot be argued over. **in•dis•put•a•bly,** *adv.* certainly.

in•dis•sol•u•ble [ɪndɪ'sɒljʊbl] *adj.* which cannot be destroyed/dissolved.

in•dis•tinct [ɪndɪ'stɪŋkt] *adj.* vague/unclear. **in•dis•tinct•ly,** *adv.* vaguely/unclearly.

in•dis•tin•guish•a•ble [ɪndɪ'stɪŋgwɪʃəbl] *adj.* which cannot be told apart from sth.

in•di•vid•u•al [ɪndɪ'vɪdjuəl] 1. *n.* (a) single person. (b) *inf.* person. 2. *adj.* (a) single. (b) belonging to a particular person. (c) for one person. **in•di•vid•u•al•ist,** *n.* person who emphasizes that he is unique and not a member of a group. **in•di•vid•u•al•is•tic,** *adj.* like an individualist. **in•di•vid•u•al•i•ty** [ɪndɪvɪdju'ælɪti] *n.* quality which makes each person different from all others. **in•di•vid•u•al•ly,** *adv.* singly/as a single person.

in•di•vis•i•ble [ɪndɪ'vɪzəbl] *adj.* which cannot be divided/separated. **in•di•vis•i•bly,** *adv.* in a way which prevents it being divided/separated.

in•doc•tri•nate [ɪn'dɒktrɪneɪt] *v.* to teach (s.o.), esp. political ideas.

æ back, ɑː farm, ɒ top, aɪ pipe, aʊ how, aɪə fire, aʊə flower, ɔː bought, ɔɪ toy, e fed, eəhair, eɪ take, ə afraid, əʊ boat, əʊə lower, vː word, iː heap, ɪ hit, ɪə hear, uː school, ʊ book, ʌ but, b back, d dog, ð then, dʒ just, f fog, g go, h hand, j yes, k catch, l last, m mix, n nut, ŋ sing, p penny, r round, s some, ʃ short, t too, tʃ chop, θ thing, v voice, w was, z zoo, ʒ treasure

in•doc•tri•na•tion [ɪndɒktrɪ'neɪʃn] *n.* teaching s.o., esp. political ideas.

in•do•lence ['ɪndələns] *n.* laziness. **in•do•lent,** *adj.* lazy.

in•dom•i•ta•ble [ɪn'dɒmɪtəbl] *adj.* which cannot be overcome.

in•door ['ɪndɔː] *adj.* done/found inside a building. **in•doors** [ɪn'dɔːz] *adv.* inside a building.

in•du•bi•ta•ble [ɪn'djuːbɪtəbl] *adj.* which cannot be doubted. **in•du•bi•ta•bly,** *adv.* certainly/definitely.

in•duce [ɪn'djuːs] *v.* (a) to persuade (s.o.) to do sth. (b) to provoke (sth)/to make (sth) happen; to make (a birth) happen. **in•duce•ment,** *n.* thing which helps persuade you to do sth.

in•duct [ɪn'dʌkt] *v.* to place (s.o.) in an office, position, etc. **in•duc•tion** [ɪn'dʌkʃn] *n.* (a) formal entry of a person into a new job, office, position, etc. (b) creation of electricity in an object by placing it near a magnet or near sth which is electrically charged. **in•duc•tive,** *adj.* (reasoning) based on known facts.

in•dulge [ɪn'dʌldʒ] *v.* (a) to spoil (s.o.). (b) (**in**) to give way to (sth enjoyable). **in•dul•gence,** *n.* being indulgent; indulgent action. **in•dul•gent,** *adj.* kind/soft; too generous. **in•dul•gent•ly,** *adv.* kindly; too generously.

in•dus•try ['ɪndəstrɪ] *n.* (a) all manufacturing processes. (b) hard work/steady work. **in•dus•tri•al** [ɪn'dʌstrɪəl] *adj.* referring to manufacturing work. **in•dus•tri•al•ist,** *n.* owner/director of a factory. **in•dus•tri•al•i•za•tion** [ɪndʌstrɪəlaɪ'zeɪʃn] *n.* changing of a society from agricultural to industrial. **in•dus•tri•al•ize** [ɪn'dʌstrɪəlaɪz] *v.* to create industries (where there were none before). **in•dus•tri•al•ly,** *adv.* (made) by industry. **in•dus•tri•ous,** *adj.* (person) who works steadily and hard. **in•dus•tri•ous•ly,** *adv.* in an industrious way.

in•e•bri•ate [ɪ'niːbrɪət] *adj.* (*formal*) (person) who is often drunk. **in•e•bri•at•ed,** *adj.* drunk. **in•e•bri•a•tion,** *n.* drunken state.

in•ed•i•ble [ɪn'edɪbl] *adj.* which you cannot eat.

in•ed•u•ca•ble [ɪn'edjukəbl] *adj.* (person) who cannot be educated.

in•ef•fa•ble [ɪn'efəbl] *adj.* (*formal*) so wonderful that it cannot be properly described.

in•ef•fec•tive [ɪnɪ'fektɪv] *adj.* which does not have any effect.

in•ef•fec•tu•al [ɪnɪ'fektjuəl] *adj.* (attempt) which is unsuccessful; (person) who is weak/incapable of asserting his authority.

in•ef•fi•cient [ɪnɪ'fɪʃnt] *adj.* not efficient; not competent. **in•ef•fi•cien•cy,** *n.* incompe-tence/lack of efficiency. **in•ef•fi•cient•ly,** *adv.* in an inefficient way.

in•el•e•gant [ɪn'elɪgənt] *adj.* not elegant.

in•el•i•gi•ble [ɪn'elɪdʒəbl] *adj.* (person) who is not qualified (**for** sth, **to** do sth).

in•ept [ɪn'ept] *adj.* stupid (remark); incapable (person). **in•ept•i•tude,** *n.* stupidity/silliness; being unable to do sth.

in•e•qual•i•ty [ɪnɪ'kwɒlɪtɪ] *n.* lack of equality.

in•eq•ui•ta•ble [ɪn'ekwɪtəbl] *adj.* unjust/not fair.

in•e•rad•i•ca•ble [ɪnɪ'rædɪkəbl] *adj.* which cannot be eradicated/removed.

in•ert [ɪ'nɜːt] *adj.* unmoving; (gas) which does not react with other substances. **in•er•tia** [ɪ-'nɜːʃə] *n.* (a) lack of motion in a body. (b) continuous movement of a body, unless checked by a force. (c) laziness.

in•es•cap•a•ble [ɪnɪ'skeɪpəbl] *adj.* which you cannot avoid.

in•es•sen•tial [ɪnɪ'senʃl] *adj. & n.* (thing) which is not absolutely necessary.

in•es•ti•ma•ble [ɪn'estɪməbl] *adj.* which cannot be estimated/calculated.

in•ev•i•ta•ble [ɪn'evɪtəbl] *adj.* which cannot be avoided. **in•ev•i•ta•bil•i•ty** [ɪnevɪtə-'bɪlɪtɪ] *n.* being inevitable. **in•ev•i•ta•bly,** *adv.* of course; with certainty.

in•ex•act [ɪnɪg'zækt] *adj.* not exact/not correct. **in•ex•act•i•tude,** *n.* error.

in•ex•cus•a•ble [ɪnɪk'skjuːzəbl] *adj.* which cannot be excused/forgiven. **in•ex•cus•a•bly,** *adv.* in an inexcusable way.

in•ex•haust•i•ble [ɪnɪg'zɔːstəbl] *adj.* which cannot be used up.

in•ex•o•ra•ble [ɪn'eksərəbl] *adj.* which cannot be changed/influenced.

in•ex•pe•di•ent [ɪnɪk'spiːdɪənt] *adj.* (action) which is not expedient.

in•ex•pen•sive [ɪnɪk'spensɪv] *adj.* cheap/not expensive.

in•ex•pe•ri•ence [ɪnɪk'spɪərɪəns] *n.* lack of experience. **in•ex•pe•ri•enced,** *adj.* with no experience/lacking experience.

in•ex•pert [ɪn'ekspɜːt] *adj.* (**at**) not expert/not skilled.

in•ex•pli•ca•ble [ɪnɪk'splɪkəbl] *adj.* which cannot be explained. **in•ex•pli•ca•bly,** *adv.* in a way which cannot be explained.

in•ex•press•i•ble [ɪnɪk'spresɪbl] *adj.* which cannot be expressed in words.

in ex•tre•mis [ɪneks'triːmɪs] *adv.* at the very end; (*of person*) when near to death.

in•ex•tri•ca•ble [ɪneks'trɪkəbl] *adj.* which you cannot get out of. **in•ex•tri•ca•bly,** *adv.* in an inextricable way.

in•fal•li•ble [ɪnˈfæləbl] adj. always correct/true; (person) who never makes mistakes. in•fal•li•bil•i•ty [ɪnfælɪˈbɪlɪtɪ] n. being infallible. in•fal•li•bly, adv. unfailingly/always.

in•fa•mous [ˈɪnfəməs] adj. very wicked (person/action). in•fa•my, n. (formal) great wickedness.

in•fant [ˈɪnfənt] n. young child. in•fan•cy, n. young childhood. in•fan•ti•cide [ɪnˈfæntɪsaɪd] n. killing of a baby. in•fan•tile [ˈɪnfəntaɪl] adj. referring to a small child; childish.

in•fan•try [ˈɪnfəntrɪ] n. section of an army which fights on foot.

in•fat•u•at•ed [ɪnˈfætjʊeɪtɪd] adj. mad (about); wildly in love (with). in•fat•u•a•tion [ɪnfætjuˈeɪʃn] n. blind love for someone.

in•fect [ɪnˈfekt] v. to make diseased. in•fec•tion, n. (a) making diseased. (b) disease which spreads. in•fec•tious, adj. (disease) which can be passed from one person to another.

in•fer [ɪnˈfɜː] v. (inferred) (a) to deduce (from). (b) to imply/to hint. in•fer•ence [ˈɪnfərəns] n. conclusion/deduction.

in•fe•ri•or [ɪnˈfɪərɪə] 1. adj. not as good. 2. n. person of a lower rank/subordinate. in•fe•ri•or•i•ty [ɪnfɪərɪˈɒrɪtɪ] n. state of being not as good as s.o. else; i. complex = exaggerated idea that one is not as good as others.

in•fer•nal [ɪnˈfɜːnl] adj. inf. like hell/hellish. in•fer•nal•ly, adv. inf. extremely.

in•fer•no [ɪnˈfɜːnəʊ] n. (-os) blaze of fire.

in•fer•tile [ɪnˈfɜːtl] adj. not fertile/not capable of having young; (land) which is not rich enough to produce crops. in•fer•til•i•ty [ɪnfəˈtɪlɪtɪ] n. being unable to bear young.

in•fest [ɪnˈfest] v. to cover/to swarm over in large numbers. in•fes•ta•tion [ɪnfesˈteɪʃn] n. being covered with pests.

in•fi•del [ˈɪnfɪdəl] n. person who is opposed to a religion, esp. Christianity.

in•fi•del•i•ty [ɪnfɪˈdelɪtɪ] n. being unfaithful.

in•fight•ing [ˈɪnfaɪtɪŋ] n. bitter argument between members of a group.

in•fil•trate [ˈɪnfɪltreɪt] v. to enter (a political or other group) secretly. in•fil•tra•tion [ɪnfɪlˈtreɪʃn] n. act of infiltrating. in•fil•tra•tor [ˈɪnfɪltreɪtə] n. person who infiltrates.

in•fi•nite [ˈɪnfɪnət] adj. endless/with no end. in•fi•nite•ly, adv. completely; much more. in•fin•i•tes•i•mal [ɪnfɪnɪˈtesɪml] adj. tiny/microscopic. in•fin•i•tive [ɪnˈfɪnɪtɪv] adj. & n. form of the verb using "to". in•fin•i•ty, n. never-ending space.

in•firm [ɪnˈfɜːm] adj. sick/weak (person). in•fir•ma•ry, n. (a) hospital. (b) place in a factory or school for the care of the sick or injured. in•fir•mi•ty, n. physical weakness.

in•flame [ɪnˈfleɪm] v. (a) (formal) to make violent. (b) to cause inflammation in. in•flam•ma•ble [ɪnˈflæməbl] adj. which catches fire easily. in•flam•ma•tion [ɪnfləˈmeɪʃn] n. swelling/redness caused by infection. in•flam•ma•to•ry [ɪnˈflæmətərɪ] adj. (speech) which makes people behave violently.

in•flate [ɪnˈfleɪt] v. to blow up (balloon/tire); to increase (prices, etc.) artificially. in•flat•a•ble, adj. which can be blown up. in•fla•tion [ɪnˈfleɪʃn] n. economic state where prices and wages are rising to keep pace with each other. in•fla•tion•ar•y, adj. (policy) which tends to increase inflation.

in•flect [ɪnˈflekt] v. to change the ending of (a word, e.g. when used in the plural). in•flec•tion, Brit. in•flex•ion, n. ending of a word which changes to indicate the plural, the gender, etc.

in•flex•i•ble [ɪnˈfleksəbl] adj. which cannot be bent/altered; (person) who cannot be persuaded to change his mind. in•flex•i•bil•i•ty [ɪnfleksɪˈbɪlɪtɪ] n. not being able to bend/to adapt. in•flex•i•bly, adv. in an unbending way.

in•flict [ɪnˈflɪkt] v. to i. pain/damage on = to cause pain/damage to; to i. oneself on s.o. = force s.o. to accept one's presence. in•flic•tion [ɪnˈflɪkʃn] n. (act of) inflicting.

in•flo•res•cence [ɪnfloˈresəns] n. group of flowers arranged on one stem.

in•flow [ˈɪnfləʊ] n. flowing in.

in•flu•ence [ˈɪnflʊəns] 1. n. (on) ability to make s.o./sth change; effect on others. 2. v. to make (s.o./sth) change. in•flu•en•tial [ɪnflʊˈenʃl] adj. so powerful as to cause change; having an effect on others.

in•flu•en•za [ɪnflʊˈenzə] n. virus disease like a bad cold with a high temperature.

in•flux [ˈɪnflʌks] n. (pl. -es) entry (of a crowd or group of people).

æ back, ɑː farm, ɒ top, aɪ pipe, aʊ how, aɪə fire, aʊə flower, ɔː bought, ɔɪ toy, e fed, eəhair, eɪ take, ə afraid, əʊ boat, əʊə lower, vː word, iː heap, ɪ hit, ɪə hear, uː school, ʊ book, ʌ but, b back, d dog, ð then, dʒ just, f fog, g go, h hand, j yes, k catch, l last, m mix, n nut, ŋ sing, p penny, r round, s some, ʃ short, t too, tʃ chop, θ thing, v voice, w was, z zoo, ʒ treasure

in•fo•mer•cial [ɪnfə'mɜːʃəl] *n.* an extended TV advertisement in an informative style.

in•form [ɪn'fɔːm] *v.* to tell officially; to give details; **to i. against s.o.** = to tell (the police, etc.) about s.o. **in•form•ant**, *n.* person who passes on information/who gives details. **in•for•mat•ics**, *n.* study of information processing. **in•for•ma•tion** [ɪnfə'meɪʃn] *n.* details/knowledge; **i. superhighway** = high-speed global computer network (the Internet); **i. technology** = technology of the communication and storage of information by computers. **in•for•ma•tive** [ɪn'fɔːmətɪv] *adj.* which tells you a lot/which conveys much detailed information. **in•formed**, *adj.* up-to-date/reliable. **in•form•er**, *n.* person who informs against his accomplices.

in•for•mal [ɪn'fɔːml] *adj.* not formal/relaxed; not following any rules; not official. **in•for•mal•ly**, *adv.* not formally/unofficially. **in•for•mal•i•ty** [ɪnfɔː'mælɪtɪ] *n.* lack of any special ceremony.

in•fo•tain•ment [ɪnfə'teɪnmənt] *n.* TV program presenting information, esp. news, in an entertaining style.

in•fra dig ['ɪnfrə'dɪg] *adv. inf.* beneath one's dignity.

in•fra-red [ɪnfrə'red] *adj.* (heat rays) which are invisible and have a longer wave-length than visible red heat rays.

in•fra•struc•ture ['ɪnfrəstrʌktʃə] *n.* basic structure; supporting framework.

in•fre•quent [ɪn'friːkwənt] *adj.* not frequent; not happening very often. **in•fre•quen•cy**, *n.* lack of frequency. **in•fre•quent•ly**, *adv.* not very often/not frequently.

in•fringe [ɪn'frɪndʒ] *v.* to break (a law). **in•fringe•ment**, *n.* breaking (**of** a law).

in•fu•ri•ate [ɪn'fjuərɪeɪt] *v.* to make furious.

in•fuse [ɪn'fjuːz] *v.* to pour hot water (on tea leaves, etc.) to make a drink. **in•fu•sion** [ɪn'fjuːʒn] *n.* drink made by pouring hot water on dried leaves, etc.

in•gen•ious [ɪn'dʒiːnɪəs] *adj.* very clever (device/person). **in•ge•nu•i•ty** [ɪndʒə'njuːɪtɪ] *n.* cleverness/skill in inventing new techniques.

in•gé•nue [ænʒeɪnjuː] *n.* supposedly simple girl.

in•gen•u•ous [ɪn'dʒenjuəs] *adj.* naive/ innocent; lacking experience. **in•gen•u•ous•ness**, *n.* being ingenuous.

in•gest [ɪn'dʒest] *v.* (*formal*) to take into the body (as food).

in•gle•nook ['ɪŋgəlnʊk] *n.* seat at the side of a very large fireplace.

in•glo•ri•ous [ɪn'glɔːrɪəs] *adj.* (*formal*) dishonorable/not glorious.

in•got ['ɪŋgət] *n.* bar (of gold, etc.).

in•grained ['ɪŋgreɪnd] *adj.* fixed.

in•gra•ti•ate [ɪn'greɪʃɪeɪt] *v.* **to i. oneself with s.o.** = make oneself liked by s.o. **in•gra•ti•at•ing**, *adj.* which will help you worm your way into s.o.'s favor.

in•grat•i•tude [ɪn'grætɪtjuːd] *n.* lack of gratitude; not being grateful.

in•gre•di•ent [ɪn'griːdɪənt] *n.* substance which is a component of sth.

in•gress ['ɪngres] *n.* (*formal*) entry.

in•grow•ing ['ɪngrəʊɪŋ] *adj.* (toenail) which grows into the flesh.

in•hab•it [ɪn'hæbɪt] *v.* to live in. **in•hab•it•a•ble**, *adj.* (place) which can be lived in. **in•hab•it•ant**, *n.* person who lives in a place.

in•hale [ɪn'heɪl] *v.* to draw (sth) into the lungs when breathing. **in•hal•ant, inhalation**, *n.* medicine which has to be inhaled. **in•hal•er**, *n.* device which makes a vapor which has to be inhaled.

in•her•ent [ɪn'hɪərənt] *adj.* natural/inborn. **in•her•ent•ly**, *adv.* naturally.

in•her•it [ɪn'herɪt] *v.* (a) to take over (money, etc.) from a person who has died; to have (characteristics) passed on from a parent. (b) to take over (a client/a problem) from a predecessor. **in•her•it•ance**, *n.* money/goods which you receive on the death of s.o. **in•her•i•tor**, *n.* person who inherits.

in•hib•it [ɪn'hɪbɪt] *v.* to restrain (s.o.) **from** doing sth. **in•hi•bi•tion** [ɪnhɪ'bɪʃn] *n.* thing which prevents you from expressing yourself freely/from letting yourself go. **in•hib•i•to•ry**, *adj.* which inhibits.

in•hos•pi•ta•ble [ɪnhɒ'spɪtəbl] *adj.* not welcoming.

in-house [ɪn'haʊs] *adj. & adv.* inside an office or factory.

in•hu•man [ɪn'hjuːmən] *adj.* not human; savage/brutal. **in•hu•mane** [ɪnhjuː'meɪn] *adj.* not humane; showing great cruelty. **in•hu•man•i•ty** [ɪnhjuː'mænɪtɪ] *n.* great cruelty. **in•hu•man•ly**, *adv.* savagely/brutally.

in•im•i•cal [ɪ'nɪmɪkl] *adj.* (*formal*) unfriendly.

in•im•i•ta•ble [ɪ'nɪmɪtəbl] *adj.* which cannot be imitated.

in•iq•ui•tous [ɪ'nɪkwɪtəs] *adj.* (*formal*) wicked. **in•iq•ui•ty**, *n.* wickedness.

in•i•tial [ɪ'nɪʃl] 1. *adj.* first. 2. *n.* **initials** = first letters (of name). 3. *v.* (**initialed, initialled**) to write your initials on (a document) to show you have read and approved it. **in•i•tial•ly**, *adv.* in the first place/at the beginning.

in•i•ti•ate [ɪ'nɪʃɪeɪt] *v.* (a) to start (sth). (b) to introduce (s.o.) **into** a secret society; to show (s.o.) the basic information about sth.

in•i•ti•a•tion [ɪnɪʃɪˈeɪʃn] *n.* introduction to a secret society. **in•i•ti•a•tive** [ɪˈnɪʃɪətɪv] *n.* decision to start sth; ability to decide. **in•i•ti•a•tor,** *n.* person who starts (a project).

in•ject [ɪnˈdʒekt] *v.* to pump a liquid into (sth/s.o.) under pressure; to put (sth new) into. **in•jec•tion,** *n.* act of injecting; liquid which has been injected.

in•ju•di•cious [ɪndʒuːˈdɪʃəs] *adj.* (*formal*) unwise.

in•junc•tion [ɪnˈdʒʌŋkʃn] *n.* (a) order (by a court) preventing s.o. from doing sth. (b) instruction; command.

in•jure [ˈɪndʒə] *v.* to hurt/to wound; **the injured party** = the party in a court case who has been offended. **the injured,** *n. pl.* people who have been wounded. **in•ju•ri•ous** [ɪnˈdʒuːərɪəs] *adj.* which can injure. **in•ju•ry,** *n.* hurt/wound.

in•jus•tice [ɪnˈdʒʌstɪs] *n.* lack of justice; not being fair.

ink [ɪŋk] 1. *n.* liquid for writing with a pen. 2. *v.* to write with a pen and ink; to mark with ink. **ink pad,** *n.* pad of cloth soaked in ink for inking date stamps, etc. **ink•well,** *n.* container to put ink in. **ink•y,** *adj.* (black) like ink; covered with ink.

ink•ling [ˈɪŋklɪŋ] *n.* suspicion/idea.

in•laid [ɪnˈleɪd] *v. see* **in•lay.**

in•land [ˈɪnlænd] *adj. & adv.* (to/of) the interior of a country.

in-laws [ˈɪnlɔːz] *n. pl. inf.* parents related to you by marriage.

in•lay [ɪnˈleɪ] 1. *n.* thing which is inlaid. 2. *v.* (**inlaid**) to insert small pieces of stone/wood/metal in (a surface) to create a pattern.

in•let [ˈɪnlet] *n.* small channel of water between islands or extending from a large body of water.

in-line skate [ɪnlaɪn ˈskeɪt] *n.* type of roller-skate in which all four wheels are set in a straight line.

in•mate [ˈɪnmeɪt] *n.* resident (of a house); person living in a hospital/prison, etc.

in•most [ˈɪnməʊst] *adj.* deepest (thoughts, etc.).

inn [ɪn] *n.* small hotel. **inn•keep•er,** *n.* person who runs an inn.

in•nards [ˈɪnədz] *n. pl. inf.* intestines; inside workings (of a machine).

in•nate [ɪˈneɪt] *adj.* inborn/natural.

in•ner [ˈɪnə] *adj.* inside; **i. room** = room leading off another room; **i. tube** = light tube containing air inside a tire; **i. ear** = space inside the head, beyond the middle ear, which controls balance and hearing. **in•ner•most,** *adj.* furthest inside.

in•ning [ˈɪnɪŋz] *n.* (*in baseball*) time when a team has a chance to score, until three batters are put out.

in•no•cent [ˈɪnəsnt] *adj.* not guilty; lacking experience/knowledge. **in•no•cence,** *n.* lack of guilt. **in•no•cent•ly,** *adv.* in a way which shows lack of experience/knowledge.

in•noc•u•ous [ɪˈnɒkjuəs] *adj.* inoffensive/harmless.

in•no•vate [ˈɪnəveɪt] *v.* to introduce changes/new methods. **in•no•va•tion** [ɪnəˈveɪʃn] *n.* invention which is new; change (in doing sth). **in•no•va•tive** [ˈɪnəveɪtɪv] *adj.* which breaks new ground/which changes everything. **in•no•va•tor,** *n.* person who introduces changes.

in•nu•en•do [ɪnjuˈendəʊ] *n.* (*pl.* **-oes**) remark which suggests criticism.

in•nu•mer•a•ble [ɪˈnjuːmərəbl] *adj.* countless/which cannot be counted.

in•oc•u•late [ɪˈnɒkjuleɪt] *v.* **to i. s.o. against** = to prevent s.o. catching a disease by injecting him/her with a vaccine. **in•oc•u•la•tion** [ɪnɒkjuˈleɪʃn] *n.* injection to stop you catching a disease.

in•of•fen•sive [ɪnəˈfensɪv] *adj.* mild/harmless.

in•op•er•a•ble [ɪnˈɒprəbl] *adj.* which cannot be operated on.

in•op•er•a•tive [ɪnˈɒprətɪv] *adj.* which is not in operation/which is not working.

in•op•por•tune [ɪnˈɒpətjuːn] *adj.* awkward/badly timed.

in•or•di•nate [ɪnˈɔːdɪnət] *adj.* excessive. **in•or•di•nate•ly,** *adv.* excessively.

in•or•gan•ic [ɔːˈgænɪk] *adj.* not relating to living organisms; **i. chemistry** = chemistry dealing with substances which are not organic.

in-pa•tient [ˈɪnˈpeɪʃnt] *n.* patient who stays in a hospital.

in•put [ˈɪnpʊt] *n.* (a) electric current put into an apparatus. (b) data/information fed into a computer.

in•quest [ˈɪŋkwest] *n.* legal inquiry into a death.

in•quire [ɪŋˈkwaɪə] *v.* (a) to ask questions (**about** sth). (b) to conduct an official investigation (**into**). **in•quir•er,** *n.* person who inquires. **in•quir•ing,** *adj.* interested in finding out information. **in•quir•ing•ly,** *adv.* in a questioning way. **in•quir•y,** *n.* (a) formal investigation (**into**). (b) question.

in•qui•si•tion [ɪŋkwɪˈzɪʃn] *n.* (a) asking very thorough questions, usu. using threats or force. (b) (*old*) Catholic tribunal for discovering heretics. **in•quis•i•tor** [ɪŋˈkwɪzɪtə] *n.* person who asks very thorough questions. **in•quis•i•tive** [ɪŋˈkwɪzətɪv] *adj.* curious/asking questions. **in•quis•i•tive•ly,** *adv.* curiously/inquiringly. **in•quis•i•tive•ness,** *n.* being inquisitive.

in•roads [ˈɪnrəudz] *n. pl.* **to make i. into sth** = to use up a large quantity of sth.

in•rush [ˈɪnrʌʃ] *n.* sudden quick pouring in of sth.

in•sa•lu•bri•ous [ɪnsəˈluːbrɪəs] *adj.* not healthy.

in•sane [ɪnˈseɪn] *adj.* mad. **in•sane•ly,** *adv.* madly. **in•san•i•ty** [ɪnˈsænɪti] *n.* madness.

in•san•i•tar•y [ɪnˈsænɪtəri] *adj.* not clean/not hygienic.

in•sa•tia•ble [ɪnˈseɪʃəbl] *adj.* which cannot be satisfied. **in•sa•tia•bly,** *adv.* in a way which cannot be satisfied.

in•scribe [ɪnˈskraɪb] *v.* to write (officially) (in a book/on a stone). **in•scrip•tion** [ɪnˈskrɪpʃn] *n.* writing inscribed on a stone, etc.

in•scru•ta•ble [ɪnˈskruːtəbl] *adj.* mysterious/which you cannot understand.

in•sect [ˈɪnsekt] *n.* small six-legged animal with a body in three parts. **in•sec•ti•cide** [ɪnˈsektɪsaɪd] *n.* liquid/powder which kills insects. **in•sec•tiv•o•rous** [ɪnsekˈtɪvərəs] *adj.* (animal) which eats insects.

in•se•cure [ɪnsɪˈkjuə] *adj.* not safe; wobbly/not firmly fixed. **in•se•cure•ly,** *adv.* not firmly. **in•se•cu•ri•ty,** *n.* feeling of not being safe.

in•sem•i•nate [ɪnˈsemɪneɪt] *v.* to introduce male seed into (a female). **in•sem•i•na•tion** [ɪnsemɪˈneɪʃn] *n.* **artificial i.** = introduction of sperm from a male into a female by a doctor or veterinarian.

in•sen•sate [ɪnˈsenseɪt] *adj.* without any feeling.

in•sen•si•ble [ɪnˈsensəbl] *adj.* (a) not conscious. (b) with no feeling. (c) very small (change); imperceptible.

in•sen•si•tive [ɪnˈsensɪtɪv] *adj.* not sensitive. **in•sen•si•tiv•i•ty** [ɪnsensɪˈtɪvɪti] *n.* lack of sensitivity/lack of awareness of how other people feel.

in•sep•a•ra•ble [ɪnˈseprəbl] *adj.* which cannot be separated; (of people) always together.

in•sert. 1. *n.* [ˈɪnsɜːt] thing which is put in. **2.** *v.*

[ɪnˈsɜːt] to put (sth) in. **in•ser•tion** [ɪnˈsɜːʃn] *n.* act of putting sth in; thing which is put in.

in•set [ˈɪnset] *n.* small piece which is put into sth larger.

in•shore [ɪnˈʃɔː] *adj. & adv.* near or toward a coast.

in•side [ɪnˈsaɪd] **1.** *n.* inner part; **i. out** = with the inner part facing outward; **to know i. out** = to know very well. **2.** *adj.* (a) indoors; which is in the interior. (b) (information) known only to people working in a certain organization. **3.** *adv.* (a) to/in the interior. (b) *inf.* in prison. **4.** *prep.* (a) to/in the interior of (sth). (b) within; **i. three hours** = in less than three hours. **in•sid•er,** *n.* person who works in an organization and therefore knows secret information; **i. trading** = illegal buying or selling of shares by people who have secret information about a company.

in•sid•i•ous [ɪnˈsɪdɪəs] *adj.* quietly treacherous; working secretly to do harm. **in•sid•i•ous•ly,** *adv.* quietly and dangerously. **in•sid•i•ous•ness,** *n.* being insidious.

in•sight [ˈɪnsaɪt] *n.* (a) clear thought. (b) deep knowledge; clear understanding.

in•sig•ni•a [ɪnˈsɪgnɪə] *n.* badge or other symbol of office or honor.

in•sig•nif•i•cant [ɪnsɪgˈnɪfɪkənt] *adj.* unimportant. **in•sig•nif•i•cance,** *n.* being insignificant.

in•sin•cere [ɪnsɪnˈsɪə] *adj.* not sincere/false. **in•sin•cer•i•ty** [ɪnsɪnˈserɪti] *n.* lack of sincerity.

in•sin•u•ate [ɪnˈsɪnjueɪt] *v.* (a) to suggest (by dropping hints); **to i. oneself** = work one's way gradually (**into** a favorable position). **in•sin•u•a•tion** [ɪnsɪnjuˈeɪʃn] *n.* (usu. cruel) hint/suggestion.

in•sip•id [ɪnˈsɪpɪd] *adj.* watery/not strong; with no flavor/no excitement. **in•sip•id•i•ty** [ɪnsɪˈpɪdɪti] *n.* being insipid.

in•sist [ɪnˈsɪst] *v.* **to i. on sth being done** = to state firmly that sth should be done. **in•sist•ence,** *n.* firm demands. **in•sist•ent,** *adj.* demanding firmly. **in•sist•ent•ly,** *adv.* in a way which demands attention.

in si•tu [ɪnˈsiːtjuː] *adv.* on the site; in its original place.

in•sole [ˈɪnsəul] *n.* soft pad which you put inside a shoe to make it more comfortable or fit better.

in•so•lent [ˈɪnsələnt] *adj.* rude. **in•so•lence,** *n.* rudeness. **in•so•lent•ly,** *adv.* rudely.

in•sol•u•ble [ɪnˈsɒljubl] *adj.* (a) (substance) which will not dissolve, usu. in water. (b) (problem) which cannot be solved.

in•sol•u•bil•i•ty [ɪnsɒljuˈbɪlɪtɪ] *n.* inability (of a chemical) to dissolve.

in•sol•vent [ɪnˈsɒlvənt] *adj.* bankrupt/unable to pay one's debts. **in•sol•ven•cy,** *n.* being insolvent.

in•som•ni•a [ɪnˈsɒmnɪə] *n.* chronic inability to sleep. **in•som•ni•ac,** *n.* person who suffers from insomnia.

in•sou•ci•ant [ɪnˈsuːsjənt] *adj.* not caring about anything. **in•sou•ci•ance,** *n.* being insouciant.

in•spect [ɪnˈspekt] *v.* to examine closely. **in•spec•tion** [ɪnˈspekʃn] *n.* examining sth closely. **in•spec•tor,** *n.* (a) person, esp. an official, who inspects. (b) officer in the police force, usu. ranking next below a superintendent. **in•spec•tor•ate,** *n.* all inspectors taken as a group.

in•spire [ɪnˈspaɪə] *v.* to make (s.o.) feel a certain sensation. **in•spi•ra•tion** [ɪnspɪˈreɪʃn] *n.* (a) sudden urge to write poems/to compose music, etc. (b) sudden good idea.

in•sta•bil•i•ty [ɪnstəˈbɪlɪtɪ] *n.* lack of stability/not being steady.

in•stall [ɪnˈstɔːl] *v.* to put (a person into a job/a machine into position for operation). **in•stal•la•tion** [ɪnstəˈleɪʃn] *n.* (a) putting (a machine in position for operation). (b) group of machines which have been put in position for operation.

in•stall•ment [ɪnˈstɔːlmənt] *n.* part (of sth which is being delivered in parts); regular payment (of part of a total sum owed); **i. plan** = system where you buy sth by paying in installments.

in•stance [ˈɪnstəns] 1. *n.* example/case; **for i.** = as an example. 2. *v.* to give as an example.

in•stant [ˈɪnstənt] 1. *n.* moment/second. 2. *adj.* immediate; **i. coffee** = coffee powder to which you add hot water to make coffee rapidly. **in•stan•ta•ne•ous** [ɪnstənˈteɪnɪəs] *adj.* immediate. **in•stan•ta•ne•ous•ly,** *adv.* immediately. **in•stant•ly,** *adv.* straight away/immediately.

in•stead [ɪnˈsted] *adv.* in the place of/rather than (sth).

in•step [ˈɪnstep] *n.* arched part of a foot.

in•sti•gate [ˈɪnstɪɡeɪt] *v.* to provoke/to start (sth). **in•sti•ga•tion** [ɪnstɪˈɡeɪʃn] *n.* suggestion. **in•sti•ga•tor,** *n.* person who stirs up trouble/who provokes action.

in•still, instil [ɪnˈstɪl] *v.* to put (an idea, etc.) into s.o.'s mind gradually.

in•stinct [ˈɪnstɪŋkt] *n.* feeling/ability for doing sth which you have from birth and have not learned. **in•stinc•tive** [ɪnˈstɪŋktɪv] *adj.* natural/inborn (reaction). **in•stinc•tive•ly,** *adv.* because of a natural impulse.

in•sti•tute [ˈɪnstɪtjuːt] 1. *n.* (a) organization set up for a purpose. (b) building which houses such an organization. 2. *v.* to set up/to start. **in•sti•tu•tion** [ɪnstɪˈtjuːʃn] *n.* (a) setting up (of an organization). (b) organization/society set up for a purpose. (c) permanent feature; longstanding custom. **in•sti•tu•tion•al,** *adj.* referring to an institution. **in•sti•tu•tion•al•ize,** *v.* to make (sth) into an institution; to put (s.o.) into an institution (such as an old people's home, etc.).

in•struct [ɪnˈstrʌkt] *v.* (a) to teach. (b) to give information or orders to. **in•struc•tion** [ɪnˈstrʌkʃn] *n.* (a) teaching. (b) **instructions** = orders; indication of how sth is to be used. **in•struc•tive,** *adj.* which teaches. **in•struc•tor, instructress,** *n.* teacher.

in•stru•ment [ˈɪnstrumənt] *n.* (a) piece of equipment. (b) formal legal document, as a contract. (c) **musical i.** = device which is blown/hit/plucked, etc., to make a musical note. **in•stru•men•tal** [ɪnstruˈmentl] *adj.* (a) responsible/playing an important role (**in** getting sth done). (b) referring to a musical instrument. **in•stru•men•tal•ist,** *n.* person who plays a musical instrument.

in•sub•or•di•nate [ɪnsəˈbɔːdɪnət] *adj.* unruly; not obeying orders. **in•sub•or•di•na•tion** [ɪnsəbɔːdɪˈneɪʃn] *n.* not obeying orders.

in•sub•stan•tial [ɪnsəbˈstænʃl] *adj.* not substantial/not solid.

in•suf•fer•a•ble [ɪnˈsʌfrəbl] *adj.* intolerable/which you cannot bear. **in•suf•fer•a•bly,** *adv.* intolerably.

in•suf•fi•cient [ɪnsəˈfɪʃnt] *adj.* not sufficient/not enough. **in•suf•fi•cien•cy,** *n.* lack. **in•suf•fi•cient•ly,** *adv.* not enough.

in•su•lar [ˈɪnsjulə] *adj.* (a) referring to an island. (b) narrow-minded. **in•su•lar•i•ty** [ɪnsjuˈlærɪtɪ] *n.* prejudice/narrowness of opinions.

in•su•late [ˈɪnsjuleɪt] *v.* to cover so as to prevent heat/electricity/sound escaping or entering. **in•su•la•tion** [ɪnsjuˈleɪʃn] *n.* act of insulating; material which insulates.

in•su•la•tor ['ɪnsjuleɪtə] *n.* material/device which insulates.

in•su•lin ['ɪnsjulɪn] *n.* hormone which regulates the use of sugar by the body, and is used to treat diabetes.

in•sult. 1. *n.* ['ɪnsʌlt] rude word said to or about a person. 2. *v.* [ɪn'sʌlt] to say rude things about (s.o.). **in•sult•ing,** *adj.* rude.

in•su•per•a•ble [ɪn'sju:prəbl] *adj.* which cannot be overcome.

in•sup•port•a•ble [ɪnsə'pɔ:təbl] *adj.* unbearable/which cannot be borne.

in•sure [ɪn'ʃʊə] *v.* to agree with a company that if you pay them a regular sum, they will compensate you for loss or damage to property or persons; **to i. a diamond ring for $5000. in•sur•ance,** *n.* agreement with a company by which you are paid compensation for loss or damage in return for regular payments of money; **i. policy** = document with the details of an insurance; **i. broker/agent** = person who arranges an insurance; **life i.** = insurance paying a sum of money when s.o. dies. **in•sur•er,** *n.* person/company which insures.

in•sur•gent [ɪn'sɜ:dʒənt] *adj. & n.* (person) in a state of revolt.

in•sur•mount•a•ble [ɪnsə'maʊntəbl] *adj.* which cannot be overcome.

in•sur•rec•tion [ɪnsə'rekʃn] *n.* uprising/revolution.

in•tact [ɪn'tækt] *adj.* in one piece/not broken.

in•tagl•io [ɪn'tɑ:lɪəʊ] *n.* design cut into a surface (as of a precious stone).

in•take ['ɪnteɪk] *n.* thing which is taken in.

in•tan•gi•ble [ɪn'tændʒəbl] *adj.* which cannot be touched/which cannot be defined.

in•te•gral ['ɪntɪgrəl] *adj.* forming (part of) a whole. **in•te•ger** ['ɪntɪdʒə] *n.* whole number (not a fraction). **in•te•grate** ['ɪntɪgreɪt] *v.* to link to form a whole; to make (people) full members of society by giving them equal opportunities, treatment, etc.; **integrated circuit** = electronic circuit on a microchip. **in•te•gra•tion** [ɪntɪ'greɪʃn] *n.* (act of) integrating.

in•teg•ri•ty [ɪn'tegrɪtɪ] *n.* honesty.

in•teg•u•ment [ɪn'tegʊmənt] *n.* (*formal*) skin.

in•tel•lect ['ɪntəlekt] *n.* ability to think or reason; brainpower. **in•tel•lec•tu•al** [ɪntə'lektjʊəl] 1. *adj.* referring to the intellect; good at using the brain. 2. *n.* person who believes that brainpower is very important/who uses his brain to make a living. **in•tel•lec•tu•al•ly,** *adv.* referring to intelligence.

in•tel•li•gence [ɪn'telɪdʒəns] *n.* (a) quickness of understanding/mental ability; **i. quotient** = number showing how intelligent you are compared to others. (b) secret information.

in•tel•li•gent, *adj.* clever/mentally able. **in•tel•li•gent•ly,** *adv.* in an intelligent way. **in•tel•li•gent•si•a** [ɪntelɪ'dʒensɪə] *n.* intellectual class of society.

in•tel•li•gi•ble [ɪn'telɪdʒəbl] *adj.* which can be understood. **in•tel•li•gi•bil•i•ty** [ɪntelɪgə'bɪlɪtɪ] *n.* being intelligible.

in•tem•per•ate [ɪn'temprət] *adj.* wild/not moderate.

in•tend [ɪn'tend] *v.* to plan to do (sth)/to mean.

in•tense [ɪn'tens] *adj.* (**-er, -est**) very strong/vigorous (action); extremely serious (person). **in•tense•ly,** *adv.* strongly. **in•ten•si•fi•ca•tion,** *n.* becoming stronger. **in•ten•si•fy,** *v.* to grow stronger/to make (sth) stronger. **in•ten•si•ty,** *n.* strength/violence (of sth). **in•ten•sive,** *adj.* very concentrated; **i. care unit** = section of a hospital dealing with seriously ill patients who need a lot of attention. **in•ten•sive•ly,** *adv.* very strongly.

in•tent [ɪn'tent] 1. *adj.* determined/absorbed. 2. *n.* **with i. to defraud** = with the aim of deceiving; **to/for all intents and purposes** = virtually/in nearly every way. **in•tent•ly,** *adv.* fixedly.

in•ten•tion [ɪn'tenʃn] *n.* aim. **in•ten•tion•al,** *adj.* done on purpose. **in•ten•tion•al•ly,** *adv.* on purpose.

in•ter [ɪn'tɜ:] *v.* (**interred**) (*formal*) to bury.

inter- ['ɪntə-] *prefix meaning* between.

in•ter•act [ɪntə'rækt] *v.* to have an effect on each other. **in•ter•ac•tion** [ɪntər'ækʃn] *n.* effect of two things on each other. **in•ter•ac•tive,** *adj.* (computer program) which allows the user to communicate with the computer.

in•ter a•li•a [ɪntə'ɑ:lɪə] among other things.

in•ter•breed [ɪntə'bri:d] *v.* (**interbred**) to breed (with an adult of another strain).

in•ter•cede [ɪntə'si:d] *v.* to plead; to make an appeal. **in•ter•ces•sion** [ɪntə'seʃn] *n.* pleading (on behalf of s.o.).

in•ter•cept [ɪntə'sept] *v.* to stop (sth) as it is passing. **in•ter•cep•tion** [ɪntə'sepʃn] *n.* stopping (of sth which is passing). **in•ter•cep•tor,** *n.* person/aircraft which intercepts.

in•ter•change ['ɪntətʃeɪndʒ] 1. *n.* (a) exchange (of ideas). (b) large road intersection where highways cross. 2. *v.* to exchange one thing for another. **in•ter•change•a•ble** [ɪntə'tʃeɪndʒəbl] *adj.* which can be substituted for each other.

in•ter•cit•y [ɪntə'sɪtɪ] *adj.* (train/plane) between two cities.

in•ter•com ['ɪntəkɒm] *n.* radio for speaking

to people over a short distance (as within a house).

in•ter•con•nect•ed [ɪntəkəˈnektɪd] *adj.* which connect with each other.

in•ter•con•ti•nen•tal [ɪntəkontɪˈnentl] *adj.* from one continent to another.

in•ter•course [ˈɪntəkɔːs] *n.* (a) reproductive act between a male and a female. (b) (*formal*) communication between people.

in•ter•dict [ˈɪntədɪkt] *n.* (*formal*) order forbidding sth.

in•ter•est [ˈɪntrəst] 1. *n.* (a) percentage return on investment; percentage payable on a loan. (b) financial share. (c) particular attention. (d) thing which you pay attention to. (e) advantage. 2. *v.* to attract s.o.'s attention. **in•ter•est•ed**, *adj.* with a personal (usu. financial) interest in sth. **in•ter•est•ing**, *adj.* which attracts attention.

in•ter•face [ˈɪntəfeɪs] *n.* area where two different systems meet and interact.

in•ter•fere [ɪntəˈfɪə] *v.* (a) to meddle/to get involved (**in/with**). (b) to affect the reception of radio/TV programs. **in•ter•fer•ence**, *n.* (a) involvement/meddling. (b) noise which affects radio/TV programs. **in•ter•fer•on**, *n.* protein which fights a virus.

in•ter•im [ˈɪntərɪm] *adj. & n.* (report) given halfway through an investigation; **in the i.** = meanwhile.

in•te•ri•or [ɪnˈtɪərɪə] *adj. & n.* inner part (of a building/car).

in•ter•ject [ɪntəˈdʒekt] *v.* to make a sudden exclamation. **in•ter•jec•tion** [ɪntəˈdʒekʃn] *n.* exclamation; word used to show surprise.

in•ter•lace [ɪntəˈleɪs] *v.* to weave together.

in•ter•lard [ɪntəˈlɑːd] *v.* to insert comments into (a text).

in•ter•leave [ɪntəˈliːv] *v.* to put (sth) between the pages of a book.

in•ter•lock [ɪntəˈlɒk] *v.* to fit together.

in•ter•loc•u•tor [ɪntəˈlɒkjutə] *n.* person who speaks to s.o. else.

in•ter•lop•er [ˈɪntələupə] *n.* person who comes in/who intrudes.

in•ter•lude [ˈɪntəluːd] *n.* quiet time between two lively periods; rest period between parts of a performance.

in•ter•mar•ry [ɪntəˈmærɪ] *v.* to marry within the same family group. **in•ter•mar•riage**, *n.* act of intermarrying.

in•ter•me•di•ar•y [ɪntəˈmiːdjərɪ] *adj. & n.*

(person) who goes between two others/who acts as messenger.

in•ter•me•di•ate [ɪntəˈmiːdjət] *adj.* halfway between two extremes.

in•ter•ment [ɪnˈtɜːmənt] *n.* (*formal*) burial.

in•ter•mez•zo [ɪntəˈmetzəu] *n.* (*pl.* -os) short piece (of music) linking two other pieces.

in•ter•mi•na•ble [ɪnˈtɜːmɪnəbl] *adj.* never-ending. **in•ter•mi•na•bly**, *adv.* without coming to an end.

in•ter•min•gle [ɪntəˈmɪŋgl] *v.* to mix together.

in•ter•mis•sion [ɪntəˈmɪʃn] *n.* (a) interval (in a play/motion picture/concert). (b) **without i.** = without a break/without stopping.

in•ter•mit•tent [ɪntəˈmɪtənt] *adj.* which takes place from time to time. **in•ter•mit•tent•ly**, *adv.* (taking place) from time to time/on and off.

in•tern. 1. *n.* [ˈɪntɜːn] recently graduated doctor who works in a hospital under supervision. 2. *v.* [ɪnˈtɜːn] to put (prisoners) in a prison without trial, esp. during a war. **in•tern•ee** [ɪntɜːˈniː] *n.* prisoner who has been interned. **in•tern•ment**, *n.* putting prisoners in a prison or camp without trial.

in•ter•nal [ɪnˈtɜːnl] *adj.* inside; **i. combustion engine** = engine in which the fuel is burned inside a closed space (as in the cylinders in a car engine). **in•ter•nal•ly**, *adv.* inside.

in•ter•na•tion•al [ɪntəˈnæʃnl] *adj.* between countries. **in•ter•na•tion•al•ly**, *adv.* (done) between countries.

in•ter•ne•cine [ɪntəˈniːsaɪn] *adj.* (*formal*) (two things) which destroy each other.

In•ter•net [ˈɪntənet] *n.* informally organized global computer network that links individual computers and computer networks and thereby transfers at high speed information, usu. located on World Wide Web sites, and services, e.g. electronic mail.

in•ter•node [ˈɪntənəud] *n.* space between two joints in a plant. **in•ter•nod•al** *adj.* between joints.

in•ter•phone [ˈɪntəfəun] *n.* telephone used to communicate between rooms or parts of a building or ship.

in•ter•plan•e•tar•y [ɪntəˈplænətrɪ] *adj.* between planets.

in•ter•play [ˈɪntəpleɪ] *n.* reaction between two forces.

In•ter•pol [ˈɪntəpɒl] *n.* international police system.

æ back, aː farm, ɒ top, aɪ pipe, aʊ how, aɪə fire, aʊə flower, ɔː bought, ɔɪ toy, e fed, eəhair, eɪ take, ə afraid, əʊ boat, əʊə lower, vː word, iː heap, ɪ hit, ɪə hear, uː school, ʊ book, ʌ but, b back, d dog, ð then, dʒ just, f fog, g go, h hand, j yes, k catch, l last, m mix, n nut, ŋ sing, p penny, r round, s some, ʃ short, t too, tʃ chop, θ thing, v voice, w was, z zoo, ʒ treasure

in•ter•po•late [ɪn'tɜːpəleɪt] v. to add (words) in between others. in•ter•po•la•tion [ɪntɜːpə'leɪʃn] n. adding of words between existing words in a text; word(s) thus added.

in•ter•pose ['ɪntəpəʊz] v. to place (sth) in between.

in•ter•pret [ɪn'tɜːprɪt] v. (a) to explain (sth) to s.o. who does not understand. (b) to translate aloud what is spoken from one language into another. in•ter•pre•ta•tion [ɪntɜːprɪ'teɪʃn] n. (a) meaning. (b) translating aloud from one language to another. in•ter•pret•er, n. person who translates aloud from one language to another.

in•ter•reg•num [ɪntə'regnəm] n. period between the reigns of successive kings; period of inactivity between one management and another.

in•ter•re•lat•ed [ɪntərɪ'leɪtɪd] adj. (several things) which are related.

in•ter•ro•gate [ɪn'terəgeɪt] v. to question severely. in•ter•ro•ga•tion [ɪntərə'geɪʃn] n. severe questioning (of a prisoner). in•ter•rog•a•tive [ɪntə'rɒgətɪv] adj. & n. questioning; i. pronoun = pronoun which asks a question; i. sentence = sentence which asks a question. in•ter•ro•ga•tor [ɪn'terəgeɪtə] n. person who questions (a prisoner) closely.

in•ter•rupt [ɪntə'rʌpt] v. to break into (a speech); to stop (sth) continuing. in•ter•rup•tion [ɪntə'rʌpʃn] n. (act of) interrupting; thing which interrupts.

in•ter•sect [ɪntə'sekt] v. to cut across; to cut across (each other). in•ter•sec•tion, n. place where lines, roads, etc. cut across each other.

in•ter•sperse [ɪntə'spɜːs] v. to scatter.

in•ter•state [ɪntə'steɪt] adj. between two states.

in•ter•stel•lar [ɪntə'stelə] adj. between stars.

in•ter•stice [ɪn'tɜːstɪs] n. small space in between other things.

in•ter•twine [ɪntə'twaɪn] v. to twist (things) together; to be twisted together.

in•ter•val ['ɪntəvl] n. period/gap (between two points/between two acts in a play); (in music) difference in pitch.

in•ter•vene [ɪntə'viːn] v. to come/to arrive in between. in•ter•ven•tion [ɪntə'venʃn] n. coming between; entry into sth.

in•ter•view ['ɪntəvjuː] 1. n. (a) discussion (on radio/TV/in the newspaper) between an important or interesting person and a journalist. (b) questioning (by one or more people) of a person applying for a job. 2. v. (a) to ask (a famous/interesting person) questions in order to publish or air the answers publicly. (b) to ask questions of (a person applying for a job). in•ter•view•ee [ɪntəvjuː'iː] n. person who is being/who is going to be interviewed. in•ter•view•er, n. person who asks the questions at an interview.

in•ter•weave [ɪntə'wiːv] v. (interwove; interwoven) to weave/to bind together.

in•tes•tate [ɪn'testeɪt] adj. not having made a will.

in•tes•tine [ɪn'testɪn] n. long tube in the body through which food passes from the stomach to the anus. in•tes•ti•nal, adj. referring to the intestine.

in•ti•mate. 1. adj. ['ɪntɪmət] (a) very close (friend); detailed (knowledge). (b) sexual (relationship). 2. n. ['ɪntɪmət] close friend. 3. v. ['ɪntɪmeɪt] to announce; to suggest. in•ti•ma•cy, n. close relationship (with s.o.). in•ti•mate•ly, adv. closely. in•ti•ma•tion [ɪntɪ'meɪʃn] n. suggestion.

in•tim•i•date [ɪn'tɪmɪdeɪt] v. to frighten (s.o.) by threats. in•tim•i•dat•ing, adj. frightening. in•tim•i•da•tion [ɪntɪmɪ'deɪʃn] n. frightening by threats.

in•to ['ɪntu] prep. (a) (movement) toward the inside. (b) so as to become; to develop as; the tadpole changed i. a frog; he burst i. tears. (c) dividing; four i. three won't go.

in•tol•er•a•ble [ɪn'tɒlərəbl] adj. which you cannot bear. in•tol•er•a•bly, adv. unbearably.

in•tol•er•ant [ɪn'tɒlərənt] adj. (person) who cannot bear people with different ideas from his own. in•tol•er•ance, n. not accepting other people's points of view.

in•to•na•tion [ɪntə'neɪʃn] n. rise or fall of the voice (in speech or singing).

in•tone [ɪn'təʊn] v. to recite (psalms, etc.) in a singing voice.

in•tox•i•cate [ɪn'tɒksɪkeɪt] v. to make (s.o.) drunk. in•tox•i•cant, n. substance which intoxicates. in•tox•i•cat•ing, adj. which makes you drunk; exciting. in•tox•i•ca•tion [ɪntɒksɪ'keɪʃn] n. drunkenness.

intra- ['ɪntrə-] prefix meaning within.

in•trac•ta•ble [ɪn'træktəbl] adj. very difficult to deal with; (problem) which is impossible to solve.

in•tran•si•gent [ɪn'trænsɪdʒənt] adj. firm; obstinate/not shifting your position/not changing your mind. in•tran•si•gence, n. firmness/being obstinate.

in transit [ɪn'trænzɪt] adv. (goods) which are being transported.

in•tran•si•tive [ɪn'trænsɪtɪv] adj. (verb) which has no object.

in•tra•u•ter•ine [ɪntrə'juːtəriːn] adj. inside the uterus; i. device = contraceptive device which is placed inside a woman's uterus.

in•tra•ve•nous [ɪntrə'viːnəs] adj. (injection) made into a vein.

in•trep•id [ɪn'trepɪd] adj. fearless/very brave. in•tre•pid•i•ty [ɪntrə'pɪdɪtɪ] n. being intrepid.

in•tri•cate ['ɪntrɪkət] adj. very complicated; made of many different parts. in•tri•ca•cy, n. complexity. in•tri•cate•ly, adv. in an intricate way.

in•trigue [ɪn'triːg] 1. n. secret plot. 2. v. (a) to plot. (b) to make (s.o.) interested.

in•trin•sic [ɪn'trɪnzɪk] adj. forming a basic part of sth. in•trin•si•cal•ly, adv. basically.

in•tro•duce [ɪntrə'djuːs] v. (a) to present (s.o.) to another person/to people who did not know him/her previously. (b) to announce (a TV/radio program, etc.). (c) to make (sth) go in; to bring (sth) in. in•tro•duc•tion [ɪntrə'dʌkʃn] n. (a) act of presenting sth; thing which presents sth. (b) making s.o. known to another person/to people who did not know him/her previously. (c) piece at the beginning of a book which explains the rest of the book. (d) elementary book about a subject; an i. to art history. in•tro•duc•to•ry, adj. (words) which introduce; i. offer = offer of a new product at a special low price.

in•troit ['ɪntrɔɪt] n. music sung at the beginning of a church service.

in•tro•spec•tive [ɪntrə'spektɪv] adj. inward-looking; thinking a lot about yourself. in•tro•spec•tion [ɪntrə'spekʃn] n. looking inward at yourself.

in•tro•vert ['ɪntrəvɜːt] n. person who thinks mainly about himself/herself. in•tro•vert•ed, adj. (person) who thinks mainly about himself/herself.

in•trude [ɪn'truːd] v. to enter where you are not wanted. in•trud•er, n. person who has intruded; in•tru•sion [ɪn'truːʒn] n. act of intruding. in•tru•sive [ɪn'truːsɪv] adj. unwanted.

in•tu•i•tion [ɪntjuː'ɪʃn] n. thinking of sth/knowing sth naturally without it being explained. in•tu•i•tive [ɪn'tjuɪtɪv] adj. based on intuition. in•tu•i•tive•ly, adv. in an intuitive way.

In•u•it ['ɪnjuːɪt] n. Eskimos.

in•un•date ['ɪnʌndeɪt] v. to flood. in•un•da•tion [ɪnʌn'deɪʃn] n. flood.

in•ure [ɪn'jʊə] v. (formal) to accustom to sth unpleasant.

in•vade [ɪn'veɪd] v. to attack and enter (a country) with an army. in•vad•er, n. person who enters a country with an army.

in•val•id 1. adj. & n. ['ɪnvəlɪd] sick/disabled (person); i. chair = small vehicle for one disabled person. 2. adj. [ɪn'vælɪd] not valid/not legal. in•val•i•da•tion [ɪnvælɪ'deɪʃn] n. making invalid. in•val•i•date [ɪn'vælɪdeɪt] v. to make (sth) invalid; to nullify. in•va•lid•i•ty, n. being an invalid; lack of validity.

in•val•u•a•ble [ɪn'væljuəbl] adj. extremely valuable.

in•var•i•a•ble [ɪn'veərɪəbl] adj. always the same/not changing. in•var•i•a•bly, adv. always.

in•va•sion [ɪn'veɪʒn] n. (a) entering a country with armed forces. (b) i. of privacy = illegal entering of a person's home in a way which intrudes on his private life.

in•vec•tive [ɪn'vektɪv] n. insulting speech/abuse.

in•veigh [ɪn'veɪ] v. (formal) to speak violently (against sth).

in•vei•gle [ɪn'veɪgl] v. to trick (s.o.) into doing sth.

in•vent [ɪn'vent] v. to create (a new process/new machine); to think up (an excuse). in•ven•tion [ɪn'venʃn] n. (a) creation (of new process/new machine). (b) new machine. in•ven•tive, adj. creative. in•ven•tive•ness, n. ability to invent. in•ven•tor, n. person who invents new processes/new machines.

in•ven•to•ry ['ɪnvəntrɪ] n. list (of contents of a house, etc.); stock (in a store/business/warehouse).

in•verse ['ɪnvɜːs] adj. & n. opposite/contrary. in•ver•sion [ɪn'vɜːʃn] n. turning sth around in a contrary way. in•vert [ɪn'vɜːt] v. to turn (sth) upside down/back to front.

in•ver•te•brate [ɪn'vɜːtɪbreɪt] adj. & n. (animal) without a backbone.

in•vest [ɪn'vest] v. to put (money) into savings/property, etc., so that it will increase in value. in•vest•ment, n. money placed so that it will increase in value. in•ves•tor, n. person who puts money into savings or property.

in•ves•ti•gate [ɪn'vestɪgeɪt] v. to study/to examine. in•ves•ti•ga•tion [ɪn'vestɪ'geɪʃn] n. examination. in•ves•ti•ga•tor, n. detective; person who investigates.

in•ves•ti•ture [ɪn'vestɪtʃə] n. ceremony where

æ back, aː farm, ɒ top, aɪ pipe, aʊ how, aie fire, aʊə flower, ɔː bought, ɔɪ toy, e fed, eəhair, eɪ take, ə afraid, əʊ boat, əʊə lower, vː word, iː heap, ɪ hit, ɪə hear, uː school, ʊ book, ʌ but, b back, d dog, ð then, dʒ just, f fog, g go, h hand, j yes, k catch, l last, m mix, n nut, ŋ sing, p penny, r round, s some, ʃ short, t too, tʃ chop, θ thing, v voice, w was, z zoo, ʒ treasure

s.o. is given a medal/where s.o. is installed in office.

in•vet•er•ate [ɪn'vetərət] *adj.* obstinate/hardened; firmly established (as by habit); **i. liar.**

in•vid•i•ous [ɪn'vɪdɪəs] *adj.* which is likely to offend people unreasonably.

in•vig•or•ate [ɪn'vɪgəreɪt] *v.* to make strong/vigorous; to make (s.o.) feel livelier.

in•vin•ci•ble [ɪn'vɪnsəbl] *adj.* which cannot be defeated. **in•vin•ci•bil•i•ty** [ɪnvɪnsə-'bɪlɪtɪ] *n.* being unbeatable.

in•vi•o•la•ble [ɪn'vaɪələbl] *adj.* which cannot be violated. **in•vi•o•la•bil•i•ty** [ɪnvaɪələ-'bɪlɪtɪ] *n.* being inviolable.

in•vis•i•ble [ɪn'vɪzəbl] *adj.* which cannot be seen. **in•vis•i•bil•i•ty** [ɪnvɪzə'bɪlɪtɪ] *n.* not being able to be seen.

in•vite [ɪn'vaɪt] *v.* (a) to ask (s.o.) to do sth. (b) to ask for (comments, etc.). **in•vi•ta•tion** [ɪnvɪ'teɪʃn] *n.* asking (s.o. to do sth). **in•vit•ing,** *adj.* attractive.

in vi•tro [ɪn'viːtrəu] *adj.* (experiment) which is carried out in a laboratory.

in•vo•ca•tion [ɪnvə'keɪʃn] *n.* (*formal*) calling on s.o. for help/support.

in•voice ['ɪnvɔɪs] 1. *n.* note sent to ask for payment for services or goods. 2. *v.* to send a note asking for payment for services or goods. **in•voic•ing,** *n.* sending of an invoice.

in•voke [ɪn'vəuk] *v.* to call on (s.o./sth) for help/support.

in•vol•un•tar•y [ɪn'vɒləntrɪ] *adj.* not voluntary/not willingly done. **in•vol•un•tar•i•ly,** *adv.* not willingly.

in•volve [ɪn'vɒlv] *v.* (a) to bring (s.o./sth) into (a dispute/a scheme). (b) to make necessary. **in•volved,** *adj.* intricate/complicated. **in•volve•ment,** *n.* contact/collaboration.

in•vul•ner•a•ble [ɪn'vʌlnərəbl] *adj.* which cannot be successfully attacked.

in•ward ['ɪnwəd] *adj.* on/to the inside. **in•ward•ly,** *adv.* on the inside. **in•ward, inwards,** *adv.* toward the inside.

i•o•dine ['aɪədiːn] *n.* (*element:* I) substance which is used in solution, e.g. as a disinfectant. **i•o•dize,** *v.* to fill with iodine.

i•on ['aɪən] *n.* atom with an electric charge. **i•on•ize,** *v.* to produce ions; to become ions. **i•on•o•sphere** [aɪ'ɒnəsfɪə] *n.* part of the atmosphere surrounding the earth which reflects radio waves back to earth.

i•o•ta [aɪ'əutə] *n.* very small piece.

IOU [aɪəu'juː] *n.* paper promising that you will pay back money which you have borrowed.

ip•e•cac [ɪpɪkæk juː'ɑːnə] *n.* drug made from the root of a plant, used as an emetic and also as cough medicine.

ip•so fac•to ['ɪpsəu'fæktəu] *adv.* because of this fact.

IQ ['aɪ'kjuː] *abbrev. for* intelligence quotient.

IRA ['aɪɑː'eɪ] *abbrev. for* Irish Republican Army; Individual Retirement Account.

I•ra•ni•an [ɪ'reɪnjən] 1. *adj.* referring to Iran. 2. *n.* person from Iran.

I•ra•qi [ɪ'rɑːkɪ] 1. *adj.* referring to Iraq. 2. *n.* (*pl.* -is) person from Iraq.

i•ras•ci•ble [ɪ'ræsɪbl] *adj.* easily becoming angry. **i•ras•ci•bil•i•ty** [ɪræsɪ'bɪlɪtɪ] *n.* being irascible.

ire ['aɪə] *n.* (*formal*) anger. **i•rate** [aɪ'reɪt] *adj.* very angry.

ir•i•des•cent [ɪrɪ'desnt] *adj.* with changing/shimmering colors. **ir•i•des•cence,** *n.* being iridescent.

i•ris ['aɪərɪs] *n.* (*pl.* -es) (a) plant with tall flat leaves and usu. yellow or purple flowers. (b) part of the eye which is colored.

I•rish ['aɪərɪʃ] 1. *adj.* referring to Ireland. 2. *n.* (a) Celtic language spoken in parts of Ireland. (b) **the I.** = people from Ireland. **I•rish•man, Irishwoman,** *n.* (*pl.* -men, -women) person from Ireland.

irk [ɜːk] *v.* to annoy/to bother. **irk•some** ['ɜːksəm] *adj.* annoying/bothersome.

i•ron ['aɪən] 1. *n. & adj.* (*element:* Fe) (a) common gray metal which can be made into a magnet; **i. ore** = iron in its natural state. (b) electric household instrument for smoothing the creases from clothes. (c) **in irons** = imprisoned with iron chains around one's ankles. (d) golf club with a metal head. 2. *v.* to press (cloth) with an iron; **to i. out** = to sort out (a problem/difficulty). **I•ron Age,** *n.* period when human beings first used iron. **I•ron Cur•tain,** *n.* imaginary border formerly existing between Communist countries in Eastern Europe and non-communist Western Europe. **i•ron•ing,** *n.* (a) pressing clothes with an electric iron. (b) clothes which need pressing. **i•ron•ing board,** *n.* high narrow table used for ironing clothes. **iron lung,** *n.* machine which encloses a patient's body, and in which pressure is increased and reduced, formerly used to make the patient breathe. **i•ron•work,** *n.* (decorative) locks/handles/gates, etc., made of iron. **i•ron•works,** *n.* factory which produces iron.

i•ro•ny ['aɪərənɪ] *n.* (a) way of referring to sth where you say the opposite of what you mean. (b) quality of happening at the wrong moment, as if deliberately planned. **i•ron•ic(al)** [aɪ'rɒnɪk(l)] *adj.* mocking/slightly funny. **i•ron•i•cal•ly,** *adv.* in a mocking way.

ir•ra•di•ate [ɪ'reɪdɪeɪt] *v.* (*of heat/light/rays*)

to shine on (sth). **ir•ra•di•a•tion** [ɪreɪdɪ-'eɪʃn] *n.* act of irradiating.

ir•ra•tion•al [ɪ'ræʃnl] *adj.* not rational/not sensible/against common-sense. **ir•ra•tion•al•ly**, *adv.* in an irrational way.

ir•rec•on•cil•a•ble [ɪrekən'saɪləbl] *adj.* which cannot be made to agree.

ir•re•cov•er•a•ble [ɪrɪ'kʌvərəbl] *adj.* which cannot be recovered.

ir•re•deem•a•ble [ɪrɪ'diːməbl] *adj.* (loss) which cannot be made good; (pledge) which cannot be redeemed.

ir•re•duc•i•ble [ɪrɪ'djuːsəbl] *adj.* which cannot be reduced.

ir•ref•u•ta•ble [ɪrɪ'fjuːtəbl] *adj.* (argument) which cannot be disproved.

ir•reg•u•lar [ɪ'regjulə] 1. *adj.* (a) not regular; not level; not happening at the same time. (b) not according to the rules; (verb) which has forms which do not fit the usual patterns of grammar. 2. *n. pl.* **irregulars** = soldiers who do not form part of a regular army. **ir•reg•u•lar•i•ty** [ɪregju'lærɪtɪ] *n.* thing which goes against the rules/the law. **ir•reg•u•lar•ly**, *adv.* not regularly.

ir•rel•e•vant [ɪ'reləvənt] *adj.* (to) not relevant/which has no connection to the subject. **ir•rel•e•vance,** *n.* having no connection with the subject.

ir•re•li•gious [ɪrɪ'lɪdʒəs] *adj.* not religious; not showing respect for religion.

ir•rep•a•ra•ble [ɪ'reprəbl] *adj.* which cannot be repaired. **ir•rep•a•ra•bly**, *adv.* in a way which cannot be repaired.

ir•re•place•a•ble [ɪrɪ'pleɪsəbl] *adj.* which cannot be replaced; (thing) for which there is no substitute.

ir•re•press•i•ble [ɪrɪ'presbl] *adj.* which cannot be held back.

ir•re•proach•a•ble [ɪrɪ'prəʊtʃəbl] *adj.* perfect/which cannot be criticized.

ir•re•sist•i•ble [ɪrɪ'zɪstəbl] *adj.* which cannot be resisted; which you cannot help accepting.

ir•res•o•lute [ɪ'rezəluːt] *adj.* undecided; (person) who hesitates/cannot decide. **ir•res•o•lute•ly**, *adv.* not knowing what to do. **ir•res•o•lu•tion**, *n.* being irresolute.

ir•re•spec•tive [ɪrɪ'spektɪv] *prep.* taking no account (**of**).

ir•re•spon•si•ble [ɪrɪ'spɒnsəbl] *adj.* wild/senseless; not responsible. **ir•re•spon•si•bly**, *adv.* with no sense of responsibility.

ir•re•triev•a•ble [ɪrɪ'triːvəbl] *adj.* which cannot be found again. **ir•re•triev•a•bly**, *adv.* hopelessly.

ir•rev•er•ent [ɪ'revrənt] *adj.* not serious; disrespectful. **ir•rev•er•ence**, *n.* being irreverent. **ir•rev•er•ent•ly**, *adv.* not in a serious way; disrespectfully.

ir•re•vers•i•ble [ɪrɪ'vɜːsəbl] *adj.* (decision) which cannot be changed.

ir•rev•o•ca•ble [ɪ'revəkəbl] *adj.* (decision) which cannot be changed.

ir•ri•gate ['ɪrɪgeɪt] *v.* (a) to water (land) by using canals and pumps. (b) to wash (a wound) with a flow of water. **ir•ri•ga•tion** [ɪrɪ'geɪʃn] *n.* watering of fields (by using canals and pumps).

ir•ri•tate ['ɪrɪteɪt] *v.* (a) to annoy. (b) to cause to burn, swell, or hurt. **ir•ri•ta•bil•i•ty** [ɪrɪtə'bɪlɪtɪ] *n.* being irritable. **ir•ri•ta•ble** ['ɪrɪtəbl] *adj.* easily annoyed. **ir•ri•ta•bly**, *adv.* in a bad-tempered way. **ir•ri•tant**, *n.* thing which irritates. **ir•ri•tat•ing**, *adj.* which irritates. **ir•ri•ta•tion** [ɪrɪ'teɪʃn] *n.* annoyance/burning, swollen, or painful condition; thing which causes this.

ir•rupt [ɪ'rʌpt] *v.* (*formal*) to appear/to come in suddenly. **ir•rup•tion** [ɪ'rʌpʃn] *n.* sudden appearance.

is [ɪz] *v. see* **be.**

Is•lam ['ɪzlæm] *n.* religion of the Muslims. **Is•lam•ic** [ɪz'læmɪk] *adj.* referring to Islam.

is•land ['aɪlənd] *n.* piece of land entirely surrounded by water; **traffic i.** = small raised piece of pavement in the center of the road where pedestrians can safely stand. **is•land•er**, *n.* person who lives on an island. **isle** [aɪl] *n.* island. **is•let**, *n.* small island.

isn't ['ɪznt] *v. short for* **is not.**

i•so•bar ['aɪsəʊbɑː] *n.* line on a weather map showing places of equal barometric pressure.

i•so•late ['aɪsəleɪt] *v.* (a) to put (sth/s.o.) in a place alone; **isolated attack** = single attack, not repeated. (b) to separate (a chemical) substance from a compound. **i•so•la•tion** [aɪsə-'leɪʃn] *n.* cutting off from communication with other people; **i. ward** = place in a hospital for people suffering from dangerous diseases. **i•so•la•tion•ism**, *n.* policy of not communicating with other countries. **i•so•la•tion•ist**, *n.* person who advocates isolationism.

i•so•mer ['aɪsəmə] *n.* chemical compound

with the same molecular formula as another, but with a different arrangement of atoms.

i•so•met•ric [aɪsəu'metrɪk] *adj.* (exercises) using muscles acting against each other or a fixed object.

i•sos•ce•les [aɪ'sɒsɪliːz] *adj.* **i. triangle** = triangle with two sides of the same length.

i•so•therm ['aɪsəuθɜːm] *n.* line on a weather map showing places with equal temperatures.

i•so•ton•ic [aɪsəu'tɒnɪk] *adj.* (drink) formulated to replenish fluid and salts lost by the body during exercise.

i•so•tope ['aɪsətəup] *n.* one of two or more forms of a chemical element which have atoms which are chemically similar but with different atomic weights.

Is•rae•li [ɪz'reɪlɪ] 1. *adj.* referring to Israel. 2. *n.* (*pl.* **-is**) person from Israel.

is•sue ['ɪʃuː] 1. *n.* (a) result. (b) problem; **to make an i. of** = have a big discussion about; **the point at i.** = the question which is being discussed; **to take i. with** = disagree with. (c) publication (of a book); putting on sale (new stamps); putting into circulation (new coins/bank notes); giving out (of uniforms/official permits, etc.). (d) one copy of a newspaper or magazine. (e) (*old*) children. 2. *v.* (a) to come out. (b) to put (new stamps) on sale; to publish (books); to put (new bank notes) into circulation; to give out/to hand out (uniforms/official permits, etc.).

isth•mus ['ɪsməs] *n.* (*pl.* **-es**) narrow piece of land connecting two larger pieces of land.

it [ɪt] *pronoun referring to a thing.* (a) (*standing in the place of thing just mentioned*) **put it down;**

it's here. (b) (*referring to nothing in particular*) **it's raining;** *inf.* **you're for it** = you are going to be in trouble.

IT ['aɪtiː] *abbrev. for* information technology.

I•tal•ian [ɪ'tæljən] 1. *adj.* referring to Italy. 2. *n.* (a) person from Italy. (b) language spoken in Italy.

i•tal•ic [ɪ'tælɪk] *adj. & n.* sloping (letter); *this is printed in italics.* **i•tal•i•cize** [ɪ'tælɪsaɪz] *v.* to print in italics.

itch [ɪtʃ] 1. *n.* (*pl.* **-es**) tickling sensation. 2. *v.* to tickle; to be very eager (to do sth). **itch•ing,** *n.* tickling sensation. **itch•y,** *adj.* making you feel you want to scratch.

i•tem ['aɪtəm] *n.* thing (in a list); **news items** = separate pieces of news on a news program. **i•tem•ize,** *v.* to make a detailed list of (things).

i•tin•er•ar•y [ɪ'tɪnərərɪ] *n.* route; list of places to be visited on a tour. **i•tin•er•ant,** *adj.* wandering/traveling.

its [ɪts] *adj.* belonging to a thing/to it.

it's [ɪts] *short for* **it is/it has.**

it•self [ɪt'self] *pronoun referring to a thing/to it.* *(a)* (*referring to an object*) **all by i.; the dog has hurt i.** (b) (*for emphasis*) **the television i.**

IUD [aɪjuː'diː] *abbrev. for* intrauterine device.

I've [aɪv] *short for* **I have.**

i•vo•ry ['aɪvərɪ] *adj. & n.* (made of) whitish substance from an elephant's tusk; **i. tower** = imaginary place where a person can avoid contact with the everyday world.

i•vy ['aɪvɪ] *n.* evergreen plant which climbs up walls and trees.

Jj

jab [dʒæb] 1. *n.* (a) sharp blow. (b) thrust with a pointed object; **j. with a needle. 2.** *v.* **(jabbed)** to poke firmly (as with a pointed object).

jab•ber ['dʒæbə] 1. *n.* quick, indistinct talk. 2. *v.* to speak quickly and indistinctly.

jac•a•ran•da [dʒækæ'rændə] *n.* tropical tree with scented pale purple flowers.

jack [dʒæk] *n.* (a) instrument for raising a heavy object (esp. a motor vehicle). (b) (*in playing cards*) the card between the queen and the ten. (c) male of certain mammals. (d) (*at bowls*) small white ball for players to aim at. **jack•boot,** *n.* high military boot. **jack•boot•ed,** *adj.* wearing jackboots. **jack•ham•mer,** *n.* power drill held in the hand. **jack-in-the-box,** *n.* box from which a toy figure springs up when the lid is opened. **jack-knife,** 1. *n.* (*pl.* **-knives**) type of large folding knife. 2. *v.* (*of vehicle pulling a trailer*) to fold in half in an accident. **jack-of-all-trades,** *n.* person who is reasonably good at a large number of jobs. **jack up,** *v.* (a) to raise with a jack. (b) *inf.* to raise (profits or prices).

jack•al ['dʒækl] *n.* wild dog, which feeds chiefly on dead flesh.

jack•ass ['dʒækæs] *n.* male donkey.

jack•daw ['dʒækdɔ:] *n.* type of small crow.

jack•et ['dʒækɪt] *n.* (a) short coat. (b) outer casing or covering; loose paper cover for a book. (c) skin (of a potato). **jack•et•ed,** *adj.* with a jacket.

jack•pot ['dʒækpɒt] *n.* **to win/to hit the j.** = win a high prize in a lottery/to enjoy particular success in sth.

Jac•o•be•an [dʒækə'bi:ən] *adj.* referring to the time of James I of England (1601–1625).

Jac•o•bite ['dʒækəbaɪt] *adj. & n.* (person) who supported James II of England or his descendants in exile.

jade [dʒeɪd] *n.* hard, usu. green, precious stone. **jade-green,** *adj.* of the bluish-green color of jade.

jad•ed ['dʒeɪdɪd] *adj.* worn out/tired.

jag [dʒæg] *n. Sl.* time of overindulgence or unrestraint in some activity.

jag•ged ['dʒægɪd] *adj.* with an irregular, rough, spiky edge.

jag•uar ['dʒægjuə] *n.* large wild cat of Central and South America.

jail [dʒeɪl] 1. *n.* prison. 2. *v.* to put (s.o.) in prison. **jail•bird,** *n.* person who has been sent to prison often. **jail•er,** *n.* person who guards prisoners in jail.

ja•lop•y [dʒə'lɒpɪ] *n. inf.* dilapidated old car.

jam [dʒæm] 1. *n.* (a) stoppage/blockage caused by too many things in too small a space. (b) *inf.* **in a j.** = in a difficult situation. (c) sweet food made by boiling together fruit, sugar, etc. 2. *v.* **(jammed)** (a) (*of machine*) to stop/to stick so that it cannot move. (b) to crowd/to force (things) into a small space. (c) to make (a radio broadcast) impossible to understand by broadcasting noise on the same wavelength. **jam•ming,** *n.* making a radio broadcast impossible to understand. **jam-packed,** *adj. inf.* packed full. **jam ses•sion,** *n.* impromptu jazz concert.

Ja•mai•can [dʒə'meɪkən] 1. *adj.* referring to Jamaica. 2. *n.* person from Jamaica.

jamb [dʒæm] *n.* side post of a door or window.

jam•bo•ree [dʒæmbə'ri:] *n.* large meeting (esp. of Scouts); big festival/party.

jan•gle ['dʒæŋgl] 1. *n.* harsh clanging noise. 2. *v.* (a) to make a harsh clanging noise. (b) to disturb/to irritate (the nerves).

jan•i•tor ['dʒænɪtə] *n.* caretaker, esp. in a school or college.

Jan•u•ar•y ['dʒænjuərɪ] *n.* 1st month of the year.

Jap•a•nese [dʒæpə'ni:z] 1. *adj.* referring to Japan. 2. *n.* (a) (*pl.* **Japanese**) person from Japan. (b) language spoken in Japan.

ja•pon•i•ca [dʒə'pɒnɪkə] *n.* flowering quince bush.

jar [dʒɑ:] 1. *n.* container for food, etc., often of glass and usu. cylindrical; **a j. of jam.** 2. *v.* **(jarred)** (a) to make a harsh/unpleasant sound. (b) to bump/to shake. (c) to affect suddenly and unpleasantly; **to j. on s.o.'s nerves.**

jar•di•nière [ʒɑːdɪnɪˈɜː] *n.* ornamental container for plants.

jar•gon ['dʒɑːgən] *n.* special form of language used by a trade/profession or particular group of people.

jas•mine ['dʒæzmɪn] *n.* shrub with sweet-smelling white or yellow flowers.

jas•per ['dʒæspə] *n.* colored quartz.

jaun•dice ['dʒɔːndɪs] *n.* sickness which makes the skin turn yellow, due to a disorder of the liver or bile. **jaun•diced,** *adj.* (a) suffering from jaundice. (b) miserable/dispirited; envious; resentful.

jaunt [dʒɔːnt] *n.* short excursion.

jaun•ty ['dʒɔːntɪ] *adj.* (-ier, -iest) cheerful/lively. **jaun•ti•ly,** *adv.* cheerfully. **jaun•ti•ness,** *n.* lively manner.

jave•lin ['dʒævlɪn] *n.* long spear used in battle or in sport.

jaw [dʒɔː] 1. *n.* (a) arrangement of bones which allow the mouth to open and shut. (b) **jaws** = two parts of a tool which grip. 2. *v. inf.* to talk (too much). **jaw•bone,** *n.* one of the two bones forming a jaw.

jay [dʒeɪ] *n.* brightly colored bird of the crow family. **jay•walk•er,** *n.* pedestrian who does not take care/pays no attention to traffic rules or signals when crossing the street. **jay•walk•ing,** *n.* being a jaywalker.

jazz [dʒæz] *n.* type of music with strong rhythm, originally played by American blacks. **jazz up,** *v. inf.* to make bright/attractive. **jazz•y,** *adj.* bright (color).

jeal•ous ['dʒeləs] *adj.* (of) feeling sorrow/anger because you want sth which belongs to s.o. else. **jeal•ous•ly,** *adv.* in a jealous way. **jeal•ous•y,** *n.* jealous feeling.

jeans [dʒiːnz] *n. pl. see* **blue jeans.**

jeep [dʒiːp] *n.* trademark for a strongly built vehicle used for traveling over rough ground.

jeer ['dʒɪə] 1. *n.* mocking/laughing in a mean, rude way. 2. *v.* (**at**) to mock/to laugh at (s.o.) in a mean, rude way.

Je•ho•vah [dʒɪˈhəʊvə] *n.* God of Israel.

je•june [dʒɪˈdʒuːn] *adj.* naive.

jell [dʒel] *v.* (*of liquid*) to become a jelly. (b) (*of plan*) to become definite. **jel•ly** ['dʒelɪ] *n.* (a) type of jam made of fruit juice boiled with sugar. (b) semi-solid substance like this. **jel•lied** ['dʒelɪd] *adj.* cooked/preserved in a jelly. **jel•ly bean,** *n.* colored candy shaped like a bean, which has a hard covering and a jellylike center. **jel•ly•fish,** *n.* sea creature with jellylike body. **jel•ly roll,** *n.* type of thin

sponge cake rolled up with cream or jam as a filling.

jen•ny ['dʒenɪ] *n.* female donkey or bird.

jeop•ard•ize ['dʒepədaɪz] *v.* to put in danger/at risk. **jeop•ard•y** ['dʒepədɪ] *n.* danger/risk.

jer•e•mi•ad [dʒerɪˈmaɪəd] *n.* (*formal*) long complaint about your problems.

jerk [dʒɜːk] 1. *n.* (a) sudden uneven movement; sharp pull. (b) *Sl.* stupid person. 2. *v.* to make a sudden movement; to pull sharply. **jerk•i•ly,** *adv.* with an abrupt/sudden movement. **jerk•i•ness,** *n.* being jerky. **jerk•y,** *adj.* abrupt/sudden.

jer•kin ['dʒɜːkɪn] *n.* short coat with no sleeves.

jer•ry-build•er ['dʒerɪbɪldə] *n.* person who builds cheap, poorly constructed, buildings. **jer•ry-built,** *adj.* (building) which is cheaply built.

jer•sey ['dʒɜːzɪ] *n.* (a) close-fitting warm upper garment. (b) **j. (cloth)** = type of loosely woven, usu. woolen, cloth. (c) type of cow.

jest [dʒest] 1. *n.* joke; thing done/said for amusement only. 2. *v.* to make jokes. **jest•er,** *n.* person who plays jokes, esp. someone employed to do this at a royal court.

jet [dʒet] 1. *n.* (a) type of black mineral which can be highly polished; **j. black** = very black. (b) long narrow spray of liquid or gas. (c) opening to allow gas to escape. (d) jet-propelled aircraft; **j. lag** = tiredness felt by travelers who fly by jet across time zones; **j. set** = wealthy people who frequently travel by jet. 2. *v.* (**jetted**) *inf.* to travel by jet. **jet en•gine,** *n.* engine which is propelled by a jet. **jet-pro•pelled,** *adj.* pushed forward by a backward movement of jets of gas. **jet pro•pul•sion,** *n.* being jet-propelled. **jet•stream,** *n.* (a) wind in the upper atmosphere. (b) stream of gases coming from a jet engine.

jet•sam ['dʒetsəm] *n.* (*no pl.*) things which have been thrown into the water from a boat.

jet•ti•son ['dʒetɪzn] *v.* to throw out (unwanted things) from a ship/balloon, etc.

jet•ty ['dʒetɪ] *n.* wall built into water, where boats can tie up.

Jew [dʒuː] *n.* person descended from the Hebrews of ancient Palestine. **Jew•ess,** *n.* Jewish woman. **Jew•ish,** *adj.* referring to Jews. **Jew•ry,** *n.* the Jews.

jew•el ['dʒuəl] *n.* (a) precious stone. (b) ornament to be worn, made from precious stones and/or precious metals, or of imitation stones. **jew•eled,** *adj.* covered with jewels. **jew•el•er,** *n.* person who makes/sells jewelry. **jew•el•ry,** *n.* ornaments to be worn, made of precious stones/metals.

jib [dʒɪb] *n.* (a) triangular sail in front of a boat. (b) arm of a crane.

jibe¹ [dʒaɪb] *n. & v. see* **gibe.**

jibe² *v.* to agree; to be in harmony; **your information jibes with mine** = it agrees with mine.

jif•fy ['dʒɪfɪ] *n. inf.* very short time.

jig [dʒɪg] 1. *n.* (a) type of fast lively dance; music for this dance. (b) instrument for guiding a tool and holding the material being worked on. 2. *v.* (**jigged**) to jump up and down; to move about jerkily. **jig•ger,** *n.* (a) small insect which lives in sand. (b) measure for serving alcohol. **jig•saw,** *n.* (a) type of saw with very fine blade for cutting out shapes. (b) **j. (puzzle)** = puzzle of irregularly shaped pieces of wood/cardboard which when fitted together form a picture.

jig•gle ['dʒɪgl] *v. inf.* to move rapidly/nervously.

jilt [dʒɪlt] *v.* to (encourage and then) reject (a lover).

jim•my ['dʒɪmɪ] *n.* flat iron bar with a curved end, used by burglars to open doors or windows.

jin•gle ['dʒɪŋgl] 1. *n.* (a) sound made by small pieces of metal knocking together. (b) verse with a very simple rhyme and/or rhythm; catchy tune advertising a product. 2. *v.* to make a tinkling sound (like pieces of metal).

jin•go•ism ['dʒɪŋgəʊɪzəm] *n.* excessive love for your country and hatred for others. **jin•go•is•tic** [dʒɪŋgəʊ'ɪstɪk] *adj.* full of jingoism.

jinks [dʒɪŋks] *n. pl.* **high j.** = lively activity; noisy fun.

jinx [dʒɪŋks] *n.* (*pl.* -es) *inf.* bad luck.

jit•ters ['dʒɪtəz] *n. pl.* **to have the j.** = to be (unnecessarily) nervous/flustered. **jit•ter•y,** *adj.* nervous/flustered.

jive [dʒaɪv] 1. *n.* type of fast rhythmic dance; music for this dance. 2. *v.* to dance to jive music.

job [dʒɒb] *n.* (a) piece of work; **to do a good j.** = to do sth well; **odd jobs** = pieces of work, esp. repairs in the house. (b) difficult task. (c) position in employment; **to be out of a j.** = to be unemployed. (d) *inf.* crime, esp. a theft. **job•ber,** *n.* wholesaler. **job•less,** 1. *adj.* with no job. 2. *n.* **the j.** = people who have no jobs. **job lot,** *n.* group of miscellaneous items sold together.

jock•ey ['dʒɒkɪ] 1. *n.* person who rides horses in races. 2. *v.* **to j. for position** = to try to improve your position, esp. by cheating or trickery. **jock•strap** ['dʒɒkstræp] *n.* support for genitals, worn, esp. by men participating in sports.

jo•cose [dʒə'kəʊs] *adj.* humorous. **joc•u•lar** ['dʒɒkjʊlə] *adj.* good humored; treating things as a joke. **joc•u•lar•i•ty** [dʒɒkju'lærɪtɪ] *n.* good humor. **joc•u•lar•ly,** *adv.* in a joking way.

joc•und ['dʒɒkənd] *adj.* (*formal*) cheerful.

jodh•purs ['dʒɒdpəz] *n. pl.* special trousers for horse riding which are narrow below the knee.

jo•ey ['dʒəʊɪ] *n.* (*in Australia*) *inf.* young kangaroo.

jog [dʒɒg] 1. *n.* (a) rather slow pace. (b) light blow, esp. from the elbow. 2. *v.* (**jogged**) (a) to move at a steady, but rather slow pace. (b) to run at an easy pace, esp. for exercise. (c) to shake/to push lightly; **it jogged his memory** = it made him remember. **jog•ger,** *n.* person who jogs for exercise. **jog•ging,** *n.* running at an easy pace for exercise. **jog•trot,** *n.* rather slow, easy pace.

jog•gle ['dʒɒgl] *v. inf.* to move rapidly/nervously.

john [dʒɒn] *n. Sl.* toilet.

join [dʒɔɪn] 1. *n.* place/line where two things come together. 2. *v.* (a) to come together/to be united; to bring together. (b) to (meet and) go along with; to meet and do sth together; **to j. forces** = to do sth by combined effort. (c) to become a member of (a club). **join•er,** *n.* person who constructs things from wood, esp. furniture and woodwork in a house. **join•er•y,** *n.* joiner's trade. **join in,** *v.* to take part. **join up,** *v.* to become a member of the armed forces.

joint [dʒɔɪnt] 1. *n.* (a) (place where) two or more pieces are attached, esp. in building or carpentry. (b) place where bones come together, allowing movement; **out of j.** = dislocated. (c) large piece of meat, esp. for roasting. (d) *inf.* low-class night club or gambling den. (e) *Sl.* cigarette containing marijuana. 2. *v.* (a) to cut up (a chicken, etc.) into pieces. (b) to provide with joints. 3. *adj.* together/combined; shared by two or more; **j. account** = bank account shared by two people; **j. author** = author who writes a book with another. **joint•ed,** *adj.* having joints. **joint•ly,** *adv.* together; by combined effort.

æ back, aː farm, ɒ top, aɪ pipe, aʊ how, aie fire, aʊə flower, ɔː bought, ɔɪ toy, e fed, eəhair, eɪ take, ə afraid, əʊ boat, əʊə lower, vː word, iː heap, ɪ hit, ɪə hear, uː school, ʊ book, ʌ but, b back, d dog, ð then, dʒ just, f fog, g go, h hand, j yes, k catch, l last, m mix, n nut, ŋ sing, p penny, r round, s some, ʃ short, t too, tʃ chop, θ thing, v voice, w was, z zoo, ʒ treasure

joist [dʒɔɪst] *n.* beam which supports a ceiling or floorboards.

joke [dʒəʊk] 1. *n.* thing said or done for amusement, to cause laughter; **practical j.** = action which makes s.o. uncomfortable for the amusement of others. 2. *v.* to tell or make jokes; to say or do sth for amusement; **I was only joking** = I did not mean it seriously. **jok•er,** *n.* (a) person who jokes. (b) extra card in a pack used as a bonus in certain games. **jok•ing•ly,** *adv.* in a joking way.

jol•ly ['dʒɒlɪ] 1. *adj.* (-ier, -iest) merry/happy. 2. *adv.* (*esp. Brit.*) *inf.* very. 3. *v. inf.* **to j. s.o. along** = to encourage s.o. by keeping him happy. **jol•li•fi•ca•tion** [dʒɒlɪfɪ'keɪʃn] *n.* enjoyment/being jolly. **jol•li•ty,** *n.* gaity.

jolt [dʒəʊlt] 1. *n.* abrupt shake/shock; violent jerk. 2. *v.* (a) to move with a jumping movement. (b) to push/to shake abruptly. (c) to give a sudden shock to.

jon•quil ['dʒɒŋkwɪl] *n.* narcissus.

joss stick ['dʒɒsstɪk] *n.* stick with incense painted on it, which burns slowly giving off a pleasant smell.

jos•tle ['dʒɒsl] *v.* to push/to bump (esp. with the elbows).

jot [dʒɒt] 1. *n.* very small amount. 2. *v.* (**jotted**) **to j. sth down** = to make (quick) notes. **jot•ter,** *n.* small pad of paper for making notes. **jot•tings,** *n. pl.* (random) notes.

joule [dʒuːl] *n.* standard unit of work and energy.

jour•nal ['dʒɜːnl] *n.* (a) diary. (b) periodical, esp. on a learned subject. (c) book for recording each day's business. **jour•nal•ese** [dʒɜːnə'liːz] *n.* style used by bad journalists. **jour•nal•ism** ['dʒɜːnəlɪzəm] *n.* profession of writing for newspapers or periodicals. **jour•nal•ist,** *n.* person who writes for newspapers or periodicals.

jour•ney ['dʒɜːnɪ] *n.* (a) long trip. (b) long distance traveled; **it's two days' j. from here.** 2. *v.* (*formal*) to make a long trip. **jour•ney•man,** *n.* (*pl.* -men) craftsman who works for s.o.

joust [dʒaʊst] *v.* to fight with spears on horseback (as an entertainment).

jo•vi•al ['dʒəʊvɪəl] *adj.* good-humored/merry. **jo•vi•al•i•ty** [dʒəʊvɪ'ælɪtɪ] *n.* good humor. **jo•vi•al•ly,** *adv.* in a jovial way.

jowl [dʒaʊl] *n.* jaw/cheek; **cheek by j.** = very close together.

joy [dʒɔɪ] *n.* (cause of) very great happiness. **joy•ful,** *adj.* very happy. **joy•ful•ly,** *adv.* very happily. **joy•less,** *adj.* very sad. **joy•ous,** *adj.* very happy. **joy•ride,** *n.* excursion for pleasure, esp. in a stolen car. **joy•stick,** *n.* (a) rod which controls the move-

ments of an aircraft. (b) device with a movable arm, which moves a cursor on a computer monitor.

JP ['dʒeɪ'piː] *abbreviation for* Justice of the Peace.

ju•bi•lant ['dʒuːbɪlənt] *adj.* full of happiness/triumph. **ju•bi•lant•ly,** *adv.* triumphantly. **ju•bi•la•tion** [dʒuːbɪ'leɪʃn] *n.* great happiness/triumph.

ju•bi•lee ['dʒuːbɪliː] *n.* (celebration of the) anniversary of an important event; **silver/golden/diamond j.** = celebration 25/50/60 or 75 years after an event took place.

Ju•da•ism ['dʒuːdeɪɪzəm] *n.* religion of the Jews.

Ju•das tree ['dʒuːdəstriː] *n.* ornamental tree with pink flowers.

judge [dʒʌdʒ] 1. *n.* (a) public official authorized to make decisions in a court of law. (b) person who decides which is the best entry in a competition. (c) person with good judgment; **he's a good j. of character.** 2. *v.* (a) to make decisions in a court of law/competition, etc. (b) to have as your opinion; to estimate. **judg•ment, judgement,** *n.* (a) making a decision. (b) sentence of a court; legal decision. (c) ability to see things clearly/to make good decisions; **against my better j.** = although I felt it was not the right thing to do.

ju•di•cial [dʒuː'dɪʃl] *adj.* referring to a legal process/to a court of law. **ju•di•ca•ture** ['dʒuːdɪkətʃə] *n.* (a) judicial system. (b) judiciary. **ju•di•cial•ly,** *adv.* legally. **ju•di•ci•ar•y** [dʒuː'dɪʃərɪ] *n.* judges as a group. **ju•di•cious,** *adj.* based on/having good judgment. **ju•di•cious•ly,** *adv.* exhibiting or using good judgment.

ju•do ['dʒuːdəʊ] *n.* modern form of Japanese wrestling.

jug [dʒʌg] *n.* (a) container with a handle, used for pouring liquids. (b) *Sl.* jail. **jugged hare,** *n.* stew made of wild rabbit soaked in wine and cooked slowly.

jug•ger•naut ['dʒʌgənɔːt] *n.* overpowering force to which people sacrifice themselves.

jug•gle ['dʒʌgl] *v.* (a) to throw and catch several objects, so that most of them are in the air at the same time. (b) to change things around, esp. in order to deceive. **jug•gler,** *n.* person who juggles.

jug•u•lar ['dʒʌgjʊlə] *n. & adj.* **j. (vein)** = main vein in the neck.

juice [dʒuːs] *n.* (a) liquid from fruit/vegetables/meat, etc; **to stew in your own j.** = to suffer the consequences of your own mistakes. (b) *inf.* fuel; electricity. **juic•i•ness,** *n.* state of being full of juice. **juic•y,** *adj.* full of juice.

ju•jit•su [dʒuːˈdʒɪtsuː] *n.* traditional Japanese unarmed combat.

ju•ju [ˈdʒuːdʒuː] *n.* African magic charm.

ju•jube [ˈdʒuːdʒuːb] *n.* type of soft candy.

juke•box [ˈdʒuːkbɒks] *n.* coin-operated record-playing machine.

ju•lep [ˈdʒuːləp] *n.* drink made of alcohol and water, usu. with a mint flavor.

Ju•ly [dʒuˈlaɪ] *n.* 7th month of the year. **Jul•ian cal•en•dar,** *n.* calendar instituted by Julius Caesar, slightly longer than the present-day calendar.

jum•ble [ˈdʒʌmbl] 1. *n.* mixture/confusion. 2. *v.* (**up**) to mix; to confuse.

jum•bo [ˈdʒʌmbəʊ] *n.* (*pl.* **-os**) anything very large, esp. a very large aircraft holding several hundred people.

jump [dʒʌmp] 1. *n.* (a) leap (in the air); (*in sports*) **long j./high j.** = competition to see how far/how high you can leap. (b) sudden movement. (c) (*in sports*) obstacle to be jumped over. 2. *v.* (a) to move suddenly, esp. upward. (b) to move by jumping; **to j. over the stream.** (c) to make a sudden movement, esp. from some emotion; **to j. to conclusions** = to make a decision too quickly; **to j. the gun** = to begin before your turn/before the correct time. **jump at,** *v.* to seize (an opportunity) eagerly. **jump•er,** *n.* (a) person who jumps. (b) article of clothing, esp. a one-piece sleeveless dress. **jumper (cable),** *n.* cable which allows two car batteries to be connected to help a car to start. **jump jet,** *n.* aircraft which can take off vertically. **jump rope,** *n.* rope which you jump over as it turns. **jump suit,** *n.* one-piece suit, with trousers attached to the shirt. **jump•y,** *adj.* (**-ier, -iest**) *inf.* nervous; excited.

junc•tion [ˈdʒʌŋkʃn] *n.* joining (place), esp. of railroad lines/roads; **j. box** = box where several electric wires join.

junc•ture [ˈdʒʌŋktʃə] *n.* (*formal*) point in time.

June [dʒuːn] *n.* 6th month of the year.

jun•gle [ˈdʒʌŋgl] *n.* (a) almost impassable tropical forest. (b) confused mass; place or circumstances where progress is difficult; **concrete j.** = area of tall impersonal buildings.

jun•ior [ˈdʒuːnɪə] 1. *adj.* (a) younger; **John Smith, Jr.** = son of John Smith Senior. (b) for younger children. (c) lower in rank. 2. *n.* (a) person who is younger/lower in rank. (b) third-year student in a school or college, next below a senior.

ju•ni•per [ˈdʒuːnɪpə] *n.* shrub with evergreen leaves and dark berries, used as flavoring for gin.

junk [dʒʌŋk] *n.* (a) large Chinese sailing boat. (b) useless articles/articles to be thrown away; **j. bonds** = bonds giving a high interest, based on the security of a company which is the target of a takeover bid. (c) (inferior) second-hand goods. (d) *Sl.* drugs, esp. heroin. **junk food,** *n.* commercially prepared food with little nutritional value. **junk•ie,** *n. Sl.* drug addict. **junk store,** *n.* store selling junk.

jun•ket [ˈdʒʌŋkɪt] 1. *n.* (a) sweet dessert made of curdled milk. (b) feast/celebration. (c) pleasure trip made by an official at public expense. 2. *v.* to have a celebration, esp. by eating and drinking.

jun•ta [ˈdʒʌntə] *n.* group of soldiers who seize power and rule a country.

ju•ris•dic•tion [dʒʊərɪsˈdɪkʃn] *n.* (legal) power.

ju•ris•pru•dence [dʒʊərɪsˈpruːdəns] *n.* study of the law.

ju•rist [ˈdʒʊərɪst] *n.* person who specializes in law.

ju•ry [ˈdʒʊərɪ] *n.* (a) group of citizens sworn to decide a verdict on the strength of evidence in a court of law. (b) group of judges in a competition. **ju•ror, juryman,** *n.* (*pl.* **-men**) member of a jury. **ju•ry•box** *n.* place where the jury sits.

just [dʒʌst] 1. *adj.* showing no favor; true/correct. 2. *adv.* (a) exactly; very nearly/almost; **j. by the door; it's j. about ready** = almost ready; **that's j. it** = that is exactly the problem. (b) (*used to indicate the immediate past or future*) **he's j. arrived; I'm j. going.** (c) only; **we're j. good friends.** (d) **j. now** = (i) at the present moment. (ii) a short time ago. (e) **j. as** = (i) exactly when; (ii) exactly in the manner that. **just•ly,** *adv.* fairly; with justice. **just•ness,** *n.* fairness.

jus•tice [ˈdʒʌstɪs] *n.* (a) quality of being fair; **to do j. to** = to treat (sth) as it deserves; **the portrait doesn't do her j.** = it is not a good likeness. (b) **to bring to j.** = to bring legal proceedings against. (c) (*esp. as title*) judge/magistrate. **Justice of the Peace,** *n.* local public official authorized to carry out some judicial duties (as performing civil marriages, trying minor cases).

jus•ti•fy [ˈdʒʌstɪfaɪ] *v.* (a) to show that sth is fair/to prove that sth is right. (b) to adjust the

---

æ back, ɑː farm, ɒ top, aɪ pipe, aʊ how, aɪe fire, aʊə flower, ɔː bought, ɔɪ toy, e fed, eəhair, eɪ take, ə afraid, əʊ boat, əʊə lower, vː word, iː heap, ɪ hit, ɪə hear, uː school, ʊ book, ʌ but, b back, d dog, ð then, dʒ just, f fog, g go, h hand, j yes, k catch, l last, m mix, n nut, ŋ sing, p penny, r round, s some, ʃ short, t too, tʃ chop, θ thing, v voice, w was, z zoo, ʒ treasure

space between characters in lines of text so that the right margin of the page is even. **jus•ti•fi•a•ble,** *adj.* which can be justified. **jus•ti•fi•a•bly,** *adv.* in a way which can be justified. **jus•ti•fi•ca•tion** [dʒʌstɪfɪˈkeɪʃn] *n.* (a) reason which shows that sth is fair. (b) making a right margin of a page of text even.

jut [dʒʌt] *v.* (**jutted**) **to j. (out)** = to stick out, usu. horizontally.

jute [dʒuːt] *n.* fiber of plants used for making sacks, etc.

ju•ve•nile [ˈdʒuːvənaɪl] 1. *adj.* of/for young people; **j. delinquent** = young person who is a criminal. 2. *n.* young person. **ju•ve•nil•i•a** [dʒuːvəˈnɪlɪə] *n.* works written when a child.

jux•ta•pose [dʒʌkstəˈpəʊz] *v.* to place side by side/very close together. **jux•ta•po•si•tion** [dʒʌkstəpəˈzɪʃn] *n.* being side by side/very close together.

Kk

K 1. *symbol for* potassium. 2. *abbrev. for* one thousand.

ka•bob [kɪ'bɑb] *n.* small cubes of meat grilled on a skewer.

kaf•tan ['kæftæn] *n. see* **caftan.**

kale [keɪl] *n.* (*no pl.*) type of cabbage with wrinkled leaves.

ka•lei•do•scope [kə'laɪdəskəʊp] *n.* tube with mirrors which reflect small pieces of colored glass and make patterns which can be seen through a viewer. **ka•lei•do•scop•ic** [kəlaɪdə'skɒpɪk] *adj.* like a kaleidoscope/with bright changing colors; frequently changing.

ka•mi•ka•ze ['kæmɪkɑːzɪ] *n. & adj.* suicidally daring (air attack).

kan•ga•roo [kæŋgə'ruː] *n.* large Australian animal, which carries its young in a pouch; **k. court** = illegal court set up by terrorists/strikers, etc., to judge one of their members.

ka•o•lin ['keɪəlɪn] *n.* fine white clay, used for making porcelain, and sometimes in medicine.

ka•pok ['keɪpɒk] *n.* kind of cotton wool, used for stuffing pillows, cushions, life jackets, etc.

ka•put [kə'pʊt] *adj. inf.* finished; broken.

kar•at ['kærət] *n.* measure of purity of gold; **18-k gold.**

ka•ra•te [kə'rɑːtɪ] *n.* Japanese style of fighting, where you hit with the side of the hand.

kar•ma ['kɑːmə] *n.* in Buddhism, the way in which a person acts which will affect his future life.

kay•ak ['kaɪæk] *n.* (a) Eskimo canoe, covered with sealskins. (b) small canoe with a narrow opening for the canoeist.

ke•bab [kɪ'bæb] *n. see* **ka•bob.**

ked•ger•ee [kedʒə'riː] *n.* spicy mixture of rice, fish and eggs.

keel [kiːl] 1. *n.* lowest timber in a ship, on which the framework is built; **on an even k.** = stable/steady. 2. *v.* **to k. over** = to fall over.

keen [kiːn] 1. *adj.* (**-er, -est**) (a) (**on**) eager/willing. (b) sharp. (c) sensitive/acute (sense). 2. *v.* to wail/to cry (because s.o. has died).

keen•ly, *adv.* sharply. **keen•ness,** *n.* being keen.

keep [kiːp] 1. *n.* (a) central tower/strongest part of a castle. (b) maintenance; **she doesn't earn her k.** = she doesn't earn enough money to pay for her food and lodging. (c) *inf.* **for keeps** = for ever. 2. *v.* (**kept** [kept]) (a) to continue to have/to possess. (b) to continue; **he kept running.** (c) to pay regard to (a promise, etc.). (d) to own/to manage (animals). (e) to maintain. (f) to support financially. (g) to have for sale/in stock. (h) to detain/to restrain. (i) to conceal. (j) to reserve. (k) to prevent (s.o. **from** doing sth). (l) to remain; **let's k. in touch** = we mustn't lose contact with each other; **she kept him company** = she stayed with him. (m) **to k. a diary** = to write notes every day about what you have done. (n) to continue to stay in good condition; **raspberries don't k.** = go rotten quickly. **keep•er,** *n.* (a) person in charge of animals in a zoo. (b) fruit which stays in good condition for a long time. **keep•ing,** *n.* (a) custody. (b) **in k. with** = in harmony with. **keep in with,** *v.* to stay on friendly terms with (s.o.). **keep on,** *v.* to continue (to do sth); **he kept on running. keep•sake,** *n.* memento; thing kept to remind you of the giver. **keep up,** *v.* to continue. **keep up with,** *v.* (a) to keep yourself informed about. (b) to go forward at the same pace; **to k. u. w. the Joneses** = to try to maintain the same social level as your neighbors.

keg [keg] *n.* small barrel; **k. beer** = beer kept in pressurized metal kegs.

kelp [kelp] *n.* large seaweed.

kel•vin ['kelvɪn] *n.* standard unit of temperature.

ken [ken] *n.* knowledge; **beyond our k.** = out of our normal range of knowledge.

ken•nel ['kenl] 1. *n.* shelter for a dog; **kennels** = place where dogs can be left when their owners go away/where dogs are bred. 2. *v.* (**kenneled, kennelled**) to keep in a kennel.

kent•ledge ['kentlɪdʒ] *n.* iron used as ballast.

æ back, ɑ: farm, ɒ: top, aɪ pipe, aʊ how, aɪe fire, aʊə flower, ɔ: bought, ɔɪ toy, e fed, eəhair, eɪ take, ə afraid, əʊ boat, əʊə lower, v: word, i: heap, ɪ hit, ɪə hear, u: school, ʊ book, ʌ but, b back, d dog, ð then, dʒ just, f fog, g go, h hand, j yes, k catch, l last, m mix, n nut, ŋ sing, p penny, r round, s some, ʃ short, t too, tʃ chop, θ thing, v voice, w was, z zoo, ʒ treasure

Ken•yan ['kenjən] 1. *adj.* referring to Kenya. 2. *n.* person from Kenya.

kept [kept] *v. see* **keep.**

ker•chief ['kɜːtʃɪf] *n.* large square scarf worn over your head.

ker•nel ['kɜːnl] *n.* (a) softer part inside the hard shell of a nut. (b) essential part/center.

ker•o•sene ['kerəsiːn] *n.* thin oil for lamps/heaters, etc.

kes•trel ['kestrəl] *n.* type of small falcon.

ketch [ketʃ] *n.* (*pl.* **-es**) two-masted sailboat.

ketch•up ['ketʃəp] *n.* sauce made from tomatoes and spices.

ket•tle ['ketl] *n.* metal container, with a lid and a spout, used for boiling water; **a fine k. of fish** = an awkward state of affairs. **ket•tle•drum,** *n.* large drum with a round bottom.

key [kiː] 1. *n.* (a) piece of metal for turning locks. (b) solution/explanation. (c) system of musical notes related to each other. (d) part of a piano/flute/typewriter/computer, etc., which you press down to make the instrument work. (e) seed case, shaped like a key. 2. *adj.* most important (thing/person). 3. *v.* (a) to link to/to make suitable for. (b) to type (words/figures) on a keyboard. **key•board.** 1. *n.* set of keys on a piano/typewriter/computer, etc. 2. *v.* to input data into a computer, using a keyboard. **keyed up,** *adj.* nervous/tense (before an examination/a battle, etc.). **key•hole,** *n.* hole in a lock into which a key is put. **key•note,** *n.* (a) dominating musical note. (b) main theme in a speech; **k. speech** = main speech (at a conference). **key•pad,** *n.* small set of keys on a computer; **numeric k.** = set of numbered keys on a computer keyboard, used for various functions. **key ring,** *n.* ring for carrying several keys together. **key•stone,** *n.* central supporting block of stone or brick in an arch; important idea on which everything else is based. **key•word,** *n.* (a) word that is the key to a code. (b) word that describes the content of a document and is used in computerized information retrieval. (c) significant or meaningful word, e.g. a password.

kg *abbrev. for* **kilogram.**

khak•i ['kɑːkɪ] *adj. & n.* dull yellow-brown (color); the color of soldiers' uniforms.

kib•butz [kɪ'bʊts] *n.* (*pl.* **-tzim** [-'tsiːm]) farming settlement in Israel.

ki•bosh ['kaɪbɒʃ] *n. Sl.* **to put the k. on sth** = to stop sth happening.

kick [kɪk] 1. *n.* (a) blow with the foot. (b) *inf.* thrill/excitement; **he did it for kicks** = to give himself a thrill. 2. *v.* to strike with the foot. **kick•back,** *n.* (a) recoil (of a gun). (b) *Sl.* bribe/illegal commission paid to s.o. who helps a business deal. **kick off,** *v.* to start a game of football. **kick-off,** *n.* start (of a football game). **kick start•(er),** *n.* pedal to start a motorcycle engine. **kick up,** *v. inf.* to make (a fuss/a row).

kid [kɪd] 1. *n.* (a) young goat. (b) *inf.* child. 2. *v.* (**kidded**) *inf.* to make (s.o.) believe sth that is not true; **I'm only kidding** = I don't mean it; **no kidding?** = is it really true? **kid•dy,** *n. inf.* child.

kid•nap ['kɪdnæp] *v.* (**kidnapped**) to steal (a child); to carry (a person) off by force illegally. **kid•nap•per,** *n.* person who kidnaps. **kid•nap•ping,** *n.* carrying away of a person by force.

kid•ney ['kɪdnɪ] *n.* one of a pair of organs in animals that extract impurities from the blood; this organ used as food; **k. bean** = type of bean with reddish seeds.

kill [kɪl] 1. *n.* putting an animal to death for sport. 2. *v.* to put to death; to make (s.o./an animal/a plant) die; **to k. time** = to spend time doing very little while waiting for sth; **to k. two birds with one stone** = to get two successful results from one action; *inf.* **my feet are killing me** = my feet hurt. **kill•er,** *n.* person who kills; **k. whale** = medium-sized black and white carnivorous whale. **kill•ing.** 1. *adj. inf.* very funny. 2. *n.* (a) putting to death. (b) large profit (on the stock market). **kill•joy,** *n.* person who stops others enjoying themselves. **kill off,** *v.* to get rid of (sth) by killing.

kiln [kɪln] *n.* oven for baking pottery or bricks.

ki•lo ['kiːləʊ] 1. *prefix meaning* one thousand. 2. *n.* (*pl.* **-os**) kilogram.

kil•o•byte ['kɪləʊbaɪt] *n.* storage unit of computer data equal to 1,024 bytes.

kil•o•cy•cle ['kɪləʊsaɪkl] *n.* one thousand cycles as a frequency of radio waves.

kil•o•gram ['kɪləʊgræm] *n.* one thousand grams.

kil•o•hertz ['kɪləʊhɜːts] *n.* one thousand hertz.

kil•o•me•ter, *Brit.* **kil•o•me•tre** [kɪ'lɒmɪtə] *n.* one thousand meters.

kil•o•volt ['kɪləʊvɒlt] *n.* one thousand volts.

kil•o•watt ['kɪləwɒt] *n.* one thousand watts.

kilt [kɪlt] *n.* pleated skirt, usu. of tartan cloth, worn by men in Scotland, and also by women. **kilt•ed,** ['kɪltɪd] *adj.* wearing a kilt.

ki•mo•no [kɪ'məʊnəʊ] *n.* (*pl.* **-os**) long, loose robe worn by Japanese women.

kin [kɪn] *n.* **next of k.** = nearest relative(s); *see also* **kith.**

kind [kaɪnd] 1. *n.* type/variety; **two of a k.** = two the same; **it's nothing of the k.** = not at all true; **payment in k.** = payment in goods or natural produce, not in money; *inf.* **k. of sorry** = rather sorry. 2. *adj.* (**-er, -est**) amiable/thoughtful;

friendly/thinking of others. **kind-heart•ed**, *adj.* thoughtful about other people. **kind•li•ness**, *n.* being kindly. **kind•ly**, *adj. & adv.* thoughtful/pleasant; in a thoughtful/pleasant way; **she doesn't take k. to** = she doesn't like; **k. shut the door** = please shut the door. **kind•ness**, *n.* being kind.

kin•der•gar•ten ['kɪndəgɑːtn] *n.* school for very young children.

kin•dle ['kɪndl] *v.* to make a fire; to catch fire. **kin•dling**, *n.* (*no pl.*) small pieces of wood used to start a fire.

kin•dred ['kɪndrɪd] *adj.* similar; **k. spirit** = person with whom you have sth in common.

ki•net•ic [kɪ'netɪk] *adj.* produced by moving; (energy) which a body has in motion.

king [kɪŋ] *n.* (a) male sovereign or hereditary ruler of a country. (b) main piece in chess; (*in cards*) card following the queen. **king•cup**, *n.* large buttercup. **king•dom**, *n.* (a) land ruled over by a king. (b) part of the world of nature. (c) **until k. come** = until the end of the world. **king•fish•er**, *n.* small brilliant blue bird that dives for fish. **king•ly**, *adj.* like a king. **king•pin**, *n.* central bolt; central person in an organization. **king-size(d)**, *adj.* very large.

kink [kɪŋk] 1. *n.* (a) knot/twist in a length of cord, wire or rope. (b) peculiar mental state. 2. *v.* to make a kink in (sth). **kink•y**, *adj. Sl.* sexually odd/peculiar.

kin•ship ['kɪnʃɪp] *n.* family relationship. **kin•folk, kinsfolk**, *n. pl.* relatives. **kins•man, kinswoman**, *n.* (*pl.* **-men, -women**) relative.

ki•osk ['kiːɒsk] *n.* small outdoor structure for the sale of newspapers/candy, etc.

kip•per ['kɪpə] *n.* split smoked herring. **kip•pered**, *adj.* smoked (fish).

kirsch [kɪəʃ] *n.* cherry brandy.

kiss [kɪs] 1. *n.* (*pl.* **-es**) touching with the lips; **she blew him a k.** = signaled to send him a kiss from a distance; **k. of life** = resuscitation by breathing into a person's mouth; **k. of death** = act which ruins (a business, etc.). 2. *v.* to touch with the lips. **kiss•er**, *n. Sl.* mouth.

kit [kɪt] *n.* (a) equipment, supplies, etc. packed for a specific purpose; **first aid k.** = supplies for the emergency treatment of injuries. (b) box containing pieces which can be put together to make a model/a piece of furniture, etc. **kit•bag**, *n.* small bag for carrying a soldier's clothes and equipment.

kitch•en ['kɪtʃɪn] *n.* room in which food is cooked. **kitch•en•ette**, *n.* very small kitchen. **kit•chen gar•den**, *n.* fruit and vegetable plot in a garden.

kite [kaɪt] *n.* (a) bird of the hawk family. (b) toy made of light wood and paper or cloth which is flown in a strong wind on the end of a string.

kith [kɪθ] *n.* **k. and kin** = friends and relatives.

kitsch [kɪtʃ] *n.* lack of artistic taste; tasteless artistic production.

kit•ten ['kɪtn] *n.* young cat. **kit•ten•ish**, *adj.* playful/like a kitten.

kit•ti•wake ['kɪtɪweɪk] *n.* type of gull.

kit•ty ['kɪtɪ] *n.* joint fund shared by a number of people for a common purpose.

ki•wi ['kiːwiː] *n.* non-flying bird, native of New Zealand. **ki•wi fruit**, *n.* small tropical fruit, with a hairy skin and green flesh.

Kleen•ex ['kliːneks] *n.* (*pl.* **-es**) trademark for a paper handkerchief.

klep•to•ma•ni•a [kleptə'meɪnɪə] *n.* irresistible tendency to steal. **klep•to•ma•ni•ac**, *n.* person who cannot stop stealing.

km *abbrev. for* kilometer.

knack [næk] *n.* talent/ability.

knack•er ['nækə] *n.* person who buys and kills useless horses.

knap•sack ['næpsæk] *n.* canvas/leather bag carried on the back.

knave [neɪv] *n.* (a) (*old*) trickster. (b) (*in cards*) jack/card between the ten and the queen.

knead [niːd] *v.* to press with the hands.

knee [niː] *n.* joint between your thigh and lower leg; **she was sitting on his k.** = sitting on his thighs. **knee•cap**. 1. *n.* bone in front of the knee. 2. *v.* to punish (s.o.) by shooting him in the kneecap. **knee-deep**, *adj.* up to the knees (in).

kneel [niːl] *v.* (**knelt** [nelt] or **kneeled**) to go on your knees. **kneel down**, *v.* to go down on your knees. **kneel•er**, *n.* hard cushion for kneeling on.

knell [nel] *n.* (*formal*) sound of a bell, rung at a solemn ceremony such as a funeral.

knelt [nelt] *v. see* **kneel**.

knew [njuː] *v. see* **know**.

knick•er•bock•ers ['nɪkəbɒkəz] *n. pl.* loose-fitting trousers which are gathered at the knees. **knick•ers** ['nɪkəz] *n. pl.* undergarment worn by a woman or girl on the lower part of the body.

knick-knack ['nɪknæk] *n.* small/light article; trinket.

æ **back**, ɑː **farm**, ɒ: **top**, aɪ **pipe**, aʊ **how**, aɪə **fire**, aʊə **flower**, ɔː **bought**, ɔɪ **toy**, e **fed**, eəhair, eɪ **take**, ə **afraid**, əʊ **boat**, əʊə **lower**, ɜː **word**, iː **heap**, ɪ **hit**, ɪə **hear**, uː **school**, ʊ **book**, ʌ **but**, b **back**, d **dog**, ð **then**, dʒ **just**, f **fog**, g **go**, h **hand**, j **yes**, k **catch**, l **last**, m **mix**, n **nut**, ŋ **sing**, p **penny**, r **round**, s **some**, ʃ **short**, t **too**, tʃ **chop**, θ **thing**, v **voice**, w **was**, z **zoo**, ʒ **treasure**

knife [naɪf] 1. *n.* (*pl.* **knives** [naɪvz]) cutting blade with a sharpened edge fixed into a handle. 2. *v.* (**knifed**) to stab (s.o.) with a knife.

knight [naɪt] 1. *n.* (a) man honored by a monarch for personal merit or services to his country (and taking the title **Sir**). (b) (*in medieval times*) brave soldier often devoted to the service of a lady. (c) piece in a chess set with a horse's head. 2. *v.* to make (s.o.) a knight. **knight•hood,** *n.* title of knight.

knit [nɪt] *v.* (a) (**knitted** or **knit**) to make (a garment) out of wool, etc., by linking two threads together with the aid of two long needles; **to k. one's brows** = to frown. (b) (**knit**) (*of broken bone*) to join together again. **knit•ter,** *n.* person who knits. **knit•ting,** *n.* woolen garment which is in the process of being made. **knit•ting ma•chine,** *n.* machine for knitting. **knit•ting nee•dle,** *n.* long needle for knitting. **knit•wear,** *n.* knitted garments.

knives [naɪvz] *n. see* **knife.**

knob [nɒb] *n.* (a) rounded bump; round lump. (b) round handle of door/drawer. **knob•by,** *adj.* bumpy; covered with knobs.

knock [nɒk] 1. *n.* sharp blow; sound of a sharp blow. 2. *v.* (a) to strike (sth) with a hard blow; **he knocked on/at the door** = hit the door with his knuckles to call attention. (b) *inf.* to criticize. (c) (*of car engine*) to make a regular/sharp noise because of misfiring. **knock a•bout,** *v.* (a) to drift aimlessly. (b) **to knock (s.o.) about** = to beat (s.o.). **knock back,** *v. inf.* to swallow quickly. **knock down,** *v.* (a) to hit (s.o./sth) to the ground. (b) to sell (an item) at an auction to a purchaser. **knock-down,** *adj.* very low (price). **knock•er,** *n.* knob or ring hinged to a door which can be struck against it to call attention. **knock•ing,** *n.* series of sharp blows; noise made by an engine which is misfiring. **knock-kneed,** *adj.* having knees that touch each other when walking. **knock off,** *v.* (a) to hit (sth) so that it falls off. (b) *inf.* **he knocked off work at 4:30** = he stopped working at 4:30. (c) **the dealer knocked $100 off the price of the car** = he reduced the price of the car by $100. **knock out,** *v.* to hit (s.o.) so hard that he loses consciousness. **knock•out,** *n.* hitting s.o. so hard that he loses consciousness.

knoll [nɒl] *n.* small hill.

knot [nɒt] 1. *n.* (a) looping the ends of string/rope, etc., and fastening them together; small group (of people). (b) hard round place in a piece of wood where a branch used to join it. (c) measurement by which a ship's/an aircraft's speed is calculated (= one nautical mile per hour). (c) type of small shore bird. 2. *v.* (**knotted**) to tie in a knot. **knot•ty,** *adj.* (**-ier, -iest**) difficult (problem).

know [nəʊ] 1. *n.* **to be in the k.** = to be well informed about sth which is not generally known. 2. *v.* (**knew** [njuː]; **has known**) (a) to have in your mind because of learning or experience; **do you k. French?** = do you speak French? (b) to recognize (s.o.). (c) to be acquainted with; **I k. him by sight/by name.** (d) **to k. what it is like to** = to have personal experience of; **to k. your own mind** = to be clear and firm in your views. **know-all,** *n.* know-it-all. **know-how,** *n. inf.* knowledge about how sth is made/is done. **know•ing,** *adj.* understanding; having knowledge. **know•ing•ly,** *adv.* deliberately. **know-it-all,** *n.* person who claims to know everything. **knowl•edge** ['nɒlɪdʒ] *n.* (a) what s.o. knows. (b) what is generally known. **knowl•edge•a•ble, knowledgable** *adj.* (person) who knows a lot about sth. **know of,** *v.* to be aware of.

knuck•le ['nʌkl] *n.* (a) finger joint. (b) (*on an animal*) joint on the leg (esp. when used as food). **knuckle down,** *v.* to apply yourself seriously to work. **knuck•le under,** *v.* to give in/to submit.

KO *abbrev. for* knock out.

ko•a•la [kəʊ'ɑːlə] *n.* **k.** (**bear**) = small Australian animal which carries its young in a pouch and lives in trees.

kohl [kəʊl] *n.* powder used to make eyelids darker.

kohl•ra•bi [kəʊl'rɑːbiː] *n.* vegetable with a thick purplish stem which is eaten.

kook•a•bur•ra ['kʊkəbʌrə] *n.* large Australian kingfisher.

kop [kɒp] *n.* (*in South Africa*) small hill.

Ko•ran [kɒ'rɑːn] *n.* holy book of the Muslims.

Ko•re•an [kə'rɪən] 1. *adj.* referring to Korea. 2. *n.* (a) person from Korea. (b) language spoken in Korea.

ko•sher ['kəʊʃə] *adj.* (food) prepared according to Jewish law.

kow•tow [kaʊ'taʊ] *v.* to show great respect (to).

kraal [krɑl] *n.* (*in South Africa*) village with a fence round it.

krill [krɪl] *n.* (*pl.* **krill**) minute shrimps living in the sea.

kryp•ton ['krɪptɒn] *n.* (*element:* Kr) rare gas.

ku•dos ['kjuːdɒs] *n.* glory/renown.

ku•du ['kuːduː] *n.* small African antelope.

kum•quat ['kʌmkwɒt] *n.* very small orange.

kung fu [kuːŋ'fuː] *n.* Chinese style of fighting.

Ll

lab [læb] *n. short for* **laboratory.**

la•bel ['leɪbl] 1. *n.* (a) piece of paper/card, etc., attached to sth to indicate price/contents/name/address, etc. (b) name under which sth is generally known. 2. *v.* (**labeled, labelled**) (a) to put a label on. (b) to name/to describe.

la•bi•al ['leɪbɪəl] *adj.* referring to the lips.

lab•o•ra•to•ry [lə'bɒrətrɪ, *Am.* 'læbrətɔːrɪ] *n.* place where scientific experiments/research are carried out.

la•bo•ri•ous [lə'bɔːrɪəs] *adj.* (a) involving a great deal of work. (b) (style) showing signs of effort. **la•bo•ri•ous•ly**, *adv.* in a laborious way.

la•bor, *Brit.* **la•bour** ['leɪbə] 1. *n.* (a) (hard) work. (b) workers/the workforce. (c) (pains of) childbirth. 2. *v.* (a) to work (hard). (b) **to l. under a delusion** = to have a (persistently) wrong impression; **to l. the point** = to argue/to discuss sth too long. **la•bored**, *adj.* (a) (*of style*) heavy/clumsy. (b) (*of breathing*) heavy/difficult. **la•bor•er**, *n.* person who does heavy manual work. **la•bor-sav•ing**, *adj.* (*of machine/gadget*) which lessens work. **la•bor un•ion**, *n.* organization which groups together workers from similar industries to represent them in bargaining for wages, benefits, etc. with employers. **la•bor un•ion•ist**, *n.* member of a labor union.

lab•ra•dor ['læbrədɔː] *n.* type of large dog, usu. black or yellow.

la•bur•num [lə'bɜːnəm] *n.* tree with bright yellow flowers and poisonous seeds in pods.

lab•y•rinth ['læbɪrɪnθ] *n.* maze; place where it is difficult to find your way about. **lab•y•rin•thine** [læbə'rɪnθaɪn] *adj.* like a labyrinth.

lace [leɪs] 1. *n.* (a) thin strip of material for tying up a shoe, etc. (b) decorative cloth with open patterns of threads. 2. *v.* (a) to tie with a lace. (b) to pour a little alcohol into (sth).

lac•er•ate ['læsəreɪt] *v.* (*formal*) to wound/to tear (flesh). **lac•er•a•tion** [læsə'reɪʃn] *n.* tearing; place where flesh has been torn.

lach•ry•mose ['lækrɪməʊs] *adj.* (*formal*) (person) who tends to cry. **lach•ry•mal**, *adj.* (gland) which produces tears.

lack [læk] 1. *n.* not having sth. 2. *v.* not to have (enough of) sth. **lack•ing**, *adj.* not enough/without.

lack•a•dai•si•cal [lækə'deɪzɪkl] *adj.* not showing any vigor/any enthusiasm.

lack•ey ['lækɪ] *n.* servant who obeys without questioning.

lack•lus•ter ['læklʌstə] *adj.* dull/not brilliant.

la•con•ic [lə'kɒnɪk] *adv.* using few words. **la•con•i•cal•ly**, *adv.* in a laconic way.

lac•quer ['lækə] 1. *n.* type of hard shiny varnish/paint, often used on metals. 2. *v.* to coat with lacquer.

la•crosse [lə'krɒs] *n.* team game played with a ball and a curved stick with a net at the end.

lac•tic ['læktɪk] *adj.* referring to milk. **lac•ta•tion** [læk'teɪʃn] *n.* (*of female*) production of milk. **lac•tose**, *n.* sugar occurring in milk. **lac•to-veg•e•tar•i•an**, *n.* vegetarian who eats dairy products and eggs.

la•cu•na [lə'kjuːnə] *n.* (*pl.* -ae) gap/space.

la•cus•trine ['lækuːstriːn] *adj.* referring to lakes.

lac•y ['leɪsɪ] *adj.* (-ier, -iest) like lace; made of a network of fine threads.

lad [læd], **lad•die** ['lædɪ] *n. inf.* boy; young man.

lad•der ['lædə] *n.* object made of horizontal bars between two uprights, used for climbing.

lad•en ['leɪdn] *adj.* (**with**) carrying a (heavy) load; (*of ship*) containing a cargo. **lad•ing**, *n.* (a) loading of ships. (b) cargo.

la•dle ['leɪdl] 1. *n.* large deep spoon for serving soup, etc. 2. *v.* (*also* **ladle out**) to serve with a ladle.

la•dy ['leɪdɪ] *n.* (a) woman, esp. of high social standing or with good manners. (b) (*as title*) *Brit.* **Lady** = feminine equivalent of Lord; title

---

æ back, aː farm, ɒ top, aɪ pipe, aʊ how, aie fire, aʊə flower, ɔː bought, ɔɪ toy, e fed, eəhair, eɪ take, ə afraid, əʊ boat, əʊə lower, vː word, iː heap, ɪ hit, ɪə hear, uː school, ʊ book, ʌ but, b back, d dog, ð then, dʒ just, f fog, g go, h hand, j yes, k catch, l last, m mix, n nut, ŋ sing, p penny, r round, s some, ʃ short, t too, tʃ chop, θ thing, v voice, w was, z zoo, ʒ treasure

of wife or sometimes daughter of a peer; title of wife of a knight or baronet. (c) **Our Lady** = the Virgin Mary. **la•dy•bug, ladybird,** *n.* type of small beetle, usu. red with black spots. **la•dy•kill•er,** *n. inf.* man who is attractive to women. **la•dy•like,** *adj.* well-mannered/polite (as a lady should be). **la•dy•ship,** *n.* *(form of address to a titled lady)* **Your Ladyship.**

lag [læg] 1. *n.* (*in time*) space/interval, esp. between two parts of an event. 2. *v.* (**lagged**) (a) to go/fall/be behind. (b) to cover (a heating appliance, pipes, etc.) to prevent heat loss or to prevent freezing. **lag•gard** ['lægəd] *n.* person who is behind the others. **lag•ging,** *n.* material for wrapping around pipes.

la•ger ['lɑːgə] *n.* type of light beer.

la•goon [lə'guːn] *n.* area of sea water almost completely surrounded by land, esp. by a coral island.

laid [leɪd] *v. see* **lay. laid-back,** *adj. inf.* unhurried/relaxed.

lain [leɪn] *v. see* **lie.**

lair ['leə] *n.* resting place of a wild animal.

laird ['leəd] *n.* (*in Scotland*) owner of a country estate.

lais•sez-faire [leseɪ'fɜə] *adj.* (economy) where the government does not interfere on principle.

la•i•ty ['leɪɪti] *n.* people who have not been trained as priests.

lake [leɪk] *n.* (a) (large) inland stretch of water. (b) type of reddish dye.

lam [læm] *v. inf.* to hit.

la•ma ['lɑːmə] *n.* Buddhist priest, esp. in Tibet. **la•ma•ser•y,** *n.* monastery for lamas.

lamb [læm] 1. *n.* (a) young sheep. (b) flesh of sheep used as food. 2. *v.* to give birth to a lamb. **lamb•ing** ['læmɪŋ] *n.* giving birth to lambs. **lambs•wool,** *n.* (*no pl.*) very soft wool.

lam•baste, lambast [læm'beɪst] *v.* to criticize (s.o.) sharply.

lame [leɪm] 1. *adj.* (**-er, -est**) (a) unable to walk properly. (b) weak/unsatisfactory. 2. *v.* to injure (s.o.) so that he cannot walk properly. **lame duck,** *n.* person/company in difficulties and having to rely on outside support. **lame•ly,** *adv.* in a weak way. **lame•ness,** *n.* being lame.

la•mé ['lɑːmeɪ] *n.* cloth with gold or silver threads.

la•mel•la [læ'melə] *n.* (*pl.* **-ae**) thin scale.

la•ment [lə'ment] 1. *n.* (a) song/music for mourning. (b) expression of grief; complaint. 2. *v.* to be very sad about (the death of s.o.). **lam•en•ta•ble** ['læməntəbl] *adj.* very bad. **lam•en•ta•bly,** *adv.* very badly.

lam•en•ta•tion [læmən'teɪʃn] *n.* expression of great sorrow.

lam•i•nat•ed ['læmɪneɪtɪd] *adj.* (a) formed in thin layers. (b) covered with a thin layer of plastic. **lam•i•na•tion** [læmɪ'neɪʃn] *n.* process of covering with a thin plastic film.

lamp [læmp] *n.* object which produces light. **lamp•light,** *n.* light from a lamp. **lamp•post,** *n.* large post which holds a street lamp. **lamp•shade,** *n.* (decorative) cover to put over a lamp.

lam•poon [læm'puːn] 1. *n.* writing which makes s.o. seem ridiculous. 2. *v.* to ridicule (s.o.) in writing.

lam•prey ['læmprɪ] *n.* edible fish, like an eel.

lance [lɑːns] 1. *n.* type of long spear. 2. *v.* to cut (a wound/an abscess, etc.) with a lancet. **lance cor•po•ral,** *n.* (*in the U.S. Marine Corps*) enlisted person above a private first class and below a corporal. **lanc•er,** *n.* soldier in a regiment which used to be armed with lances. **lan•cet,** *n.* (a) pointed two-edged surgical knife. (b) tall thin pointed window.

land [lænd] 1. *n.* (a) solid part of the earth's surface. (b) earth/soil. (c) country. (d) farm areas as distinguished from urban areas. 2. *v.* (a) to come to land; to bring to land. (b) to bring a fish out of water and onto the land; to obtain (a good job). (c) to give/to deal (a blow). (d) **to l. (up) in** = to arrive/to reach. **land•ed,** *adj.* owning land. **land•fall,** *n.* seeing land for the first time from sea or air. **land•fill,** *n.* disposing of refuse in holes in the ground. **land•ing,** *n.* (a) (*esp. of aircraft*) touching land; **l. gear** = wheels on which an aircraft lands. (b) space at the top of a flight of stairs. **land•ing net,** *n.* net at the end of a long pole, for taking fish out of water. **land•ing stage,** *n.* (floating) platform where passengers can leave boats. **land•la•dy,** *n.* (a) woman from whom you rent a house/room, etc. (b) woman who runs a hotel or inn, etc. **land•locked,** *n.* (sea/harbor) surrounded by land. **land•lord,** *n.* (a) man from whom you rent a house/room, etc. (b) man who runs a hotel or inn, etc. **land•lub•ber,** *n. inf.* person who is not used to going on ships. **land•mark,** *n.* (a) object on land which you can see easily, esp. one used by ships to find out their position. (b) outstanding/important event, etc. **landmine,** *n.* mine hidden in the ground. **land•own•er,** *n.* person who owns land. **land•scape** ['lændskeɪp] 1. *n.* (a) scenery/appearance of the countryside; **l. gardening** = making a garden more beautiful by making artificial lakes, hills, planting trees, etc. (b) painting of a country scene. 2. *v.* to improve (a garden) by creating small hills/lakes, planting trees, etc. **land•scape gar•den•er,** *n.* person who designs the layout of large gardens/pieces of land. **land•slide,** *n.* (a) slipping of large amounts of earth, etc., down a hillside. (b) overwhelming event, esp. an electoral victory in which one party is totally defeated. **land•ward,** *adj. & adv.* toward the land. **land•wards,** *adv.* toward the land.

lan•dau ['lændɔ:] *n.* horse-drawn carriage with a folding top.

lane [leɪn] *n.* (a) narrow road, often in the country. (b) way/road for traffic, usu. in a particular direction; **shipping lanes** = routes followed by ships; **bus l.** = part of a road where only buses may drive.

lan•guage ['læŋgwɪdʒ] *n.* (a) way of speaking of a country/a group of people; **l. laboratory** = room with tape recorders where students can study foreign languages. (b) way of speaking; **bad l.** = swearing. (c) human speech. (d) means of communication, esp. signs, letters and other symbols used to instruct a computer.

lan•guid ['læŋgwɪd] *adj.* slow-moving/lacking energy. **lan•guid•ly,** *adv.* lazily. **lan•guish** ['læŋgwɪʃ] *v.* to become weak/ill, often because of sorrow. **lan•guor** ['læŋgə] *n.* (a) lack of energy. (b) tender emotional mood. **lan•guor•ous,** *adj.* slow-moving/lazy.

lank [læŋk] *adj.* (a) (*of hair*) straight/dull/lifeless. (b) (*of person*) thin/drooping. **lank•i•ness,** *n.* being lanky. **lank•y,** *adj.* (-ier, iest) tall/thin/awkward (person).

lan•o•lin ['lænəlɪn] *n.* fat from sheep's wool used in skin creams.

lan•tern ['læntən] *n.* lamp with a covering to protect it, which can be carried in the hand.

lan•yard ['lænjəd] *n.* string worn around your neck or shoulder with a whistle, etc., on it.

lap [læp] 1. *n.* (a) your body from waist to knees, when you are sitting; **in the l. of luxury** = in great luxury. (b) one complete circuit (of a racecourse). 2. *v.* (**lapped**) (a) (*of animal*) to drink with the tongue. (b) (**up**) to take in greedily. (c) (*of waves*) to wash against (the shore/the edge of sth). (d) to go so fast that you are a whole lap ahead of (another competitor). (e) to fold (sth) so that it overlaps. **lap dog,** *n.* small pet dog. **lap•top,** *n.* small computer which can be held on the lap.

la•pel [lə'pel] *n.* part of collar of coat, etc., which folds back.

lap•i•dar•y ['læpɪdərɪ] *adj.* (a) referring to stones (esp. precious stones). (b) very short and precise (statement).

lap•is laz•u•li [læpɪs'læzjulaɪ] *n.* bright blue stone.

lapse [læps] 1. *n.* (a) failure to do sth properly. (b) interval of time, esp. when sth does not take place. 2. *v.* (a) to fail/to cease to do sth. (b) to cease to be valid. (c) to fall into a lower/less active state.

lap•wing ['læpwɪŋ] *n.* bird found in fields.

lar•board ['lɑ:bəd] *n.* (*old*) port side (of ship).

lar•ce•ny ['lɑ:snɪ] *n.* crime of stealing.

larch [lɑ:tʃ] *n.* (*pl.* -es) cone-bearing tree which loses its leaves in winter.

lard [lɑ:d] 1. *n.* melted down pig fat used in cooking. 2. *v.* to cover (meat) with bacon or lard; to fill (a speech) with quotations, etc.

lard•er ['lɑ:də] *n.* room/cupboard for storing food.

large [lɑ:dʒ] *adj.* (-er, -est) (a) (very) big. (b) **at l.** = (i) free/not imprisoned; (ii) in general. **large•ly,** *adv.* mostly/for the most part. **large-scale,** *adj.* in a large way/involving large numbers of people or large sums of money.

lar•gess, largesse [lɑ:'dʒes] *n.* generous giving of gifts or money.

lar•go ['lɑ:gəu] *adv. & n.* (piece of music) which is played slowly.

lar•i•at ['lærɪət] *n.* lasso.

lark [lɑ:k] 1. *n.* (a) bird which sings and flies high in the sky. (b) *inf.* prank; joke. 2. *v. inf.* to have fun/play jokes. **lark•spur,** *n.* plant with tall spikes of flowers.

lar•rup ['lærəp] *v. inf.* to beat (s.o.) up.

lar•va ['lɑ:və] *n.* (*pl.* -vae [-vi:]) early stage of development of an insect, different in form from the adult.

lar•ynx ['lærɪnks] *n.* (*pl.* -es) upper part of the windpipe, where sounds are made by the voice. **lar•yn•gi•tis** [lærɪn'dʒaɪtɪs] *n.* inflammation of the larynx causing a sore throat.

la•sa•gne [lə'zænjə] *n.* type of pasta which is made of wide flat strips.

las•civ•i•ous [lə'sɪvɪəs] *adj.* full of sexual desire. **las•civ•i•ous•ly,** *adv.* in a lascivious way. **las•civ•i•ous•ness,** *n.* being lascivious.

la•ser ['leɪzə] *n.* instrument which produces a highly concentrated beam of light; **l. printer** = printer that uses a laser beam to produce

---

æ back, ɑ: farm, ɒ: top, aɪ pipe, aʊ how, aɪə fire, aʊə flower, ɔ: bought, ɔɪ toy, ə fed, eəhair, eɪ take, ə afraid, əʊ boat, əʊə lower, ʌ: word, i: heap, ɪ hit, ɪə hear, u: school, ʊ book, ʌ but, b back, d dog, ð then, dʒ just, f fog, g go, h hand, j yes, k catch, l last, m mix, n nut, ŋ sing, p penny, r round, s some, ʃ short, t too, tʃ chop, θ thing, v voice, w was, z zoo, ʒ treasure

high-quality print; **l. treatment** = medical treatment using a laser beam.

lash [læʃ] 1. *n.* (*pl.* -es) (a) stroke with a whip. (b) flexible part of a whip. (c) eyelash. 2. *v.* (a) to beat (sth) wth a whip. (b) to make a movement like beating with a whip. (c) to fasten/to tie down tightly with rope/string. **lash•ing**, *n.* (a) whipping. (b) tying/binding with rope, etc. **lash out**, *v.* to **l. o. at** = to become (unexpectedly) very angry at/to try to hit.

lass [læs], **las•sie** ['læsɪ] *n.* (*pl.* -es) *inf.* girl; young woman.

Las•sa fe•ver ['læsə'fiːvə] *n.* fatal viral disease which originated in Africa.

las•si•tude ['læsɪtjuːd] *n.* (*formal*) tiredness.

las•so [lə'suː] 1. *n.* (*pl.* -os) rope with looped end for catching horses/cattle, etc. 2. *v.* to catch (animals) with a lasso.

last [lɑːst] 1. *adj.* (a) placed/coming at the end (of a list/line/period of time); **l. thing at night** = at the very end of the day; **l. but one** = the one before the end one; **l. but not least** = at the end of a list, but not because it is the least important; **the l. straw** = last of a series of events etc. which leads to a loss of patience, tolerance, etc.; **the l. word in hats** = the very latest fashion; **the l. person I would want to go on vacation with** = the most unlikely person. (b) most recent; **l. Monday; l. week.** 2. *n.* (a) shape on which a shoe is made or repaired. (b) final thing/period/sight; **at (long) l.** = in the end/after a long time; **to the l.** = till the very end. 3. *adv.* (a) at the end. (b) most recently. 4. *v.* to continue (to exist); to remain in good condition. **last•ing**, *adj.* which continues for a long time. **last•ly**, *adv.* at the end/finally. **Last Sup•per**, *n.* last meal take by Christ with his disciples.

latch [lætʃ] 1. *n.* (*pl.* -es) fastening for a door, etc., consisting of a small bar which fits into a catch. 2. *v.* (a) to close with a latch. (b) *inf.* to **l. on to sth** = to seize/to obtain. **latch•key**, *n.* key for a front door; **l. child** = child who has a key to the house and lets himself in when he comes home from school because both parents are at work.

late [leɪt] 1. *adj.* (-er, -est) (a) at a time after that decided/intended; **the train is ten minutes l.** (b) at/toward the end of a period of time. (c) at/toward/past the end of a season. (d) **latest** = last/most recent. (e) (*formal*) referring to s.o. who has died; **my l. father.** 2. *adv.* (-er, -est) (a) after the appointed time. (b) after a certain time. **late•com•er**, *n.* person who arrives after others/after the appointed time. **late•ly**, *adv.* during recent days/weeks. **late•ness**, *n.* being late.

la•tent ['leɪtənt] *adj.* present but not developed.

lat•er•al ['lætərəl] *adj.* referring to the side; (fin) on the side of a fish's body. **lat•er•al•ly**, *adv.* toward the side.

lat•er•ite ['lætəraɪt] *n.* hard clay, like rock.

la•tex ['leɪteks] *n.* milky juice from a rubber tree.

lath [lɑːθ] *n.* narrow thin strip of wood.

lathe [leɪð] *n.* machine for holding and turning wood/metal, so that it can be shaped.

lath•er ['lɑːðə] 1. *n.* (a) mass of (soap) bubbles. (b) (*esp. on horse*) frothy sweat; **to be in a l.** = to be upset/flustered. 2. *v.* (a) to make (sth) form a lather; to form a lather. (b) to cover with lather.

Lat•in ['lætɪn] 1. *n.* (a) language formerly spoken by the Romans. (b) person from Italy, Spain, Portugal or South America. 2. *adj.* (a) referring to the language of ancient Rome. (b) referring to Italy, Spain, Portugal and South America; **L. America** = countries in South and Central America where Spanish or Portuguese is spoken.

lat•i•tude ['lætɪtjuːd] *n.* (a) breadth of view/tolerance/scope. (b) position on the earth's surface measured in degrees north or south of the equator; **northern latitudes** = in areas north of the equator.

la•trine [lə'triːn] *n.* lavatory in a military camp or prison.

lat•te ['lætei, 'lɑːtei] *n.* coffee made with hot milk.

lat•ter ['lætə] 1. *adj.* (a) second thing mentioned (of two). (b) recent; of the final part/period. **lat•ter•ly**, *adv.* recently.

lat•tice ['lætɪs] *n.* pattern (of pieces of wood in a fence, etc.) made of crisscross diagonal lines; **l. window** = window with small panes and lead frames forming a crisscross pattern.

laud [lɔːd] *v.* (*formal*) to praise. **laud•a•ble**, *adj.* worthy of praise. **laud•a•bly**, *adv.* in a laudable way. **laud•a•to•ry**, *adj.* containing praise.

lau•da•num ['lɔːdnəm] *n.* opium in alcohol, used as a sedative.

laugh [lɑːf] 1. *n.* sound made to express amusement/happiness; **to do sth for a l.** = to do it for amusement only/as a joke. 2. *v.* (a) to make sounds which express amusement/happiness; **to l. up one's sleeve** = to laugh secretly. (b) **to l. at** = to make fun of. **laugh•a•ble**, *adj.* only worth laughing at; ridiculous. **laugh•ing gas**, *n.* gas which makes you laugh when you breathe it, used esp. by dentists as an anesthetic. **laugh•ing stock**, *n.* person whom everyone makes fun of. **laugh•ter**, *n.* (sound/act of) laughing.

launch [lɔːntʃ] 1. *n.* (*pl.* -es) (a) type of small motor boat. (b) act of launching (boat/rocket/new project, etc.). 2. *v.* (a) to put (a boat/ship) into the water, esp. for the first time. (b) to send off (a rocket into the air). (c) to give (sth/s.o.) a start. **launch•ing pad**, *n.* starting platform for a rocket, etc.

laun•dry ['lɔ:ndrɪ] *n.* (a) place where clothes/sheets, etc., are washed. (b) clothes/sheets, etc. for washing, or which have been washed. **laun•der**, *v.* (a) to wash clothes. (b) *inf.* to pass (illegal profits, etc.) into the conventional banking system. **laun•der•ette, laundrette** ['lɔ:ndret] *n.* laundry with coin-operated washing machines for public use. **Laun•dro•mat** ['lɔ:ndrəmæt] *n.* trademark for a launderette. **laun•dress**, *n.* woman who washes laundry.

lau•re•ate ['lɔ:rɪət] *n.* person who has been awarded a prize; **Poet L.** = leading poet who is asked to write commemorative verse for special occasions.

lau•rel ['lɒrəl] *n.* tree with smooth shiny evergreen leaves; **to rest on your laurels** = to enjoy your past success, without trying to gain more.

la•va ['lɑ:və] *n.* molten material flowing from a volcano which becomes solid when it cools.

lav•a•to•ry ['lævətrɪ] *n.* (a) small room with facilities for washing the hands and face and a toilet. (b) toilet.

lav•en•der ['lævɪndə] *n.* (a) plant with sweet-smelling bluish-purple flowers. (b) bluish-purple color.

lav•ish ['lævɪʃ] 1. *adj.* (a) generous/ample (helping of food, etc.). (b) extravagant/over-generous. 2. *v.* (**on** s.o.) to give (over-)generously. **lav•ish•ly**, *adv.* in a lavish way. **lav•ish•ness**, *n.* being lavish.

law [lɔ:] *n.* (a) rules by which a country is governed and the people controlled. (b) rule/controlling force; **to lay down the l.** = to state sth in a dogmatic way. (c) process of upholding the rules of a country. **law-a•bid•ing**, *adj.* obeying the law. **law•court**, *n.* court where cases are heard and justice is administered. **law•ful**, *adj.* according to law/legal. **law•ful•ly**, *adv.* in a lawful way. **law•less**, *adj.* wild/uncivilized; paying no attention to law. **law•less•ness**, *n.* being lawless. **law•suit**, *n.* legal case. **law•yer**, *n.* person who has studied law and can advise people on legal matters.

lawn [lɔ:n] *n.* (a) (area of) short grass in a garden; **l. tennis** = tennis played on grass. (b) very fine cotton material. **lawn•mow•er**, *n.* machine for cutting grass.

lax [læks] *adj.* (-er, -est) loose/not rigid. **lax•a•tive**, *adj. & n.* (substance) which helps to loosen the bowels. **lax•i•ty, laxness**, *n.* being loose/not being rigid.

lay [leɪ] 1. *adj.* (a) (person) who is not trained as a priest. (b) not belonging to a profession or specialization. 2. *n.* (*old*) short narrative poem. 3. *v.* (**laid**) (a) to place/to put, often in a horizontal position. (b) to place in the right position; **to l. a carpet.** (c) (*of bird*) to produce (an egg). (d) to make (a bet). (e) to set/to place dishes, etc. on (a table); **l. the table for three.** (f) to set (a trap/a scene). (g) *see also* **lie. lay a•side, lay by**, *v.* to put (sth) away for future use. **lay down**, *v.* to put (sth) down/to give (sth) up. **lay•er.** 1. *n.* (a) (horizontal) thickness of sth. (b) shoot which is layered. 2. *v.* to make a new plant by attaching a shoot to the ground so that it takes root. **lay fig•ure**, *n.* large doll used by artists as a model. **lay in**, *v.* to store for future use. **lay in•to**, *v. inf.* to attack/to hit (s.o.). **lay•man**, *n.* (*pl.* **-men**) person who does not belong to a particular profession or specialization. **lay off**, *v.* to dismiss (workers) temporarily. (b) *inf.* to stop doing sth. **lay-off**, *n.* temporary dismissal from work. **lay on**, *v.* to put on. **lay out**, *v.* (a) to place in an orderly way, esp. on a table, etc. (b) to make a design for (a garden/a book, etc.). (c) to spend (money). (d) to prepare (a corpse) for burial. **lay•out**, *n.* design, esp. of a garden/a book. **lay up**, *v.* (a) to store (away). (b) **to be laid up** = to be ill in bed.

lay•ette [leɪ'et] *n.* clothes for a new-born baby.

la•zy ['leɪzɪ] *adj.* (-ier, -iest) not wanting to do any work. **laze**, *v.* to do nothing or very little. **la•zi•ly**, *adv.* in a lazy way. **la•zi•ness**, *n.* being lazy. **la•zy•bones**, *n. inf.* person who does not like work/who does nothing.

lb [paʊnd] *abbrev. for* pound (in weight).

LCD *abbrev. for* liquid crystal display.

lea [li:] *n.* field used for pasture; meadow.

leach [li:tʃ] *v.* to remove a substance from soil, etc., by passing water through it.

lead[1] [led] *n.* (a) (*element:* Pb) heavy soft bluish-gray metal. (b) weight at the end of a rope, used for measuring the depth of water. (c) writing part of a pencil. **lead•en** ['ledn] *adj.* of/like lead; **l. sky** = dull gray sky.

lead[2] [li:d] 1. *n.* (a) front position/first action; **to go into the l./to take the l.** (b) (*in cards*) right to play first. (c) leash to keep a dog in control. (d) electric wire, etc., which joins an appliance to its source of power. (e) (actor who plays a) main role. (f) amount by which one is ahead. 2. *v.* (**led** [led]) (a) to go/to be ahead; to show the way; to go toward. (b) to be the first/to have the most important place. (c) to make (sth) have; to have; **it led me to think she was lying** = made me think. (d) to be at the head of/to direct. (e) (*in cards*) to play as first card; to play first. (f) to go in a particular direction. **lead•er** ['li:də] *n.* (a) person who manages/directs others. (b) chief player, esp. of the violin, in an orchestra. **lead•er•ship**, *n.* being the person who manages/directs others. **lead•ing**, *adj.* which leads; most important; **l. article** = main article in a newspaper, giving views on topics of current interest; **l. lady/man** = actress/actor taking the main role; **l. question** = question which is worded in order to get a particular answer. **lead on**, *v.* to go ahead, so that others will follow; to encourage (s.o.) to go on, esp. to do sth stupid. **lead time**, *n.* time between placing an order and receiving the goods. **lead up to**, *v.* to prepare the way for sth (in conversation).

leaf [li:f] 1. *n.* (*pl.* **leaves** [li:vz]) (a) flat, usu. green, part of a plant, growing from a stem or branch; **trees in l.** = with leaves. (b) sheet of paper forming two pages of a book; **to turn over a new l.** = to change your ways/to try to improve. (c) flat folding part (of a table). (d) very thin sheet of metal, etc. 2. *v.* **to l. through the pages of a book** = to turn them over rapidly without reading. **leaf•let**, *n.* sheet of paper, often folded, giving information as an advertisement. **leaf mold**, *n.* compost made of rotted leaves. **leaf•y**, *adj.* covered with leaves.

league [li:g] 1. *n.* (a) group joined together for some purpose; **in l. with s.o.** = working with s.o. against s.o. else. (b) association of sports clubs which play against each other. (c) (*old*) measure of distance (about 3 miles). 2. *v.* to join together/to form a group for a particular purpose.

leak [li:k] 1. *n.* (a) hole through which liquid/gas, etc., can escape or enter; **the canoe sprang a l.** = got a hole. (b) escape of secret information. 2. *v.* (a) (*of liquid/gas, etc.*) to flow away/to escape. (b) (*of container*) to allow liquid/gas, etc., to escape or enter. (c) to pass on (secret information). **leak•age**, *n.* (a) action of leaking. (b) amount of liquid, etc., which has escaped. **leak•y**, *adj.* which leaks.

lean [li:n] 1. *adj.* (**-er, -est**) (a) thin/with little flesh. (b) (*of meat*) with little fat. (c) poor/unproductive. 2. *n.* meat with little fat. 3. *v.* (**leaned,** (*esp. Brit.*) **lent** [lent]) (a) to support (yourself/sth) (**on** sth/s.o.). (b) to stand/to be in

a position at an angle. (c) to have a tendency **toward. lean•ing,** *n.* tendency **toward**/interest in. **lean•ness,** *n.* being thin. **lean o•ver,** *v.* to bend (in a particular direction); **to l. o. backward to help** = make every effort to help. **lean-to,** *n.* (small) building supported against the wall of a larger building.

leap [li:p] 1. *n.* (a) jump. (b) upward/forward movement; **to advance by leaps and bounds** = to make rapid progress; **l. in the dark** = action where you are unsure of the consequences. 2. *v.* (**leaped/leapt** [lept]) (a) to jump. (b) to rise suddenly. **leap at,** *v.* to seize/to accept eagerly. **leap•frog.** 1. *n.* game in which one person jumps over the bent back of another. 2. *v.* (**leapfrogged**) to jump over s.o.'s bent back. **leap year,** *n.* every fourth year, in which February has 29 days.

learn [lɜːn] *v.* (**learned/learnt** [lɜːnd/lɜːnt]) (a) to gain knowledge of (sth)/of how to do (sth). (b) to hear (news, etc.). **learn•ed** ['lɜːnɪd] *adj.* (a) (person) who has much knowledge. (b) (journal) for specialists. **learn•er,** *n.* person who is learning. **learn•ing,** *n.* (a) gaining knowledge of sth/of how to do sth. (b) great study/knowledge.

lease [li:s] 1. *n.* renting of a building/piece of land, etc., for a specified period; **it's given him a new l. on life** = it's made him want to make a fresh start/to live more fully. 2. *v.* (a) (*also* **lease out**) to take/to give on a lease. (b) to hold on a lease. **lease•hold.** 1. *n.* (holding of) property on a lease. 2. *adj.* held on a lease. **lease•hold•er,** *n.* person who holds a property on a lease.

leash [li:ʃ] *n.* (*pl.* **-es**) strap/cord to keep a dog in control.

least [li:st] 1. *adj. & n.* (of) the smallest/most unimportant (amount). 2. *adv.* in the smallest way.

leath•er ['leðə] *n.* skin of certain animals, used to make shoes/bags, etc. **leath•er•jack•et,** *n.* grub of a fly. **leath•er•y,** *adj.* (tough) like leather.

leave [li:v] 1. *n.* (a) permission. (b) time off; permission to be away. (c) **to take l. of** = to say goodbye to; **to take l. of one's senses** = to become quite mad. 2. *v.* (**left** [left]) (a) to go away (from). (b) to allow to remain behind/to forget to take; **l. me alone** = don't pester me; **l. it to me** = let me deal with it. (c) to abandon. (d) to give (sth) **to** s.o. in your will. (e) to have at the time of one's death. **leave behind,** *v.* to forget to take (s.o./sth) with you. **leave off,** *v.* to stop. **leave out,** *v.* to forget/to omit (sth).

leav•en ['levn] 1. *n.* substance which causes a dough to rise; thing which causes a change for the better. 2. *v.* to add leaven to (dough); to cause a change.

Leb•a•nese [lebə'ni:z] 1. *adj.* referring to Lebanon. 2. *n.* (*pl.* **Lebanese**) person from Lebanon.

lech•er ['letʃə] *n.* man who frequently indulges in sex. **lech•er•ous,** *adj.* indulging in sex. **lech•er•y,** *n.* indulgence in sex.

lec•tern ['lektən] *n.* stand with a sloping surface on which you can put a book/papers, etc., from which you are going to read aloud in public.

lec•ture ['lektʃə] 1. *n.* (a) talk, esp. to students or other group of people on a particular subject. (b) (long) scolding. 2. *v.* to give a lecture (**on** sth). **lec•tur•er,** *n.* (a) person who gives a talk on a particular subject. (b) teacher in a university or college below an assistant professor. **lec•ture•ship,** *n.* position as a lecturer.

led [led] *v. see* **lead²**.

ledge [ledʒ] *n.* flat (narrow) part which sticks out from a cliff or building.

ledg•er ['ledʒə] *n.* book in which accounts are kept. **led•ger line,** *n.* leger line.

lee [li:] *n.* side of a ship sheltered from the wind; **l. shore** = shore toward which the wind is blowing. **lee•ward,** *adj., adv. & n.* (side of a ship) sheltered from the wind. **lee•way,** *n.* extra time/extra space.

leech [li:tʃ] *n.* (*pl.* **-es**) (a) type of worm which sucks blood. (b) (*old inf.*) doctor.

leek [li:k] *n.* vegetable related to the onion, with white stem and long green leaves.

leer ['lɪə] 1. *n.* nasty sideways look, often expressing sexual desire. 2. *v.* to look with a leer (**at** s.o.).

lees [li:z] *n. pl.* sediment left at the bottom of a wine bottle, etc.

left [left] 1. *n.* (a) side of the body which normally has the weaker hand. (b) left hand/fist. (c) (*in politics*) group/policy having liberal or radical views. 2. *adj.* (a) of/on the side of the body which normally has the weaker hand; **l. bank** = bank of a river, etc., on your left when facing down stream. (b) of the left (in politics). 3. *adv.* on/to the left. 4. *see also* **leave.** **left-handed,** *adj.* using the left hand more than the right. **left•ist,** *adj. & n.* (person) who is on the left politically. **left•o•vers,** *n. pl.* what is not used, esp. food which has not been eaten. **left-wing,** *adj.* politically on the left. **left-wing•er,** *n.* person who is on the left politically.

leg [leg] 1. *n.* (a) part of the body on which a person or animal walks; **to be on one's last legs** = to be almost exhausted; **to give s.o. a l. up** = to help him to climb to a higher position; **to pull s.o.'s l.** = to joke by telling him sth untrue. (b) leg of an animal used for food. (c) part of a garment which covers the leg. (d) part of a piece of furniture which supports. (e) section of a race/journey. 2. *v. inf.* **to l. it** = to walk. **leg•ged** [legd, 'legɪd] *suffix meaning* with legs; **four-legged animal. leg•gings,** *n. pl.* thick coverings for the lower legs. **leg•gy,** *adj.* with long legs. **leg•less,** *adj.* without any legs. **leg-pull,** *n. inf.* hoax. **leg warm•ers,** *n. pl.* knitted garments for the legs, like like long socks with no feet.

leg•a•cy ['legəsɪ] *n.* what is left to a person (after s.o.'s death). **leg•a•tee** [legə'ti:] *n.* person who receives a legacy.

le•gal ['li:gl] *adj.* (a) in accordance with/obeying the law; **l. aid** = free legal representation given to people without enough money to pay lawyers' fees; **l. tender** = money which must legally be accepted if you give it in payment. (b) referring to the (processes of the) law. **le•gal•is•tic** [li:gə'lɪstɪk] *adj.* too concerned with the law. **le•gal•i•ty** [lɪ'gælɪtɪ] *n.* being allowed by law. **le•gal•ize,** *v.* to authorize (sth) by law. **le•gal•ly,** *adv.* in accordance with the law.

leg•ate ['legət] *n.* official envoy (from the Pope). **le•ga•tion** [lɪ'geɪʃn] *n.* group of officials who represent their government in a foreign country; building where they live and work.

leg•end ['ledʒənd] *n.* (a) story from the past which may not be based on fact. (b) key to symbols used on a map. **leg•end•ar•y,** *adj.* referring to a legend.

leg•er•de•main [ledʒədə'meɪn] *n.* trickery; conjuring.

leg•er line ['ledʒə'laɪn] *n.* small line on a musical score, written above or below the normal five lines.

leg•i•ble ['ledʒɪbl] *adj.* clear/able to be (easily) read. **leg•i•bil•i•ty** [ledʒɪ'bɪlɪtɪ] *n.* being easily read. **leg•i•bly,** *adv.* in a legible way.

le•gion ['li:dʒən] *n.* (a) division of an army. (b) association/body, esp. of soldiers; **the Foreign L.** = private army, organized by France, which serves overseas. (c) very large number. **le•gion•naire,** *n.* member of a legion, such as the Foreign Legion; **legionnaires' disease** =

æ back, ɑ: farm, ɒ top, aɪ pipe, aʊ how, aɪə fire, aʊə flower, ɔ: bought, ɔɪ toy, e fed, eəhair, eɪ take, ə afraid, əʊ boat, əʊə lower, ɜ: word, i: heap, ɪ hit, ɪə hear, u: school, ʊ book, ʌ but, b back, d dog, ð then, dʒ just, f fog, g go, h hand, j yes, k catch, l last, m mix, n nut, ŋ sing, p penny, r round, s some, ʃ short, t too, tʃ chop, θ thing, v voice, w was, z zoo, ʒ treasure

disease, similar to pneumonia, caused by bacteria in air-conditioning systems.

leg•is•late ['ledʒɪsleɪt] v. to make laws. **leg•is•la•tion** [ledʒɪ'sleɪʃn] n. (making of) laws. **leg•is•la•tive** ['ledʒɪslətɪv] adj. referring to laws/law-making. **leg•is•la•tor**, n. person who makes laws. **leg•is•la•ture** ['ledʒɪslətʃə] n. law-making body.

le•git•i•ma•cy [lɪ'dʒɪtɪməsɪ] n. being in accordance with the law. **le•git•i•mate**, adj. (a) legal/lawful; (child) born to married parents. (b) reasonable/justifiable. **le•git•i•mate•ly**, adv. in accordance with the law; correctly. **le•git•i•mize**, v. to make legitimate.

leg•ume ['legjuːm] n. plant (like a pea or bean) which has seeds in pods. **le•gu•mi•nous** [le-'gjuːmɪnəs] adj. (plant) which has seeds in pods.

lei•sure ['leʒə] n. time free to do what you want; **at your l.** = when there is an opportunity/without hurry; **l. pursuits** = pastimes. **lei•sured**, adj. having plenty of leisure; **l. classes** = people who do not need to work to earn money. **lei•sure•ly**, adj. without hurry.

leit•mo•tiv ['laɪtməʊtiːf] n. theme (in music) which reappears and which shows a special feeling/state.

lem•ming ['lemɪŋ] n. small Scandinavian mammal which travels in groups and is said to fall blindly over cliffs into the sea.

lem•on ['lemən] n. pale yellow sour-tasting fruit; tree which bears such fruit. **lem•on•ade** [lemə'neɪd] n. drink made with lemon juice, water, and sometimes, sugar.

le•mur ['liːmə] n. monkeylike animal with a long tail.

lend [lend] v. (**lent**) (a) to give (sth to s.o.) for a certain period of time; **will you l. me your book for a day or two?** (b) to give/to contribute (to); **to l. a hand** = to help; **to lend itself to** = to be suitable for. **lend•er**, n. person who lends (money). **lend•ing li•brar•y**, n. section of a library from which books may be taken away for a time.

length [leŋθ] n. (a) measurement of how long sth is from end to end; **he won the race by a l.** = by the length of a horse/man/boat, etc. (b) piece of sth of a particular length; **a l. of rope.** (c) being long; **a stay of some l.** = quite a long stay; **at l.** = (i) at last; (ii) for a long time. (d) **to go to great lengths** = to make great efforts. **length•en**, v. to make/to become longer. **length•i•ly**, adv. for a long time/at length. **length•i•ness**, n. being long. **length•wise, lengthways**, adv. along the length/along the longest side. **length•y**, adj. (**-ier, -iest**) (very) long.

le•ni•en•cy, lenience ['liːnjəns(ɪ)] n. being merciful/not being strict. **le•ni•ent**, adj. showing mercy/not strict or severe. **le•ni•ent•ly**, adv. in a lenient way.

lens [lenz] n. (pl. **-es**) (a) piece of glass/plastic, etc., curved so as to cause light rays to join or spread out, and used in glasses/telescopes/cameras, etc. (b) part of the eye. (c) **contact l.** = small lens worn on the eyeball to help you to see.

lent [lent] v. see **lend**.

Lent [lent] n. (in the Christian church) period before Easter when many Christians eat less/give up some luxury. **Lent•en**, adj. referring to Lent.

len•til ['lentl] n. small round dried seed used as food.

Le•o ['liːəʊ] n. one of the signs of the Zodiac, shaped like a lion. **le•o•nine** ['liːəʊnaɪn] adj. referring to a lion.

leop•ard ['lepəd] n. large spotted animal of the cat family. **leop•ard•ess**, n. female leopard.

le•o•tard ['lɪəʊtɑːd] n. skintight one-piece costume worn by ballet dancers.

lep•er ['lepə] n. person who has leprosy. **lep•ro•sy**, n. serious infectious skin disease which slowly destroys flesh and nerves. **lep•rous**, adj. like leprosy.

lep•i•dop•ter•a [lepɪ'dɒptərə] n. pl. group of insects, including butterflies and moths.

lep•re•chaun ['leprəkɔːn] n. (in Irish folklore) wicked little elf.

les•bi•an ['lezbɪən] adj. & n. (woman) who is sexually attracted to other women. **les•bi•an•ism**, n. state of being lesbian.

le•sion ['liːʒn] n. wound; change in body tissue.

less [les] 1. adj. & n. (of a) smaller quantity/size/value. 2. prep. minus/with a certain amount taken away. 3. adv. in a smaller amount/to a smaller degree. **less•en**, v. to make (sth) become less; to reduce. **less•er**, adj. smaller.

les•see [le'siː] n. person who holds a lease/who pays rent. **les•sor** [le'sɔː] n. person who gives a lease/who receives rent.

les•son ['lesn] n. (a) period of time in school, etc., during which you are taught. (b) means by which you learn; **he's learned his l.** = he is wiser; **to teach s.o. a l.** = to make s.o. wiser/to punish s.o. (c) part of the Bible which is read in church.

lest [lest] conj. (a) (formal) in order to avoid. (b) for fear that.

let [let] 1. v. (**let**) (a) to permit/to allow. (b) to lend (a house, etc.) for a period of time in return for money. 2. v. (showing command/suggestion) **let's hurry; don't let's start yet.** 3. n. inf. period of lease of a property. **let a•lone,**

adv. not to mention. **let down,** *v.* (a) to take down/to lower. (b) to fail to help/to disappoint. **let•down,** *n.* disappointment. **let go,** *v.* (a) to lose hold (**of** sth). (b) to allow (s.o.) to leave. **let in,** *v.* (a) to allow to come in. (b) **to let yourself in for** = to allow yourself to get involved in (a difficult situation). **let off,** *v.* (a) to make (a gun, etc.) fire. (b) **to let s.o. off** = not to punish s.o. after all. **let on,** *v. inf.* to tell a secret. **let out,** *v.* (a) to allow to go out/to escape. (b) to lend for a period of time in return for money. (c) to make (a garment, etc.) wider. **let up,** *v.* to stop/to become less. **let-up,** *n.* stopping/slackening.

le•thal ['liːθl] *adj.* deadly/causing death.

leth•ar•gy ['leθədʒɪ] *n.* (feeling of) unwillingness to do anything; lack of energy. **le•thar•gic** [lə'θɑːdʒɪk] *adj.* feeling/appearing unwilling to do anything; lacking energy.

let's [lets] *short for* **let us.**

let•ter ['letə] 1. *n.* (a) written/printed symbol representing a sound of speech; **to the l.** = to the last detail. (b) piece of writing sent from one person/organization to another to pass on information. (c) **letters** = literary learning. 2. *v.* to mark with letters. **let•ter•head,** *n.* printed heading on writing paper. **let•ter•ing,** *n.* (a) writing letters. (b) letters in an inscription, etc. **let•ter•press,** *n.* method of printing using metal letters.

let•tuce ['letɪs] *n.* green vegetable whose leaves are often used in salads.

leu•ko•cyte ['ljuːkəʊsaɪt] *n.* white blood cell.

leu•ke•mi•a [luːˈkiːmɪə] *n.* serious, often fatal, illness, which increases the white cells in the blood.

lev•ee ['levɪ] *n.* embankment built along the bank of a river which is liable to flood.

lev•el ['levl] 1. *n.* (a) flat/horizontal position; **on the l.** = (i) in a flat position; (ii) *inf.* straight/honest. (b) position in relation to height and depth; position on a scale/in a list. (c) instrument for testing whether sth is horizontal or not. 2. *adj.* (a) flat/even/horizontal. (b) (**with**) at the same level as. (c) calm/even; *inf.* **to do one's l. best** = one's very best. 3. *v.* (**leveled, levelled**) (a) to make/to become level; **they leveled the house to the ground** = they destroyed it completely. (b) to point/to aim (an accusation) **at** s.o. **lev•el-head•ed,** *adj.* calm/able to act sensibly. **level with,** *v. inf.* to speak frankly.

lev•er ['liːvə] 1. *n.* instrument such as a bar

which helps to raise a heavy object, or to move part of a machine, etc. 2. *v.* to move with a lever. **lev•er•age,** *n.* (a) force of a lever. (b) influence which you can use to reach your aims. **lev•er•aged buy•out,** *n.* buying a company, using the company's assets as security for the money bo:rowed to buy it.

lev•er•et ['levrət] *n.* young hare.

le•vi•a•than [lɪˈvaɪəθən] *n.* huge powerful monster or machine.

lev•i•tate ['levɪteɪt] *v.* (*of person/heavy body*) to rise into the air. **lev•i•ta•tion** [levɪˈteɪʃn] *n.* rising into the air.

lev•i•ty ['levɪtɪ] *n.* disrespectful way of considering serious things.

le•vy ['levɪ] 1. *n.* (a) demand for/collection of (a tax/a number of soldiers). (b) tax/number of soldiers (which has been collected). 2. *v.* to demand/to collect (a tax/a number of soldiers).

lewd [luːd] *adj.* (-er, -est) indecent/rude. **lewd•ly,** *adv.* in a lewd way. **lewd•ness,** *n.* lewd action.

lex•i•con ['leksɪkən] *n.* dictionary. **lex•i•cog•ra•phy** [leksɪˈkɒgrəfɪ] *n.* writing of dictionaries. **lex•i•cog•ra•pher,** *n.* person who writes dictionaries.

ley [leɪ] *n.* lea.

li•a•ble ['laɪəbl] *adj.* (a) (legally) responsible (**for** sth). (b) apt/likely (**to** do sth). **li•a•bil•i•ty** [laɪəˈbɪlɪtɪ] *n.* (a) debt; obligation; **he couldn't meet his liabilities** = he couldn't pay his debts. (b) disadvantage; handicap.

li•ai•son [lɪˈeɪzɒn] *n.* joining/relationship/connection; **l. officer** = person responsible for dealings with another group. **li•aise,** *v.* to join with others, esp. for discussion (**with** s.o.).

li•ar ['laɪə] *n.* person who tells lies.

lib [lɪb] *n. inf. short for* **liberation.**

li•ba•tion [laɪˈbeɪʃn] *n.* (*formal*) drink offered to a god.

li•bel ['laɪbl] 1. *n.* untrue statement(s) in writing, damaging to s.o.'s character. 2. *v.* (**libeled, libelled**) to damage s.o.'s character in writing. **li•bel•ous,** *adj.* (writing) which libels s.o.

lib•er•al ['lɪbrəl] 1. *adj.* (a) wide in views/meaning, etc. (b) ample/generous. (c) (*in politics*) having views/policies based on freedom of individuals, democratic reform, etc. 2. *n.* (*in politics*) person having liberal views; **Liberal** = member or supporter of a liberal party or policy. **lib•er•al•ism,** *n.* (*in politics*) liberal views/policies. **lib•er•al•i•ty** [lɪbəˈrælɪtɪ] *n.* (a) being open-minded. (b) generosity. **lib•er•al•i•za•tion** [lɪbərəlaɪˈzeɪʒn] *n.* act of liberalizing. **lib•er•al•ize** [ˈlɪbərəlaɪz] *v.* to make (laws, etc.) more liberal; to become more liberal. **lib•er•al•ly**, *adv.* in a liberal way.

lib•er•ate [ˈlɪbəreɪt] *v.* to set/to make (s.o./sth) free (**from** sth). **lib•er•a•tion** [lɪbəˈreɪʃn] *n.* setting free. **lib•er•a•tor**, *n.* person who sets s.o. free. **lib•er•tar•i•an** [lɪbəˈteərɪən] *n.* person who believes in freedom of thought and action. **lib•er•tine** [ˈlɪbətiːn] *n.* man who is sexually immoral. **lib•er•ty** [ˈlɪbətɪ] *n.* freedom; **at l.** = free/not in captivity; **to take liberties** = to do sth without permission; **to take liberties with sth/s.o.** = to treat sth./s.o. too familiarly.

li•bi•do [lɪˈbiːdəu] *n.* (*pl.* **-os**) sexual urge. **li•bid•i•nous**, *adj.* full of sexual urge.

Li•bra [ˈliːbrə] *n.* one of the signs of the zodiac, shaped like a pair of scales.

li•brar•y [ˈlaɪbrərɪ] *n.* (a) place where books are stored (to be read/borrowed/consulted). (b) collection of books. **li•brar•i•an** [laɪ-ˈbreərɪən] *n.* person who works in a library. **li•brar•i•an•ship**, *n.* art of being a librarian.

li•bret•to [lɪˈbretəu] *n.* (*pl.* **-os**) words of an opera. **li•bret•tist**, *n.* person who writes a libretto.

Lib•y•an [ˈlɪbjən] 1. *adj.* referring to Libya. 2. *n.* person from Libya.

lice [laɪs] *n. pl. see* **louse.**

li•cense [ˈlaɪsəns] 1. *n.* (a) (document giving) official permission to have/to do sth. (b) freedom, esp. when used too much or wrongly. (c) **poetic l.** = use of language in poetry which would not be acceptable in prose. 2. *v.* to give (s.o.) official permission to do sth. **li•cen•see** [laɪsənˈsiː] *n.* holder of a license. **li•cen•ti•ate** [laɪˈsenʃɪət] *n.* person who has been licensed to practice a profession.

li•cen•tious [laɪˈsenʃəs] *adj.* indulging in sex or other pleasures beyond what is normally permitted. **li•cen•tious•ness**, *n.* excessive indulgence in sex.

li•chen [ˈlaɪkən] *n.* flat gray/yellow/green plant which grows on stones or on other plants.

lic•it [ˈlɪsɪt] *adj.* legal.

lick [lɪk] 1. *n.* (a) stroke with the tongue. (b) *inf.* speed. (c) *inf.* **a l. and a promise** = a quick job of doing something. 2. *v.* (a) to taste/to stroke with the tongue; **to l. s.o.'s boots** = to behave very humbly toward s.o. to gain favor; **to l. into shape** = to put into proper form, as through hard work or discipline. (b) to beat/to hit. (c) *inf.* to defeat (in a game). **lick•ing**, *n.* (a) stroking with the tongue. (b) beating. (c) *inf.* defeat.

lic•o•rice [ˈlɪkərɪs] *n.* black substance from the root of a plant, used in medicine and in candy and liquor.

lid [lɪd] *n.* (a) covering for a container, often with a handle. (b) eyelid/covering of the eye.

lie [laɪ] 1. *n.* (a) statement which is not true; **to give the l. to** = to prove (sth) is wrong. (b) position/direction in which sth is situated. 2. *v.* (a) (**lied, lying**) to say something which is not true. (b) (**lay, lying, has lain**) to be in a horizontal position; **he lay dead on the ground.** (c) to be. **lie down**, *v.* to put yourself in a horizontal position (**on** sth); **they won't take that lying down** = they won't accept it without protest. **lie low**, *v.* to hide.

lie•der [ˈliːdə] *n.* German romantic song.

liege [liːdʒ] *n.* (*old*) lord (to whom people give service).

li•en [ˈlɪən] *n.* legal right to take and hold s.o.'s goods until a debt is paid.

lieu [ljuː] *n.* **in l. of** = instead of.

lieu•ten•ant [luːˈtenənt] *n.* rank in the armed forces (*in the army below* captain, *in the navy below* lieutenant-commander); **l.-colonel** = rank in the army below colonel; **l.-commander** = rank in the navy below commander.

life [laɪf] *n.* (*pl.* **lives** [laɪvz]) (a) state of being alive; **run for your lives** = as fast as you can; **I can't for the l. of me understand** = I can't understand at all; **not on your l.** = not under any circumstances. (b) liveliness/energy. (c) living things; **is there l. on Mars?** (d) (length of) time you are alive; **in early l.** = when he was a child; **l. insurance** = insurance paid if you die; **l. imprisonment** = imprisonment for the rest of your life. (e) story of s.o.'s life. **life•belt**, *n.* cork-filled ring to keep s.o. afloat. **life•boat**, *n.* boat used to rescue people at sea. **life cy•cle**, *n.* life of an animal/plant through various stages. **life•guard**, *n.* person who rescues people who get into difficulties while swimming. **life jack•et**, *n.* buoyant jacket to keep s.o. afloat. **life•less**, *adj.* (a) not alive. (b) not lively. **life•like**, *adj.* (*of a picture, etc.*) looking like the real person/thing. **life•line**, *n.* rope thrown to a drowning person; help given to s.o. in difficulties. **life•long**, *adj.* lasting your whole life. **life pre•serv•er**, *n.* lifebelt/life jacket. **lif•er**, *n.* person who is serving a sentence of life imprisonment. **life-sav•ing**, *n.* rescuing people from drowning. **life-size(d)**, *adj.* (statue/painting, etc.) which is the same size as the real thing or person. **life•style**, *n.* way in which s.o. or a group of people live their daily lives; **life•style busi•ness**, *n.* small business primarily run to allow the owner to pursue personal interests rather than to maximize profits. **life•time**, *n.* time when you are alive; **the chance of a l.** = the best chance you are ever likely to get.

lift [lɪft] 1. *n.* (a) (act of) raising. (b) ride in a car. (c) *Brit.* elevator; **ski l.** = device to take skiers to the top of a ski slope. 2. *v.* (a) to raise (to a higher position). (b) to take plants or tubers out of the ground. (c) to take away/to remove (a ban). (d) *inf.* to steal. (e) (*of fog/clouds*) to rise. **lift-off**, *n.* vertical take-off of a space rocket.

lig•a•ment ['lɪgəmənt] *n.* tough tissue which holds bones together.

li•ga•ture ['lɪgətʃʊə] *n.* thread used for tying in surgical operations; link between two printed letters.

light [laɪt] 1. *n.* (a) brightness which allows you to see; **don't stand in my l.** = between me and the source of light. (b) bulb/object which gives light. (c) **in l. of what he said** = in consideration of it; **to throw l. on sth** = make it clearer; **to come to l.** = be discovered. (d) appearance/aspect. (e) means of making a cigarette, etc., catch fire. (f) *pl.* **lights** = (i) lungs of certain animals used as food; (ii) traffic lights. 2. *v.* (**lit**) (a) to make (sth) start to burn. (b) to give light to. 3. *adj.* (**-er, -est**) (a) having a lot of light, allowing you to see well. (b) pale (color). (c) not heavy; **she's a l. sleeper** = wakens easily. (d) not serious; **to make l. of** = to treat as unimportant. 4. *adv.* (to travel) with little luggage. **light•en**, *v.* (a) to make lighter/not so dark. (b) to make lighter/not so heavy. **light•er**, *n.* (a) small instrument for making cigarettes, etc., burn. (b) boat used for loading other boats. **light•er•man**, *n.* (*pl.* **-men**) man who works on a lighter. **light-fin•gered**, *adj.* (person) who is likely to steal. **light-head•ed**, *adj.* dizzy; feeling excited. **light-heart•ed**, *adj.* cheerful/without a care. **light heav•y•weight**, *n.* weight in boxing between middleweight and heavyweight. **light•house**, *n.* tall building containing a light to guide ships. **light•ly**, *adv.* in a light way; **l. dressed** = wearing thin clothes; **to get off l.** = with little or no punishment. **light•ness**, *n.* being light. **light pen**, *n.* pen with a tip which is sensitive to light, and which can "read" lines or images and transfer them to a computer. **light•ship**, *n.* ship which carries a large light, acting as a floating lighthouse. **light up**, *v.* (a) to give light to (sth). (b) to become bright. (c) to start to smoke a cigar, cigarette, or pipe. **light•weight.** 1. *n.* (a)

weight in boxing between featherweight and welterweight. (b) person without much influence. 2. *adj.* (a) light (clothes). (b) not very influential/important. **light year**, *n.* distance traveled by light during one year (about six trillion miles).

light•ning ['laɪtnɪŋ] 1. *n.* flash of electricity in the sky, followed by thunder; **like l.** = very fast; **l. rod** = rod for carrying a lightning charge straight to the ground to prevent damage to buildings. 2. *adj.* extremely fast.

lig•nite ['lɪgnaɪt] *n.* brown coal.

like [laɪk] 1. *adj.* (nearly) the same/similar. 2. *prep.* in the same way as/the same as/similar to; **I feel l. some chocolate** = I would like to eat some chocolate. 3. *n.* similar thing(s). 4. *adv.* **l. as not** = probably. 5. *conj.* in the same way as. 6. *v.* (a) to have pleasant feelings about. (b) to desire/to want. **like•a•ble**, *adj.* pleasant. **like•li•hood**, *n.* probability. **like•ly.** 1. *adj.* (**-ier, -iest**) (a) probable. (b) suitable (for)/apt (to). 2. *adv.* probably; **not l.!** = certainly not. **like-mind•ed**, *adj.* (person) who has the same opinions. **lik•en** ['laɪkən] *v.* **to l. sth to sth** = to compare, by showing how one thing is similar to another. **like•ness**, *n.* thing which looks like s.o./sth. **likes**, *n. pl.* (a) **l. and dislikes** = things you like and don't like. (b) *inf.* **the l. of him** = people like him. **like•wise**, *adv.* (a) in the same way. (b) similarly/the same. **lik•ing**, *n.* pleasant feeling towards s.o.; fondness for s.o./sth.

li•lac ['laɪlək] *n.* (a) tree with clusters of (pale) purple or white flowers. (b) pale purple color.

lil•li•pu•tian [lɪlɪ'pjuːʃn] *adj.* very small.

lilt [lɪlt] 1. *n.* song/way of speaking with a light well-marked rhythm. 2. *v.* to sing/to play a tune with a light well-marked rhythm. **lilt•ing**, *adj.* (song) which has a lilt.

lil•y ['lɪlɪ] *n.* type of white flower which grows from a bulb. **lil•y-of-the-val•ley**, *n.* spring plant with small white flowers growing in clusters.

li•ma bean ['liːməbiːn] *n.* bean with flat pale seeds.

limb [lɪm] *n.* (a) leg/arm/wing. (b) branch of a tree; **out on a l.** = in a difficult/exposed situation.

lim•ber ['lɪmbə] *v.* **to l. up** = to do exercises to warm your muscles before taking part in a sporting contest.

lim•bo ['lɪmbəʊ] *n.* (a) place between heaven and hell, where unbaptized people are said to

---

æ **back**, ɑː **farm**, ɒ **top**, aɪ **pipe**, aʊ **how**, aɪə **fire**, aʊə **flower**, ɔː **bought**, ɔɪ **toy**, e **fed**, eə **hair**, eɪ **take**, ə **afraid**, əʊ **boat**, əʊə **lower**, ɜː **word**, iː **heap**, ɪ **hit**, ɪə **hear**, uː **school**, ʊ **book**, ʌ **but**, b **back**, d **dog**, ð **then**, dʒ **just**, f **fog**, g **go**, h **hand**, j **yes**, k **catch**, l **last**, m **mix**, n **nut**, ŋ **sing**, p **penny**, r **round**, s **some**, ʃ **short**, t **too**, tʃ **chop**, θ **thing**, v **voice**, w **was**, z **zoo**, ʒ **treasure**

go when they die. (b) position of not being accepted or rejected; being halfway between two stages. (c) **l. dancing** = West Indian dance where the dancer bends his body backwards parallel to the floor to pass under a horizontal bar.

lime [laɪm] *n.* (a) white substance containing calcium, used in making cement. (b) small yellowish-green tropical fruit like a lemon; tree which bears such fruit. (c) northern deciduous tree with smooth leaves and yellowish flowers. **lime green,** *adj. & n.* green color of lime. **lime•light,** *n.* attention/publicity. **lime•stone,** *n.* light-colored stone containing calcium.

lim•er•ick ['lɪmərɪk] *n.* type of amusing five-line poem.

lim•it ['lɪmɪt] 1. *n.* furthest point/extent; boundary; end (beyond which you cannot go); *inf.* **that's the l.** = too much. 2. *v.* to put a limit on/to keep within limits; not to allow (sth) to go beyond a certain point. **lim•i•ta•tion** [lɪmɪ'teɪʃn] *n.* (a) act of limiting. (b) thing which stops you going further; **to know your limitations** = to know what you are capable of doing.

limn *v.* (a) to draw or describe sth. (b) to highlight sth, esp. with bright colors.

lim•ou•sine [lɪmə'ziːn] *n.* large luxurious car, with a partition between the driver and the passenger.

limp [lɪmp] 1. *n.* way of walking unevenly. 2. *v.* to walk with an uneven step. 3. *adj.* without stiffness/soft; without energy. **limp•ly,** *adv.* in a limp way. **limp•ness,** *n.* being limp.

lim•pet ['lɪmpɪt] *n.* cone-shaped shellfish which clings to rocks.

lim•pid ['lɪmpɪd] *adj.* clear. **lim•pid•i•ty** [lɪm'pɪdɪtɪ] *n.* (*formal*) being clear.

linch•pin ['lɪnʃpɪn] *n.* (a) pin which goes through an axle to hold a wheel on. (b) very important person/piece of machinery.

lin•dane ['lɪndeɪn] *n.* powerful insecticide.

lin•den ['lɪndən] *n.* (*formal*) lime tree.

line [laɪn] 1. *n.* (a) (long) thin mark; **to draw the l. at** = to stop short of/not to do. (b) long wire/cord. (c) **telephone l.** = cable along which telephone messages are sent; **the l.'s bad** = it is difficult to make out what s.o. is saying; **crossed l.** = two telephone conversations which intermingle by error. (d) row of people/cars/words, etc.; *inf.* **to drop s.o. a l.** = to send a short letter; **l. printer** = computer printer which prints each line separately. (e) number of people or things waiting one behind the other for sth. (f) tracks on which trains run. (g) shipping/air company. (h) sequence of ancestors/descendants. (i) **lines** = shape/outline; general design. (j) direction;

method; course of action; **in l. with** = according to/following (a decision); **to take a hard l.** = to be aggressive/not to weaken in any way. (k) type of work/goods. 2. *v.* (a) to put lines on. (b) to form a line along the edge of a street, etc. (c) to put a layer of material inside (a piece of clothing); **to l. one's pockets** = to make money (usu. dishonestly). **lin•e•age** ['lɪnɪɪdʒ] *n.* line of descendants (from an ancestor). **lin•e•al** ['lɪnɪəl] *adj.* (descendant) in direct line. **lin•e•a•ments,** *n. pl.* outline of the face/features. **lin•e•ar** ['lɪnɪə] *adj.* referring to lines/to length. **line•man,** *n.* (*pl.* **-men**) man who installs or repairs electric/telephone/railroad lines. **lin•er,** *n.* (a) thing used for lining. (b) large passenger ship. **line up,** *v.* to form a line. **line-up,** *n.* row/list of people. **lin•ing,** *n.* layer of material inside sth.

lin•en ['lɪnɪn] *n.* (a) cloth made from flax. (b) **(household) l.** = sheets/pillowcases/tablecloths, etc.; **to wash your dirty l. in public** = tell shameful personal secrets.

ling [lɪŋ] *n.* (a) type of small edible fish. (b) heather.

lin•ger ['lɪŋgə] *v.* (a) to wait/to remain/to stay longer than necessary/expected. (b) (*of sick person*) to remain alive.

lin•ge•rie ['læn̈ʒərɪ] *n.* women's underwear.

lin•go ['lɪŋgəʊ] *n. Sl.* language.

lin•gua fran•ca [lɪŋgwə'fræŋkə] *n.* language used by speakers of various languages as a common means of communication.

lin•gual ['lɪŋgwəl] *adj.* referring to the tongue.

lin•guist ['lɪŋgwɪst] *n.* (a) person who knows foreign languages well. (b) person who studies linguistics. **lin•guis•tic** [lɪŋ'gwɪstɪk] *adj.* (a) referring to language(s). (b) referring to the science of language. **lin•guis•tics,** *n.* science of language.

lin•i•ment ['lɪnɪmənt] *n.* oily substance which you rub on the skin to lessen pains.

link [lɪŋk] 1. *n.* (a) ring which forms part of a chain. (b) thing which connects two parts. 2. *v.* to join. **link•age,** *n.* act of linking.

links [lɪŋks] *n. pl.* golf course.

lin•net ['lɪnɪt] *n.* small singing bird.

li•no•cut ['laɪnəʊkʌt] *n.* design printed from a block of linoleum which has been cut into a pattern. **li•no•le•um** [lɪ'nəʊlɪəm] *n.* hard smooth floor covering.

lin•seed ['lɪnsiːd] *n.* seed of flax.

lint [lɪnt] *n.* soft cloth used for putting on wounds.

lin•tel ['lɪntl] *n.* piece of wood/stone over a door or window.

li•on ['laɪən] *n.* large wild animal of the cat family, the male of which has a long mane; **the l.'s share** = the biggest part. **li•on•ess,** *n.* female lion. **li•on•ize**, *v.* to treat (s.o.) as very important.

lip [lɪp] *n.* (a) one of two fleshy parts round the outside of the mouth; **to keep a stiff upper l.** = not to show emotion in time of trouble; **to smack one's lips over** = to express great enjoyment of. (b) *Sl.* impudence/rudeness. (c) edge of a bowl/cup, etc. **lipped**, *adj.* with lips. **lip•read**, *v.* (**lipread** ['lɪpred]) (*of a deaf person*) to follow speech by watching the movements of the lips of the person speaking. **lip serv•ice**, *n.* **to pay l. s. to sth** = to give a false impression of respecting/obeying sth. **lip•stick**, *n.* (stick of) substance for coloring the lips.

lip•id ['lɪpɪd] *n.* fatty substance in the tissue in human bodies.

liq•ue•fy ['lɪkwɪfaɪ] *v.* to become liquid; to make (sth) become liquid. **liq•ue•fac•tion** [lɪkwɪ'fækʃn] *n.* making/becoming liquid.

li•queur [lɪ'kɜː] *n.* strong alcoholic drink.

liq•uid ['lɪkwɪd] 1. *n.* substance which flows easily like water, and which is neither a gas nor a solid. 2. *adj.* (a) which is neither gas nor solid, and which flows easily; **l. crystal display** = display panel, where the figures appear black. (b) (*of assets, etc.*) able to be changed easily into cash. (c) (*of sounds*) pure/clear. **liq•ui•date**, *v.* (a) (*of a company*) to settle accounts by selling assets to pay off debts. (b) to pay (a debt). (c) *inf.* to kill. **liq•ui•da•tion** [lɪkwɪ'deɪʃn] *n.* the settling of accounts by selling assets to pay off debts. **liq•ui•da•tor**, *n.* person authorized to liquidate assets. **liq•uid•i•ty** [lɪ'kwɪdɪtɪ] *n.* (*in finance*) being able to change assets into cash. **liq•uid•ize**, *v.* to reduce fruit to liquid. **liq•uid•iz•er**, *n.* machine which liquidizes.

liq•uor ['lɪkə] *n.* (a) alcoholic drink. (b) liquid produced in cooking.

liq•uo•rice ['lɪkərɪs] *n. see* **lic•o•rice.**

li•ra ['lɪrə] *n.* unit of money used in Italy.

lisle [laɪl] *n.* fine cotton (used to make shirts, stockings, etc.).

lisp [lɪsp] 1. *n.* speech defect in which "s" is pronounced as "th". 2. *v.* to speak with a lisp.

lis•som ['lɪsəm] *adj.* lithe/supple.

list [lɪst] 1. *n.* (a) number of items written/spoken one after another; **wine l.** = list of wines available in a restaurant; **to be on the danger l.** = to be dangerously ill; **l. price** = price of sth as shown in a catalog. (b) (*of ship*) leaning to one side. (c) **to enter the lists** = to become involved

in sth, as a candidate in an election. 2. *v.* (a) to say/to write (a number of items) one after the other. (b) (*of ship*) to lean over to one side.

lis•ten ['lɪsn] *v.* to pay attention (**to** s.o./sth) in order to hear. **lis•ten•er**, *n.* person who listens.

lis•te•ri•a [lɪs'tiːərɪə] *n.* bacteria found in some foods and in domestic animals, which can cause infections such as meningitis.

list•less ['lɪstləs] *adj.* (feeling) dull, without interest or energy. **list•less•ly**, *adv.* in a way which lacks show of interest. **list•less•ness**, *n.* lack of interest/energy.

lit [lɪt] *v. see* **light.**

lit•a•ny ['lɪtənɪ] *n.* form of prayer with repeated responses, used in churches.

li•tchi ['laɪtʃɪ] *n.* small Chinese fruit, with a red skin and large stone.

li•ter, *Brit.* **li•tre** ['liːtə] *n.* measurement for liquids (almost 2 pints).

lit•er•a•cy ['lɪtərəsɪ] *n.* ability to read and write. **lit•er•al** 1. *adj.* keeping to the exact meaning of the original words. 2. *n.* typesetting mistake. **lit•er•al•ly**, *adv.* in a literal way; (*to emphasize*) **his eyes were l.** popping out of his head. **lit•er•al•ness**, *n.* being literal. **lit•er•ar•y**, *adj.* referring to literature. **lit•er•ate** ['lɪtərət] *adj.* (a) able to read and write. (b) well educated, esp. in literary subjects. **lit•er•a•ti** [lɪtə'rɑːtiː] *n. pl.* literary people. **lit•er•a•ture** ['lɪtrɪtʃə] *n.* (a) books/writing, esp. novels, poetry, drama, biography, etc. (b) what has been written on a particular subject. (c) written information about sth.

lithe [laɪð] *adj.* supple/bending easily.

lith•o•graph ['lɪθəgrɑːf] 1. *n.* painting/drawing, etc., reproduced by lithography. 2. *v.* to print by lithography. **lith•o•graph•ic** [lɪθə'græfɪk] *adj.* of lithography. **lith•og•ra•phy** [lɪ'θɒgrəfɪ] *n.* method of printing using oil and ink on a flat surface such as a stone/a sheet of metal, etc.

lit•i•gate ['lɪtɪgeɪt] *v.* to go to law; to bring a lawsuit against s.o. **lit•i•gant**, *n.* person involved in a lawsuit. **lit•i•ga•tion** [lɪtɪ'geɪʃn] *n.* (a) bringing a lawsuit against s.o. (b) lawsuit. **li•ti•gious** [lɪ'tɪdʒəs] *adj.* always ready to go to law.

lit•mus ['lɪtməs] *n.* blue substance which is turned red by an acid and back to blue by an alkali. **lit•mus pa•per**, *n.* paper containing litmus, used to test for acids and alkalis.

æ back, aː farm, ɒ top, aɪ pipe, aʊ how, aɪə fire, aʊə flower, ɔː bought, ɔɪ toy, e fed, eəhair, eɪ take, ə afraid, əʊ boat, aʊə lower, vː word, i heap, ɪ hit, ɪə hear, uː school, ʊ book, ʌ but, b back, d dog, ð then, dʒ just, f fog, g go, h hand, j yes, k catch, l last, m mix, n nut, ŋ sing, p penny, r round, s some, ʃ short, t too, tʃ chop, θ thing, v voice, w was, z zoo, ʒ treasure

li•tre ['liːtə] *n. see* **li•ter**.

lit•ter ['lɪtə] 1. *n.* (a) paper, etc. left on streets. (b) stretcher/bed on which a person is carried. (c) bedding of straw, etc., for animals. (d) (*of animals*) group of young born at one time. 2. *v.* (a) to drop paper, etc. about. (b) (*of animals*) to produce young.

lit•tle ['lɪtl] 1. *adj.* (**less, least**) (a) small; **his l. sister** = his younger sister. (b) **a l.** = small amount of. (c) not much. 2. *n.* small amount; **l. by l.** = gradually. 3. *adv.* (a) (by) a small amount; **I see him very l.** = not very often. (b) **he l. thought he would win** = he had no idea that he would win.

lit•to•ral ['lɪtɒrəl] *adj. & n.* (referring to the) coast.

lit•ur•gy ['lɪtədʒɪ] *n.* form of public service in church. **li•tur•gi•cal** [lɪ'tɜːdʒɪkl] *adj.* referring to liturgy.

live. 1. *adj.* [laɪv] (a) in a living state. (b) burning. (c) (*of broadcast*) not recorded. (d) carrying an electric current; (ammunition) which has not been exploded; *inf.* **l. wire** = very lively and energetic person. 2. *v.* [lɪv] (a) to be alive/to have life; **l. and let l.** = be tolerant. (b) to have your (place of) residence. (c) to lead a certain type of life; **he lives in style;** *inf.* **to l. it up** = to lead a life of wild parties, etc. (d) **to l. on** = to get food/money, etc., from. **live down,** *v.* to cause (a disgrace) to be forgotten; **he'll never l. it down** = it will never be forgotten. **live in,** *v.* to live in the building where you work. **live•li•hood** ['laɪvlɪhud] *n.* (way of getting) your means of living. **live•li•ness** ['laɪvlɪnəs] *n.* being lively. **live•long** ['lɪvlɒŋ] *adj.* (*formal*) **the l. day** = all the day. **live•ly** ['laɪvlɪ] *adj.* (**-ier,   -iest**) bright/wide-awake/(very) active. **liv•en,** *v.* to make lively. **live•stock** ['laɪvstɒk] *n.* animals kept on a farm. **liv•ing** ['lɪvɪŋ] 1. *adj.* alive. 2. *n.* (a) (way of) life. (b) means of subsistence. (c) **the l.** = people who are alive. **liv•ing room,** *n.* room in a house for general use.

liv•er ['lɪvə] *n.* organ in the lower part of the body which helps the digestion by producing bile; animal's liver used as food. **liv•er•ish,** *adj.* feeling rather sick and unwell; irritable.

liv•er•y ['lɪvrɪ] *n.* (a) special clothing of a group of servants/of an organization. (b) care of horses for payment; **l. stable** = place where horses may be looked after and may also be hired. **liv•er•ied,** *adj.* wearing a livery.

liv•id ['lɪvɪd] *adj.* (a) of the dark gray color of lead. (b) extremely angry.

liz•ard ['lɪzəd] *n.* type of reptile with four legs and scales.

lla•ma ['lɑːmə] *n.* thick-haired camellike animal found in South America.

lo [ləu] *inter.* (*old*) look!

load [ləud] 1. *n.* (a) heavy object(s) which have to be carried. (b) (*on vehicle*) what has to be/what is being transported. (c) amount of material transported. (d) amount of power carried by an electric circuit. (e) thing which is difficult to bear; **that's a l. off my mind** = I feel much less worried. (f) *inf.* **loads of** = plenty/lots. 2. *v.* (a) to put (esp. sth heavy) **into/on to.** (b) to put ammunition into (a gun)/to put film into (a camera); to put a disk program into a computer. (c) **to l. s.o. with** = to give large quantities to. **load•ed,** *adj.* (a) *inf.* having a lot of money. (b) **l. question** = question which is worded in such a way so as to trap the person who answers. (c) (dice) which has a secret weight in it. **load•er,** *n.* person who loads.

loaf [ləuf] 1. *n.* (*pl.* **loaves** [ləuvz]) (large) piece of bread baked separately. 2. *v.* to wander about/to waste time doing nothing. **loaf•er,** *n.* (a) person who does nothing all day. (b) light casual shoe with no laces.

loam [ləum] *n.* fertile soil which crumbles easily. **loam•y,** *adj.* crumbly fertile (soil).

loan [ləun] 1. *n.* (a) lending. (b) thing lent (esp. a sum of money from a bank). 2. *v.* to lend.

loath [ləuθ] *adj.* very unwilling.

loathe [ləuð] *v.* to hate very much. **loath•ing,** *n.* feeling of hate/disgust (**for**). **loath•some,** *adj.* disgusting/horrible.

lob [lɒb] 1. *n.* ball which is hit high into the air. 2. *v.* (**lobbed**) to throw/hit (a ball) slowly in a high curve.

lob•by ['lɒbɪ] 1. *n.* entrance hall/corridor. 2. *v.* to try to influence (s.o.) (esp. in order to get a bill through a legislature).

lobe [ləub] *n.* (a) lower curved part of the ear. (b) division of the lungs/brain/liver, etc. **lo•bar,** *adj.* referring to a lobe. **lo•bot•o•my** [lə'bɒtəmɪ] *n.* operation to remove a lobe.

lo•bel•ia [lɒ'biːlɪə] *n.* low plant with blue flowers.

lob•ster ['lɒbstə] *n.* shellfish with a long body, two large claws, and eight legs, used as food. **lob•ster pot,** *n.* cage left in the sea to catch lobsters.

lo•cal ['ləukl] 1. *adj.* referring to a place/district; near at hand; **l. anesthetic** = which numbs a particular area of the body. 2. *n.* person who lives in a district, esp. the district where you live. **lo•cale** [ləu'kɑːl] *n.* place where sth takes place. **lo•cal•i•ty** [ləu'kælɪtɪ] *n.* area/district. **lo•cal•ize** ['ləukəklaɪz] *v.* to set in a particular place; to be confined to a particular area. **lo•cal•ly,** *adv.* in the (same) district. **lo•cate** [ləu'keɪt] *v.* (a) to find (the position of). (b) **to be located** = to be in a particular position. **lo•ca•tion** [ləʊ'keɪʃn] *n.* (a) finding the position of sth. (b) place/position. (c) **on l.** = (filming) which takes place in a real setting, not in a studio.

loch [lɒk] *n.* (*in Scotland*) lake; arm of the sea.

lock [lɒk] 1. *n.* (a) device for closing a door/container, etc., by means of a key; **under l. and key** = shut up securely. (b) part in a gun by which it is fired; **l., stock, and barrel** = (everything) all together. (c) section of a canal/river with barriers which can be opened or closed to control the flow of water, thus allowing boats to move up or down to different levels. (d) bundle of hair hanging together. 2. *v.* (a) to close (a door/a box, etc.) with a key. (b) to fix/to become fixed in a certain position. **lock•a•ble,** *adj.* which can be locked. **lock•er,** *n.* small compartment for personal belongings which you can close with a key; **l. room** = room in a sports stadium where players change and leave their clothes in lockers. **lock•jaw,** *n.* disease where your jaws become closed tight together. **lock•nut,** *n.* second nut, used to keep the first nut in place. **lock out,** *v.* to prevent (s.o.) from going in by locking the door. **lock•out,** *n.* industrial dispute in which employees are kept out of the factory until they agree to certain terms. **lock•smith,** *n.* person who makes/repairs locks. **lock up,** *v.* (a) to close (a building) by locking doors. (b) to keep (a person/thing) inside by locking doors, etc. **lock•up,** *n.* prison cell.

lock•et ['lɒkɪt] *n.* small ornamental case to hold a picture/lock of hair, etc., worn round the neck.

lo•co•mo•tive [ləʊkə'məʊtɪv] 1. *adj.* referring to movement. 2. *n.* engine of a train. **lo•co•mo•tion,** *n.* (power of) movement.

lo•cus ['ləʊkəs] *n.* (*pl.* **loci** ['ləʊsaɪ]) point, line, curve, etc., in a technical diagram.

lo•cust ['ləʊkəst] *n.* insect, like a large grasshopper, which destroys crops.

lode [ləʊd] *n.* vein of metal ore. **lode•star,** *n.* pole star. **lode•stone,** *n.* magnetic iron ore.

lodge [lɒdʒ] 1. *n.* (a) small house, cabin, etc. used temporarily, as during vacations or hunting season. (b) small house or cottage on an estate or in a park, where a caretaker, gardener, etc. lives. (c) meeting place for a) group of freemasons, etc. (d) home of beavers. 2. *v.* (a) to rent a room (in a boarding house). (b) to be/to remain. (c) (*formal*) to make/to place (a complaint). **lodg•er,** *n.* person who

rents a room. **lodg•ing,** *n.* (a) accommodation. (b) **lodgings** = rented rooms.

lo•ess ['ləʊəs] *n.* yellow powdery earth found in China, North America, etc.

loft [lɒft] *n.* (a) top part of a house immediately under the roof; attic. (b) upper level in a church, etc. used for a special purpose. (c) **hay l.** = top part of a barn used for storing hay.

loft•y ['lɒftɪ] *adj.* (-ier, -iest) (a) very high. (b) arrogant/proud. **loft•i•ly,** *adv.* in a proud way.

log [lɒg] 1. *n.* (a) thick piece of a tree trunk/large branch; **to sleep like a l.** = very soundly; **as easy as falling off a l.** = very easy. (b) device for calculating the speed of a ship. (c) daily detailed record of speed/position/happenings, esp. on a ship. (d) *short for* **log•a•rithm.** 2. *v.* (**logged**) (a) to write down details of (sth which has happened) in a logbook. (b) to cover a (distance)/to spend (time). **log•book,** *n.* (*on ship, etc.*) book with record of a journey. **log•ging,** *n.* cutting trees for timber.

lo•gan•ber•ry ['ləʊgənberɪ] *n.* soft fruit, a cross between a blackberry and a raspberry.

log•a•rithm ['lɒgərɪðm] *n.* one of a set of numbers listed in such a way as to help with calculations by adding and subtracting instead of multiplying and dividing. **log•a•rith•mic** [lɒgə'rɪθmɪk] *adj.* referring to logarithms.

log•ger•heads ['lɒgəhedz] *n.* **to be at l.** = to quarrel or disagree with s.o.

log•gia ['lɒdʒɪə] *n.* covered gallery which is open on one side.

log•ic ['lɒdʒɪk] *n.* science of reasoning; power of reasoning clearly. **log•i•cal,** *adj.* (a) clearly reasoned. (b) (*of person*) able to reason clearly. **log•i•cal•ly,** *adv.* in a logical/reasonable way.

lo•gis•tics [lɒ'dʒɪstɪks] *n.* organization of the movement of supplies/people, etc.

lo•go ['lɒgəʊ] *n.* (*pl.* **-os**) symbol/design used by a company to identify its products.

loin [lɔɪn] *n.* (a) (meat from the) back of an animal. (b) **loins** = part of the body between the hips. **loin•cloth,** *n.* long cloth wrapped round the hips.

loi•ter ['lɔɪtə] *v.* to wander about slowly/aimlessly; to stand about. **loi•ter•er,** *n.* person who wanders/who is standing about.

loll [lɒl] *y.* (a) to sit/stand/lie in a lazy way. (b) (*of tongue*) to hang out.

æ back, ɑ: farm, ɒ: top, aɪ pipe, aʊ how, aɪe fire, aʊə flower, ɔ: bought, ɔɪ toy, e fed, eəhair, eɪ take, ə afraid, əʊ boat, aʊə lower, vː word, iː heap, ɪ hit, ɪə hear, uː school, ʊ book, ʌ but, b back, d dog, ð then, dʒ just, f fog, g go, h hand, j yes, k catch, l last, m mix, n nut, ŋ sing, p penny, r round, s some, ʃ short, t too, tʃ chop, θ thing, v voice, w was, z zoo, ʒ treasure

270 lollipop ▪ loose

lol•li•pop ['lɒlɪpɒp] *n.* candy on the end of a stick.

lol•lop ['lɒləp] *v. inf.* to walk with long clumsy steps.

lone [ləʊn] *adj.* alone; lonely; **l. wolf** = person who likes to be alone. **lone•ly,** *adj.* (a) with few or no people. (b) feeling sad because of being alone. **lone•li•ness,** *n.* being alone; feeling sad because you are alone. **lon•er,** *n.* person who prefers to be alone. **lone•some,** *adj.* lonely/sad because of being alone.

long [lɒŋ] 1. *adj.* (-er, -est) (a) measured in space from end to end; not short. (b) measured in time; **they stayed for a l. time.** 2. *adv.* for a long time; **all night l.** = for the whole night. (b) **as l. as** = while/since. (c) **so/as l. as** = provided that. 3. *n.* long time; **before l.** = in a short time; **for l.** = for a long time. 4. *v.* **to l. for** = to want very much. **long-dis•tance,** *adj.* (a) (*in sport*) (race) run between two places which are far apart. (b) (telephone call) made over a long distance. **long•hand,** *n.* ordinary writing (not shorthand). **long•horn,** *n.* type of cow with long horns. **long•ing,** *n.* great desire (**for** sth). **long johns,** *n. pl. inf.* long underpants. **long-lived,** *adj.* (person) who lives for a long time. **long-play•ing,** *adj.* (record) which plays for about 20 minutes each side. **long-range,** *adj.* which covers a long distance. **long•shore•man,** *n.* (*pl.* **-men**) person who works at a port, loading or unloading ships. **long shot,** *n.* attempt which has little chance of being successful. **long-sight•ed,** *adj.* able to see things at a distance more clearly than things which are close. **long•stand•ing,** *adj.* which has been arranged some time before. **long-suf•fer•ing,** *adj.* patient/tolerating much. **long-term,** *adj.* lasting/planned to last for a long time. **long-wind•ed,** *adj.* (person) who talks too much in a boring way; (talk) which lasts too long.

lon•gev•i•ty [lɒn'dʒevɪtɪ] *n.* very long life.

lon•gi•tude ['lɒndʒɪtjuːd] *n.* position on the earth's surface measured in degrees east or west of an imaginary line running through Greenwich, England. **lon•gi•tu•di•nal,** *adj.* which runs lengthwise. **lon•gi•tu•di•nal•ly,** *adv.* from end to end.

loo•fah ['luːfə] *n.* type of sponge, made from a dried pod.

look [lʊk] 1. *n.* (a) turning your eyes (often quickly) to see sth. (b) search (**for** sth). (c) appearance; the way sth/s.o. appears. (d) **good looks** = beauty/pleasing personal appearance. 2. *v.* (a) (**at**) to make efforts to see. (b) to stare at; **he looked me straight in the face.** (c) seem/to have the appearance of; **he looks ill;**

she **looks the part** = looks right for the job. **look af•ter,** *v.* to take care of. **look a•head,** *v.* to make plans for the future. **look•a•like,** *n. inf.* person who looks like s.o. else. **look at,** *v.* to make efforts to see/to examine/to consider. **look back,** *v.* (a) to turn around to see what is behind you. (b) to recall the past. **look back on,** *v.* to think about (sth) in the past. **look down,** *v.* **to look down on s.o./to look down your nose at s.o./sth** = to think you are better than s.o./to regard with disdain. **look•er-on,** *n.* (*pl.* **lookers-on**) person who is watching (without taking part). **look for,** *v.* to try to find. **look for•ward,** *v.* (**to**) to think about (sth) in the future (usu. with pleasure). **look in (on),** *v. inf.* to visit (s.o.) briefly. **look•ing glass,** *n.* mirror. **look in•to,** *v.* to examine/to find out about. **look on,** *v.* (a) to watch without taking part. (b) to consider/to think of sth as. **look out,** *v.* (a) (**on**) to have a view toward. (b) (**for**) to keep looking in order to find. (c) (**for**) to be careful of. **look•out,** *n.* (a) place from which you can see what is happening. (b) careful attention. (c) affair; **that's his l.** = he must deal with it himself. (d) person who watches. **look o•ver,** *v.* to examine. **look a•round,** *v.* (a) to turn to see behind you. (b) to examine all of a place. **look through,** *v.* (a) to examine the whole of (sth) (often quickly). (b) to pretend not to see. **look to,** *v.* (a) to expect (help) from. (b) (*formal*) to take care of. **look up,** *v.* (a) to turn your eyes in an upward direction. (b) to get better. (c) to try to find (sth) in a reference book, etc. (d) to get in contact with. **look up to,** *v.* to consider with respect/admiration.

loom [luːm] 1. *n.* machine on which cloth is woven. 2. *v.* to appear/to come into sight (gradually).

loon [luː] *n.* grebe.

loon•y ['luːnɪ] *adj. & n. inf.* mad (person). **loon•y bin,** *n. inf.* lunatic asylum.

loop [luːp] 1. *n.* (a) curve formed by a piece of thread/ribbon, etc. which crosses over itself. (b) thing of this shape. 2. *v.* to make a loop/loops; (*of aircraft*) **to l. the loop** = to fly in a complete circle vertically, turning upside down at the top. **loop•hole,** *n.* (a) narrow hole in a wall for shooting through. (b) means of escape/of avoiding (a law).

loose [luːs] 1. *adj.* (-er, -est) (a) not (fully) attached/not fixed; **to be at l. ends** = to have nothing special to do. (b) not tight. (c) with pieces separated. (d) **l. change** = money in coins only. (e) (translation) which is not very exact. (f) of doubtful morals. 2. *v.* to make (sth) become untied/to let (sth) go. 3. *adv.* not tightly. **loose•ly,** *adv.* (a) not tightly. (b) in an

inexact way. **loose•leaf,** *adj.* (book) of which the pages can be removed and replaced.
loos•en, *v.* to make (sth) less tight.
loose•ness, *n.* being loose.

loot [lu:t] 1. *n.* (a) things which have been taken. (b) *Sl.* money. 2. *v.* to steal. **loot•er,** *n.* person who steals (esp. from stores during a riot).

lop [lɒp] *v.* (**lopped**) to cut off (esp. tree branches).

lope [ləup] 1. *n.* running with long strides. 2. *v.* to run with long (slow) strides.

lop-eared ['lɒpɪəd] *adj.* (rabbit) with drooping ears.

lop•sid•ed [lɒp'saɪdɪd] *adj.* with one side larger/lower/heavier than the other.

lo•qua•cious [lɒ'kweɪʃəs] *adj.* (person) who talks a lot/too much. **lo•quac•i•ty** [lɒ'kwæsɪtɪ], **loquaciousness,** *n.* talking too much.

lord [lɔ:d] 1. *n.* (a) nobleman/ruler. (b) *Brit.* title for certain peers; **House of Lords** = upper chamber of the British Parliament. (c) **the Lord** = Jesus Christ. (d) *Brit.* title for men in certain positions (such as bishops/judges, etc.). (e) expression of surprise/shock; **Good Lord!** 2. *v.* **to l. it over s.o.** = to behave as if you are superior. **lord•li•ness,** *n.* (a) nobility. (b) pride. **lord•ly,** *adj.* (a) referring to the nobility. (b) proud/arrogant. **lord•ship,** *n. Brit.* (*form of address to a lord*) **Your Lordship.**

lore [lɔ:] *n.* (*no pl.*) traditional beliefs and knowledge.

lor•gnette [lɔ:'njet] *n.* glasses which you hold in front of your eyes with a handle.

lose [lu:z] *v.* (**lost** [lɒst]) (a) to stop having/owning (sth); **she lost her gloves** = did not know where they were; **they lost sight of it** = could no longer see it; **that joke was lost on him** = he did not understand it. (b) to fail to win. (c) to cause the loss of. (d) **to get lost/to l. your way** = to be/become unable to find the way to where you were going; *Sl.* **get lost!** = go away! (e) **to l. weight** = to become lighter. (f) (*of clock/watch*) to become/to go slow. **los•er,** *n.* person who does not win; **he's a bad l.** = behaves badly when he loses a game. **lost** [lɒst] *adj.* which has been lost; **to give sth up for l.** = have no hope of ever having it again; **he looks l.** = looks bewildered.

loss [lɒs] *n.* (*pl.* -es) (a) no longer having sth. (b) thing/amount which you no longer have; **they sold it at a l.** = for less than they paid for it. (c) **to be at a l. what to do** = not to know what to do. **loss lead•er,** *n.* article which is sold at a loss to attract customers.

lost [lɒst] *v. see* **lose.**

lot [lɒt] *n.* (a) *inf.* **a lot (of)/lots (of)** = a large amount/number (of); **I've seen quite a l. of him lately** = seen him many times. (b) **the l.** = everything. (c) set of things (for selling); thing/group of things together offered at an auction sale. (d) piece of land; **parking l.** = place where cars can be parked. (e) fate/fortune. (f) **to draw lots** = to decide sth by taking pieces of paper from a box/throwing dice, etc.

loth [ləuθ] *adj.* loath.

lo•tion ['ləuʃn] *n.* liquid used to soothe/to soften/to heal the skin.

lot•ter•y ['lɒtrɪ] *n.* game of chance in which tickets are sold with prizes given for certain numbers.

lo•tus ['ləutəs] *n.* tropical water plant, with large flowers.

loud [laud] 1. *adj.* (-er, -est) (a) having a sound which is (too) easily heard. (b) (*of colors, etc.*) too striking/showy. 2. *adv.* in a way which is easily heard. **loud•ly,** *adv.* in a way which is easily heard. **loud-mouthed,** *adj.* talking indiscreetly or in a way which is too easily heard. **loud•ness,** *n.* being (too) easily heard. **loud•speak•er,** *n.* part of a radio, etc., which allows sound to be heard.

lounge [laundʒ] 1. *n.* (a) room for sitting in. (b) bar in a hotel; **departure l.** = room at an airport where passengers wait to board their planes. (c) sitting around doing nothing or very little. 2. *v.* to sit/to lie doing nothing or very little. **loung•er,** *n.* person who lounges.

louse [laus] *n.* (*pl.* **lice** [laɪs]) small insect which lives on human and animal bodies. **lous•y** ['lauzɪ] *adj.* (a) covered with lice. (b) *inf.* horrible/unfair.

lout [laut] *n.* loutish person. **lout•ish,** *adj.* awkward/rude/ill-mannered.

lou•ver, *Brit.* **lou•vre** ['lu:və] *n.* sloping wooden strips in a frame which overlap and only allow some light to enter. **lou•vered,** *adj.* with louvers.

love [lʌv] 1. *n.* (a) great liking/respect for s.o./sth; **to do sth for the l. of it** = without looking for profit; **it can't be had for l. nor money** = not at all/by any means; **there's no l. lost between them** = they hate each other. (b) great liking/passion for s.o., esp. strong sexual feeling toward s.o.; **to be in l./to fall in l. with s.o.; to make l. (to s.o.)** = have sexual intercourse

---

æ back, ɑ: farm, ɒ: top, aɪ pipe, au how, aɪə fire, auə flower, ɔ: bought, ɔɪ toy, e fed, eəhair, eɪ take, ə
afraid, əu boat, əuə lower, v: word, i: heap, ɪ hit, ɪə hear, u: school, u book, ʌ but, b back, d dog, ð then,
dʒ just, f fog, g go, h hand, j yes, k catch, l last, m mix, n nut, ŋ sing, p penny, r round, s some, ʃ short, t
too, tʃ chop, θ thing, v voice, w was, z zoo, ʒ treasure

with; **l. story** = one about sexual love; **l. affair** = (often short) sexual relationship. (c) person whom you love. (d) *inf.* form of address, esp. to a woman or child. (e) (*in tennis, etc.*) score of zero. 2. *v.* (a) to have strong feelings of affection for. (b) to have great liking/passion, esp. strong sexual feelings for (s.o.). (c) to like very much. **lov•a•ble**, *adj.* pleasant/easy to love. **love•bird**, *n.* budgerigar. **love-child**, *n.* illegitimate child. **love•less**, *adj.* without love. **love•li•ness**, *n.* being very attractive. **love•lorn**, *adj.* sad because you love s.o. who does not love you. **love•ly**, *adj.* (-ier, -iest) (a) beautiful. (b) *inf.* very pleasant. **lov•er**, *n.* (a) person (esp. a man) who is in love. (b) person who loves (sth). **love•sick**, *adj.* unhappy because of being in love. **lov•ing**, *adj.* affectionate/showing love. **lov•ing•ly**, *adv.* in a loving way.

low [ləʊ] 1. *adj.* (-er, -est) (a) at/near/toward the bottom; in a position below (others); **l. voice** = not easily heard. (b) coarse/mean; inferior. (c) feeling depressed/ill, etc. 2. *adv.* in a low direction/way/position; **to lie l.** = to keep hidden; **supplies are running l.** = are becoming scarce. 3. *n.* (a) low-pressure zone in the atmosphere, bringing bad weather. (b) **sales are at an all-time l.** = the lowest point ever. 4. *v.* to make a sound like a cow. **low•brow**, *adj. & n.* (person) without intellectual interests. **low•down**. 1. *adj.* mean/bad/to be despised. 2. *n. inf.* **to give the lowdown (on sth)** = the details (esp. confidential). **low•er**. 1. *adj.* further down; **l. deck** = deck under another deck; **l. case** = small (letter), not a capital; **l. house** = more important of two parts of a parliament. 2. *v.* (a) to make (sth) reach a position further down; **l. your voice** = speak more quietly. (b) **to l. yourself (so far as to)** = to do sth of which you should be ashamed. **low fre•quen•cy**, *n.* radio frequency which is low and can be heard. **low-grade**, *adj.* of poor quality. **low-key**, *adj.* quiet/without excitement. **low•land**, *adj.* coming from a low-lying region. **low•lands**, *n. pl.* low-lying region. **low•li•ness**, *n.* being lowly. **low•ly**, *adj.* (-ier, -iest) humble/modest. **low-ly•ing**, *adj.* (region) which is at a low altitude/almost at sea level.

low•er•ing ['laʊərɪŋ] *adj.* gloomy/threatening(-looking).

loy•al ['lɔɪəl] *adj.* (**to**) faithful/supporting (s.o./sth). **loy•al•ist**, *n.* person who is loyal. **loy•al•ly**, *adv.* in a loyal way. **loy•al•ty**, *n.* being faithful.

loz•enge ['lɒzɪndʒ] *n.* (a) diamond shape (esp. as used in heraldry). (b) flavored medicine tablet.

LP [el'piː] *abbreviation for* long-playing record.
Ltd. ['lɪmɪtɪd] *short for* limited.

lu•bri•cate ['luːbrɪkeɪt] *v.* to cover (sth) with oil or grease to make it run smoothly. **lu•bri•cant**, *adj. & n.* (substance) which makes sth run smoothly. **lu•bri•ca•tion** [luːbrɪ'keɪʃn] *n.* covering with oil or grease.

lu•cerne [luˈsɜːn] *n.* plant like clover used as fodder for cattle.

lu•cid ['luːsɪd] *adj.* (a) clear/easily understood. (b) able to think clearly. **lu•cid•i•ty** [luːˈsɪdɪtɪ] *n.* being clear. **lu•cid•ly**, *adv.* in a lucid way.

luck [lʌk] *n.* (a) chance/fortune; **as l. would have it** = as it happened; **to be down on your l.** = have bad luck. (b) good fortune; **to be out of l.** = have bad luck. **luck•i•ly**, *adv.* by good fortune. **luck•less**, *adj.* with no luck/unlucky. **luck•y**, *adj.* (-ier, -iest) (a) having good fortune/success. (b) having good fortune associated with it; **13's my l. number.**

lu•cre ['luːkə] *n. inf.* money. **lu•cra•tive** ['luːkrətɪv] *adj.* bringing in (much) money/profit.

lu•di•crous ['luːdɪkrəs] *adj.* causing laughter; ridiculous.

luff [lʌf] *v.* to sail toward the wind.

lug [lʌg] 1. *n.* small projecting piece for carrying sth or for attaching sth to it. 2. *v.* (**lugged**) to pull (sth heavy) along.

lug•gage ['lʌgɪdʒ] *n.* (*no pl.*) suitcases/bags, etc., for carrying your belongings when traveling; **l. rack** = space for bags, etc., above seats in a train, etc.

lug•ger ['lʌgə] *n.* small sailboat.

lu•gu•bri•ous [ləˈguːbrɪəs] *adj.* very miserable/mournful. **lu•gu•bri•ous•ly**, *adv.* in a lugubrious way.

luke•warm ['luːkwɔːm] *adj.* (a) slightly warm, but not hot. (b) without enthusiasm.

lull [lʌl] 1. *n.* quiet(er)/calm(er) interval. 2. *v.* to make calmer/to soothe. **lull•a•by** ['lʌləbaɪ] *n.* song/piece of music designed to make a child sleep.

lum•ba•go [lʌmˈbeɪgəʊ] *n.* pain in the lower part of the back. **lum•bar** ['lʌmbə] *adj.* referring to the lower part of the back.

lum•ber ['lʌmbə] 1. *n.* (a) wood which has been cut. (b) old articles which are not in use at the moment; junk. 2. *v.* (a) *inf.* (**with**) to give (s.o.) things he doesn't really want. (b) to move with a slow heavy step/pace. **lum•ber•jack**, *n.* person who cuts down trees. **lum•ber jack•et**, *n.* short thick working coat.

lu•men ['luːmɪn] *n.* unit of measurement of light.

lu•mi•nous ['luːmɪnəs] *adj.* giving out light (in

the dark). **lu•mi•nar•y,** *n.* learned person. **lu•mi•nes•cence,** *n.* sending out light without heat. **lu•mi•nos•i•ty** [luːmɪ'nɒsɪtɪ] *n.* being luminous.

lump [lʌmp] 1. *n.* (a) (often shapeless) mass; **l. of sugar** = solid cube of sugar; **l. sum** = money (paid) in one amount/not divided up. (b) swelling on the body. (c) *inf.* heavy, clumsy person. 2. *v.* (a) **to l. together** = to put together in one place/in one group. (b) *inf.* **he can l. it** = he'll just have to tolerate it. **lump•y,** *adj.* (-ier, -iest) having solid parts.

lu•na•cy ['luːnəsɪ] *n.* madness. **lu•na•tic,** *adj. & n.* mad (person).

lu•nar ['luːnə] *adj.* referring to the moon; **l. month** = period from one new moon to the next.

lunch [lʌnʃ] 1. *n.* (*pl.* **-es**) midday meal. 2. *v.* (*formal*) to have lunch. **lunch•eon** ['lʌnʃən] *n.* (*formal*) midday meal; **l. meat** = canned sausage or meat loaf. **lunch hour, lunchtime,** *n.* period when the midday meal is usually eaten.

lung [lʌŋ] *n.* one of two organs in the chest, with which you breathe. **lung fish,** *n.* type of fish which breathes through lungs.

lunge [lʌndʒ] 1. *n.* sudden forward movement. 2. *v.* to make a sudden movement forward.

lu•pine ['luːpaɪn] 1. *n.* garden flower with tall flower spikes. 2. *adj.* referring to a wolf.

lurch [lɜːtʃ] 1. *n.* (*pl.* **-es**) (a) sudden (unsteady) movement. (b) *inf.* **to leave in the l.** = to leave/fail in time of trouble or crisis. 2. *v.* to move with a sudden unsteady movement. **lurch•er,** *n.* dog used to retrieve game.

lure ['ljʊə] 1. *n.* (a) small object used to attract fish, etc., in order to catch them. (b) thing which traps/attracts. 2. *v.* to attract, esp. into sth bad.

lu•rid ['ljʊərɪd] *adj.* (a) which glows in an unpleasant sinister way. (b) (*of book/motion picture*) sensational/meant to shock. **lu•rid•ly,** *adv.* in a lurid way. **lu•rid•ness,** *n.* being lurid.

lurk [lɜːk] *v.* to hide/to remain hidden.

lus•cious ['lʌʃəs] *adj.* good to taste.

lush [lʌʃ] 1. *adj.* (plants) growing thickly/richly. 2. *n. Sl.* drunkard. **lush•ness,** *n.* being lush.

lust [lʌst] 1. *n.* (a) strong sexual desire. (b) great desire for sth. 2. *v.* **to l. (after)** = to have a great desire for. **lust•ful,** *adj.* full of sexual desire.

lus•ter, *Brit.* **lus•tre** ['lʌstə] *n.* shine/brilliance. **lus•trous,** *adj.* brilliant.

lust•y ['lʌstɪ] *adj.* (-ier, -iest) strong/healthy. **lust•i•ly,** *adv.* strongly. **lust•i•ness,** *n.* great strength/health.

lute [luːt] *n.* old stringed musical instrument played like a guitar.

lux•u•ri•ance [lʌg'ʒuːrɪəns] *n.* great quantity/abundance. **lux•u•ri•ant,** *adj.* growing abundantly. **lux•u•ri•ant•ly,** *adv.* in a luxuriant way. **lux•u•ri•ate,** *v.* to enjoy freely/to laze happily.

lux•u•ry ['lʌkʃərɪ] *n.* (a) great comfort. (b) thing which is pleasant to have but not necessary. **lux•u•ri•ous** [lʌg'ʒuːrɪəs] *adj.* very comfortable; very expensive. **lux•u•ri•ous•ly,** *adv.* in a luxurious way. **lux•u•ri•ous•ness,** *n.* being comfortable/expensive.

lye [laɪ] *n.* water mixed with ashes, used for washing.

ly•ing ['laɪɪŋ] *v. see* **lie.**

lymph [lɪmf] *n.* liquid found in animal tissues. **lym•phat•ic** [lɪm'fætɪk] *adj.* referring to lymph.

lynch [lɪnʃ] *v.* (*of a mob*) to kill (s.o.) without trial (esp. by hanging).

lynx [lɪŋks] *n.* (*pl.* **-es**) spotted short-tailed animal of the cat family. **lynx-eyed,** *adj.* with very good eyesight.

lyre ['laɪə] *n.* old stringed musical instrument. **lyre•bird,** *n.* tropical bird with tail feathers shaped like a lyre.

lyr•ic ['lɪrɪk] *adj. & n.* (a) (poem, etc.) concerned with feeling. (b) (poem, etc.) intended to be sung. **lyr•i•cal,** *adj.* (a) (poem) using suitable language to express feelings. (b) *inf.* eager/enthusiastic. **lyr•i•cal•ly,** *adv.* in a lyrical way. **lyr•i•cism** ['lɪrɪsɪzəm] *n.* quality of a poem which expresses feelings. **lyr•i•cist,** *n.* person who writes the words of a song. **lyr•ics,** *n. pl.* words of a song.

æ back, aː farm, ɒ: top, aɪ pipe, aʊ how, aiə fire, aʊə flower, ɔ: bought, ɔɪ toy, e fed, eəhair, eɪ take, ə afraid, əʊ boat, əʊə lower, vː word, i: heap, ɪ hit, ɪə hear, u: school, ʊ book, ʌ but, b back, d dog, ð then, dʒ just, f fog, g go, h hand, j yes, k catch, l last, m mix, n nut, ŋ sing, p penny, r round, s some, ʃ short, t too, tʃ chop, θ thing, v voice, w was, z zoo, ʒ treasure

Mm

m *abbrev. for* meter; mile.

ma [mɑ:] *n. inf.* mother.

ma'am [mɑ:m] *n.* 1. madam. 2. term used to address the Queen of England.

mac [mæk] *n. inf.* raincoat.

ma•ca•bre [mə'kɑ:br] *adj.* causing horror; gruesome.

mac•ad•am [mə'kædəm] *n.* road surface made of small pieces of broken stone. **mac•ad•am•ized**, *adj.* covered with macadam.

mac•a•ro•ni [mækə'rəʊnɪ] *n.* food made of short thick tubes of flour paste.

mac•a•roon [mækə'ru:n] *n.* small sweet almond biscuit.

ma•caw [mə'kɔ:] *n.* brightly colored South American parrot.

mace [meɪs] *n.* (a) heavy bar of wood/metal used in ceremonies to symbolize authority. (b) spice made from the outside of a nutmeg.

mac•er•ate ['mæsəreɪt] *v.* to soak in a liquid until soft.

Mach (num•ber) ['mæk('nʌmbə)] *n.* figure showing the speed of supersonic aircraft in relation to the speed of sound; **at M. one** = at the speed of sound.

ma•chet•e [mə'tʃetɪ] *n.* jungle knife used in South America.

Mach•i•a•vel•li•an [mækɪə'velɪən] *adj.* sly/clever (in political plotting).

mach•i•na•tion [mækɪ'neɪʃn] *n.* plot.

ma•chine [mə'ʃi:n] 1. *n.* (a) device in which power from a motor drives wheels/gears, etc. (b) organization; **political machine.** 2. *v.* to make/to shape with a machine. **ma•chine gun,** *n.* gun which automatically fires many bullets one after the other. **ma•chin•er•y,** *n.* (*no pl.*) mechanism; (working parts of) machines. **machine tools,** *n. pl.* tools operated by a motor and used to shape metal/wood, etc. **ma•chin•ing,** *n.* working with a machine. **ma•chin•ist,** *n.* person who works machinery, esp. machine tools.

ma•chis•mo [mə'kɪzməʊ] *n.* exaggerated sense of male pride. **ma•cho** ['mætʃəʊ] *adj.* (man) who is aggressively male.

mack•er•el ['mækrəl] *n.* (*pl.* **mackerel**) common sea fish.

mack•in•tosh ['mækɪntɒʃ] *n.* raincoat.

ma•cra•mé [mə'krɑ:meɪ] *n.* (*no pl.*) knotted string articles.

macro- ['mækrəʊ] *prefix meaning* very large/covering a wide area.

mac•ro•bi•ot•ic [mækrəʊbaɪ'ɒtɪk] *adj.* referring to a health-giving diet of cereals/vegetables, etc.

mac•ro•cosm ['mækrəʊkɒzəm] *n.* large complete system; the universe.

mad [mæd] *adj.* (**madder, maddest**) (a) not sane; wild/silly; *inf.* **like m.** = (i) very fast; (ii) very enthusiastically; **he's m. with/at you** = angry with you. (b) very enthusiastic (**about** s.o./sth). (c) (dog or other animal) suffering from rabies. **mad•cap,** *adj. & n.* wild (person). **mad cow dis•ease,** *n. inf.* bovine spongiform encephalopathy. **mad•den,** *v.* to make mad; to exasperate/to annoy. **mad•den•ing,** *adj.* exasperating. **mad•house,** *n.* place which is full of noise and people rushing about. **mad•ly,** *adv.* like a madman. **mad•man,** *n.* (*pl.* **-men**) lunatic; **he drove like a m.** = he drove very fast/furiously. **mad•ness,** *n.* being mad; lunacy. **mad•wom•an,** *n.* (*pl.* **-women**) female lunatic.

mad•am ['mædəm] *n.* (a) formal way of addressing a woman. (b) woman who keeps a brothel.

mad•der ['mædə] *n.* plant which gives a red dye.

made [meɪd] *v. see* **make.**

ma•dei•ra [mə'dɪərə] *n.* sweet dessert wine.

ma•don•na [mə'dɒnə] *n.* (picture/statue of) the Virgin Mary.

mad•ri•gal ['mædrɪgl] *n.* group song popular in the sixteenth and seventeenth centuries.

mael•strom ['meɪlstrɒm] *n.* violent whirlpool in the sea; violent confusion.

maes•tro ['maɪstrəʊ] *n.* (*pl.* **-os**) *inf.* musical genius; conductor.

ma•fi•a ['mæfɪə] *n.* secret (Italian) organization dealing in crime.

mag•a•zine [mægə'zi:n] *n.* (a) (illustrated) paper which appears at regular intervals. (b) radio/TV program made up from various items on the same theme, broadcast regularly. (c) box containing ammunition/film/slides which clips on to a gun/a camera/projector.

(d) room/building used as a store for explosives. **ma•gen•ta** [mə'dʒentə] n. & adj. dark red-purple (color).

mag•got ['mægət] n. white grub (of a bluebottle) which lives in rotting meat. **mag•got•y,** adj. full of maggots.

Ma•gi ['meidʒai] n. pl. wise men who brought gifts to the infant Christ.

mag•ic ['mædʒik] 1. n. spells/conjuring tricks, etc., which do not appear to follow normal scientific rules; **as if by m.** = suddenly/from nowhere; **black m.** = evil spells designed to harm people. 2. adj. enchanted. **mag•i•cal,** adj. produced by magic; fairylike. **mag•i•cal•ly,** adv. by magic. **mag•ic bul•let,** n. inf. any drug that targets diseased tissue without producing adverse side effects. **ma•gi•cian** [mə'dʒiʃn] n. wizard/conjuror.

mag•is•te•ri•al [mædʒi'stiəriəl] adj. with an air of authority. **mag•is•te•ri•al•ly,** adv. in a commanding way.

mag•is•trate ['mædʒistreit] n. judge in a minor court.

mag•ma ['mɑgmə] n. (a) molten rock under the earth's crust. (b) paste.

Mag•na Car•ta ['mægnə 'kɑːtə] n. charter, signed by King John of England in 1215, which gave basic rights to some subjects.

mag•nan•i•mous [mæg'næniməs] adj. very generous. **mag•na•nim•i•ty** [mægnə'nimiti] n. great generosity. **mag•nan•i•mous•ly,** adv. in a magnanimous way.

mag•nate ['mægneit] n. important businessman.

mag•ne•si•um [mæg'niːziəm] n. (element: Mg) metal which burns with a brilliant white light. **mag•ne•sia,** n. white powder made from magnesium, used in medicines.

mag•net ['mægnət] n. thing which attracts, esp. a metal object which attracts iron and steel and points roughly north and south when suspended. **mag•net•ic** [mæg'netik] adj. having a power of attraction; **m. pole/m. north** = the point to which the needle of a compass points; **m. field** = area around a magnet which is under its influence; **m. mine** = floating bomb which is attracted to the metal hull of a passing ship; **m. tape** = plastic tape for recording music/information, etc. **mag•net•i•cal•ly,** adv. by a magnet. **mag•net•ism** ['mægnətizəm] n. (a) natural

attractive power of magnets. (b) personal power of attraction. **mag•net•ize,** v. to make (a piece of metal) into a magnet.

mag•ne•to [mæg'niːtəu] n. (pl. -os) device in an engine which produces electricity used for ignition.

mag•nif•i•cent [mæg'nifisnt] adj. very fine/splendid/very luxurious. **mag•nif•i•cence,** n. splendor/luxury. **mag•nif•i•cent•ly,** adv. in a magnificent way.

mag•ni•fy ['mægnifai] v. to make (something) appear larger; **magnifying glass** = lens which makes small objects appear larger. **mag•ni•fi•ca•tion** [mægnifi'keiʃn] n. making something appear larger; degree to which things appear larger. **mag•ni•fi•er,** n. thing which magnifies.

mag•ni•tude ['mægnitjuːd] n. size; (of stars) brightness.

mag•no•lia [mæg'nəuliə] n. large tree with huge flowers.

mag•num ['mægnəm] n. very large bottle (of wine, esp. champagne).

mag•pie ['mægpai] n. common large black and white bird.

ma•ha•ra•jah [mɑːhə'rɑːdʒə] n. Indian prince. **ma•ha•ra•ni** [mɑːhə'rɑːniː] n. Indian princess.

ma•hat•ma [mə'hætmə] n. (in India) title given to a holy man.

mah•jong [mɑː'dʒɒn] n. Chinese game played with small counters.

ma•hog•a•ny [mə'hɒgəni] n. dark wood used for making furniture.

maid [meid] n. female servant; **old m.** = middle-aged unmarried woman. **maid•en.** 1. n. (formal) unmarried girl/woman. 2. adj. (a) unmarried (woman); **m. aunt** = unmarried aunt; **m. name** = surname of a woman before she is married. (b) first; **m. voyage/flight** = first voyage of a new ship/of a new aircraft. **maid•en•hair,** n. type of fern. **maid•en•hood,** n. (formal) being a maiden. **maid•en•ly,** adj. (formal) like a maiden.

mail [meil] 1. n. (a) letters delivered. (b) postal service; **m. order** = ordering and buying by mail. (c) **chain m.** = type of armor made of small interlocking metal rings. 2. v. to send (sth) by the postal service. **mail•bag,** n. large canvas bag for carrying mail. **mail•box,** n. box where letters are deposited to be picked up and delivered by the postal service.

mail•ing list, *n.* list of names and addresses of people to whom information can be sent. **mail car•ri•er,** *n.* person employed to deliver mail.

maim [meɪm] *v.* to wound; to make lame.

main [meɪn] 1. *n.* (a) (*formal*) **with might and m.** = with all your strength or power. (b) **in the m.** = generally speaking. (c) central pipe for distributing water/gas, etc. 2. *adj.* most important. **main•land** ['meɪnlənd] *n.* large solid mass of land. **main•ly,** *adv.* mostly/in a very important way. **main•mast,** *n.* most important mast on a ship. **main•sail** ['meɪnsl] *n.* most important sail on a ship. **main•spring,** *n.* (a) central spring of a watch. (b) most important force which makes you do sth. **main•stay,** *n.* principal support. **main•stream,** *n.* most important trend or dominating force.

main•tain [meɪn'teɪn] *v.* (a) to keep (order); to keep (doing sth). (b) to keep sth in working order. (c) to state/to assert. **main•te•nance,** *n.* (a) keeping. (b) money for upkeep.

mai•son•ette [meɪzə'net] *n.* apartment on two floors.

maî•tre d' [metrə'diː], **maître d'hôtel** ['metrəd əu'tel] *n.* head waiter.

maize [meɪz] *n.* corn.

maj•es•ty ['mædʒəstɪ] *n.* (a) greatness. (b) form of address to a King or Queen. **ma•jes•tic** [mə'dʒestɪk] *adj.* grand/stately. **ma•jes•ti•cal•ly,** *adv.* grandly.

ma•jor ['meɪdʒə] 1. *n.* (a) (*in the armed forces*) officer above a captain. (b) (*formal*) legally adult person. 2. *adj.* (a) bigger; more important; **the m. part of the work** = most of the work. (b) musical key where there are semitones between the third and fourth, and between the seventh and eighth notes. 3. *v.* to specialize in a subject as an undergraduate. **ma•jor•do•mo,** *n.* chief servant in a large house. **ma•jor•ette** [meɪdʒə'ret] *n.* girl or woman who leads a marching band. **ma•jor-gen•er•al,** *n.* (*in the armed forces*) army officer below a lieutenant-general. **ma•jor•i•ty** [mə'dʒɒrɪtɪ] *n.* (a) larger part. (b) larger number of voters. (c) legally adult age.

make [meɪk] 1. *n.* (a) brand; country of origin (of an object). (b) inf. **he's on the m.** = all he wants to do is to make money. 2. *v.* (**made**) (a) to prepare; to do; to construct; **to m. the beds** = to put the beds in proper order after they have been slept in. (b) to earn; **I m. $200 a week.** (c) to add up to; to score. (d) to cause (s.o.) to be; **he made himself comfortable.** (e) to force (s.o.) to do sth; **make a•way with,** *v.* to remove (sth)/to make (sth) disappear.

make-be•lieve, *n.* pretending/believing sth is true when it is not. **make do,** *v.* (**with**) to put up with (sth)/to use (sth) even if it is not suitable. **make for,** *v.* to aim; to go toward. **make good,** *v.* (a) to put (sth) right. (b) to carry out (a promise). (c) to become successful. **make of,** *v.* to consider; **what do you make of it?** = what do you think of it? **make off with,** *v.* to run away with (sth)/to steal (sth). **make out,** *v.* (a) to draw up (a list); to write (a check). (b) to distinguish/to see properly. (c) to assert/to maintain. (d) *inf.* to succeed. **make o•ver,** *v.* to transfer. **make•o•ver,** *n.* complete restyling, esp. of a person's clothes/hair, etc. **mak•er,** *n.* person who makes sth. **make•shift,** *adj. & n.* (thing) used temporarily in place of sth else. **make up,** *v.* (a) to complete/to fill up; **I can't make up my mind** = I can't decide; **to make up for lost time** = to act specially quickly. (b) to put lipstick/powder, etc., on your face. (c) to invent. (d) **to make it up to s.o.** = to compensate s.o. for sth lost/damaged, etc. **make-up,** *n.* (a) composition. (b) character. (c) lipstick/cream/powder, etc., used to beautify your face. **make•weight,** *n.* small quantity added to make up the weight of sth. **mak•ing,** *n.* formation; **it was 3 years in the m.** = it took 3 years to make; **it has the makings of** = it may develop into.

ma•lac•ca [məl'ækə] *n.* tropical cane used to make walking sticks.

mal•a•chite ['mæləkaɪt] *n.* green stone.

mal•ad•just•ed [mælə'dʒʌstɪd] *adj.* (person) who does not fit into society. **mal•ad•just•ment,** *n.* being maladjusted.

mal•ad•min•is•tra•tion [mælədmɪnɪ'streɪʃn] *n.* incompetent administration.

mal•a•droit [mælə'drɔɪt] *adj.* (*formal*) clumsy.

mal•a•dy ['mælədɪ] *n.* (*formal*) illness.

ma•laise [mæ'leɪz] *n.* (*formal*) awkward feeling; slight sickness.

mal•a•prop•ism ['mæləprɒpɪzəm] *n.* incorrect use of a word which sounds similar to the correct one.

ma•lar•i•a [mə'leərɪə] *n.* tropical fever caused by a parasite carried by mosquitoes. **ma•lar•i•al,** *adj.* referring to malaria.

Ma•lay•sian [mə'leɪʒn] 1. *adj.* referring to Malaysia. 2. *n.* person from Malaysia. **Ma•lay,** *n. & adj.* (person) from Malaysia; language spoken in Malaysia.

mal•con•tent ['mælkəntent] *n.* (*formal*) dissatisfied person.

male [meɪl] 1. *adj.* (a) referring to men/boys. (b) referring to the sex which fertilizes eggs produced by females. 2. *n.* (a) man/boy. (b) animal/insect of the sex which does not give birth to offspring.

mal•e•fac•tor ['mælɪfæktə] *n.* (*formal*) criminal.

ma•lev•o•lence [mə'levələns] *n.* (*formal*) ill-will; desire to hurt others. **ma•lev•o•lent,** *adj.* wishing (s.o.) ill.

mal•fea•sance [mæl'fiːzəns] *n.* (*formal*) an unlawful act.

mal•for•ma•tion [mælfɔː'meɪʃn] *n.* being wrongly shaped/badly formed. **mal•formed,** *adj.* bady formed/shaped.

mal•func•tion [mæl'fʌŋkʃn] 1. *n.* bad/incorrect working (of a machine/of the heart, etc.). 2. *v.* to work badly.

mal•ice ['mælɪs] *n.* unfriendly feelings; **out of m.** = to be spiteful. **ma•li•cious** [mə'lɪʃəs] *adj.* wicked/intentionally spiteful; wanting to hurt others. **ma•li•cious•ly,** *adv.* in a malicious way.

ma•lign [mə'laɪn] *v.* to say bad things about (s.o.); **he has been much maligned** = people have criticized him a lot. **ma•lig•nan•cy** [mə'lɪgnənsɪ] *n.* being malignant. **ma•lig•nant** [mə'lɪgnənt] *adj.* (a) wishing harm to someone. (b) likely to be fatal. **ma•lig•ni•ty,** *n.* malignant feeling.

ma•lin•ger [mə'lɪŋgə] *v.* to pretend to be ill (to avoid work). **ma•lin•ger•er,** *n.* person who pretends to be ill.

mall [mɔːl] *n.* shopping complex with many different kinds of retail stores and usu. restaurants and other businesses.

mal•lard ['mælɑːd] *n.* common wild duck.

mal•le•a•ble ['mælɪəbl] *adj.* soft/which can be molded into shape. **mal•le•a•bil•i•ty,** *n.* being malleable.

mal•let ['mælɪt] *n.* large wooden hammer.

mal•low ['mæləʊ] *n.* wild flower growing in marshy ground.

mal•nu•tri•tion [mælnjuː'trɪʃn] *n.* lack of enough good food.

mal•o•dor•ous [mæl'əʊdərəs] *adj.* (*formal*) which smells bad.

mal•prac•tice [mæl'præktɪs] *n.* improper or illegal conduct by a professional, as a doctor or lawyer.

malt [mɔːlt] *n.* grain which has been prepared for making beer or whisky by being allowed to sprout and then dried. **malt•ed,** *adj.* tasting of malt.

Mal•tese [mɒl'tiːz] *adj.* & *n.* (person) from Malta.

mal•treat [mæl'triːt] *v.* to treat (s.o.) badly. **mal•treat•ment,** *n.* rough treatment.

ma•ma [mə'mɑː] *n.* child's name for mother.

mam•ba ['mæmbə] *n.* poisonous African snake.

mam•bo ['mæmbəʊ] *n.* South American dance.

mam•ma [mə'mɑː] *n.* = **ma•ma.**

mam•mal ['mæml] *n.* type of animal which gives birth to live young and suckles them with milk. **mam•ma•li•an** [mə'meɪlɪən] *adj.* referring to mammals. **mam•ma•ry,** *adj.* referring to the breast.

mam•mon ['mæmən] *n.* wealth regarded as evil and the object of greedy pursuit.

mam•moth ['mæməθ] 1. *n.* very large prehistoric hairy elephant. 2. *adj.* huge.

man [mæn] 1. *n.* (*pl.* **men**) (a) adult male human being. (b) person; **the m. in the street** = the ordinary citizen; **no man's land** = land between two armies which belongs to neither side. (c) husband. (d) servant; ordinary soldier/worker. (e) piece (in chess, etc.). 2. *v.* (**manned**) to provide with men; to be the workforce for (a machine/an office, etc.). **man-eat•er,** *n.* animal which eats people. **man-eat•ing,** *adj.* (animal) which eats people. **man•ful•ly,** *adv.* like a man; in a strong/forceful way. **man•han•dle,** *v.* (a) to move (something large and heavy) by hand. (b) to handle someone roughly. **man•hole,** *n.* hole in the road or pavement through which you go down into the sewers, etc. **man•hood,** *n.* (*no pl.*) state of being an adult male. **man-hour,** *n.* work done by one person in one hour. **man•hunt,** *n.* search (for a criminal). **man•kind** [mæn'kaɪnd] *n.* (*no pl.*) the human race. **man•li•ness,** *n.* virility/male characteristics. **man•ly,** *adj.* virile/with very strong male features; brave. **man-made,** *adj.* artificial (material, etc.). **man•nish,** *adj.* (woman) who looks/dresses like a man. **man•pow•er,** *n.* work force/number of workers. **man-of-war,** *n.* (a) (*old*) battleship. (b) **Portuguese man-of-war** = type of very large jellyfish. **man•serv•ant,** *n.* male servant. **man-sized,** *adj.* very large. **man•slaugh•ter,** *n.* killing s.o. without intending to do so.

man•a•cle ['mænəkl] 1. *n.* one of two steel rings connected by a chain, which attach the wrists of a prisoner together. 2. *v.* to attach (a prisoner's) wrists together.

æ back, ɑː farm, ɒ top, aɪ pipe, aʊ how, aiə fire, aʊə flower, ɔː bought, ɔɪ toy, e fed, eəhair, eɪ take, ə afraid, əʊ boat, əʊə lower, vː word, iː heap, ɪ hit, ɪə hear, uː school, ʊ book, ʌ but, b back, d dog, ð then, dʒ just, f fog, g go, h hand, j yes, k catch, l last, m mix, n nut, ŋ sing, p penny, r round, s some, ʃ short, t too, tʃ chop, θ thing, v voice, w was, z zoo, ʒ treasure

man•age ['mænɪdʒ] v. (a) to direct. (b) to arrange to do sth; to succeed in doing sth; **can she m. all by herself?** = can she cope/can she do the work all by herself? **man•age•a•ble**, adj. which can be managed/directed. **man•age•ment**, n. (a) handling of (a tool); directing (of work). (b) group of people who direct workers; **under new m.** = with a new owner/manager. **man•ag•er**, n. (a) head of a department in a company. (b) person who manages/directs; director of a theater; organizer of a sports team/singer, etc.; person who runs a store. **man•ag•er•ess** [mænɪdʒə'res] n. (pl. -es) woman who runs a store. **man•a•ge•ri•al** [mænə'dʒɪərɪəl] adj. referring to a manager; **discussions at m. level** = discussions among managers. **man•ag•ing di•rec•tor**, n. overall director of a company.

man•a•tee [mænə'tiː] n. large plant-eating sea mammal.

man•da•mus [mæn'deməs] n. order from a higher court to a lower court.

man•da•rin ['mændərɪn] n. (a) small orange with a soft easily-peeled skin. (b) important member of a group. (c) **Mandarin** = principal form of the Chinese language.

man•date ['mændeɪt] n. power given to a person to act on behalf of s.o. else; **the government has a m. from the people to cut taxes** = people approved of the plan to cut taxes when they voted for the government. **man•dat•ed**, adj. (territory) which is entrusted to a country to administer. **man•da•to•ry** ['mændətərɪ] adj. obligatory/compulsory.

man•di•ble ['mændɪbl] n. lower jawbone (of birds/insects, etc.).

man•do•lin ['mændəlɪn] n. stringed instrument like a small guitar.

man•drel ['mændrəl] n. the turning central shaft of a lathe.

man•drill ['mændrɪl] n. large baboon.

mane [meɪn] n. long hair on neck of a lion or horse; long untidy hair.

ma•neu•ver [mə'nuːvə] n. & v. 1. n. (a) action of moving sth. 2. **maneuvers** = military exercises. 2. v. (a) to move (sth) heavy/awkward. (b) to work to put yourself in a good position. **ma•neu•ver•a•bil•i•ty** [mənuːvrə'bɪlɪtɪ] n. ability to be easily maneuvered. **ma•neu•ver•a•ble**, adj. which can be maneuvered/moved.

man•ga•nese ['mæŋgəniːz] n. (element: Mn) gray metal.

mange [meɪndʒ] n. disease of the skin of animals, which makes the hair fall out. **man•gy**, adj. dirty/diseased.

man•ger ['meɪndʒə] n. box for food for horses/cows, etc.

man•gle ['mæŋgl] 1. n. device with rollers for squeezing the water out of clothes. 2. v. (a) to squeeze water out of (clothes) by passing them through a mangle. (b) to tear; to chop up; to mess up.

man•go ['mæŋgəu] n. (pl. -oes) large tropical fruit with a big stone.

man•grove ['mæŋgrəuv] n. kind of tropical tree growing in wet areas.

ma•ni•a ['meɪnɪə] n. madness; exaggerated passion (for sth). **ma•ni•ac**, n. mad person. **ma•ni•a•cal** [mə'naɪəkl] adj. mad. **man•ic** ['mænɪk] adj. referring to mania.

man•i•cure ['mænɪkjuə] 1. n. treatment for the hands; **to have a m.** = to have your hands cleaned and nails trimmed. 2. v. to care for the hands. **manicure set,** n. small box or bag with scissors/nail file, etc. **man•i•cur•ist**, n. person who gives treatment to people's hands.

man•i•fest ['mænɪfest] 1. adj. (formal) obvious/plain to see. 2. n. list of goods in a shipment. 3. v. (formal) to appear/to show. **man•i•fes•ta•tion** [mænɪfe'steɪʃn] n. appearance. **man•i•fest•ly**, adv. (formal) obviously. **man•i•fes•to** [mænɪ'festəu] n. (pl. -oes) program of action outlined by a political party.

man•i•fold ['mænɪfəuld] 1. adj. (formal) of varying sorts. 2. n. **exhaust m.** = tubes of an exhaust pipe of a car.

man•i•kin ['mænɪkɪn] n. very small man.

ma•nil•a [mə'nɪlə] n. (also **Manila paper**) thick brown paper (used for envelopes).

man•i•oc ['mænɪɒk] n. tropical plant from which a flour is made.

ma•nip•u•late [mə'nɪpjuleɪt] v. to handle; to falsify (accounts) to make them seem more profitable. **ma•nip•u•la•tion** [mənɪpju-'leɪʃn] n. handling (of machinery); falsification (of accounts). **ma•nip•u•la•tor**, n. person who manipulates.

man•na ['mænə] n. unexpected help/food.

man•ne•quin ['mænɪkɪn] n. person or dummy wearing clothes to show them to possible buyers.

man•ner ['mænə] n. (a) way of behaving/acting; (b) **manners** = way of acting in public. (c) sort; **in a m. of speaking** = in a sort of way. **man•nered**, adj. full of mannerisms. **man•ner•ism**, n. characteristic way of acting/of doing sth. **man•ner•ly**, adj. well-behaved.

ma•nœu•vre [mə'nuːvə] n. Brit. see **ma•neu•ver.**

ma•nom•e•ter [mæ'nɒmɪtə] n. instrument for measuring pressure.

man•or ['mænə] n. main house on a country estate, etc.; **m. house** = country house.

man•sard ['mænsɑːd] *n.* **m. (roof)** = roof where the top part slopes more gently than the bottom.

man•sion ['mænʃən] *n.* very large private house.

man•tel ['mæntl] (*also* **mantelpiece** ['mæntlpiːs]) *n.* shelf above a fireplace.

man•tis ['mæntɪs] *n.* **praying m.** = large tropical insect.

man•tle ['mæntl] *n.* (a) cloak. (b) gauze cover for a gas or kerosene lamp.

man•u•al ['mænjuəl] 1. *adj.* done by hand. 2. *n.* (a) book of instructions. (b) car where the gears are changed by hand. (c) keyboard of an organ. **man•u•al•ly,** *adv.* (done) by hand.

man•u•fac•ture [mænju'fæktʃə] 1. *n.* making of a commercially produced product. 2. *v.* to make (products) commercially. **man•u•fac•tur•er,** *n.* person/company producing commercial products.

ma•nure [mə'njuə] 1. *n.* dung of animals used as a fertilizer on land. 2. *v.* to spread manure on (land).

man•u•script ['mænjuskrɪpt] *adj. & n.* (document/novel/poem) written by hand or typed, etc., but not printed.

Manx [mæŋks] *adj. & n.* (person, etc.) from the Isle of Man.

man•y ['menɪ] *adj. & n.* (**more, most**) great number; **a good m. prisoners** = quite a large number; **m. a time** = often.

Ma•o•ri ['maurɪ] 1. *adj.* referring to the original natives of New Zealand. 2. *n.* (a) language spoken by the native race of New Zealand. (b) member of the native race of New Zealand.

map [mæp] 1. *n.* diagram of an area showing features and places and their relative positions and sizes; **street m.** = diagram showing streets with their names; **physical m.** = diagram showing mountains/rivers, etc.; **political m.** = diagram showing the borders of countries/administrative districts, etc. 2. *v.* (**mapped**) to draw a diagram of (an area); **to m. out a route** = to plan a journey in advance. **map•ping,** *n.* art of making maps.

ma•ple ['meɪpl] *n.* northern tree, with sweet sap; **m. sugar/m. syrup** = sugar/syrup made from the sap of the maple tree.

mar [mɑː] *v.* (**marred**) to spoil.

mar•a•bou ['mærəbuː] *n.* large stork, with a heavy bill.

ma•rac•as [mæ'rækəs] *n. pl.* percussion instrument, formed of a pair of gourds with dried seeds inside them.

mar•a•schi•no [mærə'skiːnəu] *n.* (*pl.* **-os**) cherry used to make liqueur in desserts, cocktails, etc.

mar•a•thon ['mærəθən] *n.* long distance race; (sth) which lasts a long time.

ma•raud [mə'rɔːd] *v.* to raid; to go about looking for plunder. **ma•raud•er,** *n.* person who raids. **ma•raud•ing,** *adj.* (person) who raids.

mar•ble ['mɑːbl] *n.* (a) very hard type of limestone which can be brilliantly polished. (b) small glass ball for playing with. **mar•bled,** *adj.* with streaks of different colors.

March [mɑːtʃ] *n.* 3rd month of the year.

march [mɑːtʃ] 1. *n.* (*pl.* **-es**) (a) military walking in step; **quick m.** = rapid walking pace; **slow m.** = slow walking pace. (b) **protest m.** = mass of people walking in a line to protest about sth. (c) music for marching. (d) progress/advance of time/events. 2. *v.* (a) to walk in step; **the police marched him off to prison** = removed him quickly to prison. (b) to walk quickly and purposefully. (c) to walk in a protest march. **march•er,** *n.* person who marches.

mare ['meə] *n.* female horse; **mare's tails** = thin wispy clouds showing a change in the weather; **mare's nest** = discovery which turns out to be useless.

mar•ga•rine [mɑː'dʒə'riːn] *n.* mixture of animal or vegetable fat which is used instead of butter.

mar•gin ['mɑːdʒɪn] *n.* (a) edge/border (of a page). (b) extra space/time; **leave a m. for error** = allow extra space/time in case you have made a mistake in your calculations; **safety m.** = space/time left to allow for safety. (c) money received which is more than money paid. **mar•gin•al,** *adj.* (a) (note) in a margin. (b) slight. **mar•gin•al•ly,** *adv.* slightly.

mar•gue•rite [mɑːgə'riːt] *n.* common large white daisy.

mar•i•gold ['mærɪgəuld] *n.* common garden plant with yellow flowers.

mar•i•jua•na [mærɪ'hwɑːnə] *n.* drug made from hemp.

ma•ri•na [mə'riːnə] *n.* harbor for yachts/motor boats, etc.

mar•i•nade [mærɪ'neɪd] 1. *n.* mixture of wine and herbs, etc., in which meat or fish is soaked before cooking. 2. *v.* (*also* **marinate**) to soak (meat or fish) in a mixture of wine and herbs.

ma•rine [mə'riːn] 1. *adj.* referring to the sea. 2. *n.* (a) **the merchant m.** = the merchant ships of

æ back, ɑː farm, ɒ top, aɪ pipe, au how, aiə fire, auə flower, ɔː bought, ɔɪ toy, e fed, eəhair, eɪ take, ə afraid, əu boat, əuə lower, vː word, iː heap, ɪ hit, tə hear, uː school, u book, ʌ but, b back, d dog, ð then, dʒ just, f fog, g go, h hand, j yes, k catch, l last, m mix, n nut, ŋ sing, p penny, r round, s some, ʃ short, t too, tʃ chop, θ thing, v voice, w was, z zoo, ʒ treasure

a country. (b) soldier serving on a ship. (c) **Marine.** member of the U.S. Marine Corps. **Marine Corps,** *n.* branch of the U.S. armed forces used for combat on land, air, and sea. **mar•i•ner** ['mærɪnə] *n.* sailor.

mar•i•on•ette [mærɪə'net] *n.* string puppet.

mar•i•tal ['mærɪtl] *adj.* referring to marriage.

mar•i•time ['mærɪtaɪm] *adj.* referring to the sea.

mar•jo•ram ['mɑ:dʒərəm] *n.* common herb used as flavoring.

mark [mɑ:k] 1. *n.* (a) spot/stain; thing which can be seen. (b) target; **wide of the m.** = far from correct. (c) sign; **punctuation m.** = printing sign (such as period/comma, etc.). (d) rating given to a student to show level or quality of performance. (e) starting line in a race; **on your marks** = get ready at your places. (f) line indicating a point reached. (g) unit of money in Germany. 2. *v.* (a) to make a sign on (sth). (b) to correct and give a rating to. (c) **to m. time** = (i) to march on one spot; (ii) to stay in one place/not to advance. **mark down,** *v.* to lower the price of (sth). **marked,** *adj.* obvious/noticeable; **a m. man** = man who has been selected by the enemy as a probable target. **mark•ed•ly** ['mɑ:kɪdlɪ] *adv.* obviously. **mark•er,** *n.* thing which marks; person who notes the scores in a competition, etc.; **m. buoy** = buoy used to indicate a dangerous spot. **mark•ing,** *n.* (a) making marks. (b) **markings** = spots/stripes, etc., on a bird or animal. (c) correcting (exercises/homework, etc). **mark out,** *v.* to indicate the boundaries of (a land); to select. **marks•man,** *n.* (*pl.* -men) person who shoots well. **marks•man•ship,** *n.* ability to shoot well. **mark up,** *v.* to increase the price of (sth). **mark-up,** *n.* amount added to the cost price to give the selling price.

mar•ket ['mɑ:kɪt] 1. *n.* (a) place where produce is sold outdoors, usu. from booths. (b) sale; **on the m.** = for sale. (c) place where a product is required/could be sold; need for a product; **m. research** = examination of the possible sales of a product before it is launched; **the Common M.** = the European Economic Community; **black m.** = illegal selling at high prices. 2. *v.* to sell (products). **mar•ket•a•ble,** *adj.* which can be sold easily. **mar•ket•ing,** *n.* selling techniques (publicity/packaging, etc.) for a product. **mar•ket•place,** *n.* place where a market is held/where goods are sold.

marl [mɑ:l] *n.* soil which is a mixture of clay and lime.

mar•line•spike ['mɑ:lɪnspaɪk] *n.* pointed hook, used for unraveling rope.

mar•ma•lade ['mɑ:məleɪd] *n.* jam made from oranges/lemons or grapefruit.

mar•mo•set [mɑ:mə'zet] *n.* small South and Central American monkey.

mar•mot ['mɑ:mət] *n.* small burrowing animal.

ma•roon [mə'ru:n] 1. *adj. & n.* deep purple red (color). 2. *v.* to abandon in an awkward place.

mar•quee [mɑ:'ki:] *n.* rooflike top over an entrance, esp. to a theater.

mar•que•try ['mɑ:kətrɪ] *n.* (making) patterns on the surface of wood with inlaid pieces of different-colored wood or ivory.

mar•ram grass ['mærəm'grɑ:s] *n.* type of grass used to stabilize sand dunes.

mar•riage ['mærɪdʒ] *n.* (a) state of being legally joined as husband and wife. (b) ceremony of being married. **mar•riage•a•ble,** *adj.* suitable to become married.

mar•row ['mærəu] *n.* (a) soft interior of bones. (b) large green vegetable growing on a creeping plant. **mar•row•fat pea,** *n.* type of pea with large seeds.

mar•ry ['mærɪ] *v.* (a) to make (two people) husband and wife. (b) to become married to (s.o.). **mar•ried,** *adj.* joined as husband and wife; **m. name** = name taken by a woman when she gets married.

mar•sa•la [mɑ:'sɑ:lə] *n.* sweet Italian wine.

marsh [mɑ:ʃ] *n.* (*pl.* -es) wet/swampy land; **m. marigold** = common yellow flower growing in marshes; **m. mallow** = common pink flower growing in marshes. **marsh•mal•low,** *n.* soft and sticky white or pink candy. **marsh•y,** *adj.* (-ier, -iest) swampy/wet (land).

mar•shal ['mɑ:ʃl] 1. *n.* (a) very high-ranking military officer in certain armies. (b) organizer (of a race/a show). (c) police or fire chief. 2. *v.* (**marshaled**) to set or arrange in order.

mar•su•pi•al [mɑ:'su:pɪəl] *adj. & n.* (animal) which carries its young in a pouch.

mart [mɑ:t] *n.* market.

mar•tel•lo tow•er [mɑ:'teləu'tauə] *n.* round fort, built by the sea in the 19th century.

mar•ten ['mɑ:tɪn] *n.* small wild flesh-eating animal like a weasel.

mar•tial ['mɑ:ʃl] *adj.* referring to war; **m. music** = marches played by military bands; **m. law** = maintenance of law by the military instead of the police; **m. arts** = oriental fighting techniques using swords/sticks, etc.

Mar•tian ['mɑ:ʃn] *n.* being which is said to inhabit the planet Mars.

mar•tin ['mɑ:tɪn] *n.* small dark bird similar to a swallow.

mar•ti•net [mɑ:tɪ'net] *n.* very strict person.

mar•tin•gale ['mɑ:tɪngeɪl] *n.* strap to hold a horse's head down.

mar•ti•ni [mɑ:'ti:nɪ] *n.* drink made of gin/vodka and vermouth.

mar•tyr ['mɑːtə] 1. *n.* person killed because of his religious beliefs; **a m. to** = suffering a lot from. 2. *v.* to kill (s.o.) for their religious beliefs. **mar•tyr•dom**, *n.* death for one's beliefs.

mar•vel ['mɑːvl] 1. *n.* object of wonder. 2. *v.* (**marveled, marvelled**) to show wonder/surprise (**at** s.o./sth). **mar•vel•ous**, *adj.* wonderful/amazing.

Marx•ism ['mɑːksɪzəm] *n.* political theory of the philosopher Marx, on which communism is based. **Marx•ist**, *adj. & n.* (person) who follows Marxism.

mar•zi•pan ['mɑːzɪpæn] *n.* paste made from almonds, used for making sweets or covering cakes.

mas•car•a [mæ'skɑːrə] *n.* liquid/paste for making eyelashes dark.

mas•cot ['mæskət] *n.* object/animal which brings good luck.

mas•cu•line ['mæskjulɪn] *adj.* (a) male/manly. (b) (*in grammar*) referring to words which have a particular form to indicate the male gender. **mas•cu•lin•ist, mas•cu•list,** *n.* person (usu. man) who actively supports the rights of males. **mas•cu•lin•i•ty** [mæskju-'lɪnɪtɪ] *n.* manliness.

ma•ser ['meɪzə] *n.* device which amplifies microwaves.

mash [mæʃ] 1. *n.* (a) mixture of things crushed together. (b) food mixture for horses. (c) mixture used as the base for making beer. 2. *v.* to crush (sth) into a paste. **mash•er,** *n.* device for crushing. **mash•ie,** *n.* type of heavy metal golf club.

mask [mɑsk] 1. *n.* covering to disguise/to protect the face. 2. *v.* to cover up/to hide. **masked,** *adj.* wearing a mask. **mask•ing tape,** *n.* tape used to cover an area which is not being painted.

mas•och•ist ['mæsəkɪst] *n.* person who enjoys being hurt. **mas•och•ism,** *n.* enjoyment at being hurt. **mas•och•is•tic,** *adj.* referring to masochism.

ma•son ['meɪsn] *n.* (a) person who builds with stone. (b) member of a secret society of freemasons. **ma•son•ic** [mə'sɒnɪk] *adj.* referring to freemasons. **ma•son•ry** ['meɪsnrɪ] *n.* art of building with stone; large stones in a building.

mas•quer•ade [mɑːskə'reɪd] 1. *n.* (a) dance/party where people wear masks. (b) pretense/hiding of the truth. 2. *v.* (**as**) to pretend to be (s.o.).

mass [mæs] 1. *n.* (*pl.* **-es**) (a) Catholic communion service; **high m.** = mass with full ceremony; **low m.** = mass without ceremony; **Requiem M.** = (music for) a mass for the dead. (b) (*in physics*) solid body. (c) (*in physics*) amount of matter in a body. (d) large number/large quantity; **m. murderer** = killer of a large number of people; **m. meeting** = meeting of a lot of people; **m. production** = production of a large number of products; **m. media** = means of communicating (TV/radio/newspapers) which reach a large number of people. (e) **the masses** = the common people. 2. *v.* to group together into a mass. **mass-pro•duce,** *v.* to produce a large number of (products) at the same time.

mas•sa•cre ['mæsəkə] 1. *n.* killing of a lot of people/animals. 2. *v.* to kill a lot of people/animals.

mas•sage ['mæsɑːʒ] 1. *n.* rubbing of the body to relieve pain or to reduce weight. 2. *v.* to rub (s.o.'s body) to relieve pain or to reduce weight. **mas•seur** [mæ'sɜː] *n.* man who massages. **mas•seuse** [mæ'sɜːz] *n.* woman who massages.

mas•sive ['mæsɪv] *adj.* very large. **mas•sive•ly,** *adv.* very much. **mas•sive•ness,** *n.* being massive.

mast [mɑːst] *n.* (a) tall pole on a ship to carry the sails. (b) tall metal construction to carry an aerial. (c) (*no pl.*) seeds of beech/oak, etc., trees.

mas•tec•to•my [mæ'stektəmɪ] *n.* operation to remove a breast.

mas•ter ['mɑːstə] 1. *n.* (a) person in control; captain (of a merchant ship). (b) person with a second degree from a university. (c) skilled person; **an old m.** = painting by a great painter of the past. 2. *adj.* controlling; **m. key** = main key; **m. switch** = switch which controls all other switches; **m. bedroom** = main bedroom. 3. *v.* to become skilled at (sth); to gain control of (sth). **master-at-arms,** *n.* (*in the navy*) petty officer in charge of small arms and discipline. **mas•ter•ful,** *adj.* commanding/like a commander. **mas•ter•ful•ly,** *adv.* in a commanding way. **mas•ter•ly,** *adj.* clever; like an expert. **mas•ter•mind.** 1. *n.* very clever person. 2. *v.* to be the brains behind (a plan). **mas•ter•piece,** *n.* very fine painting/book/piece of music, etc. **mas•ter•stroke,** *n.* very clever action.

æ back, ɑː farm, ɒ top, aɪ pipe, aʊ how, aɪə fire, aʊə flower, ɔː bought, ɔɪ toy, e fed, eəhair, eɪ take, ə afraid, əʊ boat, əʊə lower, vː word, iː heap, ɪ hit, ɪə hear, uː school, ʊ book, ʌ but, b back, d dog, ð then, dʒ just, f fog, g go, h hand, j yes, k catch, l last, m mix, n nut, ŋ sing, p penny, r round, s some, ʃ short, t too, tʃ chop, θ thing, v voice, w was, z zoo, ʒ treasure

mas•ter•y, *n.* control over s.o.; complete understanding of a subject; great skill at a game.

mas•tic ['mæstɪk] *n.* gum from certain trees.

mas•ti•cate ['mæstɪkeɪt] *v.* (*formal*) to chew. **mas•ti•ca•tion** [mæstɪ'keɪʃn] *n.* chewing.

mas•tiff ['mæstɪf] *n.* large fierce breed of dog.

mas•toid ['mæstɔɪd] *n.* bone just behind the ear.

mas•tur•bate ['mæstəbeɪt] *v.* to rub the sex organs to excite them. **mas•tur•ba•tion** [mæstə'beɪʃn] *n.* exciting the sex organs by rubbing.

mat [mæt] *n.* (a) small piece of carpet/woven straw, etc. used as a floor covering; **bath m.** = small carpet to step on to when getting out of a bath. (b) small piece of cloth/wood/glass put under a plate on a table. **mat•ted**, *adj.* stuck together (like a mat). **mat•ting**, *n.* (material for making) large mats; **coconut m.** = floor covering made from coconut fibers.

mat•a•dor ['mætædɔ:] *n.* bullfighter who fights on foot.

match [mætʃ] 1. *n.* (*pl.* -es) (a) equal (person/thing); **they are a good m.** = they go well together. (b) game. (c) small piece of wood/cardboard with a chemical tip which lights when rubbed against a rough surface. (d) marriage. 2. *v.* (a) to be equal to. (b) to fit/to go with. **match•board**, *n.* tongue-and-groove board, with a projecting tongue along one edge and a corresponding groove along the other. **match•box**, *n.* small box containing matches. **match•less**, *adj.* with no equal. **match•mak•er**, *n.* person who arranges a marriage. **match•stick**, *n.* stick of wood forming a match. **match•wood**, *n.* small pieces of wood.

mate [meɪt] 1. *n.* (a) one of a pair of animals; husband or wife. (b) *inf.* friend/companion. (c) fellow worker. (d) workman's helper; assistant. (e) (*on merchant ship*) officer below a captain. (f) (*in chess*) position where the king cannot move, and the game ends. 2. *v.* (a) (*of animals*) to breed. (b) (*in chess*) to put (your opponent's king) in a position from which he cannot escape.

ma•te•ri•al [mə'tɪərɪəl] 1. *n.* (a) substance which can be used for making sth. (b) useful implements; **writing materials** = pens/pencils/ink/paper, etc. (c) cloth. (d) subject matter/notes (for a book, etc.). 2. *adj.* (a) referring to physical things. (b) important. **ma•te•ri•al•ism**, *n.* interest only in physical things/belief that only physical things are important. **ma•te•ri•al•ist**, *n.* person who believes in materialism. **ma•te•ri•al•is•tic**, *adj.* referring to materialism. **ma•te•ri•al•ize**, *v.* to become real/to ap-

pear. **ma•te•ri•al•ly**, *adv.* greatly/noticeably.

ma•ter•nal [mə'tɜ:nl] *adj.* referring to a mother; **m. grandfather** = father of your mother. **ma•ter•nal•ly**, *adv.* like a mother. **ma•ter•ni•ty**, *n.* becoming a mother; giving birth; **m. leave** = paid leave from a job while you are having a baby.

math•e•mat•ics [mæθə'mætɪks] *n.* science of numbers and measurements. **math•e•mat•i•cal**, *adj.* referring to mathematics. **math•e•mat•i•cal•ly**, *adv.* by mathematics. **math•e•ma•ti•cian** [mæθəmə'tɪʃn] *n.* expert at mathematics. **math**, *n. inf.* mathematics.

ma•tin•ée ['mætɪneɪ] *n.* afternoon performance of a play or motion picture.

mat•ins ['mætɪnz] *n. pl.* prayers said in the morning.

ma•tri•arch ['meɪtrɪɑ:k] *n.* woman who leads a family/a group. **ma•tri•ar•chal** [meɪtrɪ'ɑ:kl] *adj.* referring to a matriarch; (society) where women rule families. **ma•tri•ar•chy**, *n.* matriarchal society.

mat•ri•cide ['mætrɪsaɪd] *n.* murder of one's mother.

ma•tric•u•late [mə'trɪkjʊleɪt] *v.* to enroll in a college or university. **ma•tric•u•la•tion** [mətrɪkjʊ'leɪʃn] *n.* act of matriculating.

mat•ri•mo•ny ['mætrɪmənɪ] *n.* state of being married. **mat•ri•mo•ni•al** [mætrɪ'məʊnɪəl] *adj.* referring to marriage.

ma•trix ['meɪtrɪks] *n.* (*pl.* -trices [-trɪsi:z] -trixes) (a) plan/pattern from which copies are made. (b) mathematical arrangement of figures in a series of columns.

ma•tron ['meɪtrən] *n.* (a) woman who guards or has charge of inmates of a prison, hospital, or other institution. (b) middle-aged married woman. **ma•tron•ly**, *adj.* like a matron.

matte, matt [mæt] *adj.* dull/not shiny.

mat•ter ['mætə] 1. *n.* (a) substance/material. (b) thing/business; **that's quite another m.** = that's quite different. (c) problem. 2. *v.* to be important. **matter-of-fact**, *adj.* practical.

mat•tock ['mætək] *n.* type of pickax with a wide blade, used for breaking up soil.

mat•tress ['mætrəs] *n.* (*pl.* -es) thick, soft part of a bed made of a canvas case with various fillings.

ma•ture [mə'tjʊə] 1. *adj.* ripe; older; reasonable/adult (attitude). 2. *v.* to ripen. **mat•u•ra•tion**, *n.* becoming mature. **ma•tu•ri•ty**, *n.* ripeness/readiness.

maud•lin ['mɔ:dlɪn] *adj.* weeping/silly through drink.

maul [mɔ:l] *v.* to attack/handle roughly.

maul•stick, *n.* stick used by a painter to hold his hand steady.

maun•der ['mɔːndə] *v.* to mumble disconnected phrases.

Maun•dy Thurs•day ['mɔːndɪ'θɜːzdɪ] *n.* Thursday before Easter Sunday.

mau•so•le•um [mɔːzə'lɪəm] *n.* important burial building.

mauve [məuv] *adj. & n.* light pinkish-purple (color).

mav•er•ick ['mævərɪk] *n.* (a) animal which has not been branded and is running loose. (b) person who does not fit into the usual pattern.

maw [mɔː] *n. (of animal)* large mouth; stomach.

mawk•ish ['mɔːkɪʃ] *adj.* silly/falsely sentimental.

max•il•la [mæk'sɪlə] *n.* upper jawbone. **max•il•lar•y,** *adj.* referring to the upper jaw.

max•im ['mæksɪm] *n.* wise saying.

max•i•mum ['mæksɪməm] *adj. & n.* greatest possible (number/amount); **at m.** = at most. **max•i•mize** ['mæksɪmaɪz] *v.* to make as large as possible.

May [meɪ] *n.* 5th month of the year; **M. Day** = May 1st. **May•day,** *n.* international distress signal. **may•fly,** *n.* small fly which appears in summer. **May•pole,** *n.* tall pole around which people dance on the first of May.

may [meɪ] *v.* (**might**) (a) *used with other verbs to mean* it is possible; **you might have left it on the train** = perhaps you left it on the train. (b) *used with other verbs to mean* it is allowed.

may•be, *adv.* perhaps; **maybe not** = possibly not.

may•hem ['meɪhem] *n.* wild confusion.

may•on•naise [meɪə'neɪz] *n.* cream sauce made with egg yolks and oil.

may•or ['meə] *n.* elected leader of a town. **may•or•ess** ['meəres] *n.* wife of a mayor; woman mayor.

maze [meɪz] *n.* network of puzzling paths in which you can get lost.

Mb megabyte.

me [miː] *pron. referring to the speaker.*

ME ['em'iː] *abbrev. for* myalgic encephalomyelitis; *see* **chronic fatigue syndrome**.

mead [miːd] *n.* alcoholic drink made from honey.

mead•ow ['medəu] *n.* large green field. **mead•ow•sweet,** *n.* common wild plant with many little white flowers.

mea•ger, *Brit.* **mea•gre** ['miːgə] *adj.* (a) scanty/few. (b) thin. **mea•ger•ness,** *n.* small amount.

meal [miːl] *n.* (a) food taken at a sitting. (b) coarse flour. **meal•time,** *n.* time when you usually eat. **meal•y,** *adj.* floury. **meal•y-mouthed,** *adj.* not straightforward; (person) who tries not to offend and so doesn't say what he thinks.

mean [miːn] 1. *n.* (a) middle; average; middle point between two extremes. (b) **means** = way/method of doing sth; **by no means** = not at all; **by all means** = certainly. (c) **means** = money/resources; **it's beyond my means** = it's too expensive for me. 2. *adj.* (-er, -est) (a) average/middle. (b) miserable/low; **m. trick** = unkind trick. (c) miserly. (d) *Sl.* very good. 3. *v.* (**meant** [ment]) (a) to intend; **he means well** = he has good intentions; **do you m. Richard?** = are you talking about Richard?; **you are meant to** = you are supposed to. (b) to signify/to show. **mean•ing.** 1. *n.* signification. 2. *adj.* significant. **mean•ing•ful,** *adj.* full of meaning/significant. **mean•ing•ful•ly,** *adv.* significantly. **mean•ing•less,** *adj.* not signifying anything. **mean•ly,** *adv.* poorly. **mean•ness,** *n.* miserliness; dislike of sharing things/of spending money. **mean•spir•it•ed,** *adj.* sly/unpleasant.

me•an•der [mɪ'ændə] 1. *n.* bend in a river. 2. *v.* to wind/to wander about. **me•an•der•ing,** *adj.* wandering/very winding (path).

meant [ment] *v. see* **me•an.**

mean•time ['miːntaɪm] 1. *n.* **in the m.** = between two events. 2. *adv.* during this time.

mean•while ['miːnwaɪl] *adv.* during this time.

mea•sles ['miːzlz] *n.* children's disease which gives you a red rash; **German m.** = mild disease which gives a red rash and which can affect an unborn child if caught by a pregnant woman. **mea•sly,** *adj. inf.* miserable/small.

meas•ure ['meʒə] 1. *n.* (a) quantity; size; **made to m.** = made specially to fit. (b) unit for showing the size/quantity of sth. (c) thing for showing the size/quantity of sth; small metal cup; long tape with inches/centimeters marked on it. (d) action; **as a precautionary m.** = as a precaution. (e) seam/layer of coal. (f) plan of a new law/a bill. (g) time (in music); rhythm (in poetry). 2. *v.* to be of a certain size/length/quantity, etc.; to find out the length/quantity of (sth). **meas•ur•a•ble,** *adj.* which can be measured. **meas•ured,**

æ back, aː farm, ɒ top, aɪ pipe, aʊ how, aɪə fire, aʊə flower, ɔː bought, ɔɪ toy, e fed, eəhair, eɪ take, ə afraid, əu boat, əuə lower, vː word, iː heap, ɪ hit, ɪə hear, uː school, ʊ book, ʌ but, b back, d dog, ð then, dʒ just, f fog, g go, h hand, j yes, k catch, l last, m mix, n nut, ŋ sing, p penny, r round, s some, ʃ short, t too, tʃ chop, θ thing, v voice, w was, z zoo, ʒ treasure

adj. regular; **with m. steps** = in a slow and stately way. **meas•ure•less,** *adj.* so large that it cannot be measured. **meas•ure•ment,** *n.* (a) finding out the size/length/quantity of sth. (b) quantity/size, etc., found out when you measure. **measure up to,** *v.* to be able to do (a difficult job). **meas•ur•ing,** *n.* finding out the size/length/quantity of sth; **m. tape** = long tape with inches/centimeters marked on it; **m. cup** = cup with quantities marked on it by lines.

meat [miːt] *n.* flesh of an animal which is eaten. **meat•ball,** *n.* minced meat rolled into a ball and cooked. **meat•y,** *adj.* (a) with a lot of meat. (b) with a lot of details/information.

mec•ca ['mekə] *n.* place which attracts a large number of people.

me•chan•ic [mɪ'kænɪk] *n.* person who works on engines. **me•chan•i•cal,** *adj.* referring to a machine. **me•chan•i•cal•ly,** *adv.* by machine; like a machine; automatically. **me•chan•ics,** *n.* (a) the study of force and power. (b) the study of machines. (c) way in which sth works. **mech•an•ism** ['mekənɪzəm] *n.* (a) working parts (of a machine). (b) way in which sth works. **mech•a•ni•za•tion** [mekənaɪ'zeɪʃn] *n.* introduction of machines to take the place of manual labor. **mech•a•nize** ['mekənaɪz] *v.* to introduce machines in place of manual labor. **mech•a•nized,** *adj.* (soldiers/military unit) equipped with armored vehicles.

mech•a•tron•ics [mekə'trɒnɪks] *n.* combination of mechanics and electronics in manufacturing processes.

med•al ['medl] *n.* metal disk, usu. attached to a ribbon, made to commemorate an important occasion; **gold/silver/bronze m.** = medal for first/second/third place in competitions. **me•dal•lion** [mɪ'dæljən] *n.* large medal. **med•al•list** ['medəlɪst] *n.* person who has won a medal in a sports competition, etc.

med•dle ['medl] *v.* (**in/with**) to interfere; to get involved with. **med•dler,** *n.* person who likes to meddle. **med•dle•some,** *adj.* (person) who interferes. **med•dling.** 1. *n.* interfering. 2. *adj.* (person) who is always interfering.

me•di•a ['miːdɪə] *n. pl.* (a) means of communicating information; **the (mass) m.** = newspapers/TV/radio, etc. (b) *see also* **me•di•um.**

me•di•ae•val [medɪ'iːvl] *adj. see* **me•di•e•val.**

me•di•an ['miːdɪən] *adj. & n.* (point) which is in the middle/(line) which goes through the middle. **me•di•al,** *adj.* in the middle.

me•di•ate ['miːdɪeɪt] *v.* to intervene/to try to bring peace between two opponents.

me•di•a•tion [miːdɪ'eɪʃn] *n.* attempt to make two opponents agree. **me•di•a•tor,** *n.* person who tries to make two opponents agree.

med•i•cal ['medɪkl] 1. *adj.* referring to the study of disease; **the m. profession** = all doctors. 2. *n. inf.* examination of the body by a doctor. **med•ic,** *n. inf.* doctor. **med•i•cal•ly,** *adv.* in a medical way. **me•dic•a•ment,** *n.* (*formal*) medicine. **med•i•cate,** *v.* to add a medicine to (sth). **med•i•ca•tion,** *n.* drug.

med•i•cine ['medsɪn] *n.* (a) study of disease, ill health and their cure. (b) liquid/powder/pill taken to cure an illness; **m. ball** = large heavy ball used for physical exercises; **m. chest** = cupboard for keeping medicines in. **me•dic•i•nal** [me'dɪsɪnl] *adj.* used to treat an illness. **me•dic•i•nal•ly,** *adv.* (used) as a medicine. **med•i•cine man,** *n.* witch doctor.

me•di•e•val [medɪ'iːvl] *adj.* referring to the Middle Ages.

me•di•o•cre [miːdɪ'əʊkə] *adj.* ordinary/not good or bad. **me•di•oc•ri•ty** [miːdɪ'ɒkrɪtɪ] *n.* (a) not being good or bad/ordinariness. (b) very ordinary person with no special talents.

med•i•tate ['medɪteɪt] *v.* (**on/about**) to think deeply about (sth). **med•i•ta•tion** [medɪ'teɪʃn] *n.* long deep (often religious) thought. **med•i•ta•tive,** *adj.* thoughtful.

me•di•um ['miːdɪəm] 1. *adj.* middle/average. 2. *n.* (*pl.* **media/mediums**) (a) middle point; **happy m.** = compromise. (b) type of paint used by an artist. (c) means of doing sth/of communicating sth. (d) person who thinks the spirits of dead people can talk through him/her.

med•lar ['medlə] *n.* fruit like a brown apple; tree which bears this fruit.

med•ley ['medlɪ] *n.* mixture.

me•dul•la [medjulə] *n.* bone marrow; the soft inner part of any organ.

meek [miːk] *adj.* (-er, -est) quiet/humble. **meek•ly,** *adv.* quietly/humbly. **meek•ness,** *n.* quietness/humility.

meer•schaum ['mɪəʃəm] *n.* white substance, used to make tobacco pipes.

meet [miːt] 1. *n.* gathering, as of huntsmen or swimmers/runners for a competition. 2. *v.* (**met**) (a) to come together. (b) to become acquainted with s.o.; **we have already met** = we know each other already. (c) to satisfy (needs). **meet•ing,** *n.* (a) coming together. (b) group of people who meet for a special purpose. **meet with,** *v.* (a) to find/to come up against; to have (an accident). (b) to have a meeting.

mega- ['megə] *prefix meaning* (a) very large. (b) one million.

meg•a•byte ['megəbaɪt] *n.* unit of storage for a computer, equal to 1,048,576 bytes.

meg•a•cy•cle ['megəsaɪkl], **meg•a•hertz** ['megəhɜːts] *n.* frequency of radio waves of one million cycles per second.

meg•a•lith ['megəlɪθ] *n.* huge stone set up by prehistoric people.

meg•a•lo•ma•ni•a [megələ'meɪnɪə] *n.* mad belief that you are more important/more powerful than you really are. **meg•a•lo•ma•ni•ac,** *n.* person suffering from megalomania.

meg•a•phone ['megəfəʊn] *n.* metal trumpet which makes the voice sound louder.

meg•a•ton ['megətʌn] *n.* force of an explosion equal to the force produced by exploding one million tons of TNT.

mei•o•sis [miː'əʊsɪs] *n.* splitting of cells.

mel•an•chol•y ['melənkəlɪ] 1. *n.* great sadness. 2. *adj.* very sad. **mel•an•cho•li•a,** [melən'kəʊlɪə] *n.* (*formal*) melancholy state. **mel•an•chol•ic** [melən'kɒlɪk] *adj.* very sad.

mel•a•nin ['melənɪn] *n.* pigment which colors the hair and skin. **mel•a•no•ma,** *n.* cancer caused by sunlight.

me•lee ['meleɪ] *n.* crowd of struggling people.

mel•lif•lu•ous [me'lɪflʊəs] *adj.* soothing/pleasant (sound).

mel•low ['meləʊ] 1. *adj.* ripe (fruit); (wine) which has matured; soft/rich (voice); calm and relaxed (older person). 2. *v.* to grow ripe/to mature; to become soft/rich; **he has mellowed** = he is much less angry/unpleasant than he used to be. **mel•low•ness,** *n.* ripeness/maturity.

mel•o•dra•ma ['melədrɑːmə] *n.* extremely exciting but badly-written play which emphasizes violently alternating passions. **mel•o•dra•mat•ic** [melədrə'mætɪk] *adj.* arousing violent emotions. **me•lo•dra•mat•i•cal•ly,** *adv.* in a melodramatic way.

mel•o•dy ['melədɪ] *n.* tune. **me•lod•ic** [mɪ'lɒdɪk] *adj.* referring to tunes. **me•lo•di•ous** [mə'ləʊdɪəs] *adj.* tuneful. **me•lo•di•ous•ly,** *adv.* in a tuneful way.

mel•on ['melən] *n.* large round fruit of a creeping plant; **waterm.** = very large type of melon with red flesh and black seeds.

melt [melt] *v.* to change from solid to liquid by heating; **to m. down scrap metal** = to heat it and make it into blocks so that it can be used again; **my heart melted at the sight of the pup-** pies = became softened/less angry. **melt•ing point,** *n.* temperature at which a solid becomes liquid. **melt•ing pot,** *n.* (a) pot in which metals can be melted. (b) place where people of different origins come to live together.

mem•ber ['membə] *n.* (a) person who belongs to a group, organization, etc. (b) limb on a human body. **mem•ber•ship,** *n.* (a) belonging to a group, organization, etc.; **m. card** = card which shows you belong (to a club/party). (b) all the members of a group, organization, etc.

mem•brane ['membreɪn] *n.* thin layer of tissue in the body.

me•men•to [mə'mentəʊ] *n.* (*pl.* -os, -oes) thing kept to remind you of sth; souvenir.

mem•o ['meməʊ] *n.* (*pl.* -os) note/short message between people working in the same organization; **m. pad** = pad of paper for writing short notes.

mem•oir ['memwɑː] *n. usu.* **memoirs** = written account of what you can remember of your life.

mem•o•ran•dum [memə'rændəm] *n.* (*pl.* -dums, -da) note/short message.

mem•o•ry ['memərɪ] *n.* (a) ability to remember; **he recited the poem from m.; if my m. serves me right** = if I can remember it correctly. (b) what you remember; **in m. of** = to remind us of. (c) capacity for storing information (in a computer). **mem•o•ra•ble,** *adj.* which you cannot forget/very striking. **me•mo•ri•al** [mɪ'mɔːrɪəl] 1. *adj.* which reminds you of sth/s.o.; **m. service** = church service to remember someone who has died. 2. *n.* monument to remind you of sth/s.o. **mem•o•rize,** *v.* to learn (sth) by heart.

men [men] *n. pl. see* **man.**

men•ace ['menəs] 1. *n.* threat; bad thing; **that child's a m.** = very naughty. 2. *v.* to threaten; **menacing clouds** = clouds which threaten to bring rain. **men•ac•ing•ly,** *adv.* in a threatening way.

mé•nage [me'nɑːʒ] *n.* household.

me•nag•er•ie [mɪ'nædʒərɪ] *n.* small zoo; collection of more or less wild animals.

mend [mend] 1. *n.* (a) place where a piece of clothing has been repaired. (b) *inf.* **on the m.** = getting better. 2. *v.* to repair; to be repaired. **mend•er,** *n.* person who mends.

æ back, ɑː farm, ɒ top, aɪ pipe, aʊ how, aɪə fire, aʊə flower, ɔː bought, ɔɪ toy, e fed, eəhair, eɪ take, ə afraid, əʊ boat, əʊə lower, ɜː word, iː heap, ɪ hit, ɪə hear, uː school, ʊ book, ʌ but, b back, d dog, ð then, dʒ just, f fog, g go, h hand, j yes, k catch, l last, m mix, n nut, ŋ sing, p penny, r round, s some, ʃ short, t too, tʃ chop, θ thing, v voice, w was, z zoo, ʒ treasure

mend•ing, *n.* (a) repairing. (b) clothes which need repairing.

men•dac•i•ty [men'dæsɪtɪ] *n.* (*formal*) telling lies. **men•da•cious** [men'deɪʃəs] *adj.* not truthful.

men•di•cant ['mendɪkənt] *adj.* (person) who begs.

men•folk ['menfəʊk] *n. pl.* all the men (in a family/group, etc.).

men•hir ['menhɪə] *n.* tall standing stone, erected by prehistoric people.

me•ni•al ['miːnɪəl] *adj.* low; badly paid.

Mé•nière's dis•ease ['meɪnɪeəzdɪ'siːz] *n.* disease of the middle ear, causing dizziness.

men•in•gi•tis [menɪn'dʒaɪtɪs] *n.* inflammation of the membrane covering the brain.

me•nis•cus [me'nɪskəs] *n.* curved surface of a drop of water.

men•o•pause ['menəpɔːz] *n.* period of life (around the age of 50) when women become no longer capable of bearing children; **male m.** = difficult period in a man's life (around the age of 50).

men•stru•ate ['menstrʊeɪt] *v.* (*of women*) to lose blood through the vagina at regular periods. **men•stru•al,** *adj.* referring to the regular monthly loss of blood through the vagina. **men•stru•a•tion** [menstrʊ'eɪʃn] *n.* monthly loss of blood through the vagina.

men•su•ra•tion [mensjʊə'reɪʃn] *n.* study of measurement.

men's wear, menswear ['menzweə] *n.* (*no pl.*) clothes for men.

men•tal ['mentl] *adj.* referring to the mind; **m. arithmetic** = calculations done in the head; **m. age** = way of showing the development of a person's mind, by expressing it as the age at which such development is normal; **m. hospital** = hospital for those who suffer from illnesses of the mind. **men•tal•i•ty** [men'tælɪtɪ] *n.* (a) mental power. (b) way of thinking which is typical of s.o./of a group. **men•tal•ly,** *adv.* concerning the brain; **m. defective** = well below normal intelligence.

men•thol ['menθɒl] *n.* white substance which tastes strongly of mint. **men•tho•lat•ed,** *adj.* treated with menthol; with menthol added.

men•tion ['menʃn] 1. *n.* reference to sth. 2. *v.* to refer to (sth); **not to m.** = not forgetting/as well as.

men•tor ['mentɔː] *n.* (*formal*) person who teaches/helps another (younger) person.

men•u ['menjuː] *n.* (a) list of food available in a restaurant. (b) list of options available in a computer program.

me•ow, miaow [miː'aʊ] 1. *n.* call of a cat. 2. *v.* to call like a cat.

mer•can•tile ['mɜːkəntaɪl] *adj.* referring to commerce.

mer•ce•nar•y ['mɜːsənərɪ] 1. *adj.* (person) who is interested only in money. 2. *n.* person who serves foreigners as a soldier for money.

mer•cer•ize ['mɜːsəraɪz] *v.* to make (cotton cloth) shiny.

mer•chant ['mɜːtʃənt] *n.* businessman; person who buys and sells; **m. marine** = commercial ships of a country; **m. seaman** = seaman in the merchant marine. **mer•chan•dise,** 1. *n.* goods for sale. 2. *v.* to sell (goods) by wide and varied advertising. **mer•chant•man, merchant ship,** *n.* (*pl.* **-men**) commercial ship.

mer•cu•ry ['mɜːkjərɪ] *n.* (*element:* Hg) liquid metal used in thermometers/barometers, etc. **mer•cu•ri•al** [mɜː'kjʊərɪəl] *adj.* (person) whose temper changes frequently.

mer•cy ['mɜːsɪ] *n.* (a) compassion/pity; kindness toward unfortunate people; **to have m. on** = to forgive/not to want to punish/harm s.o.; **m. killing** = euthanasia, killing of s.o. who is very ill or in pain; (b) sth to be grateful for. **mer•ci•ful,** *adj.* (person) who forgives/who is kind. **mer•ci•ful•ly,** *adv.* thankfully; in a forgiving/kindly way. **mer•ci•less,** *adj.* harsh/cruel. **mer•ci•less•ly,** *adv.* without mercy. **mer•ci•less•ness,** *n.* lack of pity; hardness (of character).

mere ['mɪə] 1. *n.* (*old*) small lake. 2. *adj.* simply/only; **he's a m. boy** = only a boy; **the m. sight of grass makes me sneeze** = simply the sight of grass makes me sneeze. **mere•ly,** *adv.* only/simply.

mer•e•tri•cious [merɪ'trɪʃəs] *adj.* showy and cheap.

mer•gan•ser [mɜː'gænzə] *n.* type of large duck, with a crest.

merge [mɜːdʒ] *v.* to join together (**with** sth). **merg•er,** *n.* amalgamation/joining of two companies.

me•rid•i•an [mə'rɪdɪən] *n.* imaginary line drawn from the North Pole to the South Pole; **the Greenwich m.** = line passing through Greenwich, England, from which longitude is calculated.

me•ringue [mə'ræŋ] *n.* sweet baked dessert made of egg whites and sugar.

me•ri•no [mə'riːnəʊ] *n.* (*pl.* **-os**) type of long-haired sheep/fine woolen material.

mer•it ['merɪt] 1. *n.* value/quality/excellence; **to go into the merits of** = to examine the good and bad points of. 2. *v.* to be worthy of/to deserve (sth). **mer•i•to•ri•ous** [merɪ'tɔːrɪəs] *adj.* (*formal*) which is valuable/which should be rewarded.

mer•maid ['mɜːmeɪd] *n.* mythical creature,

half woman and half fish. **mer•man**, *n.* mythical creature, half man and half fish.

mer•ry ['merɪ] *adj.* (**-ier, -iest**) happy; **to make m.** = to have a good time; **the more the merrier** = the more there are the happier everything is. **mer•ri•ly**, *adv.* happily. **mer•ri•ment**, *n.* fun. **mer•ry-go-round**, *n.* platform that revolves, with wooden horses, etc., in an amusement park, etc. **mer•ry•mak•er**, *n.* person who is enjoying himself. **mer•ry•mak•ing**, *n.* festivity/celebration.

mesh [meʃ] 1. *n.* (*pl.* **-es**) space between the threads of a net. 2. *v.* (*of a cogwheel*) to link together with another toothed wheel.

mes•mer•ize ['mezməraɪz] *v.* to hypnotize.

mess [mes] 1. *n.* (*pl.* **-es**) (a) dirt; disorder/confusion; **they made a m. of the repair job** = they did the repair job badly. (b) group of soldiers/sailors, etc. who eat together; room where officers eat and sleep. 2. *v.* (**with**) to eat together. **mess a•bout**, *v.* (a) to spend your spare time doing sth. (b) to waste time. **mess•i•ly**, *adv.* in a messy way. **mess up**, *v. inf.* (a) to dirty. (b) to ruin/to spoil. **mess•y**, *adj.* (**-ier, -iest**) dirty; disorderly.

mes•sage ['mesɪdʒ] *n.* news/information sent; *inf.* **he got the m.** = he understood.

mes•sen•ger, *n.* person who brings a message.

mes•si•ah [mɪ'saɪə] *n.* (a) person whom the Jews expect will come to free them. (b) Jesus Christ. **mes•si•an•ic** [mesɪ'ænɪk] *adj.* referring to the Messiah.

Messrs. ['mesəz] *n. used formally as plural of* Mr.

met [met] *v. see* **meet**.

meta- ['metə] *prefix meaning* change.

me•tab•o•lism [me'tæbəlɪzəm] *n.* processes by which plants and animals use food to create energy. **met•a•bol•ic** [metə'bɒlɪk] *adj.* referring to metabolism.

met•a•car•pus ['metə'kɑːpəs] *n.* the bones in the hand.

met•al ['metl] *n.* usu. solid mineral substance which can conduct heat and electricity. **me•tal•lic** [mə'tælɪk] *adj.* referring to metal. **met•al•lur•gist** [me'tælədʒɪst] *n.* person who studies metals. **met•al•lur•gy** [me-'tælədʒɪ] *n.* study of metals. **met•al•work**, *n.* making things with metal; pieces of metal made into a construction/a work of art.

met•a•mor•pho•sis [metə'mɔːfəsɪs] *n.* (*pl.* **-phoses** [-fəsiːz]) change, esp. an insect's

change of form. **met•a•mor•phose** [metə-'mɔːfəuz] *v.* to change from one state to another.

met•a•phor ['metəfə] *n.* way of describing sth by suggesting it has the properties of sth else. **met•a•phor•i•cal** [metə'fɒrɪkl] *adj.* like a metaphor. **met•a•phor•i•cal•ly**, *adv.* in a metaphorical way.

met•a•phys•ics [metə'fɪzɪks] *n.* philosophical study of truth/knowledge/existence, etc. **met•a•phys•i•cal**, *adj.* referring to metaphysics.

met•a•tar•sus [metə'tɑːsəs] *n.* the bones in the foot.

me•tath•e•sis [me'tæθəsɪs] *n.* change of sounds in a word, where letters are transposed.

mete out ['miːt'aut] *v.* to give (punishment).

me•te•or ['miːtɪə] *n.* small object which flashes through space and shines brightly as it burns up on entering the earth's atmosphere. **me•te•or•ic** [miːtɪ'ɒrɪk] *adj.* like a meteor/very rapid. **me•te•or•ite** ['miːtɪəraɪt] *n.* lump of rock/iron which falls to earth from space.

me•te•or•ol•o•gy [miːtɪə'rɒlədʒɪ] *n.* study of climate and weather. **me•te•or•o•log•i•cal** [miːtɪərə'lɒdʒɪkl] *adj.* referring to the climate and weather; **m. station** = research station which notes weather conditions. **me•te•or•ol•o•gist** [miːtɪə-'rɒlədʒɪst] *n.* person who studies climate and weather.

me•ter, *Brit.* **me•tre** ['miːtə] 1. *n.* (a) device for counting how much time/water/gas, etc., has been used; **parking m.** = device into which you put money to pay for parking. (b) standard measurement of length (approximately 39.4 inches). (c) regular rhythm in poetry. 2. *v.* to count by a meter. **met•ric** ['metrɪk] *adj.* (a) referring to meter as a measurement; **the m. system** = system of measurement based on meters, liters, etc. (b) referring to meter as rhythm. **met•ri•cal**, *adj.* (poem) written in a regular rhythm. **met•ri•cate** ['metrɪkeɪt] *v.* to express in meters/centimeters, etc. **met•ri•ca•tion** [metrɪ'keɪʃn] *n.* changing of a measuring system to the metric system.

meth•ane ['miːθeɪn] *n.* colorless gas, which easily catches fire and is found naturally in the ground.

meth•a•nol ['meθənɒl] *n.* methyl alcohol.

meth•od ['meθəd] *n.* (a) way of doing sth. (b)

æ back, ɑː farm, ɒ top, aɪ pipe, au how, aiə fire, auə flower, ɔ bought, ɔɪ toy, e fed, eəhair, eɪ take, ə afraid, əu boat, əuə lower, vː word, iː heap, ɪ hit, ɪə hear, uː school, u book, ʌ but, b back, d dog, ð then, dʒ just, f fog, g go, h hand, j yes, k catch, l last, m mix, n nut, ŋ sing, p penny, r round, s some, ʃ short, t too, tʃ chop, θ thing, v voice, w was, z zoo, ʒ treasure

well-organized system. **me•thod•i•cal** [mɪ'θɒdɪkl] *adj.* ordered/regulated. **me•thod•i•cal•ly**, *adv.* in a well-organized way. **Meth•od•ist**, *n. & adj.* (person) following the teaching of John Wesley. **meth•od•ol•o•gy**, *n.* methods used in a certain process or study.

meth•yl [meθɪl] *n.* **m. alcohol** = poisonous alcohol found in wood. **meth•yl•at•ed spir•its** ['meθɪleɪtɪd'spɪrɪts] *n.* alcohol used for lighting or heating.

me•tic•u•lous [me'tɪkjʊləs] *adj.* attentive to detail (**about** doing sth). **me•tic•u•lous•ly**, *adv.* carefully/paying attention to details. **me•tic•u•lous•ness**, *n.* being meticulous.

me•tier ['metɪeɪ] *n.* profession; occupation one is good at.

me•tre ['miːtə] *n. & v. Brit. see* **me•ter.**

met•ro•nome ['metrənəum] *n.* device which beats time regularly, used when practicing/playing music.

me•trop•o•lis [mə'trɒpəlɪs] *n. (pl. -es)* large capital city. **met•ro•pol•i•tan** [metrə'pɒlɪtən] 1. *adj.* referring to a large capital city. 2. *n.* chief bishop in the Orthodox Church.

met•tle ['metl] *n.* vigor/strength of character (of a person); **to put s.o. on his m.** = to make s.o. try to do his best. **met•tle•some**, *adj.* (*formal*) vigorous/active.

mew [mju:] 1. *n.* soft cry which a cat makes. 2. *v.* to make a soft cry like a cat.

mews [mju:z] *n.* (*esp. Brit.*) (a) row of former stables or garages converted into houses. (b) stables.

Mex•i•can ['meksɪkən] 1. *adj.* referring to Mexico. 2. *n.* person from Mexico.

mez•za•nine ['metsəni:n] *n.* floor between the ground floor and the first floor.

mez•zo-so•pra•no ['metsəusə'prɑːnəu] *n.* singer or voice lower in pitch than a soprano.

mez•zo•tint ['medzəutɪnt] *n.* print made from a plate which has rough and smooth areas.

Mg *symbol for* magnesium.

mg *abbrev. for* milligram.

mi•aow [mi:'au] *see* **me•ow.**

mi•as•ma [mɪ'æzmə] *n.* unpleasant/poisonous air.

mi•ca ['maɪkə] *n.* type of mineral which splits into thin glittering layers.

mice [maɪs] *n. pl. see* **mouse.**

Mich•ael•mas ['mɪkəlməs] *n.* (*esp. Brit.*) 29th September; **M. daisy** = common autumn garden flower.

micro- ['maɪkrəu] 1. *prefix meaning* (a) very small. (b) one millionth. 2. *n.* microcomputer.

mi•crobe ['maɪkrəub] *n.* germ; tiny living organism.

mi•cro•chip ['maɪkrəutʃɪp] *n.* small piece of silicon used in electronics.

mi•cro•com•pu•ter [maɪkrəukʌm'pjuːtə] *n.* small computer for office or personal use.

mi•cro•cli•mate ['maɪkrəu'klaɪmət] *n.* climate of a small area.

mi•cro•cosm ['maɪkrəkɒzəm] *n.* miniature version.

mi•cro•fiche ['maɪkrəfi:ʃ] *n.* index card made of microfilms.

mi•cro•film ['maɪkrəfɪlm] 1. *n.* film on which sth is photographed in very small scale. 2. *v.* to make a very small-scale photograph of.

mi•cro•me•ter [maɪ'krɒmɪtə] *n.* instrument for measuring very small distances.

mi•cron ['maɪkrɒn] *n.* one millionth of a meter.

mi•cro•or•gan•ism [maɪkrəu'ɒgənɪzm] *n.* tiny living organism.

mi•cro•phone ['maɪkrəfəun] *n.* apparatus for capturing sound and passing it to a loudspeaker or recording apparatus.

mi•cro•proc•es•sor [maɪkrəu'prəusesə] *n.* small central processing unit using microchips.

mi•cro•scope ['maɪkrəskəup] *n.* apparatus which enlarges things which are very small. **mi•cro•scop•ic** [maɪkrə'skɒpɪk] *adj.* so small as to be visible only through a microscope.

mi•cro•wave ['maɪkrəweɪv] *n.* very short electric wave; **m. oven** = small oven which cooks very rapidly using microwaves.

mid- [mɪd] *prefix meaning* middle. **mid•day**, *n.* twelve o'clock noon. **mid•land**, *adj. & n.* (referring to the) central part of a country; **the Midlands** = the central part of England. **mid•night**, *n.* twelve o'clock at night. **mid•riff**, *n.* front part of the body above the waist and below the chest. **mid•ship•man**, *n. (pl. -men)* student trainee officer in the U.S. Navy. **midst**, *n.* middle; **in our m.** = among us. **mid•stream**, *n.* middle part of a river. **mid•sum•mer**, *n.* middle of the summer. **mid•way**, *adv.* half-way. **Mid•west**, *n.* central northern part of the United States. **mid•win•ter**, *n.* middle of the winter.

mid•den ['mɪdn] *n.* heap of dung.

mid•dle ['mɪdl] 1. *adj.* in the center; half-way between two things; **m. sized** = neither big nor small; **m. class** = professional class (between the upper class and the lower class); **the M. Ages** = historical period between the Dark Ages and the Renaissance (about 1000 to 1500). 2. *n.* (a) center; central point. (b) waistline. **mid•dle-aged**, *adj.* not young and not old (between 40 and 60 years of age). **Mid•dle East**, *n.* area between Egypt and

Pakistan. **Mid•dle East•ern,** *adj.* referring to the Middle East. **mid•dle•man,** *n.* (*pl.* -men) businessman who buys from one source to sell to another. **mid•dle-of-the-road,** *adj.* center/moderate (politics). **mid•dle•weight,** *n.* weight in boxing between welterweight and light heavyweight. **mid•dling,** *adj.* neither good nor bad; not very large or small.

midge [mɪdʒ] *n.* small stinging flying insect.

mid•get ['mɪdʒɪt] *n.* very small person or thing.

mid•wife ['mɪdwaɪf] *n.* (*pl.* -wives ['-waɪvz]) person (usu. a woman) trained to help deliver a baby. **mid•wife•ry** ['mɪdwɪfrɪ] *n.* work of helping deliver babies.

mien [miːn] *n.* way in which a person behaves or looks.

miff [mɪf] *v. inf.* to offend/to annoy (s.o.).

might [maɪt] 1. *v. see* **may.** 2. *n.* force/strength. **might•y.** 1. *adj.* (-ier, -iest) (a) strong. (b) great; *inf.* **you're in a m. hurry** = you are very impatient. 2. *adv. inf.* very. **might•i•ly,** *adv.* greatly.

mi•gnon•ette [mɪnjəˈnet] *n.* scented garden plant.

mi•graine ['miːɡreɪn] *n.* recurrent very bad headache.

mi•grate [maɪˈɡreɪt] *v.* to move from one place to another with the seasons. **mi•grant** ['maɪɡrənt] *adj. & n.* (bird) which moves from one place to another with the seasons; (worker) who moves from one job to another or from one country to another. **mi•gra•tion** [maɪˈɡreɪʃn] *n.* movement of birds from one country to another. **mi•gra•to•ry** ['maɪɡrətərɪ] *adj.* referring to migration.

mike [maɪk] *n. inf.* microphone.

milch [mɪltʃ] *adj.* **m. cow** = cow kept for milk.

mild [maɪld] *adj.* (-er, -est) (a) soft/not severe (punishment). (b) not harsh (weather). (c) not strong/powerful. **mild•ly,** *adj.* softly/kindly; **to put it m.** = not to say anything rude. **mild•ness,** *n.* kindness/softness; warmness (of winter weather).

mil•dew ['mɪldjuː] 1. *n.* powdery fungus on plants/paper/leather, etc. 2. *v.* to become covered with mildew. **mil•dewed,** *adj.* covered with mildew.

mile [maɪl] *n.* measure of length (1,760 yards/1.61 kilometers); *inf.* **miles of string** = very long piece of string; **it's miles too big** =

much too big. **mile•age,** *n.* (a) distance traveled in miles; **car with a low m.** = car which has not traveled as much as is normal. (b) *inf.* **to get a lot of m. out of** = to gain benefit from. **mil•er,** *n.* person who runs in a 1 mile race. **mile•stone,** *n.* stone showing distance in miles; important point (history, etc.).

mi•lieu ['miːljɜː] *n.* surroundings/environment.

mil•i•tant ['mɪlɪtənt] *adj. & n.* (person) who supports a policy of violence; (person) who is very active in supporting a cause/a political party. **mil•i•tan•cy,** *n.* activity/vigor (in supporting a political party/a cause).

mil•i•tar•y ['mɪlɪtrɪ] 1. *adj.* referring to the army or armed forces. 2. *n.* **the m.** = the armed forces. **mil•i•ta•rism,** *n.* belief in the use of the military to solve political problems. **mil•i•ta•rist,** *n.* person who believes in militarism. **mil•i•ta•ris•tic,** *adj.* believing that the military should be used to solve political problems. **mil•i•tate,** *v.* to work actively (against). **mi•li•tia** [mɪˈlɪʃə] *n.* emergency military force made of ordinary citizens rather than professional soldiers.

milk [mɪlk] 1. *n.* white liquid produced by female mammals for feeding their young, esp. the milk produced by cows; **m. shake** = milk mixed with flavoring and ice cream; **m. choco-late** = pale brown chocolate (flavored with milk); **m. teeth** = first set of teeth produced by a child. 2. *v.* (a) to take the milk from (an animal). (b) to get all the money from (s.o.). **milk•er,** *n.* (a) person who milks. (b) **good m.** = cow which produces a lot of milk. **milk•ing,** *n.* taking milk from a cow; **m. ma-chine** = machine which milks cows automatically. **milk•man,** *n.* (*pl.* -men) person who delivers the milk to houses each morning. **milk•y,** *adj.* (-ier, -iest) tasting like milk; cloudy like milk; containing milk; **the M. Way** = luminous band in the night sky composed of many stars.

mill [mɪl] 1. *n.* (a) machine for grinding corn into flour; building which contains such a machine; *inf.* **he's been through the m.** = he has suffered a great deal. (b) small instrument for grinding. (c) large factory. 2. *v.* (a) to grind (corn, etc.). (b) to put vertical lines around the edge of a coin. **mill a•bout, mill around,** *v.* to move in various directions. **mill•er,** *n.* man who runs a flour mill. **mill•pond,** *n.* water dammed to provide power for a watermill. **mill•stone,** *n.* (a) large grooved stone used

æ back, aː farm, ɒ top, aɪ pipe, aʊ how, aiə fire, aʊə flower, ɔː bought, ɔɪ toy, e fed, eəhair, eɪ take, ə afraid, əʊ boat, əʊə lower, vː word, iː heap, ɪ hit, ɪə hear, uː school, ʊ book, ʌ but, b back, d dog, ð then, dʒ just, f fog, g go, h hand, j yes, k catch, l last, m mix, n nut, ŋ sing, p penny, r round, s some, ʃ short, t too, tʃ chop, θ thing, v voice, w was, z zoo, ʒ treasure

to grind corn, etc. (b) great obstacle which causes trouble.

mil•len•ni•um [mɪ'lenɪəm] *n.* (*pl.* -**ia**) (a) period of a thousand years; **m. bug** = problems with computer software/hardware caused by the change in date to the year 2000. (b) period of great happiness.

mil•le•pede ['mɪlɪpiːd] *n.* millipede.

mil•let ['mɪlɪt] *n.* grain used for food.

milli- ['mɪlɪ] *prefix meaning* one thousandth.

mil•li•bar ['mɪlɪbɑː] *n.* unit of atmospheric pressure.

mil•li•gram ['mɪlɪgræm] *n.* one thousandth of a gram.

mil•li•me•ter ['mɪlɪmiːtə], *Brit.* **mil•li•me•tre** *n.* one thousandth of a meter.

mil•li•ner ['mɪlɪnə] *n.* person who makes/sells women's hats. **mil•li•ner•y**, *n.* hats and ribbons.

mil•lion ['mɪljən] number 1,000,000. **mil•lion•aire** [mɪljə'neə] *n.* person who has more than a million dollars. **mil•lionth, 1,000,000th,** 1. *adj.* referring to a million. 2. *n.* one of a million parts.

mil•li•pede ['mɪlɪpiːd] *n.* small creeping animal with a large number of legs.

milt [mɪlt] *n.* sperm from a male fish.

mime [maɪm] 1. *n.* (a) actor who does not speak, but conveys a story/emotions through gesture. (b) gesture used to convey a story/emotions. (c) story conveyed by gestures. 2. *v.* to convey a story/emotions through gesture.

mim•ic ['mɪmɪk] 1. *n.* person who imitates. 2. *v.* (**mimicked**) to imitate. **mim•ic•ry,** *n.* imitation.

mi•mo•sa [mɪ'məʊzə] *n.* semi-tropical tree with yellow, scented flowers.

min•a•ret [mɪnə'ret] *n.* tower attached to a mosque.

mince [mɪns] 1. *n.* meat which has been ground up into very small pieces. 2. *v.* (a) to grind up (meat/vegetables) until they are in very small pieces; **he didn't m. his words** = he said what he had to say in a straightforward way. (b) **to m. along** = to walk along in a very affected manner, taking small steps. **mince•meat,** *n.* mixture of apples, spices, dried fruit, etc.; **to make m. out of** = to defeat/destroy completely. **mince pie,** *n.* small pie filled with mincemeat, often eaten at Christmas. **minc•er,** *n.* machine for grinding up meat, etc. **minc•ing,** *adj.* (a) affected (way of walking). (b) **m. machine** = mincer.

mind [maɪnd] 1. *n.* power of thinking; memory; **keep him in m.** = remember him; **to make up your m.** = to decide what to do; **I'm in two minds about going** = I can't decide whether to go or not; **I've a good m. to do it myself** = I would very much like to do it myself; **he's changed his m. twice already** = he has changed his decision/his point of view; **what do you have in m.?** = what are you thinking of? **state of m.** = general opinion/mood/feeling; **he's got sth on his m.** = he is worried about sth; **try to take her m. off the subject** = try to stop her thinking about the subject; **not in his right m.** = mad. 2. *v.* (a) to be careful about. (b) to bother about/to be busy about; **m. your own business** = don't interfere in my affairs; **never m.** = don't bother/don't worry. (c) to object to/to be annoyed by; **would you m. shutting the door?** = please shut the door; **I wouldn't m. a cup of tea** = I would rather like a cup of tea. (d) to look after (sth) while the owner is away. **mind-bog•gling,** *adj. inf.* very surprising. **mind•ed,** *adj.* interested (in doing sth); **commercially m.** = businesslike. **mind•ful,** *adj.* remembering/thinking of sth. **mind•less,** *adj.* without thinking/stupid. **mind read•er,** *n.* person who seems to be able to guess what s.o. else is thinking.

mine [maɪn] 1. *n.* (a) deep hole in the ground for digging out minerals; **he is a m. of information** = he is full of information. (b) explosive device which is planted underground or underwater. 2. *v.* (a) to excavate/to dig for minerals. (b) to plant mines underground or under water. 3. *pron.* belonging to me; **he's a friend of m.** = one of my friends. **mine•field,** *n.* area of land/sea full of mines. **mine•lay•er,** *n.* ship which specializes in planting mines under water. **min•er,** *n.* person who works in a mine; **m.'s lamp** = special lamp worn by a miner on his helmet. **mine•sweep•er,** *n.* ship which specializes in removing mines placed under water by the enemy. **mine•work•er,** *n.* worker in a mine. **min•ing,** *n.* (a) action of extracting minerals. (b) placing mines underground or under water.

min•er•al ['mɪnrəl] *adj. & n.* (non-living substance) which is extracted from the earth; **m. water** = (i) water from a spring; (ii) non-alcoholic fizzy drink; **m. rights** = permission to dig out minerals. **min•er•al•o•gist** [mɪnə'rælədʒɪst] *n.* scientist who studies minerals. **min•er•al•o•gy,** *n.* study of minerals.

min•e•stro•ne [mɪnɪ'strəʊnɪ] *n.* type of vegetable soup.

min•gle ['mɪŋgl] *v.* to mix.

min•gy ['mɪndʒɪ] *adj. inf.* mean/not generous (with money, etc.).

min•i ['mɪnɪ] 1. *n.* miniskirt. 2. *adj. & prefix.* very small. **min•i•bus,** *n.* small bus holding about twelve people. **min•i•com** ['mɪnɪkɒm] *n.* machine enabling deaf people to send and receive typed messages by telephone. **min•i•com•put•er,** *n.* small computer, but larger than a micro. **min•i•mar•ket,** *n.* small self-service store. **min•i•skirt,** *n.* very short skirt.

min•i•a•ture ['mɪnɪtʃə] 1. *n.* very small model/portrait/painting. 2. *adj.* very small. **min•i•a•tur•ize,** *v.* to produce a very small version of (sth).

min•im ['mɪnɪm] *n.* note in music lasting half as long as a semibreve.

min•i•mum ['mɪnɪməm] *adj. & n. (pl.* **-mums, -ma)** smallest possible (quantity). **min•i•mal,** *adj.* smallest possible. **min•i•mize,** *v.* to reduce to the smallest amount; to make (sth) seem very small.

min•ion ['mɪnjən] *n.* low-grade assistant (who flatters his boss).

min•is•ter ['mɪnɪstə] 1. *n.* (a) member of a government in charge of a department. (b) Protestant members of the clergy. 2. *v.* **to m. to s.o.'s needs** = to look after s.o./to take care of s.o. **min•is•te•ri•al** [mɪnɪ'stɪərɪəl] *adj.* referring to a government minister. **min•is•tra•tion** [mɪnɪ'streɪʃn] *n.* care/aid, as given by a priest. **min•is•try,** *n.* (a) government department; offices of a government department. (b) work of a member of the clergy.

mink [mɪŋk] *n.* (a) small animal whose fur is very valuable; **m. farm** = farm where these animals are reared. (b) *inf.* mink coat.

min•now ['mɪnəʊ] *n.* small freshwater fish.

mi•nor ['maɪnə] 1. *adj.* (a) lesser; less important; **Asia M.** = Turkey. (b) (musical key) where there are semitones between the second and third, and between the fifth and sixth notes. 2. *n.* young person under the legal age, usu. 18. **mi•nor•i•ty** [maɪ'nɒrɪtɪ] *n.* (a) number/quantity less than half of a total; **the men are in the m.** = there are more women than men. (b) period when a person is less than the legal age, usu. 18 years old.

min•strel ['mɪnstrəl] *n. (old)* traveling singer or musician. (b) one of a group of performers made up to look like black people.

mint [mɪnt] 1. *n.* (a) factory where coins are made; **in m. condition** = perfect/exactly as when it was made; *inf.* **a m. (of money)** = a great deal of money. (b) common herb used as flavoring. (c) small white candy tasting of peppermint. 2. *v.* to make coins.

min•u•et [mɪnju'et] *n.* slow stately dance.

mi•nus ['maɪnəs] 1. *prep.* less; *inf.* **he came m. his wife** = without his wife. 2. *n.* sign (–) meaning less; **m. 10 degrees (–10°).**

mi•nus•cule ['mɪnəskjuːl] *adj.* very small.

min•ute¹ ['mɪnɪt] *n.* (a) one sixtieth part of an hour or of a degree in an angle; **ten minutes past three** = 3:10; **five minutes to four** = 3:55; **m. hand** = long hand on watch or clock; **m. steak** = thin slice of beef which can be cooked quickly. (b) very short space of time; **he'll be here any m. now** = any time now. (c) **minutes** = notes of what is said at a meeting. **min•ut•ed,** *adj.* put in the minutes of a meeting.

mi•nute² [maɪ'njuːt] *adj.* very small. **mi•nute•ly** [maɪ'njuːtlɪ] *adv.* in great detail. **mi•nute•ness** [maɪ'njuːtnəs] *n.* very small size. **mi•nu•ti•ae** [mɪ'njuːʃɪiː] *n. pl.* very small details.

minx [mɪŋks] *n.* naughty girl.

mir•a•cle ['mɪrəkl] *n.* marvelous thing which happens apparently by the power of God; very wonderful happening. **mi•rac•u•lous** [mɪ'rækjuləs] *adj.* wonderful/inexplicable. **mi•rac•u•lous•ly,** *adv.* wonderfully/inexplicably.

mi•rage ['mɪrɑːʒ] *n.* imaginary image caused by heat (such as water and palm trees seen in a desert).

mire ['maɪə] *n. (formal)* muddy place; mud.

mir•ror ['mɪrə] 1. *n.* glass backed by metal which reflects an image; **rear-view m.** = mirror inside a car which enables the driver to see what is behind without turning his head; **m. image** = exact copy, but reversed as in a mirror. 2. *v.* to reflect as in a mirror.

mirth [mɜːθ] *n. (formal)* gaiety/happiness.

mis- [mɪs] *prefix meaning* wrongly.

mis•ad•ven•ture [mɪsəd'ventʃə] *n.* unlucky accident.

mis•an•thrope, misanthropist ['mɪzənθrəʊp, mɪ'zænθrəpɪst] *n.* person who dislikes the human race. **mis•an•throp•ic** [mɪzən'θrɒpɪk] *adj.* (person) who dislikes the human race. **mis•an•thro•py** [mɪ'zænθrəpɪ] *n.* dislike of the human race.

mis•ap•ply [mɪsə'plaɪ] *v.* to use (sth) wrongly.

mis•ap•pre•hend [mɪsæprɪ'hend] *v.* not to understand. **mis•ap•pre•hen•sion** [mɪsæprɪ'henʃən] *n.* not understanding; **laboring under a m.** = not understanding the situation correctly.

mis•ap•pro•pri•ate [mɪsə'prəʊprɪeɪt] *v.* to

æ back, ɑː farm, ɒ top, aɪ pipe, aʊ how, aɪə fire, aʊə flower, ɔ: bought, ɔɪ toy, e fed, eəhair, eɪ take, ə afraid, əʊ boat, əʊə lower, ɜː word, iː heap, ɪ hit, ɪə hear, uː school, ʊ book, ʌ but, b back, d dog, ð then, dʒ just, f fog, g go, h hand, j yes, k catch, l last, m mix, n nut, ŋ sing, p penny, r round, s some, ʃ short, t too, tʃ chop, θ thing, v voice, w was, z zoo, ʒ treasure

use (public money) for your own purposes. **mis•ap•pro•pri•a•tion** [mɪsəprəʊprɪ'eɪʃn] *n.* using public money for your own purposes.

mis•be•have [mɪsbɪ'heɪv] *v.* to act badly/to behave badly. **mis•be•hav•ior,** *n.* bad behavior.

mis•cal•cu•late [mɪs'kælkjʊleɪt] *v.* to calculate wrongly. **mis•cal•cu•la•tion** [mɪskælkju'leɪʃn] *n.* mistake in calculating.

mis•car•ry [mɪs'kærɪ] *v.* (a) (*of plan*) to go wrong. (b) to produce a baby which is not sufficiently developed to live. **mis•car•riage** ['mɪskærɪdʒ] *n.* (a) failure (of a scheme); **m. of justice** = wrong decision by a court. (b) loss of a baby during pregnancy.

mis•cast [mɪs'kɑːst] *v.* (**miscast**) to cast (an actor/actress) in a part which is unsuitable.

mis•cel•la•ne•ous [mɪsə'leɪnɪəs] *adj.* varied/mixed. **mis•cel•la•ny** [mɪ'selənɪ] *n.* collection of varied things (usu. varied pieces of writing).

mis•chance ['mɪs'tʃɑːns] *n.* (*formal*) bad luck.

mis•chief ['mɪstʃɪf] *n.* bad behavior/bad action; **they mean m.** = they are intending to do damage; **to make m.** = to make trouble/to make two people angry with each other; **the boy is always getting into m.** = he's always doing something naughty. **mis•chief-mak•er,** *n.* person who tries to start trouble. **mis•chie•vous** ['mɪstʃɪvəs] *adj.* wicked/naughty. **mis•chie•vous•ly,** *adv.* in a mischevous way. **mis•chie•vous•ness,** *n.* tendency to cause trouble.

mis•con•cep•tion [mɪskən'sepʃən] *n.* mistaken idea.

mis•con•duct [mɪs'kɒndʌkt] *n.* bad conduct/bad behavior; **professional m.** = behavior which is not acceptable in a member of a profession.

mis•con•strue [mɪskən'struː] *v.* not to understand. **mis•con•struc•tion** [mɪskən-'strʌkʃn] *n.* wrong interpretation of an action.

mis•count [mɪs'kaʊnt] *v.* to count wrongly.

mis•cre•ant ['mɪskrɪənt] *n.* wicked person/criminal.

mis•deed [mɪs'diːd] *n.* wicked action.

mis•de•mean•or [mɪsdɪ'miːnə], *Brit.* **mis•de•mean•our** *n.* (not very serious) unlawful act.

mis•di•rect [mɪsdaɪ'rekt] *v.* to give wrong directions to.

mi•ser ['maɪzə] *n.* person who hoards money and refuses to spend it. **mi•ser•li•ness,** *n.* dislike of spending money. **mi•ser•ly,** *adj.* not wanting to spend money.

mis•er•a•ble ['mɪzrəbl] *adj.* sad/unhappy; awful/bad/unpleasant (weather); very low

(salary). **mis•er•a•bly,** *adv.* sadly/unhappily.

mis•er•i•cord [mɪ'zerɪkɔːd] *n.* seat in a medieval church which folds back to show carving on its underside.

mis•er•y ['mɪzərɪ] *n.* sadness; suffering; **her life was sheer m.** = was very unhappy; **to put a dog out of its m.** = to kill a dog because it is in pain; **to put s.o. out of his m.** = to tell s.o. the result/not to keep s.o. waiting any longer.

mis•fire [mɪs'faɪə] *v.* not to fire properly; **the car engine is misfiring** = is not igniting the fuel at the right time; **his plan misfired** = went wrong.

mis•fit ['mɪsfɪt] *n.* person who does not fit in with a group/fit into society.

mis•for•tune [mɪs'fɔːtjuːn] *n.* bad luck.

mis•giv•ing [mɪs'gɪvɪŋ] *n.* doubt/fear.

mis•guid•ed [mɪs'gaɪdɪd] *adj.* badly advised; wrongly judged; foolish.

mis•hap ['mɪshæp] *n.* slight accident.

mish•mash ['mɪʃmæʃ] *n.* disorderly collection; jumble.

mis•in•form [mɪsɪn'fɔːm] *v.* to give (s.o.) wrong information.

mis•in•ter•pret [mɪsɪn'tɜːprɪt] *v.* to interpret wrongly, not to understand correctly. **mis•in•ter•pre•ta•tion** [mɪsɪntɜːprɪ'teɪʃn] *n.* wrong interpretation; misunderstanding.

mis•judge [mɪs'dʒʌdʒ] *v.* to judge wrongly; to form a wrong opinion about (s.o./sth).

mis•lay [mɪs'leɪ] *v.* (**mislaid**) to put (sth) down and not to remember where you have put it.

mis•lead [mɪs'liːd] *v.* (**misled**) to give (s.o.) wrong information/to make (s.o.) make a mistake. **mis•lead•ing,** *adj.* wrong/erroneous; likely to cause a mistake.

mis•man•age [mɪs'mænɪdʒ] *v.* to manage wrongly/badly. **mis•man•age•ment,** *n.* bad management.

mis•match [mɪs'mætʃ] 1. *n.* bad match. 2. *v.* to match (two opponents) badly.

mis•no•mer [mɪs'nəʊmə] *n.* wrong name/wrong term.

mi•sog•y•nist [mɪ'sɒdʒɪnɪst] *n.* man who dislikes women. **mi•sog•y•ny,** *n.* hatred of women.

mis•place [mɪs'pleɪs] *v.* to put in the wrong place.

mis•print ['mɪsprɪnt] *n.* error in printing.

mis•pro•nounce [mɪsprə'naʊns] *v.* to pronounce wrongly. **mis•pro•nun•ci•a•tion** [mɪsprənʌnsɪ'eɪʃn] *n.* pronouncing wrongly.

mis•quote [mɪs'kwəʊt] *v.* to quote wrongly/incorrectly. **mis•quo•ta•tion** [mɪskwəʊ'teɪʃn] *n.* incorrect quotation.

mis•read [mɪs'riːd] *v.* (**misread** [mɪs'red]) to

read wrongly; to make a mistake when reading.

mis•rep•re•sent [mɪsreprɪ'zent] v. to show (sth) wrongly; to give a wrong idea of (sth); to distort (facts). **mis•rep•re•sen•ta•tion** [mɪsreprɪzen'teɪʃn] n. distortion of what s.o. said or wrote.

mis•rule [mɪs'ru:l] 1. n. bad rule/bad government. 2. v. to rule badly.

miss [mɪs] 1. n. (pl. **-es**) (a) failure to hit. (b) title of unmarried woman; **Miss Jones.** (c) title used to address/call s.o., as a waitress, etc. 2. v. (a) not to hit/see, etc.; **you didn't m. much** = there wasn't much to see/the performance was not very good. (b) **he just missed being killed** = he was very nearly killed. (c) to regret the absence of (s.o./sth). **miss•ing,** adj. absent/lost; stolen. **miss out on,** v. inf. not to enjoy (sth) because of being absent.

mis•sal ['mɪsl] n. book containing the text of the Catholic mass and other prayers.

mis•shap•en [mɪs'ʃeɪpn] adj. deformed/oddly shaped.

mis•sile ['mɪsl] n. (a) weapon which is thrown. (b) explosive rocket which can be guided to its target.

mis•sion ['mɪʃn] n. (a) aim/purpose for which s.o. is sent; **her m. in life is to help orphans** = her calling/her chosen task. (b) house/office of a missionary. (c) group of people sent somewhere with a particular aim. (d) embassy or consulate. **mis•sion•ar•y** ['mɪʃənrɪ] adj. & n. (person) whose duty is to try to convert people to his religion. **mis•sion state•ment,** n. formal statement of the objectives of a company/organization.

mis•sive ['mɪsɪv] n. (formal) letter.

mis•spell [mɪs'spel] v. (**mispelled/mispelt**) to spell wrongly. **mis•spell•ing,** n. spelling mistake.

mis•spent ['mɪsspent] adj. (youth) which has been wasted.

mis•state•ment [mɪs'steɪtmənt] n. wrong statement of facts.

mist [mɪst] 1. n. thin fog/haze. 2. v. to get covered with mist; **to m. up** = to become covered with condensation. **mist•i•ness,** n. being misty. **mist•y,** adj. (**-ier, iest**) (a) full of mist. (b) vague (memory).

mis•take [mɪs'teɪk] 1. n. error; wrong action. 2. v. (**mistook; mistaken**) (a) to understand (sth) wrongly. (b) **to m. s.o. for s.o.** = to assume

(s.o.) is s.o. else. **mis•tak•en,** adj. wrong. **mis•tak•en•ly,** adv. by mistake/in error.

mis•ter ['mɪstə] n. inf. form of address to a man.

mis•time [mɪs'taɪm] v. to choose the wrong time/an inconvenient time to do something.

mis•tle•toe ['mɪzltəʊ] n. parasitic plant which grows on oaks or apple trees, used as a Christmas decoration.

mis•took [mɪs'tʊk] v. see **mis•take.**

mis•treat•ment [mɪs'tri:tmənt] n. bad treatment (of prisoners, etc.).

mis•tress ['mɪstrəs] n. (pl. **-es**) (a) woman in charge/who employs/teaches; **she's her own m.** = she is independent. (b) woman who has a sexual relationship with a man without being married to him.

mis•trust [mɪs'trʌst] 1. n. wariness/lack of trust. 2. v. not to trust (s.o.)/to be doubtful about (s.o.). **mis•trust•ful,** adj. not trusting.

mis•un•der•stand [mɪsʌndə'stænd] v. (**misunderstood**) not to understand. **mis•un•der•stand•ing,** n. wrong understanding/disagreement.

mis•use 1. n. [mɪs'ju:s] wrong use. 2. v. [mɪs'ju:z] to use (sth) in a wrong way; to treat (s.o.) badly.

mite [maɪt] n. (a) very small child. (b) very small creature like a spider, living in stale food.

mi•ter, Brit. **mi•tre** ['maɪtə] n. (a) hat worn by bishops and archbishops. (b) (in woodwork) type of sloping joint/sloping edge. **mi•tred,** adj. sloping (joint/edge).

mit•i•gate ['mɪtɪgeɪt] v. to make (a crime) less serious. **mit•i•ga•tion** [mɪtɪ'geɪʃn] n. making less serious.

mi•to•sis [maɪ'təʊsɪs] n. cell division.

mi•tre ['maɪtə] n. Brit. see **mi•ter.**

mitt, mitten [mɪt, 'mɪtn] n. (a) glove without separate fingers, esp. a glove to wash with or to hold hot dishes with. (b) glove which leaves the fingers bare.

mix [mɪks] 1. n. (pl. **-es**) blend/mingling of several things. 2. v. to blend/to mingle. **mixed,** adj. made up of different things put together; **a m. marriage** = marriage between two people of different races; (in tennis) **m. doubles** = doubles match where a man and woman play against another man and woman; **I have very m. feelings about the project** = in some ways I am for it and in others I am against it; **it's a m. blessing** = in some ways it is a good thing, but

---

æ back, ɑ: farm, ɒ: top, aɪ pipe, aʊ how, aɪə fire, aʊə flower, ɔ: bought, ɔɪ toy, e fed, eəhair, eɪ take, ə afraid, əʊ boat, əʊə lower, v: word, i: heap, ɪ hit, ɪə hear, u: school, ʊ book, ʌ but, b back, d dog, ð then, dʒ just, f fog, g go, h hand, j yes, k catch, l last, m mix, n nut, ŋ sing, p penny, r round, s some, ʃ short, t too, tʃ chop, θ thing, v voice, w was, z zoo, ʒ treasure

in others it is not. **mix•er,** *n.* (a) machine for mixing. (b) person who fits in well with other people. **mix•ture** ['mɪkstʃə] *n.* blend/mingling together; **cough m.** = liquid medicine to cure a cough. **mix up,** *v.* (a) to confuse; **I always mix him up with his brother** = I always think he is his brother. (b) to involve. (c) **the speaker got all mixed up** = he got confused/lost his notes. **mix-up,** *n. inf.* confusion.

miz•zen•mast ['mɪzənmɑːst] *n.* mast nearest the stern of a ship. **miz•zen,** *n.* sail on a mizzenmast.

ml *abbrev. for* milliliter.

mm *abbrev. for* millimeter.

Mn *symbol for* manganese.

Mo *symbol for* molybdenum.

mne•mon•ic [nɪˈmɒnɪk] *adj. & n.* (rhyme) which helps you to remember certain facts.

moan [məʊn] 1. *n.* (a) low groan. (b) general complaint. 2. *v.* (a) to make a low groan. (b) to complain (**about** sth). **moan•er,** *n. inf.* person who complains.

moat [məʊt] *n.* wide ditch with water in it, surrounding a castle/old house. **moat•ed,** *adj.* with a moat.

mob [mɒb] 1. *n.* (a) crowd of unruly people. (b) *inf.* criminal gang. 2. *v.* (**mobbed**) to surround in a wild crowd. **mob•ster,** *n. inf.* member of a criminal gang.

mo•bile ['məʊbaɪl, *Am.* 'məʊbl] 1. *adj.* which can move; **he is not very m.** = he can't walk easily. 2. *n.* artistic creation using pieces of metal/paper, etc., which when hung up can move. **mo•bile phone,** *n.* portable telephone that operates on radio signals. **mo•bil•i•ty** [məʊˈbɪlɪtɪ] *n.* ability to move. **mo•bi•li•za•tion** [məʊbɪlaɪˈzeɪʃn] *n.* grouping of people together (esp. to join the armed forces). **mo•bi•lize** ['məʊbɪlaɪz] *v.* to group (people) together (esp. to join the armed forces).

moc•ca•sins ['mɒkəsɪnz] *n. pl.* soft leather shoes.

mo•cha ['mɒkə] *n.* (a) type of coffee from Arabia. (b) coffee and chocolate flavoring.

mock [mɒk] 1. *adj.* false/imitation. 2. *v.* to laugh at (s.o./sth). **mock•er•y,** *n.* (a) laughing at (s.o./sth). (b) thing which is only a bad imitation. **mock•ing,** *adj. & n.* laughing at (s.o./sth). **mock•ing•bird,** *n.* bird from the southern United States which imitates the song of other birds. **mock-up,** *n.* scale model of a new product for testing purposes.

mod [mɒd] *adj. inf. short for* **mod•ern.**

mode [məʊd] *n.* way (of doing sth). **mod•al,** *adj. & n.* (verb such as **can, must,** etc.) which is used with other verbs, and not alone.

mod•el ['mɒdl] 1. *n. & adj.* (a) small-scale

copy. (b) thing which you can take as a perfect example to be copied; **artist's m.** = person whose job is to sit while an artist draws pictures of him/her. (c) person whose job is to wear new clothes to show them to customers. (d) style of car, etc., produced in a particular period. 2. *v.* (**modeled, modelled**) (a) to make a model; to make shapes (of clay); **modeling clay** = special clay for sculpture. (b) **he modeled his way of walking on that of his father** = he imitated his father's way. (c) to wear (new clothes) to show to customers.

mo•dem ['məʊdem] *n.* device for sending data by telephone, linking a computer to the telephone lines.

mod•er•ate 1. *adj. & n.* ['mɒdərət] (a) not excessive; middling. (b) (person) without a violent political bias. 2. *v.* ['mɒdəreɪt] to diminish/to make less strong. **mod•er•ate•ly,** *adv.* quite/not excessively. **mod•er•a•tion** [mɒdəˈreɪʃn] *n.* not an excessive use; calming down. **mod•er•a•tor,** *n.* chairman of a church meeting, public discussion, etc.

mod•ern ['mɒdən] *adj.* of the present day; not ancient; **m. languages** = languages which are spoken today. **mod•ern•ism,** *n.* 20th-century rejection of former traditions in architecture/literature, etc. and in favor of new ideas/methods. **mo•der•ni•ty** [məˈdɜːnɪtɪ] *n.* being modern. **mod•ern•i•za•tion** [mɒdənaɪˈzeɪʃn] *n.* act of modernizing. **mod•ern•ize** ['mɒdənaɪz] *v.* to make modern; to renovate.

mod•est ['mɒdɪst] *adj.* (a) not boasting. (b) not demanding/not excessive. **mod•est•ly,** *adv.* in a modest way. **mod•es•ty,** *n.* (a) not being boastful. (b) not being excessive/demanding.

mod•i•cum ['mɒdɪkəm] *n.* small quantity.

mod•i•fy ['mɒdɪfaɪ] *v.* (a) to change/to alter (sth) to fit a different use. (b) to reduce. **mod•i•fi•ca•tion** [mɒdɪfɪˈkeɪʃn] *n.* change. **mod•i•fi•er,** *n.* thing which modifies; word which qualifies another word.

mod•ish ['məʊdɪʃ] *adj.* fashionable.

mod•u•late ['mɒdjuleɪt] *v.* to change the pitch of a note/a musical key. **mod•u•la•tion** [mɒdjuˈleɪʃn] *n.* change of pitch.

mod•ule ['mɒdjuːl] *n.* section of a larger combination; **lunar m.** = section of a spacecraft which lands on the moon. **mod•u•lar,** *adj.* made of various modules.

mo•dus op•e•ran•di [ˈməʊdəsɒpəˈrændɪ] *n.* way of working.

mo•dus vi•ven•di [ˈməʊdəsvɪˈvendɪ] *n.* informal way of working together.

mo•gul ['məʊgəl] *n.* bump on a ski slope.

mo•hair ['məʊheə] *n.* very soft wool from a type of goat.

moist [mɔɪst] *adj.* (**-er, -est**) slightly wet/damp. **mois•ten** ['mɔɪsn] *v.* to make moist. **moist•ness,** *n.* being moist. **mois•ture** ['mɔɪstʃə] *n.* slight wetness. **mois•tur•iz•er** ['mɔɪstʃəraɪzə] *n.* cream which makes the skin softer. **mois•tur•iz•ing,** *adj.* (cream) which makes the skin softer.

mo•lar ['məʊlə] *n.* large back tooth used for grinding food.

mo•las•ses [mə'læsɪz] *n.* thick black raw syrup removed from unrefined sugar.

mold, *Brit.* **mould** [məʊld] 1. *n.* (a) soft earth; **leaf m.** = soft earth formed from dead leaves. (b) hollow shape into which a liquid is poured, so that when the liquid becomes hard it takes that shape; **jelly m.** = shape for making jelly. (c) grayish powdery fungus. 2. *v.* to shape (sth). **mold•er.** 1. *n.* person who molds. 2. *v.* to rot away. **mold•i•ness,** *n.* being moldy/rotten. **mold•ing,** *n.* thing which has been molded. **mold•y,** *adj.* rotten/covered with mold.

mole [məʊl] *n.* (a) small black mammal which lives underground. (b) small dark spot on the skin. (c) *inf.* member of an organization who is in the pay of the opponent/enemy. (d) stone jetty/pier used as a breakwater. (e) standard measurement of the amount of a substance. **mole•hill,** *n.* little heap of earth pushed up by a mole; **to make a mountain out of a m.** = to make a fuss about sth which is really trivial. **mole•skin,** *n.* skin of a mole used for making clothes.

mol•e•cule ['mɒlɪkjuːl] *n.* smallest unit into which a substance can be divided. **mo•lec•u•lar** [mə'lekjʊlə] *adj.* referring to molecules: **m. weight** = mass of one molecule of a substance compared to that of one atom of carbon.

mo•lest [mə'lest] *v.* to attack/to beat (s.o.). **mo•les•ta•tion** [mɒlɪs'teɪʃn] *n.* (*formal*) act of molesting.

mol•li•fy ['mɒlɪfaɪ] *v.* to make (s.o.) feel less annoyed. **mol•li•fi•ca•tion** [mɒlɪfɪ'keɪʃn] *n.* act of mollifying.

mol•lusk ['mɒləsk], **mol•lusc** *n.* animal with no backbone, but usu. with a shell (such as snails/oysters, etc.).

mol•ly•cod•dle ['mɒlɪkɒdl] *v.* to spoil (s.o.)/to treat (s.o.) too softly.

Mo•lo•tov cock•tail ['mɒlətɒf'kɒkteɪl] *n.* handmade bomb, made of a bottle filled with flammable liquid, with a short wick.

molt *Brit.* **moult** [məʊlt] *v.* to lose feathers/fur. **mol•ten** ['məʊltən] *adj.* not solid; melted.

mo•lyb•de•num [mɒ'lɪbdənəm] *n.* (*element:* Mo) whitish metal.

mo•ment ['məʊmənt] *n.* (a) very short space of time; **at any m.** = very soon; **at the m.** = just now; **for the m.** = for the time being. (b) importance. **mo•men•tar•i•ly,** *adv.* for a short space of time. **mo•men•tar•y,** *adj.* shortlived/passing. **mo•men•tous** [mə'mentəs] *adj.* very important.

mo•men•tum [mə'mentəm] *n.* impetus; movement forward; **to gain/to lose m.** = to progress faster/slower.

mon•arch ['mɒnək] *n.* king or queen; ruler. **mon•ar•chi•c(al)** [mə'nɑːkɪk(l)] *adj.* referring to a monarchy. **mon•ar•chist** ['mɒnəkɪst] *n.* supporter of a monarchy. **mon•ar•chy** ['mɒnəkɪ] *n.* system of government with a hereditary ruler such as a king or queen.

mon•as•ter•y ['mɒnəstrɪ] *n.* group of buildings where monks live. **mo•nas•tic** [mɒ'næstɪk] *adj.* referring to a monastery/to monks.

Mon•day ['mʌndɪ] *n.* first day of the week/day between Sunday and Tuesday.

mon•e•tar•y ['mʌnɪtərɪ] *adj.* referring to money or currency. **mon•e•ta•rism,** *n.* belief that inflation can be checked by reducing the amount of money available in the economy. **mon•e•ta•rist,** *n.* person who believes in monetarism.

mon•ey ['mʌnɪ] *n.* coins or notes which are used for buying and selling; **to come into m.** = to inherit money; **we were offered our m. back** = a refund of what we had already paid; **we ran out of m.** = we had no money left. **money box,** *n.* box that can be locked and in which you can keep money. **mon•eyed,** *adj.* rich. **mon•ey•lend•er,** *n.* person who lends money. **mon•ey or•der,** *n.* order for passing money from one person to another via the post office.

mong•ol ['mɒŋgəl] *adj. & n.* (person) born with mongolism. **mon•gol•ism** *n.* defect in a person from birth, of which the symptoms are slanting eyes, flattened skull and low intelligence.

mon•goose ['mɒŋguːs] *n.* small tropical mammal which kills snakes.

mon•grel ['mʌŋgrəl] *adj. & n.* not pure-bred (dog)/(dog) of mixed breeds.

mon•i•tor ['mɒnɪtə] 1. *n.* (a) person who watches/surveys the progress of sth. (b) student (in a school) who has a particular duty to perform. (c) apparatus for checking the progress of sth, esp. the screen of a computer or a small television screen in a television studio. 2. *v.* to check/to survey (the progress of sth).

monk [mʌŋk] *n.* man who is a member of a religious group and lives in a monastery. **monk•ish**, *adj.* like a monk.

mon•key ['mʌŋkɪ] 1. *n.* usu. a tropical mammal which resembles a human being, but which normally has a tail; **m. nut** = peanut; **m. puzzle tree** = type of tropical pine tree with spiky branches; **m. wrench** = large spanner with an adjustable grip. 2. *inf.* **to m. about** = to play/to mess around.

mon•o ['mɒnəʊ] 1. *prefix meaning* single. 2. *n. & adj.* not stereophonic; (machine/record) which reproduces sound through a single channel.

mon•o•chrome ['mɒnəkrəʊm] *adj. & n.* (in a) single color, usu. black and white.

mon•o•cle ['mɒnəkl] *n.* eye glass/single lens worn to correct sight.

mo•noc•u•lar [mɒ'nɒkjuːlə] *adj.* (vision) as with one eye, with no sense of depth.

mo•nog•a•my [mə'nɒgəmɪ] *n.* system of marriage to one person at a time. **mo•nog•a•mous,** *adj.* (marriage) to one husband or wife.

mon•o•gram ['mɒnəgræm] *n.* design based on the initials of your name. **mon•o•grammed,** *adj.* with your initials on it.

mon•o•graph ['mɒnəgrɑːf] *n.* short book about a specialized subject.

mon•o•lith ['mɒnəlɪθ] *n.* single standing stone. **mon•o•lith•ic** [mɒnə'lɪθɪk] *adj.* solid/heavy; changeless.

mon•o•logue, monolog ['mɒnəlɒg] *n.* long speech by one actor alone on the stage.

mon•o•ma•ni•a [mɒnə'meɪnɪə] *n.* mania about a single thing.

mo•no•nu•cle•o•sis [mɒnənjuːklɪ'əʊsɪs] *n.* glandular fever.

mon•o•phon•ic [mɒnə'fɒnɪk] *adj.* not stereophonic; (record) with sound coming from a single channel.

mon•o•plane ['mɒnəpleɪn] *n.* plane with one pair of wings.

mo•nop•o•ly [mə'nɒpəlɪ] *n.* system where one person or company supplies all needs in one area without any competition. **mo•nop•o•li•za•tion** [mənɒpəlaɪ'zeɪ[n] *n.* creating of a monopoly. **mo•nop•o•lize** [mə'nɒpəlaɪz] *v.* to create a monopoly; to use

(sth) entirely for yourself; **to m. the conversation** = to do all the talking and not let anyone else speak.

mon•o•rail ['mɒnəreɪl] *n.* train which runs on a single rail.

mon•o•syl•la•ble ['mɒnəsɪləbl] *n.* word which only has one syllable. **mon•o•syl•lab•ic** [mɒnəsɪ'læbɪk] *adj.* (word) with only one syllable; (conversation) using only monosyllables.

mon•o•the•ism [mɒnəʊ'θɪɪzəm] *n.* belief that there is only one god.

mon•o•tone ['mɒnətəʊn] *n.* flat/level tone of voice. **mo•not•o•nous** [mə'nɒtənəs] *adj.* not varied/not changing/boring. **mo•not•o•nous•ly,** *adv.* in a monotonous way. **mo•not•o•ny,** *n.* lack of variety.

mon•ox•ide [mə'nɒksaɪd] *n.* chemical compound containing one atom of oxygen.

mon•sig•nor [mɒn'siːnə] *n.* title given to an important priest in the Roman Catholic church.

mon•soon [mɒn'suːn] *n.* (a) season of wind and rain in the tropics. (b) wind blowing in the Indian Ocean.

mon•ster ['mɒnstə] 1. *n.* (a) horrible/strange creature. (b) very large and terrifying animal/thing. (c) cruel/wicked person. 2. *adj.* very large. **mon•stros•i•ty** [mɒn'strɒsɪtɪ] *n.* horrible/strange/ugly thing. **mon•strous** ['mɒnstrəs] *adj.* huge/ugly/horrible.

mon•tage [mɒn'tɑːʒ] *n.* picture/piece of music, etc., made of several items brought together; action of putting several items together to make a picture/piece of music, etc.

month [mʌnθ] *n.* one of the twelve periods which form a year. **month•ly.** 1. *adj. & adv.* occurring every month. 2. *n.* magazine which appears each month.

mon•u•ment ['mɒnjumənt] *n.* (a) (**to** s.o.) stone/building/statue, etc., erected in memory of s.o. who is dead. (b) building which is very old. **mon•u•men•tal** [mɒnju'mentl] *adj.* (a) very large. (b) referring to a monument.

moo [muː] 1. *n.* sound made by a cow. 2. *v.* to make a sound like a cow.

mooch [muːtʃ] *v.* (**about**) to go about aimlessly.

mood [muːd] *n.* (a) general feeling. (b) bad temper. (c) group of forms of a verb which indicates a fact, a possibility or a condition. **mood•i•ly,** *adv.* in a moody way. **mood•i•ness,** *n.* gloomy feeling; quick change from good to bad temper. **mood•y,** *adj.* (**-ier, -iest**) often gloomy/often bad-tempered; changing quickly from good to bad temper.

moon [muːn] *n.* satellite which travels around a planet, esp. the one which travels around the earth each month and shines with reflected light from the sun; **once in a blue m.** = very rarely. **moon•beam**, *n.* ray of light from the moon. **moon•light** 1. *n.* light from the moon. 2. *v.* to work at a second job after one's regular job. **moon•light•er**, *n.* person who works at a second job after his regular job. **moon•light•ing**, *n. inf.* working at a second job (usu. in the evening) after your regular job. **moon•lit**, *adj.* lit by light from the moon. **moon•shine**, *n. inf.* (a) nonsense. (b) illegal alcohol. **moon•stone**, *n.* semi-precious stone with a white shine.

moor ['muə, mɔ:] 1. *n.* uncultivated land covered with low shrubs. 2. *v.* to attach (a boat) to a dock, etc. **moor•ing**, *n.* (a) action of attaching a boat. (b) **moorings** = place where a boat is moored; ropes, etc., used to moor a boat.

moose [mu:s] *n.* (*pl.* **moose**) American elk.

moot [mu:t] 1. *adj.* **m. point** = question which is open to discussion. 2. *v.* to raise (a question/a suggestion).

mop [mɒp] 1. *n.* brush for washing floors with a head made of soft string or foam rubber; **m. of hair** = long and untidy hair. 2. *v.* (**mopped**) (a) to wash the floor, using a mop. (b) to wipe. **mop up**, *v.* (a) to clear up (liquid) using a mop. (b) to clear up (pockets of resistance).

mope [məup] *v.* to be miserable/gloomy.

mo•ped ['məuped] *n.* two-wheeled vehicle with a low-powered motor.

mo•quette [mɒ'ket] *n.* thick cloth for covering chairs, etc.

mo•raine [mə'reɪn] *n.* heap of gravel, etc., left by a glacier.

mor•al ['mɒrəl] 1. *adj.* (a) referring to right and wrong in human behavior. (b) referring to good human behavior; **m. support** = encouragement without active help. 2. *n.* lesson to be drawn from a story. 3. **morals** = personal character and way of behaving. **mor•al•ist**, *n.* person who criticizes low moral standards. **mo•ral•i•ty** [mə'rælɪtɪ] *n.* correct way of behaving; sense of moral standards. **mor•al•ize** ['mɒrəlaɪz] *v.* to draw a lesson from a story or event. **mor•al•ly**, *adv.* according to correct human behavior.

mo•rale [mə'rɑːl] *n.* feeling of confidence.

mo•rass [mə'ræs] *n.* (*pl.* **-es**) (a) deep swamp/marsh. (b) mass of things which prevent any progress.

mor•a•to•ri•um [mɒrə'tɔ:rɪəm] *n.* (*pl.* **-ia, -iums**) temporary ban.

mo•ray eel [mɒreɪ'i:l] *n.* type of large eel.

mor•bid ['mɔ:bɪd] *adj.* (a) interested in death/unpleasant things. (b) connected with disease. **mor•bid•i•ty** [mɔ:'bɪdɪtɪ] *n.* sickly interest in death/unpleasant things. **mor•bid•ly**, *adv.* in a morbid way.

mor•dant ['mɔ:dənt] *adj.* (*formal*) cruel (sarcasm).

more [mɔ:] 1. *adj.* extra/additional. 2. *n.* extra/additional amount. 3. *adv.* (a) additionally/to a larger extent. (b) (*forming comparative*) **she is m. intelligent than her brother.** (c) **not any m.** = no longer; **m. or less** = approximately/practically. **more•o•ver** [mɔ:'rəuvə] *adv.* besides; in addition.

mor•ga•nat•ic [mɔ:gə'nætɪk] *adj.* **m. marriage** = marriage of a king or queen to s.o. of lower rank who does not take their title.

morgue [mɔ:g] *n.* building where dead bodies are kept before burial.

mor•i•bund ['mɒrɪbʌnd] *adj.* dying; going out of existence.

Mor•mon ['mɔ:mən] *adj. & n.* (member) of a Christian sect, founded in the United States in 1830.

mor•nay ['mɔ:neɪ] *adj.* cooked with a cheese sauce.

morn•ing ['mɔ:nɪŋ] *n.* early part of the day, before 12 noon; **4 in the m.** = 4 a.m.; **the m. train** = the train which leaves every morning.

mo•roc•co [mə'rɒkəu] *n.* fine soft leather.

mo•ron ['mɔ:rɒn] *n.* (a) adult with the intelligence of a child. (b) stupid person. **mo•ron•ic** [mə'rɒnɪk] *adj.* stupid.

mo•rose [mə'rəus] *adj.* gloomy and bad-tempered. **mo•rose•ly**, *adv.* in a morose way. **mo•rose•ness**, *n.* being morose.

mor•phine, morphia ['mɔ:fi:n, 'mɔ:fɪə] *n.* drug which kills pain and makes you go to sleep.

morph•ing ['mɔ:fɪŋ] *n.* computer graphics technique in which one image is gradually changed into another, used esp. in films.

mor•phol•o•gy [mɔ:'fɒlədʒɪ] *n.* (a) study of the way in which words change in the plural, or according to gender or conjugation. (b) study of the forms of plants or animals. **mor•pho•log•i•cal** [mɔ:fə'lɒdʒɪkl] *adj.* referring to morphology.

mor•ris ['mɒrɪs] *n.* **m. dance** = old English dance, danced by men in white clothes with bells on their legs.

mor•row ['mɒrəu] *n.* (*old*) next day.

æ back, ɑ: farm, ɒ: top, aɪ pipe, aʊ how, aɪə fire, aʊə flower, ɔ: bought, ɔɪ toy, e fed, eəhair, eɪ take, ə afraid, əʊ boat, əʊə lower, ʌ: word, i: heap, ɪ hit, ɪə hear, u: school, ʊ book, ʌ but, b back, d dog, ð then, dʒ just, f fog, g go, h hand, j yes, k catch, l last, m mix, n nut, ŋ sing, p penny, r round, s some, ʃ short, t too, tʃ chop, θ thing, v voice, w was, z zoo, ʒ treasure

Morse code [mɔːsˈkəʊd] *n.* system of dots and dashes for sending messages.

mor•sel [ˈmɔːsl] *n.* small piece.

mor•tal [ˈmɔːtl] 1. *adj.* (a) causing death; **m. enemy** = deadly enemy. (b) referring to the body; **m. remains** = corpse. 2. *n.* human being. **mor•tal•i•ty** [mɔːˈtælɪtɪ] *n.* (a) human state. (b) **m. rate** = number of deaths (as a percentage of population). **mor•tal•ly**, *adv.* so as to cause death.

mor•tar [ˈmɔːtə] *n.* (a) cement mixture for holding together bricks or stones when building. (b) bowl for crushing things with a pestle. (c) short cannon. **mor•tar•board**, *n.* black cap with a square top worn at academic ceremonies, as by people receiving or giving university degrees.

mort•gage [ˈmɔːgɪdʒ] 1. *n.* agreement whereby s.o. lends money on the security of a property; money lent on the security of property; **second m.** = further loan obtained on a property which is already mortgaged. 2. *v.* to give (a property) as security for a loan. **mort•ga•gee** [mɔːgɪˈdʒiː] *n.* person who loans money on mortgage. **mort•ga•gor**, **mortgager** [mɔːgɪˈdʒɔː] *n.* person who borrows money on a mortgage.

mor•tice [ˈmɔːtɪs] *n. see* **mor•tise.**

mor•ti•cian [mɔːˈtɪʃn] *n.* undertaker.

mor•ti•fy [ˈmɔːtɪfaɪ] *v.* to humiliate. **mor•ti•fi•ca•tion** [mɔːtɪfɪˈkeɪʃn] *n.* feeling of shame/humiliation.

mor•tise [ˈmɔːtɪs] *n.* hole cut in the end of a piece of wood into which another piece (a tenon) fits to form a joint; **m. lock** = lock which is fitted into a door.

mor•tu•ar•y [ˈmɔːtjʊərɪ] *n.* place where dead bodies are kept before burial.

mo•sa•ic [məˈzeɪɪk] *n.* tiny pieces of colored stone stuck to a wall or floor in patterns.

Mos•lem [ˈmɒzləm] *adj. & n.* = **Mus•lim.**

mosque [mɒsk] *n.* religious building for Muslims.

mos•qui•to [məsˈkiːtəʊ] *n.* (*pl.* **-oes**) small flying insect which sucks blood; **m. net** = thin net spread over a bed to prevent mosquitoes biting at night.

moss [mɒs] *n.* (*pl.* **-es**) primitive green plant growing in compact low clumps on the ground or on stones. **moss•y**, *adj.* covered with moss.

most [məʊst] 1. *adj.* the largest number/largest quantity (of sth). 2. *n.* the largest number/largest quantity; **to make the m. of** = get as much profit/value from sth as possible. 3. *adv.* to the largest extent. (a) (*forming superlative*) **the m. intelligent child.** (b) (*intensive*) very. **most•ly**, *adv.* in most cases/most often.

mo•tel [məʊˈtel] *n.* hotel for people traveling by car where there is a parking space for every room.

mo•tet [məʊˈtet] *n.* music for a small group of unaccompanied singers.

moth [mɒθ] *n.* flying insect with large wings like a butterfly, but flying mainly at night; **clothes m.** = type of moth of which the grub eats wool or fur. **moth•ball**, *v. inf.* to store (a ship, etc.) in working order for future use. **moth•balls**, *n. pl.* balls of a chemical substance put among clothes to keep moths away; **in m.** = stored for future use. **moth-eat•en**, *adj.* full of holes made by moths; old and decrepit.

moth•er [ˈmʌðə] 1. *n.* female parent; **m. country** = country where you or your ancestors were born; **m. tongue** = first language a child speaks; **M. Superior** = woman head of a religious community. 2. *v.* to look after (s.o.) very attentively. **moth•er•hood**, *n.* being a mother. **moth•er-in-law**, *n.* (*pl.* **mothers-in-law**) mother of your wife or husband; **mother-in-law plant** = type of house plant with a few tall stiff vertical leaves. **moth•er•less**, *adj.* with no mother. **moth•er•ly**, *adj.* maternal/like a mother. **moth•er-of-pearl**, *n.* shiny substance found on the inside of oyster shells.

mo•tif [məʊˈtiːf] *n.* distinctive repeating pattern in a design/in a piece of music.

mo•tion [ˈməʊʃn] 1. *n.* (a) movement/act of moving; **in m.** = moving. (b) gesture/movement; **to go through the motions** = to do sth for the sake of appearances, without believing in it. (c) proposal which is to be put to the vote (at a meeting); **to second a m.** = to support the person who proposed the motion. 2. *v.* to make a gesture. **mo•tion•less**, *adj.* still/not moving. **mo•tion pic•ture**, *n.* moving picture shown on a screen.

mo•tive [ˈməʊtɪv] 1. *n.* reason for doing sth. 2. *adj.* which makes sth move. **mo•ti•vate** [ˈməʊtɪveɪt] *v.* to make (s.o.) do sth; to encourage (s.o.) to do sth; **highly motivated** = eager. **mo•ti•va•tion** [məʊtɪˈveɪʃn] *n.* reason for doing sth/encouragement to do sth.

mot•ley [ˈmɒtlɪ] *adj.* varied; of varied sorts of colors.

mo•tor [ˈməʊtə] 1. *n.* (a) machine which causes motion; engine. (b) car. 2. *v.* to travel in a car. 3. *adj.* (a) operated by a motor. (b) (nerve) which links the brain to the muscles, so causing motion; **m. neuron disease** = disease of the nerves which control the muscles. **mo•tor•bike**, *n. inf.* motorcycle. **mo•tor•boat**, *n.* small boat with a motor. **mo•tor•cade**, *n.* official procession of cars. **mo•tor•cy•cle**, *n.* two-wheeled vehicle powered by a motor. **mo•tor•cy•clist,** *n.* person riding a motorcycle. **mo•tor•ing,** *n.* traveling in a car. **mo•tor•ist,** *n.* driver of a car. **mo•tor•ize,** *v.* to provide (sth) with an engine; to equip (s.o.) with motor transport.

mot•tled ['mɒtld] *adj.* spotted with different colors.

mot•to ['mɒtəʊ] *n.* (*pl.* -oes, -os) short phrase which is used to sum up an attitude.

mould [məʊld] *n., v. Brit. see* **mold.**

moult [məʊlt] *v. Brit. see* **molt.**

mound [maʊnd] *n.* small heap/hill.

mount [maʊnt] 1. *n.* (a) (*usu. in names*) mountain. (b) cardboard frame for a picture. (c) horse/donkey, etc., on which a rider sits. 2. *v.* (a) to climb on to (sth); to rise; **mounted police** = police on horseback. (b) to stand on or put on guard to protect sth. (c) to set (sth) in a cardboard frame/in a metal ring/brooch, etc. (d) to organize (an expedition). **Moun•tie,** *n. inf.* member of the Royal Canadian Mounted Police. **mount up,** *v.* to rise/to increase.

moun•tain ['maʊntn] *n.* (a) very high land; **m. sheep** = sheep which are specially bred to live on mountains; **m. ash** = common northern tree with red berries. (b) large amount; **m. of work** = large quantity of work. **moun•tain•eer** [maʊntə'nɪə] *n.* person who climbs mountains for pleasure. **moun•tain•eer•ing,** *n.* climbing of mountains as a sport. **moun•tain•ous,** *adj.* (area) full of mountains; very high (waves).

moun•te•bank ['maʊntɪbæŋk] *n.* person who persuades people to pay money by talking cleverly.

mourn [mɔːn] *v.* to regret (sth). **mourn•er,** *n.* person who grieves s.o. has died; **the mourners** = people attending a funeral. **mourn•ful,** *adj.* very sad. **mourn•ful•ly,** *adv.* in a very sad way. **mourn•ing,** *n.* (a) period of time when one grieves over the death of a relative or friend. (b) dark clothes worn as a mark of respect for someone who has died.

mouse [maʊs] *n.* (*pl.* **mice** [maɪs]) (a) small rodent with a long tail, often living in houses. (b) device which is held in the hand and moved across a flat surface, used to control a cursor on a computer monitor. **mouse•hole,** *n.* small hole in which mice live. **mous•er,** *n.* **the cat is a good m.** = good at catching mice. **mouse•trap,** *n.* trap for catching mice. **mous•y,** *adj.* (a) small and insignificant (person). (b) brownish-gray (color).

mous•sa•ka ['muːsækæ] *n.* Greek dish, made of eggplant and minced meat.

mousse [muːs] *n.* light food made of whipped eggs, cream and flavoring.

mous•tache ['mʌstɑːʃ] *n. see* **mus•tache.**

mouth 1. *n.* [maʊθ] (a) part of the head through which you take in food and drink and through which you speak. (b) wide entrance; **m. of a river** = place where a river enters the sea. 2. *v.* [maʊð] to move the mouth as if speaking, without making any sound; to speak without being heard. **mouth•ful,** *n.* (a) quantity contained in the mouth. (b) *inf.* complicated word/phrase. **mouth•or•gan,** *n.* small musical instrument played by blowing, with a series of small valves giving different notes. **mouth•piece,** *n.* (a) part of a musical instrument which goes into the mouth. (b) person who speaks on behalf of s.o. **mouth•wash,** *n.* antiseptic solution for cleaning the inside of the mouth. **mouth-wa•ter•ing,** *adj.* very delicious.

move [muːv] 1. *n.* (a) action of changing place; movement; **get a m. on!** = hurry up; *inf.* **we must make a m.** = we must act. (b) movement (of a piece in chess); **what's the next m.?** = what do we have to do next? (c) changing of place of residence. 2. *v.* (a) to change the position (of sth); to change position; **don't m.!** = stand still! *inf.* **we must be moving** = we must leave. (b) to leave one place to go to live in another. (c) to change the feelings of (s.o.). (d) to propose (a motion in a debate). **mov•a•ble, move•able** *adj.* which can be moved. **move a•bout,** *v.* to change (sth) from one place to another. **move a•way,** *v.* to change to another place further away; to change (sth) to a position further away; **we are moving away from San Francisco** = we are leaving San Francisco to live in another town. **move back,** *v.* (a) to go backward; to change (sth) to a place further back. (b) to return to a previous place. **move for•ward,** *v.* to go forward; to make (s.o.) go to a place further forward. **move in,** *v.* to settle with furniture in a new house. **move•ment,** *n.* (a) action of changing position/of not being still. (b) mechanism (of a clock). (c) main part of a large piece of music. (d) group of people working toward a certain aim. **move off,** *v.* to go away. **move on,** *v.* to go forward; to make (s.o.) go forward. **mov•er,** *n.* person who moves furniture from one house to another. **mov•ie,** *n.*

æ back, ɑː farm, ɒ top, aɪ pipe, aʊ how, aɪə fire, aʊə flower, ɔː bought, ɔɪ toy, e fed, eəhair, eɪ take, ə afraid, əʊ boat, əʊə lower, ɜː word, iː heap, ɪ hit, ɪə hear, uː school, ʊ book, ʌ but, b back, d dog, ð then, dʒ just, f fog, g go, h hand, j yes, k catch, l last, m mix, n nut, ŋ sing, p penny, r round, s some, ʃ short, t too, tʃ chop, θ thing, v voice, w was, z zoo, ʒ treasure

motion picture. **mov•ing**, *adj*. (a) which changes position/which is not still; **m. staircase** = escalator. (b) which affects your feelings.

mow [məʊ] *v*. (**has mown**) to cut (grass). **mow down**, *v*. to kill/to slaughter. **mow•er**, *n*. (a) person who cuts grass. (b) machine which cuts grass; lawnmower.

mpg *abbrev. for* miles per gallon.

mph *abbrev. for* miles per hour.

Mr. ['mɪstə] *n*. title given to a man.

Mrs. ['mɪsɪz] *n*. title given to a married woman.

Ms. [mʌz, mɪz] *n*. title given to a woman (married or unmarried).

much [mʌtʃ] 1. *adj*. a lot of. 2. *adv*. (**more/most**) to a great extent/very; *inf*. **it's a bit m.!** = it's quite unreasonable! **m. to my amazement** = to my great surprise. 3. *n*. a lot; *inf*. **not up to m.** = relatively inactive.

muck [mʌk] 1. *n*. dirt; manure. 2. *v*. **to m. out a stable** = to clean a stable; *inf*. **to m. about with** = to play about with; *inf*. **to m. up** = to ruin. **muck•rak•ing**, *n*. discovering and publishing scandalous stories about famous people. **muck•y**, *adj*. (-ier, -iest) dirty; covered with muck.

mu•cus ['mju:kəs] *n*. shiny substance which coats the inside of cavities of the body. **mu•cous**, *adj*. referring to mucus; **m. membrane** = wet membrane which lines inside passages of the body.

mud [mʌd] *n*. very wet earth. **mud•di•ness**, *n*. being muddy. **mud•dy**, 1. *adj*. (-ier, -iest) full of mud; covered with mud. 2. *v*. to put mud on sth; **to m. the waters** = to stir up trouble/confusion. **mud•flap**, *n*. flap hanging behind the wheel of a car to prevent mud and water being splashed. **mud•flats**, *n. pl*. flat muddy land covered by the sea at high tide. **mud•guard**, *n*. strip of metal over the wheel on a bicycle to stop mud and water being splashed. **mud•pack**, *n*. paste put on the face to improve the texture of the skin. **mud•sling•ing**, *n*. insults.

mud•dle ['mʌdl] 1. *n*. confusion/mixture. 2. *v*. to confuse/to mix up. **mud•dle•head•ed**, *adj*. confused. **muddle through**, *v*. to get through one's business/to succeed in a muddled way.

mues•li ['mju:zlɪ] *n*. breakfast food of flakes of cereal/dried fruit, etc., eaten with milk or yogurt.

mu•ez•zin [mu:'ezɪn] *n*. person who calls Muslims to prayer.

muff [mʌf] 1. *n*. warm covering for a particular part of the body, esp. the hands. 2. *v*. to do (sth) badly.

muf•fin ['mʌfɪn] *n*. small round cake, usu. eaten with butter.

muf•fle ['mʌfl] *v*. (a) to wrap up in clothes. (b) to deaden (a loud noise). **muf•fler**, *n*. (a) long scarf. (b) silencer (on car exhaust).

muf•ti ['mʌftɪ] *n. inf*. **in m.** = in civilian clothes; not in uniform.

mug [mʌg] 1. *n*. (a) large glass/cup with a handle. (b) *inf*. face. 2. *v*. (**mugged**) to attack and rob (in the street). **mug•ger**, *n*. person who attacks and robs s.o. in the street. **mug•ging**, *n*. robbery with violence (in the street). **mug shot**, *n. inf*. photograph of s.o.'s face.

mug•gy ['mʌgɪ] *adj. inf*. warm and wet (weather).

mu•lat•to [mju:'lætəʊ] *n*. (*pl*. -oes) person of mixed Negro and White race.

mul•ber•ry ['mʌlbərɪ] *n*. soft purple fruit; tree which bears this fruit.

mulch [mʌltʃ] 1. *n*. (*pl*. -es) covering of manure/rotten leaves, etc., spread on the ground to improve the soil. 2. *v*. to spread mulch on (the ground).

mulct [mʌlkt] *v*. to take money away from (s.o.).

mule [mju:l] *n*. (a) hybrid between a donkey and a horse; obstinate person. (b) light shoe with an open heel. **mu•le•teer** [mjulə'tɪə] *n*. person who drives mules carrying loads. **mul•ish**, *adj*. obstinate/difficult to deal with.

mull [mʌl] *v*. to heat (wine) with spices/sugar, etc. **mull o•ver**, *v*. to ponder/to think about (sth).

mul•lah ['mʊlə] *n*. Muslim religious thinker.

mul•let ['mʌlɪt] *n*. small sea fish.

mul•li•ga•taw•ny [mʌlɪgə'tɔ:nɪ] *n*. hot soup made with curry.

mul•lion ['mʌljən] *n*. vertical (wooden/metal) bar between panes of glass in a window.

multi- ['mʌltɪ] *prefix meaning* many.

mul•ti•col•ored ['mʌltɪkʌləd] *adj*. with many colors.

mul•ti•far•i•ous [mʌltɪ'feərɪəs] *adj*. very varied/in many different types.

mul•ti•lat•er•al [mʌltɪ'lætərəl] *adj*. between more than two partners.

mul•ti•me•di•a [mʌltɪ'mi:dɪə] *adj*. (a) (teaching method/advertising campaign, etc.) using several media. (b) (computer hardware/software) using data in several media, e.g. graphics/sound/text.

mul•ti•mil•lion•aire [mʌltɪmɪljə'neə] *n*. person who has several million dollars.

mul•ti•na•tion•al [mʌltɪ'næʃnl] *adj. & n*. (company) which operates in several different countries.

mul•ti•ple ['mʌltɪpl] 1. *adj*. many/repeated; **m. sclerosis** = disease of the nervous system, which gets progressively worse. 2. *n.* (a) number which contains another number several times exactly. (b) repeated groups of the same number of sth; **sold in multiples of five** = you can buy five, ten, fifteen, etc. **mul•ti•pli•ca•tion** [mʌltɪplɪˈkeɪʃn] *n.* action of multiplying; **m. sign ()** = sign used to show that numbers are to be multiplied; **m. tables** = lists of figures to learn by heart how each number is multiplied. **mul•ti•plic•i•ty** [mʌltɪˈplɪsɪtɪ] *n.* vast and varied mass. **mul•ti•ply** [ˈmʌltɪplaɪ] *v.* (a) to calculate the sum of several numbers repeated a stated number of times. (b) to increase in number.

mul•ti•ra•cial [mʌltɪˈreɪʃl] *adj.* (society) whose members come from various races.

mul•ti•sto•ry [ˈmʌltɪstɔːrɪ] *adj.* (building) with many stories.

mul•ti•tude [ˈmʌltɪtjuːd] *n.* great number/crowd. **mul•ti•tu•di•nous** [mʌltɪˈtjuːdɪnəs] *adj.* in very large numbers.

mum [mʌm] *adj.* silent; **he kept m.** = he didn't say a word.

mum•ble [ˈmʌmbl] 1. *n.* speech which you can't understand because it is indistinct. 2. *v.* to speak indistinctly.

mum•bo-jum•bo [mʌmbəʊˈdʒʌmbəʊ] *n.* nonsense/meaningless talk.

mum•mer [ˈmʌmə] *n.* member of a group acting in a traditional Christmas play.

mum•my [ˈmʌmɪ] *n.* corpse preserved with ointments and bandages as in ancient Egypt. **mum•mi•fy,** *v.* to preserve (a dead body) in a perfect state.

mumps [mʌmps] *n.* infectious illness with swelling on either side of the neck.

munch [mʌnʃ] *v.* to chew (sth crisp or dry) with large regular movements of the jaws.

Mun•chau•sen's syn•drome [ˈmʌntʃəʊzən] *n.* psychiatric condition in which s.o. feigns illness/injury to get medical treatment; **M. s. by proxy** = psychiatric condition in which s.o. inflicts injury on or claims illness in others in order to get medical treatment for that person.

mun•dane [mʌnˈdeɪn] *adj.* ordinary.

mu•nic•i•pal [mjuːˈnɪsɪpl] *adj.* referring to a town; **m. park** = park which belongs to a town. **mu•nic•i•pal•i•ty** [mjuːnɪsɪˈpælɪtɪ] *n.* self-governing city or town.

mu•nif•i•cence [mjuːˈnɪfɪsns] *n.* (*formal*) great generosity. **mu•nif•i•cent,** *adj.* (*formal*) extremely generous.

mu•ni•tions [mjuːˈnɪʃnz] *n. pl.* weapons and ammunition.

mu•ral [ˈmjʊərəl] 1. *adj.* referring to walls. 2. *n.* painting on a wall.

mur•der [ˈmɜːdə] 1. *n.* (a) illegal killing of s.o. (b) *inf.* awful or unpleasant thing. 2. *v.* (a) to kill (s.o.) illegally. (b) *inf.* to ruin (a song) by singing it badly. **mur•der•er,** *n.* person who has committed a murder. **mur•der•ess** [ˈmɜːdrəs] *n.* woman who has committed a murder. **mur•der•ous** [ˈmɜːdərəs] *adj.* likely to kill.

murk [mɜːk] *n.* (*formal*) darkness/gloominess. **murk•i•ness,** *n.* being dark/gloomy. **murk•y** [ˈmɜːkɪ] *adj.* (-ier, -iest) dark/gloomy (water).

mur•mur [ˈmɜːmə] 1. *n.* low whisper of voices/low sound. 2. *v.* to speak in a low voice; to complain in a low voice. **mur•mur•ing,** *n.* (a) speaking in a low voice. (b) **murmurings** = grumblings/complaints.

mus•cat [ˈmʌskət] *n.* type of sweet grape; wine made from this grape.

mus•ca•tel [mʌskəˈtel] *n.* type of sweet black grape, usually dried.

mus•cle [ˈmʌsl] 1. *n.* springlike parts of the body which allow the limbs to move. 2. *v. inf.* **to m. in on sth** = to push yourself forward to take part in sth which is organized by s.o. else. **mus•cu•lar** [ˈmʌskjʊlə] *adj.* referring to muscles; **m. dystrophy** = disease causing gradual weakening of the muscles.

muse [mjuːz] 1. *n.* (*formal*) goddess who inspires poets, musicians, etc. 2. *v.* to think deeply; to daydream.

mu•se•um [mjuːˈzɪəm] *n.* building in which a collection of valuable or rare objects are put on display permanently.

mush [mʌʃ] *n.* soft half-liquid mess. **mush•i•ness,** *n.* being mushy. **mush•y,** *adj.* (a) soft and partly liquid. (b) *inf.* very sentimental.

mush•room [ˈmʌʃruːm] 1. *n.* edible round white fungus. 2. *v.* to spring up rapidly.

mu•sic [ˈmjuːzɪk] *n.* sounds made by playing instruments or singing; **to face the m.** = to face sth unpleasant. **mu•si•cal.** 1. *adj.* referring to music; (person) who likes music/plays music a lot; **m. chairs** = (i) game where people try to sit on chairs when the music stops, with one chair and one person less each time; (ii) *inf.* continual movement from office to office/from job to job. 2. *n.* (*also* **musical comedy**) play with

---

æ **back,** ɑː **farm,** ɒː **top,** aɪ **pipe,** aʊ **how,** aɪə **fire,** aʊə **flower,** ɔː **bought,** ɔɪ **toy,** e **fed,** eə **hair,** eɪ **take,** ə **afraid,** əʊ **boat,** əʊə **lower,** ɜː **word,** iː **heap,** ɪ **hit,** ɪə **hear,** uː **school,** ʊ **book,** ʌ **but,** b **back,** d **dog,** ð **then,** dʒ **just,** f **fog,** g **go,** h **hand,** j **yes,** k **catch,** l **last,** m **mix,** n **nut,** ŋ **sing,** p **penny,** r **round,** s **some,** ʃ **short,** t **too,** tʃ **chop,** θ **thing,** v **voice,** w **was,** z **zoo,** ʒ **treasure**

songs and popular music. **mu•sic box,** *n.* small box with a clockwork motor which plays a tune when the box is opened. **mu•si•cal•ly,** *adv.* in a musical way. **music hall,** *n.* theater specializing in variety shows. **mu•si•cian** [mju:'zɪʃn] *n.* person who plays music professionaly/skillfully. **mu•si•col•o•gy** [mju:zɪ'kɒlədʒɪ] *n.* academic study of music. **mu•si•col•o•gist,** *n.* specialist in the study of music.

musk [mʌsk] *n.* perfume obtained from glands of a deer. **musk ox,** *n.* large wild ox, found in North America. **musk•rat,** *n.* North American water rat with fine fur. **musk rose,** *n.* old-fashioned scented rose. **musk•y,** *adj.* with a smell like musk.

mus•keg ['mʌskeg] *n.* (*in northern North America*) marsh.

mus•ket ['mʌskɪt] *n.* early portable gun with a long barrel. **mus•ket•eer,** *n.* soldier who was armed with a musket.

Mus•lim ['mʊzlɪm] *adj. & n.* (person) following the religion of the prophet Mohammed.

mus•lin ['mʌzlɪn] *n.* very fine thin cotton cloth.

muss [mʌs] *v. inf.* to disorder or ruffle (hair, etc.).

mus•sel ['mʌsl] *n.* mollusk with a dark blue shell, whose soft parts can be eaten.

must [mʌst] 1. *v.* (a) *used with verbs to mean* it is necessary. (b) *used with verbs to mean* it is probable; **it m. be the doctor** = it cannot be anyone else. 2. *n.* (a) *inf.* very necessary thing. (b) grape juice.

mus•tache, moustache ['mʌstæʃ] *n.* hair grown on the upper lip.

mus•tang ['mʌstæŋ] *n.* wild horse of the American plains.

mus•tard ['mʌstəd] *n.* (a) sharp-tasting yellow powder made from crushed seeds; paste made from this powder; **m. gas** = poisonous gas which burns the skin; **m. yellow** = dull yellow color. (b) plant whose seeds make mustard powder.

mus•ter ['mʌstə] 1. *n.* gathering; parade and inspection of soldiers, etc.; **to pass m.** = to be acceptable. 2. *v.* to gather together.

mus•ty ['mʌstɪ] *adj.* (**-ier, -iest**) smelling damp/rotten/stale; smelling old. **mus•ti•ness,** *n.* rotten/stale smell.

mu•tate [mju:'teɪt] *v.* to change genetically. **mu•ta•bil•i•ty** [mju:tə'bɪlɪtɪ] *n.* being mutable. **mu•ta•ble,** *adj.* which is likely to change/which can be changed. **mu•tant** ['mju:tənt] *n.* animal/plant which has changed genetically. **mu•ta•tion** [mju:'teɪʃn] *n.* genetic change.

mute [mju:t] 1. *adj.* (a) silent/dumb (person). (b) (letter) which is not pronounced. 2. *n.* (a)

person who cannot speak/who is dumb; **deaf m.** = person who cannot hear or speak. (b) device used to soften the sound of a musical instrument. 3. *v.* to soften the sound of (a musical instrument). **mute•ly,** *adv.* silently.

mu•ti•late ['mju:tɪleɪt] *v.* to cut off a limb/an ear, etc., from (s.o.); to damage (an object). **mu•ti•la•tion** [mju:tɪ'leɪʃn] *n.* loss of a limb; great damage.

mu•ti•ny ['mju:tɪnɪ] 1. *n.* uprising, esp. of soldiers/sailors, etc., against the orders of their officers. 2. *v.* to refuse to carry out orders/to rise up against officers. **mu•ti•neer** [mju:tɪ'nɪə] *n.* person who mutinies. **mu•ti•nous** ['mju:tɪnəs] *adj.* likely to mutiny/rebellious. **mu•ti•nous•ly,** *adv.* in a mutinous way.

mutt [mʌt] *n. Sl.* (a) idiot/stupid person. (b) dog.

mut•ter ['mʌtə] 1. *n.* low indistinct way of speaking. 2. *v.* to mumble/to speak in a low and indistinct voice. **mut•ter•ing,** *n.* speaking indistinctly.

mut•ton ['mʌtn] *n.* meat of a sheep.

mu•tu•al ['mju:tjʊəl] *adj.* felt/done by two people to each other; between two people; belonging to two people; **our m. friend** = the friend of both of us; **by m. consent** = with the agreement of both parties. **mu•tu•al•ly,** *adv.* to two people; by two people.

Mu•zak ['mju:zæk] *n.* trademark for system of playing recorded music in public places.

muz•zle ['mʌzl] 1. *n.* (a) nose of an animal. (b) device placed round the mouth of a dog to prevent it biting. (c) mouth of a gun. 2. *v.* to put a muzzle on the mouth of (a dog) to prevent it biting; **to m. the press** = to stop newspapers from printing what they want.

muz•zy ['mʌzɪ] *adj. inf.* dizzy/in a daze. **muz•zi•ness,** *n.* feeling muzzy.

my [maɪ] *adj.* belonging to me.

my•al•gi•a [maɪ'ældʒɪə] *n.* muscle pain. **my•al•gic en•ceph•a•lo•my•e•li•tis (ME)** [maɪ'ældʒɪk en'sefələʊmaɪ'laɪtɪs] *n. see* **chronic fatigue syndrome**.

my•col•o•gy [maɪ'kɒlədʒɪ] *n.* study of fungi. **my•co•log•i•cal** [maɪkə'lɒdʒɪkl] *adj.* referring to mycology.

my•e•li•tis [maɪə'laɪtɪs] *n.* inflammation of the spinal cord.

my•nah (bird) ['maɪnə'(bɜ:d)] *n.* black tropical bird which can be taught to talk.

my•o•pi•a [maɪ'əʊpɪə] *n.* short-sightedness/ not being able to see things which are far away. **my•op•ic** [maɪ'ɒpɪk] *adj.* short-sighted.

myr•i•ad ['mɪrɪəd] (*formal*) 1. *n.* very large number. 2. *adj.* very many.

myrrh [mɜː] *n.* sweet-smelling resin used to make incense, etc.

myr•tle ['mɜːtl] *n.* evergreen plant with scented flowers.

my•self [maɪ'self] *pronoun referring to* me. **all by m.** = on my own.

mys•ter•y ['mɪstrɪ] *n.* thing which cannot be explained; state of not being able to be explained. **mys•te•ri•ous** [mɪ'stɪərɪəs] *adj.* secret/which cannot be explained. **mys•te•ri•ous•ly**, *adv.* secretly/in a way which cannot be explained.

mys•tic ['mɪstɪk] 1. *n.* person who attempts to make contact with God through prayer/meditation, etc. 2. *adj.* in contact with God. **mys•ti•cal**, *adj.* in contact with God by some process which cannot be understood. **mys•ti•cism** ['mɪstɪsɪzəm] *n.* religion based on attempts to contact God by prayer and meditation.

mys•ti•fy ['mɪstɪfaɪ] *v.* to puzzle/to bewilder. **mys•ti•fi•ca•tion** [mɪstɪfɪ'keɪʃn] *n.* puzzle/bewilderment.

mys•tique [mɪ'stiːk] *n.* mysterious atmosphere about a person or thing.

myth [mɪθ] *n.* (a) ancient folk story about gods. (b) untrue, but commonly held, notion. **myth•i•cal**, *adj.* (a) referring to ancient tales of gods. (b) untrue/not existing. **myth•o•log•i•cal** [mɪθə'lɒdʒɪkl] *adj.* referring to mythology. **my•thol•o•gy** [mɪ'θɒlədʒɪ] *n.* study of myths; ancient folk stories from a particular source.

myx•o•ma•to•sis [mɪksəmə'təʊsɪs] *n.* fatal disease of rabbits.

æ back, ɑː farm, ɒ top, aɪ pipe, aʊ how, aɪe fire, aʊə flower, ɔː bought, ɔɪ toy, e fed, eəhair, eɪ take, ə afraid, əʊ boat, əʊə lower, vː word, iː heap, ɪ hit, ɪə hear, uː school, ʊ book, ʌ but, b back, d dog, ð then, dʒ just, f fog, g go, h hand, j yes, k catch, l last, m mix, n nut, ŋ sing, p penny, r round, s some, ʃ short, t too, tʃ chop, θ thing, v voice, w was, z zoo, ʒ treasure

Nn

N *symbol for* nitrogen.

Na *symbol for* sodium.

nab [næb] *v.* (**nabbed**) (a) *inf.* to snatch/to pull away (sth) suddenly/to steal. (b) *inf.* to catch (s.o.) in the act/to pounce on (s.o.).

na•dir ['neɪdɪə] *n.* lowest point.

nag [næg] 1. *n. inf.* horse. 2. *v.* (**nagged**) to try to persuade (s.o.) by saying the same thing again and again/to criticize without seeming to stop. **nag•ging**, *adj.* persistent (pain, etc.).

nai•ad ['naɪæd] *n.* goddess living in a stream.

nail [neɪl] 1. *n.* (a) hard covering at the ends of fingers and toes; **n. scissors** = curved scissors for cutting nails. (b) small metal spike with a pointed end, used to hold things together; **hard as nails** = very tough; *inf.* **to hit the n. on the head** = to make an accurate judgment/to give the right answer. 2. *v.* to attach with nails.

na•ive [naɪ'iːv] *adj.* inexperienced and innocent. **na•ive•ly**, *adv.* in a naive way. **na•ive•té**, naivety, *n.* being naive.

na•ked ['neɪkɪd] *adj.* with no clothes on; with no covering; **n. flame** = flame with no protective shield; **invisible to the n. eye** = which can only be seen using a telescope/microscope. **na•ked•ly**, *adv.* with no covering. **na•ked•ness**, *n.* being naked.

nam•by-pam•by ['næmbɪpæmbɪ] *adj.* weak and silly.

name [neɪm] 1. *n.* (a) title/word which you use to call people/things; **Christian n./first n.** = particular name given to someone as a child; **he put his n. down to join the club** = he applied to join; **to call s.o. names** = to insult s.o. (b) **in n. only** = according to the name used, but not really in fact. (c) **to have a bad n.** = a bad reputation; **to make a n. for oneself** = to become famous or successful. 2. *v.* (a) to call by a name; to give a name to. (b) to specify; **to n. the day** = to fix the date for a wedding. (c) to appoint s.o. to a post. **name•less**, *adj.* with no name; (word/name) not to be used because of disgust or in order to remain anonymous. **name•ly**, *adv.* that is to say. **name•sake**, *n.* person with the same name as another.

nan•a [næn, 'nænə] *n.* child's name for grandmother.

nan•ny ['nænɪ] *n.* (a) nurse paid to look after children in their own home. (b) **n. goat** = female goat.

nano- ['nænəʊ] *prefix meaning* one billionth; **nanometer; nanosecond.**

na•no•me•ter ['nænəʊmiːtə] *n.* one billionth of a meter.

na•no•sec•ond ['nænəʊsekənd] *n.* one billionth of a second.

na•no•tech•nol•o•gy [nænəʊtek'nɒlədʒɪ] *n.* technology used to manufacture/manipulate objects with dimensions of less than 100 nanometers.

nap [næp] 1. *n.* (a) short sleep. (b) raised surface of cloth, such as velvet. 2. *v.* to sleep for a short time; **to catch s.o. napping** = to find s.o. off guard.

na•palm ['neɪpɑːm] *n.* inflammable substance used in incendiary bombs.

nape [neɪp] *n.* back of the neck.

naph•tha ['næfθə] *n.* oil derived from coal/petroleum, used to light fires/clean clothes, etc. **naph•tha•lene** ['næfθəliːn] *n.* strong-smelling white chemical used to make mothballs.

nap•kin ['næpkɪn] *n.* square piece of cloth or paper used to protect clothes and wipe your mouth at mealtimes.

nar•cis•sus [nɑː'sɪsəs] *n.* (*pl.* **-issus**, **issuses**, **-issi** [-ɪsaɪ]) white flower similar to a daffodil. **nar•cis•sism**, *n.* great love for your own appearance. **nar•cis•sis•tic** [nɑːsɪ'sɪstɪk] *adj.* loving your own appearance.

nar•cot•ic [nɑː'kɒtɪk] *adj. & n.* (substance) which can make you feel sleepy or become unconscious; **narcotics squad** = police department dealing with drug offenses.

nar•rate [nə'reɪt] *v.* to write/to speak about events; to tell (a story). **nar•ra•tion** [nə'reɪʃn] *n.* speaking/writing about events. **nar•ra•tive** ['nærətɪv] 1. *n.* what is actually written or told. 2. *adj.* describing events which took place. **nar•ra•tor** [nə'reɪtə] *n.* person who gives an actual account; person who reads a story.

nar•row ['nærəʊ] 1. *adj.* (a) not wide; **n. escape** = escape at the last minute from an awkward or dangerous situation. (b) **n. majority** = very small margin of votes. (c) restricted (opinions). 2. *v.* to make/to become less wide; to make/to become smaller. **nar•row•ly,** *adv.* nearly/only just. **nar•row-mind•ed,** *adj.* not capable of seeing many points of view/not tolerant. **nar•row•ness,** *n.* being narrow. **nar•rows,** *n. pl.* narrow stretch of water.

nar•whal ['nɑːwəl] *n.* type of whale which lives in the Arctic and has a long tusk.

nar•y ['neɪrɪ] *adj. (old)* not one.

na•sal ['neɪzl] *adj.* referring to the nose; spoken as if through the nose. **na•sal•ly,** *adv.* in a nasal way.

nas•tur•tium [nə'stɜːʃəm] *n.* creeping plant with large orange or yellow flowers.

nas•ty ['nɑːstɪ] *adj.* (**-ier, -iest**) unpleasant/disagreeable; **to turn n.** = to become hostile/unfriendly/unpleasant. **nas•ti•ly,** *adv.* in a nasty way. **nas•ti•ness,** *n.* being nasty; nasty happening.

na•tal ['neɪtl] *adj.* referring to birth.

na•tion ['neɪʃn] *n.* people of a particular country. **na•tion•al** ['næʃnl] 1. *adj.* belonging to the people of a particular country. 2. *n.* person of a particular country. **Na•tion•al Guard,** *n.* part of the U.S. army made up of military forces from each state, used in time of war or national emergency. **na•tion•al•ism** ['næʃnəlɪzəm] *n.* feeling of pride in one's nation; desire for independence for a country. **na•tion•al•ist,** *n.* person who supports nationalism. **na•tion•al•is•tic,** *adj.* referring to nationalism. **na•tion•al•i•ty** [næʃə-'nælɪtɪ] *n.* citizenship of a country. **na•tion•al•i•za•tion** [næʃnəlar'zeɪʃn] *n.* conversion of private industries to ownership by the national government. **na•tion•al•ize** ['næʃnəlaɪz] *v.* to put (a private industry) under central government ownership and control. **na•tion•al•ly,** *adv.* in a national way; (done) all over the nation. **na•tion•al park,** *n.* area of land run by the national government for public use, where building/tourism, etc. are controlled. **na•tion•wide** ['neɪʃnwaɪd] *adj.* all over the country.

na•tive ['neɪtɪv] 1. *n.* (a) person born in a particular country. (b) uncivilized original inhabitant. (c) plant/animal which originally comes from a particular country. 2. *adj.* (a) natural; (qualities) with which a person is born. (b) unaltered/undeveloped. (c) belonging to those born in a country. (d) **n. to** = (plant/animal) which originally comes from a certain country.

na•tiv•i•ty [nə'tɪvɪtɪ] *n.* birth, esp. that of Jesus Christ; **n. play** = play describing the events surrounding the birth of Jesus Christ.

nat•ter ['nætə] 1. *n. inf.* friendly informal conversation/chat. 2. *v. inf.* to have a friendly informal chat.

nat•ty ['nætɪ] *adj.* (**-ier, -iest**) smart/tidy (personal appearance).

nat•u•ral ['nætʃrəl] 1. *adj.* (a) based on inner knowledge or instinct; not learned. (b) normal/not artificial. (c) not surprising/not unexpected. (d) dealing with (the study of) nature; **n. gas** = gas which is found in the earth. (e) (*in music*) (note) which is neither sharp nor flat. 2. *n.* person who is naturally suitable for a job/a part in a play, etc. **nat•u•ral his•to•ry,** *n.* (*also* **natural science**) study of nature. **nat•u•ral•ism,** *n.* (*in art/literature*) showing things as they really are. **nat•u•ral•ist,** *n.* person who studies animals or plants. **nat•u•ral•is•tic,** *adj.* (art, etc.) which shows things as they really are. **nat•ur•al•i•za•tion** [nætʃərəlar'zeɪʃn] *n.* act of naturalizing; being naturalized. **nat•ur•al•ize** ['nætʃərəlaɪz] *v.* (a) to introduce (a plant or animal) into another country. (b) to let cultivated plants become wild. (c) to grant (s.o.) citizenship of a country other than that in which he was born. **nat•u•ral•ly** ['nætʃrəlɪ] *adv.* (a) in a natural/unstudied way. (b) as you would expect/of course. **nat•u•ral•ness,** *n.* being natural.

na•ture ['neɪtʃə] *n.* (a) character (of a person/thing/animal); **human n.** = attitudes and behavior which are typical of human beings. (b) kind/class (of thing). (c) world of plants and animals; **the laws of n.** = what happens in the world of plants and animals. **-natured,** *suffix showing a* characteristic; **good-natured.** **na•tur•ist,** *n.* nudist.

naught [nɔːt] *n.* zero/nothing; the symbol 0; **to come to n.** = to be unsuccessful/fail.

naugh•ty ['nɔːtɪ] *adj.* (**-ier, -iest**) bad/disobedient (child). **naugh•ti•ly,** *adv.* wickedly. **naugh•ti•ness,** *n.* wickedness/bad behavior.

nau•se•a ['nɔːzɪə] *n.* feeling of sickness/of extreme dislike. **nau•se•ate,** *v.* to make (s.o.) loathe/dislike very much. **nau•se•at•ing,** *adj.* horrible/which makes you sick. **nau•seous,** *adj.* (a) which nauseates. (b) feeling unwell.

nau•ti•cal ['nɔːtɪkl] *adj.* referring to ships, sail-

æ back, ɑː farm, ɒ top, aɪ pipe, aʊ how, aɪə fire, aʊə flower, ɔː bought, ɔɪ toy, e fed, eəhair, eɪ take, ə afraid, əʊ boat, əʊə lower, vː word, iː heap, ɪ hit, ɪə hear, uː school, ʊ book, ʌ but, b back, d dog, ð then, dʒ just, f fog, g go, h hand, j yes, k catch, l last, m mix, n nut, ŋ sing, p penny, r round, s some, ʃ short, t too, tʃ chop, θ thing, v voice, w was, z zoo, ʒ treasure

ing and boating; **n. mile** = measure of length at sea (2025 yards or 1.85 kilometers).

nau•ti•lus [nɔ:'tɪləs] *n.* large type of shell fish.

na•val ['neɪvl] *adj.* referring to ships and esp. to a navy; **n. engagement** = battle at sea; **n. base** = port for warships; **n. college** = establishment for training naval officers.

nave [neɪv] *n.* main part of a church.

na•vel ['neɪvl] *n.* small hollow in the middle of your stomach where the umbilical cord was attached; **n. orange** = large seedless orange with a small hollow at the bottom.

nav•i•gate ['nævɪgeɪt] *v.* to guide/to steer (a ship or aircraft). **nav•i•ga•bil•i•ty** [nævɪgə'bɪlɪtɪ] *n.* being navigable. **nav•i•ga•ble,** *adj.* (a) steerable/seaworthy. (b) (river) deep enough for ships to sail in it. **nav•i•ga•tion** [nævɪ'geɪʃn] *n.* guiding/steering a ship/an aircraft along a certain course. **nav•i•ga•tor** ['nævɪgeɪtə] *n.* person who guides/steers a ship or an aircraft.

na•vy ['neɪvɪ] 1. *n.* all a country's warships and crews. 2. *adj. & n.* **(blue)** = dark blue.

nay [neɪ] *adv.* (*old*) no.

N.B. [en'bi:] *short for* nota bene, *meaning* please note.

NCO [ensi:'əu] *n.* non-commissioned officer.

neap [ni:p] *n.* **n. tide** = tide which does not rise or fall very much, midway between the spring tides.

Ne•a•pol•i•tan [nɪə'pɒlɪtən] *adj.* referring to Naples; **N. ice cream** = ice cream made of layers of different colors and flavors.

near ['nɪə] (**-er, -est**) 1. *adv.* close/at only a little distance in space or time. 2. *prep.* close by (an object); not far away in time. 3. *adj.* **n. relations** = closest relations; **n. miss** = (i) sth which is not quite successful; (ii) narrow escape. 4. *v.* to draw near to/to approach. **near•by,** 1. *adj.* which is situated close by. 2. *adv.* close by. **Near East,** *n.* countries at the eastern end of the Mediterranean. **near•ly,** *adv.* (a) almost. (b) closely; **not n. big enough** = far too small. **near•ness,** *n.* closeness. **near•sight•ed,** *adj.* short-sighted/only able to see clearly things which are near.

neat [ni:t] *adj.* (**-er,-est**) (a) tidy/clean. (b) (alcohol) with no water added. (c) apt/precise (words). (d) skillful/well handled. **neat•ly,** *adv.* in a neat way. **neat•ness,** *n.* tidy/clean appearance.

neb•u•la ['nebjulə] *n.* (*pl.* **-ae** [-li:], **-as**) cloud of dust in space which shines like a star at night. **neb•u•lous** ['nebjuləs] *adj.* vague.

nec•es•sar•y ['nesəsərɪ] 1. *n.* what is essential/what must be done. 2. *adj.* essential/which cannot be avoided. **nec•es•sar•i•ly** [nesə-'serəlɪ] *adv.* in an unavoidable way; **taking the**

train isn't n. more expensive than the bus** = it can be cheaper. **ne•ces•si•tate** [nɪ'sesɪteɪt] *v.* to make essential/to compel. **ne•ces•si•tous,** *adj.* (*formal*) poor. **ne•ces•si•ty,** *n.* (a) need/compulsion. (b) absolutely essential thing.

neck [nek] 1. *n.* (a) part of the body connecting the head to the shoulders; *inf.* **to be up to your n. in work** = have a lot of work to do; **to breathe down s.o.'s n.** = to watch s.o. very closely/to follow close behind s.o.; **to win by a n.** = win a race by a very short distance; **to finish n. and n.** = to be equal winners; *inf.* **a pain in the n.** = a troublesome person/thing; **to save your n.** = escape hanging/punishment; *inf.* **to get it in the n.** = to be severely criticized; *inf.* **to stick your n. out** = take a chance/to be asking for trouble. (b) narrow passage leading to a wider area; *inf.* **in this n. of the woods** = in this part of the world. (c) part of a garment which goes around your neck. (d) part of an animal eaten as food. 2. *v. inf.* to fondle/caress. **neck•lace,** *n.* string of beads/pearls, etc., worn around the neck. **neck•let,** *n.* ornament worn tightly around the neck. **neck•line,** *n.* edge of a dress, etc., around the neck. **neck•tie,** *n.* band of material worn around the neck and tied in front with a knot.

nec•ro•man•cy ['nekrəmænsɪ] *n.* art of black magic/of predicting the future by speaking to the dead. **nec•ro•man•cer,** *n.* person who practices necromancy.

ne•crop•o•lis [ne'krɒpəlɪs] *n.* large ancient cemetery.

nec•tar ['nektə] *n.* (a) sweet substance produced by flowers. (b) any extremely pleasant drink.

nec•tar•ine ['nektəri:n] *n.* fruit like a peach with a smooth skin.

nee, née [neɪ] *adj.* with the maiden name of; **Mrs. Smith, n. Taylor.**

need [ni:d] 1. *n.* (a) what is necessary. (b) **in n. of** = requiring. (c) time of difficulty/poverty; **a friend in n. is a friend indeed** = a person who helps you when you are in difficulties is a real friend. 2. *v.* to be necessary/to be required. **need•ful,** *adj.* (*old*) necessary. **need•less,** *adj.* unnecessary/not called for. **needs.** 1. *pl.* actual requirements. 2. *adv.* **if n. be** = if it has to be done. **need•y,** *adj.* (**-ier, -iest**) in need of/requiring help or food.

nee•dle ['ni:dl] 1. *n.* (a) thin metal/plastic/wooden tool with a sharp point at one end; **it's like looking for a n. in a haystack** = it's a hopeless task. (b) **hypodermic n.** = needle used for injections. (c) hand/pointer (on a dial); **compass n.** = the indicator on the dial of a compass. (d) leaf of a pine tree. 2. *v.* to irritate/to provoke (s.o.). **nee•dle•wom•an,** *n.*

woman who is good at sewing.
nee•dle•work, *n.* sewing done with needle
and thread.

ne'er-do-well ['neədu:wel] *n.* person who is
good for nothing.

ne•far•i•ous [nɪ'feərɪəs] *adj.* (*formal*) very
wicked.

ne•gate [nɪ'geɪt] *v.* to oppose/to cancel out
(sth). **ne•ga•tion** [nɪ'geɪʃn] *n.* what is canceled out/negated. **neg•a•tive** ['negətɪv] 1. *n.*
(a) reply indicating no. (b) reverse image of a
photograph. (c) one of the terminals in a battery. 2. *adj.* (a) meaning no; showing opposi-
tion/refusal. (b) without good/positive
qualities. (c) minus/less than zero. 3. *v.* to con-
tradict/to oppose (sth). **neg•a•tive
eq•ui•ty,** *n.* state of owning a property valued at less than what is owed on it as a mortgage. **neg•a•tive•ly,** *adv.* in a way which
suggests opposition.

ne•glect [nɪ'glekt] 1. *n.* disregard/lack of care
or attention. 2. *v.* (a) to fail to look after/to fail
to maintain. (b) to omit to do (sth which
should be done). **ne•glect•ed,** *adj.* not
looked after. **ne•glect•ful,** *adj.* **to be n. of** =
to forget about. **neg•li•gence** ['neglɪdʒəns]
n. absence of proper care and attention.
neg•li•gent, *adj.* not giving proper care and
attention. **neg•li•gi•ble,** *adj.* not
significant/not worth regarding.

neg•li•gee, negligé ['neglɪʒeɪ] *n.* woman's
light dressing gown.

ne•go•ti•ate [nɪ'gəʊsɪeɪt] *v.* (a) to discuss so
as to make an agreement with s.o. (b) to make
a financial arrangement. (c) to overcome an
obstacle/difficulty. **ne•go•ti•a•ble** [nɪ-
'gəʊsɪəbl] *adj.* which can be negotiated.
ne•go•ti•a•tion [nɪgəʊsɪ'eɪʃn] *n.* discuss-
ing/arranging by discussion.
ne•go•ti•a•tor [nɪ'gəʊsɪeɪtə] *n.* person who
discusses to try to reach an agreement.

Ne•gro ['ni:grəʊ, 'ni:grəs] *adj.* & *n.* (*pl.* **-oes**)
member of a dark-skinned race of people orig-
inating in Africa. **Ne•groid,** *adj.* having the
characteristics of Negroes.

neigh [neɪ] 1. *n.* sound made by a horse. 2. *v.* to
make a sound like a horse.

neigh•bor ['neɪbə], *Brit.* **neigh•bour** *n.* (a)
person who lives in a nearby
house/road/country. (b) person sitting beside
you. **neigh•bor•hood,** *n.* (a) district and its
people. (b) **in the n. of** = around/near to (in
space or amount). **neigh•bor•ing,** *adj.* next

to each other. **neigh•bor•ly,** *adj.* in a
friendly/helpful way.

nei•ther ['naɪðə, 'ni:ðə] 1. *adv.* & *conj.* **n. ... nor**
= not one ... and not the other. 2. *adj.* & *pron.*
not either of two things or persons.

nel•son ['nelsən] *n.* (*in wrestling*) way of holding the opponent, with the arms under his
armpits and the hands on the back of his neck.

nem. con. ['nem'kɔn] *adv.* with no one voting
against.

nem•e•sis ['nemɪsɪs] *n.* (*no pl.*) just punishment from which you cannot escape.

neo- ['ni:əʊ] *prefix meaning* new.

ne•o•lith•ic [ni:əʊ'lɪθɪk] *adj.* belonging to the
late Stone Age.

ne•ol•o•gism [ni:'ɒlədʒɪzəm] *n.*
newly-invented word.

ne•on ['ni:ɒn] *n.* (*element:* Ne) colorless gas
often used in tubes to make illuminated signs.

ne•o•phyte ['ni:əʊfaɪt] *n.* beginner; person
who is learning.

neph•ew ['nefju:] *n.* son of your brother or sister.

ne•phri•tis [nef'raɪtɪs] *n.* kidney disease.

nep•o•tism ['nepətɪzəm] *n.* giving members of
your family jobs for which they are not necessarily qualified.

nerve [nɜ:v] 1. *n.* (a) one of many thin threads
forming part of the body's system for conveying messages to and from the brain; **in a state
of nerves** = in a tense/anxious state; **to get on
s.o.'s nerves** = to irritate/annoy s.o. (b) cour-
age/confidence; *inf.* **he's got n.** = he's bold/im-
pudent/rude; **to have the n. to** = to be so rude
as to. (c) **to strain every n.** = to make tremen-
dous efforts. 2. *v.* **to n. yourself** = to summon
up strength/confidence. **nerve-rack•ing,**
adj. disturbing. **nerv•ous,** *adj.* (a) **the n. system** = the pattern of nerve fibers in the body;
n. breakdown = physical and mental collapse
caused by worry. (b) timid/easily dis-
turbed/easily upset. **nerv•ous•ly,** *adv.* in a
worried/frightened way. **nerv•ous•ness,** *n.*
being nervous. **nerv•y,** *adj. inf.* boldly impu-
dent/rude.

nest [nest] 1. *n.* (a) place built by birds to lay
their eggs; **to feather your n.** = to make a lot of
money (usu. fraudulently). (b) hiding
place/collecting place for people or animals.
(c) **n. of tables** = tables of different sizes fitting
under each other. 2. *v.* (*of birds*) to build a
nest. **nest egg,** *n.* investment/money put

æ back, a: farm, ɒ: top, aɪ pipe, aʊ how, aɪə fire, aʊə flower, ɔ: bought, ɔɪ toy, e fed, eəhair, eɪ take, ə
afraid, əʊ boat, əʊə lower, v: word, i: heap, ɪ hit, ɪə hear, u: school, ʊ book, ʌ but, b back, d dog, ð then,
dʒ just, f fog, g go, h hand, j yes, k catch, l last, m mix, n nut, ŋ sing, p penny, r round, s some, ʃ short, t
too, tʃ chop, θ thing, v voice, w was, z zoo, ʒ treasure

aside for future use. **nes•tling** ['neslɪŋ] *n.* small bird not yet ready to leave the nest.

nes•tle ['nesl] *v.* (a) to settle down comfortably. (b) to have close and loving contact.

net [net] 1. *n.* loosely woven material; piece of this material used for fishing/catching/fencing, etc. 2. *v.* (**netted**) (a) to catch in a net. (b) to make a true profit; **to n. a big profit** = to make a lot of money. 3. *adj.* (price/weight) left after taking away the weight of the container/the tax paid, etc.; **n. profit** = actual gain after expenses have been paid; **n. weight** = true weight without the wrappings. **net•ting**, *n.* material made of string/wire loosely woven into a regular pattern of holes. **net•work**, *n.* interconnecting system (of railroads, etc.); radio/TV system; interconnected computer system.

Net [net] *n. inf.* **the Net** = the Internet.

neth•er ['neðə] *adj.* (*formal*) lower; **n. regions** = bottom part. **neth•er•most**, *adj.* lowest.

net•i•quette ['netɪket] *n.* Internet etiquette.

ne•tsu•ke ['netskɪ] *n.* carved ivory toggle, formerly used in Japan.

net•tle ['netl] 1. *n.* (**stinging**) **n.** = weed with stinging leaves. 2. *v.* to anger/to irritate. **net•tle•rash**, *n.* skin rash caused by an allergy.

neu•ral ['njʊrəl] *adj.* referring to nerves. **neu•ral•gia** [njuˈrældʒə] *n.* nerve pains in the face or head. **neu•ral•gic**, *adj.* referring to neuralgia. **neu•ri•tis** [njuˈraɪtɪs] *n.* inflammation of nerves. **neu•ro•bi•ol•o•gy**, *n.* study of the biology of the nervous system. **neu•ro•log•i•cal** [njurəˈlɒdʒɪkl] *adj.* referring to neurology. **neu•rol•o•gist** [njuˈrɒlədʒɪst] *n.* person who studies the nervous system. **neu•rol•o•gy** [njuˈrɒlədʒɪ] *n.* study of the body's nervous system. **neu•ron**, *n.* cell in the nerve system which passes on impulses. **neu•ro•sis** [njuˈrəʊsɪs] *n.* (*pl.* -**oses** [-əʊsiːz]) mental illness caused by a nervous disorder. **neu•rot•ic** [njuˈrɒtɪk] *adj.* unbalanced (behavior). **neu•rot•ic•al•ly**, *adv.* in an unbalanced way.

neu•ter ['njuːtə] 1. *adj.* (*in grammar*) not having a masculine or feminine gender. 2. *v.* to castrate. **neu•tral.** 1. *adj.* (a) not favoring or supporting either side in a dispute. (b) not having a distinctive color. (c) neither acid or alkali. 2. *n.* (a) citizen of a neutral country. (b) **the car is in n.** = not in gear. **neu•tral•i•ty** [njuˈtrælɪtɪ] *n.* being uncommitted/neutral; not taking sides. **neu•tral•i•za•tion** [njuːtrəlaɪˈzeɪʃn] *n.* act of neutralizing. **neu•tral•ize** ['njuːtrəlaɪz] *v.* to cancel out by using an opposite. **neu•tral•ly**, *adv.* in a neutral way. **neu•tron**, *n.* basic particle with no

electric charge; **n. bomb** = nuclear bomb which kills people but does little damage to buildings.

nev•er ['nevə] *adv.* (a) not ever/not at any time. (b) (*for emphasis*) not at all. (c) (*exclamation of surprise*) surely not; **well I n.!** how surprising! **nev•er-end•ing**, *adj.* which does not stop. **nev•er•more**, *adv.* (*formal*) not any more. **nev•er•the•less** [nevəðəˈles] *adv.* despite all that/all the same. **nev•er-to-be-for•got•ten**, *adj.* memorable.

new [njuː] *adj.* (-**er, -est**) (a) completely different/not thought of before/not met before. (b) changed/different. (c) fresh/unused; **to turn over a n. leaf** = become better/start again. (d) most recent; **n. moon** = moon when it is a thin crescent. (e) just bought/just acquired. **new•born**, *adj.* just born. **new•com•er**, *n.* person who has just come to an area. **new•fan•gled**, *adj.* newly invented. **new•ly**, *adv.* most recently; **newlyweds** = people who have just gotten married. **new•ness**, *n.* being recent/fresh; not having been used. **news** [njuːz] *n.* spoken or written information about events; **it's in the n.** = it is of topical interest; **to break the n. to s.o.** = to tell s.o. bad/unwelcome news; **no n. is good n.** = the absence of bad news means things may be going well. **news•cast•er**, *n.* person who reads the news on television. **news flash**, *n.* short news item. **news•group**, *n.* Internet service that enables users to exchange electronic mail on a common theme. **news•let•ter**, *n.* printed sheet giving news to members of a church/club, etc. **news•man**, *n.* (*pl.* -**men**) journalist. **news•pa•per**, *n.* daily/weekly paper containing information and news. **news•print**, *n.* paper for printing newspapers and magazines. **news•reel**, *n.* short motion picture about current events. **news•wor•thy**, *adj.* (events) worth recording/mentioning in papers or on television. **news•y**, *adj. inf.* full of news. **New World**, *n.* North and South America. **new year**, *n.* the year which has just started; period just after 1st January. **New Year's Day**, *n.* January 1st. **New Year's Eve**, *n.* December 31st.

new•el ['njuːəl] *n.* post at the top or bottom of stairs, to which the banisters are attached.

newt [njuːt] *n.* small, lizardlike animal which can live either in or out of water.

new•ton ['njuːtən] *n.* standard measurement of force.

next [nekst] 1. *adj.* (a) (*of time/sequence*) coming after. (b) (*of place*) closest to/nearest; **she lives n. door** = in the house/apartment next to this one. 2. *adv.* coming after in place/time; **what n.?** = what other amazing or absurd things can we expect? **it costs n. to nothing** = it costs very little. 3. *n.* person/thing following; **the week after n.** = not the next week but the following one. **next-door,** *adj.* living next door. **next of kin,** *n.* (*no pl.*) nearest relative(s).

nex•us ['neksəs] *n.* link/connecting point for ideas, organizations, etc.

Ni *symbol for* nickel.

nib [nɪb] *n.* pointed writing end of a pen.

nib•ble ['nɪbl] 1. *n.* bite/very small amount eaten. 2. *v.* to take very small, cautious bites. **nib•ble a•way,** *v.* to remove gradually/in little pieces.

nice [naɪs] *adj.* (-er, -est) (a) generally pleasant. (b) precise; subtle. **nice-look•ing,** *adj.* pretty/pleasant to look at. **nice•ly,** *adv.* in a satisfactory/good manner. **nice•ness,** *n.* quality of being agreeable. **ni•ce•ty,** *n.* fine/exact detail.

niche [niːʃ] *n.* (a) hollow in a wall or pillar to put a statue/vase/decoration in; **to find your n./to find a n. for yourself** = to find a completely satisfying or suitable role/job. (b) special place in a market.

nick [nɪk] 1. *n.* small dent/notch (usu. to mark a place); *inf.* **in the n. of time** = just in time. 2. *v.* to make a small notch/cut.

nick•el ['nɪkl] 1. *n.* (a) (*element:* Ni) silver-colored metal. (b) 5-cent coin. 2. *v.* (**nickeled, nickelled**) to coat with nickel.

nick•name ['nɪkneɪm] 1. *n.* abbreviated or pet name. 2. *v.* to give (s.o.) a nickname.

nic•o•tine ['nɪkətiːn] *n.* poisonous brown liquid obtained from tobacco.

niece [niːs] *n.* daughter of your brother or sister.

nif•ty ['nɪftɪ] *adj. inf.* (a) attractive/fashionable. (b) very good; excellent (idea).

Ni•ge•ri•an [naɪ'dʒɪərɪən] 1. *adj.* referring to Nigeria. 2. *n.* person who comes from Nigeria.

nig•gard•ly ['nɪgədlɪ] *adj.* mean; very small (amount).

nig•gle ['nɪgl] *v.* to be fussy about relatively unimportant details. **nig•gling,** *adj.* unimportant/insignificant.

nigh [naɪ] *adv.* (*formal*) near.

night [naɪt] *n.* last part of each day; period of darkness from sunset to sunrise; **last n.** = yesterday after dark; **the first n.** = the official opening performance of a play or entertainment; **n. out** = evening spent outside the home. **night•cap,** (a) (*old*) cap worn in bed. (b) bed-time drink. **night•clothes,** *n. pl.* clothes worn in bed. **night•club,** *n.* club only open at night. **night•dress,** *n.* nightgown. **night•fall,** *n.* time when night starts. **night•gown,** *n.* gown worn by women in bed. **night•ie,** *n. inf.* nightgown. **night•in•gale,** *n.* small brown singing bird. **night•jar,** *n.* dark-colored bird which flies by night. **night•life,** *n.* entertainment which takes place in a town at night. **night•light,** *n.* small dim light left burning at night. **night•ly,** *adv.* every night. **night•mare,** *n.* (a) vivid frightening dream. (b) horrible event. **night•mar•ish,** *adj.* vividly frightening. **night school,** *n.* school which has classes for adults in the evening. **night•shade,** *n.* poisonous plant. **night•shirt,** *n.* long shirt worn in bed. **night soil,** *n.* human excreta, used as manure. **night•time,** *n.* period of night; **nighttime flight** = flight during the hours of darkness. **night•watch•man,** *n.* (*pl.* -men) man who guards a building at night.

ni•hil•ism ['nɪhɪlɪzəm] *n.* belief that nothing which exists is good. **ni•hil•ist,** *n.* person who believes in nihilism.

nil [nɪl] *n.* nothing/zero.

nim•ble ['nɪmbl] *adj.* (-er, -est) agile/fast-moving; physically fit and alert. **nim•bly,** *adv.* in an expert way.

nim•bus ['nɪmbəs] *n.* (a) dark raincloud. (b) shining halo.

nin•com•poop ['nɪŋkəmpuːp] *n.* silly person/fool.

nine [naɪn] *n.* number 9; **n. times out of ten** = in most cases; *inf.* **dressed to the nines** = wearing your most elaborate clothes; **possession is n. tenths of the law** = it is easy to claim ownership of something which is already in your possession. **nine•pins,** *n. pl.* skittles. **nine•teen,** *n.* number 19; **the n. hundreds** = the years after 1900. **nine•teenth, 19th,** *adj. & n.* referring to nineteen; **the n. century** = period from 1800 to 1899. **nine•ti•eth, 90th,** *adj. & n.* referring to ninety. **nine•ty,** *n.* number 90; **she's in her nineties** = she is between 90 and 99 years old. **ninth, 9th,** *adj. & n.* referring to nine; **the n. century** = period from 800 to 899.

nin•ny ['nɪnɪ] *n.* idiot.

nip [nɪp] 1. *n.* (a) small amount of alcohol. (b) short sharp bite/pinch; **a n. in the air** = a sud-

---

æ back, ɑː farm, ɒ top, aɪ pipe, aʊ how, aɪə fire, aʊə flower, ɔː bought, ɔɪ toy, e fed, eəhair, eɪ take, ə afraid, əʊ boat, əʊə lower, ʌː word, iː heap, ɪ hit, ɪə hear, uː school, ʊ book, ʌ but, b back, d dog, ð then, dʒ just, f fog, g go, h hand, j yes, k catch, l last, m mix, n nut, ŋ sing, p penny, r round, s some, ʃ short, t too, tʃ chop, θ thing, v voice, w was, z zoo, ʒ treasure

den/sharp burst of cold weather. 2. *v.* (**nipped**) to bite/to pinch sharply or suddenly. **nip•per**, *n. inf.* (a) small child. (b) **nippers** = pincers. **nip•py**, *adj. inf.* (a) sharp-tasting. (b) cold.

nip•ple ['nɪpl] *n.* (a) small projection on the tip of a breast from which, in females, the mother's milk comes. (b) short piece of pipe with threads at both ends, used for coupling two parts.

nir•va•na [nɪə'vɑːnə] *n. (for Buddhists)* happy state after death when the dead person's soul joins the divine soul.

Nis•sen hut ['nɪsən'hʌt] *n.* shed with a semi-circular roof of corrugated iron and a concrete floor.

nit [nɪt] *n.* egg of a louse. **nit-pick•ing**, *n. inf.* petty criticism/finding small faults to criticize. **nit•wit**, *n. inf.* idiot.

ni•tro•gen ['naɪtrədʒən] *n. (element:* N) gas which makes up four-fifths of the atmosphere. **ni•tro•gly•cer•ine**, *n.* liquid explosive. **ni•trate**, *n.* salt of nitric acid. **ni•tric ac•id**, *n.* acid containing nitrogen. **ni•trous**, *adj.* containing nitrogen.

nit•ty-grit•ty [nɪtɪ'grɪtɪ] *n. inf.* basic details (of a matter).

nm *abbrev. for* nanometer.

no. *abbrev. for* number.

no ['nəʊ] 1. *n. & adv.* showing the negative/opposite of yes; **the noes have it** = most people have voted no. 2. *adj.* none of/not any of; **it's n. distance** = not at all far/a very short distance away; **it's n. joke** = not funny but serious; **n. admission** = entrance not allowed; *inf.* **n. way** = certainly not. 3. *adv.* not/not at all; **n. sooner said than done** = it will be done immediately.

no•ble ['nəʊbl] 1. *n.* person of high rank by title or birth. 2. *adj.* (**-er, -est**) of high rank/dignified; worthy or praise/splendid. **no•bil•i•ty** [nə'bɪlɪtɪ] *n.* (a) titled members of society/the aristocracy. (b) high-mindedness. **no•ble•man**, *n. (pl.* **-men**) noble. **no•ble-mind•ed•ness**, *n.* high-mindedness/worthy thoughts. **no•ble•ness**, *n.* being noble; nobility. **no•ble•wom•an**, *n. (pl.* **-women**) woman of high rank. **no•bly**, *adv.* in a noble fashion/heroically.

no•bod•y ['nəʊbədɪ] 1. *n.* person of no importance. 2. *pron.* no one/no person.

noc•tur•nal [nɒk'tɜːnl] *adj.* referring to the night; (animals which are) most active at night. **noc•turne** ['nɒktɜːn] *n.* painting/piece of music conveying a feeling of night.

nod [nɒd] 1. *n.* forward movement of the head as a greeting/as a sign of agreement. 2. *v.* (**nodded**) to show agreement/to give permission/to

agree by a forward movement of the head; **to n. off** = to fall asleep; **nodding acquaintance** = (i) person you know only slightly; (ii) slight knowledge.

node [nəʊd] *n.* (a) place where leaves grow from a plant's stem. (b) knob on a root/branch/human joint. (c) point where curves cross. **nod•al**, *adj.* central/at the point where lines meet. **nod•ule** ['nɒdjuːl] *n.* small node.

No•el [nəʊ'el] *n.* Christmas.

nog [nɒg] *n.* **egg n.** = drink made of alcohol and raw eggs. **nog•gin**, *n.* small quantity of alcohol.

noise [nɔɪz] 1. *n.* loud (usu. unpleasant) sound. 2. *v.* **to n. sth about/abroad** = to make sth public/to spread the news. **noise•less**, *adj.* without any sound. **noise•less•ly**, *adv.* in a silent way. **nois•i•ly**, *adv.* in a noisy/loud way. **nois•y**, *adj.* (**-ier, -iest**) making a lot of noise; loud.

no•mad ['nəʊmæd] *adj. & n.* (member) of a wandering tribe with no fixed home. **no•mad•ic** [nəʊ'mædɪk] *adj.* not staying in one place/traveling.

no man's land ['nəʊmænzlænd] *n.* territory between two armies which belongs to neither side.

nom de plume [nɒmdə'pluːm] *n.* name used by an author in place of his own.

no•men•cla•ture [nə'menklətʃə] *n. (formal)* system of naming.

nom•i•nal ['nɒmɪnl] *adj.* (a) referring to names. (b) in name rather than in fact; **n. fee** = very small amount of money/token payment. **nom•i•nal•ly**, *adv.* in name rather than in fact.

nom•i•nate ['nɒmɪneɪt] *v. tr.* to name/to propose. **nom•i•na•tion** [nɒmɪ'neɪʃn] *n.* act of nominating; suggested name. **nom•i•na•tor**, *n.* person who nominates. **nom•i•nee** [nɒmi'niːi] *n.* person who is nominated.

nom•i•na•tive ['nɒmɪnətɪv] *n.* form of a noun when it is the subject of a verb.

non- [nɒn] *prefix meaning* not/the opposite.

non•a•ge•nar•i•an [nɒnədʒə'neərɪən] *adj. & n.* (person) who is between 90 and 99 years old.

non•ag•gres•sion [nɒnə'greʃn] *n.* agreement not to engage in war.

non•al•co•hol•ic [nɒnælkə'hɒlɪk] *adj.* not intoxicating/not containing alcohol.

non•a•ligned [nɒnə'laɪnd] *adj.* (country) which is not linked to a large and powerful bloc of countries. **non•a•lign•ment**, *n.* policy of being nonaligned.

non•cha•lant ['nɒnʃələnt] *adj.* casual/unexcited. **non•cha•lance,** *n.* being calm/unmoved. **non•cha•lant•ly,** *adv.* in a nonchalant way.

non•com•bat•ant [nɒnˈkɒmbətənt] *adj. & n.* (person) who does not fight; doctor/priest, etc., attached to an army.

non•com•mis•sioned [nɒnkəˈmɪʃnd] *adj.* **noncommissioned officer** = soldier of a lower rank than a commissioned officer.

non•com•mit•tal [nɒnkəˈmɪtl] *adj.* not favoring a definite course of action/not agreeing with either side in an argument.

non com•pos men•tis [nɒnkɒmpɒsˈmentɪs] *adj.* mad.

non•con•form•ist [nɒnkənˈfɔːmɪst] *adj. & n.* (person) who does not act in the same way as most people. **non•con•form•i•ty,** *n.* being nonconformist.

non•de•script [ˈnɒndɪskrɪpt] *adj.* very ordinary/without individual qualities.

none [nʌn] 1. *pron.* (a) not any (**of**). (b) no person/no one. 2. *adv.* (*used with* **the** *and comparative or* **too**) not at all; **n. too good; n. the worse for the accident.**

non•en•ti•ty [nɒˈnentɪtɪ] *n.* person of no importance.

none•the•less [nʌnθəˈles] *adv.* nevertheless.

non•e•vent [nɒnɪˈvent] *n.* happening which was expected to be important but which turns out not to be so.

non•ex•ist•ent [nɒnɪgˈzɪstənt] *adj.* not having any existence in fact/not real.

non•fic•tion [ˈnɒnfɪkʃn] *n.* (*no pl.*) books which are not fiction/which are factual.

non•in•ter•ven•tion [nɒnɪntəˈvenʃən] *n.* act of not interfering.

non•pay•ment [nɒnˈpeɪmənt] *n.* failing to pay what is due.

non•plussed, nonplused [nɒnˈplʌst] *adj.* puzzled/confused.

non•prof•it-mak•ing [nɒnˈprəfɪtmeɪkɪŋ] *adj.* (organization such as a charity) which is not allowed to make a profit.

non•re•fund•a•ble [nɒnrɪˈfʌndəbl] *adj.* which will not be refunded.

non•res•i•dent [nɒnˈrezɪdənt] *adj. & n.* (person) not living in/not staying very long in a place.

non•re•turn•a•ble [nɒnrɪˈtɜːnəbl] *adj.* (bottle) on which there is no deposit and which the manufacturers do not want back.

non•sense [ˈnɒnsəns] *n.* foolish ideas/ridiculous behavior. **non•sen•si•cal** [nɒnˈsensɪkl] *adj.* absurd.

non se•qui•tur [nɒnˈsekwɪtə] *n.* phrase which does not follow logically from what has gone before; conclusion drawn incorrectly from the evidence.

non•skid [nɒnˈskɪd] *adj.* which prevents skidding.

non•smok•er [ˈnɒnsməʊkə] *n.* (a) person who does not smoke. (b) place where smoking is not allowed. **non•smok•ing,** *adj.* where smoking is not allowed.

non•start•er [nɒnˈstɑːtə] *n. inf.* project/plan which never materializes.

non•stick [ˈnɒnstɪk] *adj.* (pan) covered with a substance which prevents food from sticking when cooking.

non•stop [ˈnɒnstɒp] 1. *adj.* not stopping/traveling directly from point of departure to the end of the journey. 2. *adv.* ceaselessly/without stopping.

non•un•ion [nɒnˈjuːnɪən] *adj.* not belonging to a union.

non•vi•o•lence [nɒnˈvaɪələns] *n.* absence of physical violence/of aggression.

noo•dles [ˈnuːdlz] *n. pl.* strips of paste for cooking. **noo•dle,** *n. sl.* fool.

nook [nʊk] *n.* small hiding place; **in every n. and cranny** = in every little hole and corner.

noon [nuːn] *n.* midday. **noon•day,** *n.* **the n. sun** = the sun at noon.

no one [ˈnəʊwʌn] *pron.* nobody/no person.

noose [nuːs] *n.* rope knotted to form a loop which can be tightened by pulling.

nor [nɔː] *conj.* (a) (*usu. followed by verb then subject*) not either/and not. (b) **neither…n.** = not one…and not the other.

Nor•dic [ˈnɔːdɪk] *adj.* referring to Scandinavia.

norm [nɔːm] *n.* normal/standard pattern.

nor•mal [ˈnɔːml] *adj.* usual/regular/expected. **nor•mal•i•ty** [nɔːˈmælɪtɪ] *n.* being normal/not having unusual features. **nor•mal•ly,** *adv.* in the usual way.

Nor•man [ˈnɔːmən] *adj. & n.* (person) from Normandy; (architecture, etc.) developed in England after the conquest by the Normans in 1066.

Norse [nɔːs] 1. *adj.* referring to ancient Scandinavia. 2. *n.* ancient Scandinavian language. **Norse•man,** *n.* (*pl.* -men) person from ancient Scandinavia.

north [nɔːθ] 1. *n.* one of the points of the compass, the direction to the right when you are facing the setting sun. 2. *adv.* toward the north; 3. *adj.* referring to the north. **n. wind** =

æ back, ɑː farm, ɒ top, aɪ pipe, aʊ how, aɪə fire, aʊə flower, ɔː bought, ɔɪ toy, e fed, eəhair, eɪ take, ə afraid, əʊ boat, əʊə lower, vː word, iː heap, ɪ hit, ɪə hear, uː school, ʊ book, ʌ but, b back, d dog, ð then, dʒ just, f fog, g go, h hand, j yes, k catch, l last, m mix, n nut, ŋ sing, p penny, r round, s some, ʃ short, t too, tʃ chop, θ thing, v voice, w was, z zoo, ʒ treasure

wind which blows from the north.
north•bound, *adj.* going toward the north.
north•east, *n.* direction half-way between
east and north. **north•east•er•ly,** *adj.* to-
ward/from the northeast. **north•east•ern,**
adj. referring to the northeast. **north•er•ly**
['nɔːðəlı] *adj. & n.* in/to/from the north; (wind)
from the north. **north•ern** ['nɔːðn] *adj.* referring to the north. **north•ern•er,** *n.* person
who lives in/comes from the north.
north•ward. 1. *adj.* toward the north. 2.
adv. (*also* **northwards**) toward the north.
north•ern•most, *adj.* furthest north.
north•west, *n.* direction half-way between
west and north. **north•west•er•ly,** *adj.* to-
ward/from the northwest. **north•west•ern,**
adj. referring to the northwest.

Nor•we•gian [nɔːˈwiːdʒən] 1. *adj.* referring to
Norway. 2. *n.* (a) person from Norway. (b)
language spoken in Norway.

nose [nəʊz] 1. *n.* (a) part of the face used for
breathing in air and smelling; **as plain as the n.
on your face** = very obvious; **to speak through
your n.** = speak as if your nose is blocked; *inf.* **I
paid through the n. for it** = I paid far too much
for it; **I did it under his very n.** = did it right in
front of him but he didn't notice; **to poke your
n. into** = to interfere unasked; **to cut off your n.
to spite your face** = to do sth when you are
angry which in fact harms you; **follow your n.**
= go straight on; **to keep s.o.'s n. to the grind-
stone** = to make s.o. work hard all the time; **to
look down your n. at s.o.** = to regard s.o. as inferior; **to turn up your n. at sth** = to reject sth as
not good enough. (b) good sense of smell; **a
good n. for** = an instinct for finding sth. (c)
front end of a vehicle. 2. *v.* (a) to discover by
smell. (b) *inf.* to detect/to discover. (c) (*of
boat*) to go in gently. **nose a•bout, nose
around,** *v.* to look/to search around.
nose•bag, *n.* bag of food hung around an
animal's neck. **nose•bleed,** *n.* flow of blood
from the nose. **nose cone,** *n.* round pointed
part at the top of a rocket. **nose•dive.** 1. *n.*
steep downward dive of an aircraft. 2. *v.* to
dive down steeply. **nose•gay,** *n.* small bunch
of flowers. **nos•y, nosey,** *adj.* (**-ier, -iest**) *inf.*
curious/interested in the affairs of other people; **N. Parker** = very inquisitive person.
nos•i•ly, *adv.* in a nosy way.

nosh [nɒʃ] *n. Sl.* snack.

nos•tal•gia [nɒˈstældʒɪə] *n.* longing for/senti-
mental recollection of the past. **nos•tal•gic,**
adj. encouraging nostalgia.
nos•tal•gi•cal•ly, *adv.* in a nostalgic way.

nos•tril ['nɒstrl] *n.* one of the two holes in the
nose to admit air and smells.

nos•trum ['nɒstrəm] *n.* quack medicine.

not [nɒt] *adv.* (a) (*used with verbs to make the
action negative; short form* **n't**) **he will not
come/he won't come.** (b) (*used to make negative
words/phrases/sentences*) **I think not** = I don't
think so. (c) (*providing emphasis by a form of
contrast*) **not yours but mine.** (d) (*used to show
the opposite*) **not a few** = many; **not too well** =
badly; **not sorry to leave** = glad to leave; **not
without reason** = with good reason.

no•ta be•ne ['nəʊtə'beneɪ] note well, pay attention to this.

no•ta•ble ['nəʊtəbl] 1. *adj.* worth noticing;
large. 2. *n.* important person. **no•ta•bil•i•ty**
[nəʊtə'bɪlɪtı] *n.* (a) being important. (b) nota-
ble/important person. **no•ta•bly,** *adv.*
significantly/particularly.

no•ta•ry (public) ['nəʊtərı('pʌblɪk)] *n.* person who has authority to see that legal documents are correctly written and who witnesses
their signing.

no•ta•tion [nəʊ'teɪʃn] *n.* system of symbols
used to show notes in music/to show mathematical signs.

notch [nɒtʃ] 1. *n.* (*pl.* **-es**) small cut (usu.
V-shaped) used to mark/to record. 2. *v.* (a) to
mark with notches. (b) to score (a goal/a victory).

note [nəʊt] 1. *n.* (a) music sound. (b) written
sign which indicates a musical sound. (c) key
on a piano, etc.; **to strike the right n.** = to play
the correct note/to provide the appropriate
tone/atmosphere/words in a particular situation. (d) very short letter; very brief writ-
ten/printed document. (e) bank note/piece of
paper money. (f) notice/attention/importance;
of n. = important; **to take n. of** = to pay attention to/to be aware of. (g) indication. 2. *v.* (a)
to write down. (b) to pay attention to.
note•book, *n.* book in which you write
notes. **note•book com•pu•ter,** *n.* portable
computer that is smaller than a laptop but bigger than a palmtop. **not•ed,** *adj.* fa-
mous/well-known. **note•pad,** *n.* pad of
paper for notes. **note•pa•per,** *n.* writing
paper for letters. **note•wor•thy,** *adj.* deserving attention.

noth•ing ['nʌθɪŋ] 1. *n.* (a) not anything; **to say
n. about** = to keep silent about; **there's n. in it** =
no truth in it; **to make sth out of n.** = to exaggerate sth; *inf.* **n. doing!** = I refuse; **to get sth for
n.** = get sth free; **to make n. of it** = make it seem
easy; **to have n. to do with** = not to associate
with/not to become involved in; **it's n. to do
with you** = not your concern; **to come to n.** = be
unsuccessful. (b) (*used with an adj. following*)
not anything. (c) (*used as a comparison/to suggest something inferior*) **that's n. to what I saw.**
2. *adv.* in no way/not at all. **noth•ing•ness,**
n. void/nothing at all.

no•tice ['nəʊtɪs] 1. *n.* (a) advance information/warning; warning to leave one's job. (b) **to take n. of** = to pay attention to. (c) written account/announcement; written information. (d) review in a newspaper. 2. *v.* to pay attention to. **no•tice•a•ble**, *adj.* easily seen. **no•tice•a•bly**, *adv.* in a noticeable way.

no•ti•fy ['nəʊtɪfaɪ] *v.* to announce/to declare/to advise/to inform. **no•ti•fi•ca•tion** [nəʊtɪfɪ'keɪʃn] *n.* formal information.

no•tion ['nəʊʃn] *n.* (a) vague awareness/idea/thought. (b) **notions** = small personal items, as buttons/thread/ribbons, etc. **no•tion•al**, *adj.* vague but assumed to be correct. **no•tion•al•ly**, *adv.* in a notional way.

no•to•ri•ous [nəʊ'tɔːrɪəs] *adj.* well known (usu. for doing sth bad). **no•to•ri•e•ty** [nəʊtə'raɪətɪ] *n.* bad/unfavorable reputation. **no•to•ri•ous•ly**, *adv.* unfavorably significant.

not•with•stand•ing [nɒtwɪθ'stændɪŋ] (*formal*) 1. *prep.* despite. 2. *adv.* all the same/anyway.

nou•gat ['nuːgɑː] *n.* type of white candy made with nuts, honey and egg whites.

nought [nɔːt] *n.* naught.

noun [naʊn] *n.* word used as a name of a person or thing.

nour•ish ['nʌrɪʃ] *v.* (a) to provide (sth) with food so that it will grow. (b) to keep alive (ideas/feelings). **nour•ish•ing**, *adj.* providing nourishment. **nour•ish•ment**, *n.* food which enables plants/animals to grow.

nous [naʊs] *n. inf.* common sense/ordinary intelligent reaction.

no•va ['nəʊvə] *n.* star which suddenly becomes much brighter and then fades away.

nov•el ['nɒvl] 1. *n.* long fictional story in the form of a book. 2. *adj.* new/original. **nov•el•ette** [nɒvə'let] *n.* short novel. **nov•el•ist** ['nɒvəlɪst] *n.* person who writes novels. **nov•el•ty**, *n.* (a) new/original thing. (b) small/unusual toy or trinket. (c) newness.

No•vem•ber [nə'vembə] *n.* 11th month of the year.

nov•ice ['nɒvɪs] *n.* (a) beginner; inexperienced person. (b) person who is intending to join a religious order but who has not yet taken the vows. **no•vi•ti•ate**, *n.* state of being a novice in a religious order.

now [naʊ] 1. *adv.* (a) at this moment. (b) immediately/beginning from this time. (c) **just n.** =

in the immediate past. (d) (*when relating events*) then/next/by that time. 2. *inter. showing warning/criticism;* **n. then!** 3. *conj.* as a result of/since. 4. *n.* this time; the present time. **now•a•days** ['naʊədeɪz] *adv.* at the present day/in these modern times.

no•where ['nəʊweə] *adv.* not in/at/to any place; **n. near completion** = far from being finished; **I got n.** = I was totally unsuccessful in what I was trying to do.

nox•ious ['nɒkʃəs] *adj.* unpleasant/harmful.

noz•zle ['nɒzl] *n.* special fitting at the end of a pipe or hose for controlling what comes out.

ns *abbrev. for* nanosecond.

nth [enθ] *adj.* to a very great extent.

nu•ance ['njuːɑːns] *n.* shade of meaning or color.

nub [nʌb] *n.* central point.

nu•bile ['njuːbaɪl] *adj.* (*of a young woman*) very attractive physically.

nu•cle•us ['njuːklɪəs] *n.* (*pl.* **-lei**) (a) vital central part around which things collect. (b) central part of an atom. **nu•cle•ar**, *adj.* concerned with/belonging to a nucleus, esp. of an atom; **n. energy** = energy produced by nuclear power; **n. family** = family group consisting of the parents and children. **n. reactor** = device for producing atomic energy; **n. power** = power from atomic energy; **n. submarine** = driven by nuclear power. **nu•cle•on•ics** [njuːklɪ'ɒnɪks] *n.* study of the application of nuclear energy.

nude [njuːd] 1. *n.* (a) naked person. (b) **in the n.** = naked. 2. *adj.* naked/bare. **nud•ism**, *n.* belief in the physical and mental advantages of going about naked. **nud•ist**, *n.* person who believes in going about naked; **n. colony** = club/camp for those who wish to go about naked. **nu•di•ty**, *n.* not wearing any clothes/nakedness.

nudge [nʌdʒ] 1. *n.* slight push/prod with the elbow to attract attention. 2. *v.* to attract attention, usu. by pushing with the elbow.

nu•ga•to•ry ['njuːgətrɪ] *adj.* (*formal*) worthless; useless.

nug•get ['nʌgɪt] *n.* lump of gold in its natural state; **n. of information** = piece of useful information.

nui•sance ['njuːsns] *n.* annoying or disagreeable person/thing; **public n.** = action which bothers other people in such a way as to be against the law.

null [nʌl] *adj.* without significance/canceled

æ back, ɑː farm, ɒ top, aɪ pipe, aʊ how, aiə fire, aʊə flower, ɔː bought, ɔɪ toy, e fed, eəhair, eɪ take, ə afraid, əʊ boat, əʊə lower, vː word, iː heap, ɪ hit, ɪə hear, uː school, ʊ book, ʌ but, b back, d dog, ð then, dʒ just, f fog, g go, h hand, j yes, k catch, l last, m mix, n nut, ŋ sing, p penny, r round, s some, ʃ short, t too, tʃ chop, θ thing, v voice, w was, z zoo, ʒ treasure

out; **n. and void** = no longer valid. **nul•li•fy,** *v.* to cancel out/to make invalid. **nul•li•ty,** *n.* nothingness/thing that is null.

numb [nʌm] 1. *adj.* without feeling or sensation/unable to move. 2. *v.* to make incapable of movement or feeling. **numb•ly,** *adv.* not moving because of being numb. **numb•ness,** *n.* having no feeling or sensation/being incapable of action. **numb•skull,** *n. inf.* stupid person.

num•ber ['nʌmbə] 1. *n.* (a) name of a figure; total of objects or persons; **one of their n.** = one of them; *inf.* **to take care of n. one** = to look after yourself/your own interests. (b) **numbers** = many in quantity. (c) (*in grammar*) term indicating whether a noun is singular or plural. (d) copy of a periodical/a song/a piece of played music; **back n.** = thing which is out of date; *inf.* **his number's up** = he's dying. 2. *v.* (a) to count/to include among/to total; **his days are numbered** = he hasn't much time to live. (b) to put a number/figure on. **num•ber•less,** *adj.* which cannot be counted.

nu•mer•al ['nju:mərəl] *n.* actual sign representing a number. **nu•mer•ate** ['nju:mərət] *adj.* able to calculate mathematically. **nu•mer•a•tion** [nju:mə'reɪʃn] *n.* calculation. **nu•mer•a•tor,** *n.* figure above the line in a fraction. **nu•mer•ic key•pad,** *n.* set of numbered keys on a computer keyboard. **nu•mer•i•cal** [nju:'merɪkl] *adj.* referring to numbers; **in n. order** = in order of numbers. **nu•mer•i•cal•ly,** *adv.* by/in number. **nu•mer•ous** ['nju:mərəs] *adj.* many/a lot of.

nu•mis•mat•ics [nju:mɪz'mætɪks] *n.* study of coins. **nu•mis•ma•tist** [nju:'mɪzmətɪst] *n.* person who collects/studies coins.

nun [nʌn] *n.* woman who is a member of a religious order living in a separate community or convent. **nun•like,** *adj.* very calm/good/restrained. **nun•ner•y,** *n.* convent/community where nuns live.

nun•ci•o ['nʌnsɪəu] *n.* ambassador sent by the Pope to a foreign country.

nup•tial ['nʌpʃl] *adj.* (*formal*) referring to marriage/wedding ceremonies. **nup•tials,** *n. pl.* wedding.

nurse [nɜːs] 1. *n.* (a) person trained and employed to look after the sick; **night n.** = nurse who is on duty at night. (b) woman employed to look after children. 2. *v.* (a) to look after (a sick person). (b) to look after very carefully. (c) to think about/to ponder over. (d) to hold close. **nurse•maid,** *n.* woman or girl who is paid to look after children. **nurs•er•y,** *n.* (a) room/building where babies or young children are looked after; **n. school** = school for very young children; **n. rhyme** = little poem telling a simple story told or sung to young children. (b) place where young plants are grown. **nurs•er•y•man,** *n.* (*pl.* -men) man who owns or manages a nursery for plants. **nurs•ing.** 1. *adj.* (person) who nurses/looks after; **n. mother** = mother who breast-feeds her baby; **n. staff** = hospital nurses; **n. home** = small (usu. private) hospital. 2. *n.* profession of looking after the sick.

nur•ture ['nɜːtʃə] *v.* (*formal*) to protect and bring up carefully.

nut [nʌt] 1. *n.* (a) fruit with an edible center inside a hard shell; **to crack nuts** = to open the shells to get at the edible centers; *inf.* **a tough n. to crack** = a hard person/a difficult problem. (b) small metal ring used for tightening a bolt; **wing n.** = nut with two projecting pieces for turning. (c) *inf.* head; **he's off his n.** = he's mad. (d) *inf.* **nuts about** = very keen on/enthusiastic about. (e) small lump (of butter). 2. *v.* **to go nutting** = to gather nuts. **nut case,** *n. inf.* mad person. **nut•crack•ers,** *n. pl.* pincers for cracking nuts. **nut•hatch,** *n.* small gray and brown bird which climbs up tree trunks. **nut•meg,** *n.* seed of a tropical tree, used as a spice. **nut•shell,** *n.* hard outside covering of a nut; **in a n.** = giving all the important details as briefly as possible. **nut•ty,** *adj.* (a) tasting of/full of nuts. (b) *inf.* crazy/very enthusiastic (**about** s.o./sth).

nu•tri•ment ['nju:trɪmənt] *n.* thing which nourishes. **nu•tri•ent,** *adj. & n.* (food) which feeds/nourishes. **nu•tri•tion** [nju:'trɪʃn] *n.* giving/receiving of nourishment. **nu•tri•tious** [nju:'trɪʃəs] *adj.* nourishing/providing food which is necessary for growth. **nu•tri•tive** ['nju:trətɪv] 1. *n.* food which is necessary for growth. 2. *adj.* providing food/nourishment.

nuz•zle ['nʌzl] *v.* to press the nose up to/to snuggle up to.

ny•lon ['naɪlɒn] *n.* very tough synthetic material. **ny•lons,** *n. pl.* women's stockings.

nymph [nɪmf] *n.* (a) young girl; minor goddess. (b) young insect, esp. young dragonfly. **nymph•et,** *n.* sexually desirable young girl. **nym•pho•ma•ni•a** [nɪmfə'meɪnɪə] *n.* (*in woman*) uncontrollably strong sexual desire. **nym•pho•ma•ni•ac,** *n.* woman who has uncontrollable sexual desires.

Oo

O, o [əu] zero/nothing.

O *symbol for* oxygen.

oaf [əuf] *n.* stupid/clumsy/unfeeling person. **oaf•ish**, *adj.* like an oaf.

oak [əuk] *n.* type of large deciduous tree; wood of this tree. **oak gall**, *n.* (*also* **oak apple**) round growth on oak trees caused by an insect. **oak•en**, *adj.* (*formal*) made of oak.

oa•kum ['əukəm] *n.* (*no pl.*) loose pieces of old rope formerly used for stuffing into the seams of wooden ships.

oar [ɔ:] *n.* long pole with a flat end, used for moving a boat along; *inf.* **to put in one's o.** = to interfere. **oar•lock,** *n.* metal support for oars. **oars•man,** *n.* (*pl.* **-men**) person who rows a boat. **oars•man•ship,** *n.* being skilled at rowing.

o•a•sis [əu'eisis] *n.* (*pl.* **-ses** [-si:z]) (a) place in the desert with water, where plants grow. (b) place which is pleasantly different from its surroundings.

oat•cake ['əutkeik] *n.* dry biscuit made of oatmeal.

oath [əuθ] *n.* (a) swearing that you are telling the truth. (b) promise. (c) swear word.

oat•meal ['əutmi:l] *n.* coarse flour made from oats.

oats [əuts] *n. pl.* cereal plant whose grain is used as food; **to sow one's wild o.** = behave in a very free and unruly way when young.

ob•bli•ga•to [ɒblɪ'ga:təu] *n.* (*pl.* **-os, -ti**) (*in music*) important accompanying part played by a solo instrument.

ob•du•rate ['ɒbdjurət] *adj.* stubborn/unyielding/unmoving. **ob•du•ra•cy,** *n.* being obdurate.

o•be•di•ence [ə'bi:dɪəns] *n.* being obedient. **o•be•di•ent,** *adj.* (person) who does what he is told to do. **o•be•di•ent•ly,** *adv.* in an obedient way.

o•bei•sance [əu'beisəns] *n.* sign of respect, such as a bow or curtsey.

ob•e•lisk ['ɒbəlisk] *n.* four-sided pillar which becomes narrower towards the top.

o•bese [ə'bi:s] *adj.* very fat. **o•be•si•ty** [ə-'bi:siti] *n.* being obese.

o•bey [ə'bei] *v.* to do what you are told to do (by s.o.).

ob•fus•cate ['ɒbfʌskeit] *v.* (*formal*) to make (sth) difficult to understand.

o•bit•u•ar•y [ə'bitjuəri] *n.* written report of s.o.'s death, usu. with details of his life; **o. col•umn** = part of a newspaper which gives obituaries.

ob•ject 1. *n.* ['ɒbdʒekt] (a) thing; **o. lesson** = thing which makes a course of action very clear. (b) aim; target/purpose. (c) person/thing to which feeling, etc., is directed. (d) (*in grammar*) noun/pronoun, etc., which follows directly from a verb or preposition. (e) **money is no o.** = is no obstacle/problem. 2. *v.* [əb'dʒekt] (**to**) to refuse to agree; to express unwillingness towards/disapproval (**of**). **ob•jec•tion** [ɒb'dʒekʃn] *n.* act of objecting; reason against. **ob•jec•tion•a•ble,** (a) *adj.* causing disapproval. (b) (*esp. of person*) very unpleasant. **ob•jec•tive** [ɒb'dʒektiv] 1. *adj.* (a) (*in grammar*) referring to the object. (b) referring to the external world. (c) considering matters from a general viewpoint and not just your own. 2. *n.* (a) aim/object in view. (b) lens in a microscope which is nearest to the object being examined. **ob•jec•tive•ly,** *adv.* in an objective way/without being influenced by your own feelings. **ob•jec•tiv•i•ty,** *n.* being objective. **ob•jec•tor,** *n.* person who objects; **conscientious o.** = person who refuses to join the armed forces because he feels war is wrong.

ob•jet d'art [ɒbdʒei'da:] *n.* ornament.

ob•late ['ɒbleit] *n.* person who has vowed to do religious work.

o•blige [ə'blaidʒ] *v.* (a) to make (s.o.) feel it is their duty to do sth. (b) to force (s.o.) to do sth. (c) to be useful/helpful to (s.o.). (d) **to be obliged to s.o.** = to owe s.o. gratitude.

æ back, a: farm, ɒ: top, ai pipe, au how, aie fire, auə flower, ɔ: bought, ɔi toy, e fed, eəhair, ei take, ə afraid, əu boat, əuə lower, v: word, i: heap, ɪ hit, ɪə hear, u: school, u book, ʌ but, b back, d dog, ð then, dʒ just, f fog, g go, h hand, j yes, k catch, l last, m mix, n nut, ŋ sing, p penny, r round, s some, ʃ short, t too, tʃ chop, θ thing, v voice, w was, z zoo, ʒ treasure

ob•li•gate ['ɒblɪgeɪt] v. to oblige.
ob•li•ga•tion [ɒblɪ'geɪʃn] n. (a) duty; legal bond. (b) duty to be grateful; **under an o. to s.o.** = morally obliged to help s.o.
ob•li•ga•to•ry [ə'blɪgətərɪ] adj. necessary according to rules or laws. **o•blig•ing**, adj. ready to help. **o•blig•ing•ly**, adv. in an obliging way.

o•blique [ə'bliːk] adj. (a) at a slant; **o. angle** = angle which is not a right angle. (b) from the side; not direct. **o•blique•ly**, adv. in an oblique way.

ob•lit•er•ate [ə'blɪtəreɪt] v. to wipe out/to destroy. **ob•lit•er•a•tion** [əblɪtə'reɪʃn] n. act of obliterating; being obliterated.

ob•liv•i•on [ə'blɪvɪən] n. forgetting totally; being completely forgotten. **ob•liv•i•ous**, adj. forgetful/unaware.

ob•long ['ɒblɒŋ] n. & adj. (referring to a) rectangular shape with two pairs of equal sides, one pair being longer than the other.

ob•lo•quy ['ɒblɒkwɪ] n. (formal) criticism.

ob•nox•ious [ɒb'nɒkʃəs] adj. very unpleasant/offensive.

o•boe ['əʊbəʊ] n. high-pitched woodwind instrument. **o•bo•ist**, n. person who plays the oboe.

ob•scene [ɒb'siːn] adj. offending moral standards/sensitive feelings; indecent. **ob•scene•ly**, adv. in an obscene way. **ob•scen•i•ty** [ɒb'senɪtɪ] n. (a) being obscene. (b) obscene word.

ob•scure [əb'skjʊə] 1. adj. (a) (of place) dark/gloomy. (b) not clear. (c) not well-known. 2. v. to hide, esp. by covering. **ob•scure•ly**, adv. in an obscure way. **ob•scu•ri•ty**, n. being obscure.

ob•se•qui•ous [əb'siːkwɪəs] adj. too humble; showing too much respect for/obedience to (s.o.). **ob•se•quies** ['ɒbsɪkwɪz] n. pl. funeral ceremonies. **ob•se•qui•ous•ly**, adv. in an obsequious way. **ob•se•qui•ous•ness**, n. being obsequious.

ob•serve [əb'zɜːv] v. (a) to follow/to obey (a law/rule/custom). (b) to watch/to look (at). (c) to notice. (d) to remark/to note. **ob•serv•ance**, n. (act of) observing. **ob•serv•ant**, adj. noticing (many details). **ob•ser•va•tion** [ɒbzə'veɪʃn] n. (a) (act of) observing; **under o.** = being carefully watched. (b) calculation of position of a ship. (c) remark. **ob•serv•a•to•ry**, n. place from which stars and planets can be watched. **ob•serv•er**, n. person who attends a meeting and watches (esp. without taking part).

ob•sess [ɒb'ses] v. to fill s.o.'s thoughts. **ob•ses•sion** [əb'seʃn] n. idea/subject which fills your mind constantly. **ob•ses•sive**, adj. caused by an obsession. **ob•ses•sive•ly**, adv. in an obsessive way.

ob•sid•i•an [ɒb'sɪdɪən] n. hard glasslike volcanic rock.

ob•so•lete ['ɒbsəliːt] adj. (word, custom) no longer in general use. **ob•so•les•cence**, n. being obsolescent. **ob•so•les•cent** [ɒbsə'lesənt] adj. going out of use/out of fashion.

ob•sta•cle ['ɒbstəkl] n. thing which is in the way/which prevents progress. **obstacle race**, n. race in which various obstacles have to be passed.

ob•stet•ric(al) [ɒb'stetrɪk(l)] adj. referring to obstetrics or childbirth. **ob•ste•tri•cian** [ɒbstə'trɪʃn] n. doctor who specializes in obstetrics. **ob•stet•rics**, n. branch of medicine dealing with childbirth.

ob•sti•nate ['ɒbstɪnət] adj. (a) sticking to your opinion/course of action, etc. against all arguments. (b) which will not go away. **ob•sti•na•cy**, n. being obstinate. **ob•sti•nate•ly**, adv. in an obstinate way.

ob•strep•er•ous [ɒb'strepərəs] adj. behaving in an uncontrolled/wild/loud way.

ob•struct [əb'strʌkt] v. to get in the way of (sth); to prevent/to hinder the progress of (sth). **ob•struc•tion** [ɒb'strʌkʃn] n. (a) act of obstructing. (b) thing which gets in the way. **ob•struc•tive**, adj. which obstructs; which aims to cause an obstruction.

ob•tain [ɒb'teɪn] v. (a) to get. (b) to exist as a rule. **ob•tain•a•ble**, adj. which can be obtained.

ob•trude [əb'truːd] v. (formal) to come/to put in the way; to form an obstacle. **ob•tru•sion** [əb'truːʒn] n. (a) (act of) obtruding. (b) thing which is in the way. **ob•tru•sive** [əb'truːsɪv] adj. (thing) which sticks out/which is in the way.

ob•tuse [əb'tjuːs] adj. (a) stupid/dull (person). (b) **o. angle** = angle of between 90° and 180°. **ob•tuse•ly**, adv. in an obtuse way. **ob•tuse•ness**, n. being obtuse.

ob•verse ['ɒbvɜːs] n. side of a coin with the head on it/the main side of a coin.

ob•vi•ate ['ɒbvɪeɪt] v. to avoid/to get round.

ob•vi•ous ['ɒbvɪəs] adj. clear; easily seen/easily noticed. **ob•vi•ous•ly**, adv. in an obvious way/clearly. **ob•vi•ous•ness**, n. being obvious.

oc•a•ri•na [ɒkə'riːnə] n. wind instrument, made of a small pot, with holes to be covered by the fingers.

oc•ca•sion [ə'keɪʒn] 1. n. (a) thing which causes sth else. (b) (time of a) happening; **on o.** = from time to time. (c) special event. 2. v. to cause (sth) to happen. **oc•ca•sion•al**, adj. happening now and then/not often.

oc•ca•sion•al•ly, *adv.* sometimes/not often.

Oc•ci•dent ['ɒksɪdənt] *n.* (*formal*) the West; Western countries. **oc•ci•den•tal** [ɒksɪ-'dentl] *adj.* referring to the Occident.

oc•ci•put ['ɒksɪpʌt] *n.* back of the head. **oc•cip•i•tal** [ɒk'sɪpɪtəl] *adj.* referring to the back of the head.

oc•clude [ɒ'kluːd] *v.* (*formal*) to shut up. **oc•clu•sion,** *n.* (a) movement of warm air upward, caused by the arrival of colder air. (b) blockage in a blood vessel.

oc•cult ['ɒkʌlt] *adj. & n.* (referring to the) supernatural; magic.

oc•cu•py ['ɒkjupaɪ] *v.* (a) to fill/to take up (space or time). (b) to take/to have possession of. (c) to take possession and remain in control of. (d) to give work/activity to. **oc•cu•pan•cy,** *n.* being occupied. **oc•cu•pant,** *n.* person who occupies a place/who is in a certain seat. **oc•cu•pa•tion** [ɒkju'peɪʃn] *n.* (a) (act of) occupying; being occupied. (b) job/position/employment. **oc•cu•pa•tion•al,** *adj.* referring to an occupation; **o. therapy** = treating sick people by encouraging them to do special activities. **oc•cu•pi•er,** *n.* person who lives in (a house).

oc•cur [ə'kɜː] *v.* (**occurred**) (a) to take place/to happen. (b) (**to**) to come into one's thoughts. (c) to be (found). **oc•cur•rence** [ə'kʌrəns] *n.* happening.

o•cean ['əʊʃn] *n.* large expanse of sea surrounding the land masses of the earth; a part of this sea. **o•ce•an•ic** [əʊsɪ'ænɪk] *adj.* referring to the ocean. **o•cea•nog•ra•phy** [əʊʃə-'nɒgrəfɪ] *n.* study of the sea.

oc•e•lot ['ɒsɪlɒt] *n.* leopardlike animal found in Central and South America.

o•cher, ochre ['əʊkə] *n.* yellow/red natural material used for coloring; dull yellow color.

o'•clock [ə'klɒk] *adv. phrase used with numbers meaning* the exact hour; **at six o'clock; the six o'clock train.**

oc•ta•gon ['ɒktəgən] *n.* geometrical figure with eight sides. **oc•tag•o•nal** [ɒk'tægənl] *adj.* eight-sided.

oc•tane ['ɒkteɪn] *n.* **o. number/o. rating** = number given to types of gasoline to indicate their quality.

oc•tave ['ɒkteɪv] *n.* (*in music*) space between the first and last notes of an eight-note scale.

oc•ta•vo [ɒk'teɪvəʊ] *n.* size of a book, when a sheet of paper is folded to make sixteen pages.

oc•tet [ɒk'tet] *n.* group of eight people, esp. musicians; piece of music for such a group.

Oc•to•ber [ɒk'təʊbə] *n.* 10th month of the year.

oc•to•ge•nar•i•an [ɒktədʒə'neərɪən] *adj. & n.* (person) who is between 80 and 89 years old.

oc•to•pus ['ɒktəpəs] *n.* (*pl.* **-es, -pi**) sea animal with eight arms.

oc•u•lar ['ɒkjulə] *adj.* referring to the eyes/to sight. **oc•u•list,** *n.* doctor who specializes in care of the eyes.

odd [ɒd] *adj.* (**-er, -est**) (a) (number) which cannot be divided exactly by two. (b) approximately/a little more than. (c) occasional; referring to various individual things/items; (*in an auction*) **o. lots** = groups of different items for sale. (d) referring to a member of a set or pair, when separated from the rest. (e) strange/peculiar. **odd•ball,** *n. inf.* eccentric person. **odd•i•ty,** *n.* (a) being odd. (b) odd thing/person. **odd•ly,** *adv.* in an odd way; for odd reasons. **odd•ments,** *n. pl.* bits and pieces; items left over. **odd•ness,** *n.* being odd. **odds,** *n. pl.* (a) difference between the amount which has been bet and the amount to be won; **o. of 10 to 1.** (b) more than an equal chance; **the o. are against it.** (c) to be at **o. with s.o.** = to quarrel constantly. (d) **o. and ends** = bits and pieces.

ode [əʊd] *n.* long poem often addressed to a person or thing.

o•di•ous ['əʊdɪəs] *adj.* hateful/horrible. **o•di•ous•ly,** *adv.* in an odious way. **o•di•ous•ness,** *n.* being odious. **o•di•um,** *n.* great unpopularity/hatred.

o•dom•e•ter [əʊ'dɒmɪtə] *n.* device for measuring the distance a vehicle travels.

o•don•tol•o•gy [ɒdɒn'tɒlədʒɪ] *n.* study of teeth.

o•dor, *Brit.* **o•dour** ['əʊdə] *n.* (a) scent/smell. (b) **to be in good/bad o. with** = to be in/out of favor with. **o•dor•ous,** *adj.* with a strong scent. **o•dor•less,** *adj.* without any smell.

od•ys•sey ['ɒdɪsɪ] *n.* long voyage of adventure.

oe•de•ma [ɪ'diːmə] *n. see* **edema.**

Oed•i•pus com•plex ['iːdɪpəs'kɒmpleks] *n.* feeling (in a man) of hatred for his father and love for his mother.

of [ɒv] *prep.* (a) belonging to/connected with.

æ back, aː farm, ɒ top, aɪ pipe, aʊ how, aɪə fire, aʊə flower, ɔː bought, ɔɪ toy, e fed, eəhair, eɪ take, ə afraid, əʊ boat, əʊə lower, ɜː word, iː heap, ɪ hit, ɪə hear, uː school, ʊ book, ʌ but, b back, d dog, ð then, dʒ just, f fog, g go, h hand, j yes, k catch, l last, m mix, n nut, ŋ sing, p penny, r round, s some, ʃ short, t too, tʃ chop, θ thing, v voice, w was, z zoo, ʒ treasure

(b) being a part/a quantity. (c) (who/which) is; **a child of ten.** (d) by/from; **south of the border; made of wool.** (e) about/concerning.

off [ɒf] 1. *adv.* (a) away (from); **they're o.** = they've started running; **day o.** = day away from work. (b) not on; **the deal is o.** = has been canceled. (c) no longer fresh. (d) **well/badly o.** = having plenty/not enough (money). (e) **right/straight o.** = immediately; **on and o.** = from time to time. (f) (*with verbs*) completely; **to finish o.** 2. *prep.* (a) (away) from. (b) (*at sea*) a certain distance from. (c) branching from. (d) disliking/not wanting (food). 3. *adj.* away; not on; **o. day** = one on which you are less successful; **o. season** = less busy season. **off•beat,** *adj. inf.* rather odd/unusual. **off chance,** *n.* slight possibility. **off-col•or,** *adj.* not well. **off•hand,** *adv. & adj.* (a) without preparation/without thinking carefully. (b) (*also* **offhanded**) rude/without courtesy. **off•hand•ed•ly,** *adv.* rudely. **off-line,** *adj.* (computer) which is not connected to a network or to a main system. **off-load,** *v.* (**on to**) to pass a load to sth/s.o. else. **off-peak,** *adj.* away from the busiest/most used times. **off-put•ting,** *adj. inf.* causing (mild) annoyance. **off-road,** *adj.* (vehicle) designed for use on rough terrain. **off-sea•son,** *adj. & n.* (period, usually winter) when prices are lower because fewer people travel. **off•set.** 1. *n.* [ˈɒfset] method of printing from a plate to a rubber surface and then to paper. 2. *v.* [ɒfˈset] (**offset**) to balance (one thing) against another. **off•shoot** [ˈɒfʃuːt] *n.* small side shoot of a plant; thing which branches from sth else. **off•shore,** *adj.* (away) from/at a distance from the shore. **off•spring** [ˈɒfsprɪŋ] *n.* child; young (of an animal). **off•stage,** *adv. & adj.* not on the stage/unseen by the audience.

of•fal [ˈɒfl] *n.* internal organs (heart, etc.) of animals, used as food.

of•fense [əˈfens] *n.* (a) state of offending; being offended; **to take o. at** = to be offended by. (b) crime; (act of) offending (esp. against a law). **of•fend** [əˈfend] *v.* to be/to go against (the law/opinions/wishes/feelings). **of•fend•er,** *n.* person who offends (esp. **against** a law). **of•fen•sive.** 1. *adj.* (a) which is unpleasant. (b) (*in military*) which is used in an attack. 2. *n.* (military) attack; **to take the o.** = to start the attack. **of•fen•sive•ly,** *adv.* in an offensive way. **of•fen•sive•ness,** *n.* being offensive.

of•fer [ˈɒfə] 1. *n.* (act of) indicating that you will do/give sth; thing which is offered; **special o.** = goods which are put on sale at a reduced price. 2. *v.* (a) to say/to indicate that you will do/give (sth). (b) to make/to express (an opinion, etc.). **of•fer•ing,** *n.* thing which is

offered. **of•fer•to•ry,** *n.* (a) offering of wine and bread in the communion service. (b) collection of money taken while the wine and bread are being offered.

of•fice [ˈɒfɪs] *n.* (a) room/building where business or professional activity is carried out; **doctor's o.** = room where a doctor sees patients. (b) position/function. (c) (*esp. in titles*) organization; government department. (d) help/services. **of•fi•cer,** *n.* (a) person who holds an official position. (b) person who holds one of the commissioned ranks in the armed forces, etc. (c) **police o.** = policeman. **of•fi•cial** [əˈfɪʃl] 1. *adj.* referring to an organization which is recognized by a government, etc. 2. *n.* person holding a recognized position. **of•fi•cial•dom,** *n.* bureaucracy. **of•fi•cial•ese,** *n. inf.* clumsy language used by bureaucrats. **of•fi•cial•ly,** *adv.* in an official way. **of•fi•ci•ate** [əˈfɪʃreɪt] *v.* (a) (*of clergy*) (**at**) to perform a religious ceremony. (b) to act as chairman, etc. **of•fi•cious,** *adj.* too ready to interfere or to offer help. **of•fi•cious•ly,** *adv.* in an officious way. **of•fi•cious•ness,** *n.* being officious.

off•ing [ˈɒfɪŋ] *n.* **in the o.** = coming/available soon.

of•ten [ˈɒfn] *adv.* many times; in many instances. **of•ten•times,** *adv.* often.

o•gee [ˈəʊdʒiː] *n.* S-shaped curve in architecture; an arch with two S-shaped curves, joining at a point.

o•gle [ˈəʊgl] *v.* to leer/look at (s.o.) with sexual desire.

o•gre [ˈəʊgə] *n.* cruel giant who eats human beings; cruel terrifying person.

oh [əʊ] *inter. expressing surprise/shock.*

ohm [əʊm] *n.* standard measure of electrical resistance.

oil [ɔɪl] 1. *n.* (a) thick smooth-running liquid of various kinds (used in cooking/heating/engineering/painting). (b) liquid found mainly underground and used to produce power. (c) picture painted with oil paints. 2. *v.* to put oil on/in (esp. to make a machine run more smoothly); **to o. the wheels** = to help to make things run more smoothly; *inf.* **well-oiled** = rather drunk. **oil-bear•ing,** *adj.* (rocks, etc.) which contain oil. **oil field,** *n.* area where oil is found. **oil•i•ness,** *n.* being oily. **oil rig,** *n.* structure for drilling for oil. **oil•skin(s),** *n.* (clothing of) material made waterproof with oil. **oil slick,** *n.* thin covering of oil on the surface of the sea. **oil tank•er,** *n.* large ship/large truck for carrying oil. **oil•y,** *adj.* (-**ier,** -**iest**) (a) like oil; covered with oil. (b) (*of manner*) too smooth and pleasant; insincere.

oint•ment [ˈɔɪntmənt] *n.* smooth healing or soothing substance spread on the skin.

OK, okay [əʊ'keɪ] *inf. inter. & adj.* all right. 2. *n.* sign of approval. 3. *v.* to give a sign of approval to.

o•ka•pi [ɒ'kɑːpiː] *n.* African animal, like a large black horse, with white stripes on its rear legs.

o•kra ['ɒkrə] *n.* tropical plant with edible green pods.

old [ould] *adj.* (**-er, -est**) (a) having great age; **o. wives' tale** = belief based on tradition rather than on fact. (b) having been in use for a long time. (c) being of a particular age. (d) having been in a certain state/having been done for a long time. (e) former. (f) term showing vagueness/affection/disrespect, etc.; *inf.* **the o. man** = boss/husband/father. **old-boy net•work,** *n.* system where men who were at school together or are members of a particular profession or group help each other get ahead in business, politics, etc. **old•en,** *adj.* (*formal*) old (times). **old-fash•ioned,** *adj.* not in fashion; out of date. **old•ie,** *n. inf.* old-fashioned/out of date thing. **old•ish,** *adj.* rather old. **old maid,** *n.* older woman who has never married. **old-time,** *adj.* not of the present/done in an old-fashioned way. **old tim•er,** *n.* s.o. who has been doing sth or been a member of sth for a long time. **Old World,** *n.* Europe, Asia and Africa.

o•le•ag•i•nous [ɒli'æʒɪnəs] *adj.* (*formal*) oily.

o•le•an•der [ɒlɪ'ændə] *n.* tropical shrub with pink flowers.

ol•fac•to•ry [ɒl'fæktərɪ] *adj.* (*formal*) referring to the sense of smell.

ol•i•gar•chy ['ɒlɪɡɑːkɪ] *n.* (country with a) government by a few powerful people.

ol•ive ['ɒlɪv] *n.* (a) small black or green fruit which produces oil and is used as food; tree which bears this fruit; **o. branch** = sign of peace. (b) **o. (green)** = dull green color of unripe olives; **o. skin** = yellowish skin.

O•lym•pic [ə'lɪmpɪk] *adj. & n.* **the O. Games/the Olympics** = international athletic competition held every four years. **O•lym•pi•ad,** *n.* major international sporting competition. **O•lym•pi•an,** *adj.* like a god; majestic.

om•buds•man ['ɒmbədzmən] *n.* (*pl.* **-men**) official who investigates complaints by members of the public against a government department or official.

o•me•ga ['əʊmɪɡə] *n.* last letter of the Greek alphabet.

om•e•let, om•e•lette ['ɒmlət] *n.* cooked egg mixture often with mushrooms, vegetables, cheese, etc. folded inside.

o•men ['əʊmən] *n.* thing giving an indication of the future. **om•i•nous** ['ɒmɪnəs] *adj.* threatening bad results. **om•i•nous•ly,** *adv.* in an ominous way.

o•mit [ə'mɪt] *v.* (**omitted**) (a) to leave out. (b) (**to**) not to do sth. **o•mis•sion** [ə'mɪʃn] *n.* (a) act of omitting. (b) thing omitted.

om•ni•bus ['ɒmnɪbəs] 1. *n.* (*old*) bus. 2. *n. & adj.* (book) which includes several books all together.

om•ni•di•rec•tion•al [ɒmnɪdaɪ'rekʃənəl] *adj.* (aerial which can capture signals) from any direction.

om•nip•o•tence [ɒm'nɪpətəns] *n.* quality of being all-powerful. **om•nip•o•tent,** *adj.* all-powerful.

om•ni•pres•ent ['ɒmnɪprezənt] *adj.* which is everywhere.

om•nis•cient [ɒm'nɪsɪənt] *adj.* (person) who knows everything. **om•nis•cience,** *n.* knowing everything.

om•niv•o•rous [ɒm'nɪvərəs] *adj.* eating everything; (animal) which eats both plants and other animals.

on [ɒn] 1. *prep.* (a) touching the top/outer surface of sth. (b) in/at. (c) with; **have you any money on you?** (d) belonging to/a member of; **on the staff.** (e) indicating a means of moving; **on foot.** (f) engaged in; **on business.** (g) from/by; **to live on a small income.** (h) (*indicating a time*) **on Sundays; on application** = when you apply; **on sale** = for sale; (i) approximately; **just on a year ago.** (j) because of; **to congratulate s.o. on his success.** (k) about/concerning; **a book on whales.** (l) toward/against; **an attack on s.o.** (m) *inf.* paid by; **the drinks are on me.** (n) (*as a bet*) **to put $5 on a horse** = to bet $5 that the horse will win. 2. *adv.* (a) in action; open; **the light is on.** (b) happening; **what's on for tonight?** (c) being worn; **put your shoes on** (d) (in a) continuing (way); **they worked on.** (e) (*indicating passing of time*) **later on.** (f) **on and off** = not continuously/with breaks in between; **on and on** = without stopping.

on•a•ger ['ɒnədʒə] *n.* wild Asian donkey.

once [wɒns] 1. *adv.* (a) for one time. (b) at all/ever. (c) at a (particular) time in the past. (d) **at o.** = (i) immediately; (ii) at the same time. 2. *conj.* as soon as. **once-o•ver,** *n. inf.* quick examination.

on•com•ing ['ɒnkʌmɪŋ] *adj.* coming toward you.

one [wɒn] 1. *n.* number 1. (a) first number; *inf.* **look after number o.** = look after yourself first. (b) single unit in quantity or number. (c) *inf.* **a quick o.** = a quick drink. 2. *adj.* (a) single (example of). (b) the only. (c) the same; **all of o. mind.** 3. *pron.* (a) thing/person indicated. (b) example of a type. 4. *indefinite adj.* (on) a certain; **o. night.** 5. *indefinite pron.* (a) (*pl.* **some/any**) an example of sth. (b) (*formal*) anyone/an indefinite person. **one-armed ban•dit,** *n.* gambling machine worked by a handle. **one-horse town,** *n. inf.* small town where very little happens. **one-leg•ged** ['wʌn'legɪd] *adj.* with only one leg. **one-night stand,** *n.* performance (of a play/of a show) for one night only. **one•self,** *pronoun referring to a person as an indefinite subject.* **one-sid•ed,** *adj.* treating or giving justice to one side only. **one•time,** *adj.* former. **one-track mind,** *n.* mind which concentrates on one thing at a time. **one-up•man•ship,** *n.* art of putting yourself at an advantage over others. **one-way,** *adj.* (street) for traffic in one direction only; (ticket) for one direction only.

on•er•ous ['ɒnərəs] *adj.* causing much (tiring) effort.

on•ion ['ʌnjən] *n.* strong-smelling vegetable with a round white bulb.

on-line ['ɒnlaɪn] *adv. & adj.* linked directly to a computer.

on•look•er ['ɒnlukə] *n.* person who watches.

on•ly ['əʊnlɪ] 1. *adj.* (the) single/(the) one without any others. 2. *adv.* (a) and not anyone/anything else. (b) as recently as. (c) **if o.** = expressing a strong wish/desire; **o. too** = very. 3. *conj.* but.

on•o•mas•tics [ɒnə'mæstɪks] *n.* study of names.

on•o•mat•o•poe•ia [ɒnəmætə'piːə] *n.* making/using words which imitate a sound. **on•o•mat•o•poe•ic,** *adj.* using onomatopoeia.

on•rush ['ɒnrʌʃ] *n.* rushing in/on.

on•set ['ɒnset] *n.* beginning (of an attack, etc.)

on•slaught ['ɒnslɔːt] *n.* sudden severe attack.

on•to ['ɒntuː] *prep.* to a position on sth.

on•tol•o•gy [ɒn'tɒlədʒɪ] *n.* study of reality. **on•to•log•i•cal** [ɒntə'lɒdʒɪkl] *adj.* referring to reality.

o•nus ['əʊnəs] *n.* responsibility (for a difficult task)

on•ward ['ɒnwəd] 1. *adj.* forward. 2. *adv.* (*also* **on•wards**) forward.

on•yx ['ɒnɪks] *n.* (*pl.* **-es**) multicolored precious stone.

oo•dles ['uːdlz] *n. pl. inf.* lots (**of**).

ooh [uː] *inter. showing surprise/shock.*

ooze [uːz] 1. *n.* slimy mud. 2. *v.* to flow slowly and gently.

o•pac•i•ty [ə'pæsɪtɪ] *n.* state of being opaque.

o•pal ['əʊpl] *n.* semi-precious stone with varied or changing colors. **o•pal•es•cence,** *n.* being opalescent. **o•pal•es•cent,** *adj.* shining like an opal.

o•paque [əʊ'peɪk] *adj.* which you cannot see through.

O•PEC ['əʊpek] *n.* (= Organization of Petroleum Exporting Countries) group of countries who produce and export oil.

o•pen ['əʊpn] 1. *adj.* (a) not closed. (b) which you can enter. (c) without limits. (d) **o. to** = without protection (from sth). (e) ready to accept/to be accepted. (f) with no attempt (being made) to hide sth. (g) with space between the parts. (h) with no fixed idea(s)/conditions. (i) (competition) without restrictions. 2. *v.* (a) to become open. (b) to start (up)/to set going. (c) to have an exit (**on to**). 3. *n.* unlimited area outdoors. **o•pen-air,** *adj.* not in a building. **o•pen-end•ed,** *adj.* with no definite end. **o•pen•er,** *n.* device for opening sth. **o•pen•hand•ed,** *adj.* generous. **open-heart,** *adj.* (surgery) with the chest cut open to expose the heart. **o•pen•ing.** 1. *n.* (a) act of opening. (b) beginning. (c) place where sth opens. (d) opportunity, such as a job vacancy. 2. *adj.* which opens. **o•pen let•ter,** *n.* letter published as an article in a newspaper and not sent to the addressee. **o•pen•ly,** *adv.* in an open way. **open-mind,** *n.* to have an **o. m.** = not to have a fixed opinion on sth. **o•pen•ness,** *n.* quality of being open. **open out,** *v.* to open (fully); to spread out widely. **open up,** *v.* (a) to open (completely). (b) to begin. **o•pen•work,** *n.* pattern (on a shoe, etc.) with holes in it.

o•pe•ra ['ɒprə] *n.* (a) dramatic performance with music, in which the words are partly or wholly sung. (b) company which performs operas. **op•er•a glass•es,** *n. pl.* small binoculars for looking at performers on the stage. **op•er•a house,** *n.* theater in which opera is performed. **op•er•at•ic** [ɒpə'rætɪk] *adj.* of/like/for opera. **op•er•et•ta** [ɒpə'retə] *n.* opera with a light-hearted story in which some of the words are spoken.

op•er•ate ['ɒpəreɪt] 1. *v.* (a) to act. (b) to (cause to) work. (c) **to o. on a patient** = to treat a patient by cutting open the body. **op•er•a•ble** ['ɒpərəbl] *adj.* which can be operated on. **op•er•a•tion** [ɒpə'reɪʃn] *n.* (a) (act of) operating; being operated on; **to come**

into o. = begin to be applied.
op•er•a•tion•al, *adj.* referring to the working of sth. (b) ready for use. **op•er•a•tive** [ˈɒpərətɪv] 1. *adj.* in operation. 2. *n.* worker, esp. one who operates a machine, etc. **op•er•a•tor** [ˈɒpəreɪtə] *n.* (a) person who works instruments, etc. (b) person who carries things out/organizes things; *inf.* **smart o.** = clever businessman.

oph•thal•mic [ɒfˈθælmɪk] *adj.* referring to (the medical treatment of) the eye. **oph•thal•mol•o•gist** [ɒfθælˈmɒlədʒɪst] *n.* doctor who specializes in diseases of the eye. **oph•thal•mol•o•gy**, *n.* study of the eye.

o•pi•ate [ˈəʊpɪət] *n.* drug which puts you to sleep.

o•pin•ion [əˈpɪnjən] *n.* (a) (**of**) what a person thinks/feels about sth; **public o.** = what people think/feel about sth. (b) view; piece of (usu. expert) advice. **o•pin•ion•at•ed**, *adj.* (person) with rigid opinions/who thinks he is always right.

o•pi•um [ˈəʊpɪəm] *n.* drug which puts you to sleep, made from a type of poppy.

o•pos•sum [əˈpɒsəm] *n.* small North American animal which carries its young in a pouch.

op•po•nent [əˈpəʊnənt] *n.* person/group which is against you.

op•por•tune [ˈɒpətjuːn] *adj.* coming (by chance) at the right time. **op•por•tune•ly**, *adv.* in an opportune way; at the right time. **op•por•tun•ism**, *n.* being an opportunist. **op•por•tun•ist**, *n.* person who takes advantage of opportunities, esp. at the expense of others. **op•por•tu•ni•ty** [ɒpəˈtjuːnɪtɪ] *n.* chance/circumstances which allow you to do sth.

op•pose [əˈpəʊz] *v.* to act against (s.o./sth); to try to prevent. **op•posed to**, *adj.* (a) against. (b) in contrast.

op•po•site [ˈɒpəzɪt] 1. *adj.* (a) facing. (b) at/in/toward the other side of sth; **o. number** = person who is in a similar position in another organization. (c) belonging to a completely different type/position. 2. *n.* thing which is completely different. 3. *prep.* in an opposite position to. **op•po•si•tion** [ɒpəˈzɪʃn] *n.* (a) (act of) opposing. (b) (*esp. in politics*) the party/group which opposes the party/group in power. (c) rivalry.

op•press [əˈpres] *v.* (a) to cause to suffer, esp. by harsh rule. (b) to cause depression/sadness in. **op•pres•sion** [əˈpreʃn] *n.* (act of) op-

pressing; being oppressed. **op•pres•sive**, *adj.* oppressing. **op•pres•sive•ly**, *adv.* in an oppressive way. **op•pres•sive•ness**, *n.* being oppressive. **op•pres•sor**, *n.* person who oppresses.

op•pro•bri•um [əˈprəʊbrɪəm] *n.* (*formal*) disgrace; (cause of) strong disapproval. **op•pro•bri•ous**, *adj.* disgraceful; rude.

opt [ɒpt] *v.* (**for**) to decide (in favor of). **opt out**, *v.* (**of**) to decide not to (take part).

op•ti•cal [ˈɒptɪkl] *adj.* referring to the eyes/to the eyesight; referring to optics. **op•tic**, *adj.* referring to the eye/to sight. **op•ti•cal•ly**, *adv.* referring to optics. **op•ti•cian** [ɒpˈtɪʃn] *n.* person who prescribes/makes/sells glasses or contact lenses, etc. **op•tics**, *n.* science of light; **fiber o.** = use of fine threads of glass to transmit light signals.

op•ti•mal [ˈɒptɪməl] *adj.* best.

op•ti•mism [ˈɒptɪmɪzəm] *n.* belief that everything is as good as it can be/will work out for the best; confident/cheerful attitude. **op•ti•mist** [ˈɒptɪmɪst] *n.* person who believes everything will work out for the best. **op•ti•mis•tic** [ɒptɪˈmɪstɪk] *adj.* feeling that everything will work out for the best; giving cause for optimism. **op•ti•mis•ti•cal•ly**, *adv.* in an optimistic way.

op•ti•mum [ˈɒptɪməm] 1. *n.* best way. 2. *adj.* best.

op•tion [ˈɒpʃn] *n.* (a) choice/alternative possibility. (b) **o. on sth** = opportunity to buy/sell sth within a certain time or at a certain price. **op•tion•al**, *adj.* which may or may not be chosen.

op•tom•e•trist [ɒpˈtɒmətrɪst] *n.* optician. **op•tom•e•try**, *n.* science of eyesight.

op•u•lence [ˈɒpjʊləns] *n.* being opulent. **op•u•lent**, *adj.* rich/luxurious/splendid. **op•u•lent•ly**, *adv.* in an opulent way.

o•pus [ˈəʊpəs] *n.* (*pl.* **-es** or **opera**) (a) piece of music which is given a number. (b) large work of art.

or [ɔː] *conj.* (a) the opposite/the alternative/the other (possibility). (b) approximately. (c) **or (else)** = if not.

or•a•cle [ˈɒrəkl] *n.* (a) (*in ancient Greece*) place where the gods answered questions about the future; person who answered questions about the future. (b) very wise and knowing person. **o•rac•u•lar** [ɒˈrækjʊlə] *adj.* referring to an oracle.

o•ral [ˈɔːrl] 1. *adj.* (a) by speaking. (b) taken by

the mouth. 2. *n.* examination where you answer questions by speaking. **o•ral•ly**, *adv.* (a) in/by speech. (b) by the mouth.

or•ange ['ɒrɪndʒ] 1. *n.* usu. sweet citrus fruit, reddish yellow when ripe; tree which bears this fruit. 2. *adj. & n.* color of an orange. **or•ange•ade** [ɒrɪndʒ'eɪd] *n.* orange-flavored drink.

o•rang•u•tang [əræŋuː'tæŋ] *n.* large red ape found in southeast Asia.

o•ra•tion [ə'reɪʃn] *n.* (*formal*) speech. **or•a•tor** ['ɒrətə] *n.* person who is able to speak forcefully and persuasively to large numbers of people; person making a speech. **or•a•tor•i•cal** [ɒrə'tɒrɪkl] *adj.* full of eloquence. **or•a•to•ry** ['ɒrətərɪ] *n.* (a) eloquent/forceful public speaking. (b) private chapel.

or•a•to•ri•o [ɒrə'tɔːrɪəʊ] *n.* (*pl.* -os) piece of music for orchestra, choir and soloists, often telling a religious story.

orb [ɔːb] *n.* (a) spherical object (such as a planet or an eyeball). (b) ornamental globe with a cross on top used by a king as a symbol of state power.

or•bit ['ɔːbɪt] 1. *n.* (a) curved track (of an object moving through space). (b) extent of influence. 2. *v.* to move in an orbit around sth.

or•chard ['ɔːtʃəd] *n.* field with fruit trees.

or•ches•tra ['ɔːkəstrə] *n.* (a) large group of musicians who play together. (b) part of a theater, usu. next to the stage, where the musicians sit; **o. seats** = seats in a theater very close to where the orchestra sits. **or•ches•tral** [ɔː'kestrəl] *adj.* referring to an orchestra. **or•ches•trate** ['ɔːkɪstreɪt] *v.* (a) to arrange (a piece of music) for an orchestra. (b) to organize (a demonstration, etc.). **or•ches•tra•tion** [ɔːkɪ'streɪʃn] *n.* (act of) orchestrating; being orchestrated.

or•chid, orchis ['ɔːkɪd, 'ɔːkɪs] *n.* flowering plant with showy flowers.

or•dain [ɔː'deɪn] *v.* (a) to make (s.o.) a priest/a clergyman in a formal ceremony. (b) (*formal*) to order/to command (that sth be done).

or•deal [ɔː'diːl] *n.* painful test of strength/courage; difficult period.

or•der ['ɔːdə] 1. *n.* (a) command/demand that sth should be done. (b) obeying of rules or laws without unrest or violence. (c) demand/request for goods from a customer; goods supplied to a customer; *inf.* **a tall o.** = a difficult task. (d) organization of items in succession. (e) good/correct arrangement; **in o.** = correct/valid; **out of o.** = not working. (f) rules for an assembly/meeting. (g) organization of monks/priests, etc.; **in holy orders** = being a priest. (h) organization of knighthood; group of people to whom a certain honor has been given. (i) type/kind/classification/rank. (j) paper which authorizes the transfer of money. (k) **in o. to/that** = so that/for the purpose of. 2. *v.* (a) to command/to demand/to say (that sth should be done). (b) to demand/to request (goods/services, etc.). (c) to arrange/to put in order. **or•der•li•ness** ['ɔːdəlɪnəs] *n.* (a) being in good order/tidiness. (b) being quiet/being orderly. **or•der•ly.** 1. *adj.* (a) in good order; tidy or well-arranged. (b) well-behaved. 2. *n.* person whose duty it is to carry out routine tasks (in a hospital or in the armed services).

or•di•nal ['ɔːdɪnl] *n. & adj.* (referring to a) number indicating the position in a series.

or•di•nance ['ɔːdɪnəns] *n.* laws/rule made by an authority.

or•di•nar•y ['ɔːdnrɪ] *adj.* normal/not unusual; typical of its class/not having any special characteristics; **out of the o.** = extraordinary. **or•di•nar•i•ly,** *adv.* in the usual way/usually.

or•di•na•tion [ɔːdɪ'neɪʃn] *n.* (act/ceremony of) ordaining s.o. as a priest.

ord•nance ['ɔːdnəns] *n.* (a) heavy guns. (b) (government department dealing with) military supplies.

ore [ɔː] *n.* material found in the earth from which metals are obtained.

o•reg•a•no [ɒrɪ'gɑːnəʊ] *n.* spicy herb used in cooking.

or•gan ['ɔːgən] *n.* (a) part of the body with a special function. (b) periodical which gives the views of a group/of an organization. (c) musical instrument with keyboard(s) and many pipes through which air is pumped to make a sound. **or•gan•ic** [ɔː'gænɪk] *adj.* (a) referring to an organ/to organs. (b) referring to living things; **o. chemistry** = concerned with carbon compounds; **o. farming** = using only natural fertilizers. **or•gan•i•cal•ly** [ɔː'gænɪklɪ] *adv.* in an organic way. **or•gan•ism** ['ɔːgənɪzəm] *n.* living thing. **or•gan•ist,** *n.* person who plays the organ. **or•gan•i•za•tion** [ɔːgənaɪ'zeɪʃn] *n.* (a) (act of) arranging; being arranged. (b) organized group or institution. **or•gan•ize** ['ɔːgənaɪz] *v.* to arrange/to put into a special form of order; to put into good order. **or•gan•iz•er,** *n.* person who arranges things.

or•gan•dy, organdie [ɔː'gændɪ] *n.* very thin stiff cotton cloth.

or•gan•o•phos•phate [ɔːgænəʊ'fɒsfeɪt] *n.* any organic pesticide containing phosphorus.

or•gasm ['ɔːgæzəm] *n.* climax of sexual excitement.

or•gy ['ɔːdʒɪ] *n.* uncontrolled indulgence in drinking/dancing; uncontrolled state or activity.

o•ri•el ['ɔːrɪəl] *n*. **o. window** = upstairs window which projects from the wall.

o•ri•ent ['ɔːrɪənt] 1. *n*. **the O.** = the East/Eastern countries. 2. *v*. to put in a certain direction. o•ri•en•tal [ɔːrɪ'entl] 1. *adj*. referring to the Orient. 2. *n*. person from the Orient. o•ri•en•tal•ist, *n*. person who studies the East. o•ri•en•tate ['ɒrɪənteɪt] *v*. to put in a certain direction. o•ri•en•ta•tion [ɔːrɪən-'teɪʃn] *n*. (act of) orientating/putting in a certain position/direction. o•ri•en•teer•ing [ɔːrɪən'tɪːərɪŋ] *n*. sport of finding your way across country by means of maps and compasses.

or•i•fice ['ɒrɪfɪs] *n*. (*formal*) hole/opening.

o•ri•ga•mi [ɒrɪ'gɑːmɪ] *n*. (*no pl*.) art of folding colored paper to make shapes.

or•i•gin ['ɒrɪdʒɪn] *n*. beginning/root; where sth/s.o. comes from. o•rig•i•nal [ə'rɪdʒɪnl] 1. *adj*. (a) from its beginning(s); from earliest times. (b) new/different; created for the first time/not a copy. (c) showing ideas not based on those of other people. 2. *n*. (a) thing from which other things are copied/translated, etc. (b) unusual person. o•rig•i•nal•i•ty [ɒrɪdʒɪ'nælɪtɪ] *n*. (a) being original/new/different. (b) ability to create sth which has never been done before. o•rig•i•nal•ly, *adv*. (a) in an original way. (b) at or from the beginning. o•rig•i•nate [ə'rɪdʒɪneɪt] *v*. (a) to bring into existence for the first time. (b) to begin/to have its beginning. o•rig•i•na•tion [ərɪdʒɪ'neɪʃn] *n*. act of originating. o•rig•i•na•tor, *n*. person who originates.

o•ri•ole ['ɒrɪəl] *n*. bird with black and yellow feathers.

or•mo•lu ['ɔːməluː] *n*. (*no pl*.) decorations made of bronze covered with gold leaf.

or•na•ment. 1. *n*. ['ɔːnəmənt] thing used as decoration. 2. *v*. ['ɔːnəment] to decorate/to help to make more beautiful. or•na•men•tal [ɔːnə'mentl] *adj*. acting as an ornament; being pretty rather than useful. or•na•men•ta•tion [ɔːnəmən'teɪʃn] *n*. act of ornamenting; group of ornaments.

or•nate [ɔː'neɪt] *adj*. having (too) much ornament.

or•ner•y ['ɔːnərɪ] *adj*. *inf*. bad-tempered.

or•ni•thol•o•gy [ɔːnɪ'θɒlədʒɪ] *n*. study of birds. or•ni•tho•log•i•cal [ɔːnɪθə'lɒdʒɪkl] *adj*. referring to ornithology.

or•ni•thol•o•gist [ɒnɪ'θɒlədʒɪst] *n*. person who studies birds.

o•ro•tund ['ɒrətʌnd] *adj*. pompous (speech or writing).

or•phan ['ɒːfn] 1. *n*. child who has no parents. 2. *v*. to make (s.o.) an orphan. or•phan•age ['ɔːfənɪdʒ] *n*. home where orphans are looked after.

or•rer•y ['ɒrərɪ] *n*. mechanical model of the solar system.

or•ris root ['ɒrɪs'ruːt] *n*. perfume from the dried roots of a type of iris.

or•tho•don•tics [ɔːθə'dɒntɪks] *n*. treatment to correct badly formed teeth.

or•tho•dox ['ɔːθədɒks] *adj*. (a) holding the generally accepted beliefs of a religion/a philosophy, etc. (b) (Jews) who observe traditional practices very strictly; **the O. Church** = the Christian Church of Eastern Europe. or•tho•dox•y, *n*. being orthodox.

or•thog•ra•phy [ɔː'θɒgrəfɪ] *n*. (correct) spelling. or•tho•graph•i•cal [ɔːθə'græfɪkl] *adj*. referring to orthography.

or•tho•pe•dic, orthopaedic [ɔːθə'piːdɪk] *adj*. referring to diseases and deformities of bones. or•tho•pe•dics, orthopaedics, *n*. branch of medicine dealing with bones, etc. or•tho•pe•dist, orthopaedist, *n*. doctor who specializes in orthopaedics.

or•thop•tics [ɔː'θɒptɪks] *n*. correction of squints.

o•ryx [ɒrɪks] *n*. large rare Arabian antelope.

os•cil•late ['ɒsɪleɪt] *v*. to swing from one side to the other. os•cil•la•tion [ɒsɪ'leɪʃn] *n*. (act of) oscillating. os•cil•lo•scope [ɒ-'sɪləskəʊp] *n*. device which shows oscillations on a screen.

o•sier ['əʊzɪə] *n*. type of willow tree whose branches are used to make baskets/furniture, etc.

os•mo•sis [ɒz'məʊsɪs] *n*. movement of liquid into another liquid through the porous walls of a container.

os•prey ['ɒsprɪ] *n*. large bird of prey which eats fish.

os•si•cle ['ɒsɪkəl] *n*. small bone in the middle ear.

os•si•fy ['ɒsɪfaɪ] *v*. to make into bone; to make rigid. os•si•fi•ca•tion [ɒsɪfɪ'keɪʃn] *n*. act of ossifying.

os•ten•si•ble [ɒ'stensɪbl] *adj*. which shows on the surface; which is meant to seem real. os•ten•si•bly, *adv*. seemingly.

æ back, ɑː farm, ɒ top, aɪ pipe, aʊ how, aɪə fire, aʊə flower, ɔː bought, ɔɪ toy, ə fed, eəhair, eɪ take, ə afraid, əʊ boat, əʊə lower, ɜː word, iː heap, ɪ hit, ɪə hear, uː school, ʊ book, ʌ but, b back, d dog, ð then, dʒ just, f fog, g go, h hand, j yes, k catch, l last, m mix, n nut, ŋ sing, p penny, r round, s some, ʃ short, t too, tʃ chop, θ thing, v voice, w was, z zoo, ʒ treasure

os•ten•ta•tious [ɒsten'teɪʃəs] *adj.* showy/aiming to impress. **os•ten•ta•tion,** *n.* showing off in a luxurious way which is intended to impress. **os•ten•ta•tious•ly,** *adv.* in an ostentatious way.

os•te•o•ar•thri•tis [ɒstɪəvɑː'θraɪtɪs] *n.* painful disease of the joints.

os•te•o•path ['ɒstɪəpæθ] *n.* doctor who treats diseases of the bones and muscles by moving or massaging the patient's limbs. **os•te•o•path•ic** [ɒstɪə'pæθɪk] *adj.* referring to osteopathy. **os•te•op•a•thy** [ɒstɪ'ɒpəθɪ] *n.* school of medicine that emphasizes treatment of diseases of the bones and muscles by moving or massaging limbs.

os•tra•cism ['ɒstrəsɪzəm] *n.* being cut off from a group/from society. **os•tra•cize** ['ɒstrəsaɪz] *v.* to force/to keep (s.o.) out of a group.

os•trich ['ɒstrɪtʃ] *n.* (*pl.* **-es**) large, fast-running, flightless bird found in Africa.

oth•er ['ʌðə] 1. *adj.* (a) different/not the one already mentioned/not the same. (b) second of two; **every o. week** = every second week. (c) (*expressing a vague idea*) **the o. day** = a day or two ago. 2. *pron.* (a) different person/different thing. (b) (*used to contrast two things or groups*) one after the o. 3. *adv.* **o. than** = apart from. **oth•er•wise,** *adv.* (a) in a different way/situation. (b) in other respects. (c) if not/or else. **oth•er•world•ly,** *adj.* (person) who is not interested in material things/who is vague and impractical.

o•ti•ose ['əʊtɪəʊs] *adj.* (*formal*) superfluous/unwanted.

o•ti•tis [əʊ'taɪtɪs] *n.* inflammation of the ear.

ot•ter ['ɒtə] *n.* fish-eating mammal with webbed feet living mainly by rivers.

ot•to•man ['ɒtəmən] *n.* low padded seat.

ouch [aʊtʃ] *inter. showing reaction to pain.*

ought [ɔːt] *v.* (*past tense:* **ought to have**) *used with other verbs* (a) (*expressing duty or obligation*) **you o. to go** = it is your duty to go. (b) (*expressing something which is vaguely desirable*) **you o. to hear that concert.** (c) (*expressing something which is probable*) **that horse o. to win.**

ounce [aʊns] *n.* measure of weight (=1/16 of a pound).

our ['aʊə] *adj.* belonging to us. **ours** ['aʊəz] *pron.* thing(s)/person(s) belonging to us. **our•selves** [aʊə'selvz] *pron. referring to the subject* we.

oust [aʊst] *v.* to force s.o. to leave a place/position.

out [aʊt] 1. *adv.* (a) not in (a building, etc.). (b) away from the starting point (of sth). (c) (in a direction) away from the inside/from the starting point. (d) having appeared/become

known; **her book is just o.** = has just been published. (e) **o. loud** = so that it can be heard. (f) not in the right position/state; **o. of practice** = not having had enough practice. (g) (*of fire/light*) no longer burning; (*of hairstyle/dress*) no longer fashionable. (h) finished; having reached the end. 2. *n.* **to know the ins and outs of** = to know sth in all its details. **out-and-out,** *adj. & adv.* complete(ly)/total(ly). **out•back,** *n.* (*in Australia*) area(s) away from centers of population. **out•bid,** *v.* (**outbid**) (*at auction*) to bid a higher sum than (s.o.). **out•board,** *adj.* (engine) which is attached to the outside of a boat. **out•break,** *n.* sudden occurrence of an illness or unrest. **out•build•ings,** *n. pl.* buildings standing apart from the main building. **out•burst,** *n.* sudden display of (violent) emotion. **out•cast,** *n. & adj.* (person who has been) rejected by/driven away from a society or a group. **out•class,** *v.* to be much better than. **out•come,** *n.* result. **out•crop,** *n.* rock which sticks out of the surface of the ground. **out•cry,** *n.* loud protest from a number of people. **out•dat•ed,** *adj.* old-fashioned. **out•do,** *v.* (**outdid; outdone**) to do better than. **out•door,** *adj.* in the open air. **out•doors,** *adv. & n.* (in/to) the open air. **out•er,** *adj.* farther out; on the outside; beyond the limits; **o. space** = space beyond the earth's atmosphere. **out•er•most,** *adj.* farthest out. **out•fit,** *n.* (a) set of equipment needed for a particular purpose. (b) set of clothing. (c) *inf.* organization. **out•fit•ter,** *n.* supplier of outfits. **out•flank,** *v.* to go by the side of (an enemy). **out•flow,** *n.* quantity which flows out. **out•go•ing,** *adj.* (a) which is going out. (b) open/lively (personality). **out•grow,** *v.* (**outgrew; outgrown**) to grow too big for (clothes); to leave behind as one grows up. **out•ing,** *n.* trip, usu. for pleasure. **out•land•ish,** *adj.* strange/different from the usual. **out•last,** *v.* to live/to last longer than. **out•law.** 1. *n.* person who is a fugitive from the law. 2. *v.* to declare illegal or outside the law. **out•lay,** *n.* expenditure. **out•let,** *n.* (a) means by which sth can escape. (b) place where sth can be sold or distributed. **out•line.** 1. *n.* line showing the outer edge(s) of sth; broad description without much detail. 2. *v.* to make a broad description of (a plan, etc.). **out•live,** *v.* to live longer than. **out•look,** *n.* view from a building/of the world/of the future. **out•ly•ing,** *adj.* away from the center/from the main part. **out•ma•neu•ver, out•man•œu•vre,** *v.* to beat s.o. by acting/working more cleverly. **out•mod•ed,** *adj.* old-fashioned.

out•num•ber, *v.* to be greater in number than. **out of,** *prep.* (a) outside of; away from; **o. of your mind** = mad. (b) from; **one o. of ten.** (c) made from. (d) no longer having; **o. of print** = with no printed copies left; **o. of stock** = with no stock left. **out-of-date,** *adj.* (a) no longer in fashion (b) no longer valid. **out-of-pock•et,** *adj.* having paid expenses personally. **out-of-the-way,** *adj.* (a) very far from the center. (b) unusual/extraordinary. **out•pa•tient,** *n.* person who is treated at a hospital without staying overnight. **out•post,** *n.* small group of soldiers in a distant part of an occupied territory. **out•pour•ing,** *n.* sth that flows out. **out•put,** *n.* amount which a firm/machine/person produces; information produced by a computer. **out•rank,** *v.* to be of a higher rank than (s.o.). **out•rid•er** ['aʊtraɪdə] *n.* guard on a motorcycle or horse, riding beside a car/carriage in a procession. **out•rig•ger,** *n.* long piece with a float at the end, which is attached to the side of a boat to make it more stable. **out•right** ['aʊtraɪt] *adv. & adj.* (a) complete(ly); all at once. (b) straight out/without pretending. **out•set** ['aʊtset] *n.* beginning. **out•shine** [aʊt'ʃaɪn] *v.* (**outshone**) to do much better than (s.o.). **out•side** [aʊt'saɪd] 1. *n.* (a) outer surface (of sth); what is beyond the outer surface/edge of sth. (b) **at the o.** = at the most. 2. *adj.* (a) on the outer surface. (b) the most (possible). (c) from the outside/from another group, etc. 3. *adv. & prep.* beyond the outer surface/edge of (sth). **out•sid•er,** *n.* (a) person who does not belong to a group, etc. (b) s.o./sth which is not expected to win. **out•size** ['aʊtsaɪz] *n. & adj.* (of) size which is larger than the normal or usual range. **out•skirts** ['aʊtskɜːts] *n. pl.* outer edges of a town, etc. **out•smart** [aʊt'smɑːt] *v.* to trick (s.o.) by being cleverer. **out•spo•ken** [aʊt-'spəʊkən] *adj.* speaking (too) frankly. **out•stand•ing** [aʊt'stændɪŋ] *adj.* (a) excellent; of unusual quality; of very high standard. (b) not yet fulfilled/incomplete. **out•stand•ing•ly,** *adv.* to an outstanding degree. **out•stay** [aʊt'steɪ] *v.* to stay longer than. **out•stretched,** *adj.* (arm, etc.) which is stretched out. **out•strip,** *v.* (**outstripped**) to run past (s.o.); to do better than (s.o.). **out to,** *adj.* trying to/aiming for. **out box,** *n.* receptacle for correspondence which is to be sent out. **out•vote** [aʊt'vəʊt] *v.* to defeat by having

more votes than. **out•ward** ['aʊtwəd] *adj. & adv.* (a) toward the outside; away from the center or starting point. (b) on the outside. **out•ward•ly,** *adv.* (appearing) on the outside. **out•ward, outwards,** *adv.* toward the outside. **out•weigh** [aʊt'weɪ] *v.* to be more important than (sth). **out•wit** [aʊt'wɪt] *v.* (**outwitted**) to trick (s.o.) by being cleverer. **out•rage** ['aʊtreɪdʒ] 1. *n.* offense; vigorous attack (esp. against moral standards). 2. *v.* to shock/to be a cause of moral indignation. **out•ra•geous** [aʊt'reɪdʒəs] *adj.* causing (moral) indignation/shock/offense. **out•ra•geous•ly,** *adv.* in an outrageous way.

ou•tré ['uːtreɪ] *adj.* strange/weird.

ou•zel ['uːzl] *n.* type of diving bird.

o•va ['əʊvə] *n. pl. see* **o•vum.**

o•val ['əʊvl] *n. & adj.* (of) a long rounded shape; egg-shaped(d).

o•va•ry ['əʊvəri] *n.* one of the two organs of a female mammal in which eggs are produced. **o•var•i•an** [əʊ'veərɪən] *adj.* referring to ovaries.

o•va•tion [ə'veɪʃn] *n.* great applause.

ov•en ['ʌvn] *n.* enclosed box which can be heated for cooking/for baking pottery, etc. **ov•en•ware,** *n.* (*no pl.*) dishes which can be put in a hot oven.

o•ver ['əʊvə] 1. *prep.* (a) on the top (surface) of. (b) higher than. (c) across/to the other side of. (d) from the top of. (e) on the other/on the far side of. (f) everywhere in. (g) during. (h) more than. (i) better than. (j) about. 2. *adv.* (a) in all parts of (sth). (b) repeatedly. (c) above the top of (sth). (d) downward from a previous vertical position. (e) into another position; **please turn o.** = turn the page. (f) to the other side of. (g) more/higher in number. (h) in excess/left behind. (i) past/finished. (j) *prefix meaning* too (much); **overexcited; overtired. o•ver•arm,** *adv.* with the arm higher than the shoulder. **o•ver•awe** [əʊvə'ɔː] *v.* to frighten. **o•ver•bal•ance,** *v.* to (cause to) lose balance. **o•ver•bear•ing,** *adj.* trying to dominate others. **o•ver•blown,** *adj.* (rose) which has almost finished flowering; (claim) which is excessive. **o•ver•board,** *adv.* into the water from the edge of a ship, etc.; *inf.* **to go o. for** = to be enthusiastic about. **o•ver•book,** *v.* to book more places than there are rooms/seats. **o•ver•charge,** *v.* to charge too much for sth. **o•ver•coat,** *n.*

æ back, ɑː farm, ɒ top, aɪ pipe, aʊ how, aɪə fire, aʊə flower, ɔː bought, ɔɪ toy, e fed, eə hair, eɪ take, ə afraid, əʊ boat, əʊə lower, ɜː word, iː heap, ɪ hit, ɪə hear, uː school, ʊ book, ʌ but, b back, d dog, ð then, dʒ just, f fog, g go, h hand, j yes, k catch, l last, m mix, n nut, ŋ sing, p penny, r round, s some, ʃ short, t too, tʃ chop, θ thing, v voice, w was, z zoo, ʒ treasure

(full-length) coat for outdoor wear. **o•ver•crowd•ed**, *adj.* containing too many people/animals, etc. **o•ver•do**, *v.* (**overdid; overdone**) (a) to do too much; to exaggerate. (b) to cook too much. **o•ver•dose**, *n.* too large a dose (of a drug). **o•ver•draft**, *n.* amount by which a bank account is overdrawn. **o•ver•draw**, *v.* (**overdrew; overdrawn**) to take out money (from a bank account) when there is no money there. **o•ver•drive**, *n.* mechanism in a car which gives an extra gear above the top gear. **o•ver•due**, *adj.* (debt) which has not been paid at the correct time; (book) which should have been returned to the library; (visit) which should have been made; (plane, etc.) which is late. **o•ver•eat**, *v.* (**overate; overeaten**) to eat too much. **o•ver•eat•ing**, *n.* eating too much. **o•ver•es•ti•mate**, *v.* to estimate too much; to think (sth) is larger than it is. **o•ver•ex•posed**, *adj.* (film) which has been exposed too much. **o•ver•fed**, *adj.* given too much to eat. **o•ver•flow**. 1. *v.* (a) to flow over the top. (b) to occupy greater space. 2. *n.* (a) liquid which has overflowed. (b) pipe to catch overflowing liquid. (c) amount or number which will not fit a given space. **o•ver•grown**, *adj.* covered (**with** plants, etc.). **o•ver•hang•ing**, *adj.* which juts out over. **o•ver•haul**. 1. [əʊvəˈhɔːl] *v.* (a) to examine carefully, repairing where necessary. (b) to overtake (another ship). 2. *n.* [ˈəʊvəhɔːl] (act of) overhauling. **o•ver•head**. 1. *adv.* above. 2. *adj.* above; **o. projector** = projector which projects a picture from a flat surface onto a screen. 3. *n.* general expenses incurred by a business as a whole, such as salaries/heating/rent, etc. **o•ver•heat**, *v.* to heat too much. **o•ver•joyed**, *adj.* very happy. **o•ver•kill**, *n.* excess of weapons/excessive strength for what is required. **o•ver•land**, *adv. & adj.* by land. **o•ver•lap**. 1. *v.* (**overlapped**) to cover a section of (sth). 2. *n.* amount by which sth overlaps. **o•ver•leaf**, *adv.* on the other side of a page. **o•ver•load**, *v.* to put too heavy a load on (sth). **o•ver•look**, *v.* (a) not to notice. (b) to pretend not to notice; to pay no attention to. (c) to look out on to. **o•ver•lord**, *n.* person in supreme command. **o•ver•ly**, *adv.* too much. **o•ver•man**, *v.* (**overmanned**) to have more workers than are needed for the job. **o•ver•much**, *adv.* too much. **o•ver•pass**, *n.* road which crosses over the top of another road. **o•ver•pay**, *v.* (**overpaid**) to pay (s.o.) too much. **o•ver•pay•ment**, *n.* paying too much. **o•ver•play**, *v.* **to o. your hand** = to attempt (to gain) too much in negotiations.

o•ver•pow•er, *v.* to gain control of (s.o.) by force. **o•ver•pow•er•ing**, *adv.* very strong. **o•ver•pro•duc•tion**, *n.* excess production. **o•ver•rate**, *v.* to estimate/to value (sth) higher than it is. **o•ver•reach**, *v.* **to o. yourself** = to go too far (and fail in what you are trying to do). **o•ver•re•act**, *v.* to react very violently. **o•ver•ride**, *v.* (**overrode; overridden**) (a) to pay no attention to (an order, etc.). (b) to be more important than other things. **o•ver•ripe**, *adj.* too ripe. **o•ver•rule**, *v.* to rule/to order against. **o•ver•run**, *v.* (**overran; overrun**) (a) to go into/to attack all parts of. (b) to continue beyond (a time limit). **o•ver•seas**, *adv. & adj.* across the sea. **o•ver•see**, *v.* (**oversaw; overseen**) to manage/supervise. **o•ver•seer**, *n.* person who supervises other people at work. **o•ver•shad•ow**, *v.* to hide/to make less conspicuous by greater brilliance. **o•ver•shoes**, *n. pl.* rubber/plastic shoes worn over ordinary shoes to protect them. **o•ver•shoot**, *v.* (**overshot**) to go beyond a natural stopping place. **o•ver•sight**, *n.* not doing sth because of forgetfulness/not noticing. **o•ver•sleep**, *v.* (**overslept; has overslept**) to sleep longer than you meant to. **o•ver•spend**, *n.* (**overspent**) to spend more than you should. **o•ver•state**, *v.* to state too strongly/with too much detail. **o•ver•state•ment**, *n.* act of overstating; what is overstated. **o•ver•stay**, *v.* **to o. your welcome** = to stay for such a long time that you are no longer welcome. **o•ver•step**, *v.* (**overstepped**) to go further than you ought to. **o•ver•stuffed**, *adj.* well padded (sofa). **o•ver•sub•scribed**, *adj.* which more people applied for than there were available. **o•ver•take**, *v.* (**overtook; overtaken**) to reach and go past (s.o. ahead of you); to pass (another car) which is going more slowly than you. **o•ver•tax**, *v.* to demand too much tax from; **to o. one's strength** = to do more than one is physically capable of. **o•ver-the-coun•ter**, *adj* (securities) not listed on a main Stock Exchange. **o•ver•throw**. 1. *n.* removal (of a government/dictator) from power. 2. *v.* (**overthrew; overthrown**) to defeat. **o•ver•time**. 1. *n.* (a) time worked beyond normal working hours. (b) money paid for working beyond normal hours. 2. *adv.* beyond normal hours. **o•ver•turn** [əʊvəˈtɜːn] *v.* to (cause to) fall over/to turn upside down. **o•ver•view**, *n.* general view (of a subject). **o•ver•ween•ing** [əʊvəˈwiːnɪŋ] *adj.* excessive/arrogant (pride). **o•ver•weight** [əʊvəˈweɪt] *adj.* too heavy. **o•ver•whelm** [əʊvə-

'welm] v. (a) to conquer (completely). (b) **overwhelmed with work** = having more work than you can do. **o•ver•whelm•ing,** adj. enormous; greater than all others.

o•ver•work [əuvə'wɜːk] 1. n. too much work. 2. v. to (cause to) work too hard. **o•ver•wrought** [əuvə'rɔːt] adj. very agitated/under a lot of stress.

o•ver•all ['əuvəɔːl] 1. adj. covering; taking in all aspects. 2. n. **overalls** = one-piece suit worn to protect the other clothes.

o•ver•cast [əuvə'kaːst] adj. (of sky) heavy/dull/cloudy.

o•ver•come [əuvə'kʌm] v. (**overcame; has overcome**) to gain victory over (an enemy/a problem/an emotion).

o•ver•hear [əuvə'hiə] v. (**overheard** [əuvə-'hɜːd]) to hear accidentally (what you are not meant to hear).

o•ver•night [əuvə'naɪt] 1. adv. until morning. 2. adj. for the night.

o•vert [əu'vɜːt] adj. open/not hidden.

o•ver•tones ['əuvətəunz] n. pl. suggestion of sth which is different from the general content.

o•ver•ture ['əuvətʃə] n. (a) (short) piece of music played at the beginning of an opera/concert, etc. (b) **to make overtures to s.o.** = to try to begin a conversation/negotiations with s.o.

o•vi•duct ['ɒvɪdʌkt] n. tube through which ova are passed to the womb.

o•vip•a•rous [ɒ'vɪpərəs] adj. which lays eggs.

o•void ['əuvɔɪd] adj. shaped like an egg.

o•vum ['əuvəm] n. (pl. **ova** ['əuvə]) female egg which can develop inside the mother's body when fertilized. **ov•u•late** ['ɒvjuleɪt] v. to produce female eggs. **ov•u•la•tion,** n. producing female eggs. **ov•ule,** n. part of a plant where the seeds develop.

ow [au] inter. showing pain.

owe [əu] v. (a) to be obliged; to be due to pay (s.o.). (b) **to o. sth to** = to have sth because of (s.o./sth). **ow•ing to,** prep. because of.

owl [aul] n. bird of prey which is mainly active at night. **owl•ish,** adj. like an owl.

own [əun] 1. v. (a) to have/to possess. (b) to recognize as belonging to you. (c) to admit; to say that sth is true. (d) inf. **to o. up to sth** = to admit/to say that you have done sth wrong. 2. adj. belonging to yourself (alone). 3. n. (a) **my o./his o.** = mine/his; **of your o.** = belonging to you; **to come into your o.** = to have the success which you deserve; **to hold your o.** = to remain firm against some threat. (b) **on your o.** = alone/by yourself. **own•er,** n. person who owns. **own•er•ship,** n. state of owning.

ox [ɒks] n. (pl. **oxen**) (a) large animal of the cow family. (b) castrated bull. **ox•bow,** n. bend of a river where the current no longer runs. **ox•eye,** n. daisy with large flowers. **ox•tail,** n. tail of the ox used as food.

ox•a•lis [ɒk'sælɪs] n. type of flower, which produces a poisonous substance.

ox•ide ['ɒksaɪd] n. chemical compound of oxygen. **ox•i•da•tion** [ɒksɪ'deɪʃn] n. act of oxidizing. **ox•i•dize** ['ɒksɪdaɪz] v. to (cause to) combine with oxygen.

ox•y•a•cet•y•lene [ɒksɪə'setɪliːn] n. & adj. (referring to a) mixture of oxygen and acetylene.

ox•y•gen ['ɒksɪdʒən] n. (element: O) gas which forms part of the earth's atmosphere and is essential for plant and animal life.

o•yez ['ɒ'jez] int. hear this.

oys•ter ['ɔɪstə] n. type of double-shelled shellfish highly valued as food; **o. bed** = part of the sea floor where oysters are found. **oy•ster•catch•er,** n. common black and white bird which lives on the seashore.

oz abbrev. for ounce.

o•zone ['əuzəun] n. (a) harmful form of oxygen; **o. hole** = gap which forms in the ozone layer, allowing harmful radiation from the sun to reach the earth; **o. layer** = layer of ozone in the stratosphere, formed by the action of sunlight on oxygen, which acts as protection against harmful rays from the sun. (b) inf. refreshing pure air.

æ back, a: farm, ɒ: top, aɪ pipe, au how, aie fire, auə flower, ɔ: bought, ɔɪ toy, e fed, eəhair, eɪ take, ə afraid, əu boat, əuə lower, vː word, iː heap, ɪ hit, ɪə hear, uː school, u book, ʌ but, b back, d dog, ð then, dʒ just, f fog, g go, h hand, j yes, k catch, l last, m mix, n nut, ŋ sing, p penny, r round, s some, ʃ short, t too, tʃ chop, θ thing, v voice, w was, z zoo, ʒ treasure

Pp

P *symbol for* phosphorus.

pa [pɑ:] *n. inf. child's name for* father.

p.a. *abbrev. for* per annum.

pace [peɪs] 1. *n.* (a) stride/step; distance covered by one step. (b) speed; **to keep p. with** = keep up with; (*of a runner*) **to set the p.** = to decide how fast a race should be run. 2. *v.* (a) to walk; to measure by walking. (b) to set the pace for (a runner, etc.). **pace•mak•er,** *n.* (a) runner who sets the pace in a race; person who runs alongside a runner to encourage him to run faster. (b) electric device which makes heartbeats regular.

pach•y•derm ['pækɪdɜːm] *n.* animal with a thick skin (such as an elephant).

pac•i•fy ['pæsɪfaɪ] *v.* to calm. **pa•cif•ic** [pə-'sɪfɪk] *adj.* peaceful/calm. **pa•cif•i•cal•ly,** *adv.* in a pacific way. **pac•i•fi•ca•tion** [pæsɪfɪ'keɪʃn] *n.* calming (of people in revolt). **pac•i•fi•er** ['pæsɪfaɪə] *n.* rubber nipple (for babies). **pac•i•fism,** *n.* opposition to war. **pac•i•fist,** *n.* person who believes in pacifism.

pack [pæk] 1. *n.* (a) bundle of things. (b) bag carried on the back, as when hiking. (c) group of animals/people. (d) articles put in a box for selling. (e) **face p.** = cream which is spread on your face and left on it for a time to clean the skin. (f) **ice p.** = bag of ice placed on the forehead to cure a headache, etc. 2. *v.* (a) to put (things) in order in a case/box. (b) to squeeze (many things) into a small area. **pack•age.** 1. *n.* (a) bundle of things/parcel. (b) **p. deal** = deal where several items are offered at the same time; **p. tour** = tour which is organized and paid for in advance. 2. *v.* to wrap/to present (goods) in an attractive way. **pack•ag•ing,** *n.* wrapping of goods in an attractive way. **pack•er,** *n.* person who packs goods. **pack•et,** *n.* small parcel; small box. **pack ice,** *n.* mass of ice covering the sea. **pack•ing,** *n.* (a) putting things into containers; **p. case** = special wooden box for packing goods (esp. for transport). (b) material used to protect goods which are being packed. (c) **to send s.o. p.** = to send s.o. away. **pack off,** *v.* to send (s.o.) away. **pack up,** *v.* to put things away (before closing a store/before leaving a place).

pact [pækt] *n.* agreement/treaty.

pad [pæd] 1. *n.* (a) soft part under the feet of some animals; soft protective cushion. (b) (*in sports*) protective guards for the leg; **knee p.** (c) set of sheets of paper lightly attached. (d) **launching p.** = area from which a rocket is launched. (e) *Sl.* room/apartment. 2. *v.* (**padded**) (a) to soften (sth hard) by using soft material; to walk about softly. (b) to make (a speech/an article) longer by inserting irrelevant material. **pad•ding,** *n.* (a) words added to pad a speech or article. (b) soft material used to make cushions, etc.

pad•dle ['pædl] 1. *n.* (a) short oar used to propel a canoe. (b) round bat used in table tennis. (c) device with a knob, used for moving a cursor on a computer screen. 2. *v.* (a) to make (a boat) move forward using a paddle. (b) to move the hands or feet in very shallow water. **pad•dle steam•er,** *n.* boat driven by large wheels on either side. **pad•dle wheel,** *n.* wheel on a paddle steamer.

pad•dock ['pædək] *n.* small field for horses.

pad•dy ['pædɪ] *n.* (*also* **paddy field**) field where rice is grown.

pad•lock ['pædlɒk] 1. *n.* small portable lock with a hook which can be unlocked and twisted to pass through a ring to lock a gate/a box, etc. 2. *v.* to lock with a padlock.

pa•dre ['pɑːdrɪ] *n.* priest or chaplain.

pae•an ['piːən] *n.* (*formal*) great song praising s.o.

pa•gan ['peɪgn] *adj. & n.* (person) who does not believe in one of the established religions; (person) who is not a Christian.

page [peɪdʒ] 1. *n.* (a) one of the sides of a sheet of paper in a book or magazine. (b) messenger boy in a hotel. (c) small boy who accompanies the bride at a wedding. 2. *v.* to call (s.o.) over a loudspeaker in a hotel, etc. **page•boy,** *n.* (a) (*old*) boy attendant on a medieval lord. (b) **p. hairstyle** = woman's hair cut quite short and straight.

pag•eant ['pædʒənt] *n.* grand display of people in costume. **pag•eant•ry,** *n.* grand ceremonies where people wear showy costumes.

pag•i•nate ['pædʒɪneɪt] *v.* to number the

pages in a book. **pag•i•na•tion** [pædʒɪ-'neɪʃn] *n.* act of paginating.

pa•go•da [pə'gəʊdə] *n.* tall tower made of several stories, found in the Far East.

paid [peɪd] *v. see* **pay.**

pail [peɪl] *n.* bucket.

pain [peɪn] 1. *n.* (a) sensation of being hurt. (b) **to take pains with sth/to do sth** = to take care. (c) **on p. of death** = at the risk of being sentenced to death. 2. *v.* to hurt. **pained,** *adj.* sad/sorrowful (expression). **pain•ful,** *adj.* which hurts. **pain•ful•ly,** *adv.* in a painful way. **pain•kil•ler,** *n.* painkilling drug. **pain•kil•ling,** *adj.* (drug) which stops part of your body hurting. **pain•less,** *adj.* which does not hurt. **pain•less•ly,** *adv.* in a painless way. **pain•stak•ing,** *adj.* careful/well-done (work).

paint [peɪnt] 1. *n.* liquid in various colors used to color. 2. *v.* (a) to cover with color. (b) to make a picture of (s.o./sth). **paint•er,** *n.* (a) person who paints pictures. (b) person who paints houses/cars, etc. **paint•ing,** *n.* (a) making pictures. (b) painted picture. **paint•work,** *n.* (*no pl.*) painted surfaces (doors/windows, etc.).

pair ['peə] 1. *n.* (a) two things taken together; two people. (b) two things joined together to make one. 2. *v.* (a) to join together in twos. (b) to mate.

pais•ley ['peɪzlɪ] *n.* pattern on textiles, of curved shapes.

pa•ja•mas [pə'dʒɑːməz] *n. pl.* light shirt and trousers worn in bed.

Pak•i•sta•ni [pækɪ'stɑːnɪ] 1. *adj.* referring to Pakistan. 2. *n.* person from Pakistan.

pal [pæl] *n. inf.* friend.

pal•ace ['pæləs] *n.* large building where a king/queen/president, etc., lives.

pal•an•quin ['pælənkwɪn] *n.* seat with a roof, carried by bearers.

pal•ate ['pælət] *n.* top part of the inside of the mouth. **pal•at•a•ble,** *adj.* nice to eat/tasting good.

pa•la•tial [pə'leɪʃl] *adj.* magnificent/like a palace.

pa•lav•er [pə'lɑːvə] *n. inf.* idle talk; chatter.

pale [peɪl] 1. *adj.* (**-er, -est**) light-colored. 2. *n.* **beyond the p.** = doing things which are not acceptable in society. 3. *v.* (a) to lose color; to become light. (b) to become less important. **pale•ness,** *n.* light color.

pa•le•o•gra•phy [pælɪ'ɒgrəfɪ] *n.* study of ancient writing.

pa•le•o•lith•ic [pælɪəʊ'lɪθɪk] *adj.* referring to the early part of the Stone Age.

pa•le•on•tol•o•gy [pælɪɒn'tɒlədʒɪ] *n.* study of fossils.

Pal•es•tin•i•an [pælɪ'stɪnɪən] *adj. & n.* (person) from Palestine.

pal•ette ['pælət] *n.* (a) flat board on which an artist mixes colors; **p. knife** = long flat knife with a rounded end. (b) range of colors available, esp. on a computer graphics program.

pal•i•mo•ny ['pælɪmənɪ] *n.* alimony paid to a friend when parting after years of life together.

pal•in•drome ['pælɪndrəʊm] *n.* word or phrase which is spelled the same backward and forward.

pal•ing(s) ['peɪlɪŋ(z)], **pal•i•sade** [pælɪ'seɪd] *n.* fence made of pointed pieces of wood.

pall [pɔːl] 1. *n.* (a) (*formal*) thick layer (of smoke). (b) cloth put over a coffin. 2. *v.* to become less interesting. **pall•bear•er,** *n.* person who walks beside a coffin in a funeral procession.

pal•let ['pælɪt] *n.* (a) flat platform on which goods can be stacked and moved from place to place. (b) straw-filled mattress.

pal•liasse ['pælɪæs] *n.* straw-filled mattress.

pal•li•ate ['pælɪeɪt] *v.* to try to reduce (a vice/pain); to cover up (a mistake). **pal•li•a•tive** ['pælɪətɪv] *adj. & n.* (thing) which reduces pain.

pal•lid ['pælɪd] *adj.* pale (face).

pal•lor ['pælə] *n.* paleness (of face).

palm [pɑːm] *n.* (a) soft inside surface of your hand. (b) tall tropical tree with long leaves at the top. **palm•cord•er** ['pɑːmkɔːdə] *n.* camcorder that is small enough to hold in the palm of the hand. **palm•ist,** *n.* person who tells the future by palmistry. **palm•is•try,** *n.* telling what will happen to you in the future from the lines in the palm of your hand. **palm off,** *v. inf.* (**on**) to give (sth bad) to s.o. without his knowing. **Palm Sun•day,** *n.* Sunday before Easter Sunday. **palm•top** ['pɑːmtɒp] *n.* portable computer that is small enough to hold in the palm of the hand, smaller than a notebook computer, and used esp. as a personal organizer. **palm•y,** *adj.* (**-ier, -iest**) pleasant; prosperous.

pal•pa•ble ['pælpəbl] *adj.* which can be felt/which can be easily seen. **pal•pa•bly,**

æ back, ɑː farm, ɒ top, aɪ pipe, aʊ how, aɪə fire, aʊə flower, ɔː bought, ɔɪ toy, e fed, eəhair, eɪ take, ə afraid, əʊ boat, əʊə lower, vː word, iː heap, ɪ hit, ɪə hear, uː school, ʊ book, ʌ but, b back, d dog, ð then, dʒ just, f fog, g go, h hand, j yes, k catch, l last, m mix, n nut, ŋ sing, p penny, r round, s some, ʃ short, t too, tʃ chop, θ thing, v voice, w was, z zoo, ʒ treasure

adv. in a palpable way. **pal•pa•tion** [pæl-'peɪʃn] *n.* examination of part of the body by feeling it with the hand.

pal•pi•tate ['pælpɪteɪt] *v.* to beat very quickly. **pal•pi•ta•tions** [pælpɪ'teɪʃnz] *n. pl.* rapid beating of the heart.

pal•sy ['pɒlzɪ] *n.* (a) paralysis. (b) trembling (of the hands, etc.). **pal•sied**, *adj.* with trembling limbs.

pal•try ['pɔːltrɪ] *adj.* (-ier, -iest) insignificant.

pal•u•dism ['pæljuːdɪzm] *n.* (*old*) malaria.

pam•pas ['pæmpəs] *n. pl.* grass-covered plains in South America; **p. grass** = type of tall ornamental grass.

pam•per ['pæmpə] *v.* to spoil (a child/a dog) by giving them too much food/by treating them too well.

pam•phlet ['pæmflət] *n.* small book with only a few pages, which is not bound with a hard cover. **pam•phlet•eer** [pæmflə'tɪə] *n.* person who writes political pamplets.

pan- [pæn] *prefix meaning* over a wide area; **pan-American** = including North America, South America and Central America.

pan [pæn] **1.** *n.* (a) metal cooking container with a handle. (b) metal dish; one of the dishes on a pair of scales. **2.** (**panned**) (a) to move a camera sideways to take in a wider view. (b) *inf.* to criticize. (c) **to p. for gold** = to sift mud in a stream, hoping to find gold in it. **pan•cake** ['pæŋkeɪk] *n.* thin soft flat cake made of flour, milk, eggs, etc. **pan out**, *v. inf.* to turn out/to succeed.

pan•a•ce•a [pænə'siːə] *n.* thing which cures everything/which solves every problem.

pa•nache [pə'næʃ] *n.* showy way of doing things.

pan•a•ma [pænə'mɑː] *n.* hat made of fine straw.

pan•a•tel•la [pænə'telə] *n.* long thin cigar.

pan•chro•mat•ic [pænkrə'mætɪk] *adj.* (film) which is sensitive to all colors.

pan•cre•as ['pæŋkrɪəs] *n.* (*pl.* -es) gland which produces insulin, and also a liquid which helps digest food.

pan•da ['pændə] *n.* (**giant**) **p.** = large black and white Chinese animal.

pan•dem•ic [pæn'demɪk] *adj.* (disease) which occurs over the whole world/over a large area.

pan•de•mo•ni•um [pændɪ'məunɪəm] *n.* great uproar and confusion.

pan•der ['pændə] *v.* to give in (**to** low tastes).

pane [peɪn] *n.* sheet of glass (in a window, etc.).

pan•e•gyr•ic [pænɪ'dʒɪrɪk] *n.* (*formal*) speech in praise of s.o.

pan•el ['pænl] **1.** *n.* (a) flat surface which is higher/lower/thicker, etc., than the rest of the surface. (b) section of different-colored material. (c) group of people who answer ques-

tions/who judge a competition. **2.** *v.* (**paneled, panelled**) to cover with sheets of wood. **panel game**, *n.* game (on radio/TV) where a group of people answer questions/guess answers, etc. **pan•el•ing, panelling**, *n.* sheets of wood used to cover walls, etc. **pan•el•ist**, *n.* member of a panel answering questions/judging a competition.

pang [pæŋ] *n.* sudden sharp pain.

pan•ic ['pænɪk] **1.** *n.* terror/fright. **2.** *v.* (**panicked**) to become frightened. **pan•ic-strick•en**, *adj.* wild with fright. **pan•ick•y**, *adj.* likely to panic.

pan•i•cle ['pænɪkl] *n.* cluster of flowers which hangs down.

pan•nier ['pænɪə] *n.* one of a pair of bags carried on the side of an animal or a bicycle.

pan•o•ply ['pænəplɪ] *n.* fine show/grand display of costume, etc.

pan•o•ram•a [pænə'rɑːmə] *n.* wide expanse of landscape. **pan•o•ram•ic** [pænə'ræmɪk] *adj.* wide.

pan•sy ['pænzɪ] *n.* (a) small multicolored garden flower. (b) *inf.* effeminate man.

pant [pænt] *v.* to breathe fast.

pan•the•ism ['pænθɪɪzəm] *n.* belief that God and the universe are one and the same; worship of many gods.

pan•ther ['pænθə] *n.* large black leopard.

pant•ies ['pæntɪz] *n. inf.* women's brief undergarment worn on the lower part of the body.

pan•tile ['pæntaɪl] *n.* curved tile for a roof.

pan•to•graph ['pæntəgrɑːf] *n.* metal frame on the roof of an electric locomotive which rises to touch an overhead electric wire to pick up electricity.

pan•to•mime ['pæntəmaɪm] *n.* theatrical entertainment presented without words, using only gestures and other body movements.

pan•try ['pæntrɪ] *n.* cool cupboard or room for keeping food in.

pants [pænts] *n. pl.* (a) *inf.* brief undergarment worn on the lower part of the body. (b) *inf.* trousers.

pan•ty•hose ['pæntɪ'həuz] *n. pl.* women's tights.

pap [pæp] *n.* soft food for invalids.

pa•pa [pə'pɑː] *n. child's name for* father.

pa•pa•cy ['peɪpəsɪ] *n.* position of pope. **pa•pal**, *adj.* referring to the pope.

pa•pa•ya [pə'pæjə], **pa•paw** ['pɔːpɔː] *n.* yellow fruit from a tropical tree.

pa•per ['peɪpə] **1.** *n.* (a) thin material made from rags or wood pulp, used for printing/writing, etc. (b) sheet of paper. (c) newspaper. (d) scientific/learned article. **2.** *v.* to cover (the walls of a room) with paper. **pa•per•back**, *n.* book with a paper cover.

pa•per boy, *n.* boy who delivers newspapers to houses. **pa•per clip,** *n.* piece of bent wire for holding pieces of paper together. **pa•per•knife,** *n.* (*pl.* **-knives**) long knife for cutting paper (esp. for opening envelopes). **pa•per•weight,** *n.* heavy block put on papers to prevent them from being blown away. **pa•per•work,** *n.* office work. **pa•per•y,** *adj.* thin like paper.

pa•pier-mâ•ché [pæpɪeɪ'mæʃeɪ] *n.* mixture of wet paper, used to make models, etc.

pa•pist ['peɪpɪst] *n.* (*rude*) Roman Catholic.

pa•poose [pə'puːs] *n.* North American Indian baby.

pap•ri•ka ['pæprɪkə] *n.* red spice made from powdered sweet peppers.

pa•py•rus [pə'paɪrəs] *n.* reed growing in the Middle East, used by the ancient Egyptians to make a type of paper.

par [pɑː] *n.* (a) equal level; **to be on a p. with** = to be equal to. (b) **to buy shares at p.** = at their original price or at face value. (c) (*in golf*) number of strokes usu. needed to hit the ball into the hole; **below p.** = not very well.

par•a•ble ['pærəbl] *n.* usu. religious story with a moral.

pa•rab•o•la [pə'ræbələ] *n.* curve like the path of an object which is thrown into the air and comes down again. **par•a•bol•ic** [pærə'bɒlɪk] *adj.* referring to a parabola.

par•a•chute ['pærəʃuːt] 1. *n.* large piece of thin material shaped like an umbrella, with cords and a harness attached, which allows you to float down safely from an aircraft. 2. *v.* to jump from an aircraft with a parachute. **par•a•chut•ist,** *n.* person who jumps regularly with a parachute.

pa•rade [pə'reɪd] 1. *n.* (a) military display/march; **p. ground** = square area on a military camp where parades are held. (b) series of bands/decorated cars, etc., passing in a street; **fashion p.** = display of new clothes by models. 2. *v.* to march past in ordered lines.

par•a•digm ['pærədaɪm] *n.* example to be copied.

par•a•dise ['pærədaɪs] *n.* ideal place where good people are supposed to live after death; any beautiful place.

par•a•dox ['pærədɒks] *n.* thing which appears to contradict itself but may really be true. **par•a•dox•i•cal** [pærə'dɒksɪkl] *adj.* contradictory. **par•a•dox•i•cal•ly,** *adv.* in a paradoxical way.

par•af•fin ['pærəfɪn] *n. Brit. see* **kerosene. p.**

wax = solid white substance used for making candles.

par•a•gon ['pærəgən] *n.* perfect model (of virtue, etc.).

par•a•graph ['pærəgrɑːf] *n.* section of several lines of prose, usu. starting with a short blank space at the beginning of a new line.

par•a•keet [pærə'kiːt] *n.* kind of small tropical parrot.

par•a•le•gal [pærə'liːgl] *n.* person who is not a lawyer, but who assists lawyers in legal matters.

par•al•lax ['pærəlæks] *n.* difference in the position of an object when it is seen from different points.

par•al•lel ['pærələl] 1. *adj.* (a) (**to/with**) (lines) which are side by side and remain the same distance apart without ever touching. (b) similar. 2. *n.* (a) geometrical line which runs parallel to another. (b) line running around the globe from east to west parallel to the equator. (c) closely similar situation; thing which can be compared. 3. *v.* to be similar to. **par•al•lel•o•gram** [pærə'leləgræm] *n.* four-sided figure where each side is parallel to the one opposite.

par•a•lyze, *Brit.* **par•a•lyse** ['pærəlaɪz] *v.* to make unable to move. **pa•ral•y•sis** [pə'ræləsɪs] *n.* being unable to move. **par•a•lyt•ic** [pærə'lɪtɪk] 1. *adj.* unable to move. 2. *n.* paralyzed person.

par•a•med•i•cal [pærə'medɪkl] *adj.* helping in medical treatment. **par•a•med•ic,** *n. inf.* person who is not a doctor, but who helps give medical treatment.

pa•ram•e•ter [pə'ræmɪtə] *n.* figure which shows the upper or lower level of some expected result; data which defines the limits of sth.

par•a•mil•i•tar•y [pærə'mɪlətrɪ] *adj.* organized in the same way as the army, but not a part of it.

par•a•mount ['pærəmaʊnt] *adj.* extreme/supreme.

par•a•mour ['pærəmuːə] *n.* (*old*) lover; mistress.

par•a•noi•a [pærə'nɔɪə] *n.* type of mental disease where you feel that everyone is against you. **par•a•noi•ac,** *adj. & n.* (person) who suffers from paranoia. **par•a•noid,** *adj. & n.* (person) suffering from paranoia.

par•a•pet ['pærəpet] *n.* small wall at the edge of a ledge/bridge, etc.

æ back, ɑː farm, ɒ top, aɪ pipe, aʊ how, aɪə fire, aʊə flower, ɔː bought, ɔɪ toy, e fed, eəhair, eɪ take, ə afraid, əʊ boat, əʊə lower, ɜː word, iː heap, ɪ hit, ɪə hear, uː school, ʊ book, ʌ but, b back, d dog, ð then, dʒ just, f fog, g go, h hand, j yes, k catch, l last, m mix, n nut, ŋ sing, p penny, r round, s some, ʃ short, t too, tʃ chop, θ thing, v voice, w was, z zoo, ʒ treasure

par•a•pher•na•lia [pærəfəˈneɪlɪə] *n. (no pl.)* mass of bits and pieces; equipment.

par•a•phrase [ˈpærəfreɪz] 1. *n.* writing which repeats sth in different words. 2. *v.* to repeat (what s.o. has said or written) using different words.

par•a•ple•gi•a [pærəˈpliːdʒə] *n.* paralysis of the legs and lower part of the body. **par•a•ple•gic,** *adj. & n.* (person) who suffers from paraplegia.

par•a•psy•chol•o•gy [pærəsaɪˈkɒlədʒi] *n.* study of unexplained psychological phenomena.

par•a•quat [ˈpærəkwæt] *n.* dangerous weedkiller.

par•a•site [ˈpærəsaɪt] *n.* animal/plant which lives on other animals or plants; person who does no useful work. **par•a•sit•ic** [pærəˈsɪtɪk] *adj.* (insect, etc.) which lives off others.

par•a•sol [ˈpærəsɒl] *n.* light umbrella to keep off the rays of the sun.

par•a•stat•al [pɑrəˈsteɪtl] *adj. & n.* (organization) owned by the state.

par•a•troop•er [ˈpærətruːpə] *n.* soldier who is a parachutist. **par•a•troops,** *n. pl.* paratroopers.

par•a•ty•phoid [pærəˈtaɪfɔɪd] *n.* fever which is similar to typhoid, but less dangerous.

par•boil [ˈpɑːbɔɪl] *v.* to half-cook (food) in boiling water.

par•cel [ˈpɑːsl] 1. *n.* (a) sth wrapped up; package. (b) small area of land. 2. *v.* (**parceled, parcelled**) to wrap and tie (something) up to send. **parcel out,** *v.* to divide up between several people.

parch [pɑːtʃ] *v.* to dry.

parch•ment [ˈpɑːtʃmənt] *n.* (a) skins of animals which have been treated and which can be used for writing on. (b) fine quality yellowish paper.

par•don [ˈpɑːdn] 1. *n.* (a) forgiveness. (b) freeing s.o. from prison or from punishment. 2. *v.* (a) to forgive. (b) to allow (s.o.) to leave prison; to release from punishment. **par•don•a•ble,** *adj.* which can be excused. **par•don•a•bly,** *adv.* in a way which can be excused.

pare [ˈpeə] *v.* to cut the skin/peel (off a fruit/vegetable, etc.); to cut back (expenses). **par•ings,** *n. pl.* pieces of skin cut off a fruit/vegetable, etc.

par•ent [ˈpeərənt] *n.* father or mother; (organization) which rules another. **par•ent•age,** *n.* origin. **pa•ren•tal** [pəˈrentl] *adj.* referring to parents. **par•ent•hood,** *n.* being a parent.

pa•ren•the•sis [pəˈrenθəsɪs] *n.* (*pl.* **-ses** [-siːz]) (a) phrase in the middle of a sentence which is placed in brackets or between dashes. (b) pa-

rentheses = (round) brackets. **par•en•thet•ic(al)** [pærənˈθetɪk(l)] *adj.* which is not part of a main sentence.

par•get•ing [ˈpɑːdʒetɪŋ] *n.* decorated plaster on the outside of a house.

pa•ri•ah [pəˈraɪə] *n.* person who is thrown out by civilized society.

pa•ri•e•tal [pəˈraɪətl] *adj.* referring to the walls of cavities in the body.

pa•ri pas•su [pærɪ ˈpæsuː] *adv.* equally/with equal shares.

par•ish [ˈpærɪʃ] *n.* (*pl.* **-es**) (a) administrative area around a church and under the care of a clergyman. (b) county. **par•ish•ion•er** [pəˈrɪʃənə] *n.* person who lives in or belongs to a parish.

par•i•ty [ˈpærɪti] *n.* equality.

park [pɑːk] 1. *n.* open public place usu. with grass and trees; **business p.** = area with buildings specially built for businesses; **national p.** = large area of countryside kept in a natural state. 2. *v.* to leave (one's car) in a particular place; **no parking** = don't leave your car here; **parking meter** = device into which you put money to pay for parking; **parking lot** = place where cars can be left temporarily.

par•ka [ˈpɑːkə] *n.* warm jacket with a hood.

Par•kin•son's dis•ease [ˈpɑːkɪnsənzdɪˈziːz] *n.* progressive disease, which affects the parts of the brain which control movement.

par•lance [ˈpɑːləns] *n.* (*formal*) way of speaking.

par•ley [ˈpɑːlɪ] 1. *n.* discussion between enemies with a view to agreeing to peace terms. 2. *v.* to discuss peace terms with an enemy.

par•lia•ment [ˈpɑːləmənt] *n.* group of elected representatives who vote the laws of a country. **par•lia•men•tar•i•an** [pɑːləmən-ˈteərɪən] *n. Brit.* (experienced and knowledgable) member of a parliament. **par•lia•men•ta•ry** [pɑːləˈmentərɪ] *adj.* referring to parliament.

par•lor, *Brit.* **par•lour** [ˈpɑːlə] *n.* (a) sitting room. (b) **beauty p.** = place where women can have their hair done and their faces made up.

par•lous [ˈpɑːləs] *adj.* bad/dangerous (state).

pa•ro•chi•al [pəˈrəʊkɪəl] *adj.* (a) referring to a parish. (b) restricted (view); narrow-minded (person).

par•o•dy [ˈpærədɪ] 1. *n.* imitation in order to make fun of s.o./sth. 2. *v.* to imitate in order to make fun.

pa•role [pəˈrəʊl] 1. *n.* **prisoner on p.** = prisoner let out of prison before the end of his sentence on condition that he behaves well. 2. *v.* to let (a prisoner) out of prison on condition that he behaves well.

par•ox•ysm [ˈpærəksɪzəm] *n.* wild fit (of anger, etc.).

par•quet ['pɑːkeɪ] *n.* flooring of small wooden blocks.

par•ri•cide ['pærɪsaɪd] *n.* murder of your own parent or other close relative; person who kills his parent or other close relative.

par•rot ['pærət] *n.* colorful tropical bird with a large curved beak.

par•ry ['pærɪ] *v.* to prevent (a blow) from hitting you.

parse [pɑːz] *v.* to describe the grammatical function of each word in a sentence.

par•sec ['pɑːsek] *n.* unit of measurement in astronomy (3.26 light years).

par•si•mo•ny ['pɑːsɪmənɪ] *n.* (*formal*) miserliness. **par•si•mo•ni•ous** [pɑːsɪˈməʊnɪəs] *adj.* miserly. **par•si•mo•ni•ous•ly,** *adv.* in a parsimonious way.

pars•ley ['pɑːslɪ] *n.* green herb used in cooking.

pars•nip ['pɑːsnɪp] *n.* vegetable with a long white edible root.

par•son ['pɑːsn] *n.* clergyman, esp. in a Protestant Church. **par•son•age,** *n.* house of a parson.

part [pɑːt] 1. *n.* (a) piece/bit; **in p.** = not completely; **spare parts** = replacement pieces (for a machine); **parts of speech** = types of words according to usage (noun/verb, etc.). (b) role; **take p. in** = to be active in. (c) **for my p.** = as far as I am concerned. (d) separation in the hair. 2. *adv.* not entirely; **part white.** 3. *v.* to separate. **part•ing,** *n.* leaving. **part•ly,** *adv.* not entirely. **part-time,** *adj. & adv.* not for the whole working day. **part with,** *v.* to give away.

par•take [pɑːˈteɪk] *v.* (**partook; partaken**) (*formal*) (**of**) to eat (food).

par•terre [pɑːˈteə] *n.* formal arrangement of flowerbeds.

par•tial ['pɑːʃl] *adj.* (a) (**to**) biased/with a liking for. (b) not complete. **par•ti•al•i•ty** [pɑːʃɪˈælɪtɪ] *n.* strong bias **for. par•tial•ly,** *adv.* (a) in a biased way. (b) not completely.

par•tic•i•pate [pɑːˈtɪsɪpeɪt] *v.* to take part **in** (sth). **par•tic•i•pant,** *n.* person who participates. **par•tic•i•pa•tion** [pɑːtɪsɪˈpeɪʃn] *n.* taking part in sth. **par•tic•i•pa•to•ry,** *adj.* in which you participate.

par•ti•ci•ple ['pɑːtɪsɪpl] *n.* part of a verb, used either to form compound tenses or as an adjective or noun. **par•ti•cip•i•al** [pɑːtɪˈsɪpɪəl] *adj.* referring to a participle.

par•ti•cle ['pɑːtɪkl] *n.* very small piece; minor part of speech.

par•ti•col•ored, *Brit.* **par•ti•col•oured** ['pɑːtɪkʌləd] *adj.* with one part in one color, and the other part in another.

par•tic•u•lar [pəˈtɪkjulə] 1. *adj.* (a) special; referring to one thing or person; **in p.** = as a special point. (b) fussy. 2. *n.* detail. **par•tic•u•lar•i•ty** [pɑːtɪkjuˈlærɪtɪ] *n.* particular quality. **par•tic•u•lar•ize** [pɑːtɪkjuləˈraɪz] *v.* to list details. **par•tic•u•lar•ly,** *adv.* specially.

par•ti•san [pɑːtɪˈzæn] *adj. & n.* (a) (person) who strongly supports a certain point of view. (b) (guerrilla) fighting against an army which has occupied his country. **par•ti•san•ship,** *n.* being a partisan.

par•ti•tion [pɑːˈtɪʃn] 1. *n.* (a) division into parts. (b) thin wall between two spaces, esp. splitting a large room into two. 2. *v.* to divide (by means of a partition).

part•ner ['pɑːtnə] *n.* (a) person who has a part share in a business. (b) person who plays/dances with s.o. **part•ner•ship,** *n.* business association between two or more people where the risks and profits are shared.

par•tridge ['pɑːtrɪdʒ] *n.* large brown and gray bird, shot for sport and food.

par•tu•ri•tion [pɑːtjuˈrɪʃn] *n.* giving birth.

par•ty ['pɑːtɪ] *n.* (a) enjoyable meeting of several people on invitation. (b) group of people. (c) person involved (esp. in legal matters); **third p.** = third person, in addition to the two principal people involved. (d) **p. line** = a shared telephone line. (e) (**political**) **p.** = official group of people with the same political ideas; **p. line** = official doctrine.

pas•chal ['pæskəl] *adj.* referring to passover or Easter.

pass [pɑːs] 1. *n.* (*pl.* **-es**) (a) lower area between two mountain peaks. (b) (*in football/hockey, etc.*) moving the ball/puck to another player. (c) acceptance at an examination. (d) bus/train season ticket; permit to go in or out. (e) **to make a p. at s.o.** = to try to start a sexual relationship with s.o. 2. *v.* (a) to go past. (b) to move (sth) **to** s.o. (c) to get through (an examination/inspection). (d) to vote by a majority for (a motion). (e) **to p. comments** = to make comments. (f) **to p. water** = to urinate. **pass•a•ble,** *adj.* fairly good. **pass•a•bly,** *adv.* fairly well. **pas•sage** ['pæsɪdʒ] *n.* (a) corridor. (b) section of a text. (c) **sea p.** = journey by sea. **pas•sage•way,** *n.* corridor. **pass a•way,** *v.* to die. **pass•book,** *n.* book which records how much money you put in or take out of your savings account in a bank. **pas•sen•ger** ['pæsɪndʒə] *n.* traveler (in a vehicle). **pass•er•by** [pɑːsə'baɪ] *n.* (*pl.* **passersby**) person who is walking past. **pass for**, *v.* to be thought to be. **pass•ing**, *adj.* (a) not permanent. (b) which is going past. **pass key**, *n.* main key which opens several doors. **pass off**, *v.* **to pass oneself off as** = to pretend to be. **pass on**, *v.* to die. **pass out**, *v. inf.* to faint. **pass o•ver**, *v.* (a) to go past above. (b) **to pass s.o. over for promotion** = to miss s.o. who should have been promoted. **Pass•o•ver** ['pɑːsəʊvə] *n.* Jewish festival which celebrates the freeing of the Jews from captivity in Egypt. **pass•port**, *n.* official document allowing you to pass from one country to another. **pass up**, *v. inf.* not to take (an opportunity). **pass•word**, *n.* secret word which you say to go past a guard or to access a computer file.

pass•é ['pæseɪ] *adj.* old-fashioned.

pas•sim ['pæsɪm] *adv.* throughout.

pas•sion ['pæʃn] *n.* violent emotion/enthusiasm. **pas•sion•ate**, *adj.* violently emotional. **pas•sion•ate•ly**, *adv.* violently. **pas•sion•flow•er**, *n.* climbing plant with green and purple flowers. **pas•sion•fruit**, *n.* (*no pl.*) edible tropical fruit.

pas•sive ['pæsɪv] *adj.* (a) not resisting; which allows things to happen; **p. resistance** = resisting (the police, etc.) by refusing to obey orders but not using violence. (b) (verb) which shows that the subject is being acted upon. **pas•sive•ly**, *adv.* not offering any resistance/not doing anything positive. **pas•sive•ness**, *n.* being passive. **pas•siv•i•ty** [pə'sɪvɪtɪ] *n.* being passive.

past [pɑːst] 1. *adj.* (time) which has gone by. 2. *n.* time which has gone by. 3. *prep.* after; beyond. **past mas•ter**, *n.* expert.

pas•ta ['pæstə] *n.* (*pl.* **pasta**). food of Italian origin made of flour and water, such as spaghetti/macaroni, etc.

paste [peɪst] 1. *n.* (a) thin glue, usu. made of flour and water. (b) soft substance. (c) imitation jewel. 2. *v.* to glue (paper, etc.). **paste•board**, *n.* cardboard.

pas•tel ['pæstl] *n.* (a) colored crayon like chalk; **p. colors** = soft, light shades. (b) picture done with colored crayons like chalk.

pas•tern ['pæstɜːn] *n.* part of a horse's foot above the hoof.

pas•teur•ize ['pɑːstʃəraɪz] *v.* to kill the germs in (milk) by heating. **pas•teur•i•za•tion** [pɑːstʃəraɪ'zeɪʃn] *n.* action of pasteurizing.

pas•tiche [pæ'stiːʃ] *n.* poem/piece of music,

etc., which is a deliberate imitation of the style of another artist.

pas•tille ['pæstl] *n.* small candy made of fruit-flavored jelly.

pas•time ['pɑːstaɪm] *n.* hobby/way of passing your spare time.

pas•tor ['pɑːstə] *n.* clergyman. **pas•to•ral**, *adj.* (a) referring to shepherds. (b) referring to the country or rustic life.

pas•try ['peɪstrɪ] *n.* (a) paste made of flour, fat and water which is used to make pies, etc. (b) cooked pie crust. (c) **pastries** = sweet cakes made of pastry filled with cream/fruit, etc.

pas•ture ['pɑːstʃə] 1. *n.* grassy area where cows and sheep can graze. 2. *v.* to put (cows and sheep) to graze. **pas•tur•age**, *n.* (*no pl.*) land used for pasturing.

pas•ty ['peɪstɪ] *adj.* white (face).

pat [pæt] 1. *n.* (a) light hit; **a p. on the back** = praise. (b) small piece (of butter). 2. *v.* (**patted**) to give (s.o./sth) a pat. 3. *adj. & adv.* (answer) given promptly.

patch [pætʃ] 1. *n.* (*pl.* **-es**) (a) small piece of material used for covering up holes. (b) small area. 2. *v.* to repair by attaching a piece of material over a hole. **patch•i•ly**, *adv.* in a patchy way. **patch•i•ness**, *n.* being patchy. **patch up**, *v.* to end (a quarrel). **patch•work**, *n.* small pieces of material sewn together in patterns. **patch•y**, *adj.* in small areas; not the same all through.

pate [peɪt] *n.* (*old*) head.

pâ•té ['pæteɪ] *n.* paste made of cooked meat or fish finely minced.

pa•tel•la [pə'telə] *n.* (*formal*) kneecap.

pat•ent ['peɪtənt] 1. *n.* (*also* ['pætnt]) official confirmation that you have the right to make or sell a new invention. 2. *adj.* (a) covered by an official patent; **p. medicine** = medicine made under a trade name by one company. (b) **p. leather** = extremely shiny leather. (c) obvious. 3. *v.* to obtain a patent for. **pat•ent•ee** [peɪtən'tiː] *n.* person who has obtained a patent. **pat•ent•ly**, *adv.* obviously/clearly.

pa•ter•ni•ty [pə'tɜːnɪtɪ] *n.* being a father. **pa•ter•nal**, *adj.* referring to a father; like a father; **my p. grandfather** = my father's father. **pa•ter•nal•ism**, *n.* paternalistic way of ruling a country/a company. **pa•ter•nal•is•tic** [pətɜːnə'lɪstɪk] *adj.* (way of ruling/of managing) which is kindly but does not give enough freedom or responsibility to individuals. **pa•ter•nal•ly**, *adv.* in a paternal way.

path [pɑːθ] *n.* (a) narrow way for walking/cycling, etc. (b) way in which sth moves. **path•way**, *n.* track for walking along.

pa•thet•ic [pə'θetɪk] *adj.* which makes you

feel pity or contempt. **pa•thet•i•cal•ly,** *adv.* in a pathetic way.

path•o•gen ['pæθədʒən] *n.* germ which causes a disease. **path•o•gen•ic,** *adj.* which causes a disease.

pa•thol•o•gy [pə'θɒlədʒɪ] *n.* study of disease. **path•o•log•i•cal** [pæθə'lɒdʒɪkl] *adj.* (a) referring to pathology. (b) caused by mental or physical disease. (c) unhealthy (interest). **pa•thol•o•gist** [pə'θɒlədʒɪst] *n.* doctor specializing in the study of disease; doctor who examines dead bodies to discover the cause of death.

pa•thos ['peɪθɒs] *n.* quality in sth which makes you feel pity.

pa•tience ['peɪʃns] *n.* (a) being patient. (b) card game for one person. **pa•tient.** 1. *adj.* (a) (person) who can wait for a long time/who remains calm/who doesn't lose his temper. (b) careful/painstaking. 2. *n.* person who is in a hospital or being treated by a doctor/dentist, etc. **pa•tient•ly,** *adv.* calmly.

pat•i•na ['pætɪnə] *n.* green sheen on old bronze objects; shine on old wooden furniture, etc.

pat•i•o ['pætɪəu] *n.* (*pl.* -os) paved area outside a house for sitting or eating.

pa•tis•se•rie [pə'tiːsərɪ] *n.* store selling cakes and pastries, esp. French cakes and pastries.

pat•ois ['pætwɑː] *n.* dialect spoken in a small area.

pa•tri•arch ['peɪtrɪɑːk] *n.* (a) bishop/high dignitary of an Eastern church. (b) respected old man. **pa•tri•ar•chal,** *adj.* referring to a patriarch.

pa•tri•cian [pə'trɪʃn] *adj. & n.* (referring to an) aristocrat.

pat•ri•cide ['pætrɪsaɪd] *n.* murder of your own father; person who kills his father.

pat•ri•mo•ny ['pætrɪmənɪ] *n.* inheritance/property which has been passed from father to son for generations.

pa•tri•ot ['peɪtrɪət] *n.* person who fights for/who is proud of his country. **pa•tri•ot•ic** [peɪtrɪ'ɒtɪk] *adj.* proud of your country; willing to fight for your country. **pa•tri•ot•i•cal•ly,** *adv.* in a patriotic way. **pa•tri•ot•ism** ['peɪtrɪətɪzəm] *n.* pride in your country.

pa•trol [pə'trəul] 1. *n.* (a) keeping guard by walking or driving up and down. (b) group of people keeping guard; **p. car** = police car which drives up and down the streets. (c) group of Boy Scouts or Girl Scouts. 2. *v.* (**patrolled**) to keep guard by walking or driving up and down. **pa•trol•man,** *n.* (*pl.* -men) police officer. **pa•trol wag•on,** *n.* police van used to transport prisoners.

pa•tron ['peɪtrən] *n.* (a) person who protects or supports s.o./sth; **p. saint** = saint who is believed to protect a special group of people. (b) regular customer (of a store); person who goes regularly to the theater. **pa•tron•age** ['pætrənɪdʒ] *n.* giving support/encouragement (to an artist, etc.). **pa•tron•ess,** *n.* woman patron. **pa•tron•ize** ['pætrənaɪz] *v.* (a) to support/to encourage (an artist, etc.). (b) to act in a condescending way to (s.o.). (c) to go regularly to (a store/theater). **pa•tron•iz•ing,** *adj.* condescending; (tone) which makes s.o. feel inferior.

pat•ro•nym•ic [pætrə'nɪmɪk] *n.* name which is derived from the name of a father.

pat•ten ['pætən] *n.* wooden clog with high sole and heel.

pat•ter ['pætə] 1. *n.* (a) soft repeated tapping noise. (b) rapid talk by a magician/salesman/trickster to distract attention from what he is really doing. 2. *v.* to make a soft repeated tapping noise.

pat•tern ['pætən] *n.* (a) model/example which you should copy; paper which shows how to cut out cloth to make a piece of clothing; **knitting p.** = instructions on how to knit sth. (b) design of repeated lines/pictures, etc. **pat•terned,** *adj.* with a repeated design.

pat•ty ['pætɪ] *n.* small round piece of food, as meat or candy; **hamburger p., peppermint p.**

pau•ci•ty ['pɔːsɪtɪ] *n.* (*formal*) small number/too little (of sth).

paunch [pɔːnʃ] *n.* (*pl.* -es) fat stomach.

pau•per ['pɔːpə] *n.* poor person.

pause [pɔːz] 1. *n.* short stop in work, etc. 2. *v.* to stop doing sth for a short time.

pave [peɪv] *v.* to cover (a road/path, etc.) with a hard surface; **to p. the way** = to prepare the way. **pave•ment,** *n.* (a) sidewalk. (b) hard road surface. **pav•ing stone,** *n.* large flat stone slab used for making paths/courtyards, etc.

pa•vil•ion [pə'vɪljən] *n.* (a) usu. open building in a park, public garden, etc. for an exhibition, entertainment, etc.

paw [pɔː] 1. *n.* (a) hairy foot of an animal with claws. (b) *inf.* hand. 2. *v.* to tap with a paw/hands, etc.; *inf.* to fondle.

æ back, ɑ: farm, ɒ: top, aɪ pipe, aʊ how, aɪə fire, aʊə flower, ɔ: bought, ɔɪ toy, e fed, eəhair, eɪ take, ə afraid, əʊ boat, əʊə lower, ɜ: word, i: heap, ɪ hit, ɪə hear, u: school, ʊ book, ʌ but, b back, d dog, ð then, dʒ just, f fog, g go, h hand, j yes, k catch, l last, m mix, n nut, ŋ sing, p penny, r round, s some, ʃ short, t too, tʃ chop, θ thing, v voice, w was, z zoo, ʒ treasure

pawl [pɔ:l] *n.* metal piece which catches in the teeth of a ratchet wheel.

pawn [pɔ:n] 1. *n.* (a) smallest piece on the chessboard. (b) person used by s.o. more powerful. (c) sth left in exchange for money which has been borrowed. 2. *v.* to leave (an object) in exchange for borrowing money (which you claim back when the money is repaid). **pawn•brok•er,** *n.* person who lends money in exchange for valuables left with him. **pawn•shop,** *n.* shop where goods can be pawned.

pay [peɪ] 1. *n.* wages/salary; **in the p. of** = paid by. 2. *v.* (**paid**) (a) to give money for sth. (b) to be worthwhile. (c) to suffer punishment **for.** (d) to make (a visit/a call). (e) to make/to show (attention, etc.). **pay•a•ble,** *adj.* which must be paid. **pay back,** *v.* (a) to return money to (s.o.). (b) to get your revenge on (s.o.). **pay•check,** *n.* salary payment. **pay•ee,** *n.* person who receives money. **pay•er,** *n.* person who pays money. **pay•load,** *n.* load carried by an aircraft or rocket. **pay•mas•ter,** *n.* officer who pays soldiers. **pay•ment,** *n.* giving money for sth. **pay off,** *v.* (a) to remove (a debt) by paying the money owed. (b) *inf.* to be successful. **pay•off,** *n. inf.* (a) reward. (b) final success. **pay•o•la,** *n.* bribery. **pay out,** *v.* (a) to give money to s.o. (b) to unroll a rope. **pay•roll,** *n.* list of people who receive wages. **pay up,** *v.* to pay what you owe.

Pb *symbol for* lead.

PC *abbrev. for* 1. ['pi:'si:] personal computer. 2. [pi:'si:] politically correct.

PCB [pi:si:'bi:] printed circuit board.

pea [pi:] *n.* climbing plant of which the round green seeds are eaten as vegetables; **sweet peas** = plant of the pea family grown for its scented flowers. **pea green,** *adj.* bright green. **pea jack•et,** *n.* double-breasted wool jacket, often worn by sailors.

peace [pi:s] *n.* (a) state of not being at war. (b) calm/quiet. **peace•a•ble,** *adj.* liking peace; not quarrelsome. **peace•a•bly,** *adv.* calmly/without quarreling. **peace div•i•dend,** *n.* extra public money available when defense spending is cut after a conflict/war, etc. **peace•ful,** *adj.* (a) calm. (b) liking peace; **p. coexistence** = living side by side without making war. **peace•ful•ly,** *adv.* (a) calmly. (b) without making war. **peace•ful•ness,** *n.* being peaceful. **peace•keep•ing,** *n.* maintaining of peace, esp. the enforcement of a cessation of hostilities by an international body, e.g. a UN peacekeeping force. **peace•mak•er,** *n.* person who tries to bring about peace.

peach [pi:tʃ] 1. *n.* (*pl.* **-es**) (a) sweet fruit, with a large stone and velvety skin; tree which bears peaches. (b) pinkish-yellow color. 2. *v. inf.* **to p. on s.o.** = to inform (the police) about s.o.

pea•cock ['pi:kɒk], **pea•hen** [pi:'hen] *n.* (a) large bird, of which the cock has a huge tail with brilliant blue and green feathers. (b) type of brown butterfly with round purple spots.

peak [pi:k] 1. *n.* (a) top of a mountain. (b) highest point; **p. period** = period of the day when most electricity is used/when most traffic is on the roads, etc. (c) front part of a cap which juts out. 2. *v.* to reach a high point. **peaked,** *adj.* (a) (cap) with a peak. (b) looking ill. **peak•y,** *adj.* peaked; sickly.

peal [pi:l] 1. *n.* (a) set of bells of different sizes; sound of bells ringing. (b) loud reverberating noise. 2. *v.* (*a*) to ring a peal of bells. (b) (*of thunder*) to roll/to make a loud noise.

pea•nut ['pi:nʌt] *n.* (a) nut which grows in the ground in pods like a pea; **p. butter** = paste made from crushed peanuts. (b) *inf.* **peanuts** = very little money.

pear ['peə] *n.* elongated fruit with one end fatter than the other; tree which bears pears. **pear-shaped,** *adj.* shaped like a pear.

pearl [pɜ:l] *n.* precious round white gem formed inside an oyster; **p. barley** = barley grains which have been rolled until they are shaped like pearls. **pearl div•er,** *n.* person who dives to the bottom of the sea to look for oysters with pearls in them. **pearl•y,** *adj.* shiny like a pearl.

peas•ant ['pezənt] *n.* farm laborer or small farmer living in a backward region. **peas•ant•ry,** *n.* (*no pl.*) peasants (seen as a class in society).

peat [pi:t] *n.* decayed vegetable matter cut out of a bog and used as fuel in or gardening. **peat•y,** *adj.* smelling/tasting like peat.

peb•ble ['pebl] *n.* small round stone. **peb•bly,** *adj.* covered with pebbles.

pe•can ['pi:kæn] *n.* nut from a tree which grows in the south United States.

pec•ca•dil•lo [pekə'dɪləu] *n.* (*pl.* -oes, -os) (*formal*) slight error/fault.

pec•ca•ry ['pekərɪ] *n.* wild South American pig.

peck [pek] 1. *n.* (a) bite with a bird's beak. (b) *inf.* little kiss. (c) (*old*) measurement of quantity of grain. 2. *v.* (a) to bite with a beak; **pecking order** = unwritten order of importance of people in a firm/office, etc. (b) *inf.* to give (s.o.) a little kiss.

pec•tin ['pektɪn] *n.* jellylike substance in fruit which helps jam to set hard.

pec•to•ral ['pektərəl] 1. *adj.* (*formal*) referring to the chest; **p. cross** = cross worn by a priest around the neck. 2. *n.* muscle in the chest.

pec•u•late ['pekjuleɪt] *v.* (*formal*) to embezzle

money. **pec•u•la•tion** [pekjʊ'leɪʃn] *n.* embezzlement.

pe•cu•liar [pɪ'kju:ljə] *adj.* (a) odd/strange. (b) belonging to one particular place or person. **pe•cu•li•ar•i•ty**, *n.* being peculiar; strange feature/detail which stands out. **pe•cu•liar•ly**, *adv.* oddly/strangely.

pe•cu•ni•ar•y [pɪ'kju:njərɪ] *adj.* referring to money.

ped•a•gog•i•cal [pedə'gɒdʒɪkl] *adj.* referring to teaching. **ped•a•gogue** ['pedəgɒg] *n.* pedantic person, esp. a teacher.

ped•al ['pedl] 1. *n.* lever worked by your foot. 2. *v.* (**pedaled, pedalled**) to make (a bicycle) go by pushing on the pedals.

ped•ant ['pedənt] *n.* pedantic person. **pe•dan•tic** [pɪ'dæntɪk] *adj.* paying too much attention to detail/showing off knowledge. **pe•dan•ti•cal•ly**, *adv.* in a pedantic way. **ped•ant•ry** ['pedəntrɪ] *n.* being pedantic.

ped•dle ['pedl] *v.* to go from house to house trying to sell sth. **ped•dler**, *n.* person who goes from house to house trying to sell sth.

ped•er•ast ['pedəræst] *n.* person who practices pederasty. **ped•er•as•ty**, *n.* homosexual relations with boys.

ped•es•tal ['pedɪstl] *n.* base (for a statue).

pe•des•tri•an [pə'destrɪən] 1. *n.* person who goes on foot; **p. crossing** = place where pedestrians can cross a road; **p. mall** = street or group of streets closed to traffic so that people can walk about freely. 2. *adj.* (a) referring to pedestrians. (b) heavy/unimaginative.

pe•di•a•tri•cian [pi:dɪə'trɪʃn] *n.* doctor who specializes in pediatrics. **pe•di•at•ric** [pi:dSIætrɪk] *adj.* referring to the medical care of children. **pe•di•at•rics** [pi:dɪ'ætrɪks] *n.* science of treatment of children's diseases.

ped•i•cure ['pedɪkjʊə] *n.* looking after the feet.

ped•i•gree ['pedɪgri:] *n.* table of ancestors of a person/animal; **p. animal** = animal with a certificate showing it is pure bred.

ped•i•ment ['pedɪmənt] *n.* triangular part at the top of the front of a classical building.

ped•lar ['pedlə] *n.* peddler.

pe•dom•e•ter [pe'dɒmɪtə] *n.* instrument which measures how far you have walked.

pe•dun•cle [pə'dʌŋkl] *n.* stalk of an inflorescence.

pee [pi:] 1. *n. inf.* (a) waste water from the body. (b) passing waste water from the body. 2. *v. inf.* to pass waste water from the body.

peek [pi:k] 1. *n. inf.* quick look. 2. *v. inf.* to look at sth quickly.

peel [pi:l] 1. *n.* outer skin of a fruit, etc. 2. *v.* (a) to take the outer skin off (a fruit/a vegetable). (b) to come off in layers. **peel•er**, *n.* special instrument for peeling vegetables. **peel•ings**, *n. pl.* bits of skin from vegetables. **peel off**, *v.* (a) (*of peel/paint*) to come off. (b) *inf.* to take off (clothes).

peep [pi:p] 1. *n.* (a) short/quick look. (b) cheep. 2. *v.* to look quickly and secretly. **peep•hole**, *n.* small hole in a door which you can look through to see who is outside.

peer ['pɪə] 1. *n.* (a) member of the nobility. (b) person of the same rank/class as another; **p. group** = group of people of equal (social) status. 2. *v.* to look at sth hard when you cannot see very well. **peer•age**, *n.* (*no pl.*) all nobles, taken as a group. **peer•ess**, *n.* woman peer. **peer•less**, *adj.* excellent/which has no equal.

peeved [pi:vd] *adj. inf.* annoyed/bothered. **peev•ish**, *adj.* bad-tempered/complaining. **peev•ish•ly**, *adv.* in a peevish way. **peev•ish•ness**, *n.* being peevish.

pee•wit ['pi:wɪt] *n.* lapwing.

peg [peg] 1. *n.* small wooden or metal stake/pin. 2. *v.* (**pegged**) (a) to attach with a peg. (b) to hold (prices, etc.) stable.

pe•jo•ra•tive [pə'dʒɒrətɪv] *adj.* disapproving/showing that you feel sth is bad.

Pe•king•ese, Pekinese [pɪkɪ'ni:z] *n.* breed of low flat-faced dogs.

pe•lag•ic [pə'lædʒɪk] *adj.* referring to the top and middle layers of the sea.

pel•ar•go•ni•um [pelɑː'gəʊnɪəm] *n.* flowering plant, the geranium.

pel•i•can ['pelɪkən] *n.* large white water bird, with a pouch under its beak in which it keeps the fish it has caught.

pel•let ['pelɪt] *n.* (a) small ball, as of medicine or food. (b) small lead ball, used in shotguns.

pel•li•cle ['pelɪkl] *n.* thin layer of skin.

pell-mell [pel'mel] *adv.* in disorder.

pel•lu•cid [pə'lu:sɪd] *adj.* very transparent.

pel•met ['pelmɪt] *n.* decorative strip of wood/cloth, etc., over a window which hides the curtain fittings.

pelt [pelt] 1. *n.* (a) skin of an animal with fur on it. (b) **at full p.** = going fast. 2. *v.* (a) **to p. s.o. with** = to fling things at s.o. (b) **the rain was pelting down** = pouring down.

pel•vis ['pelvɪs] *n.* (*pl.* **-es**) bones in the lower

æ back, ɑ: farm, ɒ: top, aɪ pipe, aʊ how, aɪə fire, aʊə flower, ɔ: bought, ɔɪ toy, e fed, eəhair, eɪ take, ə afraid, əʊ boat, əʊə lower, ɜ: word, i: heap, ɪ hit, ɪə hear, u: school, ʊ book, ʌ but, b back, d dog, ð then, dʒ just, f fog, g go, h hand, j yes, k catch, l last, m mix, n nut, ŋ sing, p penny, r round, s some, ʃ short, t too, tʃ chop, θ thing, v voice, w was, z zoo, ʒ treasure

part of the body forming the hips. **pel•vic**, *adj*. referring to the pelvis.

pem•mi•can ['pemɪkən] *n*. dried meat, used by explorers as rations.

pen [pen] 1. *n*. (a) small fenced area for sheep. (b) writing instrument using ink; **p. name** = name used by a writer which is not his own; **p. pal** = person whom you have never met, but with whom you exchange letters. (c) female swan. 2. *v*. (**penned**) (a) to enclose (sheep) in a pen. (b) to write with a pen.

pe•nal ['piːnl] *adj*. referring to a legal punishment; **p. system** = system of punishments relating to various crimes. **pe•nal•i•za•tion** [pɪnəlaɪ'zeɪʃn] *n*. act of penalizing. **pe•nal•ize**, *v*. to punish. **pen•al•ty** ['penəltɪ] *n*. (a) punishment. (b) punishment in sport. (c) disadvantages.

pen•ance ['penəns] *n*. punishment which a person accepts to make amends for a sin.

pence [pens] *n*. *Brit. see* **pen•ny.**

pen•chant ['pɑːnʃɑːŋ] *n*. liking (for sth).

pen•cil ['pensl] 1. *n*. instrument for writing, made of wood with a graphite center. 2. *v*. (**penciled, pencilled**) to write with a pencil. **pen•cil sharp•en•er**, *n*. instrument for sharpening pencils.

pend•ant ['pendənt] *n*. ornament which hangs from a chain worn around the neck. **pend•ent**, *adj*. hanging.

pend•ing ['pendɪŋ] *adj. & prep*. awaiting; until.

pen•du•lum ['pendjuləm] *n*. weight on the end of a rod or chain which swings from side to side, such as that which makes a clock work. **pen•du•lous**, *adj*. which hangs down heavily.

pen•e•trate ['penɪtreɪt] *v*. go into/through. **pen•e•tra•bil•i•ty** [penɪtrə'bɪlɪtɪ] *n*. ability to be penetrated. **pen•e•tra•ble**, *adj*. which can be penetrated. **pen•e•trat•ing**, *adj*. deep/searching (look); very profound (questions). **pen•e•tra•tion** [penɪ'treɪʃn] *n*. (a) getting into sth. (b) deep understanding.

pen•guin ['peŋgwɪn] *n*. Antarctic bird which swims well but cannot fly.

pen•i•cil•lin [penɪ'sɪlɪn] *n*. substance made from a mold, used to kill bacteria.

pen•in•su•la [pə'nɪnsjulə] *n*. large piece of land jutting into the sea. **pen•in•su•lar**, *adj*. referring to a peninsula.

pe•nis ['piːnɪs] *n*. (*pl*. -es) part of the male body used for urinating and for sexual intercourse.

pen•i•tent ['penɪtənt] *adj. & n*. (person) who is sorry for having done sth wrong. **pen•i•tence**, *n*. being penitent. **pen•i•ten•tial** [penɪ'tenʃl] *adj*. referring to penance. **pen•i•ten•tia•ry** [penɪ'tenʃərɪ] *n*. prison.

pen•knife ['pennaɪf] *n*. (*pl*. -knives [-naɪvz]) small folding pocket knife.

pen•nant ['penənt] *n*. long thin flag.

pen•non ['penən] *n*. small forked flag.

pen•ny ['penɪ] *n*. (*pl*. pennies; *Brit*. pennies or pence) small coin (the smallest unit in some currencies); (*in Britain*) one hundredth part of a pound. **pen•ni•less**, *adj*. with no money.

pe•nol•o•gy [piː'nɒlədʒɪ] *n*. study of punishment and crime.

pen•sion ['penʃn] 1. *n*. money paid regularly to s.o. who has retired from work/to a widow, etc. 2. *v*. **to p. s.o. off** = to make s.o. stop working and live on a pension. **pen•sion•a•ble**, *adj*. (person) who has the right to have a pension; (job) which gives you the right to have a pension; (age) at which a pension begins to be paid. **pen•sion•er**, *n*. person who gets a pension.

pen•sive ['pensɪv] *adj*. thoughtful. **pen•sive•ly**, *adv*. thoughtfully. **pen•sive•ness**, *n*. being pensive.

pent [pent] *adj*. **pent-up emotions** = emotions which are repressed.

pen•ta•gon ['pentəgən] *n*. (a) geometrical figure with five sides. (b) **the Pentagon** = the U.S. Defense Department. **pen•tag•o•nal** [pen'tægənl] *adj*. five-sided.

pen•tam•e•ter [pen'tæmitə] *n*. line of poetry with five beats.

pen•tath•lon [pen'tæθlən] *n*. athletic competition where competitors have to compete in five different sports.

pent•house ['penthaus] *n*. apartment on the top of a high building.

pe•nul•ti•mate [pe'nʌltɪmət] *adj*. next to last.

pe•num•bra [pe'nʌmbrə] *n*. edge of a shadow where only part of the light is cut off.

pen•u•ry ['penjurɪ] *n*. (*formal*) (a) extreme poverty. (b) great lack. **pe•nu•ri•ous** [pɪ'njuərɪəs] *adj*. very poor.

pe•o•ny ['pɪənɪ] *n*. perennial summer flower with large scented flowerheads.

peo•ple ['piːpl] 1. *n*. (a) (*pl*.) persons; human beings. (b) citizens (of a town or country). 2. *v*. to fill with people.

pep [pep] 1. *n*. *inf*. vigor; **p. talk** = talk designed to encourage people to work hard/to win a match, etc. 2. *v*. *inf*. **to p. up** = to make livelier and more active.

pep•per ['pepə] 1. *n*. (a) sharp spice used in cooking. (b) green or red fruit used as a vegetable. 2. *v*. (**with**) to sprinkle/to throw (things) at. **pep•per•corn**, *n*. dried seed of pepper. **pep•per•mill**, *n*. small grinder used for grinding peppercorns. **pep•per•mint,** *n.* (a) common plant with a sharp mint flavor. (b) candy flavored with peppermint. **pep•per•y,** *adj.* (a) (soup, etc.) with too much pepper in it. (b) very easily angered.

pep•tic ['peptɪk] *adj.* referring to the digestive system; **p. ulcer** = ulcer in the stomach.

per [pɜː] *prep.* (a) out of; **ten p. thousand.** (b) in; **sixty miles p. hour.** (c) for; **p. annum** = in each year; **p. capita** = for each person.

per•am•bu•late [pəˈræmbjʊleɪt] *v.* (*formal*) to walk about slowly. **per•am•bu•la•tion,** *n.* slow walk. **per•am•bu•la•tor,** *n.* (*formal*) baby carriage.

per•ceive [pəˈsiːv] *v.* to notice through the senses; to become aware of. **per•cep•ti•ble** [pəˈseptɪbl] *adj.* which can be seen/heard/smelled, etc. **per•cep•ti•bly,** *adv.* noticeably. **per•cep•tion** [pəˈsepʃn] *n.* ability to notice. **per•cep•tive,** *adj.* acute; able to notice quickly. **per•cep•tive•ly,** *adv.* in a perceptive way. **per•cep•tive•ness, perceptivity,** *n.* being perceptive.

per•cent [pəˈsent] *adv. & n.* out of each hundred. **per•cent•age** [pəˈsentɪdʒ] *n.* proportion shown as part of a hundred. **per•cen•tile** [pəˈsentaɪl] *n.* one of a hundred equal groups into which a large number can be divided.

perch [pɜːtʃ] 1. *n.* (a) (*pl.* -es) branch/ledge on which a bird can sit. (b) (*pl.* **perch**) type of freshwater fish. 2. *v.* to sit on a perch; to be set in a high place.

per•chance [pəˈtʃɑːns] *adv.* (*old*) perhaps.

per•cip•i•ent [pəˈsɪpɪənt] *adj.* perceptive/able to notice quickly. **per•cip•i•ence,** *n.* being percipient.

per•co•late ['pɜːkəleɪt] *v.* to filter (through). **per•co•la•tion** [pɜːkəˈleɪʃn] *n.* filtering. **per•co•la•tor,** *n.* coffee pot where the water boils up and filters through coffee.

per•cus•sion [pəˈkʌʃn] *n.* action of hitting together; **p. instruments** = musical instruments which are hit (drums/triangles, etc.); **p. cap** = piece of paper with a small amount of explosive powder which explodes when hit.

per•e•gri•na•tions [perɪɡrɪˈneɪʃnz] *n. pl.* (*formal*) traveling/wandering.

per•e•grine ['perɪɡrɪn] *n.* type of falcon.

per•emp•to•ry [pəˈremptərɪ] *adj.* abrupt (tone)/curt (refusal). **per•emp•to•ri•ly,** *adv.* in a peremptory way.

per•en•ni•al [pəˈrenɪəl] 1. *adj.* which continues from year to year. 2. *n.* plant which flowers every year without needing to be sown again. **per•en•ni•al•ly,** *adv.* always.

pe•re•stroi•ka [perɪˈstrɔɪkə] *n.* reconstruction (of the Russian economy).

per•fect 1. *adj.* ['pɜːfɪkt] (a) without any mistakes/flaws. (b) total (stranger). (c) **p. (tense)** = past tense of a verb which shows that the action has been completed. 2. *v.* [pəˈfekt] to make perfect. **per•fec•tion** [pəˈfekʃn] *n.* state of being perfect; **to p.** = perfectly. **per•fec•tion•ist,** *n.* person who insists that perfection is possible/that everything has to be perfect. **per•fect•ly** ['pɜːfɪktlɪ] *adv.* completely.

per•fi•dy ['pɜːfɪdɪ] *n.* (*formal*) treachery. **per•fid•i•ous** [pəˈfɪdɪəs] *adj.* (*formal*) treacherous.

per•fo•rate ['pɜːfəreɪt] *v.* to make a hole in/to pierce. **per•fo•ra•tion** [pɜːfəˈreɪʃn] *n.* (a) action of making a hole. (b) small hole.

per•force [pəˈfɔːs] *adv.* (*old*) because it is necessary.

per•form [pəˈfɔːm] *v.* (a) to carry out an action. (b) to act in public. **per•for•mance,** *n.* (a) working of a machine; action of a sportsman. (b) public show. **per•form•er,** *n.* person who gives a public show.

per•fume 1. *n.* ['pɜːfjuːm] (a) pleasant smell. (b) liquid scent. 2. *v.* [pəˈfjuːm] (a) to give a pleasant smell to (sth). (b) to pour perfume on. **per•fum•er•y,** *n.* shop which makes and sells perfumes.

per•func•to•ry [pəˈfʌŋktərɪ] *adj.* rapid and superficial. **per•func•to•ri•ly,** *adv.* in a perfunctory way.

per•go•la ['pɜːɡələ] *n.* framework of wood over which climbing plants can be trained.

per•haps [pəˈhæps] *adv.* possibly/maybe.

per•i•car•di•um [perɪˈkɑːdɪəm] *n.* membrane round the heart. **per•i•car•di•tis,** *n.* inflammation of the pericardium.

per•i•he•li•on [perɪˈhiːlɪɒn] *n.* point where a planet is nearest to the sun.

per•il ['perəl] *n.* great danger. **per•il•ous,** *adj.* very dangerous. **per•il•ous•ly,** *adv.* in a perilous way.

pe•rim•e•ter [pəˈrɪmɪtə] *n.* outside line around an enclosed area.

pe•ri•od ['pɪərɪəd] *n.* (a) length of time; **p. furniture** = antique furniture from a certain time; **p. piece** = piece of antique furniture, etc. (b)

æ back, ɑː farm, ɒ top, aɪ pipe, aʊ how, aɪə fire, aʊə flower, ɔː bought, ɔɪ toy, e fed, eəhair, eɪ take, ə afraid, əʊ boat, əʊə lower, ɜː word, iː heap, ɪ hit, ɪə hear, uː school, ʊ book, ʌ but, b back, d dog, ð then, dʒ just, f fog, g go, h hand, j yes, k catch, l last, m mix, n nut, ŋ sing, p penny, r round, s some, ʃ short, t too, tʃ chop, θ thing, v voice, w was, z zoo, ʒ treasure

class time in a school. (c) punctuation mark (.) used in writing to mark the end of a sentence. (d) regular monthly flow of blood from a woman's womb. **pe•ri•od•ic** [piːrɪ'ɒdɪk] *adj.* repeated after a regular length of time; **p. table** = list of chemical elements arranged in order of their atomic numbers. **pe•ri•od•i•cal.** 1. *adj.* periodic; repeated after a regular length of time. 2. *n.* magazine which appears regularly. **pe•ri•od•i•cal•ly,** *adv.* from time to time.

per•i•pa•tet•ic [perɪpə'tetɪk] *adj.* (person) who wanders from place to place.

pe•riph•er•y [pə'rɪfərɪ] *n.* edge. **pe•riph•er•al,** 1. *adj.* minor/not very important. 2. *n.* **peripherals** = items of hardware (such as printers) which are attached to a computer.

pe•riph•ra•sis [pə'rɪfrəsɪs] *n.* (*pl.* **-ses**) way of saying sth which is not straightforward. **per•i•phras•tic** [perɪ'fræstɪk] *adj.* not straightforward (expression).

per•i•scope ['perɪskəʊp] *n.* long tube with mirrors which allows s.o. in a submerged submarine to look above the surface of the water.

per•ish ['perɪʃ] *v.* (a) (*formal*) to die. (b) to rot. **per•ish•a•ble,** *adj.* (food) which can go bad easily; **perishables** = perishable food.

per•i•stal•sis [perɪ'stælsɪs] *n.* regular movement of the muscles in the intestine.

per•i•to•ni•tis [perɪtə'naɪtɪs] *n.* inflammation of the lining of the abdomen.

per•i•wig ['perɪwɪg] *n.* large wig, worn in the 17th and 18th centuries.

per•i•win•kle ['perɪwɪŋkl] *n.* (a) small creeping plant with blue flowers. (b) edible snail which lives in salt water.

per•jure ['pɜːdʒə] *v.* **to p. yourself** = to tell lies in a court of law when you have sworn to tell the truth. **per•jur•er,** *n.* person who has committed perjury. **per•ju•ry,** *n.* crime of perjuring yourself.

perk [pɜːk] 1. *v.* **to p. up** = to become more alert/more interested. 2. *n. inf.* valuable extras which you are given by your employer in addition to your salary. **perk•y,** *adj. inf.* lively/interested.

perm [pɜːm] 1. *n. inf.* curls or a wave put into your hair artificially. 2. *v. inf.* to put a wave or curl into (s.o.'s hair).

per•ma•cul•ture ['pɜːməkʌltʃə] *n.* agriculture/power generation, etc. that does not deplete natural resources or cause pollution.

per•ma•frost ['pɜːməfrɒst] *n.* (*no pl.*) soil in the Arctic which remains permanently frozen, even in summer.

per•ma•nent ['pɜːmənənt] *adj.* lasting forever/supposed to last for ever. **per•ma•nence, permanency,** *n.* state of being permanent. **per•ma•nent•ly,** *adv.* always.

per•man•ga•nate [pə'mæŋgəneɪt] *n.* salt containing manganese; **p. of potash** = dark purple crystals used for disinfecting.

per•me•ate ['pɜːmɪeɪt] *v.* to filter; to spread right through. **per•me•a•bil•i•ty** [pɜːmɪə'bɪlɪtɪ] *n.* being permeable. **per•me•a•ble,** *adj.* which lets liquid pass through. **per•me•a•tion** [pəːmɪ'eɪʃn] *n.* act of permeating.

per•mis•si•ble [pə'mɪsəbl] *adj.* which can be allowed. **per•mis•sion** [pə'mɪʃn] *n.* freedom which you are given to do sth. **per•mis•sive** [pə'mɪsɪv] *adj.* free; allowing many things to be done which formerly were not allowed. **per•mis•sive•ness,** *n.* being permissive.

per•mit 1. *n.* ['pɜːmɪt] paper which allows you to do sth. 2. *v.* [pə'mɪt] (**permitted**) to allow.

per•mu•ta•tion [pəːmjuː'teɪʃn] *n.* grouping of several items together in varied combinations; combination of various items in a different order.

per•ni•cious [pə'nɪʃəs] *adj.* harmful/evil.

per•nick•et•y [pə'nɪkətɪ] *adj. inf.* very fussy.

per•o•ra•tion [perə'reɪʃn] *n.* (*formal*) very long speech.

per•ox•ide [pə'rɒksaɪd] *n.* chemical used for bleaching hair or killing germs.

per•pen•dic•u•lar [pɜːpən'dɪkjʊlə] *adj. & n.* (line) standing vertically/at right angles to a base; style of late medieval English church architecture. **per•pen•dic•u•lar•ly,** *adv.* in a perpendicular way.

per•pe•trate ['pɜːpɪtreɪt] *v.* (*formal*) to commit (a crime). **per•pe•tra•tion** [pəːpɪ'treɪʃn] *n.* act of perpetrating. **per•pe•tra•tor,** *n.* person who commits (a crime).

per•pet•u•al [pə'petjʊəl] *adj.* continuous/without any end. **per•pet•u•al•ly,** *adv.* always. **per•pet•u•ate,** *v.* to make (sth) continue forever. **per•pe•tu•i•ty** [pəːpɪ'tjuːɪtɪ] *n.* (*formal*) **in p.** = forever/without any end.

per•plex [pə'pleks] *v.* to confuse/to puzzle. **per•plex•i•ty,** *n.* bewilderment/puzzled state.

per•qui•site ['pɜːkwɪzɪt] *n.* (*formal*) valuable extra which is given to you by your employer in addition to your salary.

per•ry ['perɪ] *n.* alcoholic drink made from fermented pear juice.

per se [pɜː'seɪ] *adv.* in itself.

per•se•cute ['pɜːsɪkjuːt] *v.* to torment/to treat cruelly. **per•se•cu•tion** [pɜːsɪ'kjuːʃn] *n.* relentless killing (because of religious beliefs); **p. complex** = mental disease where you feel that everyone is persecuting you. **per•se•cu•tor** ['pɜːsɪkjuːtə] *n.* person who persecutes.

per•se•vere [pɜːsɪ'vɪə] *v.* (**with/in**) to continue doing sth (in spite of obstacles). **per•se•ver•ance,** *n.* act of persevering.

Per•sian ['pɜːʃn] 1. *adj.* referring to Persia. 2. *n.* (a) person from Persia. (b) cat with long silky fur.

per•si•flage [pɜːsɪ'flɑːʒ] *n.* (*formal*) frivolous talk.

per•sist [pə'sɪst] *v.* (**in**) to continue doing sth (in spite of obstacles); to continue to exist. **per•sist•ence,** *n.* obstinacy; refusal to stop doing sth. **per•sist•ent,** *adj.* continual. **per•sist•ent•ly,** *adv.* in a persistent way. **per•sist•ent veg•e•ta•tive state,** *n.* irreversible medical condition, caused by brain damage, in which consciousness is absent.

per•son ['pɜːsn] *n.* (a) human being; **she appeared in p.** = appeared herself. (b) (*in grammar*) one of the three forms of verbs or pronouns which indicate who the speaker is; **first p.** = I or we; **second p.** = you; **third p.** = he, she, it, they. **per•so•na** [pɜː'səʊnə] *n.* a person's character as seen by others. **per•son•a•ble,** *adj.* attractive/good-looking/having a pleasant character. **per•son•age,** *n.* important person. **per•son•al,** *adj.* (a) referring to a person; (letter) addressed so that you and no one else may open it; **p. computer** = small computer used by a person at home; **p. organizer** (= electronic organizer) = computer used as a diary that is small enough to carry in a pocket. (b) rude (remarks). (c) (*in grammar*) **p. pronoun** = pronoun which refers to s.o., such as "I", "he", "she", etc. **per•son•al•i•ty** [pɜːsə'nælɪtɪ] *n.* (a) character. (b) famous person; **p. cult** = publicity given to a political leader or other famous person, making him into a kind of god. **per•son•al•ized,** *adj.* with your name or initials printed on it. **per•son•al•ly,** *adv.* (a) from your own point of view. (b) in person. (c) **don't take it p.** = don't think it was meant to criticize you. **per•so•na non gra•ta** [pɜː-'səʊnənɒn'grɑːtə] *n.* person (esp. a diplomat) who is not acceptable to a foreign country. **per•son•i•fi•ca•tion** [pəsɒnɪfɪ'keɪʃn] *n.* good example of an abstract quality in a person. **per•son•i•fy** [pə'sɒnɪfaɪ] *v.* to be a good example of. **per•son•nel** [pɜːsə'nel] *n.* staff/people employed by a company; **p. manager** = manager who looks after

pay/sick leave/administration, etc., for all the staff.

per•spec•tive [pə'spektɪv] *n.* (a) (*in art*) way of drawing objects/scenes, so that they appear to have depth or distance; **to put things in p.** = to show things in an objective way. (b) way of looking at sth.

Per•spex ['pɜːspeks] *n.* trademark for a type of tough clear plastic.

per•spi•ca•cious [pɜːspɪ'keɪʃəs] *adj.* (person) who understands clearly. **per•spi•cac•i•ty** [pɜːspɪ'kæsɪtɪ] *n.* clearness of understanding.

per•spi•cu•i•ty [pɜːspɪ'kjuːɪtɪ] *n.* clearness of expression. **per•spic•u•ous** [pə'spɪkjuəs] *adj.* clearly expressed.

per•spire [pə'spaɪə] *v.* to sweat. **per•spi•ra•tion** [pɜːspə'reɪʃn] *n.* sweat.

per•suade [pə'sweɪd] *v.* to get s.o. to do what you want by explaining or pleading. **per•sua•sion** [pə'sweɪʒn] *n.* (a) act of persuading. (b) firm (usu. religious) belief. **per•sua•sive** [pə'sweɪzɪv] *adj.* which persuades. **per•sua•sive•ly,** *adv.* in a persuasive way. **per•sua•sive•ness,** *n.* being persuasive.

pert [pɜːt] *adj.* lively; spirited.

per•tain [pə'teɪn] *v.* (*formal*) to be relevant.

per•ti•na•cious [pɜːtɪ'neɪʃəs] *adj.* obstinate. **per•ti•nac•i•ty** [pɜːtɪ'næsɪtɪ] *n.* obstinateness/stubbornness.

per•ti•nent ['pɜːtɪnənt] *adj.* relevant; to the point. **per•ti•nence,** *n.* being pertinent. **per•ti•nent•ly,** *adv.* in a pertinent way.

per•turb [pə'tɜːb] *v.* to make (s.o.) anxious. **per•tur•ba•tion** [pɜːtə'beɪʃn] *n.* anxiety/bother.

pe•ruse [pə'ruːz] *v.* (*formal*) to read carefully. **pe•rus•al,** *n.* reading.

Pe•ru•vi•an [pə'ruːvɪən] 1. *adj.* referring to Peru. 2. *n.* person from Peru.

per•vade [pə'veɪd] *v.* to spread everywhere. **per•va•sive** [pə'veɪsɪv] *adj.* penetrating. **per•va•sive•ness,** *n.* penetrating everywhere.

per•verse [pə'vɜːs] *adj.* obstinately awkward; continuing to do sth even if it is wrong. **per•verse•ly,** *adv.* in an obstinate way. **per•verse•ness,** *n.* contrariness. **per•ver•sion** [pə'vɜːʃn] *n.* corruption (of s.o. to do sth evil). **per•ver•si•ty,** *n.* being perverse. **per•vert.** 1. *n.* ['pɜːvɜːt] person who commits unnatural sexual acts. 2. *v.* [pə'vɜːt]

(a) to corrupt (s.o.) to do evil. (b) to misinterpret; distort the meaning of.

per•vi•ous ['pɜːvɪəs] *adj.* (membrane) which allows liquid to pass through.

pe•se•ta [pe'seɪtə] *n.* unit of currency used in Spain.

pe•so ['peɪzəʊ] *n.* unit of currency used in many S. American countries.

pes•sa•ry ['pesərɪ] *n.* contraceptive device placed in the vagina.

pes•si•mism ['pesɪmɪzəm] *n.* belief that only bad things will happen. **pes•si•mist** ['pesɪmɪst] *n.* pessimistic person. **pes•si•mis•tic** [pesɪ'mɪstɪk] *adj.* gloomy/believing that only bad things will happen. **pes•si•mis•ti•cal•ly**, *adv.* gloomily.

pest [pest] *n.* (a) troublesome plant, animal, or often an insect. (b) *inf.* person who annoys. **pes•ter**, *v.* to bother (s.o.). **pes•ti•cide** ['pestɪsaɪd] *n.* poison to kill pests.

pes•ti•lence ['pestɪləns] *n.* (*formal*) plague/disease. **pes•ti•len•tial** [pestɪ'lenʃl] *adj.* like a plague/very unpleasant.

pes•tle ['pesl] *n.* round-headed heavy tool for crushing things in a bowl.

pet [pet] 1. *n.* animal kept in the home to give pleasure. 2. *adj.* (a) favorite; **p. name** = special name given to s.o. you are fond of. (b) tame (animal). 3. *v.* (**petted**) to caress/to fondle.

pet•al ['petl] *n.* one of several colorful leaflike parts of a flower.

pe•tard [pə'tɑːd] *n.* (*formal*) **to be hoist with/by your own p.** = to be caught in a trap which you have set for s.o. else.

pe•ter ['piːtə] *v.* **to p. out** = to come to an end/to fade away.

pe•tite [pə'tiːt] *adj.* (*of a woman*) small and dainty.

pe•tit four [pətɪ'fʊə] *n.* small fancy cake or biscuit eaten at parties.

pe•ti•tion [pə'tɪʃn] 1. *n.* (a) official request (often signed by many people). (b) legal request. 2. *v.* to ask (s.o.) for sth/to make an official request. **pe•ti•tion•er**, *n.* person who makes a petition.

pet•rel ['petrəl] *n.* sea bird which flies long distances.

pet•ri•fy ['petrɪfaɪ] *v.* (a) to turn to stone. (b) to strike (s.o.) still with fear. **pet•ri•fac•tion, petrification**, *n.* act of petrifying.

pet•ro•chem•i•cal [petrəʊ'kemɪkl] *adj. & n.* (chemical) produced from petroleum or natural gas.

pet•ro•dol•lar [petrəʊ'dɒlə] *n.* dollar which is earned by a country selling oil.

pet•rol ['petrəl] *n. Brit.* gasoline. **pe•tro•le•um** [pə'trəʊlɪəm] *n.* raw mineral

oil (from the earth); **p. products** = substances (like gasoline/plastics, etc.) which are made from petroleum. **pe•trol•o•gy**, *n.* study of rocks.

pet•ti•coat ['petɪkəʊt] *n.* piece of women's underwear/light skirt worn under another skirt.

pet•ti•fog•ging ['petɪfɒgɪŋ] *adj.* (a) dealing with small useless details. (b) dishonest (lawyer).

pet•ty ['petɪ] *adj.* (a) insignificant/unimportant; **p. cash** = small amounts of cash (in an office); **p. officer** = non-commissioned officer in the U.S. Navy. (b) with a narrow point of view. **pet•ti•ness**, *n.* (a) unimportance. (b) narrowness of outlook.

pet•u•lant ['petjʊlənt] *adj.* irritable/bad-tempered. **pet•u•lance**, *n.* irritability. **pet•u•lant•ly**, *adv.* in a petulant way.

pe•tu•nia [pɪ'tjuːnɪə] *n.* common summer garden flower.

pew [pjuː] *n.* long bench seat in a church; *inf.* **take a p.** = sit down.

pew•ter ['pjuːtə] *n.* alloy, usu. a mixture of tin and lead, used for making mugs/plates, etc.

pH [piː'eɪtʃ] *n.* **pH factor** = measurement of how much acidity or alkalinity there is (in the soil, etc.).

pha•lanx ['fælæŋks] *n.* (a) tight mass of people (esp. marching forward). (b) bone in a finger or toe.

phal•lus ['fæləs] *n.* (*pl.* -es) (*formal*) penis in erection. **phal•lic**, *adj.* referring to a phallus; **p. symbol** = thing which resembles a penis, and is taken to symbolize male sex.

phan•tasm ['fæntæzəm] *n.* seeing sth in the imagination/seeing ghosts. **phan•tas•ma•go•ri•a** [fæntæzmə'gɒrɪə] *n.* mass of ghostly shapes.

phan•tom ['fæntəm] *n.* ghost.

phar•i•sa•ic(al) [færɪ'seɪɪk(l)] *adj.* self-righteously good; hypocritical.

phar•ma•ceu•ti•cal [fɑːmə'sjuːtɪkl] *adj.* referring to medicines. **phar•ma•cist** ['fɑːməsɪst] *n.* person who makes and sells medicines. **phar•ma•col•o•gy** [fɑːmə-'kɒlədʒɪ] *n.* study of medicines. **phar•ma•co•pe•ia, pharmacopoeia** [fɑːməkə'piːə] *n.* collection of drugs; book which lists drugs. **phar•ma•cy**, *n.* study of medicines; place which makes and sells medicines.

phar•ynx ['færɪŋks] *n.* (*pl.* -es) passage at the back of the nose leading to the esophagus. **phar•yn•gi•tis** [færɪn'dʒaɪtɪs] *n.* inflammation of the pharynx.

phase [feɪz] 1. *n.* period; stage in development of sth. 2. *v.* **to p. in/out** = to introduce/to remove gradually.

pheas•ant ['fezənt] *n.* large bright-colored bird with a long tail, shot for sport and food.

phe•no•bar•bi•tal [fi:nəʊ'bɑ:bɪtəʊn] *n.* drug which makes the patient sleep.

phe•nol ['fi:nɒl] *n.* carbon derivative, used in medicine.

phe•nom•e•non [fe'nɒmɪnɒn] *n.* (*pl.* **-mena**) thing which happens naturally; esp. remarkable thing/happening. **phe•nom•e•nal,** *adj.* remarkable. **phe•nom•e•nal•ly,** *adv.* remarkably.

phi•al ['faɪl] *n.* (*formal*) small bottle.

phi•lan•der•er [fɪ'lændərə] *n.* man who flirts with women.

phi•lan•thro•py [fɪ'lænθrəpɪ] *n.* love of/caring for human beings, shown esp. by giving money to charity. **phil•an•throp•ic** [fɪlən'θrɒpɪk] *adj.* kind (towards human beings). **phi•lan•thro•pist** [fɪ'lænθrəpɪst] *n.* person who is philanthropic.

phi•lat•e•ly [fɪ'lætəlɪ] *n.* stamp collecting. **phil•a•tel•ic** [fɪlə'telɪk] *adj.* referring to stamp collecting. **phi•lat•e•list,** *n.* person who studies or collects stamps.

-phile [faɪl] *suffix meaning* (person) who likes; **Francophile** = person who likes the French.

phil•har•mon•ic [fɪlɑ:'mɒnɪk] *adj.* liking music (used in names of orchestras/concert halls, etc.).

phi•lis•tine ['fɪlɪstaɪn] *adj. & n.* (person) who is unsympathetic to the arts.

phil•o•den•dron [fɪlə'dendrən] *n.* tropical climbing plant, often used as a house plant.

phi•lol•o•gy [fɪ'lɒlədʒɪ] *n.* study of (the history of) language. **phil•o•log•i•cal** [fɪlə-'lɒdʒɪkl] *adj.* referring to philology. **phi•lol•o•gist** [fɪ'lɒlədʒɪst] *n.* expert in philology.

phi•los•o•phy [fɪ'lɒsəfɪ] *n.* study of the meaning of human existence; study of the methods and limits of human knowledge; general way of thinking. **phi•los•o•pher,** *n.* person who studies the meaning of human existence. **phil•o•soph•i•cal** [fɪlə'sɒfɪkl] *adj.* (a) thoughtful; calm. (b) referring to philosophy. **phil•o•soph•i•cal•ly,** *adv.* thoughtfully; calmly. **phi•los•o•phize,** *v.* to think seriously (like a philosopher).

phil•ter ['fɪltə] *n.* (*old*) magic potion to make s.o. fall in love.

phle•bi•tis [flɪ'baɪtɪs] *n.* inflammation of a vein.

phlegm [flem] *n.* (a) slimy substance in the throat, etc., when you have a cold. (b) calmness. **phleg•mat•ic** [fleg'mætɪk] *adj.* calm/not easily annoyed. **phleg•mat•i•cal•ly,** *adv.* in a phlegmatic way.

phlox [flɒks] *n.* (*pl.* **phlox**) common perennial flower.

-phobe [fəʊb] *suffix meaning* (person) who does not like; **xenophobe** = person who dislikes foreigners.

pho•bi•a ['fəʊbɪə] *n.* abnormal terror/hatred of something.

phoe•nix ['fi:nɪks] *n.* mythical bird, said to die by burning and reappear from its ashes.

phone [fəʊn] 1. *n.* telephone. 2. *v.* to call (s.o.) by telephone. **phone book,** *n.* book which lists people's names, addresses and phone numbers. **phone booth,** *n.* small booth containing a public telephone.

pho•net•ic [fə'netɪk] 1. *adj.* referring to spoken sounds. 2. *n. pl.* **phonetics** = (i) study of sounds of a language; (ii) written signs which indicate sounds. **pho•net•i•cal•ly,** *adv.* using phonetics; (language spoken) in a way which closely follows the written letters. **pho•ne•ti•cian** [fəʊnə'tɪʃn] *n.* person who studies phonetics. **phon•ics** ['fɒnɪks] *n.* method of teaching reading, using letters as guides to pronunciation. **pho•nol•o•gy** [fə-'nɒlədʒi] *n.* study of sounds of speech.

pho•n(e)y ['fəʊnɪ] 1. *adj.* (**-ier, -iest**) *inf.* false. 2. *n. inf.* person who pretends to be richer/more famous, etc., than he really is.

pho•no•graph ['fəʊnəgrɑːf] *n.* machine on which records are played.

phos•phate ['fɒsfeɪt] *n.* chemical compound containing phosphorus, often used as a fertilizer.

phos•pho•res•cence [fɒsfə'resns] *n.* ability to shine in the dark after being exposed to light. **phos•pho•res•cent,** *adj.* which shines in the dark after being exposed to light. **phos•pho•rus** ['fɒsfərəs] *n.* (*element:* P) poisonous yellow substance which shines in the dark.

pho•to ['fəʊtəʊ] 1. *n.* (*pl.* **-os**) *inf.* photograph. 2. **photo-** *prefix meaning* (i) light; (ii) photograph. **pho•to•chem•i•cal,** *adj.* (chemical reaction) which is caused by light. **pho•to•cop•y** ['fəʊtəʊkɒpɪ] 1. *n.* copy (of a document) made by photographing it. 2. *v.* to copy (sth) photographically and make a print of it. **pho•to•cop•i•er,** *n.* machine which

æ back, ɑ: farm, ɒ: top, aɪ pipe, aʊ how, aɪe fire, aʊə flower, ɔ: bought, ɔɪ toy, e fed, eəhair, eɪ take, ə afraid, əʊ boat, əʊə lower, v: word, i: heap, ɪ hit, ɪə hear, u: school, ʊ book, ʌ but, b back, d dog, ð then, dʒ just, f fog, g go, h hand, j yes, k catch, l last, m mix, n nut, ŋ sing, p penny, r round, s some, ʃ short, t too, tʃ chop, θ thing, v voice, w was, z zoo, ʒ treasure

takes photocopies. **pho•to•e•lec•tric** [fəʊtəʊɪ'lektrɪk] *adj.* referring to electricity controlled by light; **p. cell** = cell which converts light into electricity or which operates a machine when a beam of light is broken. **pho•to fin•ish** ['fəʊtəʊfɪnɪʃ] *n.* very close end of a race when a photograph is used to decide who is the winner. **pho•to•gen•ic** [fəʊtəʊ'dʒiːnɪk] *adj.* (person) who looks well in photographs. **pho•to•graph** ['fəʊtəgrɑːf] 1. *n.* picture taken by a camera by means of exposing sensitive film to light. 2. *v.* to take a picture with a camera. **pho•tog•ra•pher** [fə'tɒgrəfə] *n.* person who takes photographs. **pho•to•graph•ic** [fəʊtəʊ'græfɪk] *adj.* referring to photography; **p. memory** = ability to remember things in exact detail, as if seen. **pho•tog•ra•phy** [fə'tɒgrəfɪ] *n.* (art of) taking pictures on sensitive film with a camera. **pho•to•gra•vure,** *n.* engraving of a photograph. **Pho•to•stat** ['fəʊtəʊstæt] 1. *n.* trademark for a type of photographic copy. 2. *v.* (**photostated, photostatted**) to make a photographic copy of. **pho•to•syn•the•sis,** *n.* process by which plants use sunlight to form carbohydrates.

phrase [freɪz] 1. *n.* (a) expression; short sentence; group of words taken together; **p. book** = book of translations of common expressions. (b) group of notes in a piece of music. 2. *v.* to express/to word (a sentence, etc.). **phras•al** ['freɪzl] *adj.* referring to a phrase; (verb) making a phrase. **phra•se•ol•o•gy** [freɪzɪ'ɒlədʒɪ] *n.* way of expressing sth; choice of words and phrases.

phre•nol•o•gy [fre'nɒlədʒɪ] *n.* study of the outside shape of the skull.

phut [fʌt] *adv. inf.* **to go p.** = to stop working.

phys•i•cal ['fɪzɪkl] *adj.* (a) referring to matter/energy, etc.; **p. geography** = study of rocks and earth, etc.; **p. chemistry** = study of chemical substances. (b) referring to the human body; **p. exercise** = exercise of the body. **phys•i•cal•ly,** *adv.* referring to the body or to the laws of nature.

phy•si•cian [fɪ'zɪʃn] *n.* doctor.

phys•ics ['fɪzɪks] *n.* study of matter/energy, etc. **phys•i•cist** ['fɪzɪsɪst] *n.* person who studies physics.

phys•i•og•no•my [fɪzɪ'ɒnəmɪ] *n.* human face.

phys•i•ol•o•gy [fɪzɪ'ɒlədʒɪ] *n.* study of the way in which living things work. **phys•i•o•log•i•cal** [fɪzɪə'lɒdʒɪkl] *adj* referring to physiology. **phys•i•ol•o•gist,** *n.* person who studies physiology.

phys•i•o•ther•a•py [fɪzɪəʊ'θerəpɪ] *n.* treatment of an illness, pain, etc., by exercise or rubbing. **phys•i•o•ther•a•pist,** *n.* person who practices physiotherapy.

phy•sique [fɪ'ziːk] *n.* shape of a person's body.

pi [paɪ] *n.* letter of the Greek alphabet (), symbolizing the quantity 3.14159, which is used to calculate the circumference of a circle from a known radius.

pi•a•no ['pjænəʊ] *n.* (*pl.* -os) musical instrument with keys which makes notes by striking wires with hammers; **grand p.** = large piano with horizontal wires. **player p.** = piano which plays music mechanically from a reel of perforated paper. **pi•an•ist** ['pɪənɪst] *n.* person who plays the piano. **pi•an•o•forte** ['pjænəʊfɔːtɪ] *n.* (*old*) piano.

pi•az•za [pɪ'ætsə] *n.* Italian square, often surrounded by arcades.

pi•broch ['piːbrɒk] *n.* mournful bagpipe music.

pi•ca ['paɪkə] *n.* measure of type.

pic•a•resque [pɪkə'resk] *adj.* fancifully romantic (story).

pic•ca•lil•li [pɪkə'lɪlɪ] *n.* pickle made of vegetables, such as cauliflower, onions, etc., in a mustard sauce.

pic•co•lo ['pɪkələʊ] *n.* (*pl.* -os) small wind instrument, like a little flute.

pick [pɪk] 1. *n.* (a) heavy tool (for breaking hard ground/concrete, etc.) with a long handle and a curved metal bar with pointed ends. (b) selected group; **to take your p.** = choose which one you want. 2. *v.* (a) to break up (hard ground/concrete, etc.) with a pick. (b) to remove things with your fingers/with a pointed tool; to clean the inside of (your nose) with your fingers. (c) to eat very daintily and without any appetite. (d) to choose. (e) to collect (ripe fruit); to cut (flowers). (f) to open (a lock) with a piece of wire. (g) to steal from (s.o.'s pocket). (h) **to p. s.o.'s brains** = to ask for ideas/information. **pick•ax, pickaxe,** *n.* pick. **pick•er,** *n.* person who picks. **pick•ings,** *n. pl.* bits and pieces left which people can pick up. **pick-me-up,** *n. inf.* alcoholic drink that makes s.o. feel better. **pick off,** *v.* to defeat/kill (an enemy) one by one. **pick on,** *v.* to select (s.o.) as a target for criticism/for bullying. **pick out,** *v.* to select/to choose. **pick•pock•et,** *n.* person who steals things from people's pockets. **pick up,** *v.* (a) to take (sth) which is on the ground. (b) to learn (a language, etc.) unsystematically. (c) to give (s.o.) a lift in a car; (*of a bus*) to take (passengers) on board; (*of police*) to arrest/to take to a police station; to start an acquaintanceship with (s.o.) by chance. (d) to get stronger. **pick•up,** *n.* (a) *inf.* person who has been picked up. (b) needle and arm of a record player. (c) light van with an open back.

pick•et ['pɪkɪt] 1. *n.* (a) guard. (b) pointed stake. (c) striking workman/union official who stands at the entrance to a factory to try to prevent other workmen from going to work; **p. line** = line of pickets preventing other workmen going to work. 2. *v.* to post strikers at the entrance of a factory to try to prevent workers going to work.

pick•le ['pɪkl] 1. *n.* (a) vegetables preserved in vinegar, etc. (b) *inf.* difficult or embarassing situation. 2. *v.* to preserve (vegetables, etc.) in vinegar. **pick•led,** *adj. inf.* drunk.

pic•nic ['pɪknɪk] 1. *n.* (a) pleasure trip with a meal eaten outdoors. 2. *v.* (**picknicked**) to eat a picnic. **pic•nick•er,** *n.* person who goes on a picnic.

pic•to•ri•al [pɪk'tɔːrɪəl] *adj.* referring to pictures.

pic•ture ['pɪktʃə] 1. *n.* (a) painting/drawing, etc.; *inf.* **to give s.o. the p.** = to tell them all the relevant details. (b) image (on a TV screen, etc.). 2. *v.* to imagine. **pic•tur•esque** [pɪktʃə-'resk] *adj.* which would make a good picture; very artistic.

pid•dle ['pɪdl] *v. inf.* (*child's language*) to urinate. **pid•dling,** *adj. inf.* very small.

pidg•in ['pɪdʒɪn] *n.* simple language made from several languages, used as a lingua franca; **p. (English)** = simplified form of English used in the Far East.

pie [paɪ] *n.* cooked dish, usu. of pastry with a filling of meat or fruit; **p. in the sky** = unattainable ideal. **pie chart,** *n.* diagram shaped like a circle with segments showing how sth is divided up. **pie-eyed,** *adj. inf.* drunk.

pie•bald ['paɪbɔːld] *adj.* (horse) with black and white patches.

piece [piːs] 1. *n.* (a) small part/bit; **he went to pieces** = he lost control of himself/had a nervous breakdown. (b) short composition in music. (c) one of the figures used in chess, but not usu. a pawn. (d) gun. 2. *v.* **to p. together** = to join separate parts together. **piece•meal,** *adv.* in bits; a bit at a time; separately. **piece•work,** *n.* work for which you are paid by the amount of work done and not by the hour.

pièce de ré•sis•tance [pɪesdəreɪsɪs'tɑŋs] *n.* main item.

pied [paɪd] *adj.* having two colors, usu. black and white.

pied-à-terre [pjeɪdæ'teə] *n.* small apartment/house which you use to live in from time to time when visiting a place.

pier ['pɪə] *n.* (a) construction going out into the water, used as a landing place for ships. (b) pillar (of a bridge).

pierce ['pɪəs] *v.* to make a hole. **pierc•ing,** *adj.* very loud, shrill (cry); very sharp/severe (cold or wind).

pi•e•ty ['paɪətɪ] *n.* being pious; great respect for religion.

pif•fle [pɪfl] *n. inf.* nonsense.

pig [pɪg] *n.* (a) farm animal which gives pork/bacon, etc.; various wild species of this animal. (b) *inf.* dirty/greedy person. (c) large block of metal; **p. iron** = iron in rough molded blocks. (d) *Sl.* policeman. **pig•ger•y,** *n.* place where pigs are kept. **pig•gy,** *n.* child's name for a pig. **pig•gy•back,** *n. adj. & adv.* carrying s.o. on your back with his arms round your neck. **pig•gy•bank,** *n.* child's savings bank, usu. in the shape of a pig. **pig•head•ed,** *adj. inf.* obstinate. **pig•let,** *n.* little pig. **pig•meat,** *n.* meat from a pig. **pig•skin,** *n.* leather made from the skin of a pig. **pig•sty,** *n.* shed where pigs are kept. **pig•tail,** *n.* hair hanging down in a plait at the back of the head.

pi•geon ['pɪdʒn] *n.* common grayish bird. **pi•geon•hole.** 1. *n.* small space used for filing papers/letters, etc. 2. *v.* (a) to file letters/papers, etc. (often as the best way to forget them). (b) to put (s.o./sth) into a particular category. **pi•geon-toed,** *adj.* with the feet turned inwards, towards each other.

pig•ment ['pɪgmənt] 1. *n.* coloring matter. 2. *v.* to color with pigment. **pig•men•ta•tion** [pɪgmən'teɪʃn] *n.* coloring of the skin.

Pig•my ['pɪgmɪ] *n. see* **Pyg•my.**

pike [paɪk] *n.* (a) (*pl.* pike) large ferocious freshwater fish. (b) (*old*) weapon, like a spear with a broad blade.

pi•laf, pilaff ['pɪlæf] *n.* Indian dish of meat with savory rice.

pi•las•ter [pɪ'læstə] *n.* rectangular column, usu. attached to a wall.

pi•lau ['pɪlaʊ] *n. see* **pi•laf.**

pil•chard ['pɪltʃəd] *n.* small fish similar to a herring.

pile [paɪl] 1. *n.* (a) heap; *inf.* **he's made a p. in real estate** = a lot of money. (b) large stake/concrete shaft driven into the earth to provide a foundation. (c) thickness of tufts of wool in a carpet. (d) **piles** = hemorrhoids. 2. *v.* **to p. (up)** = to heap up. **pile driv•er,** *n.* machine for

---

æ **back,** ɑː **farm,** ɒ **top,** aɪ **pipe,** aʊ **how,** aɪə **fire,** aʊə **flower,** ɔː **bought,** ɔɪ **toy,** e **fed,** eə **hair,** eɪ **take,** ə **afraid,** əʊ **boat,** əʊə **lower,** ɜː **word,** iː **heap,** ɪ **hit,** ɪə **hear,** uː **school,** ʊ **book,** ʌ **but,** b **back,** d **dog,** ð **then,** dʒ **just,** f **fog,** g **go,** h **hand,** j **yes,** k **catch,** l **last,** m **mix,** n **nut,** ŋ **sing,** p **penny,** r **round,** s **some,** ʃ **short,** t **too,** tʃ **chop,** θ **thing,** v **voice,** w **was,** z **zoo,** ʒ **treasure**

forcing piles into the earth. **pile•up**, *n.* series of cars which have smashed into each other.

pil•fer ['pɪlfə] *v.* to steal small objects or small amounts of money. **pil•fer•er**, *n.* person who pilfers. **pil•fer•age, pilfering**, *n.* stealing small objects or amounts of money.

pil•grim ['pɪlgrɪm] *n.* person who goes to visit a holy place. **pil•grim•age**, *n.* journey to visit a holy place/a famous place.

pill [pɪl] *n.* small round tablet of medicine; *inf.* **she's on the p.** = she takes contraceptive tablets. **pill•box**, *n.* (a) round box for pills. (b) concrete shelter for a small gun.

pil•lage ['pɪlɪdʒ] 1. *n.* plundering by soldiers. 2. *v.* (*of soldiers*) to plunder/to steal goods (from a captured town, etc.).

pil•lar ['pɪlə] *n.* (a) column. (b) strong supporter.

pil•lion ['pɪljən] *n.* rear saddle for a passenger on a motorcycle.

pil•lo•ry ['pɪlərɪ] 1. *n.* (*old*) wooden stand with holes for the head and hands, where criminals were placed so that the public could throw things at them. 2. *v.* to make (s.o.) appear ridiculous or foolish in public.

pil•low ['pɪləʊ] *n.* bag full of soft material which you put your head on in bed. **pil•low•case, pillowslip**, *n.* cloth bag to cover a pillow with.

pi•lot ['paɪlət] 1. *n.* (a) person who guides ships into harbor or through dangerous channels. (b) person who flies an aircraft. (c) **p. light** = small gas light on a stove/water-heater, etc., from which the main gas jets are lit. 2. *v.* (a) to guide (a ship). (b) to fly (an aircraft).

pi•mien•to [pɪmɪ'entəʊ], **pi•men•to** *n.* (*pl.* -os) green or red fruit with a hot spicy taste used as a vegetable.

pimp [pimp] 1. *n.* man who organizes and makes money from prostitutes. 2. *v.* to work as a pimp.

pim•per•nel ['pɪmpənel] *n.* wild plant with small red flowers.

pim•ple ['pɪmpl] *n.* small bump on the surface of the skin. **pim•ply**, *adj.* covered with pimples.

pin [pɪn] 1. *n.* (a) small sharp metal stick with a round head, used for attaching clothes/papers, etc., together; **safety p.** = type of bent pin where the sharp point is held by a metal shield; **pins and needles** = prickling feeling in your hand or foot after it has been numb for a time. (b) blunt wooden or metal bolt used for fastening things together. 2. *v.* (**pinned**) (a) to attach with a pin; **to p. s.o. down** = to get him to say what he really thinks/to make his mind up. (b) to hold fast. **pin•ball**, *n.* table game where a ball has to be rolled into holes. **pin•cush•ion**, *n.* round pad in which you

can stick pins. **pin mon•ey**, *n. inf.* small amount of money for buying extra items. **pin•point**, *v.* to indicate exactly. **pin•prick**, *n.* slight annoyance. **pin•stripe**, *n.* dark cloth with a very thin white line in it. **pin•up**, *n. inf.* photograph of a pretty girl which you can pin up on a wall.

pin•a•fore ['pɪnəfɔː] *n.* apron worn to cover a dress.

pince-nez ['pænsneɪ] *n. pl.* glasses which clip onto your nose.

pin•cers ['pɪnsəz] *n. pl.* (a) **(pair of) p.** = scissor-shaped tool for holding sth tight. (b) claws of a crab/lobster.

pinch [pɪnʃ] 1. *n.* (*pl.* -es) (a) squeezing tightly/nipping between finger and thumb; **in a p.** = if really necessary; **to feel the p.** = find you have less money than you need. (b) small quantity of sth held between finger and thumb. 2. *v.* (a) to squeeze tightly, using the finger and thumb. (b) to hold tight and hurt. (c) *inf.* to steal. (d) *Sl.* to arrest.

pine [paɪn] 1. *n.* type of evergreen tree; wood from a pine tree. 2. *v.* (**to**) waste away (because you want sth). **pine•ap•ple** ['paɪnæpl] *n.* large tropical fruit, shaped like a pine cone with stiff prickly leaves on top. **pine cone**, *n.* fruit of a pine tree. **pine wood**, *n.* wood of pine trees. **pin•e•al gland**, *n.* small gland, shaped like a pine cone, found in the brain.

ping [pɪŋ] 1. *n.* noise made when a small bell/a glass, etc., is hit. 2. *v.* to make a ping.

ping pong ['pɪŋpɒŋ] *n. inf.* table tennis.

pin•ion ['pɪnjən] 1. *n.* (a) large outer feather on a bird's wing. (b) toothed wheel or cogwheel. 2. *v.* to tie up (s.o.'s arms) tightly.

pink [pɪŋk] 1. *adj. & n.* (color) like pale red or flesh color. 2. *n.* (a) scented garden flower like a small carnation. (b) **in the p.** = very well/prosperous. **pink•ing shears**, *n. pl.* large scissors used by dressmakers, which give a zigzag edge to a cut.

pin•na•cle ['pɪnəkl] *n.* topmost point (of a pointed rock, of s.o.'s career); tall, thin stone spire or tower.

pint [paɪnt] *n.* liquid measure (= 16 ounces or 0.473 liter).

pi•o•neer [paɪə'nɪə] 1. *n.* person who is among the first to try to do sth/who is the first to explore/settle in a new land. 2. *v.* to be first to do (sth).

pi•ous ['paɪəs] *adj.* showing great respect for religion. **pi•ous•ly**, *adv.* in a pious way.

pip [pɪp] *n.* (a) small seed. (b) star on the shoulder showing an officer's rank in the British army.

pipe [paɪp] 1. *n.* (a) tube. (b) instrument for smoking tobacco. (c) thin metal flute; **the pipes** = bagpipes. 2. *v.* to send (water/gas, etc.)

along a pipe; **piped music** = recorded music played continuously (in a restaurant, etc.). **pipe down**, *v. inf.* to stop talking. **pipe dream**, *n.* plan which is impossible to carry out. **pipe•line**, *n.* very large tube for carrying oil/natural gas, etc., over long distances; **in the p.** = being worked on/on the way. **pip•er**, *n.* person who plays the bagpipes. **pipe up**, *v. inf.* to start talking (esp. in a high-pitched voice). **pip•ing**. 1. *n.* (a) collection of tubes; section of metal tube. (b) decoration like white tubes on a cake/on a dress. 2. *adv.* **p. hot** = extremely hot.

pi•pette [pɪ'pet] *n.* thin glass measuring tube used in laboratories.

pip•it ['pɪpɪt] *n.* small singing bird.

pip•pin ['pɪpɪn] *n.* type of sweet apple.

pi•quant ['piːkənt] *adj.* nice sharp (flavor); pleasantly interesting/amusing. **pi•quan•cy**, *n.* being piquant. **pi•quant•ly**, *adv.* in a piquant way.

pique [piːk] 1. *n.* resentment/annoyance. 2. *v.* (a) to make (s.o.) resentful. (b) to arouse s.o.'s curiosity.

pi•qué ['pikei] *n.* cotton material with ribs.

pi•ra•nha [pɪ'rɑːnə] *n.* small tropical fish which attacks animals, including man.

pi•rate ['paɪərət] 1. *n.* (a) robber (esp. at sea). (b) person who copies a patented invention or a copyrighted work. **p. radio** = illegal radio station. 2. *v.* to publish books/make recordings which are copied from those of another publisher without having the right to do so. **pi•ra•cy**, *n.* robbery (at sea); illegal publishing of books/making of records. **pi•rat•i•cal** [par'rætɪkl] *adj.* referring to a pirate.

pir•ou•ette [pɪru'et] 1. *n.* spinning around on one foot when dancing. 2. *v.* to spin around on one foot.

pis•ca•to•ri•al [pɪskə'tɔːrɪəl] *adj.* referring to fishing.

Pis•ces ['paɪsiːz] *n.* one of the signs of the zodiac, shaped like fish.

pis•ci•cul•ture [pɪsɪ'kʌltʃə] *n.* raising fish for food.

piss [pɪs] 1. *n. inf. & vulgar* (a) waste water from the body. (b) passing waste water from the body. 2. *v. inf. & vulgar* to pass waste water from the body.

pis•tach•i•o [pɪ'stæʃɪəu] *n.* (*pl.* -os) small green tropical nut.

piste [piːst] *n.* track for skiing.

pis•til ['pɪstɪl] *n.* female part of a flower, which produces seeds.

pis•tol ['pɪstl] *n.* small gun which is held in the hand.

pis•ton ['pɪstn] *n.* (*in an engine*) metal disk which moves up and down in a cylinder; **p. rod** = rod which is attached to a piston and which drives other parts of the engine.

pit [pɪt] 1. *n.* (a) deep, dark hole in the ground. (b) coalmine. (c) hole in the floor of a garage (for inspecting the underside of a car); (*at car races*) place where the cars are inspected and repaired. (d) stone of some fruit. 2. *v.* (**pitted**) (a) to try (your strength) **against.** (b) to take the stone out of (a fruit). (c) to mark with a hole.

pitch [pɪtʃ] 1. *n.* (*pl.* -es) (a) black substance which comes from tar and is used for waterproofing boats/roofs, etc. (b) level of tone in music. (c) height (of anger/of excitement). (d) angle of a sloping roof. (e) **sales p.** = smooth talk, aimed at selling sth. 2. *v.* (a) to put up (a tent). (b) to throw (a ball). (c) to set the level of a musical tone. (d) (*of boat*) to rock with the front and back going up and down. **pitch-black, pitch dark**, *adj.* very black; very dark. **pitch•blende**, *n.* mineral which produces radium. **pitched**, *adj.* **p. battle** = battle fought on a selected piece of ground; fierce argument. **pitch•er** ['pɪtʃə] *n.* (a) large container for liquids, usu. with a handle. (b) person who pitches a ball. **pitch•fork**, *n.* large fork for moving bales of hay. **pitch in•to**, *v.* to attack. **pitch pine**, *n.* type of pine which produces strong resin.

pit•fall ['pɪtfɔːl] *n.* trap/danger.

pith [pɪθ] *n.* (a) soft part in the center of a plant stem; soft white stuff under the skin of a lemon/an orange, etc. (b) important part (of an argument). **pith•i•ly**, *adv.* in a pithy way. **pith•y**, *adj.* (-ier, -iest) (a) (wood) with a soft center. (b) concise; full of serious meaning.

pi•ton ['piːtɒn] *n.* metal peg used in rock-climbing.

pit•tance ['pɪtns] *n.* low wage.

pit•ter-pat•ter ['pɪtəpætə] *n.* series of small sounds.

pi•tu•i•tar•y [pɪ'tjuɪtrɪ] *adj.* **p. gland** = gland in the brain which produces hormones which control the development and function of the body.

pit•y ['pɪtɪ] 1. *n.* feeling of sympathy for s.o. unfortunate; **to take p. on s.o.** = to be sorry for s.o. 2. *v.* to feel sympathy for (s.o.).

æ back, ɑː farm, ɒ top, aɪ pipe, aʊ how, aɪə fire, aʊə flower, ɔː bought, ɔɪ toy, e fed, eəhair, eɪ take, ə afraid, əʊ boat, əʊə lower, ɜː word, iː heap, ɪ hit, ɪə hear, uː school, ʊ book, ʌ but, b back, d dog, ð then, dʒ just, f fog, g go, h hand, j yes, k catch, l last, m mix, n nut, ŋ sing, p penny, r round, s some, ʃ short, t too, tʃ chop, θ thing, v voice, w was, z zoo, ʒ treasure

pit•e•ous ['pɪtɪəs], **pit•i•a•ble**, *adj.* which deserves pity. **pit•i•ful**, *adj.* (a) deserving pity; sad. (b) inadequate. **pit•i•ful•ly**, *adv.* in a pitiful way. **pit•i•less**, *adj.* showing no pity.

piv•ot ['pɪvət] 1. *n.* point on which sth turns. 2. *v.* to turn on a point; to depend on sth. **piv•ot•al**, *adj.* of great importance.

pix•el ['pɪksəl] *n.* tiny element of color or light on a TV screen or computer monitor. **pix•e•la•tion**, *n.* (a) appearance of the squares of color that make up a digitized image when the image is displayed at low resolution. (b) covering of a video image with a grid of colored squares, usu. to conceal s.o.'s identity.

pix•ie ['pɪksɪ] *n.* small fairy.

piz•za ['piːtsə] *n.* Italian dish, consisting of a flat round piece of dough cooked with tomatoes, onions, etc., on top. **piz•ze•ri•a**, *n.* restaurant which sells pizzas.

piz•zi•ca•to [pɪtsɪ'kɑːtəʊ] *n. & adv.* (music) played by plucking the strings instead of using the bow.

plac•ard ['plækɑːd] 1. *n.* poster. 2. *v.* to stick posters up.

pla•cate [plə'keɪt] *v.* to calm (s.o.); to make (s.o.) less angry. **pla•ca•to•ry**, *adv.* which placates.

place [pleɪs] 1. *n.* (a) location/spot. (b) house/home. (c) open area. (d) set position; **to take p.** = to happen/to be held. (e) rank (in a series); **in the first p.** = first of all. (f) job. (g) one of the first three positions in a horse race. 2. *v.* (a) to put. (b) to give (an order). (c) to put in a set position. (d) to remember who s.o. is. **place•mat**, *n.* mat which a person's plate is put on. **place•ment**, *n.* placing s.o. in a job. **place set•ting**, *n.* set of knife/fork/spoon, etc. for one person.

pla•ce•bo [plə'siːbəʊ] *n.* (*pl.* -os) harmless substance given to a patient instead of a drug to make him believe he is receiving treatment.

pla•cen•ta [plə'sentə] *n.* tissue in the womb which nourishes the unborn baby.

plac•id ['plæsɪd] *adj.* (-er, -est) calm. **pla•cid•i•ty** [plə'sɪdɪtɪ] *n.* calmness. **plac•id•ly**, *adv.* calmly.

plack•et ['plækɪt] *n.* opening with buttons at the waist of a skirt.

pla•gia•rism ['pleɪdʒərɪzəm] *n.* copying what s.o. else has written. **pla•gia•rist**, *n.* author who copies the work of s.o. else. **pla•gia•rize**, *v.* to copy the work of (another author).

plague [pleɪg] 1. *n.* (a) fatal infectious disease transmitted by fleas from rats. (b) great quantity of pests. 2. *v.* to annoy/to bother (s.o.).

plaice [pleɪs] *n.* (*pl.* **plaice**) common flat sea fish.

plaid [plæd] *n.* (a) (*in Scotland*) long piece of (tartan) cloth. (b) pattern of differently colored stripes that cross over each other; cloth with this pattern.

plain [pleɪn] 1. *adj.* (-er, -est) (a) obvious/easy to understand. (b) simple/uncomplicated. (c) not pretty. 2. *n.* large flat area of country. **plain•clothes**, *n. pl.* ordinary/everyday clothes (not uniform). **plain•ly**, *adv.* (a) obviously. (b) simply. **plain•ness**, *n.* (a) clearness. (b) simpleness. **plain•song**, *n.* medieval music for church services. **plain-spo•ken**, *adj.* (person) who speaks in a straightforward way.

plain•tiff ['pleɪntɪf] *n.* person who starts a legal action against s.o. else.

plain•tive ['pleɪntɪv] *adj.* sad.

plait [plæt] 1. *n.* (hair/wool, etc.) with three strands woven into a long rope. 2. *v.* to weave hair, etc., to form a plait.

plan [plæn] 1. *n.* (a) scheme; **according to p.** = as we had intended. (b) drawing of the way sth is to be built or constructed. (c) map of streets. 2. *v.* (**planned**) (a) to draw up a scheme to construct sth. (b) to scheme/to propose to do sth. **plan•ner**, *n.* person who draws up schemes; **town p.** = person who designs how a town should develop. **plan•ning**, *n.* making plans; **family p.** = decision by parents on how many children to have.

plane [pleɪn] 1. *n.* (a) flat surface. (b) aircraft. (c) tool for smoothing wood. (d) tree often grown in towns, of which bark comes off in large pieces. 2. *adj.* level/flat. 3. *v.* to smooth (wood) flat with a plane.

plan•et ['plænɪt] *n.* body which revolves around a star, esp. around the sun. **plan•e•tar•i•um** [plænɪ'teərɪəm] *n.* domed building in which you sit and watch as pictures of the stars are projected against the ceiling. **plan•e•tar•y** ['plænɪtrɪ] *adj.* referring to the planets.

plan•gent ['plændʒnt] *adj.* sad resonant (music).

plank [plæŋk] *n.* (a) long flat piece of wood used in building. (b) proposal in a political program. **plank•ing**, *n.* series of planks.

plank•ton ['plæŋktn] *n.* tiny organisms living in the sea.

plant [plɑːnt] 1. *n.* (a) thing which grows in the ground, is usu. green, and cannot move from one place to another. (b) factory. (c) machinery. 2. *v.* (a) to put (a plant) into the ground. (b) to put in a special position. (c) to put (sth) secretly; to put (stolen goods) secretly on s.o., in order to make it look as if he stole them. **plan•ta•tion** [plɑːn'teɪʃn] *n.* (a) area of trees specially planted. (b) tropical estate growing a particular crop. **plant•er,** *n.* (a) person in charge of a plantation. (b) decorative container to hold plants in pots.

plan•tain ['plæntɪn] *n.* (a) common weed. (b) tropical fruit.

plaque [plæk] *n.* (a) decorative plate hung on a wall; stone/metal/earthenware plate with an inscription. (b) deposit which forms on the teeth.

plas•ma ['plæzmə] *n.* liquid part of blood.

plas•ter ['plɑːstə] 1. *n.* (a) mixture of fine sand and lime which when mixed with water is used for covering walls of houses. (b) white paste, used to make molds/to make coverings to hold broken arms and legs in place. (c) **sticking p.** = adhesive cloth/tape used for holding bandages in place/for covering small wounds. 2. *v.* (a) to cover with plaster. (b) to cover thickly as if with plaster. **plas•ter cast,** *n.* (a) block of plaster put round a broken leg, etc. (b) mold made by covering sth with plaster. (c) copy of a statue made in plaster. **plas•tered,** *adj. Sl.* drunk. **plas•ter•er,** *n.* person who covers walls with plaster.

plas•tic ['plæstɪk] 1. *n.* artificial substance, which can be molded into any shape; **p. bomb** = explosive material which can be molded in the hand. 2. *adj.* soft/pliable; **p. surgery** = operation to replace damaged skin or to improve s.o.'s appearance. **plas•tic•i•ty** [plæs'tɪsɪtɪ] *n.* state of being plastic.

plate [pleɪt] 1. *n.* (a) thin flat sheet of metal/glass, etc. (b) flat dish for putting food on. (c) dishes made of gold or silver. (d) thin layer of gold/silver on a less precious metal; objects made of this. (e) book illustration on shiny paper. (f) piece of plastic with false teeth attached which fits into your mouth. 2. *v.* to cover with a thin layer of gold or silver. **plate•ful,** *n.* quantity held by a plate. **plate glass,** *n.* glass in very large sheets.

pla•teau ['plætəʊ] *n.* (*pl.* -eaus, -eaux [-əʊz]) high flat area of land.

plate•let ['pleɪtlət] *n.* small cell in the blood which helps blood to clot.

plat•en ['plætən] *n.* roller around which the paper goes in a typewriter.

plat•form ['plætfɔːm] *n.* (a) raised floor space for speakers in a hall. (b) raised pavement by the side of the rails in a railroad station so that passengers can get on and off trains easily. (c) proposals put forward by the leaders of a political party before an election. (d) computer system that requires unique versions of software.

plat•i•num ['plætɪnəm] *n.* (*element:* Pt) rare light-colored precious metal; **p. blonde** = woman with silvery blonde hair.

plat•i•tude ['plætɪtjuːd] *n.* ordinary saying, esp. one which the speaker thinks is very important.

pla•ton•ic [plə'tɒnɪk] *adj.* (love between man and woman) which is not sexual.

pla•toon [plə'tuːn] *n.* small group of soldiers/part of a company.

plat•ter ['plætə] *n.* large serving plate.

plat•y•pus ['plætɪpəs] *n.* (*pl.* -es) Australian mammal which lays eggs.

plau•dits ['plɔːdɪts] *n. pl.* applause.

plau•si•ble ['plɔːzɪbl] *adj.* which sounds as though it is correct when it often is not. **plau•si•bly,** *adv.* in a plausible way. **plau•si•bil•i•ty** [plɔːzɪ'bɪlɪtɪ] *n.* being plausible.

play [pleɪ] 1. *n.* (a) way of amusing yourself; sport. (b) theatrical performance; script of a theatrical performance. (c) freedom to move. 2. *v.* (a) to amuse yourself/to pass the time in a pleasant way. (b) to take part in a game. (c) to perform on a musical instrument. (d) to act a part in a theatrical performance. (e) to let a fish which has been caught on a hook swim until it is tired and can easily be landed. (f) to make (a record player) work. *play at, v.* (a) to work in a slack way. (b) (*of children*) to pretend to be. **play back,** *v.* to listen to (sth) which you have just recorded on tape. **play•boy,** *n.* rich man who spends his time amusing himself rather than working. **play down,** *v.* to make (sth) seem less important. **play•er,** *n.* person who plays. **play•fel•low,** *n.* playmate. **play•ful,** *adj.* liking to play. **play•ful•ly,** *adv.* in a playful way. **play•ful•ness,** *n.* being playful. **play•ground,** *n.* area, esp. around school buildings, where children can play. **play•group,** *n.* group of small children who play together under supervision. **play•house,** *n.* theater. **play•ing card,** *n.* one of a set of fifty-two cards, marked in four designs, used for playing various games. **play•ing field,** *n.* area of grass where sports can be played. **play•mate,** *n.* child another child plays with. **play off,** *v.* to p. s.o. off against s.o. = to try to benefit by making two people oppose each other. **play on,** *v.* to take

æ back, ɑː farm, ɒ top, aɪ pipe, aʊ how, aɪə fire, aʊə flower, ɔː bought, ɔɪ toy, e fed, eəhair, eɪ take, ə afraid, əʊ boat, əʊə lower, ɜː word, iː heap, ɪ hit, ɪə hear, uː school, ʊ book, ʌ but, b back, d dog, ð then, dʒ just, f fog, g go, h hand, j yes, k catch, l last, m mix, n nut, ŋ sing, p penny, r round, s some, ʃ short, t too, tʃ chop, θ thing, v voice, w was, z zoo, ʒ treasure

advantage by exciting (s.o.'s sympathy).
play•pen, *n.* type of enclosed space in which
babies can be left to play safely. **play•thing**,
n. toy. **play•time**, *n.* time in nursery school
when children can play. **play up**, *v. inf.* to
make stand out. **play•wright**, *n.* person who
writes plays.

pla•za ['plɑːzə] *n.* open area in a town.

plea [pliː] *n.* (a) answer to a charge in court; **p.
bargaining** = arrangement where an accused
person pleads guilty to some charges so as to
be let off others. (b) (*formal*) request. (c) excuse.

plead [pliːd] *v.* (a) to answer a charge in a law
court. (b) to give as an excuse. (c) **to p. with s.o.**
= to try to change s.o.'s mind by asking again
and again.

pleas•ant ['pleznt] *adj.* (**-er, -est**) agree-
able/which pleases. **pleas•ant•ly**, *adv.* in a
pleasant way. **pleas•ant•ry**, *n.* joke; pleasant remark.

please [pliːz] *v.* (a) to make (s.o.)
happy/satisfied; **p. yourself** = do as you like.
(b) *polite expression after an order or request,
meaning* if you would like. **pleased**, *adj.*
happy; satisified. **pleas•ing**, *adj.* which
pleases. **pleas•ur•a•ble** ['pleʒərəbl] *adj.*
pleasant. **pleas•ure** ['pleʒə] *n.* amuse-
ment/happiness.

pleat [pliːt] 1. *n.* vertical fold (in a skirt, etc.). 2.
v. to iron vertical folds in.

pleb•i•scite ['plebɪsɪt] *n.* general vote by the
inhabitants of a country on an important
issue.

ple•be•ian [pliːˈbiːən] 1. *n.* a member of the
common people; ordinary person. 2. *adj.* com-
mon/ordinary; of the working class. **plebs**, *n.
pl. inf.* the common people.

plec•trum ['plektrəm] *n.* small stick for plucking the strings of a guitar, etc.

pledge [pledʒ] 1. *n.* (a) object given to the
lender when borrowing money, and which will
be returned to the borrower when the money
is paid back. (b) promise. 2. *v.* (a) to give (sth)
as a pledge when borrowing money. (b) to
promise.

ple•na•ry ['pliːnərɪ] *adj.* complete; **p. session** =
session of a conference where all the delegates
meet together.

plen•i•po•ten•ti•ar•y [plenɪpəˈtenʃərɪ] *adj.
& n.* (person) who has full powers to act on behalf of his country.

plen•te•ous ['plentɪəs] *adj.* (*formal*) more
than enough.

plen•ty ['plentɪ] *n.* large quantity.
plen•ti•ful, *adj.* abundant; in large quantities.

ple•num ['pleɪnəm] *n.* general meeting.

ple•o•nasm ['plɪənæzəm] *n.* use of more
words than necessary.

ple•o•nas•tic [plɪəˈnæstɪk] *adj.* (expression)
where some words are superfluous.

pleth•o•ra ['pleθərə] *n.* (*formal*) too many
(**of**).

pleu•ra ['plʊərə] *n.* membrane covering the
lungs. **pleu•ri•sy**, *n.* disease of the membrane covering the lungs.

plex•us ['pleksəs] *n.* network of nerves.

pli•a•ble ['plaɪəbl], **pli•ant** ['plaɪənt] *adj.*
which can be bent easily; (person) who can be
easily persuaded. **pli•a•bil•i•ty, pliancy**, *n.*
being pliable/pliant.

pli•ers ['plaɪəz] *n. pl.* (**pair of**) **p.** = tool shaped
like scissors for pinching, twisting or cutting
wire.

plight [plaɪt] 1. *n.* bad state. 2. *v.* (*formal*) to
promise.

Plim•soll line ['plɪmsɒlaɪn] *n.* line along the
side of a ship which shows the level of the
water when the ship is loaded.

plinth [plɪnθ] *n.* pedestal on which a statue
stands.

plod [plɒd] *v.* (**plodded**) (a) to walk heavily. (b)
to work steadily. **plod•der**, *n.* person who
works steadily but rather slowly.

plop [plɒp] 1. *n.* noise made by a stone falling
into water. 2. *v.* (**plopped**) to make a noise like
a stone falling into water.

plot [plɒt] 1. *n.* (a) small area of land for build-
ing/for growing vegetables, etc. (b) basic story
of a book/play/motion picture. (c) wicked
plan. 2. *v.* (**plotted**) (a) to mark on a map; to
draw a graph. (b) to draw up a wicked plan.
plot•ter, *n.* person who plots.

plough [plaʊ] *n. & v. Brit. see* **plow**.

plov•er ['plʌvə] *n.* type of wading bird (found
in fields and moors).

plow, *Brit.* **plough** [plaʊ] 1. *n.* (a) farm machine for turning over soil. (b) **snow p.** = machine like a tractor with a large blade in front,
used for clearing snow from streets, etc. 2. *v.*
(a) to turn over the soil. (b) to work slowly.
plow back, *v.* to invest (profits) back in a
business. **plow•man**, *n.* (*pl.* **-men**) farm
worker who drives a plow. **plow•share**, *n.*
blade of a plow.

ploy [plɔɪ] *n.* clever trick.

pluck [plʌk] 1. *n.* courage. 2. *v.* (a) to pull out
feathers or eyebrows. (b) to pick (flowers,
etc.). (c) to pull and release the strings of a guitar to make a sound; **to p. up one's courage** = to
get ready to face a danger. **pluck•i•ly**, *adv.* in
a plucky way. **pluck•y**, *adj.* (**-ier, -iest**) brave.

plug [plʌg] 1. *n.* (a) disk which covers a hole,
esp. the hole for waste water in a bath/sink,
etc. (b) device with pins which go into the
holes in an electric socket, and allow the cur-

rent to pass through; (*in a car*) **spark p.** = device which passes electric sparks to ignite the fuel mixture. (c) *inf.* piece of publicity. (d) piece of tobacco which you chew. 2. *v.* (**plugged**) (a) to block up (a hole). (b) *inf.* to publicize. (c) *inf.* to shoot. **plug a•way**, *v. inf.* to work hard (**at**). **plug in**, *v.* to push an electric plug into a socket.

plum [plʌm] *n.* (a) gold, red or purple fruit with a smooth skin and a large stone; tree which bears this fruit; **p. pudding** = rich boiled fruit pudding, usu. eaten at Christmas. (b) deep purple color.

plum•age ['pluːmɪdʒ] *n.* feathers on a bird.

plumb [plʌm] 1. *adj.* straight; vertical. 2. *n.* lead weight for testing if sth is straight. 3. *v.* (a) to measure (the depth of water) by using a plumb line. (b) to understand or solve sth. (c) to fix the plumbing in (a house). 4. *adv.* (a) exactly (in the middle). (b) *inf.* completely. **plumb•er**, *n.* person who installs and repairs water pipes, etc. **plumb•ing**, *n.* system of water pipes in a house. **plumb line**, *n.* rope with a weight on the end, dropped over the side from a ship to find how deep the water is or held beside a wall to see if it is vertical.

plume [pluːm] *n.* tall feather (worn in a hat, etc.); tall column of smoke. **plumed**, *adj.* with a plume.

plum•met ['plʌmɪt] *v.* to fall sharply.

plump [plʌmp] 1. *adj.* (**-er, -est**) fat and tender; round fat (person). 2. *v.* (a) **to p. up** = to shake (squashed cushions) until they are fat. (b) to throw or put down with force. **plump•ness**, *n.* fatness.

plun•der ['plʌndə] 1. *n.* booty/goods seized, esp. in war. 2. *v.* to seize goods by force.

plunge [plʌndʒ] 1. *n.* dive; **to take the p.** = suddenly decide to do sth. 2. *v.* to dive deeply; to throw yourself into. **plung•er**, *n.* (a) device which goes up and down in a cylinder. (b) handle with a soft rubber head, for clearing blocked pipes by suction.

plu•per•fect [pluːˈpɜːfɪkt] *adj. & n.* (tense) showing sth which took place before a time in the past.

plu•ral ['pluərəl] *adj. & n.* (*in grammar*) form of a word showing more than one. **plu•ral•ism**, *n.* system in a country or society where groups which have different ethnic, cultural, religious, etc. backgrounds are allowed to exist. **plu•ral•i•ty** [pluəˈrælɪtɪ] *n.* majority.

plus [plʌs] 1. *prep.* in addition to. 2. *adj. & n.* (a) sign (+) meaning more than. (b) *inf.* favorable

sign. **plus-fours**, *n. pl.* baggy golfing trousers, attached at the calf.

plush [plʌʃ] 1. *n.* soft-pile cloth for furnishings. 2. *adj.* (**-er, -est**) *inf.* luxurious.

plu•to•crat ['pluːtəkræt] *n.* person who is very rich and powerful. **plu•toc•ra•cy** [pluːˈtɒkrəsɪ] *n.* government by the very rich.

plu•to•ni•um [pluːˈtəʊnɪəm] *n.* (*element:* Pu) radioactive substance, used to produce nuclear power.

ply [plaɪ] 1. *n.* (a) thickness of wood in plywood. (b) strand of wool. 2. *v.* (a) to go backward and forward. (b) **to p. s.o. with** = to force s.o. to eat/drink sth. **ply•wood**, *n.* sheet made of several thin sheets of wood stuck together.

p.m. [piːˈem] *adv.* in the afternoon/after midday.

pneu•mat•ic [njuːˈmætɪk] *adj.* driven by compressed air. **pneu•mat•i•cal•ly**, *adv.* using compressed air.

pneu•mo•nia [njuːˈməʊnɪə] *n.* illness caused by inflammation of the lungs.

PO ['piːˈəʊ] *n.* post office.

poach [pəʊtʃ] *v.* (a) to cook (eggs without their shells/fish, etc.) in gently boiling water. (b) to catch game illegally. **poach•er**, *n.* person who catches game illegally.

pock•et ['pɒkɪt] 1. *n.* (a) small bag attached to the inside of a coat/trousers, etc., for holding money/keys, etc.; **p. dictionary** = small dictionary which you can keep in your pocket; **p. money** = money given each week to a child to spend as he pleases. (b) **to be in p.** = to have made a profit; **to be out of p.** = to have lost money. (c) hole with a small bag at each corner and side of a billiard table. (d) small patch/small group in a certain place. 2. *v.* (a) to put in your pocket. (b) to send (a billiard ball) into a pocket. **pock•et•book**, *n.* woman's purse. **pock•et•ful**, *n.* amount contained in a pocket.

pock•marked ['pɒkmɑːkt] *adj.* covered with round scars.

pod [pɒd] *n.* long case in which peas/beans, etc., are formed.

podg•y ['pɒdʒɪ] *adj. inf.* (**-ier, -iest**) fat.

po•di•um ['pəʊdɪəm] *n.* raised platform (for winning sportsmen/orchestral conductors, etc., to stand on).

po•em ['pəʊɪm] *n.* piece of writing, in a particular rhythm, often with lines of a regular length which rhyme. **po•et, poetess**, *n.* person who writes poems. **po•et•ic(al)** [pəʊ-

---

æ back, ɑː farm, ɒ top, aɪ pipe, aʊ how, aɪə fire, aʊə flower, ɔː bought, ɔɪ toy, e fed, eəhair, eɪ take, ə afraid, əʊ boat, əʊə lower, ɜː word, iː heap, ɪ hit, ɪə hear, uː school, ʊ book, ʌ but, b back, d dog, ð then, dʒ just, f fog, g go, h hand, j yes, k catch, l last, m mix, n nut, ŋ sing, p penny, r round, s some, ʃ short, t too, tʃ chop, θ thing, v voice, w was, z zoo, ʒ treasure

'etɪk(l)] *adj.* referring to poetry; imaginative/rhythmic (as in a poem). **po•et•i•cal•ly,** *adv.* in a poetic way. **po•et•ry** ['pəʊətrɪ] *n.* writing of poems; poems taken as a type of literature.

po•grom ['pɒgrəm] *n.* official persecution/massacre (esp. of Jews).

poign•ant ['pɔɪnjənt] *adj.* moving/sad (thought). **poign•an•cy,** *n.* sadness. **poign•ant•ly,** *adv.* sadly/in a way which moves you to sadness.

poin•set•ti•a [pɔɪn'setɪə] *n.* plant with large green leaves, turning red at the top, used as a Christmas decoration.

point [pɔɪnt] 1. *n.* (a) sharp end (of a pin, etc.). (b) dot; **decimal p.** = dot used to indicate the division between units and decimals (such as 3.25). (c) place/spot; **p. of no return** = place where you can only go on and not go back. (d) reason/purpose. (e) meaning/argument. (f) specific time; **on the p. of** = just about to. (g) headland. (h) mark in games or competitions; mark on a scale. (i) (*in an engine*) electrical contacts. 2. *v.* (a) to aim (a gun/your finger) **at** s.o./sth. (b) to sharpen to a point. (c) to fill the spaces in between bricks with mortar. **point-blank,** *adj. & adv.* (a) at very close range. (b) sharply/directly. **point•ed,** *adj.* (a) with a sharp end. (b) obviously reproving (remark). **point•ed•ly,** *adv.* in an unfriendly way. **point•er,** *n.* (a) dog which is trained to point out game with its nose. (b) arrow/rod which points. **point•less,** *adj.* meaningless. **point•less•ly,** *adv.* meaninglessly. **point out,** *v.* to indicate/to show. **point up,** *v.* to make (sth) seem even more obvious.

poise [pɔɪz] 1. *n.* balance/graceful way of holding your head or of standing upright. 2. *v.* to balance. **poised,** *adj.* ready (**to** kill/**for** action).

poi•son ['pɔɪzn] 1. *n.* substance which kills or makes you ill if it is swallowed or if it gets into the bloodstream. 2. *v.* to kill with poison. **poi•son•er,** *n.* person who poisons. **poi•son•ous,** *adj.* which can kill or harm with poison.

poke [pəʊk] *v.* (a) to push with your finger/with a stick. (b) **to p. about/around** = to search. **pok•er,** *n.* (a) long metal rod for stirring up a fire. (b) card game in which the players gamble. **pok•er face,** *n.* expression which shows no emotion. **po•ker•faced,** *adj.* showing no emotion.

pok•y ['pəʊkɪ] *adj.* (**-ier, -iest**) *inf.* cramped/small (room).

po•lar ['pəʊlə] *adj.* referring to the North/South Poles. **po•lar bear,** *n.* white bear which lives in the Arctic. **po•lar•ize**

['pəʊləraɪz] *v.* to divide into two opposite groups. **po•lar•i•za•tion** [pəʊlərar'zeɪʃn] *n.* attraction around two opposite poles; division into main groups.

pol•der ['pɒldə] *n.* land which has been reclaimed from the sea.

pole [pəʊl] *n.* (a) one of the points at each end of the earth's axis. (b) one of the two opposing ends of a magnet; **they are poles apart** = they are very different/they will never come to an agreement. (c) long wooden/metal rod; **p. vaulting** = sport where you have to jump over a high bar with the help of a long pole. (d) **Pole** = person from Poland. **pole•ax, poleaxe.** 1. *n.* (*old*) large ax used in battle. 2. *v.* to knock (s.o.) down. **pole star,** *n.* star which appears to be near to the North Pole.

pole•cat ['pəʊlkæt] *n.* small wild flesh-eating animal, like a weasel.

po•lem•ic [pə'lemɪk] *n.* argument/attack on s.o.'s views. **po•lem•i•cal,** *adj.* controversial/likely to start an argument.

po•lice [pə'liːs] 1. *n.* group of people who keep law and order in a country; **p. force** = group of police in a certain area; **p. station** = local office of a police force. 2. *v.* to keep law and order in (a town, etc.). **po•lice•man, police-woman,** *n.* (*pl.* **-men, -women**) member of the police. **po•lice of•fi•cer,** *n.* policeman/policewoman. **po•lice state,** *n.* country which is terrorized by the police.

pol•i•cy ['pɒlɪsɪ] *n.* (a) way of acting. (b) written agreement with an insurance company.

po•li•o•my•e•li•tis [pəʊlɪəʊmaɪə'laɪtɪs] *inf.* **po•li•o** ['pəʊlɪəʊ] *n.* disease of the nerves in the spinal cord, sometimes causing paralysis.

pol•ish ['pɒlɪʃ] 1. *n.* (*pl.* **-es**) (a) shiny surface. (b) rubbing to make sth shiny. (c) substance used to make things shiny. 2. *v.* to rub (sth) to make it shiny. **pol•ished,** *adj.* (a) shiny. (b) made perfect by practice. (c) polite (manners). **pol•ish•er,** *n.* machine which polishes. **pol•ish off,** *v.* to finish off (a job) quickly/to eat (a meal) quickly. **pol•ish up,** *v. inf.* to improve.

Po•lish ['pəʊlɪʃ] 1. *adj.* referring to Poland. 2. *n.* language spoken in Poland.

Pol•it•bu•ro [pɒ'lɪtbjuːrəʊ] *n.* central committee of a communist party.

po•lite [pə'laɪt] *adj.* (**-er, -est**) not rude; courteous. **po•lite•ly,** *adv.* courteously; in a well-mannered way. **po•lite•ness,** *n.* good manners.

pol•i•tics ['pɒlɪtɪks] *n.* study of how to govern a country. **pol•i•tic** ['pɒlɪtɪk] *adj.* wise/careful. **po•lit•i•cal** [pə'lɪtɪkl] *adj.* referring to government/party politics; **p. party** = organized group of people who believe in one particular method of ruling a country. **po•lit•i•cal•ly**, *adv.* as far as politics are concerned. **po•lit•i•cal•ly cor•rect,** *adj.* referring to language or actions chosen to avoid giving offense or showing prejudice, esp. concerning race and gender. **pol•i•ti•cian** [pɒlɪ'tɪʃn] *n.* person who works in politics, esp. a member of parliament.

pol•ka ['pɒlkə] *n.* type of lively dance; **p. dots** = small round dots (as a pattern on cloth).

poll [pəʊl] 1. *n.* (a) vote/voting. (b) number of votes. (c) **public opinion p.** = questioning of a sample group of people to guess at the views of the whole population on a question. 2. *v.* (a) to vote. (b) to get a number of votes in an election. (c) to cut the horns off (a cow). **poll•ing,** *n.* voting; elections; **p. booth** = small booth in which each voter writes his vote; **p. place** = place where you vote in an election. **poll tax,** *n.* tax which is levied equally on each person.

pol•lard ['pɒləd] *v.* to cut the branches of (a tree) back to the main trunk.

pol•len ['pɒln] *n.* usu. yellow powder in flowers which fertilizes them; **p. count** = number showing the amount of pollen in the air (which can cause hayfever). **pol•li•nate** ['pɒlɪneɪt] *v.* to fertilize with pollen. **pol•li•na•tion** [pɒlɪ'neɪʃn] *n.* fertilizing with pollen.

pol•lute [pə'luːt] *v.* to make dirty. **pol•lu•tant,** *n.* substance which pollutes. **pol•lut•er,** *n.* person or company which pollutes. **pol•lu•tion** [pə'luːʃn] *n.* making dirty.

po•lo ['pəʊləʊ] *n.* (a) ball game in which the two teams ride on ponies; **water p.** = ball game played by two teams in the water. (b) **p. shirt** = pullover sports shirt, usu. with short sleeves.

pol•ter•geist ['pɒltəgaɪst] *n.* ghost which knocks things over/makes loud sounds, etc.

poly- ['pɒlɪ] *prefix meaning* several.

pol•y•an•thus [pɒlɪ'ænθəs] *n.* common garden flower, like a primrose with a large flower head.

pol•y•chrome ['pɒlɪkrəʊm] *adj.* with several colors.

pol•y•es•ter [pɒlɪ'estə] *n.* type of synthetic fiber used esp. in clothing.

po•lyg•a•my [pə'lɪgəmɪ] *n.* custom of having several wives at the same time. **po•lyg•a•mist,** *n.* man with several wives. **po•lyg•a•mous,** *adj.* referring to polygamy.

pol•y•glot ['pɒlɪglɒt] *adj. & n.* (person) who speaks several languages; (dictionary, etc.) written in several languages.

pol•y•gon ['pɒlɪgən] *n.* geometrical figure with many sides. **po•lyg•o•nal** [pə'lɪgənl] *adj.* with many sides.

pol•y•mer ['pɒlɪmə] *n.* chemical compound whose molecule is made of several single similar molecules. **po•lym•er•i•za•tion,** *n.* act of polymerizing. **po•lym•er•ize,** *v.* to make/to become a polymer.

pol•yp ['pɒlɪp] *n.* (a) small primitive water animal shaped like a tube. (b) growth inside the human body.

pol•y•sty•rene [pɒlɪ'staɪriːn] *n.* light plastic used as a heat insulator or as packing material.

pol•y•syl•la•ble ['pɒlɪsɪləbl] *n.* word with several syllables. **pol•y•syl•lab•ic** [pɒlɪsɪ'læbɪk] *adj.* (word) with several syllables.

pol•y•tech•nic [pɒlɪ'teknɪk] *n.* educational establishment giving degrees, esp. in technical subjects.

pol•y•the•ism [pɒlɪ'θiːɪzm] *n.* belief in the existence of many gods.

pol•y•thene ['pɒlɪθiːn] *n.* type of almost transparent plastic used in thin sheets.

pol•y•un•sat•u•rat•ed [pɒlʌn'sætjʊreɪtɪd] *adj.* (fat) which does not form cholesterol in the blood.

pol•y•u•re•thane [pɒlɪ'jʊərəθeɪn] *n.* type of plastic used in paints.

po•man•der [pə'mændə] *n.* (box containing) dried scented herbs; **p. ball** = dried orange with cloves stuck into it.

pome•gran•ate ['pɒmɪgrænɪt] *n.* tropical fruit with red flesh and many seeds.

pom•mel ['pɒml] *n.* high front part of a saddle.

pomp [pɒmp] *n.* splendid ceremony. **pom•pos•i•ty** [pɒm'pɒsɪtɪ] *n.* being pompous. **pomp•ous** ['pɒmpəs] *adj.* very solemn/too dignified.

pom•pom ['pɒmpɒm] *n.* small tufted ball of wool worn as an ornament on a hat, etc.

pon•cho ['pɒnʃəʊ] *n.* (*pl.* **-os**) cloak made of a single large piece of material, with a hole in the center for your head.

pond [pɒnd] *n.* small lake.

pon•der ['pɒndə] *v.* to think deeply. **pon•der•ous,** *adj.* very heavy and slow-moving. **pon•der•ous•ly,** *adv.* in a ponderous way.

æ back, ɑː farm, ɒ top, aɪ pipe, aʊ how, aɪe fire, aʊə flower, ɔː bought, ɔɪ toy, e fed, eəhair, eɪ take, ə afraid, əʊ boat, əʊə lower, vː word, iː heap, ɪ hit, ɪə hear, uː school, ʊ book, ʌ but, b back, d dog, ð then, dʒ just, f fog, g go, h hand, j yes, k catch, l last, m mim, n nut, ŋ sing, p penny, r round, s some, ʃ short, t too, tʃ chop, θ thing, v voice, w was, z zoo, ʒ treasure

pon•tiff ['pɒntɪf] *n.* the Pope. **pon•tif•i•cal** [pɒn'tɪfɪkl] *adj.* referring to the Pope. **pon•tif•i•cate** [pɒn'tɪfɪkeɪt] *v.* to speak/to write in a pompous way.

pon•toon [pɒn'tuːn] *n.* boat used to support a floating temporary bridge; **p. bridge** = one built on pontoons.

po•ny ['pəʊnɪ] *n.* small horse. **pony tail,** *n.* hairstyle where the hair is tied at the back and falls loosely.

poo•dle ['puːdl] *n.* type of curly-haired dog, usu. clipped.

poof [puːf] *n. Sl.* (*rude*) homosexual.

pooh-pooh [puː'puː] *v. inf.* to ridicule (an idea).

pool [puːl] 1. *n.* (a) small lake. (b) area of water or other liquid. (c) **swimming p.** = enclosed tank of water for swimming. (d) common supply of money/food, etc., for a group of people. (e) group where people share facilities; **car p.** = arrangement where several people share cars; **typing p.** = group of typists working for several departments. (f) (*in sports*) system of gambling where you have to forecast the results of a game or match. (g) game similar to billiards. 2. *v.* to group (resources) together. **pool•room,** *n.* public place where you can play pool.

poop [puːp] *n.* high raised stern of a ship.

poor ['pʊə, pɔː] *adj.* (**-er, -est**) (a) having little or no money; **p. in** = with very little (of sth). (b) not very good. **poor•ly.** 1. *adv.* (a) in quite a bad way. (b) without money. 2. *adj.* ill. **poor•ness,** *n.* bad quality.

pop [pɒp] 1. *n.* (a) noise like a cork coming out of a bottle. (b) *inf.* father. (c) *inf.* popular song. (d) *inf.* nonalcoholic sweet drink. 2. *v.* (**popped**) (a) to make a pop. (b) *inf.* to go quickly. (c) to put quickly. (d) to ask (a question) quickly. 3. *adj. inf.* popular. **pop•corn,** *n.* sweet corn which has been heated until it bursts. **pop•gun,** *n.* toy gun which makes a pop.

Pope [pəʊp] *n.* the head of the Roman Catholic Church.

pop•lar ['pɒplə] *n.* common tall and slender tree.

pop•lin ['pɒplɪn] *n.* strong cotton cloth used for making shirts.

pop•py ['pɒpɪ] *n.* common flower, red when wild.

pop•u•lace ['pɒpjʊləs] *n.* ordinary people.

pop•u•lar ['pɒpjʊlə] *adj.* (a) referring to the ordinary people. (b) liked by a lot of people. **pop•u•lar•i•ty** [pɒpjʊ'lærɪtɪ] *n.* being popular. **pop•u•lar•i•za•tion** [pɒpjʊlərəɪ'zeɪʃn] *n.* act of popularizing. **pop•u•lar•ize** ['pɒpjʊləraɪz] *v.* to make (sth) understood/liked by a lot of people. **pop•u•lar•ly,** *adv.* generally; by most people.

pop•u•late ['pɒpjʊleɪt] *v.* to put people to live in (a place). **pop•u•la•tion** [pɒpjʊ'leɪʃn] *n.* number of people who live in a place. **pop•u•lous** ['pɒpjʊləs] *adj.* thickly populated.

por•bea•gle ['pɔːbiːgl] *n.* type of shark.

por•ce•lain ['pɔːslɪn] *n.* fine china.

porch [pɔːtʃ] *n.* (*pl.* **-es**) shelter over a doorway.

por•cine ['pɔːsaɪn] *adj.* like a pig.

por•cu•pine ['pɔːkjʊpaɪn] *n.* rodent with long sharp spikes covering its body.

pore [pɔː] 1. *n.* small hole in the skin through which sweat passes. 2. *v.* **to p. over** = to look at (a book, etc.) very closely.

pork [pɔːk] *n.* (*no pl.*) meat from a pig. **pork•er,** *n. inf.* pig.

por•nog•ra•phy [pɔː'nɒgrəfɪ] *n.* pornographic motion pictures/books/art. **porn** [pɔːn] *n. inf.* pornography; **hard/soft p.** = extremely indecent/less indecent pornographic material. **por•no•graph•ic** [pɔːnə'græfɪk] *adj.* (book, etc.) which deals with sex in an indecent way.

po•rous ['pɔːrəs] *adj.* (solid) which allows liquid to pass through. **po•ros•i•ty** [pɔː'rɒsɪtɪ] *n.* being porous.

por•phy•ry ['pɔːfɪrɪ] *n.* type of stone with crystals in it.

por•poise ['pɔːpəs] *n.* large sea mammal which tends to swim in groups.

por•ridge ['pɒrɪdʒ] *n.* (*no pl.*) oatmeal cooked in water.

port [pɔːt] *n.* (a) harbor. (b) town with a harbor. (c) left side (when looking forward on board a ship/aircraft). (d) strong sweet wine from Portugal. (e) opening in a ship's side for a gun. (f) opening in a computer for plugging in an attachment.

port•a•ble ['pɔːtəbl] 1. *adj.* which can be carried. 2. *n.* machine, such as a small computer, which can be carried.

por•tage ['pɔːtɑːʒ] *n.* transporting a boat across country.

por•tal ['pɔːtl] *n.* imposing entrance.

port•cul•lis [pɔːt'kʌlɪs] *n.* (*pl.* **-es**) gate which was dropped to close the entrance to a medieval castle.

por•tend [pɔː'tend] *v.* (*formal*) to warn (that sth unpleasant is going to happen).

por•tent ['pɔːtənt] *n.* (*formal*) warning (that sth unpleasant is going to happen). **por•ten•tous** [pɔː'tentəs] *adj.* important/significant; warning that sth unpleasant is going to happen.

por•ter ['pɔːtə] *n.* (a) person who carries luggage for travelers. (b) doorkeeper (in a hotel).

(c) person who does general work in a restaurant, store, etc. **por•ter•age,** *n.* charge for carrying sth. **por•ter•house (steak),** *n.* piece of best quality steak.

port•fo•li•o [pɔːt'fəʊlɪəʊ] *n.* (*pl.* **-os**) (a) large cardboard case for carrying paintings, etc. (b) collection of shares. (c) (*in government*) office of minister or cabinet member.

port•hole ['pɔːthəʊl] *n.* round window in the side of a ship.

por•ti•co ['pɔːtɪkəʊ] *n.* (*pl.* **-oes, -os**) roof supported by columns forming a porch in front of the entrance to a building.

por•tion ['pɔːʃn] 1. *n.* (a) part. (b) serving of food. 2. *v.* **to p. out** = to share out.

port•ly ['pɔːtlɪ] *adj.* (**-ier, -iest**) rather fat.

port•man•teau [pɔːt'mæntəʊ] *n.* trunk for carrying clothes.

por•trait ['pɔːtreɪt] *n.* painting/photograph of a person. **por•trai•ture** ['pɔːtrətʃə] *n.* art of painting portraits. **por•tray** [pɔː'treɪ] *v.* to paint/to describe (a scene or a person). **por•tray•al,** *n.* painting; description of a scene or person.

Por•tu•guese [pɔːtju'giːz] 1. *adj.* referring to Portugal; **P. man-of-war** = type of very large jelly fish. 2. *n.* (a) person from Portugal. (b) language spoken in Portugal.

pose [pəʊz] 1. *n.* (a) way of standing/sitting. (b) way of behaving which is just a pretense. 2. *v.* (a) **to p. for s.o.** = to stand/to sit still while s.o. paints/photographs you. (b) to pretend to be. (c) to set (a problem); to put (a question). **pos•er,** *n. inf.* difficult question. **po•seur** [pəʊ'zɜː] *n.* person who behaves in a false way.

posh [pɒʃ] *adj.* (**-er, -est**) inf. very smart.

po•si•tion [pə'zɪʃn] 1. *n.* (a) way of standing/sitting. (b) place. (c) job. 2. *v.* to place.

pos•i•tive ['pɒzɪtɪv] 1. *adj.* (a) meaning yes. (b) certain; sure/convinced. (c) registering the existence of sth. (d) plus/more than zero. 2. *n.* (a) photograph printed from a negative, where the light and dark appear as they are in nature. (b) one of the terminals in a battery. **pos•i•tive•ly,** *adv.* absolutely. **pos•i•tron,** *n.* positive electron.

pos•se ['pɒsɪ] *n.* group of armed men/police.

pos•sess [pə'zes] *v.* (a) to own. (b) to occupy s.o.'s mind; **what possessed him?** = why did he do it? **pos•ses•sion** [pə'zeʃn] *n.* (a) ownership. (b) thing you own. **pos•ses•sive,** *adj.* (a) (*in grammar*) (word) which indicates possession. (b) (person) who treats another person as if he owns him. **pos•ses•sive•ly,** *adv.* in a possessive way. **pos•ses•sor,** *n.* owner.

pos•si•ble ['pɒsɪbl] *adj.* (a) which can happen. (b) likely. **pos•si•bil•i•ty** [pɒsɪ'bɪlɪtɪ] *n.* (a) chance; being likely. (b) **the plan has possibilities** = may well work. **pos•si•bly,** *adv.* (a) which may happen. (b) perhaps.

pos•sum ['pɒsəm] *n. inf.* **to play p.** = to pretend to sleep/to be dead so as to trick an opponent.

post [pəʊst] 1. *n.* (a) wooden/concrete stake fixed in the ground. (b) place where a sentry is on duty. (c) job/position. (d) small settlement far from civilization. (e) (*esp. Brit.*) mail; letters, etc., sent by mail. 2. *v.* (a) to send (s.o.) on duty. (b) (*esp. Brit.*) to send (a letter, etc.) by mail; **to keep s.o. posted** = to keep s.o. informed. (c) to stick up (a notice). **post•age,** *n.* payment for sending a letter by mail; **p. stamp** = piece of paper which you buy and stick on a letter, etc., to pay for it to be sent to its destination. **post•al,** *adj.* referring to the post office. **post•card,** *n.* card (sometimes with a picture) which you send through the mail. **post•er,** *n.* large notice stuck up on a wall, etc.; large picture/advertisement stuck on a wall. **post•haste,** *adv.* very fast. **post•man,** *n.* (*pl.* **-men**) person who delivers letters to houses. **post•mark.** 1. *n.* mark stamped on a letter to show when it was mailed. 2. *v.* to stamp (a letter) with a postmark. **post•mas•ter, postmistress,** *n.* (a) person in charge of a post office. (b) person in charge of electronic mail at a site. **post of•fice,** *n.* (a) building where mail is received/stamps sold, etc. (b) government organization which runs the postal services. **post•paid,** *adj.* (reply) with postage paid by the sender.

post- [pəʊst] *prefix meaning* later than/after. **post•date,** *v.* to put a date on (a check) which is later than the day on which you actually write it. **post•grad•u•ate,** *n.* person who has a first degree from a college or university and who is studying for a further degree. **post•hu•mous** ['pɒstjuməs] *adj.* after death. **post•hu•mous•ly,** *adv.* after death. **post•mod•ern,** *adj.* (architecture/literature, etc.) rejecting modernism, esp. by mixing styles or by drawing attention to generic conventions. **post mor•tem** [pəʊst'mɔːtəm] *adj. & n.* (examination) to find out the cause of death. **post•na•tal,** *adj.* referring to the time just after the birth of a child. **post•pone**

[pəs'pəun] v. to put off until later.
post•pone•ment, n. putting off until later.
post•pran•di•al, adj. after dinner.
post•script, n. additional note at the end of
a letter. **post•vi•ral syn•drome,** n. see
chronic fatigue syndrome. post•war,
adj. referring to the period after the war.
pos•te•ri•or [pɒ'stɪərɪə] n. behind/buttocks.
pos•ter•i•ty [pɒ'sterɪtɪ] n. generations
which will follow.
pos•tern ['pɒstən] n. (old) back door or gate.
pos•tu•late ['pɒstjʊleɪt] 1. n. basis upon which
sth is postulated. 2. v. to suppose (that sth is
true). **pos•tu•lant,** n. person who is a candidate to join a religious order.
pos•ture ['pɒstʃə] 1. n. way of sitting/standing,
etc. 2. v. to take up a particular position for
effect.
po•sy ['pəuzɪ] n. small bunch of flowers.
pot [pɒt] 1. n. (a) container made of glass or
clay. (b) inf. **to go to p.** = to become ru-
ined/useless. (c) Sl. marijuana. 2. v. (**potted**) to
put in a pot. **pot•bel•ly,** n. inf. fat stomach.
pot•boil•er, n. worthless novel written rapidly for money. **potbound,** adj. (of plant)
with roots too large for the pot. **pot•hole,** n.
(a) hole in rock worn away by water. (b) hole
in a road surface. **pot•luck,** n. **to take p.** = to
take whatever comes, with no possibility of
choice. **pot•sherd,** n. piece of broken pot.
pot•shot, n. inf. **to take a p. at s.o.** = to try to
shoot s.o. without aiming properly. **pot•ted,**
adj. preserved in a pot. **pot•ting shed,** n.
shed in a garden where you put plants in pots.
po•ta•ble ['pɒtəbl] adj. which can be drunk
safely.
pot•ash ['pɒtæʃ] n. potassium salts.
po•tas•si•um [pə'tæsɪəm] n. (element: K)
light white metallic substance.
po•ta•to [pə'teɪtəu] n. (pl. **-oes**) common vegetable, formed under the soil; **sweet p.** = yam.
po•teen [pɒ'tiːn] n. illegal distilled whiskey.
po•ten•cy ['pəutənsɪ] n. strength. **po•tent,**
adj. strong.
po•ten•tate ['pəutənteɪt] n. Eastern ruler.
po•ten•tial [pə'tenʃl] 1. adj. possible. 2. n. (a)
possibility of developing into sth valuable. (b)
(in physics) electrical property which governs
the flow of an electric charge.
po•ten•ti•al•i•ty, n. being potential.
po•ten•tial•ly, adv. possibly.
po•ten•ti•om•e•ter, n. instrument for
measuring differences in electrical potential.
po•tion ['pəuʃn] n. liquid mixture to make you
sleep, etc.
pot•pour•ri [pəupuːˈriː] n. (a) dried flow-
ers/herbs kept in a bowl to scent a room. (b)
general mixture of bits and pieces.

pot•ter ['pɒtə] 1. n. person who makes pots
out of clay. 2. v. (esp. Brit.) **to p. about** = to
putter around. **pot•ter•y,** n. (a) potter's
workshop. (b) pots; articles made of clay,
earthenware.
pot•ty ['pɒtɪ] inf. 1. n. child's toilet. 2. adj. (**-ier,
-iest**) (esp. Brit.) mad.
pouch [pautʃ] n. (pl. **-es**) (a) small bag for carrying coins/ammunition, etc. (b) bag in the skin
in front of some marsupials where the young
live and grow for some time after birth.
poul•tice ['pəultɪs] 1. n. hot wet dressing put
on a wound. 2. v. to dress (a wound) with a
poultice.
poul•try ['pəultrɪ] n. (no pl.) common farm
birds such as ducks/hens, reared for eggs or to
be eaten.
pounce [pauns] 1. n. act of pouncing. 2. v. to
jump (**on** sth).
pound [paund] 1. n. (a) measure of weight (=
approx. 16 ounces or 0.45 kilogram). (b) standard unit of money in Great Britain and several other countries. (c) place where stray
animals or illegally-parked cars are put. 2. v.
(a) to smash into little pieces; to hit hard. (b)
to run heavily. (c) (of heart) to beat fast.
pound•age ['paundɪdʒ] n. rate charged for
each pound.
pour [pɔː] v. (a) to flow out/down. (b) to transfer liquid from one container to another.
pout [paut] 1. n. (a) sulky expression where the
lips stick out. (b) type of fish. 2. v. to make a
sulky expression with the lips.
pov•er•ty ['pɒvətɪ] n. being poor; **a p. of** = a
lack of.
pow•der ['paudə] 1. n. very fine dry grains
(like flour); (**face**) **p.** = scented flourlike substance for putting on the face; **p. room** =
women's toilet. 2. v. to put powder on.
pow•dered, adj. covered with powder.
pow•der•y, adj. fine/like powder.
pow•er ['pauə] n. (a) strength. (b) ability. (c)
driving force; **p. pack** = portable source of
electricity. (d) (in mathematics) number of
times a number is multiplied by itself. (e) (in
physics) strength of a lens. (f) (also **power base**)
political/social strength (of a person/a group).
(g) political control. **pow•er•boat,** n. boat
which has a powerful engine, used for racing.
power down, v. to shut down (a computer)
in stages, finishing by switching off the
power. **power drill,** n. powerful electric
drill. **pow•ered,** adj. driven/worked.
pow•er•ful, adj. very strong.
pow•er•less, adj. unable to do anything.
pow•er sta•tion, pow•er plant, n. works
where electricity is produced. **pow•er
steer•ing,** n. steering (in a car) which is pow-

ered by the engine. **power up**, v. to switch on the power to sth, esp. a computer.

pow•wow ['pauwau] n. inf. meeting to discuss some problem.

PR [piː'ɑː] n. public relations; proportional representation.

prac•ti•ca•ble ['præktɪkəbl] adj. which can be done/which can be put into practice. **prac•ti•ca•bil•i•ty** [præktɪkə'bɪlɪtɪ] n. ability to be put into practice.

prac•ti•cal ['præktɪkl] adj. interested in practice/action rather than ideas; referring to practice rather than theory; **p. joke** = trick played on s.o. to make other people laugh. **prac•ti•cal•i•ty**, n. way in which sth works in practice. **prac•ti•cal•ly**, adv. (a) in practice. (b) almost.

prac•tice ['præktɪs] 1. n. (a) actual application; **to put sth into p.** = to apply sth/to use sth. (b) habit. (c) repeated exercise; **out of p.** = not capable because of lack of exercise. (d) business of a doctor/dentist/lawyer. (e) **practices** = ways of doing things. 2. v. (a) to put sth into practice. (b) to do repeated exercises. (c) to carry on a job as a doctor or lawyer. **prac•ticed**, adj. skilled.

prac•ti•tion•er [præk'tɪʃənə] n. doctor; **general p.** = doctor who treats all patients/all illnesses.

prag•mat•ic [præg'mætɪk] adj. dealing with fact/practical matters, not concerned with theory. **prag•mat•i•cal•ly**, adv. in a pragmatic way. **prag•ma•tism** ['prægmətɪzəm] n. pragmatic approach (to a problem). **prag•ma•tist**, n. person who is pragmatic.

prai•rie ['preərɪ] n. grass-covered plain in North America; **p. dog** = small North American mammal, living in burrows; **p. oyster** = mixture of raw egg, tomato juice and spices, taken to cure a hangover.

praise [preɪz] 1. n. admiration/expression of approval. 2. v. to express strong approval of (s.o./sth). **praise•wor•thy**, adj. which should be praised.

pra•line ['prɑːliːn] n. candy made of crushed nuts and honey.

pram [præm] n. Brit. inf. baby carriage.

prance [prɑːns] v. to jump about/to move lightly.

prank [præŋk] n. trick.

prat•tle ['prætl] 1. n. chatter. 2. v. to chatter in a childish way.

prawn [prɔːn] n. shellfish like a large shrimp.

prax•is ['præksɪs] n. practice.

pray [preɪ] v. to speak to God; to ask God for sth; (formal) **p. be seated** = please sit down. **prayer**, n. act of speaking to God; request.

pre- [prɪ] prefix meaning before.

preach [priːtʃ] v. (a) to give a sermon in church. (b) to recommend/to advise; to give moral advice. **preach•er**, n. person who gives a sermon.

pre•am•ble [priː'æmbl] n. introduction/remarks at the beginning (of a speech/treaty, etc.).

pre•ar•range [priːə'reɪndʒ] v. to arrange in advance.

pre•car•i•ous [prɪ'keərɪəs] adj. likely to fall; uncertain. **pre•car•i•ous•ly**, adv. unsafely.

pre•cau•tion [prɪ'kɔːʃn] n. care taken in advance (to avoid sth unpleasant). **pre•cau•tion•ar•y**, adj. (measure) taken to avoid sth unpleasant.

pre•cede [prɪ'siːd] v. to take place before (sth). **prec•e•dence** ['presɪdəns] n. **to take p. over** = to go before/to be more important than. **prec•e•dent** ['presɪdənt] n. thing which has happened before, and which can be a guide as to what should be done. **pre•ced•ing** [prɪ'siːdɪŋ] adj. which comes before.

pre•cen•tor [prɪ'sentɔː] n. person in charge of leading a church choir or the congregation in singing.

pre•cept ['priːsept] n. command; guiding rule.

pre•cinct ['priːsɪŋkt] n. area surrounded by a wall; administrative district of a town or city.

pre•cious ['preʃəs] adj. worth a lot of money; of great value.

prec•i•pice ['presɪpɪs] n. high cliff (not usu. near the sea). **pre•cip•i•tous** [prɪ'sɪpɪtəs] adj. very steep.

pre•cip•i•tate 1. n. [prɪ'sɪpɪtət] chemical substance which settles at the bottom of a liquid. 2. v. [prɪ'sɪpɪteɪt] (a) to make sth happen suddenly. (b) to settle at the bottom of a liquid. 3. adj. [prɪ'sɪpɪtət] rushed/hurried. **pre•cip•i•tate•ly**, adv. in a rushed way. **pre•cip•i•ta•tion** [prɪsɪpɪ'teɪʃn] n. (a) (formal) great hurry. (b) quantity of rain/snow, etc., which falls on a certain place.

pré•cis ['preɪsɪ] 1. n. (pl. précis ['preɪsiːz]) summary of the main points of a text. 2. v. to summarize.

pre•cise [prɪ'saɪs] adj. (a) exact. (b) careful. **pre•cise•ly**, adv. (a) exactly. (b) in a careful way. **pre•ci•sion** [prɪ'sɪʒn] n. accuracy.

æ back, ɑː farm, ɒ top, aɪ pipe, aʊ how, aɪə fire, aʊə flower, ɔː bought, ɔɪ toy, e fed, eəhair, eɪ take, ə afraid, əʊ boat, əʊə lower, ɜː word, iː heap, ɪ hit, ɪə hear, uː school, ʊ book, ʌ but, b back, d dog, ð then, dʒ just, f fog, g go, h hand, j yes, k catch, l last, m mix, n nut, ŋ sing, p penny, r round, s some, ʃ short, t too, tʃ chop, θ thing, v voice, w was, z zoo, ʒ treasure

pre•clude [prɪ'kluːd] v. to prevent.

pre•co•cious [prɪ'kəʊʃəs] adj. (child) who is surprisingly advanced for his/her age. **pre•co•cious•ly**, adv. in a precocious way. **pre•co•cious•ness, precocity** [prɪ'kɒsɪti] n. being precocious.

pre•con•ceive [priːkən'siːv] v. to have an idea or belief from the beginning/before sth starts. **pre•con•cep•tion** [priːkən'sepʃn] n. preconceived idea.

pre•con•di•tion [priːkən'dɪʃn] n. condition which is set in advance.

pre•cur•sor [prɪ'kɜːsə] n. thing which leads to an invention/person who goes in advance. **pre•cur•so•ry**, adj. which is in advance.

pre•date ['priːdeɪt] v. to come before in date.

pred•a•tor ['predətə] n. animal which lives by eating other animals. **pred•a•to•ry**, adj. (animal) which eats other animals; (person) who lives off other people.

pre•de•cease [priːdɪ'siːs] v. (formal) to die before (s.o.). **pred•e•ces•sor** ['priːdɪsesə] n. person who has held the same job, etc., before you.

pre•des•tine [priː'destɪn] v. to decide the fate of (s.o.) in advance. **pre•des•ti•na•tion** [priːdestɪ'neɪʃn] n. being predestined.

pre•de•ter•mine [priːdɪ'tɜːmɪn] v. to decide in advance.

pre•dic•a•ment [prɪ'dɪkəmənt] n. troubles/difficult situation.

pred•i•cate 1. n. ['predɪkət] (in grammar) statement about the subject. 2. v. ['predɪkeɪt] (formal) to base a supposition on (sth).

pred•i•ca•tive [prɪ'dɪkətɪv] adj. (adjective, etc.) which makes a statement about a noun.

pre•dict [prɪ'dɪkt] v. to foretell/to tell in advance what will happen. **pre•dict•a•ble**, adj. which could be predicted. **pre•dict•a•bly**, adv. in a way which could have been predicted. **pre•dic•tion** [prɪ'dɪkʃn] n. foretelling.

pre•di•lec•tion [priːdɪ'lekʃn] n. liking/preference.

pre•dis•pose [priːdɪ'spəʊz] v. to make (s.o.) favor sth in advance. **pre•dis•po•si•tion** [priːdɪspə'zɪʃn] n. being predisposed.

pre•dom•i•nate [prɪ'dɒmɪneɪt] v. to be bigger/stronger/more numerous. **pre•dom•i•nance**, n. being predominant. **pre•dom•i•nant** [prɪ'dɒmɪnənt] adj. most striking/obvious. **pre•dom•i•nant•ly**, adv in a predominant way.

pre•em•i•nent, pre-eminent [priː'emɪnənt] adj. excellent/much better than everything else. **pre•em•i•nence, pre-eminence**, n. being preeminent.

pre•empt, pre-empt [priː'empt] v. to get an advantage by doing sth before anyone else. **pre•emp•tion, pre-emption**, n. act of preempting. **pre•emp•tive, pre-emptive**, adj. which gains an advantage by acting before anyone else.

preen [priːn] v. (of bird) to smooth its feathers; **to p. yourself** = to smarten yourself up; **to p. yourself on sth** = to congratulate yourself.

pre•fab•ri•cat•ed [priː'fæbrɪkeɪtɪd] adj. built in advance; (house) built out of pieces which are assembled on the site. **pre•fab** ['priːfæb] n. inf. prefabricated house. **pre•fab•ri•ca•tion** [priːfæbrɪ'keɪʃn] n. building in advance.

pref•ace ['prefəs] 1. n. piece written (usu. by the author) to introduce a book. 2. v. to say/to write sth as an introduction. **pref•a•to•ry** ['prefətrɪ] adj. which acts as a preface.

pre•fect ['priːfekt] n. high official, as the administrative head of one of the departments of France.

pre•fer [prɪ'fɜː] v. (preferred) (a) **to p. sth to sth** = to like (to do) sth better than sth else. (b) (formal) to promote (s.o.). **pref•er•a•ble** ['prefrəbl] adj. which you would prefer. **pref•er•a•bly**, adv. if possible. **pref•er•ence** ['prefrəns] n. liking for one thing more than another. **pref•er•en•tial** [prefə'renʃl] adj. showing one thing is preferred to another. **pre•fer•ment** [prɪ'fɜːmənt] n. promotion to a more important post.

pre•fix ['priːfɪks] 1. n. (pl. -es) part of a word put in front of another. 2. v. to put some word in front of another/to preface.

preg•nan•cy ['pregnənsɪ] n. state of being pregnant; **p. test** = test to see if a woman is pregnant. **preg•nant**, adj. carrying an unborn child; **p. pause** = pause while everyone waits for sth to happen/for s.o. to speak.

pre•hen•sile [priː'hensaɪl] adj. which can grasp/hold on to sth.

pre•his•to•ry [priː'hɪstərɪ] n. time before written history. **pre•his•to•ri•an** [priːhɪ'stɔːrɪən] n. person who specializes in the study of prehistory. **pre•his•tor•ic** [priːhɪ'stɒrɪk] adj. belonging to prehistory.

pre•judge [priː'dʒʌdʒ] v. to judge (sth) without hearing all the facts.

prej•u•dice ['predʒədɪs] 1. n. (usu. unjust) feeling against s.o.. 2. v. (a) to make (s.o.) unfriendly toward s.o./sth. (b) to harm. **prej•u•diced**, adj. unfairly biased (against s.o.). **prej•u•di•cial** [predʒʊ'dɪʃl] adj. which might be damaging.

prel•ate ['prelət] n. person of high rank in a church.

pre•lim•i•nar•y [prɪ'lɪmɪnərɪ] adj. which

goes before. **pre•lim•i•nar•ies,** *n. pl.* things which have to be done before sth can take place.

prel•ude ['prelju:d] *n.* thing (esp. piece of music) which introduces sth more important; short piece of music on one theme.

pre•mar•i•tal [prɪ'mærɪtəl] *adj.* before marriage.

pre•ma•ture [premə'tjʊə] *adj.* which happens before the right time; (baby) born less than nine months after conception. **pre•ma•ture•ly,** *adv.* before the right time.

pre•med•i•tate [pri:'medɪteɪt] *v.* to think over/to plan in advance. **pre•med•i•ta•tion** [pri:medɪ'teɪʃn] *n.* planning in advance.

pre•mier ['premɪə] 1. *n.* prime minister. 2. *adj.* first/most important. **pre•mière** ['premɪeə] *n.* first performance of a motion picture/play, etc. **pre•mier•ship,** *n.* being prime minister; time when s.o. is prime minister.

prem•ise ['premɪs] *n.* (*pl.* **-es**) statement which is the basis for reasoning.

prem•is•es ['premɪsɪz] *n. pl.* building and land around it.

pre•mi•um ['pri:mɪəm] *n.* (a) annual amount paid for an insurance policy. (b) **at a p.** = scarce, and therefore valuable; **to put a p. on sth** = to show that sth is useful/valuable. (c) bonus.

pre•mo•lar [pri:'məʊlə] *n.* tooth between the canines and the molars.

pre•mo•ni•tion [premə'nɪʃn] *n.* feeling that sth is going to happen. **pre•mon•i•to•ry** [prɪ'mɒnɪtrɪ] *adj.* warning (sign).

pre•na•tal [pri:'neɪtl] *adj.* referring to the time before the birth of a child.

pre•oc•cu•pa•tion [pri:ɒkju'peɪʃn] *n.* only thinking about one thing. **pre•oc•cu•pied,** *adj.* thinking only about one thing; worried. **pre•oc•cu•py,** *v.* to make (s.o.) think about only one thing and worry about it.

prep [prep] *adj. inf.* (a) used in preparing for sth. (b) **p. school** = preparatory school.

pre•pare [prɪ'peə] *v.* to get ready. **prep•a•ra•tion** [prepə'reɪʃn] *n.* (a) getting ready. (b) substance which has been mixed. **pre•par•a•to•ry** [prɪ'pærətrɪ] *adj.* which prepares; **p. school** = private or parochial school that prepares students for college. **pre•pared,** *adj.* ready (**to**).

pre•pay ['pri:peɪ] *v.* (**prepaid**) to pay in ad-

vance. **pre•pay•ment,** *n.* paying in advance.

pre•pon•der•ate [prɪ'pɒndəreɪt] *v.* (*formal*) to be in a majority. **pre•pon•der•ance** [prɪ'pɒndərəns] *n.* large number. **pre•pon•der•ant,** *adj.* in a majority.

prep•o•si•tion [prepə'zɪʃn] *n.* word which is used with a noun/pronoun to show how it is linked to another word.

pre•pos•sess•ing [pri:pə'zesɪŋ] *adj.* pleasant.

pre•pos•ter•ous [pri:'pɒstərəs] *adj.* silly/absurd.

pre•pro•grammed; preprogramed [pri:-'prəʊgræmd] *adj.* which has been programmed beforehand.

pre•req•ui•site [pri:'rekwɪzɪt] *n.* thing which you must have before you can do sth.

pre•rog•a•tive [prɪ'rɒgətɪv] *n.* privilege belonging to one person or group.

presby•o•pi•a [prezbɪ'əʊpɪə] *n.* gradual failing sight (in an old person).

pres•by•ter•y ['prezbɪtərɪ] *n.* (a) Roman Catholic priest's house. (b) court of a church made of ministers and important laymen. **Pres•by•te•ri•an** [prezbɪ'ti:ərɪən] *adj. & n.* (member) of a Protestant church, ruled by a group of laymen.

pre•scient ['presɪənt] *adj.* (*formal*) (person) who can tell what is likely to take place in the future. **pre•science,** *n.* being prescient.

pre•scribe [prɪ'skraɪb] *v.* to order (sth) to be done; to tell s.o. to use (sth). **pre•scrip•tion** [prɪ'skrɪpʃn] *n.* paper on which a doctor has written out instructions for the preparation and use of a medicine to be taken by the patient. **pre•scrip•tive,** *adj.* which prescribes.

pres•ence ['prezns] *n.* (a) being present. (b) **p. of mind** = sense/calmness; ability to act quickly. (c) impressive appearance/way of acting (on the stage).

pre•sent 1. *adj.* ['preznt] (a) being at the place/at the time. (b) being here now. (c) (*in grammar*) (tense) which describes what is happening now. 2. *n.* ['preznt] *n.* (a) at the time we are in now; **at p.** = now. (b) gift. 3. *v.* [prɪ'zent] (a) to give. (b) to put on (a play/show). (c) to introduce (s.o. into society/an artist to the audience). (d) **to p. oneself** = to arrive/to come. **pre•sent•a•ble** [prɪ'zentəbl] *adj.* (person) who is suitable to appear in company. **pres•en•ta•tion** [prezən'teɪʃn] *n.* act of giving. **pres•ent-day,** *adj.* modern. **pres•ent•ly,** *adv.* (a) soon. (b) now.

æ back, a: farm, ɒ: top, aɪ pipe, aʊ how, aɪe fire, aʊə flower, ɔ: bought, ɔɪ toy, e fed, eəhair, eɪ take, ə afraid, əʊ boat, aʊə lower, v: word, i: heap, ɪ hit, ɪə hear, u: school, ʊ book, ʌ but, b back, d dog, ð then, dʒ just, f fog, g go, h hand, j yes, k catch, l last, m mix, n nut, ŋ sing, p penny, r round, s some, ʃ short, t too, tʃ chop, θ thing, v voice, w was, z zoo, ʒ treasure

pre•sen•ti•ment [prɪˈzentɪmənt] *n.* feeling that sth unpleasant will soon happen.

pre•serve [prɪˈzɜːv] 1. *n.* (a) place where game/fish, etc., are protected so that they can be killed for sport. (b) **preserves** = jam/pickles, etc. 2. *v.* (a) (*formal*) to keep/to protect. (b) to treat (food) so that it keeps for a long time. **pres•er•va•tion** [prezəˈveɪʃn] *n.* protecting. **pre•serv•a•tive** [prɪˈzɜːvətɪv] *n.* substance used to make food keep/to stop food from going bad. **pre•serv•er,** *n.* person/thing that preserves; *see also* **life preserver. pre•serv•ing pan,** *n.* very large pan for making preserves.

pre•side [prɪˈzaɪd] *v.* to sit at the head of the table (at a meeting). **pres•i•den•cy** [ˈprezɪdnsɪ] *n.* job of president. **pres•i•dent** [ˈprezɪdənt] *n.* head of a republic; chief member of a club; head of a business firm. **pres•i•den•tial** [prezɪˈdenʃl] *adj.* referring to a president. **pre•sid•i•um** [prɪˈsɪdɪəm] *n.* ruling committee (in a communist country).

press [pres] 1. *n.* (*pl.* **-es**) (a) machine which squeezes. (b) **printing p.** = machine for printing books/newspapers, etc. (c) newspapers and magazines taken as a whole. (d) crowd. 2. *v.* (a) to push down; to push against; to squeeze. (b) to iron the creases from (clothes). (c) to force (s.o.) to do sth. (d) to **p. on/forward** = to continue/to go ahead. **pressed,** *adj.* **I'm p. for time** = I haven't much time; **I'd be hard p. to do it** = I would find it difficult. **press con•fer•ence,** *n.* interview given by a famous person to several journalists. **press clip•ping,** *n.* piece cut out from a newspaper with an article which is relevant to s.o/sth. **press gang.** 1. *n.* (*old*) group of people who forced men to join the navy or army. 2. *v.* to force (s.o.) **into** doing sth. **press•ing.** 1. *adj.* urgent. 2. *n.* record/series of records. **pres•sure** [ˈpreʃə] *n.* (a) act of squeezing/pushing down; **to put p. on s.o. to do sth** = to try to force s.o. to do sth. (b) force pushing down/moving/being heavy, etc.; **blood p.** = force with which the blood is driven through the body; **p. group** = group of people who try to influence the government, etc. (c) stress. **pres•sure cook•er,** *n.* type of saucepan with a tight-fitting lid, which cooks food rapidly under pressure. **pres•sur•i•za•tion** [preʃəraɪˈzeɪʃn] *n.* keeping an aircraft cabin at a constant atmospheric pressure. **pres•sur•ize,** *v.* to put under pressure. **pres•su•rized,** *adj.* (aircraft cabin) kept at a constant atmospheric pressure.

pres•tige [preˈstiːʒ] *n.* admiration aroused by s.o. because of rank or qualifications or job. **pres•tig•ious** [preˈstɪdʒəs] *adj.* which brings prestige.

pres•to [ˈprestəʊ] *adv.* (*in music*) rapidly; **p.!** = word used by magicians when carrying out magic tricks.

pre•stressed [ˈpriːˈstrest] *adj.* which has been stressed in advance.

pre•sume [prɪˈzjuːm] *v.* (a) to suppose/to assume. (b) (**to**) to take the liberty of doing sth. (c) (*formal*) **to p. (up)on s.o.'s good nature** = to take unfair advantage of s.o.'s kindness. **pre•sum•a•bly,** *adv.* probably; as you would expect. **pre•sump•tion** [prɪˈzʌmpʃn] *n.* (a) thing which is assumed to be true. (b) rudeness. **pre•sump•tive,** *adj.* which is presumed to be true; **heir p.** = heir (to a throne) who may be displaced by the birth of s.o. with a better right. **pre•sump•tu•ous** [prɪˈzʌmptjʊəs] *adj.* rude/bold. **pre•sump•tu•ous•ly,** *adv.* in a presumptuous way.

pre•sup•pose [priːsəˈpəʊz] *v.* to assume in advance (that sth is true/that certain conditions are met). **pre•sup•po•si•tion** [prɪːsəpəˈzɪʃn] *n.* thing which is assumed in advance.

pre•tax [ˈpriːtæks] *adj.* before tax is paid.

pre•teen [ˈpriːtiːn] *adj. & n.* (boy/girl) just under the age of 13.

pre•tend [prɪˈtend] *v.* (a) to make believe so as to deceive s.o. (b) (**to**) to be bold enough to claim. **pre•tense,** *Brit.* **pre•tence** [prɪˈtens] *n.* making believe. **pre•tend•er,** *n.* person who has (false) claims to sth, usu. person who claims to be king. **pre•ten•sion** [prɪˈtenʃn] *n.* claim. **pre•ten•tious** [prɪˈtenʃəs] *adj.* very showy; claiming to be more important than you are. **pre•ten•tious•ness,** *n.* being pretentious.

pre•ter•nat•u•ral [priːtəˈnætʃrəl] *adj.* supernatural; extraordinary.

pre•text [ˈpriːtekst] *n.* excuse.

pret•ty [ˈprɪtɪ] 1. *adj.* (**-ier, -iest**) pleasant to look at; attractive. 2. *adv. inf.* quite. **pret•ti•ly,** *adv.* daintily. **pret•ti•ness,** *n.* attractiveness/pleasantness.

pret•zel [ˈpretsəl] *n.* hard salty biscuit, made in the shape of a knot.

pre•vail [prɪˈveɪl] *v.* (*formal*) (a) **to p. upon** = to persuade. (b) to be usual/common. **pre•vail•ing,** *adj.* usual/common; **p. wind** = wind which usually blows from a certain direction. **prev•a•lence** [ˈprevələns] *n.* being widespread. **prev•a•lent,** *adj.* widespread.

pre•var•i•cate [prɪˈværɪkeɪt] *v.* (*formal*) to try not to tell the truth. **pre•var•i•ca•tion** [prɪværɪˈkeɪʃn] *n.* act of prevaricating; lie. **pre•var•i•ca•tor,** *n.* person who prevaricates.

pre•vent [prɪˈvent] *v.* to stop (sth) from happening; **to p. s.o. from** = to stop (s.o.) from

doing sth. **pre•vent•a•ble**, *adj.* which could
be prevented. **pre•ven•tion** [prɪ'venʃn] *n.*
preventing. **pre•ven•ta•tive, preventive**
[prɪ'vent(ə)ɪv] *adj.* which prevents.

pre•view ['priːvjuː] *n.* showing of a motion pic-
ture/an exhibition, etc., before it is open to the
general public.

pre•vi•ous ['priːvɪəs] 1. *adj.* former, earlier. 2.
adv. **p. to** = before. **pre•vi•ous•ly**, *adv.* before.

pre•war ['priːwɔː] *adj. & adv.* existing/happen-
ing before a war.

prey [preɪ] 1. *n.* animal eaten by another; **birds
of p.** = birds which eat other birds/animals. 2.
v. **to p. (up)on** = to attack animals and eat
them; **sth is preying on his mind** = sth is worrying him.

price [praɪs] 1. *n.* quantity of money which has
to be paid to buy sth; **at a p.** = if you are willing
to pay a lot. 2. *v.* to give (sth) a price.
price•less, *adj.* (a) extremely valuable. (b)
very funny (joke). **pric•ey**, *adj. inf.* expensive.

prick [prɪk] 1. *n.* pain caused by sth sharp. 2. *v.*
(a) to jab with sth sharp; to make small holes
in (sth). (b) **to p. up your ears** = to listen attentively. **prick•le**, *n.* thorn/sharp point (on a
plant/hedgehog, etc.). **prick•li•ness**, *n.*
being prickly. **prick•ly**, *adj.* covered with
prickles; **p. pear** = type of cactus; **p. heat** = skin
rash caused by hot climate.

pride [praɪd] 1. *n.* (a) pleasure in your own abil-
ities/achievements/possessions. (b) very high
opinions of yourself. (c) group of lions. 2. **to p.
oneself on** = to be extremely proud of.

priest [priːst] *n.* person who has been ordained
to serve God/to interpret the wishes of God/to
carry out formal religious duties; **parish p.** =
priest who is in charge of a parish.
priest•ess, *n.* female priest. **priest•hood**,
n. job of being a priest. **priest•ly**, *adj.* referring to priests.

prig [prɪg] *n.* very moral and conceited person.
prig•gish, *adj.* very moral and conceited.
prig•gish•ness, *n.* being priggish.

prim [prɪm] *adj.* (**primmer, primmest**) very cor-
rect/unbending. **prim•ly**, *adj.* in a prim way.
prim•ness, *n.* being prim.

pri•ma bal•ler•i•na [priːməbælə'riːnə] *n.*
leading woman dancer in a ballet company.
pri•ma don•na [priːmə'dɒnə] *n.* leading
woman singer in opera; person who is conceited and liable to outbursts of emotion.

pri•ma•cy ['praɪməsɪ] *n.* being in first place,
being most important.

pri•ma fa•cie [praɪmə'feɪʃɪ] *adv. & adj.* based
on what seems right at first sight.

pri•mal ['praɪml] *adj.* (*formal*) primeval.

pri•ma•ry ['praɪmərɪ] 1. *adj.* basic; **p. colors** =
basic colors (red, yellow and blue) which go to
make up all the other colors; **p. election** = first
election to choose a candidate to represent a
political party in a main election; **p. school** =
school for small children (up to the age of nine
or ten). 2. *n.* primary election. **pri•ma•ri•ly**,
adv. mainly/mostly.

pri•mate *n.* (a) ['praɪmət] leading bishop. (b)
['praɪmeɪt] **the primates** = members of the
highest level of mammals (apes, human beings, etc.).

prime [praɪm] 1. *adj.* (a) most important. (b) of
best quality. (c) **p. number** = number (such as
2, 5, 11, etc.) which can only be divided by itself or by 1. 2. *n.* period when you are at your
best. 3. *v.* (a) to get (sth) prepared; to give
(wood/metal) a first coat of special paint, before giving the top coat. (b) to put water into
(a water pump)/oil into (a machine) so as to
start it working. (c) to give (s.o.) information
or instruct beforehand. **prime min•is•ter**,
n. head of the government in Britain and other
countries. **prim•er**, *n.* (a) special paint to
cover an unpainted surface. (b) elementary
textbook.

pri•me•val [praɪ'miːvl] *adj.* referring to the period at the beginning of the world.

prim•i•tive ['prɪmɪtɪv] *adj.* (a) referring to
very early/prehistoric times. (b) rough/crude.

pri•mo•gen•i•ture [praɪməʊ'dʒenɪtʃə] *n.*
rule by which the eldest son is the heir.

pri•mor•di•al [praɪ'mɔːdjəl] *adj.* (*formal*)
which existed at the beginning (a long time
ago).

prim•rose ['prɪmrəʊz] *n.* small pale yellow
wild spring flower.

prim•u•la ['prɪmjʊlə] *n.* garden flower, like a
primrose, but with many colors.

prince [prɪns] *n.* son of a king; male ruler of a
small state; male member of a royal family.
prince•ly, *adj.* like a prince; large (sum of
money/salary). **prin•cess**, *n.* daughter of a
king; female member of a royal family; female
ruler of a small state; wife of a prince.

prin•ci•pal ['prɪnsɪpl] 1. *adj.* main/most important. 2. *n.* (a) head (of a primary or secondary school); main actor (in a play). (b) money
on which interest is paid/capital which has

been invested. **prin•ci•pal•i•ty** [prɪnsɪ-'pælɪtɪ] *n.* land ruled by a prince. **prin•ci•pal•ly**, *adv.* mainly.

prin•ci•ple ['prɪnsɪpl] *n.* (a) law/general rule; **in p.** = in agreement with the general rule. (b) personal sense of truth; **on p.** = because of what you believe.

print [prɪnt] 1. *n.* (a) mark made on sth; *see also* **footprint, fingerprint.** (b) letters printed on a page; **the small p.** = conditions on a contract, usu. written in very small letters. (c) picture which has been printed; photograph which has been reproduced on paper; cloth with a design printed on it. 2. *v.* (a) to mark letters on paper by a machine. (b) to write capital letters or letters which are not joined together. (c) to reproduce a photograph/pattern, etc. **print•ed cir•cuit,** *n.* electronic circuit where the connections are printed on a board; **p.c. board** = flat board on which metal strips are printed to form a circuit. **print•er,** *n.* (a) person who prints books/newspapers, etc. (b) machine which prints automatically. **print•ing,** *n.* art of printing books/newspapers, etc.; **p. press** = machine which prints books, etc. **print•out,** *n.* printed information from a computer.

pri•on ['priːɒn] *n.* protein found in the brain, an abnormal form of which causes such diseases as bovine spongiform encephalopathy (BSE), Creutzfeldt-Jakob Disease (CJD), and scrapie.

pri•or ['praɪə] 1. *adj. & adv.* before; previous; **p. to** = before. 2. *n.* male head of a priory. **pri•or•ess,** *n.* woman head of a priory. **pri•or•i•ty** [praɪ'ɒrɪtɪ] *n.* (a) right to be first. (b) thing which has to be done first. **pri•o•ry** ['praɪərɪ] *n.* building where monks or nuns live.

prise [praɪz] *v.* to prize.

prism ['prɪzəm] *n.* glass block usu. with a triangular cross-section, which splits white light up into the colors of the rainbow. **pris•mat•ic** [prɪz'mætɪk] *adj.* referring to a prism.

pris•on ['prɪzn] *n.* place where people are kept by law after they have been found guilty of a crime. **pris•on•er,** *n.* person who is in prison; **p. of war** = soldier/airman, etc., who has been captured by the enemy.

pris•sy ['prɪsɪ] *adj.* (-ier, -iest) unpleasantly proud of being good.

pris•tine ['prɪstiːn] *adj.* (*formal*) fresh/unspoilt.

pri•vate ['praɪvət] 1. *adj.* (a) belonging to one person, not to everyone; **p. means** = personal income from investments; **p. parts** = sex organs; **p. eye** = detective employed by an ordinary person. (b) belonging to certain people, but not to the state or the general public; **showing** = preview of an exhibition for certain

invited guests. 2. *n.* (a) **in p.** = being away from other people. (b) ordinary soldier of the lowest rank. (c) **privates** = private body parts. **pri•va•cy** ['praɪvəsɪ] *n.* being away from other people. **pri•va•teer,** *n.* armed ship which belongs to a private individual. **pri•vate•ly,** *adv.* (a) in private. (b) (owned) by private individuals. **pri•va•ti•za•tion** [praɪvətaɪ'zeɪʃn] *n.* act of privatizing. **pri•va•tize** ['praɪvətaɪz] *v.* to return (a nationalized industry) to private ownership.

pri•va•tion [praɪ'veɪʃn] *n.* lack of money/food, etc.

priv•et ['prɪvɪt] *n.* common shrub, used for garden hedges.

priv•i•lege ['prɪvɪlɪdʒ] *n.* favor/right granted to some people but not to everyone. **priv•i•leged,** *adj.* having a privilege.

priv•y ['prɪvɪ] 1. *adj.* (*formal*) **to be p. to a secret** = to know the details of a secret. 2. *n. inf.* rough toilet outside a house. **priv•y coun•cil,** *n.* group of important people who advise a king or queen.

prize [praɪz] 1. *n.* (a) money or object given to a winner. (b) ship captured in war. 2. *v.* (a) to value. (b) (*also* **prise**) to life or pull with the help of a lever. **prize•fight,** *n.* boxing match where the winner wins money. **prize•fight•er,** *n.* boxer.

pro [prəʊ] 1. *prefix meaning* in favor of. 2. *n.* (a) **pros and cons of a case** = arguments for and against it. (b) *inf.* professional sportsman/actor, etc.

prob•a•ble ['prɒbəbl] *adj.* likely. **prob•a•bil•i•ty** [prɒbə'bɪlɪtɪ] *n.* likelihood. **prob•a•bly,** *adv.* likely.

pro•bate ['prəʊbeɪt] *n.* proving in law that a document (esp. a will) is valid.

pro•ba•tion [prə'beɪʃn] *n.* (a) period when s.o. is being tested. (b) period when a criminal is supervised instead of being put in prison; **p. officer** = official who looks after prisoners on probation. **pro•ba•tion•ar•y,** *adj.* (period) when s.o. is being tested. **pro•ba•tion•er,** *n.* criminal who is on probation.

probe [prəʊb] 1. *n.* (a) instrument used by doctors to examine wounds, etc. (b) thorough investigation. (c) **space p.** = spacecraft sent into space for scientific purposes. 2. *v.* to examine (sth) deeply.

pro•bi•ty ['prəʊbɪtɪ] *n.* (*formal*) total honesty.

prob•lem ['prɒbləm] *n.* thing which is difficult to solve. **prob•lem•at•ic(al)** [prɒblə-'mætɪk(l)] *adj.* doubtful; likely to cause a problem.

pro•bos•cis [prəʊ'bɒsɪs] *n.* (*pl.* -es) long sucking tube coming from the head of an animal (such as the trunk of an elephant/the sting of a mosquito).

pro•ceed [prə'siːd] v. to continue/to go further. **pro•ce•dur•al** [prə'siːdʒərəl] adj. referring to procedure. **pro•ce•dure** [prə'siːdʒə] n. (a) way in which sth ought to be carried out. (b) medical treatment. **pro•ceed a•gainst**, v. to start a lawsuit against (s.o.). **pro•ceed•ings**, n. pl. report of what takes place at a meeting. **pro•ceeds** ['prəusiːdz] n. pl. money which you receive when you sell sth.

proc•ess ['prəusɛs] 1. n. (pl. -es) (a) method of making sth. (b) **in the p. (of)** = while doing sth. 2. v. (a) to make manufactured goods using raw materials; **processed cheese** = cheese which has been treated so that it will keep for a long time. (b) to prepare (figures) for a computer; to sort out (information). **pro•cess•ing**, n. treating raw materials; sorting out information. **pro•ces•sion** [prə'sɛʃn] n. group of people marching (with a band, etc.) in line. **pro•ces•sion•al**, adj. referring to a procession. **proc•es•sor**, n. machine/person who processes; computer device which processes information.

pro•claim [prə'kleɪm] v. to state officially and in public. **proc•la•ma•tion** [prɒklə'meɪʃn] n. official public statement.

pro•cliv•i•ty [prə'klɪvɪtɪ] n. (formal) tendency.

pro•cras•ti•nate [prəu'kræstɪneɪt] (formal) v. to delay/to put sth off until later. **pro•cras•ti•na•tion** [prəkræstɪ'neɪʃn] n. delaying/putting off.

pro•cre•ate ['prəukrɪeɪt] v. (formal) to produce (young). **pro•cre•a•tion**, n. act of procreating.

proc•tor ['prɒktə] n. university official who watches over students during examinations.

pro•cure [prə'kjuə] v. (formal) (a) to obtain. (b) to provide (girls) for sex. **pro•cur•a•ble**, adj. which can be obtained. **pro•cure•ment**, n. obtaining.

prod [prɒd] 1. n. poke; **give him a p.** = nudge him/try to get him to act. 2. v. (**prodded**) to poke with a finger/stick, etc.

prod•i•gal ['prɒdɪɡl] adj. wasteful; (person) who spends a lot. **prod•i•gal•i•ty** [prɒdɪ'ɡælɪtɪ] n. being prodigal. **prod•i•gal•ly**, adv. wastefully.

prod•i•gy ['prɒdɪdʒɪ] n. remarkable person or thing. **pro•di•gious** [prə'dɪdʒəs] adj. re-markable/enormous. **pro•di•gious•ly**, adv. remarkably/enormously.

pro•duce 1. n. ['prɒdjuːs] things grown on the land. 2. v. [prə'djuːs] (a) to bring out. (b) to make/to manufacture. (c) to put on (a play/a motion picture). (d) to yield (crops, etc.). **pro•duc•er** [prə'djuːsə] n. (a) person who puts on a play/a motion picture. (b) person/country which makes/grows sth.

prod•uct ['prɒdʌkt] n. (a) thing which is manufactured/produced; **p. placement** = advertising method in which a product is used or displayed in a TV program or a film. (b) result. (c) (in mathematics) result of multiplying two numbers. **pro•duc•tion** [prə'dʌkʃn] n. (a) manufacturing. (b) putting on a play/motion picture. **pro•duc•tive** [prə'dʌktɪv] adj. which produces. **pro•duc•tiv•i•ty** [prɒdʌk'tɪvɪtɪ] n. rate of output/of production (in a factory).

pro•fane [prə'feɪn] adj. not religious; blasphemous. **pro•fane•ly**, adv. in a profane way. **pro•fan•i•ty** [prə'fænɪtɪ] n. rudeness; swearing/blasphemy.

pro•fess [prə'fes] v. to declare. **pro•fessed**, adj. declared. **pro•fess•ed•ly** [prə'fesɪdlɪ] adv. openly. **pro•fes•sion** [prə'feʃn] n. (a) work which needs special training/skill/knowledge. (b) declaration (of belief in sth). **pro•fes•sion•al**. 1. adj. (a) referring to a profession; expert; **p. athlete** = athlete who is paid to play. 2. n. (a) expert. (b) athlete who is paid to play. **pro•fes•sion•al•ism**, n. (a) expertise/skill. (b) being a professional athlete. **pro•fes•sion•al•ly**, adv. in a professional way. **pro•fes•sor**, n. (a) chief teacher in a subject at a college/university. (b) teacher of music/art, etc. **pro•fes•so•ri•al** [prɒfə'sɔːrɪəl] adj. referring to a professor. **pro•fes•sor•ship**, n. position of professor at a college/university.

prof•fer ['prɒfə] v. (formal) to offer.

pro•fi•cient [prə'fɪʃnt] adj. (at) very capable (of doing sth). **pro•fi•cien•cy**, n. skill in doing sth. **pro•fi•cient•ly**, adv. in a capable way.

pro•file ['prəufaɪl] n. (a) view of s.o.'s head from the side; **to maintain a low p.** = to be quiet/unobtrusive. (b) short biography/description of a famous person (in a newspaper).

prof•it ['prɒfɪt] 1. n. money gained; **p. margin** = percentage of money gained against money paid out. 2. v. to gain. **prof•it•a•bil•i•ty**

[prɒfɪtə'brlɪtɪ] *n.* ability to produce a profit. **prof•it•a•ble** ['prɒfɪtəbl] *adj.* likely to produce a profit. **prof•it•a•bly,** *adv.* at a profit. **prof•it•eer** [prɒfɪ'tɪə] 1. *n.* person who makes too much profit. 2. *v.* to make too much profit. **prof•it•eer•ing,** *n.* making too much profit.

prof•li•gate ['prɒflɪgət] *adj. & n. (formal)* (person) who is very extravagant/who leads a wild life. **prof•li•ga•cy** ['prɒflɪgəsɪ] *n.* extravagance/spending money wildly.

pro•for•ma [prəʊ'fɔːmə] *adj. & n.* (invoice) sent asking the purchaser to pay in advance.

pro•found [prə'faʊnd] *adj.* very serious/very deep (understanding/thought). **pro•found•ly,** *adv.* extremely. **pro•fun•di•ty** [prə'fʌndɪtɪ] *n.* depth (of thought or understanding).

pro•fuse [prə'fjuːs] *adj.* abundant/excessive. **pro•fuse•ly,** *adv.* excessively/too much. **pro•fuse•ness,** *n.* being profuse. **pro•fu•sion** [prə'fjuːʒn] *n.* very large quantity.

prog•e•ny ['prɒdʒənɪ] *n. (no pl.) (formal)* children/offspring. **pro•gen•i•tor** [prəʊ'dʒenɪtə] *n.* ancestor; animal/plant from which others are descended.

pro•ges•ter•one [prəʊ'dʒestərəʊn] *n.* hormone which stops women ovulating, and helps the uterus in the first stages of pregnancy.

prog•na•thous [prɒg'neɪθəs] *adj.* with a lower jaw which is longer than the upper.

prog•nos•ti•cate [prɒg'nɒstɪkeɪt] *v. (formal)* to foretell. **prog•no•sis** [prɒg'nəʊsɪs] *n.* forecast. **prog•nos•ti•ca•tion,** *n. (formal)* forecast.

pro•gram ['prəʊgrəm], *Brit.* **pro•gramme** ['prəʊgræm] 1. *n.* (a) list of items in an entertainment. (b) show/item on TV or radio. 2. *v.* (-mmed, -med) to arrange shows on TV/radio. **pro•gram** ['prəʊgræm] 1. *n.* instructions given to a computer. 2. *v.* to give instructions to (a computer); **programming language** = system of signs and words used to program a computer. **pro•gram•mable, programable,** *adj.* (device) which can be programmed. **pro•gram•mer, programer,** *n.* (a) person who arranges shows on TV/radio. (b) person who programs a computer.

pro•gress 1. *n.* ['prəʊgres] (*pl.* -es) movement forward; **work in p.** = work which is being done. 2. *v.* [prə'gres] to advance. **pro•gres•sion** [prə'greʃn] *n.* advance/movement forward. **pro•gres•sive,** *adj.* (a) (movement) in stages. (b) advanced (ideas). **pro•gres•sive•ly,** *adv.* by stages.

pro•hib•it [prə'hɪbɪt] *v.* to forbid. **pro•hi•bi•tion** [prəʊhɪ'bɪʃn] *n.* forbidding (esp. the sale of alcohol). **pro•hib•i•tive** [prə'hɪbɪtɪv] *adj.* (price) which is so high that you cannot pay it.

pro•ject 1. *n.* ['prɒdʒekt] (a) plan. (b) work planned by students on their own. 2. *v.* [prə'dʒekt] (a) to plan. (b) to throw (a picture on a screen). **pro•jec•tile** [prə'dʒektaɪl] *n.* thing which is thrown/shot. **pro•jecting,** *adj.* sticking/jutting/standing out. **pro•jec•tion,** *n.* (a) thing planned/forecast. (b) (*in geography*) picture of the shape of the earth on a flat surface. (c) thing which stands/sticks out. (d) action of projecting a picture on a screen. **pro•jec•tion•ist,** *n.* person who operates a projector in a movie theater. **pro•jec•tor,** *n.* apparatus for throwing pictures on a screen.

pro•lapse ['prəʊlæps] *n.* state where an organ in the body moves out of place.

pro•le•gom•e•na [prəʊle'gɒmɪnə] *pl. n. (formal)* introduction.

pro•le•tar•i•at [prəʊlɪ'teərɪət] *n.* working class. **pro•le•tar•i•an,** *adj. & n.* (member) of the working class.

pro•lif•ic [prə'lɪfɪk] *adj.* producing many children; very productive. **pro•lif•i•cal•ly,** *adv.* in a prolific way. **pro•lif•er•ate** [prə'lɪfəreɪt] *v.* to produce shoots/young, etc., rapidly. **pro•lif•er•a•tion** [prəlɪfə'reɪʃn] *n.* rapid spread.

pro•lix ['prəʊlɪks] *adj. (formal)* long-winded/using too many words. **pro•lix•i•ty** [prəʊ'lɪksɪtɪ] *n.* being prolix.

pro•logue, prolog ['prəʊlɒg] *n.* piece spoken as the introduction of a play or poem; preliminary section in a book.

pro•long [prə'lɒŋ] *v.* to lengthen. **pro•lon•ga•tion** [prəʊlɒŋ'geɪʃn] *n.* lengthening. **pro•longed,** *adj.* lasting for a long time.

prom•e•nade [prɒmə'nɑːd] 1. *n.* area where you can walk; (*on a ship*) **p. deck** = deck where passengers can stroll about. 2. *v.* to walk about. **prom** [prɒm] *n.* formal dance at a school or college at the end of a school year; **p. concerts/the proms** = promenade concerts. **prom•e•nad•er,** *n.* person who promenades.

prom•i•nence ['prɒmɪnəns] *n.* (a) standing out; thing which stands out. (b) fame. **prom•i•nent,** *adj.* (a) standing out/easily seen. (b) famous. **prom•i•nent•ly,** *adv.* so as to be easily seen.

pro•mis•cu•ous [prə'mɪskjʊəs] *adj.* (person) who does not prefer one thing to another, esp. who has sexual relations with many people. **prom•is•cu•i•ty** [prɒmɪ'skjuːɪtɪ] *n.* having sexual relations with many people. **pro•mis•cu•ous•ly**, adv. in a promiscuous way.

prom•ise ['prɒmɪs] 1. n. (a) act of promising that you will definitely do sth. (b) **to show p.** = to make people feel that you will do well in the future. 2. v. (a) to give your word that you will definitely do sth. (b) to show signs of what may happen in the future. **prom•is•ing**, adj. (person) who is likely to succeed.

prom•is•so•ry ['prɒmɪsərɪ] adj. (note) in which you promise to pay s.o. money on a certain date.

prom•on•to•ry ['prɒməntərɪ] n. piece of land jutting out into the sea.

pro•mote [prə'məʊt] v. (a) to give (s.o.) a better job. (b) to advertise. (c) to encourage. **pro•mot•er**, n. person who promotes; person who organizes a boxing match, etc. **pro•mo•tion** [prə'məʊʃn] n. (a) advancement to a better job. (b) advertising (a new product). **pro•mo•tion•al**, adj. (material) used in advertising.

prompt [prɒmpt] 1. adj. (-er, -est) done at once; quick/rapid. 2. v. (a) to suggest to (s.o.) that he should do sth. (b) to tell an actor words which he has forgotten. 3. n. message to a computer user, telling him to do sth. **prompt•er**, n. person who prompts an actor. **promp•ti•tude**, n. being prompt. **prompt•ly**, adv. immediately; rapidly. **prompt•ness**, n. quickness.

prom•ul•gate ['prɒmʌlgeɪt] v. (formal) to make (a law) known to the public. **prom•ul•ga•tion** [prɒml'geɪʃn] n. (formal) announcement of a law.

prone [prəʊn] adj. (a) (lying) flat. (b) likely (**to**).

prong [prɒŋ] n. one of the sharp points of a fork; point of an attack. **pronged**, adj. with prongs.

pro•noun ['prəʊnaʊn] n. (in grammar) word which stands in place of a noun.

pro•nounce [prə'naʊns] v. (a) to speak a series of sounds which form a word; to speak clearly. (b) to declare in a formal way. **pro•nounced**, adj. noticeable. **pro•nounce•ment**, n. official/formal statement. **pro•nun•ci•a•tion** [prənʌnsɪ'eɪʃn] n. way of pronouncing words.

pron•to ['prɒntəʊ] adv. inf. immediately.

proof [pruːf] 1. n. (a) thing which proves/which shows that sth is true. (b) percentage of alcohol in a drink. (c) test sheet of printing which

has to be corrected by the author before the book can be produced; copy of a photograph/lithograph, etc., for the artist to examine to see if it is acceptable. 2. adj. (**against**) safe from/not affected by. 3. v. to paint with a protective coat. **proof•read**, v. to read and correct proofs.

-proof [pruːf] suffix safe against/protected against.

prop [prɒp] 1. n. (a) support; stick which holds sth up. (b) **props** = articles used in the production of a play/motion picture. 2. v. (**propped**) to support.

prop•a•gan•da [prɒpə'gændə] n. spreading of (frequently false) political ideas. **prop•a•gan•dist**, n. person who spreads political ideas.

prop•a•gate ['prɒpəgeɪt] v. (a) to make (new plants) by sowing seed/taking cuttings. (b) to spread (ideas). **prop•a•ga•tion** [prɒpə'geɪʃn] n. act of propagating. **prop•a•ga•tor**, n. small glass-covered box for growing new plants.

pro•pane ['prəʊpeɪn] n. colorless gas used for heating and cooking.

pro•pel [prə'pel] v. (**propelled**) to send forward. **pro•pel•lant**, n. fuel used to propel. **pro•pel•ler**, n. mechanism with blades which turns rapidly to drive boats and aircraft.

pro•pen•si•ty [prə'pensɪtɪ] n. (formal) tendency/leaning.

prop•er ['prɒpə] adj. (a) right. (b) thorough (cleaning, etc.). (c) (in grammar) **p. noun** = noun which is a name of a person/a country, etc. (d) very correct. (e) (thing) itself exactly. **prop•er•ly**, adv. (a) rightly/correctly. (b) thoroughly.

prop•er•ty ['prɒpətɪ] n. (a) thing which belongs to s.o. (b) building or buildings. (c) **properties** = articles used in the production of a play/motion picture; **p. man** = person responsible for all the articles used in a play/motion picture. (d) quality.

proph•e•cy ['prɒfəsɪ] n. act of prophesying; thing prophesied. **proph•e•sy** ['prɒfɪsaɪ] v. to foretell what will happen in the future. **proph•et** ['prɒfɪt] n. person who foretells what will happen; religious leader. **proph•et•ess**, n. woman prophet. **proph•et•ic(al)** [prə'fetɪk(l)] adj. which is like a prophecy. **pro•phet•i•cal•ly**, adv. in a prophetic way.

pro•phy•lax•is [prɒfɪˈlæksɪs] *n.* prevention of a disease. **pro•phy•lac•tic** [prɒfɪˈlæktɪk] *adj. & n.* (substance) which prevents disease.

pro•pin•qui•ty [prɒˈpɪŋkwɪtɪ] *n.* (*formal*) closeness/nearness.

pro•pi•ti•ate [prəˈpɪʃɪeɪt] *v.* (*formal*) to appease/to make (s.o.) less angry. **pro•pi•ti•a•tion** [prəpɪʃɪˈeɪʃn] *n.* act of appeasing. **pro•pi•ti•a•to•ry** [prəˈpɪʃɪətərɪ] *adj.* which tries to appease/to make less angry. **pro•pi•tious** [prəˈpɪʃəs] *adj.* favorable. **pro•pi•tious•ly**, *adv.* in a propitious way.

pro•po•nent [prɒˈpəʊnənt] *n.* person who proposes sth.

pro•por•tion [prəˈpɔːʃn] *n.* (a) part (of a total). (b) relationship between a part and a total; **in p.** = in the right amount. (c) **proportions** = the relative height/length (of a building/picture, etc.). **pro•por•tion•al**, *adj.* which is directly related; **p. representation** = system of voting where the votes cast for each party determine the number of seats each party has in a legislative body. **pro•por•tion•al•ly**, *adv.* in proportion. **pro•por•tion•ate**, *adj.* which is in proportion. **pro•por•tion•ate•ly**, *adv.* in proportion.

pro•pose [prəˈpəʊz] *v.* (a) to suggest/to make a suggestion. (b) **to p. to s.o.** = to ask s.o. to marry you. **pro•pos•al**, *n.* (a) suggestion/thing which is suggested. (b) asking s.o. to marry you. **pro•pos•er**, *n.* person who proposes (a motion). **prop•o•si•tion** [prɒpəˈzɪʃn] *n.* (a) thing which has been proposed. (b) **tough p.** = problem which is difficult to solve.

pro•pound [prəˈpaʊnd] *v.* (*formal*) to put forward (an idea).

pro•pri•e•tor [prəˈpraɪətə] *n.* owner. **pro•pri•e•tar•y** [prəˈpraɪətrɪ] *adj.* (a) referring to a proprietor. (b) **p. medicine** = medicine which is sold under a brand name and manufactured by a particular company. **pro•pri•e•tress**, *n.* woman proprietor. **pro•pri•e•to•ri•al**, *adj.* like a proprietor.

pro•pri•e•ty [prəˈpraɪətɪ] *n.* decency; good behavior.

pro•pul•sion [prəˈpʌlʃn] *n.* moving forward.

pro ra•ta [prəʊˈrɑːtə] *adv. & adj.* in proportion.

pro•sa•ic [prəˈzeɪɪk] *adj.* ordinary; not poetic; rather dull. **pro•sa•i•cal•ly**, *adv.* in a prosaic way.

pro•sce•ni•um [prəˈsiːnɪəm] *n.* part of a stage in a theater which sticks out beyond the curtain; **p. arch** = arch above the front part of a stage in a theater.

pro•scribe [prəʊˈskraɪb] *v.* (*formal*) to forbid

by law. **pro•scrip•tion** [prɒsˈkrɪpʃn] *n.* (*formal*) act of proscribing.

prose [prəʊz] *n.* writing which is not in verse. **pros•y**, *adj.* wordy/dull in style.

pros•e•cute [ˈprɒsɪkjuːt] *v.* to bring (s.o.) to court to answer a charge. **pros•e•cu•tion** [prɒsɪˈkjuːʃn] *n.* (a) court case against s.o. (b) people who have accused s.o. of a crime in a court. **pros•e•cut•ing at•tor•ney**, *n.* public official who accuses a criminal in a law court on behalf of the state. **pros•e•cu•tor** [ˈprɒsɪkjuːtə] *n.* person who prosecutes;

pros•e•lyte [ˈprɒsɪlaɪt] *n.* person recently converted to a religion. **pros•e•lyt•ize**, *v.* to try to convert (people) to a religion.

pros•o•dy [ˈprɒsədɪ] *n.* rules of writing poetry.

pros•pect 1. *n.* [ˈprɒspekt] (a) a view. (b) **to have sth in p.** = to expect sth to happen. (c) **prospects** = future possibilities. (d) person who may become a customer. 2. *v.* [prəˈspekt] to search (a land for minerals). **pro•spec•tive**, *adj.* which may happen in the future. **pros•pec•tor**, *n.* person who searches for minerals. **pro•spec•tus** [prəˈspektəs] *n.* paper giving information about sth in the hope of attracting clients/customers.

pros•per [ˈprɒspə] *v.* to succeed; to become rich. **pros•per•i•ty** [prɒsperɪtɪ] *n.* being rich. **pros•per•ous** [ˈprɒspərəs] *adj.* wealthy/rich.

pros•tate [ˈprɒsteɪt] *n.* gland around the bladder in men.

pros•the•sis [ˈprɒsθəsɪs] *n.* (*pl.* -ses) (*formal*) artificial leg/arm, etc.

pros•ti•tute [ˈprɒstɪtjuːt] 1. *n.* person who receives money for sexual intercourse. 2. *v.* to use (your talents) in a low/unworthy way. **pros•ti•tu•tion** [prɒstɪˈtjuːʃn] *n.* offering sexual intercourse for payment.

pros•trate 1. *adj.* [ˈprɒstreɪt] (lying) flat. 2. *v.* [prəˈstreɪt] **to p.** oneself before s.o. = to fall down (in front of s.o. as a mark of respect, fear, etc.); **he was prostrated by malaria** = he had to stay lying down. **pros•tra•tion** [prəˈstreɪʃn] *n.* lying down/falling down in front of s.o.

pro•tag•o•nist [prəˈtægənɪst] *n.* main character in a play/book, etc.; leader of one side in a conflict.

pro•te•an [ˈprəʊtɪən] *adj.* which changes easily.

pro•tect [prəˈtekt] *v.* to defend against attack; to shield against dirt/germs, etc. **pro•tec•tion** [prəˈtekʃn] *n.* (a) shelter. (b) defense. **pro•tec•tive**, *adj.* which protects. **pro•tec•tive•ly**, *adv.* in a protective way. **pro•tec•tor**, *n.* person/thing which protects. **pro•tec•tor•ate**, *n.* country which is protected (and usu. controlled) by another country.

pro•té•gé ['prɒtɜʒeɪ] *n.* person (usu. young) who is supported in work with money or advice by s.o. else.

pro•tein ['prəʊtiːn] *n.* compound which is an essential part of living cells; one of the elements in food which is necessary to keep the human body working properly.

pro tem•po•re, pro tem [prəʊ'tempɒreɪ, 'prəʊ'tem] *adv.* temporarily.

pro•test 1. *n.* ['prəʊtest] statement that you object or disapprove; **p. march** = march in procession to show that you protest against sth. 2. *v.* [prə'test] (a) to object/to raise a violent objection (**against**). (b) to state solemnly. **Prot•es•tant** ['prɒtɪstənt] *adj. & n.* (member) of a Western Christian church which is not part of the Roman Catholic Church. **Prot•es•tant•ism,** *n.* beliefs of the Protestant church. **prot•es•ta•tion** [prɒtɪ-'steɪʃn] *n.* violent statement of protest.

pro•to•col ['prəʊtəkɒl] *n.* (a) correct (diplomatic) behavior. (b) draft agreement.

pro•ton ['prəʊtɒn] *n.* nucleus of a hydrogen atom, found in all atoms.

pro•to•plasm ['prəʊtəplæzəm] *n.* basic jellylike substance in all living matter.

pro•to•type ['prəʊtətaɪp] *n.* first model of a new machine, etc.

pro•to•zo•a [prəʊtəʊ'zəʊə] *n. pl.* simplest types of living creatures.

pro•tract•ed [prə'træktɪd] *adj.* very lengthy. **pro•trac•tion,** *n.* being protracted. **pro•trac•tor,** *n.* semicircular device, used for measuring angles in geometry.

pro•trude [prə'truːd] *v.* to stick out. **pro•tru•sion,** *n.* thing which protrudes.

pro•tu•ber•ance [prə'tjuːbərəns] *n.* bump/swelling. **pro•tu•ber•ant,** *adj.* which swells outwards.

proud [praʊd] *adj.* (**of**) full of pride; thinking a lot of yourself/of sth belonging to you; *inf.* **he did us p.** = he treated us generously. **proud•ly,** *adv.* with pride; with great satisfaction.

prove [pruːv] *v.* (a) to demonstrate that sth is right. (b) to turn out. **prov•a•ble,** *adj.* which can be proved. **prov•en** [prəʊvn] *adj.* which has been shown to be right.

prov•e•nance ['prɒvənəns] *n.* (*formal*) origin.

prov•en•der ['prɒvəndə] *n.* (*no pl.*) (*formal*) food.

pro•verb ['prɒvɜːb] *n.* saying which has a moral/which teaches you sth. **pro•ver•bi•al** [prə'vɜːbɪəl] *adj.* mentioned in a proverb; well-known. **pro•ver•bi•al•ly,** *adv.* in a proverbial way.

pro•vide [prə'vaɪd] *v.* (a) to supply; **to p. for** = earn enough to feed and clothe. (b) to take care of. **pro•vid•er,** *n.* person who provides. **pro•vid•ed that, providing,** *conj.* on condition that.

prov•i•dence ['prɒvɪdəns] *n.* (lucky) fate. **prov•i•dent,** *adj.* careful to think about the future and keep money/supplies for use in time of need. **prov•i•den•tial** [prɒvɪ'denʃnl] *adj.* lucky. **prov•i•den•tial•ly,** *adv.* luckily.

prov•ince ['prɒvɪns] *n.* (a) large administrative division of a country; **the provinces** = parts of a country away from the capital. (b) area of knowledge; area of responsbility. **pro•vin•cial** [prə'vɪnʃl] 1. *adj.* referring to a province/to the provinces; narrow-minded/not very worldly. 2. *n.* person from the provinces.

pro•vi•sion [prə'vɪʒn] 1. *n.* (a) thing that is provided; **to make p. for** = to see that sth is allowed for in the future. (b) *pl.* **provisions** = food. (e) condition in a document. 2. *v.* to stock up with food. **pro•vi•sion•al,** *adj.* temporary; conditional. **pro•vi•sion•al•ly,** *adv.* temporarily.

pro•vi•so [prə'vaɪzəʊ] *n.* (*pl.* -os) condition.

pro•voke [prə'vəʊk] *v.* (a) to incite (s.o.) to do sth violent. (b) to make (a reaction) start. **prov•o•ca•tion** [prɒvə'keɪʃn] *n.* action of provoking. **pro•voc•a•tive** [prɒ'vɒkatɪv] *adj.* likely to provoke a violent response. **pro•voc•a•tive•ly,** *adv.* in a provocative way. **pro•vok•ing,** *adj.* annoying.

pro•vost ['prɒvəst] *n.* (a) administrative official at a college/university. (b) **p. marshal** = head of a group of military police in the army/navy.

prow [praʊ] *n.* front end of a ship.

prow•ess ['praʊes] *n.* (*formal*) skill.

prowl [praʊl] 1. *n.* **on the p.** = creeping about. 2. *v.* to creep about quietly. **prowl•er,** *n.* person who creeps about, esp. a burglar.

prox•i•mate ['prɒksɪmət] *adj.* (*formal*) nearest/closest. **prox•im•i•ty** [prɒk'sɪmɪtɪ] *n.* closeness.

prox•y ['prɒksɪ] *n.* (a) document giving s.o. the power to act/to vote on your behalf. (b) person who acts/votes on your behalf.

æ back, ɑː farm, ɒ top, aɪ pipe, aʊ how, aiə fire, aʊə flower, ɔː bought, ɔɪ toy, e fed, eəhair, eɪ take, ə afraid, əʊ boat, əʊə lower, vː word, iː heap, ɪ hit, ɪə hear, uː school, ʊ book, ʌ but, b back, d dog, ð then, dʒ just, f fog, g go, h hand, j yes, k catch, l last, m mix, n nut, ŋ sing, p penny, r round, s some, ʃ short, t too, tʃ chop, θ thing, v voice, w was, z zoo, ʒ treasure

Pro•zac ['prəʊzæk] *n.* trademark for type of antidepressant drug.

prude [pru:d] *n.* prudish person. **prud•er•y**, **prudishness**, *n.* state of being prudish. **prud•ish**, *adj.* with strict principles and easily shocked.

pru•dence ['pru:dns] *n.* great care/caution. **pru•dent**, *adj.* very careful/very cautious. **pru•den•tial** [pru:'denʃl] *adj.* (*formal*) showing prudence. **pru•dent•ly**, *adv.* in a prudent way.

prune [pru:n] 1. *n.* dried plum. 2. *v.* to cut branches off (a tree); to cut back (a tree/shrub) to keep it in good shape or to encourage it to produce flowers; to cut back (expenditure, etc.); to cut out (parts of a book, etc.).

pru•ri•ent ['prʊərɪənt] *adj.* which causes indecent thoughts. **pru•ri•ence**, *n.* being prurient.

prus•sic ac•id ['prʌsɪk 'æsɪd] *n.* type of poisonous acid.

pry [praɪ] *v.* (a) to look inquisitively into sth. (b) to lift open or move with a lever.

P.S. [pi:'es] *short for* post scriptum, additional note at the end of a letter.

psalm [sɑːm] *n.* religious song from the Bible. **psalm•ist**, *n.* person who wrote the psalms. **psal•ter** ['sɔːltə] *n.* book of psalms with music, for use in church.

pse•phol•o•gy [se'fɒlədʒɪ] *n.* study of elections/voting patterns and opinion polls of voters. **pse•phol•o•gist**, *n.* person who specializes in psephology.

pseud [sju:d] *n. inf.* person who is not really as he pretends to be.

pseudo- ['sju:dəʊ] *prefix meaning* false.

pseu•do•nym ['sju:dənɪm] *n.* false/invented name. **pseu•don•y•mous** [sju:'dɒnɪməs] *adj.* (writer) using a pseudonym.

psit•ta•co•sis [psɪtə'kəʊsɪs] *n.* serious disease, caught by people from birds.

pso•ri•a•sis [sɔː'raɪəsɪs] *n.* itching disease which causes red patches on the skin.

psych•e•del•ic [saɪkə'delɪk] *adj.* so full of bright moving colors that you become hallucinated.

psy•chi•a•try [saɪ'kaɪətrɪ] *n.* study of mental disease. **psy•chi•at•ric** [saɪkɪ'ætrɪk] *adj.* referring to psychiatry. **psy•chi•a•trist** [saɪ'kaɪətrɪst] *n.* person who studies and treats mental disease.

psy•chic ['saɪkɪk] *adj. & n.* (person) in contact with supernatural forces. **psy•chi•cal**, *adj.* in contact with supernatural forces.

psy•cho•a•nal•y•sis [saɪkəʊə'næləsɪs] *n.* treatment of mental disorder by discussion. **psy•cho•an•a•lyze**, *Brit.* **psy•cho•a•nal•yse**, *v.* to treat (s.o.) by psy-

choanalysis. **psy•cho•an•a•lyst** [saɪkəʊ'ænəlɪst] *n.* person who treats patients by psychoanalysis.

psy•chol•o•gy [saɪ'kɒlədʒɪ] *n.* study of the human mind. **psy•cho•log•i•cal** [saɪkə-'lɒdʒɪkl] *adj.* referring to psychology. **psy•cho•log•i•cal•ly**, *adv.* mentally. **psy•chol•o•gist** [saɪ'kɒlədʒɪst] *n.* person who studies the human mind.

psy•cho•neu•ro•im•mu•nol•o•gy ['saɪ-kəʊnjʊərəʊɪmju'nɒlədʒɪ] *n.* study of the impact of psychology on the immune system.

psy•cho•path ['saɪkəpæθ] *n.* psychopathic criminal. **psy•cho•path•ic** [saɪkə'pæθɪk] *adj.* mentally unstable in a dangerous way.

psy•cho•sis [saɪ'kəʊsɪs] *n.* (*pl.* -oses [-əʊsi:z]) mental illness which changes the patient's personality. **psy•chot•ic** [saɪ'kɒtik] *adj. & n.* (person) suffering from a psychosis.

psy•cho•so•mat•ic [saɪkəʊsə'mætɪk] *adj.* (physical illness) created by a mental state.

psy•cho•ther•a•py [saɪkəʊ'θerəpɪ] *n.* treatment of mental disorder by psychological means.

Pt *symbol for* platinum.

PTA Parent Teacher Association.

ptar•mi•gan ['tɑːmɪgən] *n.* type of mountain bird.

pter•o•dac•tyl [terəʊ'dæktɪl] *n.* prehistoric flying dinosaur.

P.T.O. [pi:ti:'əʊ] *short for* please turn over (a page, etc.).

Pu *symbol for* plutonium.

pub [pʌb] *n. inf.* bar/tavern.

pu•ber•ty ['pju:bətɪ] *n.* period of adolescence when a person becomes sexually mature.

pu•bic ['pju:bɪk] *adj.* referring to the area around the sexual organs.

pub•lic ['pʌblɪk] 1. *adj.* (a) referring to the people in general; **p. holiday** = holiday for everyone. (b) **p. school** = (i) (*in the United States*) primary or secondary school supported by state and local funds; (ii) (*in Britain*) private fee-paying school which is not part of the state system. 2. *n.* people in general; **in p.** = in the open; in front of everyone. **pub•li•ca•tion** [pʌblɪ'keɪʃn] *n.* (a) making public/publishing. (b) book/paper which has been published. **pub•li•cist** ['pʌblɪsɪst] *n.* person who attracts people's attention to a product. **pub•lic•i•ty** [pʌb'lɪsɪtɪ] *n.* advertising; attracting people's attention to a product. **pub•li•cize**, *v.* to attract people's attention to sth/to make publicity for sth. **pub•lic•ly**, *adv.* in public. **pub•lic re•la•tions**, *n.* maintaining good relations between an organization and the public. **pub•lic ser•vice**, *n.* working for the government; all government

agencies and their personnel.
pub•lic-spir•it•ed, *adj.* (person) who acts
energetically for the good of the community.

pub•lish ['pʌblɪʃ] *v.* to make publicly known;
to bring out (a book/newspaper) for sale.
pub•lish•er, *n.* person who produces
books/newspapers for sale. **pub•lish•ing,** *n.*
producing books/newspapers for sale; **p.
house** = company which publishes books.

puce [pjuːs] *adj.* dark purplish red.

puck [pʌk] *n.* small disk which is hit in ice
hockey.

puck•er ['pʌkə] 1. *n.* wrinkle/fold. 2. *v.* to wrin-
kle (your brow).

puck•ish ['pʌkɪʃ] *adj.* mischievous/full of playful tricks.

pud•ding ['pudɪŋ] *n.* (a) sweet/dessert. (b)
sweet food which has been cooked or boiled.

pud•dle ['pʌdl] *n.* small pool of water (e.g. one
left after rain).

pudg•y [pʌdʒɪ] *adj.* soft and fat.

pu•er•ile ['pjuəraɪl] *adj.* childish/stupid.
pu•er•il•i•ty [pjuə'rɪlɪtɪ] *n.* being puerile.

puff [pʌf] 1. *n.* (a) small breath. (b) powder p. =
light pad for powdering the skin. (c) **p. pastry**
= light sort of pastry. 2. *v.* to blow. **puff•ball,**
n. type of round white fungus. **puff•i•ness,**
n. being puffy. **puff•y,** *adj.* swollen (face).

puf•fin ['pʌfɪn] *n.* black and white bird with a
large colored beak, living near the sea.

pug [pʌg] *n.* type of small dog, with a flat face.
pug•nosed, *adj.* with a flattened nose.

pu•gi•list ['pjuːdʒɪlɪst] *n.* (*formal*)
fighter/boxer. **pu•gi•lism,** *n.* (*formal*) boxing.

pug•na•cious [pʌg'neɪʃəs] (*formal*) *adj.* (person) who likes fighting; quarrelsome.
pug•na•cious•ly, *adv.* in a pugnacious
way. **pug•nac•i•ty** [pʌg'næsɪtɪ] *n.* being
pugnacious.

puis•ne ['pjuːnɪ] *adj.* lower in rank.

pu•is•sance ['pwiːsɑːns] *n.* power; strength.

puke [pjuːk] *v. inf.* to vomit.

puk•ka ['pʌkə] *adj. inf.* real; of good quality.

pul•chri•tude ['pʌlkrɪtjuːd] *n.* (*formal*)
beauty.

pule [pjuːl] *v.* (*of children*) to wail/to whimper.

pull [pul] 1. *n.* (a) act of dragging/moving sth toward you. (b) *inf.* influence. (c) handle (which
has to be pulled). (d) deep inhaling (of a cigarette). 2. *v.* (a) to move (sth) by dragging; to
move (sth) toward you. (b) to strain (a muscle). **pull down,** *v.* to bring (sth) down by

pulling. **pull in,** *v.* to reach a place. **pull off,**
v. (a) to take off (a piece of clothing/a handle,
etc.) by pulling. (b) *inf.* to succeed in doing
(sth). (c) to drive off a road and stop. **pull
out,** *v.* (a) to bring (sth) out by pulling. (b) to
drive away from the side of the road; to drive
towards the middle of the road. **pull
through,** *v.* to recover from an illness. **pull
to•geth•er,** *v.* **he pulled himself together** = he
became calmer/he controlled his emotions.
pull up, *v.* (a) to stop (in a vehicle). (b) to
raise by pulling.

pul•let ['pulɪt] *n.* young chicken.

pul•ley ['pulɪ] *n.* apparatus for lifting heavy
weights with a grooved wheel around which a
rope runs.

pull•man ['pulmən] *n.* sleeping car (on a train).

pull•o•ver ['puləuvə] *n.* piece of clothing made
of wool, etc., covering the top part of the body
and which you pull on over your head.

pul•mo•nar•y ['pʌlmənrɪ] *adj.* referring to
the lungs.

pulp [pʌlp] 1. *n.* squashy mass. 2. *v.* to crush to
a pulp. **pulp•y,** *adj.* in a pulp.

pul•pit ['pulpɪt] *n.* enclosed platform in a
church where the priest preaches.

pul•sar ['pʌlsə] *n.* invisible star which sends
out radio signals.

pulse [pʌls] *n.* 1. (a) regular beat of the heart.
(b) dried seed of peas/beans. 2. *v.* to pulsate.
pul•sate [pʌl'seɪt] *v.* to throb regularly.
pul•sa•tion [pʌl'seɪʃn] *n.* regular throbbing.

pul•ver•ize ['pʌlvəraɪz] *v.* to crush to powder.
pul•ver•i•za•tion [pʌlvərai'zeɪʃn] *n.* crushing to powder.

pu•ma ['pjuːmə] *n.* large wild American cat.

pum•ice (stone) ['pʌmɪs('stəʊn)] *n.* block of
light gray porous lava used for rubbing stains
off your skin.

pum•mel ['pʌml] *v.* (**pummeled, pummelled**) to
hit s.o. with many blows.

pump [pʌmp] 1. *n.* (a) machine for forcing liquids or air. (b) low-cut shoe for women. 2. *v.*
(a) to force (liquid/air) with a pump. (b) *inf.* to
ask (s.o.) searching questions.

pump•kin ['pʌmpkɪn] *n.* large round orange-colored vegetable.

pun [pʌn] 1. *n.* play with words of different
meanings. 2. *v.* (**punned**) to make puns.
pun•ster, *n.* a person who is always making
puns.

punch [pʌntʃ] 1. *n.* (*pl.* **-es**) (a) blow with the
fist; **p. line** = last sentence of a story/joke

æ back, ɑː farm, ɒ top, aɪ pipe, aʊ how, aɪə fire, aʊə flower, ɔː bought, ɔɪ toy, e fed, eəhair, eɪ take, ə
afraid, əʊ boat, əʊə lower, vː word, iː heap, ɪ hit, ɪə hear, uː school, ʊ book, ʌ but, b back, d dog, ð then,
dʒ just, f fog, g go, h hand, j yes, k catch, l last, m mix, n nut, ŋ sing, p penny, r round, s some, ʃ short, t
too, tʃ chop, θ thing, v voice, w was, z zoo, ʒ treasure

which gives the point. (b) metal tool for making holes. (c) drink made of wine or spirits and spices. 2. *v.* (a) to hit (s.o.) with your fist. (b) to make holes in (sth) with a punch. **Punch and Ju•dy,** *n.* form of children's puppet show, with traditional characters. **punch bowl,** *n.* bowl for mixing wine and spices to make punch. **punch-drunk,** *adj.* suffering from brain damage from being punched on the head too often. **punch-out,** *n. inf.* fight.

punc•til•i•ous [pʌŋk'tɪlɪəs] *adj.* attentive to detail/extremely fussy. **punc•til•i•ous•ly,** *adv.* in a punctilious way. **punc•til•i•ous•ness,** *n.* being punctilious.

punc•tu•al ['pʌŋktjʊəl] *adj.* on time. **punc•tu•al•i•ty** [pʌŋktjʊ'ælɪtɪ] *n.* being on time/never being late. **punc•tu•al•ly,** *adv.* on time.

punc•tu•ate ['pʌŋktjʊeɪt] *v.* (a) to split a sentence using punctuation marks. (b) to interrupt. **punc•tu•a•tion** [pʌŋktjʊ'eɪʃn] *n.* splitting of a sentence using punctuation marks; **p. marks** = signs used in writing (such as period, comma, dash) to show how a sentence is split up.

punc•ture ['pʌŋktʃə] 1. *n.* hole in a tire; very small hole. 2. *v.* to make a small hole in (sth).

pun•dit ['pʌndɪt] *n.* expert (esp. in political matters).

pun•gent ['pʌndʒənt] *adj.* sharp (taste, smell); sarcastic (comment). **pun•gen•cy,** *n.* being pungent. **pun•gent•ly,** *adv.* in a pungent way.

pun•ish ['pʌnɪʃ] *v.* to make (s.o.) suffer because of sth he has done. **pun•ish•a•ble,** *adj.* (offense) for which you can be punished. **pun•ish•ment,** *n.* treatment given to punish s.o. **pu•ni•tive** ['pjuːnətɪv] *adj.* which aims to punish.

punk [pʌŋk] 1. *n. inf.* (a) young hoodlum. (b) follower of punk rock. 2. *adj. inf.* bad/inferior. **punk rock,** *n.* loud music played by people wearing outrageous costumes.

punt [pʌnt] 1. *n.* (a) long flat-bottomed boat, propelled with a pole. (b) (*Ireland*) monetary unit. 2. *v.* (a) to push (a punt) with a pole. (b) to kick a ball which is in the air. (c) to bet on a horse race. **punt•er,** *n.* (a) person who gambles, esp. on horseraces. (b) person who pushes a punt along with a pole.

pu•ny ['pjuːnɪ] *adj.* (-ier, -iest) weak/feeble; very small.

pup [pʌp] 1. *n.* young of certain animals, esp. young dog; **p. tent** = small tent made of two sloping sides and a horizontal pole. 2. *v.* (**pupped**) to have pups.

pu•pa ['pjuːpə] *n.* (*pl.* -pae [-piː], -as) resting period in the life of an insect when it is changing from a grub/caterpillar to a butterfly/beetle. **pu•pal,** *adj.* referring to a pupa. **pu•pate** [pjuː'peɪt] *v.* (*of caterpillar*) to turn into a pupa.

pu•pil ['pjuːpl] *n.* (a) child at a school; person learning from a teacher. (b) hole in the central part of the eye, through which the light passes.

pup•pet ['pʌpɪt] *n.* doll which moves and which is used to give a performance; **p. show** = performance given using puppets; **p. state** = country controlled by another country. **pup•pet•eer** [pʌpɪ'tɪə] *n.* person who gives a performance using puppets.

pup•py ['pʌpɪ] *n.* young dog.

pur•blind ['pɜːblaɪnd] *adj.* partly blind.

pur•chase ['pɜːtʃəs] 1. *n.* (a) thing bought. (b) ability to grip/ability to lift sth by using a lever. 2. *v.* to buy; **purchasing power** = quantity that can be bought with a certain amount of money. **pur•chas•er,** *n.* person who buys sth.

pur•dah ['pɜːdə] *n.* seclusion of women (in Eastern countries).

pure ['pjʊə] *adj.* (-er, -est) (a) very clean; not mixed with other things. (b) innocent; with no faults. **pure•ly,** *adv.* only/solely.

pu•rée ['pjʊəreɪ] 1. *n.* semi-liquid pulp (of a vegetable/fruit). 2. *v.* to make (sth) into a purée.

pur•ga•to•ry ['pɜːgətrɪ] *n.* place where you suffer temporarily after death; (place of) suffering.

purge [pɜːdʒ] 1. *n.* (a) medicine which clears the bowels. (b) removal of political opponents. 2. *v.* (a) to clear out (waste matter). (b) to remove (political opponents). **pur•ga•tive** ['pɜːgətɪv] *adj. & n.* (medicine) which clears the bowels.

pu•ri•fy ['pjʊərɪfaɪ] *v.* to clean/to make pure. **pu•ri•fi•ca•tion** [pjʊərɪfɪ'keɪʃn] *n.* making pure. **pu•ri•fi•er,** *n.* machine that purifies. **pur•ist** ['pjʊərɪst] *n.* person who insists on everything being done in the correct way. **pu•ri•ty,** *n.* being pure/absolutely clean. **pu•ri•tan** ['pjʊərɪtən] *n.* puritanical person. **pu•ri•tan•i•cal** [pjʊəri'tænɪkl] *adj.* very strict concerning morals.

purl [pɜːl] *v.* to knit putting your needle into the back of the loop.

pur•lieus ['pɜːljuːz] *pl. n.* (*formal*) surroundings; neighborhood.

pur•loin [pɜː'lɔɪn] *v.* (*formal*) to steal.

pur•ple ['pɜːpl] *adj. & n.* reddish-blue (color). **pur•plish,** *adj.* quite purple.

pur•port [pɜː'pɔːt] (*formal*) 1. *n.* meaning. 2. *v.* to mean.

pur•pose ['pɜːpəs] *n.* aim/plan; use; **on p.** = according to what was planned; intentionally.

pur•pose•ful, *adj.* intentional; with an aim in view; (person) with set aims. **pur•pose•ful•ly**, *adv.* in a purposeful way. **pur•pose•ful•ness**, *n.* being purposeful. **pur•pose•ly**, *adv.* on purpose/intentionally.

purr [pɜː] 1. *n.* (a) noise made by a cat when pleased. (b) low noise made by a powerful engine. 2. *v.* (a) (*of cat*) to make a noise to show pleasure. (b) (*of engine*) to make a low noise.

purse [pɜːs] 1. *n.* (a) small bag for carrying money. (b) handbag. 2. **to p. your lips** = to pinch/to press your lips together to show you are displeased. **purs•er**, *n.* officer on a ship who deals with the money, supplies and the passengers' accommodation.

pur•sue [pəˈsjuː] *v.* (a) to chase (s.o./sth). (b) to continue to do (sth). **pur•su•ance**, *n.* (*formal*) carrying out of (duty, plan, etc.). **pur•su•ant to**, *adv.* relating to. **pur•su•er**, *n.* person who chases s.o. **pur•suit** [pəˈsjuːt] *n.* (a) chase; **in p. of** = looking for. (b) (*formal*) career/occupation.

pu•ru•lent [ˈpjʊərʊlənt] *adj.* (*formal*) full of pus.

pur•vey [pɜːˈveɪ] *v.* (*formal*) to supply (goods). **pur•vey•or**, *n.* person who supplies goods.

pur•view [ˈpɜːvjuː] *n.* general scope of a document.

pus [pʌs] *n.* yellowish liquid which gathers in infected wounds/spots.

push [pʊʃ] 1. *n.* (-es) (a) act of pressing sth so that it moves away from you. (b) energy; *inf.* determination to do well. 2. *v.* (a) to press; to move (sth) by pressing. (b) *inf.* **I am pushed for time** = I haven't much time to spare. (c) *Sl.* to sell (drugs) illegally. **push but•ton**, *n.* switch which is operated by pushing. **push•er**, *n. Sl.* person who sells drugs illegally. **push•ful**, *adj.* ambitious; eager to get what you want. **push off**, *v. inf.* to get going/to start a journey. **push•o•ver**, *n. inf.* easy task; person who is easily influenced. **push-up**, *n.* exercise where you lie flat on the floor and push yourself up with your hands. **push•y**, *adj. inf.* wanting to succeed/ambitious.

pu•sil•lan•i•mous [pjuːsɪˈlænɪməs] *adj.* (*formal*) timid/afraid. **pu•sil•la•nim•i•ty** [pjuːsɪləˈnɪmɪtɪ] *n.* being pusillanimous.

puss [pʊs], **pus•sy** [ˈpʊsɪ], **pus•sy•cat** [ˈpʊsɪkæt] *n.* familiar words for a cat. **pus•sy•foot**, *v. inf.* **to p. about** = to dither/to be undecided.

pus•tule [ˈpʌstjuːl] *n.* blister/spot (on the skin).

put [pʊt] *v.* (**put**; **putting**) (a) to place; *inf.* **to stay p.** = to stay where you are. (b) to express in words. (c) to estimate **at.** (d) **to p. a stop to** = to stop. (e) (*in sports*) to throw (the shot). **put a•cross**, *v.* to explain (sth) in a convincing way. **put a•way**, *v.* to clear (things) away. **put back**, *v.* to place (sth) where it was before. **put by**, *v.* to save. **put down**, *v.* (a) to place at a lower level/on the ground. (b) to land an aircraft. (c) to note. (d) to kill (a sick animal). (e) **to p. your foot down** = to be very strict/firm. **put in**, *v.* (a) to place inside. (b) **he p. in three hour's work** = he worked for three hours. (c) **to p. in for a job** = to apply. **put off**, *v.* (a) to delay. (b) to upset or repel. **put on**, *v.* (a) to place. (b) to get dressed in (a piece of clothing). (c) to switch on (a light, etc.). (d) to add (weight). **put out**, *v.* (a) to place outside. (b) to stretch out (one's hand, etc.). (c) to switch off (a light, etc.). (d) *inf.* **to be p. out** = to be annoyed. (e) (*of ships*) **to p. out to sea** = to leave harbor. **put up**, *v.* (a) to fix upright; to build. (b) to raise. (c) to offer. (d) to find a place for (s.o.) to sleep. (e) **to p. up with s.o./sth** = to accept s.o./sth, even if they are unpleasant/noisy, etc. (f) **to p. s.o. up to sth** = to encourage s.o. to do sth. **put-up•on**, *adj.* forced to do sth unpleasant.

pu•ta•tive [ˈpjuːtətɪv] *adj.* (*formal*) **the p. au•thor** = the person who is supposed to be the author.

pu•tre•fy [ˈpjuːtrɪfaɪ] *v.* to rot. **pu•tre•fac•tion** [pjuːtrɪˈfækʃn] *n.* rotting. **pu•tres•cent**, *adj.* which is rotting. **pu•trid**, *adj.* rotten; smelling rotten.

putsch [pʊtʃ] *n.* armed overthrow of a government.

putt [pʌt] 1. *n.* short shot (on a green) in golf. 2. *v.* to hit a short shot in golf. **put•ter**. 1. *n.* golf club for putting. 2. *v.* **to p. around** = not to do anything in particular/to do little jobs here and there.

put•tee [ˈpʌtɪ] *n.* long piece of cloth wound round the leg to act as protection.

put•ty [ˈpʌtɪ] *n.* soft substance which hardens after a time, used esp. for sealing the glass in windows.

puz•zle [ˈpʌzl] 1. *n.* (a) problem; thing which is difficult to solve. (b) game where you have to solve a problem. 2. *v.* to perplex/to mystify; to be a problem. **puz•zle•ment**, *n.* being puz-

---

æ back, ɑː farm, ɒ top, aɪ pipe, aʊ how, aɪə fire, aʊə flower, ɔː bought, ɔɪ toy, e fed, eəhair, eɪ take, ə afraid, əʊ boat, əʊə lower, ɜː word, iː heap, ɪ hit, ɪə hear, uː school, ʊ book, ʌ but, b back, d dog, ð then, dʒ just, f fog, g go, h hand, j yes, k catch, l last, m mix, n nut, ŋ sing, p penny, r round, s some, ʃ short, t too, tʃ chop, θ thing, v voice, w was, z zoo, ʒ treasure

zled. **puzz•ling,** *adj.* which does not make sense/which is a problem.

PVC [pi:vi:'si:] *n.* type of plastic.

PVS [pi:vi:'es] *abbrev. for* persistent vegetative state.

pyg•my ['pɪgmɪ] *adj. & n.* (type of animal) which is smaller than normal; very short (person).

py•ja•mas [pɪ'dʒɑ:məz] *n. pl. Brit.* pajamas.

py•lon ['paɪlən] *n.* tall metal tower for carrying electric cables.

py•or•rhe•a [paɪə'rɪə] *n.* infection of the gums around the teeth.

pyr•a•mid ['pɪrəmɪd] *n.* shape with a square base and four sides rising to meet at a point. **py•ram•i•dal** [pɪ'ræmɪdl] *adj.* shaped like a pyramid.

pyre ['paɪə] *n.* ceremonial fire; **funeral p.** = pile on which a dead body is cremated.

py•re•thrum [paɪ'ri:θrəm] *n.* insecticide made from a flower.

py•ri•tes [paɪ'raɪti:z] *n.* yellowish chemical substance containing a metal.

py•ro•ma•ni•ac [paɪrəu'meɪnɪæk] *n.* person who sets fire to buildings.

py•ro•tech•nics [paɪrəu'teknɪks] *n. pl.* science of fireworks. **py•ro•tech•nic(al),** *adj.* referring to fireworks.

Pyr•rhic vic•to•ry ['pɪrɪk 'vɪktrɪ] *n.* victory which costs the victor too much effort/too many losses.

py•thon ['paɪθn] *n.* large snake which kills its prey by crushing.

pyx [pɪks] *n.* box in church where consecrated bread and wine are kept.

Qq

qua [kweɪ] *adv.* acting or functioning as.

quack [kwæk] 1. *n.* (a) sound made by a duck. (b) *inf.* unqualified doctor. 2. *v.* to make a noise like a duck.

quad [kwɒd] *n. inf.* quadrangle.

quad•ran•gle [ˈkwɒdræŋgl] *n.* open square surrounded by buildings (in a school/college).

quad•rant [ˈkwɒdrənt] *n.* (a) quarter of a circle. (b) instrument used for measuring angles.

quad•ra•phon•ic [kwɒdrəˈfɒnɪk] *adj.* (sound) which is reproduced through four loudspeakers.

quad•rat•ic [kwɒdˈrætɪk] *adj.* (equation) involving the square of the unknown quantity.

quad•ren•ni•al [kwɒdˈrenɪəl] *adj.* happening every four years.

quad•ri•lat•er•al [kwɒdrɪˈlætərəl] *adj. & n.* (shape) with four sides.

quad•ru•ped [ˈkwɒdrʊped] *n.* animal with four legs.

quad•ru•ple [kwɒˈdrʊpl] *v.* to multiply four times. **quad•ru•plets** [ˈkwɒdrʊplets] *n. pl.* four babies born at the same birth. **quad•ru•pli•cate** [kwɒˈdruːplɪkət] *n.* **in q.** = in four copies. **quads** [kwɒdz] *n. pl. inf.* quadruplets.

quaff [kwɒf] *v.* to drink with large gulps.

quag•mire [ˈkwɒgmaɪə] *n.* bog/area of dangerous marsh.

quail [kweɪl] 1. *n.* small game bird. 2. *v.* to shrink back in fear; to shudder (**at** sth).

quaint [kweɪnt] *adj.* (-er, -est) picturesque/oddly old-fashioned. **quaint•ly**, *adv.* in a quaint way. **quaint•ness**, *n.* old-fashioned oddness.

quake [kweɪk] 1. *n. inf.* earthquake. 2. *v.* to shake (with fear/cold). **Quak•er**, *n. inf.* member of a Christian religious society, known as the Society of Friends.

qual•i•fy [ˈkwɒlɪfaɪ] *v.* (a) **to q. as** = to study for and obtain a license or permit which allows you to do a certain type of work. (b) **to q. for** = to pass a test/a section of a competition and so proceed to the next step. (c) to modify; to attach conditions. **qual•i•fi•ca•tion** [kwɒlɪfɪˈkeɪʃn] *n.* (a) knowledge, skill, or other proof that shows you have the necessary requirements for a job, position, etc. (b) modification/condition which limits. **qual•i•fi•er**, *n.* person who qualifies.

qual•i•ty [ˈkwɒlɪtɪ] *n.* (a) worth. (b) characteristic. **qual•i•ta•tive**, *adj.* referring to quality.

qualm [kwɑːm] *n.* feeling of guilt/worry.

quan•da•ry [ˈkwɒndrɪ] *n.* puzzle/problem; **in a q.** = puzzled/not knowing what to do.

quan•ti•fy [ˈkwɒntɪfaɪ] *v.* to calculate in quantities/in amounts. **quan•ti•fi•a•ble**, *adj.* which can be quantified.

quan•ti•ty [ˈkwɒntɪtɪ] *n.* amount; **an unknown q.** = person/thing you know nothing about. **quan•ti•ta•tive**, *adj.* referring to quantity.

quan•tum [ˈkwɒntəm] *n.* **q. theory** = theory in physics that energy exists in fixed amounts.

quar•an•tine [ˈkwɒrəntiːn] 1. *n.* period of time when an animal/a person/thing (usu. coming from another country) has to be kept apart to avoid the risk of passing on disease. 2. *v.* to put (s.o./an animal/sth) in quarantine.

quark [kwɑːk] *n.* smallest particle.

quar•rel [ˈkwɒrəl] 1. *n.* argument; **to pick a q. with s.o.** = to start an argument. 2. *v.* (**quarreled, quarrelled**) to argue (**about/over** sth). **quar•rel•ing**, *n.* arguments. **quar•rel•some**, *adj.* argumentative/often getting into quarrels.

quar•ry [ˈkwɒrɪ] 1. *n.* (a) place where stone, etc., is dug out of the ground. (b) animal which is being hunted; person/thing which is being looked for. 2. *v.* to dig (stone) out of ground.

quart [kwɔːt] *n.* measure of liquid (= 2 pints).

quar•ter [ˈkwɔːtə] 1. *n.* (a) one of four parts. (b) period of fifteen minutes before or after the hour. (c) period of three months. (d) area. (e) **quarters** = accommodation for people in the armed forces. (f) 25 cent coin. 2. *v.* (a) to cut into four equal parts. (b) to place (soldiers) in lodgings. **quarter day**, *n.* day which marks the beginning of a three month period for accounting purposes. **quar•ter•deck**, *n.* top deck of a ship near the stern. **quar•ter•fi•nal**, *n.* (*in sport*) one of four

æ back, ɑː farm, ɒ top, aɪ pipe, aʊ how, aɪə fire, aʊə flower, ɔː bought, ɔɪ toy, e fed, eəhair, eɪ take, ə afraid, əʊ boat, əʊə lower, ɜː word, iː heap, ɪ hit, ɪə hear, uː school, ʊ book, ʌ but, b back, d dog, ð then, dʒ just, f fog, g go, h hand, j yes, k catch, l last, m mix, n nut, ŋ sing, p penny, r round, s some, ʃ short, t too, tʃ chop, θ thing, v voice, w was, z zoo, ʒ treasure

matches in a competition, the winners of which go into the semi-finals. **quar•ter•ly,** *adj., adv. & n.* (magazine) which appears every three months. **quar•ter•mas•ter,** *n.* (*Military*) officer in charge of clothing, equipment, quarters, etc.

quar•tet(te) [kwɔːˈtet] *n.* (a) four people. (b) four musicians playing together. (c) piece of music for four musicians.

quar•to [ˈkwɔːtəu] *adj. & n.* size of paper one quarter of a standard sheet.

quartz [kwɔːts] *n.* hard crystalline mineral, used for making watches because of its very regular vibrations.

qua•sar [ˈkweɪsɑː] *n.* distant star which gives off intense radiation.

quash [kwɒʃ] *v.* to annul (a legal sentence).

quasi- [ˈkweɪzaɪ] *prefix meaning* almost.

quat•rain [ˈkwɒtreɪn] *n.* stanza of poetry with four lines.

qua•ver [ˈkweɪvə] 1. *n.* tremble (in the voice). 2. *v.* to tremble (of voice). **qua•ver•ing,** *adj.* trembling (voice).

quay [kiː] *n.* stone wharf/place where ships tie up to load or unload.

quea•sy [ˈkwiːzɪ] *adj.* feeling sick. **quea•si•ness,** *n.* being queasy.

queen [kwiːn] *n.* (a) wife of a king; woman ruler of a country; **q. mother** = mother of a king or queen who is the widow of a king. (b) (*at cards*) card between the jack and the king. (c) important piece in chess. (d) **q. ant/bee** = leading ant/bee in a colony. (e) the best/the most perfect woman. (f) *Sl.* male homosexual. **queen•ly,** *adj.* like a queen.

queer [kwɪə] 1. *adj.* (**-er, -est**) (a) odd/strange. (b) *Sl. adj. & n.* homosexual. (c) ill. 2. *v.* to make sth go wrong. **queer•ness,** *n.* strangeness/oddness.

quell [kwel] *v.* to calm (a riot); to hold back (your feelings).

quench [kwenʃ] *v.* **to q. your thirst** = to have a drink.

quern [kwɜːn] *n.* mill for grinding flour by hand.

quer•u•lous [ˈkwerjʊləs] *adj.* bad-tempered/peevish; always complaining. **quer•u•lous•ly,** *adv.* in a querulous way. **quer•u•lous•ness,** *n.* being querulous.

que•ry [ˈkwɪərɪ] 1. *n.* (a) question. (b) question mark. 2. *v.* to doubt whether sth is true; to ask a question.

quest [kwest] *n.* (*formal*) search.

ques•tion [ˈkwestʃn] 1. *n.* (a) sentence which requires an answer; **q. mark** = sign (?) which shows that a question is being asked. (b) problem; **the human rights q.** (c) matter; **the matter in q.** = which is being discussed; **it's out of the q.** = it's unthinkable. 2. *v.* (a) to ask (s.o.) ques-

tions. (b) to doubt. **ques•tion•a•ble,** *adj.* doubtful. **ques•tion•er,** *n.* person who asks questions. **ques•tion•naire** [kwestʃənˈneə] *n.* printed list of questions given to people to answer.

queue [kjuː] (*esp. Brit.*) 1. *n.* line of people/cars, etc., waiting one behind the other for sth. 2. *v.* (*also* **queue up**) to form a queue.

quib•ble [ˈkwɪbl] 1. *n.* argument about details; petty objection. 2. *v.* to argue about details. **quib•bler,** *n.* person who argues about details.

quiche [kiːʃ] *n.* open tart with a filling of eggs/meat/vegetables, etc.

quick [kwɪk] 1. *adj.* (**-er, -est**) (a) fast/rapid. (b) **she has a q. temper** = she loses her temper easily. 2. *n.* live flesh (esp. flesh around fingernails/toenails); **he was cut to the q.** = he was very hurt. **quick-act•ing,** *adj.* (medicine) which takes effect rapidly. **quick•en,** *v.* (a) to make (sth) go faster. (b) to stimulate. **quick•ie,** *n. inf.* (a) quick drink/question, etc. (b) quick divorce. **quick•lime,** *n.* lime. **quick•ly,** *adv.* rapidly. **quick•ness,** *n.* being quick. **quick•sand,** *n.* dangerous area of soft sand where you can sink in easily. **quick•sil•ver,** *n.* mercury. **quick•step,** *n.* dance with quick steps. **quick-tem•pered,** *adj.* (person) who loses his temper easily. **quick-wit•ted,** *adj.* intelligent (person)/(person) who understands quickly.

quid [kwɪd] *n.* lump of chewing tobacco.

quid pro quo [kwɪdprəuˈkwəu] *n.* something done in return for something else.

qui•es•cent [kwaɪˈesnt] *adj.* (*formal*) calm. **qui•es•cence,** *n.* calmness.

qui•et [ˈkwaɪət] 1. *n.* absence of noise; calm/tranquility. 2. *adj.* (**-er, -est**) (a) calm/making no noise. (b) simple; **q. color scheme** = where the colors aren't bright. 3. *v.* to calm; to stop (s.o.) being noisy. **qui•et•ly,** *adv.* without making any noise. **qui•et•ness,** *n.* calm/tranquility. **qui•e•tude,** *n.* (*formal*) quietness.

quill [kwɪl] *n.* long feather (formerly used as a pen).

quilt [kwɪlt] *n.* padded cover for a bed. **quilt•ed,** *adj.* made with a pad sewn between two layers of cloth.

quince [kwɪns] *n.* hard fruit used for making jelly; tree producing this fruit.

qui•nine [ˈkwɪniːn] *n.* drug made from the bark of a tropical tree, used to treat malaria.

quin•quen•ni•al [kwɪnˈkwenɪəl] *adj.* happening every five years.

quins [kwɪnz] *n. pl. inf.* quintuplets.

quin•sy [ˈkwɪnzɪ] *n.* (*old*) infection of the tonsils.

quin•tes•sence [kwɪn'tesns] *n.* essential part (of sth); perfect example. **quin•tes•sen•tial** [kwinti'senʃl] *adj.* which is a perfect example.

quin•tet(te) [kwɪn'tet] *n.* (a) group of five musicians playing together. (b) piece of music for five musicians.

quin•tu•ple ['kwɪntjʊpl] *v.* to multiply five times. **quin•tup•lets,** *n. pl.* five babies born at the same birth.

quip [kwɪp] 1. *n.* joke/clever remark. 2. *v.* (**quipped**) to make a joke/a clever remark.

quire ['kwaɪə] *n.* 24 or 25 sheets of paper.

quirk [kwɜːk] *n.* oddity/strange event.

quis•ling ['kwɪzlɪŋ] *n.* person who betrays his country by helping the enemy who is occupying it.

quit [kwɪt] *v.* (**quit/quitted**) (a) *inf.* to leave (a job/house, etc.). (b) *inf.* to stop. **quits,** *adj.* **to be q.** = to be equal. **quit•tance,** *n.* (*formal*) receipt. **quit•ter,** *n. inf.* person who gives up easily.

quite [kwaɪt] *adv.* (a) completely. (b) fairly/relatively; **q. a few** = several.

quiv•er ['kwɪvə] 1. *n.* (a) tremor/slight shake. (b) holder for arrows. 2. *v.* to tremble.

quix•ot•ic [kwɪk'sɒtɪk] *adj.* strange/impractical (person). **quix•ot•i•cal•ly,** *adv.* in a quixotic way.

quiz [kwɪz] 1. *n.* (*pl.* **quizzes**) series of questions; **q. show** = TV/radio program where people are asked questions. 2. *v.* (**quizzed**) to ask (s.o.) questions. **quizmaster,** *n.* person who asks the questions in a TV/radio quiz.

quiz•zi•cal ['kwɪzɪkl] *adj.* odd.

quoin [kɔɪn] *n.* block of stone making a corner of a building.

quoit [kwɔɪt] *n.* large ring used in a game to throw over pegs.

quo•rum ['kwɔːrəm] *n.* number of people who have to be present to make a vote valid.

quo•ta ['kwəʊtə] *n.* fixed amount of goods which can be supplied/share; fixed number.

quote [kwəʊt] 1. *n.* (a) passage quoted; quotation. (b) estimate. (c) *inf.* **quotes** = quotation marks. 2. *v.* (a) to repeat a number (as a reference); to repeat a text of an author; **can I q. you?** = can I repeat what you have said? (b) to indicate the beginning of a quotation (when speaking). (c) to give an estimate **for** work to be done. **quot•a•ble,** *adj.* which can be quoted; suitable to be quotable. **quo•ta•tion** [kwəʊ'teɪʃn] *n.* (a) passage quoted. (b) estimate. (c) **q. mark** = punctuation mark (" ") used to indicate what s.o. has said.

quoth [kwəʊθ] *v.* (*old*) said.

quo•tient ['kwəʊʃnt] *n.* result when one number is divided by another.

q.v. [kju:'vi:] *abbreviation for* quod vide, *meaning* which see.

qwert•y ['kwɜːtɪ] *n.* normal English keyboard for a typewriter or computer.

Rr

R [ɑ:] **the three Rs** = basic subjects in primary school (reading, writing, arithmetic).

Ra *symbol for* radium.

rab•bi ['ræbaɪ] *n.* Jewish priest. **rab•bin•i•cal** [rə'bɪnɪkl] *adj.* referring to a rabbi.

rab•bit ['ræbɪt] *n.* common wild animal with long ears and short tail which lives in burrows.

rab•ble ['ræbl] *n.* crowd/unruly mass of people.

rab•id ['ræbɪd] *adj.* (a) suffering from rabies. (b) wild/fanatic. **rab•id•i•ty** [rə'bɪdɪtɪ] *n.* being rabid. **ra•bies** ['reɪbi:z] *n.* hydrophobia.

rac•coon [rə'ku:n] *n.* type of small North American flesh-eating wild animal.

race [reɪs] 1. *n.* (a) competition to see who is the fastest; **to run a r.** (b) rush of water in a narrow channel. (c) group of human beings with similar physical characteristics; **r. relations** = relations between different racial groups in the same country. (d) species/breed of plant/animal, etc. 2. *v.* (a) to run/to drive, etc., to see who is the fastest. (b) to go very fast. **race•course,** *n.* grassy track where horse races are run. **race•horse,** *n.* horse specially bred and trained to run in races. **rac•er,** *n.* (a) person who is running in a race. (b) special bicycle/car for racing. **race•track,** *n.* track, usu. grassy, where horse races are run. **ra•cial** ['reɪʃl] *adj.* referring to race; **r. discrimination/prejudice** = discrimination/prejudice against s.o. because of race. **ra•cial•ism,** *n.* racism. **ra•cial•ist,** *adj. & n.* racist. **ra•cial•ly,** *adv.* in a racial way. **rac•ing,** *n.* competitions to see who is fastest. **rac•ism,** *n.* prejudice against a group of people because of their race. **rac•ist,** *adj. & n.* (person) who treats s.o. differently because of race. **rac•y,** *adj.* (-ier, -iest) vigorous (style of writing).

ra•ceme [rə'si:m] *n.* flowers growing along a stem.

rack [ræk] 1. *n.* (a) frame to hold things (such as letters/hats); **roof r.** = grid attached to the roof of a car for carrying luggage. (b) **to go to r. and ruin** = to become dilapidated. (c) **r. of lamb** = rib section of lamb, formed of a series of chops, roasted. 2. *v.* (a) **to r. your brains** = to think very hard. (b) to cause pain (to). (c) to draw (wine, beer) off the dregs. **rack and pin•ion,** *n.* toothed wheel which connects with a toothed bar to drive a machine (esp. a cog railway) forward. **rack rail•way,** *n.* cog railway.

rack•et ['rækɪt] 1. *n.* (a) instrument made of a light frame with tight strings across it, used for hitting the ball in tennis, squash and badminton. (b) *inf.* loud noise. (c) *inf.* illegal profit-making deal. **rack•et•eer** [rækɪ'tɪə] *n.* swindler/gangster. **rack•et•eer•ing,** *n.* crime of running a racket. **rack•et•y,** *adj.* (car) which makes a lot of noise.

rac•on•teur [rækɒn'tɜ:] *n.* person who is good at telling stories.

rac•quet ['rækɪt] *n.* (sports) racket.

ra•dar ['reɪdɑ:] *n.* system by which you can detect objects and judge their position by sending radio signals to them which are reflected back as dots on a small screen.

ra•di•ate ['reɪdɪeɪt] *v.* to send out/to give off (rays/heat); to spread out (from a central point). **ra•di•al,** *adj.* which spreads out from a central point; (tire) with grooves which give a better grip of the road surface. **ra•di•ance,** *n.* brightness. **ra•di•ant,** *adj.* bright (smile); (heat) which radiates. **ra•di•ant•ly,** *adv.* in a radiant way. **ra•di•a•tion** [reɪdɪ'eɪʃn] *n.* sending out/giving off (rays, heat). **ra•di•a•tor** ['reɪdɪeɪtə] *n.* (a) heating device in which steam or hot water passes through a series of coils or pipes. (b) water-filled metal panel for cooling a car engine.

rad•i•cal ['rædɪkl] 1. *adj.* thorough/complete; basic (difference); **r. party** = a party which believes in the necessity of making great changes in the system of running a country. 2. *n.* member of a radical party. **rad•i•cal•ly,** *adv.* in a radical way.

rad•i•cle ['rædɪkl] *n.* small root (on a pea or bean).

ra•di•o ['reɪdɪəʊ] 1. *n.* (*pl.* -os) system for sending/receiving messages using atmospheric waves; apparatus which sends out/receives messages using atmospheric waves. 2. *v.* to send (a message) using a radio. **ra•di•o•ac•tive** [reɪdɪəʊ'æktɪv] *adj.* (substance) which gives off harmful radiation through the breaking up of its atoms.

ra•di•o•ac•tiv•i•ty [reɪdɪəʊæk'tɪvɪtɪ] *n.* giving off of harmful radiation due to the breaking up of atoms. **ra•di•o•car•bon,** *n.* radioactive form of carbon; **r. dating** = calculating the age of sth. by measuring the amount of radiocarbon that has decayed. **ra•di•og•ra•pher** [reɪdɪ'ɒgrəfə] *n.* person who takes X-rays. **ra•di•og•ra•phy,** *n.* making X-rays. **ra•di•o•i•so•tope,** *n.* radioactive isotope, used in radiation treatment. **ra•di•ol•o•gist,** *n.* person who studies X-rays. **ra•di•ol•o•gy** [reɪdɪ'ɒlədʒɪ] *n.* science of X-rays and their use in medicine. **ra•di•o•tel•e•phone,** *n.* long-distance telephone (from a ship) which uses radio. **ra•di•o•ther•a•py** *n.* use of X-rays to treat disease.

rad•ish ['rædɪʃ] *n.* small red root vegetable, eaten raw.

ra•di•um ['reɪdɪəm] *n.* (*element:* Ra) radioactive metal used in treating cancer.

ra•di•us ['reɪdɪəs] *n.* (*pl.* **radii** ['reɪdɪaɪ], **radiuses**) (a) distance from the center of a circle to the circumference. (b) one of the two bones in the lower part of the arm.

ra•don ['reɪdɒn] *n.* (*element:* Rn) natural radioactive gas occurring in certain types of soil and construction materials.

raf•fi•a ['ræfɪə] *n.* (*no pl.*) strips from a palm leaf used to make baskets, etc.

raff•ish ['ræfɪʃ] *adj.* vulgar and showy; rather disreputable. **raff•ish•ness,** *n.* being raffish.

raf•fle ['ræfl] 1. *n.* lottery where you buy a numbered ticket in the hope of winning a prize. 2. *v.* to offer (a prize) for a lottery.

raft [rɑːft] *n.* flat boat made of pieces of wood/logs tied together.

raft•er ['rɑːftə] *n.* sloping beam which holds up a roof.

rag [ræg] 1. *n.* (a) piece of torn cloth; **dressed in rags** = wearing old, torn clothes; *inf.* **the r. trade/business** = clothing or fashion industry. (b) *inf.* newspaper, esp. one thought of with contempt. (c) piece of ragtime music. 2. *v.* (**ragged** [rægd]) to play jokes on (s.o.). **rag•bag,** *n.* collection of mismatched items. **rag•a•muf•fin,** *n.* dirty child wearing ragged clothes. **rag doll,** *n.* doll made of bits of cloth. **rag•ged** ['rægɪd] *adj.* (a) torn; uneven (edge). (b) (person) wearing rags. **rag rug,** *n.* rug made of strips of torn cloth sewn together. **rag•time,** *n.* music written with a strongly syncopated rhythm.

rage [reɪdʒ] 1. *n.* violent anger; *inf.* **all the r.** = very fashionable. 2. *v.* to be violently angry; to be violent.

rag•lan ['ræglən] *n.* style of coat where the sleeves continue straight to the collar, with no seam on the shoulder.

ra•gout ['ræguː] *n.* meat and vegetable stew.

raid [reɪd] 1. *n.* sudden attack. 2. *v.* to make a sudden attack on/a sudden visit to. **raid•er,** *n.* person who takes part in a raid.

rail [reɪl] 1. *n.* (a) bar of wood/metal (in a fence, etc.). (b) **rails** = metal bars along which trains run; **live r.** = rail which conducts electricity for electric trains. (c) railroad; **by r.** = on a train. (d) small bird which lives near water. 2. *v.* **to r. against** = to speak violently against. **rail•head,** *n.* end of a railroad line. **rail•ing,** *n. pl.* fence made of rails. **rail•ler•y,** *n.* making fun of s.o. **rail•road.** 1. *n.* track with two metal rails along which trains run; train system of a country. 2. *v. inf.* to force (sth) hurriedly. **rail•way,** *n.* railroad, esp. one which runs for a short distance.

rai•ment ['reɪmənt] *n.* clothing.

rain [reɪn] 1. *n.* water falling from clouds in drops. 2. *v.* to fall like rain. **rain•bow,** *n.* colored arc which appears in the sky when the sun's light falls on rain. **rain check,** *n.* agreement to have/to do sth later; **I'll take a r. check on that** = I'll not accept your offer now, but I will take it up again later. **rain•coat,** *n.* waterproof coat. **rain•drop,** *n.* drop of rain. **rain•fall,** *n.* amount of rain which falls in a certain place over a certain period. **rain for•est,** *n.* thick, lush tropical jungle where it rains frequently. **rain•wa•ter,** *n.* water which has fallen as rain. **rain•y,** *adj.* (-ier, -iest) with a lot of rain.

raise [reɪz] 1. *n.* increase in salary. 2. *v.* (a) to lift; to make (sth) higher. (b) to bring up (a subject) for discussion. (c) to rear (animals/a family). (d) to collect; **to r. money.**

rai•sin ['reɪzn] *n.* dried grape.

rai•son d'ê•tre [reɪzɒn'detr] *n.* reason for the existence of sth.

raj [rɑːdʒ] *n.* **the r.** = British rule in India. **ra•jah** ['rɑːdʒə] *n.* Indian ruler.

rake [reɪk] 1. *n.* (a) tool with a long handle and bent metal teeth, used for smoothing earth/for gathering fallen leaves, etc. (b) immoral man. (c) angle of slope. 2. *v.* (a) to smooth/to gather using a rake. (b) to slope. **rake-off,** *n. inf.* illegal payment paid as a commission. **rake up,**

æ back, ɑ: farm, ɒ: top, aɪ pipe, aʊ how, aɪə fire, aʊə flower, ɔ: bought, ɔɪ toy, e fed, eəhair, eɪ take, ə afraid, əʊ boat, əʊə lower, v: word, i: heap, ɪ hit, ɪə hear, u: school, ʊ book, ʌ but, b back, d dog, ð then, dʒ just, f fog, g go, h hand, j yes, k catch, l last, m mix, n nut, ŋ sing, p penny, r round, s some, ʃ short, t too, tʃ chop, θ thing, v voice, w was, z zoo, ʒ treasure

v. to start talking again about (sth which had been forgotten). **rak•ish,** *adj.* (that) worn at a slant/tilted sideways.

ral•ly ['rælɪ] 1. *n.* (a) gathering of members of a group/association/political party. (b) car competition where cars have to cross difficult country in a certain time. (c) return to strength (of s.o. who is ill). (d) long series of shots in tennis. 2. *v.* (a) to gather together. (b) to recover (temporarily) from an illness/a setback.

ram [ræm] 1. *n.* (a) male sheep. (b) heavy machine for pressing down hard. 2. *v.* (**rammed**) (a) to batter sth down hard. (b) to hit (another ship/car, etc.,) hard.

RAM [ræm] *n.* random access memory, memory in a computer which allows access to data.

Ram•a•dan [ræmə'dæn] *n.* 9th month of the year, when Muslims fast.

ram•ble ['ræmbl] 1. *n.* walk for pleasure in the country. 2. *v.* (a) to go for a walk. (b) to talk on and on in a confused way. **ram•bler,** *n.* (a) person who goes for walks in the country. (b) type of rose which climbs. **ram•bling,** *adj.* (a) confused (speech). (b) (house) which is full of rooms and corridors.

ram•bu•tan [ræmbu:'tæn] *n.* small reddish fruit found in S.E. Asia.

ram•e•kin ['ræməkɪn] *n.* small dish for baking food in an oven; food cooked in this way.

ram•i•fi•ca•tion [ræmɪfɪ'keɪʃn] *n.* (a) part of a large complicated system. (b) consequence; result.

ramp [ræmp] *n.* slightly sloping surface joining two different levels.

ram•page [ræm'peɪdʒ] 1. *n.* **to go on the r.** = go about breaking things/creating disorder. 2. *v.* to rush about creating disorder.

ramp•ant ['ræmpənt] *adj.* which is widespread and uncontrollable, as crime.

ram•part ['ræmpɑːt] *n.* defensive wall.

ram•rod ['ræmrod] *n.* **to stand stiff as a r.** = to stand very straight.

ram•shack•le ['ræmʃækl] *adj.* dilapidated/falling to pieces.

ran [ræn] *v. see* **run.**

ranch [rɑːntʃ] *n.* farm where horses or cattle are reared. **ranch•er,** *n.* person who owns/runs a ranch.

ran•cid ['rænsɪd] *adj.* bad/stale (butter). **ran•cid•i•ty,** *n.* being rancid.

ran•cor, *Brit.* **ran•cour** ['ræŋkə] *n.* bitterness/dislike. **ran•cor•ous,** *adj.* bitter/hateful.

rand [rɒnt] *n.* money used in South Africa.

ran•dom ['rændəm] *adj. & n.* done aimlessly/without any planning; **at r.** = aimlessly/with no selection; **r. sample** = sample for testing taken without any selection. **ran•dom•ness,** *n.* being random.

rand•y ['rændɪ] *adj.* (**-ier, -iest**) eager to have sexual intercourse. **rand•i•ness,** *n.* being randy.

rang [ræŋ] *v. see* **ring.**

range [reɪndʒ] 1. *n.* (a) series (of buildings/mountains) in line. (b) large open pasture; **free-range hens** = chickens which are allowed to run about in fields. (c) choice/series (of colors, etc.). (d) distance which a shell/bullet can reach; distance which an aircraft can fly without refueling; distance that you can see/hear. (e) large kitchen stove which has cooking surfaces and an oven. 2. *v.* to spread/to vary. **range find•er,** *n.* device (on a gun/camera) for calculating the distance of an object. **rang•er,** *n.* person who looks after a forest or park. **rang•y,** *adj.* with long legs.

rank [ræŋk] 1. *n.* (a) row of soldiers. (b) **ranks** = ordinary soldiers; **he rose from the ranks** = from being an ordinary soldier he became an officer; **the r. and file** = ordinary people. (c) position in society/in the armed forces. 2. *v.* to classify/to be classified in order of importance. 3. *adj.* (**-er, -est**) (a) (plants) which grow luxuriantly. (b) complete/total. (c) with an unpleasant smell. **rank•ness,** *n.* being rank.

ran•kle ['ræŋkl] *v.* to cause bitterness.

ran•sack ['rænsæk] *v.* to search/to turn over (a room) to find sth.

ran•som ['rænsəm] 1. *n.* payment asked for before a hostage is set free; **to hold s.o. for r.** = demand payment before s.o. is set free. 2. *v.* to pay a ransom for (s.o.).

rant [rænt] *v.* to declaim/to shout violently.

rap [ræp] 1. *n.* (a) tap/sharp blow; *inf.* **to take the r.** = to accept responsibility. (b) form of West Indian music where the singer improvises. 2. *v.* (**rapped**) (a) to tap/to give a sharp blow. (b) to sing rap music.

ra•pa•cious [rə'peɪʃəs] *adj.* greedy. **ra•pac•i•ty** [rə'pæsɪtɪ] *n.* greed.

rape [reɪp] 1. *n.* (a) act of having sexual intercourse with s.o. against their will. (b) vegetable with yellow flowers, whose seeds are used to produce oil. 2. *v.* to have sexual intercourse with (s.o.) against their will. **rap•ist,** *n.* person who rapes s.o.

rap•id ['ræpɪd] 1. *adj.* fast. 2. *n. pl.* **rapids** = place where a river runs fast over boulders and down a steep slope. **ra•pid•i•ty** [rə'pɪdɪtɪ] *n.* speed. **rap•id•ly,** *adv.* fast.

ra•pi•er ['reɪpɪə] *n.* long, thin sword for thrusting.

rap•port [ræ'pɔː] *n.* understanding/close link.

rap•proche•ment [ræ'prɒʃmɒŋ] *n.* becoming closer (of former enemies).

rapt [ræpt] *adj.* **with r. attention** = very attentively. **rapt•ly,** *adv.* attentively.

rap•tor ['ræptə] *n.* bird of prey.

rap•ture ['ræptʃə] *n.* delight; **to go into raptures over** = to be delighted by. **rap•tur•ous,** *adj.* excited and delighted (applause, etc.). **rap•tur•ous•ly,** *adv.* in a rapturous way.

rare [reə] *adj.* (**-er, -est**) (a) very unusual. (b) (meat) which is very lightly cooked. **rare•ly,** *adv.* hardly ever. **rar•e•fied** ['reərɪfaɪd] *adj.* (air) which is not very dense. **rar•i•ty,** *n.* (a) (*also* **rareness**) uncommonness. (b) rare object.

rare•bit ['reəbɪt] *n.* **Welsh r.** = cooked cheese on toast.

rar•ing ['reərɪŋ] *adj. inf.* **r. to go** = eager to go.

ras•cal ['rɑːskəl] *n.* naughty person/child. **ras•cal•ly,** *adj.* naughty.

rash [ræʃ] 1. *n.* red area/red spots on the skin; **heat r.** = spots caused by hot weather. 2. *adj.* (**-er, -est**) not cautious/thoughtless; done without thinking. **rash•ly,** *adv.* without thinking. **rash•ness,** *n.* being rash/acting rashly.

rash•er ['ræʃə] *n.* slice (of bacon or ham).

rasp [rɑːsp] 1. *n.* rough metal file used for smoothing surfaces. 2. *v.* to make a grating noise.

rasp•ber•ry ['rɑːzbrɪ] *n.* (a) common red soft fruit growing on tall canes; bush which bears this fruit. (b) *inf.* rude noise made with the mouth to show derision.

Ras•ta•far•i•an [ræstə'feərɪən] *adj. & n.* (member) of a West Indian sect.

rat [ræt] 1. *n.* (a) common gray rodent, living in cellars/sewers/on ships. (b) sly unpleasant person. 2. *v.* (**ratted**) (a) to hunt rats. (b) *inf.* (**on**) to go back on a promise/to betray (s.o.). **rat race,** *n.* competition for success in the business world. **rat•ty,** *adj. inf.* annoyed/short-tempered.

rat•a•fi•a [rætə'fiə] *n.* sweet liqueur flavored with almonds.

rat•chet (wheel) ['rætʃət('wiːl)] *n.* wheel with teeth and a catch to prevent it from turning backward.

rate [reɪt] 1. *n.* (a) number expressed as a proportion of one quantity to another; **birth r./death r.** = number of births/deaths per 1000 of population. (b) frequency at which sth is done/level of cost (as compared to a previous level). (c) speed. (d) **first r.** = very good; **second r.** = rather bad. (e) **at any r.** = in any case. 2. *v.* to value. **rat•ing,** *n.* (a) valuing. (b) **TV ratings** = comparative estimates of audiences for competing TV shows.

rath•er ['rɑːðə] *adv.* (a) relatively/quite. (b) (*used with* **would** *to show preference*) **I'd r. stay** = I would prefer to stay; **I'd r. not** = I would prefer not to. (c) **r. than** = in preference to.

rat•i•fy ['rætɪfaɪ] *v.* to approve (a treaty) officially. **rat•i•fi•ca•tion** [rætɪfɪ'keɪʃn] *n.* official approval.

ra•tio ['reɪʃɪəu] *n.* (*pl.* **-os**) proportion.

ra•ti•oc•i•nate [rætɪ'osɪneɪt] *v.* to think coherently.

ra•tion ['ræʃn] 1. *n.* amount of food/supplies allowed. 2. *v.* to allow only a certain amount of food/supplies. **ra•tion•ing,** *n.* allowing only a certain amount of food/supplies.

ra•tion•al ['ræʃənl] *adj.* reasonable/based on reason. **ra•tion•ale** [ræʃə'nɑːl] *n.* set of reasons which are the basis of a system/of a series of actions. **ra•tion•al•i•ty,** *n.* being rational. **ra•tion•al•i•za•tion** [ræʃnəlaɪ'zeɪʃn] *n.* act of rationalizing. **ra•tion•al•ize** [ræʃnə-'laɪz] *v.* to find a reason for usu. unreasonable actions. **ra•tion•al•ly,** *adv.* based on reason.

rat•tan [rə'tæn] *n.* tropical cane, used to make furniture.

rat•tle ['rætl] 1. *n.* (a) (wooden) instrument which makes a loud repeated noise. (b) repeated clattering noise. 2. *v.* (a) to make a repeated clattering noise. (b) *inf.* to worry/to upset. **rat•tle off,** *v. inf.* to speak rapidly. **rat•tle•snake,** *n.* American poisonous snake which makes a rattling noise with its tail. **rat•tling,** *adj. inf.* very good.

rau•cous ['rɔːkəs] *adj.* rough/hoarse (cough/cry). **rau•cous•ly,** *adv.* in a raucous way. **rau•cous•ness,** *n.* being raucous.

raun•chy ['rɔːntʃɪ] *adj.* (**-ier, -iest**) coarse/openly obscene.

rav•age ['rævɪdʒ] *v.* to devastate/to ruin (a town, etc.). **rav•ages,** *n. pl.* damage.

rave [reɪv] *v.* (a) to be wildly mad. (b) *inf.* to be fanatical (**about** sth). **rav•ing,** *adj.* wild (madman). **rav•ings,** *n. pl.* wild mad talk.

rav•el ['rævl] *v.* (a) to disentangle (sth which is twisted). (b) to tangle/to make sth knotted and twisted.

rav•en ['reɪvn] *n.* large black bird of the crow family.

rav•en•ous ['rævənəs] *adj.* very hungry. **rav•en•ous•ly,** *adv.* extremely (hungry).

ra•vine [rə'viːn] *n.* deep narrow valley.

ra•vi•o•li [rævɪ'əulɪ] *n.* Italian dish of small pasta squares filled with a meat stuffing.

rav•ish ['rævɪʃ] *v.* (a) to steal by force. (b) to en-

æ back, ɑ: farm, ɒ: top, aɪ pipe, aʊ how, aɪə fire, aʊə flower, ɔ: bought, ɔɪ toy, e fed, eəhair, eɪ take, ə afraid, əʊ boat, əʊə lower, vː word, iː heap, ɪ hit, ɪə hear, uː school, ʊ book, ʌ but, b back, d dog, ð then, dʒ just, f fog, g go, h hand, j yes, k catch, l last, m mix, n nut, ŋ sing, p penny, r round, s some, ʃ short, t too, tʃ chop, θ thing, v voice, w was, z zoo, ʒ treasure

chant. **rav•ish•ing,** *adj.* very beautiful/very delightful.

raw [rɔː] 1. *adj.* (**-er, -est**) (a) uncooked. (b) basic/untreated (sewage/data); untrained (recruits). (c) cold and damp (weather). (d) **r. deal** = bad/unfair treatment. (e) exposed/sensitive; **to touch a r. nerve** = to touch a sensitive spot. 2. *n.* (a) sensitive spot. (b) wild natural state. **raw•hide,** *n.* leather which has not been tanned. **raw•ness,** *n.* being raw.

ray [reɪ] *n.* (a) beam of light/heat; small quantity (of hope); **X-rays** = rays which go through the soft tissue, and allow the bones and organs in the body to be photographed. (b) large, flat sea fish.

ray•on ['reɪɒn] *n.* synthetic fiber resembling silk.

raze [reɪz] *v.* **to r. to the ground** = to demolish completely.

ra•zor ['reɪzə] *n.* instrument with a very sharp blade for removing hair. **ra•zor•bill,** *n.* type of black and white sea bird. **razor-sharp,** extremely sharp (blade/mind, etc.).

razz•ma•tazz ['ræzmətæz] *n. inf.* energetic, showy display or activity.

Rd. *short for* road.

re [riː] *prep.* concerning.

re- [riː] *prefix meaning* again.

reach [riːtʃ] 1. *n.* (*pl.* **-es**) (a) distance you can travel easily; distance you can stretch out your hand. (b) continuous section, as of a river. 2. *v.* (a) to stretch out. (b) to arrive at. (c) to come to (an agreement). **reach•a•ble,** *adj.* which can be reached.

re•act [rɪ'ækt] *v.* to do/to say sth in reply to words or an action; **to r. against** = show opposition to; **acids r. with metals** = change their chemical composition. **re•ac•tion** [rɪ'ækʃn] *n.* act of reacting; thing done/said in reply; **what was his r.?** = what did he say/do? **re•ac•tion•ar•y,** *adj. & n.* (person) who is opposed to any political change/to any reforms. **re•ac•ti•vate,** *v.* to make (sth) work again. **re•ac•tive,** *adj.* which is active chemically. **re•ac•tor,** *n.* device for producing atomic energy.

read [riːd] 1. *n. inf.* looking at and understanding writtten or printed words. 2. *v.* (**read, has read** [red]) (a) to look at and understand written words; to speak aloud words which are written; **to r. between the lines** = to understand a hidden meaning which is not immediately apparent. (b) to interpret; **to r. s.o.'s palm** = to interpret the lines on a hand as indications of what will happen in the future. **read•a•bil•i•ty,** *n.* being readable. **read•a•ble,** *adj.* (a) legible/which can be read. (b) (story) which is a pleasure to read. **read•er,** *n.* (a) person who reads. (b) profes-

sor's assistant who helps grade exams, etc. (c) school book to help children to read. (d) apparatus for reading microfilms. (e) person who reads manuscripts/proofs to check them. **read•ing,** *n.* (a) act of looking at and understanding printed words. (b) interpretation. **read•ing room,** *n.* room (in a library) set aside for reading.

re•ad•dress [riːə'dres] *v.* to put another address on (an envelope/package).

re•ad•just [riːə'dʒʌst] *v.* to adjust again; to put back to the original position. **re•ad•just•ment,** *n.* act of readjusting.

read•y ['redɪ] *adj.* (**-ier, -iest**) (a) prepared (**to**). (b) fit to be used. (c) quick/rapid; **he has a r. answer to everything** = he always has an answer. (d) **r. cash** = cash which is immediately available. **read•i•ly,** *adv.* willingly. **read•i•ness,** *n.* willingness; **to hold sth in r.** = to keep sth ready for use. **ready-cooked,** *adj.* (food) which has been cooked in advance. **read•y•made,** **ready-to-wear,** *adj.* (clothes) which are made by mass production, to fit any person of a certain size.

re•a•gent [rɪ'eɪdʒnt] *n.* substance used in a chemical reaction.

re•al [rɪəl] *adj.* (a) true/not imitation; (sth) which exists. (b) **r. estate** = land or buildings which are bought or sold. **re•al•ism,** *n.* (a) facing facts/accepting life as it is. (b) showing things (in writing/painting) as they really are. **re•al•ist,** *n.* (a) artist/writer who shows things as they really are. (b) person who accepts life as it really is, and doesn't idealize it. **re•al•is•tic** [rɪə'lɪstɪk] *adj.* (a) which looks as if it is real. (b) accepting life as it really is. **re•al•is•ti•cal•ly,** *adv.* in a realistic way. **re•al•i•ty** [rɪ'ælɪtɪ] *n.* what is real/not imaginary. **re•al•ly,** *adv.* truly. **re•al time,** *n.* action of a computer which takes place at the same time as the problem it is solving.

re•a•lign [riːə'laɪn] *v.* to set in a new direction; to set in a new group. **re•a•lign•ment,** *n.* change in a series of alliances between countries or political parties.

re•al•ize ['rɪəlaɪz] *v.* (a) to come to understand clearly. (b) to sell property for (money). (c) to make real; to make (sth) come true. **re•al•i•za•tion** [rɪəlaɪ'zeɪʃn] *n.* (a) gradual understanding. (b) conversion of property into money. (c) carrying out of a plan.

realm [relm] *n.* (a) kingdom. (b) general area.

Re•al•po•li•tik [reɪ'ælpɒlɪtɪk] *n.* politics based on real situations, not on moral principles.

re•al•tor ['rɪəltə] *n.* person who arranges the sale of houses and land. **re•al•ty,** *n.* real estate.

ream [riːm] n. (a) 500 sheets of paper. (b) **reams** = very large quantity (of paper).

re•an•i•mate [rɪˈænɪmeɪt] v. to bring back to life.

reap [riːp] v. to harvest (corn, etc.). **reap•er,** n. person/machine which harvests corn, etc.

re•ap•pear [riəˈpɪə] v. to appear again. **re•ap•pear•ance,** n. second appearance.

re•ap•prais•al [riəˈpreɪzl] n. fresh examination of sth to see if your former opinion was correct.

rear [ˈrɪə] 1. n. back part; **to bring up the r.** = march behind. 2. adj. at the back; **r. view mirror** = mirror in a car in which you can see what is behind you without turning around. 3. v. (a) to breed/to raise (animals). (b) to lift (part of the body). (c) (of horse, etc.) to stand up on its back legs. **rear ad•mi•ral,** n. high-ranking naval officer (below vice-admiral). **rear guard,** n. soldiers defending the back part of an army. **rear•most,** adj. farthest at the back.

re•arm [rɪˈɑːm] v. to arm/to stock up with weapons again. **re•ar•ma•ment** [rɪˈɑːməmənt] n. arming again.

re•ar•range [riəˈreɪnʒ] v. to arrange again. **re•ar•range•ment,** n. new arrangement.

rea•son [ˈriːzn] 1. n. (a) cause/explanation for why sth happens. (b) power of thought; commonsense. 2. v. (a) to think/to plan carefully and logically. (b) **to r. with s.o.** = to try to calm s.o./to make s.o. change his mind. **rea•son•a•ble,** adj. (a) not extravagant/moderate. (b) sensible. **rea•son•a•bly,** adv. in a reasonable way. **rea•son•ing,** n. putting your mind to use; **I don't follow your r.** = I can't see how you reached this conclusion.

re•as•sem•ble [riəˈsembl] v. (a) to put back together. (b) to gather together again.

re•as•sure [riəˈʃʊə] v. to calm (s.o.)/to make (s.o.) less afraid/less doubtful. **re•as•sur•ance,** n. act of reassuring.

re•bate [ˈriːbeɪt] n. (a) reduction in the amount of money which should be paid; money which is returned to the person who paid it. (b) groove cut into a piece of wood to hold the tongue on another piece.

reb•el 1. n. [ˈrebəl] person who fights against the government/against the person in charge. 2. v. [rɪˈbel] (**rebelled**) to fight (**against** s.o./sth). **re•bel•lion** [rɪˈbeljən] n. revolt/fight against the government/against authority. **re•bel•lious** [rɪˈbeljəs] adj. fighting against the government/against authority.

re•boot [riːˈbuːt] v. to restart (a computer).

re•bound 1. n. [ˈriːbaʊnd] bouncing back; **on the r.** = (i) as it bounces back; (ii) while still shocked by a dissappointment. 2. v. [riːˈbaʊnd] to bounce back.

re•buff [rɪˈbʌf] 1. n. refusal. 2. v. to refuse.

re•build [riːˈbɪld] v. (**rebuilt**) to build again.

re•buke [rɪˈbjuːk] (formal) 1. n. blame/reproof. 2. v. to blame/to scold.

re•bus [ˈriːbʌs] n. trick, where pictures are used to represent words.

re•but [rɪˈbʌt] v. (**rebutted**) to reject/to disprove (an argument). **re•but•tal,** n. act of rebutting.

re•cal•ci•trant [rɪˈkælsɪtrənt] adj. (formal) difficult/disobedient. **re•cal•ci•trance,** n. being recalcitrant.

re•call [rɪˈkɔːl] 1. n. calling back. 2. v. (a) to call/to summon back (an ambassador/defective cars). (b) to remember.

re•cant [rɪˈkænt] v. to admit that your former beliefs were wrong. **re•can•ta•tion** [rɪkænˈteɪʃn] n. act of recanting.

re•ca•pit•u•late [riːkəˈpɪtjuleɪt] inf. **re•cap** [ˈriːkæp] v. to repeat the main points of an argument. **re•ca•pit•u•la•tion** [riːkəpɪtjuˈleɪʃn] inf. **re•cap,** n. repeating the main points.

re•cap•ture [riːˈkæptʃə] 1. n. act of recapturing. 2. v. to catch again (an escaped prisoner); to take again (a seat in an election).

re•cast [riːˈkɑːst] v. to make again; to write a statement) again in a different way.

recd. abbrev. for received.

re•cede [rɪˈsiːd] v. to go away/to retreat. **re•ced•ing,** adj. (forehead) which slopes backward; (hair) which begins to disappear from the front of the forehead.

re•ceipt [rɪˈsiːt] n. (a) receiving; **on r. of** = when you receive. (b) paper showing that you have paid/that you have received sth. (c) **receipts** = money taken in a business.

re•ceive [rɪˈsiːv] v. (a) to get sth which has been sent; inf. **he was on the receiving end of a lot of criticism** = he had to suffer a lot of criticism. (b) to greet/to welcome; to entertain. **re•ceiv•er,** n. (a) person who accepts stolen goods. (b) person put in charge of a bankrupt company or person. (c) part of a telephone which you can lift and listen to. (d) part of a radio which receives broadcast programs.

æ back, ɑː farm, ɒ top, aɪ pipe, aʊ how, aɪə fire, aʊə flower, ɔː bought, ɔɪ toy, e fed, eəhair, eɪ take, ə afraid, əʊ boat, əʊə lower, ɜː word, iː heap, ɪ hit, ɪə hear, uː school, ʊ book, ʌ but, b back, d dog, ð then, dʒ just, f fog, g go, h hand, j yes, k catch, l last, m mix, n nut, ŋ sing, p penny, r round, s some, ʃ short, t too, tʃ chop, θ thing, v voice, w was, z zoo, ʒ treasure

re•cent ['ri:sənt] *adj.* which took place not very long ago. **re•cent•ly**, *adv.* not long ago/only a short time ago.

re•cep•ta•cle [rɪ'septəkl] *n.* container.

re•cep•tion [rɪ'sepʃn] *n.* (a) welcome. (b) (*in a hotel*) desk where you check in. (c) big party held to welcome special guests. (d) quality of sound of a radio/TV broadcast. **re•cep•tion•ist**, *n.* person in a hotel/doctor's office, etc., who meets visitors and answers the telephone. **re•cep•tive**, *adj.* eager to take in new ideas. **re•cep•tive•ness, re•ceptivity** [risep'tiviti] *n.* being receptive. **re•cep•tor**, *n.* cell at the end of a nerve, which receives impulses.

re•cess [rɪ'ses] *n.* (*pl.* **-es**) (a) alcove/part of the wall of a room which is set back. (b) temporary stopping of usual business or activity, as of a legislature. (c) recreation period at school. (d) inaccessible part. **re•cessed**, *adj.* set back. **re•ces•sive**, *adj.* (*of genes*) not likely to predominate.

re•ces•sion [rɪ'seʃn] *n.* collapse of world economy/of trade.

re•cher•ché [re'ʃeəʃeɪ] *adj.* chosen with care.

re•cid•i•vist [rə'sɪdɪvɪst] *n.* hardened criminal/person who commits a crime repeatedly.

rec•i•pe ['resɪpɪ] *n.* (a) instructions for cooking. (b) effective way to do sth; **it's a r. for disaster** = it's bound to lead to disaster.

re•cip•i•ent [rɪ'sɪpɪənt] *n.* person who receives.

re•cip•ro•cate [rɪ'sɪprəkeɪt] *v.* to do the same thing in return. **re•cip•ro•cal.** 1. *adj.* mutual; **r. trade agreement** = agreement on two-way trade between countries. 2. *n.* (*in math*) quantity produced when 1 is divided by a figure. **re•cip•ro•cal•ly**, *adv.* in a reciprocal way. **rec•i•proc•i•ty** [resɪ'prɒsɪtɪ] *n.* mutual interchange between countries, states or groups.

re•cite [rɪ'saɪt] *v.* to speak (verse, etc.) aloud in public. **re•cit•al**, *n.* reciting in public sth which has been written. (b) performance of music by one or a few musicians. **rec•i•ta•tion** [resɪ'teɪʃn] *n.* thing recited from memory; recital. **rec•i•ta•tive** [resɪtə'ti:v] *n.* (*in an opera*) speech sung in a rhythmic way.

reck•less ['rekləs] *adj.* foolish/rash/not thinking. **reck•less•ly**, *adv.* in a reckless way. **reck•less•ness**, *n.* foolishness/rashness.

reck•on ['rekn] *v.* (a) to calculate/to estimate; (b) to think. (c) **to r. on** = to count on/to depend on. (d) **to r. with** = to have to deal with. **reck•on•er**, *n.* book with tables to help calculations. **reck•on•ing**, *n.* calculation; **day**

of **r.** = time when you have to pay for your mistakes.

re•claim [rɪ'kleɪm] *v.* to make (useless land) fit for use; to take back (land) from the sea. **rec•la•ma•tion** [reklə'meɪʃn] *n.* reclaiming (of land).

re•cline [rɪ'klaɪn] *v.* to lie back.

rec•luse [rɪ'klu:s] *n.* person who lives alone and hidden away.

rec•og•nize ['rekəgnaɪz] *v.* (a) to know (s.o./sth) because you have seen him/it before. (b) to admit (a mistake). (c) to admit (the value of sth). (d) **to r. a government** = to accept that a new government is the legal authority in a country; **to r. a union** = to agree that a union can officially represent workers in a factory. **rec•og•ni•tion** [rekəg'nɪʃn] *n.* recognizing; **he's changed beyond all r.** = so much that you can't recognize him. **rec•og•niz•a•ble** [rekəg'naɪzəbl] *adj.* which can be recognized. **re•cog•ni•zance** [re'kɒgnɪzəns] *n.* money given as a pledge to a court that s.o. will obey the conditions laid down by the court.

re•coil 1. *n.* ['ri:kɔɪl] sudden movement backward of a gun when it is fired. 2. *v.* [rɪ'kɔɪl] to move backward suddenly; to shrink back from sth unpleasant.

rec•ol•lect [rekə'lekt] *v.* to remember. **rec•ol•lec•tion** [rekə'lekʃn] *n.* remembering.

rec•om•mend [rekə'mend] *v.* (a) to advise s.o. to do sth. (b) to praise (sth/s.o.). **rec•om•men•da•tion** [rekəmen'deɪʃn] *n.* (a) advice. (b) praise; thing which is in your favor.

rec•om•pense ['rekəmpens] 1. *n.* payment for sth done/for the time lost, etc. 2. *v.* to pay s.o. for sth done/for time lost, etc.

rec•on•cile ['rekənsaɪl] *v.* (a) to make two enemies become friendly. (b) **to reconcile oneself to** = to accept. (c) to make (two accounts/statements) agree. **rec•on•cil•i•a•tion** [rekənsɪlɪ'eɪʃn] *n.* bringing together of two enemies, so that they become friends; making two accounts/statements agree.

rec•on•dite [rɪ'kɒndaɪt] *adj.* (*formal*) obscure (information).

re•con•di•tion [rɪkən'dɪʃn] *v.* to overhaul thoroughly.

re•con•nais•sance [rɪ'kɒnɪsns] *n.* survey of land for military information.

re•con•noi•ter, *Brit.* **re•con•noi•tre** [rekə'nɔɪtə] *v.* to make a survey to get information/to make a reconnaissance.

re•con•sid•er [ri:kən'sɪdə] *v.* to think over again.

re•con•sti•tute [rɪ'kɒnstɪtjut] *v.* to form (sth) again as it was before.

re•con•struct [ri:kən'strʌkt] v. (a) to build again. (b) to work out how (a crime) must have been committed. re•con•struc•tion, n. act of reconstructing; thing reconstructed.

re•con•vene [ri:kən'vi:n] v. to meet again.

re•cord 1. n. ['rekɔ:d] (a) report of sth which has happened; he is on r. as saying = he is accurately reported as saying; she spoke off the r. = in private/what she said is not to be made public. (b) note/written account. (c) flat plastic disk on which sound is fixed by a recording instrument. (d) description of s.o.'s past career. (e) sporting achievement which is better than any other; at r. speed = very fast. 2. v. [rɪ'kɔ:d] (a) to report; to make a note. (b) to fix sound on a plastic disk or tape. rec•ord-break•ing, adj. which breaks records. re•cord•er [rɪ'kɔ:də] n. (a) person whose job is to take notes and keep records. (b) instrument which records. (c) wooden flute held forward when played. re•cord•ing, n. (a) act of fixing sounds on tape/on disk. (b) music/speech which has been recorded. re•cord•ist, n. person who records sounds on tape or disk. rec•ord play•er, n. machine for playing back music/speech, etc., from a record.

re•count 1. n. ['ri:kaunt] counting votes again (when the result is very close). 2. v. (a) [rɪ'kaunt] to tell (a story). (b) [ri:'kaunt] to count again.

re•coup [rɪ'ku:p] v. to r. your losses = to get back money which you have lost.

re•course [rɪ'kɔ:s] n. to have r. to sth = to use sth in an emergency.

re•cov•er [rɪ'kʌvə] v. (a) to get back (sth which has been stolen/lost). (b) (from) to get well again after an illness. (c) (from) to get over (a shock). (d) [ri:'kʌvə] to put a new cover (on a chair). re•cov•er•a•ble, adj. which can be gotten back. re•cov•ered mem•o•ry, n. apparent recollection, usu. by s.o. in psychotherapy, of an alleged childhood trauma, the memory of which had previously been suppressed. re•cov•er•y, n. (a) getting back (stolen property). (b) getting well again. (c) return to good condition.

rec•re•a•tion [rekrɪ'eɪʃn] n. pleasant occupation for your spare time. rec•re•a•tion•al, adj. referring to recreation.

re•crim•i•nate [rɪ'krɪmɪneɪt] v. to accuse (s.o.) who has accused you. re•crim•i•na•tion [rɪkrɪmɪ'neɪʃn] n. accu-

sation made by s.o. who is accused. re•crim•i•na•to•ry [rɪ'krɪmɪnətrɪ] adj. (remarks) which accuse s.o.

re•cru•des•cence [ri:kru:'desəns] n. (formal) breaking out again (of a disease).

re•cruit [rɪ'kru:t] 1. n. new soldier; new member of a club, etc. 2. v. to encourage (s.o.) to join the armed forces/a club, etc. re•cruit•ment, n. encouraging people to join the armed forces/a club, etc.

rec•tal ['rektəl] adj. referring to the rectum.

rec•tan•gle ['rektæŋgl] n. four-sided shape with right angles and two sets of opposite and equal sides. rec•tan•gu•lar [rek'tæŋgjʊlə] adj. like a rectangle.

rec•ti•fy ['rektɪfaɪ] v. to correct/to make right. rec•ti•fi•a•ble, adj. which can be corrected. rec•ti•fi•ca•tion [rektɪfɪ'keɪʃn] n. correction.

rec•ti•lin•e•ar [rektɪ'lɪnɪə] adj. with straight lines.

rec•ti•tude ['rektɪtju:d] n. (esp. moral) correctness.

rec•to ['rektəu] n. right/main side (of a piece of paper, page of a book, etc.).

rec•tor ['rektə] n. (a) priest in charge of a parish. (b) head of certain schools/colleges/universities. rec•to•ry, n. house of a rector.

rec•tum ['rektəm] n. lower part of the intestine, leading to the anus.

re•cum•bent [rɪ'kʌmbənt] adj. (formal) lying down.

re•cu•per•ate [rɪ'kju:pəreɪt] v. to recover/to get better after an illness or a loss. re•cu•per•a•tion [rɪkju:pə'reɪʃn] n. getting better. re•cu•per•a•tive, adj. which helps recuperation.

re•cur [rɪ'kɜ:] v. (recurred) to happen again. re•cur•rence [rɪ'kʌrəns] n. reappearance/happening again. re•cur•rent [rɪ'kʌrənt], re•curr•ing [rɪ'kɜ:rɪŋ] adj. (a) which happens again. (b) (decimal figure) which is repeated for ever.

rec•u•sant ['rekjuzənt] adj. & n. (old) (person) who refuses to comply, esp. one who refused to accept the Anglican Church in England.

re•cy•cle [ri:'saɪkl] v. to process (waste material) so that it can be used again.

red [red] adj. & n. (redder, reddest) (color) like blood or fire; inf. see r. = get very angry; inf. to be in the r. = to be in debt; r. carpet = official welcome; r. tape = official rules which stop you doing sth quickly; r. herring = false

---

æ back, a: farm, ɒ: top, aɪ pipe, au how, aie fire, auə flower, ɔ: bought, ɔɪ toy, e fed, eə hair, eɪ take, ə afraid, əu boat, əuə lower, v: word, i: heap, ɪ hit, ɪə hear, u: school, u book, ʌ but, b back, d dog, ð then, dʒ just, f fog, g go, h hand, j yes, k catch, l last, m mix, n nut, ŋ sing, p penny, r round, s some, ʃ short, t too, tʃ chop, θ thing, v voice, w was, z zoo, ʒ treasure

track/sth which leads you away from the main problem; *inf.* **the Reds** = the Communists. **red-blood•ed,** *adj.* strong, vigorous. **red•breast,** *n.* robin. **Red Cres•cent,** *n.* organization similar to the Red Cross, working in Muslim countries. **Red Cross,** *n.* international organization which cares for the sick and injured, and also organizes relief work. **red cur•rant,** *n.* common red soft fruit growing in small clusters; bush which bears this fruit. **red•den,** *v.* to turn red/to blush. **red•dish,** *adj.* rather red. **red flag,** *n.* flag of the communist party. **red-hand•ed,** *adj.* **they caught him red-handed** = as he was committing a crime. **red•head,** *n.* person with red hair. **red-hot,** *adj.* (*of metal*) very hot. **Red In•dian,** *n.* (*rude*) North American Indian. **red-let•ter day,** *n.* very special day. **red•ness,** *n.* being red. **red•shank,** *n.* large sandpiper. **red•start,** *n.* small singing bird with red feathers beneath the tail. **red•wood,** *n.* type of very tall coniferous tree growing on the west coast of North America.

re•dec•o•rate [riː'dekəreɪt] *v.* to decorate/to paint again.

re•deem [rɪ'diːm] *v.* (a) to buy back (sth which you have pledged to borrow money); to pay off (a debt). (b) to compensate. (c) to save from sin. **Re•deem•er,** *n.* Jesus Christ. **re•deem•ing,** *adj.* which compensates. **re•demp•tion** [rɪ'dempʃn] *n.* (a) payment of a debt. (b) being saved from sin.

re•de•ploy [riːdɪ'plɔɪ] *v.* to move (workers/soldiers) from one place to another. **re•de•ploy•ment,** *n.* act of redeploying.

re•di•rect [riːdaɪ'rekt] *v.* to change the direction or movement of.

red•o•lent ['redələnt] *adj.* which smells (**of** sth); which reminds you (**of** sth). **red•o•lence,** *n.* being redolent.

re•dou•ble [riː'dʌbl] *v.* **to r. your efforts** = to try even harder.

re•doubt [rɪ'daʊt] *n.* small fort. **re•doubt•a•ble** [rɪ'daʊtəbl] *adj.* formidable/bold.

re•dound [rɪ'daʊnd] *v.* (*formal*) **it will r. to your credit** = will make you more admired.

re•dress [rɪ'dres] 1. *n.* compensation done to make up for something wrong. 2. *v.* to correct/to compensate/to repair; **to r. a wrong** = to make things right again.

re•duce [rɪ'djuːs] *v.* (a) to make smaller/lower; **to r. s.o. to the ranks** = to punish an officer by making him an ordinary soldier; **to r. one's weight** = to get thinner. (b) to force (s.o.) to do sth humiliating. **re•duc•i•ble,** *adj.* which

can be reduced. **re•duc•tion** [rɪ'dʌkʃn] *n.* lowering (of price/speed/standards).

re•dun•dant [rɪ'dʌndənt] *adj.* more than necessary; excess. **re•dun•dan•cy,** *n.* state of being redundant.

re•du•pli•cate [rɪ'djuplɪkeɪt] *v.* to repeat (sth).

re•ech•o, re-echo [riː'ekəʊ] *v.* to echo again.

reed [riːd] *n.* (a) marsh plant with tall stem. (b) part of a wind instrument which vibrates to make a note. **reed•i•ness,** *n.* being reedy. **reed•y,** *adj.* (a) high-pitched (voice). (b) (marsh) which is full of reeds.

reef [riːf] 1. *n.* (a) ridge of rock in the sea. (b) **r. knot** = type of flat knot which does not come undone easily. 2. *v.* to reduce the size of (a sail) by rolling part of it up. **reef•er,** *n.* (a) sailor's short coat. (b) *Sl.* marijuana cigarette.

reek [riːk] 1. *n.* strong smell. 2. *v.* to smell strongly (**of**).

reel [riːl] 1. *n.* (a) spool for winding thread/string/film around. (b) lively Scottish dance. 2. *v.* (a) to wind around a reel. (b) **to r. off** = to quote at length. (c) to stagger.

re•el•ect [riːɪ'lekt] *v.* to elect again. **re•e•lec•tion** [riːɪ'lekʃn] *n.* being reelected.

re•em•ploy [riːem'plɔɪ] *v.* to employ (s.o.) again.

re•en•ter [riː'entə] *v.* to enter again. **re•en•try** [riː'entrɪ] *n.* entering again.

ref [ref] *n. inf.* (*in sports*) referee.

re•fec•to•ry [rɪ'fektərɪ] *n.* dining hall (in a school, etc.); **r. table** = long narrow dining table.

re•fer to [rɪ'fɜː] *v.* (**referred**) (a) to mention. (b) to look into sth for information. (c) to pass (a problem) to s.o. to decide. (d) to tell (s.o.) to see s.o. else. **ref•er•ee** [refə'riː] 1. *n.* (*in sports*) person who sees that the game is played according to the rules/who judges between two sides. 2. *v.* to act as a referee in a sports match. **ref•er•ence** ['refrəns] *n.* (a) (**to**) mention; **with r. to** = concerning/about. (b) direction for further information; **r. book** = book (such as dictionary/encyclopedia) where you can look up information; **r. library** = library of reference books. (c) statement about s.o.'s character, etc. **re•fer•ral** [rɪ'fɜːrl] *n.* act of referring.

ref•er•en•dum [refə'rendəm] *n.* (*pl.* **-da/-dums**) vote by all the people of a country or state on a proposed or current law to let them decide.

re•fill 1. *n.* ['riːfɪl] container with a fresh quantity of liquid/ink, etc.; another drink. 2. *v.* [riː'fɪl] to fill again.

re•fine [rɪ'faɪn] *v.* to make better/more pure. **re•fined,** *adj.* very elegant/polite.

re•fine•ment, *n.* (a) elegance. (b) improvement. **re•fin•er**, *n.* business/person that refines. **re•fin•er•y**, *n.* factory where sth is refined.

re•fit 1. *n.* ['ri:fɪt] repairs (to a ship). 2. *v.* [ri:'fɪt] (**refitted**) to repair (a ship).

re•flate [ri:'fleɪt] *v.* to stimulate (an economy which has previously been deflated). **re•fla•tion** [ri:'fleɪʃn] *n.* action of stimulating a deflated economy. **re•fla•tion•ar•y**, *adj.* likely to cause reflation.

re•flect [rɪ'flekt] *v.* (a) to send back (light/heat/an image). (b) to think back into the past/to ponder. (c) **to r. on** = to be a criticism of. **re•flec•tion**, *Brit.* **re•flex•ion** [rɪ'flekʃn] *n.* (a) sending back of light/heat; reflected image (in a mirror). (b) thought; **on r.** = on thinking more about it. (c) criticism. **re•flec•tive**, *adj.* thoughtful. **re•flec•tor**, *n.* apparatus which reflects.

re•flex ['ri:fleks] 1. *n.* (*pl.* **-es**) automatic action/instinctive response. 2. *adj.* (a) which is automatic; **r. action** = action done instinctively. (b) which returns as a reflection; **r. camera** = camera where the picture is reflected from the lens to the viewfinder exactly as it will appear on the photograph; **r. angle** = angle of more than 180°. **re•flex•ive** [rɪ'fleksɪv] *adj.* (*in grammar*) verb or pronoun which refers back to the subject.

re•float [ri:'fləʊt] *v.* to float again (a ship which has gone aground).

re•flux ['ri:flʌks] *n.* flowing back.

re•form [rɪ'fɔ:m] 1. *n.* improving/improvement. 2. *v.* (a) to correct/to improve. (b) to become good/to stop committing crime or doing wrong. **ref•or•ma•tion** [refə'meɪʃn] *n.* act of reforming; **the Reformation** = religious movement in sixteenth century Europe which brought about the creation of the Protestant churches. **re•form•a•to•ry** [rɪ'fɔ:mətrɪ] *n.* type of prison school where young criminals are sent in the hope that they will be reformed. **re•form•er**, *n.* person who tries to improve (a system).

re•fract [rɪ'frækt] *v.* to bend (rays of light, etc.) as they pass through the surface of water. **re•frac•tion** [rɪ'frækʃn] *n.* bending of light as it goes from one substance to another (such as into water). **re•frac•tive**, *adj.* producing refraction. **re•frac•tor**, *n.* object/substance which refracts.

re•frac•to•ry [rɪ'fræktərɪ] *adj.* difficult/disobedient.

re•frain [rɪ'freɪn] 1. *n.* chorus which is repeated after each section of a song or poem. 2. *v.* **to r. from** = to keep from doing sth.

re•fresh [rɪ'freʃ] *v.* to make fresh again; to make less tired; **let me r. your memory** = help you to remember sth which you seem to have forgotten. **re•fresh•er (course)**, *n.* lessons which bring your knowledge of sth up to date. **re•fresh•ing**, *adj.* (a) which refreshes. (b) new and invigorating. **re•fresh•ment**, *n.* refreshments = food and drink.

re•frig•er•a•tor [rɪ'frɪdʒəreɪtə] *n.* box or room for keeping things (esp. food) cold by ice or mechanical means. **re•frig•er•ant**, *n.* substance used to make other substances very cold. **re•frig•er•at•ed**, *adj.* kept cold. **re•frig•er•a•tion** [rɪfrɪdʒə'reɪʃn] *n.* keeping things cold.

re•fu•el [ri:'fjʊəl] *v.* (**refueled, refuelled**) to put more fuel into (a ship/plane/car, etc.).

ref•uge ['refju:dʒ] *n.* place to hide/to shelter; **to take r.** = to shelter. **ref•u•gee** [refju:'dʒi:] *n.* person who has been driven out of his own country and needs shelter; **political r.** = person who has left his country for political reasons.

re•fund 1. *n.* ['ri:fʌnd] repayment of money. 2. *v.* [ri:'fʌnd] to pay back (money).

re•fur•bish [rɪ'fɜ:bɪʃ] *v.* to polish up again.

re•fuse 1. *n.* ['refju:s] things to be thrown out; garbage; rubbish. 2. *v.* [rɪ'fju:z] (a) to say that you do not accept/that you will not do sth. (b) not to give s.o. (permission). **re•fus•al** [rɪ'fju:zl] *n.* (a) saying no; **to meet with a flat r.** = to be refused completely. (b) **to give s.o. first r. of sth** = to let them have first choice of buying sth.

re•fute [rɪ'fju:t] *v.* to prove that (sth) is wrong. **ref•u•ta•tion** [refju:'teɪʃn] *n.* proof that sth is wrong.

re•gain [ri:'geɪn] *v.* to get back.

re•gal ['ri:gl] *adj.* referring to a king/queen; royal. **re•ga•li•a** [rɪ'geɪlɪə] *n.* *pl.* robes/crown, etc., worn by a king/queen/mayor. **re•gal•ly**, *adv.* like a king/queen.

re•gale [rɪ'geɪl] *v.* to entertain.

re•gard [rɪ'gɑ:d] 1. *n.* (a) concern. (b) esteem. (c) **regards** = best wishes. 2. *v.* (a) to consider. (b) **as regards** = concerning. **re•gard•ing**, *prep.* concerning. **re•gard•less**, *adj.* paying

---

æ back, ɑ: farm, ɒ top, aɪ pipe, aʊ how, aɪə fire, aʊə flower, ɔ: bought, ɔɪ toy, e fed, eəhair, eɪ take, ə afraid, əʊ boat, əʊə lower, v: word, i: heap, ɪ hit, ɪə hear, u: school, ʊ book, ʌ but, b back, d dog, ð then, dʒ just, f fog, g go, h hand, j yes, k catch, l last, m mix, n nut, ŋ sing, p penny, r round, s some, ʃ short, t too, tʃ chop, θ thing, v voice, w was, z zoo, ʒ treasure

no attention to; **carry on r.** = carry on in spite of everything.

re•gat•ta [rɪˈgætə] n. series of boat races (for either yachts or rowboats).

re•gen•er•ate [rɪˈdʒenəreɪt] v. to start up again. **re•gen•er•a•tion** [rɪdʒenəˈreɪʃn] n. growing again/starting again.

re•gent [ˈriːdʒənt] n. person who rules in place of a king or queen. **re•gen•cy**, n. period when a regent is ruling.

reg•gae [ˈregeɪ] n. type of West Indian music.

reg•i•cide [ˈredʒɪsaɪd] n. person who kills a king.

re•gime [reˈʒiːm] n. system of government/administration.

reg•i•men [ˈredʒɪmən] n. planned course of action to improve your health.

reg•i•ment [ˈredʒɪmənt] 1. n. group of soldiers, usu. commanded by a colonel or lieutenant-colonel. 2. v. to keep (s.o.) under strict discipline. **reg•i•men•tal** [redʒɪˈmentl] adj. belonging to a regiment. **reg•i•men•tals**, n. pl. military uniform of a certain regiment. **reg•i•men•ta•tion** [redʒɪmenˈteɪʃn] n. very strict discipline.

re•gion [ˈriːdʒən] n. area; **the metropolitan r.** = area around a city; **in the r. of $10,000** = about $10,000. **re•gion•al**, adj. referring to a region.

reg•is•ter [ˈredʒɪstə] 1. n. (a) list (of names). (b) range of notes covered by a voice/a musical instrument. (c) **cash r.** = device which records sales/money taken in a store. (d) (in printing) fitting of several printing plates in such a way that various colors correspond exactly on the paper. (e) level of language (such as formal/colloquial, etc.). 2. v. (a) to write (a name) officially in a list; **to r. at a hotel** = to write your name and address when you arrive at the hotel. (b) to record (a temperature, etc.). **reg•is•tered**, adj. which has been officially recorded. **reg•is•trar** [ˈredʒɪstrɑː] n. person who keeps official records; person who keeps the records of a school/college/university. **reg•is•tra•tion** [redʒɪˈstreɪʃn] n. (a) act of registering. (b) official document proving that sth has been registered; **car registration.** **reg•is•try** [ˈredʒɪstrɪ] n. place where official records are kept.

re•gress [rɪˈgres] v. to go back to an earlier, and usu. worse, condition. **re•gres•sion**, n. going back. **re•gres•sive**, adj. which regresses.

re•gret [rɪˈgret] 1. n. sorrow; **much to my r.** = I am very sorry. 2. v. (**regretted**) to be sorry that sth has happened. **re•gret•ful**, adj. sorry/sad. **re•gret•ful•ly**, adv. sadly. **re•gret•ta•ble**, adj. which must be regret-

ted. **re•gret•ta•bly**, adv. in a regrettable way.

reg•u•lar [ˈregjulə] 1. adj. (a) habitual/done at the same time each day. (b) usual/ordinary. (c) **r. army** = permanent, professional army; **r. officer** = professional officer. (d) (in grammar) **r. verb** = verb which has no unusual parts. 2. n. (a) inf. customer who always shops in a particular store/who always drinks in a certain bar, etc. (b) professional soldier. **reg•u•lar•i•ty** [regjuˈlærɪtɪ] n. being regular. **reg•u•lar•i•za•tion** [regjuləraɪˈzeɪʃn] n. act of regularizing. **reg•u•lar•ize** [ˈregjuləraɪz] v. to make legal. **reg•u•lar•ly**, adv. in a regular way. **reg•u•late** [ˈregjuleɪt] v. to adjust (a machine) so that it works regularly. **reg•u•la•tion** [regjuˈleɪʃn] n. act of regulating; rule. **reg•u•la•tor**, n. person/instrument which regulates a machine.

re•gur•gi•tate [rɪˈgɜːdʒɪteɪt] v. (formal) to spout out (food which has already been swallowed/information which has already been learned). **re•gur•gi•ta•tion** [rigɜːdʒɪˈteɪʃn] n. act of regurgitating.

re•ha•bil•i•tate [riːhəˈbɪlɪteɪt] v. to train (a disabled person/an ex-prisoner, etc.) to lead a normal life and fit into society. **re•ha•bil•i•ta•tion** [riːhəbɪlɪˈteɪʃn] n. act of rehabilitating.

re•hash 1. n. [ˈriːhæʃ] thing rehashed. 2. v. [riːˈhæʃ] to bring out (an old story/book, etc.) in more or less the same form as before.

re•hearse [rɪˈhɜːs] v. to practice (a play/a concert, etc.) before a public performance. **re•hears•al** [rɪˈhɜːsəl] n. practice of a play/concert, etc., before a public performance; **dress r.** = last rehearsal of a play, etc., when everyone is in costume.

re•house [riːˈhauz] v. to put (s.o.) into a new house or apartment.

reign [reɪn] 1. n. period when a king/queen/emperor rules; **r. of terror** = period when law and order have broken down. 2. v. to rule.

re•im•burse [riːɪmˈbɜːs] v. to pay (s.o.) back the money he has spent. **re•im•burse•ment**, n. act of reimbursing; money reimbursed.

rein [reɪn] 1. n. strap which controls a horse; **to keep on a tight r.** = under strict control. 2. v. **to r. in** = to pull on the reins to control (a horse).

re•in•car•nate [riːɪnˈkɑːneɪt] v. (formal) to make (the soul of a dead person) be born again in another body. **re•in•car•na•tion** [riːɪnkɑːˈneɪʃn] n. survival of a person's soul born again in another body after death.

rein•deer [ˈreɪndɪə] n. (pl. **reindeer**) type of deer which lives in the Arctic.

re•in•force [riːɪnˈfɔːs] v. to strengthen/to consolidate; **reinforced concrete** = concrete

strengthened with metal rods.
re•in•force•ment, *n.* (a) act of reinforcing.
(b) **reinforcements** = new soldiers to support
others already fighting.

re•in•state [riːɪnˈsteɪt] *v.* to put back into a
former position or condition.
re•in•state•ment, *n.* putting back into a
former position or condition.

re•in•sure [riːɪnˈʃuːə] *v.* to spread the risk of insurance, by insuring part of the risk with another insurer.

re•in•vest [riːɪnˈvest] *v.* to invest again.

re•it•er•ate [riːˈɪtəreɪt] *v.* to repeat.
re•it•er•a•tion [riːɪtəˈreɪʃn] *n.* repetition.

re•ject 1. *n.* [ˈriːdʒekt] thing which has been
thrown away as not satisfactory; **rejects** = sub-
standard goods sold at a reduced price. 2. *v.*
[rɪˈdʒekt] to refuse to accept (sth); to throw
(sth) away as not satisfactory. **re•jec•tion**
[rɪˈdʒekʃn] *n.* refusal.

re•jig•ger [riːˈdʒɪg] *v.* (**rejiggered**) *inf.* to arrange in a different way.

re•joice [rɪˈdʒɔɪs] *v.* to be very happy.
re•joic•ing, *n.* great happiness.

re•join [rɪˈdʒɔɪn] *v.* (a) to join again. (b) (*formal*) to reply. **re•join•der,** *n.* (*formal*) reply.

re•ju•ve•nate [rɪˈdʒuːvəneɪt] *v.* to make (s.o.)
young again; to give (sth) new strength.
re•ju•ve•na•tion [rɪdʒuːvəˈneɪʃn] *n.* act of
rejuvenating.

re•kin•dle [riːˈkɪndl] *v.* to light again.

re•lapse [rɪˈlæps] 1. *n.* becoming ill again (after
a temporary improvement); getting back into
old bad habits. 2. *v.* to become ill again; to get
back into old bad habits.

re•late [rɪˈleɪt] *v.* (a) to tell (a story). (b) to connect (two things). (c) to have a successful relationship (**with** s.o.). **re•lat•ed,** *adj.* (a)
linked. (b) belonging to the same family.
re•la•tion [rɪˈleɪʃn] *n.* (a) story. (b) link-
ing/links (between two things); **public relations**
= maintaining good connections with the
public, esp. to put across a point of view/to
publicize a product. (c) member of a family.
re•la•tion•ship, *n.* link/connection; being
related.

rel•a•tive [ˈrelətɪv] 1. *n.* person who is related
to s.o.; member of a family. 2. *adj.* (a) which is
compared to sth; **their r. poverty** = their poverty compared with really wealthy people or
with the wealth they used to have. (b) (*in
grammar*) **r. pronoun** = pronoun (such as
"who" and "which") which connects two

clauses. **rel•a•tive•ly,** *adv.* compara-
tively/more or less. **rel•a•tiv•i•ty** [relə-
ˈtɪvɪtɪ] *n.* (*in physics*) relationship between objects and time and speed.

re•lax [rɪˈlæks] *v.* (a) to slacken/to decrease tension; to make less strict. (b) to rest from work.
re•lax•a•tion [riːlækˈseɪʃn] *n.* (a) slackening
of a rule, etc. (b) rest. **re•laxed,** *adj. inf.*
happy/not upset.

re•lay 1. *n.* [ˈriːleɪ] (a) shift of people working.
(b) **r. race** = running race by teams in which
one runner passes a baton to another who
then runs on. 2. *v.* [rɪˈleɪ] to pass on (a message); to pass on (a TV/radio broadcast)
through a relay station. **re•lay sta•tion,** *n.*
transmitting station which receives signals
from a main transmitter and broadcasts them
further.

re•lease [rɪˈliːs] 1. *n.* (a) setting free. (b) new re-
cord/piece of information which is made pub-
lic. 2. *v.* (a) to set free. (b) to make public.

rel•e•gate [ˈrelɪgeɪt] *v.* to put into a worse position. **rel•e•ga•tion** [relɪˈgeɪʃn] *n.* moving
into a worse position.

re•lent [rɪˈlent] *v.* to change your mind about a
strict decision you have taken/to be less strict.
re•lent•less, *adj.* pitiless. **re•lent•less•ly,**
adv. with no pity.

rel•e•vant [ˈrelɪvənt] *adj.* which relates/has to
do with sth being spoken of. **rel•e•vance,** *n.*
being relevant.

re•li•a•ble [rɪˈlaɪəbl] *adj.* which can be relied
on/which can be trusted. **re•li•a•bly,** *adv.* in
a way which can be trusted. **re•li•a•bil•i•ty**
[rɪlaɪəˈbɪlɪtɪ] *n.* being reliable. **re•li•ance,** *n.*
trust/confidence. **re•li•ant,** *adj.* which relies
on sth.

rel•ic [ˈrelɪk] *n.* object which has been left over
from the past; holy remains (such as the bones
of a saint). **rel•ict,** *n.* (*formal*) widow.

re•lief [rɪˈliːf] *n.* (a) reducing pain/tension. (b)
help; **r. fund** = money collected to help victims
of a disaster. (c) person/thing that takes over
from another. **a r. nurse.** (d) carving in which
the details of design stand out; **in r.** = standing
out/prominent; **r. map** = map where mountains are drawn so that an impression of
height is given. **re•lieve** [rɪˈliːv] *v.* (a) to reduce (pain/tension); **to r. oneself** = to urinate
or defecate. (b) to help. (c) to take over from
(s.o.). (d) to remove a weight from (s.o.).

re•li•gion [rɪˈlɪdʒən] *n.* belief in gods or in one
God; system of worship. **re•li•gious,** *adj.* re-

æ back, ɑ: farm, ɒ: top, aɪ pipe, aʊ how, aɪə fire, aʊə flower, ɔ: bought, ɔɪ toy, ə fed, eəhair, eɪ take, ə
afraid, əʊ boat, əʊə lower, ɜ: word, i: heap, ɪ hit, ɪə hear, u: school, ʊ book, ʌ but, b back, d dog, ð then,
dʒ just, f fog, g go, h hand, j yes, k catch, l last, m mix, n nut, ŋ sing, p penny, r round, s some, ʃ short, t
too, tʃ chop, θ thing, v voice, w was, z zoo, ʒ treasure

ferring to religion. **re•li•gious•ly**, *adv.* regularly/at a fixed time of day.

re•lin•quish [rɪ'lɪŋkwɪʃ] *v.* (*formal*) to leave/to let go.

rel•i•quar•y ['relɪkweri] *n.* container for holy relics.

rel•ish ['relɪʃ] 1. *n.* (*pl.* -es) (a) a seasoning/flavor; spicy pickles/spicy sauce. (b) enjoyment. 2. *v.* to enjoy.

re•lo•cate [riːlə'keɪt] *v.* to set (offices) in a new location; move to another place. **re•lo•ca•tion** [riːlə'keɪʃn] *n.* act of relocating.

re•luc•tant [rɪ'lʌktənt] *adj.* not eager/not willing. **re•luc•tant•ly**, *adv.* not willingly. **re•luc•tance**, *n.* lack or eagerness.

re•ly [rɪ'laɪ] *v.* (on) to trust.

re•main [rɪ'meɪn] *v.* (a) to stay. (b) **it remains to be seen** = we will see in due course. **re•main•der**. 1. *n.* (a) what is left over. (b) **remainders** = books which are sold off cheaply. 2. *v.* to sell off (new books) cheaply. **re•mains**, *n. pl.* (a) dead body. (b) things left over/left behind.

re•mand [rɪ'mɑːnd] *v.* to order (a prisoner) back into custody to appear at a later hearing of a trial when more evidence will be produced.

re•mark [rɪ'mɑːk] 1. *n.* comment/observation. 2. *v.* to notice/to comment. **re•mark•a•ble**, *adj.* unusual/which you might comment on. **re•mark•a•bly**, *adv.* unusually.

rem•e•dy ['remədɪ] 1. *n.* thing which may cure. 2. *v.* to make (sth) better/to put (sth) right. **re•me•di•al** [rɪ'miːdɪəl] *adj.* which cures/which makes sth better; **r. reading** = class of special instruction for students who are weak in reading.

re•mem•ber [rɪ'membə] *v.* (a) to call back into your mind (sth which you have seen/read/heard, etc., before). (b) to send good wishes to s.o. (c) **he remembered me in his will** = he left me sth in his will. **re•mem•brance**, *n.* memory.

re•mind [rɪ'maɪnd] *v.* **to r. s.o. of sth** = to make (s.o.) remember sth. **re•mind•er**, *n.* thing which reminds you of sth.

rem•i•nis•cence [remɪ'nɪsəns] *n.* memory of sth from the past. **rem•i•nisce** [remɪ'nɪs] *v.* to talk about memories of the past. **rem•i•nis•cent**, *adj.* which reminds you of the past.

re•miss [rɪ'mɪs] *adj.* careless.

re•mis•sion [rɪ'mɪʃn] *n.* pardon (for your sins).

re•mit 1. *n.* ['riːmɪt] orders; area of responsibility. 2. *v.* [ri'mit] (**remitted**) (a) to pardon (sins).

(b) to send (money). **re•mit•tance**, *n.* sending money; money which is sent.

rem•nant ['remnənt] *n.* piece/quantity left over.

re•mon•strate ['remənstreɪt] *v.* to protest **against** sth. **re•mon•strance** [rɪ'mɒnstrəns] *n.* act of remonstrating.

re•morse [rɪ'mɔːs] *n.* regret about sth wicked which you have done. **re•morse•ful**, *adj.* full of remorse. **re•morse•less**, *adj.* pitiless/cruel. **re•morse•less•ly**, *adv.* in a remorseless way.

re•mote [rɪ'məʊt] *adj.* (-er, -est) (a) distant; **r. control** = (a) control (of a model plane, etc.) by radio signals. (b) device used to control the operation of sth, as a TV, from a distance. (c) slight (possibility). (d) uncommunicative (person). **re•mote•ly**, *adv.* distantly. **re•mote•ness**, *n.* being remote.

re•mold ['riːməʊld] *v.* to mold again.

re•mount [ri'maʊnt] *v.* to get back on to (a horse/bicycle, etc.).

re•move [rɪ'muːv] 1. *n.* step or grade; **one r. from** = one grade up/down from. 2. *v.* (a) to take away. (b) to dismiss (s.o.) from a job. **re•mov•a•ble**, *adj.* which can be removed. **re•mov•al**, *n.* changing of location, as of a business. **re•mov•er**, *n.* thing which removes; **paint r.** = liquid which removes old paint.

re•mu•ner•ate [rɪ'mjuːnəreɪt] *v.* (*formal*) to pay (s.o.). **re•mu•ner•a•tion** [rɪmjuːnə'reɪʃn] *n.* payment. **re•mu•ner•a•tive** [rɪ'mjuːnərətɪv] *adj.* well paid.

ren•ais•sance [re'neɪsəns] *n.* rebirth/starting again; **the Renaissance** = artistic movement in late medieval Europe based on a renewal of interest in the Greek and Roman civilizations.

re•nal ['riːnl] *adj.* referring to the kidneys.

re•nas•cent [rɪ'neɪsənt] *adj.* which is rising again.

rend [rend] *v.* (**rent**) to tear.

rend•er ['rendə] *v.* (a) to give (back); to send in (an account). (b) to translate. (c) **to r. (down)** = to melt (fat). (d) to cover (a wall) with a coating of plaster. (e) to make (s.o.) be (speechless, etc.). **rend•er•ing**, *n.* translation; performance (of a song, etc.).

ren•dez•vous ['rɒndeɪvuː] 1. *n.* meeting place/appointment; meeting. 2. *v.* (**rendezvoused** ['rɒndeɪvuːd]) to arrange to meet.

ren•di•tion [ren'dɪʃn] *n.* performance (of a song, etc.).

ren•e•gade ['renɪgeɪd] *adj. & n.* (person) who gives up a faith/a belief to adopt another; (person) who leaves one group to join another.

re•nege [rɪ'neɪg] *v.* **to r. on** = to fail to do sth which you had promised to do.

re•new [rɪ'njuː] v. to start again; to replace (sth old) with sth new. **re•new•a•ble**, adj. which can be renewed. **re•new•al**, n. act of renewing.

ren•net ['renɪt] n. substance which when added to milk makes it curdle and so form cheese.

re•nounce [rɪ'naʊns] v. to give up officially. **re•nounce•ment**, n. act of renouncing.

ren•o•vate ['renəveɪt] v. to make (sth) like new. **ren•o•va•tion** [renə'veɪʃn] n. making like new. **ren•o•va•tor**, n. person/machine that renovates.

re•nown [rɪ'naʊn] n. fame. **re•nowned**, adj. famous (for sth).

rent [rent] 1. n. (a) money paid for the use of an apartment/house/office, etc. (b) tear/slit (in cloth). 2. v. (a) to pay money to live in (a house/apartment, etc.). (b) to give use of (a house/apartment, etc.) for money. (c) see also **rend. ren•tal**, n. rent/money paid to live in a room/apartment/office, etc.

re•nun•ci•a•tion [rɪnʌnsɪ'eɪʃn] n. giving up/renouncing of a claim.

re•o•pen [riː'əʊpən] v. (a) to open again. (b) to start to investigate a case again.

re•or•gan•ize [riː'ɔːgənaɪz] v. to organize in a new way. **re•or•gan•i•za•tion** [rɪɔːgənaɪ'zeɪʃn] n. act of reorganizing.

re•or•i•ent [rɪ'ɔːrɪenteɪt] v. to set (s.o.) in another direction.

rep [rep] n. inf. (a) traveling salesman. (b) repertory theater. (c) strong corded material used in upholstery.

re•paid [riː'peɪd] v. see **re•pay**.

re•pair [rɪ'peə] 1. n. (a) mending. (b) **to be in a good state of r./in good r.** = to be in good condition. 2. v. (a) to mend. (b) (old) to go. **re•pair•er**, n. person who mends. **re•pair•a•ble**, adj. which can be mended. **rep•a•ra•tion** [repə'reɪʃn] n. thing/money which makes up for a wrong.

rep•ar•tee [repɑː'tiː] n. series of witty answers in a conversation.

re•past [rɪ'pɑːst] n. (formal) meal.

re•pa•tri•ate [riː'pætrɪeɪt] v. to bring/to send (s.o.) back to their home country. **re•pa•tri•a•tion** [rɪpætrɪ'eɪʃn] n. act of repatriating.

re•pay [riː'peɪ] v. (repaid) to pay back. **re•pay•a•ble**, adj. which can be repaid. **re•pay•ment**, n. paying back.

re•peal [rɪ'piːl] 1. n. abolition of a law, so that it is no longer valid. 2. v. to do away with (a law).

re•peat [rɪ'piːt] 1. n. & adj. performance which is repeated. 2. v. to say/to do (sth) again. **re•peat•a•ble**, adj. which can be repeated. **re•peat•ed•ly** [rɪ'piːtɪdlɪ] adv. over and over again. **re•peat•er**, n. old pocket watch which rings the hours; gun which can fire several times without being reloaded.

re•pel [rɪ'pel] v. (repelled) (a) to drive back (an attack). (b) to disgust/to be so unpleasant that you drive people away. **re•pel•ling**, adj. disgusting. **re•pel•lent**, adj. & n. (thing) which drives away/which repels; **insect r.** = spray which keeps insects away.

re•pent [rɪ'pent] v. to be very sorry. **re•pent•ance**, n. great regret. **re•pent•ant**, adj. full of repentance.

re•per•cus•sion [rɪpɜː'kʌʃn] n. result/effect.

rep•er•toire ['repətwɑː] n. works which s.o. can play/sing by heart; works which a theater company has ready for performance.

rep•er•to•ry ['repətrɪ] n. (a) **r. theater** = theater with a permanent group of actors who present a series of plays, changing them at regular intervals. (b) store (of information/stories, etc.).

rep•e•ti•tion [repɪ'tɪʃn] n. act of repeating; thing which is repeated. **rep•e•ti•tious**, **re•petitive** [rɪ'petɪtɪv] adj. which repeats sth too frequently.

re•place [riː'pleɪs] v. (a) to put (sth) back in place. (b) to put (sth) in place of sth else. **re•place•a•ble**, adj. which can be replaced. **re•place•ment**, n. (a) putting back; replacing sth with sth else. (b) thing which is used to replace; **r. parts** = spare parts (of an engine) used to replace parts which have worn out.

re•play ['riːpleɪ] n. (a) (in sports) second match between teams, competitors, etc. (b) **instant r.** = section of a sporting event which is shown again on TV at a slower speed, so that the action can be appreciated.

re•plen•ish [rɪ'plenɪʃ] v. to fill up again. **re•plen•ish•ment**, n. act of replenishing; thing which replenishes.

re•plete [rɪ'pliːt] adj. (formal) full and satisfied.

rep•li•ca ['replɪkə] n. exact copy.

re•ply [rɪ'plaɪ] 1. n. answer. 2. v. to answer.

re•port [rɪ'pɔːt] 1. n. (a) description/story of what has happened. (b) comments by teachers on a child's progress in school; comments by a commission on a problem. (c) explosion. 2. *v.* (a) to write a description of what happened; **you must r. the burglary to the police** = give them the details. (b) to make a complaint about (s.o.). (c) to present oneself officially; **to r. for work.** (d) **to r. to** = be responsible to. **re•port•age** [repɔ:'tɑ:ʒ] *n.* reporting of news (esp. for a magazine or TV). **re•port•ed•ly,** *adv.* according to what has been reported. **re•port•er,** *n.* journalist who writes articles for a newspaper on events.

re•pose [rɪ'pəuz] 1. *n.* (*formal*) calm/resting. 2. *v.* (*formal*) (a) to rest. (b) to place (trust) in s.o.

re•pos•i•to•ry [rɪ'pɒzɪtrɪ] *n.* store (of information, etc.).

re•pos•sess [ri:pə'zes] *v.* to take back (goods) when the purchaser cannot pay the payments.

re•pous•sé [rə'pu:seɪ] *adj. & n.* (metalwork) which is hammered into relief from the back.

rep•re•hend [rɪprɪ'hend] *v.* to criticize. **rep•re•hen•si•ble** *adj.* which can be criticized. **rep•re•hen•si•bly,** *adv.* in a reprehensible way.

rep•re•sent [reprɪ'zent] *v.* (a) to mean/to show. (b) to speak on behalf of (s.o./a group of people). (c) to sell goods on behalf of (s.o.). **rep•re•sen•ta•tion** [reprɪzen'teɪʃn] *n.* (a) being represented. (b) **representations** = complaints/protests. **rep•re•sen•ta•tive** [reprɪ'zentətɪv] 1. *adj.* typical. 2. *n.* person who represents; traveling salesman; member of the lower house of the U.S. Congress; **the House of Representatives.**

re•press [rɪ'pres] *v.* to keep down/to control. **re•pressed,** *adj.* kept under strict control. **re•pres•sion** [rɪ'preʃn] *n.* keeping under control. **re•pres•sive,** *adj.* severe/sharp.

re•prieve [rɪ'pri:v] 1. *n.* pardon given to a prisoner. 2. *v.* to pardon.

rep•ri•mand ['reprɪmɑ:nd] 1. *n.* severe rebuke. 2. *v.* to criticize (s.o.) severely.

re•print 1. *n.* ['ri:prɪnt] book which has been printed again. 2. *v.* [ri:'prɪnt] to print (a book) again.

re•pris•al [rɪ'praɪzl] *n.* punishment of people in revenge for sth.

re•pro ['ri:prəu] *n.* (*also* **reproproof**) proof which is photographed to make a printing film.

re•proach [rɪ'prəutʃ] 1. *n.* (a) thing which is a disgrace. (b) **beyond r.** = blameless. (c) rebuke. 2. *v.* **to r. s.o. with sth** = to blame s.o. for sth. **re•proach•ful,** *adj.* which blames. **re•proach•ful•ly,** *adv.* in a reproachful way.

rep•ro•bate ['reprəbeɪt] *n.* wicked person/scoundrel.

re•pro•duce [ri:prə'dju:s] *v.* (a) to copy. (b) to produce young. **re•pro•duc•tion** [ri:prə'dʌkʃən] *n.* (a) copy (of a painting, etc.); **the r. is bad on this recording** = the quality of the sound is bad. (b) production of young. **re•pro•duc•tive,** *adj.* (organs) which produce young.

re•proof [rɪ'pru:f] *n.* (*formal*) blame/criticism. **re•prove** [rɪ'pru:v] *v.* (*formal*) to criticize/to blame (someone). **re•prov•ing,** *adj.* criticizing.

rep•tile ['reptaɪl] *n.* cold-blooded animal which lays eggs and is covered with scales. **rep•til•i•an** [rep'tɪlɪən] *adj.* like a reptile.

re•pub•lic [rɪ'pʌblɪk] *n.* system of government where final authority is given to all citizens entitled to vote and is carried out by representatives elected directly or indirectly by these citizens. **re•pub•li•can,** *adj. & n.* referring to a republic; (supporter) of a republic. **Re•pub•li•can,** *adj. & n.* (member) of one of the two main political parties in the United States. **re•pub•li•can•ism,** *n.* belief in the republic as a means of government.

re•pu•di•ate [rɪ'pju:dɪeɪt] *v.* to reject/to refuse to accept. **re•pu•di•a•tion** [rɪpju:dɪ'eɪʃn] *n.* rejection.

re•pug•nant [rɪ'pʌgnənt] *adj.* unpleasant/nasty. **re•pug•nance,** *n.* feeling of distaste/dislike.

re•pulse [rɪ'pʌls] *v.* to push back. **re•pul•sion** [rɪ'pʌlʃn] *n.* (a) act of repulsing. (b) feeling of dislike/distaste. **re•pul•sive,** *adj.* unpleasant/nasty.

re•pute [rɪ'pju:t] *n.* reputation/general opinion; **of good r. rep•u•ta•ble** ['repjutəbl] *adj.* well thought of/with a good reputation. **rep•u•ta•tion** [repju'teɪʃn] *n.* general opinion (of s.o.); **I only know her by r.** = I have never met her, but I know what people think of her. **re•put•ed** [rɪ'pju:tɪd] *adj.* supposed. **re•put•ed•ly** [rɪ'pju:tɪdlɪ] *adv.* according to most people.

re•quest [rɪ'kwest 1. *n.* asking/demand; **on r.** = if asked for. 2. *v.* to ask/to demand politely.

req•ui•em ['rekwɪəm] *v.* mass for the dead; music to be sung at a requiem.

re•quire [rɪ'kwaɪə] *v.* (a) to demand/to request. (b) to need. **re•quire•ment,** *n.* what is needed.

req•ui•si•tion [rekwɪ'zɪʃn] 1. *n.* official order. 2. *v.* to demand/to order that sth should be handed over; to demand and take (supplies) for an army; to order (supplies) for a school. **req•ui•site** ['rekwɪzɪt] *adj. & n.* (thing) which is necessary. etc.

rere•dos ['rɪədɒs] *n.* carved screen behind an altar.

re•run ['ri:rʌn] *n.* second showing of a program or motion picture on TV.

re•sale [ri:'seɪl] *n.* selling to s.o. goods which you have bought.

re•scind [rɪ'sɪnd] *v.* to annul/to cancel (a law).

res•cue ['reskju:] 1. *n.* saving; **r. squad** = group of people who are going to save s.o. 2. *v.* to save. **res•cu•er,** *n.* person who rescues or tries to rescue.

re•search [rɪ'sɜːtʃ] 1. *n.* scientific study/trying to find out facts. 2. *v.* to study/to try to find out facts. **re•search•er,** *n.* person who researches.

re•sem•ble [rɪ'zembl] *v.* to be similar to. **re•sem•blance,** *n.* looking like s.o.

re•sent [rɪ'zent] *v.* to feel annoyed at a real or imaginary injury. **re•sent•ful,** *adj.* annoyed. **re•sent•ful•ly,** *adv.* in a resentful way. **re•sent•ment,** *n.* annoyance.

re•serve [rɪ'zɜːv] 1. *n.* (a) quantity kept back for future special use; **in r.** = waiting to be used. (b) (*in sports*) extra player; **reserves** = part-time troops kept to help the regular army if necessary. (c) area of land set aside for a particular purpose; **nature r.** = area where animals and vegetation are protected. (d) shyness; not speaking openly. (e) (*at an auction*) price which an item must reach before the owner will allow it to be sold. 2. *v.* to keep back for a special use; to book (a seat/a table). **res•er•va•tion** [rezə'veɪʃn] *n.* (a) booking (of a seat/table). (b) doubt. (c) area of land set aside for a particular purpose; area set aside by the U.S. government for North American Indians to live. **re•served,** *adj.* (a) booked. (b) shy; (person) who does not speak openly. **re•serv•ist** [rɪ'zɜːvist] *n.* part-time soldier who is a member of the army reserves.

res•er•voir ['rezəvwɑː] *n.* (a) large (usu. artificial) lake where water is kept for pumping to a town or city. (b) container (for storing liquids); mass (of information/facts) which can be used if necessary.

re•side [rɪ'zaɪd] *v.* (*formal*) to live/to have a house. **res•i•dence** ['rezɪdəns] *n.* (a) place where you live. (b) act of living in a place; **r. hall** = building with rooms where students live. **res•i•den•cy,** *n.* act of residing. **res•i•dent** ['rezɪdənt] 1. *adj.* living permanently in a place. 2. *n.* person who lives in a place. **res•i•den•tial** [rezɪ'denʃl] *adj.* (part of a town) with houses rather than stores or factories.

res•i•due ['rezɪdju:] *n.* what is left over. **re•sid•u•al** [re'zɪdjʊəl] *adj.* remaining. **re•sid•u•ar•y,** *adj.* (*formal*) residual (part of an estate).

re•sign [rɪ'zaɪn] *v.* (a) to give up a job or position. (b) **to r. yourself to** = to accept. **res•ig•na•tion** [rezɪg'neɪʃn] *n.* (a) giving up a job; **he tendered/handed in his r.** = he resigned. (b) acceptance that sth has to happen. **re•signed,** *adj.* accepting that sth has to happen. **re•sign•ed•ly** [rɪ'zaɪnɪdlɪ] *adv.* patiently/calmly/without complaining.

re•sil•ient [rɪ'sɪlɪənt] *adj.* (material) which easily returns to its original shape (after being crushed); (person) who is strong/able to recover easily from a blow. **re•sil•ience,** *n.* being resilient.

res•in ['rezɪn] *n.* sticky sap, esp. from pine trees. **res•in•ous,** *adj.* like resin; made of resin.

re•sist [rɪ'zɪst] *v.* to oppose/not to give in to (sth). **re•sist•ance,** *n.* (a) opposition/fight against sth; **r. movement** = movement of ordinary people against an invader of a country; **he took the line of least r.** = he did it the easiest way. (b) (*in physics*) force which opposes sth; ability not to conduct electricity/heat, etc. **re•sist•ant,** *adj.* which resists. **re•sis•tiv•i•ty,** *n.* ability to resist the flow of an electric current. **re•sis•tor,** *n.* device which increases the resistance to an electric current/which prevents a current from flowing.

re•skill [ri:'skɪl] *v.* to train (a workforce/worker) in new skills.

res•o•lute ['rezəlu:t] *adj.* determined/having made up your mind. **res•o•lute•ly,** *adv.* in a resolute way. **res•o•lu•tion** [rezə'lu:ʃn] *n.* (a) decision reached at a meeting; proposal to be decided at a meeting. (b) (*also* **resoluteness**) determination (to do sth)/strength of character. (c) solving (of a problem). (d) splitting up into separate parts. (e) clearness of a computer image (calculated as the number of pixels per unit of area).

re•solve [rɪ'zɒlv] 1. *n.* determination (to do sth). 2. *v.* (a) to decide to do sth. (b) to solve (a problem). (c) to split up into separate parts.

res•o•nant ['rezənənt] *adj.* which sounds/rings/echoes loudly. **res•o•nance,** *n.* deep loud ringing tone.

re•sort [rɪ'zɔːt] 1. *n.* (a) place where people go on vacations. (b) **as a last r.** = when everything

---

æ back, ɑ: farm, ɒ: top, aɪ pipe, aʊ how, aɪe fire, aʊə flower, ɔ: bought, ɔɪ toy, e fed, eəhair, eɪ take, ə afraid, əʊ boat, əʊə lower, vː word, iː heap, ɪ hit, rə hear, uː school, ʊ book, ʌ but, b back, d dog, ð then, dʒ just, f fog, g go, h hand, j yes, k catch, l last, m mix, n nut, ŋ sing, p penny, r round, s some, ʃ short, t too, tʃ chop, θ thing, v voice, w was, z zoo, ʒ treasure

else fails. 2. *v.* **to r. to** = to use sth in a difficult situation/when everything else has failed.

re•sound [rɪˈzaʊnd] *v.* to make a loud, echoing, deep noise. **re•sound•ing,** *adj.* great/complete; **r. success.**

re•source [rɪˈsɔːs] *n.* source of supply for what is needed/used; **natural resources** = minerals/oil/trees; **left to one's own resources** = left to look after oneself. **re•source•ful,** *adj.* good at looking after yourself/at dealing with problems. **re•source•ful•ly,** *adv.* in a resourceful way. **re•source•ful•ness,** *n.* being resourceful.

re•spect [rɪˈspekt] 1. *n.* (a) admiration/regard. (b) concern/detail; **with r. to** = concerning; **in some respects** = in some ways. (c) **respects** = polite good wishes. 2. *v.* (a) to admire/to honor (s.o.). (b) to pay attention to (sth). **re•spect•a•bil•i•ty** [rɪspektəˈbɪlɪtɪ] *n.* being respectable. **re•spect•a•ble** [rɪˈspektəbl] *adj.* (a) proper/worthy of respect. (b) quite large/fairly large. **re•spect•a•bly,** *adv.* properly. **re•spect•er,** *n.* person who respects others. **re•spect•ful,** *adj.* full of respect. **re•spect•ful•ly,** *adv.* showing respect. **re•spect•ing,** *prep.* concerning. **re•spec•tive,** *adj.* referring to each one separately. **re•spec•tive•ly,** *adv.* referring to each one separately.

re•spire [resˈpaɪə] *v.* (*formal*) to breathe. **res•pi•ra•tion** [respɪˈreɪʃn] *n.* breathing in of air; **to give s.o. artificial r.** = to force s.o. (who is almost dead from drowning) to breathe. **res•pi•ra•tor** [ˈrespɪreɪtə] *n.* device which helps you to breathe, esp. a mask worn as protection against gas, smoke, etc. **res•pi•ra•to•ry,** *adj.* referring to breathing.

res•pite [ˈrespaɪt] *n.* rest; **without r.** = without stopping.

re•splend•ent [rɪˈsplendənt] *adj.* very splendid.

re•spond [rɪˈspɒnd] *v.* to reply/to react (**to**); **he responded to treatment** = he began to get better. **re•spond•ent,** *n.* defendant in a law suit, esp. in a divorce case. **re•sponse,** *n.* (a) answer. (b) reply made by the congregation to the clergyman in a church service. **re•spon•si•bil•i•ty** [rɪspɒnsɪˈbɪlɪtɪ] *n.* (a) being responsible; **he has taken on a lot of r.** = he has agreed to be responsible for many things. (b) thing which you are responsible for. **re•spon•si•ble,** *adj.* (a) (**for**) causing. (b) (person) taking decisions for sth/directing sth. (c) **r. to s.o.** = being under the authority of s.o. who expects you to carry out the work well. (d) trustworthy (person). (e) **r. position** = job where decisions have to be made. **re•spon•si•bly,** *adv.* in a responsible way.

re•spon•sive, *adj.* (person) who reacts quickly/who shows sympathy. **re•spon•sive•ness,** *n.* sensitivity.

rest [rest] 1. *n.* (a) sleep/calm state; **to set s.o.'s mind at r.** = to calm s.o.'s worries. (b) stop; **the wagon came to r. at the bottom of the hill** = stopped moving. (c) (*in music*) short break between notes. (d) support; **arm r.** = part of a chair which you put your arms on; **head r.** = cushion to support your head (usu. attached to a seat in a car). (e) **the r.** = remains/what is left over/other people. 2. *v.* (a) to sleep/to be calm. (b) to make (sth) be calm. (c) **to let the matter r.** = not to deal with the problem any more. **rest•ful,** *adj.* calm/which makes you feel calm. **rest•less,** *adj.* agitated; always on the move. **rest•less•ly,** *adv.* in a restless way. **rest•less•ness,** *n.* being restless. **rest•room, rest room** *n.* room having a sink and toilet, for use by the public or employees, as in a restaurant, store, etc.

res•tau•rant [ˈrestrɒnt] *n.* place where you can buy a meal; **self-service r.** = where you serve yourself. **res•tau•ra•teur** [restəræˈtəː] *n.* person who runs a restaurant.

res•ti•tu•tion [restɪˈtjuːʃn] *n.* compensation/paying back.

res•tive [ˈrestɪv] *adv.* nervous/agitated. **res•tive•ness,** *n.* agitation.

re•store [rɪsˈtɔː] *v.* (a) to give back. (b) to repair/to make (sth) new again. **res•to•ra•tion** [restəˈreɪʃn] *n.* (a) giving back. (b) reparing sth/making sth look like new again. **re•stor•a•tive** [rɪˈstɒrətɪv] *adj.* & *n.* (medicine) which makes you stronger. **re•stor•er,** *n.* person who restores old paintings, etc.

re•strain [rɪˈstreɪn] *v.* to hold back; to prevent/to try and stop. **re•strained,** *adj.* controlled/calm. **re•straint,** *n.* control; **with great r.** = without losing your temper; **lack of r.** = (excessive) freedom.

re•strict [rɪˈstrɪkt] *v.* to limit. **re•strict•ed,** *adj.* limited; **r. area** = area where only certain people are allowed. **re•stric•tion** [rɪˈstrɪkʃn] *n.* limitation. **re•stric•tive,** *adj.* which restricts/limits.

re•sult [rɪˈzʌlt] 1. *n.* (a) thing which happens because of sth; outcome. (b) score (in a game); grades (in an exam). 2. *v.* **to r. from** = to happen because of sth which has been done; **to r. in** = to produce as an effect. **re•sult•ant,** *adj.* which results.

re•sume [rɪˈzjuːm] *v.* to start again after an interruption. **re•sump•tion** [rɪˈzʌmpʃn] *n.* starting again.

ré•su•mé [ˈrezumeɪ] *n.* (a) short summing up of the main points. (b) summary of biographical details, esp. details of education and work experience, used in applying for a job.

re•sur•face [riːˈsɜːfəs] v. (a) to put a new surface (on a road). (b) to reappear on the surface.

re•sur•gent [rɪˈsɜːdʒənt] adj. which is rising again/becoming more powerful again. **re•sur•gence,** n. reappearance/rising again.

res•ur•rect [rezəˈrekt] v. to bring back to use; to start up again. **res•ur•rec•tion** [rezəˈrekʃn] n. bringing back to life.

re•sus•ci•tate [rɪˈsʌsɪteɪt] v. to bring (someone who is almost dead) back to life. **re•sus•ci•ta•tion** [rɪsʌsɪˈteɪʃn] n. bringing back to life.

re•tail [ˈriːteɪl] 1. n. selling small quantities of goods to an ordinary customer; **r. outlet** = shop which sells goods direct to the customer. 2. v. (a) to sell (goods) direct to customers who will not sell them again; **to r. at** = to sell for (a certain price). (b) to pass on (gossip). **re•tail•er,** n. owner of a store which sells goods to consumers.

re•tain [rɪˈteɪn] v. to keep; **to r. a lawyer to act for you** = to agree with a lawyer that he will act for you (and usu. to pay him in advance); **retaining wall** = wall which holds back a mass of earth/the water in a reservoir, etc. **re•tain•er,** n. (a) money paid in advance to s.o. for work he will do later. (b) (old) servant.

re•tal•i•ate [rɪˈtælɪeɪt] v. to hit back/to attack (s.o.) in revenge. **re•tal•i•a•tion** [rɪtælɪˈeɪʃn] n. **in r. for** = as a reprisal for. **re•tal•i•a•to•ry** [rɪˈtælɪətrɪ] adj. (measures) taken in retaliation.

re•tard [rɪˈtɑːd] v. to make slow/to delay the progress of. **re•tar•da•tion** [rɪtɑːˈdeɪʃn] n. act of retarding. **re•tard•ed,** adj. mentally slower than s.o. of the same age. **re•tard•ed•ness,** n. being retarded.

retch [retʃ] v. to have spasms in the throat as if you were about to vomit.

re•ten•tion [rɪˈtenʃn] n. keeping/holding. **re•ten•tive,** adj. (memory) which retains well.

re•think [riːˈθɪŋk] 1. n. inf. second thought about a problem. 2. v. (**rethought**) to think again/to reconsider.

ret•i•cent [ˈretɪsənt] adj. uncommunicative/not willing to talk about sth. **ret•i•cence,** n. unwillingness to talk.

ret•i•na [ˈretɪnə] n. layer on the inside of the surface of the eye, which is sensitive to light.

ret•i•nue [ˈretɪnjuː] n. group of people following an important person.

re•tire [rɪˈtaɪə] v. (a) to stop work (and usu. draw a pension); to make (s.o.) stop work (and draw a pension). (b) to go away into a place by yourself. (c) **to r. to bed for the night** = to go to bed. **re•tire•ment,** n. (a) act of retiring from work. (b) period of life when you are retired. **re•tir•ing,** adj. quiet and reserved (person).

re•tort [rɪˈtɔːt] 1. n. (a) sharp reply. (b) glass bottle with a long, thin bent neck used for distilling. 2. v. to reply sharply.

re•touch [riːˈtʌtʃ] v. to improve (a picture/a photograph) by adding or removing lines by hand.

re•trace [riːˈtreɪs] v. to go back to the origins of (sth); **to r. one's steps** = go back over the same path again.

re•tract [rɪˈtrækt] v. to pull back; to withdraw (sth said). **re•tract•a•ble,** adj. (undercarriage of a plane) which folds up into the body of the plane. **re•trac•tion** [rɪˈtrækʃn] n. pulling back; folding up. **re•trac•tor,** n. surgical instrument used to hold back the flesh during an operation.

re•tread 1. n. [ˈriːtred] tire which has had its surface renewed. 2. v. [riːˈtred] to renew the surface of a tire.

re•treat [rɪˈtriːt] 1. n. (a) withdrawing of an army from a battle. (b) quiet place. (c) period of calm meditation (in a religious establishment). 2. v. to withdraw from a battle.

re•trench [rɪˈtrentʃ] v. to economize/to cut back on expenditure. **re•trench•ment,** n. reduction of expenditure.

re•tri•al [riːˈtraɪəl] n. second trial.

ret•ri•bu•tion [retrɪˈbjuːʃn] n. well-deserved punishment. **re•trib•u•tive** [reˈtrɪbjuːtɪv] adj. acting as a punishment.

re•trieve [rɪˈtriːv] v. to get back (sth) which was lost; to bring back (sth). **re•triev•a•ble,** adj. which can be retrieved. **re•triev•al,** n. getting back; **r. system** = system (in a catalog/in a computer program) to allow information to be retrieved. **re•triev•er,** n. type of dog trained to fetch birds which have been shot.

ret•ro•ac•tive [retrəʊˈæktɪv] adj. which takes effect from a time in the past; **r. to last April** = which takes effect from last April.

ret•ro•grade [ˈretrəgreɪd] adj. backward.

ret•ro•gress [retrəʊˈgres] v. to move back-

æ back, ɑː farm, ɒ top, aɪ pipe, aʊ how, aɪə fire, aʊə flower, ɔː bought, ɔɪ toy, e fed, eəhair, eɪ take, ə afraid, əʊ boat, əʊə lower, ɜː word, iː heap, ɪ hit, ɪə hear, uː school, ʊ book, ʌ but, b back, d dog, ð then, dʒ just, f fog, g go, h hand, j yes, k catch, l last, m mix, n nut, ŋ sing, p penny, r round, s some, ʃ short, t too, tʃ chop, θ thing, v voice, w was, z zoo, ʒ treasure

ward. **ret•ro•gres•sion,** *n.* moving backward.

ret•ro•rock•et ['retrəurɒkɪt] *n.* rocket which slows down a space vehicle/a plane.

ret•ro•spect ['retrəspekt] *n.* **in r.** = when you look back. **ret•ro•spec•tive** [retrə'spektɪv] *adj. & n.* which looks back on past events; (exhibition) of works of art covering the whole career of an artist.

re•trous•sé [rə'truːseɪ] *adj.* turned up (nose).

ret•si•na [re'tsiːnə] *n.* Greek wine flavored with resin.

re•turn [rɪ'tɜːn] 1. *n.* (a) going back/coming back; **on my r. home** = when I got back home; **r. ticket** = ticket which allows you to go to one place and come back; **many happy returns of the day** = best wishes for a happy birthday; **by r. mail** = by the next mail service back. (b) profit/income from money invested. (c) sending back. (d) report of results of an election; **tax r.** = official statement of income, etc., to a government agency. (e) (*in tennis, etc.*) sending back of a ball. (f) **r. match** = match played between two teams who have played each other recently. (g) key on a computer keyboard which shows that data has been completely entered. 2. *v.* (a) to come back/to go back. (b) to give back/to send back. (c) to elect (s.o.) to a legislative body, etc. **re•turn•a•ble,** *adj.* which can be returned.

re•un•ion [riː'juːnɪən] *n.* meeting of people who have not met for a long time. **re•u•nite** [riːjuː'naɪt] *v.* to join (two things) together again.

re•us•a•ble [riː'juːzəbl] *adj.* which can be used again.

rev [rev] 1. *n. inf.* revolution. 2. *v.* (**revved**) *inf.* (*also* **rev up**) to make (a car engine) go quickly while the car is standing still.

Rev. ['revrənd] *abbrev. for* Reverend.

re•val•ue [riː'væljuː] *v.* to value again (usu. at a higher value). **re•val•u•a•tion** [rɪvæljuː'eɪʃn] *n.* revaluing/recalculating the value.

re•vamp [riː'væmp] *v. inf.* to improve the appearance of (sth which is slightly old-fashioned).

re•veal [rɪ'viːl] *v.* to show (sth) which was hidden. **rev•e•la•tion** [revə'leɪʃn] *n.* surprise.

rev•eil•le [rɪ'vælɪ] *n.* (*in the military*) signal to soldiers to get up in the morning.

rev•el ['revəl] 1. *n.* **revels** = merrymaking/happy celebrations. 2. *v.* (**reveled, revelled**) to take delight (**in**); to have a happy time. **rev•el•er,** *Brit.* **rev•el•ler,** *n.* person who is celebrating. **rev•el•ry,** *n.* celebration.

re•venge [rɪ'venʒ] 1. *n.* action to harm s.o. in return for harm he has caused you. 2. *v.* to harm s.o. in return for harm he has caused you. **re•venge•ful,** *adj.* wanting revenge.

rev•e•nue ['revənjuː] *n.* money which is received; taxes which a government receives.

re•ver•ber•ate [rɪ'vɜːbəreɪt] *v.* to echo/to ring out loudly in an echo. **re•ver•ber•a•tion** [rɪvɜːbə'reɪʃn] *n.* echoing.

re•vere [rɪ'vɪə] *v.* to worship/to respect (s.o.) very highly. **rev•er•ence** ['revrəns] *n.* (a) great respect. (b) bow (as a mark of respect). **rev•er•end,** *adj.* (a) worthy of respect. (b) **Reverend** = title given to members of the clergy or religious orders; **Reverend Mother** = title given to the head of a convent. **rev•er•ent,** *adj.* showing respect. **rev•er•en•tial,** *adj.* extremely respectful. **rev•er•ent•ly,** *adv.* in a reverent way.

rev•er•ie ['revərɪ] *n.* daydream.

re•vers [rɪ'vɪə] *n.* edge of a coat collar, etc., which is turned back to form the lapel.

re•ver•sal [rɪ'vɜːsəl] *n.* change to sth opposite; **r. of fortune** = bad luck.

re•verse [rɪ'vɜːs] 1. *adj.* opposite; **in r. order** = backward. 2. *n.* (a) the opposite. (b) gear of a car which makes you go backward. (c) defeat (in battle). 3. *v.* (a) to do the opposite; to make a car go backward; (*on the phone*) **to r. the charges** = to ask the person you are calling to pay for the call. (b) to change a decision to the opposite. **re•vers•i•ble,** *adj.* cloth/coat which can be worn with either side out. **re•ver•sion** [rɪ'vəːʃn] *n.* return to an original state/to an original owner or his heirs. **re•ver•sion•ar•y,** *adj.* (property) which passes to the original owner or his heirs on the death of the existing one.

re•vert [rɪ'vɜːt] *v.* to go back/to come back (**to**); **to r. to type** = to go back to an original state; **to r. to a subject** = to start talking about the subject again.

re•vet•ment [rɪ'vetmənt] *n.* stone facing to a wall.

re•view [rɪ'vjuː] 1. *n.* (a) written opinion of a book/play/motion picture, etc. (b) magazine which contains articles about new books/motion pictures/plays. (c) general examination. (d) general inspection of soldiers/naval vessels, etc. 2. *v.* (a) to write your opinion of (a book/play/motion picture, etc.). (b) to inspect (soldiers/naval vessels). (c) to consider generally. **re•view•er,** *n.* person who writes opinions of books/play/motion pictures.

re•vile [rɪ'vaɪl] *v.* (*formal*) to insult; to criticize sharply.

re•vise [rɪ'vaɪz] *v.* (a) to read/to study a lesson again. (b) to correct/to change. **re•vi•sion** [rɪ'vɪʒən] *n.* act of revising; thing revised. **re•vi•sion•ism,** *n.* revising the original pure concept (of a political movement, esp. communism).

re•vive [rɪ'vaɪv] *v.* to come back/to bring back

to life again. **re•viv•al**, *n.* bringing back to life; renewal of interest in sth. **re•viv•al•ist**, *n.* person who leads a religious revival.

re•voke [rɪ'vəuk] *v.* to cancel. **rev•o•ca•tion** [revə'keɪʃn] *n.* act of revoking.

re•volt [rɪ'vəult] 1. *n.* uprising against authority. 2. *v.* (a) to rise up **against** authority. (b) to disgust. **re•volt•ing**, *adj.* (a) in revolt. (b) disgusting/which makes you feel ill.

rev•o•lu•tion [revə'lu:ʃn] *n.* (a) rotation/turning around a central point. (b) uprising against a government. **rev•o•lu•tion•ar•y.** 1. *adj.* (a) aiming to change things completely/very new. (b) referring to a political revolution. 2. *n.* person who takes part in an uprising against a government. **rev•o•lu•tion•ize**, *v.* to change completely.

re•volve [rɪ'vɒlv] *v.* (a) to turn around. (b) to be centered on. **re•volv•er**, *n.* small hand gun with a cartridge chamber which turns after each shot is fired. **re•volv•ing**, *adj.* which turns around.

re•vue [rɪ'vju:] *n.* stage show with satirical sketches/songs, etc.

re•vul•sion [rɪ'vʌlʃn] *n.* (*formal*) disgust.

re•ward [rɪ'wɔ:d] 1. *n.* money/present given to s.o. as a prize or for information or the return of sth. 2. *v.* to give (s.o.) money/a present as a prize or for giving information or returning sth. **re•ward•ing**, *adj.* which gives moral satisfaction.

re•write ['ri:raɪt] 1. *n. inf.* act of rewriting. 2. *v.* (**rewrote, rewritten**) to write (sth) again in different words.

Rh *abbrev. for* Rh factor.

rhap•so•dy ['ræpsədɪ] *n.* poetry/music/song showing great excitement/passion. **rhap•sod•i•cal** [ræp'sɒdɪkl] *adj.* excited/passionate. **rhap•so•dize**, *v.* (**over**) to praise (sth) extravagantly.

rhe•o•stat ['rɪəstæt] *n.* device for making lights lower by cutting down the flow of electric current gradually.

rhe•sus ['ri:səs] *adj.* **r. monkey** = small monkey, often used in laboratories for scientific research; **r. factor** = Rh factor.

rhet•o•ric ['retərɪk] *n.* art of speaking forcefully and eloquently. **rhe•tor•i•cal** [rɪ'tɒrɪkl] *adj.* referring to rhetoric; **r. question** = question to which you do not expect an answer.

rheu•ma•tism ['ru:mətɪzəm] *n.* disease causing pains in the joints or muscles.

rheu•mat•ic [ru:'mætɪk] *adj.* referring to rheumatism; **r. fever** = serious disease of children and young people where the joints swell. **rheu•mat•ic**, *adj.* referring to or having rheumatism. **rheu•ma•toid ar•thri•tis**, *n.* continuing disease of the joints where they become stiff, swollen and painful.

Rh fac•tor [ ] *n.* substance in the blood (or absent from it) which can affect newborn babies and people having blood transfusions; **Rh positive** = having an Rh factor; **Rh negative** = with no Rh factor.

rhine•stone ['raɪnstəun] *n.* imitation colorless precious stone.

rhi•noc•er•os [raɪ'nɒsərəs], *inf.* **rhi•no** ['raɪnəu] *n.* (*pl.* **-es, -os**) huge Asiatic or African animal with a thick skin and one or two horns on its head.

rhi•zome ['raɪzəum] *n.* thick stem which lies on the ground like a root and produces shoots.

rho•do•den•dron [rəudə'dendrən] *n.* large evergreen shrub with clusters of huge colorful flowers.

rhom•bus ['rɒmbəs] *n.* shape with four equal sides but with no right angles. **rhom•boid.** 1. *adj.* shaped like a rhombus/diamond-shaped. 2. *n.* four-sided shape with opposite sides equal in length and no right angles.

rhu•barb ['ru:bɑ:b] *n.* garden plant with large poisonous leaves, whose stalks are cooked as a dessert.

rhyme [raɪm] 1. *n.* (a) sameness of sounds between two words (used in poetry). (b) little piece of poetry; **nursery r.** = (often nonsensical) piece of poetry for children. 2. *v.* (**with**) to have the same sound as.

rhythm ['rɪðəm] *n.* regular beat in music/poetry, etc. **rhyth•mic(al)** ['rɪðmɪk(l)] *adj.* with a regular beat. **rhyth•mi•cal•ly**, *adv.* in a rhythmical way.

rib [rɪb] 1. *n.* (a) one of several bones forming a cage across the chest. (b) piece of meat with the rib attached to it; **spare ribs** = cooked pork ribs in a usu. spicy sauce. (c) curved timber whch is part of the structure of a ship; one of the spokes of an umbrella. (d) thicker part in a leaf. (e) thicker line of stitches in knitting. 2. *v. inf.* to tease (s.o.). **rib•bed**, *adj.* with ribs. **rib cage**, *n.* all the ribs in an animal.

rib•ald ['rɪbəld] *adj.* rude (song/joke). **rib•ald•ry**, *n.* rude jokes.

rib•bon ['rɪbn] *n.* long flat thin piece of material for tying or decoration; **typewriter r.** = flat piece of material covered with ink, which is struck by the letters in a typewriter.

ri•bo•fla•vin [raibəʊ'fleivin] *n.* type of vitamin B.

ri•bo•nu•cle•ic ac•id [riːbəʊnjuː'kleɪɪk 'æsɪd] *n.* substance in cells which takes information from the DNA and converts it to enzymes and proteins.

rice [raɪs] *n.* common tropical cereal, grown in wet ground or water; **brown r.** = rice which still has its outer covering; **wild r.** = plant of North America, which resembles rice; **r. pudding** = dessert made of rice, milk and sugar; **r. paper** = very thin paper which you can eat and which is used in cooking.

rich [rɪtʃ] 1. *adj.* **(-er, -est)** (a) having a great deal of money. (b) (food) with a lot of cream/fat/eggs, etc. in it. (c) deep and resonant (voice); dark (color). (d) fertile (soil). (e) **r. in** = with many resources. 2. *n.* **the r.** = rich people. **rich•es** ['rɪtʃɪz] *n.* wealth. **rich•ly**, *adv.* splendidly; **which you so r. deserve** = which you deserve very much. **rich•ness**, *n.* wealth; being rich.

Rich•ter scale ['rɪXtə'skeɪl] *n.* scale for measuring earthquakes.

rick [rɪk] 1. *n.* (a) large pile of straw or hay in a field. (b) sprain. 2. *v.* to twist/sprain (ankle, back).

rick•ets ['rɪkɪts] *n.* disease of children (caused by lack of vitamins) where bones become bent. **rick•et•y**, *adj.* wobbly (chair).

rick•shaw, ['rɪkʃɔː] *n.* light wheeled chair pulled by a man.

ric•o•chet ['rɪkəʃeɪ] *v.* **(ricocheted** ['rɪkəʃeɪd]**)** to bounce off a surface at an angle.

rid [rɪd] *v.* **(rid)** to clear away; **to get r. of sth** = to dispose of sth/to throw sth away. **rid•dance**, *n.* **good r.** = I am glad to get rid of it.

-ridden [rɪdn] *suffix meaning* filled with/affected by.

rid•dle ['rɪdl] 1. *n.* (a) guessing game where you have to guess the answer to a deliberately puzzling question. (c) large sieve for separating soil from stones. 2. *v.* (a) to put (soil) through a sieve. (b) **to r. with bullets** = to shoot many times. **rid•dled with**, *adj.* full of.

ride [raɪd] 1. *n.* (a) trip/journey on horseback/on a bicycle/in a car, etc.; *Sl.* **he was taken for a r.** = (i) they tricked him; (ii) they murdered him. (b) a vehicle or device which people ride on or in for fun at a fair or amusement park. 2. *v.* **(rode, has ridden)** (a) to go for a trip on horseback/on a bicycle/in a car, etc. (b) *(of ships)* **to r. at anchor** = to float; **the ships rode out the storm** = they remained at anchor during the storm. **rid•er**, *n.* (a) person who rides. (b) additional clause to a contract.

rid•er•less, *adj.* (horse) with no rider. **ride up**, *v.* *(of dress, etc.)* to move upward through movement of the body. **ri•ding**, *n.* sport of going on horseback; **r. school** = school where you learn to ride a horse. **rid•ing lights**, *n. pl.* lights on a ship at anchor.

ridge [rɪdʒ] *n.* long narrow raised part. **ridged**, *adj.* with ridges.

rid•i•cule ['rɪdɪkjuːl] 1. *n.* mocking/laughing at s.o.; **to hold s.o. up to r.** = to laugh at s.o. 2. *v.* to laugh at (s.o./sth). **ri•dic•u•lous**, *adj.* silly/which can be laughed at. **ri•dic•u•lous•ly**, *adv.* in a silly way. **ri•dic•u•lous•ness**, *n.* silliness.

rife [raɪf] *adj.* common.

rif•fle ['rɪfl] *v.* to turn quickly **(through** the pages of a book).

riff•raff ['rɪfræf] *n.* *(no pl.)* worthless ordinary people.

ri•fle ['raɪfl] 1. *n.* hand gun with a long barrel with spiral grooves inside. 2. *v.* (a) to search and to steal from. (b) to make spiral grooves inside a gun barrel.

rift [rɪft] *n.* split/crack.

rig [rɪg] 1. *n.* (a) way in which a ship's sails are arranged. (b) metal construction for drilling for minerals. (c) *inf.* set of clothes. 2. *v.* **(rigged)** (a) to fit out a ship with sails. (b) to arrange a dishonest result. **rig•ging**, *n.* ropes on a ship. **rig up**, *v.* to arrange/to construct (sth) quickly.

right [raɪt] 1. *adj.* (a) good/honest. (b) correct. (c) **to get on the r. side of s.o.** = to make s.o. favor you; *inf.* **on the r. side of forty** = less than forty years old. (d) **r. angle** = angle of 90°. (e) straight/in order; **is he in his r. mind?** = is he sane? **she's all r. again** = she's better. (f) not left; referring to the hand which most people use for writing. 2. *n.* (a) what is correct/good; **in the r.** = not to be criticized. (b) legal title to sth; **she has no r. to be here** = she should not be here; **civil rights** = legal entitlements of every citizen; **by rights** = if things were done properly. (c) the right-hand side/the right-hand direction; **the r.** = political parties which are conservative. 3. *adj.* (a) **r. on** = straight on. (b) **r. away** = immediately. (c) completely. (d) correctly; **it serves you r.** = you deserved it. (e) to the right-hand side. 4. *v.* to correct; to make (sth) return to its correct position. 5. *inter.* (a) agreed/OK. (b) *inf.* do you understand? **right-an•gled**, *adj.* with a 90° angle. **right•eous** ['raɪtʃəs] *adj.* virtuous/very good. **right•eous•ly**, *adv.* in a righteous way. **right•eous•ness**, *n.* virtue/goodness. **right•ful**, *adj.* legally correct. **right•ful•ly**, *adv.* in a rightful way. **right-hand**, *adj.* referring to the right hand; **right-hand man** = most important assistant. **right-hand•ed,** *adj.* (person) who uses the right hand for writing/working, etc. **right•ist,** *n.* member of a conservative political group. **right•ly,** *adv.* correctly; **I can't r. say** = I am not very sure. **right-mind•ed,** *adj.* (person) who has correct ideas/who thinks in the way most people think. **right•ness,** *n.* correctness. **right of way,** *n.* (a) right to walk over s.o. else's property. (b) right (of one vehicle) to go first at an intersection. **right•size,** *v.* to reduce a company's workforce to the optimum size in order to reduce costs and maximize efficiency, without excessive downsizing. **right-wing,** *adj.* belonging to the conservative political parties. **right-wing•er,** *n.* person who is on the right politically.

rig•id ['rɪdʒɪd] *adj.* stiff/unbending/inflexible. **rig•id•ly,** *adv.* stiffly. **ri•gid•i•ty** [rɪ'dʒɪdɪtɪ] *n.* being rigid.

rig•ma•role ['rɪgmərəʊl] *n.* long incoherent speech/meaningless jumble of words.

rig•or, *Brit.* **rig•our** ['rɪgə] *n.* severity (of the law, etc.); harshness (of the climate). **rig•or mor•tis** [-'mɔːtɪs] *n.* stiffening of a body after death. **rig•or•ous,** *adj.* very strict. **rig•or•ous•ly,** *adv.* in a rigorous way.

rile [raɪl] *v. inf.* to annoy.

rill [rɪl] *n.* small stream.

rim [rɪm] *n.* edge of a wheel/of a cup; frame of glasses. **rim•less,** *adj.* (glasses) with no frame. **rimmed,** *adj.* with a rim.

rime [raɪm] *n.* white frost.

rind [raɪnd] *n.* skin on fruit/meat/cheese.

ring [rɪŋ] 1. *n.* (a) circular piece of metal/wood, etc., with a hole in the center. (b) anything shaped like a circle; *inf.* **to run rings around s.o.** = to do things more efficiently than s.o. (c) group of people (usu. criminals). (d) center of a circus where performances take place; square place where a boxing/wrestling match takes place. (e) sound of a bell. (f) call on the telephone. 2. *v.* **(rang, has rung)** (a) to make a sound of a bell; *inf.* **it rings a bell** = it reminds me of sth. (b) **my ears are ringing** = there is a sound like that of bells in my ears. (c) (*esp. Brit.*) to telephone; **to r. s.o. up** = to call s.o. on the telephone; **to r. back** = to phone in reply to a phone call; **to r. off** = to stop the telephone call/to put down the receiver. 3. *v.* **(ringed)** (a) to put a ring on the leg of a wild bird for marking purposes. (b) to mark with a circle. **ring•er,** *n.* (a) person who rings church bells.

(b) *inf.* **dead r.** = person/horse exactly similar to another. **ring•lead•er,** *n.* head of a gang or group/person who organizes a crime. **ring•let,** *n.* long curl (of hair). **ring•mas•ter,** *n.* master of ceremonies in a circus. **ring•side,** *adj.* by the side of a boxing/wrestling ring. **ring•worm,** *n.* disease of the skin which causes round red patches.

rink [rɪŋk] *n.* place where you can roller-skate or ice-skate; surface for skating.

rinse [rɪns] 1. *n.* (a) putting soapy laundry/soapy dishes/soapy hair through clean water to remove the soap. (b) colored liquid for the hair. 2. *v.* to put (soapy/dirty things) into clean water to remove the soap/the dirt.

ri•ot ['raɪət] 1. *n.* (a) noisy, violent disorder among crowds of people; **to run r.** = to become disordered/to get out of control; **to read s.o. the r. act** = to warn s.o. to stop being disorderly. (b) mass (of sounds/colors). (c) very amusing motion picture/play, etc. 2. *v.* to take part in a riot/to get out of control. **ri•ot•er,** *n.* person who takes part in a riot. **ri•ot•ing,** *n.* riots/outbreaks of civil disorder. **ri•ot•ous,** *adj.* wild/out of control. **ri•ot•ous•ly,** *adv.* in a riotous way. **ri•ot po•lice,** *n.* police specially equipped to deal with rioters.

rip [rɪp] 1. *n.* tear (in cloth). 2. *v.* **(ripped)** to tear; *inf.* **to let r.** = to allow sth to go freely. **rip cord,** *n.* cord you pull to make a parachute open. **rip off,** *v.* (a) to tear off. (b) *Sl.* **to rip s.o. off** = to cheat s.o./to make s.o. pay too much. **rip-off,** *n. Sl.* bad deal/thing which costs too much. **rip-roar•ing,** *adj.* wild/noisy (party); great (success). **rip•saw,** *n.* saw with large teeth, for rough cutting.

RIP [ɑːaɪ'piː] *short for* Rest in Peace, Requiescat in Pace.

ri•par•i•an [rɪ'perɪən] *adj.* (*formal*) referring to the banks of a river.

ripe [raɪp] *adj.* (-er, -est) ready to eat/to be harvested; **to a r. old age** = until very old; **the time is r. for sth** = it is the right time to do sth. **rip•en,** *v.* to become ripe. **ripe•ness,** *n.* readiness; state of being ripe.

ri•poste [rɪ'pɒst] 1. *n.* quick, sharp reply. 2. *v.* to make a quick, sharp reply.

rip•ple ['rɪpl] 1. *n.* little wave. 2. *v.* to make little waves.

rise [raɪz] 1. *n.* (a) movement upward; slope upward. (b) **to give r. to sth** = to start sth. 2. *v.* **(rose, has risen)** (a) to move upward; to get up;

æ back, ɑː farm, ɒ top, aɪ pipe, aʊ how, aɪə fire, aʊə flower, ɔː bought, ɔɪ toy, e fed, eəhair, eɪ take, ə afraid, əʊ boat, əʊə lower, ʌ word, iː heap, ɪ hit, ɪə hear, uː school, ʊ book, ʌ but, b back, d dog, ð then, dʒ just, f fog, g go, h hand, j yes, k catch, l last, m mix, n nut, ŋ sing, p penny, r round, s some, ʃ short, t too, tʃ chop, θ thing, v voice, w was, z zoo, ʒ treasure

to get out of bed. (b) (*of a court or legislative body*) to stop meeting. (c) **to r. in revolt/to r. against s.o.** = to riot/to rebel. **ris•er,** *n.* (a) **early r.** = person who gets up early in the morning. (b) vertical board holding up the tread of a staircase. **ris•ing.** 1. *adj.* which is moving upward/which is increasing; **r. genera-tion** = new generation which will follow the present one; **r. forty** = nearly forty years old. 2. *n.* (a) movement upward. (b) rebellion/revolt.

ris•i•ble ['rɪzɪbl] *adj.* laughable.

risk [rɪsk] 1. *n.* possible harm; dangerous chance; **they run the r. of being caught** = they may well be caught. 2. *v.* to chance/to do sth which may possibly cause harm. **risk•i•ly,** *adv.* in a risky way. **risk•i•ness,** *n.* being risky. **risk•y,** *adj.* (**-ier, -iest**) danger-ous/which may cause harm.

ri•sot•to [rɪ'sɒtəu] *n.* Italian dish of cooked rice with meat/fish/vegetables in it.

ris•qué ['ri:skeɪ] *adj.* slightly indecent.

ris•sole ['rɪsəul] *n.* fried ball of meat/fish, etc.

rite [raɪt] *n.* religious ceremony; **last rites** = communion for s.o. who is dying. **rit•u•al** ['rɪtjuəl] *adj. & n.* (referring to) a religious cer-emony. **rit•u•al•ly,** *adv.* in a ritual way.

ri•val ['raɪvl] 1. *n. & adj.* (person) who com-petes. 2. *v.* (**rivaled, rivalled**) to compete with s.o.; to be of similar quality. **ri•val•ry,** *n.* competition.

riv•en ['rɪvn] *adj.* (*formal*) split.

riv•er ['rɪvə] *n.* large stream of water which goes into another stream, or into the sea. **riv•er•side,** *adj.* on the banks of a river.

riv•et ['rɪvɪt] 1. *n.* nail which fastens metal plates together. 2. *v.* (a) to fasten metal plates together. (b) to attract s.o.'s attention.

Riv•i•er•a [rɪvɪ'eərə] *n.* beautiful south coast, esp. along the Mediterranean.

riv•u•let ['rɪvjulət] *n.* little stream.

Rn *symbol for* radon.

RNA [ɑ:en'eɪ] *abbrev. for* ribonucleic acid.

roach [rəutʃ] *n.* (a) (*pl.* **roaches, roach**) small freshwater fish. (b) (*pl.* **roaches**) *inf.* cock-roach.

road [rəud] *n.* (a) path for cars and other vehi-cles; way of getting somewhere; **the r. to suc-cess** = the path which leads to success; **on the r.** = traveling from place to place (as a sales-man/worker). (b) **roads** = part of the sea near a port where ships can lie at anchor. **road•block,** *n.* barrier put across a road by the police. **road hog,** *n. inf.* dangerous driver who takes up two lanes. **road•house,** *n.* inn, tavern, etc. along a main road. **road•ie,** *n. inf.* person who organizes a traveling musical or theatrical group. **road•kill,** *n.* animal(s) killed on a road by motor vehicles.

road•rage, *n.* aggressive behavior by driv-ers. **road•side,** *n.* by the side of a road. **road•stead,** *n.* part of the sea near a port where ships can lie at anchor. **road•way,** *n.* main surface of a road. **road•works,** *n. pl.* repairs to a road. **road•wor•thi•ness,** *n.* being roadworthy. **road•wor•thy,** *adj.* in a fit state to be driven on a road.

roam [rəum] *v.* to wander.

roan [rəun] *adj. & n.* (brown horse) with gray hairs in its coat.

roar [rɔ:] 1. *n.* loud, deep call; loud shouting. 2. *v.* to make a loud call. **roar•ing.** 1. *adj.* wild (success); **to do a r. business in** = to sell sth rap-idly. 2. *n.* sound of loud, deep calls.

roast [rəust] 1. *n.* meat which has been/which will be cooked in an oven. 2. *v.* to cook over a fire/in an oven. 3. *adj.* which has been roasted; **r. beef. roast•ing,** *adj.* (chicken) which is ready to be roasted.

rob [rɒb] *v.* (**robbed**) to steal from s.o. **rob•ber,** *n.* person who steals money from s.o. **rob•ber•y,** *n.* stealing.

robe [rəub] *n.* 1. long, loose garment (for men or women), as worn by judges; long garment worn over pajamas or a nightgown. 2. *v.* to dress in a robe.

rob•in ['rɒbɪn] *n.* common small brown bird with a red breast; **round r.** = letter of com-plaint signed by many people.

ro•bot ['rəubɒt] *n.* machine which works like a human being; (*in science fiction*) machine which looks a little like a human being and which can act like one. **ro•bot•ics** [rəu-'bɒtɪks] *n.* science of electronic robots.

ro•bust [rə'bʌst] *adj.* strong/vigorous. **ro•bust•ly,** *adv.* in a robust way. **ro•bust•ness,** *n.* being robust.

rock [rɒk] 1. *n.* (a) stone/solid part of the earth's surface. (b) large piece of stone; *inf.* **on the rocks** = (i) bankrupt; (ii) (whisky) with ice; **r. plant** = alpine plant. (c) music with a strong rhythm. 2. *v.* to sway from side to side; to make (sth) sway from side to side; *inf.* **don't r. the boat** = don't disturb what has been ar-ranged. **rock bot•tom,** *n.* the lowest point. **rock•er,** *n.* (a) semicircular wooden piece which a rocking chair or rocking horse stands on. (b) rocking chair; *inf.* **off one's r.** = mad. **rock gar•den** (*also* **rockery**) *n.* garden planted around a collection of rocks. **rock•ing,** *adj.* swaying; **rocking horse** = child's wooden horse on rockers; **rocking chair** = chair which rocks backward and forward on rockers. **rock•y,** *adj.* (a) full of rocks. (b) *inf.* wobbly.

rock•et ['rɒkɪt] 1. *n.* (a) type of firework which, when lit, flies up into the sky; spacecraft; type of bomb which is shot through space at an enemy. (b) engine driven by burning gas, which powers a spacecraft or bomb. 2. *v.* to shoot upward very fast. **rock•et•ry,** *n.* (*no pl.*) science of space rockets.

ro•co•co [rə'kəukəu] *adj. & n.* ornate flowery (style of architecture of the 18th century).

rod [rɒd] *n.* (a) long stick. (b) **fishing r.** = long stick with a line attached, used for fishing.

rode [rəud] *v. see* **ride.**

ro•dent ['rəudənt] *n.* animal which chews and gnaws (such as a mouse/rat, etc.).

ro•de•o [rəu'deɪəu] *n.* (*pl.* -os) display of skill by cowboys.

roe [rəu] *n.* (a) fish eggs. (b) type of small deer. **roe•buck,** *n.* male roe deer.

roent•gen ['rʌntjən] *adj.* referring to X-rays.

rog•er ['rɒdʒə] *inter. & signal meaning* message received and understood.

rogue [rəug] *adj. & n.* (a) wicked/dishonest person. (b) **r. elephant** = elephant driven out of the herd by the other elephants. **ro•guer•y,** *n.* roguish behavior. **ro•guish,** *adj.* wicked/dishonest.

roist•er•er ['rɔɪstərə] *n.* person who celebrates noisily. **roist•er•ing,** *n.* noisy celebrations.

role [rəul] *n.* part played by s.o. (in a play, motion picture, or real life).

roll [rəul] 1. *n.* (a) thing which has been turned over and over to make a tube; **jelly r.** = cake rolled up with jam in it; **sausage r.** = small pastry with a sausage inside. (b) very small loaf of bread. (c) list of names; **r. of honor** = list of prizewinners/list of soldiers who have died during a war. (d) movement from side to side. (e) rumble (of drums). 2. *v.* (a) to make a tube out of sth flat. (b) to flatten by using a roller. (c) to make (sth) move forward by turning it over and over; *inf.* **rolling in money** = having a great deal of money. (d) to rock from side to side. (e) **to r. one's r's** = when speaking the letter "r", to make the tip of the tongue vibrate. (f) to make a low rumbling noise. (g) *inf.* to rob (s.o.), esp. when he is asleep. **roll•call,** *n.* calling names from a list. **roll•er,** *n.* (a) round object which rolls; **steam r.** = machine for flattening new road surfaces. (b) large wave in the sea. (c) **r. towel** = continuous towel hanging on a horizontal bar. (d) plastic tube used for rolling hair into curls. **Roll•er•blade** ['rəuləbleɪd] *n.* trademark for a type of roller skate. *see* **in-line skate. roll•er coast•er,** *n.* railroad in an amusement park which goes

up and down steep slopes. **roll•er skate,** *n.* shoe or device with wheels which you strap to your foot so as to glide along fast on a surface. **roll•er-skate** *v.* to glide on roller skates. **roll•er-skat•ing,** *n.* sport of going on roller skates. **roll•ing,** *adj.* (countryside) which is a mass of small hills; **r. pin** = wooden roller with handles, for flattening pastry; **r. stock** = passenger cars, engines, etc. used on a railroad. **roll-top,** *adj.* **r. desk** = desk with a cover made of slats of wood which slide upward to open it.

roll•ick•ing ['rɒlɪkɪŋ] *adj.* noisy and jolly.

ro•ly-po•ly ['rəulɪ'pəulɪ] *adj. & n. inf.* fat (person).

ROM [rɒm] *n.* read-only memory computer memory with data programmed into it, which can only be read, but not changed.

Ro•man ['rəumən] *adj.* referring to Rome; **roman** = printing type with straight letters; **R. candle** = type of firework giving a brilliant fountain of light; **R. numerals** = numbers written in the Roman style (I, II, III, IV, etc.). **Ro•man Cath•o•lic,** *adj. & n.* (person) belonging to the Christian church of which the Pope is the head. **Ro•man Cath•ol•i•cism,** *n.* beliefs of the Roman Catholic church.

ro•mance [rə'mæns] 1. *n.* (a) **r. language** = language which has derived from Latin, as French and Italian. (b) love affair. (c) love story. (d) invented story. 2. *v.* to invent/to make up a story. **ro•man•tic** [rə'mæntɪk] *adj.* (*a*) full of mystery and romance. (b) (literary/artistic style) which is very imaginative/based on personal emotions. **ro•man•ti•cal•ly,** *adv.* in a romantic way. **ro•man•ti•cism,** *n.* romantic literary style. **ro•man•ti•cize,** *v.* to turn (sth) into a romantic story.

Ro•man•esque [rəumə'nesk] *adj. & n.* architectural style with round arches and vaults found in Europe in the early Middle Ages.

Ro•ma•ni•an [ru:'meɪnɪən] 1. *adj.* referring to Romania. 2. *n.* (a) person from Romania. (b) language spoken in Romania.

Rom•a•ny ['rəumənɪ] *n.* (a) gypsy. (b) language spoken by gypsies.

romp [rɒmp] 1. *n.* (a) energetic play. (b) easy win. 2. *v.* (a) to play energetically. (b) to win easily. **romp•ers,** *n.* one-piece suit for a baby.

ron•do ['rɒndəu] *n.* (*pl.* -os) piece of music where the same theme is repeated several times.

æ back, a: farm, ɒ: top, aɪ pipe, au how, aie fire, auə flower, ɔ: bought, ɔɪ toy, e fed, eəhair, eɪ take, ə afraid, əu boat, əuə lower, v: word, i: heap, ɪ hit, ɪə hear, u: school, u book, ʌ but, b back, d dog, ð then, dʒ just, f fog, g go, h hand, j yes, k catch, l last, m mix, n nut, ŋ sing, p penny, r round, s some, ʃ short, t too, tʃ chop, θ thing, v voice, w was, z zoo, ʒ treasure

rood [ru:d] *n.* **r. screen** = screen built across a church, separating the chancel from the nave.

roof [ru:f] 1. *n.* (a) covering over a building. (b) top of the inside of the mouth. (c) top of a car/bus/truck, etc.; **sun r.** = roof of a car which you can open in good weather; **r. rack** = grid fixed to the roof of a car for carrying luggage. 2. *v.* to put a roof on (a building).

rook [rʊk] 1. *n.* (a) large black bird of the crow family. (b) (*in chess*) piece shaped like a castle. 2. *v. Sl.* to cheat. **rook•er•y**, *n.* place where rooks nest; colony of penguins/seals.

rook•ie ['rʊkɪ] *n. inf.* new recruit in the armed forces/in the police.

room [ru:m] 1. *n.* (a) one of the divisions inside a house. (b) space; **to make r. for** = squeeze up to give space for; **there's r. for improvement** = things could be improved. 2. *v.* to live in furnished rooms. **room•ing-house**, *n.* house with furnished rooms to rent. **room•mate**, *n.* person with whom you share a room. **room•y**, *adj.* (-ier, -iest) spacious.

roost [ru:st] 1. *n.* perch for a bird; **to rule the r.** = be in charge/be the boss. 2. *v.* to perch. **roost•er**, *n.* male bird (esp. a domestic chicken).

root [ru:t] 1. *n.* (a) part of a plant which goes down into the ground, and which takes nourishment from the soil; part of a hair/a tooth which goes down into the skin; **to take r.** = to start to grow; **to put down roots** = to begin to feel at home in a place. (b) source. (c) (*in language*) word which is a base for other words. (d) **square r.** = number which if multiplied by itself gives the number you have; **cube r.** = number which if multiplied by itself twice gives the number you have. 2. *v.* to make roots; **deeply rooted fear** = fear which is very strongly felt. (b) (**for**) to dig (sth) up/to look for (sth); **to r. for a team** = to cheer a team on. **root beer**, *n.* dark sweet drink, flavored with roots. **root crop**, *n.* crop which is grown for its edible roots (such as carrots, turnips, etc.). **root•less**, *adj.* with no roots. **root•stock**, *n.* plant on which another is grafted. **root up**, **root out**, *v.* to pull up (a plant) by its roots; to remove (sth) completely.

rope [rəʊp] 1. *n.* thick string/thick cord; *inf.* **he knows the ropes** = he knows all about it/how to go about doing it. 2. *v.* to tie together with a rope; **to r. s.o. in** = to get s.o. to help/to join; **to r. off** = to stop people going into a place by putting a rope around it. **rop•y**, *adj.* (-ier, -iest) forming thick threads, as a liquid.

ro•sa•ry ['rəʊzərɪ] *n.* string of beads used by Catholics when saying prayers.

rose [rəʊz] 1. *n.* (a) scented flower which grows on a prickly bush. (b) pink color; *inf.* **wearing r. colored glasses** = seeing things as being very

good, when they are not. (c) piece of metal/plastic with many holes in it, which is attached to the spout of a watering can, so that the water comes out in a spray. 2. *v. see* **rise**. **ro•se•ate** ['rəʊzɪət] *adj.* deep pink. **rose•bud**, *n.* flower bud of a rose. **rose win•dow**, *n.* large round decorated window found usu. in the west wall of a church. **rose•wood**, *n.* fragrant hard red wood, used for making furniture. **ros•i•ness**, *n.* being rosy. **ros•y**, *adj.* (-ier, -iest) (a) bright pink. (b) very favorable.

ro•sé [rəʊ'seɪ] *n.* pink wine.

rose•mar•y ['rəʊzmərɪ] *n.* common evergreen herb with scented leaves.

ro•sette [rə'set] *n.* ribbon bunched to look like a flower, used as a decoration or as a badge.

ros•in ['rɒzɪn] *n.* solid resin used to rub a violin bow.

ros•ter ['rɒstə] *n.* list of duties which have to be done and the people who do them.

ros•trum ['rɒstrəm] *n.* raised stand for a speaker.

rot [rɒt] 1. *n.* (a) decay; **dry r.** = decay in house timbers caused by a fungus. (b) nonsense. 2. *v.* (**rotted**) to decay; to go bad. **rot•ten**, *adj.* decayed; *inf.* **to feel r.** = (i) to feel ill; (ii) to feel ashamed.

ro•ta ['rəʊtə] *n.* roster.

ro•tate [rəʊ'teɪt] *v.* to turn around. **ro•ta•ry** ['rəʊtərɪ] *adj.* which turns/rotates; **r. printing press** = one where the paper passes around large rollers. **ro•ta•tion** [rəʊ'teɪʃn] *n.* turning/taking turns; **r. of crops** = growing different crops in turn. **ro•ta•to•ry**, *adj.* turning (motion). **ro•tor**, *n.* piece of machinery which rotates; the blades of a helicopter.

rote [rəʊt] *n.* learning by heart.

ro•tis•ser•ie [rəʊ'ti:sərɪ] *n.* electric machine for turning meat on a spit in front of heat.

ro•tund [rə'tʌnd] *adj.* round/fat. **ro•tun•da**, *n.* circular building with a dome. **ro•tun•di•ty**, *n.* being rotund.

rou•ble ['ru:bl] *n.* ruble.

rouge [ru:ʒ] *n.* pink cream/powder which you put on your face to give yourself more color. **rouged**, *adj.* wearing rouge.

rough [rʌf] 1. *adj.* (-er, -est) (a) not smooth/bumpy/uneven; **to give s.o. a r. time** = treat s.o. badly. (b) unfinished; approximate (translation). 2. *n.* (a) area of long grass on a golf course. (b) unfinished design. 3. *adv.* brutally/harshly. 4. *v.* **to r. out** = to make a rough design; **to r. it** = to live uncomfortably; **to r. s.o. up** = to beat/to attack s.o. **rough•age**, *n.* coarse stuff, such as bran, which you eat to help digestion. **rough and read•y**, *adj.* approximate; not completely finished.

rough-and-tum•ble, *adj.* disorderly and often violent; **rough and tumble life, rough and tumble game. rough•cast,** *n.* covering for the outside of the walls of a house, made of small stones. **rough•en,** *v.* to make/to become rough. **rough•ly,** *adv.* in a rough way. **rough•neck,** *n.* coarse, rowdy person. **rough•ness,** *n.* being rough. **rough•shod,** *adj.* **to ride r. over s.o.'s feelings** = to pay no attention to s.o.'s feelings.

rou•lette [ruːˈlet] *n.* game of chance where bets are made on the number of a box where a small ball will stop in a rotating wheel; **Russian r.** = game played with a revolver containing a single bullet which is spun around and then fired at the player's head.

round [raʊnd] 1. *adj.* (**-er, -est**) (a) circular/shaped like a circle. (b) **r. trip** = trip to a destination and back. (c) exact (number). 2. *n.* (a) circle. (b) complete or regular course or route; **r. of golf** = going around all the holes in a golf course. (c) part of a contest/of a boxing match. (d) **r. of drinks** = series of drinks bought by one person; **r. of applause** = burst of clapping. (e) one bullet; one shell. (f) song for several voices, each starting at a different point. 3. *adv.* (a) around. (b) completely; **all year r.** = during the whole year. 4. *prep.* around; approximately. 5. *v.* (a) (*also* **round off**) to make round. (b) to go around (a corner). (c) **to r. up** = to gather together. (d) to make a whole number; **to r. a number up** = to increase it to the nearest whole number above. **round•a•bout,** *adj.* not straight; indirect. **round•ed,** *adj.* with smooth/round corners or edges. **Round•head,** *n.* supporter of Parliament in the English Civil War in the 17th century. **round•house,** *n.* circular building for repairing railroad engines. **round•ly,** *adv.* sharply/critically; totally. **round•up,** *n.* gathering together.

rouse [raʊz] *v.* to wake (s.o.) who is sleeping; to get (s.o.) to act. **rous•ing,** *adj.* loud/exciting.

roust•a•bout [ˈraʊstəbaʊt] *n.* laborer on an oil rig.

rout [raʊt] 1. *n.* complete defeat (of an army). 2. *v.* (a) to defeat completely. (b) to search; **to r. s.o. out** = to pull s.o. out from where he is hidden.

route [ruːt] 1. *n.* way to be followed to get to a destination; **bus r.** = normal way which a bus follows. 2. *v.* to send (s.o.) along a route.

rou•tine [ruːˈtiːn] 1. *n.* (a) normal/regular way of doing things; **daily r.** = things which you do every day. (b) instructions which carry out a task as part of a computer program. 2. *adj.* normal/everyday. **rou•tine•ly,** *adv.* (done) as a routine.

roux [ruː] *n.* mixture of fat and flour cooked to make a base for a sauce.

rove [rəʊv] *v.* to wander.

row¹ [rəʊ] 1. *n.* (a) line (of chairs, etc.). (b) short trip in a rowboat. 2. *v.* to make a boat go forward by using oars. **row•boat,** *n.* small boat for rowing. **row•er,** *n.* person who rows. **row•ing,** *n.* making a boat move by the use of oars.

row² [raʊ] 1. *n.* (a) loud noise. (b) loud argument. 2. *v.* to argue loudly.

row•an [ˈrəʊən] *n.* mountain ash.

row•dy [ˈraʊdɪ] 1. *adj.* making a great deal of noise. 2. *n.* rough person, who makes a lot of noise. **row•di•ly,** *adv.* in a rowdy way. **row•di•ness,** *n.* rowdy behavior.

row•el [ˈraʊəl] *n.* little wheel with spikes, attached to a spur.

roy•al [ˈrɔɪəl] *adj.* referring to a king or queen; **r. blue** = bright dark blue. **roy•al•ist,** *n.* person who is a political supporter of a king. **roy•al•ly,** *adv.* splendidly/with great pomp. **roy•al•ty,** *n.* state of being royal; members of a king's family. (b) money paid to the author of a book/the owner of land where oil is found, etc., as a percentage of the receipts of sale.

RSVP [ɑːesviːˈpiː] *abbrev. for* répondez s'il vous plaît *meaning* please reply.

RTA [ˈɑːtiːˈeɪ] *abbrev. for* road traffic accident.

rub [rʌb] *v.* (**rubbed**) (a) to move sth across the surface of sth else. (b) *inf.* **to r. s.o. the wrong way** = to make s.o. irritable. **rub•bing,** *n.* action of rubbing; **r. alcohol** = pure alcohol used as an antiseptic. **rub down,** *v.* to rub (s.o./a horse) vigorously. **rub in,** *v.* to make (a cream) enter the skin by rubbing; *inf.* **don't rub it in** = don't go on talking about my mistake. **rub out,** *v.* to remove or erase (as a pencil mark).

rub•ber [ˈrʌbə] *n.* (a) elastic material made from the sap of a tree; **r. plant** = type of indoor plant with thick shiny green leaves. (b) **rubbers** = rubber/plastic shoes worn over ordinary shoes to protect them. (c) number of games of bridge. (d) piece of rubber used for removing pencil marks. **rub•ber band,** *n.* thin loop of

æ back, ɑː farm, ɒ top, aɪ pipe, aʊ how, aɪə fire, aʊə flower, ɔː bought, ɔɪ toy, e fed, eəhair, eɪ take, ə afraid, əʊ boat, əʊə lower, ɜː word, iː heap, ɪ hit, ɪə hear, uː school, ʊ book, ʌ but, b back, d dog, ð then, dʒ just, f fog, g go, h hand, j yes, k catch, l last, m mix, n nut, ŋ sing, p penny, r round, s some, ʃ short, t too, tʃ chop, θ thing, v voice, w was, z zoo, ʒ treasure

rubber for holding things together. **rub•ber•ize**, *v.* to coat with rubber. **rub•ber•neck**, *v. inf.* to stare with curiosity while straining the neck to do so. **rub•ber stamp**. 1. *n.* stamp made of rubber, with words or figures cut on it, which is used for stamping documents. 2. *v.* to agree to (sth) automatically without examining it. **rub•ber•y**, *adj.* flexible and strong like rubber.

rub•bish ['rʌbɪʃ] *n.* (*no pl.*) (a) things which are to be thrown away; trash. (b) nonsense. **rub•bish•y**, *adj.* useless/stupid.

rub•ble ['rʌbl] *n.* small stones/broken bricks, etc. used in constructing paths, etc.

ru•bel•la [ru:'belə] *n.* (*formal*) German measles.

ru•bi•cund ['ru:bɪkənd] *adj.* (*formal*) red (face).

ru•bric ['ru:brɪk] *n.* (a) written instruction; direction. (b) written heading to a piece of writing, sometimes in red.

ru•by ['ru:bɪ] 1. *n.* red precious stone. 2. *adj.* dark red (color).

ruche [ru:ʃ] *n.* cloth gathered into folds. **ruched**, *adj.* gathered in folds.

ruck [rʌk] 1. *n.* crease in cloth. 2. *v.* to form creases.

ruck•sack ['rʌksæk] *n.* bag carried on the back by a walker, bicyclist, etc.

ruck•us ['rʌkəs] *n. inf.* fight.

ruc•tion ['rʌkʃənz] *n. inf.* argument/angry scene.

rud•der ['rʌdə] *n.* flat plate at the stern of a boat/on the tail of an aircraft, used for steering.

rud•dy ['rʌdɪ] *adj.* (-ier, -iest) red/fire-colored.

rude [ru:d] *adj.* (-er, -est) (a) impolite; obscene. (b) having coarse manners or behavior. (c) rough/primitive. **rude•ly**, *adv.* not politely. **rude•ness**, *n.* being rude.

ru•di•ments ['ru:dɪmənts] *n.* simple/elementary facts. **ru•di•men•ta•ry** [ru:dɪ'mentərɪ] *adj.* basic; not fully developed.

rue [ru:] 1. *n.* bitter herb. 2. *v.* to regret. **rue•ful**, *adj.* sorry/regretful. **rue•ful•ly**, *adv.* in a rueful way.

ruff [rʌf] *n.* (a) wide collar of ruffled lace. (b) bird with a ring of colored feathers around its neck.

ruf•fi•an ['rʌfɪən] *n.* tough/violent person.

ruf•fle ['rʌfl] 1. *n.* material/lace gathered into a bunch and used as decoration on clothes/curtains, etc. 2. *v.* to disturb (feathers/water/s.o.'s hair); *inf.* **ruffled** = flustered.

rug [rʌg] *n.* small carpet.

Rug•by ['rʌgbɪ] *n.* type of football played with an oval ball, which can be passed from hand to hand as well as being kicked.

rug•ged ['rʌgɪd] *adj.* (a) rough/uneven. (b) strict; sturdy. **rug•ged•ly**, *adv.* in a rugged way. **rug•ged•ness**, *n.* being rugged.

ru•in ['ru:ɪn] 1. *n.* (a) wreck; complete loss of all your money. (b) **ruins** = remains of collapsed buildings. 2. *v.* (a) to wreck/to spoil completely. (b) to bring to financial collapse. **ru•in•a•tion** [ruɪ'neɪʃn] *n.* act of ruining. **ru•ined**, *adj.* in ruins. **ru•in•ous**, *adj.* so expensive as to cause ruin. **ru•in•ous•ly**, *adv.* extremely (expensive).

rule [ru:l] 1. *n.* (a) general way of conduct; **as a r.** = generally/usually. (b) strict order of the way to behave. (c) government. (d) ruler (for measuring, etc.). (e) straight line (in printing). 2. *v.* (a) to govern/to control. (b) to give an official/legal decision. (c) to draw a straight line using a ruler; **ruled paper** = paper with lines on it. **rul•er**, *n.* (a) person who governs. (b) strip of wood/plastic with measurements marked on it, used for drawing straight lines, measuring, etc. **rul•ing**. 1. *adj.* (party) which governs. 2. *n.* legal decision. **rule out**, *v.* to leave (sth) out/not to consider (sth).

rum [rʌm] *n.* alcoholic drink made from the juice of sugar cane.

rum•ba ['rʌmbə] *n.* Caribbean dance with a strong rhythm.

rum•ble ['rʌmbl] 1. *n.* (a) low rolling noise. (b) *inf.* street fight. 2. *v.* to make a low rolling noise.

ru•mi•nate ['ru:mɪneɪt] *v.* (a) to chew over food which has already been swallowed once (as a cow does). (b) to think over a problem. **ru•mi•nant** ['ru:mɪnənt] *adj. & n.* animal (like a cow) which chews its cud. **ru•mi•na•tion** [ru:mɪ'neɪʃn] *n.* deep thought. **ru•mi•na•tive**, *adj.* thoughtful.

rum•mage ['rʌmɪdʒ] 1. *n.* (a) searching about for sth. (b) miscellaneous things; **r. sale** = sale of unwanted objects. 2. *v.* to search about for sth.

rum•my ['rʌmɪ] *n.* card game where each player tries to collect sets of similar cards or several cards in sequence.

ru•mor, *Brit.* **ru•mour** ['ru:mə] *n.* story passed on from one person to another without necessarily being true. **ru•mored**, *adj.* spread by rumor.

rump [rʌmp] *n.* back part of an animal.

rum•ple ['rʌmpl] *v.* to crush/to dishevel.

rum•pus ['rʌmpəs] *n.* (*pl.* -es) noisy disturbance; fuss.

run [rʌn] 1. *n.* (a) act of going quickly on foot; **on the r.** = running away; **the soldiers broke into a r.** = started to run; **go for a r.** = to exercise by running; **take a r.** = to go for a short trip in a car. (b) period; **in the long r.** = eventually. (c) access to; **he has the r. of the house** = he can go anywhere in the house. (d) track for running, skiing, etc. (e) caged area where animals (as dogs or chickens) are kept. (f) point made in baseball. (g) long hole in a stocking. (h) excessive demand; sudden selling of sth. (i) carrying out of a task by a computer. 2. *v.* **(ran, has run)** (a) to go very quickly on foot; to race. (b) to travel (fast). (c) *(of motor, transport)* to work. (d) to amount to. (e) to go in a direction. (f) to direct; **he runs his own business.** (g) **to r. a bath** = to fill a bath (h) *(of liquid)* to flow; **this color won't r.** = will not come out if put in water; **his nose is running** = liquid is coming from his nose (because he has a cold). **run a•cross,** *v.* (a) to cross quickly on foot. (b) to find/to meet by chance. **run a•long,** *v.* to go alongside. **run a•way,** *v.* to escape. **run•a•way.** 1. *n.* person who has escaped. 2. *adj.* escaping from control; **r. horse. run down,** *v.* (a) to go down quickly on foot. (b) *(of clock, machine)* to go slower. (c) to criticize (s.o.). (d) to knock down (with a vehicle). (e) **to be r.-down** = to feel unwell/tired. **run•down.** 1. *adj.* delapidated/not looked after. 2. *n.* summary. **run for,** *v.* to be a candidate for (an office). **run in,** *v.* (a) to work (a new engine) slowly until it works properly. (b) *inf.* to arrest (s.o.). **run in•to,** *v.* to meet (s.o.) by chance. **run•ner,** *n.* (a) person who is running (in a race). (b) shoot of a plant which makes roots where it touches the soil. (c) sharp blade of a skate/a sled. (d) narrow carpet. **run•ner-up,** *n.* *(pl.* **runners-up)** person who comes after the winner in a race. **run•ning.** 1. *adj.* (a) which runs; **r. commentary** = commentary on an action while the action is taking place; **r. total** = total which is carried from one column of figures to the next. (b) used in running a race. (c) **for three days r.** = one after another. 2. *n.* (a) race; **in the r. for** = a candidate for. (b) working. **run off,** *v.* (a) to escape/to flee. (b) **to run off several photocopies** = to make several photocopies. **run-of-the-mill,** *adj.* ordinary. **run on,** *v.* (a) to continue. (b) to use (sth) as a fuel. **run out,** *v.* *(of goods/supplies)* to become used up. **run out of,** *v.* to be short of. **run o•ver,** *v.* (a) to go over (sth) quickly; review. (b) to knock (s.o.) down with a car. **run up,** *v.* (a) to go up quickly on foot. (b) **to run up against sth** = to meet with or find. (c) to sew (sth)

quickly. **run•way,** *n.* track on which aircraft land.

runes [ruːnz] *pl. n.* ancient form of writing, used by early Germans. **ru•nic,** *adj.* referring to runes; magic.

rung [rʌŋ] 1. *n.* one of the bars on a ladder. 2. *v. see* **ring.**

run•nel ['rʌnl] *n.* small stream.

run•ny ['rʌnɪ] *adj.* liquid; **he's got a r. nose** = his nose is running (because he has a cold).

runt ['rʌnt] *n.* small person or animal.

ru•pee [ruːˈpiː] *n.* money used in India and other countries.

rup•ture ['rʌptʃə] 1. *n.* (a) break (in negotiations/friendly relations); burst/break (of part of the body). (b) hernia. 2. *v.* (a) to break off (negotiations/friendly relations). (b) to burst through; **he ruptured himself lifting a heavy box** = the strain caused a hernia.

ru•ral ['ruərəl] *adj.* referring to the countryside.

ruse ['ruːz] *n.* clever trick.

rush [rʌʃ] 1. *n. (pl.* **-es)** (a) type of wild grass growing in water. (b) fast movement; **r. hour** = time of day when traffic is heaviest/when trains are full. (c) **rushes** = first prints of a motion picture, before it has been edited. 2. *v.* (a) to go forward fast; **don't r. me** = don't hurry me. (b) to attack suddenly.

rusk [rʌsk] *n.* hard biscuit given to babies to suck.

rus•set ['rʌsɪt] 1. *n.* type of sweet brown apple. 2. *adj. & n.* reddish-brown (color).

Rus•sian ['rʌʃn] 1. *adj.* referring to Russia. 2. *n.* (a) person from Russia. (b) language spoken in Russia.

Russo- ['rʌsəu] *prefix meaning* between Russia and another country.

rust [rʌst] 1. *n.* (a) red substance formed on iron or steel which is left in damp air. (b) red fungus disease of plants. (c) reddish-brown (color). 2. *v.* to get rusty. **rust belt,** *n.* depressed area where heavy industry is in decline. **rust•i•ness,** *n.* being rusty. **rust•less,** *adj.* with no rust. **rust•proof,** *adj.* (metal) which will not rust. **rust•y,** *adj.* (-ier, -iest) (a) covered with rust. (b) not in practice; (person) who lacks practice.

rus•tic ['rʌstɪk] 1. *adj.* rough/of country style. 2. *n.* country/unsophisticated person. **rus•ti•cate,** *v.* to send to live in the country.

rus•tle ['rʌsl] 1. *n.* noise of dry leaves/silk, etc. rubbing together. 2. *v.* (a) to make a soft crackling noise. (b) to steal cattle. **rus•tler,** *n.*

æ back, aː farm, ɒː top, aɪ pipe, aʊ how, aie fire, aʊə flower, ɔː bought, ɔɪ toy, e fed, eəhair, eɪ take, ə afraid, əʊ boat, əʊə lower, vː word, iː heap, ɪ hit, ɪə hear, uː school, ʊ book, ʌ but, b back, d dog, ð then, dʒ just, f fog, g go, h hand, j yes, k catch, l last, m mix, n nut, ŋ sing, p penny, r round, s some, ʃ short, t too, tʃ chop, θ thing, v voice, w was, z zoo, ʒ treasure

cattle thief. **rustle up,** *v. inf.* to get (sth) ready quickly. **rust•ling,** *n.* stealing (of cattle).

rut [rʌt] *n.* (a) long deep track made in soft earth by a wheel; **to get into a r.** = to start to lead a dull life with no excitement or career prospects. (b) period when a male deer is sexually excited. **rut•ted,** *adj.* (path) full of ruts. **rut•ting,** *adj.* (deer) in rut.

ru•ta•ba•ga [ˈruːtəbɑːgə] *n.* type of root vegetable like a yellow turnip.

ruth•less [ˈruːθləs] *adj.* pitiless/cruel. **ruth•less•ly,** *adv.* cruelly. **ruth•less•ness,** *n.* cruelty.

rye [raɪ] *n.* (a) type of dark brown cereal. (b) type of whisky made from rye. **rye•grass,** *n.* type of grass grown in pastures.

Ss

S *symbol for* sulfur.

Sab•bath ['sæbəθ] *n.* seventh day of the week; religious day of rest; (*for Jews*) Saturday; (*for Christians*) Sunday.

sab•bat•i•cal [sə'bætɪkl] *n. & adj.* (leave) granted to teachers, etc., for study and travel after a period of work.

sa•ble ['seɪbl] *n.* small brown-furred arctic animal; fur from this animal.

sab•o•tage ['sæbətɑːʒ] 1. *n.* malicious/deliberate destruction. 2. *v.* to destroy/to render useless deliberately. **sab•o•teur** [sæbə'tɜː] *n.* person who commits sabotage.

sa•ber, *Brit.* **sa•bre** ['seɪbə] *n.* sword with curved blade.

sac [sæk] *n.* baglike part of an animal/plant.

sac•cha•rin ['sækərɪn] *n.* extremely sweet substance used as a substitute for sugar. **sac•cha•rine,** *adj.* too sweet/sickly.

sac•er•do•tal [sæsə'dəʊtl] *adj.* referring to priests.

sa•chet ['sæʃeɪ] *n.* small bag (a fragrant substance), used to perfume drawers, closets, etc.

sack [sæk] 1. *n.* (a) plundering (of a town). (b) large bag made of strong rough cloth. (c) *inf.* dismissal; **to get/to be given the s.** = to be dismissed from a job. (d) *inf.* bed. 2. *v.* (a) to plunder. (b) *inf.* to dismiss (s.o.) from a job. **sack•cloth,** *n.* **s. and ashes** = (i) clothes worn at times of penitence; (ii) symbol of repentance. **sack•ful,** *n.* amount held in a sack. **sack•ing,** *n.* coarse material from which sacks are made; old sacks.

sac•ra•ment ['sækrəmənt] *n.* (a) Christian religious ceremony. (b) the consecrated bread (and wine) taken at Communion. **sac•ra•men•tal** [sækrə'mentl] *adj.* referring to sacrament.

sa•cred ['seɪkrəd] *adj.* (a) associated with religion. (b) holy. (c) respected. **sa•cred cow,** *n. inf.* belief/idea which is not to be criticized. **sa•cred•ness,** *n.* being sacred.

sac•ri•fice ['sækrɪfaɪs] 1. *n.* (a) killing of animal/person as an offering to a god. (b) animal killed as an offering to a god. (c) thing given up at personal cost in order to achieve sth else. 2. *v.* (a) to offer (sth) as a sacrifice. (b) to give up/to devote. **sac•ri•fi•cial** [sækrɪ'fɪʃl] *adj.* as a sacrifice.

sac•ri•lege ['sækrɪlɪdʒ] *n.* using sth sacred in a disrespectful way. **sac•ri•le•gious** [sækrɪ-'lɪdʒəs] *adj.* referring to sacrilege.

sac•ris•ty ['sækrɪstɪ] *n.* room in a church where vestments/ vessels, etc., are kept. **sac•ris•tan,** *n.* person who looks after a church, esp. the vestments/holy vessels, etc.

sac•ro•sanct ['sækrəʊsæŋkt] *adj.* very sacred/protected by religious respect.

sac•rum ['seɪkrəm] *n.* triangular bone at the base of the spine.

sad [sæd] *adj.* (**sadder, saddest**) unhappy/sorrowful. **sad•den,** *v.* to make unhappy. **sad•ly,** *adv.* unhappily. **sad•ness,** *n.* being sad.

sad•dle ['sædl] 1. *n.* (a) rider's seat on a bicycle/on the back of a horse; **in the s.** = in control. (b) ridge between two mountains. (c) **s. of lamb** = joint of meat from the back of a sheep. 2. *v.* (a) to put a saddle on (a horse, etc.). (b) to burden (s.o.) **with** a task or responsibility. **sad•dle•bag,** *n.* bag attached to a bicycle; one of a pair of bags on a horse. **sad•dler,** *n.* maker of saddles and other equipment for horses. **sad•dler•y,** *n.* shop making/selling saddles.

sa•dism ['seɪdɪzəm] *n.* pleasure derived from being cruel or watching cruelty. **sa•dist** ['seɪdɪst] *n.* person who delights in sadism. **sa•dis•tic** [sə'dɪstɪk] *adj.* referring to sadism. **sa•dis•ti•cal•ly,** *adv.* in a sadistic way.

SAD ['eseɪ'diː] *abbrev. for* seasonal affective disorder.

S.A.E. self-addressed envelope.

sa•fa•ri [sə'fɑːrɪ] *n.* hunting expedition in Africa; **s. park** = park where large wild animals run free, and visitors can look at them from their cars.

æ back, aː farm, ɒ top, aɪ pipe, aʊ how, aɪe fire, aʊə flower, ɔː bought, ɔɪ toy, e fed, eəhair, eɪ take, ə afraid, əʊ boat, əʊə lower, ɜː word, iː heap, ɪ hit, ɪə hear, uː school, ʊ book, ʌ but, b back, d dog, ð then, dʒ just, f fog, g go, h hand, j yes, k catch, l last, m mix, n nut, ŋ sing, p penny, r round, s some, ʃ short, t too, tʃ chop, θ thing, v voice, w was, z zoo, ʒ treasure

safe [seɪf] 1. *n.* (a) strong, usu. fireproof, box for valuables. (b) ventilated cupboard for food. 2. *adj.* (**-er, -est**) (a) uninjured. (b) secure/out of danger. (c) certain/to be relied upon. **safe•con•duct**, *n.* paper which allows s.o. to go through enemy territory. **safe-de•pos•it box**, *n.* box (in a bank) in which you can store valuables. **safe•guard** ['seɪfgɑːd] 1. *n.* protection. 2. *v.* to guard/to protect. **safe•ly**, *adv.* without any danger; without being harmed. **safe•ty** ['seɪftɪ] *n.* freedom from danger or risk; **road s.** = care to be taken by pedestrians and drivers; **s. belt** = belt worn in a car/in an aircraft as protection in case of accident; **s. catch** = lock which stops a gun being fired by accident; **s. curtain** = fireproof barrier between the stage and the auditorium in a theater; **s. pin** = type of bent pin whose point is protected by a guard; **s. valve** = valve as in a steam boiler, which lets out excess pressure automatically.

saf•flow•er ['sæflaʊə] *n.* plant which produces an oil used in cooking.

saf•fron ['sæfrən] 1. *n.* orange-colored powder made from crocus flowers, from which coloring and flavoring are obtained. 2. *adj.* orange-colored.

sag [sæg] 1. *n.* bending under weight or pressure. 2. *v.* (**sagged**) to sink/to bend (in the middle) under weight or pressure.

sa•ga ['sɑːgə] *n.* (a) story of heroic achievement or adventure. (b) series of books telling the history of a family.

sa•ga•cious [sə'geɪʃəs] *adj.* (*formal*) wise/shrewd. **sa•ga•cious•ly**, *adv.* wisely. **sa•gac•i•ty** [sə'gæsɪtɪ] *n.* exceptional intelligence/wisdom.

sage [seɪdʒ] 1. *n.* (a) aromatic herb used in cookery; **s. green** = grayish green color. (b) very wise man. 2. *adj.* wise/discreet. **sage•ly**, *adv.* in a wise way.

Sag•it•tar•i•us [sædʒɪ'teərɪəs] *n.* one of the signs of the zodiac, shaped like an archer.

sa•go ['seɪgəʊ] *n.* white powder used as food; **s. palm** = palm tree whose pith yields sago.

said [sed] *v. see* **say.**

sail [seɪl] 1. *n.* (a) piece of canvas/nylon, etc., attached to the mast of a boat to catch the wind. (b) trip in a boat. (c) arm of a windmill which turns with the wind. 2. *v.* (a) to travel on water. (b) to travel in a sailboat; **to s. close to the wind** = to sail nearly against the wind. (c) to control (a sailboat). **sail•boat**, *n.* boat which has sails for propulsion. **sail•cloth**, *n.* canvas for making sails. **sail•ing.** 1. *adj.* (ship) which uses sails. 2. *n.* journey by ship; **easy s.** = straightforward progress with no problems. **sail•or** ['seɪlə] *n.* seaman/person who sails;

good/bad s. = person who is liable/not liable to seasickness.

saint [seɪnt] *n.* (a) (*abbreviated with names to* **St.** [snt]) person recognized by the Christian church as having led an exceptionally holy life, and canonized after death. (b) very good/devoted person. **saint•hood**, *n.* being a saint. **saint•li•ness**, *n.* holiness/piety. **saint•ly**, *adj.* holy.

sake¹ [seɪk] *n.* **for the s. of s.o./sth** = out of consideration for/in the interest of.

sake² ['sɑːkɪ] *n.* Japanese rice wine.

sa•laam [sə'lɑːm] 1. *n.* bow made in Eastern countries to greet s.o. 2. *v.* to make a salaam.

sa•la•cious [sə'leɪʃəs] *adj.* erotic/obscene. **sa•la•cious•ly**, *adv.* in a salacious way. **sa•la•cious•ness, salacity** [sə'læsɪtɪ] *n.* being salacious.

sal•ad [sæləd] *n.* cold dish of various cooked or raw vegetables; cold meat served with a dressing and lettuce; **s. dressing** = mixture of oil/vinegar, etc., used on salad; **fruit s.** = mixture of chopped fresh fruit.

sal•a•man•der ['sæləmændə] *n.* small animal like a lizard.

sa•la•mi [sə'lɑːmɪ] *n.* salty Italian sausage, eaten cold.

sal•a•ry ['sælərɪ] *n.* fixed payment made to an employee at regular intervals. **sal•a•ried**, *adj.* (person) who is paid a salary.

sale [seɪl] *n.* (a) exchange of sth for money; **on/for s.** = ready to be sold. (b) goods sold at reduced/special prices for a short period of time. (c) organized selling of goods; **tag s.** = selling of unwanted household goods. (d) **sales** = money received in a business. **sal•a•ble, saleable**, *adj.* fit for sale. **sales•girl**, *n.* woman in a store who sells goods to customers. **sales•la•dy**, *n.* saleswoman. **sales•man**, *n.* (*pl.* **-men**) (a) person who sells a producer's goods to a store. (b) man in a store who sells goods to customers. **sales•man•ship**, *n.* the art of selling. **sales•per•son**, *n.* person who sells goods in a store. **sales•wom•an**, *n.* (*pl.* **-women**) woman in a store who sells goods to customers.

sa•li•ent ['seɪlɪənt] 1. *n.* projecting part of a fortification/of a line of battle. 2. *adj.* prominent/conspicuous/most important.

sa•line ['seɪlaɪn] *adj.* containing salt. **sa•lin•i•ty** [sə'lɪnɪtɪ] *n.* amount of salt.

sa•li•va [sə'laɪvə] *n.* liquid formed in the mouth to help digestion. **sal•i•var•y**, *adj.* **s. gland** = gland which produces saliva. **sal•i•vate** ['sælɪveɪt] *v.* to make saliva. **sal•i•va•tion** [sælɪ'veɪʃn] *n.* act of salivating.

sal•low ['sæləʊ] *adj.* (**-er, -est**) sickly yellow (complexion).

sal•ly ['sælɪ] 1. *n.* (a) sudden rush (of soldiers) out of a defended position. (b) witticism. 2. *v.* (*also* **sally forth**) to go out.

salm•on ['sæmən] 1. *n.* (*pl.* **salmon**) large pink-fleshed fish. 2. *adj. & n.* orange-pink (color). **salmon trout,** *n.* large sea trout with pink flesh.

Sal•mo•nel•la [sælmə'nelə] *n.* type of bacteria which grows on meat, eggs, and fish, and causes food poisoning.

sa•lon ['sælɒn] *n.* hairdresser's/dressmaker's business; room/building housing a hairdresser's or dressmaker's.

sa•loon [sə'luːn] *n.* (a) large lounge in a ship. (b) public bar.

sal•si•fy ['sælsɪfɪ] *n.* vegetable with a long white root.

salt [sɔːlt] 1. *n.* (a) white substance (sodium chloride) used to season and preserve food; *inf.* **to take sth with a grain of s.** = not to believe sth completely. (b) (*in chemistry*) combination of a metal with an acid; (c) *inf.* **old s.** = experienced sailor. 2. *adj.* containing salt; cured/preserved/seasoned with salt. 3. *v.* to add salt to. **salt a•way,** *v.* to put (sth) aside for the future. **salt•cel•lar,** *n.* small dish or shaker containing salt to be sprinkled on food. **salt-free,** *adj.* without salt. **salt•i•ness, saltness,** *n.* being salty. **salt lick,** *n.* block of salt put in a field for animals to lick. **salt pan,** *n.* enclosure where salt is formed as sea water evaporates. **salt•pe•ter,** *Brit.* **salt•pe•tre** [sɔːlt'piːtə] *n.* potassium nitrate/powder used to make gunpowder. **salt•y,** *adj.* (**-ier, -iest**) containing salt.

sa•lu•bri•ous [sə'luːbrɪəs] *adj.* (*formal*) healthy. **sa•lu•bri•ty,** *n.* healthiness.

sa•lu•ki [sə'luːkɪ] *n.* breed of hound.

sa•lute [sə'luːt] 1. *n.* gesture expressing respect/homage/recognition. 2. *v.* to give a salute to (s.o.).

sal•u•tar•y ['sæljutərɪ] *adj.* useful/helpful; which has a good effect. **sal•u•ta•tion** [sælju'teɪʃn] *n.* words spoken/written in praise of s.o./to greet s.o.

sal•vage ['sælvɪdʒ] 1. *n.* (a) payment made for saving a ship/its cargo from loss by wreck. (b) objects saved (from a boat/fire, etc.). 2. *v.* to save (from wreck/fire, etc.).

sal•va•tion [sæl'veɪʃn] *n.* saving of the soul from sin; saving of a person from evil.

Sal•va•tion Ar•my, *n.* religious organization run on military lines which specializes in missionary and welfare work among poor people.

salve [sælv] 1. *n.* healing ointment; **lip s.** = ointment which prevents lips cracking in cold weather. 2. *v.* **to s. one's conscience** = to do sth to ease one's conscience.

sal•ver ['sælvə] *n.* large tray (usu. made of silver).

sal•vi•a ['sælvɪə] *n.* common summer garden plant with red or purple flowers.

sal•vo ['sælvəʊ] *n.* (*pl.* **-os, -oes**) (a) simultaneous firing of several guns in a battle at sea or as a salute. (b) round of applause.

sal vo•la•ti•le [sælvə'lætəlɪ] *n.* smelling-salts.

Sa•mar•i•tan [sə'mærɪtən] *n.* person who helps s.o. in trouble.

same [seɪm] 1. *adj.* identical; unchanging; **it's all the s. to me** = I don't mind. 2. *pron.* the identical thing. 3. *adv. inf.* **all the s./just the s.** = nevertheless. **same•ness,** *n.* (a) being the same. (b) monotony.

sam•o•var ['sæməʊvɑː] *n.* urn used in Russia for boiling water for tea.

sam•pan ['sæmpæn] *n.* small Chinese boat.

sam•phire ['sæmfaɪə] *n.* type of European fern which grows near the sea.

sam•ple ['sɑːmpl] 1. *n.* specimen. 2. *v.* (a) to test/to try (by taking a small amount). (b) to ask a group of people questions to find out a general reaction. **sam•pler,** *n.* decorated tapestry panel (usu. with letters, numbers and simple pictures) made to show skill in sewing stitches.

sam•u•rai ['sæmuraɪ] *n.* medieval Japanese warrior.

san•a•to•ri•um [sænə'tɔːrɪəm] *n.* hospital for the treatment of invalids, esp. people suffering from tuberculosis.

sanc•ti•fy ['sæŋktɪfaɪ] *v.* to consecrate/to make holy. **sanc•ti•fi•ca•tion** [sæŋktɪfɪ'keɪʃn] *n.* making holy. **sanc•ti•mo•ni•ous** [sæŋktɪ'məʊnɪəs] *adj.* pretending to be holy. **sanc•ti•mo•ni•ous•ly,** *adv.* in a sanctimonious way. **sanc•ti•ty** ['sæŋktɪtɪ] *n.* holiness of life/saintliness.

sanc•tion ['sæŋkʃn] 1. *n.* (a) official permission or approval. (b) penalty for breaking a rule; **economic sanctions** = restrictions on trade with a country in order to try to influence its political development. 2. *v.* (a) to approve. (b) to permit.

sanc•tu•ar•y ['sæŋktjʊərɪ] *n.* (a) holy place.

æ back, ɑː farm, ɒ top, aɪ pipe, aʊ how, aɪə fire, aʊə flower, ɔː bought, ɔɪ toy, e fed, eəhair, eɪ take, ə afraid, əʊ boat, əʊə lower, vː word, iː heap, ɪ hit, ɪə hear, uː school, ʊ book, ʌ but, b back, d dog, ð then, dʒ just, f fog, g go, h hand, j yes, k catch, l last, m mix, n nut, ŋ sing, p penny, r round, s some, ʃ short, t too, tʃ chop, θ thing, v voice, w was, z zoo, ʒ treasure

(b) part of a church where the high altar is placed. (c) place for the protection of wild animals or birds. (d) refuge.

sanc•tum ['sæŋktəm] *n.* (a) holy place. (b) private room; **inner s.** = most private/secret office.

sand [sænd] 1. *n.* (a) mass of tiny fragments of worn-down rock, etc., found on seashores/river beds/deserts, etc. 2. *v.* (a) (*also* **sand down**) to rub smooth with sandpaper. (b) to spread sand on (icy roads). **sand•bag.** 1. *n.* bag filled with sand and used as a defense/as ballast. 2. *v.* (**-bagged**) (a) to protect (sth) with a wall of sandbags. (b) to knock (s.o.) out by hitting him with a sandbag. **sand•bank,** *n.* ridge of sand, as on a hillside. **sand•blast,** *v.* to clean (the exterior of a building) by directing a powerful jet of sand on to it. **sand•box,** *n.* place with sand where children can play. **sand•er,** *n.* machine/person who sands. **sandpa•per.** 1. *n.* paper with a coating of sand for smoothing. 2. *v.* to rub (sth) smooth with sandpaper. **sand•pi•per,** *n.* small bird with a long bill which lives on beaches. **sands,** *n.pl.* sandy place. **sand•stone,** *n.* rock made of compressed sand. **sand•storm,** *n.* high wind in a desert blowing clouds of sand. **sand•y,** *adj.* like sand; made of sand.

san•dal ['sændl] *n.* light open shoe worn in the summer. **san•dal•wood,** *n.* (a) tropical tree; fragrant wood from this tree. (b) scent from this tree.

sand•wich ['sændwɪtʃ] 1. *n.* (*pl.* **-es**) two slices of bread with meat, cheese or other filling between the slices. 2. *v.* to insert (sth) between two others. **sand•wich board,** *n.* pair of boards worn over the shoulders in the street to advertise sth. **sandwich man,** *n.* man who carries a sandwich board.

sane [seɪn] *adj.* (**-er, -est**) reasonable/not mad. **sane•ly,** *adv.* in a sane way. **san•i•ty** ['sænɪtɪ] *n.* being sane.

sang [sæŋ] *v. see* **sing.**

sang•froid [sɑːŋ'frwɑː] *n.* calmness when in danger.

san•gui•nar•y ['sæŋgwɪnərɪ] *adj.* delighting in bloodshed or killing.

san•guine ['sæŋgwɪn] *adj.* confident/optimistic.

san•i•ta•tion [sænɪ'teɪʃn] *n.* hygiene/conditions affecting health. **san•i•tar•y** ['sænɪtərɪ] *adj.* referring to sanitation/hygiene; **s. napkin** = pad of material worn by women to absorb blood lost during menstruation.

sank [sæŋk] *v. see* **sink.**

San•skrit ['sænzkrɪt] *n.* classical language of India.

sans ser•if ['sænz'serɪf] *n.* typeset character with no serifs.

San•ta Claus ['sæntə'klɔːz] *n.* man dressed in red robes with a long white beard who is believed to bring gifts to children on Christmas Day.

sap [sæp] 1. *n.* (a) juice circulating in plants and trees. (b) (*in warfare*) tunnel dug to get near to the enemy. (c) *inf.* silly person. 2. *v.* (**sapped**) (a) to weaken/to drain away. (b) to undermine/to make insecure by removing foundations.

sap•ling ['sæplɪŋ] *n.* young tree.

sap•phire ['sæfaɪə] 1. *n.* blue precious stone. 2. *adj.* clear blue (color).

sap•ro•phyte ['sæprəʊfaɪt] *n.* fungus which lives on decaying plants. **sap•ro•phyt•ic** [sæprəʊ'fɪtɪk] *adj.* living on decaying plants.

sar•a•band ['særəbænd] *n.* slow Spanish dance.

sar•casm ['sɑːkæzəm] *n.* making sharp unpleasant remarks. **sar•cas•tic** [sɑː'kæstɪk] *adj.* scornful, with sarcasm. **sar•cas•ti•cal•ly,** *adv.* in a sarcastic way.

sar•co•ma [sɑː'kəʊmə] *n.* kind of malignant tumor.

sar•coph•a•gus [sə'kɒfəgəs] *n.* (*pl.* **-gi** [gaɪ]) stone coffin often decorated with sculpture.

sar•dine [sɑː'diːn] *n.* small fish of the herring family; **packed like sardines** = very tightly.

sar•don•ic [sɑː'dɒnɪk] *adj.* scornful/cynical. **sar•don•i•cal•ly,** *adv.* in a sardonic way.

sar•don•yx ['sɑːdɒnɪks] *n.* semiprecious stone, with red layers.

Sar•gas•so Sea [sɑː'gæsəʊ'siː] *n.* area of the Atlantic Ocean, with few currents, covered with drifting weed.

sa•ri ['sɑːrɪ] *n.* long piece of cloth worn by Indian women.

sa•rong [sə'rɒŋ] *n.* cloth worn wrapped round the lower part of the body by S.E. Asian men and women.

sar•sa•pa•ril•la [sɑːspə'rɪlə] *n.* drink made from the root of a tropical American plant.

sar•to•ri•al [sɑː'tɔːrɪəl] *adj.* (*formal*) referring to men's clothes.

sash [sæʃ] *n.* (*pl.* **-es**) (a) ornamental scarf or band, as worn by military officers. (b) wooden frame holding panes of glass. **sash cord,** *n.* rope in a sash window which allows the frames to slide up and down smoothly. **sash win•dow,** *n.* window made of panes of glass set in two frames which slide up and down.

sa•shay [sə'ʃeɪ] *v.* to walk confidently.

sat [sæt] *v. see* **sit.**

Sa•tan ['seɪtən] *n.* the devil. **sa•tan•ic** [sə'tænɪk] *adj.* diabolical/like the devil.

satch•el ['sætʃəl] *n.* small leather/canvas bag, sometimes worn on the shoulders.

sate [seɪt] *v.* (*formal*) to satisfy (s.o.) by giving him too much.

sa•teen [sə'tiːn] *n.* type of fine cotton cloth which looks like satin.

sat•el•lite ['sætəlaɪt] *n.* (a) heavenly body which goes around a planet. (b) artificial body which was launched from and which goes around the earth; **s. broadcast** = radio/TV broadcast which is transmitted via a satellite; **s. dish** = aerial, shaped like a dish, used to capture satellite broadcasts. **satellite state,** *n.* country controlled by a more powerful one. **satellite town,** *n.* small town dependent on a larger town near by.

sa•ti•ate ['seɪʃeɪt] *v.* to satisfy totally/to fill to overflowing. **sa•ti•a•tion,** *n.* act of satiating. **sa•ti•e•ty** [sə'taɪətɪ] *n.* being satiated.

sat•in ['sætɪn] 1. *n.* silk fabric with a glossy surface. 2. *adj.* made of satin. **sat•in•wood,** *n.* type of hard tropical wood. **sat•in•y,** *adj.* smooth and shiny, like satin.

sat•ire ['sætaɪə] *n.* (a) attacking s.o. in speech/writing by making them seem ridiculous. (b) humorously critical piece of writing. **sa•tir•ic, satirical** [sə'tɪrɪkl] *adj.* humorously critical. **sa•tir•i•cal•ly,** *adv.* in a satirical way. **sat•i•rist** ['sætɪrɪst] *n.* writer of satires. **sat•i•rize** ['sætɪraɪz] *v.* to attack (sth) in a more or less amusing way.

sat•is•fac•tion [sætɪs'fækʃn] *n.* (a) payment of debt; compensation (for damage). (b) good feeling; sense of comfort/happiness. **sat•is•fac•to•ry,** *adj.* causing satisfaction; quite good. **sat•is•fac•to•ri•ly,** *adv.* in a satisfactory way. **sat•is•fy** ['sætɪsfaɪ] 1. *v.* (a) to comply with/to fulfill. (b) to show adequate proof. (c) to make (s.o.) content/pleased. (d) to convince/to rid of doubt. **sat•is•fy•ing,** *adj.* which satisfies.

sat•u•rate ['sætʃureɪt] 1. *v.* to make very wet. **sat•u•rat•ed fat,** *n.* fat (such as animal fat) which contains the largest amount of hydrogen possible. **sat•u•ra•tion** [sætʃu'reɪʃn] *n.* complete filling; **s. point** = point at which a substance cannot absorb any more liquid.

Sat•ur•day ['sætədeɪ] *n.* sixth day of the week; day between Friday and Sunday.

sat•ur•na•li•a [sætə'neɪlɪə] *n.* wild orgy.

sat•ur•nine ['sætənaɪn] *adj.* gloomy character.

sa•tyr ['sætə] *n.* classical god living in woods, with a human body, but with legs and ears like a goat's.

sauce [sɔːs] *n.* (a) liquid poured over food. (b) *inf.* impertinence. **sauce•boat,** *n.* vessel in which sauce is served. **sauce•pan,** *n.* deep cooking pot with a long handle. **sau•ci•ly,** *adv. inf.* insolently. **sau•ci•ness,** *n. inf.* being saucy. **sau•cy,** *adj.* (-ier, -iest) *inf.* insolent.

sau•cer ['sɔːsə] *n.* shallow dish placed under a cup; **flying s.** = object shaped like a saucer which people say they have seen in the sky.

Sa•u•di (A•ra•bi•an) ['saudɪ(ə'reɪbɪən)] *adj. n.* (person) from Saudi Arabia.

sau•er•kraut ['sauəkraut] *n.* German dish of pickled cabbage.

sau•na ['sɔːnə] *n.* (a) very hot steam bath. (b) room where you can have a sauna bath.

saun•ter ['sɔːntə] 1. *n.* stroll/leisurely walk. 2. *v.* to walk in a leisurely way/to stroll.

sau•ri•an ['sɔːrɪən] *adj. & n.* (animal) like a lizard.

sau•sage ['sɒsɪdʒ] *n.* tube of edible skin full of minced and seasoned pork or other meat. **sausage roll,** *n.* small piece of sausage cooked in pastry.

sau•té ['səuteɪ] 1. *adj.* fried in a little fat. 2. *v.* (**sautéed**) to fry in a little fat.

sav•age ['sævɪdʒ] 1. *adj.* (a) uncivilized/primitive. (b) fierce/ferocious. 2. *n.* wild/uncivilized human being. 3. *v.* to attack with teeth. **sav•age•ly,** *adv.* in a savage way. **sav•age•ness, savagery,** *n.* being savage.

sa•van•na(h) [sə'vænə] *n.* grassy plain in a tropical country.

sa•vant ['sævɒn] *n.* learned person; **idiot s.** = person of limited intelligence, but with a highly developed skill in a single faculty (such as memorizing numbers).

save [seɪv] 1. *v.* (a) to rescue from misfortune. (b) to keep for future use/to reserve; (*computers*) to keep data in storage after it has been keyboarded. (c) to economize/to not spend. (d) (*in sports*) to prevent opponents from scoring by keeping a ball or puck out of one's goal. (e) to gain (time). (f) to avoid (trouble). 2. *prep. & conj.* except. **sav•er,** *n.* person who saves money. **sav•ing.** 1. *n.* economy. 2. *adj.* redeeming. 3. *prep.* (*old*) except. **sav•ings,** *n.* money saved. **sav•ings bank,** *n.* bank which gives interest on deposits of money.

sav•ior, *Brit.* **sav•iour** ['seɪvjə] *n.* person who saves; **our Savior** = Jesus Christ.

sa•vor•y ['seɪvərɪ] *n.* herb used in cooking.

æ back, aː farm, ɒ top, aɪ pipe, au how, aiə fire, auə flower, ɔː bought, ɔɪ toy, e fed, eəhair, eɪ take, ə afraid, əu boat, əuə lower, vː word, iː heap, ɪ hit, ɪə hear, uː school, u book, ʌ but, b back, d dog, ð then, dʒ just, f fog, g go, h hand, j yes, k catch, l last, m mix, n nut, ŋ sing, p penny, r round, s some, ʃ short, t too, tʃ chop, θ thing, v voice, w was, z zoo, ʒ treasure

sa•vor, *Brit.* **savour** ['seɪvə] 1. *n.* characteristic taste. 2. *v.* (a) to appreciate (food and wine). (b) **to s. of** = to suggest. **sa•vor•i•ness**, *Brit.* **sa•vour•i•ness**, *n.* appetizing taste or smell. **sa•vor•y**, *Brit.* **sa•vour•y**, *adj.* (a) appetizing. (b) spicy/not sweet.

sa•voy [sə'vɔɪ] *n.* curly winter cabbage.

saw [sɔ:] 1. *n.* (a) steel tool with a blade with a serrated edge, used for cutting wood/metal etc. (b) old saying. 2. *v.* (**sawed; sawn**) (a) to cut (wood, etc.) with a saw. (b) *see also* **see**. **saw•dust**, *n.* powder produced from sawing wood. **saw•fish**, *n.* large sea fish with a nose shaped like a saw. **saw•mill**, *n.* place where wood is sawed mechanically. **saw•yer**, *n.* person who saws wood.

sax [sæks] *n. inf.* saxophone.

sax•i•frage ['sæksɪfreɪdʒ] *n.* low alpine plant with pink flowers.

sax•o•phone ['sæksəfəʊn] *n.* brass musical instrument with keys. **sax•o•phon•ist** [sæk-'sɒfɒnɪst] *n.* saxophone player.

say [seɪ] 1. *n.* right to decide. 2. *v.* (**said** [sed]) (a) to speak. (b) to give (an opinion); to put an idea into words. (c) to suggest. **say•ing**, *n.* proverb/phrase which is often used.

scab [skæb] *n.* (a) dry rough crust formed over a wound while it is healing. (b) *inf.* workman who refuses to take part in a strike. **scab•by**, *adj.* covered with scabs.

scab•bard ['skæbəd] *n.* sheath/holder for a dagger or sword.

sca•bies ['skeɪbi:z] *n.* (*no pl.*) skin disease which makes you itch.

sca•bi•ous ['skeɪbɪəs] *n.* perennial plant with pincushion-shaped flowers.

scab•rous ['skeɪbrəs] *adj.* (*formal*) with a rough surface.

scaf•fold ['skæfəld] *n.* platform on which executions take place. **scaf•fold•ing**, *n.* structure of poles and planks providing workmen with a platform to stand on while working.

scal•a•wag [skæl'əwæg] *n.* naughty person; rascal.

scald [skɔ:ld] 1. *n.* burn caused by boiling liquid. 2. *v.* to injure with hot liquid or steam. **scald•ing.** 1. *n.* being burned by a hot liquid. 2. *adj.* very hot.

scale [skeɪl] 1. *n.* (a) thin horny plate protecting the skin of fish and snakes; **s. insect** = insect which sucks sap from plants and covers itself with a scale. (b) hard deposit stuck to a surface. (c) arrangement of musical notes in order. (d) graded system. (e) relative measurements of a small object which are exactly similar to those of a larger object. 2. *v.* (a) to remove scales from. (b) to remove deposit from (teeth). (c) to drop off in thin layers. (d) to climb up/to climb over. (e) **to s. up/down** = to increase/to reduce proportionally. **scale•a•ble**, *adj.* which can be scaled. **scale**, **scales**, *n.* instrument for weighing. **scal•y**, *adj.* covered with scales.

scal•lion ['skælɪɒn] *n.* young onion.

scal•lop ['skɒləp] *n.* (a) type of shellfish with a semi-circular ridged shell. (b) ornamental edging of material in small semicircles. **scal•loped**, *adj.* with scallops along the edge.

scal•ly•wag ['skælɪwæg] *n.* scalawag.

scalp [skælp] 1. *n.* skin and hair on the top of the head. 2. *v.* (a) to cut off the scalp of (s.o.). (b) *inf.* to sell tickets at a very high price. **scalp•er**, *n. inf.* person who sells tickets at a very high price.

scal•pel ['skælpl] *n.* small surgical knife.

scam [skæm] *n.* fraud.

scamp [skæmp] 1. *n.* rascal. 2. *v.* to do (sth) in an unsatisfactory way.

scamp•er ['skæmpə] 1. *n.* quick run. 2. *v.* to run quickly.

scam•pi ['skæmpɪ] *n. pl.* large prawns.

scan [skæn] 1. *v.* (**scanned**) (a) to test the rhythm of (a line of poetry); (*of poetry*) to fit a regular rhythm. (b) to look intently all over. (c) to pass a radar beam over (an area); to pass X-rays through part of the body. 2. *n.* action of passing a radar beam or X-ray over an area; **brain s.** = examining the inside of the brain by passing X-rays through the head. **scan•ner**, *n.* machine for carrying out scanning.

scan•dal ['skændl] *n.* (a) unkind gossip. (b) thing that produces a general feeling of anger. **scan•dal•ize**, *v.* to shock. **scan•dal•ized**, *adj.* shocked. **scan•dal•mon•ger**, *n.* person who spreads gossip. **scan•dal•ous**, *adj.* shameful. **scan•dal•ous•ly**, *adv.* terribly.

Scan•di•na•vi•an [skændɪ'neɪvɪən] *n. & adj.* (person) from Scandinavia.

scan•sion ['skænʃn] *n.* art of scanning poetry.

scant [skænt] *adj.* hardly enough. **scant•i•ly**, *adj.* **s. dressed** = with very few clothes on. **scant•i•ness**, *n.* lack; meagerness. **scant•y**, *adj.* (**-ier, -iest**) meager/not sufficient.

scape•goat ['skeɪpgəʊt] *n.* person who carries the blame for s.o. else.

scap•u•la ['skæpjulə] *n.* shoulder blade.

scar [skɑ:] 1. *n.* mark left after a wound has healed. 2. *v.* (**scarred**) (a) to wound (s.o.) causing a permanent mark. (b) to leave a mark on the mind of.

scar•ab ['skærəb] *n.* carved beetle.

scarce [skeəs] *adj.* (**-er, -est**) insufficient for the demand/hard to find; *inf.* **to make oneself s.** = to disappear/to keep out of the way.

scarce•ly, *adv.* hardly/only just.
scarce•ness, scarcity, *n.* lack/insufficiency.

scare [skeə] 1. *n.* fright/terror. 2. *v.* (a) to frighten. (b) to be alarmed. **scared,** *adj.* frightened. **scare•crow,** *n.* figure looking like a man set up in a field to frighten off birds. **scare•mon•ger,** *n.* person who likes to alarm others. **scare•mon•ger•ing,** *n.* spreading of alarm. **scar•y,** *adj.* (-ier, -iest) frightening.

scarf [skɑːf] *n.* (*pl.* **scarves**) long strip or square of material worn around the neck to keep you warm or for ornament.

scar•i•fy ['skærɪfaɪ] *v.* to make slits in (sth).

scar•let ['skɑːlət] *adj.* brilliant red color. **scar•let fe•ver,** *n.* (*also* **scarlatina**) infectious disease producing a bright red rash.

scarp [skɑːp] *n.* steep hillside.

Scart, SCART [skɑːt] *n.* electronic plug and socket system, used to carry signals in cables for TV/video, etc.

scath•ing ['skeɪðɪŋ] *adj.* very critical.

scat•ter ['skætə] 1. *v.* (a) to throw here and there. (b) to go/to run in all directions. **scat•ter•brain,** *n.* forgetful person. **scat•ter•brained,** *adj.* forgetful/careless. **scat•tered,** *adj.* spread out.

scaup [skɔːp] *n.* type of wild duck.

scav•en••ger ['skævɪndʒə] *n.* (a) animal which feeds on dead animals. (b) person who looks for useful things among things thrown away. **scav•enge,** *v.* to look for useful things among things thrown away.

sce•nar•i•o [sɪ'nɑːrɪəʊ] *n.* (*pl.* -os) written version of a play with details of characters/scenes, etc.

scene [siːn] *n.* (a) subdivision of an act in a play; **behind the scenes** = without being obvious/without many people knowing. (b) place in which events actually occur. (c) view/surroundings. (d) display of temper. (e) *inf.* **it's not my s.** = it doesn't interest me/it is not the sort of thing I usually do. **scen•er•y,** *n.* (a) painted cloth backgrounds and other props used in a theater to make the stage resemble the supposed scene of action. (b) view of the countryside. **sce•nic,** *adj.* referring to scenery; **s. route** = road running through beautiful countryside.

scent [sent] 1. *n.* pleasant smell. (b) characteristic smell; **on the s. of** = following a trail. (c) perfume. (d) sense of smell. 2. *v.* (a) to find out by smelling. (b) to begin to suspect. (c) to make fragrant.

scep•tic ['skeptɪk] *n.* skeptic.

scep•ter, *Brit.* **scep•tre** ['septə] *n.* gold stick covered with precious stones carried by a king or queen.

sched•ule ['ʃedjuːl, *Am.* 'skedʒuːl] 1. *n.* (a) timetable. (b) program/list of events. (c) plan. (d) appendix to a document. 2. *v.* (a) to list officially. (b) to plan (sth) for a particular time.

scheme [skiːm] 1. *n.* (a) plan/arrangement. (b) plot. 2. *v.* to plot. **sche•mat•ic** [skɪ'mætɪk] *adj.* laid out like a diagram. **sche•mat•i•cal•ly,** *adv.* in a schematic way. **schem•er,** *n.* person who plots. **schem•ing,** *adj.* (person) who plots.

scher•zo ['skeətsəʊ] *n.* (*pl.* -os, -zi) lively section of a longer piece of music.

schism ['skɪzəm] *n.* division of a religious community into factions. **schis•mat•ic** [skɪz'mætɪk] *adj.* tending to break away.

schist [ʃɪst] *n.* rock which splits into thin layers.

schiz•o•phre•ni•a [skɪtsəʊ'friːnɪə] *n.* mental illness where thoughts, feelings and actions are all disconnected. **schiz•oid** ['skɪtsɔɪd] *adj. & n.* (person) suffering from schizophrenia. **schiz•o•phren•ic** [skɪtsəʊ'frenɪk] *adj.* referring to schizophrenia.

schmaltz [ʃmɒlts] *n.* too much sentimentality (in writing/music, etc.).

schnapps [ʃnæps] *n.* colorless German alcohol.

schnit•zel ['ʃnɪtzl] *n.* thin flat piece of veal fried in breadcrumbs.

schol•ar ['skɒlə] *n.* (a) person who studies. (b) learned person. (c) student at a school, college or university who has a scholarship. **schol•ar•li•ness,** *n.* being scholarly. **schol•ar•ly,** *adj.* learned/seeking to learn. **schol•ar•ship,** *n.* (a) profound learning. (b) money given to a student to help pay for the cost of studying at a school, college or university. **scho•las•tic** [skə'læstɪk] *adj.* referring to schools or teaching.

school [skuːl] 1. *n.* (a) place for teaching (usu. children); department of a college or university. (b) followers of a philosopher/artist, etc. (c) large group of fish or sea animals. 2. *v.* to teach/to train. **school•book,** *n.* book used in school. **school•boy, schoolgirl,** *n.* child who goes to school. **school•chil•dren,** *n.pl.* children who go to school. **school•ing,** *n.* education at school level. **school•mas•ter,**

æ back, ɑː farm, ɒ top, aɪ pipe, aʊ how, aɪə fire, aʊə flower, ɔː bought, ɔɪ toy, e fed, eəhair, eɪ take, ə afraid, əʊ boat, əʊə lower, vː word, iː heap, ɪ hit, ɪə hear, uː school, ʊ book, ʌ but, b back, d dog, ð then, dʒ just, f fog, g go, h hand, j yes, k catch, l last, m mix, n nut, ŋ sing, p penny, r round, s some, ʃ short, t too, tʃ chop, θ thing, v voice, w was, z zoo, ʒ treasure

schoolmistress, *n.* schoolteacher.
school•teach•er, *n.* person who teaches in a school.

schoon•er ['sku:nə] *n.* (a) sailing ship with two or more masts and sails running lengthwise down the ship. (b) tall glass for beer, etc.

sci•at•i•ca [saɪ'ætɪkə] *n.* pain in the back and legs. **sci•at•ic nerve,** *n.* nerve in the hip.

sci•ence ['saɪəns] *n.* (a) knowledge obtained from observation and arranged into a system. (b) study based on observation and experiment (such as chemistry/biology, etc.). **sci•ence fic•tion,** *n.* stories on the subject of space travel/life in the future. **sci•en•tif•ic** [saɪən'tɪfɪk] *adj.* referring to science. **sci•en•tif•i•cal•ly,** *adv.* according to scientific experiment. **sci•en•tist** ['saɪəntɪst] *n.* person who studies science.

scim•i•tar ['sɪmɪtə] *n.* short sword with a curved blade.

scin•til•late ['sɪntɪleɪt] *v.* to sparkle. **scin•til•lat•ing,** *adj.* sparkling. **scin•til•la•tion** [sɪntɪ'leɪʃn] *n.* wit/sparkle.

sci•on ['saɪən] *n.* piece of a plant which is grafted on to another; young member of a noble family.

scis•sors ['sɪzəz] *n.pl.* (**a pair of**) **s.** = instrument for cutting fabric/paper etc. constructed of two blades with handles for thumb and fingers.

scle•ro•sis [sklə'rəʊsɪs] *n.* hardening of soft tissue; **multiple s.** = gradual disease where hardening of tissue causes general paralysis.

scoff [skɒf] *v.* (a) **to s. at** = to make fun of in a nasty way. (b) *inf.* to eat greedily. **scoff•er,** *n.* person who scoffs. **scoffing,** *adj.* mocking. **scoff•ing•ly,** *adv.* mockingly.

scold [skəʊld] *v.* to speak to (s.o.) angrily. **scold•ing,** *n.* rebuke.

sconce ['skɒns] *n.* decorated bracket which holds a light.

scone [skɒn] *n.* small soft cake usu. eaten with cream and jam.

scoop [sku:p] 1. *n.* (a) short-handled shovel/spoon; round spoon for serving ice cream. (b) portion of ice cream, etc. (c) piece of news which is published in one newspaper before any other. 2. *v.* (a) to lift, using a scoop; **to s. out the inside of sth** = to remove the inside of sth with a spoon, etc. (b) **to s. a newspaper** = to print a news item before another paper does.

scoot•er ['sku:tə] *n.* (a) child's two-wheeled vehicle with footboard and a long steering handle, pushed along with one foot. (b) **motor s.** = motorized two-wheel bicycle with a curving shield in front and a platform for the feet. **scoot,** *v. inf.* to go quite fast.

scope [skəʊp] *n.* (a) reach of observation/action. (b) opportunity, as for expression.

scor•bu•tic [skɔː'bu:tɪk] *adj.* suffering from scurvy.

scorch [skɔːtʃ] 1. *v.* to burn slightly/to brown; **scorched-earth policy** = tactics in war where all the resources are destroyed before retreating and giving up territory to the enemy. **scorch•er,** *n. inf.* very hot day. **scorch•ing,** *adj.* very hot/which scorches.

score [skɔː] 1. *n.* (a) scratch/line/mark (in paint, etc.). (b) debt; **to settle old scores** = to finally get even with s.o. (c) number of points made in a game; *inf.* **he knows the s.** = he knows all the facts of the case. (d) piece of music written out showing the parts for each instrument or voice. (e) twenty; **scores of** = many. (f) question/matter. 2. *v.* (a) to scratch. (b) to make a point in a game. (c) to write down the score in a game. (d) to write out (a piece of music) with parts for each instrument or voice. **score•board,** *n.* large board showing the score in a tennis match, etc. **scor•er,** *n.* person who makes a point in a game; person who writes down the scores in a game.

scorn [skɔːn] 1. *n.* feeling of looking down/disrespect. 2. *v.* to look down on/not respect. **scorn•ful,** *adj.* disrespectful. **scorn•ful•ly,** *adv.* in a scornful way.

Scor•pi•o ['skɔːpɪəʊ] *n.* one of the signs of the zodiac, shaped like a scorpion.

scor•pi•on ['skɔːpɪən] *n.* poisonous tropical insect which stings with a long curved tail.

Scot [skɒt] *n.* person from Scotland. **Scots.** 1. *adj.* referring to Scotland. 2. *n.* form of English spoken in Scotland. **Scots•man, Scotswoman,** *n.* (*pl.* **-men, -women**) person from Scotland. **Scot•tish,** *adj.* referring to Scotland; **S. terrier** = type of black or white terrier.

Scotch [skɒtʃ] 1. *adj.* referring to Scotland; (**Scottish** *is preferred in Scotland, but* **Scotch** *is always used in the following*) **S. broth** = soup made with mutton, barley, etc.; **S. mist** = thick mist and rain; **S. terrier** = Scottish terrier; **S. whisky** = whisky made in Scotland. 2. *n.* (a) (*pl.* **-es**) Scotch whisky; a glass of this drink. (b) **S. tape** = trademark for a type of transparent sticky tape. 3. *v.* **to s.** = to try to stop (a rumor).

scot-free [skɒt'fri:] *adj.* **to get off s.** = without being punished.

scoun•drel ['skaʊndrəl] *n.* wicked person.

scour ['skaʊə] *v.* (a) to clean by scrubbing with a hard material. (b) to search everywhere. **scour•er,** *n.* pad of steel wool for cleaning pans.

scourge [skɜːdʒ] 1. *n.* thing which causes suffering. 2. *v.* to cause suffering.

scout [skaʊt] 1. *n.* (a) person sent out to look

for information. (b) boy who belongs to the Boy Scouts; **the Scouts** = the Boy Scouts. 2. *v.* to reconnoiter; **to s. around for** = to search for. **scout•mas•ter,** *n.* leader of a group of Boy Scouts.

scowl [skaʊl] 1. *n.* angry look made by wrinkling the forehead. 2. *v.* to make a scowl.

scrab•ble ['skræbl] *v.* **to s. (about)** = to scratch wildly with your hands or feet.

scrag [skræg] *n.* lean end of a sheep's neck used to make soup. **scrag•gy** ['skrægɪ] *adj.* (**-ier, -iest**) thin and bony.

scram [skræm] *inter. meaning* go away!

scram•ble ['skræmbl] 1. *n.* (a) act of scrambling (up sth). (b) rush. 2. *v.* (a) to hurry along on hands and knees. (b) to try to get somewhere by pushing. (c) **scrambled eggs** = eggs mixed together and stirred as they are cooked in butter. (d) to mix up (a radio signal/telephone link) so that it cannot be understood without an apparatus for unmixing it. **scram•bler,** *n.* machine for scrambling radio signals.

scrap [skræp] 1. *n.* (a) small piece. (b) waste materials; **scraps** = bits of waste food/waste material; **s. heap** = heap of sth to be thrown away, esp. metal; **s. metal/paper** = waste metal/paper. (c) *inf.* fight. 2. *v.* (**scrapped**) (a) to throw away as waste. (b) to give up (plans). (c) to fight. **scrap•book,** *n.* large book with blank pages for sticking photographs/newspaper cuttings, etc., into. **scrap•py,** *adj.* (**-ier, -iest**) made of bits and pieces.

scrape [skreɪp] 1. *n.* (a) mark made by sth hard being pulled across a surface. (b) awkward situation/trouble. 2. *v.* to scratch with a hard object being pulled across a surface; **s. together** = to collect with difficulty; **s. through** = to get through (an examination, etc.) with difficulty. **scrap•er,** *n.* instrument for scraping. **scrap•ie,** *n.* usu. fatal disease of the nervous system in sheep, caused by an abnormal prion protein in the brain. **scrap•ings,** *n.pl.* pieces which have been scraped off.

scratch [skrætʃ] 1. *n.* (*pl.* **-es**) (a) long slight wound/mark made by a sharp point. (b) sound of a sharp point being pulled across a surface. (c) act of scratching a part of the body which itches. (d) **to start from s.** = to start at the beginning/with no previous preparation; **up to s.** = satisfactory. 2. *adj.* **s. player** = player who starts with no handicap. 3. *v.* (a) to make a long wound/mark with a sharp pointed instrument; **to s. the surface** = to deal with only

the first part of the problem and not to get down to the basic details. (b) to make a sound by pulling a sharp point across a surface. (c) to rub with your fingernails (a part of the body which itches). (d) (*of competitor*) to cross one's name off the list of entrants for a race. **scratch•y,** *adj.* which makes a scratching noise.

scrawl [skrɔ:l] 1. *n.* bad/careless handwriting. 2. *v.* to write badly/carelessly.

scrawn•y ['skrɔ:nɪ] *adj.* (**-ier, -iest**) thin and bony.

scream [skri:m] 1. *n.* (a) loud/piercing cry. (b) **screams of laughter** = loud/piercing laughter. (c) *inf.* very funny thing/person. 2. *v.* (a) to make loud/piercing cries. (b) **s. with laughter** = laugh uproariously. **scream•ing•ly,** *adv.* **s. funny** = extremely funny.

scree [skri:] *n.* loose stones on a mountainside.

screech [skri:tʃ] 1. *n.* (*pl.* **-es**) piercing cry (of an animal). 2. *v.* to make a piercing cry. **screech owl,** *n.* type of owl which screeches.

screed [skri:d] *n.* very long document.

screen [skri:n] 1. *n.* (a) flat surface which protects/divides. (b) thing which acts as protection against draft/fire/noise, etc. (c) flat white surface for projecting movies/slides. (d) device like a large sieve for sifting sand/gravel into varying sizes. 2. *v.* (a) to protect from draft/fire/noise, etc. (b) to show a movie/slides on a screen. (c) to question/to examine (people) to find out if they have a disease/if they have committed a crime. (d) to sift (sand/gravel) into varying sizes. **screen•play,** *n.* scenario of a motion picture. **screen•writ•er,** *n.* person who writes screenplays.

screw [skru:] 1. *n.* (a) metal pin with a groove winding up from the point to the head, so that when twisted it goes into a hard surface. (b) act of turning a screw with a screwdriver. (c) twisting motion. (d) *Sl.* prison guard. 2. *v.* (a) to attach with screws. (b) to attach by twisting. (c) to twist/distort. **screw•ball,** *n. inf.* odd/crazy person. **screw•driv•er,** *n.* tool with a long handle and small flat end which is used for turning screws. **screw-top jar,** *n.* jar with a top which screws on and off. **screw•y,** *adj.* (**-ier, -iest**) *inf.* mad.

scrib•ble ['skrɪbl] 1. *n.* (a) (child's) meaningless marks. (b) bad writing. 2. *v.* (a) to make meaningless marks. (b) to write badly/hurriedly. **scrib•bly,** *adj.* scribbled (writing).

æ back, ɑ: farm, ɒ: top, aɪ pipe, aʊ how, aɪə fire, aʊə flower, ɔ: bought, ɔɪ toy, e fed, eəhair, eɪ take, ə afraid, əʊ boat, əʊə lower, ɜ: word, i: heap, ɪ hit, ɪə hear, u: school, ʊ book, ʌ but, b back, d dog, ð then, dʒ just, f fog, g go, h hand, j yes, k catch, l last, m mix, n nut, ŋ sing, p penny, r round, s some, ʃ short, t too, tʃ chop, θ thing, v voice, w was, z zoo, ʒ treasure

scribe [skraɪb] n. (old) person who writes copies (of letters/books, etc.) by hand.

scrim•mage ['skrɪmɪdʒ] n. wild struggle.

scrimp [skrɪmp] v. to use as little as possible (of sth).

scrim•shaw ['skrɪmʃɔ:] n. carvings made by sailors on whalebone or ivory.

scrip [skrɪp] n. (no pl.) new shares issued by a company instead of paying a dividend.

script [skrɪpt] n. (a) style of handwriting. (b) thing written by hand/manuscript. (c) written version of words which are spoken in a motion picture/play.

scrip•ture ['skrɪptʃə] n. holy writing; the Bible. **scrip•tur•al**, adj. referring to scripture.

scroll [skrəʊl] 1. n. (a) roll of paper with writing on it. (b) curved shape. 2. v. to move text up or down on a computer screen.

scro•tum ['skrəʊtəm] n. bag containing the testicles. **scro•tal**, adj. referring to the scrotum.

scrounge [skraʊndʒ] v. to try to get (sth) from s.o. without paying for it. **scroung•er**, n. person who scrounges.

scrub [skrʌb] 1. n. (a) (area of land covered by) small bushes. (b) action of cleaning with a stiff brush. 2. v. (**scrubbed**) to clean by rubbing with a stiff brush. **scrub brush**, n. (also **scrubbing brush**) stiff brush with no handle, for scrubbing floors, etc. **scrub•by**, adj. (**-ier**, **-iest**) inf. shabby, small and unpleasant.

scruff [skrʌf] n. skin at the back of the neck. **scruff•i•ly**, adv. in a scruffy way. **scruff•i•ness**, n. being scruffy. **scruff•y**, adj. (**-ier**, **-iest**) untidy/dirty.

scrump•tious ['skrʌmʃəs] adj. inf. very good to eat or pleasant to look at, etc.

scrunch [skrʌntʃ] v. inf. to crush.

scru•ple ['skru:pl] 1. n. doubt about whether sth is right which stops you from doing it. 2. v. to have scruples about doing sth. **scru•pu•lous** ['skru:pjʊləs] adj. very careful. **scru•pu•lous•ly**, adv. in a scrupulous way. **scru•pu•lous•ness**, n. being scrupulous.

scru•ti•nize ['skru:tɪnaɪz] v. to examine very carefully. **scru•ti•ny**, n. careful examination/very close look.

scu•ba ['sku:bə] n. underwater breathing apparatus.

scud [skʌd] v. (**scudded**) (of clouds) to rush past.

scuff [skʌf] v. to scrape the outside surface/the soles of (shoes) when walking.

scuf•fle ['skʌfl] 1. n. small fight. 2. v. to fight.

scull [skʌl] 1. n. one of two short oars used by a single rower. 2. v. to row a boat with two oars.

scul•ler•y ['skʌləri] n. (esp. Brit.) small room at the back of a kitchen, used for washing up.

sculpt [skʌlpt] v. to carve (figures, etc.) out of wood/metal/stone. **sculp•tor** ['skʌlptə] n. person who makes figures/artistic constructions out of wood/metal/stone. **sculp•ture** ['skʌlptʃə] 1. n. (a) art of sculpting. (b) figure made by a sculptor. 2. v. to sculpt.

scum [skʌm] n. (a) thick dirty foam layer on the surface of a liquid. (b) people of the worst type; worthless person. **scum•my**, adj. covered with scum.

scup•per ['skʌpə] n. hole in the side of a ship to let water run off the deck.

scurf [skɜ:f] n. dandruff/bits of dead skin in the hair.

scur•ril•ous ['skʌrɪləs] adj. very insulting/rude. **scur•ril•ous•ly**, adv. in a scurrilous way. **scur•ril•ous•ness**, **scurrility** [skʌ'rɪlɪtɪ] n. being scurrilous.

scur•ry ['skʌrɪ] 1. n. fast movement. 2. v. to run fast, taking short steps.

scur•vy ['skɜ:vɪ] n. disease caused by lack of Vitamin C which is found in fruit and vegetables.

scut [skʌt] n. little tail (of a rabbit/deer).

scut•tle ['skʌtl] 1. n. type of bucket for keeping coal in the house. 2. v. (a) to sink (a ship) intentionally by opening holes in the bottom to allow water to come in. (b) **to s. off** = to run away fast.

scythe [saɪð] 1. n. tool with a wide blade on the end of a long handle, used for cutting grass. 2. v. to cut (grass) with a scythe.

sea [si:] n. (a) area of salt water; inf. **at s.** = not understanding what is happening. (b) salt water. (c) waves; **a heavy s.** = very large waves. (d) mass (of faces in a crowd). **sea a•nem•o•ne**, n. primitive sea animal which looks like a flower. **sea bird**, n. bird which lives by the sea. **sea•board**, n. land by the edge of the sea. **sea•borne**, adj. (troops, etc.) brought by sea. **sea breeze**, n. light wind blowing inland from the sea. **sea•coast**, n. land along the edge of the sea. **sea•far•er**, n. person who travels/works on the sea. **sea•far•ing**, adj. which works/travels on the sea. **sea•food**, n. fish and shellfish which can be eaten. **sea front**, n. area with buildings, running along the edge of the sea at a resort town. **sea•go•ing**, adj. (boat) which is used on the sea. **sea•gull**, n. white sea bird. **sea horse**, n. small black fish which looks like a horse. **sea legs**, n. **he's got his s. legs** = he is used to traveling by sea and isn't seasick. **sea lev•el**, n. the level of the sea, taken as a point for measuring altitude. **sea li•on**, n. large type of seal. **sea•man**, n. (pl. **-men**) sailor; person who travels/works on the sea. **sea•man•ship**, n. art of sailing a ship. **sea•plane**, n. plane with floats which can

land on water. **sea•port,** *n.* port.
sea•scape, *n.* painting of the sea. **sea•shell,**
n. shell of a shellfish which lives in the sea.
sea•shore, *n.* land along the edge of the sea.
sea•sick, *adj.* ill because of the motion of a
ship. **sea•sick•ness,** *n.* being seasick.
sea•side, *n.* land by the side of the sea. **sea
ur•chin,** *n.* type of small spiny sea animal.
sea•ward, *adj.* toward the sea. **sea•ward,**
seawards, *adv.* toward the sea. **sea•weed,**
n. plant which grows in the sea.
sea•wor•thy, *adj.* (boat) which is fit to go to
sea.

seal [siːl] 1. *n.* (a) large animal living mainly in
the sea, with flippers for swimming. (b) piece
of hard red wax with a design stamped on it,
used for showing that a document has been
officially approved or for closing an enve-
lope/package so that it cannot be opened secretly. (c) metal stamp with a design, used for
sealing with wax. (d) tight fit (of a bottle, etc.).
2. *v.* *(a)* to attach and stamp a piece of hard
wax to show that a document has been
officially approved/to prevent an envelope
being opened. (b) to close (sth) tightly so that
something cannot be opened. (c) to agree on
the terms of (an agreement/bargain).
seal•ant, *n.* substance used for sealing.
seal•ing wax, *n.* hard red wax used for making official seals. **seal off,** *v.* to close off so as
to prevent anyone entering. **seal•skin,** *n.* skin
of a seal.

seam [siːm] *n.* (a) line where two pieces of cloth
are sewn together/where two pieces of metal
are welded together. (b) layer (of coal, etc.).
seam•less, *adj.* (stockings, etc.) with no
seam. **seam•stress** ['semstrəs] *n.* woman
who sews. **seam•y,** *adj.* (-ier, -iest) **s. side of
life** = the unpleasant parts of life.

sé•ance ['seɪɑːns] *n.* meeting where people try
to get in touch with the spirits of dead people.

sear ['sɪə] *v.* to burn severely/to scorch.

search [sɜːtʃ] 1. *n.* (*pl.* **-es**) trying to find sth; **s.
engine** = Internet service that allows users to
search for specified items; **s. warrant** = official
permit to carry out a search; **s. party** = group
of people sent to look for s.o. 2. *v.* (a) to examine carefully in order to find sth. (b) **to s. for** =
try to find. **search•er,** *n.* person who
searches. **search•ing,** *adj.* very careful (examination). **search•light,** *n.* powerful light
used to try to see things, esp. aircraft, at night.
sea•son ['siːzn] 1. *n.* (a) one of four parts into

which a year is divided. (b) any period of the
year when sth usually takes place. 2. *v.* (a) to
add spices to (food). (b) to dry (wood) until it
is ready to be used. **sea•son•a•ble,** *adj.*
which fits the season. **sea•son•a•bly,** *adv.*
as is usual for the season. **sea•son•al,** *adj.*
which only lasts for a season; (work) for the
(summer) season only; **s. affective disorder
(SAD)** = depressive condition affecting some
people in late autumn/winter, thought to be
caused by lack of sunlight. **sea•soned,** *adj.*
(wood) which has been dried; (traveler) who
has much experience of traveling.
sea•son•ing, *n.* spices which are added to
food.

seat [siːt] 1. *n.* (a) thing you sit on. (b) place (on
a committee/town council, etc.). (c) part of a
chair on which you sit. (d) part of a pair of
trousers which covers the buttocks. (e) **s. of
government** = place where the government is
carried on. (f) way of sitting on a horse. 2. *v.*
(a) to make (s.o.) sit down. (b) to have room
for people to sit down. **seat belt,** *n.* belt worn
in a car/in an aircraft as protection in case of
accident. **seat•ing,** *n.* giving seats to people.

se•ba•ceous [sɪ'beɪʃəs] *adj.* which produces
fat.

se•cant ['siːknt] *n.* line which crosses a curve.

se•cede [sɪ'siːd] *v.* (*formal*) to break away from
a group. **se•ces•sion** [sɪ'seʃn] *n.* act of seced-
ing.

se•clud•ed [sɪ'kluːdɪd] *adj.* (place) which is
quiet/away from crowds. **se•clu•sion** [sɪ-
'kluːʒn] *n.* quiet/solitude.

sec•ond ['sekənd] (*as a number can be written
2nd*) 1. *n.* (a) sixtieth part of a minute; a moment; **s. hand** = long fast-moving hand on a
watch. (b) sixtieth part of a degree. (c) per-
son/thing which comes after the first. (d) person who helps a boxer/wrestler. (e) **seconds** =
articles which are not perfect and are sold
cheaply. (f) second gear. 2. *adj.* (a) coming
next after the first; **s. class** = ordinary railroad
travel, etc., which is not as luxurious or
expensive as first class; **s. in command** =
person directly under the commanding
officer/managing director, etc.; **the s. century**
= period from A.D. 100 to 199. (b) **every s. day**
= every other day/on alternate days. 3. *v.* to
support (a proposal). **sec•ond•ar•y**
['sekəndrɪ] *adj.* (a) second in importance/in
position. (b) **s. school** = school between primary school and a college or university. (c) **s.
colors** = colors made by mixing primary col-

æ back, ɑː farm, ɒ top, aɪ pipe, aʊ how, aɪə fire, aʊə flower, ɔː bought, ɔɪ toy, e fed, eəhair, eɪ take, ə
afraid, əʊ boat, əʊə lower, vː word, iː heap, ɪ hit, ɪə hear, uː school, ʊ book, ʌ but, b back, d dog, ð then,
dʒ just, f fog, g go, h hand, j yes, k catch, l last, m mix, n nut, ŋ sing, p penny, r round, s some, ʃ short, t
too, tʃ chop, θ thing, v voice, w was, z zoo, ʒ treasure

ors. **sec•ond•ar•i•ly**, *adv.* in second place in importance. **sec•ond best**, *adj. & adv.* in second place; not as good as the best. **sec•ond child•hood**, *n.* period in old age when old people seem to act like children. **sec•ond•er**, *n.* person who supports a motion. **second half**, *n.* second section (as of a football game). **sec•ond hand**, *adj. & adv.* not new/used; **I heard it at s. h.** = not from the original source of the news. **sec•ond•ly**, *adv.* in second place. **sec•ond na•ture**, *n.* **it is s. n. to him** = he does it quite naturally. **sec•ond-rate**, *adj.* not of good quality. **sec•ond sight**, *n.* being able to tell what will happen in the future. **sec•ond thoughts**, *n. pl.* **to have s. t. about** = to change one's mind. **sec•ond wind**, *n.* **he got his s. w.** = he could breathe again easily after having lost his breath.

se•cret ['siːkrət] 1. *adj.* hidden from other people; not known. 2. *n.* thing which is not known/which is kept hidden; **in s.** = without anyone knowing. **se•cre•cy**, ['siːkrəsɪ] *n.* keeping sth secret. **se•cre•tive**, *adj.* liking to keep things secret. **se•cre•tive•ly**, *adv.* in a secretive way. **se•cre•tive•ness**, *n.* being secretive. **se•cret•ly**, *adv.* in secret. **se•cret serv•ice**, *n.* government department which deals in espionage.

sec•re•taire [sekrə'teə] *n.* desk with many little drawers.

sec•re•tar•y ['sekrətərɪ] *n.* (a) person who writes letters/files documents, etc., for s.o. (b) person who deals with correspondence/arranges meetings, etc., in a club/society. (c) official in charge of a government department. (d) official in an embassy; **first s.** = senior official in an embassy. **Sec•re•tar•y Gen•er•al**, *n.* chief administrative officer of an international organization. **sec•re•tar•i•al** [sekrə'teərɪəl] *adj.* referring to a secretary. **sec•re•tar•i•at**, *n.* group of officials who administer a large office.

se•crete [sɪ'kriːt] *v.* (a) to hide. (b) to produce (a liquid). **se•cre•tion** [sɪ'kriːʃn] *n.* liquid produced by an organ/a plant.

sect [sekt] *n.* religious group. **sec•tar•i•an** [sek'teərɪən] *adj.* referring to a religious group.

sec•tion ['sekʃn] *n.* (a) cutting; cutting tissue in an operation. (b) part. (c) picture of sth showing what it is like when cut through. (d) part of sth which, when joined to other parts, goes to make up a whole. **sec•tion•al**, *adj.* (a) (diagram) showing a section through sth. (b) (built) in sections.

sec•tor ['sektə] *n.* (a) section of a circle between two lines drawn from the center to the circum-

ference; section of the surface of a computer disk. (b) **private s.** = part of industry which is privately owned; **public s.** = nationalized industries and the civil service.

sec•u•lar ['sekjulə] *adj.* not religious/not connected with religion. **sec•u•lar•ize**, *v.* to make secular.

se•cure [sɪ'kjuːə] 1. *adj.* (a) safe. (b) firmly fixed; **s. job** = where you can't be fired. (c) confident. 2. *v.* (a) to make firm/to fasten. **se•cure•ly**, *adv.* in a secure way. **se•cu•ri•ty**, *n.* (a) safety. (b) protection against criminals/against hardship; **airport s.** = measures to protect aircraft against hijackers. (c) thing given to s.o. who has lent you money and which is returned when the loan is repaid. (d) **securities** = stocks and bonds. **Se•cu•ri•ty Coun•cil**, *n.* ruling body of the United Nations.

se•dan [sɪ'dæn] *n.* covered car which has two or four doors. **se•dan chair**, *n.* (*old*) seat in a box carried on long poles by bearers.

se•date [sɪ'deɪt] 1. *adj.* serious/dignified. 2. *v.* to give (a patient) sedatives. **se•date•ly**, *adv.* in a calm/serious way. **se•date•ness**, *n.* being sedate. **sed•a•tive** ['sedətɪv] *adj. & n.* (medicine) which makes you calm/which makes you go to sleep. **se•da•tion** [sɪ'deɪʃn] *n.* giving medicine to calm a patient or make him go to sleep.

sed•en•tar•y ['sedəntrɪ] *adj.* always sitting down.

sedge [sedʒ] *n.* type of grass which grows in water.

sed•i•ment ['sedɪmənt] *n.* solid which forms at the bottom of a liquid. **sed•i•men•ta•ry** [sedr'mentərɪ] *adj.* (rocks) which were formed from mud deposited at the bottom of the sea/rivers, etc. **sed•i•men•ta•tion**, *n.* action of depositing solid particles at the bottom of liquid.

se•di•tion [sə'dɪʃn] *n.* encouraging people to rebel against the government. **se•di•tious**, *adj.* which encourages people to rebel.

se•duce [sɪ'djuːs] *v.* (a) to persuade (s.o.) to do sth which is perhaps wrong. (b) to persuade (s.o.) to have sexual intercourse. **se•duc•er**, *n.* person who seduces. **se•duc•tion** [sɪ'dʌkʃn] *n.* act of seducing. **se•duc•tive** [sɪ'dʌktɪv] *adj.* attractive.

sed•u•lous ['sedjuləs] *adj.* very careful and persistent. **sed•u•lous•ly**, *adv.* in a sedulous way.

se•dum ['siːdəm] *n.* succulent rock plant.

see [siː] 1. *n.* area over which a bishop rules. 2. *v.* (**saw** [sɔː], **seen**) (a) to sense with your eyes. (b) to accompany; **to s. s.o. home.** (c) to understand. (d) to examine. (e) to make sure (**that**).

(f) to visit/to meet. (g) to go to a performance of (a play/motion picture, etc.). **see•ing,** *n.* action of sensing with the eyes; **s. that** = since.

see through, *v.* (a) to understand s.o.'s plans to trick you. (b) to work on (sth) until it is finished. **see-through,** *adj.* transparent. **see to,** *v.* to busy yourself about sth; **see to it** = make sure (**that**).

seed [siːd] 1. *n.* (a) part of a plant which appears after the flowers and then can produce a new plant; **to go/to run to s.** = produce flowers and seeds which are not needed; **he's gone to s.** = he's lost energy, power, etc.; deteriorated. (b) tennis player selected as one of the best players in a tournament (before the tournament starts). 2. *v.* (a) to produce seeds. (b) to select (the best players) in a tennis tournament and arrange them so that they do not play each other until the later rounds. **seed•bed,** *n.* special area of fine soil where you can sow seeds. **seed•less,** *adj.* (fruit) with no seeds in it. **seed•ling,** *n.* very young plant. **seed•y,** *adj.* (-ier, -iest) worn-out (clothes); shabby (person).

seek [siːk] *v.* (**sought** [sɔːt]) (a) to look for. (b) to ask for. **seek•er,** *n.* person who seeks.

seem [siːm] *v.* to appear. **seem•ing,** *adj.* not real, though appearing to be. **seem•ing•ly,** *adj.* apparently. **seem•ly,** *adj.* decent/correct.

seen [siːn] *v. see* **see.**

seep [siːp] *v.* (*of a liquid*) to pass through a crack. **seep•age,** *n.* act of seeping; liquid which has seeped.

seer ['siːə] *n.* (*old*) person who sees into the future.

seer•suck•er ['sɪəsʌkə] *n.* cotton cloth with a wrinkled surface.

see•saw ['siːsɔː] 1. *n.* children's toy made of a plank with seats at each end, balanced in the middle, so that when one end goes up the other goes down. 2. *v.* to go up and down.

seethe [siːð] *v.* (a) to be very angry. (b) to move about like boiling water. **seeth•ing,** *adj.* very angry.

seg•ment ['segmənt] *n.* part of sth (which seems to form a natural division); part of a circle or sphere. **seg•men•ta•tion** [segmən-'teɪʃn] *n.* being segmented. **seg•ment•ed** [seg'mentɪd] *adj.* with segments.

seg•re•gate ['segrɪgeɪt] *v.* to divide one group from another. **seg•re•ga•tion** [segrɪ'geɪʃn] *n.* division of one group from another; **racial s.**

= splitting of a population into groups according to race or color.

seine [seɪn] *n.* type of fishing net.

seis•mic ['saɪzmɪk] *adj.* referring to earthquakes. **seis•mo•graph,** *n.* instrument for recording earthquakes. **seis•mo•log•i•cal** [saɪzmə'lɒdʒɪkl] *adj.* referring to seismology. **seis•mol•o•gy** [saɪz'mɒlədʒɪ] *n.* study of earthquakes.

seize [siːz] *v.* (a) to grab/to hold tight. (b) to confiscate/to take by force. **seize up,** *v.* (*of an engine*) to stop working/to become blocked. **sei•zure** ['siːʒə] *n.* (a) confiscation of goods by the police. (b) stroke/illness caused by lack of blood to the brain.

sel•dom ['seldəm] *adv.* rarely/not often.

se•lect [sɪ'lekt] 1. *v.* to choose. 2. *adj.* (a) of top quality. (b) **s. group** = group which only lets in certain people. **se•lec•tion** [sɪ'lekʃn] *n.* (a) choice. (b) things chosen. **se•lec•tive,** *adj.* which chooses (carefully). **se•lec•tive•ly,** *adv.* in a selective way. **se•lec•tiv•i•ty,** *n.* being able to choose carefully.

self [self] *n.* (*pl.* **selves**) your own person or character. **self-ad•dressed,** *adj.* (envelope) on which you have written your own address. **self-as•ser•tive,** *adj.* (person) who makes others do what he wants. **self-as•sur•ance,** *n.* being self-assured. **self-as•sured,** *adj.* sure you are capable of doing sth. **self-cen•tered,** *adj.* (person) who only thinks of himself. **self-con•fi•dence,** *n.* being self-confident. **self-con•fi•dent,** *adj.* sure you are capable of doing sth. **self-con•scious,** *adj.* embarrassed because you feel you have certain faults. **self-con•scious•ly,** *adv.* with embarrassment. **self-con•scious•ness,** *n.* being self-conscious. **self-con•trol,** *n.* keeping your feelings under control. **self-de•feat•ing,** *adj.* (plan) which works in such a way that it defeats its own purpose. **self-de•fense,** *n.* protecting yourself. **self-de•ni•al,** *n.* refusing to give yourself sth/going without sth which you would like. **self-de•ter•mi•na•tion,** *n.* choosing your own political future. **self-ed•u•cat•ed,** *adj.* (person) who has taught himself everything he knows and who has not been to school. **self-ef•fac•ing,** *adj.* (person) who tries to be inconspicuous/who does not want people to notice him. **self-em•ployed,** *adj.* (person) who works for himself, and is not an employee

---

æ back, ɑː farm, ɒ top, aɪ pipe, aʊ how, aiə fire, aʊə flower, ɔː bought, ɔɪ toy, e fed, eəhair, eɪ take, ə afraid, əʊ boat, əʊə lower, ɜː word, iː heap, ɪ hit, ɪə hear, uː school, ʊ book, ʌ but, b back, d dog, ð then, dʒ just, f fog, g go, h hand, j yes, k catch, l last, m mix, n nut, ŋ sing, p penny, r round, s some, ʃ short, t too, tʃ chop, θ thing, v voice, w was, z zoo, ʒ treasure

receiving a salary from s.o. else. **self-es•teem,** *n.* pride in yourself. **self-ev•i•dent,** *adj.* obvious. **self-ex•plan•a•to•ry,** *adj.* obvious/which explains itself. **self-gov•ern•ing,** *adj.* (country) which governs itself. **self-gov•ern•ment,** *n.* control of a country by its own people, not by another country. **self-help,** *n.* improving one's condition by one's own efforts. **self-im•por•tant,** *adj.* (person) who feels he is very important when he really is not. **self-in•dul•gent,** *adj.* (person) who gives himself everything he wants. **self-in•ter•est,** *n.* working for one's own benefit. **self-made man,** *n.* person who has become rich or successful entirely through his own efforts. **self-pit•y,** *n.* pity for yourself. **self-por•trait,** *n.* painting which an artist has made of himself. **self-pos•sessed,** *adj.* calm/not bothered. **self-ris•ing flour,** *n.* flour which contains baking powder to make cakes rise. **self-re•li•ance,** *n.* being self-reliant. **self-re•li•ant,** *adj.* independent/relying only on yourself. **self-re•spect,** *n.* pride in yourself/concern that you have a good character and work well. **self-right•eous,** *adj.* feeling sure that you are doing what is right. **self-rule,** *n.* self-government. **self-sac•ri•fice,** *n.* giving up sth which you would like, so that others may enjoy it. **self-sac•ri•fic•ing,** *adj.* (person) who gives up pleasures, so that others may enjoy them. **self-sat•is•fac•tion,** *n.* being self-satisfied. **self-sat•is•fied,** *adj.* contented with what you have done. **self-seek•ing,** *adj.* (person) who works to his own advantage, at the expense of others. **self-serv•ice,** *n. & adj.* (store, restaurant, gas station, etc.) where you help yourself and pay at a cashier's desk. **self-styled,** *adj.* (person) who has given himself a title. **self-suf•fi•cien•cy,** *n.* being self-sufficient. **self-suf•fi•cient,** *adj.* producing enough food, etc., for all needs. **self-sup•port•ing,** *adj.* providing for one's own needs, with no help from others. **self-taught,** *adj.* (person) who has taught himself a certain skill. **self-willed,** *adj.* obstinate/always wanting to have your own way.

self•ish ['selfɪʃ] *adj.* only interested in yourself/doing sth only for yourself. **self•ish•ly,** *adv.* (done) only for yourself. **self•ish•ness,** *n.* being selfish.

self•less ['selfles] *adj.* not selfish/thinking only of others.

self•same ['selfseɪm] *adj.* exactly the same.

sell [sel] 1. *n.* act of selling; **hard s.** = forceful selling of a product. 2. *v.* (**sold, has sold**) (a) to give goods to s.o. in exchange for money. (b) *inf.* to betray. **sell date,** *n.* date on a package of food, which is the last date on which the food is guaranteed to be good. **sell•er,** *n.* (a) person who sells. (b) **good s.** = thing that sells well. **sell off,** *v.* to sell (sth) cheaply to get rid of it. **sell out,** *v.* (a) to sell so many things that you have none left. (b) *inf.* to abandon your principles. **sell-out,** *n.* (a) show/play, etc. where all the tickets have been sold. (b) *inf.* abandoning of principles.

sel•vage, selvedge ['selvɪdʒ] *n.* edge of a piece of cloth which does not fray.

se•man•tics [sɪ'mæntɪks] *n.* study of the meaning of language. **se•man•ti•cal•ly,** *adv.* in a way which refers to semantics.

sem•a•phore ['semǝfɔː] *n.* way of signaling using two arms (and flags) in different positions for each letter.

sem•blance ['semblǝns] *n.* appearance.

se•men ['siːmǝn] *n.* liquid in which male sperm floats.

se•mes•ter [sǝ'mestǝ] *n.* division of an academic year, usu. 15 to 18 weeks.

semi- ['semɪ] *prefix meaning* half. **sem•i•cir•cle,** *n.* half a circle. **sem•i•cir•cu•lar,** *adj.* like a half circle in shape. **sem•i•co•lon,** *n.* punctuation mark (;) showing a pause. **sem•i•con•duc•tor,** *n.* material (such as silicon) which is partly able to conduct electricity. **sem•i•con•scious,** *adj.* half conscious. **sem•i•de•tached,** *adj.* (house) which is joined to another similar house on one side, but is not joined on the other. **sem•i•fi•nal,** *n.* one of two matches in a competition, the winners of which go into the final game. **sem•i•fi•nal•ist,** *n.* team/player in a semifinal. **sem•i•of•fi•cial,** *adj.* not quite official. **sem•i•pre•cious,** *n.* (stone) which is quite valuable, but not in the same class as diamonds/rubies/sapphires, etc. **sem•i•skilled,** *adj.* (worker) who has been trained to a certain level. **sem•i•tone,** *n.* (*in music*) half a tone on the scale.

sem•i•nal ['semɪnl] *adj.* which acts as the starting point for sth new.

sem•i•nar ['semɪnɑː] *n.* meeting of a small group of students with a teacher to have discussions and report on research findings, etc.

sem•i•nar•y ['semɪnǝrɪ] *n.* college for priests.

Se•mit•ic [sǝ'mɪtɪk] *adj.* referring to a group of races including Jews and Arabs.

sem•o•li•na [semǝ'liːnǝ] *n.* hard crushed wheat, used to make spaghetti and milk puddings.

sen•ate ['senǝt] *n.* (a) governing or lawmaking group. (b) upper house of the legislature of the

United States, most U.S. states and certain other countries. **sen•a•tor**, *n*. member of a senate.

send [send] *v.* (**sent**) (a) to tell (s.o.) to go somewhere; to make (sth) go from one place to another. (b) to give (s.o.) a sensation; **it sends chills up my spine**. (c) to put out (roots, etc.). (d) *inf.* to make (s.o.) excited. **send a•way**, *v.* (a) to make (s.o./sth) go away. (b) **to s. a. for** = to write asking s.o. to send sth to you. **send back**, *v.* to return (sth). **send•er**, *n.* person who sends. **send for**, *v.* to pass a message to (s.o.) asking them to come. **send off**, *v.* (a) to make (s.o./sth) go off. (b) to mail; **to s. o. for** = send away for. **send-off**, *n.* party to say goodbye to s.o. leaving on a trip, starting a new job, etc. **send out**, *v.* to make (s.o./sth) go out. **send up**, *v.* to make (s.o./sth) go up.

se•nile ['siːnaɪl] *adj.* old and mentally weak. **se•nil•i•ty** [sə'nɪlɪtɪ] *n.* being senile.

sen•ior ['siːnjə] 1. *adj.* (a) older; **J. Smith S.** = father of J. Smith Junior; **s. citizen** = older person esp. one living on a pension. (b) more important (rank, etc.). 2. *n.* (a) older person. (b) student in his final year of school. **sen•ior•i•ty** [siːnɪ'ɒrɪtɪ] *n.* being senior.

sen•na ['senə] *n.* **s. pods** = dried pods used as a laxative.

sen•sa•tion [sen'seɪʃn] *n.* (a) feeling. (b) (thing/person that causes) great excitement. **sen•sa•tion•al**, *adj.* very exciting. **sen•sa•tion•al•ly**, *adv.* in a sensational way.

sense [sens] 1. *n.* (a) one of the five ways in which you notice sth; **sixth s.** = ability to feel that sth has taken place/will take place, without using any of the five senses. (b) feeling. (c) **senses** = power of reasoning; **to come to one's senses** = become reasonable. (d) meaning; **to make s.** = to have a meaning; **to make s. of** = to understand. (e) reasonableness/good judgment. 2. *v.* to feel. **sense•less**, *adj.* (a) stupid. (b) unconscious. **sense•less•ness**, *n.* stupidity.

sen•si•ble ['sensɪbl] *adj.* (a) reasonable/showing good judgment. (b) (person) who has common sense. (c) **s. walking shoes** = strong, but not fashionable, walking shoes. (d) (*formal*) **s. of** = aware of. **sen•si•bil•i•ty** [sensɪ'bɪlɪtɪ] *n.* being capable of delicate feeling. **sen•si•bly**, *adv.* in a sensible way.

sen•si•tive ['sensɪtɪv] *adj.* (a) able to feel keenly/sharply. (b) (instrument) which measures very accurately. (c) (substance) which reacts to light, etc. **sen•si•tiv•i•ty** [sensɪ'tɪvɪtɪ], **sen•si•tive•ness**, *n.* being sensitive. **sen•si•tive•ly**, *adv.* in a sensitive way. **sen•si•tize** ['sensɪtaɪz] *v.* to make sensitive (to light, etc.).

sen•sor ['sensə] *n.* apparatus which detects sth by sense of heat/light/smell of smoke, etc. **sen•so•ry**, *adj.* referring to the senses.

sen•su•al ['sensjʊəl] *adj.* referring to pleasures of the body, not of the mind. **sen•su•al•i•ty**, *n.* experience of sensual pleasure. **sen•su•al•ly**, *adv.* in a sensual way.

sen•su•ous ['sensjʊəs] *adj.* which gives pleasure to the senses. **sen•su•ous•ly**, *adv.* in a sensuous way.

sent [sent] *v. see* **send**.

sen•tence ['sentəns] 1. *n.* (a) words put together to form a complete separate statement. (b) decision of a judge which gives the details of punishment. 2. *v.* to condemn (s.o.) to a certain punishment.

sen•ten•tious [sen'tenʃəs] *adj.* too full of moral sense. **sen•ten•tious•ly**, *adv.* in a sententious way.

sen•tient ['senʃnt] *adj.* able to feel.

sen•ti•ment ['sentɪmənt] *n.* (a) show of feeling. (b) **sentiments** = opinions. **sen•ti•men•tal** [sentɪ'mentəl] *adj.* full of emotion/full of feeling. **sen•ti•men•tal•i•ty** [sentɪmən'tælɪtɪ] *n.* playing on the emotions (in literature/music). **sen•ti•men•tal•ly**, *adv.* by feeling.

sen•ti•nel ['sentɪnl] *n.* person or thing that watches or guards.

sen•try ['sentrɪ] *n.* sentinel, esp. a soldier on duty at a gate, etc. who watches and alerts others of danger. **sen•try box**, *n.* wooden shelter for a sentry.

se•pal ['sepəl] *n.* green leaf under the petals of a flower.

sep•a•rate 1. *adj.* ['seprət] detached/not together. 2. *v.* ['sepəreɪt] to detach/to divide. 3. *n.* **separates** = pieces of women's clothing (skirts/blouse/sweater, etc.) which can be worn in different combinations. **sep•a•ra•ble** ['seprəbl] *adj.* which can be separated. **sep•a•rate•ly**, *adv.* in a separate way. **sep•a•ra•tion** [sepə'reɪʃn] *n.* dividing/living apart. **sep•a•ra•tism** ['sepərətɪzəm] *n.* political ideal of separating from a large country. **sep•a•ra•tist**, *adj.* &

æ back, ɑː farm, ɒ top, aɪ pipe, aʊ how, aiə fire, aʊə flower, ɔː bought, ɔɪ toy, e fed, eəhair, eɪ take, ə afraid, əʊ boat, əʊə lower, vː word, iː heap, ɪ hit, ɪə hear, uː school, ʊ book, ʌ but, b back, d dog, ð then, dʒ just, f fog, g go, h hand, j yes, k catch, l last, m mix, n nut, ŋ sing, p penny, r round, s some, ʃ short, t too, tʃ chop, θ thing, v voice, w was, z zoo, ʒ treasure

n. (person) who wants his region to separate from a large country. **sep•a•ra•tor,** *n.* person/machine that separates.

se•pi•a ['si:piə] *n.* brown color.

sep•sis ['sepsis] *n.* being septic.

Sep•tem•ber [sep'tembə] *n.* 9th month of the year.

sep•ten•ni•al [sep'teniəl] *adj.* for seven years.

sep•tet [sep'tet] *n.* group of seven musicians; piece of music for seven instruments.

sep•tic ['septik] *adj.* (wound) which has gone bad/become poisoned; **s. tank** = underground tank near a house for collecting sewage.

sep•ti•ce•mi•a, septicaemia [septɪ'si:mɪə] *n.* poisoning of the blood.

sep•tu•a•ge•nar•i•an [septjuədʒə'neərɪən] *n.* person who is between seventy and seventy-nine years old.

sep•tum ['septəm] *n.* (*pl.* **-ta**) wall between two sections of the body/a plant.

sep•ul•cher, *Brit.* **sep•ul•chre** ['sepəlkə] *n.* tomb. **se•pul•chral** [se'pʌlkrəl] *adj.* referring to a sepulcher; very deep gloomy (voice).

se•quel ['si:kwəl] *n.* (a) continuation of a story, play, etc. (b) result.

se•quence ['si:kwəns] *n.* (a) series of things happening; series of numbers which follow each other. (b) scene in a motion picture. **se•quen•tial,** *adj.* in sequence. **se•quen•tial•ly,** *adv.* in sequence.

se•ques•ter [sɪ'kwestə] *v.* (*formal*) to seclude. **se•ques•trate** ['sekwɪstreɪt] *v.* (*formal*) to confiscate (property). **se•ques•tra•tor,** *n.* person who seizes property on the orders of a court.

se•quin ['si:kwɪn] *n.* small round shiny metal ornament. **se•quined,** *adj.* covered with sequins.

se•quoi•a [sɪ'kwɔɪə] *n.* redwood.

se•ragl•io [se'ræljəu] *n.* harem.

ser•aph ['seræf] *n.* (*pl.* **seraphs, seraphim**) highest angel. **se•raph•ic, seraphical,** *adj.* like a seraph.

ser•e•nade [serə'neɪd] 1. *n.* love song. 2. *v.* to sing a love song to (s.o.).

ser•en•dip•i•ty [serən'dɪpɪtɪ] *n.* pleasure which you get from finding things by accident.

se•rene [sə'ri:n] *adj.* calm/not worried. **se•rene•ly,** *adv.* in a serene way. **se•ren•i•ty** [sə'renɪtɪ] *n.* being serene.

serf [sɜːf] *n.* peasant/slave working on a farm. **serf•dom,** *n.* state of being a serf.

serge [sɜːdʒ] *n.* type of thick cloth.

ser•geant ['sɑːdʒənt] *n.* (a) noncommissioned officer in the army/air force/marine corps. (b) police officer below a captain.

se•ri•al ['sɪərɪəl] 1. *adj.* (number) of a series. 2. *n.* story/TV play which is told in several installments. **se•ri•al•ize,** *v.* to make (a novel, etc.) into a serial. **se•ri•al mo•nog•a•my,** *n.* practice of having a succession of long-lasting romantic sexual relationships.

se•ri•a•tim [sɪərɪ'ɑːtɪm] *adv.* in order; in a series.

se•ries ['sɪərɪːz] *n.* (*pl.* **series**) (a) group of things which come one after the other in a set order. (b) group of things that go together.

ser•if ['serɪf] *n.* little line added to the end of a stroke in a typeset character.

se•ri•ous ['sɪərɪəs] *adj.* (a) not humorous. (b) important/grave. **se•ri•ous•ly,** *adv.* in a serious way. **se•ri•ous•ness,** *n.* being serious.

ser•mon ['sɜːmən] *n.* serious speech made in church. **ser•mon•ize,** *v.* to preach to (s.o.).

ser•pent ['sɜːpənt] *n.* snake. **ser•pen•tine,** *adj.* like a snake; winding.

ser•rat•ed [sə'reɪtɪd] *adj.* toothed (blade); with a zigzag edge. **ser•ra•tion,** *n.* being serrated; serrated edge.

ser•ried ['serɪd] *adj.* **in s. ranks** = in ranks close together.

se•rum ['sɪərəm] *n.* yellow liquid in the blood, which can be injected into s.o.'s body to fight disease.

serve [sɜːv] 1. *n.* act of serving the ball in tennis. 2. *v.* (a) to provide/to give (food); to put (food) before/at a table in a restaurant, etc.; (*of a recipe*) to make enough food for. (b) to work for. (c) to be useful (**as**). (d) to deal with (a customer). (e) to undergo punishment. (f) to start a game of tennis by hitting the ball first. (g) **it serves you right** = you deserve the punishment you got. (h) to assist a priest (at mass). **serv•ant,** *n.* (a) person who is paid to work in the house. (b) **civil s.** = government employee. **serv•er,** *n.* (a) person who serves at a table. (b) large flat knife for serving food; spoon/fork for serving fish or salad. (c) person who helps a priest (at mass). (d) computer hardware/software that distributes files/databases to other computers on a network.

serv•ice ['sɜːvɪs] 1. *n.* (a) working for s.o.; **military s.** = period which you spend in the armed forces; **s. charge** = charge added to a bill for sth done; **s. road** = road which runs alongside a major highway, giving access to stores and houses. (b) group of people working together; **civil s.** = all the government employees; **the foreign s.** = people who represent their country abroad; **the services** = the armed forces. (c) providing basic essentials which people require; **bus s.** = regularly passing bus. (d) regular religious ceremony. (e) act of starting a game of tennis by hitting the ball first. (f) set of china for use at meals. (g) repairs to a machine, done on a regular basis; **the car needs a**

s. = examination by the garage; **s. area** = place along a highway where you can stop and buy fuel/get food, etc. 2. *v.* to do any repairs which need doing to (a car, etc.). **serv•ice•a•ble,** *adj.* practical; which will be useful. **serv•ice•man,** *n.* (*pl.* **-men**) member of the armed forces of a country. **serv•ice sta•tion,** *n.* place which sells fuel/oil, etc. **serv•ice•wom•an,** *n.* (*pl.* **-women**) woman member of the armed forces of a country.

ser•vile ['sɜː.vail] *adj.* like a slave. **ser•vile•ly,** *adv.* in a servile way. **ser•vil•i•ty** [sɜː'vɪlɪtɪ] *n.* acting like a slave. **ser•vi•tude** ['sɜː.vɪtjuːd] *n.* slavery.

servo- ['sɜː.vəu] *prefix meaning* power-assisted.

ses•a•me ['sesəmiː] *n.* tropical plant whose seeds produce oil or are eaten.

ses•sion ['seʃn] *n.* (a) meeting of a committee/legislative body, etc.; **in s.** = in the process of meeting. (b) meeting to study/to practice.

set [set] 1. *n.* (a) group of things which go together; (*in mathematics*) group of numbers, etc., which are linked. (b) apparatus for sending or receiving radio, television, or other communication. (c) one of the main parts of a tennis match. (d) group of people. (e) scenery on a stage. (f) position/direction. (g) arranging of hair. 2. *v.* (**set**) (a) to put/to place; **to s. the table** = put the knives and forks, etc. on the table. (b) to arrange/to fix (a machine, etc.). (c) to arrange in place. (d) to make (free, etc.). (e) to become solid. (f) (*of sun/stars*) to go down. (g) to write music to go with (a poem, etc.). (h) to place scenery on a stage; to put (the action of a story) in a certain period. (i) to arrange letters in rows for printing. 3. *adj.* (a) fixed/which cannot be changed. (b) ready. **set a•bout,** *v.* to start doing (sth). **set a•side,** *v.* (a) to put to one side/to reject. (b) to keep (for future use). **set back,** *v.* (a) to make late. (b) *inf.* **it s. me back $10** = it cost me $10. **set•back,** *n.* holding back of progress. **set down,** *v.* to write down on paper. **set forth,** *v.* (a) to start a journey. (b) to write out (a list, etc.). **set in,** *v.* to start. **set off,** *v.* (a) to start a journey (b) to light (fireworks); to make (a bomb) explode; to start (a reaction). (c) to show up; make prominent. **set out,** *v.* (a) to put out. (b) to start a journey. **set•ting,** *n.* (a) action of setting. (b) background for a story; frame in which a diamond or other stone is fixed. (c) **place s.** = set of knives/forks/spoons, etc., for one person. **set to,** *v.* to get to work.

set-to, *n. inf.* argument/fight. **set up,** *v.* to build/to establish. **set•up,** *n. inf.* arrangement/organization. **set up•on,** *v.* to attack.

set•tee [sə'tiː] *n.* sofa.

set•ter ['setə] *n.* hunting dog trained to point out game by standing still.

set•tle ['setl] 1. *n.* long wooden bench with a back. 2. *v.* (a) to arrange/to agree; to end (a dispute); **to s. up** = pay the bill; **to s. on/for** = to decide on/to choose. (b) (*also* **settle down**) to place yourself in a comfortable position/to rest. (c) to go to live in a new country. (d) (*of sediment*) to fall to the bottom of a liquid; (*of building*) to sink into the ground. (e) to pass money, etc. to s.o. by a formal or legal process. **set•tled,** *adj.* fixed/unchanging. **set•tle•ment,** *n.* (a) payment (of a bill); agreement in a dispute. (b) place where a group of people has settled. (c) settling money, etc., on s.o. (d) (*of building*) act of sinking into the ground. **set•tler,** *n.* person who goes to settle in a new country.

sev•en ['sevn] *n.* number 7. **sev•en•teen,** *n.* number 17. **sev•en•teenth, 17th,** *adj. & n.* referring to seventeen; **the s. century** = period from 1600 to 1699. **sev•enth, 7th,** *adj. & n.* referring to seven. **sev•en•ti•eth, 70th,** *adj. & n.* referring to seventy. **sev•en•ty,** *n.* number 70.

sev•er ['sevə] *v.* to cut off. **sev•er•ance,** *n.* cutting off; **s. pay** = money paid as compensation to s.o. who is losing a job.

sev•er•al ['sevrəl] *adj. & pron.* more than a few, but not very many. **sev•er•al•ly,** *adv.* separately.

se•vere [sə'vɪə] *adj.* (**-er, -est**) (a) very strict. (b) very bad (illness, weather, etc.). **se•vere•ly,** *adv.* (a) strictly. (b) badly. **se•ver•i•ty** [sə'verɪtɪ] *n.* being severe.

sew [səu] *v.* (**sewn**) to attach/to mend by using a needle and thread; to make (with a needle and thread). **sew•ing,** *n.* (a) action of attaching/mending with needle and thread. (b) work which s.o. is in the process of sewing. **sew•ing ma•chine,** *n.* machine which sews. **sew up,** *v.* (a) to close (a hole) by sewing. (b) *inf.* to settle (a deal).

sew•er ['suə] *n.* large tube in the ground used for taking away waste and dirty water from houses and other buildings. **sew•age** ['suːɪdʒ] *n.* waste and dirty water. **sew•er•age,** *n.* system of sewers for removing waste and dirty water.

æ back, ɑː farm, ɒ top, aɪ pipe, aʊ how, aɪə fire, aʊə flower, ɔː bought, ɔɪ toy, e fed, eəhair, eɪ take, ə afraid, əʊ boat, əʊə lower, ɜː word, iː heap, ɪ hit, ɪə hear, uː school, ʊ book, ʌ but, b back, d dog, ð then, dʒ just, f fog, g go, h hand, j yes, k catch, l last, m mix, n nut, ŋ sing, p penny, r round, s some, ʃ short, t too, tʃ chop, θ thing, v voice, w was, z zoo, ʒ treasure

sex [seks] 1. *n.* (*pl.* -es) (a) one of two groups (male and female) into which animals and plants can be divided; **s. appeal** = attractiveness to members of the other sex. (b) **to have s. with s.o.** = to have sexual intercourse. 2. *v.* **to s. chickens** = to tell whether chickens are male or female. **sex•ism**, *n.* bias against one sex. **sex•ist**, *adj. & n.* (person) who is biased against one of the sexes. **sex•less**, *adj.* without sex; not involving sexual feeling. **sex•o•log•i•cal**, *adj.* referring to sexology. **sex•ol•o•gist**, *n.* person who studies sexual behavior. **sex•ol•o•gy** [sek'sɒlədʒi] *n.* study of sexual behavior. **sex•u•al** ['seksjʊəl] *adj.* referring to sex; **s. intercourse** = reproductive act between a male and female. **sex•u•al•i•ty**, *n.* interest in sexual intercourse. **sex•u•al•ly**, *adv.* in a sexual way. **sex•y**, *adj.* sexually attractive.

sex•a•ge•nar•i•an [seksədʒə'neəriən] *adj. & n.* (person) who is between sixty years and sixty-nine years old.

sex•tant ['sekstənt] *n.* instrument for calculating the position of a ship by referring to the stars.

sex•tet [seks'tet] *n.* (a) group of six musicians playing together. (b) piece of music for six musicians.

sex•ton ['sekstən] *n.* man who works in a church/rings the bells/digs graves, etc.

sh [ʃ] *inter.* used to make silence.

shab•by ['ʃæbɪ] *adj.* (-ier, -iest) poor/worn out (clothes); mean (trick). **shab•bi•ly**, *adv.* in a shabby way. **shab•bi•ness**, *n.* being shabby.

shack [ʃæk] 1. *n.* rough wooden hut. 2. *v. Sl.* **to s. up with s.o.** = to go to live with s.o.

shack•le ['ʃækl] 1. *n.* thing which hampers movement; **shackles** = chains (for attaching a prisoner). 2. *v.* to attach (s.o.) with a chain.

shade [ʃeɪd] 1. *n.* (a) dark place which is not in the sunlight. (b) dark part of a picture. (c) cover put on a lamp; blind on a window. (d) type of color; slight difference. (e) little bit. (f) *inf.* **shades** = sunglasses. (g) (*formal*) ghost. 2. *v.* (a) to protect (sth) from sunlight. (b) to make (a picture) darker. (c) (*also* **shade off**) to change from one color to another gradually. **shad•i•ness**, *n.* being shady. **shad•ing**, *n.* action of making shade; making part of a picture darker. **shad•y**, *adj.* (-ier, -iest) (a) full of shade. (b) dishonest/disreputable.

shad•ow ['ʃædəʊ] 1. *n.* (a) shade made by an object in light; **five o'clock s.** = dark tint on a man's chin as his beard begins to grow. (b) small amount. (c) person who follows s.o. 2. *v.* to follow (s.o.). **shad•ow•y**, *adj.* vague/indistinct.

shaft [ʃɑːft] *n.* (a) long stick which is the main part of an arrow/a javelin, etc.; long pole in front of a cart to which a horse is attached. (b) ray of light. (c) rod which turns in an engine. (d) pillar. (e) deep hole in the ground; **elevator s.** = hole down the center of a building in which an elevator moves up and down.

shag [ʃæg] *n.* (a) thick tobacco. (b) type of black sea bird.

shag•gy ['ʃægɪ] *adj.* (-ier, -iest) with long hair; **s. dog story** = very long story with an unexpectedly silly ending.

shake [ʃeɪk] 1. *n.* (a) act of moving from side to side or up and down. (b) drink made by mixing milk and flavoring. 2. *v.* (**shook** [ʃuːk]; **shaken**) to move from side to side or up and down; **to s. one's head** = to move one's head from side to side to indicate "no". **shake down**, *v.* to cause to settle. **shake•down**, *n.* rough bed. **shak•en**, *adj.* very upset/disturbed. **shake off**, *v.* to get rid of (sth unpleasant). **shak•er**, *n.* person/machine which shakes; container for mixing cocktails. **shake-up**, *n. inf.* total change. **shak•i•ly**, *adv.* in a shaky way. **shak•i•ness**, *n.* being shaky. **shak•y**, *adj.* (-ier, -iest) (a) wobbly; trembling. (b) not very reliable.

shale [ʃeɪl] *n.* type of rock which splits into soft thin slices.

shall [ʃæl] *v.* used with **I** and **we** to form future (*past* **should**) (a) (*suggestion/request*) **s. we sit down?** (b) (*emphasis in the future*) yes I s.! (*note: except for* (a) **shall** *is gradually being replaced by* **will**); *see also* **should**.

shal•lot [ʃə'lɒt] *n.* type of small onion which grows in clusters.

shal•low ['ʃæləʊ] 1. *adj.* (-er, -est) (a) not deep. (b) superficial (mind). 2. *n.* **shallows** = water which is not deep. **shal•low•ness**, *n.* being shallow.

sham [ʃæm] 1. *adj.* false. 2. *n.* thing which is false. 3. *v.* (**shammed**) to pretend.

sham•ble ['ʃæmbl] *v.* **to s. along** = to wander along dragging your feet.

sham•bles ['ʃæmblz] *n.* disorder/mess.

shame [ʃeɪm] 1. *n.* (a) feeling caused by being guilty/being ashamed. (b) **what a s.** = what a pity/how sad. 2. *v.* **to s. s.o. into** = to make s.o. ashamed so that he does sth. **shame•faced**, *adj.* embarrassed/ashamed. **shame•fac•ed•ly**, *adv.* in embarrassment. **shame•ful**, *adj.* scandalous/disgraceful. **shame•ful•ly**, *adv.* in a shameful way. **shame•less**, *adj.* without shame. **shame•less•ly**, *adv.* in a shameless way.

sham•poo [ʃæm'puː] 1. *n.* liquid soap for washing your hair/a carpet, etc. 2. *v.* to wash (your hair/the carpet, etc.) with a shampoo.

sham•rock ['ʃæmrɒk] *n.* small cloverlike plant with leaves which are split into three parts.

shang•hai [ʃæŋ'haɪ] *v.* (**shanghaied**) to capture (s.o.) and force them to obey your orders, esp. to force s.o. to join the crew of a ship.

shank [ʃæŋk] *n.* (a) straight shaft. (b) leg.

shan't [ʃɑːnt] *v. contraction of* shall not.

shan•ty ['ʃæntɪ] *n.* (a) rough wooden hut; **s. town** = group of huts belonging to poor people. (b) chantey.

shape [ʃeɪp] 1. *n.* (a) form; **the picture is taking s.** = is beginning to look like sth. (b) mold or pattern for forming sth into a shape. (c) condition. 2. *v.* (a) to form/to make into a shape. (b) **to s. up well** = turn out well. **shape•less,** *adj.* with no definite shape. **shape•less•ness,** *n.* being shapeless. **shape•li•ness,** *n.* being shapely. **shape•ly,** *adj.* with an attractive shape.

shard [ʃɑːd] *n.* piece of broken pottery.

share ['ʃeə] 1. *n.* (a) part which belongs to someone. (b) contribution which each person makes. (c) one of the parts into which a company's capital is divided. (d) plowshare, the metal blade of a plow. 2. *v.* (a) to divide up among several people. (b) **to s. sth with s.o.** = to allow s.o. to use sth which you also use. (c) to have/to use (sth) in common. **share•hold•er,** *n.* person who owns shares in a company. **share•hold•ing,** *n.* group of shares in a company owned by one person.

shark [ʃɑːk] *n.* (a) large dangerous fish which can kill a man. (b) *inf.* crook/swindler.

sharp [ʃɑːp] 1. *adj.* (**-er, -est**) (a) with a fine cutting edge. (b) very cutting/harsh. (c) with a very acute angle. (d) bitter. (e) clever/intelligent. (f) with a highly-developed sense. (g) high-pitched (sound). (h) (*in music*) (note) which is slightly higher than the correct pitch. (i) clear (image). 2. *n.* note in music which is a semitone higher. 3. *adv.* (a) acutely. (b) exactly. (c) (*in music*) higher than the correct pitch. **sharp•en,** *v.* to make sharp. **sharp•en•er,** *n.* pencil s. = instrument for sharpening pencils. **sharp•er,** *n.* (*also* **sharpie**) person who cheats at cards. **sharp•ly,** *adv.* (a) acutely. (b) completely. (c) harshly. **sharp•ness,** *n.* being sharp. **sharp•shoot•er,** *n.* person who can shoot very accurately. **sharp-wit•ted,** *adj.* clever.

shat•ter ['ʃætə] *v.* to break into little pieces; to upset (s.o.) very badly.

shave [ʃeɪv] 1. *n.* act of cutting off the hair on your face, legs, etc. with a razor; **close s.** = near miss. 2. *v.* (a) to cut off the hair on your face, legs, etc. (b) to slice very thin pieces off (sth). **shav•en,** *adj.* (*old*) shaved. **shav•er,** *n.* razor; machine for shaving. **shav•ing,** *n.* (a) act of cutting off hair; **s. cream** = cream which you put on your face before shaving. (b) **shavings** = small thin slices of wood cut off by a plane.

shawl [ʃɔːl] *n.* large square of warm material for wrapping around your shoulders/your head.

she [ʃiː] (a) *pron. referring to a female person.* (b) *prefix meaning* female; **she-wolf.**

sheaf [ʃiːf] *n.* (*pl.* **sheaves** [ʃiːvz]) bundle of corn/of papers.

shear ['ʃɪə] *v.* (**sheared/shorn** [ʃɔːn]) to cut the wool off (sheep, etc.); to cut (**through** sth). **shear•er,** *n.* person who cuts the wool off sheep. **shears,** *n.* cutting tool like large scissors. **shear•wa•ter,** *n.* type of small dark sea bird.

sheath [ʃiːθ] *n.* (a) holder (for a knife, etc.). (b) rubber contraceptive. **sheathe** [ʃiːð] *v.* to put a knife back into its sheath. **sheath knife,** *n.* (*pl.* **-knives**) knife kept in a sheath.

sheaves [ʃiːvz] *n. see* sheaf.

shed [ʃed] 1. *n.* wooden building. 2. *v.* (**shed**) (a) to lose (leaves); to lose/to take off (clothes). (b) to let flow (blood, tears, light); **to s. light on** = to make clearer.

sheen [ʃiːn] *n.* brilliant shining surface.

sheep [ʃiːp] *n.* (*pl.* **sheep**) farm animal, reared for wool or for meat. **sheep dip,** *n.* bath of disinfectant into which sheep are put to kill parasites. **sheep•dog,** *n.* type of dog specially trained for herding sheep. **sheep•ish,** *adj.* ashamed/embarrassed. **sheep•ish•ly,** *adv.* with a sheepish air. **sheep•ish•ness,** *n.* being sheepish. **sheep•shank,** *n.* knot tied to make a rope shorter. **sheep•skin,** *n.* skin of a sheep with the wool attached.

sheer ['ʃɪə] 1. *adj.* (a) complete/total. (b) very steep. (c) very fine (stockings, etc.). 2. *adv.* straight up or down. 3. *v.* to swerve.

sheet [ʃiːt] *n.* (a) large piece of thin cloth which is put on a bed. (b) large flat piece (of paper/cardboard/plywood, etc.); **s. feed** = device which allows separate sheets of paper to be fed into a printer. **s. lightning** = lightning which appears as a sheet and not as a single flash. (c) rope for attaching a sail. **sheet an•chor,** *n.* large anchor used if a ship is in difficulties.

æ back, ɑː farm, ɒ top, aɪ pipe, aʊ how, aiə fire, aʊə flower, ɔː bought, ɔɪ toy, e fed, eəhair, eɪ take, ə afraid, əʊ boat, əʊə lower, ɔː word, iː heap, ɪ hit, ɪə hear, uː school, ʊ book, ʌ but, b back, d dog, ð then, dʒ just, f fog, g go, h hand, j yes, k catch, l last, m mix, n nut, ŋ sing, p penny, r round, s some, ʃ short, t too, tʃ chop, θ thing, v voice, w was, z zoo, ʒ treasure

sheik [ʃeɪk] *n.* Arab leader. **sheik•dom** ['ʃeɪkdəm] *n.* country ruled by a sheik.

shel•drake, shelduck ['ʃeldreɪk, 'ʃeldʌk] *n.* type of wild duck.

shelf [ʃelf] *n.* (*pl.* **shelves** [ʃelvz] (a) plank attached to a wall/in a cupboard on which things can be put; *inf.* **on the s.** = (i) left behind/forgotten about; (ii) not married (when all your friends are married); **s. life** = length of time food can be kept in a store before it goes bad. (b) narrow ledge of rock.

shell [ʃel] 1. *n.* (a) hard outside of some animals. (b) hard outside of an egg/a nut. (c) exterior of a car/building. (d) metal tube full of explosive fired from a gun. 2. *v.* (a) to take (peas) out of their pods/(a hardboiled egg) out of its shell. (b) to bombard with shells. **shell•fish,** *n.* (*no pl.*) sea animal with a shell (such as a crab/mussel, etc.). **shell out,** *v. inf.* to pay money. **shell shock,** *n.* illness in soldiers caused by being in battle.

shel•lac ['ʃelæk] *n.* resin used to make varnish.

shel•ter ['ʃeltə] 1. *n.* place where you can go for protection. 2. *v.* to give (s.o.) protection; to take shelter. **shel•tered,** *adj.* protected from wind/cold/unpleasant happenings.

shelve [ʃelv] 1. *v.* (a) to put off discussing a problem. (b) to slope down. (c) to put (sth) on a shelf. 2. *n. pl. see* **shelf. shelv•ing,** *n.* set of shelves.

she•nan•i•gans [ʃɪ'nænɪgənz] *n. pl. inf.* (a) mischief. (b) dishonest trick.

shep•herd ['ʃepəd] 1. *n.* man who looks after sheep; **s.'s pie** = minced meat cooked with mashed potatoes on top. 2. *v.* to guide. **shep•herd•ess,** *n.* woman who looks after sheep.

sher•bet ['ʃɜːbət] *n.* frozen dessert made with fruit juice, water and either milk or egg white.

sher•iff ['ʃerɪf] *n.* county police officer.

sher•ry ['ʃerɪ] *n.* type of strong wine, originally from Spain.

shib•bo•leth ['ʃɪbəleθ] *n.* slogan/policy formerly considered important.

shield [ʃiːld] 1. *n.* (a) large protective plate carried by riot police/knights in armor, etc. (b) protection against sth dangerous. 2. *v.* to protect.

shift [ʃɪft] 1. *n.* (a) change of place/of direction; **s. key** = key on a typewriter/computer which makes capital letters. (b) group of workers who work for a period and whose place is then taken by another group. (c) loose dress. 2. *v.* (a) to change position/direction; to move. (b) *inf.* **to s. for yourself** = to look after yourself. **shift•i•ness,** *n.* dishonesty. **shift•less,** *adj.* lazy. **shift•y,** *adj.* (-ier, -iest) looking dishonest.

shil•le•lagh [ʃɪ'leɪlɪ] *n.* (*in Ireland*) thick stick.

shil•ling ['ʃɪlɪŋ] *n.* currency used in Kenya and some other countries; old British coin worth 12 pence.

shil•ly-shal•ly ['ʃɪlɪ'ʃælɪ] *v.* to hesitate.

shim•mer ['ʃɪmə] 1. *n.* soft quivering light. 2. *v.* to quiver with light.

shin [ʃɪn] 1. *n.* front of the bottom part of your leg. 2. *v.* (shinned) **to s. up a tree** = to climb up.

shin•dig, shindy ['ʃɪndɪg, ʃɪndɪ] *n. inf.* row/noisy party.

shine [ʃaɪn] 1. *n.* (a) brightness. (b) act of polishing. 2. *v.* (shone [ʃɒn]) (a) to glint brightly. (b) to be brilliant. (c) to polish. **shin•ing,** *adj.* brilliant. **shin•y,** *adj.* (-ier, -iest) bright/polished.

shin•gle ['ʃɪŋgl] *n.* (a) mass of small stones on a beach. (b) flat piece of wood/slate, etc. nailed on a wall or roof as a covering. (c) **shingles** = disease related to chickenpox causing a painful rash. **shin•gly,** *adj.* covered with small stones.

ship [ʃɪp] 1. *n.* large boat for carrying goods/passengers. 2. *v.* (shipped) (a) to put/to take on board a ship. (b) to send (goods), not necessarily on a ship. **ship•build•er,** *n.* person who builds ships. **ship•build•ing,** *n.* building of ships. **ship•mate,** *n.* sailor on the same ship as you. **ship•ment,** *n.* (a) sending of goods. (b) quantity of goods shipped. **ship•own•er,** *n.* person who owns a ship. **ship•per,** *n.* person who sends goods. **ship•ping,** *n.* (a) sending of goods; **s. company** = which specializes in the sending of goods. (b) (group of) ships; **s. lanes** = routes across the sea which are regularly used by ships. **ship•shape,** *adj.* neat/tidy. **ship•wreck,** *n.* wrecking of a ship. **ship•wrecked,** *adj.* (person) involved in a shipwreck. **ship•yard,** *n.* works where ships are built.

shire ['ʃaɪə] *n. Brit.* county.

shirk [ʃɜːk] *v.* to try not to do sth/not to work. **shirk•er,** *n.* person who shirks.

shirr [ʃɜː] *v.* (a) to gather (cloth) by running threads through it. (b) to bake (beaten eggs).

shirt [ʃɜːt] *n.* piece of light clothing worn on the top part of the body; *inf.* **keep your s. on!** = keep calm/don't lose your temper or patience. **shirt•sleeves,** *n.* **in one's s.** = not wearing a jacket. **shirt•waist,** *n.* woman's dress where the top part looks like a shirt. **shirt•y,** *adj. inf.* angry.

shish•ke•bab ['ʃɪʃkɪbæb] *n.* small pieces of meat and vegetables cooked on a skewer.

shit [ʃɪt] 1. *n.* (*vulgar*) (a) excreta/solid waste matter from the body. (b) *Sl* dirt. (c) *Sl* nonsense. 2. *v.* (*vulgar*) to pass solid waste matter from the body.

shiv•er ['ʃɪvə] 1. *n.* tremble (with cold/fear). 2. *v.* (a) to tremble (with cold/fear/fever). (b) to break into tiny pieces. **shiv•er•y,** *adj.* trembling (esp. with fever).

shoal [ʃəʊl] *n.* (a) (*also* **shoals**) bank of sand under the water. (b) group of fish swimming about.

shock [ʃɒk] 1. *n.* (a) untidy mass (of hair). (b) sudden (unpleasant) surprise. (c) mental/physical collapse (after a blow/a sudden surprise). (d) **electric s.** = sudden painful passing of electric current through the body; **electric s. treatment** = medical treatment of mental illness using electric shocks. (e) great blow; **s. absorbers** = part of a car/aircraft which reduces the effect of bumps. 2. *v.* to give (s.o.) a sudden (unpleasant) surprise. **shock•er,** *n. inf.* shocking person/thing. **shock•head•ed,** *adj.* with a mass of hair. **shock•ing,** *adj.* upsetting/unpleasant. **shock•ing•ly,** *adv.* in a shocking way. **shock jock** *n. inf.* radio disc jockey who is intentionally outrageous. **shock•proof,** *adj.* (watch, etc.) which is not affected by shocks. **shock troops,** *n.* soldiers specially trained to attack violently.

shod [ʃɒd] *adj.* wearing shoes.

shod•dy ['ʃɒdɪ] 1. *n.* poor quality cloth. 2. *adj.* (**-ier, -iest**) (a) badly made. (b) low/nasty (trick). **shod•di•ly,** *adv.* in a shoddy way. **shod•di•ness,** *n.* bad quality.

shoe [ʃuː] 1. *n.* (a) article of clothing which you wear on your feet both inside and outside the house, not covering your ankles; **in his shoes** = in his place/in the situation he is in. (b) ring of metal nailed under a horse's hoof. (c) **brake shoes** = curved metal blocks which tighten around a wheel. 2. *v.* (**shod/shoed**) to attach metal horseshoes to the hooves of (a horse). **shoe•horn,** *n.* curved piece of plastic/metal which you put into the heel of a shoe to make it easier to put on. **shoe•lace,** *n.* lace for tying up shoes. **shoe•mak•er,** *n.* person who makes and mends shoes. **shoe•shine,** *n.* polishing of shoes. **shoe•string,** *n.* shoelace; **on a s.** = with only a little money. **shoe•tree,** *n.* device which is put in a shoe to help keep its shape.

shone [ʃɒn] *v. see* **shine.**

shoo [ʃuː] 1. *inter. meaning* go away. 2. *v.* **to s. away** = to frighten away (birds/small children, etc.).

shook [ʃʊk] *v. see* **shake.**

shoot [ʃuːt] 1. *n.* (a) new growth on a plant. (b) expedition to kill wild animals with guns; **turkey s.** 2. *v.* (**shot** [ʃɒt]) (a) to fire a bullet from a gun/an arrow from a bow; to kill (s.o./an animal) with a bullet or an arrow. (b) to rush/to go fast; **to s. the rapids** = to race through rapids in a light boat. (c) (*in sports*) to kick or throw a ball, etc.; to score (a goal). (d) to make (a motion picture). **shoot down,** *v.* to make (an aircraft) crash by hitting it with a shell. **shoot•ing.** 1. *n.* action of shooting with a gun; **s. stick** = walking stick with a handle which unfolds to make a seat. 2. *adj.* which goes very fast; **s. star** = meteor. **shoot up,** *v.* to go up fast.

shop [ʃɒp] 1. *n.* (a) store, usu. small, where you can buy goods. (b) workshop/place where goods are made; **closed s.** = works where all the workers have to belong to a single union; **to talk s.** = to talk about your job/about your office. 2. *v.* (**shopped**) to buy things in a store; **to s. around** = to go to various stores and compare prices before buying what you want. **shop•keep•er,** *n.* person who owns or runs a shop. **shop•lift•er,** *n.* person who steals things from a store. **shop•lift•ing,** *n.* stealing from a store. **shop•per,** *n.* person who buys goods from a store. **shop•ping,** *n.* (a) goods which you have bought in a store. (b) action of buying things in a store. **shop•worn,** *adj.* made dirty by being on display in a store. **shop stew•ard,** *n.* elected union representative in a factory/office, etc.

shore [ʃɔː] 1. *n.* (a) land at the edge of the sea or a lake; beach. (b) prop. 2. *v.* to hold **up** (sth) which might fall down.

shorn [ʃɔːn] *adj.* cut off; *see also* **shear.**

short [ʃɔːt] 1. *adj.* (**-er, est**) (a) not long. (b) not long in time; **in s.** = briefly. (c) not tall. (d) rude. (e) not enough/not as much as is needed (**of**); **s. weight** = not quite as much in weight as supposed. (f) light/crumbly (pastry). 2. *n.* (a) short motion picture. (b) short-circuit. (c) *pl.* **shorts** = trousers not going below the knee. 3. *adv.* (a) abruptly; **to stop s.** (b) not far enough; **to fall s.** 4. *v.* to short-circuit. **short•age,** *n.* lack. **short•bread,** *n.* thick sweet crumbly biscuit. **short•cake,** *n.* (a) shortbread. (b) dessert made with biscuits or cake with fruit and cream. **short•change,** *v.* to cheat (s.o.). **short-cir•cuit.** 1. *n.* jump of electric current between two points, missing out part of the normal circuit. 2. *v.* (a) to make a short-circuit. (b) to get through difficulties by

æ back, aː farm, ɒ top, aɪ pipe, aʊ how, aɪə fire, aʊə flower, ɔː bought, ɔɪ toy, e fed, eəhair, eɪ take, ə afraid, əʊ boat, əʊə lower, ɜː word, iː heap, ɪ hit, ɪə hear, uː school, ʊ book, ʌ but, b back, d dog, ð then, dʒ just, f fog, g go, h hand, j yes, k catch, l last, m mix, n nut, ŋ sing, p penny, r round, s some, ʃ short, t too, tʃ chop, θ thing, v voice, w was, z zoo, ʒ treasure

taking a short cut. **short•com•ing**, *n.* fault/defect. **short•cut**, *n.* way which is shorter than usual; quicker way of reaching your destination. **short•en**, *v.* to make/to become shorter. **short•en•ing**, *n.* lard/cooking fat. **short•fall**, *n.* amount which is missing to make up an expected total. **short•hand**, *n.* way of writing fast by using a system of signs. **short-hand•ed**, *adj.* not having enough workers. **short•horn**, *n.* type of cattle with short horns. **short list**, *n.* list of some of the people who have applied for a job, and who have been chosen to come for an interview. **short-list**, *v.* to make a short list of (candidates) for a job; to put (s.o.'s name) on a short list. **short-lived**, *adj.* which does not last long. **short•ly**, *adv.* (a) soon. (b) abruptly/rudely. **short•ness**, *n.* (a) state of being short. (b) rudeness. **short or•der**, *n.* food cooked on the spot in a restaurant (such as ham and eggs). **short•sight•ed**, *adj.* (a) (person) who can only see near objects. (b) not paying attention to what may happen in the future. **short•sight•ed•ness**, *n.* being shortsighted. **short-sleeved**, *adj.* (shirt, etc.) with short sleeves. **short-staffed**, *adj.* with not enough workers. **short-tem•pered**, *adj.* (person) who easily gets angry. **short-term**, *adj.* not lasting long. **short time**, *n.* shorter working hours than usual. **short wave**, *n.* radio wave about 50 meters long.

shot [ʃɒt] 1. *adj.* (silk) which changes color according to the light. 2. *n.* (a) (*no pl.*) small pellets/bullets fired from a gun. (b) large heavy ball thrown in a competition; **to put the s.** = throw the weight in a competition. (c) act of shooting; the sound of shooting; **like a s.** = very rapidly. (d) person who shoots. (e) *inf.* attempt. (f) *Sl.* injection. (g) *Sl.* small drink of alcohol. (h) *inf.* photograph. *see also* **shoot**. **shot•gun**, *n.* gun which fires small pellets.

should [ʃʊd] *v. used to show certain moods.* (a) ought; **they s. have arrived by now** = they ought to have arrived. (b) must; **why s. I be the one to go?** = why must I be the one? (c) **who s. we meet but my aunt** = what a surprise we had when we met my aunt. (d) (*tentative suggestion*) **s. I try again?** (e) (*future after* that) **it is strange that he s. want to go.**

shoul•der ['ʃəʊldə] 1. *n.* (a) part of the body at the top of the arm/between the top of the arm and the neck. (b) part of a piece of clothing between the top of the arm and the neck. (c) top part of the front leg of an animal. (d) reinforced side part of a road. 2. *v.* (a) to put on your shoulder. (b) to push with your shoulder. (c) to take on (a burden). **shoulder bag**, *n.* bag which can be carried over the shoulder.

shoul•der blade, *n.* large flat bone in the shoulder.

shout [ʃaʊt] 1. *n.* loud cry. 2. *v.* to make a loud cry; **to s. s.o. down** = to shout so loudly that s.o. cannot speak.

shove [ʃʌv] 1. *n. inf.* sharp push. 2. *v. inf.* to give a push to. **shove off**, *v. inf.* to go away.

shov•el ['ʃʌvl] 1. *n.* tool with a wide blade and a long handle, used for lifting dirt, snow, etc. 2. *v.* (**shoveled, shovelled**) to lift up with a shovel. **shov•el•ful**, *n.* contents of a shovel. **shov•el•er**, *n.* wild duck with a wide flat beak.

show [ʃəʊ] 1. *n.* (a) exhibition/display. (b) performance; **s. business** = actors/actresses/producers etc. (considered as a group); the entertainment world. (c) pretense. 2. *v.* (**shown**) (a) to make (sth) seen; to allow s.o. to see (sth); to be seen. (b) to indicate. (c) to point out/to direct. (d) to prove/to demonstrate. **show•case**, *n.* case or box with a glass front or a glass top for putting things on show in a store or museum. **show•down**, *n.* final argument which will solve a crisis. **show•i•ly**, *adv.* in a showy way. **show•i•ness**, *n.* being showy. **show-jump•er**, *n.* horse specially trained for show-jumping. **show-jump•ing**, *n.* riding competition where horses have to jump over different obstacles in a short time. **show•man**, *n.* (*pl.* **-men**) person who puts on shows (such as circuses, etc.); person who is good at presenting things. **show•man•ship**, *n.* art of putting on attractive shows. **show off**, *v.* (a) to display (sth) to great effect. (b) to try to make people look at you by doing sth which will attract their attention. **show-off**, *n. inf.* person who shows off. **show•piece**, *n.* important item in an exhibition. **show•room**, *n.* room where goods are shown to customers. **show up**, *v.* (a) to reveal/to show (s.o.'s/sth's faults). (b) to stand out. (c) *inf.* to arrive. **show•y**, *adj.* (**-ier, -iest**) too bright (colors); too ostentatious.

show•er ['ʃaʊə] 1. *n.* (a) light fall of rain/small stones, etc. (b) (*also* **showerhead**) spray device in a bathroom for washing your whole body. (c) (*also* **shower bath**) bath taken in a spray of water from above. (d) party where presents are given to a girl about to get married. 2. *v.* (a) (*also* **shower down**) to pour/to fall in a quantity. (b) to wash under a spray. **show•er•proof**, *adj.* (coat) which can protect against light rain. **shower stall**, *n.* separate unit with a shower in it. **show•er•y**, *adj.* with many showers.

shrank [ʃræŋk] *v. see* **shrink**.

shrap•nel ['ʃræpnl] *n.* (*no pl.*) pieces of metal from an exploded shell or bomb, etc.

shred [ʃred] 1. *n.* (a) long strip torn off sth. (b) small piece. 2. *v.* (**shredded**) to tear into long strips; to cut into very thin strips. **shred•der**, *n.* machine for tearing waste paper into long strips; device for cutting vegetables into long thin strips.

shrew [ʃruː] *n.* (a) animal like a mouse with a long nose. (b) unpleasant bad-tempered woman who is always criticizing. **shrew•ish**, *adj.* bad-tempered (woman).

shrewd [ʃruːd] *adj.* (**-er, -est**) clever/wise. **shrewd•ly**, *adv.* in a shrewd way. **shrewd•ness**, *n.* being shrewd.

shriek [ʃriːk] 1. *n.* loud high-pitched cry. 2. *v.* to make a shriek.

shrift [ʃrɪft] *n.* **to get short s.** = to be treated curtly.

shrike [ʃraɪk] *n.* bird which pins insects to spines before eating them.

shrill [ʃrɪl] *adj.* (**-er, -est**) high-pitched. **shril•ly**, *adv.* in a shrill way. **shrill•ness**, *n.* being shrill.

shrimp [ʃrɪmp] *n.* (a) small shellfish with a long tail. (b) *inf.* small person. **shrimp•ing**, *n.* fishing for shrimps.

shrine [ʃraɪn] *n.* tomb/chapel where a saint is buried.

shrink [ʃrɪŋk] 1. *n. Sl.* psychiatrist. 2. *v.* (**shrank; shrunk**) (a) to make smaller; to get smaller. (b) to move back (**from**). **shrink•age**, *n.* action of shrinking; amount by which sth shrinks.

shriv•el [ˈʃrɪvl] *v.* (**shriveled, shrivelled**) to make/to become dry and wrinkled.

shroud [ʃraʊd] 1. *n.* (a) long cloth covering a dead body. (b) **shrouds** = ropes from a mast to the sides of a ship. 2. *v.* to cover up.

Shrove Tues•day [ˈʃrəʊvˈtjuːzdeɪ] *n.* the Tuesday before Lent.

shrub [ʃrʌb] *n.* small bush. **shrub•ber•y**, *n.* planting of shrubs.

shrug [ʃrʌg] 1. *n.* raising the shoulders to show you are not interested. 2. *v.* (**shrugged**) **to s. your shoulders** = to raise your shoulders to show you are not interested. **shrug off**, *v.* to treat (sth) as if it is not a cause of worry.

shrunk [ʃrʌŋk] *v. see* **shrink.**

shrunk•en [ˈʃrʌŋkən] *adj.* wrinkled; dried up.

shuck [ʃʌk] 1. *n.* shell/outer covering. 2. *v.* to take the shell off (sth).

shud•der [ˈʃʌdə] 1. *n.* tremble of horror. 2. *v.* to tremble with horror.

shuf•fle [ˈʃʌfl] *v.* (a) to walk dragging your feet. (b) to mix (playing cards). **shuf•fle**

play, *n.* function on a CD player that randomly selects and plays tracks from any of several loaded CDs.

shun [ʃʌn] *v.* (**shunned**) to avoid.

shunt [ʃʌnt] *v.* to move (a train) into a siding; to move (s.o.) to the side; get out of the way.

shush [ʃuʃ] *inf. inter. meaning* be quiet.

shut [ʃʌt] *v.* (**shut**) (a) to close. (b) to lock up (sth) so that it cannot escape. (c) to close for business. **shut down**, *v.* to make (a factory) stop working. **shut•down**, *n.* closure of a factory. **shut•eye**, *n. inf.* sleep. **shut in**, *v.* to lock inside; to surround. **shut off**, *v.* to switch off (an engine/the water supply, etc.). **shut out**, *v.* (a) to block. (b) to lock (s.o.) outside. **shut•ter**, *n.* (a) folding wooden/metal cover which covers a window. (b) (*in camera*) part which opens and closes very rapidly to allow the light to go on to the film. **shut•tered**, *adj.* with shutters. **shut up**, *v.* (a) to close. (b) *inf.* to be quiet; to make (s.o.) be quiet.

shut•tle [ˈʃʌtl] 1. *n.* part of a loom which carries the thread from side to side; **s. service** = bus/plane which goes backward and forward between two places; **s. diplomacy** = action of a diplomat going backward and forward between two countries to try to make them reach agreement. 2. *v.* to go backward and forward; to send (s.o.) backward and forward. **shut•tle•cock**, *n.* light ball with feathers stuck in it, which is hit in badminton.

shy [ʃaɪ] 1. *adj.* timid/afraid to do sth. 2. *n.* throwing (of a ball). 3. *v.* (a) to throw. (b) (*of horse*) to jump with fear. **shy•ly**, *adv.* timidly. **shy•ness**, *n.* being shy. **shy•ster**, *n. Sl.* dishonest businessman.

SI *abbrev. for* Système International, the international system of units for measuring physical properties, such as weight, speed, heat, etc.

Si•a•mese [saɪəˈmiːz] *adj.* referring to Siam; **S. twins** = twins born with parts of their bodies joined together; **S. cat** = type of cat with pale fawn fur, dark brown face and blue eyes.

sib•i•lant [ˈsɪbɪlənt] *adj. & n.* (sound) like a hiss.

sib•ling [ˈsɪblɪŋ] *n.* brother or sister.

sic [sɪk] *adv.* this (used to indicate a mistake).

sick [sɪk] *adj.* (a) ill/not well; **s. leave** = time off work because of illness. (b) vomiting; feeling ready to vomit. (c) (**of**) showing disgust/dislike. **sick•bay**, *n.* hospital ward (esp. on a ship). **sick•bed**, *n.* bed where a sick person is lying. **sick•en,** v. to make or become ill. **sick•en•ing,** adj. which makes you sick. **sick•ly,** adj. (-ier, -iest) not well; weak. **sick•ness,** n. (a) illness. (b) feeling of being about to vomit. **sick pay,** n. wages paid to s.o. who is ill and cannot work. **sick•room,** n. room where a sick person is in bed.

sick•le ['sɪkl] n. tool with a semicircular blade, used for cutting corn.

side [saɪd] 1. n. (a) edge; area near the edge; **on the s.** = (i) apart from one's usual job; (ii) dishonestly. (b) one of four parts which (with the top and bottom) make a box, etc.; wall (of a house). (c) part of the body between the hips and the shoulder; **s. by s.** = close together (in a row). (d) surface. (e) slope (of a mountain); surface/part. (f) team. (g) group holding a particular point of view; **to take sides** = to support one party or another in a quarrel. (h) family connection. 2. adj. (a) secondary/less important (road, etc.). (b) at the side (not the front or back). 3. v. **to s. with s.o.** = to support s.o. in an argument. **side•board,** n. piece of dining room furniture with shelves and drawers for holding plates, etc. **side•burns,** n. short whiskers down the side of a person's face. **side•car,** n. small compartment for one passenger attached to the side of a motorcycle. **side ef•fects,** n. secondary and unexpected effects (as of a drug). **side is•sue,** n. secondary problem. **side•kick,** n. inf. companion/helper. **side•light,** n. (a) incidental information. (b) small light, as on the side of a boat. **side•line,** n. (a) business which is extra to your normal work. (b) pl. **sidelines** = lines at the edge of a football field, tennis court, etc. **side•long,** adj. from one side. **side•sad•dle,** adv. (of woman) (to ride) with both legs on the same side of the horse. **side•show,** n. small show in addition to the main show, as at a circus. **side•step,** v. (side-stepped) to avoid. **side•swipe,** v. inf. (of car) to hit another vehicle in passing. **side•track,** v. to attract s.o.'s attention away from the main problem. **side•walk,** n. path at the side of a road, usu. paved. **side•ward, side-wards,** adv. to the side. **side•ways,** adv. to the side; with the side in front. **side•whisk•ers,** n. pl. long whiskers down the side of a person's face. **sid•ing,** n. minor railroad line where trains are kept until needed.

si•de•re•al [saɪ'dɪərɪəl] adj. referring to the stars.

si•dle ['saɪdl] v. to walk sideways, not directly forward.

siege [siːdʒ] n. act of surrounding an enemy town with an army to make it surrender.

si•en•na [sɪ'enə] n. **burnt s.** = reddish-brown color; **raw s.** = yellowish-brown color.

si•es•ta [sɪ'estə] n. afternoon rest.

sieve [sɪv] 1. n. kitchen utensil with very small holes for passing liquid through to hold back lumps/for sorting out large pieces in flour, sugar, etc. 2. v. to pass (a liquid/a powder) through a sieve to sort out large lumps.

sift [sɪft] v. (a) to sieve. (b) to examine carefully. **sift•er,** n. container with small holes in the lid for sprinkling sugar or flour.

sigh [saɪ] 1. n. deep breath, showing sadness/relief, etc. 2. v. to breathe deeply showing sadness, relief, etc.

sight [saɪt] 1. n. (a) one of the five senses, the ability to see. (b) glimpse; act of seeing. (c) range of vision. (d) spectacle; thing which you ought to see. (e) funny/odd thing. (f) part of a gun through which you look to take aim. (g) inf. **a s. more** = a lot more. 2. v. (a) to see for the first time. (b) to aim a gun. **sight•less,** adj. blind. **sight-read,** v. to play written music without having practiced it. **sight•see•ing,** n. visiting the sights of a place. **sight•se•er,** n. tourist/person seeing the sights of a place.

sign [saɪn] 1. n. (a) movement (of hand/head, etc.) which means sth; **s. language** = signs of the hands used by deaf and dumb people to communicate. (b) mark. (c) indication/thing which suggests that sth may happen. (d) trace. (e) board advertising the name of a product, store, service, etc.; plate or board giving information, directions, warning, etc. 2. v. (a) to write your signature at the end of (a letter or on a document, etc.). (b) to make a movement which has a meaning. **sign a•way,** v. to give up possession of (sth) by signing a document. **sign•board,** n. board with a sign. **sign off,** v. to end a letter/a radio broadcast. **sign on,** v. to join the armed services for a period; to start work. **sign•post,** 1. n. post with a sign showing directions to a place. 2. v. to indicate a direction with signs. **sign up,** v. (a) to join the armed services for a period. (b) to volunteer or register for sth.

sig•nal ['sɪgnl] 1. n. (a) movement of the hand/head, etc., which tells s.o. to do sth. (b) lights/mechanical flags, etc., used to announce or warn of sth. (c) sound heard on a radio receiver. 2. adj. (formal) remarkable. 3. v. (**signaled, signalled**) to make signs to tell s.o. to do sth. **sign•al•er,** n. person who signals. **sig•nal•ly,** adv. (formal) remarkably. **sig•nal•man,** n. (pl. **-men**) person who controls railroad signals.

sig•na•to•ry ['sɪgnətrɪ] n. person who signs (a treaty, etc.).

sig•na•ture ['sɪgnətʃə] n. (a) name which has

been signed. (b) group of pages of a book (usually 32 or 64) which are folded out of one sheet of paper. (c) **s. tune** = theme song.

sig•net ['sɪgnɪt] *n.* seal (for sealing with wax); **s. ring** = ring worn on the little finger with a design carved on to it to use as a seal.

sig•ni•fy ['sɪgnɪfaɪ] *v.* (a) to mean. (b) to show; make known. (c) to be of importance. **sig•nif•i•cance,** *n.* (a) meaning. (b) importance. **sig•nif•i•cant,** *adj.* which is important/which has a lot of meaning. **sig•nif•i•cant•ly,** *adv.* in a significant way. **sig•ni•fi•ca•tion,** *n.* meaning.

si•lage ['saɪlɪdʒ] *n.* green crops fermented in a silo and used to feed animals.

si•lence ['saɪləns] 1. *n.* (a) lack of noise. (b) not saying anything. 2. *v.* (a) to make (s.o.) stop talking. (b) to stop (sth) making a noise. **si•lenc•er,** *n.* apparatus attached to a gun to stop the noise of it being fired. **si•lent,** *adj.* quiet. **si•lent•ly,** *adv.* in a silent way.

sil•hou•ette [sɪluː'et] 1. *n.* black outline of s.o.'s head or sth in profile. 2. *v.* to stand out in profile.

sil•i•ca ['sɪlɪkə] *n.* mineral compound of silicon. **sil•i•ca gel,** *n.* hard crystals used to keep things dry in humid conditions. **sil•i•cate,** *n.* common silicon compound.

sil•i•con ['sɪlɪkən] *n.* (*element:* Si) common element which is not a metal, and which is usu. found in compounds; **s. chip** = small piece of silicon used in transistors and very small electronic devices.

sil•i•cone ['sɪlɪkəʊn] *n.* chemical substance used in making oils.

sil•i•co•sis [sɪlɪ'kəʊsɪs] *n.* disease of the lungs caused by breathing in dust.

silk [sɪlk] *n.* thread which is produced by a caterpillar; cloth woven from this thread. **silk•en,** *adj.* soft and shiny. **silk•screen pro•cess,** *n.* method of printing by forcing colors through a taut piece of cloth. **silk•worm,** *n.* caterpillar which produces silk. **silk•y,** *adj.* soft and shiny.

sill [sɪl] *n.* ledge beneath a window/a door.

sil•ly ['sɪlɪ] *adj.* (-ier, -iest) stupid/idiotic. **sil•li•ness,** *n.* being silly.

si•lo ['saɪləʊ] *n.* (*pl.* -os) (a) large tower for storing grain/for storing green crops (as food for animals). (b) deep hole in the ground in which rockets are kept.

silt [sɪlt] 1. *n.* fine mud washed down by a river. 2. *v.* **to s. up** = to fill with silt.

sil•ver ['sɪlvə] *n.* (a) (*element:* Ag) precious white metal; **s. jubilee** = 25th anniversary of an important event; **s. wedding** = anniversary of 25 years of marriage. (b) **s. foil** = sheet of thin shiny metal which looks like silver, used for wrapping food in. (c) coins made of white metal. (d) light shining color like silver. **sil•ver birch,** *n.* common northern tree with white bark. **sil•ver•fish,** *n.* small silvery insect found in kitchens, etc. **sil•ver•smith,** *n.* craftsman who makes things in silver. **sil•ver•ware,** *n.* (*no pl.*) articles made of silver. **sil•ver•y,** *adj.* (a) shiny like silver. (b) light ringing (sound).

sim•i•an ['sɪmɪən] *adj.* like a monkey.

sim•i•lar ['sɪmɪlə] *adj.* very alike but not quite the same. **sim•i•lar•ly,** *adv.* in a similar way. **sim•i•lar•i•ty,** *n.* sameness/likeness.

sim•i•le ['sɪmɪlɪ] *n.* comparison using "like" or "as".

sim•mer ['sɪmə] *v.* to boil gently; **to s. down** = to become calmer.

sim•per ['sɪmpə] 1. *n.* silly affected smile. 2. *v.* to say with a simper.

sim•ple ['sɪmpl] *adj.* (-er, -est) (a) not complicated; not difficult. (b) *inf.* not very intelligent. (c) **s. interest** = interest calculated on the original sum without adding each year's interest to the capital. (d) plain/ordinary. **sim•ple•mind•ed,** *adj.* not very intelligent. **sim•ple•ton,** *n.* person who is not very intelligent. **sim•plic•i•ty** [sɪm'plɪsɪtɪ] *n.* being simple. **sim•pli•fi•ca•tion** [sɪmplɪfɪ'keɪʃn] *n.* making simple. **sim•pli•fy** ['sɪmplɪfaɪ] *v.* to make (sth) simple. **sim•ply,** *adv.* (a) without complication. (b) absolutely. (c) purely/only.

sim•u•late ['sɪmjuleɪt] *v.* to pretend. **sim•u•la•tion** [sɪmju'leɪʃn] *n.* pretense. **sim•u•la•tor** ['sɪmjuleɪtə] *n.* machine which allows a learner to experience simulated conditions (as in a car/aircraft, etc.).

si•mul•ta•ne•ous [sɪməl'teɪnɪəs] *adj.* happening at the same time. **si•mul•ta•ne•ous•ly,** *adv.* at the same time.

sin [sɪn] 1. *n.* wicked deed; action which goes against the rules of religion; **to live in s.** = to live together without being married. 2. *v.* (sinned) to do sth wicked/wrong. **sin•ful,** *adj.* wicked (person/action). **sin•ner,** *n.* person who has sinned.

since [sɪns] 1. *adv.* from then onward. 2. *prep.*

from a certain time. 3. *conj.* (a) from a certain time. (b) because.

sin•cere [sɪn'sɪə] *adj.* very honest/open. **sin•cere•ly**, *adv.* really/truly; **s. yours** = greeting written at the end of a letter. **sin•cer•i•ty** [sɪn'serɪtɪ] *n.* honesty.

sine [saɪn] *n.* (*in mathematics*) ratio between the length of one of the shorter sides opposite an acute angle to that of the hypotenuse in a right-angled triangle.

si•ne•cure ['saɪnɪkjʊə] *n.* job for which you get paid but which does not involve much work.

si•ne di•e ['sɪneɪdɪeɪ] *adv.* to a later date, which is unspecified.

si•ne qua non ['sɪneɪkwɑː'nɒn] *n.* condition without which something cannot function.

sin•ew ['sɪnjuː] *n.* strong cord which joins a muscle to a bone. **sin•ew•y**, *adj.* very strong.

sing [sɪŋ] *v.* (**sang, sung**) (a) to make music with your mouth. (b) to make a buzzing noise. **sing•er**, *n.* person who sings. **sing•song**, *adj.* (voice) with a rising and falling tone.

singe ['sɪndʒ] *v.* to burn slightly.

sin•gle ['sɪŋgl] 1. *adj.* (a) alone/one by itself. (b) for one person. (c) unmarried. 2. *n.* (a) **singles** = tennis game played between two people. (b) small phonograph record with only one piece of music on each side. 3. *v.* **to s. out** = to select. **sin•gle-breast•ed**, *adj.* (coat) which does not fold over widely in the front to button. **sin•gle-hand•ed**, *adj.* all by yourself. **sin•gle-mind•ed**, *adj.* thinking only of one aim. **sin•gle-mind•ed•ness**, *n.* being single-minded. **sin•gle•ness**, *n.* (a) being single. (b) **s. of purpose** = having only one aim. **sin•gly**, *adv.* one by one.

sin•gu•lar ['sɪŋgjʊlə] 1. *adj. & n.* referring to one person/thing. 2. *adj.* (a) odd/peculiar. (b) remarkable. **sin•gu•lar•i•ty** [sɪŋgjʊ'lærɪtɪ] *n.* oddness/peculiarity. **sin•gu•lar•ly**, *adv.* (a) strangely. (b) particularly.

sin•is•ter ['sɪnɪstə] *adj.* looking evil; which promises evil.

sink [sɪŋk] 1. *n.* (a) basin for washing as in a kitchen. (b) place where substances pass to be absorbed out of the atmosphere. 2. *v.* (**sank; sunk**) (a) to (cause to) go to the bottom of water/mud, etc. (b) to go down. (c) to make (a well). (d) **to s. your teeth into** = to bite. (e) to invest. **sink•er**, *n.* lead weight used to pull down a fishing line into the water. **sink in**, *v.* to become fixed in the mind.

Sino- ['saɪnəʊ] *prefix meaning* Chinese/between China and another country.

sin•u•ous ['sɪnjʊəs] *adj.* winding. **sin•u•os•i•ty** [sɪnjʊ'ɒsɪtɪ] *n.* (a) being sinuous. (b) bend (in a pipe or road).

si•nus ['saɪnəs] *n.* (*pl.* **-es**) hole in the bones of the head connected with the nose and air passages. **si•nus•i•tis** [saɪnə'saɪtɪs] *n.* infection of the sinuses.

sip [sɪp] 1. *n.* small quantity of liquid. 2. *v.* (**sipped**) to drink taking only a small quantity at a time.

si•phon ['saɪfn] 1. *n.* (a) device for aerating water. (b) bent tube to allow you to take liquid from one container to another placed at a lower level. 2. *v.* (a) to remove (liquid) by using a siphon. (b) to remove (money) from a source illegally.

sir [sɜː] *n.* (a) respectful way of addressing a man (usu. an older or more important man). (b) title given to a knight or baronet. (c) way of addressing a man in a formal letter.

sire ['saɪə] 1. *n.* (a) male horse which is a father. (b) (*old*) Sire = way of addressing a king. 2. *v.* (*of a horse*) to be father of.

si•ren ['saɪrən] *n.* loud warning signal which wails.

sir•loin ['sɜːlɔɪn] *n.* best cut of beef from the back of the animal.

si•sal ['saɪsl] *n.* rope made from fibers from a tropical plant.

sis•kin ['sɪskɪn] *n.* small finch.

sis•sy ['sɪsɪ] *n.* weak girlish man/boy.

sis•ter ['sɪstə] 1. *n.* (a) female child whose parents are the same as yours. (b) nun; title given to nuns. 2. *adj.* similar/identical; **s. ship** = ship of the same design. **sis•ter•hood**, *n.* state of being a sister. **sis•ter-in-law**, *n.* (*pl.* **sisters-**) wife of your brother; sister of your husband or wife. **sis•ter•ly**, *adj.* like a sister.

sit [sɪt] *v.* (**sat**) (a) to be seated; to make (s.o.) be seated; to rest in a seated position with your behind on a chair/on the ground, etc.; **to s. for your portrait** = to pose (not necessarily in a seated position). (b) to be in session/to meet. (c) to be a member of. (d) (*of bird*) to sit on her eggs. **sit back**, *v.* to be seated and lean backward. **sit down**, *v.* to take a seat. **sit-down**, *adj.* (a) **sit-down dinner** = meal where you sit at a table. (b) **sit-down strike** = strike where workers do not move from their place of work. **sit-in**, *n.* occupation of a place, as by workers/students, etc. **sit on**, *v.* (a) to be a member of (a committee). (b) *inf.* to delay (a request). **sit•ter**, *n.* person who sits/poses for a painter; **baby-sitter** = person who looks after a child when its parents are out. **sit tight**, *v.* to stay where you are/to refuse to move. **sit•ting**, *n.* act of sitting; session. **sit•ting-room**, *n.* small living room. **sit up**, *v.* (a) to straighten yourself on your chair. (b) to stay up/not to go to bed.

site [saɪt] 1. *n.* (a) place where a building/town is situated. (b) place where an event took place.

(c) Internet location devoted to a particular subject. 2. *v.* to place (a building/town) on a particular piece of land.

sit•u•ate ['sɪtjueɪt] *v.* to place. **sit•u•a•tion** [sɪtjuˈeɪʃn] *n.* (a) place where a building is. (b) state of affairs. (c) job.

sitz bath ['sɪtsbɑːθ] *n.* small low bath in which a person can sit, but not lie down.

six [sɪks] *n.* number 6; *inf.* **they're all at sixes and sevens** = they're very disorganized/they can't agree. **six•teen,** *n.* number 16. **six•teenth, 16th,** *adj. & n.* referring to sixteen. **sixth, 6th,** *adj. & n.* referring to six. **six•ti•eth, 60th,** *adj. & n.* referring to sixty. **six•ty,** *n.* number 60; **she's in her sixties** = she is aged between 60 and 69.

size [saɪz] 1. *n.* (a) largeness of sth. (b) measurements. (c) type of pastelike glue. 2. *v.* (a) **to s. s.o. up** = to judge s.o.'s capabilities. (b) to cover with glue. **size•a•ble,** *adj.* quite large.

siz•zle ['sɪzl] *v.* to make a hissing sound when frying; *inf.* to be very hot.

skate [skeɪt] 1. *n.* (a) (*pl.* **skate**) large flat fish with white flesh. (b) sharp blade under boots worn for gliding on ice. 2. *v.* to glide on ice wearing skates. **skate•board,** *n.* board with two pairs of wheels which you stand on to glide about. **skat•er,** *n.* person who goes skating.

ske•dad•dle [skɪˈdædl] *v. inf.* to go quickly.

skein [skeɪn] *n.* length of wool loosely wound around and around into a loop.

skel•e•ton ['skelɪtn] *n.* (a) bones inside a body; **s. in the closet** = secret that a family or person is trying to keep hidden. (b) **s. staff** = few staff left to carry on essential work while the others are away. (c) **s. key** = key which will fit any lock in a building. (d) rough outline. **skel•e•tal,** *adj.* like a skeleton.

skep [skep] *n.* straw beehive.

skep•tic ['skeptɪk] *n.* (a) person who doubts the truth of religion. (b) person who always doubts the truth of what he is told. **skep•ti•cal,** *adj.* doubtful/(person) who doubts. **skep•ti•cal•ly,** *adv.* doubtfully/distrustfully. **skep•ti•cism,** *n.* doubt/uncertainty.

sketch [sketʃ] 1. *n.* (*pl.* -es) (a) rough drawing. (b) short amusing play. 2. *v.* to make a rough drawing/a rough plan of. **sketch•book,** *n.* book of drawing paper for sketching. **sketch•i•ly,** *adv.* in a sketchy way. **sketch•i•ness,** *n.* being sketchy. **sketch**

map, *n.* roughly drawn map. **sketch pad,** *n.* pad of paper for sketching. **sketch•y,** *adj.* (-ier, -iest) rough/incomplete.

skew [skjuː] *adj.* not straight.

skew•bald ['skjuːbɔːld] *adj.* (horse) with patches of white with another color, but not black.

skew•er ['skjuə] 1. *n.* long thin metal rod for putting through pieces of meat when cooking. 2. *v.* to stick a long metal rod through (sth).

ski [skiː] 1. *n.* long flat narrow piece of wood, etc., which you attach under your boot for moving over snow; **water skis** = similar pieces of wood for gliding over water. 2. *v.* to travel on skis; **to go skiing** = to travel on skis as a sport. **ski boots,** *n. pl.* special boots for skiing. **ski•er,** *n.* person traveling on skis. **ski jump,** *n.* slope with a sudden drop at the bottom to allow a skier to jump high in the air. **ski lift,** *n.* device to take skiers to the top of a slope.

skid [skɪd] 1. *n.* sliding sideways. (b) plank for sliding heavy objects along. 2. *v.* (**skidded**) to slide sideways in a vehicle with the wheels not gripping the surface.

skiff [skɪf] *n.* light sailboat or rowboat.

skill [skɪl] *n.* cleverness/ability to do something. **skill•ful,** *adj.* clever/very able. **skill•ful•ly,** *adv.* in a skillful way. **skilled,** *adj.* having/requiring a particular skill.

skil•let ['skɪlɪt] *n.* frying pan.

skim [skɪm] *v.* (**skimmed**) (a) to remove things floating on the surface of (a liquid). (b) to dash over the surface of sth; **to s. through a book** = to read a book quickly.

skimp [skɪmp] *v.* (a) to do a job badly. (b) not to give enough of; **they s. on food** = they don't spend much money of food. **skimp•y,** *adj.* (-ier, -iest) insufficient (meal); tight/short (clothes).

skin [skɪn] 1. *n.* (a) outer surface of an animal's body; **by the s. of their teeth** = only just. (b) outer surface. 2. *v.* (**skinned**) to remove the skin of. **skin-deep,** *adj.* on the surface/superficial. **skin div•er,** *n.* person who goes skin diving. **skin div•ing,** *n.* sport of swimming underwater with breathing apparatus but without special clothing. **skin•flint,** *n.* miser. **skin•ny,** *adj.* (-ier, -iest) *inf.* thin. **skin•tight,** *adj.* (clothes) which are close-fitting.

skip [skɪp] 1. *n.* act of skipping. 2. *v.* (**skipped**) (a) to jump over a rope; to run along half hop-

---

æ back, ɑː farm, ɒ top, aɪ pipe, aʊ how, aɪə fire, aʊə flower, ɔː bought, ɔɪ toy, e fed, eə hair, eɪ take, ə afraid, əʊ boat, əʊə lower, ɜː word, iː heap, ɪ hit, ɪə hear, uː school, ʊ book, ʌ but, b back, d dog, ð then, dʒ just, f fog, g go, h hand, j yes, k catch, l last, m mix, n nut, ŋ sing, p penny, r round, s some, ʃ short, t too, tʃ chop, θ thing, v voice, w was, z zoo, ʒ treasure

ping and half jumping. (b) to miss out (part of a book).

skip•per ['skɪpə] 1. *n.* captain (of a ship/of a team). 2. *v.* to be the captain of (a team).

skirl [skɜːl] *n.* wailing sound made by bagpipes.

skir•mish ['skɜːmɪʃ] *n.* (*pl.* **-es**) slight battle between opposite sides.

skirt [skɜːt] 1. *n.* piece of woman's clothing covering the lower part of the body from the waist to the knees or ankles. 2. *v.* to go around/to avoid going through or dealing with.

skit [skɪt] *n.* short humorous play/story.

skit•tish ['skɪtɪʃ] *adj.* (*of horse, etc.*) liable to jump about unexpectedly.

skit•tle ['skɪtl] *n.* bottle-shaped wooden object used with a ball in a game.

sku•a ['skjuːə] *n.* type of large sea bird.

skul•dug•ger•y [skʌl'dʌgərɪ] *n. inf.* deceitful or dishonest actions; trickery.

skulk [skʌlk] *v.* (a) to hide away (because you are planning sth wicked). (b) to creep about mysteriously.

skull [skʌl] *n.* bony part of the head. **skull•cap**, *n.* tight-fitting small round hat.

skunk [skʌŋk] *n.* American mammal with black and white fur, which produces a bad smell when frightened or attacked.

sky [skaɪ] *n.* area above the earth which is blue during the day, and where the moon and stars appear at night. **sky-blue**, *adj. & n.* bright light blue (color). **sky di•ver**, *n.* person who jumps from an aircraft, and falls freely for some time before opening his parachute. **sky-high**, *adv.* as high as the sky; very high; **to blow sth sky-high** = to blow sth up with a powerful explosive. **sky•lark**, 1. *n.* small singing bird which sings as it flies upward. 2. *v.* to play; frolic. **sky•light**, *n.* window in a roof or ceiling. **sky•line**, *n.* horizon; shape of buildings silhouetted against the sky. **sky•scrap•er**, *n.* very tall building.

slab [slæb] *n.* thick flat rectangular block.

slack [slæk] 1. *adj.* (**-er, -est**) (a) not taut/not tight. (b) not busy. (c) lazy/not working well. 2. *n.* (a) looseness; loose part of a rope. (b) very small pieces of coal. (c) **slacks** = trousers. 3. *v.* **to s. (off)** = to be lazy/to do less work. **slack•en**, *v.* (a) to loosen. (b) **to s. off** = to work less. **slack•er**, *n.* person who doesn't work hard. **slack•ly**, *adv.* (a) loosely. (b) lazily. **slack•ness**, *n.* being slack.

slag [slæg] *n.* waste material left after metal has been extracted from ore; **s. heap** = mountain of slag left near a metal works or coalmine.

slain [sleɪn] *v. see* **slay.**

slake [sleɪk] *v.* (a) **to s. your thirst** = to drink to remove your thirst. (b) to mix lime with water.

sla•lom ['slɑːləm] *n.* race in skiing, where you have to ski fast between a series of posts.

slam [slæm] 1. *n.* (a) banging of a door. (b) **grand s.** = winning all the card games in a competition. 2. *v.* (**slammed**) (a) to bang. (b) *inf.* to criticize very unfavorably.

slan•der ['slɑːndə] 1. *n.* untrue thing said about a person which hurts his reputation; crime of saying such things. 2. *v.* to say untrue things about a person. **slan•der•ous**, *adj.* (statement) which is slander.

slang [slæŋ] *n.* words or phrases used by certain groups of people in popular speech which are not used in correct or written language. **slang•y**, *adj. inf.* using slang.

slant [slɑːnt] 1. *n.* (a) slope; **on the s.** = sloping. (b) point of view. 2. *v.* (a) to slope. (b) to show (news or information) in a biased way. **slant•ing**, *adj.* sloping. **slant•wise, slantways**, *adv.* at an angle; on a slope.

slap [slæp] 1. *n.* smack with your hand flat. 2. *v.* **slapped**) (a) to hit with your hand flat. (b) to bring (sth) down flat on to a surface; **to s. down** = criticize sharply. 3. *adv.* **to run s. into the wall** = right into the wall. **slap•dash**, *adj.* careless. **slap•hap•py**, *adj. inf.* happily careless. **slap•stick**, *adj. & n.* rough (comedy) which depends on physical jokes.

slash [slæʃ] 1. *n.* (*pl.* **-es**) long cut. 2. *v.* (a) to make a long cut. (b) to shorten; to reduce (a price) drastically.

slat [slæt] *n.* thin flat piece of wood. **slat•ted**, *adj.* made of slats.

slate [sleɪt] 1. *n.* (a) dark-gray stone which splits into thin sheets; piece of this stone used as a roof covering or for writing on; **to start a clean s.** = to start again (without any faults held against you). (b) group of candidates in an election. 2. *v. inf.* to criticize severely; censure. **slate gray**, *adj. & n.* very dark blue-gray (color).

slat•tern ['slætən] *n.* dirty woman. **slat•tern•ly**, *adj.* (*of a woman*) dirty.

slaugh•ter ['slɔːtə] 1. *n.* (a) killing of animals for meat. (b) killing of people (in war). 2. *v.* (a) to kill (animals) for meat. (b) to kill (many people) in war. **slaugh•ter•house**, *n.* place where animals are slaughtered.

slave [sleɪv] 1. *n.* person who belongs to and works for s.o. 2. *v.* (*also* **slave away**) to work hard. **slave driv•er**, *n. inf.* employer who makes his workers work very hard. **slav•er•y**, *n.* being a slave; buying and selling slaves. **slav•ish**, *adj.* exact (imitation) without any imagination. **slav•ish•ly**, *adv.* (to obey rules) exactly without exercising any imagination.

slav•er ['sleɪvə] 1. *n.* liquid which dribbles out

of your mouth. 2. *v.* to dribble/to let liquid trickle out of your mouth.

slay [sleɪ] *v.* (*formal*) (**slew** [sluː], **slain**) to kill.

slea•zy ['sliːzɪ] *adj.* (**-ier, -iest**) *inf.* dirty/disreputable.

sled [sled] 1. *n.* small vehicle with runners for sliding over snow. 2. *v.* **to go sledding** = to play on the snow using a sled.

sledge [sledʒ] *n. & v. see* **sled. sledge•ham•mer,** *n.* very large heavy hammer.

sleek [sliːk] 1. *adj.* (**-er, -est**) smooth/shiny; well-kept. 2. *v.* to smooth down (hair) with oil. **sleek•ly,** *adv.* in a sleek way. **sleek•ness,** *n.* being sleek.

sleep [sliːp] 1. *n.* state of resting naturally and unconsciously; **to go/to get to s.** = to start sleeping; **to send s.o. to s.** = to make s.o. go to sleep (from boredom/by hypnosis); **to put to s.** = to kill; **my foot has gone to s.** = has become numb. 2. *v.* (**slept**) (a) to be in a state of natural rest and unconsciousness; **I'll s. on it** = I will make a decision on the problem in the morning; **to s. sth off** = to get rid of the effects of sth by sleeping; **to s. with s.o.** = to have sexual intercourse with s.o. (b) to have enough beds for. **sleep•er,** *n.* (a) person who is asleep. (b) sleeping car. (c) overnight train with sleeping cars. **sleep•i•ly,** *adv.* in a sleepy way. **sleep•i•ness,** *n.* being sleepy. **sleep•ing.** 1. *adj.* asleep. 2. *n.* being asleep; **s. pill** = medicine which makes you go to sleep; **s. car** = railroad car on a train with beds where passengers can sleep; **s. bag** = quilted bag for sleeping in a tent, etc.; **s. sickness** = tropical disease which affects the nervous system. **sleep•less,** *adj.* with no sleep. **sleep•less•ness,** *n.* having no sleep; not able to get to sleep. **sleep•walk,** *v.* to walk about when you are asleep. **sleep•walk•er,** *n.* person who sleepwalks. **sleep•y,** *adj.* (**-ier, -iest**) half asleep; ready to go to sleep.

sleet [sliːt] 1. *n.* mixture of snow and rain. 2. *v.* **it is sleeting** = snow and rain are falling together.

sleeve [sliːv] *n.* (a) part of clothing which covers the arm; **to have sth up your s.** = to have a plan which you are keeping secret. (b) cover for a piece of machinery. (c) square cardboard cover for a phonograph record. **sleeve•less,** *adj.* with no sleeves.

sleigh [sleɪ] *n.* large sled pulled by horses or reindeer, etc.

sleight [slaɪt] *n.* **s. of hand** = quickness of a ma-

gician's movements when performing a card trick.

slen•der ['slendə] *adj.* (a) very thin/slim. (b) not strong; not large. **slen•der•ness,** *n.* being slender.

slept [slept] *v. see* **sleep.**

sleuth [sluːθ] *n. inf.* detective.

slew [sluː] *v. see* **slay.**

slice [slaɪs] 1. *n.* (a) thin piece cut off sth. (b) **fish s.** = flat broad knife for serving fish. (c) (*in games*) stroke which makes the ball spin toward the right. 2. *v.* (a) to cut into slices. (b) to cut sharply. (c) to hit a ball so that it spins toward the right. **slic•er,** *n.* machine for slicing meat/bread, etc.

slick [slɪk] 1. *adj.* (**-er, -est**) clever (in a way which tricks people). 2. *n.* **oil s.** = layer of oil which has spilled on the sea from a tanker or oil rig. 3. *v.* **to s. down** = to make (hair) sleek.

slid [slɪd] *v. see* **slide.**

slide [slaɪd] 1. *n.* (a) action of slipping on a smooth surface. (b) slippery surface for sliding, esp. a metal slope for children to slide down. (c) thin glass plate to put under a microscope. (d) plastic transparent photograph which can be projected on a screen. 2. *v.* (**slid** [slɪd]) (a) to move smoothly. (b) **to let things s.** = to allow things to become worse/not to care if things get worse. **slide rule,** *n.* device for calculating, made of a ruler marked with numbers and a central part which slides sideways. **slid•ing scale,** *n.* system of marks/points/taxes, etc., which vary according to a scale.

slight [slaɪt] 1. *adj.* (**-er, -est**) (a) thin/slender (person). (b) not very large; not very important. 2. *n.* insult. 3. *v.* to insult/to be rude to (s.o.). **slight•ing•ly,** *adv.* rudely/insultingly. **slight•ly,** *adv.* not very much.

slim [slɪm] 1. *adj.* (**slimmer, slimmest**) (a) thin/slender/not fat. (b) small. 2. *v.* (**slimmed**) to diet in order to become thin. **slim•mer,** *n.* person who is trying to lose weight. **slim•ness,** *n.* being slim.

slime [slaɪm] *n.* thin mud; dirty, sticky liquid. **slim•i•ness,** *n.* being slimy. **slim•y,** *adj.* (**-ier, -iest**) unpleasantly muddy/slippery/sticky.

sling [slɪŋ] 1. *n.* (a) device for throwing a stone. (b) carrying strap; bandage tied around your neck to hold your wounded arm steady. (c) apparatus made of ropes and pulleys for hoisting and carrying goods. 2. *v.* (**slung**) (a) to throw. (b) to hold up/to hang by a sling.

æ back, aː farm, ɒː top, aɪ pipe, aʊ how, aiə fire, aʊə flower, ɔː bought, ɔɪ toy, e fed, eəhair, eɪ take, ə afraid, əʊ boat, əʊə lower, ɜː word, iː heap, ɪ hit, ɪə hear, uː school, ʊ book, ʌ but, b back, d dog, ð then, dʒ just, f fog, g go, h hand, j yes, k catch, l last, m mix, n nut, ŋ sing, p penny, r round, s some, ʃ short, t too, tʃ chop, θ thing, v voice, w was, z zoo, ʒ treasure

sling•shot, *n.* catapult/strong elastic band on a forked stick, used for throwing stones.

slink [slɪŋk] *v.* (**slunk**) to creep about furtively. **slink•y,** *adj.* (**-ier, -iest**) smooth (shape); tight, smooth (clothes).

slip [slɪp] 1. *n.* (a) action of sliding by mistake. (b) mistake; **s. of the tongue** = mistake in speaking. (c) **to give s.o. the s.** = to escape from s.o. (d) **pillow s.** = pillowcase. (e) small piece of paper. (f) petticoat. (g) **slips** = long smooth slope on which ships are built. (h) mixture of clay and water which is used in pottery. 2. *v.* (**slipped**) (a) to slide by mistake. (b) to go quietly. (c) (*of machinery*) to miss/not to connect; **slipped disk** = painful state where one of the cushioning disks in the spine has become displaced. **slip•per,** *n.* light comfortable shoe worn indoors. **slip•per•y,** *adj.* (a) so smooth that one can easily slip on it. (b) *inf.* (person) who cannot be trusted. **slip•py,** *adj. inf.* slippery. **slip•shod,** *adj.* badly carried out (work); careless (dress). **slip•stream,** *n.* air blown backward by an aircraft engine; point just behind a fast-moving vehicle. **slip up,** *v. inf.* to make a mistake. **slip-up,** *n. inf.* mistake. **slip•way,** *n.* smooth slope on which ships are built or repaired.

slit [slɪt] 1. *n.* long cut; narrow opening. 2. *v.* (**slit**) to make a slit.

slith•er ['slɪðə] *v.* to slide along, down, or in various directions.

sliv•er ['slɪvə] *n.* thin piece of wood or meat.

slob [slɒb] *n. inf.* sloppy/untidy person. **slob•ber** ['slɒbə] *v.* to dribble saliva from your mouth. **slob•ber•y,** *adj.* covered with saliva.

sloe [sləʊ] *n.* bitter wild fruit like a plum; tree which bears this fruit.

slog [slɒg] 1. *n.* difficult work; difficult walk. 2. *v.* (**slogged**) to work hard at sth difficult. **slog•ger,** *n.* person who works hard.

slo•gan ['sləʊgn] *n.* phrase used in publicity for a product/for a political party, etc.

sloop [sluːp] *n.* type of small ship.

slop [slɒp] *v.* (**slopped**) to spill. **slop•pi•ly,** *adv.* in a sloppy way. **slop•pi•ness,** *n.* being sloppy. **slop•py,** *adj.* (**-ier, -iest**) (a) untidy; badly done (work). (b) stupidly sentimental. **slops,** *n. pl.* (a) waste food given to pigs. (b) liquid refuse.

slope [sləʊp] 1. *n.* slanting surface; angle of a slanting surface; slanting piece of ground. 2. *v.* to slant upward or downward. **slop•ing,** *adj.* (roof, etc.) which slopes.

slosh [slɒʃ] *v.* to splash. **sloshed,** *adj. inf.* drunk.

slot [slɒt] 1. *n.* narrow opening (for putting a coin, mail, etc. into); **s. machine** = vending machine. 2. *v.* (**slotted**) **to s. into** = to fit into (a slot).

sloth [sləʊθ] *n.* (a) (*formal*) laziness. (b) slow-moving South American mammal, like a bear. **sloth•ful,** *adj.* (*formal*) lazy.

slouch [slaʊtʃ] *v.* to stand/to sit in a bad position/with bent shoulders; **to s. along** = to walk along bending forward. **slouch hat,** *n.* hat with a wide brim which can be turned down.

slough 1. *n.* (a) [slʌf] old skin of a snake. (b) [slaʊ] marshy place. 2. *v.* [slʌf] (*of a snake*) to lose (its skin).

slov•en•ly ['slʌvənlɪ] *adj.* untidy; careless (work). **slov•en•li•ness,** *n.* being slovenly.

slow [sləʊ] 1. *adj.* (**-er, -est**) (a) not fast. (b) (*of clock, etc.*) **to be s.** = to show a time which is earlier than the correct time. (c) not quick to learn; *inf.* **to be s. on the uptake** = not to understand quickly. 2. *adv.* not fast; **to go s.** = to advance less quickly. 3. *v.* **to s. down** = to make (sth) go slowly; to go more slowly. **slow•down,** *n.* slowing down (of business activity). **slow•ly,** *adv.* in a slow way. **slow mo•tion,** *n.* (*in motion pictures*) action which appears to take place very slowly because the film speed has been slowed down. **slow•ness,** *n.* being slow. **slow•worm,** *n.* snakelike lizard.

sludge [slʌdʒ] *n.* wet mud; wet refuse.

slug [slʌg] 1. *n.* (a) common garden animal like a snail with no shell. (b) small metal pellet. 2. *v.* (**slugged**) *inf.* to hit (s.o.) a heavy blow. **slug•gard,** *n.* lazy person. **slug•gish,** *adj.* lazy/slow-moving. **slug•gish•ly,** *adv.* in a slow way.

sluice [sluːs] 1. *n.* channel for taking water around a dam. 2. *v.* to wash (sth) with lots of water. **sluice gate,** *n.* gate which allows water to enter the sluice channel.

slum [slʌm] *n.* poor, rundown area of a town. **slum•ming,** *n.* visiting slums; visiting people who you think are of a lower class or less rich than yourself.

slum•ber ['slʌmbə] 1. *n.* gentle sleep. 2. *v.* to sleep gently. **slum•ber•er,** *n.* person who slumbers.

slump [slʌmp] 1. *n.* collapse (of prices); economic collapse (of a country). 2. *v.* (a) to fall suddenly. (b) to sit/to lie clumsily/heavily.

slung [slʌŋ] *v. see* **sling.**

slunk [slʌŋk] *v. see* **slink.**

slur [slɜː] 1. *n.* (a) insult. (b) slurring of several notes; mark on a musical score to show that notes should be slurred. 2. *v.* (**slurred**) (a) to speak words indistinctly. (b) (*in music*) to play several notes without a break between them.

slurp [slɜːp] *v. inf.* to drink noisily.

slur•ry ['slʌrɪ] *n.* (*no pl.*) watery mud/cement.

slush [slʌʃ] *n.* (a) half-melted snow. (b) sentimentality. **slush fund**, *n. inf.* money kept for the purposes of bribery. **slush•y**, *adj.* (a) covered with half-melted snow. (b) very sentimental.

slut [slʌt] *n. inf.* dirty, untidy woman. **slut•tish**, *adj.* like a slut.

sly [slaɪ] *adj.* (**-er, -est**) cunning (person); **on the s.** = without anyone knowing. **sly•ly**, *adv.* in a sly way. **sly•ness**, *n.* being sly.

smack [smæk] 1. *n.* (a) blow with the flat of the hand. (b) loud kiss. (c) slight taste or hint of sth. 2. *v.* (a) to hit (s.o.). (b) **to s. one's lips** = make a loud noise (as if hungry). (c) to smell/to taste; **that smacks of bribery** = it sounds as though bribery is involved. 3. *adv. inf.* straight/directly. **smack•er**, *n. inf.* dollar.

small [smɔːl] 1. *adj.* (**-er, -est**) (a) not large; little. (b) delicate/soft (voice). (c) not imposing. (d) petty/thinking only of trivial things. 2. *n.* **the s. of the back** = the lower part of the back. 3. *adv.* into little bits. **small hours**, *n.* period after midnight. **small-mind•ed**, *adj.* thinking only of yourself/of trivial things. **small•ness**, *n.* being small. **small•pox**, *n.* dangerous infectious disease causing a rash which leaves marks on the skin. **small talk**, *n.* general conversation about sth unimportant. **small-time**, *adj.* unimportant.

smarm•y [ˈsmɑːmɪ] *adj.* (**-ier, -iest**) (person) who is unpleasantly smooth. **smarm•i•ness**, *n.* being smarmy.

smart [smɑːt] 1. *n.* sharp pain (from a wound). 2. *v.* to hurt/to feel as if burning. 3. *adj.* (**-er, -est**) (a) sharp (blow). (b) rapid/efficient. (c) clever. (d) well-dressed/elegant. **smart•en**, *v.* **to s. yourself up** = to make yourself look smart. **smart•ly**, *adv.* in a smart way. **smart•ness**, *n.* being smart.

smash [smæʃ] 1. *n.* (*pl.* **-es**) (a) crash (of a car). (b) financial collapse. (c) powerful shot (in tennis). 2. *v.* (a) to break (sth) to pieces. (b) to hit sth hard. (c) to hit (a ball) hard. **smash hit**, *n. inf.* play/motion picture, etc., which is very successful. **smash•ing**, *adj. inf.* very good/fantastic.

smat•ter•ing [ˈsmætrɪŋ] *n.* small knowledge (of a language).

smear [smɪə] 1. *n.* (a) dirty mark; thing which is smeared (esp. a small amount of sth for examining under a microscope). (b) insult; **s. campaign** = campaign to discredit s.o. by spreading gossip about his private life. 2. *v.* (a)

to make dirty marks on sth. (b) to spread (sth greasy).

smell [smel] 1. *n.* (a) one of the five senses, felt through the nose. (b) thing which you can sense through the nose. (c) unpleasant thing which you can sense through the nose. 2. *v.* (**smelled/smelt**) (a) to notice (sth) by the nose. (b) to sniff in order to sense the smell. (c) to give off a smell. **smell•ing salts**, *n. pl.* crystals of a compound of ammonia, which are smelled to cure faintness. **smell•y**, *adj.* (**-ier, -iest**) which gives off an unpleasant smell.

smelt [smelt] 1. *n.* (*pl.* **smelt**) small edible fish. 2. *v.* (a) to produce metal by melting ore. (b) *see also* **smell. smelter**, *n.* works where metal is extracted from ore. **smelt•ing**, *n.* production of metal by heating ore with coke and limestone.

smid•gen [ˈsmɪdʒn] *n. inf.* very small amount.

smile [smaɪl] 1. *n.* expression of pleasure with the mouth turned up at the corners. 2. *v.* to make an expression of happiness by turning up the corners of the mouth. **smil•ey**, *n.* symbol of a smile/frown, esp. those sent in electronic mail.

smirk [smɜːk] 1. *n.* unpleasant superior smile. 2. *v.* to give a smirk.

smite [smaɪt] *v.* (**smote, has smitten**) (*formal*) to hit; **smitten with** = liking.

smith [smɪθ] *n.* person who works in metal. **smith•y** [ˈsmɪðɪ] *n.* workshop where a blacksmith works.

smith•er•eens [smɪðəˈriːnz] *n.* very small bits.

smit•ten [ˈsmɪtn] *v. see* **smite.**

smock [smɒk] *n.* long loose overall worn over clothes to protect them. **smock•ing**, *n.* embroidery on gathered material.

smog [smɒg] *n.* mixture of fog and exhaust fumes of cars.

smoke [sməʊk] 1. *n.* (a) vapor and gas given off when sth burns. (b) action of smoking a cigarette. 2. *v.* (a) to send out clouds of vapor and gas. (b) to cure (bacon/fish, etc.) by hanging in wood smoke. (c) to suck in smoke from a burning cigarette/pipe, etc. **smoke•less**, *adj.* which makes no smoke. **smok•er**, *n.* (a) person who smokes cigarettes, etc. (b) railroad car where you can smoke. **smoke•screen**, *n.* thick smoke made so that the enemy cannot see; anything which is deliberately used to hide what is going on. **smok•y**, *adj.* (**-ier, -iest**) full of cigarette smoke.

smol•der, *Brit.* **smoul•der** [ˈsməʊldə] *v.* to burn slowly.

æ back, ɑː farm, ɒ top, aɪ pipe, aʊ how, aɪə fire, aʊə flower, ɔː bought, ɔɪ toy, e fed, eəhair, eɪ take, ə afraid, əʊ boat, əʊə lower, ɜː word, iː heap, ɪ hit, ɪə hear, uː school, ʊ book, ʌ but, b back, d dog, ð then, dʒ just, f fog, g go, h hand, j yes, k catch, l last, m mix, n nut, ŋ sing, p penny, r round, s some, ʃ short, t too, tʃ chop, θ thing, v voice, w was, z zoo, ʒ treasure

smooth [smuːð] 1. *adj.* (**-er, -est**) (a) (surface) with no bumps/no roughness. (b) with no bumps/jolts. (c) with no hair. (d) too pleasant (person). 2. *v.* to make smooth; **to s. the way for sth** = to make it easy; **to s. things over** = to settle an argument. **smooth•ly**, *adv.* in a smooth way. **smooth•ness**, *n.* being smooth.

smor•gas•bord [ˈsmɔːɡəsbɔːd] *n.* Swedish buffet of many cold dishes.

smote [sməʊt] *v. see* **smite**.

smoth•er [ˈsmʌðə] *v.* (a) to stifle and kill (s.o.). (b) to cover.

smudge [smʌdʒ] 1. *n.* dirty (ink) stain. 2. *v.* to make a mark, such as by rubbing ink which is not dry. **smudg•y**, *adj.* (paper) with a dirty mark on it.

smug [smʌɡ] *adj.* (**smugger, smuggest**) self-satisfied. **smug•ly**, *adv.* in a way which shows you are pleased with yourself. **smug•ness**, *n.* being smug.

smug•gle [ˈsmʌɡl] *v.* to take (goods) past a customs check without declaring them for duty; to take (sth) into or out of a prison without the guards seeing. **smug•gler**, *n.* person who smuggles goods.

smut [smʌt] 1. *n.* (a) small black mark. (b) indecent stories. **smut•ty**, *adj.* (**-ier, -iest**) indecent.

Sn *symbol for* tin.

snack [snæk] *n.* light meal. **snack•bar**, *n.* restaurant where you can have a light meal, usu. sitting at a counter.

snaf•fle [ˈsnæfl] *n.* horse's bit.

snag [snæɡ] 1. *n.* (a) obstacle; thing which prevents you from doing sth. (b) sharp point; place where a piece of clothing has been caught on a sharp point. 2. *v.* (**snagged**) to catch and tear (your clothes) on a sharp point.

snail [sneɪl] *n.* common slimy animal with a shell; **at a s.'s pace** = extremely slowly. **snail mail**, *n. inf.* conventional mail system, slow when compared to almost instantaneous electronic mail.

snake [sneɪk] 1. *n.* long, sometimes poisonous, reptile which wriggles along the ground. 2. *v.* to wriggle like a snake.

snap [snæp] 1. *n.* (a) sudden dry noise. (b) **cold s.** = sudden spell of cold weather. (c) type of crisp cracker. (d) snapshot. (e) fastening for clothes, made of two small metal studs which fit into each other. 2. *adj.* (decision) taken hurriedly. 3. *v.* (**snapped**) (a) to try to bite. (b) to speak sharply. (c) to break sharply; to make a dry noise (in breaking). (d) to take a photograph of (s.o.). (e) **to s. up** = to buy quickly. (f) *inf.* **to s. out of it** = to get out of a state of depression. **snap•drag•on**, *n.* antirrhinum. **snap•per**, *n.* type of fish. **snap•pi•ly**, *adv.*

in a snappy way. **snap•py**, *adj.* (**-ier, -iest**) (a) irritable/short-tempered. (b) *inf.* **make it s.!** = do it quickly. **snap•shot**, *n.* informal photograph taken quickly.

snare [sneə] 1. *n.* trap for catching animals made with a noose which is pulled tight. 2. *v.* to catch with a snare.

snarl [snɑːl] 1. *n.* (a) angry growl. (b) tangle. 2. *v.* (a) to growl angrily. (b) to make tangled.

snatch [snætʃ] 1. *n.* (*pl.* **-es**) (a) grabbing sth. (b) short piece (of a song, etc.). 2. *v.* to grab (sth) rapidly.

snaz•zy [ˈsnæzɪ] *adj.* (**-ier, -iest**) *inf.* smart/in fashion.

sneak [sniːk] 1. *n. inf.* dishonest person. 2. *v.* to creep without being seen. **sneak•ers**, *n. pl.* soft sports shoes with rubber soles. **sneak•ing**, *adj.* secret. **sneak•y**, *adj. inf.* deceitful/not open.

sneer [snɪə] 1. *n.* sarcastic smile; unpleasant smile. 2. *v.* to give s.o. a sarcastic smile to show contempt; to speak in a contemptuous way.

sneeze [sniːz] 1. *n.* sudden blowing out of air through your mouth and nose because of irritation in your nose. 2. *v.* make a sneeze; *inf.* **it's nothing to s. at** = you should not refuse it/despise it.

snick [snɪk] 1. *n.* small cut (with a knife). 2. *v.* to hit (a ball) a sharp glancing blow. **snick•er** [ˈsnɪkə] 1. *n.* quiet unpleasant laugh. 2. *v.* to laugh quietly in an unpleasant way. **snick•er•ing**, *n.* hidden laughter.

snide [snaɪd] *adj. inf.* unpleasant/envious (remark).

sniff [snɪf] 1. *n.* short intake of air through the nose. 2. *v.* to take in air rapidly through the nose. **sniff•er**, *n.* person who sniffs. **snif•fle**. 1. *n.* slight cold in the head. 2. *v.* to keep on sniffing because of a cold.

snig•ger [ˈsnɪɡə] *n. & v. see* **snick•er**.

snip [snɪp] 1. *n.* piece which has been cut off. 2. *v.* (**snipped**) to cut with scissors. **snip•pet**, *n.* little bit (of cloth, etc.).

snipe [snaɪp] 1. *n.* large marsh bird with a long beak. 2. *v.* **to s. at s.o.** = to shoot at s.o. from a hiding place/to make continuous criticism of s.o. **snip•er**, *n.* hidden soldier who shoots at the enemy.

snitch [snɪtʃ] *v. inf.* to steal.

sniv•el [ˈsnɪvl] *v.* (**sniveled, snivelled**) (a) to have a runny nose. (b) to cry and complain.

snob [snɒb] *n.* person who likes people who are of a higher social class than himself; **intellectual s.** = person who looks down on those who are not as well-educated as he feels he is himself. **snob•ber•y, snobbishness**, *n.* being a snob. **snob•bish**, *adj.* referring to a snob.

snood [snuːd] *n.* (*old*) ornamental bag-shaped

net for holding a woman's hair at the back of the head.

snook•er ['snuːkə] n. game like billiards played on a table with twenty-two balls of various colors.

snoop [snuːp] v. to creep about investigating sth secretly. **snoop•er,** n. person who spies on s.o. secretly.

snoot•y ['snuːtɪ] adj. (-ier, -iest) inf. superior (air/expression). **snoot•i•ly,** adv. in a snooty way. **snoot•i•ness,** n. being snooty.

snooze [snuːz] 1. n. short sleep. 2. v. to sleep lightly for a short time.

snore [snɔː] 1. n. loud noise in the throat made by breathing air when you are asleep. 2. v. to make a snore. **snor•er,** n. person who snores.

snor•kel ['snɔːkl] n. tube which goes from the mouth or mask of an underwater swimmer to the surface to allow him to breathe in air. **snor•kel•ing,** n. **to go s.** = to go swimming with a snorkel.

snort [snɔːt] 1. n. (a) snorting noise. (b) inf. small drink. 2. v. to make a loud noise blowing air out through the nose.

snot [snɒt] n. inf. mucus in the nose.

snout [snaut] n. nose of an animal (esp. a pig).

snow [snəu] 1. n. water vapor which freezes and falls in light white flakes. 2. v. to fall in flakes of snow; **snowed under** = overwhelmed. **snow•ball.** 1. n. ball of snow. 2. v. (a) to throw snowballs. (b) to get bigger and bigger. **snow•blind•ness,** n. painful lack of sight caused by the brightness of snow. **snow•drift,** n. heap of snow which has been piled up by the wind. **snow•drop,** n. small spring bulb with little white flowers. **snow•fall,** n. amount of snow which has fallen. **snow•flake,** n. flake of snow. **snow line,** n. point on a high mountain above which there is always snow. **snow•man,** n. (pl. -men) figure of a man made out of snow. **snow•mo•bile** ['snəuməbiːl] n. vehicle with caterpillar tracks specially designed for driving on snow. **snow•plow,** n. heavy vehicle with a plow on the front for clearing snow off roads/railroads, etc. **snow•shoes,** n. pl. frames shaped like tennis rackets, with a light web, which are tied under the feet for walking on snow. **snow•storm,** n. storm which brings snow. **snow-white,** adj. pure white. **snow•y,** adj. (-ier, -iest) covered with snow; white like snow.

snub [snʌb] 1. n. insult; insulting refusal to speak to s.o. 2. v. (**snubbed**) to insult (s.o.) by refusing to speak to them/by not paying any attention to them. 3. adj. **s. nose** = small nose which is turned up at the end.

snuff [snʌf] 1. n. powdered tobacco which is sniffed into the nose. 2. v. to put out (a candle).

snuf•fle ['snʌfl] 1. n. loud sniff. 2. v. to sniff noisily.

snug [snʌg] adj. (**snugger, snuggest**) warm and comfortable. **snug•gle,** v. to curl yourself up to be warm; to curl up close to s.o. for warmth. **snug•ly,** adv. in a snug way.

so [səu] 1. adv. (a) to such an extent. (b) in this way. (c) true/correct; **I think s.** = I think it is true. (d) in the same way. (e) **or s.** = approximately. (f) **and s. on** = and in a similar way; etcetera. 2. conj. (a) therefore. (b) **s. that/s. as to** = for the purpose of. **so-and-so,** n. (a) somebody (whom you do not want to name). (b) hated person. **so-called,** adj. wrongly called. **so-so,** adj. & adv. inf. not very well.

soak [səuk] 1. n. being very wet. 2. v. to put (sth) in a liquid so as to be completely covered; to get/to make very wet. **soak•ing.** 1. n. (action of) being soaked. 2. adj. & adv. wet through. **soak up,** v. to absorb (a liquid).

soap [səup] 1. n. material made of oil and fat used for washing. 2. v. to wash with soap. **soap•box,** n. box on which a speaker stands to talk to a meeting outdoors. **soap op•er•a,** n. trite serial story on television. **soap•stone,** n. type of soft gray stone which can be easily carved. **soap•suds,** n. pl. foam made from soap. **soap•y,** adj. full of soap; covered with soap.

soar [sɔː] v. (a) to fly high into the air; (of bird) to glide without beating its wings. (b) to rise rapidly.

sob [sɒb] 1. n. short breath like a hiccup when crying. 2. v. (**sobbed**) to weep, taking short breaths like hiccups.

so•ber ['səubə] 1. adj. (a) not drunk. (b) serious. (c) dark (color). 2. v. **to s. up** = to recover from drunkenness. **so•ber•ly,** adv. seriously. **so•ber•ness, sobriety** [sə'braɪɪtɪ] n. being sober.

so•bri•quet ['səubrɪkeɪ] n. nickname.

soc•cer ['sɒkə] n. form of football played between two teams of eleven players who can only kick or bounce the ball off a point of the body.

so•cia•ble ['səuʃəbl] adj. friendly/liking the

æ back, ɑː farm, ɒ top, aɪ pipe, au how, aiə fire, auə flower, ɔː bought, ɔɪ toy, e fed, eəhair, eɪ take, ə afraid, əu boat, əuə lower, vː word, iː heap, ɪ hit, ɪə hear, uː school, u book, ʌ but, b back, d dog, ð then, dʒ just, f fog, g go, h hand, j yes, k catch, l last, m mix, n nut, ŋ sing, p penny, r round, s some, ʃ short, t too, tʃ chop, θ thing, v voice, w was, z zoo, ʒ treasure

company of other people. **so•cia•bil•i•ty** [səuʃə'bɪlɪtɪ] n. being sociable.

so•cial ['səuʃl] 1. adj. (a) referring to society; **s. science** = study of the problems of society; **s. security** = system of old-age, unemployment, or disability insurance provided by the U.S. government through regular payments made by an employer and employee; **s. services** = state services to help people's problems; **s. worker** = person who works to help families in need. (b) living in groups. 2. n. party. **so•cial•ism** n. political system where the state owns and runs the wealth of the country; belief that all property should belong to the state and that every citizen is equal. **so•cial•ist**, adj. & n. (person) who believes in socialism; (policies) which follow the principles of socialism. **so•cial•ite**, n. person who moves in high society. **so•cial•ize**, v. (a) to be friendly with other people (at a party). (b) to organize (a country) along the principles of socialism. **so•cial•ly**, adv. in a social way. **so•ci•e•ty** [sə'saɪɪtɪ] n. (a) way in which people are organized; group of people who live in the same way. (b) group/club/association of people with the same interests. (c) (also **high society**) top class of people. **so•ci•ol•o•gy** [səusɪ'ɒlədʒɪ] n. study of society and how people live in society. **so•ci•o•log•i•cal** [səusɪə'lɒdʒɪkl] adj. referring to society and the way in which society changes. **so•ci•ol•o•gist** [səusɪ'ɒlədʒɪst] n. person who studies society and how people live in it.

sock [sɒk] 1. n. covering for the foot and lower part of the leg. 2. v. inf. to hit.

sock•et ['sɒkɪt] n. hole(s) into which sth is fitted; **electric s.** = one which a plug/bulb can be fitted into.

sod [sɒd] n. piece of soil with grass growing on it.

so•da ['səudə] n. compound of sodium; **s. (water)** = water aerated by putting gas into it; **ice cream s.** = sweet drink mixed with ice cream. **so•da foun•tain**, n. bar where sweet drinks and ice cream are served.

sod•den ['sɒdn] adj. very wet.

so•di•um ['səudɪəm] n. (element: Na) white soft metal, which can catch fire, and is usu. found in combination with other substances.

sod•om•y ['sɒdɒmɪ] n. anal or oral sexual intercourse, esp. between men.

so•fa ['səufə] n. long seat with a soft back for several people.

sof•fit ['sɒfɪt] n. underside of an arch.

soft [sɒft] adj. (-er, -est) (a) not hard; (pencil) which makes wide blurred marks. (b) quiet (voice). (c) not strict. (d) inf. stupid. (e) (water) with little calcium in it; (drink) which is not alcoholic; (drugs) which are not addictive.

soft-boiled, adj. (egg) which has not been boiled very much. **soft•en** ['sɒfn] v. to make/to become soft; **to s. up** = to make weak before attacking or before asking for a favor. **soft•en•er**, n. **water s.** = apparatus for making hard water soft. **soft-heart•ed**, adj. not strict/too kind. **soft•ly**, adv. in a soft way. **soft•ness**, n. being soft. **soft soap**, n. inf. flattery. **soft•ware**, n. computer programs (as opposed to the machines). **soft•wood**, n. wood from pine and fir trees.

sog•gy ['sɒgɪ] adj. (-ier, -iest) wet and soft. **sog•gi•ness**, n. being soggy.

soil [sɔɪl] 1. n. earth. 2. v. to make dirty.

so•journ ['sʌdʒən] 1. n. (formal) stay. 2. v. (formal) to stay.

sol•ace ['sɒləs] n. (formal) comfort.

so•lar ['səulə] adj. referring to the sun; **s. energy/s. power** = electricity produced from the radiation of the sun; **s. heating** = heating system run by light from the sun; **s. system** = series of planets orbiting the sun; **s. plexus** = (i) group of nerves behind the bottom of the lungs and the stomach; (ii) inf. the lower part of the body where the stomach is. **so•lar•i•um** [sə'leərɪəm] n. room where you can enjoy real or artificial sunlight.

sold [səuld] v. see **sell**.

sol•der ['səuldə] 1. n. soft metal used to join metal surfaces together when it is melted. 2. v. to join (metal surfaces together) with solder. **sol•der•ing i•ron**, n. tool which is heated to apply solder.

sol•dier ['səuldʒə] 1. n. member of the army. 2. v. (a) to be on military service. (b) **to s. on** = to continue doing a hard job. **sol•dier•y**, n. soldiers.

sole [səul] 1. n. (a) underside of the foot; bottom part of a shoe. (b) flat sea fish. 2. v. to put a new sole on (a shoe). 3. adj. (a) only. (b) belonging to one person; **he has the s. right to** = he is the only person allowed to. **sole•ly**, adv. only.

sol•e•cism ['sɒlɪsɪzəm] n. embarrassing mistake made in speaking.

sol•emn ['sɒləm] adj. (a) special and religious (ceremony). (b) very serious. **so•lem•ni•ty** [sə'lemnɪtɪ] n. being solemn. **sol•em•ni•za•tion** [sɒləmnaɪ'zeɪʃn] n. celebration (of a marriage/of a religious ceremony). **sol•em•nize** ['sɒlemnaɪz] v. to celebrate/to perform (a marriage/a religious ceremony). **sol•emn•ly**, adv. in a solemn way.

so•le•noid ['sɒlənɔɪd] n. coiled wire which produces a magnetic field when an electric current passes through it.

sol-fa [sɒl'fɑː] *n.* system of indicating tones in music by syllables (*doh-ray-me*, etc.).

so•lic•it [sə'lɪsɪt] *v.* to ask for. **so•lic•i•ta•tion** [səlɪsɪ'teɪʃn] *n.* soliciting. **so•lic•i•tor,** *n.* lawyer who gives advice to people on legal problems. **so•lic•i•tous,** *adj.* worried/anxious about sth. **so•lic•i•tous•ly,** *adv.* in a solicitous way. **so•lic•i•tude,** *n.* anxiety/worry about sth.

sol•id ['sɒlɪd] 1. *adj.* (**-er, -est**) (a) not liquid. (b) not hollow. (c) made all of one material; **for eight hours s.** = without stopping. (d) trustworthy. 2. *n.* (a) solid sustance. (b) three-dimensional shape. **sol•i•dar•i•ty** [sɒlɪ'dærɪtɪ] *n.* common interest with s.o. **so•lid•i•fi•ca•tion** [sɒlɪdɪfɪ'keɪʃn] *n.* act of solidifying. **so•lid•i•fy** [sə'lɪdfaɪ] *v.* to (make sth) become solid. **so•lid•i•ty** [sə'lɪdɪtɪ] *n.* being solid. **sol•id•ly,** *adv.* completely. **sol•id-state,** *adj.* (TV set, etc.) which uses transistors and not valves.

so•lil•o•quy [sə'lɪləkwɪ] *n.* speech spoken by a character alone on the stage. **so•lil•o•quize,** *v.* to speak all alone.

sol•i•taire [sɒlɪ'teə] *n.* (a) game for one person, as any of various card games or a game played on a board with balls which have to be jumped from hole to hole removing the intervening balls one at a time. (b) single diamond (in a ring, etc.).

sol•i•tar•y ['sɒlɪtrɪ] *adj.* (a) single/sole. (b) lonely; **s. confinement** = imprisonment alone in a cell. **sol•i•tude,** *n.* being alone.

so•lo ['səuləu] 1. *n.* (*pl.* **-os, -li**) piece of music for one person. 2. *adj. & adv.* carried out by one person. **so•lo•ist,** *n.* musician who plays a solo.

sol•stice ['sɒlstɪs] *n.* **summer s.** = period of the longest day (June 21st); **winter s.** = period of the longest night (December 21st).

sol•u•ble ['sɒljubl] *adj.* (a) which can be dissolved. (b) (problem) which can be solved. **sol•u•bil•i•ty** [sɒlju'bɪlɪtɪ] *n.* ability to be dissolved/solved. **so•lu•tion** [sə'luːʃn] *n.* (a) liquid in which sth has been dissolved. (b) act of solving a problem; answer to a problem.

solve [sɒlv] *v.* to find the answer to (a problem). **solve•a•ble,** *adj.* which can be solved. **solv•er,** *n.* person who solves a problem.

sol•ven•cy ['sɒlvənsɪ] *n.* state of being solvent. **sol•vent.** 1. *adj.* having enough money to pay your debts. 2. *n.* liquid which dissolves another substance.

so•ma•to•tro•pin [səmɑːtəu'trɒfɪn] *n.* growth hormone.

som•ber, *Brit.* **som•bre** ['sɒmbə] *adj.* dark and gloomy. **som•ber•ly,** *adv.* in a somber way.

som•bre•ro [səm'breərəu] *n.* (*pl.* **-os**) hat with a wide brim worn in South America.

some [sʌm] 1. *adj.* (a) not a particular one. (b) certain; (c) several/a few; a little. (d) *inf.* wonderful; **that was s. party!** 2. *pron.* several out of a group; part of a whole. 3. *adv.* approximately. **some•bod•y** ['sʌmbədɪ] *pron.* (a) a particular unknown person. (b) *inf.* important person. **some•how** ['sʌmhau] *adv.* in one way or another. **some•one** ['sʌmwʌn] *pron.* somebody. **some•place** ['sʌmpleɪs] *adv.* somewhere. **some•thing** ['sʌmθɪŋ] *pron.* (a) a particular unknown thing. (b) (*replacing a forgotten detail*) **the 4 s. train** = the train which leaves at some time after 4 o'clock. **some•time** ['sʌmtaɪm] *adv.* (a) at a particular unknown time. (b) (*old*) formerly. **some•times** ['sʌmtaɪmz] *adv.* from time to time/at times. **some•what** ['sʌmwɒt] *adv.* rather. **some•where** ['sʌmweə] *adv.* at some particular unknown place.

som•er•sault ['sʌməsɔːlt] 1. *n.* rolling over, with your head underneath and feet over your head. 2. *v.* to do a somersault/to roll over.

som•nam•bu•lism [sɒm'næmbjulɪzəm] *n.* walking in your sleep. **som•nam•bu•list** [sɒm'næmbjulɪst] *n.* person who walks when asleep.

som•no•lence ['sɒmnələns] *n.* (*formal*) being sleepy/sleepiness. **som•no•lent,** *adj.* sleepy.

son [sʌn] *n.* male child of a parent. **son-in-law** *n.* (*pl.* **sons-in-law**) husband of a daughter.

so•nar ['səunɑː] *n.* device for finding underwater objects by using sound waves.

so•na•ta [sə'nɑːtə] *n.* piece of music in three or four movements for one or two instruments.

sonde [sɒnd] *n.* device attached to a balloon, used for taking samples of the atmosphere.

son et lu•mi•ère [sɒneɪluːmɪ'ɜː] *n.* sound-and-light show.

song [sɒŋ] *n.* (a) singing. (b) words and music to be sung; **for a s.** = for very little money; *inf.* **he gave us a great s. and dance about it** = a great fuss. **song•bird,** *n.* bird which sings particularly well. **song•ster,** *n.* person or bird that sings.

son•ic ['sɒnɪk] *adj.* referring to sound waves; **s.**

æ back, ɑː farm, ɒ top, aɪ pipe, au how, aiə fire, auə flower, ɔː bought, ɔɪ toy, e fed, eəhair, eɪ take, ə afraid, əu boat, əuə lower, vː word, iː heap, ɪ hit, ɪə hear, uː school, u book, ʌ but, b back, d dog, ð then, dʒ just, f fog, g go, h hand, j yes, k catch, l last, m mix, n nut, ŋ sing, p penny, r round, s some, ʃ short, t too, tʃ chop, θ thing, v voice, w was, z zoo, ʒ treasure

boom = bang made by an aircraft traveling faster than the speed of sound.

son•net ['sɒnɪt] *n.* poem with fourteen lines.

son•ny ['sʌnɪ] *n. inf.* way of addressing a boy.

so•no•rous ['sɒnərəs] *adj.* which makes a loud ringing noise.

soon [su:n] *adv.* (**-er, -est**) (a) in a very short time; **sooner or later** = at some time to come. (b) **I would as s./sooner stay than go away** = I would rather stay.

soot [sʊt] *n.* black carbon dust which collects in chimneys. **soot•y,** *adj.* (**-ier, -iest**) black; covered with soot.

soothe [su:ð] *v.* to calm. **sooth•ing,** *adj.* which calms. **sooth•ing•ly,** *adv.* in a soothing way.

sooth•say•er ['su:θseɪə] *n.* person who foretells the future.

sop [sɒp] 1. *n.* (a) piece of bread dipped in liquid. (b) sth given as a bribe to make s.o. keep quiet. 2. *v.* (**sopped**) to soak in liquid; to soak up (a liquid). **sop•ping,** *adj.* **s. wet** = soaked. **sop•py,** *adj.* soaked.

so•phis•ti•ca•tion [səfɪstɪˈkeɪʃn] *n.* (a) cultured way of life. (b) advanced ideas behind the construction of a machine. **so•phis•ti•cat•ed,** *adj.* (a) cultured. (b) complicated/advanced (machine).

soph•ist•ry ['sɒfɪstrɪ] *n.* clever argument which is probably wrong.

soph•o•more ['sɒfəmɔ:] *n.* second-year student at a school, college, or university.

sop•o•rif•ic [sɒpəˈrɪfɪk] *adj. & n.* (medicine) which makes you go to sleep.

so•pran•o [səˈprɑ:nəʊ] *n.* (*pl.* **-os**) high-pitched singing voice; woman or boy with such a voice.

sor•bet ['sɔ:beɪ] *n.* water ice.

sor•cer•y ['sɔ:sərɪ] *n.* witchcraft/magic. **sor•cer•er, sorceress,** *n.* person who makes magic.

sor•did ['sɔ:dɪd] *adj.* unpleasant/dirty. **sor•did•ly,** *adv.* in a sordid way. **sor•did•ness,** *n.* being sordid.

sore [sɔ:] 1. *adj.* (**-er, -est**) (a) painful/which hurts. (b) *inf.* upset/annoyed. 2. *n.* painful spot on the skin. **sore•ly,** *adv.* very much. **sore•ness,** *n.* being sore.

sor•ghum ['sɔ:gəm] *n.* type of grass, used as a cereal.

so•ror•i•ty [səˈrɒrɪtɪ] *n.* student society for women.

sor•rel ['sɒrəl] *n.* (a) common sour-tasting edible plant. (b) (horse which is) a reddish brown color.

sor•row ['sɒrəʊ] *n.* sadness. **sor•row•ful,** *adj.* very sad. **sor•row•ful•ly,** *adv.* in a sorrowful way. **sor•ry,** *adj.* (**-ier, -iest**) (a) regretting

sth. (b) feeling pity/sympathy **for** s.o. (c) pitiful.

sort [sɔ:t] 1. *n.* type/variety; **good s.** = pleasant type of person; *inf.* **s. of tired** = rather tired; **a meal of sorts** = not a very good meal; **out of sorts** = slightly unwell. 2. *v.* to arrange in different groups. **sort•er,** *n.* person who sorts; **mail s.** = person who sorts letters in a post office.

sort•ie ['sɔ:ti:] *n.* sudden attack; bombing raid (by aircraft).

SOS [esəʊˈes] *n.* international code for showing that you are in distress.

souf•flé ['su:fleɪ] *n.* light cooked dish, made from beaten eggs.

sought [sɔ:t] *v. see* **seek. sought after,** *adj.* which people want.

soul [səʊl] *n.* (a) the spirit in a person (as opposed to the body). (b) spirited or animating part. (c) **she is the s. of honor** = a fine example of honor. (d) person. **soul•ful,** *adj.* with a lot of feeling. **soul•ful•ly,** *adv.* in a soulful way. **soul•less,** *adj.* very dull/inhuman. **soul mu•sic,** *n.* popular music played by black musicians, which conveys deep feelings. **soul-search•ing,** *n.* examination of your own motives/conscience.

sound [saʊnd] 1. *n.* (a) noise; **s. wave** = wave in the air which carries sound; **s. barrier** = the speed of sound. 2. *v.* (a) to make a noise. (b) **to s. like** = to be similar in sound to (sth). (c) **to s. s.o. out** = to talk to s.o. to test his opinion. (d) to measure the depth of water. 3. *adj.* (**-er, -est**) (a) healthy/not rotten. (b) reasonable/trustworthy. (c) deep (sleep). **sound-and-light show,** *n.* entertainment consisting of sound and lighting effects, shown in the open air at night. **sound ef•fects,** *n. pl.* noises made in a play/motion picture, etc., which imitate real sounds (such as thunder/gunfire, etc.). **sound•ing,** *n.* (a) making of noise; **s. board** = (i) board (as above a pulpit) which reflects sound; (ii) way of spreading ideas. (b) measuring the depth of water. **sound•less,** *adj.* which does not make any noise. **sound•less•ly,** *adv.* not making any noise. **sound•ly,** *adv.* thoroughly/deeply. **sound•ness,** *n.* being sound. **sound off,** *v. inf.* to start talking loudly **about** sth. **sound•proof.** 1. *adj.* made so that sound cannot get through. 2. *v.* to make (a building) soundproof. **sound•track,** *n.* part of a motion picture where the sound is recorded.

soup [su:p] *n.* liquid food usu. eaten at the beginning of a meal; *inf.* **in the s.** = in real trouble. **soup kitch•en,** *n.* place where soup and other food is given to the poor/to victims of a disaster. **soup up,** *v. inf.* to increase the power of (an engine).

soupçon ['suːpsɒn] *n.* slight taste; very small amount.

sour ['savə] 1. *adj.* (**-er, -est**) (a) not sweet; sharp-tasting; *inf.* **s. grapes** = saying unpleasant things because of envy. (b) (milk) which has gone bad. (c) bad-tempered/unpleasant (person). 2. *v.* to make bad. **sour•ly,** *adv.* in a bad-tempered way. **sour•ness,** *n.* being sour. **sour•puss,** *n. inf.* unpleasant bad-tempered person.

source [sɔːs] *n.* place of origin/place where something starts or comes from.

souse [saus] *v.* (a) to soak in water. (b) to pickle (herrings, etc.) in salt water.

south [sauθ] 1. *n.* one of the points of the compass; (*in areas north of the equator*) the direction of the sun at midday. 2. *adj.* of the south. 3. *adv.* toward the south. **south•bound,** *adj.* going toward the south. **south•east,** *adj, adv. & n.* direction between south and east. **south•east•er•ly, southeastern,** *adj.* referring to the southeast. **south•er•ly** ['sʌðəlɪ] *adj.* (a) (wind) from the south. (b) **in a s. direction** = toward the south. **south•ern** ['sʌðən] *adj.* referring to the south. **south•ern•er** ['sʌðənə] *n.* person who lives in the south. **south•ern•most,** *adj.* farthest south. **south•paw,** *n. inf.* (*in sports*) player/boxer who is left-handed. **south•ward.** 1. *adj.* toward the south. 2. *adv.* (*also* **southwards**) toward the south. **south•west,** *adj., adv. & n.* direction between south and west. **south•west•er•ly, south•west•ern,** *adj.* referring to the south-west.

sou•ve•nir [suːvə'nɪə] *n.* thing which reminds you of a place/an event.

sou'•west•er [sau'westə] *n.* waterproof hat, worn esp. by sailors.

sov•er•eign ['sɒvrɪn] 1. *n.* (a) ruler/king or queen. (b) former British gold coin worth one pound sterling. 2. *adj.* (a) powerful (remedy). (b) self-governing. **sov•er•eign•ty,** *n.* total power; self-government.

So•vi•et ['səuvɪət] *adj. & n.* (a) (person) from Russia/the Commonwealth of Independent States (formerly the Soviet Union). (b) council/committee in a Communist country. **So•vi•et Un•ion,** *n.* former name for government of Russia/the Commonwealth of Independent States.

sow 1. *n.* [sau] female pig. 2. *v.* [səu] (**sowed, sown**) to put seed into earth so that it grows. **sow•er** ['səuə] *n.* person who sows seed.

soy [sɔɪ, 'sɔjə] *n.* (*also* **soy bean**) kind of very nutritious tropical bean; **s. sauce** = salty Chinese sauce made from soy beans.

soz•zled ['sɒzld] *adj. inf.* drunk.

spa [spɑː] *n.* place where mineral water comes out of the ground naturally and where people go to drink or bathe in the water because of its medicinal properties.

space [speɪs] 1. *n.* (a) place; empty area between two objects/on a sheet of paper, etc. (b) short period of time; **s. bar** = key on a typewriter/computer which makes a space between letters. (c) (*also* **outer space**) area beyond the earth's atmosphere. 2. *v.* **to s. out** = to time (things) at intervals; to place (things) with gaps between them. **space•craft,** *n.* rocket in which astronauts travel in space. **space•man,** *n.* (*pl.* **-men**) person who travels in space. **space-sav•ing,** *adj.* (piece of furniture, etc.) which is compact or which folds, and so saves space. **space•ship,** *n.* rocket in which astronauts travel in space. **space•suit,** *n.* special clothes worn by spacemen. **spa•cious** ['speɪʃəs] *adj.* very large/with lots of space. **spa•cious•ness** ['speɪʃəsnəs] *n.* state of being spacious.

spade [speɪd] *n.* (a) long-handled tool for digging holes in the ground; **to call a s. a s.** = to say what you think without trying to hide your opinions. (b) **spades** = one of the four suits in a pack of cards. **spade•work,** *n.* preliminary work.

spa•ghet•ti [spə'getɪ] *n.* Italian food formed of long strips of pasta.

spam [spæm] *v.* (**spamming, spammed**) to send an unsolicited electronic mail message, e.g. sales literature, to members of Internet newsgroups.

span [spæn] 1. *n.* (a) width (of wings/an arch, etc.). (b) arch of a bridge. (c) length of time. 2. *v.* (**spanned**) to stretch across.

span•drel ['spændrəl] *n.* wall between adjoining arches.

span•gle ['spæŋgl] *n.* small piece of bright metal which is sewn on a dress as an ornament. **span•gled,** *adj.* covered with spangles.

Span•iard ['spænjəd] *n.* person from Spain.

span•iel ['spænjəl] *n.* type of dog with large hanging ears.

æ back, ɑː farm, ɒ top, aɪ pipe, au how, aiə fire, auə flower, ɔː bought, ɔɪ toy, e fed, eəhair, eɪ take, ə afraid, əu boat, əuə lower, vː word, iː heap, ɪ hit, ɪə hear, uː school, u book, ʌ but, b back, d dog, ð then, dʒ just, f fog, g go, h hand, j yes, k catch, l last, m mix, n nut, ŋ sing, p penny, r round, s some, ʃ short, t too, tʃ chop, θ thing, v voice, w was, z zoo, ʒ treasure

Span•ish ['spænɪʃ] 1. *adj.* referring to Spain. 2. *n.* language spoken in Spain and Latin America.

spank [spæŋk] *v.* to smack on the behind. **spank•ing.** 1. *adj. inf.* (a) fast (pace). (b) bright new. 2. *n.* series of smacks on the behind.

spar [spɑ:] 1. *n.* (a) ship's mast or a wooden beam for holding the sails. (b) type of mineral crystal. 2. *v.* (**sparred**) to practice boxing. **spar•ring part•ner,** *n.* person a boxer spars with.

spare ['speə] 1. *adj.* (a) not used/extra; **s. parts** = replacement parts for a machine; **s. tire** = tire carried to replace one that has a puncture. *inf.* **s. tire** = fold of fat around the waist of a plump person. (b) thin (person/body). 2. *n.* extra thing/replacement. 3. *v.* (a) to do without. (b) to give up; not to need. (c) **to s. s.o.'s life** = not to kill s.o. whom you have defeated; to have mercy on s.o. (d) **he was spared the embarrassment** = it saved him from being embarrassed. **spare ribs,** *n. pl.* cooked pork ribs in a spicy sauce. **spar•ing,** *adj.* **to be s. with** = to economize. **spar•ing•ly,** *adv.* using little.

spark [spɑ:k] 1. *n.* little flash of fire/of electricity/of life. 2. *v.* to send out sparks/to make electric sparks. **spark plug,** *n.* (*in a car engine*) device which produces a spark which ignites the mixture of gasoline and air. **spar•kle** ['spɑ:kl] 1. *n.* bright shiny light; small spark. 2. *v.* to glitter/to shine brightly; **sparkling wine** = wine which bubbles. **spar•kler,** *n.* type of firework which sends out sparks.

spar•row ['spærəu] *n.* common small brown and gray bird. **spar•row•hawk,** *n.* common small European hawk.

sparse [spɑ:s] *adj.* (**-er, -est**) not thick; thinly spread. **sparse•ly,** *adv.* with few (things); thinly. **sparse•ness, sparsity,** *n.* being sparse.

spar•tan ['spɑ:tən] *adj.* harsh/hard (discipline)/uncomfortable (conditions).

spasm ['spæzəm] *n.* (a) sudden uncontrollable pulling of muscles. (b) sudden fit (of energy, activity, etc.) **spas•mod•ic** [spæz'mɒdɪk] *adj.* coming in spasms/from time to time. **spas•mod•i•cal•ly,** *adv.* from time to time.

spas•tic ['spæstɪk] *adj. & n.* (person) who has suffered from brain damage which causes partial paralysis.

spat [spæt] 1. *n.* (a) small gaiter which just covers the shoe. (b) minor argument. 2. *v. see* **spit.**

spate [speɪt] *n.* sudden rush (of orders, etc.).

spathe [speɪθ] *n.* leaf which encloses a flower.

spa•tial ['speɪʃəl] *adj.* referring to space. **spa•tial•ly,** *adv.* in a spatial way.

spat•ter ['spætə] *v.* to splash with little spots of liquid.

spat•u•la ['spætjulə] *n.* wide flat blunt flexible knife.

spawn [spɔ:n] 1. *n.* eggs (of a fish/frog, etc.); **mushroom s.** = material like seeds from which mushrooms grow. 2. *v.* to produce eggs.

spay [speɪ] *v.* to make (a female animal) sterile by removing her ovaries.

speak [spi:k] *v.* (**spoke, spoken**) (a) to say words and phrases; **I know him to s. to** = I know him enough to get into conversation with him. (b) to talk in public. (c) to be able to say things in (a foreign language). **speak•er,** *n.* (a) person who speaks. (b) chairman of the U.S. House of Representatives, the British House of Commons, and certain other legislative bodies. (c) loudspeaker. **speak for,** *v.* to plead on s.o.'s behalf. **speak•ing,** *n.* action of talking; **we're not on s. terms** = we have quarreled and don't speak to each other. **speak up,** *v.* (a) to speak louder. (b) **to s. up for** = to support.

spear ['spɪə] 1. *n.* long pointed throwing weapon. 2. *v.* to jab (s.o./sth) with a spear. **spear•head.** 1. *n.* front part of a force of attackers. 2. *v.* to be in the front of an attacking force. **spear•mint,** *n.* common type of mint, often used in chewing gum.

spec [spek] *n. inf.* **to buy on s.** = without being sure of the value/condition.

spe•cial ['speʃəl] 1. *adj.* (a) particular/referring to one particular thing. (b) extraordinary/rare/unusual. 2. *n.* (a) particular edition of a newspaper. (b) particular dish on a menu. (c) article reduced in price. **spe•cial•ist,** *n.* person who has studied sth very deeply. **spe•cial•i•ty** [speʃɪ'ælɪtɪ] *n.* particular interest; subject which you have studied/thing you are known for. **spe•cial•i•za•tion** [speʃəlaɪ'zeɪʃn] *n.* act of specializing; thing you specialize in. **spe•cial•ize** ['speʃəlaɪz] *v.* **to s. in sth** = to study/to produce sth in particular. **spe•cial•ly,** *adv.* particularly; unusually.

spe•cies ['spi:ʃɪz] *n.* (*pl* **species**) (a) group of animals/plants which are closely similar, and which can breed together. (b) *inf.* sort. **spe•cie,** *n. pl.* (*formal*) coins.

spec•i•fy ['spesɪfaɪ] *v.* to state clearly what is required. **spe•cif•ic** [spe'sɪfɪk] *adj.* particular/precise (details). **spe•cif•i•cal•ly,** *adv.* particularly. **spec•i•fi•ca•tion** [spesɪfɪ'keɪʃn] *n.* detailed plan/information. **spec•i•fic grav•i•ty,** *n.* density of a substance divided by the density of water.

spec•i•men ['spesɪmən] *n.* (a) sample which is

selected for study or exhibition. (b) sample/example.

spe•cious ['spiːʃəs] *adj.* not really true as it seems. **spe•cious•ly**, *adv.* in a specious way. **spe•cious•ness**, *n.* being specious.

speck [spek] *n.* tiny spot. **speck•le**, *n.* small (usu. brown) spot. **speck•led**, *adj.* covered with speckles.

specs [speks] *n. pl. inf.* eyeglasses.

spec•ta•cle ['spektəkl] *n.* (a) show. (b) eyeglasses. **spec•tac•u•lar** [spek'tækjulə] *adj.* impressive (show/display). **spec•tac•u•lar•ly**, *adv.* in a spectacular way. **spec•ta•tor**, *n.* person who watches a show/a sports event, etc.

spec•ter, *Brit.* **spec•tre** ['spektə] *n.* (a) ghost. (b) fear. **spec•tral**, *adj.* like a ghost.

spec•trum ['spektrəm] *n.* bands of colors varying from red to blue (as seen in a rainbow); range (of ideas, etc.). **spec•trog•ra•phy**, *n.* recording of a spectrum, used to analyze the chemical composition of a substance.

spec•u•late ['spekjuleɪt] *v.* (a) **to s. about** = to make guesses about. (b) to gamble by buying things whose value you hope will rise. **spec•u•la•tion** [spekju'leɪʃn] *n.* (a) guesses made about sth. (b) gambling by buying things whose value you hope will rise. **spec•u•la•tive** ['spekjulətɪv] *adj.* (a) made by guessing. (b) gambling; **s. venture** = one whose outcome is uncertain. **spec•u•la•tor** ['spekjuleɪtə] *n.* person who buys goods in the hope or reselling them again at a profit.

spec•u•lum ['spekjuləm] *n.* (a) reflector in a telescope. (b) tube for inspecting the interior of the body.

sped [sped] *v. see* **speed.**

speech [spiːtʃ] *n.* (*pl.* -es) (a) ability to talk. (b) spoken language; **the parts of s.** = different groups of words (nouns/verbs, etc.) which are used in a similar way in language. (c) talk given in public. **speech•i•fy**, *v. inf.* to make long speeches. **speech•less**, *adj.* incapable of saying anything.

speed [spiːd] 1. *n.* (a) quickness of movement. (b) rate of movement. 2. *v.* (**sped** or **speeded**) (a) to go fast. (b) to drive a car faster than the legal speed; to make (progress) go faster. **speed•boat**, *n.* racing motor boat. **speed•i•ly**, *adv.* very fast. **speed•i•ness**, *n.* being speedy. **speed•om•e•ter** [spiː-'dɒmɪtə] *n.* dial which shows you how fast you

are driving. **speed up**, *v.* to go faster; to make (sth) go faster. **speed•way**, *n.* racing track for automobiles or motorcycles. **speed•well**, *n.* small wild plant with blue flowers. **speed•y**, *adj.* (-ier, -iest) very fast.

spe•le•ol•o•gy [spiːlɪ'ɒlədʒɪ] *n.* climbing down into caves or holes in the ground. **spe•le•o•log•i•cal**, *adj.* referring to speleology. **spe•le•ol•o•gist**, *n.* person who climbs in or explores caves and holes in the ground.

spell [spel] 1. *n.* (a) magic curse; words which may have a magic effect. (b) period of time. 2. *v.* (**spelled/spelt**) (a) to say aloud/to write correctly the letters which form a word; **to s. out** = (i) to write out all the letters of; (ii) to explain very clearly. (b) to mean. **spell•bind•er**, *n.* thing which enchants/attracts and keeps the attention. **spell•bound**, *adj.* bewitched/enchanted. **spell check**, *v.* to check the spelling of text, using a computer program. **spell•er**, *n.* person who spells. **spell•ing**, *n.* way in which a word is spelled; writing words correctly. **spell•ing check•er**, *n.* computer program which checks spelling.

spen•cer ['spensə] *n.* type of sleeved vest worn by women in the 19th century.

spend [spend] *v.* (**spent**) (a) to pay (money) in exchange for sth. (b) to pass (time). (c) **to s. oneself** = to tire oneself out. **spend•er**, *n.* person who spends. **spend•ing**, *n.* action of using money to buy sth. **spend•thrift**, *adj. & n.* (person) who spends money fast.

spent [spent] *adj.* used; **s. fuel** = fuel which has been used in a nuclear reactor; *see also* **spend.**

sperm [spɜːm] *n.* (a) male fluid which fertilizes the eggs of a female. (b) **s. whale** = large whale which provides oil. **sper•ma•cet•i** [spɜːmə'setɪ] *n.* (*no pl.*) white substance taken from a sperm whale, and used as a base for perfumes. **sper•ma•to•zo•a** [spɜːmətə'zəʊə] *n. pl.* sperms. **sper•mi•cid•al**, *adj.* which kills sperm.

spew [spjuː] *v. inf.* **to s. (out)** = to vomit; to pour out.

sphag•num ['sfægnəm] *n.* type of moss.

sphere ['sfɪə] *n.* (a) object which is perfectly round. (b) area (of influence); society. **spher•i•cal** ['sferɪkl] *adj.* shaped like a sphere/perfectly round.

sphinc•ter ['sfɪŋktə] *n.* circular muscle which controls an opening.

æ back, aː farm, ɒ top, aɪ pipe, aʊ how, aɪə fire, aʊə flower, ɔː bought, ɔɪ toy, ə fed, eəhair, eɪ take, ə afraid, əʊ boat, əʊə lower, vː word, iː heap, ɪ hit, ɪə hear, uː school, ʊ book, ʌ but, b back, d dog, ð then, dʒ just, f fog, g go, h hand, j yes, k catch, l last, m mix, n nut, ŋ sing, p penny, r round, s some, ʃ short, t too, tʃ chop, θ thing, v voice, w was, z zoo, ʒ treasure

sphinx [sfɪŋks] n. (pl. -es, -ges) legendary animal in Egypt with the head of a woman and the body of a lion; large stone monument of this animal.

spice [spaɪs] 1. n. (a) flavoring made from seeds/leaves of plants, etc. (b) thing which excites interest. 2. v. to add spices to (a dish). **spic•i•ness**, n. being spicy. **spic•y**, adj. (a) with a lot of spices. (b) rather rude (story).

spick-and-span ['spɪkən'spæn] adj. very clean/tidy.

spi•der ['spaɪdə] n. eight-legged animal, which makes a web and eats flies; **s. plant** = common house plant, with long yellow and green leaves. **spi•der web, spider's web**, n. web made by a spider. **spi•der•y**, adj. thin and scrawling (handwriting).

spiel [spi:l] n. inf. long flow of talk (aimed at persuading).

spig•ot ['spɪgət] n. tap/faucet (in a barrel).

spike [spaɪk] 1. n. (a) long sharp point. (b) **spikes** = sharp points in the soles of sports or running shoes. 2. v. (a) to attach spikes to. (b) to jam (a gun). (c) to cut (another player/runner) with your spikes. **spiked**, adj. covered with spikes. **spik•y**, adj. standing up in sharp points.

spill [spɪl] 1. (a) fall. (b) long thin piece of wood for lighting cigarettes/candles, etc. 2. v. (**spilled/spilt**) to pour (liquid) out of a container by mistake. **spill•age**, n. action of spilling; amount of liquid spilt.

spin [spɪn] 1. n. (a) action of turning around and around. (b) short fast trip. 2. v. (**spun**) (a) to turn around and around very fast; to make (a ball) turn as it goes through the air. (b) to twist (raw wool/cotton, etc.) to form a thread. **spin-dri•er**, n. machine for drying laundry by turning it around very fast. **spin-dry**, v. to dry (laundry) in a spin-drier. **spin•ner**, n. person who spins thread. **spin•ner•et** [spɪnə'ret] n. part of the spider which spins the threads to make a web. **spin•ning wheel**, n. apparatus for twisting and winding wool. **spin-off**, n. secondary result; useful by-product. **spin out**, v. inf. to make (sth) last a long time.

spi•na bif•i•da [spaɪnə'bɪfɪdə] n. condition from birth, where the spine is badly formed allowing the membrane covering the spinal cord to protrude.

spin•ach ['spɪnɪtʃ] n. common green-leaved vegetable.

spin•dle ['spɪndl] n. (a) pin used for twisting thread in a spinning machine. (b) central pin around which sth turns.

spin•dly ['spɪndlɪ] adj. (-ier, -iest) long, thin and weak.

spin•drift ['spɪndrɪft] n. spray which is blown from breaking waves.

spine [spaɪn] n. (a) backbone. (b) back of a book. (c) prickle (on a cactus/hedgehog, etc.). **spi•nal**, n. referring to the spine; **s. column** = backbone; **s. cord** = group of nerves running down the inside of the spine. **spine•less**, adj. (person) who is weak and indecisive. **spin•y**, adj. covered with prickles.

spin•et [spɪ'net] n. old musical instrument, like a small rectangular harpsichord.

spin•na•ker ['spɪnəkə] n. large balloonlike sail on the front of a racing yacht.

spin•ster ['spɪnstə] n. unmarried woman (usu. middle-aged).

spi•ral ['spaɪərəl] 1. n. (a) thing which is twisted around and around like a spring. (b) thing which turns around and around getting higher or lower all the time. 2. adj. twisted around and around like a spring. 3. v. (**spiraled, spiralled**) to go around and around and rise at the same time. **spi•ral•ly**, adv. in a spiral shape.

spire ['spaɪə] n. pointed construction on top of a church tower.

spir•it ['spɪrɪt] 1. n. (a) soul. (b) ghost; **Holy S.** = the third person of the Christian Trinity. (c) energetic way of doing sth. (d) real meaning (not always expressed in words). (e) **spirits** = strong alcoholic drink (whisky/gin, etc.). 2. v. **to s. away** = to remove as if by magic. **spir•it•ed**, adj. very vigorous. **spir•it•ed•ly**, adv. in a spirited way. **spir•it lev•el**, n. tool for testing if a surface is level using a glass tube containing an airbubble. **spir•it•u•al**. 1. adj. referring to the spirit; dealing with the soul. 2. n. religious song sung by blacks in the southern United States. **spir•it•u•al•ism**, n. belief that you can communicate with the spirits of dead people. **spir•it•u•al•ist**, n. person who tries to communicate with the spirits of dead people. **spir•it•u•al•i•ty**, n. state of being spiritual. **spir•it•u•al•ly**, adv. in a spiritual way. **spir•it•u•ous**, adj. alcoholic.

spit [spɪt] 1. n. (a) long metal rod passed through meat which turns so that the meat is evenly cooked. (b) long thin stretch of land going out into the sea. (c) liquid formed in the mouth; **s. and polish** = excessive cleaning; inf. **he is the dead s. and image of his father** = he looks exactly like his father. 2. v. (a) (**spitted**) to put (meat) on a spit to roast. (b) (**spit, spat**) to send liquid out of the mouth; inf. **he is the spitting image of his father** = he looks exactly like his father. (c) to send sparks out; to rain slightly. **spit•tle** ['spɪtl] n. saliva. **spit•toon** [spɪ'tu:n] n. dish for spitting into.

spite [spaɪt] 1. n. (a) bad feeling against s.o./desire to hurt s.o. (b) **in s. of sth** = without bothering about. 2. *v.* to try to annoy. **spite•ful**, *adj.* full of bad feeling/wishing to hurt s.o. **spite•ful•ly**, *adv.* in a spiteful way. **spite•ful•ness**, *n.* being spiteful.

splash [splæʃ] 1. *n.* (*pl.* -es) (a) noisy throwing of liquid; sound of liquid being thrown noisily. (b) mark made by dirty liquid being scattered. (c) bright patch of color. (d) short spurt (of soda water, etc.). (e) sudden show; sudden spending of money. 2. *v.* (*of liquid*) to make a noise while hitting (a solid). (b) to send dirty liquid on to. (c) to display. **splash down**, *v.* (*of space capsule*) to land in the sea. **splash•down**, *n.* landing (of a spacecraft) in the sea. **splash•y**, *adj.* which splashes.

splat•ter ['splætə] *v.* to splash.

splay [spleɪ] 1. *adj.* turned outward. 2. *v.* to slant outward.

spleen [spliːn] *n.* organ near the stomach which keeps the blood in good condition.

splen•did ['splendɪd] *adj.* magnificent/wonderful. **splen•did•ly**, *adv.* wonderfully/extremely well. **splen•dor**, *Brit.* **splen•dour**, *n.* magnificence.

sple•net•ic [splə'netɪk] *adj.* violently angry.

splice [splaɪs] 1. *n.* joint which links two pieces of rope. 2. *v.* to join (two pieces of rope) by twisting the threads together; to join (two pieces of film) together. **splic•er**, *n.* device for joining pieces of film together.

splint [splɪnt] *n.* stiff bar tied to a broken leg, etc., to keep it straight.

splin•ter ['splɪntə] 1. *n.* small pointed piece (of wood/metal); **s. group** = group of people who have separated from a main group. 2. *v.* to split into thin pointed pieces.

split [splɪt] 1. *n.* (a) thin crack; sharp break. (b) **the splits** = gymnastic exercise where you sit on the floor with one leg stretched out in front, and the other behind you. (c) **banana s.** = dessert of bananas, whipped cream, ice cream and nuts. 2. *v.* (**split**) to divide (sth) into parts; to make (sth) divide/crack; *inf.* **my head is splitting** = I have a bad headache. 3. *adj.* which has been cracked; **s. peas** = dried peas broken in half; **in a s. second** = very fast; **to have a s. personality** = to have two ways of behaving which are quite different in varying circumstances. **split-lev•el**, *adj.* (house) having a room or rooms with part of the floor higher than the rest. **split up**, *v.* to divide.

splotch [splɒtʃ] *n.* dirty mark; oddly-shaped spot of color.

splurge [splɜːdʒ] 1. *n. inf.* spending spree. 2. *v. inf.* to spend money extravagantly.

splut•ter ['splʌtə] *v.* (a) to spit when speaking; to speak rapidly. (b) to sputter (when cooking).

spoil [spɔɪl] 1. *v.* (**spoiled/spoilt**) (a) to ruin/to make bad. (b) to treat (a child) so leniently that it ruins his character. 2. *n. pl.* **spoils** (a) booty, goods taken by soldiers from a defeated enemy. (b) waste material from a mine. **spoil•er**, *n.* decorative panel at the front or back of a car, which is intended to slow the vehicle down. **spoil for**, *v.* to be eager for sth. **spoil•sport**, *n.* person who spoils other people's enjoyment.

spoke [spəʊk] 1. *n.* one of the rods running from the axle of a wheel to the rim. 2. *v. see also* **speak**. **spokeshave**, *n.* tool with a curved blade for smoothing sth round.

spo•ken ['spəʊkn] *v. see* **speak**.

spokes•man, **spokeswoman**, **spokesperson** ['spəʊksmən, -wuːmən, -pɜːsən] *n.* (*pl.* -men, -women) person who speaks on behalf of s.o.

spo•li•a•tion [spəʊlɪ'eɪʃn] *n.* (*formal*) act of plundering.

spon•dee ['spɒndeɪ] *n.* measure (two long syllables) used in Latin poetry.

sponge [spʌndʒ] 1. *n.* (a) soft skeleton of a sea animal/block of synthetic material full of small holes, which soaks up water and is used for washing; **s. bath** = washing a patient in bed, using a sponge; *inf.* **to throw up/in the s.** = to give in/to admit you are beaten. (b) act of washing with a sponge. (c) **s. cake** = light soft cake. 2. *v.* (a) to wash with a sponge. (b) *inf.* **to s. sth from s.o.** = to get by begging or borrowing from s.o. **spong•er**, *n.* person who doesn't work but gets money by begging for or borrowing it from friends. **spon•gy**, *adj.* soft and full of holes.

spon•sor ['spɒnsə] 1. *n.* (a) person who helps s.o./sth by taking responsibility. (b) person or firm who pays for a television show/sports event, etc., as a form of advertisement. (c) person who pays money to a charity if s.o. else walks, swims, runs, a certain distance, etc. 2. *v.* to be a sponsor; to be responsible for (a bill in a legislative body); to pay for (a television show/a sports event, etc.); (*of godparent*) **to s. a child at baptism** = to promise to help the child to lead a Christian life. **spon•sor•ship**, *n.* action of sponsoring.

spon•ta•ne•ous [spɒn'teɪnɪəs] *adj.* which

æ back, ɑː farm, ɒ top, aɪ pipe, aʊ how, aɪə fire, aʊə flower, ɔː bought, ɔɪ toy, e fed, eəhair, eɪ take, ə afraid, əʊ boat, əʊə lower, ɜː word, iː heap, ɪ hit, ɪə hear, uː school, ʊ book, ʌ but, b back, d dog, ð then, dʒ just, f fog, g go, h hand, j yes, k catch, l last, m mix, n nut, ŋ sing, p penny, r round, s some, ʃ short, t too, tʃ chop, θ thing, v voice, w was, z zoo, ʒ treasure

happens freely/which is not forced. **spon•ta•ne•ous•ly**, *adv.* in a spontaneous/natural way. **spon•ta•ne•i•ty** [spɒntə-'nɪətɪ] *n.* acting in a natural way.

spoof [spu:f] *n. inf.* hoax/amusing imitation.

spook [spu:k] *n.* ghost. **spook•y**, *adj. inf.* frightening; (place) which is likely to be haunted.

spool [spu:l] *n.* cylinder around which sth is wound.

spoon [spu:n] 1. *n.* eating utensil with a small bowl and a long handle. 2. *v.* **to s. sth up/into** = to lift sth up/to put sth in with a spoon. **spoon•bill**, *n.* large white bird with a spoon-shaped end to its bill. **spoon-feed**, *v.* to give (a baby) food with a spoon; to teach (people) by giving them answers to questions and not allowing them to work by themselves; to provide everything for (s.o.) so that they need do nothing to help themselves. **spoon•ful**, *n.* amount contained in a spoon.

spoon•er•ism ['spu:nərɪzəm] *n.* exchanging letters of words by mistake (**queer old dean** for *dear old queen*).

spoor ['spuə] *n.* (*no pl.*) tracks left by an animal.

spo•rad•ic [spə'rædɪk] *adj.* which happens at irregular intervals. **spo•rad•i•cal•ly**, *adv.* in a sporadic way.

spore [spɔ:] *n.* plant cell which reproduces without requiring to be fertilized.

spor•ran ['spɒrən] *n.* leather bag worn by Scotsmen in front of the kilt.

sport [spɔ:t] 1. *n.* (a) game (such as soccer/hockey/tennis, etc.); **blood sports** = hunting animals as a sport; **sports car** = light fast open car; **sports jacket/sports coat** = man's casual jacket. (b) *inf.* **good s.** = pleasant person always willing to help. (c) animal/plant which is very different from its parents. 2. *v.* to wear. **sport•ing**, *adj.* (person) who plays according to the rules/who is pleasant and willing to help; **s. chance** = a good or fair chance. **spor•tive**, *adj.* playful. **sports•man**, *n.* (*pl.* -men) (a) person who takes part in a sport. (b) person who plays properly. **sports•man•like**, *adj.* (playing a game) in a proper way/according to the rules; not cheating. **sports•man•ship**, *n.* quality of being a good sportsman/of not cheating. **sports•wear**, *n.* (*no pl.*) clothes worn to play sports or for casual wear. **sports•wom•an**, *n.* (*pl.* -women) woman who takes part in a sport. **sport•y**, *adj.* interested in or engaged in sports.

spot [spɒt] 1. *n.* (a) place; **on the s.** = on duty/at your post; **in a s.** = in a difficult position; **to put s.o. on the s.** = in a position where he has to act. (b) pimple. (c) usu. round colored mark. (d) *inf.* small amount. (e) spotlight/bright light

which only shines on one spot. 2. *v.* (**spotted**) (a) to mark with a spot. (b) to notice. **spot check**, *n.* surprise check (on items at random). **spot•less**, *adj.* very clean. **spot•less•ly**, *adj.* **s. clean** = extremely clean. **spot•light**. 1. *n.* bright light which shines on one small area. 2. *v.* to highlight/to draw attention to (sth). **spot•ter**, *n.* person who notes or watches for things. **spot•ty**, *adj.* (-ier, -iest) full of spots.

spouse ['spauz] *n.* (*formal*) husband or wife.

spout [spaut] 1. *n.* tube for pouring liquid out of a pitcher, etc.; tube for sending waste water/rainwater away from the wall of a building. 2. *v.* (a) to come out in a stream. (b) *inf.* to speak continuously.

sprain [spreɪn] 1. *n.* twist of a joint. 2. *v.* to twist (a joint).

sprang [spræŋ] *v. see* **spring.**

sprat [spræt] *n.* very small herringlike fish.

sprawl [sprɔ:l] 1. *n.* irregular spread; **urban s.** = unregulated spread of houses built over what formerly was countryside. 2. *v.* (a) to lie with arms and legs spread out. (b) to spread out in an irregular way.

spray [spreɪ] 1. *n.* (a) branch with flowers on it. (b) liquid in the form of tiny drops/in a mist. (c) sprayer. 2. *v.* to send out liquid in a fine mist. **spray•er**, *n.* machine for spraying. **spray gun**, *n.* tool shaped like a pistol with a small container attached (used for spraying paint/insecticide, etc.).

spread [spred] 1. *n.* (a) wide expanse; width. (b) act of sending out over a wide area. (c) *inf.* feast. (d) soft food of meat/cheese for spreading on bread, crackers, etc. (e) **double-page s.** = text which runs over two facing pages in a book or newspaper. 2. *v.* (**spread**) (a) to send out/to go out over a wide area. (b) to space out over a period of time. (c) to cover with a layer of sth. **spread-ea•gled**, *adj.* lying flat with arms and legs stretched out. **spread•sheet**, *n.* computer printout of tables of figures.

spree [spri:] *n.* happy time; **to go on a spending s.** = to have a happy time spending money.

sprig [sprɪg] *n.* (a) small branch. (b) design of small branches.

spright•ly ['spraɪtlɪ] *adj.* (-ier, -iest) light and vigorous. **spright•li•ness**, *n.* being sprightly.

spring [sprɪŋ] 1. *n.* (a) small stream of water coming out of the ground. (b) season of the year following winter when plants begin to grow and put out leaves. (c) leap in the air. (d) coiled wire which returns to its original shape after being stretched or compressed. (e) bounciness. 2. *v.* (**sprang, has sprung**) (a) to leap/to bounce. (b) to set (sth) off/to make (sth) happen suddenly. (c) to come **from**. (d) **to**

s. a leak = to start taking in water through a crack. **spring•board,** *n.* long flexible board used to give an impetus to a diver or jumper. **spring•bok** ['sprɪŋbok] *n.* type of African deer. **spring-clean,** *v.* to clean thoroughly after the winter. **spring fe•ver,** *n.* feeling of excitement at the coming of spring. **spring•i•ness,** *n.* being springy. **spring•like,** *adj.* (weather) which is mild like in spring. **spring tide,** *n.* tide which rises and falls very sharply, and occurs at the new and full moon. **spring•time,** *n.* spring/the season after winter. **spring•y,** *adj.* (-ier, -iest) flexible; (board) which bends; (carpet/grass) which is very soft.

sprin•kle ['sprɪŋkl] *v.* to scatter water/sand, etc. **sprin•kler,** *n.* device for sprinkling; **s. system** = system of automatic fire control which sprinkles water on a fire and is set off by rising heat. **sprin•kling,** *n.* (a) action of scattering water/sand, etc. (b) small quantities.

sprint [sprɪnt] 1. *n.* short fast running race. 2. *v.* to run very fast over a short distance. **sprint•er,** *n.* runner who specializes in sprint races.

sprit [sprɪt] *n.* small spar which goes diagonally across a sail. **sprit•sail,** *n.* sail held by a sprit.

sprite [spraɪt] *n.* fairy.

sprock•et ['sprokɪt] *n.* small tooth on a wheel. **sprock•et wheel,** *n.* toothed wheel which connects with a chain.

sprout [spraʊt] 1. *n.* young shoot of a plant; **Brussels sprouts** = edible shoots from a type of cabbage. 2. *v.* to send out (shoots/horns).

spruce [spruːs] 1. *n.* type of fir tree. 2. *adj.* smart. 3. *v.* to **s. yourself up** = to make yourself neat. **spruce•ly,** *adv.* in a spruce way. **spruce•ness,** *n.* being spruce.

sprung [sprʌŋ] *v. see* **spring.**

spry [spraɪ] *adj.* (old person) who is vigorous and active. **spry•ly,** *adv.* in a spry way. **spry•ness,** *n.* being spry.

spud [spʌd] *n. inf.* potato.

spume [spjuːm] *n.* foam (on the sea).

spun [spʌn] *v. see* **spin.**

spunk [spʌŋk] *n. inf.* courage.

spur [spɜː] 1. *n.* (a) metal point attached to the heels of a rider's boots which pricks a horse to make it go faster; **to win your spurs** = to show for the first time how good you are. (b) low hill running from a higher range of mountains; minor road/railroad line leading off a

main one. (c) impetus/stumulus; **on the s. of the moment** = without planning in advance. 2. *v.* (**spurred**) to urge (s.o.) **on.**

spurge ['spɜːdʒ] *n.* common weed with bitter white sap.

spu•ri•ous ['spjʊərɪəs] *adj.* false. **spu•ri•ous•ly,** *adv.* in a spurious way. **spu•ri•ous•ness,** *n.* being spurious.

spurn [spɜːn] *v.* to reject (an offer) scornfully.

spurt [spɜːt] 1. *n.* (a) jet of liquid. (b) sudden effort. 2. *v.* (a) **to s. out** = to come out in a jet. (b) to show sudden energy.

sput•ter ['spʌtə] *v.* to spit/to send out sparks or fat.

spu•tum ['spjuːtəm] *n.* mucus which is spit out of the mouth.

spy [spaɪ] 1. *n.* person who is paid to try to find out what the enemy/a criminal gang/a rival company is planning to do. 2. *v.* to see; **to s. on s.o.** = to try, in secret, to find out what s.o. is doing. **spy•ing,** *n.* trying to find out information about the enemy. **spy out,** *v.* to try to find out (sth) secretly.

squab [skwob] *n.* small pigeon.

squab•ble ['skwobl] 1. *n.* quarrel/argument. 2. *v.* to argue.

squad [skwod] *n.* (a) small group of soldiers; **firing s.** = group of soldiers who shoot s.o. who has been condemned to death. (b) small group of workmen/police; **s. car** = police car on patrol. (c) (sports) team.

squad•ron ['skwodrən] *n.* group of soldiers; group of aircraft; group of naval ships.

squal•id ['skwolɪd] *adj.* sordid/unpleasant/dirty. **squal•id•ly,** *adv.* in a squalid way. **squal•or,** *n.* dirt; dirty state.

squall [skwoːl] 1. *n.* sudden gust of wind. 2. *v.* to cry loudly. **squal•ly,** *adj.* accompanied by gusts of wind.

squan•der ['skwondə] *v.* to waste (money/energy).

square ['skweə] 1. *n.* (a) shape with four equal sides and four right angles; *inf.* **we're back to s. one** = we'll have to start planning again from the beginning. (b) open area in a town, surrounded by buildings. (c) instrument for drawing right angles. (d) a number multiplied by itself. 2. *adj.* (a) shaped like a square. (b) **s. corner** = corner with a right angle. (c) fair/straightforward; **s. deal** = honest treatment; **s. meal** = a good filling meal. (d) straight. (e) multiplied by itself; **s. mile** = area of one mile multiplied by one mile; **s. root** =

æ back, ɑː farm, ɒ top, aɪ pipe, aʊ how, aɪə fire, aʊə flower, ɔː bought, ɔɪ toy, e fed, eəhair, eɪ take, ə afraid, əʊ boat, əʊə lower, ɜː word, iː heap, ɪ hit, ɪə hear, uː school, ʊ book, ʌ but, b back, d dog, ð then, dʒ just, f fog, g go, h hand, j yes, k catch, l last, m mix, n nut, ŋ sing, p penny, r round, s some, ʃ short, t too, tʃ chop, θ thing, v voice, w was, z zoo, ʒ treasure

number which when multiplied by itself produces the number you have. 3. *adv.* (a) in a level/straight way. (b) directly. 4. *v.* (a) to make (a round stone, etc.) square; **squared paper** = paper with squares drawn on it (for making graphs, etc.). (b) to balance (accounts); to pay (s.o.) what is owed; to pay (s.o.) a bribe. (c) to multiply (sth) by itself. (d) to straighten (your shoulders); **to s. off with s.o.** = to prepare to fight. **square•ly,** *adv.* in a straightforward way.

squash [skwɒʃ] 1. *n.* (a) fast game played with rackets in a court with high walls. (b) vegetable like a pumpkin, etc. 2. *v.* (a) to crush. (b) to stop (a revolt) by force; to stop (s.o.) speaking by being rude to them. **squash court,** *n.* court for playing squash. **squash•y,** *adv.* (**-ier, -iest**) soft and wet.

squat [skwɒt] 1. *n.* action or position of squatting. 2. *v.* (**squatted**) (a) to crouch down, sitting on your heels. (b) to occupy an empty house without the permission of the owner. 3. *adj.* (**squatter, squattest**) short and thick. **squat•ter,** *n.* person who occupies an empty house without the permission of the owner.

squaw [skwɔ:] *n.* North American Indian woman.

squawk [skwɔ:k] 1. *n.* short harsh cry. 2. *v.* to make short harsh cries.

squeak [skwi:k] 1. *n.* little high-pitched cry (like that of a mouse); high-pitched sound (like a rusty hinge). 2. *v.* to make a squeak. **squeak•y,** *adj.* (gate) which squeaks.

squeal [skwi:l] 1. *n.* long loud high-pitched cry. 2. *v.* to make long loud high-pitched cries.

squeam•ish ['skwi:mɪʃ] *adj.* easily made sick/easily shocked. **squeam•ish•ness,** *n.* being squeamish.

squee•gee ['skwi:dʒi:] *n.* implement for removing water from floors, windows, etc. made of a wad of sponge attached to a hinged plate.

squeeze [skwi:z] 1. *n.* (a) pressure; crushing. (b) **s. of lemon** = few drops of lemon juice. 2. *v.* (a) to crush/to force/to press. (b) to push together; to push to get into/through a small space. **squeez•er,** *n.* device for pressing citrus fruit to get the juice out.

squelch [skweltʃ] 1. *n.* noise made by a wet sticky substance. 2. *v.* to make a wet sucking noise.

squib [skwɪb] *n.* (a) small firework which bangs. (b) short saying or piece of writing, often witty or satirical.

squid [skwɪd] *n.* sea animal like a small octopus.

squig•gle ['skwɪgl] 1. *n.* illegible curly marks/handwriting. 2. *v.* to make squiggles.

squint [skwɪnt] 1. *n.* (a) state where your two

eyes look in different directions. (b) act of squinting. 2. *v.* (a) to have eyes which look in different directions. (b) to half-close your eyes when looking at sth.

squire ['skwaɪə] *n.* (a) (*in England*) gentleman living in the country, often the owner of a large house. (b) male escort for a woman.

squirm [skwɜ:m] *v.* to wriggle about; **it makes me s.** = it makes me very embarrassed.

squir•rel ['skwɪrəl] *n.* common small mammal with a large bushy tail, living in trees.

squirt [skwɜ:t] 1. *n.* (a) sharp jet of liquid. (b) *inf.* **little s.** = small insignificant person. 2. *v.* to send out a sharp jet of liquid.

squish•y ['skwɪʃɪ] *adj.* soft and squashy.

Sr *symbol for* strontium.

St. [snt; stri:t] *short form of* Saint or Street.

stab [stæb] 1. *n.* wound made with a sharp knife; **s. in the back** = attack by s.o. who is thought to be loyal; *inf.* **to have a s. at** = to try to do. 2. *v.* (**stabbed**) to wound with a sharp knife; **to s. s.o. in the back** = to attack s.o. who thinks you are his friend.

sta•ble ['steɪbl] 1. *n.* (a) building for keeping a horse. (b) **stables** = place where horses are kept for breeding/racing, etc. 2. *v.* to keep (a horse) in a stable. 3. *adj.* (**-er, -est**) solid; steady/not wobbly. (b) (*in chemistry*) (compound) which does not change or decompose easily. **sta•bil•i•ty** [stə'bɪlɪtɪ] *n.* steadiness. **sta•bi•li•za•tion** [steɪbɪlaɪ'zeɪʃn] *n.* making stable. **sta•bi•lize** ['steɪbɪlaɪz] *v.* to make steady. **sta•bi•liz•er,** *n.* (a) fin attached to the hull of a ship to prevent rolling. (b) substance added to processed food to keep it in a stable condition. **sta•ble•boy,** *n.* man who looks after horses in a stable. **sta•bly,** *adv.* in a stable way.

stac•ca•to [stə'ka:təʊ] *adj. & n.* sharp (noise).

stack [stæk] 1. *n.* (a) heap; *inf.* lots (of). (b) brick structure housing a chimney. (c) inner part of a library where books are kept without being open to the public. 2. *v.* (a) to pile up. (b) (*of aircraft*) to circle around waiting in turn for permission to land at a busy airport.

sta•di•um ['steɪdɪəm] *n.* large building for sports events.

staff [stɑ:f] 1. *n.* (a) long thick stick. (b) people working in a school/college/company, etc. (c) officers who help the commander organize a military force; **general s.** = officers who work at headquarters. (d) (*pl.* **staves**) set of five lines on which musical notes are written. 2. *v.* to provide employees for (a company, etc.). **staff•er,** *n.* member of a staff.

stag [stæg] *n.* male deer; **s. party** = party for men only. **stag bee•tle,** *n.* large black beetle with horns.

stage [steɪdʒ] 1. *n.* (a) platform (on which a

play is acted, etc.); **s. directions** = notes in the script of a play showing what the actors have to do; **s. fright** = nervousness before appearing before an audience; **s. whisper** = loud whisper which everyone can hear; **to go on the s.** = to become an actor. (b) period/phase. (c) each of the parts of a rocket. (d) part of a journey. 2. *v.* (a) to put on/to arrange (a performance of a play, etc.). (b) to make/to organize. **stage•coach**, *n.* (*old*) horsedrawn passenger coach which ran regularly along certain routes. **stage•craft**, *n.* art of the theater. **stage•hand**, *n.* person who moves scenery/prepares the stage (in a theater). **stage-man•age**, *v.* to arrange/to organize (a performance); to plan (a trick/a coup). **stage man•ag•er**, *n.* person who organizes a performance of a play/opera, etc. **stag•er**, *n. inf.* **old s.** = old experienced person. **stag•ing**, *n.* putting on (of a play). **stag•y**, *adj.* unreal; looking too much as if being acted on a stage.

stag•fla•tion [stæg'fleɪʃn] *n.* period when the economy stagnates but inflation increases.

stag•ger ['stægə] *v.* (a) to walk unsteadily. (b) to astonish. (c) to arrange things so that they do not coincide exactly. **stag•ger•ing**, *adj.* astonishing. **stag•ger•ing•ly**, *adv.* astonishingly.

stag•nant ['stægnənt] *adj.* (a) (water) which does not flow/which is not pure enough to drink. (b) (business) which does not make increased sales. **stag•nate** [stæg'neɪt] *v.* to stay static; not advance. **stag•na•tion** [stæg'neɪʃn] *n.* being stagnant.

staid [steɪd] *adj.* serious/not adventurous.

stain [steɪn] 1. *n.* (a) dirty mark which is difficult to remove. (b) liquid used to change the color of wood. 2. *v.* (a) to make a dirty mark on (sth). (b) to change the color of (wood, etc.); **stained glass** = colored glass for windows (esp. in church). **stain•less**, *adj.* without any stain; **s. steel** = steel which contains nickel and chromium so that it does not rust in contact with air or water.

stair ['steə] *n.* (a) step (on a staircase) (b) (**flight of**) **stairs** = series of steps leading from one floor of a building to the next. **stair car•pet**, *n.* long narrow piece of carpet for covering stairs. **stair•case**, *n.* flight of stairs (usu. with a handrail). **stair rod**, *n.* metal rod which keeps a stair carpet in place. **stair•way**, *n.* staircase.

stake [steɪk] 1. *n.* (a) strong pointed stick. (b)

money which is gambled; **he has a s. in the company** = he has invested some money in the company, hoping to make a profit; **at s.** = which may be lost. 2. *v.* (a) to put a stick in the ground; **to s. your claim to** = to suggest that you hold the right to own sth. (b) to bet (money, etc.).

sta•lac•tite ['stæləktaɪt] *n.* long point of limestone hanging from the ceiling of a cave, formed by mineral deposits from dripping water.

sta•lag•mite ['stæləgmaɪt] *n.* long point of limestone rising from the floor of a cave formed by mineral deposits from dripping water.

stale [steɪl] *adj.* (**-er, -est**) (a) no longer fresh; (joke) that has been repeated many times. (b) **to grow s.** = to become bored/tired so that you are no longer working well. **stale•mate**, *n.* (a) (*in chess*) position where a player cannot move without being checkmated. (b) situation where neither side will compromise. **stale•ness**, *n.* being stale.

stalk [stɔːk] 1. *n.* (a) thin stem of a plant. (b) small part of the stem which attaches a fruit to the plant. 2. *v.* (a) to try to get close enough to an animal to shoot it. (b) to march along proudly. **stalk•er**, *n.* person who stalks animals.

stall [stɔːl] 1. *n.* (a) compartment for one animal in a stable, etc. (b) **stalls** = seats in church for the choir and clergy. (c) booth or table with goods laid out for sale; small moveable store. 2. *v.* (a) (*of a car engine*) to stop unintentionally. (b) (*of an aircraft*) to go so slowly that it falls suddenly. (c) to put off making a decision.

stal•lion ['stæljən] *n.* male horse, esp. one kept for breeding.

stal•wart ['stɒlwət] 1. *adj.* strong/vigorous/brave. 2. *n.* strong/vigorous/brave person.

sta•men ['steɪmən] *n.* one of the thin spikes in the center of a flower which carry the pollen.

stam•i•na ['stæmɪnə] *n.* ability to do sth for a long time.

stam•mer ['stæmə] 1. *n.* unintentional repetition of sounds when speaking. 2. *v.* to repeat sounds when speaking. **stam•mer•er**, *n.* person who stammers.

stamp [stæmp] 1. *n.* (a) banging your foot on the ground. (b) object for making a mark on sth. (c) device for cutting out a design. (d) small piece of gummed paper for sticking on an envelope/package, etc., to pay for it to be

---

æ **back**, ɑ: **farm**, ɒ: **top**, aɪ **pipe**, aʊ **how**, aɪə **fire**, aʊə **flower**, ɔ: **bought**, ɔɪ **toy**, e **fed**, eəhair, eɪ **take**, ə **afraid**, əʊ **boat**, əʊə **lower**, ɜ: **word**, i: **heap**, ɪ **hit**, ɪə **hear**, u: **school**, ʊ **book**, ʌ **but**, b **back**, d **dog**, ð **then**, dʒ **just**, f **fog**, g **go**, h **hand**, j **yes**, k **catch**, l **last**, m **mix**, n **nut**, ŋ **sing**, p **penny**, r **round**, s **some**, ʃ **short**, t **too**, tʃ **chop**, θ **thing**, v **voice**, w **was**, z **zoo**, ʒ **treasure**

sent by mail; **s. machine** = machine which sells stamps automatically. (e) any small piece of gummed paper used to show you have made a payment. (f) mark made by a rubber stamp. 2. *v.* (a) to bang your foot hard on the ground. (b) to make a mark on sth. (c) to stick a stamp on (sth); **stamped self-addressed envelope** = envelope with your own name, address and a stamp, which you enclose in a letter so that the person you are writing to can reply. **stamp out,** *v.* to stop/to eradicate.

stam•pede [stæm'piːd] 1. *n.* mad rush (of animals/people). 2. *v.* to rush madly.

stance [stɑːns] *n.* (a) way of standing. (b) attitude/position.

stanch [stɑːnʃ] *v.* to stop blood flowing.

stan•chion ['stænʃn] *n.* vertical post/bar which holds sth up.

stand [stænd] 1. *n.* (a) position; **to make a s. against** = to resist. (b) support; thing which holds sth up; flat base. (c) arrangement of shelves/posters, etc., at an exhibition. (d) **stands** = series of seats for spectators at a sports event. (e) **witness s.** = place where a witness sits in a law court. (f) **taxi s.** = place where taxis wait. (g) **one-night s.** = stop for a single performance (of a play/by a musical group) before moving to another location the following night. 2. *v.* (**stood**) to be/to place in an upright position. (b) to be on your feet/not be sitting down. (c) to stay/to remain. (d) to bear/to accept. **stand a•side,** *v.* to step to one side. **stand back,** *v.* to step backward; to be behind. **stand by,** *v.* (a) to be ready. (b) to stand at one side without taking part in the action. (c) to support/to be faithful. **stand•by,** *n.* (a) thing which is ready to go into action if necessary. (b) waiting; **he is on s.** = he is waiting to see if he is needed; (*at an airport*) traveler waiting for a ticket to become available because of a cancellation. **stand for,** *v.* (a) to mean. (b) to be in favor of. **stand in for,** *v.* to take s.o.'s place. **stand-in,** *n.* person who takes s.o.'s place. **stand•ing.** 1. *n.* (a) being on your feet; **s. room only** = room for people to stand, not to sit. (b) social position. 2. *adj.* (a) upright/not lying or sitting. (b) permanent; **s. order** = permanent order always in effect; **it is a s. joke** = it is sth we always laugh about. **stand•off•ish,** *adj.* (person) who is cold/who does not make friends. **stand•off•ish•ness,** *n.* unfriendliness. **stand out,** *v.* to be obvious. **stand o•ver,** *v.* to supervise s.o. very closely. **stand•pipe,** *n.* upright pipe connected to the water main in the street, with a tap which allows water to be taken off when the supply to buildings has been cut. **stand•point,** *n.* point of view/position from which you look at a problem.

stand•still, *n.* state of being stopped. **stand to,** *v.* (*in army, etc.*) to be ready to go into action. **stand up,** *v.* (a) to get to your feet. (b) **s. up straight!** = hold yourself straight. (c) **to s. up for sth** = to defend/to support; **to s. up to s.o.** = to fight or confront s.o. bravely; **to s. s.o. up** = to fail to meet s.o. at a rendezvous. **stand-up,** *adj.* **stand-up buffet** = buffet where you eat standing up; **stand-up fight** = real fight where people come to blows.

stand•ard ['stændəd] 1. *n.* (a) model with which sth is compared. (b) excellent quality which is set as a target. (c) large flag. (d) tree/bush grown with a single tall trunk. 2. *adj.* (a) normal/usual; **s. pronunciation** = pronunciation which is generally used by educated speakers. (b) **s. rose** = rose grown with a single tall trunk. (c) which is taken as a measure. **stand•ard•i•za•tion** [stændədaɪ'zeɪʃn] *n.* setting of a standard; making sure that everything conforms to a standard. **stand•ard•ize** ['stændədaɪz] *v.* to make everything conform to a standard.

stank [stæŋk] *v. see* **stink.**

stan•za ['stænzə] *n.* section of a poem made up of a series of lines.

sta•pes ['steɪpiːz] *n.* one of the ossicles in the ear.

staph•y•lo•coc•cus [stæfɪlə'kɒkəs] *n.* (*pl.* **-cocci** [-kɒkaɪ]) type of bacterium which causes food poisoning and infection in the blood.

sta•ple ['steɪpl] 1. *n.* piece of strong bent wire used to hold things in place; small wire clip for attaching papers together by being passed through them and then bent over. 2. *adj.* main product of a country/town, etc. (b) **s. diet** = main part of what you eat. 3. *v.* to attach with a staple. **sta•pler,** *n.* small instrument for stapling.

star [stɑː] 1. *n.* (a) body in the sky like a very distant sun which shines at night. (b) the sign of the zodiac which marks your birth; *inf.* **thank your lucky stars** = consider yourself very lucky. (c) shape with several regular points. (d) asterisk. (e) actor/actress who is very well known to the public. 3. *v.* (**starred**) (a) to play an important part (**in** a play, motion picture, etc.). (b) to have (a famous actor) playing. (c) to mark with a star. **star•dom,** *n.* being a star in motion pictures, etc. **star•fish,** *n.* sea animal shaped like a star. **star•less,** *adj.* (night) when no stars are visible. **star•let,** *n.* young actress, esp. in motion pictures. **star•light,** *n.* light from the stars. **star•lit,** *adj.* (night) lit by the light of the stars. **star•ry,** *adj.* covered with stars. **star•ry-eyed,** *adj.* wildly hopeful. **Stars and Stripes,** *n.* the flag of the United States.

star•board ['stɑːbəd] *n. & adj.* right side of a ship when facing forward.

starch [stɑːtʃ] 1. *n.* (a) white energy-giving carbohydrate in bread/potatoes/rice, etc. (b) white powder mixed with water to make cloth stiff. 2. *v.* to make (cloth) stiff with starch. **starch•y,** *adj.* (a) full of starch. (b) very formal (manner).

stare ['steə] 1. *n.* fixed look from the eyes. 2. *v.* to look at s.o./sth with a fixed gaze; *inf.* **it's staring you in the face** = it is very obvious. **star•ing,** *adj., adv.* with a fixed look.

stark [stɑːk] 1. *adj.* (-er, -est) (a) total/pure (nonsense). (b) bare (landscape/details). 2. *adv.* completely (naked); **s. raving mad** = completely mad. **stark•ly,** *adv.* in a stark way. **stark•ness,** *n.* being stark.

star•ling ['stɑːlɪŋ] *n.* common dark bird with a green sheen to its feathers.

start [stɑːt] 1. *n.* (a) beginning; **for a s.** = in the first place. (b) **to give s.o. two meters' s.** = to place them at the beginning of a race two meters in front of you. (c) sudden jump/sudden movement; **by fits and starts** = at odd moments. 2. *v.* (a) to begin. (b) to (cause to) begin to work. (c) to set (sth) going. (d) to jump (in surprise). **start•er,** *n.* (a) person or animal who starts. (b) person who gives the signal for the start of a race. (c) *inf.* first course in a meal. (d) machine which starts a car engine. **start•ing,** *n.* beginning (of a race, etc.); **starting point** = point from which everything begins. **start off, start out,** *v.* to begin to do/to go. **start up,** *v.* to make (an engine, etc.) begin to work.

star•tle ['stɑːtl] *v.* to make (s.o.) jump in surprise. **star•tling,** *adj.* remarkable/surprising.

starve [stɑːv] *v.* to deprive of food; to die from lack of food; *inf.* **I'm starving** = I am very hungry; **starved for** = not having enough of. **star•va•tion** [stɑːˈveɪʃn] *n.* lack of food.

stash [stæʃ] *v. inf.* **to s. away** = to store in a safe place.

state [steɪt] 1. *n.* (a) condition; *inf.* **in a s.** = very angry. (b) government of a nation; **state-owned** = owned by the country/government (not privately owned). (c) independent country. (d) one of the semi-independent parts of a federal country. 2. *adj.* belonging to/run by/given by the government. 3. *v.* to say clearly/to claim. **stat•ed,** *adj.* fixed/regulated. **State De•part•ment,** *n.* section of the U.S. government dealing with foreign

affairs. **state•less,** *adj.* (person) who is not a citizen of any state. **state•li•ness,** *n.* being stately. **state•ly,** *adj.* noble/dignified. **state•ment,** *n.* declaration clearly written or spoken. **state-of-the-art,** *adj.* very advanced technically. **state•room,** *n.* large cabin on a ship. **state•side,** *adj. & adv.* in/to the United States of America. **states•man,** *n.* (*pl.* -men) person who is or was a member of a government. **states•man•like,** *adj.* like a statesman. **states•man•ship,** *n.* skill in government of a country.

stat•ic ['stætɪk] 1. *adj.* not moving; **s. electricity** = electricity which stays in one place (in a car/cloth). 2. *n.* electrical interference in the air which disturbs a radio signal. **stat•ics,** *n.pl.* study of physical forces in equilibrium or of motionless bodies.

sta•tion ['steɪʃn] 1. *n.* (a) place where trains stop to pick up and put down passengers; place where buses begin or end their journeys. (b) central building for some sort of service. (c) **radio s./TV s.** = broadcasting headquarters with its own frequency. (d) position in society. (e) **sheep s.** = large sheep farm in Australia. 2. *v.* to place (s.o.) at a spot. **sta•tion•ar•y,** *adj.* not moving. **sta•tion•mas•ter,** *n.* person in charge of a railroad station. **sta•tion wag•on,** *n.* long car with a part at the back for carrying goods.

sta•tion•er ['steɪʃənə] *n.* person who sells stationery. **sta•tion•er•y,** *n.* materials for writing, such as paper/pens/ink.

sta•tis•tic [stəˈtɪstɪk] *n.* fact given in the form of a figure; **statistics** = study of facts given in the form of figures. **sta•tis•ti•cal,** *adj.* referring to statistics. **sta•tis•ti•cal•ly,** *adv.* in a statistical way. **stat•is•ti•cian** [stætɪsˈtɪʃn] *n.* person who studies/analyzes statistics.

sta•tue ['stætjuː] *n.* figure of a person or thing carved in stone/made of metal, etc. **stat•u•ar•y,** *n.* collection of statues. **stat•u•esque** [stætjuˈesk] *adj.* (woman) who is beautiful but large and dignified. **stat•u•ette** [stætjuˈet] *n.* small statue.

stat•ure ['stætʃə] *n.* (a) height. (b) importance.

sta•tus ['steɪtəs] *n.* (*no pl.*) (a) legal position. (b) importance/position in the eyes of other people; **s. symbol** = object which may make other people think more highly of you. **sta•tus quo** ['steɪtəs'kwəʊ] *n.* state of things as they are at the moment.

stat•ute ['stætjuːt] *n*. law. **stat•u•to•ry** ['stætjutrɪ] *adj*. legal; officially imposed.

staunch [stɔːnʃ] 1. *adj*. (**-er, -est**) firm (friend). 2. *v*. to stop (a flow of blood). **staunch•ly,** *adv*. firmly.

stave [steɪv] 1. *n*. (a) curved piece of wood which forms part of a barrel. (b) set of five lines on which music is written. 2. *v*. (a) (**staved/stove**) **to s. in** = to batter a hole in a boat/a barrel. (b) **to s. off** = to hold off/to prevent.

stay [steɪ] 1. *n*. (a) time which you spend in a place. (b) **s. of execution** = delay ordered by a governor in carrying out a sentence. (c) strong rope which supports, e.g. a mast on a ship. (d) (*old*) **stays** = corset. 2. *v*. to stop in a place. **stay-at-home,** *n*. person who does not go out much. **stay a•way,** *v*. to keep away. **stay in,** *v*. to stay at home. **stay out,** *v*. not to come home. **stay up,** *v*. to postpone going to bed.

stead [sted] *n*. (a) **it stood him in good s.** = it was very useful to him. (b) **in your s.** = in place of you.

stead•fast ['stedfɑːst] *adj*. firm/constant. **stead•fast•ly,** *adv*. firmly/constantly.

stead•y ['stedɪ] 1. *adj*. (**-ier, -iest**) (a) firm/not wobbling. (b) continuing regularly. (c) (person) who is not easily upset. 2. *n*. *inf*. boyfriend/girlfriend with whom you go out regularly. 3. *inter*. be careful. 4. *v*. to make/to keep firm. **Stead•i•cam** ['stedɪkæm] *n*. trademark for a device for steadying a hand-held camera. **stead•i•ly,** *adv*. (a) firmly. (b) regularly/continuously. **stead•i•ness,** *n*. being steady.

steak [steɪk] *n*. (a) thick slice of meat, esp. beef, cut from the best part of the animal. (b) thick slice of fish. **steak•house,** *n*. restaurant serving steak and other grilled food.

steal [stiːl] *v*. (**stole; stolen**) (a) to take (sth which does not belong to you). (b) **to s. a glance at** = to look at quickly and secretly. (c) **to s. a march on s.o.** = to do sth stealthily before s.o. can do it. (d) to creep very quietly (into).

stealth [stelθ] *n*. **by s.** = in a secret way/without anyone knowing. **stealth•i•ly,** *adv*. in a stealthy way. **stealth•i•ness,** *n*. being stealthy. **stealth•y** *adj*. (**-ier, -iest**) without anyone knowing or seeing.

steam [stiːm] 1. *n*. (a) vapor which comes off hot water/from warm breath; **s. engine** = engine which runs on steam pressure. (b) *inf*. **to let off s.** = (i) to use up your excess energy; (ii) to explode with anger. 2. *v*. (*a*) to cook by steam. (b) to send out steam. (c) to move by steam power. (d) (*of window*) **to s. up** = to be covered by a mist; *inf*. **to get steamed up about** = to get very annoyed. **steam•boat,** *n*. boat powered by steam. **steam•er,** *n*. (a) large passenger ship (powered by steam). (b) type of pan with holes in the bottom which is placed over boiling water for steaming vegetables, etc. **steam•roll•er,** *n*. vehicle with a very heavy roller for flattening newly laid road surfaces. **steam•ship,** *n*. large passenger ship (powered esp. by steam). **steam•y,** *adj*. full of steam.

ste•a•tite ['strətaɪt] *n*. soft gray stone which can be carved.

steed [stiːd] *n*. (*in literature*) horse.

steel [stiːl] 1. *n*. (a) hard flexible metal made from iron and carbon; **s. band** = West Indian band which plays music on steel drums of varying sizes. (b) bar of rough steel for sharpening knives. 2. *v*. **to s. yourself to do sth** = to get up enough courage to do sth. **steel•i•ness,** *n*. being steely. **steel wool,** *n*. very fine steel wire used in wads for cleaning metal. **steel•works,** *n*. factory which produces steel. **steel•y,** *adj*. sharp/hard like steel.

steep [stiːp] 1. *adj*. (**-er, -est**) (a) which rises or falls sharply. (b) *inf*. excessive. 2. *v*. to soak in a liquid for a long time. **steep•en,** *v*. to become steeper. **steep•ly,** *adv*. (rising) sharply. **steep•ness,** *n*. being steep.

stee•ple ['stiːpl] *n*. church tower with the top rising to a point. **stee•ple•chase,** *n*. race run across open country, over fences, hedges, etc.; race on a track over hurdles. **stee•ple•chas•er,** *n*. person/horse that runs in a steeplechase. **stee•ple•jack,** *n*. person who climbs towers/factory chimneys, etc., to do repairs.

steer ['stɪə] 1. *n*. young bull raised for meat. 2. *v*. to guide/to make (a vehicle) go in a certain direction; **to s. clear of** = to avoid. **steer•age,** *n*. (a) act of steering. (b) cheapest accommodation in a passenger ship. **steer•ing,** *n*. mechanism in a car which steers it; **s. wheel** = wheel which is turned by the driver to alter the direction of a car; **s. column** = metal tube to which the steering wheel is attached; **s. committee** = small committee which does detailed work on the agenda for a large committee meeting. **steers•man,** *n*. (*pl.* **-men**) man who steers a ship.

ste•le [stiːl] *n*. carved slab of stone, placed upright.

stel•lar ['stelə] *adj*. referring to stars.

stem [stem] 1. *n*. (a) long stalk on which flowers and leaves grow. (b) thin part of a wine glass/of a tobacco pipe. (c) basic part of a word to which endings or prefixes are added. (d) **from s. to stern** = from the bows to the stern of a boat. 2. *v*. (**stemmed**) (a) to result **from.** (b) to stop/to prevent (a flow, etc.).

stench [stentʃ] n. strong unpleasant smell.

sten•cil ['stensl] 1. n. sheet of cardboard or metal with a pattern cut out of it, so that if it is placed on a surface and color is passed over it, the pattern will appear on the surface; pattern/letters/numbers, etc., which are painted in this way. 2. v. (stenciled, stencilled) (a) to mark with a stencil. (b) to make using a stencil.

sten gun ['stengʌn] n. British small machine gun.

ste•nog•ra•pher [stə'nɒgrəfə] n. person who can take shorthand. **ste•nog•ra•phy** [stə-'nɒgrəfɪ] n. shorthand.

ste•no•sis [sten'əʊsɪs] n. condition where an artery becomes narrow.

sten•to•ri•an [sten'tɔːrɪən] adj. (formal) very loud (voice).

step [step] 1. n. (a) single movement of the foot when walking/running; distance covered by this movement; **s. by s.** = little by little. (b) sound made by moving a foot forward. (c) regular movement of the feet; **keep in s.** = move at the same pace as everyone else; **out of s.** = not moving at the same pace as everyone else. (d) action. (e) stair (on a staircase); flat rung (on a ladder). 2. v. (stepped) to make a movement with a foot; **to s. on the brakes** = to push the brake pedal hard. **Step,** n. aerobic exercise system that involves repeatedly stepping on and off a specially-designed box. **step in,** v. to involve yourself/to interfere. **step•lad•der,** n. ladder with flat rungs. **step•ping•stone,** n. one of a series of stones in a stream which allow you to cross it. **step up,** v. to increase.

step- [step] prefix showing a family relationship which is through a parent who has remarried. **step•broth•er,** n. male child of your stepfather or stepfather. **step•daugh•ter,** n. daughter of your wife/husband by another marriage. **step•fa•ther,** n. husband of your mother who is not your father. **step•moth•er,** n. wife of your father, who is not your mother. **step•sis•ter,** n. female child of your stepfather or stepmother. **step•son,** n. son of your wife/husband by another marriage.

steppe [step] n. wide grass-covered plain in Russia and Asia.

stereo- ['sterɪəʊ] prefix referring to sth which has two dimensions.

ster•e•o ['sterɪəʊ] n. & adj. (machine) which reproduces sound through two different channels and loudspeakers.

ster•e•o•phon•ic [sterɪəʊ'fɒnɪk] adj. referring to sound which comes from two places at once.

ster•e•o•scope ['sterɪəʊskəʊp] n. apparatus which shows a picture which appears to have depth and be three-dimensional. **ster•e•o•scop•ic** [sterɪə'skɒpɪk] adj. referring to seeing in three dimensions; **s. vision** = ability to see the same object with both eyes, and so judge distance.

ster•e•o•type ['sterɪətaɪp] n. pattern for certain types of person. **ster•e•o•typed,** adj. fitting certain patterns.

ster•ile ['steraɪl] adj. (a) not capable of bearing fruit/children. (b) so clean that no germs/bacteria can grow. **ste•ril•i•ty** [ste'rɪlɪtɪ] n. inability to grow fruit/to produce children or ideas. **ster•i•li•za•tion** [sterɪlaɪ'zeɪʃn] n. action of sterilizing. **ster•i•lize** ['sterɪlaɪz] v. (a) to make (s.o.) incapable of producing children. (b) to make so clean that bacteria/germs cannot grow. **ster•i•liz•er,** n. apparatus for sterilizing.

ster•ling ['stɜːlɪŋ] 1. adj. of a certain standard/of good quality; **s. silver** = silver of a certain high purity. 2. n. standard measure of British currency.

stern [stɜːn] 1. adj. (-er, -est) harsh/strict. 2. n. rear part of a ship. **stern•ly,** adv. in a stern way. **stern•ness,** n. being stern. **stern•wheel•er,** n. large pleasure ship with a paddle wheel at the stern.

ster•num ['stɜːnəm] n. central bone on the chest. **ster•nal,** adj. referring to the sternum.

ste•roid ['stɪərɔɪd] n. one of a group of natural substances in plants and animals, including hormones.

ster•to•rous ['stɜːtərəs] adj. making a snoring sound.

stet [stet] v. word showing that a correction should not be made.

steth•o•scope ['steθəskəʊp] n. doctor's instrument for listening to a patient's chest.

stet•son ['stetsən] n. tall cowboy hat with a wide brim.

ste•ve•dore ['stiːvədɔː] n. person who works at a port, unloading or loading ships.

stew [stjuː] 1. n. dish of meat and vegetables cooked together for a long time; inf. **in a s.** = in an agitated state. 2. v. to cook for a long time in liquid. **stewed,** adj. Sl. drunk.

æ back, aː farm, ɒ top, aɪ pipe, aʊ how, aɪə fire, aʊə flower, ɔː bought, ɔɪ toy, e fed, eəhair, eɪ take, ə afraid, əʊ boat, əʊə lower, ɜː word, iː heap, ɪ hit, ɪə hear, uː school, ʊ book, ʌ but, b back, d dog, ð then, dʒ just, f fog, g go, h hand, j yes, k catch, l last, m mix, n nut, ŋ sing, p penny, r round, s some, ʃ short, t too, tʃ chop, θ thing, v voice, w was, z zoo, ʒ treasure

stew•ard ['stjʊəd] *n*. (a) man who serves meals or drinks on a ship/aircraft/in a club. (b) person who organizes a meeting; person who looks after a farm or estate for the owner. (c) **shop s.** = elected union representative. **stew•ard•ess**, *n*. woman who looks after passengers on a ship or aircraft.

stick [stɪk] 1. *n*. (a) piece of wood; strong piece of wood with a handle used as a support when walking; **hockey s.** = stick with a curved end, used in playing hockey. (b) long piece. 2. *v*. **(stuck)** (a) to jab or push (sth sharp) **into** sth. (b) to glue; to attach. (c) to stay close/to keep **(to)**. (d) to be fixed/not to be able to move. **stick•er**, *n*. small piece of paper or plastic which you can stick on a surface as a decoration or advertisement. **stick•i•ly**, *adv*. in a sticky way. **stick•i•ness**, *n*. state of being sticky. **stick•ing plas•ter**, *n*. strip of cloth which can be stuck to the skin to cover a wound. **stick-in-the-mud**, *n*. *inf*. person who will not accept new ideas. **stick-on**, *adj*. (label) which sticks on to a surface. **stick out** *v*. *(a)* to push out; to be further out than usual. (b) to be easily seen. **stick up**, *v*. (a) to put up (a notice, etc.); **s. them up!** = put your hands up (to show you surrender). (b) *inf*. **to s. up for s.o.** = to defend s.o. **stick•y**, *adj*. **(-ier, -iest)** (a) covered with glue; which sticks easily. (b) *inf*. difficult/awkward/unpleasant; **s. wicket** (*esp*. *Brit*.) = difficult situation.

stick•le•back ['stɪklbæk] *n*. common small freshwater fish with spines along its back.

stick•ler ['stɪklə] *n*. **(for)** person who attaches great importance to sth.

stiff [stɪf] *adj*. **(-er, -est)** (a) which cannot be bent or moved easily; (brush) with hard bristles; starched (collar); **bored s.** = very bored. (b) solid/thick (paste). (c) strong (breeze). (d) difficult/hard (examination, penalty). (e) (whisky, etc.) with not much water added. (f) high (price). (g) unfriendly/unsociable. **stiff•en**, *v*. (a) to become/make stiff. (b) to become cautious/unfriendly. (c) (*of wind*) to become stronger. (d) to make (resistance) stronger. **stiff•en•er**, *n*. thing which stiffens. **stiff•ly**, *adv*. in a stiff way. **stiff-necked**, *adj*. obstinate. **stiff•ness**, *n*. being stiff.

sti•fle ['staɪfl] *v*. (a) to prevent (s.o.) from breathing. (b) to hold back (a yawn, etc.). **sti•fling**, *adj*. suffocating; extremely hot.

stig•ma ['stɪgmə] *n*. (a) disgrace; feeling of shame. (b) top of the center of a flower which receives pollen to make seeds. **stig•ma•tize** ['stɪgmətaɪz] *v*. to give a bad name to (sth).

stile [staɪl] *n*. steps which allow people, but not animals, to get over a wall or fence.

sti•let•to [stɪ'letəʊ] *n*. **(pl. -os)** (a) long thin dagger. (b) **s. heels** = high thin heels on women's shoes.

still [stɪl] 1. *n*. (a) apparatus for producing alcohol. (b) one picture from a motion-picture film. 2. *adj*. **(-er, -est)** calm/motionless; **s. life** = picture of flowers or objects, not people or animals. 3. *adv*. (a) up until this/that moment. (b) even. (c) however. **still•birth**, *n*. birth of a dead child. **still•born**, *adj*. (child) which is born dead; (idea) which is never put into practice. **still•ness**, *n*. calm. **still•room**, *n*. pantry/storage area in a large house.

stilts [stɪlts] *n*. *pl*. poles to raise (sth) above the ground; **pair of stilts** = two poles with foot rests to enable you to walk high in the air. **stilt•ed**, *adj*. (style of writing) which is very formal/not natural.

stim•u•late ['stɪmjʊleɪt] *v*. to excite/to encourage; to make more active. **stim•u•lant**, *n*. drug which makes you more active. **stim•u•la•tion** [stɪmjʊ'leɪʃn] *n*. being stimulated. **stim•u•lus**, *n*. **(pl. -li** [-laɪ]**)** thing that encourages further activity.

sting [stɪŋ] 1. *n*. (a) tiny needle in the tail of an insect/leaf of a plant which injects poison. (b) wound made by an insect or plant. (c) burning feeling. 2. *v*. **(stung** [stʌŋ]**)** (a) to wound with a sting. (b) to have a burning feeling. (c) to hurt (s.o.) so that he reacts. (d) *inf*. to cheat (s.o.) of money. **sting•ing net•tle**, *n*. common wild plant which causes a rash. **sting•ray**, *n*. large flat fish with a sting in its tail.

stin•gy ['stɪndʒɪ] *adj*. **(-ier, -iest)** *inf*. mean; not free with money. **stin•gi•ness**, *n*. meanness.

stink [stɪŋk] 1. *n*. unpleasant smell; *inf*. **to create a s.** = to object vigorously. 2. *v*. **(stank; stunk)** to make an unpleasant smell.

stint [stɪnt] 1. *n*. (a) amount of time spent doing sth. (b) **without s.** = in large quantities/with no restriction. 2. *v*. to give in very small amounts.

sti•pend ['staɪpend] *n*. fixed salary. **sti•pen•di•ar•y** [staɪ'pendjərɪ] *adj*. person who is paid a stipend.

stip•ple ['stɪpl] *v*. to color with small dots.

stip•u•late ['stɪpjʊleɪt] *v*. to insist; to make a condition. **stip•u•la•tion** [stɪpjʊ'leɪʃn] *n*. condition (in a contract).

stir [stɜː] 1. *n*. (a) mixing up a liquid. (b) fuss/agitation. 2. *v*. **(stirred)** (a) to mix up (a liquid). (b) to cause fuss/agitation. (c) to move. **stir•ring**, *adj*. exciting. **stir up**, *v*. to cause (trouble).

stir•rup ['stɪrəp] *n*. metal loop hanging from the saddle into which the rider puts his foot; **s. cup** = drink taken on horseback before setting off on a ride.

stitch [stɪtʃ] 1. *n*. **(pl. -es)** (a) small loop of cotton or wool made with a needle in sewing or knitting; *inf*. **I haven't got a s. to wear** = I have no suitable clothes. (b) small loop of thread used by a surgeon to attach a wound together. (c) sharp pain in the side of the body which comes after you have been running; *inf.* **in stitches** = laughing uproariously. 2. *v.* to attach with a needle and thread.

stoat [stəʊt] *n.* small brown flesh-eating animal whose fur turns white in winter.

stock [stɒk] 1. *n.* (a) plant on which other plants are grafted. (b) race/family. (c) handle of a rifle. (d) **stocks** = frame which a boat rests on when being built. (e) **stocks** = wooden frame with holes for the feet, in which criminals were placed. (f) quantity of things for use; quantities of goods for sale; **to take s.** = (i) to count what you have in stock; (ii) to assess a situation. (g) farm animals. (h) liquid made from boiling bones, etc., in water, used as a base for soups and sauces. (i) common scented garden flower. (j) capital invested in a business; **s. market** = buying and selling of shares; **s. exchange** = building in which shares are bought and sold. 2. *v.* (a) to keep (goods) for sale. (b) to provide with goods/animals/plants, etc. 3. *adj.* usual; **s. size** = normal size; **s. argument** = one which is frequently used. **stock•breed•er,** *n.* farmer who specializes in breeding animals. **stock•breed•ing,** *n.* breeding animals. **stock•brok•er,** *n.* agent who buys shares on the stock exchange. **stock•car,** *n.* car adapted for brutal racing. **stock•hold•er,** *n.* owner of stocks in a company. **stock•i•ness,** *n.* being stocky. **stock-in-trade,** *n.* things needed to carry on a business; habitual way of acting. **stock•man,** *n.* (*pl.* **-men**) man who looks after farm animals. **stock•pile.** 1. *n.* supplies kept in reserve (in case of an emergency). 2. *v.* to collect supplies in case of emergency. **stock•pot,** *n.* large pot for making soup. **stock•room,** *n.* room where stocks are kept. **stock-still,** *adv.* without moving. **stock•tak•ing,** *n.* counting of goods in stock at the end of a period. **stock up on,** *v.* to buy supplies for use in the future. **stock•y,** *adj.* (**-ier, -iest**) short and strong (person). **stock•yard,** *n.* place where animals are kept before they are slaughtered or shipped.

stock•ade [stɒ'keɪd] *n.* strong fence made of thick upright poles.

stock•i•nette, stockinet [stɒki'net] *n.* elastic material.

stock•ing ['stɒkɪŋ] *n.* long close-fitting piece

of clothing to cover your leg and foot; **in his s. feet** = without his shoes on.

sto•ic ['stəʊɪk] *n.* person who accepts problems or pain without complaining. **sto•i•cal,** *adj.* accepting problems or pain without complaining. **sto•i•cal•ly,** *adv.* in a stoical way. **sto•i•cism** ['stəʊɪsɪzəm] *n.* being stoical.

stoke [stəʊk] *v.* to put fuel in (a furnace). **stok•er,** *n.* person who stokes a furnace; seaman who looks after the engines.

stole [stəʊl] 1. *n.* wide light scarf worn around the shoulders. 2. *v. see* **steal.**

sto•len ['stəʊlən] *v. see* **steal.**

stol•id ['stɒlɪd] *adj.* slow and heavy; not excitable. **sto•lid•i•ty** [stɒ'lɪdɪtɪ] *n.* being stolid. **stol•id•ly,** *adv.* in a stolid way.

sto•ma ['stəʊmə] *n.* (*pl.* **-ata, -as**) pore in a plant.

stom•ach ['stʌmək] 1. *n.* (a) bag inside the body in which food is digested; **s. ache** = pain in the stomach. (b) part of the body lower than the chest. (c) desire. 2. *v.* to put up with/to tolerate.

stomp [stɒmp] *v.* to stamp/to walk with a heavy tread.

stone [stəʊn] 1. *n.* (a) small piece of rock. (b) piece of rock which has been cut for building, etc.; **Stone Age** = prehistoric period when humans made tools out of stone; **precious s.** = rare mineral which is very valuable. (c) hard seed inside some types of fruit. (d) hard piece of mineral which forms inside the body (in the kidneys, etc.) and causes pain. (e) measure of weight (= 14 pounds or 6.35 kilograms). 2. *adv.* completely (deaf); **s. broke** = with no money. 3. *v.* (a) **to s. (s.o.) to death** = to throw stones at (s.o.) and kill him. (b) to take the pits/stones out of (fruit). **stone•chat,** *n.* small dark bird with a red breast. **stone•crop,** *n.* type of plant which grows among stones. **stoned,** *adj. Sl.* (a) drunk. (b) drugged. **stone•ma•son,** *n.* person who cuts and builds with stone. **stone•wall,** *v.* to be uncooperative, as by refusing to answer when questioned. **stone•ware,** *n.* (*no pl.*) pottery made of rough clay and fired at high temperatures. **stone•work,** *n.* walls, etc., made of stone. **ston•i•ly,** *adv.* with no feeling. **ston•y,** *adj.* (**-ier, -iest**) (a) covered with stones. (b) hard; with no feeling. (c) *inf.* **s. broke** = stone broke.

stood [stʊd] *v. see* **stand.**

stooge [stuːdʒ] 1. *n. inf.* (a) person who does

æ back, a: farm, ɒ: top, aɪ pipe, aʊ how, aɪə fire, aʊə flower, ɔ: bought, ɔɪ toy, e fed, eəhair, eɪ take, ə afraid, əʊ boat, əʊə lower, v: word, i: heap, ɪ hit, ɪə hear, u: school, ʊ book, ʌ but, b back, d dog, ð then, dʒ just, f fog, g go, h hand, j yes, k catch, l last, m mix, n nut, ŋ sing, p penny, r round, s some, ʃ short, t too, tʃ chop, θ thing, v voice, w was, z zoo, ʒ treasure

what he is told to do. (b) the stupid one of a pair of comedians. 2. *v.* to act as a stooge.

stook [stʌk] *n.* (*esp. Brit.*) group of sheaves of corn, leaning together.

stool [stuːl] *n.* (a) seat with no back. (b) lump of waste matter passed from the bowels. **stool•pi•geon**, *n.* criminal who helps the police to trap another criminal.

stoop [stuːp] 1. *n.* bending forward. 2. *v.* (a) to bend forward. (b) **he stoops** = he has a permanently bent back. (c) **to s. to do sth** = to allow yourself to do sth which you feel is beneath you.

stop [stɒp] 1. *n.* (a) act of not moving/not doing sth. (b) place where a bus, etc., usually stops to pick up or let out passengers. (c) block which prevents a door, etc., closing. (d) knob on an organ which switches on a different set of pipes; set of pipes on an organ which produce a particular sound; **to pull out all the stops** = to do everything possible. 2. *v.* (**stopped**) (a) to make (sth which is moving) come to a halt; to come to a halt. (b) to make (sth) cease working; to cease working/doing sth. (c) to stay in a place. (d) to block; to fill (a gap). (e) to cut off (supply); to prevent (money) being paid; **to s. a check** = to tell the bank not to pay a check which you have written; **to s. s.o.'s wages** = not to pay s.o. **stop by**, *v. inf.* to visit s.o. for a short time. **stop•cock**, *n.* tap which stops the supply of water. **stop down**, *v.* to make the aperture of a lens smaller. **stop•gap**, *n. & adj.* thing which is used temporarily while waiting for sth more suitable to turn up. **stop off**, *v.* to make a stop on a long journey. **stop o•ver**, *v.* to make an overnight stop on a long journey. **stop•o•ver**, *n.* overnight stop on a long journey. **stop•page**, *n.* action of stopping/blocking. **stop•per**, *n.* piece of glass/cork, etc., which fits the mouth of a jar to close it. **stop•watch**, *n.* watch which can be started and stopped by pressing a button, used for timing races.

store [stɔː] 1. *n.* (a) supply of food, etc., kept for later use; **to set great s. by sth** = think that sth is very important. (b) place where you buy goods. 2. *v.* (a) to keep (sth) for future use. (b) to put (sth) in a warehouse. **stor•age**, *n.* (a) act of keeping/putting in store. (b) memory, the part of a computer where data is stored. **store•house**, *n.* place where things are stored. **store•keep•er**, *n.* person who owns a store. **store•room**, *n.* room where things are stored.

sto•ry, *Brit.* **sto•rey** ['stɔːrɪ] *n.* whole floor in a building. **sto•ried**, *Brit.* **sto•reyed**, *adj.* with several stories.

stork [stɔːk] *n.* large, usu. white, bird with long legs and long beak.

storm [stɔːm] 1. *n.* (a) period of bad weather with wind. (b) **s. of applause** = loud burst of clapping and cheering. (c) sudden violent attack; **s. troops** = soldiers who are specially trained to attack and capture. 2. *v.* (a) to be violently angry. (b) to attack and capture. **storm•y**, *adj.* referring to a storm; like a storm.

sto•ry ['stɔːrɪ] *n.* (a) tale of what has happened. (b) piece of fiction. (c) *inf.* lie. **sto•ry•line**, *n.* plot of a novel/motion picture, etc. **sto•ry•tell•er**, *n.* (a) person who tells a story. (b) *inf.* person who tells lies.

stoup [stuːp] *n.* bowl for holy water in a church.

stout [staut] 1. *adj.* (**-er, -est**) (a) fat. (b) strong/thick (material). (c) brave. 2. *n.* strong dark beer. **stout-heart•ed**, *adj.* brave. **stout•ly**, *adv.* (a) vigorously. (b) solidly/strongly. **stout•ness**, *n.* being stout.

stove [stəuv] *n.* machine for heating or cooking. **stove•pipe**, *n.* metal chimney which carries the smoke from a stove.

stow [stəu] *v.* to put away; to pack. **stow a•way**, *v.* (a) to pack. (b) to travel secretly on a ship/aircraft without paying the fare. **stow•a•way**, *n.* person who stows away.

stra•bis•mus [strə'bɪzməs] *n.* squint.

strad•dle ['strædl] *v.* to stand with legs apart, and your feet on either side of (sth).

strafe [strɑːf] *v.* to attack (sth) by shooting at it from a low-flying plane.

strag•gle ['strægl] *v.* to hang/to walk in an untidy way. **strag•gler**, *n.* person who walks well behind the main group of people. **strag•gling, straggly**, *adj.* which grows untidily.

straight [streɪt] 1. *adj.* (**-er, -est**) (a) not curved; **s. hair** = not curly. (b) honest/frank. (c) simple/not complicated; (whisky, etc.) with nothing added. (d) tidy; not crooked. (e) serious (actor/play); **to keep a s. face** = to stop yourself smiling. (f) *Sl.* not homosexual. 2. *n.* **the s.** = part of a racecorse (usu. near the finish) which is not curved. 3. *adv.* (a) in a straight line. (b) immediately. (c) directly. (d) honestly; *inf.* **to go s.** = to lead an honest life after having been a criminal. **straight•a•way**, *adv.* immediately/at once. **straight•en**, *v.* to make/to become straight. **straight•for•ward**, *adj.* frank/honest. **straight•for•ward•ly**, *adv.* in an honest way. **straight•ness**, *n.* being straight. **straight off**, *adv.* at once. **straight out**, *adv.* directly.

strain [streɪn] 1. *n.* (a) act of pulling tight; tension. (b) hurt caused by pulling a muscle too hard. (c) stress; mental/physical tension. (d) way of speaking. (e) breed. (f) tune. 2. *v.* (a) to pull/to work too hard. (b) to make a great 'effort (**to**). (c) to put too much stress on (credulity/patience). (d) to pass (a liquid) through a sieve to separate it from solids. **strained,** *adj.* (a) which has been pulled/worked too hard. (b) tense/unfriendly. **strain•er,** *n.* sieve for separating liquids from solids.

straits [streɪts] *n. pl.* (a) narrow piece of sea water between two masses of land. (b) money difficulties. **strait•ened,** *adj.* **in s. circumstances** = not having enough money to live on. **strait•jack•et,** *n.* (a) strong coat whose sleeves are tied behind the back to prevent a mad person from attacking people. (b) thing which prevents you from acting freely. **strait•laced,** *adj.* with very strict ideas about correct moral behavior.

strake [streɪk] *n.* plank which runs along a ship lengthwise.

strand [strænd] 1. *n.* (a) long piece of hair/thread, etc. (b) (*formal*) shore. 2. *v.* to leave (your ship) on the shore. **strand•ed,** *adj.* alone and helpless.

strange [streɪnʒ] *adj.* (**-er, -est**) (a) odd/bizarre. (b) which you have never seen/heard before. **strange•ly,** *adv.* oddly/curiously. **strange•ness,** *n.* being strange. **stran•ger,** *n.* person whom you do not know; **you're quite a s.** = I haven't seen you for a long time; **he is a s. to the town** = he does not know it well.

stran•gle ['stræŋgl] *v.* to kill (s.o.) by pressing on his throat so that he cannot breath; to crush (initiative/a plan). **stran•gle•hold,** *n.* control which prevents you doing what you want to do. **stran•gler,** *n.* person who strangles. **stran•gu•la•tion** [stræŋgju'leɪʃn] *n.* being strangled.

strap [stræp] 1. *n.* long flat piece of leather or material for attaching sth. 2. *v.* (**strapped**) (a) to attach with a strap. (b) to hit (s.o.) with a strap. **strap•hang•ing,** *n.* traveling standing in a crowded bus/train, holding onto a strap attached to the roof. **strap•less,** *adj.* with no straps. **strap•ping,** *adj.* big/strong (young man/girl).

stra•ta ['strɑːtə] *n. see* **stra•tum**.

strat•a•gem ['strætədʒəm] *n.* clever plan to trick an enemy.

stra•te•gic, strategical [strə'tiːdʒɪk(l)] *adj.* referring to strategy; (position) which gives an advantage over the enemy. **stra•te•gi•cal•ly,** *adv.* according to strategy. **strat•e•gist** ['strætədʒɪst] *n.* officer who plans military attacks. **strat•e•gy** ['strætədʒɪ] *n.* planning of war/of an action.

strat•i•fy ['strætɪfaɪ] *v.* to form layers; to be arranged in layers. **strat•i•fi•ca•tion** [strætɪfɪ'keɪʃn] *n.* forming layers; arranging in layers.

strat•o•sphere ['strætəsfɪə] *n.* upper layer of the earth's atmosphere.

stra•tum ['strɑːtəm] *n.* (*pl.* **-ta** [-tə], **-ums**) layer (esp. of rock); **social strata** = levels of society.

stra•tus ['strɑːtəs] *n.* **s. clouds** = low flat clouds.

straw [strɔː] *n.* (a) dry stalks of plants like corn. (b) one single dry stalk of a plant; thin plastic tube for sucking liquid; *inf.* **that's the last s.** = that is all I can stand/as much as I can take; **s. vote/poll** = random questioning to test the general opinion of the public/of a group.

straw•ber•ry ['strɔːberɪ] *n.* common red summer fruit growing on low plants; **s. mark** = red mark on the skin, which is present from birth.

stray [streɪ] 1. *adj. & n.* (animal, etc.) which is wandering away from home. 2. *adj.* (bullet, etc.) wandering off course. 3. *v.* to wander.

streak [striːk] 1. *n.* (a) band/line (of color); flash (of light). (b) quality of character. 2. *v.* (a) to rush. (b) *inf.* to run about naked in public as a joke. **streak•y,** *adj.* with smudges of color or dirt.

stream [striːm] 1. *n.* (a) small flow of water; small river. (b) continuous flow. (c) current. 2. *v.* to flow. **stream•er,** *n.* long thin flag; long paper or ribbon used as a decoration. **stream•ing,** *adj.* act of flowing. **stream•line,** *v.* (a) to design (a car/plane/boat, etc.) so that it can move easily through water or air. (b) to make more efficient; to modernize.

street [striːt] *n.* road in a town, with houses or businesses on each side; **the man in the s.** = the ordinary citizen; **at s. level** = on the same level as the street. **street•car,** *n.* form of public transportation, consisting of vehicles running on rails laid in the street.

strength [streŋθ] *n.* (a) being strong. (b) number of people in a force or group. (c) **on the s. of** = because of. **strength•en,** *v.* to make stronger.

stren•u•ous ['strenjʊəs] *adj.* energetic. **stren•u•ous•ly,** *adv.* vigorously. **stren•u•ous•ness,** *n.* being strenuous.

strep•to•coc•cus [streptə'kɒkəs] *n.* (*pl.* **-cocci** [-kɒkaɪ]) bacterium which causes infections,

---

æ back, ɑ: farm, ɒ: top, aɪ pipe, aʊ how, aɪə fire, aʊə flower, ɔ: bought, ɔɪ toy, e fed, eəhair, eɪ take, ə afraid, əʊ boat, əʊə lower, ʋ: word, i: heap, ɪ hit, ɪə hear, u: school, ʋ book, ʌ but, b back, d dog, ð then, dʒ just, f fog, g go, h hand, j yes, k catch, l last, m mix, n nut, ŋ sing, p penny, r round, s some, ʃ short, t too, tʃ chop, θ thing, v voice, w was, z zoo, ʒ treasure

such as a sore throat. **strep•to•my•cin** [streptəˈmaɪsɪn] *n.* type of antibiotic.

stress [stres] 1. *n.* (*pl.* **-es**) (a) force; pressure. (b) nervous strain. (c) emphasis. 2. *v.* to emphasize; to put stress on (sth).

stretch [stretʃ] 1. *n.* (*pl.* **-es**) (a) act of being pulled out. (b) act of putting out your arms and legs as far as they will go. (c) long piece (of road); long period (of time); *Sl.* time spent in prison. 2. *v.* (a) to pull out (sth elastic). (b) to pull (sth) out too far. (c) to be able to be pulled out. (d) to put out your arms or legs as far as they will go. (e) to extend for a great distance. (f) to relax (a rule). **stretch•er,** *n.* (a) portable bed with handles at each end for carrying sick people; **s. bearer** = person who lifts one end of a stretcher. (b) thing which stretches.

strew [struː] *v.* (**strewn**) to scatter.

stri•at•ed [straɪˈeɪtɪd] *adj.* marked with parallel furrows. **stri•a•tion,** *n.* furrow/ridge parallel to several others.

strick•en [ˈstrɪkn] *adj.* hit/struck by disease/emotion, etc.

strict [strɪkt] *adj.* (**-er, -est**) (a) exact (meaning). (b) (orders) which must be obeyed. (c) severe/harsh; (person) who insists that rules are obeyed. **strict•ly,** *adv.* in a strict way. **strict•ness,** *n.* being strict. **stric•ture** [ˈstrɪktʃə] *n.* criticism/words of blame.

stride [straɪd] 1. *n.* long step with your legs. 2. *v.* (**strode** [strəʊd]) to take long steps.

stri•dent [ˈstraɪdənt] *adj.* unpleasantly loud harsh high (sound). **stri•den•cy,** *n.* being strident. **stri•dent•ly,** *adv.* in a strident way.

strife [straɪf] *n.* fighting; trouble between people.

strike [straɪk] 1. *n.* (a) stopping of work by workers (because of disagreement with management). (b) **air s.** = rapid attack from the air. (c) **oil s.** = discovery of oil. 2. *v.* (**struck** [strʌk]) (a) to hit. (b) to light (a match); to make (a coin/a medal); to make/to agree (a bargain). (c) **to be struck down with flu** = to have a sudden attack of flu. (d) to make an impression on (s.o.). (e) to discover (oil, etc.). (f) to lower (a flag); to pack up (a tent). (g) to make (a note) sound in music; (*of clock*) to ring (the hour). (h) to go in a certain direction. (i) to stop working because of disagreement or in protest. **strike•bound,** *adj.* closed because of a strike. **strike•break•er,** *n.* worker who continues to work when his colleagues are on strike. **strike off,** *v.* to cross off (a list). **strike out,** *v.* to cross off (a list). **strike ben•e•fit/pay,** *n.* wages paid to striking workers by their union. **strik•er,** *n.* person who goes on strike. **strike up,** *v.* (a) to start playing a piece of music. (b) **to s. up an acquaintance with s.o.** = to start getting to know

s.o. **strik•ing,** *adj.* remarkable. **strik•ing•ly,** *adv.* remarkably.

string [strɪŋ] 1. *n.* (a) thin rope for tying things together; *inf.* **strings** = hidden conditions; *inf.* **to pull strings** = to try to obtain sth through influential friends. (b) series of things tied together. (c) thin wire in a musical instrument; **the strings** = part of an orchestra playing stringed instruments. (d) tough thread (in meat/vegetables). 2. *v.* (**strung** [strʌŋ]) (a) to tie together in a series. (b) to put a string in (a musical instrument). (c) **highly strung** = excitable; very nervous. **string a•long,** *v.* (a) to agree with s.o. (b) to make (s.o.) promises to get him to cooperate. **string bag,** *n.* shopping bag made of a net of knotted string. **string bean,** *n.* type of bean. **string course,** *n.* horizontal line of projecting bricks. **stringed,** *adj.* (musical instrument) with strings. **string out,** *v.* to put (things) in a long line. **string up,** *v.* to hang up with a string; *inf.* to hang (s.o.). **string•y,** *adj.* (meat/vegetables) with tough threads.

strin•gent [ˈstrɪndʒənt] *adj.* strict/severe. **strin•gen•cy,** *n.* being stringent. **strin•gent•ly,** *adv.* in a stringent way.

strip [strɪp] 1. *n.* long narrow piece; **cartoon s./comic s.** = cartoon story made of a series of small drawings side by side. 2. *v.* (**stripped**) (a) to make naked; to take off your clothes. (b) to remove (sth). **strip down,** *v.* to take (an engine) to pieces. **strip•per,** *n.* (a) liquid for removing old paint, wax, etc. (b) person who performs a striptease. **strip•tease,** *n.* entertainment where s.o. takes their clothes off piece by piece.

stripe [straɪp] *n.* (a) long strip of color. (b) strip of colored cloth sewn to a uniform to show a certain rank in the armed forces. **striped,** *adj.* with stripes. **strip•y,** *adj.* covered with many stripes.

strip•ling [ˈstrɪplɪŋ] *n.* very young man.

strive [straɪv] *v.* (**strove** [strəʊv]; **has striven**) to try very hard (**to**).

strobe [strəʊb] *n.* light which flashes on and off very rapidly. **stro•bo•scope,** *n.* device which makes lights flash on and off (on a dance floor).

strode [strəʊd] *v. see* **stride.**

stroke [strəʊk] 1. *n.* (a) gentle touch. (b) line made by a pen/brush, etc. (c) blow. (d) illness/paralysis caused by damage to part of the brain. (e) one movement; **s. of luck** = piece of luck. (f) particular style of swimming. (g) one ring of a bell. (h) rower seated in the stern who gives the time for all the others in a boat. 2. *v.* (a) to run your hands gently over. (b) to set the time for the other rowers in a boat.

stroll [strəul] 1. *n.* short leisurely walk. 2. *v.* to walk slowly along. **stroll•er,** *n.* (a) person who strolls. (b) light carriage for babies.

strong [strɒŋ] 1. *adj.* (**-er, -est**) (a) powerful. (b) large (in numbers). (c) with a powerful smell/noise, etc.; **s. drink** = alcohol. 2. *adv. inf.* **still going s.** = still working well after a long time. **strong•box,** *n.* small safe for keeping jewels. **strong•hold,** *n.* fortress; place which is difficult to capture. **strong•ly,** *adv.* powerfully. **strong•man,** *n.* powerful/influential man. **strong-mind•ed** *adj.* with clear fixed ideas. **strong point,** *n.* good quality/characteristic. **strong•room,** *n.* room with thick walls and door where money/jewels, etc. are kept. **strong-willed,** *adj.* with a strong character.

stron•ti•um ['strɒntɪəm] *n.* (*element:* Sr) white radioactive metal.

strop [strɒp] 1. *n.* leather strap for sharpening razors. 2. *v.* (**stropped**) to sharpen (a razor) on a strop.

strove [strəuv] *v. see* **strike.**

struck [strʌk] *v. see* **strike.**

struc•ture ['strʌktʃə] 1. *n.* (a) way in which things are put together. (b) building. 2. *v.* to arrange in a certain way. **struc•tur•al,** *adj.* referring to a structure. **struc•tur•al•ly,** *adv.* referring to a structure.

strug•gle ['strʌgl] 1. *n.* bitter/violent fight. 2. *v.* to fight violently.

strum [strʌm] *v.* (**strummed**) to play (a guitar, etc.) in an informal way.

strung [strʌŋ] *v. see* **string.**

strut [strʌt] 1. *n.* (a) bar of wood, metal, etc., which supports sth. (b) strutting way of walking. 2. *v.* (**strutted**) to walk in a proud and important way.

strych•nine ['strɪkniːn] *n.* bitter poison.

stub [stʌb] 1. *n.* (a) small piece left after sth has been used. (b) piece of paper left after a check or a ticket has been torn out of a book. 2. *v.* (**stubbed**) (a) to hurt (your toe) by hitting it against a rock. (b) to put out (a cigarette) by pressing the stub against sth. **stub•by,** *adj.* short and fat (fingers).

stub•ble ['stʌbl] *n.* (a) short stems left after corn has been cut. (b) short hairs which grow if a man does not shave for several days. **stub•bly,** *adj.* covered with short bristles.

stub•born ['stʌbən] *adj.* obstinate; (person) who will only do what he wants to do; (thing) which will not do what you want it to do.

stub•born•ly, *adv.* obstinately. **stub•born•ness,** *n.* being stubborn.

stuc•co ['stʌkəu] *n.* plaster put on walls and painted; plaster used to make molded decorations in buildings. **stuc•coed,** *adj.* covered with stucco.

stuck [stʌk] *v. see* **stick. stuck-up,** *adj. inf.* thinking very highly of oneself; conceited.

stud [stʌd] *n.* (a) nail head or other metal object sticking out from a surface, often for decoration. (b) type of button with two heads for passing through two holes to fasten a shirt. (c) horses which are kept for breeding; (*also* **stud farm**) farm where horses are kept for breeding; **s. book** = register of pedigree horses, etc. 2. *v.* (**studded**) to cover with nails, etc. **stud•ded,** *adj.* covered (**with** nails/stars, etc.).

stu•dent ['stjuːdənt] *n.* person who is studying at a school/college/university.

stu•di•o ['stjuːdɪəu] *n.* (*pl.* **-os**) (a) place where artists paint/where photographers take photographs. (b) place where motion pictures/broadcasts/recordings are made. (c) very small apartment, having one room and a bathroom and kitchen area.

stu•di•ous ['stjuːdɪəs] *adj.* (a) showing careful study. (b) careful. **stu•di•ous•ly,** *adv.* carefully. **stu•di•ous•ness,** *n.* being studious.

stud•y ['stʌdɪ] 1. *n.* (a) act of examining sth carefully to learn more about it. (b) room in which s.o. works/studies. (c) piece of music which aims to improve the player's technique; work of art in which new ideas are practiced. 2. *v.* (a) to examine (sth) in detail to learn more about it. (b) to follow a course at a college or university. **stud•ied,** *adj.* done very carefully; done on purpose.

stuff [stʌf] 1. *n.* (a) material of which sth is made. (b) *inf.* equipment/belongings; **that's the s.** = that's it! 2. *v.* (a) to fill (sth) very full. (b) to block (a hole). (c) to fill the skin of a dead animal with material to make it look lifelike. (d) to put stuffing into (a chicken, etc.). **stuff•ing,** *n.* (a) seasoned mixture put inside a chicken, etc., before cooking. (b) material used to fill cushions/chair seats, etc.

stuff•y ['stʌfɪ] *adj.* (**-ier, -iest**) (a) (room) full of bad air from lack of ventilation. (b) prudish; old-fashioned. **stuff•i•ly,** *adv.* in a stuffy way. **stuff•i•ness,** *n.* being stuffy.

stul•ti•fy ['stʌltɪfaɪ] *v.* (*formal*) to make (s.o.) stupid. **stul•ti•fi•ca•tion** [stʌltɪfɪˈkeɪʃn] *n.* act of stultifying.

æ back, aː farm, ɒ top, aɪ pipe, aʊ how, aɪə fire, aʊə flower, ɔː bought, ɔɪ toy, e fed, eəhair, eɪ take, ə afraid, əʊ boat, əʊə lower, vː word, iː heap, ɪ hit, ɪə hear, uː school, ʊ book, ʌ but, b back, d dog, ð then, dʒ just, f fog, g go, h hand, j yes, k catch, l last, m mix, n nut, ŋ sing, p penny, r round, s some, ʃ short, t too, tʃ chop, θ thing, v voice, w was, z zoo, ʒ treasure

stum•ble ['stʌmbl] 1. *n.* tripping over; awkward step. 2. *v.* (a) to trip over sth; to walk awkwardly. (b) to **s. across** = to find by chance. **stum•bling block**, *n.* thing which prevents you from doing sth.

stump [stʌmp] 1. *n.* (a) short piece left after sth has been finished or cut down. (b) one of the three sticks placed in the ground as a target in cricket. 2. *v.* (a) to **s. along** = to walk along heavily. (b) *inf.* to puzzle. (c) (*in cricket*) to put (a batsman) out by touching the stumps with the ball when he is not in the hitting area. **stump•y**, *adj.* (-ier, -iest) *inf.* short and squat.

stun [stʌn] *v.* (**stunned**) to knock out; to shock completely. **stun•ning**, *adj.* extraordinary/marvelous.

stung [stʌŋ] *v. see* **sting.**

stunk [stʌŋk] *v. see* **stink.**

stunt [stʌnt] 1. *n.* trick; dangerous action done to attract attention. 2. *v.* to shorten/to prevent (sth) from growing. **stunt man**, *n.* person who carries out dangerous actions in motion pictures in place of the star.

stu•pe•fy ['stjuːpɪfaɪ] *v.* (a) to make stupid. (b) to astonish. **stu•pe•fac•tion** [stjuːpɪ'fækʃn] *n.* astonishment.

stu•pen•dous [stjuː'pendəs] *adj.* extraordinary/magnificent.

stu•pid ['stjuːpɪd] *adj.* (a) not very intelligent; with no sense. (b) dull; with a dull mind. **stu•pid•i•ty** [stjuː'pɪdɪ tɪ] *n.* being stupid. **stu•pid•ly**, *adv.* in a stupid way. **stu•por** ['stjuːpə] *n.* being in a daze; being half senseless.

stur•dy ['stɜːdɪ] *adj.* (-ier, -iest) strong and vigorous. **stur•di•ly**, *adv.* in a sturdy way. **stur•di•ness**, *n.* being sturdy.

stur•geon ['stɜːdʒən] *n.* (*pl.* sturgeon) large edible fish whose eggs are caviar.

stut•ter ['stʌtə] 1. *n.* speech defect where you stutter. 2. *v.* to repeat the same sounds when speaking.

sty [staɪ] *n.* (a) shed in which a pig lives. (b) (*also* **stye**) infected pimple near the eye.

style [staɪl] 1. *n.* (a) way/manner of doing sth; **in s.** = very grandly. (b) fashion. (c) elegance. 2. *v.* (a) to name. (b) to give a certain style to (hair, etc.). **styl•ish**, *adj.* elegant/fashionable. **styl•ish•ly**, *adv.* in a stylish way. **styl•ish•ness**, *n.* fashion/elegance. **styl•ist**, *n.* person who gives (a) style to sth; **hair s.** = hairdresser. **sty•lis•tic** [staɪ'lɪstɪk] *adj.* referring to style in art. **sty•lis•ti•cal•ly**, *adv.* referring to style in art. **sty•lis•tics**, *n.* study of style of writing. **styl•i•za•tion** [staɪlaɪ'zeɪʃn] *n.* showing sth in a stylized way. **styl•ize**, *v.*

to show (sth) according to a fixed pattern/not in a natural way.

sty•lus ['staɪləs] *n.* needle of a record player.

sty•mie ['staɪmɪ] *v.* to block (a plan).

styp•tic ['stɪptɪk] *adj.* which stops bleeding; **s. pencil** = small stick of white substance (alum) which stops bleeding from cuts.

suave [swɑːv] *adj.* (-er, -est) extremely polite with very smooth manners (but often with an unpleasant character). **suave•ly**, *adv.* in a suave way. **suav•i•ty**, *n.* being suave.

sub [sʌb] 1. *n. inf.* (a) substitute. (b) submarine. 2. *v.* (**subbed**) *inf.* to act as a substitute. 3. *prefix* **sub–** = below/under.

sub•al•tern ['sʌbəltən] *n. & adj.* (person) in a subordinate position.

sub•com•mit•tee ['sʌbkəmɪti] *n.* small committee which is part of a large committee.

sub•con•scious [sʌb'kɒnʃəs] 1. *adj.* (idea/feeling) which you have in your mind without being aware of it. 2. *n.* part of your mind which has subconscious ideas or feelings. **sub•con•scious•ly**, *adv.* in a subconscious way.

sub•con•ti•nent [sʌb'kɒntɪnənt] *n.* mass of land which is part of a continent.

sub•con•tract 1. *n.* [sʌb'kɒntrækt] agreement between a main contractor and another person or company who will do part of the work which the contractor has agreed to do. 2. *v.* [sʌbkən'trækt] to agree with another person or company that they will do part of the work which you have agreed to do. **sub•con•trac•tor**, *n.* person/company who does work for a contractor.

sub•cu•ta•ne•ous [sʌbkjuː'teɪnɪəs] *adj.* (*formal*) under the skin.

sub•di•vide [sʌbdɪ'vaɪd] *v.* to divide (sth) which has already been divided. **sub•di•vi•sion**, *n.* (a) division of sth into smaller units. (b) land which has been divided up into plots for houses.

sub•due [sʌb'djuː] *v.* (a) to overcome/to conquer. (b) to make quiet; to make less bright. **sub•dued**, *adj.* (a) overcome/beaten. (b) low (light); **s. colors** = (i) dull colors; (ii) pastel shades.

sub•head•ing ['sʌbhedɪŋ] *n.* secondary heading.

sub•hu•man [sʌb'hjuːmən] *adj.* less advanced than a human.

sub•ject 1. *n.* ['sʌbdʒɪkt] (a) person who belongs to a country. (b) (*in grammar*) word which shows the person or thing which does an action. (c) thing which is being discussed. (d) thing which is being studied. 2. *adj.* ['sʌbdʒɪkt] (a) belonging to; under the power of (a state, king, etc.). (b) **s. to** = (i) likely to be ruled by/to suffer from; (ii) depending on. 3. *v.*

[sʌb'dʒekt] (**to**) to make (sth/s.o.) undergo sth unpleasant. **sub•jec•tion** [sʌb'dʒekʃn] *n.* being subjected. **sub•jec•tive** [sʌb'dʒektɪv] *adj.* seen from your own point of view. **sub•jec•tive•ly**, *adv.* in a subjective way. **sub•jec•tiv•i•ty**, *n.* being subjective. **sub•ject mat•ter**, *n.* subject dealt with in a book/TV program.

sub•join [sʌb'dʒɔɪn] *v.* to add (sth) at the end.

sub ju•di•ce [sʌb'dʒuːdɪsɪ] *adv.* being considered in a court of law.

sub•ju•gate ['sʌbdʒugeɪt] *v.* (*formal*) to bring (a country) under your control. **sub•ju•ga•tion** [sʌbdʒu'geɪʃn] *n.* act of subjugating.

sub•junc•tive [sʌb'dʒʌŋktɪv] *adj. & n.* (referring to) a form of a verb used to show doubt/desire, etc.

sub•lease [sʌb'liːs] 1. *n.* lease of a building/house/apartment which is already leased. 2. *v.* to sublet.

sub•let [sʌb'let] *v.* (**sublet**) to lease (a building/house/apartment) which you yourself rent.

sub•li•mate. 1. *n.* ['sʌblɪmət] substance formed when a substance is changed from solid to vapor. 2. *v.* ['sʌblɪmeit] (a) to change a substance from solid to vapor. (b) (*formal*) to channel (crude energy/emotion) into an activity which is accepted in society. **sub•li•ma•tion**, *n.* act of sublimating.

sub•lime [sə'blaɪm] *adj.* grand/wonderful; noble; very great. **sub•lime•ly**, *adv.* wonderfully.

sub•lim•i•nal [sʌb'lɪmɪnl] *adj.* below the consciousness of the senses.

sub•ma•chine gun [sʌbmə'fiːngʌn] *n.* light machine gun.

sub•ma•rine [sʌbmə'riːn] 1. *adj.* which lives/takes place under the water. 2. *n.* ship which can travel under the water. **sub•ma•rin•er** [sʌb'mærɪnə] *n.* member of the crew of a submarine.

sub•merge [sʌb'mɜːdʒ] *v.* (a) to (make sth) go under the surface of the water. **sub•mer•gence, submersion** [sʌb'mɜːʃn] *n.* being submerged.

sub•mis•sion [sʌb'mɪʃn] *n.* (a) state of giving in/giving way. (b) evidence/document/opinion submitted to s.o. **sub•mis•sive** [sʌb'mɪsɪv] *adj.* meek (person) who gives in easily. **sub•mis•sive•ly**, *adv.* in a submissive way. **sub•mis•sive•ness**, *n.* meekness.

sub•mit, *v.* (a) to give way; to yield. (b) to give (evidence/documents/opinion) for s.o. to examine.

sub•nor•mal [sʌb'nɔːml] *adj.* less than normal; below normal standard.

sub•or•di•nate 1. *adj. & n.* [sə'bɔːdnət] (person) who is under the control of s.o. else; **s. clause** = phrase in a sentence which cannot stand alone, and which is dependent on another clause. 2. *v.* [sə'bɔːdɪneɪt] to put (sth) in a less important position; to consider (sth) as less important. **sub•or•di•na•tion** [sʌbɔːdɪ'neɪʃn] *n.* act of subordinating.

sub•orn [sə'bɔːn] *v.* (*formal*) to bribe (s.o.) to commit perjury.

sub•poe•na [sʌb'piːnə] 1. *n.* order to come to a court. 2. *v.* to order (s.o.) to come to a court.

sub•scribe [sʌb'skraɪb] *v.* (a) to give money (to a charity). (b) to pay for a series of issues of a magazine/for a series of tickets to concerts, etc. (c) **to s. to an opinion** = to agree with it. **sub•scrib•er**, *n.* person who subscribes to a charity/to a magazine; person who subscribes to a particular service. **sub•scrip•tion** [sʌb'skrɪpʃn] *n.* (a) money paid to a charity. (b) money paid to a magazine/to a club for a a series of issues/a year's membership.

sub•sec•tion ['sʌbsekʃn] *n.* part of a section.

sub•se•quent ['sʌbsɪkwənt] *adj.* which follows later. **sub•se•quent•ly**, *adv.* later.

sub•ser•vi•ent [səb'sɜːvɪənt] *adj.* weak/always giving in to s.o. **sub•ser•vi•ent•ly**, *adv.* in a subservient way. **sub•ser•vi•ence**, *n.* being subservient.

sub•side [sʌb'saɪd] *v.* (a) to sink down. (b) to become less violent or active. **sub•sid•ence** [sʌb'saɪdəns] *n.* sinking down (of the ground).

sub•sid•i•ar•y [sʌb'sɪdjərɪ] *adj. & n.* (thing) which is less important; **s. (company)** = company which is controlled by another.

sub•si•dy ['sʌbsɪdɪ] *n.* contribution of money. **sub•si•dize** ['sʌbsɪdaɪz] *v.* to help by giving money.

sub•sist [sʌb'sɪst] *v.* to exist (with difficulty). **sub•sist•ence** [sʌb'sɪstəns] *n.* existence; survival with very little money or food; **s. level** = having only just enough to live on.

sub•soil ['sʌbsɔɪl] *n.* layer of soil under the topsoil.

sub•son•ic ['sʌbsɒnɪk] *adj.* (plane) which flies at a speed less than the speed of sound.

sub•stance ['sʌbstəns] *n.* (a) matter/material of which things can be made. (b) basis (of an

æ back, aː farm, ɒ top, aɪ pipe, aʊ how, aiə fire, aʊə flower, ɔː bought, ɔɪ toy, e fed, eəhair, eɪ take, ə afraid, əʊ boat, əʊə lower, ɜː word, iː heap, ɪ hit, ɪə hear, uː school, ʊ book, ʌ but, b back, d dog, ð then, dʒ just, f fog, g go, h hand, j yes, k catch, l last, m mix, n nut, ŋ sing, p penny, r round, s some, ʃ short, t too, tʃ chop, θ thing, v voice, w was, z zoo, ʒ treasure

argument/report). (c) **a man of s.** = a wealthy man. **sub•stan•tial** [sʌb'stænʃl] *adj.* (a) large/important.   (b)   large/solid. **sub•stan•tial•ly**, *adv.* mostly/mainly. **sub•stan•ti•ate** [sʌb'stænʃıeıt] *v.* to justify; to prove that (sth) is true. **sub•stan•ti•a•tion** [sʌbstænʃı'eıʃn] *n.* act of substantiating.

sub•stand•ard [sʌb'stændəd] *adj.* second-rate; below the normal standard.

sub•stan•tive ['sʌbstəntıv] 1. *adj.* real; existing. 2. *n.* noun.

sub•sta•tion ['sʌbsteıʃn] *n.* small local electricity station.

sub•sti•tute ['sʌbstıtjuːt] 1. *n.* person/thing taking the place of s.o./sth else. 2. *v.* to put (sth/s.o.) in the place of (s.o./sth). **sub•sti•tu•tion** [sʌbstı'tjuːʃn] *n.* act of substituting.

sub•stra•tum [sʌb'strɑːtəm] *n.* (*pl.* **-ta**) a layer, as of earth, that lies under another.

sub•sume [səb'sjuːm] *v.* (*formal*) to include in a certain category.

sub•ten•ant [sʌb'tenənt] *n.* person to whom a building/house/apartment has been sublet. **sub•ten•an•cy**, *n.* act of subletting.

sub•ter•fuge ['sʌbtəfjuːdʒ] *n.* trick; clever plot.

sub•ter•ra•ne•an [sʌbtə'reınıən] *adj.* under the ground.

sub•ti•tle ['sʌbtaıtl] 1. *n.* (a) secondary title on a book. (b) **subtitles** = translation of the dialogue of a foreign motion picture which is shown on the bottom of the screen. 2. *v.* to give a subtitle or subtitles to (sth).

sub•tle ['sʌtl] *adj.* (a) difficult to explain; very delicate (scent). (b) cunning. **sub•tle•ty** ['sʌtltı] *n.* thing which is difficult to explain/to describe. **sub•tly**, *adv.* in a subtle way.

sub•to•tal ['sʌbtəutl] *n.* total of one section of a set of figures.

sub•tract [sʌb'trækt] *v.* to take away (sth from a group). **sub•trac•tion** [sʌb'trækʃn] *n.* act of subtracting.

sub•trop•i•cal [sʌb'trɒpıkl] *adj.* referring to the subtropics. **sub•trop•ics**, *n.* areas of the world between the tropics and the temperate zones.

sub•urb ['sʌbɜːb] *n.* residential area on the outskirts of a city or town; **the suburbs** = area made up of suburbs. **sub•ur•ban** [sə'bɜːbən] *adj.* referring to the suburbs. **sub•ur•bi•a** [sə'bɜːbıə] *n. inf.* the suburbs.

sub•ven•tion [sʌb'venʃn] *n.* subsidy.

sub•ver•sion [sʌb'vɜːʃn] *n.* act of subverting. **sub•ver•sive** [sʌb'vɜːsıv] *adj.* which tries to subvert. **sub•vert** [sʌb'vɜːt] *v.* to try to destroy the authority of (the government).

sub•way ['sʌbweı] *n.* underground railroad system.

sub-ze•ro [sʌb'zıərəʊ] *adj.* (temperature) below zero degrees.

suc•ceed [sək'siːd] *v.* (a) to follow on; to take the place of. (b) to do well; to do what you have been trying to do. **suc•cess** [sək'ses] *n.* (*pl.* **-es**) (a) doing what you have been trying to do. (b) thing/person who does well. **suc•cess•ful**, *adj.* which succeeds. **suc•cess•ful•ly**, *adv.* in a successful way. **suc•ces•sion** [sək'seʃn] *n.* (a) series. (b) right to take s.o.'s place; act of taking s.o.'s place. **suc•ces•sive** [sək'sesıv] *adj.* one after the other. **suc•ces•sive•ly**, *adv.* one after the other. **suc•ces•sor**, *n.* person who takes s.o.'s place.

suc•cinct [sək'sıŋkt] *adj.* concise/not using many words. **suc•cinct•ly**, *adv.* in a succinct way.

suc•cor, *Brit.* **suc•cour** ['sʌkə] 1. *n.* (*formal*) help. 2. *v.* (*formal*) to help.

suc•cu•lent ['sʌkjulənt] 1. *adj.* juicy/full of juice. 2. *n.* type of plant with thick fleshy leaves and stems (like a cactus).

suc•cumb [sə'kʌm] *v.* (**to**) to give in/to yield; to die (from).

such [sʌtʃ] 1. *adj.* (a) like/similar. (b) so large/so great. (c) of this type. 2. *pron.* thing/person of a certain kind; **s. as it is** = although it is not very good. **such and such**, **such-and-such**, *pron.* a particular/a certain. **such•like**, *adj. pron.* similar (people/things).

suck [sʌk] 1. *n.* action of drawing in liquid through the mouth. 2. *v.* (a) to pull (liquid) into your mouth. (b) to pull in (sth) by suction. **suck•er**, *n.* (a) shoot which sprouts from an underground stem or root. (b) thing which sticks onto a surface by suction. (c) *inf.* person who is easily tricked. **suck•le**, *v.* to give (a child) milk from the breast. **suck•ling**, *n.* young animal/child still taking milk from its mother. **suck up to**, *v. Sl.* to try to make (s.o.) like you (by giving presents/making compliments, etc.). **suc•tion** ['sʌkʃn] *n.* action of sucking in air/liquid, so that sth will be pulled in/will stick to a surface because of the vacuum created; **s. cup** = small concave pad which will stick to a surface if pressed hard; **s. pump** = pump which sucks up liquid when air is pulled out of it.

su•crose ['suːkrəuz] *n.* sugar found in plants.

sud•den ['sʌdn] *adj.* which happens rapidly/unexpectedly; **all of a s.** = suddenly. **sud•den•ly**, *adv.* rapidly/unexpectedly. **sud•den•ness**, *n.* being rapid/unexpected.

suds [sʌdz] *n. pl.* foam made with soap.

sue [suː] *v.* to take (s.o.) to court/to start a lawsuit against (s.o.).

suede [sweɪd] *n.* soft leather with a rough/furry surface.

su•et ['sʊɪt] *n.* hard fat from an animal, used in cooking. **su•et•y,** *adj.* made of suet; like suet.

suf•fer ['sʌfə] *v.* (a) to feel pain; to be in a difficult situation. (b) to put up with. (c) to undergo. **suf•fer•ance,** *n.* **he is only here on s.** = we allow him to be here but we don't really want him. **suf•fer•er,** *n.* person who suffers. **suf•fer•ing,** *n.* feeling pain.

suf•fice [sə'faɪs] *v.* (*formal*) to be enough. **suf•fi•cien•cy** [sə'fɪʃənsɪ] *n.* enough supplies. **suf•fi•cient** [sə'fɪʃənt] *adj.* enough. **suf•fi•cient•ly,** *adv.* enough.

suf•fix ['sʌfɪks] *n.* (*pl.* **-es**) part added after a word to make another word.

suf•fo•cate ['sʌfəkeɪt] *v.* to not be able to breathe; to kill/to die by stopping breathing. **suf•fo•ca•tion** [sʌfə'keɪʃn] *n.* not being able to breathe.

suf•fra•gan ['sʌfrəgən] *n.* bishop who helps another bishop run a large diocese.

suf•frage ['sʌfrɪdʒ] *n.* right to vote in elections. **suf•fra•gette,** *n.* (*old*) woman who campaigned for the right to vote.

suf•fuse [sə'fjuːz] *v.* to cover with (color). **suf•fu•sion,** *n.* act of suffusing.

sug•ar ['ʃʊgə] 1. *n.* sweet substance made from the juice of a sugar cane or from sugar beet. 2. *v.* (a) to put sugar into. (b) to make sth more pleasant or more acceptable. **sug•ar beet,** *n.* plant with a large root which when crushed gives sugar. **sug•ar cane,** *n.* tropical plant whose stalks when crushed give sugar and rum. **sug•ar•coat•ed,** *adj.* covered with a coating of hard sugar. **sug•ar dad•dy,** *n.* old man who entertains young girls, and gives them presents. **sug•ar•y,** *adj.* with too much sugar.

sug•gest [sə'dʒest] *v.* (a) to propose (an idea). (b) to hint/to insinuate. **sug•gest•i•ble,** *adj.* (person) who can easily be influenced. **sug•ges•tion,** *n.* proposal. **sug•ges•tive,** *adj.* (a) which suggests. (b) which gives an impression of indecency. **sug•ges•tive•ly,** *adv.* in a suggestive way.

su•i•cide ['sʊɪsaɪd] *n.* (a) killing yourself; **to commit s.** = to kill yourself. (b) person who has killed himself. **su•i•cid•al** [sʊɪ'saɪdl] *adj.* referring to suicide.

suit [suːt] 1. *n.* (a) two or three pieces of clothing made of the same cloth (jacket/vest and trousers or skirt). (b) lawsuit/court case. (c) one of the four groups with the same symbol in a pack of cards; **to follow s.** = to do what s.o. else has done. 2. *v.* (a) to go together; be appropriate for each other. (b) to be completely acceptable/convenient; **s. yourself** = do what you want. (c) to fit s.o.'s appearance. **suit•a•bil•i•ty** [suːtə'bɪlɪtɪ] *n.* being suitable. **suit•a•ble** ['suːtəbl] *adj.* convenient; (thing) which fits. **suit•a•bly,** *adv.* in a convenient/fitting way. **suit•case,** *n.* box with a handle for carrying clothes in when you are traveling. **suit•or,** *n.* person who wants to marry a certain girl.

suite [swiːt] *n.* (a) series of rooms/pieces of furniture which make a set. (b) group of people accompanying a king, queen or other important person. (c) several short pieces of music which are played together as a group. (d) **en s.** ['ɒn'swiːt] = attached.

sul•fa, *Brit.* **sul•pha** ['sʌlfə] *n.* **s. drug** = sulfonamide.

sul•fur, *Brit.* **sul•phur** ['sʌlfə] *n.* (*element:* S) solid substance, usu. found as a yellow powder. **sul•fate,** *n.* salt formed from sulfuric acid. **sul•fide,** *n.* combination of sulfur with another substance. **sul•fon•a•mide,** *n.* drug used against bacteria. **sul•fu•ric ac•id** [sʌl'fjʊərɪk'æsɪd] *n.* very strong acid containing sulfur. **sul•fur•ous** ['sʌlfərəs] *adj.* like sulfur.

sulk [sʌlk] 1. *n.* **sulks** = being grumpy/annoyed in silence. 2. *v.* to show you are annoyed by not saying anything. **sulk•i•ly,** *adv.* in a sulky way. **sulk•i•ness,** *n.* being sulky. **sulk•y,** *adj.* bad-tempered/grumpy.

sul•len ['sʌln] *adj.* silently angry; unpleasant. **sul•len•ly,** *adv.* in a sullen way.

sul•ly ['sʌlɪ] *v.* (*formal*) to dirty (a reputation).

sul•pha ['sʌlfə] *n. Brit. see* **sul•fa.**

sul•phur ['sʌlfə] *n. Brit. see* **sul•fur.**

sul•tan ['sʌltən] *n.* Muslim prince. **sul•tan•a** [sʌl'tɑːnə] *n.* (a) wife of a sultan. (b) type of seedless raisin. **sul•tan•ate,** *n.* country ruled by a sultan.

sul•try ['sʌltrɪ] *adj.* (**-ier, -iest**) (a) hot/heavy (weather). (b) attractive in a dark way; passionate. **sul•tri•ness,** *n.* being sultry.

sum [sʌm] 1. *n.* (a) total of numbers added together; **the s. total** = the total of several sums added together. (b) quantity of money. (c) arithmetic problem. 2. *v.* (**summed**) **to s. up** =

æ **back,** ɑː **farm,** ɒ **top,** aɪ **pipe,** aʊ **how,** aɪə **fire,** aʊə **flower,** ɔː **bought,** ɔɪ **toy,** e **fed,** eə**hair,** eɪ **take,** ə **afraid,** əʊ **boat,** əʊə **lower,** ɜː **word,** iː **heap,** ɪ **hit,** ɪə **hear,** uː **school,** ʊ **book,** ʌ **but,** b **back,** d **dog,** ð **then,** dʒ **just,** f **fog,** g **go,** h **hand,** j **yes,** k **catch,** l **last,** m **mix,** n **nut,** ŋ **sing,** p **penny,** r **round,** s **some,** ʃ **short,** t **too,** tʃ **chop,** θ **thing,** v **voice,** w **was,** z **zoo,** ʒ **treasure**

to give a summary/to tell briefly what has happened. **sum•ma•rize** ['sʌməraɪz] *v.* to give a brief account of (sth). **sum•ma•ry.** 1. *n.* short account of what has happened; short version of sth longer. 2. *adj.* (a) brief. (b) done quickly without wasting too much time. **sum•mar•i•ly,** *adv.* quickly. **sum•ma•tion,** *n.* summary of evidence given by both attorneys at the end of a trial. **sum•ming-up,** *n.* summarizing statement or summation.

sum•mer ['sʌmə] *n.* season of the year following spring, when plants begin to make fruit; the warmest season; **s. vacation** = main/longest vacation during a school year; **s. school** = classes held at a school/university/college during the summer vacation. **sum•mer•house,** *n.* small house in a garden where you can sit in the summer. **sum•mer•time,** *n.* summer season. **sum•mer•y,** *adj.* like the summer.

sum•mit ['sʌmɪt] *n.* (a) top (of a mountain). (b) **s. (meeting)** = meeting of heads of government to discuss international problems. **sum•mit•ry,** *n. inf.* diplomacy carried on at summit meetings.

sum•mon ['sʌmən] *v.* (a) to call. (b) **to s. up courage** = to get together courage to do sth. **sum•mons.** 1. *n.* (a) official demand to go to see s.o. (b) official legal order to appear in court. 2. *v.* to order (s.o.) to appear in court.

sump [sʌmp] *n.* pit in which water collects.

sump•tu•ous ['sʌmtʃʊəs] *adj.* very luxurious/splendid. **sump•tu•ous•ly,** *adv.* in a sumptuous way.

sun [sʌn] 1. *n.* (a) very hot body around which the earth revolves and which provides heat and daylight. (b) light from the sun. 2. *v.* (sunned) **to s. yourself** = to sit in the sun. **sun•bathe,** *v.* to lie in the sun to get your body brown. **sun•beam,** *n.* ray of sunlight. **sun•burn,** *n.* painful inflammation of the skin caused by being in the sun for too long. **sun•burned,** *adj.* made brown or red by the sun. **sun•deck,** *n.* deck where people can sit in the sun. **sun•di•al,** *n.* round clock face with a central pointer whose shadow points to the time when the sun shines on it. **sun•down,** *n.* moment when the sun goes down. **sun•drenched,** *adj.* (always) very sunny. **sun•flow•er,** *n.* very large yellow flower on a tall stem; **s. oil** = oil made from its seeds. **sun•glass•es,** *n.* dark glasses to protect your eyes from the sun. **sun•lamp,** *n.* lamp which gives off ultraviolet rays like the sun, used to give a suntan indoors. **sun•less,** *adj.* with no sun. **sun•light,** *n.* light from the sun. **sun•lit,** *adj.* lit by the sun. **sun•ni•ly,** *adv.* in a happy way. **sun•ny,** adj. (-ier, -iest)

full of sunlight; happy (character); *inf.* **s. side up** = (egg) fried without being turned over. **sun•rise,** *n.* time at which the sun rises. **sun•roof,** *n.* part of a roof of a car which slides open. **sun•set,** *n.* time when the sun goes down behind the horizon; colorful sky as the sun goes down. **sun•shade,** *n.* light bright-colored umbrella to protect from the sun. **sun•shine,** *n.* light from the sun. **sun•shine roof,** *n.* sunroof. **sun•spot,** *n.* dark spot which appears on the surface of the sun. **sun•stroke,** *n.* illness caused by being overly exposed to the sun's rays or extreme heat. **sun•tan,** *n.* brown color of the skin caused by the sun. **sun•tanned,** *adj.* with a skin made brown by the sun. **sun•up,** *n.* sunrise.

sun•dae ['sʌndɪ] *n.* dessert of ice cream, whipped cream, chopped nuts and fruit.

Sun•day ['sʌndɪ] *n.* last day of the week; day between Saturday and Monday; **S. best** = best clothes; **S. school** = school for teaching religion to children, usu. held on a Sunday.

sun•der ['sʌndə] *v.* (*formal*) to split into parts.

sun•dew ['sʌndju:] *n.* wild plant which catches insects for food.

sun•dry ['sʌndrɪ] 1. *adj.* various. 2. *n.* (a) **all and s.** = everyone. (b) **sundries** = various small articles/small items on a list.

sung [sʌŋ] *v. see* **sing.**

sunk [sʌŋk] *adj.* ruined/lost; *see also* **sink. sunken,** *adj.* (a) which is beneath the surface. (b) lower than the surrounding area.

sup [sʌp] 1. *n.* mouthful of liquid. 2. *v.* (supped) to drink in small mouthfuls.

su•per ['su:pə] 1. *adj. inf.* wonderful. 2. *n. inf.* (a) superintendent. (b) extra actor. 3. **super-** *prefix meaning* more/greater/of better quality.

su•per•a•bun•dance [su:pərə'bʌndəns] *n.* great abundance; very large quantity. **su•per•a•bun•dant,** *adj.* very abundant/in very large quantities.

su•per•an•nu•at•ed [su:pə'rænjueɪtɪd] *adj.* too old to work properly; old-fashioned. **su•per•an•nu•a•tion** [su:pərænju'eɪʃn] *n.* (a) retirement of workers when they reach a certain age. (b) pension paid to s.o. who has retired.

su•perb [su:'pɜːb] *adj.* marvelous/wonderful. **su•perb•ly,** *adv.* wonderfully.

su•per•charged ['su:pətʃɑːdʒd] *adj.* (motor/person) with much increased energy. **su•per•charg•er,** *n.* apparatus on a car engine for increasing the power.

su•per•cil•i•ous [su:pə'sɪlɪəs] *adj.* looking down on others; considering others as inferior. **su•per•cil•i•ous•ly,** *adv.* in a supercilious way. **su•per•cil•i•ous•ness**, *n.* being supercilious.

su•per•fi•cial [suːpəˈfɪʃl] *adj.* touching only the top surface; not going deeply beneath the surface. **su•per•fi•ci•al•i•ty** [suːpəfɪʃɪˈælɪtɪ] *n.* being superficial. **su•per•fi•cial•ly**, *adv.* in a superficial way.

su•per•fine [suːpəˈfaɪn] *adj.* very fine.

su•per•flu•ous [suːˈpəːfluəs] *adj.* which is more than is needed. **su•per•flu•i•ty** [suːpəˈfluːɪtɪ] *n.* being superfluous/more than is needed; excess. **su•per•flu•ous•ly**, *adv.* in a superfluous way.

su•per•high•way [suːpəˈhaɪweɪ] *n.* main highway, usu. having more than one line per direction.

su•per•hu•man [suːpəˈhjuːmən] *adj.* more than is normal in human beings.

su•per•im•pose [suːpəɪmˈpəʊz] *v.* to place on top of sth.

su•per•in•tend [suːpərɪnˈtend] *v.* to be in charge. **su•per•in•tend•ent**, *n.* (a) person in charge. (b) senior police officer.

su•pe•ri•or [suːˈpɪərɪə] 1. *adj.* (a) of better quality; of a larger quality. (b) higher in rank. (c) thinking yourself to be better than others. 2. *n.* (a) person of higher rank. (b) leader of a religious community. **su•pe•ri•or•i•ty** [suːpɪərɪˈɒrɪtɪ] *n.* being superior.

su•per•la•tive [suːˈpɜːlətɪv] 1. *adj.* of the best quality. 2. *n.* form of an adjective or adverb showing the highest level of comparison. **su•per•la•tive•ly**, *adv.* extremely well.

su•per•man [ˈsuːpəmæn] *n.* (*pl.* -men) man who has superhuman strength/power/ability.

su•per•mar•ket [ˈsuːpəmɑːkɪt] *n.* large store selling mainly food, where you serve yourself.

su•per•nat•u•ral [suːpəˈnætʃərəl] *adj. & n.* (things) which happen not in accordance with the laws of nature. **su•per•nat•u•ral•ly**, *adv.* in a supernatural way.

su•per•no•va [ˈsuːpənəʊvə] *n.* large star which explodes and suddenly appears in the sky.

su•per•nu•mer•ar•y [ˈsuːpəˈnjuːmərərɪ] *adj. & n.* (person) who is in addition to the usual number of people.

su•per•phos•phate [suːpəˈfɒsfeɪt] *n.* fertilizer based on phosphates.

su•per•pow•er [ˈsuːpəpaʊə] *n.* extremely powerful country.

su•per•scrip•tion [suːpəˈskrɪpʃn] *n.* words written above sth.

su•per•sede [suːpəˈsiːd] *v.* to take the place of (sth which is older or less efficient).

su•per•son•ic [suːpəˈsɒnɪk] *adj.* faster than the speed of sound.

su•per•sti•tion [suːpəˈstɪʃn] *n.* belief in magic and the supernatural. **su•per•sti•tious** [suːpəˈstɪʃəs] *adj.* believing in magic and the supernatural.

su•per•struc•ture [ˈsuːpəstrʌktʃə] *n.* top structure of a ship; structure built on top of sth else.

su•per•tank•er [ˈsuːpətæŋkə] *n.* very large oil tanker.

su•per•vene [suːpəˈviːn] *v.* to happen as something extra, usu. causing change.

su•per•vise [ˈsuːpəvaɪz] *v.* to watch over work, etc., to see that it is well done. **su•per•vi•sion** [suːpəˈvɪʒn] *n.* act of supervising. **su•per•vi•sor** [ˈsuːpəvaɪzə] *n.* person who supervises. **su•per•vi•so•ry** [suːpəˈvaɪzərɪ] *adj.* as a supervisor.

su•per•wom•an [ˈsuːpəwʊmən] *n.* (*pl.* -women) woman who has superhuman strength/power/ability.

su•pine [ˈsuːpaɪn] *adj.* (*formal*) (a) lying flat on your back. (b) uninterested/lazy.

sup•per [ˈsʌpə] *n.* evening meal.

sup•plant [səˈplɑːnt] *v.* to take (s.o.'s) place by cunning maneuvers.

sup•ple [ˈsʌpl] *adj.* flexible/which bends easily. **sup•ple•ness**, *n.* being supple. **sup•ply** [ˈsʌplɪ], **supplely** *adv.* in a supple way.

sup•ple•ment 1. *n.* [ˈsʌplɪmənt] (a) thing which is in addition. (b) addition to a book; magazine which is part of a newspaper. 2. *v.* [ˈsʌplɪment] to add to. **sup•ple•men•ta•ry** [sʌplɪˈmentrɪ] *adj.* in addition.

sup•pli•ant [ˈsʌplɪənt] *n.* person who begs for help.

sup•pli•cate [ˈsʌplɪkeɪt] *v.* (*formal*) to beg for sth. **sup•pli•cant**, *n.* person who begs for help. **sup•pli•ca•tion** [sʌplɪˈkeɪʃn] *n.* (*formal*) begging for help.

sup•ply [səˈplaɪ] 1. *n.* (a) providing sth which is needed. (b) stock of sth which has been provided. (c) **supplies** = food, etc., which has been stocked/which is going to be provided. 2. *v.* (a) to provide (sth which is necessary). (b) **to s. s.o. with sth** = to provide sth to s.o. (c) to satisfy. 3. *adv.* [ˈsʌplɪ] *see* **sup•ple**. **sup•pli•er** [səˈplaɪə] *n.* person/store/country which supplies.

sup•port [səˈpɔːt] 1. *n.* (a) thing which supports. (b) moral/financial encouragement. 2. *v.* (a) to hold up. (b) to provide/to earn money so that s.o. can live. (c) to encourage/to agree with. **sup•port•er**, *n.* person who encourages a plan/a sports team, etc. **sup•port•ing cast**, *n.* group of actors who play the minor parts in a play.

sup•pose [sə'pəuz] *v.* (a) to assume sth to be correct (even if it is not). (b) to think. (c) what happens if? **sup•pos•ed•ly** [sə'pəuzɪdlɪ] *adv.* as it is assumed. **sup•pos•ing**, *conj.* what happens if? **sup•po•si•tion** [sʌpə'zɪʃn] *n.* thing which is assumed; guess.

sup•pos•i•to•ry [sə'pɒzɪtərɪ] *n.* tablet of medicinal material which is put into the rectum or vagina where it melts.

sup•press [sə'pres] *v.* (a) to crush; to stop (a revolution). (b) to forbid the publication of (sth). (c) to hide (feelings). **sup•pres•sion** [sə'preʃn] *n.* act of suppressing.

sup•pu•rate ['sʌpjʊreɪt] *v.* (*formal*) to produce pus.

supra- ['su:prə] *prefix.* beyond.

su•pra•na•tion•al [su:prə'næʃnl] *adj.* over/beyond the interests of a single nation or several nations.

su•preme [sʊ'pri:m] *adj.* highest; total (indifference). **su•preme•ly**, *adv.* totally/completely. **su•prem•a•cy** [sʊ'preməsɪ] *n.* highest power.

sur•charge 1. *n.* ['sɜ:tʃɑ:dʒ] extra charge. 2. *v.* [sɜ:'tʃɑ:dʒ] to charge an extra amount.

surd [sɜ:d] *n.* (*in mathematics*) quantity (like a root) which cannot be expressed as a whole number.

sure [ʃɔ:, 'ʃʊə] 1. *adj.* (**-er, -est**) (a) without any doubt; certain; **for s.** = for certain. (b) reliable. (c) **s. of yourself** = confident. 2. *adv.* certainly. **sure•fire**, *adj. inf.* absolutely certain to work; which cannot fail. **sure•foot•ed**, *adj.* able to walk on slippery rocks/narrow ledges without slipping. **sure•ly**, *adv.* (a) carefully. (b) naturally/of course. **sure•ness**, *n.* being sure. **sure•ty**, *n.* (a) person who takes the responsibility that s.o. will do sth. (b) money paid as a guarantee that s.o. will appear in court.

surf [sɜ:f] 1. *n.* line of breaking waves along a shore; foam from breaking waves. 2. *v.* (a) to ride on breaking waves on a board. (b) **to s. the Internet** = to browse through the information on the Internet, usu. with no definite objective. **surfboard**, *n.* board which you stand on to ride on breaking waves. **surf boat**, *n.* light boat for riding on surf. **surf•er**, *n.* person who surfs. **surf•ing, surfriding**, *n.* riding on breaking waves as a sport.

sur•face ['sɜ:fəs] 1. *n.* top layer; outside of sth.

2. *v.* (a) to come up from under/to appear on the top of water, etc. (b) to cover (a road, etc.) with a hard substance. **sur•face mail**, *n.* mail which travels by truck/train/ship, etc., and not by air.

sur•feit ['sɜ:fɪt] 1. *n.* (*formal*) too much. 2. *v.* to feed (s.o.) too much.

surge [sɜ:dʒ] 1. *n.* (a) rising up of water into waves. (b) sudden increase. 2. *v.* (a) to rise up. (b) move (forward) in a mass.

sur•geon ['sɜ:dʒən] *n.* doctor who performs operations. **sur•ger•y**, *n.* treatment of disease or wounds by cutting open part of the body. **sur•gi•cal** ['sɜ:dʒɪkl] *adj.* referring to surgery; **s. gloves** = gloves worn by a surgeon. **sur•gi•cal•ly**, *adv.* in a surgical way.

sur•ly ['sɜ:lɪ] *adj.* (**-ier, -iest**) grumpy/sullen. **sur•li•ness**, *n.* being surly.

sur•mise [sə'maɪz] 1. *n.* guess/supposition. 2. *v.* to guess.

sur•mount [sɜ:'maʊnt] *v.* (a) to overcome (an obstacle). (b) to be on top of (sth). **sur•mount•a•ble**, *adj.* which can be surmounted.

sur•name ['sɜ:neɪm] *n.* family name.

sur•pass [sə'pɑ:s] *v.* to do better than.

sur•plice ['sɜ:plɪs] *n.* long white robe worn by clergy/choirboys.

sur•plus ['sɜ:pləs] *adj. & n.* (*pl.* **-es**) extra (stock); (material) left over.

sur•prise [sə'praɪz] 1. *n.* shock caused by sth unexpected. 2. *v.* (a) to give (s.o.) a surprise/an unexpected shock. (b) to catch (s.o.) unexpectedly. **sur•pris•ing**, *adj.* astonishing/unusual. **sur•pris•ing•ly**, *adv.* in an unusual way.

sur•re•al•ism [sə'rɪəlɪzəm] *n.* 20th century art movement in which an artist depicts realistic objects in an unreal environment, emphasizing the meaning he sees beyond reality. **sur•re•al•ist**, *adj. & n.* (artist) following the principles of surrealism. **sur•re•al•is•tic**, *adj.* very strange/totally unreal.

sur•ren•der [sə'rendə] 1. *n.* (a) giving in (to an enemy). (b) giving up (of goods); giving up (of an insurance policy); **s. value** = amount of money you will receive if you end an insurance policy before the normal completion date. 2. *v.* (a) to give in (**to** an enemy). (b) to give up (a ticket/insurance policy, etc.).

sur•rep•ti•tious [sʌrəp'tɪʃəs] *adj.* done in secret. **sur•rep•ti•tious•ly**, *adv.* in secret.

sur•ro•gate ['sʌrəgɪt] *n.* deputy/person who acts in place of s.o.

sur•round [sə'raʊnd] 1. *n.* border; edge. 2. *v.* to be/to come all around (sth). **sur•round•ing**, *adj.* which surrounds. **sur•round•ings**, *n.pl.* area around a place/person.

sur•tax ['sɜːtæks] *n.* extra tax, as on incomes over a certain amount.

sur•veil•lance [sɜː'veɪləns] *n.* strict watch.

sur•vey 1. *n.* ['sɜːveɪ] (a) general view. (b) careful examination of sth. (c) taking measurements of land heights/distances/roads/buildings, etc., to produce accurate plans or maps. 2. *v.* [sə'veɪ] (a) to look at/to talk about (sth) in a general way. (b) to make a survey of sth. (c) to measure (land) in order to produce an accurate plan or map. **sur•vey•or,** *n.* person who surveys land.

sur•vive [sə'vaɪv] *v.* (a) to continue to live (after an accident, etc.). (b) to live longer than (s.o.). **sur•viv•al,** *n.* continuing to live. **sur•vi•vor,** *n.* person who survives.

sus•cep•ti•ble [sə'septɪbl] *adj.* (a) **s. to** = likely to catch (a disease). (b) easily upset. **sus•cep•ti•bil•i•ty** [səseptə'bɪlɪtɪ] *n.* being susceptible.

sus•pect 1. *adj. & n.* ['sʌspekt] (person) who is thought to have committed a crime; (food) which might be poisonous. 2. *v.* [sə'spekt] (a) **to s. s.o. of** = to think that (s.o.) may have committed a crime. (b) to guess/to think.

sus•pend [sə'spend] *v.* (a) to hang; to make (sth) hang in a liquid. (b) to stop (sth) for a time. (c) to take (sth) away as a punishment; to stop (s.o.) from doing sth. **sus•pend•ers,** *n.pl.* (a) elastic straps to hold up stockings or socks. (b) elastic straps worn over the shoulders to hold up trousers. **sus•pense,** *n.* impatient wait for sth to happen or for a decision to be reached. **sus•pen•sion,** *n.* (a) act of suspending; being suspended; **s. bridge** = one which hangs by ropes/chains, etc., from tall towers. (b) system of springs, etc., in a car which attaches the chassis to the axles.

sus•pi•cion [sə'spɪʃn] *n.* (a) feeling that sth is wrong or that s.o. has committed a crime. (b) guess; general feeling. (c) slight hint. **sus•pi•cious,** *adj.* which can be suspected. **sus•pi•cious•ly,** *adv.* (a) in a suspicious way. (b) as if suspecting sth.

sus•tain [sə'steɪn] *v.* (a) to keep (sth) going. (b) to suffer. (c) to support. **sus•tain•a•ble,** *adj.* referring to the use of natural resources in such a way that the environment is preserved, e.g. forestry that replaces each tree felled. **sus•tained,** *adj.* which continues for a long time. **sus•tain•ing,** *adj.* which will support or nourish. **sus•te•nance** ['sʌstənəns] *n.* (a) food. (b)

means of s. = way of keeping alive/of keeping strong.

su•ture ['suːtʃə] *n.* thread used for stitching wounds together; stitching (of a wound); stitch made to hold a wound together.

su•ze•rain ['suːzəreɪn] *n.* (*formal*) overlord. **su•ze•rain•ty,** *n.* rule over (a state).

svelte [svelt] *adj.* slim and graceful.

swab [swɒb] 1. *n.* (a) large mop for wiping floors, decks, etc. clear of water. (b) piece of material used for cleaning a wound or for taking samples of infection for analysis. (c) sample of infection taken for analysis. 2. *v.* (**swabbed**) to clean (a floor, deck, etc.) with a swab.

swad•dle ['swɒdl] *v.* (*old*) to wrap (a baby) in pieces of cloth.

swag [swæg] *n. inf.* stolen goods (esp. jewelry/silver, etc.).

swag•ger ['swægə] 1. *n.* proud way of walking. 2. *v.* to walk in a proud way, swinging your body.

swal•low ['swɒləʊ] 1. *n.* (a) mouthful of liquid which you drink in one movement; act of swallowing. (b) common fast-flying bird with long wings and tail. 2. *v.* (a) to make (food/liquid) pass down your throat from your mouth to the stomach. (b) to accept (a story) as true. (c) to make disappear.

swam [swæm] *v. see* **swim.**

swamp [swɒmp] 1. *n.* area of wet soft land. 2. *v.* to fill (a boat) with water; **swamped with** = having so much (work, etc.) that it is impossible to deal with. **swamp•y,** *adj.* (**-ier, -iest**) wet (land) like a marsh.

swan [swɒn] *n.* large white water bird with a long curved neck. **swan dive,** *n.* dive where the arms are stretched out sideways from the shoulder at the start. **swan song,** *n.* last performance by an artist (esp. a singer); last work by a writer.

swank [swæŋk] 1. *n. inf.* showing off. 2. *v. inf.* to show off; to show that you think a lot of yourself. **swank•y,** *adj. inf.* pretentious; (acting) in a swanking way.

swap, swop [swɒp] 1. *n. inf.* exchange. 2. *v.* (**swapped/swopped**) *inf.* to exchange (sth **for** sth).

sward [swɑːd] *n.* soft grassy surface.

swarm [swɔːm] 1. *n.* large group of insects, etc., flying about together. 2. *v.* (a) to move about in a large group. (b) (**up**) to climb using your hands and feet like a monkey.

æ back, ɑː farm, ɒ top, aɪ pipe, aʊ how, aɪə fire, aʊə flower, ɔː bought, ɔɪ toy, e fed, eəhair, eɪ take, ə afraid, əʊ boat, əʊə lower, ɜː word, iː heap, ɪ hit, ɪə hear, uː school, ʊ book, ʌ but, b back, d dog, ð then, dʒ just, f fog, g go, h hand, j yes, k catch, l last, m mix, n nut, ŋ sing, p penny, r round, s some, ʃ short, t too, tʃ chop, θ thing, v voice, w was, z zoo, ʒ treasure

swarth•y ['swɔːðɪ] *adj.* (**-ier, -iest**) with a dark complexion.

swash•buck•ling ['swɒʃbʌklɪŋ] *adj.* daring; living dangerously.

swas•ti•ka ['swɒstɪkə] *n.* ancient sign, shaped like a cross with each arm bent at right angles.

swat [swɒt] *v.* (**swatted**) to hit and kill (a fly, etc.). **swat•ter**, *n.* (*also* **fly swatter**) flat piece of stiff netting, plastic, etc. on a handle for killing flies and other insects.

swatch [swɒtʃ] *n.* (*pl.* **-es**) small sample of fabric.

swath [swɒθ] *n.* strip cut by a scythe/harvester/mower.

swathe [sweɪð] *v.* to wrap up.

sway [sweɪ] 1. *n.* (a) power. (b) act of swaying. 2. *v.* (a) to (cause to) move from side to side. (b) to influence.

swear ['sweə] *v.* (**swore** [swɔː]; **sworn** [swɔːn]) (a) to promise solemnly. (b) to (make s.o.) take an oath. (c) to curse. (d) **to s. by** = to believe completely or enthusiastically in. **swear word**, *n.* word used as a curse or to show annoyance.

sweat [swet] 1. *n.* drops of liquid which come through your skin when you are hot. 2. *v.* to produce sweat; **we'll have to s. it out** = keep on with it, even if it is unpleasant/difficult. **sweat•band**, *n.* band of fabric worn around your head or wrist to stop sweat trickling down. **sweat•er**, *n.* piece of clothing made of wool, cotton, etc. covering the top part of the body which you wear. pull on over your head. **sweat•shirt**, *n.* loose long-sleeved cotton shirt with no collar or buttons. **sweat shop**, *n.* factory using people who work hard for little money under poor conditions. **sweat•y**, *adj.* damp with sweat.

Swede [swiːd] *n.* person from Sweden. **Swed•ish**. 1. *adj.* referring to Sweden. 2. *n.* language spoken in Sweden.

sweep [swiːp] 1. *n.* (a) act of sweeping (with a brush); act of swinging (a sword or your hand); **to make a clean s.** = to clear sth away completely/to win completely. (b) wide stretch (of water, etc.). (c) person who cleans chimneys. (d) sweepstakes. 2. *v.* (**swept** [swept]) (a) to clean with a brush. (b) to win completely. (c) to clear up (dust/snow, etc.) with a brush. (d) to make a wide movement. (e) to move rapidly; to carry (sth) along rapidly. **sweep•er**, *n.* person/machine that sweeps. **sweep•ing**, *adj.* wide-ranging/far-reaching; **s. statement** = statement which is partly true but too general. **sweep•stakes**, *n.* form of gambling where the holders of the winning tickets take all the money which has been bet.

sweet [swiːt] 1. *adj.* (**-er, -est**) (a) tasting like sugar; not sour; **s. tooth** = liking for sweet things. (b) pleasant; **s. pea** = pea with scented flowers. (c) fresh (air). 2. *n.* small piece of sweet food, made with sugar or chocolate. **sweet•bread**, *n.* pancreas of an animal eaten as food. **sweet corn**, *n.* corn, eaten as food. **sweet•en**, *v.* (a) to make sweet. (b) *inf.* to give (s.o.) a bribe to make sure he is favorable to you. **sweet•en•er**, *n.* (a) thing/material which sweetens. (b) *inf.* bribe. **sweet•en•ing**, *n.* act of making sweet; substance which makes sweet. **sweet•heart**, *n.* darling; boy/girl friend. **sweet•ie**, *n. inf.* (a) sweet. (b) darling. **sweet•ly**, *adv.* in a sweet way. **sweet•meat**, *n.* (*old*) sweet. **sweet•ness**, *n.* being sweet. **sweet po•ta•to**, *n.* yam. **sweet wil•liam**, *n.* type of common scented garden flower.

swell [swel] 1. *n.* (a) rising movement of the sea. (b) increasing loudness. 2. *adj.* fine. 3. *v.* (**swelled/swollen**) (a) to increase. (b) **to s. (up)** = to become larger/to increase in size. (c) **to s. (out)** = to become/to make (sails) fully rounded. **swell•ing**, *n.* part of the body which has swollen.

swel•ter ['sweltə] *v.* to be very hot. **swel•ter•ing**, *adj.* very hot.

swept [swept] *v. see* **sweep.**

swerve [swɜːv] 1. *n.* movement to the side. 2. *v.* to move to one side.

swid•den ['swɪdən] *n.* type of farming, where forest is cut and burned to create space for growing crops.

swift [swɪft] 1. *adj.* (**-er, -est**) fast. 2. *n.* fast-flying bird like a swallow but with shorter wings and tail. **swift•ly**, *adv.* fast. **swift•ness**, *n.* rapidity.

swig [swɪg] 1. *n. inf.* large mouthful of liquid. 2. *v.* (**swigged**) *inf.* to drink in large mouthfuls.

swill [swɪl] 1. *n.* food for pigs. 2. *v. inf.* to drink a lot of alcohol, etc.

swim [swɪm] 1. *n.* act of moving in the water using arms/legs/flippers, etc.; **in the s.** = up to date/knowing what's going on. 2. *v.* (**swam; swum**) (a) to move in water using arms, legs, flippers, etc. (b) to cross (a river, etc.) by swimming. (c) to be covered with liquid. (d) (*of head, room*) to seem to turn. **swim•mer**, *n.* person who swims. **swim•ming**, *n.* action of swimming. **swim•ming•ly**, *adv. inf.* very well. **swim•ming pool**, *n.* pool for swimming. **swim•suit**, *n.* one- or two-piece garment worn for swimming.

swin•dle ['swɪndl] 1. *n.* trick to get money from s.o. 2. *v.* to get money from (s.o.) by a trick. **swin•dler**, *n.* person who swindles s.o.

swine [swaɪn] *n.* (*no pl.*) (a) pig. (b) *inf.* unpleasant person. **swine fe•ver**, *n.* infectious disease of pigs. **swine•herd**, *n.* (*old*) person who looks after pigs.

swing [swɪŋ] 1. *n.* (a) movement from side to side or forward and backward; movement of voters to vote for a certain party. (b) **in full s.** = going very well. (c) seat on the end of two ropes which you can sit on and swing backward and forward. 2. *v.* (**swung** [swʌŋ]) (a) to move from side to side or forward and backward. (b) to make (sth) turn around; to turn around. (c) to move in a rhythmic way with a regular motion. **swing bridge,** *n.* bridge which can be made to turn to allow ships to pass underneath. **swing•er,** *n.* person who is fashionably modern. **swing•ing,** 1. *n.* action of moving backward and forward. 2. *adj.* (a) moving backward and forward. (b) *inf* lively; fashionably modern. **swing•ing door,** *n.* door which is not attached with a catch, and which opens when you push it. **swing-wing,** *adj.* (aircraft) with adjustable wings.

swipe [swaɪp] 1. *n. inf.* sweeping hit/blow. 2. *v.* (a) *inf.* to hit (s.o.) with a sweeping blow. (b) *Sl.* to steal.

swirl [swɜːl] 1. *n.* whirling/twisting movement. 2. *v.* to move with a whirling/twisting motion.

swish [swɪʃ] 1. *n.* soft rustle (of a dress/of dead leaves); whistle (of a stick). 2. *v.* to make a whistling noise with a whip/stick.

Swiss [swɪs] 1. *adj.* referring to Switzerland. 2. *n.* (*pl.* **Swiss**) person from Switzerland.

switch [swɪtʃ] 1. *n.* (*pl.* **-es**) (a) apparatus for starting or stopping an electric current. (b) sudden change. (c) whip made of a thin stick. (d) tuft of hair at the end of an animal's tail, as a cow. 2. *v.* (a) to send (a train, etc.) in a different direction; to do sth quite different. (b) to hit with a switch. **switch•back,** *n.* road or railroad having many curves. **switch•board,** *n.* central telephone panel where calls can be transferred to different rooms. **switch off,** *v.* to stop an electric current. **switch on,** *v.* to start an electric current flowing. **switch o•ver to,** *v.* to change to sth quite different.

swiv•el ['swɪvl] 1. *n.* joint between two parts which enables either part to turn without the other. 2. *v.* (**swiveled, swivelled**) to turn around; to pivot. **swiv•el chair,** *n.* chair which pivots, so that the seat can turn while the legs stay stationary.

swiz•zle•stick ['swɪzlstɪk] *n.* small stick used to stir an alcoholic drink.

swol•len ['swəʊlən] *adj.* blown up; increased in size; *see also* **swell.**

swoon [swuːn] *v.* to faint.

swoop [swuːp] 1. *n.* coming rapidly down from a height to attack; sudden attack; **at/in one fell s.** = in a sudden move/all at once. 2. *v.* to come down rapidly to attack; to attack suddenly.

swop [swɒp] *n. & v. see* **swap.**

sword [sɔːd] *n.* weapon with a long sharp blade held by a handle; **to cross swords with** = to get into an argument with. **sword•fish,** *n.* fish with a long pointed upper jaw like a sword. **swords•man,** *n.* (*pl.* **-men**) person who fights well with a sword.

swore [swɔː] *v. see* **swear.**

sworn [swɔːn] *adj.* **s. enemies** = total enemies; *see also* **swear.**

swum [swʌm] *v. see* **swim.**

swung [swʌŋ] *v. see* **swing.**

syb•a•rite ['sɪbəraɪt] *n.* person who enjoys luxury. **syb•a•rit•ic** [sɪbə'rɪtɪk] *adj.* very comfortable and luxurious.

syc•a•more ['sɪkəmɔː] *n.* common deciduous tree with very large leaves.

syc•o•phant ['sɪkəfænt] *n.* person who flatters s.o. in power. **syc•o•phan•tic** [sɪkə-'fæntɪk] *adj.* which flatters excessively.

syl•la•ble ['sɪləbl] *n.* unit of sound which forms a whole word or part of a word. **syl•lab•ic** [sɪ'læbɪk] *adj.* referring to a syllable.

syl•la•bub ['sɪləbʌb] *n.* dessert made of cream whipped with wine.

syl•la•bus ['sɪləbəs] *n.* (*pl.* **-es, -bi**) list of subjects to be studied.

syl•lo•gism ['sɪlədʒɪzəm] *n.* logical reasoning where a conclusion is reached from two statements.

sylph [sɪlf] *n.* thin girl. **sylph•like,** *adj.* very slim.

syl•van ['sɪlvən] *adj.* (*formal*) referring to woods.

sym•bi•o•sis [sɪmbɪ'əʊsɪs] *n.* state where two living organisms live close together and depend on each other to a certain extent. **sym•bi•ot•ic** [sɪmbaɪ'ɒtɪk] *adj.* referring to symbiosis.

sym•bol ['sɪmbl] *n.* sign/letter/picture/object which represents sth/which is a short way of indicating sth. **sym•bol•ic(al)** [sɪm'bɒlɪk(l)] *adj.* which acts as a symbol. **sym•bol•i•cal•ly,** *adv.* used as a symbol. **sym•bol•ism,** *n.* (a) movement in literature and art which used symbols to express emotion, etc. (b) using symbols to express emotion, etc. **sym•bol•ist,** *adj. & n.* (follower) of symbolism. **sym•bol•ize** ['sɪmbəlaɪz] v. to represent (sth) by a symbol; to be a symbol for (sth).

sym•me•try ['sɪmətrɪ] n. state where two sides of sth are exactly alike. **sym•met•ri•cal** [sɪ-'metrɪkl] adj. referring to symmetry.

sym•pa•thy ['sɪmpəθɪ] n. (a) feeling of pity or sorrow for s.o. who has problems. (b) common feeling; sharing ideas. **sym•pa•thet•ic** [sɪmpə'θetɪk] adj. showing sympathy. **sym•pa•thet•i•cal•ly**, adv. in a sympathetic way. **sym•pa•thize**, v. (with) (a) to show sympathy to (s.o. in trouble). (b) to approve; to agree. **sym•pa•thiz•er**, n. person who sympathizes with s.o.'s political views.

sym•pho•ny ['sɪmfənɪ] n. piece of music in several parts for a full orchestra. **sym•phon•ic** [sɪm'fɒnɪk] adj. referring to a symphony.

sym•po•si•um [sɪm'pəuzɪəm] n. (pl. -ia) organized meeting to discuss a specific subject; collection of articles written on a specific subject.

symp•tom ['sɪmptəm] n. thing which shows visibly that feelings exist/that changes are taking place. **symp•to•mat•ic** [sɪmptə'mætɪk] adj. (of) which shows visibly that changes are taking place or that feelings exist.

syn•a•gogue ['sɪnəgɒg] n. building where Jews worship.

syn•apse ['sɪnæps] n. point in the nervous system where neurons join.

sync [sɪŋk] n. inf. synchronization; **out of s.** = not synchronized.

syn•chro•mesh ['sɪŋkrəmeʃ] n. type of gear system where the gears revolve at the same speeds before being engaged.

syn•chro•nize ['sɪŋkrənaɪz] v. to adjust (watches) to the same time; to arrange (things) so that they happen at the same time. **syn•chro•ni•za•tion** [sɪŋkrənaɪ'zeɪʃn] n. act of synchronizing.

syn•co•pate ['sɪŋkəpeɪt] v. (in music) to stress (a beat) which would not normally be stressed and so change the rhythm. **syn•co•pa•tion** [sɪŋkə'peɪʃn] n. act of syncopating.

syn•co•pe ['sɪŋkəpɪ] n. fainting attack.

syn•di•cal•ism ['sɪndɪkəlɪzm] n. form of socialism, where control is in the hands of the labor unions.

syn•di•cate 1. n. ['sɪndɪkət] group of people or companies working together to make money. 2. v. ['sɪndɪkeɪt] to produce (an article/a cartoon) which is then sold to a series of newspapers. **syn•di•ca•tion** [sindi'keiʃn] n. act of syndicating.

syn•drome ['sɪndrəum] n. (a) series of symptoms which show an illness. (b) symptoms which show a general feeling/way of approaching a problem, etc.

syn•er•gy ['sɪnədʒɪ] n. (of two organizations) working together better than working separately.

syn•od ['sɪnəd] n. meeting of religious leaders.

syn•o•nym ['sɪnənɪm] n. word which means the same thing as another word. **syn•on•y•mous** [sɪ'nɒnɪməs] adj. which has the same meaning.

syn•op•sis [sɪ'nɒpsɪs] n. (pl. -ses) summary (of main points made in a book or article).

syn•o•vi•tis ['saɪnəu'vaɪtɪs] n. inflammation of the membrane covering a joint.

syn•tax ['sɪntæks] n. grammatical rules for putting words together into sentences. **syn•tac•tic** [sɪn'tæktɪk] adj. referring to syntax.

syn•the•sis ['sɪnθəsɪs] n. (pl. -ses) bringing several parts together to form a whole. **syn•the•size** ['sɪnθəsaɪz] v. to combine (several things) together to make a whole. **syn•the•siz•er**, n. electronic device which can make musical sounds similar to those of different instruments.

syn•thet•ic [sɪn'θetɪk] 1. n. artificial/man-made material. 2. adj. artificial; made in such a way that it looks natural. **syn•thet•i•cal•ly**, adv. in a synthetic way.

syph•i•lis ['sɪfɪlɪs] n. serious disease transmitted by sexual intercourse or inherited. **syph•i•lit•ic**, adj. & n. (person) suffering from syphilis.

Syr•i•an ['sɪrɪən] adj. & n. (person) from Syria;

sy•rin•ga [sɪ'rɪŋgə] n. tall shrub with scented white flowers.

sy•ringe [sɪ'rɪndʒ] 1. n. tube with a piston or rubber bulb so that liquids can be sucked into it then squeezed out, as in giving injections. 2. v. to clean by blowing liquid with a syringe.

syr•up ['sɪrəp] n. thick sweet liquid; thick golden juice from sugar. **syr•up•y**, adj. like syrup; very sweet.

sys•tem ['sɪstəm] n. (a) arrangement of things which work together. (b) way of organizing things to work together. (c) method. (d) body. **sys•tem•at•ic** [sɪstə'mætɪk] adj. orderly/methodical. **sys•tem•at•i•cal•ly**, adv. in a methodical way. **sys•tem•a•tize** ['sɪstəmətaɪz] v. to organize into a system. **sys•tem•ic** [sɪs'temɪk] adj. which affects the whole system. **sys•tems a•nal•y•sis**, n. use of a computer to forecast needs, etc., by analyzing the way in which a system is actually operating. **sys•tems an•a•lyst**, n. person who specializes in systems analysis.

sys•to•le [sɪs'təulɪ] n. phase in the heartbeat, when the heart contracts and pumps blood out.

Tt

T, t [ti:] *inf.* **it suits him to a T** = it suits him perfectly; **to dot one's i's and cross one's t's** = to settle the final details (of an agreement)/to be very careful about sth; **T-bone steak** = type of beef steak with a bone shaped like a T in it. **T shirt** = light short-sleeved shirt with no buttons or collar; **T square** = device shaped like a T for drawing right angles.

tab [tæb] *n.* (a) small loop of cloth for hanging up a coat/for pulling open a box. (b) little colored marker attached to cards in an index so that they can be found easily; *inf.* **to pick up the t.** = to pay the bill; **to keep tabs on s.o.** = to keep watch on s.o.

tab•ard ['tæbɑːd] *n.* short sleeveless coat worn by knights over their armor.

ta•bas•co [tə'bæskəu] *n.* trademark for a hot red sauce.

tab•by (cat) ['tæbi(kæt)] *n.* striped black, brown, and gray cat.

tab•er•nac•le ['tæbənækl] *n.* (a) place of worship. (b) ornamental box for consecrated bread and wine.

ta•ble ['teɪbl] 1. *n.* (a) piece of furniture with a flat top and legs, used for eating at/for working at, etc.; **to set the t.** = to get the table ready for a meal; **to clear the t.** = to remove dirty plates/knives, etc. after a meal; **to turn the tables on s.o.** = to put yourself in a superior position, where before you were in an inferior one. (b) printed list of figures/facts; **multiplication tables** = lists of figures to learn by heart how each number is multiplied. **t. of contents** = list of contents of a book. 2. *v.* to put aside for future consideration; **to t. a proposal.**

ta•ble•cloth, *n.* cloth for covering a table during a meal. **ta•ble•land,** *n.* high flat land. **ta•ble lin•en,** *n.* tablecloths/napkins, etc. **ta•ble man•ners,** *n. pl.* polite way of eating according to the rules of society. **ta•ble•spoon,** *n.* large spoon for serving food at the table. **ta•ble•spoon•ful,** *n.* quantity held in a tablespoon. **ta•ble ten•nis,** *n.* game played on a large table with a net across the center, using small round paddles and a very light white ball.

ta•ble•ware, *n.* knives, forks, spoons, plates, etc.

tab•leau ['tæbləu] *n.* (*pl.* -eaux [-əuz], -eaus) scene where actors represent a historic occasion, etc., without moving.

ta•ble d'hôte ['tɑːblədəut] *n.* menu which has a restricted number of dishes at a reduced price.

tab•let ['tæblət] *n.* (a) small round pill of medicine. (b) flat stone with an inscription on it. (c) bar (of soap/chemical, etc.).

tab•loid ['tæblɔɪd] *n.* popular newspaper with a small page size, usu. with a large number of pictures.

ta•boo [tə'buː] 1. *adj.* forbidden (by religion/by custom). 2. *n.* (religious) custom which forbids sth.

ta•bor ['teɪbɔː] *n.* small drum beaten with the hand.

tab•u•lar ['tæbjulə] *adj.* arranged in a table. **tab•u•late** ['tæbjuleɪt] *v.* to arrange (figures) in a table. **tab•u•la•tion** [tæbju'leɪʃn] *n.* arrangement (of figures) in a table. **tab•u•la•tor,** *n.* device on a typewriter/in a computer program which allows the typist to make columns automatically.

tach•o•graph ['tækəgrɑːf] *n.* machine placed in the cab of a truck which records details of the mileage and time spent on a journey.

tach•y•car•di•a [tækɪ'kɑːdɪə] *n.* rapid heartbeat.

tac•it ['tæsɪt] *adj.* (agreement, etc.) which is understood, but not actually given. **tac•it•ly,** *adv.* (agreement given) without speaking, but nevertheless understood. **tac•i•turn,** *adj.* (person) who does not say much. **tac•i•tur•ni•ty** [tæsɪ'tɜːnɪtɪ] *n.* silence/not saying much.

tack [tæk] 1. *n.* (a) small nail (with a large head); *inf.* **to get down to brass tacks** = to talk real business/to start discussing the real problem. (b) (*in sewing*) light stitch to hold cloth in place and which can be taken out later. (c) diagonal movement of a ship so that it is sailing against the wind; **on the wrong t.** = in error. (d) saddle and equipment for riding a horse. 2. *v.* (a) to nail (sth) using tacks; (b) to make a light temporary stitch. (c) to change direction so that you are sailing into the wind; **they were tacking up the river** = they sailed in a zigzag way up the river against the wind. **tack on,** *v.* to add (sth) at the end.

tack•le ['tækl] 1. *n.* (a) equipment. (b) **block and t.** = arrangement of ropes, pulleys and hooks for lifting heavy weights. (c) (*in football, etc.*) grabbing an opposing player so that he falls to the ground and releases the ball. 2. *v.* (a) to grab (s.o./sth); to try to deal with (a problem). (b) (*in football, etc.*) to grab (an opposing player) so that he falls to the ground. **tack•ler,** *n.* person who tackles.

tack•y ['tækɪ] *adj.* (**-ier, -iest**) sticky. **tack•i•ness,** *n.* being tacky.

tact [tækt] *n.* care in your relationships with people so that you do not offend them. **tact•ful,** *adj.* using tact. **tact•ful•ly,** *adv.* in a tactful way. **tact•less,** *adj.* lacking tact/unintentionally offensive. **tact•less•ly,** *adv.* in a tactless way. **tact•less•ness,** *n.* lack of tact.

tac•tic ['tæktɪk] *n.* (*often pl.*) way of doing sth so as to be at an advantage; way of placing troops/guns, etc., so as to be in a better position than the enemy. **tac•ti•cal,** *adj.* referring to tactics; **t. error** = mistake in planning. **tac•ti•cal•ly,** *adv.* in a tactical way. **tac•ti•cian** [tæk'tɪʃn] *n.* person who is expert at tactics. **tac•tile** ['tæktaɪl] *adj.* sensitive to touch; referring to the sense of touch.

tad•pole ['tædpəʊl] *n* baby frog/toad in its first stage after hatching.

taf•fe•ta ['tæfɪtə] *n.* thin shiny stiff cloth.

taff•rail ['tæfreɪl] *n.* guard rail round the stern of a ship.

taf•fy ['tæfɪ] *n.* sticky chewy candy made with sugar and butter.

tag [tæg] 1. *n.* (a) small loop of cloth; metal piece at the end of a shoelace. (b) label. (c) common old saying. (d) children's game where you have to try to touch another child who chases the others in his turn. 2. *v.* (**tagged**) *inf.* **to t. after s.o.** = to stay close to s.o.; **to t. along behind** = to follow closely.

tai•ga ['taɪgæ] *n.* forest in north Siberia.

tail [teɪl] 1. *n.* (a) part of an animal at the rear of its body, usu. sticking out at the back; **to turn t.** = run away. (b) back part of a long coat/of a shirt, etc.; **wearing tails** = wearing evening-dress. (c) back part (of a line of people, etc.); back (of a car). (d) **tails** = reverse side of a

coin/the side of a coin without the head of a person, etc., on it. (e) *inf.* detective who is following s.o. closely. 2. *v.* to follow (s.o.) closely. **tail•gate, tail•board,** *n.* hinged board at the back of a truck, station wagon, etc., which can be let down to load or unload the contents. **tail coat,** *n.* man's black evening jacket with a long tail at the back. **tail end,** *n.* back part (of a line); last part (of a motion picture, etc.). **tail•less,** *adj.* (animal) with no tail. **tail•light,** *n.* rear light (of a car, etc.). **tail off,** *v.* to die away/to fade away. **tail•pipe,** *n.* exhaust pipe of a motor vehicle or aircraft. **tail•spin,** *n.* dive by an aircraft, where the machine turns around and around. **tail wind,** *n.* wind blowing behind an aircraft, making it go faster.

tai•lor ['teɪlə] 1. *n.* person who makes outer clothes (suits/coats, etc.) usu. for men. 2. *v.* (a) to make clothes which fit. (b) to make (sth) fit particular circumstances. **tai•lor-made,** *adj.* made to fit.

taint [teɪnt] 1. *n.* slight trace of evil/of corruption. 2. *v.* to infect/to corrupt; **tainted food** = food which has become rotten (by touching other rotten food).

take [teɪk] 1. *n.* (a) one scene of a motion picture which has been filmed. (b) money taken in a store/in a business. 2. *v.* (**took; has taken**) (a) to hold/to grasp/to carry. (b) to remove/to steal. (c) to buy/to rent/to occupy; to have a (newspaper) delivered to your house regularly; **to t. a seat** = sit down; **to t. the chair** = to act as chairman (at a meeting). (d) to win (a prize). (e) to be a candidate for (an examination). (f) to eat/to drink (usually); **do you t. sugar in your tea?** (g) to make (a photograph). (h) to accept; **t. it from me** = believe what I say; **t. my advice** = do as I suggest. (i) to need; **it took three men to lift the piano; we took two days/it took us two days to get the work done.** (j) to lead; to go (in a direction); **can you t. me to the station?** = can you drive me to the station? (k) to hold; (*of machine*) to accept/to be able to work with. (l) to do (a certain action); **to t. a walk/a bath/a vacation.** (m) to stand/to put up with. (n) to be successful/to have effect; **the kidney transplant has taken** = has been successful; **the cuttings have taken** = have sprouted roots. **take af•ter,** *v.* to be like (a parent). **take aw•ay,** *v.* (a) to remove. (b) to subtract. **take back,** *v.* (a) to return. (b) **I take it all back** = I withdraw what I said and apologize for having said it. **take down,** *v.* (a) to lower (sth which is hanging). (b) to write down (what s.o. says). (c) to demolish. **take-home pay,** *n.* amount of money you actually receive out of your wages, after tax, etc., has been deducted. **take in,** *v.* (a) to accept/to bring inside. (b) to include. (c) to trick (s.o.). (d) to understand. (e) to make (a skirt, etc.) smaller. **ta•ken with,** *adj. inf.* attracted by. **take off,** *v.* (a) to remove (clothes). (b) to fly into the air. (c) *inf.* to imitate. **take•off,** *n.* (a) departure (of an aircraft). (b) *inf.* imitation. **take on,** *v.* (a) to agree to do (some work). (b) to agree to employ (s.o.). (c) to fight; to play against. **take out,** *v.* (a) to pull (sth) out. (b) to invite (s.o.) to go out. (c) **to t. o. an insurance policy on** = to start to insure. (d) **to take it out on s.o.** = to make s.o. suffer to help relieve your own feelings. (c) **the heat takes it out of me** = makes me very tired. **take•out,** *n. & adj.* (place where you can buy) food to take and eat elsewhere. **take o•ver,** *v.* (a) to buy (a business). (b) **to t. o. from s.o.** = to start to do sth in place of s.o. else. **take•o•ver,** *n.* buying of a business; **t. bid** = offer to buy a business. **tak•er,** *n.* person who wants to take or buy sth. **take to,** *v.* (a) to do sth, usu. to help you out of a bad situation; **he took to the woods** = went into the woods to hide; **she took to drink** = started to drink alcohol regularly. (b) to start to like (s.o.). **take up,** *v.* (a) to pick up; **they've taken up the carpeting** = removed the carpeting. (b) to occupy (space). (c) to start to do (a sport/a craft). (d) to start to work on (an idea); to start to discuss (a case). (e) to make (a skirt, etc.) shorter. (f) *inf.* **to take s.o. up on sth** = to accept a suggestion which s.o. has made. **take up with,** *v.* to become friendly with (s.o.). **tak•ings,** *n. pl.* money received in a store/in a business.

talc [tælk] *n.* smooth soft mineral used to make powder to put on the body; powder made from this mineral. **tal•cum pow•der,** *n.* powder made from talc.

tale [teɪl] *n.* story; **old wives' t.** = superstitious belief.

tal•ent ['tælənt] *n.* (a) natural gift/ability. (b) people with natural ability. **t. contest** = contest to find new singers/comedians, etc. **tal•ent•ed,** *adj.* very gifted.

tal•is•man ['tælɪzmən] *n.* object kept because it supposedly brings good luck.

talk [tɔːk] 1. *n.* (a) spoken words; **idle t.** = gossip; **double t.** = saying one thing and thinking the opposite. (b) conversation. (c) lecture/informal speech. 2. *v.* (a) to speak (a language). *inf.* **now you're talking** = that's a good idea. (b) to gossip. (c) to give information (usu. unwillingly). **talk•a•tive,** *adj.* (person) who likes to

chat/to gossip. **talk down,** *v.* (a) to speak in a condescending way/in an exaggeratedly simple way (**to s.o.**). (b) to give instructions over the radio to a pilot for landing his aircraft when visibility is bad. **talk•er,** *n.* person who talks. **talk•ing,** *n.* speech, conversation; **he did all the t.** = the others said nothing. **talk•ing point,** *n.* thing which supports one side in a disagreement or debate. **talk•ing-to,** *n. inf.* scolding. **talk into,** *v.* **to talk s.o. into doing sth** = to persuade. **talk o•ver,** *v.* **come and talk it over** = come and discuss it. **talk a•round,** *v.* **I talked him around** = I persuaded him to change his mind; **we just talked around the subject** = we never discussed the main problem.

tall [tɔːl] *adj.* (**-er, -est**) (a) high. (b) *inf.* unbelievable (story); **t. order** = command which is extremely difficult to carry out. **tall•boy,** *n.* type of tall chest of drawers.

tal•low ['tæləʊ] *n.* fat from animals, used to make candles.

tal•ly ['tælɪ] 1. *n.* note/account. 2. *v.* to agree (**with**).

tal•on ['tælən] *n.* claw (of a bird).

tam•a•risk ['tæmərɪsk] *n.* shrub with feathery evergreen leaves, which is often grown near the sea.

tam•bo•rine [tæmbə'riːn] *n.* small drum with metal pieces loosely attached to the rim, so that they jangle when it is beaten.

tame [teɪm] 1. *adj.* (**-er, -est**) (a) (animal) which is not wild/which can be approached by human beings. (b) not very exciting. 2. *v.* to make (an animal) tame; to make safe. **tame•ness,** *n.* being tame. **tam•er,** *n.* person who tames wild animals.

tam-o'-shan•ter [tæmə'ʃæntə] *n.* flat Scottish cap, like a beret.

tamp [tæmp] *v.* to press down.

tam•per ['tæmpə] *v.* **to t. with** = to meddle with.

tam•pon ['tæmpɒn] *n.* pad of cotton or similar material used to soak up blood.

tan [tæn] 1. *n. & adj.* brownish yellow (color). 2. *n.* brown color of the skin after being in the sun. 3. *v.* (**tanned**) to treat (animal skin) to make leather. (b) to get brown by sitting in the sun. **tan•ner,** *n.* person who makes animal skins into leather. **tan•ner•y,** *n.* factory where skins are made into leather.

tan•dem ['tændəm] *n.* bicycle for two people; **in t.** = in pairs/together.

æ back, ɑː farm, ɒ top, aɪ pipe, aʊ how, aɪə fire, aʊə flower, ɔː bought, ɔɪ toy, e fed, eəhair, eɪ take, ə afraid, əʊ boat, əʊə lower, ɜː word, iː heap, ɪ hit, ɪə hear, uː school, ʊ book, ʌ but, b back, d dog, ð then, dʒ just, f fog, g go, h hand, j yes, k catch, l last, m mix, n nut, ŋ sing, p penny, r round, s some, ʃ short, t too, tʃ chop, θ thing, v voice, w was, z zoo, ʒ treasure

tang [tæŋ] *n.* sharp smell/taste. **tang•y,** *adj.* with a sharp taste/smell.

tan•gent ['tændʒənt] *n.* line which touches a curve without cutting through it; **to go off on/at a t.** = to change direction/to follow another line of thought. **tan•gen•tial** [tæn-'dʒənʃl] *adj.* referring to a tangent.

tan•ge•rine ['tændʒə'riːn] *n.* small orange with soft skin which peels easily.

tan•gi•ble ['tændʒəbl] *adj.* which can be touched; real. **tan•gi•bil•i•ty** [tændʒɪ'bɪlɪti] *n.* being tangible. **tan•gi•bly,** *adv.* in a real/definite way.

tan•gle ['tæŋgl] 1. *n.* mix of threads/string/hair; **in a t.** = all mixed up. 2. *v.* to mix (things) together in knots; **to t. with s.o.** = to get into an argument.

tan•go ['tæŋgəu] *n.* (*pl.* **-os**) dance where you glide sideways.

tank [tæŋk] *n.* (a) large (metal) container for liquids. (b) **t. truck** = truck having a tank for carrying gas or liquids. (c) armored vehicle with caterpillar tracks and a powerful gun. **tank•er,** *n.* (a) special ship for carrying liquids (esp. oil). (b) special truck for carrying gas or liquids. **tank up,** *v. inf.* to drink a lot.

tan•kard ['tæŋkəd] *n.* large covered mug for drinking beer.

tan•nin ['tænɪn] *n.* red-brown liquid (found in the bark of trees/in tea) which is used to make leather. **tan•nic,** *adj.* **t. acid** = tannin.

tan•sy ['tænzɪ] *n.* herb with yellow flowers.

tan•ta•lize ['tæntəlaɪz] *v.* to tease (s.o.) by offering him sth which he can't have. **tan•ta•liz•ing,** *adj.* which tantalizes. **tan•ta•liz•ing•ly,** *adv.* in a tantalizing way.

tan•ta•mount ['tæntəmaunt] *adj.* equivalent/equal (to).

tan•trum ['tæntrəm] *n.* attack of uncontrollable bad temper.

tap [tæp] 1. *n.* (a) apparatus with a twisting knob and a valve which, when you turn it, allows liquid to come out of a pipe/container; **t. water** = water which comes from the mains and not from a well; **on t.** = readily available. (b) slight blow; light knock. 2. *v.* (**tapped**) (a) to run liquid out of (a barrel) by fixing a tap; to cut a hole in so that the sap flows out; **to t. a sugar maple.** (b) to attach a secret listening device to (a telephone). (c) to start to exploit (sth new). (d) to hit lightly. **tap dance,** *n.* dance done by beating time to the music with metal-soled shoes. **tap danc•er,** *n.* dancer who specializes in tap dancing. **tap danc•ing,** *n.* dancing with special shoes with metal soles, so that the dancer beats time to the music. **tap•root,** *n.* main root (of a tree) which goes straight down into the soil.

tape [teip] 1. *n.* (a) long thin flat strip (of cloth/plastic, etc.); **adhesive t.** = glued plastic strip for sticking things together, etc.; **insulating t.** = sticky tape for wrapping round electrical connections: **measuring tape** = long strip marked in inches/centimeters, etc. for measuring; **magnetic t.** = sensitive plastic tape for recording. (b) long string held across the finishing line of a race. 2. *v.* (a) to attach with a tape. (b) to record (sth) on magnetic tape. **tape deck,** *n.* apparatus which plays tape and records on tape, but does not have its own amplifier or loudspeakers. **tape meas•ure,** *n.* long strip of cloth/metal marked in inches/centimeters, etc., used for measuring. **tape•re•cord,** *v.* to record (sth) on tape. **tape re•cord•er,** *n.* apparatus which records on tape and plays back these tapes. **tape re•cord•ing,** *n.* recording done on tape. **tape•worm,** *n.* long flatworm which lives in the intestines of human beings and other animals.

tap•er ['teipə] 1. *n.* long slender candle, made of a wick covered with a thin layer of wax. 2. *v.* to make (sth) become thinner at the end; (*also* **taper off**) to become thinner at the end.

tap•es•try ['tæpɪstrɪ] *n.* thick woven cloth with a picture or design, usu. hung on walls or used to cover chairs.

tap•i•o•ca [tæpɪ'əukə] *n.* white starchy powder which comes from a tropical plant and is used to make puddings.

ta•pir ['teipə] *n.* South American animal like a pig with a short trunk.

tap•pet ['tæpɪt] *n.* small projecting piece which opens or closes a valve by tapping on it.

tar [tɑː] 1. *n.* (a) black oily substance which comes from coal and is used for covering roads. (b) *inf.* sailor. 2. *v.* (**tarred**) to cover with tar; **tarpaper** = thick brown waterproof paper with an inner layer of tar; **to t. and feather s.o.** = to cover s.o. with hot tar and feathers as a punishment; **to be tarred with the same brush** = to have the same weaknesses/to make the same mistakes (as s.o.).

ta•ran•tu•la [tə'ræntjulə] *n.* large mildly poisonous tropical spider.

tar•dy ['tɑːdɪ] *adj.* (**-ier, -iest**) (*formal*) late. **tar•di•ly,** *adv.* late. **tar•di•ness,** *n.* being tardy.

tare [teə] *n.* (a) allowance made for the weight of the truck, etc., in calculating transport costs. (b) (*old*) weed.

tar•get ['tɑːgɪt] *n.* thing which you aim at; **t. practice** = practicing at shooting at a target.

tar•iff ['tærɪf] *n.* (a) tax to be paid for importing goods; **to lift t. barriers** = to reduce import taxes. (b) list of prices (as of public transportation).

tar•mac ['tɑːmæk] *n.* (a) trademark for a hard surface of a road made of tar mixed with small stones. (b) runway of an airport. **tar•macked,** *adj.* covered with tarmac.

tarn [tɑːn] *n.* small mountain lake.

tar•nish ['tɑːnɪʃ] *v.* (*of metal*) to become discolored; to ruin (a reputation).

ta•rot ['tærəʊ] *n.* set of cards designed for use in telling fortunes.

tar•pau•lin [tɑː'pɔːlin] *n.* large waterproof cloth.

tar•ra•gon ['ærəgən] *n.* common herb used in cooking.

tar•ry ['tærɪ] *v.* (*old*) to stay behind.

tar•sus ['tɑːsəs] *n.* set of bones in the ankle.

tart [tɑːt] 1. *n.* (a) small pastry shell filled with cooked fruit, vegetables, etc. (b) *Sl.* prostitute. 2. *adj.* (**-er, -est**) (a) bitter (taste). (b) sharp (answer). 3. *v. inf.* **to t. yourself up** = to dress, esp. in a flashy manner. **tart•ly,** *adv.* sharply. **tart•ness,** *n.* sourness (of taste).

tar•tan ['tɑːtən] *n. & adj.* (cloth) woven into a special pattern for one of the Scottish clans; distinctive pattern in such a cloth.

tar•tar ['tɑːtə] *n.* (a) hard substance which forms on teeth. (b) **cream of t.** = white powder used in cooking and in medicine. (c) *inf.* fierce person. **tar•tar•ic** [tɑː'tærɪk] *adj.* **t. acid** = acid used in cooking.

tar•tar(e) sauce [tɑːtɑː'sɔːs] *n.* mayonnaise containing finely chopped pieces of vegetables.

task [tɑːsk] *n.* (a) work which has to be done. (b) **to take s.o. to t.** = to criticize. **task force,** *n.* special group (esp. of soldiers) chosen to carry out a hard task. **task•mas•ter,** *n.* person who sets a hard task.

tas•sel ['tæsl] *n.* group of threads tied together at one end to form a ball, with the other ends hanging free. **tas•seled,** *adj.* with tassels.

taste [teɪst] 1. *n.* (a) sense by which you can tell differences of flavor between things you eat; **t. buds** = cells on the tongue which enable you to tell differences in flavor. (b) flavor of food or drink. (c) very small quantity (of food/drink); **he's had a t. of prison** = he has been in prison once. (d) liking (for sth); **expensive tastes** = liking for expensive things. (c) **good/bad t.** = ability/inability to judge what is fine/beautiful/refined. 2. *v.* (a) to sense the flavor of (sth). (b) to have a flavor (**of**). (c) to try (sth); to experience (freedom). **taste•ful,** *adj.* showing good taste. **taste•ful•ly,** *adv.* in good taste.

taste•less, *adj.* (a) with no particular flavor. (b) showing bad taste. **taste•less•ly,** *adv.* in a tasteless way. **tast•er,** *n.* person whose job is to taste food to test its quality. **tast•y,** *adj.* (**-ier, -iest**) with a particular pleasant flavor.

tat•ters ['tætəz] *n.* **in t.** = (i) torn (clothes); (ii) (person) wearing old torn clothes. **tat•tered** ['tætəd] *adj.* torn and old.

tat•ting ['tætɪŋ] *n.* type of lace made by hand.

tat•tle ['tætl] *v.* (*formal*) to gossip.

tat•too [tə'tuː] 1. *n.* (a) rapid beating (of drums). (b) decoration on skin made by pricking with a needle and putting color into the wound. 2. *v.* to make decorations on s.o.'s skin by pricking it and putting color into the wound.

tat•ty ['tætɪ] *adj.* (**-ier, -iest**) untidy/shabby.

taught [tɔːt] *v. see* **teach.**

taunt [tɔːnt] 1. *n.* sarcastic jeering. 2. *v.* to jeer at (s.o.) sarcastically.

Tau•rus ['tɔːrəs] *n.* one of the signs of the zodiac, shaped like a bull.

taut [tɔːt] *adj.* stretched tight. **taut•en,** *v.* to make tight; to become tight. **taut•ly,** *adv.* tightly. **taut•ness,** *n.* being taut.

tau•tol•o•gy [tɔː'tɒlədʒɪ] *n.* unnecessary use in a phrase of different words which mean the same thing. **tau•to•log•i•cal,** *adj.* using tautology.

tav•ern ['tævən] *n.* inn/bar.

taw [tɔː] *n.* big fancy marble.

taw•dry ['tɔːdrɪ] *adj.* (**-ier, -iest**) cheap and in bad taste.

taw•ny ['tɔːnɪ] *adj.* (**-ier, -iest**) orange brown.

tax [tæks] 1. *n.* (*pl.* **-es**) (a) money taken by the government from incomes/sales, etc., which pays for government services and its support; **t.-free** = without having to pay any tax. (b) burden; **it's a severe t. on our resources** = it strains our resources. 2. *v.* (a) to put a tax on (sth/s.o.). (b) to strain. (c) (*formal*) **to t. s.o. with** = to accuse s.o. of. **tax•a•ble,** *adj.* which can be taxed. **tax•a•tion** [tæk'seɪʃn] *n.* (a) (system of) imposing taxes. (b) money raised from taxes. **tax•pay•er,** *n.* person who pays taxes. **tax re•turn,** *n.* form to be filled in to report your earnings and allowances to the government.

tax•i ['tæksɪ] 1. *n.* car which can be hired; **t. stand** = place in the street where taxis can wait. 2. *v.* (*of aircraft*) to go along the ground before take-off or after landing. **tax•i•cab,** *n.* taxi.

æ back, a: farm, ɒ: top, aɪ pipe, aʊ how, aɪə fire, aʊə flower, ɔ: bought, ɔɪ toy, e fed, eəhair, eɪ take, ə afraid, əʊ boat, əʊə lower, v: word, i: heap, ɪ hit, ɪə hear, u: school, ʊ book, ʌ but, b back, d dog, ð then, dʒ just, f fog, g go, h hand, j yes, k catch, l last, m mix, n nut, ŋ sing, p penny, r round, s some, ʃ short, t too, tʃ chop, θ thing, v voice, w was, z zoo, ʒ treasure

tax•i•me•ter, *n.* machine fitted inside a taxi which shows the price for the journey.

tax•i•der•my ['tæksɪdɜːmɪ] *n.* art of stuffing the skins of dead animals so that they look lifelike. **tax•i•der•mist,** *n.* person who stuffs the skins of dead animals so that they look lifelike.

tax•on•o•my [tæk'sɒnəmɪ] *n.* scientific classification (esp. of plants and animals). **tax•on•o•mist,** *n.* person who specializes in taxonomy.

TB ['tiː'biː] *abbreviation for* tuberculosis.

tea [tiː] *n.* (a) dried leaves of a tropical plant which are used to make a common drink. (b) drink made by pouring boiling water on to dried leaves of the tea plant. (c) any hot drink made in a similar way; **herb t.** = tea made with the dried flowers or leaves of herbs. (d) *Brit.* afternoon meal; **t. service/t. set** = plates/cups/ saucers, etc., used at tea; **high tea** = large meal eaten in the early evening in the North of England and Scotland. **tea•bag,** *n.* small paper bag full of tea which is put into the pot instead of loose tea. **tea-cad•dy,** *n.* small wooden box or can for holding tea. **tea co•zy,** *n.* cover for putting over a teapot to keep it warm. **tea•cup,** *n.* large cup for tea. **tea par•ty,** *n.* party (held in the afternoon or early evening) when you drink tea, eat cakes, etc. **tea•pot,** *n.* special pot with a handle and spout for making tea in. **tea•room,** *n.* small restaurant which serves mainly tea and light meals. **tea•spoon,** *n.* small spoon for stirring tea. **tea•spoon•ful,** *n.* quantity contained in a teaspoon. **tea•time,** *n.* time when you have tea (about 4 o'clock in the afternoon). **tea tow•el,** *n.* cloth for drying dishes. **tea trol•ley,** *n.* small table on wheels from which you can serve food.

teach [tiːtʃ] *v.* (**taught** [tɔːt]) to give (s.o.) information; to give lessons (in a school); to show (s.o.) how to do sth; *inf.* **that'll t. him to be so rude** = will punish him for being rude. **teach•a•ble,** *adj.* which can be taught. **teach•er,** *n.* person who teaches. **teach-in,** *n. inf.* informal lengthy period of discussions on a topic. **teach•ing,** *n.* (a) action of giving knowledge/giving lessons; **the t. profession** = teachers as a group. (b) (*also* **teachings**) political or moral ideas/philosophy.

teak [tiːk] *n.* large tropical tree; hard wood of this tree, which does not warp, and is used for making furniture, etc.

teal [tiːl] *n.* (*pl.* **teal**) small type of wild duck.

team [tiːm] 1. *n.* (a) group of people playing together/working together. **t. spirit** = good feeling among those who play or work well together as a team. (b) group of animals working together. 2. *v.* **to t. up with s.o.** = to join s.o. to work together. **team•ster,** *n.* truck driver. **team•work,** *n.* ability to work together as a group; working together as a group.

tear¹ ['tɪə] *n.* drop of water formed in the eyes when you cry; **he burst into tears** = suddenly started to cry; **in tears** = crying. **tear•drop,** *n.* one tear. **tear•ful,** *adj.* sad/crying. **tear•ful•ly,** *adv.* in a tearful way. **tear gas,** *n.* gas which makes you cry, used to control crowds of rioters. **tear•jerk•er,** *n. inf.* motion picture/novel which makes you cry. **tear-stained,** *adj.* (face) with the marks of tears.

tear² ['teə] 1. *n.* (a) hole torn in a piece of cloth; (b) **wear and t.** = normal usage (of a house/car, etc.) which wears sth away. 2. *v.* (**tore** [tɔː]; **has torn** [tɔːn]) (a) to make a hole in (sth) by pulling; **torn between** = unable to decide between. (b) to pull to pieces; **to t. into s.o.** = to attack s.o.; **they tore up the road** = dug up the road surface; **to t. oneself away from** = to leave reluctantly. (c) *inf.* to go fast; **to t. down the road** = to drive very fast.

tease [tiːz] 1. *n.* person who annoys/irritates people on purpose. 2. *v.* (a) to annoy (s.o.)/to irritate (s.o.) on purpose. (b) to disentangle threads (with a comb); to brush (cloth) to make it soft. **teas•er,** *n. inf.* problem which is difficult to solve/question which is difficult to answer.

tea•sel ['tiːzl] *n.* tall plant with prickly flower heads.

teat [tiːt] *n.* (a) projection on a cow's udder through which milk passes. (b) rubber cap put on a baby's feeding bottle through which the baby sucks milk.

tech•ni•cal ['teknɪkl] *adj.* (a) referring to a particular industry/trade/profession, etc.; **t. term** = term used by specialists; **t. school** = school where technical skills are taught. (b) referring to a fixed interpretation of the rules; **t. knockout** = where the referee stops the fight because a boxer is too hurt to continue. **tech** [tek] *n. inf.* technician. **tech•ni•cal•ly,** *adv.* (a) in a technical way; (b) strictly speaking. **tech•ni•cal•i•ty** [teknɪ'kælɪtɪ] *n.* (a) technical detail. (b) strict interpretation of rules/of laws. **tech•ni•cian** [tek'nɪʃn] *n.* person who is specialized in industrial or scientific work. **tech•nique** [tek'niːk] *n.* skilled way of doing sth. **tech•no•crat** ['teknəkræt] *n.* person with particular technical/organizational skills, brought in to run a country/an organization. **tech•no•log•i•cal** [teknə'lɒdʒɪkl] *adj.* referring to technology. **tech•no•log•i•cal•ly,** *adv.* in a technological way. **tech•nol•o•gist,** *n.* specialist in technology. **tech•nol•o•gy** [tek'nɒlədʒɪ] *n.*

knowledge/study of new industrial or scientific skills.

tec•ton•ics [tek'tɒnɪks] *n.* study of the earth's crust and its movements.

ted•dy (bear) ['tedɪ('beə)] *n.* child's toy bear.

te•di•ous ['tiːdɪəs] *adj.* boring. **te•di•ous•ly,** *adv.* in a boring way. **te•di•ous•ness, tedium** ['tiːdɪəm] *n.* boredom/being boring.

tee [tiː] 1. *n.* (a) spot on a golf course where the ball is placed before you hit it. (b) little peg, on which the golf ball is placed. 2. *v.* **to t. off** = to hit the ball from a tee.

teem [tiːm] *v.* (a) to be full of/covered with sth; (b) *inf.* **it's teeming** = it's pouring (rain).

teens [tiːnz] *n. pl.* age between 13 and 19. **teen•age** ['tiːneɪdʒ] *adj.* adolescent; referring to s.o. aged between 13 and 19. **teen•ag•er,** *n.* person aged between 13 and 19.

tee•ny(-wee•ny) ['tiːnɪ('wiːnɪ)] *adj. inf.* very small.

tee-shirt ['tiːʃɜːt] *n.* light short-sleeved shirt with no buttons or collar.

tee•ter ['tiːtə] *v.* to wobble. **tee•ter-tot•ter,** *n.* seesaw.

teeth [tiːT] *n. see* tooth. **teethe** [tiːð] *v.* to grow your first teeth. **teeth•ing,** *n.* time when a baby grows its first teeth.

tee•to•tal [tiː'təʊtl] *adj.* (person) who never drinks any alcohol. **tee•to•tal•er,** *n.* person who never drinks any alcohol.

Tef•lon ['teflɒn] *n.* trademark for a non-stick surface, used on frying pans, etc.

tele- ['teliː] *prefix meaning* over a distance.

tel•e•cast ['telɪkɑːst] *n.* TV broadcast.

tel•e•com•mu•ni•ca•tions [telɪkəmjuːnɪ'keɪʃnz] *n. pl.* system of passing messages over a great distance (such as telephone/radio, etc.).

tel•e•com•mute ['telɪkɒmjuːt] *v.* to work (for an employer) from home by using communications technology, such as computers, to keep in touch with colleagues, managers, customers, etc.

tel•e•con•fer•ence ['telɪkɒnfərəns] *n.* conference between people located in different places via telephone links.

tel•e•gram ['telɪgræm] *n.* message sent by telegraph.

tel•e•graph ['telɪgrɑːf] 1. *n.* system of sending messages along wires; **t. line** = wire along which telegraph messages are sent; **t. pole** = pole which holds up a telegraph line. 2. *v.* to send (a message) along wires. **te•leg•ra•pher** [tə'legrəfə] *n.* person who

sends messages by telegraph.

tel•e•graph•ese, *n.* abbreviated language used when writing telegrams.

tel•e•graph•ic [telɪ'græfɪk] *adj.* referring to telegraph. **te•leg•ra•phy** [tə'legrəfɪ] *n.* sending messages by telegraph.

tel•ep•a•thy [tə'lepəTɪ] *n.* sending feelings/sympathy/mental images from one person to another without the use of the senses. **tel•e•path•ic** [telɪ'pæTɪk] *adj.* referring to telepathy.

tel•e•phone ['telɪfəʊn] 1. *n.* device/system for speaking to s.o. over a distance usu. using electric current running along wires; **on the t.** = speaking into the telephone; **t. banking** = banking services provided over the telephone; **t. booth** = outdoor booth with a public telephone in it. 2. *v.* to speak to (s.o.) by telephone. **tel•e•phon•ic** [telɪ'fonɪk] *adj.* referring to the telephone. **tel•e•phon•ist** [tə'lefənɪst] *n.* person who connects telephone calls at a switchboard. **te•leph•o•ny,** *n.* science of telephones.

tel•e•pho•to lens [telɪ'fəʊtəʊ'lenz] *n.* lens for a camera which gives a large picture of sth which is at a distance.

tel•e•print•er ['telɪprɪntə] *n.* teletypewriter.

tel•e•sales [telɪ'seɪlz] *n.* sales made by telephone.

tel•e•scope ['telɪskəʊp] 1. *n.* tube with a series of lenses for looking at very distant objects; **radio t.** = apparatus which detects radio signals from stars and follows their movements. 2. *v.* to push together, so that one piece slides into another; to crush together. **tel•e•scop•ic** [telɪ'skɒpɪk] *adj.* (a) referring to a telescope. (b) (parts) which slide together like a telescope.

tel•e•type•writ•er [telɪ'taɪprɑːtə] *n.* apparatus like a typewriter which sends out and receives messages by telegraph, and which prints them when they are received.

tel•e•vi•sion [telɪ'vɪʒn] *n.* system for sending pictures by radio waves; **t. (set)** = apparatus for showing pictures sent by radio waves. **tel•e•vise** ['telɪvaɪz] *v.* to broadcast (sth) by television. **televised live** = shown direct/not recorded and broadcast later.

tel•ex ['teleks] 1. *n. (pl. -es)* system of sending messages by teletypewriter; message sent by teletypewriter. 2. *v.* to send a message to (s.o.), using the teletypewriter.

tell [tel] *v.* (**told**) (a) to say. (b) to pass on information. (c) to give instructions (**how to do**

sth). (d) to make out (the difference) **between** two things); to notice a quality. (e) to have an effect; **his age told in the end** = finally he lost because he was older than the other competitors. (g) to count (money/votes, etc.); **all told** = altogether. **tell•er** ('telə) *n.* person who counts votes; clerk in a bank who counts money and pays it out to customers. **tell•ing**, *adj.* which has an effect. **tell•ing•ly**, *adv.* in a telling way. **tell off**, *v. inf.* to reprimand/to criticize (s.o.). **tell on**, *v. inf.* **to tell on s.o.** = to let out a secret about someone. **tell•tale**. 1. *n.* person who gives away a secret. 2. *adj.* (thing) which gives away a secret.

te•mer•i•ty [tə'merɪtɪ] *n.* audacity; daring to do sth.

temp [temp] 1. *n. inf. short for* temporary secretary. 2. *v. inf.* to work as a temp.

tem•per ['tempə] 1. *n.* (a) usually calm state of mind; **he lost his t.** = he became very angry; **she kept her t.** = she stayed calm and did not get angry. (b) (good/bad) state of mind. (c) fit of anger. (d) hardness of a metal due to beating. 2. *v.* (a) to harden (steel). (b) to moderate/to make less strong.

tem•per•a ['tempərə] *n.* type of thick paint which can be diluted with water.

tem•per•a•ment ['temprəmənt] *n.* state of mind; nature of a person. **tem•per•a•men•tal** [temprə'mentl] *adj.* (person) likely to change his state of mind frequently; likely to get easily excited or depressed. **tem•per•a•men•tal•ly**, *adv.* according to a state of mind.

tem•per•ance ['tempərəns] *n.* (a) being moderate/controlled. (b) not drinking alcohol; **t. movement** = group of people who try to persuade others not to drink alcohol.

tem•per•ate ['temprət] *adj.* (a) moderate/sober (language/habits). (b) (climate) which is neither extremely hot nor cold. **tem•per•a•ture** ['temprətʒə] *n.* (a) amount of heat measured in degrees. (b) state where the temperature of the body is higher than it should be.

tem•pest ['tempɪst] *n.* storm. **tem•pes•tu•ous** [tem'pestjʊəs] *adj.* violently stormy/very wild.

tem•plate ['templeɪt] *n.* thin sheet used as a pattern for cutting pieces of wood/metal, etc., to an exact shape.

tem•ple ['templ] *n.* (a) flat part of the front of the head on each side of the forehead. (b) building for worship (not usu. Christian or Muslim).

tem•po ['tempəu] *n.* (*pl.* -os/tempi ['tempi:]) rhythm; beat (of music, etc.).

tem•po•ral ['temprəl] *adj.* (a) referring to the temple/the flat part of the side of the head near the forehead. (b) referring to this world/not eternal/not spiritual. (c) referring to time.

tem•po•rar•y ['temprərɪ] *adj.* which only lasts a short time/which is meant to last a short time. **tem•po•rar•i•ly** ['temprərəlɪ] *adv.* for a short time. **tem•po•rize**, *v.* to try to gain time.

tempt [temt] *v.* (a) to attract (s.o.); to try to persuade (s.o.) to do sth. (b) **I am tempted to accept** = I think I will accept. (c) **to t. fate** = to take a great risk. **temp•ta•tion** [tem'teɪʃn] *n.* state of being tempted; thing which attracts you. **tempt•er, temptress**, *n.* person who tempts. **tempt•ing**, *adj.* attractive.

ten [ten] *n.* number 10; *inf.* **t. to one he finds out** = he's very likely to find out.

ten•a•ble ['tenəbl] *adj.* (theory) which can be held/supported.

te•na•cious [tɪ'neɪʃəs] *adj.* which holds on to sth tightly; obstinate; determined. **te•na•cious•ly**, *adv.* in a tenacious way. **te•nac•i•ty** [tə'næsɪtɪ] *n.* holding to sth too tightly.

ten•ant ['tenənt] *n.* person who rents a room/apartment/house/land. **ten•an•cy**, *n.* period during which a tenant rents a property.

tench [tentʃ] *n.* (*pl.* tench) type of small fish.

tend [tend] *v.* (a) to look after. (b) to be likely (to do sth). (c) to lean (in a certain direction). **ten•den•cy**, *n.* being likely to do sth. **ten•den•tious** [ten'denʃəs] *adj.* (book/article/speech) which puts over a strong point of view which is not generally approved.

tend•er ['tendə] 1. *n.* (a) boat which brings supplies to a large ship. (b) offer to do work at a certain price. (c) **legal t.** = coins/notes which are legally acceptable when offered in payment. 2. *adj.* (a) soft/delicate; **t. meat** = which can be chewed/cut easily. (b) **t. plants** = which cannot stand frost; **child of t. years** = very young child. (c) **a t. heart** = very compassionate/very loving. (d) painful; *inf.* **you've touched him on a t. spot** = you have mentioned sth which he is very touchy about. 3. *v.* (a) (*formal*) to offer. (b) (**for**) to offer to do work at a certain price. **ten•der•foot**, *n.* inexperienced person. **ten•der•heart•ed**, *adj.* kind. **ten•der•ize**, *v.* to make (meat) tender. **ten•der•loin** ['tendəlɔːn] *n.* piece of tender beef or pork from the side of the backbone. **ten•der•ly**, *adv.* gently; with kindness. **ten•der•ness**, *n.* being tender.

ten•don ['tendən] *n.* strong cord of tissue attaching a muscle to a bone.

ten•dril ['tendrəl] *n.* thin curling part with which a plant clings to a support.

ten•e•ment ['tenəmənt] *n.* large (often dilapidated) building which is divided into apartments.

ten•et ['tenet] *n.* basic principle/belief.

ten•fold ['tenfəuld] *adv.* ten times as much.

ten•ner ['tenə] *n. inf.* ten-dollar bill.

ten•nis ['tenɪs] *n.* game for two players or two pairs of players who use rackets to hit a ball backward and forward over a net; **t. court** = specially marked ground for playing tennis; **t. elbow** = painful condition of the elbow joint caused by strain.

ten•on ['tenən] *n.* small projection from the end of a piece of wood which fits into a corresponding mortise in another piece to form a joint.

ten•or ['tenə] *n.* (a) man who sings with the highest normal male voice. (b) highest male voice; musical instrument with a high pitch. (c) (*formal*) general meaning or condition.

tense [tens] 1. *n.* form of a verb which shows when the action takes place. 2. *adj.* (-er, -est) (a) stretched tight. (b) nervous and anxious. (c) warlike (state between countries). 3. *v.* to make/to become tense. **tense•ly,** *adv.* in a tense way. **tense•ness,** *n.* being tense.

ten•sile ['tensail] *adj.* referring to tension; **t. strength** = force needed to stretch sth until it breaks. **ten•sion** ['tenʃn] *n.* (a) tightness; being stretched. (b) nervous anxiety. (c) state of aggravation (between countries). (d) electric power; **high-t. wires.**

tent [tent] *n.* small canvas shelter held up by poles and attached to the ground with pegs and ropes; **to pitch a t.** = to put up a tent; **oxygen t.** = cover put up over a sick person's bed to allow oxygen to be pumped in.

ten•ta•cle ['tentəkl] *n.* long arm with suckers (such as that of an octopus).

ten•ta•tive ['tentətɪv] *adj.* uncertain; done as a trial; **t. offer** = made to find out what the response is. **ten•ta•tive•ly,** *adv.* in a tentative way.

ten•ter•hooks ['tentəhuːks] *n. pl.* **on t.** = impatiently waiting/anxious and uncertain.

tenth [tenT], **10th,** *adj. & n.* referring to ten; **the t. century** = period from 900 to 999.

ten•u•ous ['tenjuəs] *adj.* thin; not strong. **ten•u•ous•ly,** *adv.* in a tenuous way. **ten•u•ous•ness,** *n.* being tenuous.

ten•ure ['tenjə] *n.* (a) right to hold property/to have employment; holding of a property or employment. (b) right to hold a job permanently.

te•pee ['tiːpiː] *n.* cone-shaped tent of North American Indians.

tep•id ['tepɪd] *adj.* slightly warm.

te•qui•la [te'kiːlə] *n.* Mexican alcoholic drink.

ter•a•flop ['terəflɒp] *n.* measure of computer processing speed.

ter•cen•ten•ar•y [tɜːsen'tiːnərɪ] *n.* tricentennial.

term [tɜːm] 1. *n.* (a) length of time; **in the long t./in the short t.** = for a long period from now/for a short period from now. (b) end of a period of time; **she was approaching her t.** = nearly at the end of her pregnancy. (c) part of a school/college/university year. (d) conditions; **to come to terms with** = to accept as inevitable; **they came to terms** = they reached agreement; **terms of payment** = way in which a payment shall be made; **our terms are ninety days** = we allow 90 days' credit. (e) relationship; **on good/bad terms** = having a friendly/unfriendly relationship. (f) particular word. (g) expressing; **in terms of health** = regarding health; **I'm thinking in terms of weekly payments** = my idea is that the payments should be made each week. 2. *v.* to call.

ter•ma•gant ['tɜːməgənt] *n.* noisy woman who bullies people.

ter•min•al ['tɜːmɪnl] 1. *adj.* (a) at the end; **t. shoot** = shoot at the end of a branch. (b) in the last period of life; **t. case** = patient who is soon going to die. 2. *n.* (a) building at an airport where passengers arrive or depart. (b) **bus t.** = building in the center of a town where buses arrive or depart. (c) **electric t.** = one of the connecting points in an electric circuit. (d) apparatus which can be used for putting information into and getting information from a distant computer (to which it is linked by cable). **ter•mi•na•ble,** *adj.* which can be terminated. **ter•mi•nal•ly,** *adv.* in a terminal way; **t. ill** = in the last stages of an illness before death. **ter•mi•nate** ['tɜːmɪneɪt] *v.* to finish/to bring (sth) to an end. **ter•mi•na•tion** [tɜːmɪ'neɪʃn] *n.* bringing to an end.

ter•mi•nol•o•gy [tɜːmɪ'nɒlədʒɪ] *n.* special words or phrases used in a particular science, art or subject. **ter•mi•no•log•i•cal** [tɜːmɪnə'lɒdʒɪkl]] *adj.* referring to terminology.

ter•mi•nus ['tɜːmɪnəs] *n.* (*pl.* **-ni** [-naɪ], **-nuses**) either end of a railroad line.

ter•mite ['tɜːmaɪt] *n.* destructive white insect, rather like an ant, which lives in tropical countries.

tern [tɜːn] *n.* white sea bird similar to a gull.

ter•race ['terəs] 1. *n.* (a) flat area which is raised above another area. (b) row of houses built along the top of a sloping area. 2. *v.* to make a flat raised area.

ter•ra•cot•ta [terə'kɒtə] *n.* red clay used to make small statues; statue made of red clay.

ter•ra fir•ma ['terə'fɜːmə] *n.* dry land.

ter•rain [tə'reɪn] *n.* area of country.

ter•ra•pin ['terəpɪn] *n.* type of small American turtle.

ter•rar•i•um [te'reɪrɪəm] *n.* glass box in which plants are grown.

ter•raz•zo [te'rætsəu] *n.* polished surface, made of little chips of stone embedded in mortar.

ter•res•tri•al [tə'restrɪəl] *adj.* referring to the earth.

ter•ri•ble ['terɪbl] *adj.* (a) awful/which makes you very frightened. (b) *inf.* very bad. **ter•ri•bly**, *adv.* (a) frighteningly. (b) *inf.* very.

ter•ri•er ['terɪə] *n.* small dog (originally used in hunting).

ter•rif•ic [tə'rɪfɪk] *adj. inf.* (a) extremely great/wonderful. (b) causing fear; awful. **ter•rif•i•cal•ly**, *adv. inf.* wonderfully/greatly/awfully. **ter•ri•fy** ['terɪfaɪ] *v.* to frighten completely. **ter•ri•fy•ing**, *adj.* frightening.

ter•rine [tə'riːn] *n.* type of pâté.

ter•ri•to•ry ['terɪtrɪ] *n.* (a) land which belongs to a country; large stretch of land. (b) area which an animal/bird, etc. considers as its own. (c) area visited by a traveling salesman. **ter•ri•to•ri•al** [terɪ'tɔːrɪəl] *adj.* referring to a territory; **t. waters** = area of sea around a country which that country controls.

ter•ror ['terə] *n.* (a) extreme fear. (b) thing which causes fear. (c) *inf.* naughty/uncontrollable person. **ter•ror•ism**, *n.* policy of using violence in a political cause. **ter•ror•ist**, *adj.* & *n.* (person) who practices terrorism. **ter•ror•ize**, *v.* to frighten (s.o.) very much. **ter•ror-strick•en, terror-struck**, *adj.* extremely frightened.

ter•ry ['terɪ] *n.* type of cloth where uncut loops stand above the surface.

terse [tɜːs] *adj.* concise/short; using few words. **terse•ly**, *adv.* briefly/concisely. **terse•ness**, *n.* being terse.

ter•ti•ar•y ['tɜːʃərɪ] *adj.* referring to a third stage or period.

tes•sei•at•ed ['tesəleɪtɪd] *adj.* covered with mosaic.

test [test] 1. *n.* (a) examination to see if sth works well/is reliable/if s.o. is healthy. **t. pilot** = pilot who flies a new aircraft to see if it works well. (b) short written or practical examination to see if s.o. knows information/knows how to do sth; **intelligence t./aptitude t.** = test to show how intelligent/how capable you are; **driving t.** = to see if you can drive a car. (c) **to put sth/s.o. to the t.** = to try sth/s.o. out to see if they can stand up to certain conditions. 2. *v.* (a) to examine (sth) to see if it is working well; to examine (s.o.) to see if he is healthy. (b) to give (s.o.) a short examination.

test case, *n.* court case where the decision sets a precedent for other similar cases to follow. **test-drive,** *v.* to drive (a new car) before you buy it to see if it works well. **test tube,** *n.* small round-bottomed glass tube used in a laboratory for making chemical tests; **t.-t. baby** = baby born through artificial insemination.

tes•ta•ment ['testəmənt] *n.* (a) **last will and t.** = document written by a person before death to indicate what should happen to his property after he dies. (b) **Old T./New T.** = the two main sections of the Bible. **tes•ta•men•ta•ry,** [testə'mentərɪ] *adj.* referring to a will.

tes•tate ['testeɪt] *adj.* (person who has died) leaving a will. **tes•ta•tor, testatrix** [tes-'teɪtə, -teɪtrɪks] *n.* (*pl.* **-trices** [-trɪsiːz]) man/woman who makes a will.

tes•ti•cle ['testɪkl] *n.* one of two male glands which produce sperm.

tes•ti•fy ['testɪfaɪ] *v.* to give evidence that sth is true. **tes•ti•mo•ni•al** [testɪ'məunɪəl] *n.* (a) statement showing what you know of a person's qualities. (b) thing done for a person/given to a person to show appreciation; **t. dinner** = dinner organized to give a present to s.o. **tes•ti•mo•ny** ['testɪmənɪ] *n.* evidence that sth is true.

tes•tis ['testɪs] *n.* (*pl.* **testes** ['testiːz]) (*formal*) testicle.

tes•tos•ter•one [tes'tɒstərəun] *n.* male sex hormone.

tes•ty ['testɪ] *adj.* irritable; easily made angry. **tes•ti•ly**, *adv.* irritably/angrily.

tet•a•nus ['tetənəs] *n.* serious disease caused by infection in a wound, which can make esp. the jaw muscles stiffen.

tetch•y ['tetʃɪ] *adj.* (**-ier, -iest**) bad-tempered. **tetch•i•ly**, *adv.* in a tetchy way.

tête-à-tête [teɪtɑː'teɪt] *n.* private conversation between two people.

teth•er ['teðə] 1. *n.* rope which attaches an animal to a post; **he's at the end of his t.** = he can't stand any more/he has lost all patience. 2. *v.* to attach (an animal) to a post with a rope.

tet•ra•he•dron [tetrə'hiːdrən] *n.* solid shape with four sides, each of which is a triangle.

Teu•ton•ic [tjuː'tɒnɪk] *adj.* German.

text [tekst] *n.* (a) main written part of a book

(not the notes or pictures, etc.). (b) original words of a speech. (c) quotation from the Bible used as a moral guide. **text•book,** *n.* book which students read for information about the subject they are studying. **tex•tu•al,** *adj.* referring to a text.

tex•tile ['tekstaɪl] *adj. & n.* (referring to) cloth.

tex•ture ['tekstʃə] *n.* quality which can be felt; degree of fineness. **tex•tured,** *adj.* with a certain feel.

than [ðæn, ðən] *conj. & prep. used to introduce the second part of comparisons and clauses;* **I have less t. you; there are more t. twenty people in the room; no sooner had we arrived t. the music started.**

thank [Tæŋk] *v.* **to t. s.o. for** = to show gratitude to (s.o.). **thank•ful,** *adj.* showing gratitude; glad because an anxiety has gone. **thank•ful•ly,** *adv.* showing relief that an anxiety has gone. **thank•ful•ness,** *n.* being thankful. **thank•less,** *adj.* (work) for which no one will thank you; difficult/hopeless (task). **thank•less•ly,** *adv.* in a thankless way. **thank•less•ness,** *n.* being thankless. **thanks,** *n.pl.* (a) word which shows you are grateful. (b) thank you; **no, t.** = no, thank you. (c) **t. to** = as a result of. **thanks•giv•ing,** *n.* day for giving thanks to God; **Thanksgiving** = national holiday celebrated in the United States on the 4th Thursday of November and in Canada on the 2nd Monday of October in commemoration of the harvest feast of the Pilgrims. **thank you,** *inter. showing* gratitude (for); **t.-y. letter** = letter in which you thank s.o. for sth.

that [ðæt] 1. *adj. & pron.* (*pl.* **those** [ðəʊz]) *used to indicate* something further away (*as opposed to* **this**) 2. *pron. linking a subject or object to a verb* **where is the letter t. he sent you?** 3. *adv. inf.* to such an extent; so much; **I knew they were going to be early, but not t. early.** 4. *conj. introducing a clause* **he knew t. we were late.**

thatch [Tætʃ] 1. *n.* reeds/straw, etc., used to make a roof. 2. *v.* to cover (a house) with a roof of reeds/straw, etc. **thatch•er,** *n.* a person who thatches houses.

thaw [Tɔ:] 1. *n.* warm weather (which results in the melting of snow/ice). 2. *v.* (a) to melt; to unfreeze (sth which is frozen). (b) to get less unfriendly/less shy/become friendlier.

the [ðə] (*before a vowel or when stressed* [ði:]). 1. *definite article.* (a) (*referring to a particular person or thing*) **the man with t. red nose.** (b) (*referring to something in general*) **t. Russians are lively people.** (c) (*stressed*) **it is t. store for furniture.** 2. *adv.* (*in comparisons*) **it will be all t. easier** = that much easier; **the sooner t. better.**

the•a•ter, *Brit.* **the•a•tre** ['Tɪətə] *n.* (a) building in which plays are performed. (b) place where motion pictures are shown. (c) art of acting/of producing plays; business of putting on plays. (d) collection of plays. (e) place where important events happen. **the•a•ter•go•er,** *n.* person who goes to the theater. **the•at•ri•cal** [Tɪ'ætrɪkl] *adj.* (a) referring to the theater. (b) very dramatic/not acting naturally. **the•at•ri•cal•ly,** *adv.* in a theatrical way. **the•at•ri•cals,** *n.pl.* amateur **t.** = performances of a play by amateurs.

thee [ði:] *pron.* (*old*) you.

theft [Teft] *n.* stealing.

their ['ðeə] *adj.* belonging to them.

theirs ['ðeəz] *pron.* belonging to them; **she's a friend of t.**

the•ism ['Ti:ɪzəm] *n.* belief that a god exists. **the•ist,** *n.* person who believes that a god exists.

them [ðem] *pron. referring to persons/things which are objects of a verb.* **them•selves** [ðem'selvz] *pron. referring to a plural subject;* **all by t.** = without any help from anyone else.

theme [Ti:m] *n.* (a) subject (of book/article). (b) main tune in a piece of music; **t. song** = catchy tune/song played several times in a motion picture or TV serial which makes the audience recognize it. **the•mat•ic** [Tɪ'mætɪk] *adj.* referring to a theme.

then [ðen] 1. *adv.* (a) at that time; **t. and there** = immediately; **now and t.** = from time to time. (b) afterward. (c) also/in any case. (d) therefore; the result is. 2. *n.* that time. 3. *adj.* existing at that time; **the t. president.**

thence [ðens] *adv.* (*formal*) (a) from that place; from there. (b) so/therefore. **thence•forth,** *adv.* (*formal*) from that time onward.

the•od•o•lite [Tɪ'ɒdəlaɪt] *n.* device for measuring angles when surveying land.

the•ol•o•gy [Tɪ'ɒlədʒɪ] *n.* study of belief in God; study of God and God's relations with human beings. **the•o•lo•gian** [Tɪə'ləʊdʒɪən] *n.* person who specializes in the study of God/in the interpretation of religion. **the•o•log•i•cal** [Tɪə'lɒdʒɪkl] *adj.* referring to theology; **t. college** = college where people study to become priests.

æ back, a: farm, ɒ: top, aɪ pipe, aʊ how, aie fire, aʊə flower, ɔ: bought, ɔɪ toy, e fed, eəhair, eɪ take, ə afraid, əʊ boat, əʊə lower, v: word, i: heap, ɪ hit, ɪə hear, u: school, ʊ book, ʌ but, b back, d dog, ð then, dʒ just, f fog, g go, h hand, j yes, k catch, l last, m mix, n nut, ŋ sing, p penny, r round, s some, ʃ short, t too, tʃ chop, θ thing, v voice, w was, z zoo, ʒ treasure

the•o•log•i•cal•ly, *adv.* in a theological way.

the•o•rem ['Tiːərəm] *n.* thing which has to be proved in mathematics.

the•o•ry ['Tɪərɪ] *n.* (a) explanation of sth which has not been proved but which you believe is true. (b) statement of general principles (which may not apply in practice); **in t. it should work** = if you follow general principles. the•o•ret•i•cal [Tɪə'retɪkl] *adj.* referring to a theory; not proved in practice. the•o•ret•i•cal•ly, *adv.* in theory, but not in practice. the•o•re•ti•cian, the•o•rist [Tɪərə'tɪʃn, 'Tɪərɪst] *n.* person who forms (political) theories. the•o•rize ['Tɪəraɪz] *v.* to make up a theory about sth.

the•os•o•phy [Tɪ'ɒsəfɪ] *n.* philosophical or religious system which states that the working of God and divine nature can be understood through mystical insight.

ther•a•py ['Terəpɪ] *n.* treatment of illness (esp. without using medicine); **speech t.** = treatment of difficulty in speaking; **occupational t.** = treatment by getting patients to do things; **group t.** = treatment by getting patients together in groups to discuss their problems. ther•a•peu•tic [Terə'pjuːtɪk] *adj.* which may cure. ther•a•peu•ti•cal•ly, *adv.* in a therapeutic way. ther•a•peu•tics, *n. pl.* study of curing diseases. ther•a•pist, *n.* person who applies therapy.

there ['ðeə] 1. *adv.* in that place/to that place; *inf.* **t. she goes again** = that is her doing it again. 2. *inter. showing various feelings* **t., t., don't cry.** 3. *pron. used as subject of a clause usually with the verb* **to be,** *when the real subject follows the verb* **there's a big car coming up the hill; t. weren't very many people at the meeting; t. appears to be a mistake.** there•a•bout(s) [ðeərə'baut(s)] *adv.* approximately. there•af•ter [ðeər'ɑːftə] *adv.* (*formal*) after that. there•by [ðeə'baɪ] *adv.* (*formal*) by doing that. there•fore ['ðeəfɔː] *adv.* consequently; for this reason. there•up•on [ðeərə'pɒn] *adv.* (*formal*) immediately after that.

therm [Tɜːm] *n.* measure of heat. ther•mal 1. *adj.* referring to heat; **t. baths** = baths of natural hot water; **t. underwear** = which keeps you warm; **t. current** = current of warm air/water. 2. *n.* current of warm air.

thermo- ['Tɜːməu] *adj.* referring to heat.

ther•mo•dy•nam•ics [Tɜːməudaɪ'næmɪks] *n.* study of heat and its relationship to power.

ther•mom•e•ter [Tɜː'mɒmɪtə] *n.* instrument for measuring the temperature.

ther•mo•nu•cle•ar [Tɜːməu'njuːklɪə] *adj.* referring to the high temperature caused by atomic fusion.

ther•mo•plas•tic [Tɜːmə'plæstɪk] *adj. & n.* (material) which becomes soft when heated and hard when cold.

ther•mos (bot•tle) ['Tɜːməs'] *n.* former trademark for a type of vacuum bottle.

ther•mo•stat ['Tɜːməstæt] *n.* instrument which controls the temperature by setting off heating or cooling devices. ther•mo•stat•ic [Tɜːmə'stætɪk] *adj.* referring to a thermostat. ther•mo•stat•i•cal•ly, *adv.* (controlled) by a thermostat.

the•sau•rus [Tə'sɔːrəs] *n.* (*pl.* -es, -ri) book with words collected according to their similar meanings, and not in alphabetical order.

these [ðiːz] *adj. & pron. see* **this**.

the•sis ['Tiːsɪs] *n.* (*pl.* -ses [-siːz] (a) long piece of written research done for a college/university degree. (b) particular point of view.

Thes•pi•an ['Tespɪən] *n.* actor, actress.

thews [Tjuːz] *n.pl.* strength.

they [ðeɪ] *pron. subject* (a) *referring to several persons or things* (b) (*referring to people in general*) **t. say it's going to rain.**

thi•a•mine ['Taɪəmiːn] *n.* Vitamin B, found in cereals, liver and pork.

thick [Tɪk] 1. *adj.* (-er, -est) (a) fat/not thin/with a large distance between the two surfaces. (b) with a large diameter. (c) dense/packed close together. (d) (liquid) which does not flow easily. (e) (voice) which is not clear. (f) *inf.* **that's a bit t.** = that's very unrealistic; exaggerated. (g) *inf.* stupid; **she's a bit t.** (h) *inf.* very friendly. 2. *n.* (a) center (of a battle). (b) **through t. and thin** = through times of difficulty as well as through easy times. 3. *adv.* in a thick layer; *inf.* **to lay it on t.** = to praise s.o. excessively. thick•en, *v.* to make thick/to become thick. thick•et ['Tɪkɪt] *n.* small wood of trees and bushes growing close together. thick•ly, *adv.* in a thick way. thick•ness, *n.* being thick; distance between sides. thick•set, *adj.* (a) (hedge) planted with bushes close together. (b) short stocky (person). thick-skinned, *adj.* (a) (fruit) with a thick skin. (b) (*of person*) insensitive/not easily hurt.

thief [Tiːf] *n.* (*pl.* thieves [Tiːvz]) person who steals. thieve, *v.* to steal. thiev•er•y, *n.* stealing. thiev•ing, *n.* act of stealing. thiev•ish, *adj.* like a thief.

thigh [Taɪ] *n.* thick top part of the leg between the knee and the hip.

thim•ble ['Tɪmbl] *n.* small cover worn to protect the end of your finger when sewing. thim•ble•ful, *n. inf.* very small quantity (of liquid).

thin [Tɪn] 1. *adj.* (**thinner, thinnest**) not

thick/with only a small distance between the two surfaces. (b) not fat. (c) with a small diameter. (d) not very dense/not close together. (e) very watery (liquid). 2. *adv.* in a thin way. 3. *v.* **(thinned)** (a) to become thin. (b) to make liquid thin. (c) to make less dense; to become less dense. **thin down,** *v.* to reduce; to make (sth) thinner. **thin•ly,** *adv.* in a thin way. **thin•ner,** *n.* substance used to thin paint. **thin•ness,** *n.* being thin. **thin out,** *v.* to remove (seedlings) to give more room to those which are left. **thin-skinned,** *adj.* (a) (fruit) with a thin skin. (b) (*of person*) sensitive/easily hurt.

thine [ðaɪn] *pron.* (*old*) your.

thing [θɪŋ] *n.* (a) object. (b) *inf.* person/animal. (c) **things** = clothes/equipment. (d) item; unspecified subject; object referred to; **it's just one t. after another** = one problem after another; **it's a good t. you came with us** = it's lucky. (e) **first t. in the morning/last t. at night** = as soon as you get up/just before you go to bed. (f) *inf.* **to have a t. about sth** = to like/dislike sth irrationally. (g) *inf.* **he wants to do his own t.** = to do what he really feels like doing. **thing•a•ma•jig, thing•a•ma•bob** *n. inf.* some object/person whose name you have forgotten.

think [θɪŋk] 1. *n.* time when you have thoughts/when you consider plans in your mind; *inf.* **you've got another t. coming** = you'll have to change your ideas, as this idea won't work. 2. *v.* **(thought** [θɔːt]**)** (a) to use your mind; **to t. aloud** = to speak your thoughts as they come into your mind. (b) to believe; to have as your opinion. (c) to expect. (d) to plan; **to t. again** = to change your mind; *inf.* **t. big!** = consider only large-scale projects. **think•a•ble,** *adj.* which can be thought. **think a•bout,** *v.* (a) to consider (sth) in your mind. (b) to plan (sth). (c) to have an opinion. **think back,** *v.* to remember. **think•er,** *n.* person who thinks; **great t.** = philosopher. **think•ing,** *n.* reasoning; **to my way of t.** = my opinion is. **think of,** *v.* (a) to consider (sth) in your mind. (b) to plan (sth). (c) to remember. (d) to have an opinion; **I told him what I thought of him** = I criticized him; **he thinks highly of his teacher** = has a high opinion of him; **she thinks nothing of working 12 hours a day** = she finds it easy; **think nothing of it** = don't bother to thank me for it; **he thought better of it** = changed his mind. **think out,** *v.* to consider carefully all the details. **think**

o•ver, *v.* to consider (sth) seriously. **think tank,** *n.* group of experts who advise the government on matters of general policy. **think through,** *v.* to consider carefully all the details. **think up,** *v.* to invent.

third, 3rd [θɜːd] *n. & adj.* referring to three; **t. person** = pronoun or part of a verb referring to a person or thing who is being referred to. **the car went up the hill in t.** = in third gear; **the Third World** = countries with no strong connections to the superpowers. **third de•gree,** *n.* hard questioning (by the police). **third par•ty,** *n.* any person who is not one of the two parties involved in a contract; person (usu. s.o. injured in an accident) who is not the driver of the car or the insurance company which insured it. **t. party insurance** = insurance which covers s.o. not named in it; **third-rate,** *adj.* very bad.

thirst [θɜːst] 1. *n.* (a) wanting to drink. (b) desire (**for**). 2. *v.* (*formal*) to desire (**after/for** sth). **thirst•y,** *adj.* (**-ier, -iest**) wanting to drink; **t. work** = hard/hot work which makes you thirsty. **thirst•i•ly,** *adv.* in a thirsty way.

thir•teen [θɜː'tiːn] *n.* number 13; **the t. hundreds** = years between 1300 and 1399. **thir•teenth, 13th,** *adj. & n.* referring to thirteen; **the t. century** = period from 1200 to 1299.

thir•ty ['θɜːtɪ] *n.* number 30; **she's in her thirties** = she is more than thirty years old but less than forty. **thir•ti•eth, 30th,** *adj. & n.* referring to thirty.

this [ðɪs] 1. *adj. & pron.* (*pl.* **these** [ðiːz]) *used to indicate* something near (*as opposed to* **that**). (a) **t. is the book I meant, not that one.** (b) **t. morning/t. evening** = today in the morning/evening. 2. *adv. inf.* to such an extent; **I didn't expect you to be t. late** = so late.

this•tle ['θɪsl] *n.* large prickly weed with purple flowers. **this•tle•down,** *n.* soft white feathery substance attached to thistle seeds.

thith•er ['ðɪðə] *adv.* (*formal*) to that place.

thole [θəʊl] *n.* peg used as oarlock.

thong [θɒŋ] *n.* (a) thin leather strap used for tying. (b) light sandal, held by a strap between the toes.

tho•rax ['θɔːræks] *n.* part of the body between the neck and the abdomen; chest (of an animal/a person); part of an insect's body to which the wings and legs are attached. **tho•rac•ic** [θɔː'ræsɪk] *adj.* referring to a thorax.

æ back, ɑː farm, ɒ top, aɪ pipe, aʊ how, aɪə fire, aʊə flower, ɔː bought, ɔɪ toy, e fed, eəhair, eɪ take, ə afraid, əʊ boat, əʊə lower, ɜː word, iː heap, ɪ hit, ɪə hear, ʌ but, b back, d dog, ð then, dʒ just, f fog, g go, h hand, j yes, k catch, l last, m mix, n nut, ŋ sing, p penny, r round, s some, ʃ short, t too, tʃ chop, θ thing, v voice, w was, z zoo, ʒ treasure

thorn [Tɔːn] *n.* spike (of a prickly plant); **a t. in one's side** = a constant annoyance. **thorn•y,** *adj.* (**-ier, -iest**) covered with thorns; (problem) which is difficult to solve.

thor•ough ['TʌrƏ] *adj.* (a) very careful/detailed. (b) complete. **thor•ough•bred,** *adj. & n.* pure-bred (horse). **thor•ough•fare,** *n.* way through which the public can go. **thor•ough•go•ing,** *adj.* complete. **thor•ough•ly,** *adv.* completely/totally. **thor•ough•ness,** *n.* completeness.

those [ðƏuz] *adj. & pron. see* **that.**

thou [ðau] *pron.* (*old*) you.

though [ðƏu] 1. *conj.* although; in spite of the fact that; **strange t. it may seem** = although it may seem strange; **as t.** = as if. 2. *adv.* in spite of this.

thought [Tɔːt] 1. *n.* (a) action of thinking; **he was lost in t.** = thinking so hard that you could not attract his attention. (b) considering in your mind; **after much t.** = after considering (the plan) for a long time; **on second t.** = having considered everything a second time. (c) plan. (d) regard. 2. *v. see* **think. thoughtful,** *adj.* (a) thinking hard. (b) considerate to other people. (c) showing deep thought. **thought•ful•ly,** *adv.* in a thoughtful way. **thought•ful•ness,** *n.* being thoughtful. **thought•less,** *adj.* without thinking; not thinking about. **thought•less•ly,** *adv.* in a thoughtless way. **thought•less•ness,** *n.* being thoughtless.

thou•sand ['Tauzənd] *n.* number 1000. **thou•sandth, 1000th.** 1. *adj.* referring to thousand. 2. *n.* one of a thousand parts.

thrall [Trɔːl] *n.* (*formal*) **in t.** = in slavery.

thrash [Træʃ] *v.* (a) to beat (with a stick). (b) to beat (another team) decisively. **thrash a•bout,** *v.* to move/to wave your arms and legs violently. **thrash•ing,** *n.* beating. **thrash out,** *v.* to discuss in detail.

thread [Tred] 1. *n.* (a) long thin piece of cotton/silk, etc.; **his life hangs by a t.** = he is very likely to die. (b) **to lose the t. of a conversation** = to miss what the conversation is about. (c) spiral ridge going around a screw/a bolt or inside a nut. 2. *v.* (a) to put a piece of cotton, etc., through the eye of a needle; to pass (a magnetic tape) through a slit. (b) to put (beads, etc.) on a string. (c) **to t. your way through a crowd** = to squeeze through a crowd carefully. **thread•bare,** *adj.* worn out (clothes). **thread•like,** *adj.* long and thin like a thread. **thread•worm,** *n.* long thin worm which lives in human intestines.

threat [Tret] *n.* (a) warning that sth unpleasant will happen or will be done. (b) person/thing which may harm. **threat•en,** *v.* to warn that

sth unpleasant will be done/that some action will be taken. **threat•en•ing•ly,** *adv.* menacingly.

three   [Triː]   *n.*   number   3. **three-di•men•sion•al,** *adj.* (picture) which has depth as well as length and breadth. **three•fold,** *adv.* three times as much. **three-piece,** *adj.* with three parts; (suit) with jacket, trousers and vest; (suite of living room furniture) consisting of a sofa and two armchairs. **three-ply,** *adj.* (wool) with three threads twisted together; (plywood) made of three layers stuck together. **three-quar•ter(s),** *adj.* referring to three fourths of a whole. **three•score,** *adj.* sixty. **three•some,** *n.* group of three people, esp. three players playing a game.

thren•o•dy ['Trenədɪ] *n.* (*formal*) funeral song.

thresh [Treʃ] *v.* to beat (corn) so that the grain falls out; **threshing machine** = machine which threshes corn automatically. **thresh•er,** *n.* person/machine that threshes.

thresh•old ['Treʃəuld] *n.* (a) bar across the floor of a doorway. (b) edge/beginning of sth. (c) limit; **t. of pain** = point at which pain becomes felt.

threw [Truː] *v. see* **throw.**

thrice [Traɪs] *adv.* three times.

thrift [Trɪft] *n.* (a) saving (money) by wise use and restricting spending. (b) type of seashore plant with small tufts of pink flowers. **thrift•i•ly,** *adv.* in a thrifty way. **thrift•i•ness,** *n.* being thrifty. **thrift•y,** *adj.* (**-ier, -iest**) careful with money.

thrill [Trɪl] 1. *n.* (shudder of) excitement. 2. *v.* to give (s.o.) a shudder of excitement; to be excited. **thrill•er,** *n.* exciting novel/motion picture, etc. (usu. about crime). **thrill•ing,** *adj.* very exciting.

thrips [Trɪps] *n.pl.* small insects which live on plants.

thrive [Traɪv] *v.* (**thrived/throve** [TrƏuv]) to grow well/to be strong.

throat [TrƏut] *n.* (a) front part of your neck below the chin. (b) pipe running from the back of your mouth down the inside of your neck; **to clear your t.** = to give a short cough; *inf.* **he's always ramming his opinions down my t.** = telling me his opinions. **throat•i•ly,** *adv.* in a throaty voice. **throat•y,** *adj.* **t. voice** = low, rough-sounding voice.

throb [Trɒb] 1. *n.* beating (of heart/machine). 2. *v.* (**throbbed**) to beat regularly; to have a regular pain.

throes [TrƏuz] *n.pl.* **death t.** = great suffering just before death; **in the t. of** = in the middle.

throm•bo•sis [Trɒm'bəʊsɪs] *n.* clot in a blood vessel, esp. in the heart.

throne [Trəʊn] *n.* ceremonial chair for a king/queen, etc.; **the t.** = the position of king/queen, etc.

throng [Trɒŋ] 1. *n.* great crowd of people. 2. *v.* to crowd together.

throt•tle ['Trɒtl] 1. *n.* valve on a pipe which allows variable quantities of steam/gas, etc., to pass into an engine; **to open up the t.** = to make the engine go faster. 2. *v.* to strangle (s.o.) by squeezing the neck, and preventing breathing. **throt•tle back, throttle down**, *v.* to reduce the supply of fuel to an engine, making it go more slowly.

through [Tru:] 1. *prep.* (a) crossing sth on the inside/going in at one side and coming out at the other. (b) during. (c) up to and including; **Monday t. Friday** = from Monday to Friday inclusively. (d) by means of. (e) because of. 2. *adv.* (a) from one side to another. (b) completely/to the finish; **we must see the plan t.** = see that it is completed. 3. *adj.* (a) which goes from one side to the other without stopping; **t. ticket** = ticket for a whole journey, with no stops or changes; **t. traffic** = traffic going through a town without stopping. (b) finished/completed; *inf.* **I'm t. with her** = I've broken off our friendship. **through and through**, *adv.* completely. **through•out** [Tru:'aʊt] 1. *prep.* in every part; at all times; from beginning to end. 2. *adv.* everywhere; at all times. **through•way**, *n.* thruway.

throve [Trəʊv] *v. see* **thrive.**

throw [Trəʊ] 1. *n.* (a) sending sth through the air. (b) distance sth is sent through the air; **they live a stone's t. away** = quite close. 2. *v.* (**threw; has thrown**) (a) to send (sth) through the air. (b) to shine (a light) **on**; **can you t. any light on the problem?** = make the problem clearer. (c) to make (a pot) with clay on a wheel. (d) *inf.* to hold (a party). (e) *inf.* to surprise/to confuse (s.o.). **throw a•way**, *v.* (a) to get rid of (sth) which you no longer need. (b) to waste. **throw•a•way**, *adj.* which can be discarded. **throw•back**, *n.* person/animal showing characteristics of distant ancestors; thing which shows a connection with the past. **throw•er**, *n.* person who throws. **throw in**, *v.* to add. **throw off**, *v.* to get rid of (sth). **throw out**, *v.* (a) to put (sth/s.o.) outside using force. (b) to send out (heat). (c) to reject. **throw o•ver**, *v.* to reject (a lover). **throw**

up, *v.* (a) to send up into the air. (b) to vomit. (c) to give up/to abandon.

thru [Tru:] *prep., adv. & adj. inf.* = **through**. **thru•way**, *n.* toll highway, usu. having more than one lane per direction.

thrum [Trʌm] *v.* (**thrummed**) to make a continuous low-pitched sound.

thrush [Trʌʃ] *n.* (a) (*pl.* **-es**) common brown bird with a speckled breast. (b) infectious throat disease caused by the bacterium *candida*.

thrust [Trʌst] 1. *n.* (a) push; force which pushes. (b) stab with a sword or dagger. 2. *v.* (**thrust**) (a) to push energetically. (b) **to t. yourself on s.o.** = to force s.o. to accept you as a guest/companion, etc.

thud [Tʌd] 1. *n.* dull, heavy noise. 2. *v.* (**thudded**) to make a dull noise.

thug [Tʌg] *n.* rough/violent person.

thumb [Tʌm] 1. *n.* (a) short thick finger which is placed apart from the other four fingers on each hand; **he is all thumbs** = he is awkward with his hands; **it's a useful rule of t.** = (i) a useful way of calculating approximately; (ii) a practical way of approaching a problem; **to be under s.o.'s t.** = to be dominated by s.o.; *inf.* **thumbs up (sign)** = gesture to show that everything is all right; *inf.* **thumbs down (sign)** = gesture to show disapproval. (b) part of a glove into which the thumb goes. 2. *v.* (a) **to t. through** = to look through (a book, etc.) quickly using your thumb; **well-thumbed book** = one which has been used often. (b) **to t. a ride** = to get a ride from a passing car by making a sign with your thumb. **thumb•nail**, *n.* nail on a thumb; **t. sketch** = rapid, very small sketch/description. **thumb in•dex**, *n.* series of notches cut in the edges of the pages of a book so that you can easily see where a new letter starts. **thumb-in•dex**, *v.* to give a book a thumb index. **thumb•screw**, *n.* machine for torturing, which squeezes the victim's thumb. **thumb•tack**, *n.* pin with a large flat head for pinning paper to a wall, etc.

thump [Tʌmp] 1. *n.* (a) dull noise. (b) punch; heavy blow with the fist. 2. *v.* (a) to hit with the fist. (b) to make a dull noise. **thump•ing**, *adj. inf.* very large.

thun•der ['Tʌndə] 1. *n.* (a) rumbling noise in the air caused by lightning; **to steal s.o.'s t.** = to take the credit for sth done by s.o. else/to do sth remarkable so that no one notices what another person has done. (b) loud rumbling noise. 2. *v.* (a) to make a rumbling noise. (b) to

---

æ back, ɑ: farm, ɒ: top, aɪ pipe, aʊ how, aɪə fire, aʊə flower, ɔ: bought, ɔɪ toy, e fed, eəhair, eɪ take, ə afraid, əʊ boat, əʊə lower, v: word, i: heap, ɪ hit, ɪə hear, u: school, ʊ book, ʌ but, b back, d dog, ð then, dʒ just, f fog, g go, h hand, j yes, k catch, l last, m mix, n nut, ŋ sing, p penny, r round, s some, ʃ short, t too, tʃ chop, θ thing, v voice, w was, z zoo, ʒ treasure

speak loudly. **thun•der•bolt**, *n.* (a) flash of lightning and thunder. (b) sudden (unpleasant) surprise. **thun•der•clap**, *n.* sudden noise of thunder. **thun•der•cloud**, *n.* large black cloud which will bring thunder and lightning. **thun•der•ing**, *adj. inf.* very big/great. **thun•der•ous**, *adj.* very loud (applause). **thun•der•storm**, *n.* rainstorm with thunder and lightning. **thun•der•struck**, *adj.* astonished. **thun•der•y**, *adj.* (weather) when thunder is likely.

Thurs•day ['Tɜːzdeɪ] *n.* fourth day of the week/day between Wednesday and Friday.

thus [ðʌs] *adv.* (*formal*) (a) in this way. (b) and so.

thwack [Twæk] 1. *n.* sound made when hitting sth hard. 2. *v.* to hit (sth) hard.

thwart [Twɔːt] *n.* seat for a rower in a boat. 2. *v.* to prevent (s.o.) doing sth.

thy [ðaɪ] *adj.* (*old*) your. **thy•self**, *pron.* (*old*) yourself.

thyme [taɪm] *n.* common herb used as flavoring.

thy•mus ['Taɪməs] *n.* lymph gland at the base of the neck.

thy•roid (gland) ['Taɪrɔɪd('glænd)] *n.* gland in the neck which influences the growth, etc., of the body. **thy•roi•dec•to•my**, *n.* operation to remove the thyroid.

Ti *symbol for* titanium.

ti•ar•a [tɪ'ɑːrə] *n.* headpiece with jewels, like a small crown.

tib•i•a ['tɪbɪə] *n.* one of the two large bones between the knee and the ankle.

tic [tɪk] *n.* twitch of the muscles which cannot be controlled.

tick [tɪk] 1. *n.* (a) mark on paper to indicate that sth is correct. (b) small insect or similar creature which lives on the skin of birds and animals. (c) small click made by a clock/watch, etc. 2. *v.* (a) to mark with a tick. (b) to make a small clicking noise; *inf.* **what makes s.o. t. =** what is the reason for his behavior. **tick a•way**, *v.* (*of time*) to pass. **tick•er**, *n. inf.* (a) watch. (b) heart. **tick•er tape**, *n.* long paper tape which carries information printed automatically by telegraph. **tick off**, *v.* (a) to mark with a tick. (b) *inf.* to make (s.o.) angry or annoyed.

tick•et ['tɪkɪt] 1. *n.* (a) piece of paper/card allowing you to travel, to go into a theater/cinema, etc.; piece of paper showing a price/information; **parking t. =** piece of paper showing that you have parked illegally and must pay a fine. (b) license held by the captain of a ship or an airplane pilot which shows he is qualified. (c) list of candidates sponsored by a political party. 2. *v.* to stick a ticket on (sth for sale).

tick•ing ['tɪkɪŋ] *n.* thick cloth for covering mattresses, etc.

tick•le ['tɪkl] 1. *n.* irritation which makes you laugh/cough. 2. *v.* (a) to irritate mildly (a part of s.o.'s body) in order to make him laugh; *inf.* **tickled pink =** very pleased and amused. (b) to itch/to be irritated. **tick•lish**, *adj.* (a) (person) who is easily made to laugh by tickling. (b) *inf.* difficult (problem). **tick•ly**, *adj.* irritated so as to make you want to scratch.

tic-tac-toe [tɪktæk'təʊ] *n.* game for two players where each puts an X or a O in one of nine squares in turn, the object being to be the first to make a line of three X's or O's.

tid•bit, *Brit.* **tit•bit** ['tɪdbɪt] *n.* special little piece (of food or information).

tid•dly•winks, *n.* game where small disks have to be flicked into a little cup.

tide [taɪd] 1. *n.* (a) regular rising and falling movement of the sea. (b) movement (of public opinion, etc.); **to swim against the t. =** to go against what most people think. 2. *v.* **to t. s.o. over =** to help him get past a difficult period. **tid•al**, *adj.* referring to the tide; **t. wave =** huge wave in the sea. **tide•mark**, *n.* mark showing the top limit of a tide. **tide•way**, *n.* channel caused by the tide running.

ti•dings ['taɪdɪŋz] *n. pl.* (*formal*) news.

ti•dy ['taɪdɪ] 1. *adj.* (-ier, -iest) (a) neat/in good order. (b) *inf.* quite large (sum). 2. *n.* small container for putting things in to keep them tidy. 3. *v.* to make (sth) neat. **ti•di•ly**, *adv.* in a tidy way. **ti•di•ness**, *n.* being tidy. **ti•dy up**, *v.* to make (sth) completely tidy; to remove (a mess).

tie [taɪ] 1. *n.* (a) thing which attaches/which restricts; **the ties of friendship.** (b) band of cloth which is worn knotted around the neck under the shirt collar; **a school t. =** particular tie which shows which school you went to. (c) linking mark in music to show that several notes are to be played as one long note. (d) equal score in a competition/election; **there was a t. for second place =** two people were equal second. 2. *v.* (a) to attach/to fasten; **she's tied to her work =** can never get away from it. (b) to make (a knot). (c) to be equal in a competition. **tie•break•er**, *n.* (*in tennis*) game to decide the winner of a set, played when the score is 6-6. **tie down**, *v.* to attach (to the floor/ground); **to tie s.o. down =** to limit s.o.'s activities. **tie-dyed**, *adj.* (shirt, etc.) which has been tied and then dyed to give a mottled effect. **tie•pin**, *n.* pin for attaching a tie. **tie up**, *v.* (a) to attach/to fasten. (b) to keep motionless; *inf.* **tied up =** busy. (c) to use (money) to purchase sth, so that it is not available for other purposes. **tie-up**, *n.* link/connection.

tier ['tɪə] *n.* one of a series of steps, usu. a row of seats in a theater; **wedding cake with four tiers** = made of four separate cakes placed one on top of the other. **ti•ered,** *adj.* with tiers.

tiff [tɪf] *n.* small argument/quarrel.

ti•ger ['taɪgə] *n.* (a) large striped catlike wild animal; **t. lily** = lily with spotted orange flowers; **paper t.** = thing which seems fierce but is really harmless. (b) country, esp. in East Asia, with a rapidly expanding economy; **t. market** = any of four key Pacific rim markets (Hong Kong/Singapore/Taiwan/South Korea), less important only than Japan. **ti•gress,** *n.* female tiger.

tight [taɪt] 1. *adj.* (-er, -est) (a) which fits (too) closely; (b) closely packed together; (schedule) which allows no spare time. (c) stretched taut. (d) *inf.* (money) which is difficult to get. (e) *inf.* drunk. 2. *adv.* (a) closely/firmly (shut). (b) closely packed. (c) *inf.* **to sit t.** = to stay where you are. **tight•en,** *v.* to make/to become tight; **we must t. our belts** = be prepared to eat less/to spend less. **tight•fis•ted,** *adj. & n.* mean/not generous. **tight•fi•tting,** *adj.* which fits tightly. **tight-lipped,** *adj.* with the mouth firmly closed; (person) who refuses to speak. **tight•ly,** *adv.* in a tight way. **tight•ness,** *n.* being tight. **tight•rope,** *n.* rope stretched between two poles on which s.o. can walk/can perform tricks. **tights,** *n.pl.* close-fitting piece of clothing worn by girls, women, dancers, etc., on the legs and lower part of the body.

tile [taɪl] 1. *n.* flat piece of baked clay used to cover floors/walls/roofs; **carpet tiles** = square pieces of carpet which can be laid on a floor like tiles. 2. *v.* to cover (a roof/a floor/a wall) with tiles. **til•er,** *n.* person who tiles (a roof, etc.).

till [tɪl] 1. *n.* drawer for keeping cash in a store, etc. 2. *v.* to cultivate (land). 3. *prep.* until/up to (the time of). 4. *conj.* to the time when/until.

till•er ['tɪlə] *n.* handle which is attached to a rudder and so steers a boat.

tilt [tɪlt] 1. *n.* (a) slope/slant. (b) **at full t.** = at full speed. 2. *v.* to slope; to place at a slope.

tilth [tɪlθ] *n.* good crumbly soil.

tim•ber ['tɪmbə] *n.* (a) cut wood ready for building. (b) growing trees which could be cut down and used for building. (c) large beam/plank used in building. **tim•bered,** *adj.* (house) made of wooden beams.

tim•bre ['tæmbə] *n.* quality of sound (of voice/musical instrument).

time [taɪm] 1. *n.* (a) existence for a period (such as years/centuries, etc.); **t. alone will tell** = the result will only become apparent later; **to have t. on your hands** = to have a period with nothing to do; **there's no t. to be lost** = we must hurry; **to make up for lost t.** = to do things rapidly because time has been wasted. (b) period between two happenings; **in three weeks' t.** = three weeks from now; **all the t.** = continuously. (c) particular period; *inf.* **to do t.** = to serve a prison sentence. (d) **times** = age/period; **behind the times** = out of date. (e) particular point at which sth took place; **I was away at the t.** = when it happened; **at the present t.** = now; **by the t. I got there** = when I got there; **from t. to t./at times** = occasionally; **for the t. being** = temporarily. (f) point expressed in hours and minutes; **Greenwich Mean Time** = internationally accepted correct time system. (g) hour at which sth usually happens; **the train arrived on t.** = at the right time; **we were in t.** = we were early enough. (h) (pleasant/bad) period. (i) one of several occasions. (j) **times** = multiplied by. (k) rhythm. 2. *v.* (a) to choose the right moment. (b) to calculate the time sth takes. **time bomb,** *n.* bomb with a clock attached, which sets off the bomb at a particular moment. **time-hon•ored,** *adj.* (custom) observed for a long time, and therefore respected. **time•keep•er,** *n.* (a) person who times a race. (b) watch or clock. **time-lag,** *n.* delay. **time•less,** *adj.* permanent; untouched by time. **time•less•ness,** *n.* being timeless. **time lim•it,** *n.* period during which sth should be done. **time•li•ness,** *n.* being timely. **time•ly,** *adj.* which happens at the right moment. **time•piece,** *n.* watch or clock. **tim•er,** *n.* (a) person/device which times; **egg t.** = device which times how long an egg boils. (b) device which can be set to start a machine/to stop a light, etc. at a particular time. **time•sav•ing,** *adj.* (device) which saves time. **time•serv•er,** *n.* person who changes his opinions to match those of people in power. **time•shar•ing,** *n.* system where several people buy shares in a property, each one being allowed to use it for a limited period each year. **time-sig•nal,** *n.* accurate radio signal showing the exact time. **time•ta•ble.** 1. *n.* list which shows the times of trains/aircraft/classes in school/appointments. 2. *v.* to draw up a list of times; to appear on a list of times. **time•work,** *n.* work which is paid for at a rate of money by the hour or day. **time zone,** *n.* zone of the earth in which a uniform time is kept. **tim•ing**, *n.* (a) action of recording the time (of a race). (b) controlling the time at which sth happens.

tim•id ['tɪmɪd] *adj.* afraid/frightened. **ti•mid•i•ty** [tɪˈmɪdɪtɪ] *n.* being timid. **tim•id•ly** ['tɪmɪdlɪ] *adv.* in a timid way. **tim•or•ous** ['tɪmərəs] *adj.* very frightened.

tim•pa•ni ['tɪmpənɪ] *n.pl.* group of kettledrums in an orchestra. **tim•pa•nist**, *n.* person who plays the timpani.

tin [tɪn] 1. *n.* (a) (*element:* Sn) silvery metal. (b) metal covered with a thin layer of tin. (c) (usu. round) metal box for keeping food in; **cookie t.** = tin for keeping cookies in. 2. *v.* to cover with tin. **tin•foil**, *n.* thin metal sheet used esp. to wrap food up. **tin•ny** ['tɪnɪ] *adj.* (**-ier, -iest**) weak, metallic (sound); (car) which rattles. **tin pan alley**, *n. inf.* area where publishers of popular music have offices. **tin plate** ['tɪnpleɪt] *n.* thin sheet of iron covered with tin. **tin•pot**, *adj. inf.* not of good quality.

tinc•ture ['tɪŋktʃə] *n.* medicine dissolved in alcohol.

tin•der ['tɪndə] *n.* very dry material for starting a fire.

tine [taɪn] *n.* prong of a fork.

tinge [tɪndʒ] 1. *n.* slight color/taste, etc., of sth. 2. *v.* to give a slight color/taste to (sth).

tin•gle ['tɪŋgl] 1. *n.* sharp prickling feeling. 2. *v.* to have a sharp prickling feeling; **tingling with excitement** = very excited.

tin•ker ['tɪŋkə] 1. *n.* mender of pots, pans, etc. who travels from place to place. 2. *v.* **to t. with sth** = to try to make sth work better.

tin•kle ['tɪŋkl] 1. *n.* ringing (like a little bell). 2. *v.* to make a little ringing noise.

tin•ni•tus [tɪˈnaɪtəs] *n.* ringing noise in the ears.

tin•sel ['tɪnsl] *n.* thin strips of glittering metal used for decorating Christmas trees, etc.

tint [tɪnt] 1. *n.* slight shade of color. 2. *v.* to give a slight shade of color; **tinted glass** = glass which has a slight shade of brown/blue, etc.

ti•ny ['taɪnɪ] *adj.* (**-ier, -iest**) very small.

tip [tɪp] 1. *n.* (a) pointed end; **the t. of the iceberg** = small part of sth (usu. unpleasant) which makes you eventually discover the rest. (b) money given to a waiter, etc., to show thanks for his services. (c) piece of helpful information; **racing tips** = suggestions as to which horses are likely to win; **take a t. from me** = take my advice. 2. *v.* (**tipped**) (a) to put a tip on (sth); (b) to make (sth) slope/lean. (c) to pour out/to empty (sth). (d) to give (a waiter, etc.) a small gift of money. (e) to give (s.o.) a piece of helpful information; **to t. s.o. off** = to warn s.o. **tip-off**, *n. inf.* piece of useful information; warning. **tip o•ver**, *v.* to lean and fall over; to

make (sth) lean and fall over. **tip•ster**, *n.* person who gives advice on which horse is likely to win a race. **tip•toe**. 1. *n.* **on t.** = quietly on the tips of your toes. 2. *v.* to walk quietly on the tips of your toes. **tip•top**, *adj. inf.* excellent.

tip•ple ['tɪpl] 1. *n. inf.* drink. 2. *v. inf.* to drink alcohol regularly.

tip•sy ['tɪpsɪ] *adj.* (**-ier, -iest**) *inf.* rather drunk. **tip•si•ly**, *adv.* in a tipsy way. **tip•si•ness**, *n.* being tipsy.

ti•rade [taɪˈreɪd] *n.* long angry speech.

tire [taɪə] 1. *n. Brit.* tyre. thick rubber cover around a wheel; **flat t.** = tire with a hole in it through which the air leaks out. 2. *v.* (a) to become/to make weary; to need a rest after physical exercise. (b) (**of**) to lose interest in doing sth. **tired**, *adj.* (a) feeling sleepy/in need of rest. (b) **t. of sth** = bored with sth/having no patience with sth. **tired•ness**, *n.* feeling in need of rest. **tire•less**, *adj.* full of energy/never needing to rest. **tire•less•ly**, *adv.* in a tireless way. **tire•some**, *adj.* annoying/bothering. **tir•ing**, *adj.* which makes you tired.

ti•ro ['taɪrəʊ] *n.* (*pl.* **-os**) *see* **ty•ro**.

tis•sue ['tɪʃuː] *n.* (a) group of cells which make up a part of an animal or plant. (b) thin cloth. (c) soft paper handkerchief. (d) **t. of lies** = mass of lies. **tis•sue pa•per**, *n.* thin soft paper used for wrapping delicate objects.

tit [tɪt] *n.* (a) type of common small bird. (b) *Sl.* teat; breast. (c) **t. for tat** = paying back a blow with another blow.

ti•tan ['taɪtn] *n.* very large/strong person. **ti•tan•ic** [taɪˈtænɪk] *adj.* very large.

ti•ta•ni•um [tɪˈteɪnɪəm] *n.* (*element:* Ti) light gray metal.

tit•bit ['tɪtbɪt] *n. Brit. see* **tid•bit.**

tithe [taɪð] *n.* one-tenth part of produce or income paid to the church.

tit•il•late ['tɪtɪleɪt] *v.* to excite. **tit•il•la•tion**, *n.* act of titillating.

tit•i•vate ['tɪtɪveɪt] *v. inf.* **to t. (yourself)** = to make yourself look smart.

ti•tle ['taɪtl] *n.* (a) name of a book/play/motion picture, etc.; **t. page** = page at the beginning of a book, where the title is written in large letters; **t. role** = part in a play/motion picture which gives the name to the play/motion picture. (b) word (usu. put in front of a name) to indicate an honor/a qualification. (c) (*in sports*) position of champion. (d) right to own (property); **t. deed** = paper showing that you are the owner of a property. **ti•tled**, *adj.* with a title (such as Lord, Sir, etc.) to show that you are a nobleman.

tit•mouse ['tɪtmaʊs] *n.* (*pl.* -mice) type of small bird.

ti•trate [taɪ'treɪt] *v.* to analyze the concentration of a chemical solution. **ti•tra•tion** [taɪ-'treɪʃn] *n.* act of titrating.

tit•ter ['tɪtə] 1. *n.* little laugh. 2. *v.* to give a little laugh.

tit•tle-tat•tle ['tɪtl'tætl] *n. inf.* gossip.

tit•u•lar ['tɪtjʊlə] *adj.* holding a title but without direct power.

tiz•zy ['tɪzɪ] *n. inf.* bother/nervous state.

TNT ['ti:en'ti:] *abbreviation for* trinitrotoluene, common high explosive.

to [tu:] 1. *prep.* (a) (*showing direction or position*) he went to France; **move to the right.** (b) (*showing time*) **from day to day; it's ten to six** = ten minutes before six o'clock. (c) (*showing person who receives something*) **give it to me.** (d) (*showing relationship*) **is this the key to the box? secretary to the managing director.** (e) concerning; **there's nothing to it** = there's no difficulty in doing it. (f) (*showing ratio*) **they lost by six goals to four; the rate is two dollars to the pound.** (g) (*showing comparison*) **I prefer butter to margarine.** 2. *adv.* (a) **he came to** = he regained consciousness. (b) **pull the door to** = pull it until it is almost shut. 3. (*forming infinitive*) (a) **after verbs they came to help us.** (b) *after adjectives* **good to eat.** (c) after nouns **he made no attempt to run away.** (d) *when the verb is a subject* **to refuse the invitation would have been rude. to and fro,** *adv.* backward and forward. **-to-be** *suffix showing something in the near future* **a mother-to-be.**

toad [təʊd] *n.* amphibian like a large frog, which lives mostly on land. **toad•stool,** *n.* fungus shaped like a mushroom, but usu. not edible, and sometimes poisonous. **toad•y.** 1. *n.* person who flatters s.o. (in the hope of getting sth in return). 2. *v.* to flatter (s.o.).

toast [təʊst] 1. *n.* (a) slices of bread which have been grilled brown. (b) taking a drink and wishing s.o. success. 2. *v.* (a) to grill (bread, etc.) until it is brown; to warm. (b) to drink and wish s.o. success. **toast•er,** *n.* electric device for toasting bread. **toast•mas•ter,** *n.* person (at a banquet) who calls on people to speak and announces the toasts.

to•bac•co [tə'bækəʊ] *n.* (dried leaves of a) plant used for smoking in cigarettes/cigars and in pipes. **to•bac•co•nist,** *n.* person who sells tobacco/cigarettes, etc.

to•bog•gan [tə'bɒgən] 1. *n.* long sled curved upward at the front. 2. *v.* to slide on a toboggan. **to•bog•gan•ing,** *n.* sport of sliding on a toboggan.

to•by jug ['təʊbɪ 'dʒʌg] *n.* small mug made in the shape of a head.

toc•ca•ta [tɒ'kɑːtə] *n.* piece of music for the organ or piano.

toc•sin ['tɒksɪn] *n.* warning bell.

to•day [tə'deɪ] *adv. & n.* (a) this present day; **a week t.** = in exactly seven days' time. (b) this present time.

tod•dle ['tɒdl] *v.* to walk unsteadily. **tod•dler,** *n.* child who is just learning to walk.

tod•dy ['tɒdɪ] *n.* alcohol and hot water and sugar.

to-do [tə'duː] *n. inf.* excitement/confusion/bother.

toe [təʊ] 1. *n.* (a) one of the five parts like fingers at the end of your foot; **big t./little t.** = the largest/smallest of the five toes; **to be on your toes** = to be ready/prepared. (b) end part of a shoe/a sock. 2. *v.* to touch with the toe; **to t. the line** = to do what you should or are told to do. **toe•hold,** *n.* grip with the toes; small foothold. **toe•nail,** *n.* nail at the end of a toe.

tof•fee ['tɒfɪ] *n.* taffy.

to•ga ['təʊgə] *n.* robe worn by men in ancient Rome.

to•geth•er [tə'geðə] *adv.* (a) in a group/all at the same time; **get t.** = meet. (b) into contact one with another; **stick the pieces t. to•geth•er•ness,** *n.* being together with other people.

togs [tɒgz] *n. pl. inf.* clothes.

tog•gle ['tɒgl] *n.* short piece of wood attached to a coat with string, used in place of a button.

toil [tɔɪl] 1. *n.* hard work. 2. *v.* to work hard.

toi•let ['tɔɪlət] *n.* (a) washing and dressing. (b) bowl with a seat on which you sit to pass waste matter from the body; room with this bowl in it; **t. paper** = soft paper for wiping your anus after getting rid of waste matter; **t. water** = scented water. **toi•let•ries,** *n. pl.* deodorant/soap/perfume, etc., used in cleaning or grooming.

to•ken ['təʊkən] *n.* (a) visible thing which is a mark/sign (of respect, etc.); **by the same t.** = in a similar way; **t. payment** = a small symbolic payment; **t. woman/black** = woman/black person appointed to a position (on a committee, etc.) to placate rights movements. (b) piece of

---

æ **back,** ɑː **farm,** ɒ **top,** aɪ **pipe,** aʊ **how,** aɪə **fire,** aʊə **flower,** ɔː **bought,** ɔɪ **toy,** e **fed,** eəhair, eɪ **take,** ə **afraid,** əʊ **boat,** əʊə **lower,** ɜː **word,** iː **heap,** ɪ **hit,** ɪə **hear,** uː **school,** ʊ **book,** ʌ **but,** b **back,** d **dog,** ð **then,** dʒ **just,** f **fog,** g **go,** h **hand,** j **yes,** k **catch,** l **last,** m **mix,** n **nut,** ŋ **sing,** p **penny,** r **round,** s **some,** ʃ **short,** t **too,** tʃ **chop,** θ **thing,** v **voice,** w **was,** z **zoo,** ʒ **treasure**

paper/card/plastic which is used to replace money.

told [təʊld] v. see **tell**.

tol•er•ate ['tɒləreɪt] v. (a) to suffer (noise, etc.) without complaining. (b) to allow (sth which you do not agree with) to exist. **tol•er•a•ble** ['tɒlərəbl] adj. (a) bearable. (b) fairly good. **tol•er•a•bly**, adv. in a fairly good way. **tol•er•ance**, n. (a) putting up with (unpleasantness, etc.); allowing (sth which you do not agree with) to exist. (b) amount by which a measurement can vary from what is specified on a plan. (c) ability to stand the effect of a drug/a poison. **tol•er•ant**, adj. (person) who tolerates. **tol•er•ant•ly**, adv. in a tolerant way. **tol•er•a•tion** [tɒlə'reɪʃn] n. allowing (sth which you do not agree with) to exist.

toll [təʊl] 1. n. (a) payment for using a road/a bridge/a ferry; **t. bridge** = one where a toll is paid. (b) loss/damage; **death t.** = number of deaths. (c) solemn ringing of a bell. 2. v. to ring (a bell) solemnly as for a funeral. **toll call**, n. long-distance telephone call for which there is a higher charge than for a local call. **toll free**, adv. without having to pay the charge for a long-distance call. **toll•gate**, n. gate across a road where a toll has to be paid. **toll•house**, n. house where the tollkeeper lives. **toll•keep•er**, n. person who takes the toll on a road/bridge, etc.

tom•(cat) ['tɒm(kæt)] n. male cat.

tom•a•hawk ['tɒməhɔːk] n. light North American Indian ax.

to•ma•to [tə'meɪtəʊ] n. (pl. -oes) red fruit growing on annual plants and used in salads; plant which bears tomatoes; **t. sauce** = sauce made with tomatoes.

tomb [tuːm] n. large grave (usu. with an underground vault in which to put a dead person). **tomb•stone**, n. large stone placed on a grave with the name of the dead person written on it.

tom•boy ['tɒmbɔɪ] n. girl who plays rough games like a boy.

tome [təʊm] n. (formal) large book.

tom•fool ['tɒmfuːl] adj. inf. idiotic. **tom•fool•er•y**, n. stupid behavior.

Tom•my gun ['tɒmɪgʌn] n. small machine gun.

to•mor•row [tə'mɒrəʊ] adv. & n. (a) the day which follows today. (b) the future.

tom-tom ['tɒmtɒm] n. small drum beaten with your hands.

ton [tʌn] n. (a) weight equal to 2000 pounds; **metric t.** = 1000 kilograms. (b) space in a ship equivalent to 100 cubic feet. (c) inf. **tons of** = lots. **ton•nage**, n. (a) space in a ship mea-

sured in tons. (b) total number of ships in a navy/belonging to a company, calculated by adding together their individual sizes. **tonne** [tʌn] n. metric ton.

tone [təʊn] 1. n. (a) quality of sound of music/voice. (b) (in music) difference between two notes which have one note between them on the piano. (c) way of speaking/writing which shows a particular emotion. (d) shade of color. (e) strength of the body and muscles. (f) general quality or appearance. 2. v. to **t. (in) with** = to fit in well/to harmonize. **tone•al** ['təʊnl] adj. referring to tone. **to•nal•i•ty** [tə-'nælɪtɪ] n. quality of tone (in the colors of a painting/in a piece of music). **tone-deaf**, adj. not able to recognize differences in musical pitch. **tone down**, v. to reduce in intensity; moderate. **tone•less**, adj. with no variation in tone. **ton•er**, n. chemical used in laser printers and photocopiers. **tone up**, v. to make fitter.

tongs [tɒŋz] n. pl. **(pair of) t.** = instrument for picking things up, with small claws on the end of two arms; **sugar t.** = tongs for picking up lumps of sugar.

tongue [tʌŋ] n. (a) long, movable piece of muscular flesh in the mouth, which is used for tasting and speaking; **with t. in cheek** = not really meant seriously; **to hold one's t.** = not to speak; **it's on the tip of my t.** = I will remember it in a moment. (b) piece of movable flesh in an animal's mouth, used as food. (c) language; **mother t.** = first language. (d) loose piece of leather under the laces in a shoe. (e) long, thin flame/piece of land. **tongue-and-groove joint**, n. type of interlocking joint in which a board with a projecting tongue along one edge fits into a corresponding groove along the edge of the next board. **tongue-tied**, adj. so shy as to be unable to say anything. **tongue twist•er**, n. phrase (like **red truck, yellow truck**) which is difficult to say quickly.

ton•ic ['tɒnɪk] 1. adj. (a) referring to a musical tone; **t. solfa** = system of writing the tones in music using syllables (doh-ray-me, etc.). (b) referring to physical strength/well-being. 2. n. (a) note which sets the key to a scale of music. (b) anything (such as medicine) which strengthens the body; **to act as a t. on s.o.** = make s.o. more energetic. (c) **t. (water)** = aerated drink containing quinine.

to•night [tə'naɪt] adv. & n. the night of the present day.

ton•nage ['tʌnɪdʒ] n. see **ton**.

tonne [tʌn] n. see **ton**.

ton•sil ['tɒnsl] n. one of two soft lumps of flesh at the back of your throat. **ton•sil•lec•to•my**, n. operation to remove the tonsils. **ton•sil•li•tis** [tɒnsɪ'laɪtɪs] *n.* painful infection of the tonsils.

ton•sure ['tɒnʃə] *n.* shaving off all or part of the hair of people becoming monks; part of the head which has been shaved. **ton•su•red,** *adj.* with a tonsure.

ton•tine ['tɒntiːn] *n.* type of investment where the survivors each receive more as investors die.

too [tuː] *adv.* (a) more than necessary. (b) as well/also. (c) *inf.* very; **t. bad!** = it's a shame!

took [tʊk] *v. see* **take.**

tool [tuːl] 1. *n.* instrument for doing work (such as hammer/spade, etc.); person used by s.o. else. 2. *v.* to decorate using a tool. **tool up,** *v.* to equip (a factory) with machinery.

toot [tuːt] 1. *n.* short sound made by a horn. 2. *v.* to blow a horn sharply.

tooth [tuːT] *n.* (*pl.* **teeth** [tiːT]) (a) one of a set of bony structures in the mouth, used by animals for chewing and biting; **milk teeth** = first set of teeth grown by a baby, and replaced by permanent teeth as a child; **false teeth** = set of artificial teeth to replace teeth which have been taken out; **in the teeth of** = running against/into; **long in the t.** = old; **armed to the teeth** = fully armed. (b) part of a saw/of a comb/of a cogwheel shaped like a tooth. **tooth•ache** ['tuːTeɪk] *n.* pain in a tooth. **tooth•brush,** *n.* small brush with a long handle used for cleaning your teeth. **toothed** *adj.* with teeth; **t. wheel** = cogwheel. **tooth•less,** *adj.* with no teeth. **tooth•paste,** *n.* paste used with a toothbrush for cleaning your teeth. **tooth•pick,** *n.* small pointed piece of wood/metal, etc., for pushing between the teeth to remove pieces of food. **tooth•some,** *adj.* good to eat. **tooth•y,** *adj.* showing a lot of teeth.

too•tle ['tuːtl] 1. *n. inf.* little toot, as on a flute. 2. *v. inf.* (a) to make a tootle. (b) to go (**along/off**).

top [tɒp] 1. *n.* (a) highest point; **on t. of everything else** = in addition to everything else. (b) upper surface. (c) roof (of a car). (d) highest/most important place. (e) **big t.** = large circus tent. (f) **at the t. of his voice** = as loud as possible. (g) child's toy which spins when twisted sharply. (h) piece of clothing covering the upper part of the body. 2. *adj.* (a) highest. (b) most important. 3. *v.* (**topped**) (a) to cut the top off. (b) to put sth on top. (c) to go higher than; *inf.* **to t. it all** = in addition to everything

else. **top•coat,** *n.* light overcoat. **top dog,** *n. Sl.* winner. **top dress•ing,** *n.* scattering fertilizer on the surface of the soil; fertilizer to be scattered in this way. **top flight,** *adj. inf.* excellent/of very high quality. **top hat,** *n.* man's tall black hat. **top-heav•y,** *adj.* unstable because the top part is heavier than the bottom. **top•knot,** *n.* small bunch of hair tied on the top of the head. **top•less,** *adj.* (*of woman*) wearing nothing on the top part of the body. **top-lev•el,** *adj.* (talks) involving important people. **top•most,** *adj.* highest. **top notch,** *adj.* top flight. **top•per,** *n. inf.* top hat. **top•ping,** *n.* cream, sauce, etc., put on the top of food. **top se•cret,** *adj.* very secret. **top•soil,** *n.* layer of good light soil on the surface (of a field, etc.).

to•paz ['təʊpæz] *n.* yellow semi-precious stone.

to•pee, topi ['təʊpɪ] *n.* helmet worn in hot countries (like India) to protect your head from the sun.

to•pi•ar•y ['təʊpjərɪ] *n.* art of cutting bushes into odd shapes for ornament.

top•ic ['tɒpɪk] *n.* subject (for discussion/of a conversation). **top•i•cal,** *adj.* which is of interest at the present time. **top•i•cal•i•ty,** *n.* being topical. **top•i•cal•ly,** *adv.* in a topical way.

to•pog•ra•phy [tə'pɒɡrəfɪ] *n.* description of land mentioning rivers, mountains, roads, buildings, etc. **to•pog•ra•pher,** *n.* person who studies topography. **top•o•graph•i•cal** [tɒpə'ɡræfɪkl] *adj.* which describes land.

to•pol•o•gy [tə'pɒlədʒɪ] *n.* study of the properties of geometrical shapes which remain the same even when the shapes change.

top•ple ['tɒpl] *v.* to make a government/dictator lose power. **top•ple o•ver** ['tɒpl'əʊvə] *v.* to make (sth) fall down; to fall down.

top•sy-tur•vy ['tɒpsɪ'tɜːvɪ] *adj. & adv.* upside down/in confusion.

toque [təʊk] *n.* round hat (for a woman) with no brim.

tor [tɔː] *n.* rocky hill.

torch [tɔːtʃ] *n.* (*pl.* **-es**) (a) (*esp. Brit.*) portable electric light which you can hold in your hand. (b) flaming piece of wood. **torch•light,** *n.* light from a flaming torch; **t. parade** = procession of people carrying flaming torches.

tore [tɔː] *v. see* **tear.**

tor•e•a•dor ['tɒrɪədɔː] *n.* Spanish bullfighter.

tor•ment 1. *n.* ['tɔːmənt] extreme pain; **in t.** =

in great pain. 2. *v.* [tɔː'ment] to make (s.o.) suffer. **tor•men•tor**, *n.* person who torments.

torn [tɔːn] *v. see* **tear.**

tor•na•do [tɔː'neɪdəʊ] *n.* (*pl.* -oes) violent whirlwind.

tor•pe•do [tɔː'piːdəʊ] 1. *n.* (*pl.* -oes) self-propelled missile which travels through the water. 2. *v.* to sink (a ship) using a torpedo; to ruin (s.o.'s plans). **tor•pe•do boat**, *n.* small fast naval ship which carries torpedoes.

tor•pid ['tɔːpɪd] *adj.* half asleep with heat; dull; sluggish. **tor•por**, *n.* being half asleep/sluggish.

torque [tɔːk] *n.* (a) mechanical force to make sth rotate. (b) prehistoric necklace made of twisted gold or silver.

tor•rent ['tɒrənt] *n.* (a) fast rushing stream. (b) fast flow. **tor•ren•tial** [tə'renʃəl] *adj.* like a torrent.

tor•rid ['tɒrɪd] *adj.* (a) very hot. (b) intense (passion).

tor•sion ['tɔːʃn] *n.* being twisted; strain caused by twisting.

tor•so ['tɔːsəʊ] *n.* (*pl.* -os, -si) body (excluding the head, arms and legs).

tort [tɔːt] *n.* act which is the subject of a civil action in court.

tor•til•la [tɔː'tiːjæ] *n.* type of Spanish omelette, with vegetables.

tor•toise ['tɔːtəs] *n.* reptile covered with a hard domed shell, which moves very slowly and can live to a great age. **tor•toise•shell**, *adj. & n.* speckled brown material (from the shell of a tortoise) or something like it used for making combs/frames for glasses, etc.; **t. cat** = brown, yellow and black cat; **t. butterfly** = common brown and red butterfly.

tor•tu•ous ['tɔːtjʊəs] *adj.* which twists and turns. **tor•tu•ous•ly**, *adv.* in a tortuous way.

tor•ture ['tɔːtʃə] 1. *n.* pain inflicted on s.o. as a punishment or to make them reveal a secret. 2. *v.* to inflict torture on s.o. **tor•tur•er**, *n.* person who tortures.

To•ry ['tɔːrɪ] *adj. & n.* (member) of the Conservative party in Great Britain or Canada.

toss [tɒs] 1. *n.* (*pl.* -es) (a) action of throwing sth into the air; **t. of a coin** = throwing a coin up to see which side is on top when it comes down; (*in sports*) **to win the t.** = guess correctly which side of the coin comes down on top and so play first. (b) sharp disdainful movement of the head. 2. *v.* (a) to throw (sth) into the air; **to t. a coin** = to throw a coin to see which side is on top when it comes down; **let's t. for it** = the person who guesses right, starts to play first/has first choice. (b) to move (sth) about; to mix (a salad); **she tossed her head** = made a sharp disdainful movement of her head.

toss•up, *n. inf.* **it's a t. which one will win** = you can't tell which one will win.

tot [tɒt] 1. *n.* (a) little child. (b) *inf.* small glass of alcohol. 2. *v.* (**totted**) **to t. up** = to add up.

to•tal ['təʊtl] 1. *adj. & n.* complete/whole (amount). 2. *v.* (**totaled, totalled**) to add up (to). **to•tal•i•ty** [təʊ'tælɪtɪ] *n.* whole amount. **to•tal•ize**, *v.* to add up (figures). **to•tal•ly**, *adv.* completely.

to•tal•i•tar•i•an [təʊtælɪ'teərɪən] *adj.* (state) governed by a single party/group which refuses to allow the existence of any opposition.

to•tal•i•za•tor ['təʊtəlaɪzeɪtə] *n.* machine which calculates the amount to be paid to people who bet on a winning horse.

tote [təʊt] 1. *n. inf.* **the t.** = totalizator. 2. *v.* to carry. **tote bag**, *n.* large carrying bag.

to•tem pole ['təʊtəmpəʊl] *n.* tall carved pole on which North American Indians carve figures of gods.

tot•ter ['tɒtə] *v.* to walk unsteadily/to wobble. **tot•ter•y**, *adj.* wobbly/likely to fall.

tou•can ['tuːkæn] *n.* American tropical bird with a huge colored beak.

touch [tʌtʃ] 1. *n.* (*pl.* -es) (a) sense by which you feel sth. (b) way of bringing your fingers into contact with sth; **she's lost her t.** = she isn't as successful/capable as she was. (c) slight tap. (d) slight stroke (of a paintbrush); **to put the finishing touches to sth** = to finish sth off. (e) contact; **to get in t. with/to lose t. with** = to contact/to lose contact with. (f) slight taste/trace. 2. *v.* (a) to feel (with the fingers); to come into contact; **I wouldn't t. it** = I wouldn't have anything to do with it; **don't t. my things** = don't interfere with them/don't move them. (b) **to t. on** = to refer to (a subject). (c) to eat or drink (*usu. negative*); **I don't t. alcohol.** (d) to affect the emotions of (s.o.). (e) to reach the same level as (s.o.). (f) *inf.* to ask (s.o.) **for** a loan. **touch-and-go**, *adj.* **it was touch-and-go** = it was doubtful. **touch down**, *v.* (*of plane*) to land. **touch•down**, *n.* (a) landing (of a plane). (b) (*in football*) scoring of six points for having possession of the ball on or behind the opponent's goal. **tou•ché** ['tuːʃeɪ] *inter. meaning* you have scored a point against me. **touched**, *adj.* (a) grateful/pleased with. (b) slightly mad. **touch•i•ness**, *n.* being susceptible/easily offended. **touch•ing.** 1. *adj.* which affects the emotions. 2. *prep.* concerning/about. **touch off**, *v.* to set off (an explosion, etc.). **touch on**, *v.* to refer to (a question) briefly. **touch pa•per**, *n.* chemically treated paper used as a fuse to light a firework. **touch•screen**, *n.* computer screen which is sensitive to touch, and where a cursor can be positioned by touching the screen.

touch•stone, *n.* thing used as a standard to test other things against. **touch-tone,** *adj.* (of a telephone dialing system) transmitting instructions/information in the form of tones produced by pressing the telephone's buttons. **touch-type,** *v.* to type without looking at the keys on the typewriter. **touch up,** *v.* to add little strokes of paint to improve the appearance of sth. **touch•y,** *adj. inf.* highly susceptible/easily offended.

tough [tʌf] 1. *adj.* (**-er, -est**) (a) hard; difficult to chew/to cut/to break; *inf.* **it's as t. as shoe leather** = extremely tough. (b) strong/hardy. (c) difficult; **to get t. with s.o.** = to deal roughly/harshly with s.o. (d) *inf.* **t. luck!** = hard luck! 2. *n. inf.* rough criminal. **tough•en,** *v.* to make tough; **toughened glass** = specially strengthened glass. **tough•ness,** *n.* being tough.

tou•pee ['tuːpeɪ] *n.* small wig.

tour ['tuə] 1. *n.* journey which goes around various places and returns to its starting point; **package t.** = one which has been totally organized in advance. 2. *v.* to visit; to go on a tour; **touring company** = theater company which goes from one town to another. **tour•ism,** *n.* business of providing lodging and entertainment for tourists. **tour•ist,** *adj. & n.* person who goes on vacation to visit places; **t. class** = type of seating in an aircraft which is cheaper than first class; **t. trap** = place whch overcharges tourists.

tour de force [tuːədə'fɔːs] *n.* act showing remarkable skill.

tour•ma•line ['tuəməliːn] *n.* type of semiprecious stone.

tour•na•ment ['tuənəmənt] *n.* (a) (*old*) contest between groups of knights. (b) sporting competition with many games which eliminate competitors.

tour•ne•dos ['tuənədəu] *n.* piece of fillet steak.

tour•ni•quet ['tuənɪkeɪ] *n.* tight bandage put around an arm or leg to stop bleeding from a wound.

tou•sle ['tauzl] *v.* to make (hair) untidy.

tout [taut] 1. *n.* person who tries to sell something to people he meets. 2. *v.* (a) to try to persuade people to vote/to buy things, etc. (b) to praise highly; **to t. a new restaurant.**

tow [təu] 1. *n.* (a) pulling a car/a ship, etc. behind you; **he had his family in t.** = coming behind him. (b) short, coarse pieces of flax. 2. *v.* to pull (a car/a ship, etc.) which cannot move

by itself. **tow•bar,** *n.* bar fitted to a car, to attach a trailer, etc. **tow-head•ed,** *adj.* with very light, almost white, blond hair. **tow-line, tow-rope,** *n.* rope which attaches a car/a ship, etc. to sth being towed. **tow•path,** *n.* path along the bank of a river/canal (along which horses used to walk to tow barges).

to•ward [tə'wɔːdz] *prep.* (*also* **towards**) (a) in the direction of. (b) to (a person/a country, etc.). (c) as part payment for. (d) near (a time).

tow•el ['tauəl] 1. *n.* piece of soft absorbent cloth for drying; **to throw in the t.** = to give up/not to continue a contest. 2. *v.* (**toweled, towelled**) to rub dry with a towel. **tow•el•ing,** *n.* soft cloth used for making towels.

tow•er ['tauə] 1. *n.* tall building; **control t.** = tall airport building containing the control room; **t. of strength** = very strong and sympathetic person. 2. *v.* to rise very high (**above**). **tow•er•ing,** *adj.* (a) very tall. (b) very great (rage).

town [taun] *n.* place where people live and work, with houses, stores, offices and factories (as opposed to the country); **t. clerk** = administrative official in a town who keeps records and issues licenses. **t. council** = elected committee which runs a town; **t. hall** = offices of the town council; public building used for meetings; **t. planning** = science of planning the development of a town; *inf.* **to go to t. over sth** = to spend a lot of money/time on sth; *inf.* **to paint the t. red** = to have a party; celebrate. **town•ie,** *n. inf.* person who lives in a town. **town house,** *n.* (a) house in a town or city. (b) expensive house in a city for one family. **towns•folk,** *n. pl.* people who live in a town. **town•ship,** *n.* (a) (*in the United States and Canada*) small town and the administrative area around it. (b) (*in South Africa*) area where black people live near a large town. **towns•man, townswoman,** *n.* (*pl.* **-men, -women**) person who lives in a town. **towns•peo•ple,** *n. pl.* people who live in a town.

tox•e•mi•a, *Brit.* **tox•ae•mi•a** [tɒk'siːmɪə] blood poisoning. **tox•ic** ['tɒksɪk] *adj.* poisonous. **tox•ic•i•ty,** *n.* being toxic. **tox•i•col•o•gist** [tɒksɪ'kɒlədʒɪst] *n.* scientist who studies poisons. **tox•i•col•o•gy,** *n.* scientific study of poisons. **tox•in,** *n.* poisonous substance.

æ back, ɑ: farm, ɒ: top, aɪ pipe, au how, aie fire, auə flower, ɔ: bought, ɔɪ toy, ə fed, eəhair, eɪ take, ə afraid, əu boat, əuə lower, ɜ: word, i: heap, ɪ hit, ɪə hear, u: school, u book, ʌ but, b back, d dog, ð then, dʒ just, f fog, g go, h hand, j yes, k catch, l last, m mix, n nut, ŋ sing, p penny, r round, s some, ʃ short, t too, tʃ chop, θ thing, v voice, w was, z zoo, ʒ treasure

tox•oph•i•ly [tɒk'sɒfɪlɪ] n. (formal) archery.

toy [tɔɪ] 1. adj. & n. thing which children play with. 2. v. **to t. with** = (i) to eat (food) reluctantly; (ii) to turn over (an idea) in your mind.

toy•shop, n. shop which sells toys.

trace [treɪs] 1. n. (a) **traces** = set of tracks/footprints left by an animal. (b) small amount; **he's vanished without a t.** = leaving nothing behind to show where he has gone. (c) **traces** = straps by which a horse is attached to a carriage; **to kick over the traces** = to rebel (against authority). 2. v. (a) to follow the tracks left by (sth); to try to find where (s.o./sth) is. (b) to copy (a picture/a map) by placing a piece of thin transparent paper over it and drawing on it. **trace•a•ble**, adj. which can be traced. **trace el•e•ment**, n. chemical element of which a tiny amount is needed by a plant or animal to grow properly. **trac•er**, n. type of bullet/shell which leaves a visible stream of sparks/smoke as it flies. **trac•er•y**, n. delicate stone patterns holding the glass in a church window. **trac•ing**, n. drawing done by tracing; **t. paper** = thin transparent paper for tracing drawings.

tra•che•a [trə'kiːə] n. windpipe. **tra•che•ot•o•my** [trækɪ'ɒtəmɪ] n. operation to make a hole in the windpipe from the outside of the neck.

tra•cho•ma [trə'kəumə] n. eye disease caused by a virus.

track ['træk] 1. n. (a) footprints of animal/marks of wheels, etc.; **the police are on the t. of the criminal** = they are following him; **to keep t. of** = to keep an account/to keep oneself informed of; **to lose t. of sth** = not to know where it is any longer; **to make tracks for home** = to set off for home. (b) path; **on the wrong t.** = working wrongly/making a wrong assumption. (c) course for racing; **t. events** = running competitions in an athletics tournament; **t. suit** = type of warm two-piece suit worn by sportsmen when practising; **t. shoes** = running shoes with spikes in the soles; **he has a good t. record** = he has been very successful in the past. (d) line of rails for a train, streetcar, etc.; inf. **to have a one-t. mind** = to think on only one thing/have only one interest. (e) endless belt on which a caterpillar tractor/tank, etc., runs. (f) part of a magnetic tape on which sth can be recorded. (g) set of grooves on a phonograph record, etc. 2. v. to follow (an animal); to follow (a moving subject) with a camera. **track•ball, track•er•ball**, n. device that consists of a small ball mounted on bearings within a socket, which can be freely rotated by the fingers to control a cursor on a computer monitor. **track down**, v. to follow and catch (an animal/a criminal). **track•er**, n. animal/person who follows tracks. **track•less**, adj. with no paths.

tract [trækt] n. (a) wide stretch of countryside. (b) short (religious or political) pamphlet. (c) system of organs in the body which are linked together.

trac•ta•ble ['træktəbl] adj. which can be tamed/made to do what is necessary. **trac•ta•bil•i•ty** [træktə'bɪlɪtɪ] n. being tractable.

trac•tion ['trækʃn] n. (a) pulling force. (b) pulling (a broken leg, etc.) up with pulleys.

trac•tor ['træktə] n. farm vehicle with large back wheels for pulling a plow, etc.; **t. feed** = paper feed in a printer, where the paper is pulled by sprocket wheels.

trade [treɪd] 1. n. (a) business; buying and selling. (b) people who buy and sell a particular type of goods/who work in a particular industry. (c) job. 2. v. (a) to carry on a business. (b) to exchange (sth for sth). **trade in**, v. to exchange an old car, etc., as part payment for a new one. **trade-in**, n. exchange of an old car, etc., for a newer one. **trade•mark**, n. particular name, symbol, etc., which has been officially registered by a manufacturer and which cannot be copied by other manufacturers. **trade name**, n. name, often registered as a trademark, used by a manufacturer to distinguish his products from those of competitors. **trade on**, v. to exploit/to profit from. **trad•er**, n. person who buys and sells. **trades•man**, n. (pl. -men) person engaged in a trade. **trades•peo•ple**, n. pl. people engaged in a trade. **trade un•ion**, n. labor union which groups together workers in a particular trade. **trade un•ion•ist**, n. member of a trade union. **trade wind**, n. tropical wind blowing toward the equator. **trad•ing**, n. business.

tra•di•tion [trə'dɪʃn] n. customs/habits/stories which are passed from generation to generation. **tra•di•tion•al**, adj. referring to tradition. **tra•di•tion•al•ist**, n. person who does things in a traditional way. **tra•di•tion•al•ly**, adv. according to tradition.

tra•duce [trə'djuːs] v. (formal) to slander (s.o.).

traf•fic ['træfɪk] 1. n. (a) movement of vehicles, esp. cars/trucks/buses, etc., on the roads; **t. jam** = blockage of traffic on a road; **t. circle** = place where several roads meet and traffic moves in a circle; **air t.** = aircraft flying. (b) illegal international business. 2. v. (**trafficked**) to deal in (drugs) illegally. **traf•fic lights**, n. red, green and amber lights which regulate the movement of traffic. **traf•fick•er**, n. person who traffics (in drugs).

trag•e•dy ['trædʒədɪ] *n.* play/motion picture/story with a sad story; unhappy event. **tra•ge•di•an** [trə'dʒiːdɪən] *n.* person who acts in tragedies. **trag•ic**, *adj.* referring to tragedy; very sad. **trag•i•cal•ly**, *adv.* very sadly.

trail [treɪl] 1. *n.* (a) tracks left by an animal. (b) path. (c) thing which stretches a long way behind. 2. *v.* (a) to let (sth) drag behind you. (b) to follow the tracks of (an animal/a person). (c) **trailing plant** = one which hangs or creeps along the ground. **trail•er**, *n.* (a) vehicle pulled behind a car, truck, etc. for transporting goods, etc. (b) van with beds, tables, washing and cooking facilities, etc. which can be towed by a car. (c) short motion picture showing parts of a full-length motion picture as an advertisement.

train [treɪn] 1. *n.* (a) series of cars pulled by a railroad engine. (b) series of events; line of animals carrying goods; retinue (of an important person); **t. of thought** = series of thoughts following one another. (c) long fuse (to light an explosive). (d) part of a dress which hangs down and trails along the ground at the back. 2. *v.* (a) to teach (s.o./an animal) to do sth; to learn how to do sth. (b) to practice (for a sport). (c) to point (a rifle/a telescope) at sth. **train•a•ble**, *adj.* which can be trained. **train•ee** [treɪ'niː] *n.* person who is being taught. **train•er**, *n.* (a) person who trains animals/sportsmen. (b) small aircraft in which you learn to fly. **train•ing**, *n.* action of being taught/of practicing; **in t.** = (i) practicing (for a sport); (ii) fit/in good physical condition.

traipse [treɪps] *v. inf.* to walk about in an aimless, idle way.

trait [treɪ(t)] *n.* particular point of s.o.'s character.

trai•tor ['treɪtə] *n.* person who sides with the enemy/who gives away secrets to the enemy. **trai•tor•ous**, *adj.* like a traitor.

tra•jec•to•ry [trə'dʒektrɪ] *n.* curved course taken by sth which has been thrown through the air.

tram [træm] *n. Brit.* streetcar. **tram•line**, *n. pl. Brit.* system of rails along which a tram runs.

tram•mel ['træml] 1. *n.* (a) (*also* **trammel net**) type of fishing net. (b) thing which prevents you from doing sth. 2. *v.* (**trammeled, trammelled**) (*formal*) to prevent (s.o.) from doing sth.

tramp [træmp] 1. *n.* (a) noise of feet hitting the ground heavily. (b) long energetic walk. (c) person who has nowhere to live and walks from place to place begging for food or money. 2. *v.* (a) to walk heavily. (b) to trample on (sth); to crush (grapes) by stepping on them to extract the juice. **tramp steam•er**, *n.* cargo boat which goes from port to port, but not on a regular route.

tram•ple ['træmpl] *v.* (**on**) to crush (by walking).

tram•po•line ['træmpəliːn] *n.* frame with a large sheet of elastic material on which you can bounce/perform exercises, etc.

trance [trɑːns] *n.* state when you are not fully conscious, and do not notice what is going on.

tran•quil ['træŋkwɪl] *adj.* calm/peaceful. **tran•quil•li•ty, tranquility** [træŋ'kwɪlɪtɪ] *n.* calm. **tran•quil•ize** ['træŋkwɪlaɪz] *v.* to make (s.o.) calm (by giving drugs). **tran•quil•iz•er**, *n.* drug which makes a person calm. **tran•quil•ly, tranquily** *adv.* in a tranquil way.

trans- [trænz] *prefix meaning* through/across.

trans•act [træn'zækt] *v.* to carry out (a piece of business). **trans•ac•tion**, *n.* piece of business; **cash t.** = piece of business paid for in cash; **transactions** = published report of what takes place at a meeting of a learned/scientific society.

trans•at•lan•tic [trænzət'læntɪk] *adj.* across the Atlantic; from the other side of the Atlantic; involving countries on both sides of the Atlantic.

trans•ceiv•er ['trænzsiːvə] *n.* transmitter and receiver.

tran•scend [træn'send] *v.* to go beyond/further than sth. **tran•scend•ent**, *adj.* which transcends. **tran•scen•den•tal** [trænsən'dentl] *adj.* which rises above the level of ordinary thought or reasoning.

trans•con•ti•nen•tal [trænzkɒntɪ'nentl] *adj.* across a continent.

tran•scribe [træn'skraɪb] *v.* to write out the text (of sth which is heard); to write out in full (what has been written down in shorthand); to rewrite (a piece of music) for another instrument than the one for which it was originally written. **tran•script** ['trænskrɪpt] *n.* written text of what was said (on the radio/at a trial, etc.). **tran•scrip•tion**, *n.* act of transcribing.

tran•sept ['trænsept] *n.* one of the two branches at right angles to the nave and choir in a cross-shaped church.

trans-fat•ty ac•id [trænz'fætɪ 'æsɪd] *n.* poly-

æ back, ɑː farm, ɒ top, aɪ pipe, aʊ how, aie fire, aʊə flower, ɔː bought, ɔɪ toy, e fed, eəhair, eɪ take, ə afraid, əʊ boat, əʊə lower, vː word, iː heap, ɪ hit, ɪə hear, uː school, ʊ book, ʌ but, b back, d dog, ð then, dʒ just, f fog, g go, h hand, j yes, k catch, l last, m mix, n nut, ŋ sing, p penny, r round, s some, ʃ short, t too, tʃ chop, θ thing, v voice, w was, z zoo, ʒ treasure

unsaturated fatty acid, used in manufacturing margarine.

trans•fer 1. *n.* ['trænsfə] (a) movement of sth/s.o. to a new place. (b) design which can be stuck on to a surface. 2. *v.* [træns'fɜː] (**transferred**) to move (sth/s.o.) to another place. **trans•fer•a•ble** [trænz'fɜːrəbl] *adj.* which can be transferred; **not t.** = (ticket) which can only be used by the person to whom it was issued. **trans•fer•ence,** *n.* act of transferring.

trans•fig•ure [trænz'fɪgə] *v.* to change for the better (the appearance of sth/s.o.). **trans•fig•u•ra•tion,** *n.* act of transfiguring.

trans•fix [trænz'fɪks] *v.* to prevent (s.o.) from moving (by giving a shock).

trans•form [trænz'fɔːm] *v.* to change completely. **trans•for•ma•tion** [trænzfə'meɪʃn] *n.* complete change of appearance. **trans•form•er** [trænz'fɔːmə] *n.* apparatus for changing the voltage of an alternating electric current.

trans•fuse [trænz'fjuːz] *v.* to move liquid from one container to another. **trans•fu•sion** [trænz'fjuːʒn] *n.* moving of liquid from one container to another; **blood t.** = giving blood to a sick patient.

trans•gress [trænz'gres] *v.* (*formal*) to go against (a rule). **trans•gres•sion,** *n.* act of transgressing. **trans•gres•sor,** *n.* person who transgresses.

tran•ship [træns'ʃɪp] *v. see* **trans•ship.**

tran•sience ['trænzɪəns] *n.* state of not being permanent. **tran•sient** ['trænzɪənt] *adj. & n.* which will not last; **transients** = people who stay in a hotel for a short time.

tran•sis•tor [træn'zɪstə] *n.* (a) device made of semi-conductors which can increase an electric current. (b) **t. (radio)** = small pocket radio which uses transistors. **tran•sis•tor•ize,** *v.* to put transistors into (sth).

tran•sit ['trænzɪt] 1. *n.* (a) movement of passengers/goods (on the way to another destination). (b) moving of a planet across the face of the sun or other planet. 2. *v.* (*formal*) to go across. **tran•si•tion** [træn'zɪʃn] *n.* movement between one state or condition and another. **tran•si•tion•al,** *adj.* referring to transition. **tran•si•tive** ['trænzɪtɪv] *adj.* (verb) which has an object.

tran•si•to•ry ['trænzɪtrɪ] *adj.* which does not last for long.

trans•late [trænz'leɪt] *v.* (a) to put (words) into another language. (b) to move (a bishop) to another see. **trans•lat•a•ble,** *adj.* which can be translated. **trans•la•tion** [trænz'leɪʃn] *n.* text which has been translated; action of translating; **simultaneous t.** = translating directly into another language what a speaker is saying. **trans•la•tor,** *n.* person who translates.

trans•lit•er•ate [trænz'lɪtəreɪt] *v.* to put (words) into the letters of a different alphabet. **trans•lit•er•a•tion,** *n.* act of transliterating.

trans•lu•cent [trænz'luːsnt] *adj.* which light can pass through, but which you cannot see through. **trans•lu•cence,** *n.* being translucent.

trans•mi•gra•tion [trænzmaɪ'greɪʃn] *n.* moving of a soul from a dead body to a living one.

trans•mit [trænz'mɪt] *v.* (**transmitted**) (a) to pass (from one person to another). (b) to send out by radio/TV. **trans•mis•sion** [trænz'mɪʃn] *n.* (a) passing (of disease) from one person to another. (b) sending out by radio/TV; a radio/TV broadcast. (c) (*in a car*) series of moving parts which pass the power from the engine to the wheels. **trans•mit•ter,** *n.* apparatus for sending out radio/TV signals.

trans•mog•ri•fy [trænz'mɒgrɪfaɪ] *v.* to change (sth) totally, usu. grotesquely.

trans•mute [trænz'mjuːt] *v.* to make (sth) change its shape or substance. **trans•mu•ta•tion,** *n.* act of transmuting.

tran•som ['trænsəm] *n.* (a) cross beam in a window; beam across the top of a door. (b) stern piece of a boat.

trans•par•en•cy [træns'pærənsɪ] *n.* (a) being transparent. (b) photograph which is printed on transparent film so that it can be projected onto a screen. **trans•par•ent,** *adj.* (a) which you can see through. (b) obvious (lie). **trans•par•ent•ly,** *adv.* obviously.

tran•spire [træn'spaɪə] *v.* (a) to happen. (b) to pass moisture through the surface of the skin/of a leaf, etc. **tran•spi•ra•tion** [trænspɪ'reɪʃn] *n.* act of transpiring.

trans•plant 1. *n.* ['trɑːnsplɑːnt] (a) act of taking an organ from one person and grafting it into another's body. (b) plant which is moved to another place to grow. 2. *v.* [træns'plɑːnt] (a) to graft (an organ) into s.o.'s body. (b) to plant (plants) in another place where they will grow permanently.

trans•port 1. *n.* ['trænspɔːt] (a) movement of goods/people; means of moving goods/people; **public t. system** = system of buses/subways/streetcars for moving the public. (b) ship/aircraft which carries goods or soldiers. (c) great emotion. 2. *v.* [træn'spɔːt] (a) to move (goods/people) from one place to another. (b) **transported with joy** = very happy. (c) (*old*) to send (a criminal) to a prison in a colony. **trans•port•a•ble,** *adj.* which can be transported. **trans•por•ta•tion** [trænspɔː'teɪʃn] *n.* (a) movement of goods/people; means of moving goods/people. (b) (*old*) sending of a

criminal to a prison in a colony.
trans•port•er [træn'spɔːtə] *n.* large truck
for carrying large loads; **t. bridge** = platform
which is suspended from a bridge and moves
across a river on cables, carrying cars, etc.

trans•pose [træn'spəuz] *v.* to make (two
things) change places. **trans•po•si•tion**
[trænspə'zɪʃn] *n.* act of transposing.

trans•ship [træns'ʃɪp] *v.* (**transshipped**) to
move (goods) from one ship/truck/railroad
car to another.

tran•sub•stan•ti•a•tion [trænsʌbstænʃɪ-
'eɪʃn] *n.* belief that the wine and bread become
the blood and body of Christ at the Communion service.

trans•u•ran•ic [trænzju'rænɪk] *adj.* (element)
which has atoms heavier than those of uranium.

trans•verse ['trænzvɜːs] *adj.* which lies across.

trans•ves•tite [trænz'vestaɪt] *n.* person who
wants to wear the clothes of the opposite sex.
trans•ves•tism [trænz'vestɪzəm] *n.* desire to
wear the clothes of the opposite sex.

trap [træp] 1. *n.* (a) device to catch an animal;
plan to catch (s.o.)/to take (s.o.) by surprise;
radar t. = device used by police to catch a motorist who is driving too fast. (b) **t. door** = door
in a floor/in a ceiling. (c) bend in a waste pipe
which is filled with water, and so stops unpleasant smells coming back up the pipe from
a sewer. (d) *Sl.* mouth. 2. *v.* (**trapped**) to catch.
trap•per, *n.* person who catches wild animals for their fur.

tra•peze [træ'piːz] *n.* bar which hangs from
ropes, and which acrobats use in a circus.

tra•pe•zi•um [træ'piːzɪəm] *n.* (a) four-sided
shape, where no two sides are parallel. (b)
Brit. trapezoid. (c) little bone in the wrist.
trap•e•zoid ['træpɪzɔɪd] *n.* (a) four-sided
shape, where two of the sides are parallel. (b)
Brit. trapezium.

trap•pings ['træpɪŋz] *n. pl.* orna-
ments/clothes/decorations which are suitable
for a particular occasion.

trash [træʃ] *n.* things to be thrown away; refuse.
trash can, *n.* container for household trash.
trash•y, *adj.* (**-ier, -iest**) very bad/completely
worthless.

trau•ma ['trɔːmə] *n.* (a) terrible shock/unpleas-
ant experience which affects your mental outlook. (b) injury. **trau•mat•ic** [trɔː'mætɪk]
adj. which gives a terrible and unpleasant
shock. **trau•mat•i•cal•ly,** *adv.* in a trau-
matic way.

trav•el ['trævl] 1. *n.* moving from one country
to another/from one place to another. 2. *v.*
(**traveled, travelled**) (a) to move from one
country to another/from one place to another.
(b) to be a sales representative (in an area).
trav•el a•gen•cy, *n.* office which arranges
tickets/hotel reservations, etc., for you when
you are making a journey. **trav•el a•gent,**
n. person who runs or works in a travel
agency. **trav•el•er,** *n.* person who is traveling from one place to another; **traveler's
checks** = checks which you can buy at your
bank and which can then be cashed in a foreign country. **trav•e•logue,** *n.* motion picture describing travel.

trav•erse 1. *n.* ['trævɜːs] (a) crossing. (b) thing
which crosses another. (c) (*in mountaineering*)
crossing of a dangerous flat rock face. 2. *v.*
[trə'vɜːs] to cross.

trav•es•ty ['trævəstɪ] 1. *n.* parody; ridiculous
copy/poor imitation. 2. *v.* to imitate (sth) in a
ridiculous way.

trawl [trɔːl] 1. *n.* long net shaped like a bag,
pulled at sea by a trawler. 2. *v.* to fish with a
trawl. **trawl•er,** *n.* fishing boat which uses a
trawl.

tray [treɪ] *n.* (a) flat board for carrying
glasses/cups and saucers, etc. (b) flat open
box/basket for papers (as on a desk).

treach•er•y ['tretʃərɪ] *n.* act of betray-
ing/being a traitor to your friends, etc.
treach•er•ous, *adv.* (a) likely to betray. (b)
dangerous. **treach•er•ous•ly,** *adv.* in a
treacherous way.

trea•cle ['triːkl] *n.* thick dark-brown syrup
produced when sugar is refined. **trea•cly,**
adj. thick and sticky like treacle.

tread [tred] 1. *n.* (a) way of walking. (b) sound
of a footstep. (c) part of a step (on stairs/an escalator) on which you put your foot. (d) surface of a tire marked with a pattern of lines. 2.
v. (**trod** [trɒd]; **has trodden**) (a) to walk. (b) to
trample on/to crush with your feet; **to t. water**
= to keep afloat in water by moving your legs
up and down. **trea•dle** ['tredl] 1. *n.* foot
pedal which makes a machine turn. 2. *v.* to
push a treadle with the foot. **tread•mill,** *n.*
(a) device turned by people/animals as they
walk around a circular path or inside a large
wheel. (b) dull routine work.

trea•son ['triːzn] *n.* betraying your coun-
try/giving your country's secrets to the enemy.
trea•son•a•ble, *adj.* which can be considered as treason.

æ back, aː farm, ɒ top, aɪ pipe, aʊ how, aiə fire, aʊə flower, ɔː bought, ɔɪ toy, e fed, eəhair, eɪ take, ə
afraid, əʊ boat, əʊə lower, ɜː word, iː heap, ɪ hit, ɪə hear, uː school, ʊ book, ʌ but, b back, d dog, ð then,
dʒ just, f fog, g go, h hand, j yes, k catch, l last, m mix, n nut, ŋ sing, p penny, r round, s some, ʃ short, t
too, tʃ chop, θ thing, v voice, w was, z zoo, ʒ treasure

treas•ure ['treʒə] 1. *n.* (a) store of money/jewels/gold, etc.; **t.-trove** = buried treasure found by accident which then becomes the property of the state; **t. hunt** = game where you follow clues from place to place until you find a prize. (b) thing which is highly valued. 2. *v.* to value (sth) very highly. **treas•ur•er**, *n.* person who looks after the finances of a club, etc. **treas•ur•y**, *n.* (a) place where treasure is kept. (b) government department which deals with the nation's money.

treat [tri:t] 1. *n.* special meal/outing, etc., which should give pleasure; **a t. in store** = a special future surprise; **this is my t.** = I am paying the bill. 2. *v.* (a) to deal with; to write about (a subject). (b) **to t. s.o. to** = to give (s.o.) a special meal/outing as a surprise gift. (c) to look after (a sick person) or deal with (a disease). (d) to pass (a substance) through a certain process. (e) (*formal*) to negotiate (**with** an enemy). **treat•ment**, *n.* (a) way of dealing with sth. (b) way of looking after a sick person or dealing with a disease.

trea•tise ['tri:tɪz] *n.* long learned piece of writing on a subject.

trea•ty ['tri:tɪ] *n.* (a) agreement between two or more countries. (b) any agreement, as between private people.

tre•ble ['trebl] 1. *n.* voice which sings high-pitched notes; high-pitched musical instrument. 2. *adj.* (a) three times as large. (b) high (voice/note); **t. clef** = sign in music showing that the notes are in a high pitch. 3. *v.* to increase by three times. **tre•bly**, *adv.* three times as much.

tree [tri:] *n.* (a) large plant with a wooden stem and branches. (b) **family t.** = diagram showing the development of a family over a long period of time. **tree creep•er**, *n.* small bird which creeps up the trunk of trees, looking for insects. **tree•less**, *adj.* with no trees. **tree line**, *n.* line at a certain altitude above which trees do not grow. **treen**, *n.* (*no pl.*) small spoons/rings, etc., made of wood. **tree•top**, *n.* top of a tree.

tre•foil ['tri:fɔɪl] *n.* design/leaf shaped in three equal parts like that of a clover.

trek [trek] 1. *n.* long and difficult journey. 2. *v.* (**trekked**) to make a long and difficult journey.

trel•lis ['trelɪs] *n.* (*pl.* -es) openwork fence made of thin pieces of wood in a crisscross pattern.

trem•ble ['trembl] 1. *n.* shaking/shuddering. 2. *v.* (a) to shake/to quiver. (b) to be very worried. **trem•bly**, *adj.* shaky/shaking.

tre•men•dous [trɪ'mendəs] *adj.* (a) enormous/very large. (b) wonderful. **tre•men•dous•ly**, *adv.* greatly.

trem•o•lo ['tremələʊ] *n.* (*pl.* -os) trembling note in music.

trem•or ['tremə] *n.* shaking; **earth t.** = slight earthquake.

trem•u•lous ['tremjʊləs] *adj.* shaking/quivering.

trench [trentʃ] 1. *n.* (*pl.* -es) long narrow ditch in the ground. 2. *v.* to dig a long narrow ditch. **trench coat**, *n.* belted waterproof coat.

trench•ant ['trentʃənt] *adj.* sharp/biting (remark); vigorous (style).

trench•er ['trentʃə] *n.* (*old*) wooden plate for food. **trench•er•man**, *n.* person who eats a lot.

trend [trend] *n.* general tendency. **trend•i•ness**, *n.* being trendy. **trend-set•ter**, *n.* person who sets the fashion. **trend•y**. 1. *adj.* (-ier, -iest) *inf.* following fashion; fashionable. 2. *n. inf.* person who follows fashion.

tre•pan, trephine [trɪ'pæn, trɪ'fi:n] 1. *n.* saw for cutting out round pieces of bone. 2. *v.* (**trepanned**) to cut a round piece of bone out of (esp. the skull).

trep•i•da•tion [trepɪ'deɪʃn] *n.* anxiety.

tres•pass ['trespəs] *v.* (**on**) to go into or onto s.o.'s property without permission. **tres•pass•er**, *n.* person who trespasses.

tres•ses ['tresɪz] *n. pl.* long hair.

tres•tle ['tresl] *n.* support made of a horizontal bar supported by four transverse legs; **t. table** = table with a top resting on a trestle.

tri- [traɪ] *prefix meaning* three.

tri•ad ['traɪæd] *n.* group of three people or things.

tri•al ['traɪəl] *n.* (a) court case to judge a criminal; **to stand t.** = to appear in court. (b) test; **on t.** = being tested to see if it is acceptable; **t. and error** = testing and rejecting various things until you find the one which works.

tri•an•gle ['traɪæŋgl] *n.* (a) geometrical shape with three sides and three angles; **eternal t.** = situation where s.o. is in love with s.o. who is in love with a third person. (b) musical instrument made of a piece of metal bent into the shape of a triangle. **tri•an•gu•lar** [traɪ'æŋgjʊlə] *adj.* shaped like a triangle. **tri•an•gu•la•tion** [traɪæŋgjʊ'leɪʃn] *n.* method of measuring land to produce maps.

tribe [traɪb] *n.* (a) group of people ruled by a chief. (b) *inf.* large family/group. **trib•al**, *adj.* referring to a tribe. **trib•al•ism**, *n.* customs and beliefs of tribes. **tribes•man**, *n.* (*pl.* -men) member of a tribe.

trib•u•la•tion [trɪbjʊ'leɪʃn] *n.* (*formal*) great misery.

tri•bu•nal [traɪ'bju:nl] *n.* court of justice.

trib•une ['trɪbjuːn] n. leader who upholds the rights of the people.

trib•ute ['trɪbjuːt] n. (a) money paid to a conqueror by people who have been conquered. (b) words/gifts, etc., to show thanks/praise; **to pay t. to** = to praise. **trib•u•tar•y.** 1. adj. (person) who pays tribute. 2. n. river which flows into a larger river.

trice [traɪs] n. **in a t.** = very rapidly.

tri•cen•ten•ni•al [traɪsen'tenɪəl] n. anniversary of 300 years.

tri•chol•o•gy [trɪk'bɪlədʒɪ] n. study of the diseases of the hair. **tri•chol•o•gist,** n. person who studies the diseases of the hair.

trick [trɪk] 1. n. (a) clever action which can deceive/confuse s.o.; **to play a t. on s.o.** = to deceive/confuse s.o.; inf. **tricks of the trade** = clever dealings which are associated with a certain trade; **card tricks/magic tricks** = clever games with cards/with hats, handkerchiefs, etc., to amuse an audience; inf. **that should do the t.** = should do what is wanted/should make it work; inf. **he doesn't miss a t.** = he is very alert. (b) (in card games) points won at the end of a round. 2. adj. which deceives; **t. question** = one which is intended to cause s.o. to make a mistake. 3. v. to deceive/to confuse; **to t. s.o. into doing sth** = to deceive s.o. so that he does sth which he did not intend to do. **trick•er•y,** n. act of deceiving. **trick•i•ness,** n. being tricky. **trick•ster,** n. person who tricks, esp. s.o. who cheats. **trick•y,** adj. (-ier, -iest) (a) difficult/awkward. (b) inf. sly/deceitful/untrustworthy.

trick•le ['trɪkl] 1. n. small flow of water; **t. charger** = device which charges a car battery slowly. 2. v. to flow/move in a small quantity. **trick•le-down ef•fect,** n. supposed indirect benefit to the poor, claimed by some economists, that results from implementing economic policies that directly benefit the rich, as such policies may boost the economy generally.

tri•col•or ['trɪkələ] n. flag with three bands of color, esp. the national flag of France.

tri•cy•cle ['traɪsɪkl] n. three-wheeled pedal vehicle like a bicycle with two back wheels.

tri•dent ['traɪdənt] n. spear with three prongs.

tried [traɪd] v. see **try.**

tri•en•ni•al [traɪ'enɪəl] adj. happening every three years.

tri•er ['traɪə] n. person who tries.

tri•fle ['traɪfl] 1. n. (a) small insignificant thing. (b) small amount. (c) dessert made of cake/biscuits/jelly/jam/sherry and whipped cream. 2. v. (with) to play with/not to treat (sth) seriously. **tri•fler,** n. person who trifles with s.o./sth. **tri•fling,** adj. slight/very small.

trig•ger ['trɪgə] 1. n. small metal lever on a gun which you pull to fire it. 2. v. **to t. off** = to start (a series of things) happening. **trig•ger-hap•py,** adj. ready to shoot/ready to act quickly without thinking.

trig•o•nom•e•try [trɪgə'nɒmɪtrɪ] n. science which deals with the relationships between the sides and angles of triangles.

trike [traɪk] n. inf. tricycle.

tri•lat•er•al [traɪ'lætrəl] adj. with three sides.

tri•lin•gual [traɪ'lɪŋgwəl] adj. (person) who can speak three languages.

trill [trɪl] 1. n. (a) warbling song (like a bird). (b) (in music) two notes rapidly repeated. 2. v. to warble/to sing like a bird.

tril•lion ['trɪljən] n. (a) one and 12 zeros. (b) esp. Brit. one and 18 zeros.

tri•lo•bite ['traɪəbaɪt] n. ancient shellfish found in fossils.

tril•o•gy ['trɪlədʒɪ] n. novel/play in three separate related parts.

trim [trɪm] 1. n. (a) state of fitness or preparedness. (b) cutting (of hair/bush, etc.). (c) decoration (on a car). 2. adj. (trimmer, trimmest) neat. 3. v. (trimmed) (a) to cut (sth) so that it is tidy. (b) to cut back; to reduce. (c) to ornament/to decorate. (d) (on a sailboat) to put sails into the best position. (e) to change your (political) opinions to fit the current popular trend. **trim•ly,** adv. in a trim way. **trim•mer,** n. person/device which trims; **hedge t.** = electric cutter for hedges. **trim•ming,** n. (a) ornament added to decorate sth; **roast pork with all the trimmings** = with the usual sauces and vegetables. (b) **trimmings** = pieces cut off (a hedge, etc.) when it is being trimmed. **trim•ness,** n. being trim.

tri•ma•ran ['traɪməræn] n. yacht with three parallel hulls.

tri•ni•tro•tol•u•ene [traɪnaɪtrəʊ'tɒljuːn] n. high explosive/TNT.

trin•i•ty ['trɪnɪtɪ] n. (a) group of three. (b) **the T.** = the three persons in the Christian God—the Father, Son and Holy Ghost.

trin•ket ['trɪŋkɪt] n. cheap ornament.

tri•o ['triːəʊ] n. (pl. -os) (a) piece of music for three instruments. (b) three musicians; group of three people.

trip [trɪp] 1. n. (a) journey; **day t.** = journey lasting one day. (b) switch which activates a motor/light, etc. (c) *Sl.* trance caused by drugs. 2. *v.* (**tripped**) (a) **to t. along** = to go along with light footsteps. (b) to catch your foot so that you stagger and fall. (c) to set off (a switch). (d) *Sl.* to go into a trance induced by drugs. **trip•me•ter,** *n.* dial on a car dashboard which shows how far you go on one particular journey. **trip•per,** *n.* person on a short (usu. one day) trip. **trip up,** *v.* **to t. s.o. up** = (i) to make s.o. fall down; (ii) to force s.o. to make a mistake. **trip•wire,** *n.* wire stretched low above the ground, which, when you touch it, sets off a gun/camera, etc.

tri•par•tite [traɪˈpɑːtaɪt] *adj.* with three parts; (agreement) between three countries.

tripe [traɪp] *n.* (a) part of a cow's/sheep's stomach used as food. (b) *inf.* worthless speech or writing/nonsense.

tri•ple [ˈtrɪpl] 1. *adj.* made of three parts; three times as big. 2. *v.* to become three times as large; to make (sth) three times as large. **tri•plet,** *n.* (a) (*in music*) three notes played quickly together. (b) one of three children born at the same birth. **tri•plex,** *adj.* with three layers. **trip•li•cate,** *n.* **in t.** = in three copies.

tri•pod [ˈtraɪpɒd] *n.* stand with three legs.

trip•tych [ˈtrɪptɪk] *n.* religious picture formed of three parts, often placed on or above an altar.

trite [traɪt] *adj.* very ordinary/unexciting (remark). **trite•ly,** *adv.* in a trite way. **trite•ness,** *n.* being trite.

tri•umph [ˈtraɪəmf] 1. *n.* (a) great victory. (b) celebration of a victory. 2. *v.* (a) **to t. over s.o.** = to win a victory over s.o. (b) to show that you are very glad that you won a victory. **tri•um•phal** [traɪˈʌmfl] *adj.* referring to triumph; **t. arch** = archway set up to celebrate a victory. **tri•um•phant,** *adj.* victorious. **tri•um•phant•ly,** *adv.* in victory.

tri•um•vi•rate [traɪˈʌmvɪrət] *n.* group of three people who rule/manage.

triv•et [ˈtrɪvət] *n.* (a) small three-legged stand for a kettle, pot, etc. over a fire. (b) stand for putting under a hot plate, pot, etc. to protect a table.

triv•i•al [ˈtrɪvɪəl] *adj.* not important; ordinary. **triv•i•a,** *n. pl.* unimportant details. **triv•i•al•i•ty** [trɪvɪˈælɪti] *n.* being unimportant; unimportant detail. **triv•i•al•ize,** *v.* to make (sth) trivial. **triv•i•al•ly,** *adv.* in a trivial way.

tro•chee [ˈtrəʊkiː] *n.* poetic measure made of one strong beat followed by a weak one. **tro•cha•ic** [trəʊˈkeɪɪk] *adj.* referring to trochee.

trod, trodden [trɒd, ˈtrɒdn] *v. see* **tread.**

trog•lo•dyte [ˈtrɒglədaɪt] *n.* person who lives in a cave.

troi•ka [ˈtrɔɪkə] *n.* (a) Russian carriage pulled by three horses. (b) three people holding power together (usu.) in Communist countries).

troll [trəʊl] *n.* (*in Scandinavia*) bad-tempered dwarf.

trol•ley [ˈtrɒlɪ] *n.* trolley car. **trol•ley car,** *n.* car which works on electricity taken from overhead wires by contact poles.

trol•lop [ˈtrɒləp] *n.* immoral woman.

trom•bone [trɒmˈbəʊn] *n.* brass wind instrument with a sliding tube. **trom•bon•ist,** *n.* person who plays the trombone.

troop [truːp] 1. *n.* (a) group of people. (b) group of Boy Scouts. (c) **troops** = soldiers; **t. ship/t. train** = ship/train which carries soldiers. 2. *v.* to move in a large group. **troop•er,** *n.* (a) cavalry soldier. (b) state police officer.

tro•phy [ˈtrəʊfɪ] *n.* (a) prize given for winning a competition. (b) thing taken from the enemy and kept as a prize.

trop•ic [ˈtrɒpɪk] *n.* (a) **T. of Cancer/of Capricorn** = two imaginary lines running around the earth, parallel to the equator, and about 23° north/south of it. (b) **the tropics** = the hot areas of the world lying between these two imaginary lines. **trop•i•cal,** *adj.* very hot; (plant, etc.) growing in the tropics.

tro•pism [ˈtrɒpɪzəm] *n.* growth of a plant towards or away from sth.

trop•o•sphere [ˈtrɒpəsfɪə] *n.* layer of atmosphere between the surface of the earth and the stratosphere.

trot [ˈtrɒt] 1. *n.* running with short regular steps; **they broke into a t.** = started to run. 2. *v.* (**trotted**) to run with short regular steps; *inf.* **to t. out** = to produce or bring out for display, etc. **trot•ter,** *n.* pig's foot cooked for food.

troth [trəʊθ] *n.* (*old*) promise.

trou•ba•dour [ˈtruːbəduːə] *n.* wandering medieval singer.

trou•ble [ˈtrʌbl] 1. *n.* (a) misfortune. (b) problem/difficult situation; **it's just asking for t.** = that type of behavior will simply cause problems for you; **he's in t. with the police** = has been accused by the police of a crime; **to get s.o. into t.** = (i) to cause s.o. to be accused of doing sth wrong; (ii) to make s.o. pregnant. (c) care which is put into an action. (d) illness; mechanical defect. 2. *v.* (a) to worry (s.o.). (b) to create problems for (s.o.); to bother (s.o.). (c) to bother (**to do sth**). **trou•ble•mak•er,** *n.* person who creates problems/who stirs up unrest. **trou•ble•shoot•er,** *n.* person whose job is to sort out problems. **trou•ble•some,** *adj.* causing trouble. **trou•ble spot,** *n.* area where trouble is likely to occur.

trough [trɒf] *n.* (a) large container for animal food or drink; **horse t./water t.** = container for water for horses to drink. (b) low place; low point between two peaks (on a graph); low-pressure area in the atmosphere; low part of the sea between two waves.

trounce [traʊns] *v.* to beat (s.o.) soundly.

troupe [truːp] *n.* company (of actors/circus clowns, etc.). **troup•er,** *n.* member of a troupe.

trou•sers ['traʊzəz] *n. pl.* **(pair of) t.** = outer clothes which cover the legs and the lower part of the body.

trous•seau ['truːsəʊ] *n.* clothes and linen collected by the bride before her wedding.

trout [traʊt] *n.* (*pl.* **trout**) type of edible freshwater fish.

trove [trəʊv] *adj. see* **treas•ure.**

trow•el ['traʊəl] *n.* (a) small hand spade used in gardening. (b) tool with a flat blade used for spreading mortar between bricks.

troy [trɔɪ] *n.* **t. weight** = system for weighing gold/silver/precious gems.

tru•ant ['truːənt] *adj. & n.* (child) who is absent from school without permission. **tru•an•cy** ['truːənsɪ] *n.* being away from school without permission.

truce [truːs] *n.* period when two armies/enemies, etc., agree to stop fighting temporarily.

truck [trʌk] *n.* (a) large motor vehicle for carrying goods, etc. (b) small hand cart. (c) **to have no t. with** = not to have anything to do with. (d) fruit and vegetables grown for sale in the market. **truck•driv•er, trucker,** *n.* driver of a truck. **truck•ing,** *n.* transport of goods, etc. by truck. **truck•load,** *n.* amount carried in a truck.

truck•le ['trʌkl] *v.* to give in (**to** s.o.) weakly. **truck•le bed,** *n.* (*also* **trundle bed**) low bed which can be pushed under another bed when not in use.

truc•u•lence ['trʌkjʊləns] *n.* being truculent. **truc•u•lent,** *adj.* threatening/fierce; eager to quarrel. **truc•u•lent•ly,** *adv.* in a truculent way.

trudge [trʌdʒ] 1. *n.* tiring walk. 2. *v.* to walk heavily.

true [truː] 1. *adj.* (-**er,** -**est**) (a) correct. (b) real. (c) correctly adjusted; **t. north** = north toward the north pole, and not the magnetic north. (d) faithful. 2. *adv.* correctly; **to come t.** = to happen as forecast. 3. *n.* **out of t.** = not quite straight/not correctly adjusted. **true-blue,**

adj. totally loyal. **true•ness,** *n.* being true. **tru•ly,** *adv.* really; **yours t.** = ending of a slightly formal letter.

truf•fle ['trʌfl] *n.* (a) type of round black or white edible fungus found under the earth. (b) soft chocolate-covered candy (usu. flavored with rum, champagne, etc.).

trug [trʌg] *n.* (*esp. Brit.*) long shallow basket for picking flowers.

tru•ism ['truːɪzəm] *n.* saying which is quite obviously true and therefore need not be said.

trump [trʌmp] 1. *n.* (*in card games*) suit which is chosen as being of higher value than the other suits; **t. card** = advantage which is kept ready for use to win an argument. 2. *v.* (a) **to t. a card** = to play a card of the suit which is trumps, and so win. (b) **to t. up** = to invent; **trumped-up charge** = false charge.

trump•er•y ['trʌmpərɪ] *adj.* (*formal*) useless and showy.

trum•pet ['trʌmpɪt] 1. *n.* brass musical instrument with three keys. 2. *v.* (a) to play the trumpet. (b) to make a loud noise. (c) (*of elephant*) to call. **trum•pet•er,** *n.* person who plays the trumpet.

trun•cat•ed [trʌn'keɪtɪd] *adj.* cut off; shortened.

trun•cheon ['trʌnʃn] *n.* short, heavy stick used by police officers.

trun•dle ['trʌndl] *v.* to roll/to push along (sth heavy). **trun•dle bed,** *n. see* **truck•le bed.**

trunk [trʌŋk] *n.* (a) main stem (of a tree); body (of a person). (b) long nose (of an elephant). (c) large box for sending/storing clothes, etc., in. (d) back part of a car (where luggage, etc. can be put). (e) **trunks** = men's shorts for swimming.

truss [trʌs] 1. *n.* (*pl.* -**es**) (a) beam holding up a bridge/a roof. (b) belt to support a hernia. 2. *v.* (a) to support with a truss. (b) to tie up (a chicken) ready for the oven; to tie up (a prisoner).

trust [trʌst] 1. *n.* (a) confidence that sth is correct/is good/will work well, etc.; **to take on t.** = without examining to see if it is all right. (b) hope. (c) responsibility. (d) passing of goods/money to s.o. who will look after it; **t. fund** = money/property, etc. administered by a trustee for the benefit of a person, company, or institution. (e) illegal grouping of business companies to eliminate competition, control prices, etc. 2. *v.* (a) to be sure of (s.o.); to have confidence in (s.o.); *inf.* **t. him to be late** = as usual, he is late. (b) to hope. **trust•ee** [trʌs'tiː]

æ **back,** ɑː **farm,** ɒ **top,** aɪ **pipe,** aʊ **how,** aɪə **fire,** aʊə **flower,** ɔː **bought,** ɔɪ **toy,** e **fed,** eə **hair,** eɪ **take,** ə **afraid,** əʊ **boat,** əʊə **lower,** ɜː **word,** iː **heap,** ɪ **hit,** ɪə **hear,** uː **school,** ʊ **book,** ʌ **but,** b **back,** d **dog,** ð **then,** dʒ **just,** f **fog,** g **go,** h **hand,** j **yes,** k **catch,** l **last,** m **mix,** n **nut,** ŋ **sing,** p **penny,** r **round,** s **some,** ʃ **short,** t **too,** tʃ **chop,** θ **thing,** v **voice,** w **was,** z **zoo,** ʒ **treasure**

n. person who has charge of money/property, etc. held in trust for a person/company, or institution. **trust•ee•ship,** *n.* position of trustee. **trust•ful, trust•ing,** *adj.* full of confidence (in s.o.). **trust•ful•ly, trust•ing•ly,** *adv.* in a trustful/trusting way. **trust•wor•thi•ness,** *n.* being trustworthy. **trust•wor•thy,** *adj.* which can be depended upon. **trust•y** ['trʌstɪ] 1. *n.* prisoner who is given certain responsibilities and privileges because he can be trusted. 2. *adj.* (-ier, -iest) which can be depended upon.

truth [truːT] *n.* thing which is true; true story; **to tell s.o. a few home truths** = to tell s.o. what you think of them/to criticize s.o.'s behavior/character. **truth•ful,** *adj.* (person) who always tells the truth. **truth•ful•ly,** *adv.* in a truthful way. **truth•ful•ness,** *n.* being truthful.

try [traɪ] 1. *n.* attempt (to do sth). 2. *v.* (a) to test. (b) to attempt. (c) to judge (a case/a person) in court. **try•ing,** *adj.* difficult to put up with. **try on,** *v.* to put (clothes) on to see if they fit. **try out,** *v.* to test (sth).

try•pan•o•some [trɪ'pænəsəʊm] *n.* parasite, carried by the tsetse fly, causing sleeping sickness.

tryst [trɪst] *n.* (old) lovers' meeting.

tsar [zɑː] *n.* former title of the emperor of Russia.

tset•se ['tsetsɪ] *n.* type of African fly which transmits disease by biting.

tub [tʌb] *n.* (a) round (wooden) container; small, round cardboard or plastic box for ice cream, butter, etc. (b) bathtub. (c) *inf.* old ship. **tub•bi•ness,** *n.* being tubby. **tub•by,** *adj.* (-ier, -iest) *inf.* fat.

tu•ba ['tjuːbə] *n.* large bass brass instrument.

tube [tjuːb] *n.* (a) long pipe for carrying liquids or gas; **inner t.** = rubber tube holding air inside a tire. (b) long pipe (in the body); **bronchial tubes** = tubes leading to the lungs. (c) soft pipe with a screw top which contains toothpaste, etc. (d) (*esp. Brit.*) subway. (e) glass bulb in a television set which projects the picture on the screen. **tube•less,** *adj.* (tire) with no inner tube. **tub•ing,** *n.* tubes made of metal/plastic, etc. **tu•bu•lar** ['tjuːbjʊlə] *adj.* like a tube.

tu•ber ['tjuːbə] *n.* thick piece of root which can be planted to make a new plant grow. **tu•ber•ous,** *adj.* (root) which produces tubers.

tu•ber•cle ['tjuːbəkl] *n.* rounded bump on the skin; scar caused by tuberculosis. **tu•ber•cu•lo•sis** [tjʊbɜːkjuˈləʊsɪs] *n.* disease of the lungs. **tu•ber•cu•lar** [tjuːˈbɜːkjʊlə] *adj.* suffering from tuberculosis. **tu•ber•cu•lin-test•ed,** *adj.* (milk/cow)

which has been tested to show that it is free from tuberculosis.

tuck [tʌk] 1. *n.* little fold/pleat in a piece of cloth. 2. *v.* (a) to fold (a blanket) around s.o. and push the ends underneath. (b) to fold cloth into little pleats. **tuck in,** *v.* (a) to push the edge of a piece of cloth underneath s.o. to keep them warm. (b) *inf.* (also **tuck away**) to eat a large quantity of food. **tuck up,** *v.* to **tuck s.o. up (in bed)** = to push the edge of the bedclothes around (s.o.) to keep them warm.

Tues•day ['tjuːzdeɪ] *n.* second day of the week/day between Monday and Wednesday.

tu•fa ['tjuːfə] *n.* type of porous volcanic rock.

tuft [tʌft] *n.* small bunch of grass/hair, etc. **tuft•ed,** *adj.* with tufts.

tug [tʌg] 1. *n.* (a) sudden pull. (b) tugboat. 2. *v.* (**tugged**) to pull hard. **tug•boat,** *n.* powerful boat used for towing barges/ships. **tug-of-war,** *n.* (a) competition where two teams pull against each other on a strong rope. (b) bitter struggle between opposing forces.

tu•i•tion [tjuˈɪʃn] *n.* charge for teaching/instruction, as at a private school or college.

tu•lip ['tjuːlɪp] *n.* common spring bulb with brilliant flowers shaped like cups. **tu•lip tree,** *n.* large evergreen tree, with big shiny leaves and large white flowers.

tulle [tjuːl] *n.* thin silk/artificial material like a veil.

tum•ble ['tʌmbl] 1. *n.* fall. 2. *v.* (a) to fall (**down**). (b) to come down in confusion. **tum•ble-down,** *adj.* (house) which is falling down/coming to pieces. **tum•bler,** *n.* round, straight glass for drinking. **tum•ble-dry,** *v.* to put laundry in a machine which dries it with warm air.

tu•mes•cent [tjuːˈmesənt] *adj.* swollen.

tum•my ['tʌmɪ] *n. inf.* stomach. **tum•my ache,** *n. inf.* pain in the stomach.

tu•mor, *Brit.* **tu•mour** ['tjuːmə] *n.* abnormal growth in or on the body.

tu•mult ['tjuːmʌlt] *n.* loud, excited noise (of a crowd). **tu•mul•tu•ous** [tjuˈmʌltjʊəs] *adj.* noisy/excited.

tu•mu•lus ['tjuːmjʊləs] *n.* (*pl.* -li) mound of earth covering an ancient tomb.

tun [tʌn] *n.* large barrel (for wine/beer).

tu•na ['tjuːnə] *n.* (*pl.* **tuna**) large sea fish (used for food).

tun•dra ['tʌndrə] *n.* Arctic plain with no trees.

tune [tjuːn] 1. *n.* (a) series of musical notes which make a recognizable melody; **he's changed his t.** = he has changed his way of thinking; *inf.* **to the t. of $100** = at least $100. (b) **in t.** = with the correct musical tone; **in t. with** = harmonizing with/similar to. 2. *v.* (a) to adjust (a musical instrument) so that it has the correct tone. (b) to adjust (an engine) so that it works more efficiently. **tune•ful,** *adj.* full of catchy tunes. **tune in,** *v.* to adjust a radio to a particular station. **tun•er,** *n.* piano t. = person who tunes pianos. **tune up,** *v.* (a) to adjust instruments before playing. (b) to adjust (an engine) so that it works more efficiently. **tun•ing fork,** *n.* metal fork which gives a correct note when it is hit.

tung•sten ['tʌŋstən] *n. (element:* W) hard gray metal used to make steel and electric light filaments.

tu•nic ['tjuːnɪk] *n.* (a) loose top garment. (b) (*esp. Brit.*) short jacket worn by soldiers/policemen, etc.

tun•nel ['tʌnl] 1. *n.* long hole in the ground. 2. *v.* (**tunneled, tunnelled**) to make a long passage under the ground.

tur•ban ['tɜːbən] *n.* long piece of cloth wrapped around the head to cover the hair.

tur•bid ['tɜːbɪd] *adj.* muddy (water). **tur•bid•i•ty** [tɜːˈbɪdɪtɪ] *n.* being turbid.

tur•bine ['tɜːbaɪn] *n.* engine driven by the force of water/steam which turns a wheel with blades.

tur•bo•jet ['tɜːbəʊˈdʒet] *n.* jet engine driven by a turbine; aircraft powered by this engine. **tur•bo•prop** ['tɜːbəʊˈprɒp] *n.* jet and propeller engine driven by a turbine; aircraft powered by this engine.

tur•bot ['tɜːbət] *n.* (*pl.* **turbot**) large flat edible sea fish.

tur•bu•lent ['tɜːbjulənt] *adj.* (a) disturbed/violently moving (water/air). (b) likely to riot. **tur•bu•lence,** *n.* disturbance in the air causing an aircraft to rock suddenly; disturbance in water.

turd [tɜːd] *n. Sl.* (*vulgar*) lump of human excreta.

tu•reen [tjuˈriːn] *n.* large bowl for serving soup.

turf [tɜːf] 1. *n.* (a) stretch of grassy area. (b) (*pl.* **turves** [tɜːvz]) piece of grass with soil around its roots which can be planted to form a lawn; (*in Ireland*) block of peat for burning. (c) **the t.** = the world of horse racing. 2. *v.* to make a lawn with turf.

tur•gid ['tɜːdʒɪd] *adj.* swollen; grand-sounding, meaningless (words). **tur•gid•ly,** *adv.* in a turgid way.

Turk [tɜːk] *n.* person from Turkey.

tur•key ['tɜːkɪ] *n.* large domestic bird, often eaten at Thanksgiving and Christmas.

Turk•ish ['tɜːkɪʃ] 1. *adj.* referring to Turkey; **T. bath** = steam bath after which you plunge into cold water. **T. delight** = scented sweet jelly eaten in lumps. 2. *n.* language spoken in Turkey.

tur•mer•ic ['tɜːmərɪk] *n.* yellow spice, used esp. in curries.

tur•moil ['tɜːmɔɪl] *n.* wild disorder.

turn [tɜːn] 1. *n.* (a) circular movement (of a wheel, etc.); **the meat is done to a t.** = properly cooked all through. (b) change of direction/condition; **to take a t. for the better/for the worse** = suddenly to start to get better/worse; **at the t. of the century** = about 1900. (c) sudden attack (of fear, shock, etc.). (d) chance to do sth in order; (*of several people*) **to take (it in) turns to do sth** = to do sth, each person doing it in order. (e) way of speaking/thinking/acting. (f) **to do s.o. a good t.** = to do sth to help them. (g) performance (in a variety show). 2. *v.* (a) to go around; to make (sth) go around in a circle. (b) to change direction; (*of tide*) to start to rise/fall; **his luck turned** = changed. (c) to change (**into** sth else); (*of milk*) to go sour. (d) to aim (a gun). (e) **to t. s.o.'s head** = to make s.o. very proud/vain; **to t. s.o.'s stomach** = to make s.o. feel sick. (f) to shape (a round piece of wood) by carving it on a lathe. (g) to pass a particular point in time; **it's turned seven** = it is past seven o'clock; **he's turned fifty** = he's more than fifty years old. **turn•a•bout,** *n.* act of turning to face in another direction.

turn a•side, *v.* to move to one side. **turn a•way,** *v.* (a) to move away. (b) to send (s.o.) away. **turn back,** *v.* (a) to turn and go back in the opposite direction. (b) to send (s.o.) back. **turn•coat,** *n.* person who switches from one opinion to another. **turn down,** *v.* (a) to refuse. (b) to reduce. (c) to fold back (a sheet on a bed), so that the pillow is uncovered. **turn•er,** *n.* person who makes chair legs, etc., on a lathe. **turn•e•ry,** *n.* (a) trade of a turner. (b) articles which are turned on a lathe. **turn in,** *v.* (a) to hand back (equipment) to s.o. in authority. (b) *inf.* to go to bed. (c) **to t. oneself in** = to give oneself up to the police. **turn•ing,** *n.* (a) action of moving in a circle/of changing direction. (b) point where sth turns. **turn•ing point,** *n.* important/decisive moment. **turn off,** *v.* (a) to switch off. (b) to change direction away from a straight line. **turn on,** *v.* (a) to switch on. (b) to attack. **turn out,** *v.* (a) to throw (s.o.) out. (b) to produce. (c) to switch off. (d) to happen. (e) to come out (in a crowd); show up. (g) **well turned-out** = well dressed. **turn•out,** *n.*

æ back, aː farm, ɒ top, aɪ pipe, aʊ how, aie fire, aʊə flower, ɔː bought, ɔɪ toy, e fed, eəhair, eɪ take, ə afraid, əʊ boat, əʊə lower, vː word, iː heap, ɪ hit, ɪə hear, uː school, ʊ book, ʌ but, b back, d dog, ð then, dʒ just, f fog, g go, h hand, j yes, k catch, l last, m mix, n nut, ŋ sing, p penny, r round, s some, ʃ short, t too, tʃ chop, θ thing, v voice, w was, z zoo, ʒ treasure

crowd of people who turn out. **turn o•ver,** v. (a) to move (the page of a book) so that you can read the next one; **to t. o. a new leaf** = to be better behaved. (b) to think about. (c) to roll over. (d) (of engine) to run gently. (e) to have sales of (a certain amount). (f) to hand (a criminal) to the police. **turn•o•ver,** n. (a) type of pie made with pastry turned over a filling. (b) change (in staff). (c) amount of sales. **turn•pike,** n. highway with tolls. **turn•stile,** n. gate which turns around on a pivot, allowing only one person to go through at a time. **turn•ta•ble,** n. (a) flat part of a record player which turns with the record on it. (b) flat turning platform with rails on it, to enable railroad locomotives to go off in a different direction. **turn up,** v. (a) to arrive; to be found. (b) to increase. (c) to roll or fold up the bottom of a garment to shorten it. (d) to unfold/unroll (a collar).

tur•nip ['tɜːnɪp] n. common vegetable, with a round white root.

tur•pen•tine ['tɜːpəntaɪn] n. oil which comes from fir trees, used for removing or thinning paint. **turps** [tɜːps] n. inf. turpentine.

tur•pi•tude ['tɜːpɪtjuːd] n. (formal) wickedness.

tur•quoise ['tɜːkwɔɪz] 1. n. green-blue precious stone. 2. adj. green-blue (color).

tur•ret ['tʌrɪt] n. small tower; small armored construction housing a gun (on a ship/tank,etc.). **tur•ret•ed,** n. with turrets.

tur•tle ['tɜːtl] n. sea reptile with a hard shell like a tortoise; **to turn t.** = to capsize. **tur•tle•dove,** n. type of wild pigeon with a soft, cooing call. **tur•tle•neck,** n. sweater with a high, usu. rolled, neck.

turves [tɜːvz] n. see **turf.**

tusk [tʌsk] n. long tooth coming far out from the mouth of some animals (such as elephants/walruses, etc.). **tusk•er,** n. inf. elephant.

tus•sah [tʌsə] n. type of coarse silk from India.

tus•sle ['tʌsl] 1. n. fight/argument. 2. v. to fight/to struggle.

tus•sock ['tʌsək] n. large tuft of grass.

tus•sore ['tʌsə] n. tussah.

tu•te•lage ['tjuːtəlɪdʒ] n. being responsible for s.o.; training/instruction given to a student.

tu•tor ['tjuːtə] 1. n. teacher (who teaches a student, esp. privately). 2. v. to act as a tutor to. **tu•to•ri•al** [tjuːˈtɔːrɪəl] n. discussion meeting between a tutor and a student or small group of students.

tut•ti-frut•ti ['tʊtɪˈfrʊtɪ] n. ice cream with pieces of preserved fruit in it.

tut-tut [tʌtˈtʌt] 1. n. sound made to show you disapprove. 2. v. (**tut-tutted**) to make disapproving sounds.

tu•tu ['tuːtuː] n. girl ballet dancer's short stiff skirt.

tux•e•do [tʌkˈsiːdəʊ] n. (pl. -os) man's dinner jacket or an outfit including this jacket.

TV [tiːˈviː] n. (a) television. (b) television set.

twad•dle ['twɒdl] n. inf. silly talk/nonsense.

twain [tweɪn] n. (formal) two things.

twang [twæŋ] 1. n. (a) sound made, such as when a guitar string is pulled and released. (b) **nasal t.** = accent made by speaking through the nose. 2. v. to make a twang.

tweak [twiːk] 1. n. sharp pull. 2. v. to pull suddenly.

tweed [twiːd] n. rough woolen cloth made of strands of different colors. **tweeds,** n. pl. clothes made of tweed.

tweet [twiːt] 1. n. little sound made by a small bird. 2. v. to make a little sound like a bird. **tweet•er,** n. loudspeaker which reproduces high sounds.

tweez•ers ['twiːzəz] n. pl. (**pair of**) **t.** = small pincers.

twelve [twelv] n. number 12. **twelfth** [twelfT] **12th,** adj. & n. referring to twelve; **the t. century** = period from 1100 to 1199.

twen•ty ['twentɪ] n. number 20; **she's in her twenties** = she is over twenty but under thirty years old. **twen•ti•eth, 20th,** adj. & n. referring to twenty; **the t. century** = period from 1900 to 1999.

twerp [twɜːp] n. Sl. stupid person.

twice [twaɪs] adv. two times; double; **he's t. my age** = two times as old as I am.

twid•dle ['twɪdl] v. to turn/to twist with no particular aim; **to t. your thumbs** = holding your hands together, to turn your thumbs around and around as a sign of not having anything to do.

twig [twɪg] n. little branch.

twi•light ['twaɪlaɪt] n. (period of) weak light between night and sunrise or between sunset and night.

twill [twɪl] n. thick cloth woven in diagonal lines.

twin [twɪn] 1. adj. & n. (child) born at the same birth as another; **identical twins** = two children born at the same time who look very similar. 2. adj. & prefix made of two similar parts. 3. v. (**twinned**) (**with**) to join or be combined.

twine [twaɪn] 1. n. thick rough string. 2. v. to twist around and around.

twinge [twɪndʒ] n. short sharp pain; small worry; **t. of guilt.**

twin•kle ['twɪŋkl] 1. n. little flicker of light; **with a t. in his eye** = with his eyes shining with amusement. 2. v. (a) to glitter. (b) (of eyes) to shine (with amusement/wickedness, etc.).

twin•kling, *n.* little flicker; **in the t. of an eye** = very fast.

twirl [twɜːl] 1. *n.* (a) spinning movement. (b) spiral shape. 2. *v.* (a) to spin around. (b) to twist in your fingers.

twirp [twəːp] *n.* twerp.

twist [twɪst] 1. *n.* (a) thing which has a twisted shape. (b) curve or turn; **t. in the road.** (c) act of twisting; **a new t. to the story** = an unexpected change. 2. *v.* (a) to turn around and around. (b) to wind (sth) around sth. (c) to bend in the wrong way; to sprain (an ankle); *inf.* **to t. s.o.'s arm** = to persuade s.o. to do what you want. (d) to change the meaning of (words). **twist•er,** *n.* (a) person or thing that twists. (b) whirlwind or tornado. **twist•y,** *adj.* which twists.

twit [twɪt] 1. *n. Sl.* silly person. 2. *v.* (**twitted**) to make fun of (s.o.).

twitch [twɪtʃ] 1. *n.* (*pl.* **-es**) sudden jerk/sudden movement. 2. *v.* to jerk suddenly/to make a sudden movement.

twit•ter ['twɪtə] 1. *n.* little calls made by birds; **she was all in a t.** = very excited. 2. *v.* to make little sounds (like birds).

twixt [twɪkst] *prep.* (*old*) between.

two [tuː] *n.* number 2. (a) **one or t.** = a few; **to put t. and t. together** = to come to a conclusion by comparing various facts; **to be of t. minds about sth** = not to be able to decide. **two-bit,** *adj. inf.* cheap/second-rate. **two-edged,** *adj.* (a) (knife) with two sharp edges. (b) (remark/action) which has two results (one good, one bad). **two-faced,** *adj.* deceitful. **two•fold,** *adv.* twice as much. **twoleg•ged** [tuːˈlegɪd] *adj.* with two legs. **two•pen•ny** ['tʌpnɪ] *adj.* costing or having a value of two pennies. **two-piece,** *adj.* made of two pieces; **t.-p. suit** = suit made of a jacket and skirt/trousers. **two-ply,** *adj.* made of two threads/two pieces. **two-seat•er,** *n.* car/aircraft with only two seats. **two•some,** *n.* two people (playing a game); game for two people. **two•step,** *n.* dance with smooth steps. **two-stroke,** *adj.* (engine) with two pistons. **two-time,** *v. inf.* to be unfaithful (to a girlfriend/boyfriend). **two- tim•er,** *n. inf.* unfaithful person. **two-tone,** *adj.* colored with two tones of the same color. **two-way,** *adj.* going in two directions.

ty•coon [taɪˈkuːn] *n.* wealthy businessman.

ty•ing ['taɪɪŋ] *v. see* **tie.**

tyke [taɪk] *n.* child, esp. a small boy.

tym•pa•num [tɪmˈpɑːnəm] *n.* (*formal*) eardrum.

type [taɪp] 1. *n.* (a) sort/kind. (b) example; **a real conservative t.** = a good example of a conservative. (c) small pieces of metal with letters molded on them, used for printing; collection of pieces of metal for printing. 2. *v.* to write with a typewriter. **type•cast,** *v.* (**typecast**) to give (an actor) the same type of part all the time. **type•script,** *n.* document typed on a typewriter. **type•set•ter,** *n.* person who sets manuscripts in type ready for printing. **type•set•ting,** *n.* action of setting type; type which has been set. **type•writ•er,** *n.* machine which prints letters on a piece of paper when you press the keys. **type•writ•ten,** *adj.* (document) which has been written with a typewriter. **typ•ing,** *n.* (a) action of writing letters with a typewriter; **t. pool** = group of typists who work for several departments in a company; **t. paper** = special paper for typewriters. (b) action of classifying into types; **blood t.** = classification of blood into certain groups. **typ•ist,** *n.* person whose job is to type letters on a typewriter. **ty•pog•ra•pher,** *n.* specialist in typography. **ty•po•graph•ic(al)** [taɪpəˈgræfɪk(l)] *adj.* referring to typography. **ty•pog•ra•phy** [taɪˈpɒgrəfɪ] *n.* (a) art of arranging material for printing/of designing a printed page. (b) study of the appearance of printed characters.

ty•phoid ['taɪfɔɪd] *adj. & n.* **t. (fever)** = serious disease caused by infected food or drink.

ty•phoon [taɪˈfuːn] *n.* tropical storm (in the Far East).

ty•phus ['taɪfəs] *n.* serious fever, where the virus is carried by lice.

typ•i•cal ['tɪpɪkl] *adj.* obviously belonging to a particular group; characteristic; **that's t. of him** = that's exactly what he always does. **typ•i•cal•ly,** *adv.* in a typical way. **typ•i•fy,** *v.* to be an excellent example of.

ty•po ['taɪpəʊ] *n.* typesetting mistake.

tyr•an•ny ['tɪrənɪ] *n.* cruel rule by an undemocratic government/ruler. **ty•ran•ni•cal, tyr•annous** [tɪˈrænɪkl, 'tɪrənəs] *adj.* cruel. **tyr•an•nize,** *v.* to rule (s.o.) in a cruel way. **ty•rant** ['taɪrənt] *n.* cruel, undemocratic ruler.

tyre ['taɪə] *n. Brit. see* **tire.**

ty•ro, tiro ['taɪrəʊ] *n.* (*pl.* **-os**) complete beginner/person with no experience.

æ back, ɑ: farm, ɒ: top, aɪ pipe, aʊ how, aɪə fire, aʊə flower, ɔ: bought, ɔɪ toy, e fed, eəhair, eɪ take, ə afraid, əʊ boat, əʊə lower, ɜ: word, i: heap, ɪ hit, ɪə hear, u: school, ʊ book, ʌ but, b back, d dog, ð then, dʒ just, f fog, g go, h hand, j yes, k catch, l last, m mix, n nut, ŋ sing, p penny, r round, s some, ʃ short, t too, tʃ chop, θ thing, v voice, w was, z zoo, ʒ treasure

Uu

U, u [juː]; **U-turn** = turn made by a car in a road so that it faces in the opposite direction; **to do a U-turn** = change policy completely. **U-boat,** *n.* German submarine.

U *symbol for* uranium.

u•biq•ui•tous [juːˈbɪkwɪtəs] *adj.* (thing) which is/which seems to be everywhere. **u•biq•ui•ty,** *n.* being everywhere.

ud•der [ˈʌdə] *n.* bag producing milk which hangs under the body of a cow or goat.

UFO [juːefˈəʊ] *n. abbrev. for* unidentified flying object.

ugh [ɜː] *inter. showing a feeling that something is unpleasant.*

ug•ly [ˈʌglɪ] *adj.* (**-ier, -iest**) (a) not pleasant to look at. (b) dangerous (mood). **ug•li•ness,** *n.* being ugly.

UHF [juːeɪtʃˈef] *abbrev. for* ultrahigh frequency.

UHT [juːeɪtʃˈtiː] *adj. abbrev. for* ultrahigh temperature.

U.K. [juːˈkeɪ] *abbrev. for* United Kingdom.

u•ku•le•le [juːkəˈleɪlɪ] *n.* very small guitar.

ul•cer [ˈʌlsə] *n.* sore on the body. **ul•cer•ate,** *v.* to cover with ulcers; to become covered with ulcers. **ul•cer•a•tion,** *n.* being covered with ulcers; place where an ulcer is. **ul•cer•ous,** *adj.* covered with ulcers.

ul•lage [ˈʌlɪdʒ] *n.* amount of missing liquid which would make a container full.

ul•na [ˈʌlnə] *n.* one of the two bones of the lower arm.

ul•te•ri•or [ʌlˈtɪərɪə] *adj.* hidden/secret; **u. motive** = reason for doing sth. which anticipates the result of the action.

ul•ti•mate [ˈʌltɪmət] *adj.* final. **ul•ti•mate•ly,** *adv.* finally.

ul•ti•ma•tum [ʌltɪˈmeɪtəm] *n.* message sent to an opponent stating that unless demands are met by a certain time, violent action (usu. war or a strike) will start.

ultra- [ˈʌltrə] *prefix meaning* extremely/very. **ul•tra•ma•rine** [ʌltrəməˈriːn] *adj. & n.* (color) of deep sea blue. **ul•tra•mod•ern,** *adj.* extremely modern. **ul•tra•son•ic,** *adj.* (sound waves) which cannot be heard by humans. **ul•tra•sound,** *n.* very high frequency sound wave, used to detect objects in the body or under water. **ul•tra•vi•o•let** [ʌltrə-ˈvaɪələt] *adj.* (light rays) which are beyond the violet of the spectrum and which tan the skin. **ul•tra vi•res,** *adv.* (acting) beyond one's powers.

um•bel [ˈʌmbl] *n.* flower head made of many single flowers on long stalks. **um•bel•lif•er•ous** [ʌmbəˈlɪfərəs] *adj.* (plant) with umbels.

um•ber [ˈʌmbə] *adj. & n.* brown (color) like earth; **burnt u.** = reddish-brown (color).

um•bil•i•cal [ʌmˈbɪlɪkl] *adj.* **u. cord** = tube joining the mother to her baby before birth, and through which nourishment passes.

um•bra [ˈʌmbrə] *n.* (*formal*) shadow.

um•brage [ˈʌmbrɪdʒ] *n.* **to take u. at** = to feel insulted by.

um•brel•la [ʌmˈbrelə] *n.* round shade of folded cloth which opens on a frame and is held over your head to keep off the rain; **u. organization** = large organization which includes small ones.

um•pire [ˈʌmpaɪə] 1. *n.* person who acts as a judge in tennis/baseball, etc., to see if the game is played according to the rules. 2. *v.* to act as umpire.

ump•teen [ʌmˈtiːn] *adj. & n. inf.* very large number. **ump•teenth,** *adj. inf.* referring to umpteen.

un- [ʌn] *prefix meaning* not; the opposite.

un, 'un [ʌn] *pron. inf.* one.

UN [ˈjuːˈen] *abbrev. for* United Nations.

un•a•bashed [ʌnəˈbæʃt] *adj.* not ashamed/not timid.

un•a•bat•ed [ʌnəˈbeɪtɪd] *adj.* with no loss of vigor.

un•a•ble [ʌnˈeɪbl] *adj.* not able.

un•a•bridged [ʌnəˈbrɪdʒd] *adj.* (text) which has not been shortened.

un•ac•cept•a•ble [ʌnəkˈseptəbl] *adj.* which cannot be accepted.

un•ac•com•pa•nied [ʌnəˈkʌmpnɪd] *adj.* alone; (singer/instrument) without any accompaniment.

un•ac•count•a•ble [ʌnəˈkaʊntəbl] *adj.* which cannot be explained. **un•ac•count•a•bly,** *adv.* without explanation. **un•ac•count•ed for,** *adj.* lost, with no explanation for the loss.

un•ac•cus•tomed [ʌnə'kʌstəmd] *adj.* not accustomed.

un•ac•quaint•ed [ʌnə'kweɪntɪd] *adj.* **to be u. with** = not knowing.

un•a•dul•ter•at•ed [ʌnə'dʌltəreɪtɪd] *adj.* pure; with nothing added.

un•af•fect•ed [ʌnə'fektɪd] *adj.* sincere/natural.

un•aid•ed [ʌn'eɪdɪd] *adj.* without help.

un•al•loyed [ʌnə'lɔɪd] *adj.* pure.

un•al•ter•a•ble [ʌn'ɒltrəbl] *adj.* which cannot be altered. **un•al•tered,** *adj.* which has not changed.

un•am•big•u•ous [ʌnæm'bɪgjʊəs] *adj.* clear/not ambiguous.

u•nan•i•mous [jʊ'nænɪməs] *adj.* where everyone agrees. **u•nan•i•mous•ly,** *adv.* all agreeing together. **u•na•nim•i•ty** [junə-'nɪmɪtɪ] *n.* being unanimous.

un•an•nounced [ʌnə'naʊnst] *adj.* which has not been announced.

un•ap•pe•tiz•ing [ʌn'æpɪtaɪzɪŋ] *adj.* which does not make you want to eat/which takes away your appetite.

un•ap•proach•a•ble [ʌnə'prəʊtʃəbl] *adj.* (person) who is very formal; (place) which cannot be approached easily.

un•armed [ʌn'ɑːmd] *adj.* with no weapons.

un•a•shamed [ʌnə'ʃeɪmd] *adj.* not ashamed.

un•asked [ʌn'ɑːskt] *adj.* without being asked.

un•as•sum•ing [ʌnə'sjuːmɪŋ] *adj.* quiet/modest.

un•at•tached [ʌnə'tætʃt] *adj.* not attached; not married.

un•at•tain•a•ble [ʌnə'teɪnəbl] *adj.* which cannot be reached.

un•at•tend•ed [ʌnə'tendɪd] *adj.* alone; not looked after.

un•at•trac•tive [ʌnə'træktɪv] *adj.* not attractive.

un•au•thor•ized [ʌn'ɔːɪəraɪzd] *adj.* which is not permitted.

un•a•void•a•ble [ʌnə'vɔɪdəbl] *adj.* which cannot be avoided. **un•a•void•a•bly,** *adv.* in an unavoidable way.

un•a•ware [ʌnə'weə] *adj.* (of) not knowing/not aware. **un•a•wares,** *adv.* without noticing; **to catch s.o. u.** = by surprise.

un•bal•anced [ʌn'bælənst] *adj.* erratic/slightly mad.

un•bear•a•ble [ʌn'beərəbl] *adj.* intolerable. **un•bear•a•bly,** *adv.* so much that you cannot bear it.

un•beat•a•ble [ʌn'biːtəbl] *adj.* which cannot be beaten. **un•beat•en,** *adj.* which has not been beaten.

un•be•com•ing [ʌnbɪ'kʌmɪŋ] *adj.* which is not decent.

un•be•known [ʌnbɪ'nəʊn] *adj.* (*also* **unbeknownst**) *inf.* **u. to anyone** = without anyone knowing.

un•be•liev•a•ble [ʌnbɪ'liːvəbl] *adj.* incredible/which you cannot believe. **un•be•liev•a•bly,** *adv.* incredibly/amazingly. **un•be•liev•er,** *n.* person who does not believe in god.

un•bend [ʌn'bend] *v.* (**unbent**) to stop being stiff and start behaving naturally. **un•bend•ing,** *adj.* inflexible/harsh (rule).

un•bi•ased [ʌn'baɪəst] *adj.* impartial/not biased.

un•bid•den [ʌn'bɪdn] *adj.* (*formal*) without having been asked.

un•bleached [ʌn'bliːtʃt] *adj.* (cloth, etc.) which has not been bleached.

un•block [ʌn'blɒk] *v.* to take a blockage away from (sth).

un•blush•ing [ʌn'blʌʃɪŋ] *adj.* showing no shame.

un•bolt [ʌn'bəʊlt] *v.* to pull back the bolt on (a door).

un•born [ʌn'bɔːn] *adj.* not yet born.

un•bos•om [ʌn'buzəm] *v.* **to u. oneself to s.o.** = tell all one's private thoughts and troubles.

un•bound•ed [ʌn'baʊndɪd] *adj.* with no limits.

un•break•a•ble [ʌn'breɪkəbl] *adj.* which cannot be broken.

un•bri•dled [ʌn'braɪdld] *adj.* (passion) which is not controlled.

un•bro•ken [ʌn'brəʊkn] *adj.* which has not been broken.

un•bur•den [ʌn'bɜːdn] *v.* **to u. yourself to s.o.** = to tell (s.o.) all your troubles/secrets.

un•but•ton [ʌn'bʌtn] *v.* to undo the buttons on.

un•called-for [ʌn'kɔːldfɔː] *adj.* not necessary; not deserved.

un•can•ny [ʌn'kænɪ] *adj.* mysterious/which seems unnatural.

un•cared-for [ʌn'keədfɔː] *adj.* not looked after.

un•ceas•ing [ʌn'siːsɪŋ] *adj.* ceaseless; without any stopping.

un•cer•e•mo•ni•ous [ʌnserɪ'məʊnɪəs] *adj.* not dignified; not polite.

æ back, ɑː farm, ɒ top, aɪ pipe, aʊ how, aɪe fire, aʊə flower, ɔː bought, ɔɪ toy, ə fed, eəhair, eɪ take, ə afraid, əʊ boat, əʊə lower, ɜː word, iː heap, ɪ hit, ɪə hear, uː school, ʊ book, ʌ but, b back, d dog, ð then, dʒ just, f fog, g go, h hand, j yes, k catch, l last, m mix, n nut, ŋ sing, p penny, r round, s some, ʃ short, t too, tʃ chop, θ thing, v voice, w was, z zoo, ʒ treasure

un•cer•e•mo•ni•ous•ly, *adv.* in an undignified way.

un•cer•tain [ʌn'sɜːtən] *adj.* (a) not certain/not sure. (b) which cannot be forecast. **un•cer•tain•ty,** *n.* being uncertain; lack of certainty.

un•chal•lenged [ʌn'tʃælənʒd] *adj.* without a challenge; **to let sth pass u.** = to let sth be said or written without questioning it.

un•char•ac•ter•is•tic [ʌnkærəkte'rɪstɪk] *adj.* not in character.

un•char•i•ta•ble [ʌn'tʃærɪtəbl] *adj.* unkind. **un•char•i•ta•bly,** *adv.* in an uncharitable way.

un•checked [ʌn'tʃekt] *adj.* with no check.

un•chris•tian [ʌn'krɪstʃn] *adj.* not kind/generous, etc.

un•ci•al ['ʌnsiəl] *adj. & n.* (rounded) letters used in early medieval manuscripts.

un•civ•i•lized [ʌn'sɪvɪlaɪzd] *adj.* not civilized; barbarous.

un•claimed [ʌn'kleɪmd] *adj.* which has not been claimed.

un•clas•si•fied [ʌn'klæsɪfaɪd] *adj.* not classified/not secret.

un•cle ['ʌŋkl] *n.* brother of your father or mother; husband of your aunt. **Un•cle Sam,** *n. inf.* person symbolizing the United States.

un•clean [ʌn'kliːn] *adj.* dirty.

un•cloud•ed [ʌn'klaʊdɪd] *adj.* not troubled/clear (liquid).

un•clut•tered [ʌn'klʌtəd] *adj.* tidy.

un•coil [ʌn'kɔɪl] *v.* to unwind.

un•com•fort•a•ble [ʌn'kʌmftəbl] *adj.* (a) not comfortable. (b) embarrassed; ill at ease. **un•com•fort•a•bly,** *adv.* in an uncomfortable way.

un•com•mit•ted [ʌnkə'mɪtɪd] *adj.* with no strong beliefs; (country) which has not decided which group to support; (voter) who has not decided which way to vote.

un•com•mon [ʌn'kɒmən] *adj.* (-er, -est) strange/odd; rare. **un•com•mon•ly,** *adv.* in an uncommon way; *inf.* very.

un•com•mu•ni•ca•tive [ʌnkə'mjuːnɪkətɪv] *adj.* silent/not talkative.

un•com•pli•men•ta•ry [ʌnkɒmplɪ'mentərɪ] *adj.* rude/not complimentary.

un•com•pro•mis•ing [ʌn'kɒmprəmaɪzɪŋ] *adj.* unwilling to give in or to change ideas.

un•con•cealed [ʌnkən'siːld] *adj.* open; not hidden.

un•con•cerned [ʌnkən'sɜːnd] *adj.* not worried/not bothered.

un•con•di•tion•al [ʌnkən'dɪʃnl] *adj.* without any conditions. **un•con•di•tion•al•ly,** *adv.* without insisting on conditions.

un•con•nect•ed [ʌnkə'nektɪd] *adj.* with no connection.

un•con•scious [ʌn'kɒnʃəs] 1. *adj.* (a) not conscious. (b) not aware. 2. *n.* **the u.** = deep level of the mind, with thoughts or feelings of which you are not conscious. **un•con•scion•a•ble** [ʌn'kɒnʃnəbl] *adj. inf.* unreasonable/excessive. **un•con•scious•ly,** *adv.* in an unconscious way. **un•con•scious•ness,** *n.* being unconscious.

un•con•sti•tu•tion•al [ʌnkɒnstɪ'tjuːʃənl] *adj.* going against the constitution.

un•con•test•ed [ʌnkən'testɪd] *adj.* (divorce) which is not disputed.

un•con•trol•la•ble [ʌnkən'trəʊləbl] *adj.* which cannot be controlled.

un•con•ven•tion•al [ʌnkən'venʃnl] *adj.* not usual.

un•cooked [ʌn'kʊkt] *adj.* not cooked.

un•co•op•er•a•tive [ʌnkəʊ'ɒpərətɪv] *adj.* not helpful/not cooperative.

un•cork [ʌn'kɔːk] *v.* to take the cork out of (a bottle).

un•cor•rob•o•rat•ed [ʌnkə'rɒbəreɪtɪd] *adj.* (evidence) which has not been confirmed.

un•cou•ple [ʌn'kʌpl] *v.* to detach (things) which are coupled.

un•couth [ʌn'kuːɪ] *adj.* rude/badly brought up.

un•cov•er [ʌn'kʌvə] *v.* (a) to take the cover off. (b) to find (sth hidden).

un•crit•i•cal [ʌn'krɪtɪkl] *adj.* (person) who does not think critically.

un•crowned [ʌn'kraʊnd] *adj.* (king) who has not been crowned; (leader) who is like a king.

un•crush•a•ble [ʌn'krʌʃəbl] *adj.* (material) which does not make creases if it is crushed.

unc•tion ['ʌŋkʃn] *n.* putting oil on a person in a religious ceremony. **unc•tu•ous** ['ʌŋkjʊəs] *adj.* extremely and unpleasantly polite. **unc•tu•ous•ly,** *adv.* in an unctuous way.

un•cul•ti•vat•ed [ʌn'kʌltɪveɪtɪd] *adj.* (land) which has not been cultivated.

un•cut [ʌn'kʌt] *adj.* which has not been cut; (motion picture) which has not been censored; (book) with pages still joined together at the edges.

un•daunt•ed [ʌn'dɔːntɪd] *adj.* bold/with no fear.

un•de•cid•ed [ʌndɪ'saɪdɪd] *adj.* (person) who has not made up his mind.

un•de•clared [ʌndɪ'kleəd] *adj.* which has not been declared.

un•de•fend•ed [ʌndɪ'fendɪd] *adj.* not defended.

un•de•mand•ing [ʌndɪ'mɑːndɪŋ] *adj.* not difficult.

un•dem•o•crat•ic [ˌʌndeməˈkrætɪk] *adj.* not democratic.

un•de•ni•a•ble [ˌʌndɪˈnaɪəbl] *adj.* which cannot be denied/which is quite clearly true.

un•der [ˈʌndə] 1. *prep.* (a) in a place which is directly below. (b) less than; **u. an hour** = less than an hour. (c) being ruled/managed/commanded by s.o. (d) because of/according to (terms). (e) in a state of; **u. repair** = being repaired; **u. lock and key** = locked up; **u. treatment** = being treated; **u. control** = controlled. 2. *adv.* in a lower place; **to go u.** = to fail/to go bankrupt; *inf.* **down u.** = in Australia and New Zealand. 3. *adj.* lower/bottom. 4. **under-** *prefix meaning* less important; not enough.

un•der•a•chieve [ˌʌndərəˈtʃiːv] *v.* to do less well than expected. **un•der•a•chiev•er,** *n.* student who does not do as well as expected.

un•der•age [ˌʌndərˈeɪdʒ] *adj.* younger than the legal age.

un•der•arm [ˈʌndərɑːm] *adv. & adj.* (thrown) with the hand kept lower than the shoulder.

un•der•car•riage [ˈʌndəkærɪdʒ] *n.* aircraft's wheels and supports.

un•der•charge [ʌndəˈtʃɑːdʒ] *v.* to charge less than you should.

un•der•clothes [ˈʌndəkləʊðz] *n. pl.* clothes worn next to the skin, under other clothes.

un•der•coat [ˈʌndəkəʊt] *n.* first coat of paint.

un•der•cov•er [ˈʌndəkʌvə] *adj.* secret; **u. agent** = spy.

un•der•cur•rent [ˈʌndəkʌrənt] *n.* (a) current of water under the surface. (b) hidden feelings.

un•der•cut [ˈʌndəkʌt] *v.* (**undercut**) to sell more cheaply than (s.o.).

un•der•de•vel•oped [ˌʌndədɪˈveləpt] *adj.* not developed; not industrially advanced.

un•der•dog [ˈʌndədɒg] *n.* person who is weaker/who always loses.

un•der•done [ˈʌndədʌn] *adj.* not cooked enough; not too cooked.

un•der•es•ti•mate 1. *n.* [ˌʌndərˈestɪmət] estimate which is less than the real quantity. 2. *v.* [ˌʌndərˈestɪmeɪt] to estimate at less than the real quantity.

un•der•ex•posed [ˌʌndərɪkˈspəʊzd] *adj.* (film) which has not been exposed sufficiently.

un•der•fed [ʌndəˈfed] *adj.* with not enough to eat.

un•der•foot [ʌndəˈfʊt] *adv.* under the feet/in the way.

un•der•gar•ment [ˈʌndəgɑːmənt] *n.* piece of clothing worn next to the skin, under other clothes.

un•der•go [ʌndəˈgəʊ] *v.* (**underwent, undergone**) to suffer/to experience.

un•der•grad•u•ate [ʌndəˈgrædjʊət] *n.* student at a college or university who has not yet received a degree.

un•der•ground 1. *adv.* [ʌndəˈgraʊnd] (a) under the ground. (b) in hiding. 2. *adj.* [ˈʌndəgraʊnd] (a) under the ground. (b) secret; against the ruling authorities. 3. *n.* [ˈʌndəgraʊnd] (a) (*esp. Brit.*) subway. (b) secret organization.

un•der•growth [ˈʌndəgrəʊT] *n.* bushes which grow thickly together under trees.

un•der•hand(ed) [ʌndəˈhænd(ɪd)] *adj.* cunning; deceitful.

un•der•lay [ˈʌndəleɪ] *v. see* **un•der•lie.**

un•der•lie [ʌndəˈlaɪ] *v.* (**underlay, underlain**) to be underneath; to be the basic cause (of sth). **un•der•ly•ing,** *adj.* basic (cause).

un•der•line [ˈʌndəlaɪn] *v.* to write a line under (a word); to emphasize.

un•der•ling [ˈʌndəlɪŋ] *n.* person who works for s.o. else.

un•der•manned [ʌndəˈmænd] *adj.* with not enough staff.

un•der•mine [ʌndəˈmaɪn] *v.* to weaken.

un•der•neath [ʌndəˈniːT] 1. *prep.* under/beneath. 2. *adv.* under. 3. *n.* the bottom part.

un•der•nour•ished [ʌndəˈnʌrɪʃt] *adj.* not having enough to eat.

un•der•paid [ʌndəˈpeɪd] *adj.* not paid enough.

un•der•pants [ˈʌndəpænts] *n. pl.* men's undergarment for the lower part of the body.

un•der•pass [ˈʌndəpɑːs] *n.* (*pl.* **-es**) place where one road goes under another.

un•der•pin [ʌndəˈpɪn] *v.* (**underpinned**) to support. **un•der•pin•ning,** *n.* support.

un•der•priv•i•leged [ʌndəˈprɪvɪlɪdʒd] *adj.* not having the same opportunities as other people.

un•der•rate [ʌndəˈreɪt] *v.* to value (sth) less than you ought.

un•der•score [ʌndəˈskɔː] *v.* to underline.

un•der•sea [ˈʌndəsiː] *adj. & adv.* under the sea.

un•der•sec•re•tar•y [ʌndəˈsekrətrɪ] *n.* official who is subordinate to a secretary of a government department.

un•der•sell [ʌndəˈsel] *v.* (**undersold**) to sell more cheaply than (s.o.).

un•der•shirt [ˈʌndəʃɜːt] *n.* men's light undergarment for the top half of the body.

un•der•side [ˈʌndəsaɪd] *n.* side which is underneath.

un•der•signed [ˈʌndəsaɪnd] *n.* **the u.** = people who have signed a letter.

un•der•size(d) [ˈʌndəsaɪz(d)] *adj.* smaller than normal.

un•der•slung [ˈʌndəslʌŋ] *adj.* (car chassis) which hangs below the axles.

un•der•staffed [ʌndəˈstɑːft] *adj.* with not enough staff.

un•der•stand [ʌndəˈstænd] *v.* (**understood**) (a) to know; to see the meaning of (sth). (b) to be an expert in (sth). (c) to think/to have an impression. (d) to take sth for granted, even if it is not written or spoken. (e) to know why (sth is done) and accept it. **un•der•stand•a•ble**, *adj.* which can be understood. **un•der•stand•a•bly**, *adv.* in a way which can be understood.

un•der•stand•ing. 1. *n.* (a) ability to understand. (b) sympathy for another person's problems. (c) private agreement. 2. *adj.* sympathetic.

un•der•state [ʌndəˈsteɪt] *v.* to make (sth) seem less important than it really is. **un•der•state•ment,** *n.* statement which does not tell the facts forcefully enough.

un•der•stood [ʌndəˈstʊd] *v. see* **un•der•stand.**

un•der•stud•y [ˈʌndəstʌdɪ] 1. *n.* actor who learns a part in the play so as to be able to act it if the main actor is ill. 2. *v.* to be the understudy of (an actor).

un•der•take [ʌndəˈteɪk] *v.* (**undertook, has undertaken**) to promise to do (sth); to accept to do (sth). **un•der•tak•er,** *n.* person who organizes funerals. **un•der•tak•ing,** *n.* (a) business. (b) promise. (c) job; **quite an u.** = very difficult job.

un•der•tone [ˈʌndətəʊn] *n.* (a) quiet voice. (b) hidden feeling.

un•der•tow [ˈʌndətəʊ] *n.* strong current under the surface of water, which flows in a different direction to that on the surface.

un•der•val•ue [ʌndəˈvæljuː] *v.* to value at less than the true rate.

un•der•wa•ter [ʌndəˈwɔːtə] *adj.* below the surface of the water.

un•der•wear [ˈʌndəweə] *n.* (*no pl.*) clothes worn next to your skin under other clothes.

un•der•weight [ʌndəˈweɪt] *adj.* which weighs less than usual.

un•der•went [ʌndəˈwent] *v. see* **un•der•go.**

un•der•world [ˈʌndəwɜːld] *n.* (a) (*in mythology*) place inhabited by the dead. (b) criminal world; **u. killing** = murder of a criminal by other criminals.

un•der•write [ʌndəˈraɪt] *v.* (**underwrote, has underwritten**) to insure (esp. ships); to accept responsibility for (sth). **un•der•writ•er** [ˈʌndəraɪtə] *n.* person who insures (esp. ships).

un•de•served [ʌndɪˈzɜːvd] *adj.* not deserved. **un•de•serv•ed•ly** [ʌndɪˈzɜːvɪdlɪ] *adv.* in an undeserved way.

un•de•sir•a•ble [ʌndɪˈzaɪərəbl] 1. *adj.* not wanted; not pleasant. 2. *n.* person who is not wanted/ who is considered a bad influence. **un•de•sir•a•bil•i•ty** [ʌndɪzaɪərəˈbɪlɪtɪ] *n.* being undesirable.

un•de•tect•ed [ʌndɪˈtektɪd] *adj.* not noticed. **un•de•tect•a•ble,** *adj.* which cannot be detected.

un•de•terred [ʌndɪˈtɜːd] *adj.* not put off.

un•de•vel•oped [ʌndɪˈveləpt] *adj.* which has not been developed.

un•did [ʌnˈdɪd] *v. see* **un•do.**

un•dies [ˈʌndɪz] *n. pl. inf.* (women's) underwear.

un•dig•ni•fied [ʌnˈdɪɡnɪfaɪd] *adj.* not dignified.

un•di•lut•ed [ʌndaɪˈljuːtɪd] *adj.* without any water added.

un•dis•charged [ʌndɪsˈtʃɑːʒd] *adj.* (debt) which has not been paid.

un•dis•tin•guished [ʌndɪsˈtɪŋgwɪʃt] *adj.* ordinary.

un•di•vid•ed [ʌndɪˈvaɪdɪd] *adj.* complete/not split.

un•do [ʌnˈduː] *v.* (**undid, has undone**) (a) to untie (a knot); to unbutton. (b) to ruin. **un•do•ing,** *n.* ruin. **un•done,** *adj.* (a) unfastened. (b) not complete.

un•doubt•ed [ʌnˈdaʊtɪd] *adj.* certain. **un•doubt•ed•ly,** *adv.* certainly.

un•dreamt-of [ʌnˈdremtɒv] *adj.* which no one can imagine.

un•dress [ʌnˈdres] *v.* to take off (usu. all your) clothes. **un•dressed,** *adj.* not wearing clothes.

un•drink•a•ble [ʌnˈdrɪŋkəbl] *adj.* (liquid) which is so unpleasant/so polluted that you cannot drink it.

un•due [ˈʌndjuː] *adj.* excessive/too much. **un•du•ly** [ʌnˈdjuːlɪ] *adv.* excessively/too much.

un•du•lant [ˈʌndjuːlənt] *adj.* **u. fever** = brucellosis.

un•du•late [ˈʌndjʊleɪt] *v.* to rise and fall like waves. **un•du•la•tion** [ʌndjʊˈleɪʃn] *n.* rise and fall (of land, etc.).

un•dy•ing [ʌnˈdaɪɪŋ] *adj.* (emotion) which lasts for ever.

un•earned [ˈʌnɜːnd] *adj.* (income) from investments/rents, etc.

un•earth [ʌnˈɜːT] *v.* to dig up; to discover.

un•earth•ly, *adj.* supernatural; *inf.* very early/late (hour).

un•eas•y [ʌn'iːzɪ] *adj.* (-ier, -iest) worried. un•eas•i•ly, *adv.* in an uneasy way. un•eas•i•ness, *n.* worry/anxiety.

un•eat•a•ble [ʌn'iːtəbl] *adj.* (food) which is so unpleasant that you cannot eat it.

un•ec•o•nom•ic(al) [ʌniːkə'nɒmɪk(l)] *adj.* which is not economic/which does not make a profit.

un•ed•u•cat•ed [ʌn'edjʊkeɪtɪd] *adj.* not educated; (person) who has not been well brought up; (way of speaking) which is not refined.

un•em•ployed [ʌnɪm'plɔɪd] *adj.* without any permanent work; **the u.** = people with no jobs. un•em•ploy•ment [ʌnɪm'plɔɪmənt] *n.* lack of jobs; **mass u.** = situation where large numbers of people are out of work.

un•end•ing [ʌn'endɪŋ] *adj.* ceaseless/with no end.

un•en•light•ened [ʌnɪn'laɪtənd] *adj.* lacking knowledge.

un•en•vi•a•ble [ʌn'envɪəbl] *adj.* which no one would envy.

un•e•qual [ʌn'iːkwəl] *adj.* (a) not equal. (b) **u. to** = not good/strong enough for. un•e•qualed, *adj.* which has no equal.

un•e•quiv•o•cal [ʌnɪ'kwɪvəkl] *adj.* clear; easily understood; which cannot be misunderstood.

un•err•ing [ʌn'ɜːrɪŋ] *adj.* faultless/making no mistake.

un•eth•i•cal [ʌn'eTɪkl] *adj.* (conduct) which does not follow the usual rules of a profession.

un•e•ven [ʌn'iːvn] *adj.* (a) bumpy/not flat. (b) not always very good. un•e•ven•ness, *n.* being uneven.

un•e•vent•ful [ʌnɪ'ventfəl] *adj.* without any particularly exciting incidents.

un•ex•am•pled [ʌnɪg'zɑːmpld] *adj.* extraordinary; of which there is no other example.

un•ex•cep•tion•a•ble [ʌnɪk'sepʃənəbl] *adj.* very satisfactory.

un•ex•cep•tion•al [ʌnɪk'sepʃnəl] *adj.* ordinary.

un•ex•pect•ed [ʌnɪk'spektɪd] *adj.* which was not expected. un•ex•pect•ed•ly, *adv.* in an unexpected way.

un•ex•plored [ʌnɪk'splɔːd] *adj.* which has never been explored.

un•ex•posed [ʌnɪk'spəuzd] *adj.* (film) which has not been used.

un•ex•pur•gat•ed [ʌn'ekspɜːgeɪtɪd] *adj.* (book, etc.) which has not had offensive parts removed.

un•fail•ing [ʌn'feɪlɪŋ] *adj.* which never fails. un•fail•ing•ly, *adv.* without fail.

un•fair [ʌn'feə] *adj.* not fair.

un•faith•ful [ʌn'feɪTfəl] *adj.* not faithful (to your husband or wife).

un•fa•mil•iar [ʌnfə'mɪlɪə] *adj.* not familiar.

un•fas•ten [ʌn'fɑːsn] *v.* to undo (sth which is fastened).

un•fath•om•a•ble [ʌn'fæðəməbl] *adj.* (mystery) which cannot be solved.

un•fa•vor•a•ble [ʌn'feɪvrəbl] *adj.* not favorable.

un•feel•ing [ʌn'fiːlɪŋ] *adj.* insensitive; not sympathetic to s.o.

un•fet•tered [ʌn'fetəd] *adj.* free.

un•fit [ʌn'fɪt] *adj.* (a) (person) who is not fit/not in good physical condition. (b) not suitable.

un•flag•ging [ʌn'flægɪŋ] *adj.* tireless.

un•flap•pa•ble [ʌn'flæpəbl] *adj.* (person) who is always calm.

un•flinch•ing [ʌn'flɪntʃɪŋ] *adj.* brave. un•flinch•ing•ly, *adv.* bravely.

un•fold [ʌn'fəuld] *v.* (a) to spread out (a newspaper). (b) (*of story*) to become clear/be told.

un•fore•seen [ʌnfɔː'siːn] *adj.* not foreseen/not anticipated.

un•for•get•ta•ble [ʌnfə'getəbl] *adj.* which cannot be forgotten.

un•for•tu•nate [ʌn'fɔːtʃənət] *adj.* (a) unlucky. (b) sad; to be regretted. un•for•tu•nate•ly, *adv.* sadly.

un•found•ed [ʌn'faundɪd] *adj.* without any basis in truth.

un•freeze [ʌn'friːz] *v.* (unfroze, unfrozen) to warm (sth) so that it stops being frozen.

un•fre•quent•ed [ʌnfrɪ'kwentɪd] *adj.* (place) where few people go.

un•friend•ly [ʌn'frendlɪ] *adj.* (-ier, -iest) not like a friend.

un•frock [ʌn'frɒk] *v.* to remove (a priest) from holy orders.

un•furl [ʌn'fɜːl] *v.* to unroll (like a flag).

un•fur•nished [ʌn'fɜːnɪʃt] *adj.* (house) with no furniture in it.

un•gain•ly [ʌn'geɪnlɪ] *adj.* awkward/clumsy (way of walking).

un•gen•tle•man•ly [ʌn'dʒentəlmənlɪ] *adj.* (behavior) not like that of a true gentleman.

un•god•ly [ʌn'gɒdlɪ] *adj.* wicked; unpleasant/dreadful. *inf.* very early/late (hour).

æ back, ɑː farm, ɒ top, aɪ pipe, aʊ how, aɪə fire, aʊə flower, ɔː bought, ɔɪ toy, e fed, eəhair, eɪ take, ə afraid, əʊ boat, əʊə lower, ɜː word, iː heap, ɪ hit, ɪə hear, uː school, ʊ book, ʌ but, b back, d dog, ð then, dʒ just, f fog, g go, h hand, j yes, k catch, l last, m mix, n nut, ŋ sing, p penny, r round, s some, ʃ short, t too, tʃ chop, θ thing, v voice, w was, z zoo, ʒ treasure

un•gra•cious [ʌnˈgreɪʃəs] *adj.* not gracious/not polite.

un•gram•mat•i•cal [ˌʌngrəˈmætɪkl] *adj.* which goes against the rules of grammar.

un•grate•ful [ʌnˈgreɪtfəl] *adj.* not grateful.

un•guard•ed [ʌnˈgɑːdɪd] *adj.* careless; **in an u. moment** = without thinking about the consequences.

un•guent [ˈʌngwənt] *n.* (*formal*) ointment.

un•gu•late [ˈʌngjuleɪt] *n.* animal with hooves.

un•hap•py [ʌnˈhæpɪ] *adj.* (**-ier, -iest**) sad. **un•hap•pi•ly**, *adv.* sadly/unfortunately. **un•hap•pi•ness**, *n.* being unhappy.

un•harmed [ʌnˈhɑːmd] *adj.* safe.

un•health•y [ʌnˈhelθɪ] *adj.* (**-ier, -iest**) (a) not healthy. (b) unnatural.

un•heard-of [ʌnˈhɜːdɒv] *adj.* strange/odd.

un•heat•ed [ʌnˈhiːtɪd] *adj.* which has no heating.

un•help•ful [ʌnˈhelpfəl] *adj.* not helpful.

un•her•ald•ed [ʌnˈherəldɪd] *adj.* not announced/publicized beforehand.

un•hinged [ʌnˈhɪndʒd] *adj.* extremely upset/mad.

un•ho•ly [ʌnˈhəʊlɪ] *adj. inf.* unpleasant.

un•hook [ʌnˈhʊk] *v.* to take (sth) off a hook; to unfasten (sth) which is attached with hooks.

un•hoped-for [ʌnˈhəʊptfɔː] *adj.* unexpected.

un•horse [ʌnˈhɔːs] *v.* to make (s.o.) fall off his horse.

un•hurt [ʌnˈhɜːt] *adj.* not hurt; safe and sound.

un•hy•gi•en•ic [ˌʌnhaɪˈdʒiːnɪk] *adj.* dirty/not hygienic.

u•ni•cam•er•al [juːnɪˈkæmərəl] *adj.* having only one legislative chamber, house or branch.

u•ni•corn [ˈjuːnɪkɔːn] *n.* mythical animal like a horse, with one long, straight horn.

un•i•den•ti•fied [ˌʌnaɪˈdentɪfaɪd] *adj.* which has not been identified; **u. flying object** = mysterious object in the sky which cannot be identified.

u•ni•fi•ca•tion [juːnɪfɪˈkeɪʃn] *n.* act of unifying; joining together into one.

u•ni•form [ˈjuːnɪfɔːm] 1. *n.* specially designed clothing worn by all members of a group. 2. *adj.* all the same; never changing. **u•ni•form•i•ty** [juːnɪˈfɒmɪtɪ] *n.* being uniform. **u•ni•form re•source lo•ca•tor**, *n.* standardized address of a site on the Internet. **u•ni•form•ly**, *adv.* in a uniform way.

u•ni•fy [ˈjuːnɪfaɪ] *v.* to join together into one.

u•ni•lat•er•al [juːnɪˈlætərəl] *adj.* on one side only; done by one side only. **u•ni•lat•er•al•ly**, *adv.* (done) by one side only.

un•im•ag•i•na•tive [ˌʌnɪˈmædʒɪnətɪv] *adj.* lacking flair.

un•im•paired [ˌʌnɪmˈpeəd] *adj.* not damaged.

un•im•peach•a•ble [ˌʌnɪmˈpiːtʃəbl] *adj.* which can be trusted completely.

un•im•por•tant [ˌʌnɪmˈpɔːtənt] *adj.* not important.

un•in•formed [ˌʌnɪnˈfɔːmd] *adj.* without full knowledge.

un•in•hab•it•a•ble [ˌʌnɪnˈhæbɪtəbl] *adj.* which cannot be lived in. **un•in•hab•it•ed**, *adj.* not lived in.

un•in•hib•it•ed [ˌʌnɪnˈhɪbɪtɪd] *adj.* free; not bound by the customs of society.

un•in•i•ti•at•ed [ˌʌnɪˈnɪʃɪeɪtɪd] *n.* **the u.** = people who are not experts.

un•in•tel•li•gi•ble [ˌʌnɪnˈtelɪdʒəbl] *adj.* which cannot be understood.

un•in•ter•rupt•ed [ˌʌnɪntəˈrʌptɪd] *adj.* with no breaks; continuous.

un•in•vit•ed [ˌʌnɪnˈvaɪtɪd] *adj.* without an invitation. **un•in•vit•ing**, *adj.* not very attractive.

un•ion [ˈjuːnɪən] *n.* (a) being joined together; countries or states which are joined together. (b) (*formal*) marriage. (c) group of people working in the same type of industry joined together for mutual protection; labor union. **un•ion•ist**, *n.* member of a labor union. **un•ion•ize**, *v.* to form a labor union in (a factory/a group of workers). **Un•ion Jack**, *n.* national flag of the United Kingdom.

u•nique [juˈniːk] *adj.* so special that there is nothing similar to it. **u•nique•ly**, *adv.* in a special or unique way.

u•ni•sex [ˈjuːnɪseks] *adj.* which can be used by both men and women.

u•ni•son [ˈjuːnɪsn] *n.* **in u.** = (i) singing the same note all together; (ii) in total agreement.

u•nit [ˈjuːnɪt] *n.* (a) one part (of a larger whole); one cupboard/one set of shelves, etc., which can be matched with others to form a whole. (b) one part (of an army). (c) standard measurement by which sth is counted. (d) number one; single number. **u•ni•tar•y**, *adj.* referring to a unit.

u•nite [juˈnaɪt] *v.* to join together as a whole. **u•ni•ty** [ˈjuːnɪtɪ] *n.* being one whole.

u•ni•valve [ˈjuːnɪvælv] *n.* animal (such as a snail) with a single shell.

u•ni•verse [ˈjuːnɪvɜːs] *n.* all that exists, including the earth, the planets and the stars. **u•ni•ver•sal** [juːnɪˈvɜːsəl] *adj.* which is everywhere; which affects everyone; **u. joint** = mechanical joint made so that each of two connected rods can move in any direction; **u. suffrage** = situation where all adults have the right to vote. **u•ni•ver•sal•ly**, *adv.* everywhere; by everyone.

u•ni•ver•si•ty [juːnɪˈvɜːsɪtɪ] *n.* place of higher

learning, where degrees are given to successful students, and a wide range of specialized subjects are taught.

un•just [ʌn'dʒʌst] *adj.* not fair. **un•just•ly**, *adv.* in an unjust way.

un•jus•ti•fied [ʌn'dʒʌstɪfaɪd] *adj.* which is not justified.

un•kempt [ʌn'kemt] *adj.* disheveled/untidy.

un•kind [ʌn'kaɪnd] *adj.* (-er, -est) harsh/cruel. **un•kind•ly**, *adv.* in a cruel way.

un•known ['ʌnnəʊn] *adj.* not known.

un•lad•en [ʌn'leɪdn] *adj.* without a load.

un•la•dy•like [ʌn'leɪdɪlaɪk] *adj.* (behavior) which is not like that of a lady.

un•law•ful [ʌn'lɔːfəl] *adj.* against the law.

un•lead•ed [ʌn'ledɪd] *adj.* (gasoline) without lead additives.

un•leash [ʌn'liːʃ] *v.* to unfasten the leash (of a dog); to set free/to set loose.

un•leav•ened [ʌn'levnd] *adj.* (bread) made without yeast.

un•less [ʌn'les] *conj.* (a) if…not. (b) except if.

un•like ['ʌnlaɪk] *adj. & prep.* not similar to; different from; **it is u. him to be rude** = he is not usually rude. **un•like•ly** [ʌn'laɪklɪ] *adj.* improbable; (story) which is probably not true.

un•lim•it•ed [ʌn'lɪmɪtɪd] *adj.* with no limits.

un•lined [ʌn'laɪnd] *adj.* (a) without lines. (b) without a lining.

un•list•ed [ʌn'lɪstɪd] *adj.* not included in a list.

un•load [ʌn'ləʊd] *v.* to remove a load from (a vehicle). **un•load•ed**, *adj.* (gun) with no bullets in it.

un•lock [ʌn'lɒk] *v.* to open (sth) which was locked.

un•looked-for [ʌn'lʌkdfɔː] *adj.* not expected.

un•luck•y [ʌn'lʌkɪ] *adj.* (-ier, -iest) not lucky; bringing bad luck. **un•luck•i•ly**, *adv.* unfortunately.

un•man•age•a•ble [ʌn'mænɪdʒəbl] *adj.* difficult to control.

un•manned [ʌn'mænd] *adj.* without a crew/without any staff.

un•man•ner•ly [ʌn'mænəlɪ] *adj.* with no manners.

un•mar•ried ['ʌnmærɪd] *adj.* not married; **u. mother** = woman who has a child but is not married.

un•mask [ʌn'mɑːsk] *v.* to remove a mask; to show (s.o.) as they really are.

un•matched [ʌn'mætʃt] *adj.* which has no equal.

un•men•tion•a•ble [ʌn'menʃnəbl] *adj.* which you must not talk about because it is so indecent/unpleasant, etc.

un•mis•tak•a•ble [ʌnmɪs'teɪkəbl] *adj.* which is easily recognized/which cannot be mistaken.

un•mit•i•gat•ed [ʌn'mɪtɪgeɪtɪd] *adj.* total/complete.

un•moved [ʌn'muːvd] *adj.* not touched/not affected.

un•mu•si•cal [ʌn'mjuːzɪkl] *adj.* not interested in music; not able to play a musical instrument.

un•named [ʌn'neɪmd] *adj.* (person) who has not been named.

un•nat•u•ral [ʌn'nætʃərəl] *adj.* which is not natural; which does not follow the usual pattern.

un•nec•es•sar•y [ʌn'nesəsərɪ] *adj.* which is not necessary. **un•nec•es•sar•i•ly**, *adv.* uselessly; for no good reason.

un•nerve [ʌn'nɜːv] *v.* to make (s.o.) lose his nerve/his courage.

un•no•ticed [ʌn'nəʊtɪst] *adj.* not noticed; without anyone noticing.

un•num•bered [ʌn'nʌmbəd] *adj.* with no numbers; which cannot be counted.

un•ob•serv•ant [ʌnəb'zɜːvənt] *adj.* not observant; (person) who does not notice things.

un•ob•struct•ed [ʌnəb'strʌktɪd] *adj.* with nothing in the way.

un•ob•tain•a•ble [ʌnəb'teɪnəbl] *adj.* which cannot be obtained.

un•ob•tru•sive [ʌnəb'truːsɪv] *adj.* not obvious; not easily noticed.

un•oc•cu•pied [ʌn'ɒkjupaɪd] *adj.* not occupied; empty.

un•of•fi•cial [ʌnə'fɪʃl] *adj.* not official; (strike) which has not been officially approved by a union. **un•of•fi•cial•ly**, *adv.* in an unofficial way.

un•op•posed [ʌnə'pəʊzd] *adj.* with no opposition.

un•or•tho•dox [ʌn'ɔːθədɒks] *adj.* not usual.

un•pack [ʌn'pæk] *v.* to take (things) out of containers in which they were transported.

un•paid [ʌn'peɪd] *adj.* (person) who is not paid a salary; (bill) which has not been settled.

un•pal•at•a•ble [ʌn'pælətəbl] *adj.* not pleasant to the taste; unpleasant (fact).

un•par•al•leled [ʌn'pærəleld] *adj.* with no parallel or no equal.

un•par•don•a•ble [ʌn'pɑːdnəbl] *adj.* which cannot be excused.

un•pa•tri•ot•ic [ˌʌnpætrɪˈɒtɪk] *adj.* not patriotic.

un•per•son [ˈʌnpɜːsən] *n.* person who is treated as if he did not exist (because of opposition to the government).

un•pleas•ant [ʌnˈplezənt] *adj.* not pleasing. **un•pleas•ant•ness,** *n.* argument/disagreement.

un•pop•u•lar [ʌnˈpɒpjulə] *adj.* not popular. **un•pop•u•lar•i•ty** [ʌnpɒpjuˈlærɪtɪ] *n.* being unpopular.

un•prec•e•dent•ed [ʌnˈpresɪdentɪd] *adj.* which has never happened before.

un•prej•u•diced [ʌnˈpredʒudɪst] *adj.* fair; not prejudiced.

un•pre•med•i•tat•ed [ʌnprɪˈmedɪteɪtɪd] *adj.* which has not been planned.

un•pre•pared [ʌnprɪˈpeəd] *adj.* not ready.

un•pre•pos•ses•sing [ʌnpriːpəˈzesɪŋ] *adj.* not very attractive.

un•pre•ten•tious [ʌnprɪˈtenʃəs] *adj.* modest/not showing off.

un•prin•ci•pled [ʌnˈprɪnsɪpld] *adj.* without any moral standards.

un•print•a•ble [ʌnˈprɪntəbl] *adj.* (words) so rude that you cannot print them.

un•pro•duc•tive [ʌnprəˈdʌktɪv] *adj.* (discussion) which does not produce any result; (land) which does not produce any crops.

un•pro•fes•sion•al [ʌnprəˈfeʃnəl] *adj.* (conduct) which is not of the sort you would expect from a member of a particular profession.

un•prof•it•a•ble [ʌnˈprɒfɪtəbl] *adj.* which does not make a profit; which is useless.

un•prompt•ed [ʌnˈprɒmptɪd] *adj.* without anyone suggesting it.

un•pro•nounce•a•ble [ʌnprəˈnaʊnsəbl] *adj.* (name) which is difficult to say.

un•pro•voked [ʌnprəˈvəʊkt] *adj.* (action) which was not provoked.

un•qual•i•fied [ʌnˈkwɒlɪfaɪd] *adj.* (a) (person) who does not have the necessary skills, etc. to qualify for a job, position, etc. (b) total/complete (success).

un•ques•tion•a•ble [ʌnˈkweʃtjənəbl] *adj.* which is certain/not doubtful. **un•ques•tion•a•bly,** *adv.* certainly. **un•ques•tion•ing,** *adj.* without doubting.

un•quote [ˈʌnkwəʊt] *v.* to indicate the end of a quotation (when speaking).

un•rav•el [ʌnˈrævl] *v.* (**unraveled, unravelled**) to disentangle (sth knotted); to solve (a mystery).

un•read•a•ble [ʌnˈriːdəbl] *adj.* (book) which is so boring that you cannot read it.

un•re•al [ʌnˈriːl] *adj.* not like the real world. **un•re•al•is•tic** [ʌnrɪəˈlɪstɪk] *adj.* impractical/not facing facts.

un•rea•son•a•ble [ʌnˈriːznəbl] *adj.* not reasonable/too large.

un•rec•og•niz•a•ble [ʌnrekəgˈnaɪzəbl] *adj.* which cannot be recognized.

un•reel [ʌnˈriːl] *v.* to undo (sth wound round a reel).

un•re•fined [ʌnrɪˈfaɪnd] *adj.* (sugar/oil) which has not been refined.

un•re•lat•ed [ʌnrɪˈleɪtɪd] *adj.* not related/with no connection.

un•re•lent•ing [ʌnrɪˈlentɪŋ] *adj.* which never stops/weakens.

un•re•li•a•ble [ʌnrɪˈlaɪəbl] *adj.* which cannot be relied on.

un•re•lieved [ʌnrɪˈliːvd] *adj.* not lessened.

un•re•mit•ting [ʌnrɪˈmɪtɪŋ] *adj.* never ceasing.

un•re•quit•ed [ʌnrɪˈkwaɪtɪd] *adj.* (love) which is not returned.

un•re•served [ʌnrɪˈzɜːvd] *adj.* not reserved. **un•re•serv•ed•ly** [ʌnrɪˈzɜːvɪdlɪ] *adv.* definitely.

un•rest [ʌnˈrest] *n.* being restless/dissatisfied; agitation to get political/industrial change.

un•ri•valed, *Brit.* **un•ri•valled** [ʌnˈraɪvəld] *adj.* with no equal.

un•roll [ʌnˈrəʊl] *v.* to undo (sth which is rolled up).

un•ruf•fled [ʌnˈrʌfld] *adj.* calm/not anxious.

un•ru•ly [ʌnˈruːlɪ] *adj.* wild/with no discipline. **un•ru•li•ness,** *n.* wild behavior.

un•safe [ʌnˈseɪf] *adj.* (**-er, -est**) dangerous.

un•said [ʌnˈsed] *adj.* **better left u.** = better not to say it.

un•salt•ed [ʌnˈsɒltɪd] *adj.* (butter, etc.) with no salt.

un•sat•is•fac•to•ry [ʌnsætɪsˈfæktrɪ] *adj.* not satisfactory.

un•sat•is•fied [ʌnˈsætɪsfaɪd] *adj.* not satisfied.

un•sat•u•rat•ed [ʌnˈsætjuːreɪtɪd] *adj.* (fat) which contains little hydrogen, and so can be broken down easily in the body.

un•sa•vor•y, *Brit.* **un•sa•vour•y** [ʌnˈseɪvərɪ] *adj.* unpleasant/disgusting.

un•scathed [ʌnˈskeɪðd] *adj.* not harmed.

un•sched•uled [ʌnˈʃedjuːld] *adj.* not on a schedule.

un•schooled [ʌnˈskuːld] *adj.* not taught; without any experience (**in**).

un•sci•en•tif•ic [ʌnsaɪənˈtɪfɪk] *adj.* not scientific.

un•scram•ble [ʌnˈskræmbl] *v.* to put back in order; to put (a coded message) back into plain language.

un•screw [ʌnˈskruː] *v.* to open by twisting a screw or a screw lid anticlockwise.

un•scru•pu•lous [ʌn'skruːpjʊləs] *adj.* not worrying too much about honesty.

un•sealed [ʌn'siːld] *adj.* (envelope, etc.) which has not been sealed.

un•sea•son•a•ble [ʌn'siːzənəbl] *adj.* not usual for the season.

un•seat [ʌn'siːt] *v.* to make (s.o.) fall off a horse; to remove from political office at an election.

un•seem•ly [ʌn'siːmlɪ] *adj.* offensive/rude (behavior).

un•seen [ʌn'siːn] *adj.* not seen/invisible.

un•sel•fish [ʌn'selfɪʃ] *adj.* not selfish/thinking of others before yourself.

un•ser•vice•a•ble [ʌn'səːvɪsəbl] *adj.* not in a good enough state to be used.

un•set•tle [ʌn'setl] *v.* to upset. **un•set•tled,** *adj.* (weather) which changes often.

un•shak•a•ble, unshakeable [ʌn'ʃeɪkəbl] *adj.* solid/firm (belief/faith).

un•sight•ly [ʌn'saɪtlɪ] *adj.* ugly.

un•signed [ʌn'saɪnd] *adj.* not signed.

un•skilled ['ʌnskɪld] *adj.* (worker) who has no particular skill.

un•so•cia•ble [ʌn'səʊʃəbl] *adj.* not friendly; not wishing to make friends.

un•so•lic•it•ed [ʌnsə'lɪsɪtɪd] *adj.* which has not been asked for.

un•solved [ʌn'sɒlvd] *adj.* (problem) which has not been solved.

un•so•phis•ti•cat•ed [ʌnsə'fɪstɪkeɪtɪd] *adj.* simple; not sophisticated.

un•sound ['ʌnsaʊnd] *adj.* (a) **of u. mind** = mad. (b) (reasoning) not based on fact or logic.

un•spar•ing [ʌn'speərɪŋ] *adj.* generous; not reluctant.

un•speak•a•ble [ʌn'spiːkəbl] *adj.* extremely unpleasant.

un•spoiled, unspoilt ['ʌnspɔɪlt] *adj.* (countryside) which has not been spoiled.

un•sta•ble [ʌn'steɪbl] *adj.* (a) not stable; changeable; (government) which is likely to fall at any moment. (b) dangerously mad.

un•stead•y [ʌn'stedɪ] *adj.* not steady; wobbly.

un•stick [ʌn'stɪk] *v.* (**unstuck**) to remove sth which is stuck on; **to come unstuck** = to go badly wrong.

un•stop•pa•ble [ʌn'stɒpəbl] *adj.* which cannot be stopped.

un•suc•cess•ful [ʌnsək'sesfəl] *adj.* not successful.

un•suit•a•ble [ʌn'suːtəbl] *adj.* not suitable.

un•sul•lied [ʌn'sʌlɪd] *adj.* pure.

un•sung [ʌn'sʌŋ] *adj.* (hero) who is not famous.

un•sure [ʌn'ʃʊə] *adj.* not sure; **u. of oneself** = lacking self-confidence.

un•sus•pect•ed [ʌnsəs'pektɪd] *adj.* which is not suspected to exist. **un•sus•pect•ing,** *adj.* (person) who does not realize sth/that a danger is imminent.

un•sweet•ened [ʌn'swiːtənd] *adj.* (food) with no sugar added.

un•swerv•ing [ʌn'swɜːvɪŋ] *adj.* (loyalty) which does not change.

un•sym•pa•thet•ic [ʌnsɪmpə'Tetɪk] *adj.* not sympathetic.

un•tan•gle [ʌn'tæŋgl] *v.* to disentangle.

un•tapped [ʌn'tæpt] *adj.* not previously used.

un•ten•a•ble [ʌn'tenəbl] *adj.* (position/theory) which cannot be defended.

un•think•a•ble [ʌn'Tɪŋkəbl] *adj.* which cannot be considered or thought of. **un•think•ing** [ʌn'Tɪŋkɪŋ] *adj.* done without thinking. **un•thought-of,** *adj.* which no one has thought possible.

un•ti•dy [ʌn'taɪdɪ] *adj.* (**-ier, -iest**) not tidy/in disorder. **un•ti•di•ly,** *adv.* in an untidy way. **un•ti•di•ness,** *n.* being untidy.

un•tie [ʌn'taɪ] *v.* to unfasten (sth which is tied with a knot).

un•til [ʌn'tɪl] *prep. & conj.* up to (a certain time).

un•time•ly [ʌn'taɪmlɪ] *adj.* (a) happening too soon. (b) not suitable.

un•to ['ʌntu] *prep.* (*old*) to.

un•told [ʌn'təʊld] *adj.* very large; so large that it cannot be counted.

un•touch•a•ble [ʌn'tʌtʃəbl] 1. *adj.* which cannot be touched. 2. *n.* person from the lowest caste in India.

un•to•ward [ʌntə'wɔːd] *adj.* unlucky/inconvenient; **nothing u. took place** = everything went off well.

un•trained [ʌn'treɪnd] *adj.* (person) who has had no training.

un•tried [ʌn'traɪd] *adj.* which has not been tested.

un•true [ʌn'truː] *adj.* wrong/not true.

un•trust•wor•thy [ʌn'trʌstwɜːðɪ] *adj.* (person) who cannot be trusted.

un•truth [ʌn'truːT] *n.* lie. **un•truth•ful,** *adj.* (person) who does not tell the truth; (statement) which is wrong.

un•us•a•ble [ʌn'juːzəbl] *adj.* which cannot be used.

æ back, aː farm, ɒ top, aɪ pipe, aʊ how, aie fire, aʊə flower, ɔː bought, ɔɪ toy, e fed, eəhair, eɪ take, ə afraid, əʊ boat, əʊə lower, vː word, iː heap, ɪ hit, ɪə hear, uː school, ʊ book, ʌ but, b back, d dog, ð then, dʒ just, f fog, g go, h hand, j yes, k catch, l last, m mix, n nut, ŋ sing, p penny, r round, s some, ʃ short, t too, tʃ chop, θ thing, v voice, w was, z zoo, ʒ treasure

un•used *adj.* (a) [ʌn'juːzd] new/clean; which has not been used. (b) [ʌn'juːsd] not accustomed (to).

un•u•su•al [ʌn'juːʒʊəl] *adj.* strange/extraordinary. **un•u•su•al•ly**, *adv.* strangely/extraordinarily.

un•ut•ter•a•ble [ʌnʌ'tərəbl] *adj.* so terrible that it cannot be expressed.

un•var•nished [ʌn'vɑːnɪʃt] *adj.* with no varnish; plain/simple (truth).

un•veil [ʌn'veɪl] *v.* to uncover (a new statue/a new plan, etc.).

un•versed [ʌn'vɜːst] *adj.* with no experience (in).

un•want•ed [ʌn'wɒntɪd] *adj.* which is not wanted.

un•war•rant•ed [ʌn'wɒrəntɪd] *adj.* which is not justified.

un•war•y [ʌn'weərɪ] *adj.* (person) who does not take care.

un•well [ʌn'wel] *adj.* sick/ill.

un•whole•some [ʌn'həʊlsəm] *adj.* not healthy/which might harm.

un•wield•y [ʌn'wiːldɪ] *adj.* large and awkward.

un•will•ing [ʌn'wɪlɪŋ] *adj.* reluctant; not willing.

un•wind [ʌn'waɪnd] *v.* (**unwound** [ʌn'waʊnd]) (a) to undo (sth which has been wound). (b) *inf.* to relax.

un•wise [ʌn'waɪz] *adj.* rash/imprudent; not wise.

un•wit•ting [ʌn'wɪtɪŋ] *adj.* not knowing/intending. **un•wit•ting•ly**, *adv.* without intending to; not intentionally.

un•wont•ed [ʌn'wɒntɪd] *adj.* not usual.

un•work•a•ble [ʌn'wɜːkəbl] *adj.* (plan) which will not work in practice.

un•wor•thy [ʌn'wɜːðɪ] *adj.* (of) (a) which does not deserve (sth). (b) not as good as one might expect from (a person).

un•wound [ʌn'waʊnd] *v. see* **un•wind**.

un•wrap [ʌn'ræp] *v.* (**unwrapped**) to take the wrapping off (sth).

un•writ•ten [ʌn'rɪtən] *adj.* **u. law** = custom which has grown up over a period of time but which is not written down.

un•zip [ʌn'zɪp] *v.* (**unzipped**) to undo a zipper.

up [ʌp] 1. *adv.* (a) toward a higher place; **hands u.!** = lift your hands into the air to show you surrender. (b) in a higher place; **this side u.** = this side must be on top. (c) toward the north. (d) to a higher level. (e) to the end; completely. (f) not in bed. (g) close to. 2. *prep.* (a) toward a higher part of (sth). (b) along; toward the source of (a river); **to walk u. and down** = backward and forward. 3. *adj.* (a) which is going up. (b) which is in a higher position; completely built; **the house is u.** = completely built.

(c) not in bed. (d) finished; **your time is u.** = you have to stop now; **his leave is u.** = he has to go back to the army. (e) *inf.* **what's u.** = what is the matter? 4. *n.* **ups and downs** = good and bad periods. 5. *v.* (**upped**) (a) to raise (prices, etc.). (b) *inf.* to get up suddenly.

up-and-com•ing [ʌpən'kʌmɪŋ] *adj.* (person) who looks as though he might succeed.

up-and-up [ʌpən'ʌp] *n.* **to be on the u.-and-u.** = to be honest/trustworthy. **up•com•ing**, *adj.* imminent/likely to happen soon. **up for**, *prep.* ready for; **u. f. sale** = on sale.

up•mar•ket, *adj.* aiming at the expensive end of the market. **up to**, *prep.* (a) as many as. (b) capable enough to do (sth). (c) **it's u. t. you** = it is your responsibility. (d) doing (sth bad).

up-to-date, *adj. & adv.* modern/using the most recent information, etc.

up•braid [ʌp'breɪd] *v.* (*formal*) to scold.

up•bring•ing ['ʌpbrɪŋɪŋ] *n.* education; training of a child.

up•date [ʌp'deɪt] *v.* to revise (sth) so that it is more up-to-date.

up•end [ʌp'end] *v.* to stand (sth) on its end.

up•grade [ʌp'greɪd] *v.* to put (s.o.) into a more important job; to improve the quality of (sth).

up•heav•al [ʌp'hiːvəl] *n.* great change/disturbance.

up•hill [ʌp'hɪl] 1. *adj.* going upward; difficult. 2. *adv.* upward.

up•hold [ʌp'həʊld] *v.* (**upheld**) to support; to say that (a decision) is right.

up•hol•ster [ʌp'həʊlstə] *v.* to cover (chairs, etc.) with padded seats and covers. **up•hol•ster•er**, *n.* person who upholsters. **up•hol•ster•y**, *n.* (a) covering chairs, etc. with padded seats and covers. (b) covers for chairs; padded seats and cushions.

up•keep [ʌp'kiːp] *n.* (cost of) keeping a house/a car, etc., in good condition.

up•land [ʌp'lənd] *n.* mountainous area (of a country).

up•lift 1. *n.* ['ʌplɪft] (a) thing which gives a feeling of happiness or goodness. (b) increase/raising. 2. *v.* [ʌp'lɪft] to lift up/to raise.

up•load [ʌp'ləʊd] *v.* to bring information from the Internet into a personal computer.

up•on [ʌ'pɒn] *prep.* (*formal*) on; **battle u. battle** = one battle after another.

up•per ['ʌpə] 1. *adj.* (a) higher. (b) further up. (c) more important; of higher rank; **the u. classes** = the nobility; (*in school*) **the u. grades** = grades with older pupils; **u. case** = capital (letters); **u. house/chamber** = one of two branches of a legislature, as the U.S. Senate; senate; **to get the u. hand** = begin to win. 2. *n.* top part of a shoe. **up•per•cut**, *n.* blow with the fist upward on the chin. **up•per•most.**

1. *adj.* (a) highest. (b) furthest up. (c) most important. 2. *adv.* **what is u. in their minds** = the subject they think about most. **up•pish, up•pi•ty,** *adj. inf.* feeling superior to other people.

up•right ['ʌpraɪt] 1. *adj.* (a) vertical. (b) very honest. 2. *n.* (a) vertical post. (b) piano with the strings and body vertical.

up•ris•ing ['ʌpraɪzɪŋ] *n.* revolt (against authority).

up•roar ['ʌprɔː] *n.* loud noise/disturbance. **up•roar•i•ous** [ʌp'rɔːrɪəs] *adj.* noisy.

up•root [ʌp'ruːt] *v.* (a) to dig up (a plant) with its roots. (b) to make (a family) move to a totally new area.

up•set 1. *n.* ['ʌpset] (a) complete change for the worse. (b) great worry/cause of unhappiness. (c) slight illness. 2. *v.* [ʌp'set] (**upset**) (a) to knock over; to fall over. (b) to change completely (for the worse). (c) to make (s.o.) worried/unhappy. (d) to make (s.o.) slightly ill. 3. *adj.* [ʌp'set] (a) very worried/unhappy/anxious. (b) made ill.

up•shot ['ʌpʃɒt] *n.* result.

up•side down ['ʌpsaɪd'daʊn] *adv.* with the top turned to the bottom.

up•stage [ʌp'steɪdʒ] 1. *adv.* at the back of the stage. 2. *v.* (a) to move nearer the front of the stage than (s.o.). (b) to take attention away from (s.o. who feels he ought to have it).

up•stairs [ʌp'steəz] 1. *adv.* toward the upper part of a house. 2. *adj.* on the upper floors of a house. 3. *n.* the upper floors of a house.

up•stand•ing [ʌp'stændɪŋ] *adj.* strong/honest.

up•start [ʌp'stɑːt] *n.* inexperienced person who has become unexpectedly important.

up•stream [ʌp'striːm] *adv. & adj.* (moving) toward the source or a river, against the flow of the current.

up•surge ['ʌpsɜːdʒ] *n.* sudden increase (of emotion).

up•take ['ʌpteɪk] *n.* **slow/quick on the u.** = slow/quick to understand.

up•tight ['ʌptaɪt] *adj. inf.* nervous and annoyed.

up•turn ['ʌptɜːn] *n.* movement upward (in sales, etc.). **up•turned,** *adj.* (boat, etc.) turned upside down.

up•ward ['ʌpwəd] *adj.* moving toward a higher level. **up•ward, upwards,** *adv.* toward a higher level. **up•wards of,** *prep.* more than.

u•ra•ni•um [juˈreɪnɪəm] *n.* (*element:* U) radioactive metal used in producing atomic energy.

ur•ban ['ɜːbən] *adj.* (a) referring to towns. (b) living in towns. **ur•ban•i•za•tion,** *n.* act of urbanizing. **ur•ban•ize,** *v.* to make (an area) into a town; to make (sth/s.o. from the country) become accustomed to the town.

ur•bane [ɜːˈbeɪn] *adj.* very polite. **ur•ban•i•ty** [əˈbænɪtɪ] *n.* being urbane.

ur•chin ['ɜːtʃɪn] *n.* dirty little boy; **sea u.** = small sea creature with a round shell covered with spikes.

u•re•a [juːˈriːə] *n.* substance produced by the liver and excreted into the urine.

u•re•ter [juːˈriːtə] *n.* tube taking urine from the kidneys to the bladder.

u•re•thra [juːˈriːˈrə] *n.* tube taking urine from the bladder out of the body.

urge [ɜːdʒ] 1. *n.* strong desire. 2. *v.* (a) to encourage; to push (s.o.) to do sth. (b) to suggest strongly. **ur•gen•cy** ['ɜːdʒənsɪ] *n.* being urgent; need for sth to be done quickly; **what's the u.?** = why are you hurrying? **ur•gent,** *adj.* which needs to be done quickly. **ur•gent•ly,** *adv.* quickly/immediately.

u•rine ['juərɪn] *n.* liquid waste matter from the body. **u•ri•nal** [juəˈraɪnəl] *n.* place where men can pass waste liquid from the body; bowl to catch waste liquid passed from the body. **u•ri•nar•y** ['juərɪnərɪ] *adj.* referring to urine; **u. tract** = organs which create and excrete urine. **u•ri•nate,** *v.* to pass waste liquid from the body.

URL [juːɑːˈel] *abbrev. for* uniform resource locator; standardized address of sites on the Internet.

urn [ɜːn] *n.* very large vase; **coffee u.** = large metal container with a tap, in which large quantities of coffee can be made.

us [ʌs] *pron. referring to* we.

U.S., U.S.A. ['juːes, juːesˈeɪ] *abbreviations for* United States (of America).

use 1. *n.* [juːs] (a) being used; way in which sth is used. (b) ability to be used. (c) usefulness. 2. *v.* [juːz] (a) to put to a purpose. (b) to take advantage of (s.o.). (c) *inf.* **I could use a beer** = I would like a beer. (d) [juːs] to do sth regularly in the past; **she used to smoke. us•a•ble** ['juːzəbl] *adj.* which can be used. **us•age** ['juːsɪdʒ] *n.* (a) custom; way of doing things. (b) way of using a word. **used,** *adj.* (a) [juːzd] not new; which has been put to a purpose. (b)

æ back, ɑː farm, ɒ top, aɪ pipe, aʊ how, aɪə fire, aʊə flower, ɔː bought, ɔɪ toy, e fed, eə hair, eɪ take, ə afraid, əʊ boat, əʊə lower, vː word, iː heap, ɪ hit, ɪə hear, uː school, ʊ book, ʌ but, b back, d dog, ð then, dʒ just, f fog, g go, h hand, j yes, k catch, l last, m mix, n nut, ŋ sing, p penny, r round, s some, ʃ short, t too, tʃ chop, θ thing, v voice, w was, z zoo, ʒ treasure

[juːsd] accustomed (**to**). **use•ful** ['juːsfəl] *adj.* which helps; **to make oneself u.** = to do helpful things. **use•ful•ly**, *adv.* in a helpful way. **use•ful•ness**, *n.* being useful. **use•less** ['juːsləs] *adj.* which does not help; *inf.* **she is quite u.** = of no help at all. **use•less•ness**, *n.* being useless. **us•er** ['juːzə] *n.* person who uses. **us•er-friend•ly**, *adj.* (program/machine) which a user finds easy to use. **use up**, *v.* to finish.

ush•er ['ʌʃə] 1. *n.* person who shows people to their seats (in a theater/in a church). 2. *v.* **to u. in** = (i) to bring (s.o.) in; (ii) to be the beginning of. **ush•er•ette** [ʌʃə'ret] *n.* girl who shows people to their seats in a theater.

U.S.S.R. [juˈeses'ɑː] *abbreviation for* former Union of Soviet Socialist Republics, now referred to as Russia/the Commonwealth of Independent States.

u•su•al ['juːʒʊəl] *adj.* ordinary; which happens often. **u•su•al•ly**, *adv.* mostly/ordinarily.

u•su•rer ['juːzjʊrə] *n.* person who lends money for high interest. **u•su•ri•ous** [juːˈzjʊərɪəs] *adj.* excessively high (interest rate). **u•su•ry**, *n.* lending money for high interest.

u•surp [juːˈzɜːp] *v.* to take the place of (s.o.). **u•sur•pa•tion** [juːzɜː'peɪʃn] *n.* act of usurping. **u•surp•er**, *n.* person who usurps (a throne).

u•ten•sil [juːˈtensl] *n.* tool/pan/knife, etc., used for work in the kitchen.

u•ter•us ['juːtərəs] *n.* part of a female body where an unborn baby is carried. **u•ter•ine** ['juːtəraɪn] *adj.* referring to the uterus.

u•til•i•ty [juːˈtɪlɪtɪ] *n.* (a) usefulness; **u. room** = room, esp. in a house, where you put the washing machine/freezer, etc. (b) **utilities** = essential public services (such as electricity/gas/water, etc.). **u•til•i•tar•i•an** [juːtɪlɪ'teərɪən] *adj.* used for a practical purpose, not decoration. **u•ti•liz•a•ble** [juːtɪ-'laɪzəbl] *adj.* which can be used. **u•ti•li•za•tion** [juːtɪlaɪ'zeɪʃn] *n.* making use of sth. **u•ti•lize** ['juːtɪlaɪz] *v.* to use; to make use of (sth) for profit.

ut•most ['ʌtməʊst] *adj.* (a) greatest that can be. (b) farthest.

u•to•pi•a [juˈtəʊpɪə] *n.* imaginary perfect world. **u•to•pi•an**, *adj.* very perfect (ideas).

ut•ter ['ʌtə] 1. *adj.* complete/total. 2. *v.* to speak; to make (a sound). **ut•ter•ance**, *n.* thing spoken. **ut•ter•ly**, *adv.* completely. **ut•ter•most**, *adj.* (a) greatest that can be. (b) farthest.

UV ['juːˈviː] *abbrev. for* ultraviolet.

u•vu•la ['juːvjʊlə] *n.* small lump of flesh hanging down at the back of the mouth.

ux•o•ri•ous [ʌk'sɔːrɪəs] *adj.* (man) who is very fond of his wife.

Vv

V,v [viː]. **V-chip** = device fitted to a TV that can block reception of programs that have been classified as unsuitable for children; **V-neck** = neckline shaped like a V; **V sign** = sign made with two fingers raised in the air (usu. meaning victory).

v. ['vɜːsəs] *prep.* against; *see* **ver•sus**.

va•can•cy ['veɪkənsɪ] *n.* (a) being vacant. (b) empty place/room/job. **va•cant**, *adj.* (a) empty/not occupied. (b) (expression) showing no interest/liveliness. **va•cant•ly**, *adv.* with a vacant expression. **va•cate** [və'keɪt] *v.* to leave/to make (sth) empty. **va•ca•tion** [və'keɪʃn] 1. *n.* (a) period of time when a person does not engage in a regular activity, as work or study. (b) act of vacating (an office, etc.). 2. *v.* to go on a vacation.

vac•ci•nate ['væksɪneɪt] *v.* **to v. s.o. against a disease** = to put a vaccine into s.o.. so that his body will react against it and thus protect him from catching the disease. **vac•ci•na•tion** [væksɪ'neɪʃn] *n.* act of vaccinating. **vac•cine** ['væksiːn] *n.* substance which contains the virus of a disease which when injected, gives protection against the disease.

vac•il•late ['væsɪleɪt] *v.* to waver/to hesitate. **vac•il•la•tion** ['væsɪ'leɪʃn] *n.* hesitation/wavering.

vac•u•ous ['vækjuəs] *adj.* with no meaning/sense; silly/vacant (expression). **va•cu•i•ty** [və'kjuɪtɪ], **vac•u•ous•ness**, *n.* emptiness of meaning/silliness.

vac•u•um ['vækjuəm] 1. *n.* space from which all matter, including air, has been removed; **vacuum-packed** = (food) packed in a vacuum, so that no air can enter the package. 2. *v. inf.* to clean with a vacuum cleaner. **vac•uum clean•er**, *n.* cleaning machine which sucks up dust. **vac•u•um bot•tle**, *n.* bottle or flask with double walls to keep liquids warm or cold.

vag•a•bond ['vægəbɒnd] *adj. & n.* (person) who wanders about/who has no home.

va•gar•y ['veɪgərɪ] *n.* oddity/strange behavior.

va•gi•na [və'dʒaɪnə] *n.* tube in a female mammal connecting the uterus to the vulva and through which a baby is born. **vag•i•nal**, *adj.* referring to the vagina.

va•grant ['veɪgrənt] *adj. & n.* (tramp/person) who wanders from place to place with no home or work. **va•gran•cy**, *n.* being a vagrant.

vague [veɪg] *adj.* (-er, -est) not clear/not precise; **I haven't the vaguest idea** = I have no idea at all. **vague•ly**, *adv.* more or less; in a vague way. **vague•ness**, *n.* being vague.

vain [veɪn] *adj.* (-er, -est) (a) useless; meaningless; (b) very proud of one's appearance. (c) **in v.** = without any success/result. **vain•ly**, *adv.* with no success/with no result.

val•ance ['væləns] *n.* short curtain.

vale [veɪl] *n.* valley.

val•e•dic•tion [vælɪ'dɪkʃn] *n.* (*formal*) farewell. **val•e•dic•to•ry**, *adj.* which says farewell.

val•ence, valency ['veɪləns, 'veɪlənsɪ] *n.* (*in chemistry*) power of an atom to combine.

val•en•tine ['væləntaɪn] *n.* (a) person chosen as a loved one on 14th February (St. Valentine's Day). (b) card or gift sent to someone you love on 14th February.

va•le•ri•an [və'lɪərɪən] *n.* type of wild plant with pink flowers.

val•et ['væleɪ, 'vælɪt] *n.* male servant who looks after his master's clothes; **v. service** = cleaning service in a hotel.

val•e•tu•di•nar•i•an [vælɪtjuːdɪ'neərɪən] *n.* person who likes to feel he is an invalid.

val•iant ['vælɪənt] *adj.* brave. **val•iant•ly**, *adv.* bravely.

val•id ['vælɪd] *adj.* (a) which is acceptable because it is true. (b) which can be lawfully used for a time. **val•i•date**, *v.* to make valid. **val•i•da•tion** [vælɪ'deɪʃn] *n.* act of validating. **va•lid•i•ty** [və'lɪdɪtɪ] *n.* (a) legal force. (b) truth.

æ back, aː farm, ɒ top, aɪ pipe, aʊ how, aɪə fire, aʊə flower, ɔː bought, ɔɪ toy, e fed, eəhair, eɪ take, ə afraid, əʊ boat, əʊə lower, vː word, iː heap, ɪ hit, ɪə hear, u: school, ʊ book, ʌ but, b back, d dog, ð then, dʒ just, f fog, g go, h hand, j yes, k catch, l last, m mix, n nut, ŋ sing, p penny, r round, s some, ʃ short, t too, tʃ chop, θ thing, v voice, w was, z zoo, ʒ treasure

val•ley ['vælɪ] *n.* long stretch of low land through which a river runs.

val•or, *Brit.* **val•our** ['vælə] *n.* bravery.

val•ue ['vælju:] 1. *n.* (a) worth (in money or esteem); **to get v. for one's money** = to get a good bargain. (b) usefulness. (c) **values** = principles/important things in life. 2. *v.* (a) to put a price in money on (an object). (b) to set a high value on (sth). **val•u•a•ble.** 1. *adj.* worth a lot of money; very useful. 2. *n.* **valuables** = objects of great value. **val•u•a•tion** [vælju'eɪʃn] *n.* estimate of the worth of sth; act of estimating the worth of sth. **val•ue-add•ed tax,** *n.* tax imposed on the value of goods or services. **val•ue•less,** *adj.* worthless/with no value.

valve [vælv] *n.* (a) mechanical device which allows air/liquid to pass through in one direction only; **safety v.** = valve which allows gas/steam, etc. to escape if the pressure is too great. (b) flap in a tube in the body which allows air/blood, etc. to circulate in one direction only. (c) part of a brass musical instrument which lengthens the tube. (d) single shell (of a shellfish). **val•vu•lar** ['vælvjulə] *adj.* referring to a valve in the heart.

vamp [væmp] *n.* (a) front part of the upper of a shoe or boot. (b) (*old*) flirtatious woman.

vam•pire ['væmpaɪə] *n.* person who supposedly sucks blood from his victims. **vam•pire bat,** *n.* type of small bat which sucks blood from animals.

van [væn] *n.* covered vehicle for carrying or moving goods, furniture, etc.

van•dal ['vændl] *n.* person who destroys property for the pleasure of destruction. **van•dal•ism,** *n.* meaningless destruction of property. **van•dal•ize,** *v.* to smash (sth) for no reason at all.

vane [veɪn] *n.* one of the blades on a water wheel/pump, etc.

van•guard ['vænɡɑːd] *n.* front part of an army; **in the v.** = in the front (of a movement).

va•nil•la [və'nɪlə] *n.* flavoring made from the seed pods of a tropical plant.

van•ish ['vænɪʃ] *v.* to disappear/to go out of sight; **to v. into thin air** = disappear completely. **van•ish•ing cream,** *n.* scented cream rubbed into the skin to make it soft. **van•ish•ing point,** *n.* point in a drawing where the horizontal lines seem to meet at eye level.

van•i•ty ['vænɪtɪ] *n.* (a) pride/feeling that you are more handsome etc. than you really are; conceit. (b) uselessness. **van•i•ty case,** *n.* small bag for carrying makeup/toiletries, etc. **van•i•ty pub•lish•ing,** *n.* practice of an author paying to have his/her book published.

van•quish ['væŋkwɪʃ] *v.* to defeat.

van•tage point ['vɑːntɪdʒpɔɪnt] *n.* place from which you can see well.

vap•id ['væpɪd] *adj.* dull (conversation). **va•pid•i•ty** [və'pɪdɪtɪ] *n.* dullness.

va•por•ize ['veɪpəraɪz] *v.* to turn into vapor. **va•por•i•za•tion** [veɪpəraɪ'zeɪʃn] *n.* changing into vapor. **va•por•iz•er,** *n.* machine which turns liquids (esp. water) into vapor. **va•por,** *Brit.* **va•pour,** *n.* gas form of a liquid, usu. caused by heating; **v. trail** = line of white vapor left in the sky by an aircraft.

var•i•a•bil•i•ty [veərɪə'bɪlɪtɪ] *n.* being variable. **var•i•a•ble** ['veərɪəbl] 1. *adj.* which varies/changes all the time. 2. *n.* thing which varies. **var•i•ance** ['veərɪəns] *n.* **to be at v. with** = to disagree. **var•i•ant,** *adj. & n.* (version/spelling, etc.) which is slightly different. **var•i•a•tion** [veərɪ'eɪʃn] *n.* (a) act of varying. (b) amount by which sth varies. (c) **variations** = pieces of music which repeat the same theme but written in a different fashion.

var•i•cel•la [værɪ'selæ] *n.* chickenpox.

var•i•col•ored ['vɜːrɪkʌləd] *adj.* variegated.

var•i•cose vein ['værɪkəʊs'veɪn] *n.* swollen vein, esp. in the leg.

var•i•e•gat•ed ['veərɪɡeɪtɪd] *adj.* (plant which is) striped/marked in contrasting colors. **var•i•e•ga•tion** [veərɪ'ɡeɪʃn] *n.* irregular marking in contrasting colors.

va•ri•e•ty [və'raɪətɪ] *n.* (a) being of different sorts; **for a v. of reasons** = for several different reasons. (b) different type (of plant). (c) **v. show** = entertainment which includes several different types of performer (such as singers/magicians/ventriloquists, etc.). **va•ri•e•tal,** *adj.* referring to a variety of plant. **var•i•ous** ['veərɪəs] *adj.* different/several. **var•i•ous•ly,** *adv.* in different ways.

var•i•fo•cal [veərɪ'fəʊkl] *adj. & n.* **v. glasses/varifocals** = glasses with a graduated lens in each frame, allowing the correction of more than one defect of vision with only one lens.

var•nish ['vɑːnɪʃ] 1. *n.* (a) liquid which when painted on sth gives it a shiny surface. (b) shiny surface made by painting with varnish. 2. *v.* (a) to paint with a liquid varnish; to give a shiny surface to sth. (b) to make seem more acceptable, better than it is, etc. in order to fool s.o.; **to v. the truth.**

var•y ['veərɪ] *v.* (a) to make different; to be different; **you ought to v. your diet** = eat different sorts of food. (b) to deviate **from. var•ied,** *adj.* of various kinds/different.

vas [væs] *n.* tube in the body.

vas•cu•lar ['væskjulə] *adj.* referring to veins, etc., which carry blood or sap.

vase [vɑːz] *n.* container for cut flowers or for decoration.

vas•ec•to•my [vəˈsektəmɪ] *n.* operation on a man to cut the tubes through which sperm flows and so to make him sterile.

vas•sal [ˈvæsl] *n.* (a) servant. (b) **v. state** = country which is under the rule of another.

vast [vɑːst] *adj.* very large. **vast•ly**, *adv.* very much. **vast•ness**, *n.* large size.

vat [væt] *n.* large container for liquids (esp. wine).

VAT [væt, viːeɪˈtiː] *abbrev. for* Value-Added Tax, government tax on goods or services.

vaude•ville [ˈvɔːdəvɪl] *n.* variety show.

vault [vɔːlt] 1. *n.* (a) arched stone ceiling. (b) underground room (for keeping things safe). (c) underground room for burying people. (d) high jump; **pole v.** = leap over a high bar, using a pole to swing you up. 2. *v.* to jump over (sth) by putting one hand on it to steady yourself. **vault•ed**, *adj.* with a stone arch.

vaunt [vɔːnt] *v.* to boast about (sth).

VD [ˈviːˈdiː] *abbrev. for* venereal disease.

VDU [viːdiːˈjuː] *abbrev. for* visual display unit.

veal [viːl] *n.* meat from a calf.

vec•tor [ˈvektə] *n.* (*in mathematics*) (a) thing which has both direction and size. (b) insect, etc., which carries disease.

veer [vɪə] *v.* to turn.

veg•e•ta•ble [ˈvedʒɪtəbl] *adj. & n.* (a) (referring to) plants; **the v. kingdom** = all plant life. (b) plant grown for food, not usu. sweet. (c) person who is more or less incapable of movement or thought. **veg•e•tar•i•an** [vedʒɪˈteərɪən] *adj. & n.* (person) who does not eat meat; (restaurant) which does not serve meat. **veg•e•tar•i•an•ism**, *n.* belief that not eating meat is good for you. **veg•e•tate**, *v.* to live like a vegetable, not moving or doing anything. **veg•e•ta•tion** [vedʒɪˈteɪʃn] *n.* (a) act of vegetating. (b) plants.

ve•he•mence [ˈvɪəməns] *n.* forceful way (of saying what you think). **ve•he•ment** [ˈvɪəmənt] *adj.* forceful. **ve•he•ment•ly**, *adv.* in a forceful way.

ve•hi•cle [ˈvɪəkl] *n.* (a) machine on wheels which travels along the road; rocket which travels in space. (b) **v. for** = means of expressing (sth). **ve•hic•u•lar** [vɪˈɪkjulə] *adj.* referring to vehicles.

veil [veɪl] 1. *n.* light cloth which can cover a woman's head or face; **to take the v.** = to become a nun. 2. *v.* to cover with a veil; **veiled** = hidden or disguised.

vein [veɪn] *n.* (a) small tube in the body along which blood runs to the heart. (b) thin line on the leaf of a plant. (c) thin layer of a mineral in a rock. (d) mood; **humorous v. veined**, *adj.* covered with veins.

veldt [velt] *n.* grass-covered plain in South Africa.

vel•lum [ˈveləm] *n.* (a) good quality writing paper. (b) skin of an animal made very thin and used for binding books or writing on.

ve•loc•i•ty [vəˈlɒsɪtɪ] *n.* speed.

ve•lour [vəˈluə] *n.* thick, soft cloth with a soft surface like velvet.

ve•lum [ˈviːləm] *n.* soft membrane. **ve•lar**, *adj.* referring to a soft membrane.

vel•vet [ˈvelvət] *adj. & n.* (a) cloth (made from silk, etc.) with a soft surface of cut threads. (b) soft skin covering a deer's antlers. **vel•vet•een**, *n.* velvet made of cotton. **vel•vet•y**, *adj.* with soft surface like velvet.

ve•nal [ˈviːnəl] *adj.* (person) who will take a bribe; (act) which is dishonest/which is done for a bribe. **ve•nal•i•ty** [vɪˈnælɪtɪ] *n.* being venal.

ven•det•ta [venˈdetə] *n.* private quarrel between families/persons.

vend•ing [ˈvendɪŋ] *n.* selling; **v. machine** = machine which provides cigarettes/chocolate, etc., when money is put into a slot. **ven•dor** [ˈvendə] *n.* person who sells.

ve•neer [vəˈnɪə] 1. *n.* (a) thin layer of expensive wood glued to the surface of ordinary wood. (b) thin layer of politeness/knowledge which covers a person's bad qualities. 2. *v.* to cover (wood) with a veneer.

ven•er•ate [ˈvenəreɪt] *v.* to respect greatly. **ven•er•a•ble**, *adj.* very old and likely to be respected. **ven•er•a•tion** [venəˈreɪʃn] *n.* respect.

ve•ne•re•al [vəˈnɪərɪəl] *adj.* (disease) transmitted during sexual intercourse.

ve•ne•tian blind [vəˈniːʃn'blaɪnd] *n.* blind to shut out light, made of horizontal strips of plastic/wood, etc., which can be opened or shut or raised and lowered by pulling a string.

venge•ance [ˈvendʒəns] *n.* harm caused to s.o. in return for harm they have caused you; *inf.* **with a v.** = very strongly.

ve•ni•al [ˈviːnɪəl] *adj.* slight (mistake); (sin) which can be excused. **ve•ni•al•i•ty** [viːnɪˈælɪtɪ] *n.* being venial.

æ back, ɑː farm, ɒ top, aɪ pipe, aʊ how, aɪə fire, aʊə flower, ɔː bought, ɔɪ toy, e fed, eə hair, eɪ take, ə afraid, əʊ boat, əʊə lower, ɜː word, iː heap, ɪ hit, ɪə hear, uː school, ʊ book, ʌ but, b back, d dog, ð then, dʒ just, f fog, g go, h hand, j yes, k catch, l last, m mix, n nut, ŋ sing, p penny, r round, s some, ʃ short, t too, tʃ chop, θ thing, v voice, w was, z zoo, ʒ treasure

ven•i•son ['venizn] *n.* meat from a deer.

ven•om ['venəm] *n.* (a) poison (from a snake, etc.). (b) bitter hatred. **ven•om•ous,** *adj.* (a) poisonous. (b) bitterly spiteful.

ve•nous ['vi:nəs] *adj.* referring to veins (in the body).

vent [vent] 1. *n.* (a) hole through which air/gas can escape. (b) slit in the back of a coat. (c) **to give v. to** = to let (an emotion) come out. 2. *v.* **he vented his anger on her** = he made her the target of his anger.

ven•ti•late ['ventɪleɪt] *v.* (a) to allow fresh air to come into. (b) to discuss (a question) in the open. **ven•ti•la•tion** [ventɪ'leɪʃn] *n.* bringing in fresh air; **v. shaft** = tube which allows fresh air to go down into a coal mine. **ven•ti•la•tor** ['ventɪleɪtə] *n.* opening which allows fresh air to come in; machine which pumps in fresh air.

ven•tral ['ventrəl] *adj.* (*formal*) referring to the abdomen.

ven•tri•cle ['ventrɪkl] *n.* space in the heart which fills up with blood and then pumps it out into the arteries.

ven•tril•o•quist [ven'trɪləkwɪst] *n.* person who can make his voice appear to come from a puppet. **ven•tril•o•quism,** *n.* act of being a ventriloquist.

ven•ture ['ventʃə] 1. *n.* commercial deal which involves risk. 2. *v.* to dare/to be bold enough to do sth dangerous or risky. **ven•ture•some,** *adj.* (person) who dares to take a risk.

ven•ue ['venju] *n.* agreed place where sth will take place.

ve•ra•cious [və'reɪʃəs] *adj.* truthful. **ve•rac•i•ty** [və'ræsɪtɪ] *n.* truth.

ve•ran•da(h) [və'rændə] *n.* covered terrace along the side of a house with no outside wall.

verb [vɜːb] *n.* part of speech which shows how s.o./sth acts or feels. **ver•bal,** *adj.* (a) referring to a verb. (b) spoken; not written down. **ver•bal•ize,** *v.* to express in words. **ver•bal•ly,** *adv.* in spoken words.

ver•ba•tim [vɜː'beɪtɪm] *adj. & adv.* word for word; in exactly the same words.

ver•be•na [vɜː'biːnə] *n.* type of scented herb, used to make soap or in hot drinks.

ver•bi•age ['vɜːbɪɪdʒ] *n.* excess, useless words.

ver•bose [və'bəus] *adj.* using more words than necessary. **ver•bos•i•ty** [və'bɒsɪtɪ] *n.* being verbose.

ver•dant ['vɜːdənt] *adj.* (*formal*) green (grass).

ver•dict ['vɜːdɪkt] *n.* (a) judgment/decision by a judge or jury. (b) opinion.

ver•di•gris ['vɜːdɪgrɪs] *n.* green discoloring of copper, etc., through contact with the atmosphere over a period of time.

ver•dure ['vɜːdjuə] *n.* (*formal*) green vegetation.

verge [vɜːdʒ] 1. *n.* edge of sth; **on the v. of** = near to. 2. *v.* **to v. on** = to be near to.

ver•i•fy ['verɪfaɪ] *v.* to check/to see if (a statement) is correct. **ver•i•fi•a•ble** [verɪ'faɪəbl] *adj.* which can be verified. **ver•i•fi•ca•tion** [verɪfɪ'keɪʃn] *n.* checking that sth is correct.

ver•i•ly ['verɪlɪ] *adv.* (*old*) truly.

ver•i•si•mil•i•tude [verɪs'mɪlɪtjuːd] *n.* appearance of being true/sth having the appearance of being true.

ver•i•ta•ble ['verɪtəbl] *adj.* true/real.

ver•mi•cel•li [vɜːmɪ'selɪ] *n.* type of very thin spaghetti.

ver•mic•u•lite [vɜː'mɪkjuːlaɪt] *n.* grains of silica, used as a growing medium for some types of pot plants.

ver•mi•form [və:mɪfɔ:m] *adj.* shaped like a worm.

ver•mil•ion [və'mɪlɪən] *adj. & n.* bright red (color).

ver•min ['vɜːmɪn] *n.* unwanted, disgusting animals, esp. those which are pests, as cockroaches, rats, etc. **ver•min•ous,** *adj.* covered with vermin.

ver•mouth ['vɜːməθ] *n.* type of strong wine flavored with herbs.

ver•nac•u•lar [və'nækjulə] *adj. & n.* (referring to) the ordinary spoken language of a country or region.

ver•nal ['vɜːnl] *adj.* (*formal*) referring to the spring.

ve•ron•i•ca [və'rɒnɪkə] *n.* low creeping plant with blue flowers.

ver•ru•ca [və'ruːkə] *n.* wart.

ver•sa•tile ['vɜːsətaɪl] *adj.* (person/machine) able to do various things equally well; (musician) who can play many different instruments. **ver•sa•til•i•ty** [vɜːsə'tɪlɪtɪ] *n.* ability to do various things with equal skill.

verse [vɜːs] *n.* (a) group of lines of poetry which form a part of a poem. (b) poetry; lines of writing with a rhythm and sometimes rhyme. (c) one line of a poem. (d) short (numbered) sentence from the Bible; **to give chapter and v. for sth** = to quote exactly the origin of a statement. **versed,** *adj.* **well v. in** = knowing a lot about/being well skilled in. **ver•si•fi•ca•tion** [vɜːsɪfɪ'keɪʃn] *n.* making of poetry; way in which a poem is written. **ver•si•fy** ['vɜːsɪfaɪ] *v.* to write poetry.

ver•sion ['vɜːʃn] *n.* (a) story of what happened as seen from a particular point of view. (b) translation.

ver•so ['vɜːsəu] *n.* left side/back (of a piece of paper/a page of a book, etc.).

ver•sus ['vɜːsəs] *prep.* (*usu. written* **v.**) (*in a civil court case/in sports*) against.

ver•te•bra ['vɜːtɪbrə] *n. (pl.* **-brae** [-briː]) one of the bones which form the spine. **ver•te•brate** ['vɜːtɪbrət] *adj. & n.* (animal) which has a backbone.

ver•tex ['vɜːteks] *n. (pl.* **-texes, -tices** [-tɪsiːz]) top; angle at the top of a triangle.

ver•ti•cal ['vɜːtɪkl] 1. *adj.* upright. 2. *n.* upright line (in geometry). **ver•ti•cal•ly**, *adv.* straight up/down.

ver•ti•go ['vɜːtɪgəʊ] *n.* dizziness caused by heights. **ver•tig•i•nous** [vɜː'tɪdʒɪnəs], *adj.* which makes one dizzy.

verve [vɜːv] *n.* enthusiasm/feeling of liveliness.

ver•y ['verɪ] 1. *adv.* (a) to a high degree; **v. much the same** = almost the same. (b) exactly; **the v. same** = exactly the same. 2. *adj.* (a) exactly the same. (b) exact; precise; **at the v. beginning** = right at the beginning.

ve•si•cle ['vesɪkl] *n.* small hollow in the body (usu. filled with liquid). **ve•sic•u•lar** [ve-'sɪkjʊlə] *adj.* referring to a vesicle.

ves•pers ['vespəz] *n.* church service in the evening.

ves•sel ['vesl] *n.* (a) container (for liquid); **blood v.** = tube which carries blood around the body. (b) ship.

vest [vest] *n.* short, close-fitting sleeveless garment which goes over a shirt and usu. under a jacket. **vest•ed,** *adj.* **v. interest** = sth which is to s.o.'s advantage, and makes him want to avoid changes, because it is in his interest to keep the present system.

ves•ti•bule ['vestɪbjuːl] *n.* entrance hall.

ves•tige ['vestɪdʒ] *n.* trace/remains. **ves•tig•i•al** [ves'tɪdʒəl] *adj.* which exists as a vestige; **v. tail** = very small tail.

vest•ments ['vestmənts] *n. pl.* clergyman's robes.

ves•try ['vestrɪ] *n.* clergyman's room in a church.

vet [vet] 1. *n. inf. short for* veterinarian. 2. *v.* (**vetted**) to examine carefully.

vetch [vetʃ] *n. (pl.* **-es**) type of wild pea.

vet•er•an ['vetrən] *n.* (a) person who has given long service and has much experience. (b) person who has served in the armed forces.

vet•er•i•nar•y ['vetrɪnrɪ] *adj.* referring to the medical and surgical treatment of animals. **vet•er•i•nar•i•an** [vetərɪ'neərɪən] *n.* doctor who specializes in veterinary medicine.

ve•to ['viːtəʊ] 1. *n. (pl.* **-oes**) power to reject sth. 2. *v.* to reject.

vex [veks] *v.* to annoy. **vex•a•tion** [vek'seɪʃn]

n. annoyance. **vex•a•tious** [vek'seɪʃəs] *adj.* annoying; **v. litigation** = legal action brought for no real reason, meant only to annoy. **vexed,** *adj.* (a) annoyed. (b) (question) which is often discussed but which has not been solved.

VHF [viːeɪtʃ'ef] *abbreviation for* very high frequency.

vi•a ['vaɪə] *prep.* (traveling) through.

vi•a•ble ['vaɪəbl] *adj.* (a) able to work in practice. (b) (*of new-born young*) sufficiently developed to survive. **vi•a•bil•i•ty** [vaɪə'bɪlɪtɪ] *n.* being viable.

vi•a•duct ['vaɪədʌkt] *n.* long bridge carrying a road/railroad over a wide valley.

vi•al ['vaɪəl] *n.* small glass bottle.

vi•ands ['vaɪəndz] *n. pl.* (*formal*) food.

vibes [vaɪbz] *n. pl. inf.* (a) vibraharp. (b) sensations.

vi•brate [vaɪ'breɪt] *v.* to shudder/to shake. **vi•bra•harp,** *n.* (*also* **vibraphone**) instrument like a xylophone with an amplifier. **vi•bran•cy,** *n.* being vibrant. **vi•brant** ['vaɪbrənt] *adj.* full (of energy). **vi•bra•tion** [vaɪ'breɪʃn] *n.* act of vibrating; rapid movement. **vi•bra•to** [vɪ'brɑːtəʊ] *n.* (*in music*) trembling effect. **vi•bra•tor,** *n.* machine which vibrates. **vi•bra•to•ry,** *adj.* which vibrates.

vi•bur•num [vaɪ'bɜːnəm] *n.* common shrub with pink or white flowers.

vic•ar ['vɪkə] *n.* (a) (*in the Church of England*) clergyman in charge of a parish. (b) (*in the Protestant Episcopal Church*) clergyman in charge of a chapel in a parish. (c) (*in the Roman Catholic Church*) prelate who represents the pope or a bishop. **vic•ar•age** ['vɪkrɪdʒ] *n.* vicar's house.

vi•car•i•ous [vɪ'keərɪəs] *adj.* felt through imagining what another person feels; (pleasure) felt because you imagine how s.o. is enjoying sth. **vi•car•i•ous•ly**, *adv.* in a vicarious way.

vice [vaɪs] *n.* (a) sexual wickedness/immorality; **v. squad** = police department dealing with prostitution, etc. (b) great wickedness. (c) bad habit. (d) vise.

vice- [vaɪs] *prefix meaning* deputy; second in rank.

vice-pres•i•dent [vaɪs'prezɪdənt] *n.* deputy to a president.

vice•roy ['vaɪsrɔɪ] *n.* person who represents a

king or queen. **vice•re•gal** [vais'ri:gl] *adj.* referring to a viceroy.

vice ver•sa [vaisə'vɜːsə] *adv.* the other way round.

vi•cin•i•ty [vɪ'sɪnɪtɪ] *n.* area around sth; **in the v. (of)** = near (by); approximately.

vi•cious ['vɪʃəs] *adj.* (a) wicked. (b) **v. circle** = interlocking chain of bad circumstances from which it is impossible to escape. **vi•cious•ly,** *adv.* in a wicked/spiteful way.

vi•cis•si•tude [vɪ'sɪsɪtjuːd] *n.* (*formal*) variation in luck.

vic•tim ['vɪktɪm] *n.* person who suffers an attack/an accident. **vic•tim•i•za•tion** [vɪktɪmaɪ'zeɪʃn] *n.* act of victimizing. **vic•tim•ize** ['vɪktɪmaɪz] *v.* to choose (s.o.) as a victim; to treat s.o. more harshly than others. **vic•tim•ol•o•gy,** *n.* study of the psychological impact of crime on its victims.

vic•tor ['vɪktə] *n.* person who wins (a game/a battle). **Vic•to•ri•an** [vɪk'tɔːrɪən] *adj.* referring to the reign of Queen Victoria of England (1837–1901). **vic•to•ri•ous** [vɪk'tɔːrɪəs] *adj.* (person/general) who has won a game/a battle. **vic•to•ry** ['vɪktrɪ] *n.* win; winning of a battle.

vict•ual ['vɪtl] (*formal*) 1. *n.* **victuals** = food. 2. *v.* to supply (a ship/an army) with food.

vi•cu•na [vɪ'kjuːnə] *n.* soft wool from a South American animal.

vi•de ['vɪdeɪ] *Latin word meaning* see.

vid•e•o ['vɪdɪəʊ] *adj. & n.* (system) which shows pictures on a television screen. **vid•e•o•cas•sette,** *n.* small cassette containing a videotape. **vid•e•o•con•fer•ence,** *n.* conference between people located in different places via video and sound links. **vid•e•o•disk,** *n.* disk which contains recorded sound and pictures. **vid•e•o•re•cord•er,** *n.* machine which records television pictures on tape, so that they can be played back later. **vid•e•o•tape.** 1. *n.* magnetic tape which can record pictures and sound for playing back through a television set. 2. *v.* to record (pictures, etc.) on magnetic tape.

vie [vaɪ] *v.* **to v. with s.o.** = to rival/to try to beat s.o.

view [vjuː] 1. *n.* (a) scene (which you can see from a certain place). (b) sight/action of looking at sth; **on v.** = on show for people to look at. (c) opinion. **I share your v.** = I agree with your opinion; **to take a dim v. of** = to disapprove of. (d) **in v. of** = when you consider. (e) intention/what you hope to do; **with a v. to** = planning to. 2. *v.* (a) to look at (sth)/to consider (a problem). (b) to watch television; **the viewing public** = people who watch television.

view•er, *n.* (a) person who watches television. (b) small device for looking at color slides. **view•find•er,** *n.* small window in a camera which you look through when taking a picture, and which shows the exact picture you are about to take. **view•point,** *n.* way of looking at things/of considering things.

vig•il ['vɪdʒɪl] *n.* keeping awake/on guard all night. **vig•i•lance,** *n.* being watchful/on guard. **vig•i•lant,** *adj.* watchful/on guard. **vig•i•lan•te** [vɪdʒɪ'læntɪ] *n.* person who tries to enforce law and order, esp. when the police find it impossible to do so.

vi•gnette [vɪ'njet] *n.* small sketch.

vig•or, *Brit.* **vig•our** ['vɪgə] *n.* energy. **vig•or•ous,** *adj.* energetic/very active; strong. **vig•or•ous•ly,** *adv.* in a vigorous way.

vile [vaɪl] *adj.* extremely unpleasant/bad. **vile•ly,** *adv.* in a vile way. **vile•ness,** *n.* being vile.

vil•i•fy ['vɪlɪfaɪ] *v.* to say extremely bad things about (s.o.). **vil•i•fi•ca•tion** [vɪlɪfɪ'keɪʃn] *n.* act of vilifying.

vil•la ['vɪlə] *n.* large country (or seaside) house (usu. in a warm country).

vil•lage ['vɪlɪdʒ] *n.* small group of houses (usu. smaller than a town) in the country. **vil•lag•er,** *n.* person who lives in a village.

vil•lain ['vɪlən] *n.* wicked person. **vil•lain•ous,** *adj.* wicked. **vil•lain•y,** *n.* wickedness.

vil•lein ['vɪleɪn] *n.* medieval agricultural laborer.

vim [vɪm] *n.* *inf.* energy.

vin•ai•grette [vɪneɪ'gret] *n.* (a) small bottle of smelling salts. (b) sauce made of oil and vinegar.

vin•di•cate ['vɪndɪkeɪt] *v.* to justify; to show that (s.o.) was right. **vin•di•ca•tion** [vɪndɪ'keɪʃn] *n.* (**of**) proving that sth was right.

vin•dic•tive [vɪn'dɪktɪv] *adj.* wanting to take revenge; spiteful. **vin•dic•tive•ly,** *adv.* spitefully. **vin•dic•tive•ness,** *n.* spite; desire to take revenge.

vine [vaɪn] *n.* (a) climbing plant which bears grapes. (b) climbing plant.

vin•e•gar ['vɪnɪgə] *n.* liquid made from sour wine/cider, used in cooking and for preserving food. **vin•e•gar•y,** *adj.* (wine, etc.) tasting like vinegar; bad-tempered (person).

vine•yard ['vɪnjəd] *n.* field of vines for producing wine.

vi•no ['viːnəʊ] *n.* *Sl.* wine, esp. red Italian wine.

vi•nous ['vaɪnəs] *adj.* referring to wine.

vin•tage ['vɪntɪdʒ] *n.* (a) collecting of grapes to make wine; grapes which are collected. (b) fine wine made in a particular year; **v. wine/v.**

port = fine/expensive old wine/port. (c) year of make. (d) of typical high quality.

vint•ner ['vɪntnə] *n.* person who makes or sells wine.

vi•nyl ['vaɪnl] *n.* type of plastic sheet which looks like leather/tiles, etc.

vi•ol ['vaɪəl] *n.* early stringed instrument.

vi•o•la [vaɪ'əʊlə] *n.* (a) small pansylike garden flower. (b) stringed instrument slightly larger than a violin.

vi•o•late ['vaɪəleɪt] *v.* (a) to break/to go against (the law/a treaty). (b) (*formal*) to rape. **vi•o•la•tion** [vaɪə'leɪʃn] *n.* act of violating; **in v. of an agreement** = against the terms of an agreement. **vi•o•la•tor,** *n.* person who violates.

vi•o•lence ['vaɪələns] *n.* (a) force/strength. (b) rough action. **vi•o•lent,** *adj.* (a) strong. (b) rough. **vi•o•lent•ly,** *adv.* strongly; roughly.

vi•o•let ['vaɪələt] *n. & adj.* (a) small wild plant with bluish purple flowers. (b) bluish purple (color).

vi•o•lin [vaɪə'lɪn] *n.* stringed musical instrument played with a bow. **vi•o•lin•ist,** *n.* person who plays the violin. **vi•o•lon•cel•lo** [vaɪələn'tʃeləʊ] *n.* (*pl.* -os) (*formal*) cello.

VIP [viːaɪ'piː] *abbreviation for* very important person; **VIP treatment** = being treated like a very important person.

vi•per ['vaɪpə] *n.* adder/poisonous snake.

vi•ra•go [vɪ'rɑːgəʊ] *n.* (*pl.* -oes, -os) fierce loud-mouthed woman.

vi•ral ['vaɪrəl] *adj.* referring to a virus.

vir•gin ['vɜːdʒɪn] 1. *n.* (a) person who has never had sexual intercourse. (b) **the V. (Mary)** = the mother of Jesus Christ. 2. *adj.* pure/untouched. **vir•gin•al,** *adj.* pure like a virgin. **vir•gin•als,** *n. pl.* type of 16th century harpsichord. **vir•gin•i•ty** [vɜː'dʒɪnɪtɪ] *n.* being a virgin; **to lose your v.** = to have sexual intercourse for the first time.

vir•gin•i•a creep•er [vɜː'dʒɪnɪə'kriːpə] *n.* common climbing plant which grows on walls, with leaves which turn bright red in autumn.

Vir•go ['vɜːgəʊ] *n.* one of the signs of the zodiac, shaped like a girl.

vir•ile ['vɪraɪl] *adj.* manly; masculine. **vi•ril•i•ty** [vɪ'rɪlɪtɪ] *n.* being virile; strength; manliness.

vi•rol•o•gy [vaɪ'rɒlədʒɪ] *n.* study of viruses. **vi•rol•o•gist,** *n.* scientist who studies viruses.

vir•tu•al ['vɜːtjʊəl] *adj.* almost, if not in fact. **vir•tu•al•ly,** *adv.* almost. **vir•tu•al re•al•i•ty,** *n.* artificial three-dimensional environment, generated by interactive computer software.

vir•tue ['vɜːtjuː] *n.* (a) particular goodness (of character); good quality. (b) special quality. (c) **by v. of** = because of. **vir•tu•ous,** *adj.* very good/very honest. **vir•tu•ous•ly,** *adv.* in a virtuous way.

vir•tu•o•so [vɜːtjʊ'əʊzəʊ] *n.* (*pl.* -os/-si [-siː]) person who is skilled in an art, esp. who can play a musical instrument extremely well. **vir•tu•os•i•ty** [vɜːtjʊ'ɒsɪtɪ] *n.* ability to play a musical instrument/sing, etc., extremely well.

vir•u•lence ['vɪrjʊləns] *n.* (*of a disease*) great strength. **vir•u•lent,** *adj.* very bad (attack of disease); very harsh (attack). **vir•u•lent•ly,** *adv.* in a virulent way.

vi•rus ['vaɪrəs] *n.* (*pl.* -es) (a) germ which is smaller than bacteria and which causes colds/pneumonia, etc. (b) hidden routine placed in a computer program, which corrupts or destroys files.

vi•sa ['viːzə] *n.* special mark on a passport/special paper allowing you to enter a country; **30-day v.** = visa which allows you to stay in a country for 30 days.

vis-à-vis [viːzə'viː] *prep.* (a) in relation to. (b) compared with.

vis•cer•a ['vɪsərə] *n. pl.* organs inside the body, esp. the intestines. **vis•cer•al,** *adj.* referring to the viscera.

vis•cos•i•ty [vɪs'kɒsɪtɪ] *n.* state of being viscous. **vis•cose** ['vɪskəʊz] *n.* artificial silk material, made from viscous cellulose. **vis•cid,** **viscous** ['vɪsɪd, 'vɪskəs] *adj.* thick/sticky (liquid).

vis•count ['vaɪkaʊnt] *n.* title of a nobleman below an earl. **vis•count•ess,** *n.* (*pl.* -es) wife of a viscount.

vise [vaɪs] *n.* tool with jaws that screw tight to hold sth. **vise•like,** *adj.* tight, as in a vise.

vis•i•ble ['vɪzɪbl] *adj.* which can be seen. **vis•i•bil•i•ty** [vɪzɪ'bɪlɪtɪ] *n.* ability to be seen clearly; **good v.** = ability for things to be seen at long distances because the air is clear. **vis•i•bly,** *adv.* obviously; in a way which can be seen.

vi•sion ['vɪʒn] *n.* (a) ability to see; **field of v.** = range from one side to another over which you can see clearly; **tunnel v.** = very narrow or prejudiced way of looking at things; narrow-mindedness. (b) ability to look and plan ahead. (c) thing which you imagine; **he has visions of himself as president** = he imagines he will be president one day. (d) ghost; strange sight. **vi•sion•ar•y**. 1. *adj.* idealistic/impracticable (plan). 2. *n.* person whose plans are idealistic and impracticable.

vis•it ['vɪzɪt] 1. *n.* short stay; **to pay a v. to** = to go to see (s.o.)/to stay a short time in (a place). 2. *v.* to stay a short time (in a place/with s.o.); **visiting hours** = times when you can visit patients in a hospital; **visiting team** = opposing team who has come to play on the home ground. **vis•it•ant,** *n.* ghost. **vis•it•a•tion** [vɪzɪ'teɪʃn] *n.* (a) trouble which is thought to be sent as a divine punishment. (b) official visit. **vis•i•tor** ['vɪzɪtə] *n.* person who visits.

vi•sor ['vaɪzə] *n.* moveable part of a helmet, which drops down to protect the face; folding shield above the windshield which protects the driver of a car from bright sunshine.

vis•ta ['vɪstə] *n.* wide view.

vis•u•al ['vɪzjʊəl] *adj.* referring to what can be seen; **v. arts** = painting/sculpture, etc. (as opposed to music); **v. aids** = slides/motion pictures used for teaching purposes. **vis•u•al•ize** ['vɪzjʊəlaɪz] *v.* to picture/to see (sth) in your mind. **vis•u•al•ly,** *adv.* in a visual way.

vi•tal ['vaɪtl] *adj.* (a) very important. (b) vigorous/energetic (person). (c) (organs in the body) which are essential to life. **vi•tal•ly,** *adv.* in a very important way. **vi•tal•i•ty** [vaɪ'tælɪtɪ] *n.* great energy. **vi•tal•ize,** *v.* to make (sth) more energetic. **vi•tals,** *n. pl.* important organs in a body. **vi•tal sta•tis•tics,** *n.* (a) official statistics concerning populations, births, deaths, etc. (b) *inf.* measurements of bust, waist and hips of a woman.

vi•ta•min ['vɪtəmɪn] *n.* chemical substance occurring in food which is important for the development or health of the human body.

vi•ti•ate ['vɪʃɪeɪt] *v.* to make bad/to make weak. **vi•ti•a•tion** [vɪʃɪ'eɪʃn] *n.* act of vitiating.

vit•re•ous ['vɪtrɪəs] *adj.* like glass. **vit•ri•fi•ca•tion** [vɪtrɪfɪ'keɪʃn] *n.* act of vitrifying. **vit•ri•fy** ['vɪtrɪfaɪ] *v.* to make into glass; to become like glass.

vit•ri•ol ['vɪtrɪəl] *n.* sulfuric acid. **vit•ri•ol•ic** [vɪtrɪ'ɒlɪk] *adj.* very violent/very rude (attack).

vi•tu•per•a•tion [vɪtjʊpə'reɪʃn] *n.* (*formal*) abuse; insulting words. **vi•tu•per•a•tive,** *adj.* (*formal*) insulting/abusive.

vi•va vo•ce ['vaɪvə 'vəʊsɪ] *adj.* orally.

vi•va•cious [vɪ'veɪʃəs] *adj.* full of life/full of excitement. **vi•va•cious•ly,** *adv.* in a vivacious way. **vi•va•cious•ness, vivacity** [vɪ'væsɪtɪ] *n.* being vivacious.

viv•id ['vɪvɪd] *adj.* (a) very bright (light/color). (b) very lifelike (description); very lively (imagination). **viv•id•ly,** *adj.* in a vivid way. **viv•id•ness,** *n.* being vivid.

vi•vip•a•rous [vɪ'vɪpərəs] *adj.* (animal) which produces live young (that is, which does not lay eggs).

viv•i•sec•tion [vɪvɪ'sekʃən] *n.* operating on a live animal for the purpose of scientific research.

vix•en ['vɪksn] *n.* female fox.

viz. [vɪz *or* 'neɪmlɪ] *adv.* namely.

vo•cab•u•lar•y [və'kæbjʊlərɪ] *n.* (a) words used by a person or group of persons. (b) printed list of words.

vo•cal ['vəʊkl] 1. *adj.* (a) referring to the voice; **v. cords** = muscles in the throat which produce sounds. (b) very loud/insistent (opposition). 2. *n. pl.* **vocals** = popular songs performed with a group. **vo•cal•ic** [vəʊ'kælɪk] *adj.* referring to vowels. **vo•cal•ist,** *n.* singer. **vo•cal•ize,** *v.* to make a sound with your voice. **vo•cal•ly,** *adv.* in a loud way.

vo•ca•tion [və'keɪʃn] *n.* job which you feel you have been called to do/for which you have a special talent; **she missed her v.** = she should be in another job for which she is better suited. **vo•ca•tion•al,** *adj.* referring to a vocation; **v. training** = training for a particular job.

vo•cif•er•ate [və'sɪfəreɪt] *v.* (*formal*) to shout protests against sth. **vo•cif•er•ous,** *adj.* loud/shouting. **vo•cif•er•ous•ly,** *adv.* loudly.

vod•ka ['vɒdkə] *n.* colorless alcohol made originally in Russia or Poland.

vogue [vəʊg] *n.* fashion; popularity; **in v.** = fashionable.

voice [vɔɪs] 1. *n.* (a) sounds made by a person speaking or singing; **she's lost her v.** = she can't speak (because of a cold); **in a low v.** = quietly; **don't raise your v.** = don't talk so loudly. (b) right to express an opinion. (c) **active v./passive v.** = forms of a verb which show whether the subject is doing sth or having sth done to it. 2. *v.* to express (an opinion). **voice•less,** *adj.* silent; with no voice. **voice mail,** *n.* electronic answering system that records telephone messages.

void [vɔɪd] 1. *adj.* (a) empty. (b) **null and v.** = not valid. 2. *n.* emptiness. 3. *v.* to empty.

voile [vɔɪl] *n.* very thin cotton or silk material.

vol•a•tile ['vɒlətaɪl] *adj.* (a) (liquid) which can easily change into vapor. (b) (person) who changes his mind/his mood frequently. **vol•a•til•i•ty** [vɒlə'tɪlɪtɪ] *n.* being volatile.

vol-au-vent [vɒləʊ'vɒn] *n.* small pastry case

with a filling of meat, vegetables, or fish inside.

vol•ca•no [vɒl'keɪnəʊ] *n.* (*pl.* **-oes, -os**) mountain with a hole on the top through which lava, ash and gas can come. **vol•can•ic** [vɒl-'kænɪk] *adj.* referring to volcanoes. **vol•can•ol•o•gy** [vɒlkə'nɒlədʒɪ] *n.* study of volcanoes.

vole [vəʊl] *n.* small animal, resembling a mouse.

vo•li•tion [və'lɪʃn] *n.* (*formal*) wish/will. **of one's own v.** = because one wants to and not because one is told to.

vol•ley ['vɒlɪ] 1. *n.* (a) series of shots/missiles which are fired/thrown at the same time. (b) (*in sports*) hitting the ball before it touches the ground. 2. *v.* (a) to fire several shots/throw several missiles at the same time. (b) (*in sports*) to hit the ball before it touches the ground. **vol•ley•ball,** *n.* team game in which a large ball is thrown across a high net, and must not touch the ground.

volt [vɒlt] *n.* standard unit of electric potential. **volt•age,** *n.* amount of electric force. **volt•me•ter,** *n.* instrument for measuring voltage.

volte-face ['vɒlt'fæs] *n.* sudden unexpected change of opinion.

vol•u•ble ['vɒljʊbl] *adj.* speaking easily with a lot of words. **vol•u•bil•i•ty** [vɒlju'bɪlɪtɪ] *n.* use of a lot of words. **vol•u•bly,** *adj.* with a lot of words.

vol•ume ['vɒljuːm] *n.* (a) book (esp. one book of a series). (b) space taken up by sth. (c) amount, esp. large. (d) loudness. **vo•lu•mi•nous** [və'ljuːmɪnəs] *adj.* large; taking up a lot of space.

vol•un•teer [vɒlən'tɪə] 1. *n.* (a) person who offers to do sth without being told to do it. (b) soldier who has joined the military of his own free will. 2. *v.* (a) to offer to do sth; to join the armed forces of your own free will. (b) to give (information) without being forced to do so. **vol•un•tar•i•ly,** *adv.* freely. **vol•un•tar•y** ['vɒləntrɪ] 1. *adj.* done of your own free will. 2. *n.* organ v. = solo piece of music played on the organ during or at the beginning or end of a church service.

vo•lup•tu•ous [və'lʌptjʊəs] *adj.* absorbed in/evoking sensual pleasure. **vo•lup•tu•ar•y,** *n.* person who enjoys sensual pleasure. **vo•lup•tu•ous•ly,** *adv.* in a voluptuous way.

vom•it ['vɒmɪt] 1. *n.* food vomited. 2. *v.* to

bring up food through your mouth when you are sick.

voo•doo ['vuːduː] *n.* witchcraft practiced in the West Indies. **voo•doo•ism,** *n.* belief in voodoo.

vo•ra•cious [və'reɪʃəs] *adj.* greedy; wanting to eat a lot; **v. reader** = person who reads a lot. **vo•ra•cious•ly,** *adv.* greedily. **vo•ra•cious•ness, voracity** [vɒ'ræsɪtɪ] *n.* being voracious.

vor•tex ['vɔːteks] *n.* (*pl.* **-texes, -tices** [-tɪsiːz]) matter which is turning around and around very fast.

vo•ta•ry ['vəʊtrɪ] *n.* (*formal*) person who worships/who admires sth fervently.

vote [vəʊt] 1. *n.* (a) expressing your opinion by marking a paper/by holding up your hand/by speaking. (b) action of voting; **to put sth to the v.** = to ask people to vote on sth. (c) the right to vote in an election/to vote on a proposal; **to give s.o. the v.** 2. *v.* (a) to express an opinion by marking a paper/by holding up your hand/by speaking. (b) **he was voted on to/off the committee** = he was elected/was not re-elected a member of the committee. **vot•er,** *n.* person who votes/who has the right to vote.

vo•tive ['vəʊtɪv] *adj.* (offering) given to fulfill a promise made to a god or to a saint.

vouch [vaʊtʃ] *v.* **to v. for sth** = to guarantee sth. **vouch•er,** *n.* paper which guarantees payment. **vouch•safe** [vaʊtʃ'seɪf] *v.* (*formal*) to ensure/to guarantee (that s.o. can do sth).

vow [vaʊ] 1. *n.* solemn promise (esp. one sworn to God). 2. *v.* to make a solemn promise.

vow•el ['vaʊəl] *n.* sound made without using the teeth, tongue or lips; one of the letters (a, e, i, o, u and sometimes y) which represent these sounds.

voy•age ['vɔɪɪdʒ] 1. *n.* long journey (esp. by water). 2. *v.* to make a long journey (by water). **voy•ag•er,** *n.* person who voyages.

vo•yeur [vwɑː'jɜː] *n.* person who watches people making love.

VR ['viː'ɑː] *abbrev. for* virtual reality.

vul•can•ize ['vʌlkənaɪz] *v.* to treat rubber with sulfur so that it is made stronger, harder and more elastic. **vul•can•ite,** *n.* vulcanized rubber. **vul•can•i•za•tion,** *n.* process of vulcanizing.

vul•can•ol•o•gy [vʌlkə'nɒlədʒɪ] *n.* volcanology.

vul•gar ['vʌlgə] *adj.* (a) rude/indecent. (b) not in good taste. (c) **v. fraction** = fraction written

---

æ back, ɑː farm, ɒ top, aɪ pipe, aʊ how, aɪə fire, aʊə flower, ɔː bought, ɔɪ toy, e fed, eəhair, eɪ take, ə afraid, əʊ boat, əʊə lower, ɜː word, iː heap, ɪ hit, ɪə hear, uː school, ʊ book, ʌ but, b back, d dog, ð then, dʒ just, f fog, g go, h hand, j yes, k catch, l last, m mix, n nut, ŋ sing, p penny, r round, s some, ʃ short, t too, tʃ chop, θ thing, v voice, w was, z zoo, ʒ treasure

as one number above and another below a line. **vul•gar•i•an** [vʌl'geərɪən] *n.* vulgar person. **vul•gar•ism**, *n.* rude expression.. **vul•gar•i•ty** [vʌl'gærɪtɪ] *n.* rudeness; lack of good taste. **vul•gar•i•za•tion**, *n.* making common/popular. **vul•gar•ly**, *adv.* in a rude/indecent way.

vul•ner•a•ble ['vʌlnərəbl] *adj.* which can be easily attacked/easily hurt.

vul•ner•a•bil•i•ty [vʌlnərə'bɪlɪtɪ] *n.* being vulnerable.

vul•pine ['vʌlpaɪn] *adj.* referring to foxes.

vul•ture ['vʌltʃə] *n.* large tropical bird that eats mainly dead flesh.

vul•va ['vʌlvə] *n.* part of female body around the opening of the vagina.

Ww

wack•y ['wækɪ] *adj.* (**-ier, -iest**) *inf.* crazy/silly.

wad [wɒd] 1. *n.* (a) thick piece of soft material. (b) thick pile of banknotes/papers. 2. *v.* (**wadded**) to form/to press into a wad. **wad•ding,** *n.* thick, soft material used for lining, packing or padding.

wad•dle ['wɒdl] 1. *n.* walk swaying from side to side like a duck. 2. *v.* to walk with a waddle.

wade [weɪd] *v.* to walk through deep water or mud; **to w. through** = to find (a book) difficult to read; **to w. into a pile of work** = to start dealing with a pile of work vigorously. **wad•er,** *n.* (a) bird which spends most of its time in shallow water or mud. (b) **waders** = long waterproof boots worn by fishermen.

wa•fer ['weɪfə] *n.* (a) thin sweet cookie eaten with ice cream. (b) thin disk of bread eaten at communion or mass.

waf•fle ['wɒfl] 1. *n.* (a) type of crisp cake cooked in an iron mold and eaten with syrup. (b) ambivalent, unclear speech/writing. 2. *v.* to speak or write in an ambivalent, unclear way. **waf•fle i•ron,** *n.* iron mold used for making waffles.

waft [wɒft] 1. *n.* gentle smell. 2. *v.* to carry (sth) gently through the air.

wag [wæg] 1. *n.* (a) movement from side to side or up and down. (b) *inf.* person who likes making jokes/facetious remarks. 2. *v.* (**wagged**) to move from side to side or up and down. **wag•gish,** *adj.* joking (remark).

wage [weɪdʒ] 1. *n.* (*also* **wages**) weekly payment given for work done; **w. freeze** = period of standstill in wages. 2. *v.* to fight (a war); **to w. war (on** sth) = to fight against sth. **wage earn•er,** *n.* person who works for wages.

wa•ger ['weɪdʒə] 1. *n.* bet/money which you promise to pay if sth you expect to happen does not take place. 2. *v.* to bet.

wag•gle ['wægl] *v.* to move from side to side.

wag•on, *Brit.* **wag•gon** ['wægn] *n.* (a) four-wheeled vehicle pulled by horses and used for carrying heavy loads. (b) *inf.* **to be on** the w. = to drink only non-alcoholic drinks. **wag•on•er,** *n.* person who drives a wagon.

wag•tail ['wægteɪl] *n.* small bird which wags its tail up and down as it walks.

waif [weɪf] *n.* homeless child or animal.

wail [weɪl] 1. *n.* high-pitched sad cry. 2. *v.* to make a high-pitched mournful cry.

wain•scot(ing) ['weɪnzkət(ɪŋ)] *n.* wood paneling covering the lower part of a wall in a house. **wain•scot•ed,** *adj.* with a wainscot.

waist [weɪst] *n.* (a) narrow part of the body between the chest and the hips. (b) narrow part (of a bottle, etc.). **waist•band,** *n.* band of cloth around the waist of a pair of trousers/skirt. **waist•line,** *n.* measurement around the waist.

wait [weɪt] 1. *n.* act of staying until sth happens or s.o. arrives; **to lie in w. for s.o.** = to hide waiting for s.o. to pass by in order to attack him. 2. *v.* (a) (**for**) to stay somewhere until sth happens or s.o./sth arrives. (b) **to w. on s.o.** = to serve food to s.o. at a table, as in a restaurant. **wait•er,** *n.* man who serves food to people in a restaurant; **head w.** = person in charge of other waiters; **dumb w.** = (i) small table (usu. with wheels) for keeping food on; (ii) apparatus for carrying food from one floor to another. **wait•ing room,** *n.* room where travelers wait for their trains/buses, etc./where patients wait to see a doctor, etc. **wait•ing list,** *n.* list of people waiting to see s.o. or do sth. **wait•ress,** *n.* (*pl.* **-es**) woman who serves food to people in a restaurant. **wait up,** *v.* to stay up/not to go to bed.

waive [weɪv] *v.* to give up (a right/a claim). **waiv•er,** *n.* giving up (of a right/claim).

wake [weɪk] 1. *n.* (a) waves left by a boat, etc., moving through water; **in the w. of** = immediately behind. (b) staying up all night with a dead body before a funeral. 2. *v.* (**waked** or **woke** [wəuk]; **has woken**) to stop (s.o.) sleeping; to stop sleeping. **wake•ful,** *adj.* not at all sleepy/not able to go to sleep. **wak•en,** *v.* to

---

æ back, ɑː farm, ɒ top, aɪ pipe, aʊ how, aɪə fire, aʊə flower, ɔː bought, ɔɪ toy, e fed, eəhair, eɪ take, ə afraid, əu boat, əuə lower, vː word, iː heap, ɪ hit, ɪə hear, uː school, ʊ book, ʌ but, b back, d dog, ð then, dʒ just, f fog, g go, h hand, j yes, k catch, l last, m mix, n nut, ŋ sing, p penny, r round, s some, ʃ short, t too, tʃ chop, θ thing, v voice, w was, z zoo, ʒ treasure

stop (s.o.) sleeping. **wake up,** v. (a) to stop sleeping. (b) **to w. u. to** = to realize.

walk [wɔːk] 1. n. (a) journey on foot. (b) way of walking. (c) wide path in a park or garden. (d) **w. of life** = social position or occupation. 2. v. (a) to move along on the feet at a normal speed. (b) to accompany (s.o./an animal) on foot. **walk•er,** n. person who walks, or who is fond of walking. **walk•ie-talk•ie,** n. portable two-way radio-telephone. **walk in,** v. to enter. **walk-in,** adj. (closet) which you can walk into. **walk•ing stick,** n. stick used to rest on when walking; cane. **walk in•to,** v. (a) to enter. (b) to hit by accident. **walk off,** v. (a) to go away; **to walk off with** = (i) to win (a prize) easily; (ii) to steal. (b) **to walk off your dinner** = to go for a walk after a big dinner to help you digest it. **walk on,** v. to continue walking. **walk-on,** n. & adj. (part) in a play where the actor doesn't have to speak. **walk out,** v. (a) to go out. (b) to leave angrily. (c) to go on strike. (d) **to w. o. on s.o.** = to leave s.o. suddenly. **walk•out,** n. strike of workers. **walk o•ver,** v. to walk across; to cross (a room) **to** see s.o./to go up to s.o. **walk•o•ver,** n. inf. easy victory. **walk up,** v. (a) to climb (on foot). (b) **to w. u. (to s.o.)** = to approach/to go to speak (to s.o.). **walk•way,** n. passage/path where you can walk.

wall [wɔːl] n. structure of brick/stone, etc., forming the side of a room/building, or the boundary of a piece of land; **w. painting** = mural; **to go to the w.** = to be defeated; inf. **he sends me up the w.** = he makes me furious. **walled,** adj. with walls. **wall•eyed,** adj. (person) who squints badly. **wall•flow•er,** n. (a) garden flower with a sweet scent. (b) (at a dance) inf. woman who is not asked to dance and is left sitting alone. **wall in,** v. to surround with walls. **wall•pa•per,** n. decorative paper stuck on the walls of a room. 2. v. to stick paper on the walls of (a room). **Wall Street,** n. major U.S. financial center, in New York City. **wall-to-wall,** adj. (carpet) which covers all the floor space of a room. **wall up,** v. to close/to block with a wall.

wal•la•by ['wɒləbɪ] n. Australian animal like a small kangaroo.

wal•let ['wɒlɪt] n. small leather case used for holding paper money, credit cards, etc. in a pocket.

wal•lop ['wɒləp] 1. n. inf. hard blow. beer. 2. v. inf. to hit hard. **wal•lop•ing,** adj. inf. huge.

wal•low ['wɒləʊ] 1. n. mud hollow where animals can roll. 2. v. (a) (of animals) to roll delightedly around in mud. (b) (of person) to take too much pleasure in.

wal•nut ['wɒlnʌt] n. (a) hard round nut with a wrinkled shell. (b) tree on which walnuts grow. (c) wood from a walnut tree.

wal•rus ['wɔːlrʌs] n. (pl. -es) Arctic animal like a large seal with two long tusks pointing downward; **w. mustache** = mustache whose long ends point downward.

waltz [wɒls] 1. n. (pl. -es) (a) dance in which a man and woman turn around together as they move forward. (b) music suitable for such a dance. 2. v. (a) to dance together. (b) inf. to walk smoothly/happily.

wan [wɒn] adj. pale/looking ill. **wan•ly,** adv. in a wan way. **wan•ness,** n. being wan.

wand [wɒnd] n. (a) slim stick used by magicians. (b) hand-held electronic device that is passed over a printed item, e.g. a bar code, to read the data represented there.

wan•der ['wɒndə] v. (a) to walk about with no special purpose or direction. (b) **to w. off** = to walk away from the correct path. (c) to go away from the subject when talking. (d) to be confused because of illness or old age. **wan•der•er,** n. person who wanders. **wan•der•ings,** n. long random journeys. **wan•der•lust,** n. passion for going off on journeys and adventures.

wane [weɪn] 1. n. **the moon is on the w.** = appears to be getting smaller; **his influence is on the w.** = is diminishing. 2. v. to appear smaller; to decrease.

wan•gle ['wæŋgl] 1. n. inf. trick/thing dishonestly obtained. 2. v. inf. to get (sth) by trickery. **wan•gler,** n. inf. person who gets things by trickery.

want [wɒnt] 1. n. (a) state of being without; **for w. of sth better** = as sth better is not available. (b) desire/wish. (c) **wants** = things needed. 2. v. (a) to wish/to desire/to long for. (b) to need/to require. **want•ed,** adj. (a) desired/needed. (b) searched for by the police, usu. because of a crime. **want•ing,** adj. (a) needing. (b) having very little of sth.

wan•ton ['wɒntn] adj. wild/undisciplined.

war [wɔː] n. (a) fighting carried on between two or more nations; **civil w.** = war between two groups in one country. (b) fight/battle; **w. of words** = bitter argument. **war cry,** n. loud shout given when going into battle; slogan used in a political campaign. **war dance,** n. dance before the start of a battle. **war•fare,** n. fighting a war; type of war. **war•head,** n. explosive top of a missile. **war-horse,** n. (a) heavy, strong horse formerly used for carrying soldiers into battle. (b) old soldier/politician who has seen many battles. **war•like,** adj. liking or ready for war. **war•lord,** n. military leader who rules part of a country. **war•mon•ger,** n. person who wants to start a war. **war paint,** n. bright color put on the face and body before battle to make the enemy afraid. **war•path**, *n. inf.* **to be on the w.** = to be angry and looking for a fight. **war•ring**, *adj.* at war. **war•ship**, *n.* armed fighting ship. **war•time**, *n.* time of war.

war•ble ['wɔːbl] 1. *n.* trembling song (of a bird). 2. *v.* to sing with a trembling note. **war•bler**, *n.* type of bird which sings with a trembling note.

ward [wɔːd] 1. *n.* (a) young person in the care of s.o. other than his parents; **w. of the court** = child who is under the protection of the court. (b) large room in a hospital; section of a hospital. (c) part of a town for election purposes. 2. *v.* **to w. (sth) off** = to keep away. **war•den**, *n.* (a) person in charge of persons, animals, or things. (b) official in charge of a prison.

ward•robe ['wɔːdrəʊb] *n.* (a) large piece of furniture in which clothes may be hung. (b) a person's clothes. (c) costumes in a theater; **w. mistress** = woman in charge of the costumes in a theater.

ward•room [wɔːdrʊm] *n.* general living-room of officers on a warship.

ware ['weə] *n.* (a) *suffix meaning* goods made of a certain material/for a special purpose. (b) *pl.* **wares** = things that have been made and are for sale. **ware•house** ['weəhaʊs] 1. *n.* large building for storing goods. 2. *v.* to store (goods) in a large building. **ware•house•man**, *n.* (*pl.* **-men**) person who works in a warehouse.

warm [wɔːm] 1. *adj.* (**-er, -est**) (a) quite hot/pleasantly hot; (*in a game*) **you're getting w.** = you're near the right answer. (b) kind and friendly (welcome). 2. *n.* being/keeping warm; warm place. 3. *v.* to make hot or hotter; **to w. up to s.o.** = to feel more and more friendly toward s.o. **warm-blood•ed**, *adj.* having warm blood. **warm-heart•ed**, *adj.* friendly and welcoming. **warm•ing pan**, *n.* metal container in which hot coals were put and which was used to warm beds. **warm•ly**, *adv.* in a warm way. **warmth**, *n.* (a) heat/state of being warm. (b) enthusiasm. **warm up**, *v.* (a) to heat/to make warm again; to become warm again. (b) to exercise before a game/a contest.

warn [wɔːn] *v.* to tell of possible danger; to inform (s.o.) in advance; **to w. s.o. off sth** = to advise s.o. not to eat/drink/touch sth. **warn•ing**. 1. *n.* (a) notice of danger. (b) **without w.** = suddenly. 2. *adj.* which tells of danger.

warp [wɔːp] 1. *n.* (a) twisting out of shape of a piece of wood. (b) threads running lengthwise in a piece of material. (c) heavy rope used for moving boats along. 2. *v.* (a) to twist out of shape. (b) to make (mind/character) evil. (c) (*of boats*) to move by pulling on a rope. **warped**, *adj.* twisted (wood/character).

war•rant ['wɒrənt] 1. *n.* (a) written official paper permitting or certifying sth. (b) **w. officer** = highest non-commissioned officer in the U.S. armed forces. 2. *v.* (a) to guarantee/to promise. (b) to justify/to deserve. **war•ran•ty**, *n.* written guarantee promising that a machine will work, etc.

war•ren ['wɒrn] *n.* land with rabbit burrows.

war•ri•or ['wɒrɪə] *n.* person who fights in a war.

wart [wɔːt] *n.* small, hard, dark lump on the skin; **warts and all** = with all faults known. **wart•hog**, *n.* type of wild African pig.

war•y ['weərɪ] *adj.* (**-ier, -iest**) careful/cautious. **war•i•ly**, *adv.* cautiously/looking around all the time. **war•i•ness** ['weərɪnəs] *n.* being wary.

was [wɒz] *v. see* be.

wash [wɒʃ] 1. *n.* (*pl.* **-es**) (a) act of cleaning with water or another liquid; *inf.* **it will all come out in the w.** = it will all be made clear in due course. (b) clothes which are being washed. (c) movement of the sea or water. (d) waves left behind a boat. (e) thin mixture of liquid; **color w.** = thin pale mixture of paint and water. 2. *v.* (a) to clean with water or another liquid. (b) to be able to be washed; *inf.* to be believable. (c) (*of water*) to flow past. (d) to be carried by water. (e) **to be washed overboard** = to be swept off the deck of a ship by a wave. **wash a•way**, *v.* to remove by water. **wash•a•ble**, *adj.* able to be washed. **wash•bowl, wash•ba•sin**, *n.* container, esp. when fixed and having faucets, for holding water for washing the hands and face. **wash•cloth**, *n.* small piece of cloth for washing the face or body. **wash•day**, *n.* day when the clothes are washed. **wash down**, *v.* (a) to clean with a lot of water. (b) **to w. down medicine with a drink of water** = to drink water to help swallow medicine. **wash•down**, *n.* complete wash all over. **wash•er**, *n.* (a) person who washes. (b) steel or rubber ring under a bolt or nut; rubber ring inside a faucet which prevents water escaping when the faucet is turned off. (c) machine for washing. (d) **windshield w.** = attachment on a car which squirts water onto the windshield to clean the glass.

wash•er•wom•an, *n.* (*pl.* **-women**) woman who washes clothes. **wash•ing,** *n.* (a) act of cleaning with water. (b) clothes which are to be washed/which have just been washed. **wash•ing ma•chine,** *n.* machine for washing clothes. **wash•ing-up,** *n.* washing of cups/plates/knives and forks, etc., after a meal. **wash•leath•er,** *n.* piece of soft leather used for cleaning windows. **wash off,** *v.* to clean away with water. **wash out,** *v.* (a) to clean/to be cleaned with water. (b) **washed out** = tired and without energy. **wash•out,** *n. inf.* (a) useless person. (b) thing that has failed. (c) removal of pollutants by the rain. **wash•room,** *n.* room where you can wash your hands and use the toilet. **wash•stand,** *n.* (a) (*old*) table on which a washbowl and jug of water stood in a bedroom. (b) fixed bowl, with faucets, for holding water for washing the hands and face. **wash up,** *v.* (a) to clean with water the cups/plates/knives and forks, etc., used during a meal. (b) to wash yourself. (c) (*of the sea*) to throw (wreckage) onto the shore.

wasp [wɒsp] *n.* striped insect, like a bee, which can sting but which does not make honey; **w. waist** = (woman's) very slim waist. **WASP,** *n.* White Anglo-Saxon Protestant. **wasp•ish,** *adj.* irritable/quick-tempered. **wasp•ish•ly,** *adv.* in a waspish way.

waste [weɪst] 1. *n.* (a) wild/uncultivated land. (b) unnecessary use (of time/money). (c) garbage; refuse; **w. pipe** = pipe which takes dirty water from a sink to the drains. 2. *v.* (a) to use more than necessary/to use badly. **w. not, want not** = don't throw anything away, you may need it later. (b) **to w. away** = to become thin/to lose weight. 3. *adj.* (a) (*of land*) uncultivated/not used for any particular purpose; **to lay w.** = to destroy the crops and houses in an area, esp. in time of war. (b) old and useless; **w. paper basket** = small container where useless papers can be put. **wast•age,** *n.* (a) loss due to waste. (b) amount lost by waste. **waste•ful,** *adj.* extravagant/which wastes a lot. **waste•ful•ly,** *adv.* in an extravagant way. **wast•er,** *n.* person/thing which wastes a lot. **wast•rel,** *n.* person who is useless and idle.

watch [wɒtʃ] 1. *n.* (*pl.* **-es**) (a) act of looking at s.o./sth; close observation. (b) person or group of people who guards or patrols an area. (c) period of duty for sailors on a ship. (d) small clock worn on the arm or carried in a pocket; **digital w.** = watch which shows the time in numbers (10:27) rather than on a circular dial. 2. *v.* (a) to look at/to observe. (b) to be careful. **neighborhood watch,** *n.* group of people in a neighborhood who make sure

that people and houses are safe at night. **watch•dog,** *n.* (a) dog which guards a house or other buildings. (b) person/committee which examines public spending/public morals, etc. **watch•er,** *n.* person who watches/observes. **watch•ful,** *adj.* very careful. **watch•ful•ly,** *adv.* very carefully. **watch•ing,** *n.* act of looking/observing. **watch•mak•er,** *n.* person who makes and repairs clocks and watches. **watch•man,** *n.* (*pl.* **-men**) person who guards a building, usu. when it is empty. **watch out,** *v.* to be careful; **to w. o. for** = to be careful to avoid. **watch•tow•er,** *n.* tower from the top of which you can see if the enemy is coming. **watch•word,** *n.* slogan/password.

wa•ter [ˈwɔːtə] 1. *n.* (a) compound of hydrogen and oxygen; liquid that is in rain/rivers/lakes and the sea; **drinking w.** = water that is safe to drink; **hot w. bottle** = rubber bottle filled with hot water and used to warm a bed or a part of the body; **by w.** = on a boat; **to be under w.** = to be covered by water; **high w./low w.** = high/low tide; **to keep your head above w.** = (i) to swim with your head out of the water; (ii) to be able to keep out of difficulties; **to pass w.** = to urinate. (b) **waters** = the water of a lake, sea, etc.; **to take the waters** = to drink mineral water at a spa. (c) *inf.* **w. on the brain** = illness where liquid forms on the brain, causing mental deficiency. (d) mixture of water with other substances. (e) (*old*) (*of diamonds/precious stones*) brilliance; **of the first w.** = of the finest quality. 2. *v.* (a) to give water to. (b) (**down**) to add water to (wine or spirits); to make (a statement) less forceful. (c) (*of eyes/mouth*) to fill with water. (d) (*of boats*) to take in supplies of drinking water. **wa•te•rbed,** *n.* mattress made of a plastic or rubber bag filled with water. **wa•ter bis•cuit,** *n.* thin hard biscuit eaten with cheese. **wa•ter boat•man,** *n.* insect which skims across the surface of lakes/rivers, etc. **wa•ter•borne,** *adj.* (troops) carried in boats; (disease) carried in water. **water brash,** *n.* bitter liquid which comes up from the stomach into the mouth. **wa•ter buf•fa•lo,** *n.* large Asian animal, with a hump, which is used for farm work. **wa•ter can•non,** *n.* machine for sending strong jets of water (for dispersing rioters, etc.). **wa•ter clos•et,** *n.* room with a toilet. **wa•ter•col•or,** *n.* (a) paint used by artists which is mixed with water, not oil. (b) picture painted in watercolors. **wa•ter•course,** *n.* path of a stream/river. **wa•ter•cress,** *n.* creeping plant grown in water and eaten in salads. **wa•tered,** *adj.* (silk) with wavy markings in it. **wa•ter•fall,** *n.* fall of a river, etc., from a high level over the edge of a cliff.

wa•ter•fowl, *n.pl.* birds which like to live around ponds and lakes (such as ducks/geese, etc.). **wa•ter•front,** *n.* bank of a river/shore of the sea and the buildings along it. **wa•ter hole,** *n.* pond in the desert, where wild animals come to drink. **water ice,** *n.* type of light ice cream made of water and flavoring. **wa•ter•ing,** *n.* (a) act of giving water. (b) **w. down** = dilution (of wine or spirits) by adding water. (c) filling of the eyes with water. **wa•ter•ing can,** *n.* container with a long spout used for giving water to plants, etc. **wa•ter•ing hole,** *n. inf.* bar where a group of people often get together. **wa•ter•less,** *adj.* without water. **wa•ter lev•el,** *n.* level of water. **wa•ter lil•y,** *n.* plant with round leaves and big flowers, growing in water. **water line,** *n.* line where the water reaches on the hull of a ship. **wa•ter•logged,** *adj.* very wet/full of water. **Wa•ter•loo,** *n. inf.* **to meet one's W.** = to have a disaster/be completely defeated. **wa•ter main,** *n.* principal pipe carrying water underground along a road, and into buildings. **wa•ter•man,** *n.* (*pl.* -**men**) man who ferries people in a rowing boat. **wa•ter•mark,** *n.* (a) faint design put in paper to show who made it. (b) mark showing where the water reaches or has reached. **wa•ter mead•ow,** *n.* meadow often flooded by a river. **wa•ter•mel•on,** *n.* large juicy fruit with red flesh. **water mill,** *n.* mill driven by the power of water running over a large wheel. **wa•ter pis•tol,** *n.* toy gun which squirts water when the trigger is pressed. **wa•ter po•lo,** *n.* ball game played in water between two teams. **wa•ter pow•er,** *n.* power/energy of running water, used to drive machines. **wa•ter•proof.** 1. *adj.* which will not let water through. 2. *v.* to make (sth) waterproof. **wa•ter rat,** *n.* small mammal living in holes in a river bank. **wa•ter•shed,** *n.* (a) area drained by a river, stream, etc. (b) point where the situation changes permanently. **wa•ter•side,** *n.* bank of a river/lake/sea. **wa•ter-ski•er,** *n.* person who goes in for water-skiing. **wa•ter-ski•ing,** *n.* sport of gliding along the surface of water standing on a pair of skis pulled by a fast boat. **wa•ter sof•ten•er,** *n.* chemical/device for removing the hardness in water. **wa•ter•spout,** *n.* (a) pipe carrying rainwater away from a roof. (b) tornado at sea when the water rises in a high column.

wa•ter sup•ply, *n.* system of pipes/tanks, etc., bringing water to people's homes; amount of water in the system. **wa•ter ta•ble,** *n.* natural level of water below ground. **wa•ter•tight,** *adj.* (a) fitting so tightly that water cannot get in or out. (b) sth so strong that it cannot be defeated, disproved, avoided; **w. argument; w. case.** **wa•ter tow•er,** *n.* tower holding a large tank of water. **wa•ter•way,** *n.* canal or deep river along which boats can easily travel. **wa•ter•weed,** *n.* weed which grows in water. **wa•ter•wheel,** *n.* wheel which is turned by water and so makes a machine work. **wa•ter wings,** *n.* inflatable rings attached to the arms of children learning to swim. **wa•ter•works,** *n.* buildings from which water is piped to houses and factories; **to turn on the w.** = to cry. **wa•ter•y,** *adj.* which has a lot of water.

watt [wɒt] *n.* standard unit of electrical power. **watt•age** ['wɒtɪdʒ] *n.* amount of electricity in watts.

wat•tle ['wɒtl] *n.* (a) woven twigs/laths used to make light walls; **w. and daub** = type of medieval construction consisting of woven strips of wood covered with mud. (b) type of Australian tree. (c) fold of red skin hanging under the throat of some birds (such as turkeys).

wave [weɪv] 1. *n.* (a) ridge on the surface of the sea. (b) up-and-down movement; **a w. of the hand.** (c) ridge on the surface; **permanent w.** = treatment which makes hair wave and curl. (d) sudden feeling; sudden spell (of hot/cold weather). 2. *v.* (a) to move up and down; **to w. to s.o.** = to signal to s.o. with the hand; **to w. s.o. aside** = to dismiss s.o. with a movement of the hand; **to w. s.o. on** = to tell s.o. to go on by a movement of the hand. (b) to have/to make ridges on the surface. **wave band,** *n.* group of wavelengths which are close together. **waved,** *adj.* (*of hair*) treated to look wavy. **wave•length,** *n.* distance between similar points on radio waves; *inf.* **they're not on the same w.** = they do not understand each other at all. **wav•y,** *adj.* (-**ier,** -**iest**) which goes up and down.

wa•ver ['weɪvə] *v.* (a) to tremble/to move from side to side. (b) to hesitate. **wa•ver•er,** *n.* person who hesitates. **wa•ver•ing,** *adj.* trembling/hesitant.

wax [wæks] 1. *n.* (a) solid substance made by bees to build the cells of their honeycomb. (b) solid substance similar to this. 2. *v.* (a) to put

---

polish on (furniture, etc.). (b) (*of the moon*) to grow bigger. **wax•en,** *adj.* pale (like wax). **wax•wing,** *n.* small bird with bright marks on its wings. **wax•works,** *n.* exhibition of wax models of famous people. **wax•y,** *adj.* like wax.

way [weɪ] 1. *n.* (a) road/path; **to make your w. through a crowd** = to push through a crowd; **w. in** = entrance; **w. out** = exit; **by the w.** = incidentally/in passing; **by w. of** = (i) via; (ii) as a method of. (b) right direction/right road; **to go out of your w. to help s.o.** = to make a special effort to help s.o. (c) particular direction; **one-way street** = street where the traffic can only move in one direction. (d) method/means/manner; **she always gets her own w.** = she gets what she wants; **to have a w. with** = know how to amuse and please; **I know all his ways** = I know all the odd little things he does; **w. out of a difficulty** = solution to a problem. (e) distance (from one place to another); **he'll go a long w.** = he will be very successful. (f) space in which s.o. wants to move. (g) state/condition; **in the ordinary w.** = usually; **out of the w.** = unusual; **in many ways** = in lots of aspects/points; **(in) no w.** = not at all. (h) progress/movement forward; **under w.** = moving forward; **to make your w. in the world** = to be successful; **to pay your w.** = to pay for yourself. 2. *adv. inf.* away/far. **way•bill,** *n.* list of goods carried, as on a railroad. **way•far•er,** *n.* (*formal*) traveler. **way•lay** [weɪˈleɪ] *v.* (**waylaid**) to wait for (s.o.) in order to attack/to ambush. **way-out,** *adj. Sl.* strange/unusual. **way•side,** *adj. & n.* (referring to the) side of the road. **way•ward,** *adj.* (child) who wants to do what he wants. **way•ward•ness,** *n.* being difficult/uncontrollable.

WC [ˈdʌbljuˈsiː] *n. short for* water closet.

we [wiː] *pron.* (a) referring to people who are speaking/to the person speaking and others. (b) *inf.* you.

weak [wiːk] *adj.* (**-er, -est**) (a) not strong in body or in character. (b) (*of a liquid*) watery/not strong. (c) not good **at** (a subject). (d) (*in grammar*) (verb) which forms its past tense using a suffix. **weak•en,** *v.* to make/to become weak. **weak-kneed,** *adj.* soft/timid/cowardly. **weak•ling,** *n.* weak person. **weak•ly.** 1. *adj.* not strong. 2. *adv.* not strongly/feebly. **weak-mind•ed,** *adj.* not strong in character. **weak•ness,** *n.* (a) being weak. (b) *inf.* liking (**for**).

weal [wiːl] *n. see* **wheal.**

wealth [welθ] *n.* (a) riches. (b) large amount. **wealth•y,** *adj. & n.* (**-ier, -iest**) very rich (person).

wean [wiːn] *v.* to make (a baby) start to eat solid food after only drinking milk; **to w. s.o. off/away from sth** = to get s.o. to drop a (bad) habit.

weap•on [ˈwepən] *n.* object with which you fight. **weap•on•ry,** *n.* (*no pl.*) weapons.

wear [ˈweə] 1. *n.* (a) act of carrying on your body as a piece of clothing; **normal w. and tear** = normal use. (b) clothes. (c) damage through much use. (d) ability to stand much use. 2. *v.* (**wore** [wɔː]; **has worn** [wɔːn]) (a) to carry on your body as a piece of clothing. (b) to become damaged through much use. (c) to stand up to much use/to last a long time. (d) to have (an expression) or your face. **wear•a•ble,** *adj.* able to be worn. **wear a•way, wear down,** *v.* to disappear/to make (sth) disappear by rubbing or much use. **wear•er,** *n.* person who wears clothes. **wear•ing,** *adj.* tiring. **wear off,** *v.* to disappear gradually; to make (sth) disappear. **wear on,** *v.* (*of time*) to pass. **wear out,** *v.* (a) to become useless through much use; to make (sth) become useless through much use. (b) **to wear yourself out/to be worn out** = to become tired through doing a lot.

wear•y [ˈwɪrɪ] 1. *adj.* (**-ier, -iest**) very tired/tiring. 2. *v.* to become tired/to make tired. **wear•i•ly,** *adv.* in a tired way. **wear•i•ness,** *n.* tiredness. **wear•i•some,** *adj.* tiring/boring.

wea•sel [ˈwiːzl] *n.* small animal with a long thin body and short legs, which kills and eats rabbits, etc.

weath•er [ˈweðə] 1. *n.* state of the air and atmosphere at a certain time; **in all weathers** = in every sort of instance, good or bad; **under the w.** = miserable/unwell. 2. *v.* (a) (*of seal/frost/wind, etc.*) to wear down (rocks, etc.). (b) to season (planks of wood); to make (wood) suitable for use by leaving it outside for several years. (c) to survive (a storm/crisis). **weath•er-beat•en,** *adj.* (a) marked by the weather. (b) (*of face*) tanned/made brown by the wind, rain and sun. **weath•er bu•reau, weather center,** *n.* office where the weather is forecast. **weath•er•cock,** *n.* weather vane in the shape of a cock. **weath•er fore•cast, weather report,** *n.* description of the weather about to come in the next few hours or days. **weath•er•man,** *n.* (*pl.* **-men**) *inf.* expert who describes the coming weather, usu. on TV or radio. **weath•er•proof,** *adj.* able to keep out the wind and the rain. **weath•er sta•tion,** *n.* place where weather conditions are recorded. **weath•er strip(ping),** *n.* strip of wood, metal, etc. which is attached to the inside of a window frame to prevent drafts. **weath•er**

vane, *n.* metal pointer on a high building which turns around to show the direction of the wind.

weave [wi:v] 1. *n.* pattern of cloth; way in which cloth has been woven. 2. *v.* (**wove** [wəuv] or **weaved, has woven** or **wove**) (a) to make cloth by winding threads in and out. (b) to make (sth) by a similar method, using straw, etc. (c) to twist and turn. **weav•er,** *n.* person who weaves. **weav•ing,** *n.* action of making cloth by winding threads in and out.

web [web] *n.* (a) thing that is woven. (b) net spun by spiders. (c) skin between the toes of a water bird, etc. (d) *inf.* **the Web** = the World Wide Web. **webbed,** *adj.* with skin between the toes. **web•bing,** *n.* strong tape used in upholstery. **web•foot•ed,** *adj.* with webbed feet. **web•site,** *n.* group of linked pages on the Internet devoted to a particular subject.

wed [wed] *v.* (**wedded** or **wed**) (a) (*formal*) to marry (s.o.); to become husband and wife. (b) **to be wedded to an idea** = to be firmly attached to an idea. **wed•ding,** *n.* marriage ceremony; **silver/golden w.** = anniversary of 25/50 years of marriage; **w. ring** = ring which is put on the finger during the wedding ceremony. **wed•lock,** *n.* being married.

wedge [wedʒ] 1. *n.* (a) V-shaped piece of wood/metal, used for splitting wood. (b) V-shaped piece, as of pie. 2. *v.* (a) to split with a wedge. (b) to fix firmly with a wedge. (c) to become tightly fixed.

Wednes•day ['wenzdɪ, 'wedənzdeɪ] *n.* third day of the week/day between Tuesday and Thursday.

wee [wi:] 1. *adj.* very small. 2. *n.* (*child's word*) (*also* **wee-wee**) urine. 3. *v.* (*child's word*) (*also* **wee-wee**) to urinate.

weed [wi:d] 1. *n.* (a) plant that you do not want in a garden. (b) **weeds** = black clothes worn by a widow. (c) *inf.* thin, skinny person. (d) *inf.* tobacco; *Sl.* marijuana. 2. *v.* (a) to pull out unwanted plants from. (b) **to w. out** = to remove. **weed-kill•er,** *n.* chemical which kills unwanted plants. **weed•y,** *adj.* (-ier, -iest) (a) covered with weeds. (b) thin and skinny (person).

week [wi:k] *n.* (a) period of seven days. **a w. from now/a w. today** = this day next week; **yesterday w.** = a week ago yesterday. (b) part of a seven day period; **he works a 35-hour w.** = he works 35 hours every week. **week•day,** *n.* any day of the week except Sunday (and sometimes Saturday). **week•end,** *n.* period from Friday evening or Saturday morning until Sunday evening or Monday morning. **week•ly.** 1. *adv. & adj.* once a week. 2. *n.* magazine published once a week.

wee•nie, weeny ['wi:nɪ] *adj. inf.* very small.

weep [wi:p] *v.* (**wept** [wept]) to cry. **weep•ing,** *adj.* (a) crying. (b) (*of tree*) with branches hanging down.

wee•vil ['wi:vl] *n.* type of beetle which eats plants, grain, etc.

weft [weft] *n.* threads going across a length of material.

weigh [weɪ] *v.* (a) to measure how heavy sth is. (b) to have a certain heaviness; **time weighs heavily on his hands** = he has nothing to do. (c) **to w. anchor** = to lift the anchor of a ship in order to sail away. (d) **to w. the pros and cons** = to examine all the arguments for and against. **weigh•bridge,** *n.* large machine for weighing heavy trucks and their goods. **weigh down,** *v.* (a) to press down. (b) to make (s.o.) gloomy. **weigh in,** *v.* (*of boxers/jockeys*) to be weighed before a fight or race. **weigh•ing ma•chine,** *n.* device for weighing.

weight [weɪt] 1. *n.* (a) heaviness (of sth); **to lose/put on w.** = to get thinner/fatter; **to pull your w.** = to do your share. (b) piece of metal used to measure the exact heaviness of sth else. (c) heavy object; **that's a w. off my mind!** = I no longer need to worry about that. (d) importance; *inf.* **to throw your w. about** = to use your authority in an arrogant way. 2. *v.* (a) to attach a weight to (sth). (b) to add (a quantity) to a sum to produce a certain result. **weight•less,** *adj.* with no weight. **weight•less•ness,** *n.* having no weight. **weight•lift•er,** *n.* person who lifts heavy weights as a sport. **weight•lift•ing,** *n.* sport of lifting heavy weights. **weight•y,** *adj.* (-ier, -iest) (a) heavy. (b) important (problem, etc.).

weir ['wɪə] *n.* (a) small dam built across a river to control the flow of water. (b) fence across a lake or river to trap fish.

weird ['wɪəd] *adj.* (-er, -est) strange/odd. **weird•ly,** *adv.* in a strange way. **weird•ness,** *n.* being weird. **weird•o** ['wɪədəu] *n.* (*pl.* -os) *inf.* strange/odd person; person who behaves in a strange way.

wel•come ['welkəm] 1. *n.* greeting/reception. 2. *v.* (a) to greet (s.o.) as he arrives. (b) to hear (news) with pleasure. 3. *adj.* (a) pleasing/received with pleasure. (b) (**to**) willingly permit-

---

æ **back,** a: **farm,** ʊ: **top,** aɪ **pipe,** aʊ **how,** aɪə **fire,** aʊə **flower,** ɔ: **bought,** ɔɪ **toy,** e **fed,** eə **hair,** eɪ **take,** ə **afraid,** əʊ **boat,** əʊə **lower,** v: **word,** i: **heap,** ɪ **hit,** ɪə **hear,** u: **school,** ʊ **book,** ʌ **but,** b **back,** d **dog,** ð **then,** dʒ **just,** f **fog,** g **go,** h **hand,** j **yes,** k **catch,** l **last,** m **mix,** n **nut,** ŋ **sing,** p **penny,** r **round,** s **some,** ʃ **short,** t **too,** tʃ **chop,** θ **thing,** v **voice,** w **was,** z **zoo,** ʒ **treasure**

ted. (c) *inf.* (*as a reply to* **thank you**) **you're w.** = it was a pleasure to do it.

weld [weld] 1. *n.* joint made by joining two pieces of metal together by first heating, then pressing. 2. *v.* to join (two pieces of metal) together by first heating, then pressing. **weld•er,** *n.* person/machine that welds metal. **weld•ing,** *n.* process of joining two pieces of metal together; place where two pieces are welded.

wel•fare ['welfeə] *n.* happiness/comfort/freedom from want; **W. State** = state which looks after the health and well-being of its citizens; **child w.** = health and well-being of children.

wel•kin ['welkɪn] *n.* (*old*) sky.

well [wel] 1. *n.* (a) deep hole at the bottom of which is water or oil. (b) deep hole; space in the center of a building where the staircase or elevator is. 2. *v.* **to w. up** = to start to flow. 3. *adv.* (**better, best**) (a) in a good way/properly; **to do w.** = to prosper; **to go w.** = (i) to be successful/to have good results; (ii) to fit/to suit; **to speak w. of** = to praise/to say nice things about. (b) to a large degree; **w. after 7 o'clock** = a long time after 7 o'clock; **pretty w. all the family** = almost all the family. (c) lucky/desirable; **you may w. be right** = you probably are right; **all's w. that ends w.** = if the result is fine then everything is fine; **to wish s.o. w.** = to wish them good luck. (d) **as w.** = also/too. 4. *adj.* healthy and in good condition. 5. *inter. starting a sentence and meaning nothing in particular or showing surprise.* **well-ad•vised,** *adj.* wise. **well-ap•point•ed,** *adj.* luxuriously furnished. **well-bal•anced,** *adj.* steady/sensible. **well-be•haved,** *adj.* good/having good manners. **well-be•ing,** *n.* health and happiness. **well•born,** *adj.* of an aristocratic family. **well-bred,** *adj.* polite/well-educated. **well-con•nect•ed,** *adj.* with influential friends or family. **well-dis•posed,** *adj.* kindly. **well-done,** *adj.* (meat) which has been cooked a long time. **well-earned,** *adj.* which has been deserved. **well-found•ed,** *adj.* (fears) which are justified. **well-groomed,** *adj.* clean and tidy (person). **well-ground•ed,** *adj.* (fears) which are justified. **well-heel•ed,** *adj. inf.* rich. **well-in•formed,** *adj.* knowing a lot about a subject. **well-in•ten•tioned,** *adj.* (person) with good intentions. **well-knit,** *adj.* strong (body). **well-known,** *adj.* famous/known by many people. **well-man•nered,** *adj.* polite/with good manners. **well-mean•ing,** *adj.* (person) who does sth with good intentions. **well-meant,** *adj.* (action) done with good intentions. **well-nigh,** *adv.* (*formal*) almost. **well-off,** *adj. inf.* rich. **well-oiled,** *adj.*

Sl. drunk. **well-read,** *adj.* having read many books and therefore knowing a lot. **well-spo•ken,** *adj.* (person) who speaks politely and correctly. **well-timed,** *adj.* which happens at the right time. **well-to-do,** *adj. inf.* wealthy. **well-wish•er,** *n.* person who is friendly toward another. **well-worn,** *adj.* used a lot.

wel•ling•ton boots, wellingtons, *inf.* **wel•lies** ['welɪŋtən'buːts, 'welɪŋtənz, 'welɪz] *n. pl.* rubber waterproof boots.

Welsh [welʃ] 1. *adj.* referring to Wales; **W. rarebit** = toasted cheese on bread. 2. *n.* (a) *pl.* **the W.** = the people of Wales. (b) language spoken in Wales. 3. *v.* **to w. on s.o.** = (i) to break a promise made to s.o.; (ii) to not pay s.o. a debt, esp. a gambling debt. **Welsh•man, Welshwoman,** *n.* person from Wales.

welt [welt] *n.* (a) leather edging for attaching the upper part of a shoe to the sole. (b) strong edge along a seam. (c) wheal.

wel•ter ['weltə] *n.* confused mass. **wel•ter•weight,** *n.* medium weight in boxing between middleweight and lightweight.

wen [wen] *n.* tumor.

wench [wenʃ] *n.* (*pl.* **-es**) (*old*) young woman.

wend [wend] *v.* **to w. one's way** = to go.

went [went] *v. see* **go.**

wept [wept] *v. see* **weep.**

were [wɜː] *v. see* **be.**

were•wolf ['wɪəwʊlf] *n.* (*pl.* **-wolves**) person who changes into a wolf.

west [west] 1. *n.* (a) one of the points of the compass, the direction in which the sun sets; **w. wind** = wind coming from the west. (b) **the W.** = the non-communist world. 2. *adv.* toward the west. **west•bound,** *adj.* going toward the west. **west•er•ly,** *adj.* (a) (wind) from the west. (b) toward the west. **west•ern.** 1. *adj.* of the west. 2. *n.* novel/motion picture about cowboys and Indians in the western United States. **west•ern•er,** *n.* person who lives in the west. **west•ern•i•za•tion,** *n.* act of westernizing. **west•ern•ize,** *v.* to make more European or American. **west•ern•most,** *adj.* furthest west. **West In•dian,** *n. & adj.* (person) from the West Indies. **west•ward** 1. *adj.* toward the west. 2. *adv.* (*also* **westwards**) toward the west.

wet [wet] 1. *adj.* (**wetter, wettest**) (a) covered or soaked with water or other liquid; **I'm w. through/soaking w.** = all my clothes are very wet; *inf.* **w. blanket** = person who spoils any fun. (b) rainy. 2. *n.* rain. 3. *v.* (**wetted**) to dampen with water. **wet•lands,** *n.* marshy areas which are often covered by water. **wet•ness,** *n.* being wet. **wet suit,** *n.* suit worn by divers which keeps the body warm with a layer of warm water. **wet•ting,** *n.* soaking/getting wet.

weth•er ['weðə] *n.* castrated ram.

whack [wæk] 1. *n.* (a) hard, noisy blow. (b) *inf.* **let's have a w. at it!** = let's try to do it. 2. *v.* to hit hard, making a loud noise. **whack•ing,** *adj. inf.* huge.

whale [weɪl] *n.* (a) huge sea mammal. (b) *inf.* **we had a w. of a time** = we enjoyed ourselves very much. **whale•boat,** *n.* boat used when hunting whales. **whale•bone,** *n.* thin bone taken from the jaws of whales and formerly used in corsets. **whal•er,** *n.* (a) boat used when hunting whales. (b) person who hunts whales. **whal•ing,** *n.* hunting of whales.

wharf [wɔːf] *n.* (*pl.* **wharves** [wɔːvz], **wharfs**) place in a dock where a ship can tie up and load or unload. **wharf•in•ger,** *n.* person who is in charge of a wharf.

what [wɒt] 1. *adj.* (a) that which. (b) (*asking a question*) which? **w. good is this to us?** = what is the use of this? (c) (*showing surprise*) how much/how great/how strange. 2. *pron.* (a) that which; **come w. may** = whatever happens. (b) (*asking a question*) which thing or things; **w. is the German word for table? what's the use of learning Latin?** = why learn Latin? **w. about stopping for lunch now?** = do you think we should stop for lunch now?; **w. did you say?/**(*not polite*) **w.?** = I didn't hear what you said, please say it again; **w. if?** = what will happen if; **he knows what's w.** = he knows what the situation is and what to do. 3. *inter. showing surprise.* **whats-it, what-d'you-call-it,** *n. inf.* thing of which you have forgotten the name for the moment. **what•ev•er** [wɒ'evə] 1. *pron.* anything at all. 2. *adj.* (a) (*strong form of* **what**) (b) **none w.** = none at all. **what for,** *pron.* (a) why. (b) what is the purpose of. (c) *inf.* **to give s.o. what for** = to be angry with s.o. **what•not,** *n.* stand with shelves for small books and ornaments. **what•so•ev•er** [wɒtsəu'evə] *adj. & pron.* (*strong form of* **whatever**) **none w.** = none at all.

wheal [wiːl] *n.* raised mark left on the skin by a blow from a whip or stick.

wheat [wiːt] *n.* cereal plant. **wheat•ear,** *n.* brown bird living in fields. **wheat•en,** *adj.* made of wheat. **wheat germ,** *n.* central part of a grain of wheat. **wheat meal,** *n.* brown flour containing most of the grain. **wheat**

sheaf, *n.* large bundle of stalks of wheat bound together.

whee•dle ['wiːdl] *v.* to ask s.o. for sth in a flattering way.

wheel [wiːl] 1. *n.* (a) circular frame which turns around a central axis (as a support for cars/trains/bicycles, etc.). (b) any similar circular object; **steering w.** = wheel which the driver of a car holds and turns to follow the road; **to take the w.** = to drive; **potter's w.** = horizontal disk on which a potter throws the clay to make pottery. 2. *v.* (a) to push along (sth) that has wheels. (b) **to w. around** = to turn around suddenly. (c) to fly in circles; **seagulls wheeling above the fishing boats.** (d) **to w. and deal** = to be involved in a number of different activities all to one's own advantage. **wheel•bar•row,** *n.* small handcart used by builders and gardeners, which has one wheel in front, and two handles behind. **wheel•base,** *n.* distance between the front and rear axles of a car/truck, etc. **wheel•chair,** *n.* chair on wheels used by people who cannot walk. **wheel•er-deal•er,** *n.* businessman who lives by making deals. **wheel•wright,** *n.* man who makes wheels.

wheeze [wiːz] 1. *n.* noisy breathing. 2. *v.* to breathe noisily and with difficulty. **wheez•i•ly,** *adv.* in a wheezy way. **wheez•i•ness,** *n.* being wheezy. **wheez•y,** *adj.* (person) who wheezes.

whelk [welk] *n.* type of edible sea snail.

whelp [welp] 1. *n.* young of a dog. 2. *v.* to give birth to a young dog.

when [wen] 1. *adv.* (*asking a question*) at what time. 2. *conj.* (a) at the time that. (b) if. **when•ev•er** [we'nevə] *adv.* at any time that.

whence [wens] *adv.* (*formal*) from where.

where ['weə] 1. *adv.* (*asking a question*) in/at/to what place? 2. *adv.* in the place. **where•a•bouts.** 1. *n. pl.* ['weərəbauts] place where s.o./sth is. 2. *adv.* [weərə'bauts] in what place? **where•as** [weər'æz] *conj.* on the other hand/while/in contrast with the fact that. **where•by** [wɛə'baɪ] *adv.* (*formal*) by which; according to which. **where•fore,** *adv.* (*old*) why? **where•in** [wɛər'ɪn] *adv.* (*formal*) in which way? **where•up•on** [weərə'pɒn] *conj.* at that point/after that. **wher•ev•er** [weər'evə] *conj.* in every place. **where•with•al,** *n.* (*formal*) necessary money.

wher•ry ['werɪ] *n.* small rowboat.

whet [wet] *v.* (**whetted**) (a) to sharpen (a knife).

æ back, aː farm, ɒ top, aɪ pipe, aʊ how, aiə fire, aʊə flower, ɔː bought, ɔɪ toy, e fed, eəhair, eɪ take, ə afraid, əʊ boat, əʊə lower, vː word, iː heap, ɪ hit, ɪə hear, uː school, ʊ book, ʌ but, b back, d dog, ð then, dʒ just, f fog, g go, h hand, j yes, k catch, l last, m mix, n nut, ŋ sing, p penny, r round, s some, ʃ short, t too, tʃ chop, θ thing, v voice, w was, z zoo, ʒ treasure

(b) **to w. your appetite** = to make you more interested in sth by giving you a little taste of it.
whet•stone, *n.* stone used to sharpen knives, etc.

wheth•er ['weðə] *conj.* (a) if. (b) either.

whey [weɪ] *n.* liquid left when milk is made into cheese.

which [wɪtʃ] 1. *adj.* what (person/thing). 2. *pron.* (a) (*asking a question*) what person/what thing. (b) (*only used with things not persons*) that/the thing that. **which•ev•er,** *pron. & adj.* (a) anything that. (b) no matter which.

whiff [wɪf] *n.* slight smell.

while [waɪl] 1. *n.* length of time; **quite a w./a good w.** = a fairly long time; **once in a w.** = from time to time. 2. *v.* **to w. away the time** = to make the time pass while you are waiting for something. 3. *conj.* (a) during/as long as. (b) although. (c) whereas/in contrast with. **whilst** [waɪlst] *conj.* while.

whim [wɪm] *n.* sudden wish or desire. **whim•si•cal** ['wɪmzɪkl] *adj.* odd/fanciful. **whim•si•cal•i•ty,** *n.* being whimsical. **whim•sy,** *n.* strange/fanciful idea.

whim•per ['wɪmpə] 1. *n.* sad/weak cry. 2. *v.* (*of small dogs*) to cry weakly.

whine [waɪn] 1. *n.* complaint/moan. 2. *v.* to moan/to complain in a long high voice.

whin•ny ['wɪnɪ] 1. *n.* sound which a horse makes when pleased. 2. *v.* (*of a horse*) to make a neigh.

whip [wɪp] 1. *n.* (a) long, thin piece of leather fixed to a handle and used for hitting animals. (b) **party w.** = member of a legislative body whose job it is to secure votes and assist in formulating party policy. 2. *v.* (**whipped**) (a) to hit with a whip. (b) to beat sharply. (c) to beat (cream, eggs, etc.) until firm. (d) to wind string around (the end of a piece of rope). (e) *inf.* to move quickly; **to w. out a gun** = to pull a gun out quickly. **whip•cord,** *n.* type of corduroy. **whip hand,** *n.* advantage. **whip•lash,** *n.* (a) piece of thin leather which is part of a whip. (b) neck injury, caused by the head moving back suddenly. **whip off,** *v.* to move quickly; to do/remove quickly. **whip•per•snap•per,** *n.* boy/young man who is too sure of himself. **whip•ping,** *n.* beating. **whip a•round,** *v.* to turn around quickly. **whip up,** *v.* to encourage/to make (sth) increase.

whip•pet ['wɪpɪt] *n.* breed of small thin dog trained for racing.

whirl [wɜːl] 1. *n.* (a) rapid turning movement. (b) giddy/dizzy feeling. 2. *v.* (a) to turn around quickly/to spin. (b) to move quickly. **whirl•i•gig,** *n.* something which turns around rapidly (like a top). **whirl•pool,** *n.*

water which turns rapidly around and around. **whirl•wind,** *n.* (a) wind blowing around and around in a circle. (b) confused rush; **w. engagement** = very rapid engagement before marriage.

whir, whirr [wɜː] *n.* noise of sth spinning around quickly. 2. *v.* to make a spinning noise.

whisk [wɪsk] 1. *n.* (a) swift movement. (b) kitchen utensil used for beating eggs/cream, etc. 2. *v.* (a) to move quickly. (b) to beat (eggs/cream) very quickly. **whisk broom,** *n.* small brush with a short handle, for removing lint, etc. from clothes.

whisk•er ['wɪskə] *n.* (a) long stiff hair at the side of an animal's mouth. (b) **whiskers** = mustache and beard on the side of a man's face. **whisk•er•y,** *adj.* covered with whiskers.

whis•key, whisky ['wɪskɪ] *n.* alcoholic drink distilled from grain; glass of this drink.

whis•per ['wɪspə] 1. *n.* (a) quiet sound/words quietly spoken. (b) rumor. 2. *v.* (a) to speak very quietly. (b) to make a very quiet sound.

whist [wɪst] *n.* card game for four people.

whis•tle ['wɪsl] 1. *n.* (a) simple instrument played by blowing; **penny w./tin w.** = cheap metal flute. (b) small pipe which gives a loud shrill noise when blown. (c) musical sound made by almost closing the lips and blowing air through the small hole; **to wet one's w.** = to have a drink. 2. *v.* (a) to blow through the lips and make a musical or shrill sound; *inf.* **you can w. for it** = you will never get it. (b) to make a shrill sound. **whis•tle•stop tour,** *n.* election tour where a candidate stops for a brief period in many different towns.

whit [wɪt] *n.* very small amount; **not a w. more** = nothing more.

white [waɪt] 1. *adj.* (-er, -est) color of snow; **w. Christmas** = Christmas with snow on the ground. 2. *n.* (a) color of snow. (b) person whose skin is not black, brown, yellow or red. (c) light-colored meat (on a chicken); **w. of an egg** = part of the egg which is not yellow. **white ant,** *n.* termite. **white•bait,** *n.* (*pl.* **whitebait**) small young fish eaten fried. **white-col•lar work•er,** *n.* office worker. **white el•e•phant,** *n.* thing which is big and expensive but useless to its owner. **white flag,** *n.* symbol of surrender. **white goods,** *n.* household linen (sheets, pillowcases, etc.); household machines, such as refrigerators and washing machines, which are usually white. **white-haired,** *adj.* with white hair. **white heat,** *n.* very high temperature, when white light is produced by heated metal. **white hot,** *adj.* extremely hot. **White House,** *n.* house of the President of the United States; *inf.* the U.S. government. **white knight,** *n.* person/company which rescues another threatened with a takeover. **white lie,** *n.* innocent lie. **whit•en,** *v.* to make white. **whit•en•er, whitening,** *n.* white liquid for making shoes, etc., white. **white•ness,** *n.* being white. **white•out,** *n.* blinding conditions caused by wind and snow. **white pa•per,** *n.* official government report. **white sale,** *n.* sale of sheets/pillowcases, etc. **white slave,** *n.* woman captured and sent abroad as a prostitute. **white slav•er•y,** *n.* trade in white slaves. **white•wash.** 1. *n.* (a) mixture of water and lime used for painting the walls of houses. (b) attempt to cover up mistakes. 2. *v.* (a) to paint with a mixture of water and lime. (b) to attempt to cover up (mistakes). **white•wood,** *n.* unpainted soft wood, such as pine. **whit•ish,** *adj.* quite white.

whith•er ['wɪðə] *adv.* (*formal*) to which place.

whit•ing ['waɪtɪŋ] *n.* (*pl.* whiting) type of small sea fish.

whit•low ['wɪtləu] *n.* infected spot near a nail.

Whit•sun ['wɪtsən] *n.* Whitsunday or Whitsuntide. Christian festival on the seventh Sunday after Easter. **Whit•sun•tide,** *n.* the week which begins with Whitsunday, esp. the first three days.

whit•tle ['wɪtl] *v.* (a) to shape (a piece of wood) by cutting off small pieces with a knife. (b) **to w. sth away/down** = to make sth gradually smaller.

whiz [wɪz] *v.* (**whizzed**) to move very fast. **whiz kid,** *n. inf.* brilliant, successful young business person.

who [huː] *pron.* (a) (*asking a question*) which person/which people? (b) the person/people that. **who•dun•it** [huːˈdʌnɪt] *n. inf.* detective story. **who•ev•er,** *pron.* anyone who/no matter who.

WHO *abbrev. for* World Health Organization.

whoa [wəu] *inter.* used to tell a horse to stand still.

whole [həul] 1. *adj.* complete; not broken/not damaged; **he ate the w. cake** = he ate all the cake; **he ate the cookie w.** = he put it all in his mouth at once and ate it, without breaking it up. 2. *n.* all; **as a w.** = altogether; **on the w.** = for the most part. **whole•heart•ed,** *adj.* complete/total. **whole•heart•ed•ly,** *adv.* completely/totally. **whole num•ber,** *n.* number which is not a fraction. **whole•sale.** 1. *n. & adj.* sale of goods in large quantities to shops which then sell them to people in small quantities. 2. *adj.* in large quantities/on a large scale.

whole•sal•er, *n.* person who buys and sells goods in large quantities. **whole•some,** ['həulsəm] *adj.* healthy/good; **w. food** = food that is good for your health. **whole•some•ness,** *n.* being wholesome. **whole•wheat,** *n.* brown flour containing all the grain. **whol•ly,** *adv.* completely/altogether.

whom [huːm] *pron.* (a) (*formal*) (*object in questions*) which person/which persons. (b) (*object in statements*) the person/persons that.

whoop [wuːp] *n.* loud cry. **whoop•ee** [wuˈpiː] *inter. showing excitement*; **to make w.** = to enjoy yourself noisily. **whoop•ing cough** ['huːpɪŋkɒf] *n.* children's illness which causes coughing and loud noises when the child tries to breathe. **whoops,** *inter. showing surprise.*

whoosh [wuːʃ] *n.* sound of air blowing past.

whop•per ['wɒpə] *n. inf.* (a) very large thing. (b) very big lie. **whop•ping,** *adj. inf.* very large.

whore ['hɔː] *n.* (*formal*) prostitute.

whorl [wɜːl] *n.* coiled/spiral shape.

whose [huːz] *pron.* (a) (*asking a question*) of who. (b) belonging to who. **who•so•ev•er** [huːsəuˈevə] *pron.* whoever.

why [waɪ] 1. *adv.* (*asking a question*) for what reason. 2. *n.* the reason. 3. *inter. showing surprise.*

wick [wɪk] *n.* length of string in the middle of a candle/piece of material in an oil lamp which is lit and burns slowly.

wick•ed ['wɪkɪd] *adj.* very bad/very nasty. **wick•ed•ly,** *adv.* in a wicked way. **wick•ed•ness,** *n.* evil; being wicked.

wick•er ['wɪkə] *n.* thin twigs used to make furniture or baskets. **wick•er•work,** *n.* (*no pl.*) objects made of thin twigs woven together.

wick•et ['wɪkɪt] *n.* (a) small door set in or next to a larger one (as in a castle gate or city wall). (b) position on the counter in a post office/bank, etc. (c) (*in cricket*) set of three sticks put in the ground and used as the target; main playing area between two sets of these sticks; *inf.* **a sticky w.** = an awkward/difficult situation. **wick•et-keep•er,** *n.* (*in cricket*) player standing behind the wicket to stop the balls that the batsman does not hit.

wide [waɪd] 1. *adj.* (-**er,** -**est**) (a) stretching far from side to side. (b) measurement from side to side. (c) enormous (range). 2. *adv.* (a) greatly/a long way apart/far. (b) **to fall w. of the target** = miss the target. **wide-an•gle,**

æ **back,** ɑː **farm,** ɒ **top,** aɪ **pipe,** au **how,** aɪə **fire,** auə **flower,** ɔː **bought,** ɔɪ **toy,** ə **fed,** eəhair, eɪ **take,** ə afraid, əu **boat,** əuə **lower,** vː **word,** iː **heap,** ɪ **hit,** ɪə **hear,** uː **school,** u **book,** ʌ **but,** b **back,** d **dog,** ð **then,** dʒ **just,** f **fog,** g **go,** h **hand,** j **yes,** k **catch,** l **last,** m **mix,** n **nut,** ŋ **sing,** p **penny,** r **round,** s **some,** ʃ **short,** t **too,** tʃ **chop,** θ **thing,** v **voice,** w **was,** z **zoo,** ʒ **treasure**

adj. (lens) which takes in a wider area than an ordinary lens. **wide a•wake,** *adj.* very much awake/not at all sleepy. **wide•ly,** *adv.* (a) greatly; **w. read** = (i) (book) which many people have read; (ii) (person) who has read many books. **wid•en,** *v.* to make larger/to become wide. **wide-rang•ing,** *adj.* (discussion) which covers a wide field of subjects. **wide•spread,** *adj.* far/over a large area.

widg•eon ['wɪdʒn] *n.* (*pl.* widgeons or widgeon) type of small wild duck.

wid•ow ['wɪdəu] *n.* woman whose husband has died. **wid•owed,** *adj.* (woman) who has become a widow; (man) who has become a widower. **wid•ow•er,** *n.* man whose wife has died. **wid•ow•hood,** *n.* being a widow.

width [wɪdT] *n.* (a) measurement from side to side. (b) piece of material (cut right across a roll).

wield ['wiːld] *v.* (a) to hold (sth), usu. by the handle, and use it. (b) to use/to control (power).

wie•ner ['wiːnə] *n.* frankfurter. **wie•ner schnit•zel,** *n.* veal escalope, fried in breadcrumbs.

wife [waɪf] *n.* (*pl.* wives) woman to whom a man is married. **wife•ly,** *adj.* like a wife.

wig [wɪg] *n.* false hair worn on the head.

wig•gle ['wɪgl] *v. inf.* to move slightly up and down or from side to side. **wig•gly,** *adj. inf.* wavy; (line) which goes up and down.

wig•wam ['wɪgwæm] *n.* cone-shaped tent of the North American Indians.

wild [waɪld] 1. *adj.* (-er, -est) (a) not tame/free to live naturally. (b) (plant) which is not a garden plant. (c) stormy/rough (sea/wind). (d) savage/angry/fierce (animal); **to be w. with excitement** = to be over-excited; *inf.* **w. about** = very enthusiastic about. (e) rough/uncivilized (country). (f) rash/reckless (plan); badly aimed (shot). 2. *n.* **in the w.** = in country which is uninhabited and where animals can live freely. **wild•cat.** 1. *n.* small wild animal of the cat family. 2. *adj.* risky/reckless; **w. strike** = unofficial strike/strike of workers without the union's permission. **wil•der•ness** ['wɪldənəs] *n.* uncultivated/uninhabited country; desert. **wild•fire,** *n.* **like w.** = very quickly. **wild•fowl,** *n. pl.* wild birds shot for sport (such as ducks and geese). **wild-goose chase,** *n.* hopeless search. **wild•life,** *n.* (*no pl.*) birds/plants/animals living free, untouched by human beings; **w. preserve** = place where wild animals are allowed to run wild. **wild•ly,** *adv.* in a wild way; **w. inaccurate** = completely wrong. **wild•ness,** *n.* being wild.

wil•de•beest ['wɪldɪbrːst] *n.* large African antelope.

wiles [waɪlz] *n. pl.* clever tricks.

wil•ful ['wɪlful] *adj.* willful.

will [wɪl] 1. *n.* (a) strength of mind and character. (b) wish; **of one's own free w.** = not forced; **at w.** = as you wish. (c) written instructions made by s.o. as to what should happen to his belongings when he dies. 2. *v.* (a) **to w. s.o. to do sth** = to suggest strongly to s.o. else by power of mind. (b) to leave (your belongings) after death to others by writing down your wishes. 3. *v.* (*used with an infinitive*) (a) to wish; **do what you w.** (b) (*polite form of asking someone to do something*) **would you please sit down?/won't you sit down?** (c) (*stressed*) to be certain to happen. 4. *used with verbs forming future tense.* **will•ing,** *adj.* wanting (**to** do sth); eager (to help). **will•ing•ly,** *adv.* eagerly. **will•ing•ness,** *n.* eagerness. **will pow•er,** *n.* strength of will.

will•ful ['wɪlfəl] *adj.* (a) (person) determined to do what he wants. (b) done on purpose; **w. murder** = murder which was planned. **will•ful•ly,** *adv.* intentionally/on purpose.

wil•lies ['wɪlɪz] *n. pl. inf.* **it gives me the w.** = it makes me scared.

will-o'-the-wisp ['wɪlədəwɪsp] *n.* bluish light caused in marshes by burning methane gas.

wil•low ['wɪləu] *n.* tree with thin supple branches often found along river banks. **wil•low pat•tern,** *n.* china with a blue and white Chinese design on it. **wil•low•y,** *adj.* tall and slender.

wil•ly-nil•ly ['wɪlɪ'nɪlɪ] *adv.* whether you want to or not.

wilt [wɪlt] 1. *n.* disease of plants which makes them droop. 2. *v.* to become weak and droop.

wil•y ['waɪlɪ] *adj.* (-ier, -iest) crafty/full of tricks. **wil•i•ness,** *n.* being wily.

wimp [wɪmp] *n.* weak individual.

wim•ple ['wɪmpl] *n.* linen covering worn by nuns over their heads.

win [wɪn] 1. *n.* action of beating s.o. in a competition/game. 2. *v.* (won [wʌn]) (a) to defeat s.o. in a contest/race, etc.; to be first in a race/competition. (b) to gain/to get (a prize). **win back,** *v.* to get back/to regain. **win•ner,** *n.* (a) person who has won a race/a prize, etc. (b) *inf.* thing which is (certain to be) successful. **win•ning.** 1. *adj.* (a) which wins. (b) attractive (smile). 2. *n.* (a) victory. (b) **winnings** = money, etc., which has been won at a game of chance. **win o•ver,** *v.* to persuade. **win out,** *v.* to succeed in the end after many difficulties.

wince [wɪns] 1. *n.* movement which shows you feel pain. 2. *v.* to show signs of pain, esp. by moving the face.

winch [wɪnʃ] 1. *n.* (*pl.* -es) device which pulls

things up by winding a rope around a drum. 2. *v.* to pull up/to lift by using a winch.

wind[1] [wɪnd] 1. *n.* (a) moving air; **high winds** = very strong winds; **to sail close to the w.** = (i) to sail a boat almost directly into the wind; (ii) to be very near to being dishonest or rude; **to take the w. out of s.o.'s sails** = to spoil s.o.'s plans, usually by doing what he was going to do. (b) breath; **to get your second w.** = to get enough breath again after being tired; to be able to make a second effort. (c) smell/scent, when hunting; **to get w. of** = to hear a rumor about. (d) gas in the stomach. (e) (*also* **wind instruments, wind section**) woodwind instruments in an orchestra. 2. *v.* (a) to make (s.o.) breathless, esp. by hitting him in the chest. (b) to smell/scent when hunting. **wind•bag**, *n. inf.* person who talks too much. **wind•break**, *n.* fence/hedge which protects sth against the wind. **wind•burn**, *n.* inflammation of the skin caused by cold wind. **wind•break•er**, *n.* short jacket, to keep out the wind. **wind•chill fac•tor**, *n.* air temperature including the effect of the wind. **wind•fall**, *n.* (a) fruit which has been blown to the ground from a fruit tree. (b) unexpected good fortune. **wind gauge**, *n.* instrument for measuring the force of the wind. **wind•jam•mer**, *n.* (*old*) large sailing ship. **wind•less**, *adj.* with no wind. **wind•mill**, *n.* mill driven by sails pushed around by the wind. **wind•pipe**, *n.* pipe leading from the nose and mouth to the lungs. **wind•shield**, *n.* glass window in the front of a car/truck, etc. **windsock**, *n.* tube of material at the end of a tall pole, which shows the direction of the wind at an airfield. **wind•surf•er**, *n.* person who does windsurfing. **wind•surf•ing**, *n.* sport of riding on the sea on a surfboard with a sail attached. **wind•swept**, *adj.* blown by strong winds. **wind•ward**, *adj., adv. & n.* (side of a ship) from which the wind blows. **wind•y**, *adj.* (-ier, -iest) (a) having much wind. (b) full of empty talk.

wind[2] [waɪnd] 1. *n.* bend/twist/turn. 2. *v.* (**wound** [waʊnd]) (a) to turn. (b) to roll up/to roll around. (c) to turn a key of (a watch/clock) until the spring is tight. **wind•ing**. 1. *adj.* turning/twisting. 2. *n.* action of turning/rolling. **wind up**, *v.* (a) to roll up. (b) to tighten a spring on a watch/clockwork toy, etc. (c) to finish; bring to an end. (d) *inf.* **to be wound up** = to be nervous/tense. **wind•lass** ['wɪndləs] *n.* (*pl.* **-es**) hand winch for

pulling sth up by winding a rope around a drum.

win•dow ['wɪndəʊ] *n.* (a) opening in a wall/door, etc., filled with glass; **stained-glass w.** = window made of small pieces of colored glass, found esp. in churches. (b) section of a computer screen reserved for a special purpose. **win•dow box**, *n.* long box for plants kept on an outside window ledge. **win•dow dress•ing**, *n.* (a) displaying goods in an artistic way in a store window. (b) putting on a display to hide the real state of affairs. **window ledge, window sill**, *n.* ledge/flat piece of wood, etc., inside and outside a window. **win•dow•pane**, *n.* single piece of glass, used as part of a whole window. **win•dow shop•ping**, *n.* looking at goods in store windows without buying them.

wine [waɪn] 1. *n.* (a) alcoholic drink made from the juice of grapes; **w. list** = list of wines which are available at a restaurant. (b) alcoholic drink made from the juice of fruit or flowers. 2. *v.* **to w. and dine s.o.** = to take s.o. out for an expensive dinner and drinks. **wine cel•lar**, *n.* cool room underground where wine is kept. **wine•glass**, *n.* glass used for drinking wine. **wine-grow•ing**, *adj.* (district) where vines are grown to produce wine. **wine mer•chant**, *n.* person who sells wines and spirits in a shop. **wine stew•ard**, *n.* person in charge of serving the wines in a restaurant.

wing [wɪŋ] 1. *n.* (a) one of the two limbs which a bird/butterfly, etc., use to fly; **to take s.o. under your w.** = to protect/to look after. (b) one of the two flat projecting parts on an aircraft. (c) side part of a large building which leads off the main part. (d) part of an army which stretches to one side; part of a political party which has a certain tendency. (e) unit of the U.S. air force; **w. commander** = officer in charge of a wing. (f) **wings** = side of the stage in a theater where actors wait before going on stage. (g) **wings** = pilot's badge. (h) (*in hockey/soccer*) forward player on the side of the center. 2. *v.* (a) to fly. (b) to shoot (in the wing/arm). **winged**, *adj.* with wings. **wing•er**, *n. suffix showing* person on the right/left of a political party. **wing•less**, *adj.* having no wings. **wing nut**, *n.* nut with two projecting parts for screwing easily. **wing•span**, *n.* distance from the tip of one wing to the tip of another (of a bird/aircraft, etc.).

æ back, ɑ: farm, ɒ: top, aɪ pipe, aʊ how, aɪə fire, aʊə flower, ɔ: bought, ɔɪ toy, e fed, eəhair, eɪ take, ə afraid, əʊ boat, əʊə lower, v: word, i: heap, ɪ hit, ɪə hear, u: school, ʊ book, ʌ but, b back, d dog, ð then, dʒ just, f fog, g go, h hand, j yes, k catch, l last, m mix, n nut, ŋ sing, p penny, r round, s some, ʃ short, t too, tʃ chop, θ thing, v voice, w was, z zoo, ʒ treasure

wink [wɪŋk] 1. *n.* act of quickly shutting and opening one eye; *inf.* **to have forty winks** = to have a short sleep. 2. *v.* (a) to shut one eye and then quickly open it again. (b) (*of lights/stars*) to shine on and off.

win•now ['wɪnəu] *v.* to separate the grain from chaff, by allowing the wind to blow the chaff away.

win•some ['wɪnsəm] *adj.* pleasant/charming.

win•ter ['wɪntə] 1. *n.* coldest season of the year; **w. sports** = sports which are played on snow or ice. 2. *v.* to spend the cold months of the year. **win•try,** *adj.* like winter; unfriendly/cold (smile).

wipe [waɪp] 1. *n.* act of cleaning or drying with a cloth. 2. *v.* to clean/to dry with a cloth. **wipe a•way,** *v.* to clean away. **wipe out,** *v.* (a) to clean and dry the inside of (sth). (b) to kill/to destroy. **wip•er,** *n.* thing that wipes; device on a car which wipes rain away from the windshield; **rear w.** = device for wiping the rain from the rear window of a car.

wire ['waɪə] 1. *n.* (a) thin metal line or thread; **w. netting** = pieces of wire twisted together to make a net; **barbed w.** = wire with sharp pieces of metal twisted in at intervals, used to stop animals or people from getting in or out; **live w.** = (i) wire which carries an electrical current; (ii) person who is full of energy; **telegraph/telephone w.** = wire along which telegraph/telephone messages are sent; *inf.* **we must have our wires crossed** = we must have misunderstood each other; **w. service** = news agency sending news to subscribers by teleprinter; **w. tapping** = listening to other people's telephone conversations with special equipment. (b) *inf.* telegram. 2. *v.* (a) to fasten with wires. (b) to put in wires to carry electricity to (a house). (c) to send a telegram. **wire•less.** 1. *n.* (*esp. Brit.*) radio. 2. *adj.* without wires. **wire•worm,** *n.* type of small insect which attacks plants. **wir•ing,** *n.* system of wires used to carry electricity. **wir•y,** *adj.* (-ier, -iest) (a) (*of person*) thin but strong. (b) (*of hair*) stiff and strong, not easily combed.

wis•dom ['wɪzdəm] *n.* intelligence/knowledge/common sense; **w. tooth** = one of four back teeth which grow when you are an adult.

wise [waɪz] *adj.* (-er, -est) having intelligence and common sense/knowing a great deal/prudent; **no one will be any the wiser** = no one will know anything about it; **I'm none the wiser** = I know no more than I did before. **wise•crack.** 1. *n.* clever remark. 2. *v.* to make a joke/a wisecrack. **wise guy,** *n.* person who pretends to know more than anyone else. **wise•ly,** *adv.* (a) in a wise way. (b) prudently.

wish [wɪʃ] 1. *n.* (*pl.* -es) want/desire. (b) **good wishes** = kind feelings/greetings. 2. *v.* (a) to

want/to desire sth which is unlikely to happen. (b) to express a desire or a hope. **wish•bone,** *n.* V-shaped bone in a chicken's breast, which you are supposed to pull with your partner, each having made a wish, the person who holds the larger piece getting his wish. **wish•ful,** *adj.* **w. thinking** = believing sth because you would like it to happen.

wish•y-wash•y ['wɪʃɪwɒʃɪ] *adj.* watery; not strong (color/character, etc.).

wisp [wɪsp] *n.* small strand; little piece. **wisp•y,** *adj.* thin/slight.

wis•te•ri•a, wistaria [wɪ'stɪərɪə, wɪ'steərɪə] *n.* climbing plant with sweet-smelling blue flowers.

wist•ful ['wɪstfəl] *adj.* longing for sth, but sad as there is no hope of getting it. **wist•ful•ly,** *adv.* in a wistful way. **wist•ful•ness,** *n.* being wistful.

wit [wɪt] 1. *n.* (a) (*usu.* wits) intelligence; **at your wit's end** = not knowing what to do next; **to keep your wits about you** = to keep calm in a difficult situation and think hard what to do next. (b) ability to say clever/funny things. (c) person who says clever and funny things. 2. *v.* (*old*) **to w.** = namely/that is.

witch [wɪtʃ] *n.* (*pl.* -es) woman believed to have evil magic powers. **witch•craft,** *n.* art of magic. **witch doc•tor,** *n.* man in a primitive tribe who appears to cure illnesses by magic. **witch•er•y,** *n.* witchcraft. **witch ha•zel,** *n.* shrub with tiny yellow flowers blooming in early spring. **witch hunt,** *n.* cruel investigation of people who are supposed to be politically unreliable.

with [wɪð, wɪT] *prep.* (a) accompanied by/together/beside. (b) having/possessing. (c) in spite of (faults). (d) using. (e) from/because of. (f) showing (an emotion). (g) (*used after many verbs to show a connection*) **to part w. sth** = to give sth away; **to meet w.** = to have/to experience unexpectedly; **I can do nothing w. him** = I can't change him; **to have nothing to do w.** = to have no connection with; **I'm w. you there!** = (i) I agree with you! (ii) I understand you; *inf.* **to be w. it** = to be fashionable/modern.

with•draw [wɪT'drɔ:] *v.* (**withdrew; withdrawn**) to move back/to take back/to pull back; to take (money) out of a bank account; to retract (sth which has been said). **with•draw•al,** *n.* taking back; removing of money (from a bank account); **w. symptoms** = symptoms shown by s.o. who is trying to stop taking a drug/smoking, etc. **with•drawn,** *adj.* shy; (person) who does not like meeting other people.

with•er ['wɪðə] *v.* (a) (*of plants*) to grow weaker and dry up. (b) to make (sth) grow weaker and dry up; to make (s.o.) feel embarrassed by looking disapprovingly.

with•er•ing, *adj.* scornful/disapproving (look).

with•ers ['wɪðəz] *n. pl.* part of a horse's back just below the neck.

with•hold [wɪT'həʊld] *v.* (**withheld**) to keep back/to refuse to give.

with•in [wɪ'ðɪn] *prep.* inside.

with•out [wɪ'ðaʊt] *prep.* not having/not with; **to go w.** = not to have (sth); **it goes w. saying that** = it hardly needs to be said that.

with•stand [wɪT'stænd] *v.* (**withstood**) to resist/to endure.

withy ['wɪðɪ] *n.* thin willow twig used to tie things together.

wit•ness ['wɪtnəs] 1. *n.* (*pl.* **-es**) (a) person who sees sth happening. (b) **to bear w. to** = to be evidence of. (c) person who witnesses s.o.'s signature. 2. *v.* (a) to see (sth) happen. (b) to sign your name on a legal paper to say that s.o.'s signature is genuine. (c) to give evidence in court. **wit•ness stand,** *n.* place where a witness sits in a law court.

wit•ting•ly ['wɪtɪŋlɪ] *adv.* on purpose/intentionally.

wit•ty ['wɪtɪ] *adj.* (**-ier, -iest**) clever and funny. **wit•ti•cism** ['wɪtɪsɪzəm] *n.* clever/funny remark.

wives [waɪvz] *n. see* **wife.**

wiz•ard ['wɪzəd] *n.* (a) man who is believed to have magic powers. (b) clever person/expert. **wiz•ard•ry,** *n.* being a wizard; cleverness.

wiz•ened ['wɪzənd] *adj.* dried up and wrinkled (face).

woad [wəʊd] *n.* wild plant with blue flowers, used to make a blue dye.

wob•ble ['wɒbl] 1. *n.* shaking movement. 2. *v.* to shake/to move unsteadily. **wob•bly,** *adj.* unsteady/shaking.

woe [wəʊ] *n.* sadness/trouble. **woe•be•gone,** *adj.* very sad (look). **woe•ful,** *adj.* full of sadness. **woe•ful•ly,** *adv.* sadly.

woke, woken [wəʊk, wəʊkn] *v. see* **wake.**

wold [wəʊld] *n.* (*esp. Brit.*) area of gently rounded hills.

wolf [wʊlf] 1. *n.* (*pl.* **wolves**) (a) wild animal like a dog, usu. living in a large group in cold northern regions; **pack of wolves** = group of wolves living together; **lone w.** = person who prefers to be alone/who does not associate with other people; **she-wolf** = female wolf; **w. cub** = young wolf; **w. in sheep's clothing** = person who seems inoffensive but really is wicked; **to keep the w. from the door** = to have

enough food to live on; **to cry w.** = to raise a false alarm. (b) *inf.* man who chases women. 2. *v.* to eat quickly. **wolf•hound,** *n.* large hunting dog. **wolf•ish,** *adj.* like a wolf.

wol•ver•ine ['wʊlvəri:n] *n.* dark-furred North American carnivorous mammal.

wom•an ['wʊmən] *n.* (*pl.* **women** ['wɪmɪn]) (a) female adult human being; **Women's Lib** = movement to give women equal status with men in business, education, society, etc. (b) female. **wom•an•hood,** *n.* state of being a woman. **wom•an•ish,** *adj.* (man) who behaves like a woman. **wom•an•ize,** *v.* to try to seduce women often. **wom•an•iz•er,** *n.* man who womanizes. **wom•an•kind,** *n.* all women. **wom•an•li•ness,** *n.* being womanly. **wom•an•ly,** *adj.* feminine, like a woman. **wom•en•folk,** *n. pl.* all women (in a family, etc.).

womb [wu:m] *n.* uterus.

wom•bat ['wɒmbət] *n.* small Australian animal.

won [wʌn] *v. see* **win.**

won•der ['wʌndə] 1. *n.* (a) amazing thing; **no w.** = it isn't surprising. (b) astonishment/surprise. 2. *v.* (a) to be surprised/to marvel (**at**). (b) to want to know/to ask yourself (why). (c) (*used when asking someone politely to do something*) **I w. if you could open the door. won•der•ful,** *adj.* marvelous/very good/exciting. **won•der•ful•ly,** *adv.* in a wonderful way. **won•der•land,** *n.* marvelous place. **won•der•ment,** *n.* astonishment/wonder. **won•drous,** *adj.* wonderful.

wont [wəʊnt] *n.* (*formal*) habit; **as is his w.** = as he usually does. **wont•ed,** *adj.* (*formal*) habitual.

won't [wəʊnt] *v.* will not.

woo [wu:] *v.* to try to attract (a woman) to marry you; to try to get (s.o.) to support you/to vote for you, etc. **woo•er,** *n.* person who woos.

wood [wʊd] *n.* (a) (*also* **woods**) large group of trees/small forest; **we're not out of the w. yet** = our problems are not over. (b) material that a tree is made of. **wood•bine,** *n.* wild climbing plant. **wood•burn•ing stove,** *n.* stove which is designed to use wood as a fuel. **wood•carv•ing,** *n.* (i) art of sculpture in wood; (ii) wooden sculpture. **wood•chuck,** *n.* North American rodent. **wood•cock,** *n.* small brown bird shot for sport or food. **wood•craft,** *n.* skill at finding your way

æ back, a: farm, ɒ: top, aɪ pipe, aʊ how, aɪe fire, aʊə flower, ɔ: bought, ɔɪ toy, e fed, eəhair, eɪ take, ə afraid, əʊ boat, əʊə lower, v: word, i: heap, ɪ hit, ɪə hear, u: school, ʊ book, ʌ but, b back, d dog, ð then, dʒ just, f fog, g go, h hand, j yes, k catch, l last, m mix, n nut, ŋ sing, p penny, r round, s some, ʃ short, t too, tʃ chop, θ thing, v voice, w was, z zoo, ʒ treasure

about woods and forests and living in them. **wood•cut**, *n.* print made from a carved wooden plate. **wood•ed**, *adj.* covered in trees. **wood•en**, *adj.* (a) made of wood. (b) stiff/showing no feeling. **wood•en•ly**, *adv.* stiffly. **wood•land**, *n.* land covered in woods. **wood•louse**, *n.* (*pl.* -**lice**) very small animal with a hard shell, which curls up when attacked, and lives in rotten wood, etc. **wood•peck•er**, *n.* bird with a long sharp beak which finds insects under the bark of trees. **wood•pig•eon**, *n.* common European wild pigeon. **wood pulp**, *n.* fragments of wood made into a pulp, used for making paper. **wood•shed**, *n.* small shed/hut used for storing wood. **wood(s)•man**, *n.* (*pl.* -**men**) man who works in woods and forests. **wood•winds**, *n.* wind instruments in an orchestra which are usu. made of wood. **wood•work**, *n.* (a) carpentry. (b) interior wooden parts of a building. **wood•worm**, *n.* small grub which bores holes in wood. **wood•y**, *adj.* (-**ier**, -**iest**) like wood; made of wood.

woof [wuf] 1. *n.* (a) weft. (b) sound of a dog's bark. 2. *v.* (*of dog*) to bark. **woof•er**, *n.* loudspeaker which reproduces low sounds.

wool [wʊl] *n.* (a) short, thick hair of a sheep/goat, etc. (b) long threads of twisted hair, used to make clothes/carpets, etc.; cloth woven from hair; **to pull the w. over s.o.'s eyes** = to deceive s.o. (c) material which looks like sheep's wool; **steel w. wool•gath•er•ing**, *n.* daydreaming/not thinking of what you are doing. **wool•en**, **woollen**, *adj.* made of wool. **wool•ens**, **wool•lens**, *n. pl.* clothing made of knitted wool. **wool•li•ness**, *n.* being woolly. **wool•ly**, **wooly**, 1. *adj.* (-**ier**, -**iest**) (a) made of wool/like wool. (b) vague/not clear. 2. *n. inf.* sweater, etc. made of wool.

wooz•y ['wu:zɪ] *adj. inf.* dizzy/in a daze.

word [wɜːd] 1. *n.* (a) unit of speech either spoken or written; **to have words with s.o.** = to quarrel with s.o.; **to have a w. with s.o.** = to have a short talk with s.o.; **in other words** = explaining sth in a different way; **you've taken the words out of my mouth** = you've said what I was going to say; **without a w.** = without speaking; **w. for w.** = exactly as is said or written. (b) message/news; **by w. of mouth** = by spoken message. (c) promise; **to give one's w.** = to promise; **he kept his w.** = he did what he promised to do; **I'll take your w. for it** = I'll believe what you say. (d) **my w.!** *inter. expressing* surprise. 2. *v.* to put in words, either written or spoken. **word•i•ly**, *adv.* in a wordy way. **word•i•ness** *n.* being wordy. **word•ing**, *n.*

choice of words. **word proc•es•sor**, *n.* typewriter with a computer memory and a screen on which the text can be displayed. **word•y**, *adj.* (-**ier**, -**iest**) *adj.* using too many words.

wore ['wɔ:] *v. see* **wear**.

work [wɜːk] 1. *n.* (a) mental or physical activity; **to have one's w. cut out** = find it difficult (to do sth). (b) job; **out of w.** = with no job. (c) thing that has been made by s.o. (d) **works** = factory. (e) **road w.** = repairs to a road. (f) **works** = moving parts of a machine; *inf.* **to give s.o. the works** = to give s.o. everything/the full treatment. 2. *v.* (a) to use energy/to make s.o. use energy in carrying out an activity. (b) (*of machine*) to operate/to move. (c) to make (a machine) function. (d) to have a job. (e) to be successful. (f) to embroider/to sew. (g) **to w. one's way** = to move gradually; **he was working himself into a rage** = he was becoming more and more angry. (h) to take coal/copper, etc., from (a mine); **worked out** = (mine) where all the ore has been extracted. **work•a•ble**, *adj.* able to be worked. **work•a•day**, *adj.* plain/ordinary. **work•a•hol•ic**, *n. inf.* person who cannot stop working. **work•book**, *n.* book of excercises to help teach a subject. **worked up**, *adj.* excited/annoyed (**about**). **work•er**, *n.* (a) person who works. (b) member of the working class. (c) type of female bee which works to provide the queen with honey, but which is sterile. **work force**, *n.* all the workers (in a factory). **work•horse**, *n.* person who can work hard. **work•ing**. 1. *adj.* which works; referring to work; **w. class** = people who work with their hands/who earn wages not salaries. 2. *n.* (*usu. pl.* **workings**) (a) place where mineral has been dug. (b) way sth works. **work•man**, *n.* (*pl.* -**men**) man who works with his hands. **work•man•like**, *adj.* skillful/expert. **work•man•ship**, *n.* skill of a good workman. **work off**, *v.* to get rid of (sth) by working. **work on**, *v.* (a) to continue to work. (b) to be busy doing sth. (c) to try to influence/to persuade. **work out**, *v.* (a) to succeed/to do well. (b) to plan (sth) in detail/to find an answer to (sth). (c) (**at**) to amount to (a price). **work•out**, *n.* exercise/practice before an athletic event. **work•room**, *n.* room where work is done. **work•shop**, *n.* place in a small factory or house where things are made. **work sta•tion**, *n.* desk with terminal, monitor, keyboard, etc., where a computer operator works. **work up**, *v.* to develop/to reach slowly.

world [wɜːld] *n.* (a) the earth; particular part of the earth; **the Old W.** = Europe, Asia and Africa; **the New W.** = North and South America; **the Third W.** = countries with no strong connections to the superpowers; **W. War** = war in which many countries all over the world take part. (b) people on Earth; everything; **to come into the w.** = to be born; **to be all alone in the w.** = to have no family; **out of this w.** = magnificent; **to think the w. of s.o.** = to think very highly of s.o.; **it will do you the w. of good** = it will help you greatly. (c) people with a particular interest/things which form a particular group. **world-fa•mous,** *adj.* known everywhere. **world•li•ness,** *n.* being worldly/not being idealistic. **world•ly,** *adj.* (a) of the material world. (b) not idealistic. **world•ly-wise,** *adj.* wise about worldly things. **world•wide,** *adj. & adv.* throughout the whole world. **World Wide Web,** *n.* global network of linked hypertext files containing information that can be accessed by an Internet user.

worm [wɜːm] 1. *n.* (a) small, spineless burrowing creature which looks like a very small snake and lives in earth. (b) similar animal which lives in the intestines of animals. (c) woodworm. (d) spiral thread of a screw. 2. *v.* to move slowly like a worm; **to w. yourself into s.o.'s favor** = to make s.o. like you by being especially nice to them; **to w. information out of s.o.** = to get information by asking many persistent questions. **worm•eat•en,** *adj.* which has been eaten by worms. **worm•wood,** *n.* bitter plant.

worn [wɔːn] *adj.* much used; *see also* **wear.** **worn out,** *adj.* (a) used so much that it is now useless. (b) tired.

wor•ry [ˈwʌrɪ] 1. *n.* (a) thing which makes you anxious. (b) being anxious. 2. *v.* (a) to be upset/anxious; to make (s.o.) upset/anxious. (b) (*of dogs*) to shake and tear with the teeth. **wor•ried,** *adj.* anxious/troubled. **wor•ri•er,** *n.* person who worries. **wor•ri•some,** *adj.* which makes you worried/anxious.

worse [wɜːs] 1. *adj.* (a) more inferior in quality, condition, etc. (b) in less good health; sicker. 2. *adv.* in a worse way. **wors•en,** *v.* to become or make worse. **worse off,** *adj.* in a worse condition.

wor•ship [ˈwɜːʃɪp] 1. *n.* (a) praise and honor shown to God. (b) praise and honor shown to s.o./sth. 2. *v.* (**worshipped**) (a) to praise and love (God). (b) to take part in a church service. (c) to praise and love (s.o./sth). **wor•ship•er,** *n.* person who worships; **sun w.** = person who loves sunbathing.

worst [wɜːst] 1. *adj.* very bad/worse than anyone/anything else. 2. *n.* most awful thing. 3. *adv.* very badly/worse than anyone/anything else.

wor•sted [ˈwʊstɪd] *n.* fine woolen cloth.

worth [wɜːT] 1. *adj.* (a) having a value/price. (b) useful; giving satisfaction; **it is w. (your) while** = it is worth the effort. (c) having riches/money, etc; **for all you are w.** = as much as possible. 2. *n.* value. **wor•thi•ly,** *adv.* in a worthy way. **wor•thi•ness,** *n.* being worthy. **worth•less,** *adj.* having no worth/no use. **worth•while** [wɜːˈTwaɪl] *adj.* which is worth doing. **wor•thy** [ˈwɜːðɪ] 1. *adj.* (**-ier, -iest**) deserving. 2. *n.* notable person (in a town).

would [wʊd] *v. see* **will.**

wound [wuːnd] 1. *n.* (a) cut/damage to the skin, usu. received in a fight. (b) hurt to the feelings. 2. *v.* (a) to hurt. (b) to hurt the fellings of (s.o.). (c) [waʊnd] *see also* **wind**[2].

wove, woven [wəʊv, ˈwəʊvn] *v. see* **weave.**

wow [waʊ] 1. *n. inf.* (a) great success. (b) fluctuation of sound in a record-player. 2. *v. inf.* (*of a singer, etc.*) to excite (the audience).

wraith [raɪT] *n.* ghost.

wran•gle [ˈræŋgl] 1. *n.* argument/dispute. 2. *v.* to argue.

wrap [ræp] 1. *n.* shawl; *inf.* **to keep sth under wraps** = to keep sth a secret. 2. *v.* (**wrapped**) to cover (sth) all around with paper/cloth, etc. **wrap up,** *v.* (a) to cover up completely. (b) to wear warm clothes. (c) **to be wrapped up in your work** = to think only of the work and take no notice of other things. **wrap•per,** *n.* piece of paper used to cover sth. **wrap•ping,** *n.* paper/cardboard/plastic, etc., used to wrap things; **w. paper** = paper used to wrap presents.

wrasse [ræs] *n.* type of sea fish.

wrath [rɒT] *n.* great anger. **wrath•ful,** *adj.* angry.

wreak [riːk] *v.* to carry out/to do (sth violent).

wreath [riːT] *n.* (a) circle of flowers or leaves esp. given at a funeral in memory of the dead person. (b) winding clouds (of smoke/mist). **wreathe** [riːð] *v.* (a) to put a circle of flowers on (s.o./sth). (b) to cover with twisting clouds of smoke/mist.

wreck [rek] 1. *n.* (a) ship which has been sunk/badly damaged on rocks, etc. (b) action of being wrecked. (c) anything which has been damaged and is useless. (d) person who, be-

æ back, ɑː farm, ɒ top, aɪ pipe, aʊ how, aie fire, aʊə flower, ɔː bought, ɔɪ toy, e fed, eəhair, eɪ take, ə afraid, əʊ boat, əʊə lower, vː word, iː heap, ɪ hit, ɪə hear, uː school, ʊ book, ʌ but, b back, d dog, ð then, dʒ just, f fog, g go, h hand, j yes, k catch, l last, m mix, n nut, ŋ sing, p penny, r round, s some, ʃ short, t too, tʃ chop, θ thing, v voice, w was, z zoo, ʒ treasure

cause of illness, can do very little. 2. v. to cause severe damage to (sth); to ruin (sth).

wreck•age, n. broken remains of a building/ship, etc., after a disaster. **wreck•er,** n. (a) person who destroys a building/plan, etc., on purpose, or tries to make a ship crash on to rocks. (b) person who is employed to destroy old buildings/break up old cars, etc. (c) truck which goes to help cars which have broken down on the road; engine which goes to help a train which has broken down on the track.

wren [ren] n. very small brown songbird.

wrench [renʃ] 1. n. (pl. -es) (a) violent twisting movement. (b) tool for turning bolts, nuts, etc. (c) sadness at leaving. 2. v. to turn and pull (sth) violently.

wrest [rest] v. (formal) to twist/to wrench away.

wres•tle ['resl] v. (a) to fight with s.o. in a contest by trying to throw him to the ground. (b) to fight/struggle with (a problem). **wres•tler,** n. person who wrestles in contests. **wres•tling,** n. **w. match** = contest of wrestlers watched by crowds of people.

wretch [retʃ] n. (pl. -es) (a) person who looks poor and miserable. (b) despicable/annoying person. **wretch•ed** ['retʃɪd] adj. (a) miserable and poor; **to feel w.** = to feel ill. (b) terrible/annoying. **wretch•ed•ly,** adv. miserably. **wretch•ed•ness,** n. being wretched.

wrig•gle ['rɪgl] v. to twist and turn; **to w. out of** = to get out of (a difficult situation) by trickery.

wring [rɪŋ] v. (**wrung**) to twist (sth), esp. to get water out of it; **to w. information from** = to manage to get information with difficulty; **to w. one's hands** = to twist and turn one's hands, showing sadness and emotion. **wring•er,** n. machine for squeezing the water out of wet washing. **wring•ing,** adj. very (wet).

wrin•kle ['rɪŋkl] 1. n. (a) line/fold of the skin. (b) line or crease in cloth. 2. v. to make lines/creases in.

wrist [rɪst] n. joint between the arm and the hand; **w. watch** = small watch worn on a strap around the wrist. **wrist•let,** n. band worn around the wrist.

writ [rɪt] n. legal paper ordering s.o. to do/not to do wth. **Holy Writ,** n. the Bible.

write [raɪt] v. (**wrote** [rəʊt], **has written**) (a) to put down words on paper. (b) to be the author of books/music, etc.. (c) to put a letter in writing and send it to s.o. inf. **that's nothing to w. home about** = it's nothing special. **write in,** v. (a) to ask for by sending a letter. (b) to vote for a candidate whose name does not appear on the ballot, by writing the name there. **write off,** v. to remove (sth) from a written list; to cancel (a debt); to see (sth) as a failure; **the car was written off** = the insurance company considered it a total loss. **write-off,** n. inf. total loss. **writ•er,** n. person who writes, esp. to earn money. **write up,** v. to describe fully in writing. **write-up,** n. inf. article in a newspaper. **writ•ing,** n. (a) thing that is written; **w. paper** = paper used for writing letters. (b) handwriting. **writ•ings,** n. pl. books, etc., written by an author.

writhe [raɪð] v. to twist and turn (in agony).

wrong [rɒŋ] 1. adj. (a) bad/not right. (b) not right/incorrect. (c) **what's w.?** = what is the matter? **I hope nothing's w.** = I hope nothing bad has happened. 2. n. bad/incorrect thing; **to be in the w.** = to have made a mistake. 3. adv. badly/incorrectly; **to go w.** = to break down/not to work properly. 4. v. to treat (s.o.) unfairly. **wrong•do•er,** n. person who has committed a sin/crime. **wrong•do•ing,** n. crime/unlawful/evil act. **wrong•ful,** adj. unjust/unlawful. **wrong•ful•ly,** adv. in a wrongful way. **wrong•head•ed,** adj. mistaken but refusing to admit it. **wrong•ly,** adv. incorrectly/badly.

wrote [rəʊt] v. see **write.**

wrought [rɔːt] adj. **w. iron** = hammered, twisted and bent iron used for making decorative gates/balconies, etc.

wrung [rʌŋ] v. see **wring.**

wry [raɪ] adj. showing dislike by twisting the mouth.

WWW abbrev. for World Wide Web.

WYS•I•WYG ['wɪzɪwɪg] what-you-see-is-what-you-get (when the text on a computer screen is exactly the same as the printed output).

Xx

X, x [eks]. **X-ray. 1.** *n.* (a) ray which will pass through solids and is used esp. in hospitals for photographing the inside of the body. (b) photograph taken with X-rays. **2.** *v.* to take an X-ray photograph of.

xen•o•phobe ['zenəfəʊb] *n.* person who hates, dislikes, or fears foreigners. **xen•o•pho•bi•a** [zenə'fəʊbɪə] *n.* hatred, dislike, or fear of foreigners. **xen•o•pho•bic,** *adj.* hating, disliking, or fearing foreigners.

Xe•rox ['zɪərɒks] **1.** *n.* (a) (*pl* **-es**) trademark for a type of photocopier. (b) (*also* **xerox**) photocopy made with this machine. **2.** *v.* (*also* **xerox**) to make a photocopy with a Xerox machine.

Xmas ['krɪsməs, 'eksməs] *n. short for* **Christmas.**

xy•lo•phone ['zaɪləfəʊn] *n.* musical instrument consisting of wooden bars of different lengths which make different notes when they are tapped with a hammer.

æ back, aː farm, ɒː top, aɪ pipe, aʊ how, aie fire, aʊə flower, ɔː bought, ɔɪ toy, e fed, eəhair, eɪ take, ə afraid, əʊ boat, əʊə lower, vː word, iː heap, ɪ hit, ɪə hear, uː school, ʊ book, ʌ but, b back, d dog, ð then, dʒ just, f fog, g go, h hand, j yes, k catch, l last, m mix, n nut, ŋ sing, p penny, r round, s some, ʃ short, t too, tʃ chop, θ thing, v voice, w was, z zoo, ʒ treasure

Yy

yacht [jɒt] *n.* boat used for pleasure and sport; **y. club** = sailing club. **yacht•ing,** *n.* art of sailing a yacht. **yachts•man,** *n.* (*pl.* -men) person who sails a yacht.

ya•hoo ['jɑːhuː] *n. inf.* crude boorish person.

yak [jæk] *n.* long-haired ox from Asia. 2. *v. inf.* to talk incessantly.

yam [jæm] *n.* tropical plant with an edible root.

yank [jæŋk] 1. *n. inf.* short sharp pull. 2. *v. inf.* to pull hard and sharply. **Yank, Yank•ee,** *n. inf.* American (esp. from a northern U.S. state).

yap [jæp] 1. *n.* short sharp bark of a dog. 2. *v.* (**yapped**) to make short sharp barks.

yard [jɑːd] *n.* (a) measure of length (= 3 feet or 36 inches or 0.91 meter). (b) piece of wood attached to the mast holding a sail. (c) enclosed space behind a house or other building. (d) enclosed space used for a certain purpose; **train y.** = place where trains are stored or repaired; **Scotland Y.** *inf.* **the Y.** = headquarters of the London Metropolitan Police. **yard•age,** *n.* length in yards or area in square yards. **yard•arm,** *n.* end of the yard holding a sail. **yard•stick,** *n.* standard for measurement.

yarn [jɑːn] 1. *n.* (a) long thread of wool/fiber used in knitting or weaving. (b) *inf.* long story. 2. *v. inf.* to tell stories.

yar•row ['jærəu] *n.* wild plant with clusters of small white flowers.

yash•mak ['jæʃmæk] *n.* veil worn by Muslim women in public.

yaw [jɔː] *v.* (*of ship/aircraft*) to go away from the course.

yawl [jɔːl] *n.* type of two-masted sailboat.

yawn [jɔːn] 1. *n.* movement of opening the mouth when tired; **to stifle a y.** = to try to stop yawning. 2. to open the mouth wide when feeling sleepy, and to breathe in and out. **yawning,** *adj.* open wide; **y. hole** = deep wide hole.

yaws [jɔːz] *n. pl.* tropical skin disease.

yd *abbreviation for* yard.

ye [yiː] 1. *pron.* (*old*) you. 2. *article used in false old names* the.

yea [jeɪ] *adv.* (*old*) yes.

year ['jɜː] *n.* (a) period of twelve months starting on January 1st and ending on December 31st; **the New Y.** = the first few days of the year; **to see the New Y. in** = to stay up until midnight on December 31st and celebrate with a party the beginning of the next year; **calendar y.** = year beginning on January 1st and ending on December 31st; **leap y.** = year with 366 days in it, one more than the normal year. (b) any period of twelve months; **the project took two years; all (the) y. round** = through the whole year; **y. in, y. out** = happening regularly over a long period of time. (c) **his early years** = his childhood; **getting on in years** = quite old; **I haven't seen him for (donkey's) years** = I haven't seen him for a long time. **year•book,** *n.* reference book which comes out each year with up-to-date information. **year•ling,** *n.* one year old animal. **year•ly,** *adj. & adv.* every year; once a year.

yearn [jɜːn] *v.* to long **for** sth/to want sth. **yearn•ing,** *n.* desire/longing.

yeast [jiːst] *n.* living fungus used to make bread and beer. **yeast•y,** *adj.* like yeast; referring to yeast.

yell [jel] 1. *n.* loud shout. 2. *v.* to shout loudly.

yel•low ['jeləu] 1. *n. & adj.* (a) color of the sun/of gold; **y. fever** = type of tropical fever; **y. pages** = section of a telephone directory giving a classified list of businesses. (b) cowardly. 2. *v.* to turn yellow. **yel•low•ham•mer,** *n.* small bird with a yellow breast. **yel•low•ish,** *adj.* rather yellow.

yelp [jelp] 1. *n.* cry of pain. 2. *v.* (*usu. of animals*) to cry out in pain.

yen [jen] *n.* (a) currency of Japan. (b) *inf.* strong desire.

yeo•man ['jəumən] *n.* (*pl.* -men) (*Brit.*) farmer with his own land; **to do y. service** = work long and hard. **yeo•man•ry,** *n.* (*old*) all yeomen.

yes [jes] *adv. & inter.* expression of agreement. **yes man,** *n.* person who always agrees with a person in authority.

yes•ter•day ['jestədeɪ] *adv. & n.* (a) the day before today; **the day before y.** = two days before today. (b) recent times. **yes•ter•year,** *adv. & n.* (*formal*) times past.

yet [jet] 1. *adv.* (a) up till now/up till this time. (b) in spite of everything. (c) even. 2. *conj.* still/but.

yet•i ['jetɪ] *n.* large animal, like an ape or bear, which is said to exist in the snows of the Himalayas.

yew [juː] *n.* evergreen tree with small cones and poisonous red berries.

Yid•dish ['jɪdɪʃ] *n.* language spoken by European Jews.

yield [jiːld] 1. *n.* crop/product; return on your

investment. 2. v. (a) to give/to produce. (b) to produce money. (c) (to) to give up/to surrender. (d) to give way when pressed. (e) (to) (of traffic) to allow other vehicles to pass first.

yo•del ['jəʊdl] v. to sing with quick changes from low to high notes. yo•del•er, n. person who yodels.

yo•ga ['jəʊgə] n. system of exercises and meditation practiced by Hindu thinkers, and now popular in western countries.

yo•gurt, yo•ghurt ['jɒgət] n. fermented milk often sweetened or flavored.

yo•gi ['jəʊgɪ] n. Hindu thinker who practices yoga.

yoke [jəʊk] 1. n. (a) piece of wood placed over the neck of a pair of animals when they are used for plowing, etc.; y. of oxen = two oxen attached together. (b) part of a dress which covers the shoulders and upper chest. 2. v. to join together (with a yoke).

yo•kel ['jəʊkl] n. stupid person from the country.

yolk [jəʊk] n. yellow part of an egg.

yon, yon•der [jɒn, 'jɒndə] adj. & adv. (which is) over there.

yore [jɔː] n. (formal) in days of y. = in the past.

York•shire pud•ding ['jɔːkʃə'pʊdɪŋ] n. baked batter eaten with roast beef.

you [juː] pron. (a) (referring to the person/persons to whom we are speaking). (b) (referring to anybody/people in general).

young [jʌŋ] 1. adj. (-er, -est) not old/recently born. 2. n. (a) young animals or birds. (b) young people. young•ster, n. young person.

your ['jɔː] adj. belonging to you. yours ['jɔːz] pron. belonging to you. your•self, your•selves [jɔːˈself, jɔːˈselvz] pron. referring to the subject you.

youth [juːT] n. (a) time when you are young. (b) young man. (c) young people; y. club = club where young people meet; y. hostel = building where young walkers, etc., can spend the night cheaply. youth•ful, adj. young. youth•ful•ness, n. being youthful.

yowl [jaʊl] v. (esp. of animals) to howl/to cry out loudly.

yo-yo ['jəʊjəʊ] n. toy made of a circular piece of wood/metal with a groove around the edge, which can be made to run up and down a string.

yuc•ca ['jʌkə] n. type of large succulent plant.

yuck•y [jʌkɪ] adj. inf. unappealing; distasteful.

Yu•go•slav ['juːgəʊslɑːv] adj. & n. (person) from Yugoslavia.

yuk•ky ['jʌkɪ] adj. inf. see yuck•y.

yule [juːl] n. Christmas; y. log = log burned at Christmas. yule•tide, n. the Christmas period.

yum-yum ['jʌmjʌm] inter. showing liking for food. yum•my, adj. inf. nice to eat; tasting good.

æ back, aː farm, ɒ top, aɪ pipe, aʊ how, aiə fire, aʊə flower, ɔː bought, ɔɪ toy, e fed, eəhair, eɪ take, ə afraid, əʊ boat, əʊə lower, vː word, iː heap, ɪ hit, ɪə hear, uː school, ʊ book, ʌ but, b back, d dog, ð then, dʒ just, f fog, g go, h hand, j yes, k catch, l last, m mix, n nut, ŋ sing, p penny, r round, s some, ʃ short, t too, tʃ chop, θ thing, v voice, w was, z zoo, ʒ treasure

Zz

za•ny ['zeɪnɪ] *adj.* (-**ier**, -**iest**) *inf.* wildly mad.

zap [zæp] *v.* (**zapped**) *inf.* to hit/kill.

zeal ['ziːl] *n.* keenness/eagerness. **zeal•ous** ['zeləs] *adj.* eager. **zeal•ot** ['zelət] *n.* person who is too enthusiastic about religion or politics.

ze•bra ['zebrə] *n.* African animal similar to a horse, but with a striped coat; **z. crossing** = pedestrian crossing painted with white stripes.

ze•nith ['zenɪθ] *n.* (a) point of the sky directly overhead. (b) highest point.

zeph•yr ['zefə] *n.* (*formal*) gentle (often westerly) breeze.

ze•ro ['zɪərəu] *n.* (a) number 0/nothing/nil. (b) temperature on a thermometer corresponding to zero. **zero hour**, *n.* time fixed to start sth important. **zero in on**, *v.* to aim at (sth)/to go straight to (sth). **zero tol•er•ance**, *n.* policy of rigorously enforcing a law/code by punishing very minor infringements in order to deter others.

zest [zest] *n.* (a) enthusiasm/enjoyment. (b) added pleasure/spice. (c) thin piece of orange or lemon peel. **zest•ful**, *adj.* enthusiastic.

zig•zag ['zɪgzæg] 1. *adj. & n.* (line) which turns sharply one way, then the opposite way. 2. *v.* (**zigzagged**) to move in a zigzag.

zilch [zɪltʃ] *n. Sl.* nothing/zero.

zinc [zɪŋk] *n.* (*element:* Zn) hard bright light-colored metal.

zin•ni•a ['zɪnjə] *n.* annual garden plant with bright flowers.

zip [zɪp] 1. *n.* (a) whistling sound made by a bullet as it goes through the air. (b) *inf.* energy. 2. *v.* (**zipped**) (a) to go fast; to whistle by. (b) **to z. up** = to close a zipper on sth. (c) to compress a computer file, by using a zip program, so that it takes up less memory. **zip code**, *n.* system of numbers written on a letter; package, etc. after the address to identify the U.S. postal area to which it is to be delivered. **zip disk**, *n.* computer disk holding compressed files. **zip•per**, *n.* device for closing openings on trousers/dresses, etc., consisting of two rows of teeth which lock together. **zip•py**, *adj. inf.* quick and lively.

zir•co•ni•um [zɜː'kəunɪəm] *n.* (*element:* Zr) rare metal used in alloys.

zith•er ['zɪðə] *n.* flat musical instrument played by plucking strings.

Zn *symbol for* zinc.

zo•di•ac ['zəudɪæk] *n.* part of the sky (divided into twelve imaginary sections) through which the sun and planets are supposed to travel during the year; **signs of the z.** = twelve signs named after groups of stars. **zo•di•a•cal** [zəu'daɪəkəl] *adj.* referring to the zodiac.

zom•bie ['zɒmbɪ] *n.* (a) (West Indian) dead body which is revived and controlled by witchcraft. (b) *inf.* person who is half-asleep/moving slowly.

zone [zəun] 1. *n.* (a) region/area/part (of a country/town). (b) region of the Earth showing a particular type of climate. 2. *v.* to divide (a town) into parts for planning purposes. **zon•al**, *adj.* of a zone. **zon•ing**, *n.* the splitting up (of a town or area) into zones.

zoo [zuː] *n.* place where wild animals are kept in enclosures and which the public can visit. **zo•ol•o•gy** [zuː'ɒlədʒɪ] *n.* study of animals. **zo•o•log•i•cal** [zuːə'lɒdʒɪkl] *adj.* referring to the study of animals; **z. gardens** = zoo. **zo•ol•o•gist** [zuː'ɒlədʒɪst] *n.* person who studies animals.

zoom [zuːm] 1. *n.* deep buzzing noise made by sth traveling fast. 2. *v.* (a) to make a deep buzzing noise when moving fast. (b) (*of prices, etc.*) to rise suddenly and steeply. (c) **to z. in on sth** = to focus a camera lens so that it makes a distant object appear to come closer. **zoom lens**, *n.* camera lens which allows you to change quickly from distant to close-up shots while still keeping in focus.

zo•on•o•sis [zəuə'nəusɪs] *n.* disease which can be caught from animals.

zuc•chi•ni [zu'kiːnɪ] *n.* green squash shaped like a cucumber.

zwie•back ['zwiːbæk] *n.* type of hard crumbly cookie.

Information
Section

SI UNITS

Base and Supplementary SI Units

Physical quantity	SI unit	Symbol
length	meter	m
mass	kilogram	kg
time	second	s
electric current	ampere	A
thermodynamic temperature	kelvin	K
luminous intensity	candela	cd
amount of substance	mole	mol
plane angle (supplementary unit)	radian	rad
solid angle (supplementary unit)	steradian	sr

Derived SI Units with Special Names

Physical quantity	SI unit	Symbol
frequency	hertz	Hz
energy	joule	J
force	newton	N
power	watt	W
pressure	pascal	Pa
electric charge	coulomb	C
electric potential difference	volt	V
electric resistance	ohm	Ω
electric conductance	siemens	S
electric capacitance	farad	F
magnetic flux	weber	Wb
inductance	henry	H
magnetic flux density (magnetic induction)	tesla	T
luminous flux	lumen	lm
illuminance	lux	lx
absorbed dose	gray	Gy
activity	becquerel	Bq
dose equivalent	sievert	Sv

Decimal Multiples and Submultiples used with SI Units

Submultiple	Prefix	Symbol
10^{-1}	deci-	d
10^{-2}	centi-	c
10^{-3}	milli-	m
10^{-6}	micro-	μ
10^{-9}	nano-	n
10^{-12}	pico-	p
10^{-15}	femto-	f
10^{-18}	atto-	a
10^{-21}	zepto-	z
10^{-24}	yocto-	y

Multiple	Prefix	Symbol
10	deca-	da
10^2	hecto-	h
10^3	kilo-	k
10^6	mega-	M
10^9	giga-	G
10^{12}	tera-	T
10^{15}	peta-	P
10^{18}	exa-	E
10^{21}	zetta-	Z
10^{24}	yotta-	Y

Computer Storage Capacity

kilo-	$= 2^{10}$	1 kilobyte	= 1,024 bytes
mega-	$= 2^{20}$	1 megabyte	= 1,024 kilobytes
giga-	$= 2^{30}$	1 gigabyte	= 1,024 megabytes

Note: in all other computing contexts the prefixes retain their usual meanings.

WEIGHTS AND MEASURES

Metric Measures

Length

1 millimeter (mm)		= 0.0394 in.
1 centimeter (cm)	= 10 mm	= 0.3937 in.
1 meter (m)	= 100 cm	= 1.0936 yd.
1 kilometer (km)	= 1,000 m	= 0.6214 mile

Imperial Measures

Length

1 inch		= 2.54 cm
1 foot (ft.)	= 12 inches	= 0.3048 m
1 yard (yd.)	= 3 feet	= 0.9144 m
1 rod	= 5.5 yards	= 5.0292 m
1 chain	= 22 yards	= 20.117 m
1 furlong	= 220 yards	= 201.17m
1 mile	= 1,760 yards	= 1.6093 km
1 nautical mile	= 6,080 feet	= 1.8532 km

Weight

1 milligram (mg)		= 0.0154 grain
1 gram (g)	= 1,000 mg	= 0.0353 oz.
1 kilogram (kg)	= 1,000 g	= 2.2046 lb.

Weight

1 ounce (oz.)	= 437.5 grains	= 28.350 g
1 pound (lb.)	= 16 ounces	= 0.4536 kg
1 stone	= 14 pounds	= 6.3503 kg
1 hundred-weight (cwt.)	= 100 pounds	= 45.359 kg
1 ton	= 20 cwt.	= 2,000 lb.

Area

1 cm^2	= 100 mm^2	= 0.1550 sq. in.
1 m^2	= 10,000 cm^2	= 1.1960 sq. yd.
1 are (a)	= 100 m^2	= 119.60 sq. yd.
1 hectare (ha)	= 100 ares	= 2.4711 acres
1 km^2	= 100 hectares	= 0.3861 sq. mi.

Area

1 sq. inch		= 6.4516 cm^2
1 sq. foot	= 144 sq. in.	= 0.0929 m^2
1 sq. yard	= 9 sq. ft.	= 0.8361 m^2
1 acre	= 4,840 sq. yd.	= 4,046.9 m^2
1 sq. mile	= 640 acres	= 259.0 hectares

Capacity

1 cm^3		= 0.0610 cu. in.
1 dm^3	= 1,000 cm^3	= 0.0351 cu. ft.
1 m^3	= 1,000 dm^3	= 1.3080 cu. yd.
1 liter	= 1 dm^3	= 0.2200 gallons
1 hectoliter	= 100 liters	= 2.7497 bushels

Capacity

1 cu. inch		=16.387 cm^3
1 cu. foot	= 1,728 cu. in.	= 0.0283 m^3
1 cu. yard	= 27 cu. ft.	= 0.7646 m^3
1 pint (pt)	= 4 gills	= 0.5683 liters
1 quart	= 2 pints	= 1.1365 liters
1 gallon	= 8 pints	= 4.5461 liters
1 bushel	= 8 gallons	= 36.369 liters
1 fluid ounce	= 8 fl. drachms	= 28.413 cm^3
1 pint	= 20 fl. oz.	= 568.26 cm^3

American and British Measures

Dry Measures

1 pint	= 0.9689 U.K. pt.	= 0.5506 liter
1 bushel	= 0.9689 U.K. bu.	= 35.238 liters

Liquid Measures

1 fluid ounce	= 1.0408 U.K. fl. oz.	
		= 0.0296 liter
1 pint (16 oz.)	= 0.8327 U.K. pt.	
		= 0.4732 liter
1 gallon	= 0.8327 U.K. gal.	
		= 3.7853 liters

CONVERSION TABLES

Length

centimeters	cm or inches	inches
2.54	1	0.39
5.08	2	0.79
7.62	3	1.18
10.16	4	1.58
12.70	5	1.97
15.24	6	2.36
17.78	7	2.76
20.32	8	3.15
22.86	9	3.54
25.40	10	3.94
50.80	20	7.87
76.20	30	11.81
101.60	40	15.75
127.00	50	19.69
152.40	60	23.62
177.80	70	27.56
203.20	80	31.50
228.60	90	35.43
254.00	100	39.37

kilometers	km or miles	miles
1.61	1	0.62
3.22	2	1.24
4.83	3	1.86
6.44	4	2.49
8.05	5	3.11
9.66	6	3.73
11.27	7	4.35
12.88	8	4.97
14.48	9	5.59
16.09	10	6.21
32.19	20	12.43
48.28	30	18.64
64.37	40	24.86
80.47	50	31.07
96.56	60	37.28
112.65	70	43.50
128.75	80	49.71
144.84	90	55.92
160.93	100	62.14

CONVERSION TABLES (CONTINUED)

Weight

kilograms	kg or pounds	pounds
0.45	1	2.20
0.91	2	4.41
1.36	3	6.61
1.81	4	8.82
2.27	5	11.02
2.72	6	13.23
3.18	7	15.43
3.63	8	17.64
4.08	9	19.84
4.54	10	22.05
9.07	20	44.09
13.61	30	66.14
18.14	40	88.19
22.68	50	110.23
27.22	60	132.28
31.75	70	154.32
36.29	80	176.37
40.82	90	198.41
45.36	100	220.46

Area

hectares	hectares or acres	acres
0.41	1	2.47
0.81	2	4.94
1.21	3	7.41
1.62	4	9.88
2.02	5	12.36
2.43	6	14.83
2.83	7	17.30
3.24	8	19.77
3.64	9	22.24
4.05	10	24.71
8.09	20	49.42
12.14	30	74.13
16.19	40	98.84
20.23	50	123.56
24.28	60	148.27
28.33	70	172.98
32.38	80	197.69
36.42	90	222.40
40.47	100	247.11

CONVERSION TABLES (CONTINUED)

Capacity

liters	liters or gallons	gallons
3.85	1	0.26
7.69	2	0.44
11.54	3	0.78
15.38	4	1.04
19.23	5	1.30
23.08	6	1.56
26.92	7	1.82
30.77	8	2.08
34.61	9	2.34
38.46	10	2.60
76.92	20	5.20
115.38	30	7.80
153.85	40	10.40
192.31	50	13.00
230.77	60	15.60
269.23	70	18.20
307.69	80	20.80
346.15	90	23.40
348.61	100	26.00

Temperature Conversion

To convert a Fahrenheit temperature to Celsius (centigrade), subtract 32, then multiply by 5/9.

To convert a Celsius (centigrade) temperature to Fahrenheit, multiply by 9/5, then add 32.

TABLE OF CHEMICAL ELEMENTS

Element	Symbol	atomic number	atomic weight	Element	Symbol	atomic number	atomic weight
actinium	Ac	89	227*	molybdenum	Mo	42	95.94
aluminum	Al	13	26.982	neodymium	Nd	60	144.24
americium	Am	95	243*	neon	Ne	10	20.179
antimony	Sb	51	112.76	neptunium	Np	93	237.048
argon	Ar	18	39.948	nickel	Ni	28	58.69
arsenic	As	33	74.92	niobium	Nb	41	92.91
astatine	At	85	210	nitrogen	N	7	14.0067
barium	Ba	56	137.327	nobelium	No	102	259*
berkelium	Bk	97	247*	osmium	Os	76	190.23
beryllium	Be	4	9.012	oxygen	O	8	15.9994
bismuth	Bi	83	208.98	palladium	Pd	46	106.42
bohrium	Bh	107	262*	phosphorus	P	15	30.9738
boron	B	5	10.811	platinum	Pt	78	195.08
bromine	Br	35	79.904	plutonium	Pu	94	244*
cadmium	Cd	48	112.411	polonium	Po	84	209*
calcium	Ca	20	40.078	potassium	K	19	39.098
californium	Cf	98	251*	praseodymium	Pr	59	140.91
carbon	C	6	12.011	promethium	Pm	61	145*
cerium	Ce	58	140.115	protactinium	Pa	91	231.036
cesium	Cs	55	132.905	radium	Ra	88	226.025
chlorine	Cl	17	35.453	radon	Rn	86	222*
chromium	Cr	24	51.996	rhenium	Re	75	186.21
cobalt	Co	27	58.933	rhodium	Rh	45	102.91
copper	Cu	29	63.546	rubidium	Rb	37	85.47
curium	Cm	96	247*	ruthenium	Ru	44	101.07
dubnium	Db	105	262*	rutherfordium	Rf	104	261*
dysprosium	Dy	66	162.50	samarium	Sm	62	150.36
einsteinium	Es	99	252*	scandium	Sc	21	44.956.
erbium	Er	68	167.26	seaborgium	Sg	106	263*
europium	Eu	63	151.965	selenium	Se	34	78.96
fermium	Fm	100	257*	silicon	Si	14	28.086
fluorine	F	9	18.9984	silver	Ag	47	107.868
francium	Fr	87	223*	sodium	Na	11	22.9898
gadolinium	Gd	64	157.25	strontium	Sr	38	87.62
gallium	Ga	31	69.723	sulfur	S	16	32.066
germanium	Ge	32	72.61	tantalum	Ta	73	180.948
gold	Au	79	196.967	technetium	Tc	43	99*
hafnium	Hf	72	178.49	tellurium	Te	52	127.60
hassium	Hs	108	265*	terbium	Tb	65	158.925
helium	He	2	4.0026	thallium	Tl	81	204.38
holmium	Ho	67	164.93	thorium	Th	90	232.038
hydrogen	H	1	1.008	thulium	Tm	69	168.934
indium	In	49	114.82	tin	Sn	50	118.71
iodine	I	53	126.904	titanium	Ti	22	47.867
iridium	Ir	77	192.217	tungsten	W	74	183.84
iron	Fe	26	55.845	uranium	U	92	238.03
krypton	Kr	36	83.80	vanadium	V	23	50.94
lanthanum	La	57	138.91	xenon	Xe	54	131.29
lawrencium	Lr	103	262*	ytterbium	Yb	70	173.04
lead	Pb	82	207.19	yttrium	Y	39	88.906
lithium	Li	3	6.941	zinc	Zn	30	65.39
lutetium	Lu	71	174.967	zirconium	Zr	40	91.22
magnesium	Mg	12	24.305				
manganese	Mn	25	54.938				
meitnerium	Mt	109	266*				
mendelevium	Md	101	258*				
mercury	Hg	80	200.59				

* *mass number of most stable isotope*

Note: elements 110–118 have not been included here as they have not yet been officially named.

THE PERIODIC TABLE

Group	1	2	3	4	5	6	7	8	9	10	11	12	13	14	15	16	17	18	n	Period
	1 H																	2 He	1	1
	3 Li	4 Be											5 B	6 C	7 N	8 O	9 F	10 Ne	2	2
	11 Na	12 Mg											13 Al	14 Si	15 P	16 S	17 Cl	18 Ar	3	3
	19 K	20 Ca	21 Sc	22 Ti	23 V	24 Cr	25 Mn	26 Fe	27 Co	28 Ni	29 Cu	30 Zn	31 Ga	32 Ge	33 As	34 Se	35 Br	36 Kr	4	4
	37 Rb	38 Sr	39 Y	40 Zr	41 Nb	42 Mo	43 Tc	44 Ru	45 Rh	46 Pd	47 Ag	48 Cd	49 In	50 Sn	51 Sb	52 Te	53 I	54 Xe	5	5
	55 Cs	56 Ba	57-71 La-Lu	72 Hf	73 Ta	74 W	75 Re	76 Os	77 Ir	78 Pt	79 Au	80 Hg	81 Tl	82 Pb	83 Bi	84 Po	85 At	86 Rn	6	6
	87 Fr	88 Ra	89-103 Ac-Lr	104 Unq	105 Unp	106 Unh	107 Uns	108 Uno	109 Une	110 Uun	111 Uuu	112 Uub	113 Uut	114 Uuq	115 Uup	116 Uuh	117 Uus	118 Uuo	7	7

	3	4	5	6	7	8	9	10	11	12	13	14	15	16	17	Period
Lanthanoids	57 La	58 Ce	59 Pr	60 Nd	61 Pm	62 Sm	63 Eu	64 Gd	65 Tb	66 Dy	67 Ho	68 Er	69 Tm	70 Yb	71 Lu	6
Actinoids	89 Ac	90 Th	91 Pa	92 U	93 Np	94 Pu	95 Am	96 Cm	97 Bk	98 Cf	99 Es	100 Fm	101 Md	102 No	103 Lr	7

Correspondence of recommended group designations to other designations in recent use

	1	2	3	4	5	6	7	8	9	10	11	12	13	14	15	16	17	18
IUPAC Recommendations 1990	1	2	3	4	5	6	7	8	9	10	11	12	13	14	15	16	17	18
Usual European Convention	IA	IIA	IIIA	IVA	VA	VIA	VIIA	VIII (or VIIIA)			IB	IIB	IIIB	IVB	VB	VIB	VIIB	0 (or VIIIB)
Usual US Convention	IA	IIA	IIIB	IVB	VB	VIB	VIIB	VIII (or VIIIB)			IB	IIB	IIIA	IVA	VA	VIA	VIIA	VIIIA (or 0)

SYMBOLS USED IN MATHEMATICS, LOGIC, AND ELECTRONICS

Operation	Symbol	Operation	Symbol
AND operation, conjunction	$\wedge$.	integral, with limits	$\int_a^b dx$
OR operation, disjunction	$\vee +$	elements of vector v	v_i
NOT operation, negation	$' - \sim$	elements of matrix A	a_{ij}
NAND operation	$|\Delta$	transpose of matrix A	A^T
NOR operation	$\uparrow \nabla$	inverse of matrix A	A^{-1}
EXOR operation	$\veebar$	equivalence	$\leftrightarrow \equiv$
		biconditional	$\leftrightarrow \equiv$
		conditional	$\rightarrow \Rightarrow$
For set S and/or set T:		general binary operation	$\circ$
		universal quantifier	$\forall$
x is a member of S	$x \in S$	existential quantifier	$\exists$
x is not a member of S	$x \notin S$	union of S and T	$S \cup T$
S is a subset of T	$S \subseteq T$	intersection of S and T	$S \cap T$
S is a proper subset of T	$S \subset T$	Cartesian product of S and T	$S \times T$
complement of S	$S' \sim S \bar{S}$	set of all x for which $p(x)$ is true	$\{x|p(x)\}$
relation	R	greater than	$>$
function of x	$f(x)$	greater than or equal to	$\geq$
function f from set X to set Y	$f{:}X{\rightarrow}Y$	less than	$<$
inverse function	f^{-1}	less than or equal to	$\leq$
inverse relation	R^{-1}	approx. equal to	$\cong$
sum, with limits	$\sum_{i=1}^{n}$	not equal to	$\neq$
		infinity	∞

THE SOLAR SYSTEM

	Approximate distance from sun		Diameter	
	millions of miles	*(millions of km)*	*miles*	*(km)*
Sun	—	—	864,950	(1,392,000)
Mercury	36	(58)	3,032	(4,880)
Venus	67	(108)	7,500	(12,100)
Earth	93	(150)	7,908	(12,755)
Mars	141	(228)	4,220	(6,790)
Jupiter	484	(778)	89,000	(143,000)
Saturn	887	(1,427)	75,000	(120,000)
Uranus	1,780	(2,870)	32,560	(52,400)
Neptune	2,794	(4,497)	30,760	(49,500)
Pluto	3,658	(5,900)	1,800	(3,000)

	Rotation period on its axis			Revolution around the sun
	days	*hours*	*minutes*	
Sun	25	09	00	—
Mercury	59	00	00	88.00 days
Venus	243	00	00	224.70 days
Earth	00	23	56	365.25 days
Mars	00	24	37	1.88 years
Jupiter	00	09	50	11.86 years

THE SOLAR SYSTEM (CONTINUED)

	Rotation period on its axis			Revolution around the sun
	days	*hours*	*minutes*	
Saturn	00	10	14	29.45 years
Uranus	00	11	00	84.00 years
Neptune	00	10	00	164.79 years
Pluto	6	09	14	248.50 years

PLANETARY SATELLITES

Planet & satellite*	Year of discovery	Diameter (km)**	Planet & satellite	Year of discovery	Diameter (km)
Earth					
			Dione	1684	1120
Moon	—	3476	Helene	1980	$36 \times 32 \times 30$
Mars			Rhea	1672	1530
			Titan	1655	5150
Phobos	1877	$27 \times 22 \times 19$	Hyperion	1848	$405 \times 260 \times 220$
Deimos	1877	$15 \times 12 \times 11$	Iapetus	1671	1440
Jupiter			Phoebe	1898	$230 \times 220 \times 210$
Metis	1979	40	*Uranus*		
Adrastea	1979	$25 \times 20 \times 15$	Ophelia	1986	30
Amalthea	1892	$270 \times 166 \times 150$	Bianca	1986	42
Thebe	1979	110×90	Cressida	1986	62
Io	1610	$3660 \times 3637 \times 3631$	Desdemona	1986	54
Europa	1610	3138	Juliet	1986	84
Ganymede	1610	5262	Portia	1986	108
Callisto	1610	4800	Rosalind	1986	54
Himalia	1904	186	Belinda	1986	66
Lysithea	1938	36	Puck	1985	154
Elara	1905	76	Miranda	1948	472
Ananke	1951	30	Ariel	1851	1158
Carme	1938	40	Umbriel	1851	1172
Pasiphae	1908	50	Titania	1787	1580
Sinope	1914	36	Oberon	1787	1524
Saturn			*Neptune*		
Atlas	1980	$37 \times 34 \times 27$	Naiad	1989	54
Prometheus	1980	$148 \times 100 \times 68$	Thalassa	1989	80
Pandora	1980	$110 \times 88 \times 62$	Despina	1989	150
Epimetheus	1978	$194 \times 190 \times 154$	Galatea	1989	160
Janus	1978	$276 \times 220 \times 160$	Larissa	1989	208×178
Mimas	1789	$421 \times 395 \times 385$	Proteus	1989	$436 \times 416 \times 402$
Enceladus	1789	$512 \times 495 \times 488$	Triton	1846	2700
Tethys	1684	1050	Nereid	1949	340
Telesto	1980	$34 \times 28 \times 26$	*Pluto*		
Calypso	1980	$34 \times 22 \times 22$	Charon	1978	1186

*Only major named satellites are shown.
**For satellites with irregular shapes, measurements along principal axes are given.

THE PLANT KINGDOM (SIMPLIFIED)

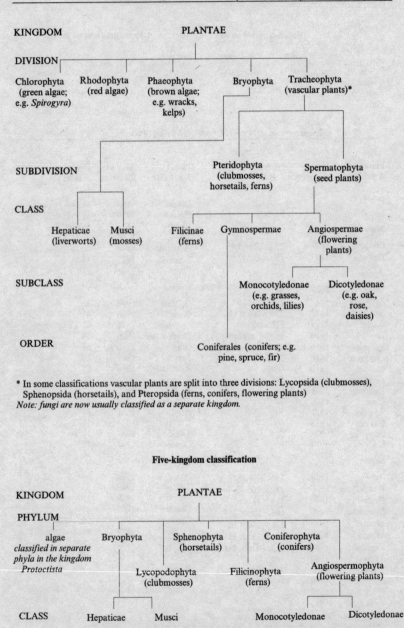

* In some classifications vascular plants are split into three divisions: Lycopsida (clubmosses), Sphenopsida (horsetails), and Pteropsida (ferns, conifers, flowering plants)
Note: fungi are now usually classified as a separate kingdom.

Five-kingdom classification

THE ANIMAL KINGDOM (SIMPLIFIED)

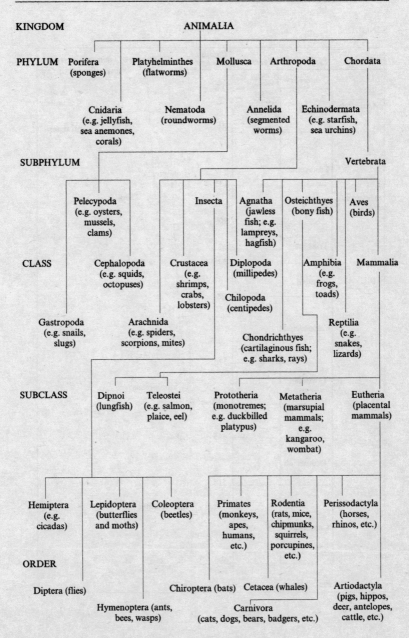

GEOLOGICAL TIME SCALE

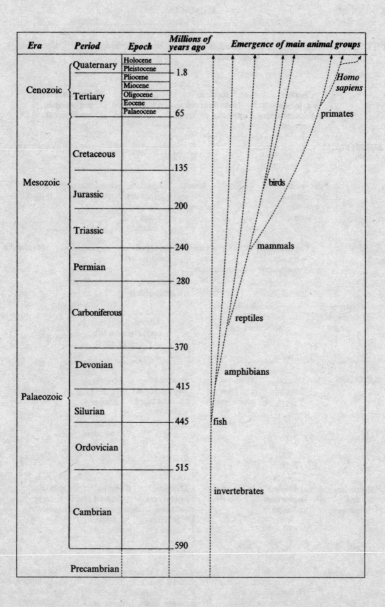

COUNTRIES OF THE WORLD

The Americas

America, United
  States of
Antigua and
  Barbuda
Argentina
Bahamas, The
Barbados
Belize
Bolivia
Brazil
Canada
Chile
Colombia
Costa Rica
Cuba
Dominica
Dominican Republic
Ecuador
El Salvador
Grenada
Guatemala
Guyana
Haiti
Honduras
Jamaica
Mexico
Nicaragua
Panama
Paraguay
Peru
St. Kitts and Nevis
St. Lucia
St. Vincent
Suriname
Trinidad and Tobago
Uruguay
Venezuela

Europe

Albania
Andorra
Austria
Belarus
Belgium
Bosnia and
  Hercegovina
Bulgaria
Croatia
Czech Republic
Denmark
Estonia
Finland
France
Germany
Greece

Hungary
Iceland
Ireland
Italy
Latvia
Liechtenstein
Lithuania
Luxembourg
Macedonia,
  Former Yugoslav
  Republic of
Malta
Moldavia
Monaco
Netherlands, The
Norway
Poland
Portugal
Romania
Russia
San Marino
Slovakia
Slovenia
Spain
Sweden
Switzerland
Ukraine
United Kingdom
Vatican City
Yugoslavia

Asia

Afghanistan
Armenia
Azerbaijan
Bahrain
Bangladesh
Bhutan
Brunei
Cambodia
China
Cyprus
Georgia
India
Indonesia
Iran
Iraq
Israel
Japan
Jordan
Kazakhstan
Kuwait
Kyrgyzstan
Laos
Lebanon

Malaysia
Maldives, The
Mongolia
Myanmar
Nepal
North Korea
Oman
Pakistan
Philippines
Qatar
Saudi Arabia
Singapore
South Korea
Sri Lanka
Syria
Taiwan
Tajikistan
Thailand
Turkey
Turkmenistan
United Arab
  Emirates
Uzbekistan
Vietnam
Yemen

Africa

Algeria
Angola
Benin
Botswana
Burkina-Faso
Burundi
Cameroon
Cape Verde
Central African
  Republic
Chad
Comoros
Congo
Congo, Democratic
  Republic of the
Côte d'Ivoire
Djibouti
Egypt
Equatorial Guinea
Eritrea
Ethiopia
Gabon
Gambia, The
Ghana
Guinea
Guinea-Bissau
Kenya
Lesotho

Liberia
Libya
Madagascar
Malawi
Mali
Mauritania
Mauritius
Morocco
Mozambique
Namibia
Niger
Nigeria
Rwanda
São Tomé and
  Príncipe
Senegal
Seychelles
Sierra Leone
Somalia
South Africa
Sudan, The
Swaziland
Tanzania
Togo
Tunisia
Uganda
Zambia
Zimbabwe

Australasia and Oceania

Australia
Fiji
Kiribati
Marshall Islands
Micronesia,
  Federated States of
Nauru
New Zealand
Palau
Papua New Guinea
Samoa
Solomon Islands
Tonga
Tuvalu
Vanuatu

THE AMERICAN STATES

State	Abbreviation	Capital	State	Abbreviation	Capital
Alabama	AL	Montgomery	New Hampshire	NH	Concord
Alaska	AK	Juneau	New Jersey	NJ	Trenton
Arizona	AZ	Phoenix	New Mexico	NM	Santa Fe
Arkansas	AR	Little Rock	New York	NY	Albany
California	CA	Sacramento	North Carolina	NC	Raleigh
Colorado	CO	Denver	North Dakota	ND	Bismarck
Connecticut	CT	Hartford	Ohio	OH	Columbus
Delaware	DE	Dover	Oklahoma	OK	Oklahoma City
Florida	FL	Tallahassee			
Georgia	GA	Atlanta	Oregon	OR	Salem
Hawaii	HI	Honolulu	Pennsylvania	PA	Harrisburg
Idaho	ID	Boise	Rhode Island	RI	Providence
Illinois	IL	Springfield	South Carolina	SC	Columbia
Indiana	IN	Indianapolis	South Dakota	SD	Pierre
Iowa	IA	Des Moines	Tennessee	TN	Nashville
Kansas	KS	Topeka	Texas	TX	Austin
Kentucky	KY	Frankfort	Utah	UT	Salt Lake City
Louisiana	LA	Baton Rouge			
Maine	ME	Augusta	Vermont	VT	Montpelier
Maryland	MD	Annapolis	Virginia	VA	Richmond
Massachusetts	MA	Boston	Washington	WA	Olympia
Michigan	MI	Lansing	West Virginia	WV	Charleston
Minnesota	MN	St. Paul	Wisconsin	WI	Madison
Mississippi	MS	Jackson	Wyoming	WY	Cheyenne
Missouri	MO	Jefferson City	*District of Columbia	DC	(Washington)
Montana	MT	Helena			
Nebraska	NE	Lincoln	*(Washington, D.C. is the capital of the United States.)		
Nevada	NV	Carson City			

THE CANADIAN PROVINCES

The Provinces

Province	Capital
Alberta	Edmonton
British Columbia	Victoria
Manitoba	Winnipeg
New Brunswick	Fredericton
Newfoundland	St. John's
Nova Scotia	Halifax
Ontario	Toronto
Prince Edward Island	Charlottetown
Quebec	Quebec
Saskatchewan	Regina

The Territories

Territory	Capital
Yukon Territory	Whitehorse
Northwest Territories	Yellowknife

Semiautonomous Region

Nunavut	Iqaluit

THE WORLD'S TEN HIGHEST MOUNTAINS

Peak	Range	Location	Height	
			feet	*meters*
Everest	Himalayas	Nepal-Tibet	29,023	8,846
Godwin Austen (K-2)	Karakoram	Kashmir	28,250	8,611
Kanchenjunga	Himalayas	Nepal-Sikkim	28,208	8,598
Lhotse	Himalayas	Nepal-Tibet	27,890	8,501
Makalu	Himalayas	Tibet-Nepal	27,790	8,470
Dhaulagiri I	Himalayas	Nepal	26,810	8,172
Manaslu	Himalayas	Nepal	26,760	8,156
Cho Oyu	Himalayas	Nepal	26,750	8,153
Nanga Parbat	Himalayas	Kashmir	26,660	8,126
Annapurna I	Himalayas	Nepal	26,504	8,078

THE WORLD'S TEN LONGEST RIVERS

River	*Source*	*Outflow*
Nile	Tributaries of Lake Victoria, Africa	Mediterranean Sea
Amazon	Glacier-fed lakes, Peru	Atlantic Ocean
Mississippi-Missouri Red Rock	Source of Red Rock, Montana	Gulf of Mexico
Yangtze Kiang	Tibetan plateau, China	China Sea
Ob	Altai Mts., Russia	Gulf of Ob
Huang Ho (Yellow)	Eastern part of Kunlan Mts., west China	Gulf of Chihli
Yenisei	Tannu-Ola Mts., western Tuva, Russia	Arctic Ocean
Paraná	Confluence of Paranaiba and Grande Rivers	Rio de la Plata
Irtish	Altai Mts., Russia, Kazakhstan, Mongolia, China	Ob River
Congo	Confluence of Lualab and Luapula Rivers, Democratic Republic of Congo	Atlantic Ocean

THE LARGEST LAKES IN THE WORLD

	Continent	*Area*	
		sq. mi.	*sq. km*
Caspian Sea	Asia	152,239	394,299
Lake Superior	North America	31,820	82,414
Lake Victoria	Africa	26,828	69,485
Aral Sea	Asia	25,659	66,457
Lake Huron	North America	23,010	59,596
Lake Michigan	North America	22,400	58,016
Lake Tanganyika	Africa	12,700	32,893
Lake Baikal	Asia	12,162	31,500
Great Bear Lake	North America	12,000	31,080
Lake Nyasa	Africa	11,600	30,044
Great Slave Lake	North America	11,170	28,930

THE LARGEST OCEANS AND SEAS IN THE WORLD

Name	Area		Average depth		Greatest known depth	
	sq. mi.	*sq. km*	*feet*	*meters*	*feet*	*meters*
Pacific Ocean	64,000,000	165,760,000	13,215	4,028	36,198	11,033
Atlantic Ocean	31,815,000	82,400,000	12,880	3,926	30,246	9,219
Indian Ocean	25,300,000	65,526,700	13,002	3,963	24,460	7,455
Arctic Ocean	5,440,200	14,090,000	3,953	1,205	18,456	5,625
Mediterranean Sea	1,145,100	2,965,800	4,688	1,429	15,197	4,632
Caribbean Sea	1,049,500	2,718,200	8,685	2,647	22,788	6,946
South China Sea	895,400	2,319,000	5,419	1,652	16,456	5,016
Bering Sea	884,900	2,291,900	5,075	1,547	15,659	4,773
Gulf of Mexico	615,000	1,592,800	4,874	1,486	12,425	3,787
Okhotsk Sea	613,800	1,589,700	2,749	838	12,001	3,658

TIME ZONES

The following list gives corresponding times to 12:00 noon, eastern standard time.

Adelaide	2:30 A.M. *	Mexico City	11:00 A.M.
Algiers	6:00 P.M.	Montevideo	2:00 P.M.
Amsterdam	6:00 P.M.	Montreal	12:00 noon
Ankara	7:00 P.M.	Moscow	8:00 P.M.
Athens	7:00 P.M.	Nairobi	8:00 P.M.
Beijing	1:00 A.M. *	New Orleans	11:00 A.M.
Belgrade	6:00 P.M.	New York	12:00 noon
Berlin	6:00 P.M.	Oslo	6:00 P.M.
Bombay	10:30 P.M.	Ottawa	12:00 noon
Brisbane	3:00 A.M. *	Panama	12:00 noon
Brussels	6:00 P.M.	Paris	6:00 P.M.
Bucharest	7:00 P.M.	Perth	1:00 A.M. *
Budapest	6:00 P.M.	Prague	6:00 P.M.
Buenos Aires	2:00 P.M.	Quebec	12:00 noon
Cairo	7:00 P.M.	Rangoon	11:30 P.M.
Calcutta	10:30 P.M.	Rio de Janeiro	2:00 P.M.
Cape Town	7:00 P.M.	St. Louis	11:00 A.M.
Caracas	1:00 P.M.	St. Petersburg	8:00 P.M.
Chicago	11:00 A.M.	San Francisco	9:00 A.M.
Colombo	10:30 P.M.	Santiago	1:00 P.M.
Copenhagen	6:00 P.M.	Singapore	12:30 A.M. *
Delhi	10:30 P.M.	Stockholm	6:00 P.M.
Denver	10:00 A.M.	Sydney	3:00 A.M. *
Dublin	5:00 P.M.	Tehran	8:30 P.M.
Helsinki	7:00 P.M.	Tokyo	2:00 A.M. *
Hobart	3:00 A.M. *	Toronto	12:00 noon
Hong Kong	1:00 A.M. *	Vancouver	9:00 A.M.
Istanbul	7:00 P.M.	Vienna	6:00 P.M.
Jerusalem	7:00 P.M.	Warsaw	6:00 P.M.
Lima	12:00 noon	Wellington	5:00 A.M. *
Lisbon	6:00 P.M.		
London	5:00 P.M.	* Next day	
Los Angeles	9:00 A.M.		
Madrid	6.00 P.M.		

UNITS OF MONEY USED IN VARIOUS COUNTRIES

Country	Unit	Country	Unit
Argentina	new peso	Kuwait	dinar
Australia	dollar	Lebanon	pound
Austria	schilling	Libya	dinar
Belgium	franc	Malaysia	ringgit
Brazil	real	Malta	lira
Canada	dollar	Mexico	peso
Chile	peso	Netherlands	guilder
China	yuan	New Zealand	dollar
Croatia	kuna	Nigeria	naira
Cuba	peso	Norway	krone
Cyprus	pound	Pakistan	rupee
Czech Republic	koruna	Peru	sol
Denmark	krone	Philippines	peso
Egypt	pound	Poland	zloty
Finland	markka	Portugal	escudo
France	franc	Romania	leu
Georgia	lari	Russia	new rouble
Germany	Deutschmark	Saudi Arabia	riyal
Ghana	cedi	Slovakia	koruna
Greece	drachma	Slovenia	tolar
Hungary	forint	South Africa	rand
India	rupee	Spain	peseta
Iran	rial	Sri Lanka	rupee
Iraq	dinar	Sweden	krona
Ireland	punt (pound)	Switzerland	franc
Israel	shekel	Syria	pound
Italy	lira	Thailand	baht
Jamaica	dollar	Tunisia	dinar
Japan	yen	Turkey	lira
Kenya	shilling	United Kingdom	pound
North and South		United States	dollar
Korea	won	Zambia	kwacha

CLASSIFICATION OF LANGUAGES (SIMPLIFIED)

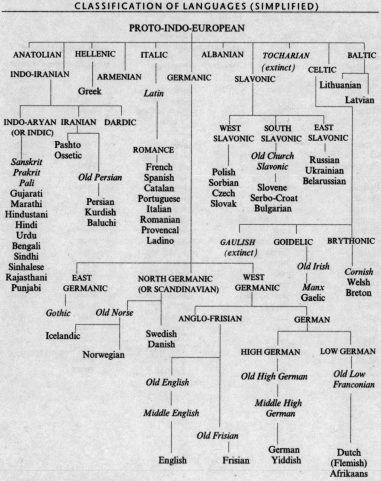

Italicized languages are no longer spoken

DEVELOPMENT OF THE ROMAN ALPHABET

Phoenician	𐤊𐤆𐤂𐤀𐤄𐤉𐤅𐤁𐤇𐤈𐤈𐤊𐤋𐤌𐤍𐤎𐤏𐤐𐤑𐤒𐤓𐤔𐤕𐤖𐤗𐤘𐤙𐤚
Hebrew	𐤀𐤁𐤂𐤃𐤄𐤅𐤆𐤇𐤈𐤉𐤊𐤋𐤌𐤍𐤎𐤏𐤐𐤑𐤒𐤓𐤔𐤕
Classical Greek	Α Β Γ Δ Ε Γ Η Ι ͥ Ι Κ Λ Μ Ν Ο Π Ρ Σ Τ Υ Υ Υ Ξ Ζ
Russian-Cyrillic	А Б Г П Е Ф Г И І К Л М Н О П Р С Т У З
Modern Roman	A B C D E F G H I J K L M N O P Q R S T U V W X Y Z

FOREIGN ALPHABETS

Greek Alphabet

Character		Name
A	α	alpha
B	β	beta
Γ	γ	gamma
Δ	δ	delta
E	ε	epsilon
Z	ζ	zeta
H	η	eta
Θ	θ	theta
I	ι	iota
K	κ	kappa
Λ	λ	lambda
M	μ	mu
N	ν	nu
Ξ	ξ	xi
O	o	omicron
Π	π	pi
P	ρ	rho
Σ	σ, ς	sigma
T	τ	tau
Y	υ	upsilon
Φ	φ	phi
X	χ	chi
Ψ	ψ	psi
Ω	ω	omega

Hebrew Alphabet

Character	Name
א	aleph
ב	beth
ג	gimel
ד	daleth
ה	he
ו	vav
ז	zayin
ח	cheth
ט	teth
י	yod
כ	kaph
ל	lamed
מ	mem
נ	nun
ס	samekh
ע	ayin
פ	pe
צ	ṣadie
ק	koph
ר	resh
ש	shin
ש	śin
ת	tav

German Gothic Alphabet

Character		Roman Character
𝔄	𝔞	Aa
𝔅	𝔟	Bb
ℭ	𝔠	Cc
𝔇	𝔡	Dd
𝔈	𝔢	Ee
𝔉	𝔣	Ff
𝔊	𝔤	Gg
ℌ	𝔥	Hh
ℑ	𝔦	Ii
𝔍	𝔧	Jj
𝔎	𝔨	Kk
𝔏	𝔩	Ll
𝔐	𝔪	Mm
𝔑	𝔫	Nn
𝔒	𝔬	Oo
𝔓	𝔭	Pp
𝔔	𝔮	Qq
𝔊	𝔯	Rr
𝔖	𝔰	Ss
𝔗	𝔱	Tt
𝔘	𝔲	Uu
𝔙	𝔳	Vv
𝔚	𝔴	Ww
𝔛	𝔵	Xx
𝔜	𝔶	Yy
𝔷	𝔷	Zz

ACCENTS AND DIACRITICAL MARKS

Accent	Name	Example	Accent	Name	Example
´	acute	é	ˇ	háček	č
/	bar	ø	‘	hamza	‘a
°	bol	å	¯	macron	ō
˘	breve	ŏ	~	tilde	ñ
˒	cedilla	ç	¨	umlaut	ü
^	circumflex	ê			
¨	diaeresis	oë			
`	grave	à			

PROOFREADERS' MARKS

Instruction	Textual mark	Marginal Mark
Insert in text the matter indicated in margin	⋏ or ∧	*New matter followed by* /
Delete	Strike through characters to be deleted	δ
Delete and close up	Strike through characters to be deleted and use linking marks	⌢̲δ̲
Leave as printed	... under characters to remain	*stet*
Change to italic	__ under characters to be altered	*ital*
Change to even small capitals	= under characters to be altered	*s.c.*
Change to capital letters	≡ under characters to be altered	*caps*
Use capital letters for initial letters and small capitals for rest of words	≡ under initial letters and = under the rest of the words	*c. & s.c.*
Change to bold type	~~ under characters to be altered	*bold*
Change to lower case	Encircle characters to be altered	*l.c.*
Change to roman type	Encircle characters to be altered	*rom*
Underline word or words	__ under words affected	*underline*
Substitute or insert character(s) under which this mark is placed, in 'superior' position	/ through character or ⋏ where required	y under character (e.g. ỹ)
Substitute or insert character(s) over which this mark is placed, in 'inferior' position	/ through character or ⋏ where required	∧ over character (e.g. ⱥ)
Change damaged character(s)	Encircle character(s) to be altered	X
Close up – delete space between characters	⌢ linking characters	⌢
Insert space	⋏	#
Transpose	⊔⊓ between characters or words	*trs*
Move matter to right	⊂| at left side of group to be moved	⊂|
Move matter to left	|⊃ at right side of group to be moved	|⊃
Raise lines	⊤ over lines to be moved ⌄ under lines to be moved	*raise*
Lower lines	⊓ over lines to be moved ⊥ under lines to be moved	*lower*
Correct the vertical alignment	‖	‖
Straighten lines	= through lines to be straightened	=
Begin a new paragraph	⊏ before first word of new paragraph	*n.p.*
No fresh paragraph here	⌇ between paragraphs	*run on*
Insert en (half-em) rule	⋏	*en*
Insert one-em rule	⋏	*em*

MUSIC

Notes and rests

Note	Rest	American	British
𝅗	▬	double-whole note	breve
o	▬	whole note	semibreve
♩	▬	half note	minim
♩	𝄽 *or* 𝄼	quarter note	crotchet
♪	𝄾	eighth note	quaver
♬	𝄿	sixteenth note	semiquaver
♬	𝅀	thirty-second note	demisemiquaver
♬	𝅁	sixty-fourth note	hemidemisemiquaver

Clefs

Fixed note	Position of middle C	Clef
		G *or* treble clef
		F *or* bass clef
		C (soprano) clef
		C (alto) clef
		C (tenor) clef

Ornaments and decorations

	acciaccatura		
	upper mordent	played	
	lower mordent	played	
	appoggiatura		
	turn	played	
	inverted turn	played	
	trill or shake		
	tremolo; rapid repetition		

MUSIC (CONTINUED)

Accidentals

♯	sharp; raising note one semitone
𝄪	double sharp; raising note one tone
♭	flat; lowering note one semitone
♭♭	double flat; lowering note one tone
♮	natural; restoring note to normal pitch after sharp or flat

Time signatures

Simple duple

$\frac{2}{2}$ or ¢   two half-note beats

$\frac{2}{4}$ two quarter-note beats

$\frac{2}{8}$ two eighth-note beats

Compound duple

$\frac{6}{4}$ two dotted half-note beats

$\frac{6}{8}$ two dotted quarter-note beats

$\frac{6}{16}$ two dotted eighth-note beats

Simple triple

$\frac{3}{2}$ three half-note beats

$\frac{3}{4}$ three quarter-note beats

$\frac{3}{8}$ three eighth-note beats

Compound triple

$\frac{9}{4}$ three dotted half-note beats

$\frac{9}{8}$ three dotted quarter-note beats

$\frac{9}{16}$ three dotted eighth-note beats

Simple quadruple

$\frac{4}{2}$ four half-note beats

$\frac{4}{4}$ or 𝄴   four quarter-note beats

$\frac{4}{8}$ four eighth-note beats

Compound quadruple

$\frac{12}{4}$ four dotted half-note beats

$\frac{12}{8}$ four dotted quarter-note beats

$\frac{12}{16}$ four dotted eighth-note beats

Staccato marks and signs of accentuation

mezzo-staccato: shorten note by about $\frac{1}{4}$

staccato: shorten note by about $\frac{1}{2}$

staccatissimo: shorten note by about $\frac{3}{4}$

detached: accented

attack

Irregular rhythms

duplet or couplet

triplet

quadruplet

quintuplet

Dynamics

crescendo

diminuendo

Curved lines

 tie or bind; two notes played as one

slur or legato; play smoothly (in one bow on stringed instrument)

Other

repeat preceding section

end of section or piece

⌢   pause

8ᵉ   play an octave above notes written

Keys and Key Signatures

Major key	Relative minor key	Key signature (sharp keys)	Key signature (flat keys)
C	A		
G	E		
D	B		
A	F#		
E	C#		
B = C♭	G#		
F# = G♭	E♭		
C# = D♭	B♭		
A♭	F		
E♭	C		
B♭	G		
F	D		

Range of various orchestral instruments

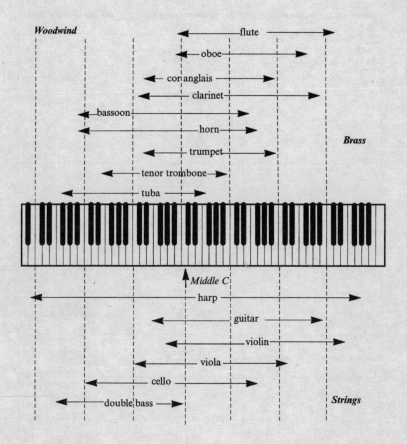

PRESIDENTS OF THE UNITED STATES

Name	Term	Name	Term
George Washington	1789–97	Grover Cleveland	1885–89
John Adams	1797–1801	Benjamin Harrison	1889–93
Thomas Jefferson	1801–09	Grover Cleveland	1893–97
James Madison	1809–17	William McKinley	1897–1901
James Monroe	1817–25	Theodore Roosevelt	1901–09
John Quincy Adams	1825–29	William Howard Taft	1909–13
Andrew Jackson	1829–37	Woodrow Wilson	1913–21
Martin Van Buren	1837–41	Warren Gamaliel Harding	1921–23
William Henry Harrison	1841	Calvin Coolidge	1923–29
John Tyler	1841–45	Herbert Clark Hoover	1929–33
James Knox Polk	1845–49	Franklin Delano Roosevelt	1933–45
Zachary Taylor	1849–50	Harry S. Truman	1945–53
Millard Fillmore	1850–53	Dwight David Eisenhower	1953–61
Franklin Pierce	1853–57	John Fitzgerald Kennedy	1961–63
James Buchanan	1857–61	Lyndon Baines Johnson	1963–69
Abraham Lincoln	1861–65	Richard Milhous Nixon	1969–74
Andrew Johnson	1865–69	Gerald Rudolph Ford	1974–77
Ulysses Simpson Grant	1869–77	James Earl Carter, Jr.	1977–81
Rutherford Hayes	1877–81	Ronald Wilson Reagan	1981–89
James Abram Garfield	1881	George Herbert Walker Bush	1989–93
Chester Alan Arthur	1881–85	William Jefferson Clinton	1993–

VICE PRESIDENTS OF THE UNITED STATES

Name	Term	Name	Term
John Adams	1789–97	Garret A. Hobart	1897–99
Thomas Jefferson	1797–1801	Theodore Roosevelt	1901
Aaron Burr	1801–05	Charles W. Fairbanks	1905–09
George Clinton	1805–12	James S. Sherman	1909–12
Elbridge Gerry	1813–14	Thomas R. Marshall	1913–21
Daniel D. Thompkins	1817–25	Calvin Coolidge	1921–23
John C. Calhoun	1825–32	Charles G. Dawes	1925–29
Martin Van Buren	1833–37	Charles Curtis	1929–33
Richard M. Johnson	1837–41	John Nance Garner	1933–41
John Tyler	1841	Henry Agard Wallace	1941–45
George M. Dallas	1845–49	Harry S. Truman	1945
Millard Fillmore	1849–50	Alben W. Barkley	1949–53
William R. King	1853	Richard Milhous Nixon	1953–61
John C. Breckinridge	1857–61	Lyndon Baines Johnson	1961–63
Hannibal Hamlin	1861–65	Hubert H. Humphrey	1965–69
Andrew Johnson	1865	Spiro T. Agnew	1969–73
Schuyler Colfax	1869–73	Gerald Rudolph Ford	1973–74
Henry Wilson	1873–75	Nelson A. Rockefeller	1974–77
William A. Wheeler	1877–81	Walter F. Mondale	1977–81
Chester Alan Arthur	1881	George Herbert Walker Bush	1981–89
Thomas A. Hendricks	1885	James Danforth Quayle	1989–93
Levi P. Morton	1889–93	Albert Gore, Jr.	1993–
Adlai E. Stevenson	1893–97		

KINGS AND QUEENS OF ENGLAND FROM 1066

The House of Normandy

William I	1066–87
William II	1087–1100
Henry I	1100–35
Stephen	1135–54

The House of Anjou or Plantagenet

Henry II	1154–89
Richard I	1189–99
John	1199–1216
Henry III	1216–72
Edward I	1272–1307
Edward II	1307–27
Edward III	1327–77
Richard II	1377–99

The House of Lancaster
   (sub-division of Plantagenet)

Henry IV	1399–1413
Henry V	1413–22
Henry VI	1422–61

The House of York
   (sub-division of Plantagenet)

Edward IV	1461–83
Edward V	1483
Richard III	1483–85

The House of Tudor

Henry VII	1485–1509
Henry VIII	1509–47

The House of Tudor (continued)

Edward VI	1547–53
Mary I	1553–58
Elizabeth I	1558–1603

The House of Stuart

James I	1603–25
Charles I	1625–49
The Commonwealth	1649–59
Charles II	1660–85
James II	1685–88
Mary II	1689–94
& William III	1689–1702
Anne	1702–14

The House of Hanover

George I	1714–27
George II	1727–60
George III	1760–1820
George IV	1820–30
William IV	1830–37
Victoria	1837–1901

The House of Saxe–Coburg

Edward VII	1901–10

The House of Windsor

George V	1910–36
Edward VIII	1936
George VI	1936–52
Elizabeth II	1952–

PRIME MINISTERS OF THE U.K.

Name	Term
Robert Walpole	1721–42
Spencer Compton, Earl of Wilmington	1742–43
Henry Pelham	1743–54
Thomas Pelham-Holles, Duke of Newcastle	1754–56
William Cavendish, Duke of Devonshire	1756–57
Thomas Pelham-Holles, Duke of Newcastle	1757–62
John Stuart, Earl of Bute	1762–63
George Granville	1763–65
Charles Watson-Wentworth, Marquis of Rockingham	1765–66
William Pitt, Earl of Chatham	1766–68
Augustus Henry Fitzroy, Duke of Grafton	1768–70
Frederick North	1770–82
Charles Watson-Wentworth, Marquis of Rockingham	1782
William Petty, Earl of Shelburne	1782–83
William Henry Cavendish Bentinck, Duke of Portland	1783
William Pitt (the Younger)	1783–1801
Henry Addington	1801–04
William Pitt	1804–06
William Wyndham Grenville, Baron Grenville	1806–07
William Bentinck, Duke of Portland	1807–09

PRIME MINISTERS OF THE U. K. (CONTINUED)

Name	Term	Name	Term
Spencer Perceval	1809–12	William Ewart Gladstone	1886
Robert Banks Jenkinson,		Robert Gascoyne-Cecil, Marquis	
Earl of Liverpool	1812–27	of Salisbury	1886–92
George Canning	1827	William Ewart Gladstone	1892–94
Frederick John Robinson,		Archibald Philip Primrose,	
Viscount Goderich	1827–28	Earl of Rosebery	1894–95
Arthur Wellesley, Duke of		Robert Gascoyne-Cecil, Marquis	
Wellington	1828–30	of Salisbury	1895–1902
Charles Grey, Earl Grey	1830–34	Arthur James Balfour	1902–05
William Lamb, Viscount		Henry Campbell-Bannerman	1905–08
Melbourne	1834	Herbert Henry Asquith	1908–16
Robert Peel	1834–35	David Lloyd George	1916–22
William Lamb, Viscount		Andrew Bonar Law	1922–23
Melbourne	1835–41	Stanley Baldwin	1923–24
Robert Peel	1841–46	James Ramsay MacDonald	1924
John Russell	1846–52	Stanley Baldwin	1924–29
Edward George Geoffrey Smith		James Ramsay MacDonald	1929–35
Stanley, Earl of Derby	1852	Stanley Baldwin	1935–37
George Hamilton Gordon,		Neville Chamberlain	1937–40
Earl of Aberdeen	1852–55	Winston Churchill	1940–45
Henry John Temple, Viscount		Clement Richard Attlee	1945–51
Palmerston	1855–58	Winston Churchill	1951–55
Edward Stanley, Earl of Derby	1858–59	Anthony Eden	1955–57
Henry Temple, Viscount		Harold Macmillan	1957–63
Palmerston	1859–65	Alec Douglas-Home	1963–64
John Russell, Earl Russell	1865–66	Harold Wilson	1964–70
Edward Stanley, Earl of Derby	1866–68	Edward Heath	1970–74
Benjamin Disraeli	1868	Harold Wilson	1974–76
William Ewart Gladstone	1868–74	James Callaghan	1976–79
Benjamin Disraeli, Earl of		Margaret Thatcher	1979–90
Beaconsfield (ennobled in 1876)	1874–80	John Major	1990–97
William Ewart Gladstone	1880–85	Tony Blair	1997–
Robert Gascoyne-Cecil, Marquis			
of Salisbury	1885–86		

PRIME MINISTERS OF CANADA

Name	Term	Name	Term
John A. Macdonald	1867–73	Richard B. Bennett	1930–35
Alexander Mackenzie	1873–78	W. L. Mackenzie King	1935–48
John A. Macdonald	1878–91	Louis Stephen St. Laurent	1948–57
John J. C. Abbott	1891–92	John George Diefenbaker	1957–63
John S. D. Thompson	1892–94	Lester B. Pearson	1963–68
Mackenzie Bowell	1894–96	Pierre Elliott Trudeau	1968–79
Charles Tupper	1896	Joseph Clark	1979–80
Wilfrid Laurier	1896–1911	Pierre Elliott Trudeau	1980–84
Robert L. Borden	1911–20	John Turner	1984
Arthur Meighen	1920–21	Brian Mulroney	1984–93
W. L. Mackenzie King	1921–26	Kim Campbell	1993
Arthur Meighen	1926	Jean Chrétien	1993–
W. L. Mackenzie King	1926–30		

BOOKS OF THE BIBLE

Old Testament

Genesis
Exodus
Leviticus
Numbers
Deuteronomy
Joshua
Judges
Ruth
1 Samuel
2 Samuel
1 Kings
2 Kings
1 Chronicles
2 Chronicles
Ezra
Nehemiah
Esther
Job
Psalms
Proverbs
Ecclesiastes
Song of Solomon
Isaiah
Jeremiah
Lamentations
Ezekiel
Daniel
Hosea
Joel
Amos
Obadiah
Jonah
Micah

Nahum
Habakkuk
Zephaniah
Haggai
Zechariah
Malachi

New Testament

Matthew
Mark
Luke
John
The Acts
Romans
1 Corinthians
2 Corinthians
Galatians
Ephesians
Philippians
Colossians
1 Thessalonians
2 Thessalonians
1 Timothy
2 Timothy
Titus
Philemon
Hebrews
James
1 Peter
2 Peter
1 John
2 John
3 John
Jude
Revelation